Web Services Research for Emerging Applications:
Discoveries and Trends

Liang-Jie Zhang
IBM T.J. Watson Research, USA

INFORMATION SCIENCE REFERENCE
Hershey · New York

Director of Editorial Content: Kristin Klinger
Director of Book Publications: Julia Mosemann
Acquisitions Editor: Lindsay Johnston
Development Editor: Julia Mosemann
Publishing Assistant: Deanna Zombro and Sean Woznicki
Typesetter: Deanna Zombro
Quality control: Jamie Snavely
Cover Design: Lisa Tosheff
Printed at: Yurchak Printing Inc.

Published in the United States of America by
Information Science Reference (an imprint of IGI Global)
701 E. Chocolate Avenue
Hershey PA 17033
Tel: 717-533-8845
Fax: 717-533-8661
E-mail: cust@igi-global.com
Web site: http://www.igi-global.com/reference

Library of Congress Cataloging-in-Publication Data

Web services research for emerging applications : discoveries and trends / Liang-Jie Zhang, editor.
p. cm.
Includes bibliographical references and index.
Summary: "This book provides a comprehensive assessment of the latest developments in Web services research, focusing on composing and coordinating Web services, XML security, and service oriented architecture, and presenting new and emerging research in the Web services discipline"--Provided by publisher.
ISBN 978-1-61520-684-1 (hardcover) -- ISBN 978-1-61520-685-8 (ebook) 1. Web services. 2. Service-oriented architecture (Computer science) 3. Application software--Development. 4. XML (Document markup language) 5. Computer security. I. Zhang, Liang-Jie.
TK5105.88813.W386 2010
006.7'8--dc22

2009053447

British Cataloguing in Publication Data
A Cataloguing in Publication record for this book is available from the British Library.

All work contributed to this book is new, previously-unpublished material. The views expressed in this book are those of the authors, but not necessarily of the publisher.

Adances in Web Services Research Book Series (AWSR)

ISBN: 1935-3685

Editor-in-Chief: Liang-Jie Zhang, IBM Research, USA

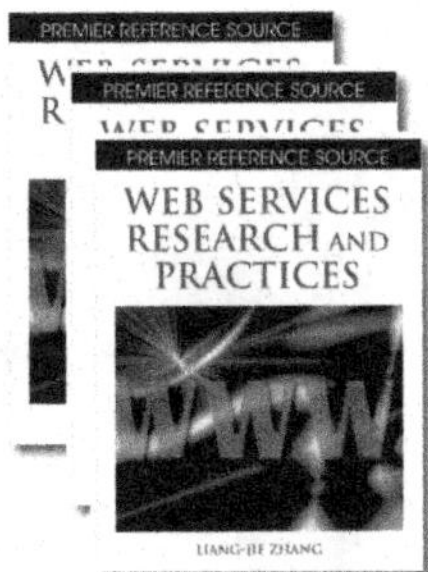

Web Services Research and Practices
Liang-Jie Zhang, IBM Research, USA

CyberTech Publishing • copyright 2008 • 278pp • H/C (ISBN: 978-1-59904-904-5)

Web services is rapidly becoming one of the most valued aspects of information technology services, as Web-based technological advancements continue to grow at an exponential rate.
Web Services Research and Practices provides researchers, scholars, and practitioners in a variety of settings essential up-to-date research in this demanding field, addressing issues such as communication applications using Web services; Semantic services computing; discovery, modeling, performance, and enhancements of Web services; and Web services architecture, frameworks, and security.

The Advances in Web Services Research (AWSR) Book Series features only the latest research findings and industry solutions dealing with all aspects of Web services technology. The overall scope of this book series will cover the advancements in the state of the art, standards, and practice of Web services, as well as to identify the emerging research topics and define the future of Services computing, including Web services on Grid computing, Web services on multimedia, Web services on communication, etc. AWSR provides an open, formal series for high quality books developed by theoreticians, educators, developers, researchers and practitioners for professionals to stay abreast of challenges in Web services technology.

Web services are network-based application components with services-oriented architecture using standard interface description languages and uniform communication protocols. Due to the importance of the field, standardization organizations such as WS-I, W3C, OASIS and Liberty Alliance are actively developing standards for Web services. Considering these developments, the Advances in Web Services Research (AWSR) Book Series seeks to further emphasize the importance of web services research and expand the availability of comprehensive resources in the advancing field.

Hershey • New York
Order online at www.igi-global.com or call 717-533-8845 x 10 –
Mon-Fri 8:30 am - 5:00 pm (est) or fax 24 hours a day 717-533-8661

Table of Contents

Preface xxii

Chapter 1
SOA Reference Architecture 1
Liang-Jie Zhang, IBM T.J. Watson Research, USA
Jia Zhang, Northern Illinois University, USA

Chapter 2
WSMoD: A Methodology for Qos-Based Web Services Design 16
M. Comerio, Università di Milano Bicocca, Milano, Italy
F. De Paoli, Università di Milano Bicocca, Milano, Italy
S. Grega, Università di Milano Bicocca, Milano, Italy
A. Maurino, Università di Milano Bicocca, Milano, Italy
C. Batini, Università di Milano Bicocca, Milano, Italy

Chapter 3
A Metamorphic Testing Methodology for Online SOA Application Testing 45
W. K. Chan, City University of Hong Kong, Hong Kong
S. C. Cheung, Hong Kong University of Science and Technology, Hong Kong
Karl R. P. H. Leung, Hong Kong Institute of Vocational Education, Hong Kong

Chapter 4
Integrated Design of eBanking Architecture 67
Tony C. Shan, Keane Inc., USA
Winnie W. Hua, CTS Inc., USA

Chapter 5
A Similarity Measure for Process Mining in Service Oriented Architecture 87
Joonsoo Bae, Chonbuk National Univ, South Korea
Ling Liu, Georgia Institute of Technology, USA
James Caverlee, Georgia Institute of Technology, USA
Liang-Jie Zhang, IBM T.J. Watson Research Center, USA
Hyerim Bae, Pusan National Univ, South Korea

Chapter 6
Rapid Development of Adaptable Situation-Aware Service-Based Systems 104
S. S. Yau, Arizona State University, USA
S. Mukhopadhyay, Louisiana State University, USA
H. Davulcu, Arizona State University, USA
D. Huang, Arizona State University, USA
R. Bharadwaj, Naval Research Laboratory, USA
K. Shenai, University of Toledo, USA

Chapter 7
Object-Oriented Architecture for Web Services Eventing 140
Krzysztof Ostrowski, Cornell University, USA
Ken Birman, Cornell University, USA
Danny Dolev, The Hebrew University of Jerusalem, Israel

Chapter 8
Composing and Coordinating Transactional Web Services 185
Frederic Montagut, SAP Schweiz AG, Switzerland, and Institut Eurecom, France
Refik Molva, Institut Eurecom, France
Silvan Tecumseh Golega, Hasso-Plattner-Institut, Germany

Chapter 9
Security Personalization for Internet and Web Services 205
George O.M. Yee, National Research Council Canada, Canada
Larry Korba, National Research Council Canada, Canada

Chapter 10
XML Security with Binary XML for Mobile Web Services 230
Jaakko Kangasharju, Helsinki Institute for Information Technology, Finland
Tancred Lindholm, Helsinki Institute for Information Technology, Finland
Sasu Tarkoma, Helsinki Institute for Information Technology, Finland

Chapter 11
Efficient and Effective XML Encoding 250
Christian Werner, University of Lübeck, Germany
Carsten Buschmann, University of Lübeck, Germany
Ylva Brandt, University of Lübeck, Germany
Stefan Fischer, University of Lübeck, Germany

Chapter 18
Service-Oriented Architecture for Migrating Legacy Home Appliances to Home Network System: Principle and Applications 422
Masahide Nakamura, Graduate School of Engineering, Kobe University, Japan
Hiroshi Igaki, Graduate School of Engineering, Kobe University, Japan
Akihiro Tanaka, Graduate School of Information Science, Nara Institute of Science and Technology, Japan
Haruaki Tamada, Graduate School of Information Science, Nara Institute of Science and Technology, Japan
Ken-ichi Matsumoto, Graduate School of Information Science, Nara Institute of Science and Technology, Japan

Chapter 19
Broadening JAIN-SLEE with a Service Description Language and Asynchronous Web Services 442
Paolo Falcarin, Politecnico di Torino, Italy
Claudio Venezia, Telecom Italia, Italy
José Felipe Mejia Bernal, Politecnico di Torino, Italy

Chapter 20
Workflow Discovery: Requirements from E-Science and a Graph-Based Solution 465
Antoon Goderis, University of Manchester, UK
Peter Li, University of Manchester, UK
Carole Goble, University of Manchester, UK

Chapter 21
An Access Control Framework for WS-BPEL Processes 492
Federica Paci, Università degli Studi di Trento, Italy
Elisa Bertino, Purdue University, USA
Jason Crampton, University of London, UK

Chapter 22
Business Process Control-Flow Complexity: Metric, Evaluation, and Validation 516
Jorge Cardoso, University of Madeira, Portugal and SAP AG Research, Germany

Chapter 23
Pattern-Based Translation of BPMN Process Models to BPEL Web Services 545
Chun Ouyang, Queensland University of Technology, Australia
Marlon Dumas, Queensland University of Technology, Australia and University of Tartu, Estonia
Arthur H.M. ter Hofstede, Queensland University of Technology, Australia
Wil M.P. van der Aalst, Queensland University of Technology, Australia and Eindhoven University of Technology, The Netherlands

Chapter 24
DSCWeaver: Synchronization-Constraint Aspect Extension to Procedural Process Specification Languages 567
Qinyi Wu, Georgia Institute of Technology, USA
Calton Pu, Georgia Institute of Technology, USA
Akhil Sahai, HP Labs, USA
Roger Barga, Microsoft Research, USA

Chapter 25
A Reservation-Based Extended Transaction Protocol for Coordination of Web Services within Business Activities 590
Wenbing Zhao, Cleveland State University, USA
Firat Kart, University of California, Santa Barbara, USA
L. E. Moser, University of California, Santa Barbara, USA
P. M. Melliar-Smith, University of California, Santa Barbara, USA

Compilation of References 620

About the Contributors 657

Index 637

Detailed Table of Contents

SOA Reference Architecture (SOA-RA) aims to provide a normative guidance for software engineers to design and develop enterprise-level Service Oriented Architecture (SOA)-based solutions. Its basis is SOA Solution Stack (S3) that defines a conceptual view of a service-oriented architecture in the context of solution design and delivery. S3 is then extended by introducing conceptual architectural building blocks (ABBs) that serve as design templates to make S3-based solutions more configurable, reusable, and goal-aligned. On top of an extendable metamodel, SOA-RA decomposes an SOA solution view into an enterprise view, an IT system view, and a services view. These view models allows software designers to establish a comprehensive overview of an expected SOA solution. This chapter first analyzes the architectural style and metamodel of S3, then describes the various view models, and then describes an end-to-end SOA solution design and modeling framework and methodology.

Web services are increasingly used as an effective means to create and streamline processes and collaborations among governments, businesses, and citizens. As the number of available web services is steadily increasing, there is a growing interest in providing methodologies that address the design of web services according to specific qualities of service (QoS) rather than functional descriptions only. This chapter presents WSMoD (Web Services MOdeling Design), a methodology that explicitly addresses this issue. Furthermore, it exploits general knowledge available on services, expressed by ontologies describing services, their qualities, and the context of use, to help the designer in expressing service requirements in terms of design artifacts. Ontologies are used to acquire and specialize common knowledge among the entities involved in service design, and to check the consistency of the web service model with constraints defined by provider and customer requirements. To improve the effectiveness of the process, the authors propose a Platform Independent Model that includes the description of specific context of service provision, without considering implementation details. The discussion of a QoS-based web service design within a real case study bears evidence of the potentials of WSMoD.

Testing the correctness of service integration is a step toward assurance of the quality of applications. These applications however may bind dynamically to their supportive services using the SOA pattern that share the same service interface, yet the latter services may behave differently. In addition, a service may implement a business strategy, such as best pricing, relative to the behaviors of its competitors and the dynamic market conditions. As such, defining a test oracle that specifies the absolute expected outcomes for individual test cases is hard. Many existing works ignore these issues to address the problem of identifying failures from test results. This chapter studies an approach to online testing. Service testing is divided into two steps. In the spirit of metamorphic testing, the offline step determines a set of successful test cases to construct their corresponding follow-up test cases for the online step. These test cases will be executed by metamorphic services that encapsulate the services as well as applicable metamorphic relations. Thus, any failure revealed by the approach will be a failure of the service under test.

This chapter describes a service-oriented framework for integrated design of eBanking architecture (IDEA) in the financial services industry. A pragmatic approach is developed to help facilitate sustainable design practices in migrating conventional n-tier online systems to a service-oriented computing paradigm, composed of Service-Oriented Architecture (SOA), Integration (SOI), Process (SOP) and Management (SOM). This comprehensive model comprises 5 modules, namely, Hybrid Methodology, Architecture Baseline Model, Service Patterns, Enterprise Service Model, and Domain-specific Model. A hybrid methodology is designed to leverage the benefits of both top-down and bottom-up approaches, in which a converging layer is conceived to incorporate the latest technologies such as portal, mashup, RIA, process orchestration, service aggregations, collaborations, choreography, business rule engine, virtualization, cloud computing, Web 2.0/3.0, and so on. A multi-tier architecture baseline model is constructed to cope with the architecture complexity in a disciplined manner. E-business patterns are applied to categorize diverse banking services, which form the foundation for subsequent selection justifications of appropriate technologies, platforms, products, tools, and infrastructure. Furthermore, common business functionalities are built in the enterprise service model as shared services to be reused across lines of business as well as delivery channels, along with the sharable technical services and infrastructure services. A domain-specific model for the Internet Channel is defined by operationalizing the hybrid methodology in a particular portfolio. In addition, a holistic reusable application platform is introduced to address the key design considerations and concerns in the implementation of service-oriented solutions. Various challenges and best-practice recommendations are also articulated in the context.

Chapter 5
A Similarity Measure for Process Mining in Service Oriented Architecture...................................... 87
Joonsoo Bae, Chonbuk National Univ, South Korea
Ling Liu, Georgia Institute of Technology, USA
James Caverlee, Georgia Institute of Technology, USA
Liang-Jie Zhang, IBM T.J. Watson Research Center, USA
Hyerim Bae, Pusan National Univ, South Korea

Business processes continue to play an important role in today's service-oriented enterprise computing systems. Mining, discovering, and integrating process-oriented services has attracted growing attention in the recent years. This chapter presents a quantitative approach to modeling and capturing the similarity and dissimilarity between different process designs. The authors derive the similarity measures by analyzing the process dependency graphs of the participating workflow processes. They first convert each process dependency graph into a normalized process matrix. Then they calculate the metric space distance between the normalized matrices. This distance measure can be used as a quantitative and qualitative tool in process mining, process merging, and process clustering, and ultimately it can reduce or minimize the costs involved in design, analysis, and evolution of workflow systems.

Chapter 6
Rapid Development of Adaptable Situation-Aware Service-Based Systems 104
S. S. Yau, Arizona State University, USA
S. Mukhopadhyay, Louisiana State University, USA
H. Davulcu, Arizona State University, USA
D. Huang, Arizona State University, USA
R. Bharadwaj, Naval Research Laboratory, USA
K. Shenai, University of Toledo, USA

Service-based systems have many applications, such as collaborative research and development, e-business, health care, military applications and homeland security. In these systems, it is necessary to provide users the capability of composing appropriate services into workflows offering higher-level functionality based on declaratively specified goals. In a large-scale and dynamic service-oriented computing environment, it is desirable that the service composition is automated and situation-aware so that robust and adaptive workflows can be generated. However, existing languages for web services are not expressive enough to model services with situation awareness and side effects. This chapter presents an approach to rapid development of adaptable situation-aware service-based systems. This approach is based on the α-logic and α-calculus, and a declarative model for situation awareness (SAW). This approach consists of four major components: (1) analyzing SAW requirements using the authors'

The growth of the Internet has been accompanied by the growth of Internet services (e.g., e-commerce, e-health). This proliferation of services and the increasing attacks on them by malicious individuals have highlighted the need for service security. The security requirements of an Internet or Web service may be specified in a security policy. The provider of the service is then responsible for implementing the security measures contained in the policy. However, a service customer or consumer may have security preferences that are not reflected in the provider's security policy. In order for service providers to attract and retain customers, as well as reach a wider market, a way of personalizing a security policy to a particular customer is needed. This chapter derives the content of an Internet or Web service security policy and proposes a flexible security personalization approach that will allow an Internet or Web service provider and customer to negotiate to an agreed-upon personalized security policy. In addition, this chapter presents two application examples of security policy personalization, and an overview of the design of the authors' security personalization prototype.

In the wireless world, there has recently been much interest in alternate serialization formats for XML data, mostly driven by the weak capabilities of both devices and networks. However, it is difficult to make an alternate serialization format that is compatible with XML security features such as encryption and signing. This chapter considers ways to integrate an alternate format with security, and presents a solution that the authors see as a viable alternative. In addition to this, the chapter presents extensive performance measurements, including ones on a mobile phone on the effect of an alternate format when using XML-based security. These measurements indicate that, in the wireless world, reducing message sizes is the most pressing concern, and that processing efficiency gains of an alternate format are a much smaller concern. The authors also make specific recommendations on security usage based on their measurements.

Compared to other middleware approaches like CORBA or Java RMI the protocol overhead of SOAP is very high. This fact is not only disadvantageous for several performance-critical applications, but especially in environments with limited network bandwidth or resource-constrained computing devices. Although recent research work concentrated on more compact, binary representations of XML data only very few approaches account for the special characteristics of SOAP communication. This chapter will discuss the most relevant state-of-the-art technologies for compressing XML data. Furthermore, it will present a novel solution for compacting SOAP messages. In order to achieve significantly better compression rates than current approaches, the compressor described in this chapter utilizes structure information from an XML Schema or WSDL document. With this additional knowledge on the "grammar" of the exchanged messages, this compressor generates a single custom pushdown automaton, which can be used as a highly efficient validating parser as well as a highly effective compressor. The main idea is to tag the transitions of the automaton with short binary identifiers that are then used to encode the path through the automaton during parsing. The authors' approach leads to extremely compact data representations and is also usable in environments with very limited CPU and memory resources.

The business needs, the availability of huge volumes of data and the continuous evolution in Web services functions derive the need of application of data mining in the Web service domain. This chapter recommends several data mining applications that can leverage problems concerned with the discovery and monitoring of Web services. This chapter then presents a case study on applying the clustering data mining technique to the Web service usage data to improve the Web service discovery process. This chapter also discusses the challenges that arise when applying data mining to Web services usage data and abstract information.

Different from traditional software applications, Web services are defined independently from any execution context. Their consequent inherent autonomy and heterogeneity fostered by a continuous evolution in business context and requirements make ensuring the execution of a composite service as intended a challenging task. This chapter presents a reengineering approach to ensure transactional reliability of composite services. Contrary to previous approaches which check correctness properties based on the composition model, the authors start from executions' log to improve services' recovery mechanisms. Basically, the chapter proposes a set of mining techniques to discover the transactional behavior from an event based log. Then, based on this mining step, the authors use a set of rules in order to improve services' reliability.

Chapter 14
Karma2: Provenance Management for Data-Driven Workflows 317
Yogesh L. Simmhan, Microsoft Research, USA
Beth Plale, Indiana University, USA
Dennis Gannon, Indiana University, USA

The increasing ability for the sciences to sense the world around us is resulting in a growing need for data-driven e-Science applications that are under the control of workflows composed of services on the Grid. The focus of this work is on provenance collection for these workflows that are necessary to validate the workflow and to determine quality of generated data products. The challenge the authors address is to record uniform and usable provenance metadata that meets the domain needs while minimizing the modification burden on the service authors and the performance overhead on the workflow engine and the services. The framework is based on generating discrete provenance activities during the lifecycle of a workflow execution that can be aggregated to form complex data and process provenance graphs that can span across workflows. The implementation uses a loosely coupled publish-subscribe architecture for propagating these activities, and the capabilities of the system satisfy the needs of detailed provenance collection. A performance evaluation of a prototype finds a minimal performance overhead (in the range of 1% for an eight-service workflow using 271 data products).

Chapter 15
Result Refinement in Web Services Retrieval Based on Multiple Instances Learning........................ 340
Yanzhen Zou, Peking University, China
Lu Zhang, Peking University, China
Yan Li, Peking University, China
Bing Xie, Peking University, China
Hong Mei, Peking University, China

Web services retrieval is a critical step for reusing existing services in the SOA paradigm. In the UDDI registry, traditional category-based approaches have been used to locate candidate services. However, these approaches usually achieve relatively low precision because some candidate Web Services in the result set cannot provide actually suitable operations for users. This chapter presents a new approach to improve this kind of category-based Web Services retrieval process which can refine the coarse matching results step by step. The refinement is based on the idea that operation specification is very important to service reuse. Therefore, a Web Service is thus investigated via multiple instances view in this approach, which indicates that a service is labeled as positive if and only if at least one operation provided by this service is usable to the user. Otherwise, it is labeled as negative. Experimental results demonstrate that this approach can increase the retrieval precision to a certain extent after one or two rounds of refinement.

Chapter 16
A Model-Driven Development Framework for Non-Functional Aspects in Service Oriented Architecture.. 358
Hiroshi Wada, University of Massachusetts - Boston, USA
Junichi Suzuki, University of Massachusetts - Boston, USA
Katsuya Oba, OGIS International, Inc., USA

Service Oriented Architecture (SOA) is an emerging style of software architectures to reuse and integrate existing systems for designing new applications. Each application is designed in an implementation independent manner using two major abstract concepts: services and connections between services. In SOA, non-functional aspects (e.g., security and fault tolerance) of services and connections should be described separately from their functional aspects (i.e., business logic) because different applications use services and connections in different non-functional contexts. This chapter proposes a model-driven development (MDD) framework for non-functional aspects in SOA. The proposed MDD framework consists of (1) a Unified Modeling Language (UML) profile to graphically model non-functional aspects in SOA, and (2) an MDD tool that accepts a UML model defined with the proposed profile and transforms it to application code. This chapter also demonstrates how the proposed framework is used in model-driven development of service-oriented applications. Empirical evaluation results show that the proposed MDD framework improves the reusability and maintainability of service-oriented applications by hiding low-level implementation technologies in UML models.

Service-Oriented Computing (SOC) has been marked as the technology trend that caters for interoperability among the components of a distributed system. However, the emergence of various incompatible instantiations of the SOC paradigm, e.g. Web or Peer-to-Peer services, and the divergences encountered within each of these instantiations state clearly that interoperability is still an open issue, mainly due its multi-dimensional nature. This chapter addresses the interoperability problem by first presenting its multiple dimensions and then by describing a conceptual model called Generic Service Model (GeSMO), which can be used as a basis for the development of languages, tools and mechanisms that support interoperability. The authors illustrate how GeSMO has been utilized for the provision of a Peer-to-Peer (P2P) service description language and a P2P invocation mechanism which leverages interoperability between heterogeneous P2P services and between P2P services and Web services.

This chapter presents a practical framework that adapts the conventional home electric appliances with the infrared remote controls (legacy appliances) to the emerging home network system (HNS). The proposed method extensively uses the concept of service-oriented architecture to improve programmatic interoperability among multi-vendor appliances. The authors first prepare APIs that assist a PC to send infrared signals to the appliances. Then the APIs are aggregated within self-contained service components, so that each of the components achieves a logical feature independent of device/vendor-specific operations. The service components are finally exhibited to the HNS as Web services. As a result, the legacy appliances can be used as distributed components with open interfaces. To demonstrate the effectiveness, the authors implement an actual HNS and integrated services with multi-vendor legacy appliances. The authors also show practical applications implemented on the developed HNS.

Chapter 19
Broadening JAIN-SLEE with a Service Description Language and Asynchronous Web Services 442
Paolo Falcarin, Politecnico di Torino, Italy
Claudio Venezia, Telecom Italia, Italy
José Felipe Mejia Bernal, Politecnico di Torino, Italy

Meshing up telecommunication and IT resources seems to be the real challenge for supporting the evolution towards the next generation of Web Services. In the telecom world, JAIN-SLEE (JAIN Service Logic Execution Environment) is an emerging standard specification for Java service platforms targeted to host value added services, composed of telecom and IT services. This chapter describes the StarSLEE platform which extends JAIN-SLEE in order to compose JAIN-SLEE services with Web services and the StarSCE service creation environment which allows exporting value added services as communication Web services. It analyzes open issues that must be addressed to introduce Web Services in new telecom service platforms.

Chapter 20
Workflow Discovery: Requirements from E-Science and a Graph-Based Solution 465
Antoon Goderis, University of Manchester, UK
Peter Li, University of Manchester, UK
Carole Goble, University of Manchester, UK

Much has been written on the promise of Web service discovery and (semi-) automated composition. In this discussion, the value to practitioners of discovering and reusing existing service compositions, captured in workflows, is mostly ignored. This chapter presents the case for workflows and workflow discovery in science and develop one discovery solution. Through a survey with 21 scientists and developers from the myGrid/Taverna workflow environment, workflow discovery requirements are elicited. Through a user experiment with 13 scientists, an attempt is made to build a benchmark for workflow ranking. Through the design and implementation of a workflow discovery tool, a mechanism for ranking workflow fragments is provided based on graph sub-isomorphism detection. The tool evaluation, drawing on a corpus of 89 public workflows and the results of the user experiment, finds that, for a simple showcase, the average human ranking can largely be reproduced.

Business processes –the next generation workflows- have attracted considerable research interest in the last fifteen years. More recently, several XML-based languages have been proposed for specifying and orchestrating business processes, resulting in the WS-BPEL language. Even if WS-BPEL has been developed to specify automated business processes that orchestrate activities of multiple Web services, there are many applications and situations requiring that people be considered as additional participants that can influence the execution of a process. Significant omissions from WS-BPEL are the specification of activities that require interactions with humans to be completed, called human activities, and the specification of authorization information associating users with human activities in a WS-BPEL business process and authorization constraints, such as separation of duty, on the execution of human activities. This chapter addresses these deficiencies by introducing a new type of WS-BPEL activity to model human activities and by developing RBAC-WS-BPEL, a role based access control model for WS-BPEL and BPCL, a language to specify authorization constraints.

Organizations are increasingly faced with the challenge of managing business processes, workflows, and recently, Web processes. One important aspect of business processes that has been overlooked is their complexity. High complexity in processes may result in poor understandability, errors, defects, and exceptions, leading processes to need more time to develop, test, and maintain. Therefore, excessive complexity should be avoided. Business process measurement is the task of empirically and objectively assigning numbers to the properties of business processes in such a way so as to describe them. Desirable attributes to study and measure include complexity, cost, maintainability, and reliability. In This chapter focuses on investigating process complexity. A metric to analyze the control-flow complexity of business processes is presented and described. The metric is evaluated in terms of Weyuker's properties in order to guarantee that it qualifies as good and comprehensive. To test the validity of the metric, this chapter describes the experiment that was carried out for empirically validating the metric.

The business process modeling notation (BPMN) is a graph-oriented language primarily targeted at domain analysts and supported by many modeling tools. The business process execution language for Web services (BPEL) on the other hand is a mainly block-structured language targeted at software developers and supported by several execution platforms. Translating BPMN models into BPEL code is a necessary step towards standards-based business process development environments. This translation is challenging since BPMN and BPEL represent two fundamentally different classes of languages. Existing BPMN-to-BPEL translations rely on the identification of block-structured patterns in BPMN models that are mapped onto structured BPEL constructs. This chapter advances the state of the art in BPMN-to-BPEL translation by defining methods for identifying not only perfectly block-structured fragments in BPMN models, but quasi-structured fragments that can be turned into perfectly structured ones and flow-based acyclic fragments that can be mapped onto a combination of structured constructs and control links. Beyond its direct relevance in the context of BPMN and BPEL, this chapter addresses issues that arise generally when translating between graph-oriented and block-structured flow definition languages

Correct synchronization among activities is critical in a business process. Current process languages such as BPEL specify the control flow of processes procedurally, which can lead to inflexible and tangled code for managing a crosscutting aspect—synchronization constraints that define permissible sequences of execution for activities. This chapter presents DSCWeaver, a tool that enables a synchronization-aspect extension to procedural languages. It uses DSCL (directed-acyclic-graph synchronization constraint language) to achieve three desirable properties for synchronization modeling: fine granularity, declarative syntax, and validation support. DSCWeaver then automatically generates executable code for synchronization. The authors demonstrate the advantages of their approach in a service deployment process written in BPEL and evaluate its performance using two metrics: lines of code (LoC) and places to visit (PtV). Evaluation results show that this approach can effectively reduce the development effort of process programmers while providing performance competitive to unwoven BPEL code.

This chapter describes a novel reservation-based extended transaction protocol for coordination of tasks within a business activity. With the advance of Web Services, the authors anticipate that business activities will be implemented as Web Services and that the automation of business activities across multiple enterprises over the Internet will become a reality. Classical extended transaction protocols are not well suited for this new breed of business activity, because of their use of compensation transactions. The authors' reservation-based extended transaction protocol employs an explicit reservation phase and an explicit confirmation/cancellation phase to eliminate the need for compensation transactions. The authors show how their Reservation Protocol maps to the Web Services Coordination specification and describe their implementation of the Reservation Protocol.

Preface

The emergence and growth of Web technologies and applications has resulted in the need for specific methods for their integration. This collection, entitled *Web Services Research for Emerging Applications: Discoveries and Trends*, provides a comprehensive assessment of the latest developments in Web services research. Individual chapters focus on composing and coordinating Web services, XML security, and service oriented architecture, presenting new and emerging research in the Web services discipline.

Chapter 1, "*SOA Reference Architecture*," by Liang-Jie Zhang and Jia Zhang first analyzes the architectural style and metamodel of SOA Solution Stack (S3), then describes the various view models, and then describes an end-to-end SOA solution design and modeling framework and methodology.

Chapter 2, "*WSMoD: A Methodology for QoS-Based Web Services Design*," by M. Comerio, F. De Paoli, S. Grega, A. Maurino, and C. Batini presents WSMoD (Web Services MOdeling Design), a methodology that explicitly addresses this issue. Furthermore, it exploits general knowledge available on services, expressed by ontologies describing services, their qualities, and the context of use, to help the designer in expressing service requirements in terms of design artifacts.

Chapter 3, "*A Metamorphic Testing Methodology for Online SOA Application Testing*," by W. K. Chan, S. C. Cheung, and Karl R. P. H. Leung studies an approach to online testing. Service testing is divided into two steps. In the spirit of metamorphic testing, the offline step determines a set of successful test cases to construct their corresponding follow-up test cases for the online step. These test cases will be executed by metamorphic services that encapsulate the services as well as applicable metamorphic relations. Thus, any failure revealed by the approach will be a failure of the service under test.

Chapter 4, "*Integrated Design of eBanking Architecture*," by Tony C. Shan and Winnie W. Hua describes a service-oriented framework for integrated design of eBanking architecture (IDEA) in the financial services industry.

Chapter 5, "*A Similarity Measure for Process Mining in Service Oriented Architecture*," by Joonsoo Bae, Ling Liu, James Caverlee, Liang-Jie Zhang, and Hyerim Bae presents a quantitative approach to modeling and capturing the similarity and dissimilarity between different process designs. The authors derive the similarity measures by analyzing the process dependency graphs of the participating workflow processes. They first convert each process dependency graph into a normalized process matrix. Then they calculate the metric space distance between the normalized matrices. This distance measure can be used as a quantitative and qualitative tool in process mining, process merging, and process clustering, and ultimately it can reduce or minimize the costs involved in design, analysis, and evolution of workflow systems.

Chapter 6, "*Rapid Development of Adaptable Situation-Aware Service-Based Systems*," by S. S. Yau, S. Mukhopadhyay, H. Davulcu, D. Huang, R. Bharadwaj, and K. Shenai presents an approach to rapid development of adaptable situation-aware service-based systems. This approach is based on the α-logic and α-calculus, and a declarative model for situation awareness (SAW). This approach consists of four major components: (1) analyzing SAW requirements using the authors' declarative model for SAW, (2) translating the model representation to α-logic specifications and specifying a control flow graph in α-logic as the goal for situation-aware service composition., (3) automated synthesis of α-calculus terms that define situation-aware workflow agents for situation-aware service composition, and (4) compilation of α-calculus terms to executable components on an agent platform. An example of applying a framework in developing a distributed control system for intelligently and reliably managing a power grid is given.

Chapter 7, "*Object-Oriented Architecture for Web Services Eventing,*" by Krzysztof Ostrowski, Ken Birman, and Danny Dolev proposes an architecture based on object-oriented design principles that is free of such limitations, extremely modular and extensible, and that can serve as a basis for extending and complementing the existing standards. The new approach emerges from the authors' work on Live Distributed Objects, a new programming model that brings object-orientation into the realm of distributed computing.

Chapter 8, "*Composing and Coordinating Transactional Web Services,*" by Frederic Montagut, Refik Molva, and Silvan Tecumseh Golega proposes a new process to automate the design of transactional composite Web services. This solution for Web services composition does not take into account functional requirements only but also transactional ones based on the Acceptable Termination States model. The resulting composite Web service is compliant with the consistency requirements expressed by business application designers and its execution can easily be coordinated using the coordination rules provided as an outcome of the authors' approach. An implementation of these theoretical results augmenting an OWL-S matchmaker is further detailed as a proof of concept.

Chapter 9, "*Security Personalization for Internet and Web Services,*" by George O.M. Yee and Larry Korba derives the content of an Internet or Web service security policy and proposes a flexible security personalization approach that will allow an Internet or Web service provider and customer to negotiate to an agreed-upon personalized security policy. In addition, this chapter presents two application examples of security policy personalization, and an overview of the design of the authors' security personalization prototype.

Chapter 10, "*XML Security with Binary XML for Mobile Web Services,*" by Jaakko Kangasharju, Tancred Lindholm, and Sasu Tarkoma considers ways to integrate an alternate format with security, and presents a solution that the authors see as a viable alternative. In addition to this, the chapter presents extensive performance measurements, including ones on a mobile phone on the effect of an alternate format when using XML-based security. These measurements indicate that, in the wireless world, reducing message sizes is the most pressing concern, and that processing efficiency gains of an alternate format are a much smaller concern. The authors also make specific recommendations on security usage based on their measurements.

Chapter 11, "*Efficient and Effective XML Encoding,*" by Christian Werner, Carsten Buschmann, Ylva Brandt, and Stefan Fischer discusses the most relevant state-of-the-art technologies for compressing XML data. Furthermore, it presents a novel solution for compacting SOAP messages. In order to achieve significantly better compression rates than current approaches, the compressor described in this chapter utilizes structure information from an XML Schema or WSDL document. With this additional knowledge on the "grammar" of the exchanged messages, this compressor generates a single custom pushdown automaton, which can be used as a highly efficient validating parser as well as a highly effective compressor. The main idea is to tag the transitions of the automaton with short binary identifiers that are then used to encode the path through the automaton during parsing. The authors' approach leads to extremely compact data representations and is also usable in environments with very limited CPU and memory resources.

Chapter 12, "*Data Mining in Web Services Discovery and Monitoring*," by Richi Nayak recommends several data mining applications that can leverage problems concerned with the discovery and monitoring of Web services. This chapter then presents a case study on applying the clustering data mining technique to the Web service usage data to improve the Web service discovery process. This chapter also discusses the challenges that arise when applying data mining to Web services usage data and abstract information.

Chapter 13, "*A Reengineering Approach for Ensuring Transactional Reliability of Composite Services*," by Sami Bhiri, Walid Gaaloul, and Claude Godart presents a reengineering approach to ensure transactional reliability of composite services. Contrary to previous approaches which check correctness properties based on the composition model, the authors start from executions' log to improve services' recovery mechanisms. Basically, the chapter proposes a set of mining techniques to discover the transactional behavior from an event based log. Then, based on this mining step, the authors use a set of rules in order to improve services' reliability.

Chapter 14, "*Karma2: Provenance Management for Data-Driven Workflows*," by Yogesh L. Simmhan, Beth Plale, and Dennis Gannon discusses the growing need for data-driven e-Science applications that are under the control of workflows composed of services on the Grid. The focus of this work is on provenance collection for these workflows that are necessary to validate the workflow and to determine quality of generated data products. The challenge the authors address is to record uniform and usable provenance metadata that meets the domain needs while minimizing the modification burden on the service authors and the performance overhead on the workflow engine and the services. The framework is based on generating discrete provenance activities during the lifecycle of a workflow execution that can be aggregated to form complex data and process provenance graphs that can span across workflows. The implementation uses a loosely coupled publish-subscribe architecture for propagating these activities, and the capabilities of the system satisfy the needs of detailed provenance collection. A performance evaluation of a prototype finds a minimal performance overhead (in the range of 1% for an eight-service workflow using 271 data products).

Chapter 15, "*Result Refinement in Web Services Retrieval Based on Multiple Instances Learning*," by Yanzhen Zou, Lu Zhang, Yan Li, Bing Xie, and Hong Mei presents a new approach to improve this kind of category-based Web Services retrieval process which can refine the coarse matching results step by step. The refinement is based on the idea that operation specification is very important to service reuse. Therefore, a Web Service is thus investigated via multiple instances view in this approach, which indicates that a service is labeled as positive if and only if at least one operation provided by this service is usable to the user. Otherwise, it is labeled as negative. Experimental results demonstrate that this approach can increase the retrieval precision to a certain extent after one or two rounds of refinement.

Chapter 16, "*A Model-Driven Development Framework for Non-Functional Aspects in Service Oriented Architecture*," by Hiroshi Wada, Junichi Suzuki, and Katsuya Oba proposes a model-driven development (MDD) framework for non-functional aspects in SOA. The proposed MDD framework consists of (1) a Unified Modeling Language (UML) profile to graphically model non-functional aspects in SOA, and (2) an MDD tool that accepts a UML model defined with the proposed profile and transforms it to application code. This chapter also demonstrates how the proposed framework is used in model-driven development of service-oriented applications. Empirical evaluation results show that the proposed MDD framework improves the reusability and maintainability of service-oriented applications by hiding low-level implementation technologies in UML models.

Chapter 17, "*Interoperability Among Heterogeneous Services: The Case of Integration of P2P Services with Web Services*," by Aphrodite Tsalgatidou, George Athanasopoulos, and Michael Pantazoglou addresses the interoperability problem by first presenting its multiple dimensions and then by describing a conceptual model called Generic Service Model (GeSMO), which can be used as a basis for the development of languages, tools and mechanisms that support interoperability. The authors illustrate how GeSMO has been utilized for the provision of a Peer-to-Peer (P2P) service description language and a P2P invocation mechanism which leverages interoperability between heterogeneous P2P services and between P2P services and Web services.

Chapter 18, "*Service-Oriented Architecture for Migrating Legacy Home Appliances to Home Network System: Principle and Applications*," by Masahide Nakamura, Hiroshi Igaki, Akihiro Tanaka, Haruaki Tamada, and Ken-ichi Matsumoto presents a practical framework that adapts the conventional home electric appliances with the infrared remote controls (legacy appliances) to the emerging home network system (HNS). The proposed method extensively uses the concept of service-oriented architecture to improve programmatic interoperability among multi-vendor appliances. The authors first prepare APIs that assist a PC to send infrared signals to the appliances. Then the APIs are aggregated within self-contained service components, so that each of the components achieves a logical feature independent of device/vendor-specific operations. The service components are finally exhibited to the HNS as Web services. As a result, the legacy appliances can be used as distributed components with open interfaces. To demonstrate the effectiveness, the authors implement an actual HNS and integrated services with multi-vendor legacy appliances. The authors also show practical applications implemented on the developed HNS.

Chapter 19, "*Broadening JAIN-SLEE with a Service Description Language and Asynchronous Web Services*," by Paolo Falcarin, Claudio Venezia, and José Felipe Mejia Bernal describes the StarSLEE platform which extends JAIN-SLEE in order to compose JAIN-SLEE services with Web services and the StarSCE service creation environment which allows exporting value added services as communication Web services. It analyzes open issues that must be addressed to introduce Web Services in new telecom service platforms.

Chapter 20, "*Workflow Discovery: Requirements from E-Science and a Graph-Based Solution*," by Antoon Goderis, Peter Li, and Carole Goble presents the case for workflows and workflow discovery in science and develop one discovery solution. Through a survey with 21 scientists and developers from the myGrid/Taverna workflow environment, workflow discovery requirements are elicited. Through a user experiment with 13 scientists, an attempt is made to build a benchmark for workflow ranking. Through the design and implementation of a workflow discovery tool, a mechanism for ranking workflow fragments is provided based on graph sub-isomorphism detection. The tool evaluation, drawing on a corpus of 89 public workflows and the results of the user experiment, finds that, for a simple showcase, the average human ranking can largely be reproduced.

Chapter 21, "*An Access Control Framework for WS-BPEL Processes*," by Federica Paci, Elisa Bertino, and Jason Crampton intoduces a new type of WS-BPEL activity to model human activities and by developing RBAC-WS-BPEL, a role based access control model for WS-BPEL and BPCL, a language to specify authorization constraints.

Chapter 22, "*Business Process Control-Flow Complexity: Metric, Evaluation, and Validation*", by Jorge Cardoso focuses on investigating process complexity. A metric to analyze the control-flow complexity of business processes is presented and described. The metric is evaluated in terms of Weyuker's properties in order to guarantee that it qualifies as good and comprehensive. To test the validity of the metric, this chapter describes the experiment that was carried out for empirically validating the metric.

Chapter 23, "*Pattern-Based Translation of BPMN Process Models to BPEL Web Services*," by Chun Ouyang, Marlon Dumas, Arthur H.M. ter Hofstede, and Wil M.P. van der Aalst advances the state of the art in BPMN-to-BPEL translation by defining methods for identifying not only perfectly block-structured fragments in BPMN models, but quasi-structured fragments that can be turned into perfectly structured ones and flow-based acyclic fragments that can be mapped onto a combination of structured constructs and control links. Beyond its direct relevance in the context of BPMN and BPEL, this chapter addresses issues that arise generally when translating between graph-oriented and block-structured flow definition languages.

Chapter 24, "*DsCWeaver: Synchronization-Constraint Aspect Extension to Procedural Process Specification Languages*," by Qinyi Wu, Calton Pu, Akhil Sahai, and Roger Barga presents DSCWeaver, a tool that enables a synchronization-aspect extension to procedural languages. It uses DSCL (directed-acyclic-graph synchronization constraint language) to achieve three desirable properties for synchronization modeling: fine granularity, declarative syntax, and validation support. DSCWeaver then automatically generates executable code for synchronization. The authors demonstrate the advantages of their approach in a service deployment process written in BPEL and evaluate its performance using two metrics: lines of code (LoC) and places to visit (PtV). Evaluation results show that this approach can effectively reduce the development effort of process programmers while providing performance competitive to unwoven BPEL code.

Chapter 25, "*A Reservation-Based Extended Transaction Protocol for Coordination of Web Services within Business Activities*," by Wenbing Zhao, Firat Kart, L. E. Moser, and P. M. Melliar-Smith describes a novel reservation-based extended transaction protocol for coordination of tasks within a business activity. With the advance of Web Services, the authors anticipate that business activities will be implemented as Web Services and that the automation of business activities across multiple enterprises over the Internet will become a reality. Classical extended transaction protocols are not well suited for this new breed of business activity, because of their use of compensation transactions. The authors' reservation-based extended transaction protocol employs an explicit reservation phase and an explicit confirmation/cancellation phase to eliminate the need for compensation transactions. The authors show how their Reservation Protocol maps to the Web Services Coordination specification and describe their implementation of the Reservation Protocol.

Web Services Research for Emerging Applications: Discoveries and Trends aims to provide contemporary coverage of Web services with a focus on how these systems help to define the future of computing and communication. Through investigations of different applications, processes, and protocols, this collection aims to inform researchers of new and emerging trends in the development and research of Web services.

Chapter 1
SOA Reference Architecture

Liang-Jie Zhang
IBM T.J. Watson Research, USA

Jia Zhang
Northern Illinois University, USA

ABSTRACT

SOA Reference Architecture (SOA-RA) aims to provide a normative guidance for software engineers to design and develop enterprise-level Service Oriented Architecture (SOA)-based solutions. Its basis is SOA Solution Stack (S3) that defines a conceptual view of a service-oriented architecture in the context of solution design and delivery. S3 is then extended by introducing conceptual architectural building blocks (ABBs) that serve as design templates to make S3-based solutions more configurable, reusable, and goal-aligned. On top of an extendable metamodel, SOA-RA decomposes an SOA solution view into an enterprise view, an IT system view, and a services view. These view models allows software designers to establish a comprehensive overview of an expected SOA solution. This chapter first analyzes the architectural style and metamodel of S3, then describes the various view models, and then describes an end-to-end SOA solution design and modeling framework and methodology.

INTRODUCTION

"What is SOA?" To a software architect, a Service Oriented Architecture (SOA) refers to an architectural style comprising a set of highly reusable components equipped with standard interfaces, connectors, constraints, composition criteria, and containers. In other words, in an SOA-based software system, comprising components are services.

Each service implies a service provider and some service consumers. SOA decouples the service provider and service consumers using a service description that covers both the interfaces (e.g., what the service can do and how to access the service) and policies (e.g., requirements and constraints) needed to describe an abstract specification of

DOI: 10.4018/978-1-61520-684-1.ch001

both functional and non-functional attributes of the service. Some of the specifications may be executable.

To provide normative guidance for software engineers to design and develop enterprise-level SOA-based solutions in a systematic manner, SOA Reference Architecture (SOA-RA) establishes a logical reference architecture that helps IT architects design the overall architecture of an SOA solution.

The foundation of SOA-RA is IBM SOA Solution Stack (S3) (Arsanjani, A., Zhang, L.-J., Ellis, M., Allam, A., & Channabasavaiah, K., 2007) that defines a conceptual view of a service-oriented architecture in the context of solution design and delivery. Nine layers are identified organizing into a two-dimensional architecture with five horizontal layers and four vertical layers. The horizontal dimension (Operational System layer, Services Component layer, Service layer, Business Process layer, and Service Consumer layer) implements functional requirements, and the vertical dimension (Integration layer, Data Architecture layer, Quality of Service (QoS) layer, and Governance layer) provides system-support facilities and enablement.

S3 provides an enterprise architectural template that guides the creation of an SOA solution at the enterprise level. Starting from the reference model, software engineers can customize and refine it, based on the needs of a service domain, to develop application-specific SOA solutions for one or more lines of business. For example, an Enterprise Service Bus (ESB) can be adopted to realize the Integration layer of the reference model to develop an ESB-based SOA solution. In other words, S3 allows us to develop and deliver SOA business services faster and easier.

S3 is also an answer to the question "If I build an SOA, what would it look like conceptually and what abstraction would be present?" It enumerates the fundamental elements of an SOA solution. Moreover, it presents the architectural foundation of an SOA solution, from which various perspectives can be derived: tooling, standards, industry specification, and so on.

However, S3 alone is coarse grained to be advisory for enterprise-level SOA solution design and development. It provides high-level guidance for developers to design an SOA solution (i.e., in nine layers) without detailed normative guidance. To provide a uniform mechanism for building configurable and reusable SOA solutions on top of S3, this chapter discusses S3-based SOA reference architecture, including S3 metamodel, enterprise view, and end-to-end SOA solution modeling. Instead of focusing on any detailed SOA method, this chapter focuses on how to design activities, roles, and work products that are critical to build an SOA-based solution.

Especially, we introduce a concept of Architectural Building Block (ABB) as the fundamental unit of an SOA solution (Zhang, L.-J., Zhang, J., & Allam, A., 2008). An ABB is an autonomous component that encapsulates internal states and functions and can be configured and extended. Each layer in S3 is comprised of multiple ABBs, which collaborate to carry all expected activities. Based on industry best practice, our previous work concluded a comprehensive collection of fine-grained ABB templates for each of the nine layers in S3, which will be discussed in detail in the following chapters.

In this chapter, we first analyze the architectural style and metamodel of S3, then we describe various view models comprised in SOA-RA. Finally, we describe an end-to-end SOA solution design and modeling framework and methodology.

S3: ARCHITECTURAL STYLE OF AN SOA

S3: A Solution View

SOA Solution Stack (S3) (Arsanjani, A., Zhang, L.-J., Ellis, M., Allam, A., & Channabasavaiah, K., 2007) includes. It provides a high-level abstraction of an SOA factored into layers, each addressing specific value propositions within SOA.

As a matter of fact, S3 is a "partially-layered" architecture, meaning that a layer in S3 is not strictly hidden from the layers above it. For example, a consumer may choose to access a service through either the business process layer or the service layer. A service may also choose to leverage two styles of service implementation: namely, service components like EJBs or .NET components or packaged applications such as SAP, or Siebel, or other SOA-enabled legacy applications.

Our logical view of an SOA comprises a set of layers, ABBs (Architectural Building Blocks), architectural and design decisions, and so on. This helps in the understanding and implementation of separation of concerns and assists in the process of creating an SOA solution. The S3 defines a blueprint that can be used to define the layers, ABBs within the layers, options available at each layer, and typical architectural decisions that need to be made (see meta model in Figure 2).

Note that there may be various ways to realize SOA (Arsanjani, A., 2005), in addition to S3. Some examples are: business process (business services)-driven approach, tool-based model-driven approach, message-based application integration through SOI (integration services), data access-based (information services) approach, legacy encapsulation and wrapping, and legacy componentization and transformation. Comparing to other approaches, SOA-RA leads to an architecture-driven SOA solution design and development methodology at enterprise level.

Figure 1 shows an abstraction of how to construct an SOA as a set of logical layers. Note that this representation is not designed to imply a strictly layered architectural style in which one layer solely depends upon the layer below it. Rather, an S3 is a *partially* layered architecture in which a company has a set of layers that are more service consumer-oriented (consumer layer, business process layer, and service layer) and a set of layers that are more service provider-oriented

Figure 1. Layers of the SOA solution stack reference architecture

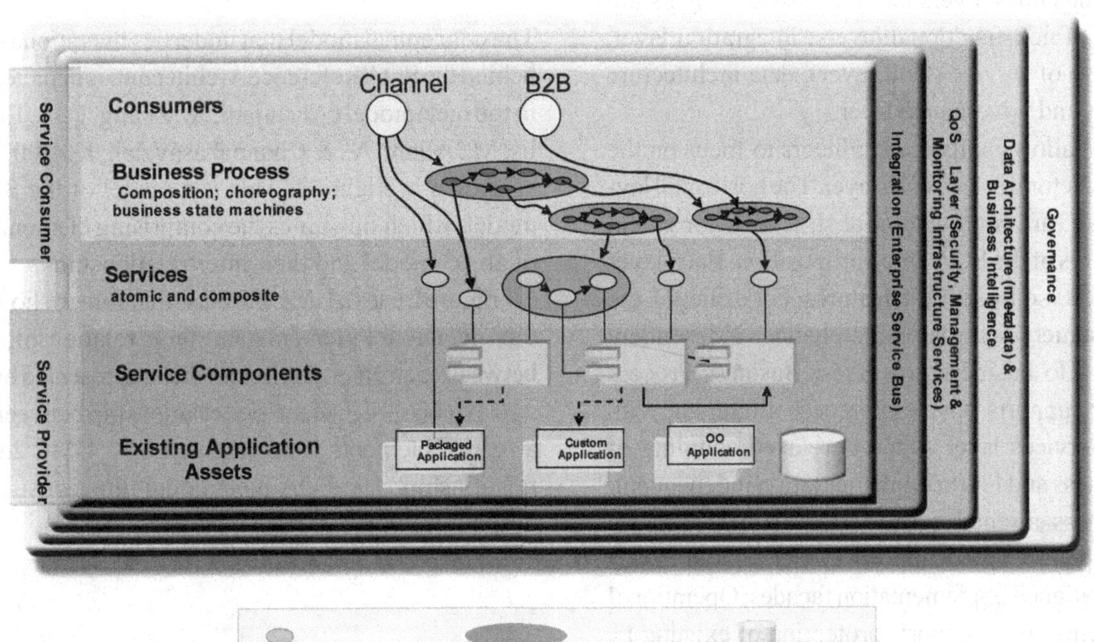

Figure 2. Metamodel for the SOA reference architecture

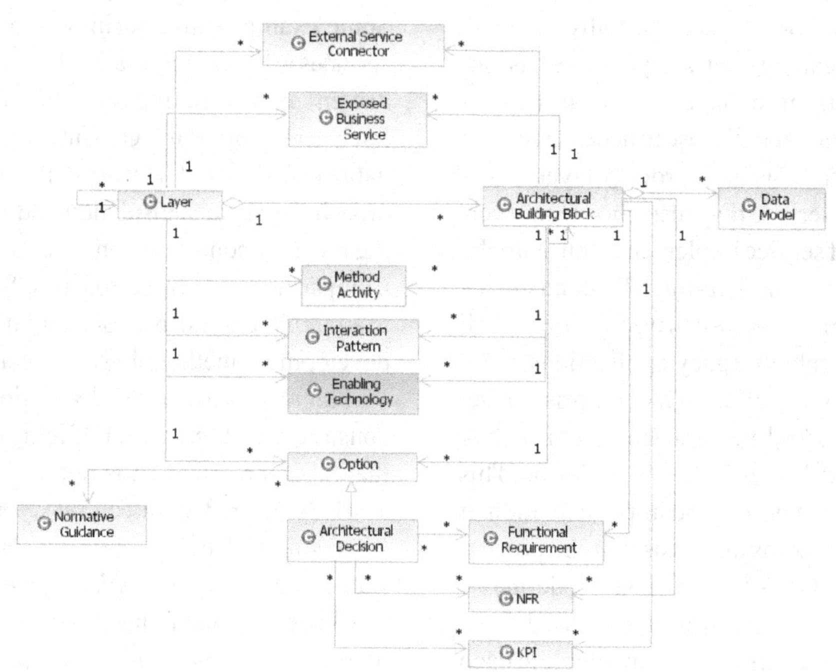

(service layer, service component layer, and Existing Application Asset layer). Cutting across both the consumer layers and the provider layers are a set of non-functional layers: integration layer, quality of service (QoS layer), data architecture layer, and governance layer.

S3 allows software engineers to focus on the architectural role of each layer. The horizontal layers in S3 are 'architectural abstractions' for salient features of the SOA value proposition. Each layer supports some specific features. For example, the Consumers layer supports channel-independent access to business processes; Business Process layer supports business process alignment with IT; Services layer supports relaxed coupling of business and IT via implementation independent, business aligned service abstractions; Service Component layer supports IT flexibility via service-aligned implementation façades; Operational Systems layer supports protection of existing IT investment.

The SOA Reference Architecture Metamodel

The conceptual model that underlies the rationale behind the SOA Reference Architecture is depicted in the metamodel (Arsanjani, A., Zhang, L.-J., Ellis, M., Allam, A., & Channabasavaiah, K., 2007) as shown in Figure 2. This is a model of the S3 model, which illustrates the comprising elements of an S3 model and their inter-relationships.

Figure 2 uses a UML 2.0 class diagram to show the metamodel elements and their relationships between each other. Each element is represented by a UML class; each identified relationship between a pair of elements is represented by a UML 2.0 relationship. The SOA metamodel thus consists of the following fourteen elements:

Layers

It is an abstraction of the nine layers of S3, which contains a set of components such as ABBs, architectural decisions, interactions among ABBs and interactions among layers.

The reason why layers are important is that the separation of concerns groups the responsibilities, interaction patterns and options at each layer, in terms of software platforms to be used, protocols, design and architectural patterns and other design principles and guidelines.

Options

It is a collection of high-level solution-level patterns that impact other artifacts. For example, options may guide to choose appropriate architectural decisions and interaction patterns. There are options in each layer, as to what the ABBs are, what their instantiations are in terms of software and platforms, what best practices are in terms of their interaction patterns.

Note that we use *options* to represent high-level design decisions, for example, how many layers should be used for a given SOA solution, which question can neither be answered and covered by architectural decisions that focus on ABB identification and selection, nor be covered by interaction patterns that focus on interactions among ABBs.

In summary, options focus on solution-level patterns or principles that an SOA solution architect should consider and make decisions up-front. Key options include deciding which SOA methodology to use, for example, starting from legacy transformation from bottom-up, starting from business process re-engineering, starting from message-driven (B2B) methodology (using a dedicated integration layer with message routing), starting from top-down business process decomposition, starting from user-centric solution design (define channels to be used), or starting from open composition approach (starting with the Service layer to identify services to be used first).

Note that options are different from architectural decisions, and governance. The former is oriented to low-level decisions, while the latter is oriented to specific scenarios (e.g., industry-specific scenarios require specific governance as normative guidance). In contrast with architectural decisions and governance, options represent high-level decision making points. In other words, options can be viewed as generalization (i.e., super class) of architectural decisions and governance.

In addition, options have many perspectives, which also include selection of enabling technology that decides which products and technologies to be used to realize an SOA solution. The latter selection is also knows as product and technology mapping.

Architectural Decisions

It is one type of options specific for architectural designs of an SOA solution. The architectural decision involves ABBs, functional requirements, Key Performance Indicators (KPIs) and Non-Functional Requirements (NFRs) to provide information on configuration and usage of ABBs. Existing architectural decisions may also be reusable by other layers or ABBs. As discussed earlier, comparing to options that consider high-level decisions, architectural decisions consider low-level decisions specific to architectural designs, for example, how to choose each ABB. Architectural decisions have to be made as to which one we will adopt for a given set of circumstances. This context and the forces that reside in the problem space shape a pattern that defines the architectural decisions typically encountered in a layer, across layers and across ABBs.

Note: As a starting point, in S3 Version 2.0, we will provide architectural design decision points and recommended options and solutions for the Consumer layer. Once the S3 model is used in practice, we will keep on adding more architectural design decision sections for each layer in the S3 model.

Normative Guidance

It is one type of options specific for scenario-specific normative guidance. In general, normative guidance may cover several layers of meanings: ABB-level guidance, layer-level guidance, and high-level guidance. ABB-level guidance refers to low-level guidance at ABB levels, such as how to implement an ABB. Layer-level guidance refers to guidance at S3 layer levels,such as how to integrate several layers into an SOA solution. High-level guidance refers to solution-level guidance such as how to linkage business service architecture and IT service architecture to into a specific SOA solution.

In general, we provide normative guidance in two levels, one as generic normative guidance that serves as high-level over all guidance to an entire SOA solution development; the other one as layer-specific normative guidance that serves as specific guidance for a specific layer in the S3 model.

It should be noted that it is not required that every layer in the S3 model has normative guidance. For some layers, we do provide layer-level normative guidance. Once the S3 model is used in practice, gradually we will keep on adding more normative guidance associated with the corresponding architectural design decisions into the "normative guidance" section of each layer.

Method Activities

It is a collection of steps that involve one or multiple ABBs to form a process in a layer.

Architectural Building Blocks

To provide a uniform mechanism for building configurable and reusable SOA solutions on top of S3, we introduced a concept of Architectural Building Block (ABB) as the fundamental unit of an SOA solution (Zhang, L.-J., Zhang, J., & Allam, A., 2008). An ABB is an autonomous component that encapsulates internal states and functions and can be configured and extended. Each layer in S3 is comprised of multiple ABBs, which collaborate to carry all expected activities. Based on industry best practice, our previous work concluded a comprehensive collection of fine-grained ABB templates for each of the nine layers in S3, which will be discussed in detail in the following chapters.

A set of ABBs reside in a layer that contains attributes, dependencies and constraints as well as relationships with other ABBs in the same layer or different layers. These components of each layer are the constituent elements of that layer that provide the essential functionality and deliver the responsibility assigned to that layer. They depict the "types" of things that can reside in that specific layer.

The introduction of conceptual ABBs make S3-based solutions be more configurable, reusable, and goal-aligned. Considering the adaptive feature of business scenarios, each project may have to configure and customize the layered ABB template library to apt to proprietary requirements and constraints. In addition, the ABB templates imply certain relationships between some ABBs.

Interaction Patterns

It is an abstraction of the various relationships among ABBs (patterns and diagrams) within and across layers.

Key Performance Indicators

It is a set of key performance indicators (KPIs) constraints that involve in ABBs and put concerns on making architectural decisions.

Non-Functional Requirement Constraints

It is a set of non-functional requirement constraints (NFRs) that involve in ABBs and put concerns on making architectural decisions.

Enabling Technology

It is a technical realization of ABBs in a specific layer by selecting which technology, e.g., whether an IBM technology or an Independent Software Vendor (ISV) technology, should be selected to fulfill the enablement. It shouls be noted that unlike other components included in the meta-model as logical concepts, enabling technology indicates actual physical realization of a speicific SOA solution.

Exposed Business Services

Exposed business services (a.k.a. externalized business solution elements) refer to entities that expose business processes or composite business applications as business services that can be reused as service assets. This construct enables a new way to quickly compose existing service assets using business processes and expose the composed business processes as new business services for future reuse.

External Service Connectors

External service connectors refer to adaptors (e.g., transformers) for exploiting external services for business connections and business integrations. Business services developed by different business entities may use different technologies so that there might exist inconsistency between them, including interface inconsistency such as parameter inconsistency and method name inconsistency. In order to link together these individually developed business services, adaptation is necessary and required. These adaptors are meant for enable business service interoperability between different business entities. Of course, adaptors are typically designed for selected solution scenarios.

Data Models

It models data contents associated with ABBs including data exchange between layers and external services.

Functional Requirements

It models the functional requirements that one layer or ABB must fulfill.

In this chapter and following chapters (2-5), we will use the above elements of the metamodel to describe the characteristics of the SOA Reference Model, the layers and the building blocks and architectural decisions about each layer.

SOA-RA VIEW MODELS

Based on S3, SOA Reference Architecture (SOA-RA) represents a logical reference architecture describing a generic architectural model for an enterprise-level SOA solution. It provides a guidance for IT architects to design the overall architecture of an SOA solution The logical view of an SOA-RA depicts an SOA solution as a combination of a set of layers, Architectural Building Blocks (ABBs) within each layer, options and recommendations for architectural and design decisions, use case model, component model, operational model, user profiles, non-functional requirements, and system context.

SOA-RA decomposes the solution view of S3 into three view models for IT architects to communicate a simple, brief, clear, and understandable overview of the target SOA solution. Three types of view models are produced at three levels: enterprise level, IT system level, and services level.

An enterprise-level view model describes the vision of the business, the IT capabilities required by the organization, and defines the key characteristics and requirements. An IT system-level view model describes the layered architectural model of SOA-RA from the IT perspective. It can be used as a very high-level architectural blueprint at very early stage in an SOA project, possibly as a pre-proposal. Such a model can guide the configuration of the initial component model and operational model. A services-level view model describes how SOA-RA can be used to enable and deliver services as software, as well as software as services.

The major purposes of the three view models are: to communicate a conceptual understanding of the target IT system, to provide a high-level shared vision of the architecture and scope of the proposed IT system, to explore and evaluate alternative architectural options, to enable early recognition and validation of the implications of the architectural approach, to facilitate effective communication between different communities of stakeholders and developers, and to vacilitate orientation for new people who join the project.

Enterprise View Model

As shown in Figure 3, the enterprise view model depicts the high-level business layer and components of an SOA solution within the business contexts. This view is mainly for high-level business people, such as C-level people. Key enterprise-level architectural concepts are discussed as follows.

Presentation

A presentation element of an SOA solution provides the link between solution users and the

Figure 3. Enterprise view model

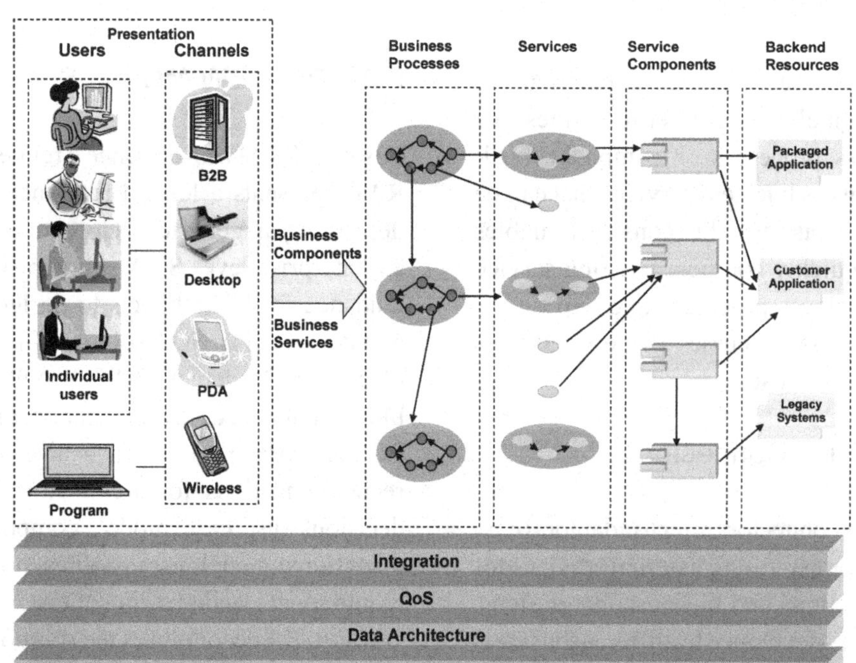

solution system. In more detail, it allows users to access the system functions through various channels. In other words, the presentation element includes two major parts: users and channels.

As shown in Figure 3, users of an SOA solution include both individual users (e.g., users, administrators, and enterprise representatives) and programs for Business-to-Business (B2B, a.k.a., machine-to-machine) interactions. In other words, an SOA solution typically supports two types of users, individual users who access the solution manually or machine programs that access the solution through an automatic manner.

As shown in Figure 3, an SOA solution typically supports a variety of communication channels, including: (1) personal computer (desktop or laptop) equipped with an Internet browser over the Internet, (2) Personal Digital Assistant (PDA), (3) wireless cell phones, and (4) servers for B2B communications. Other channels may be added if necessary.

BUSINESS PROCESS

A business process element refers to workflows representing an enterprise-specific business-related procedure. As shown in Figure 3, a business service can contain multiple business processes. Similar to business services, business processes are technology-independent. As shown in Figure 3, existing business components and business services can be optional input. As shown in Figure 3, a business process may dependent on other business processes and services.

Service

A service element refers to reusable Web services that can be configured to construct business processes. These Web services have published interfaces in *ad hoc* standard languages (e.g., WSDL) and can be universally accessed through the Internet. Web services are hosted by their corresponding service providers. Comparing with business services and business processes, Web services are technology-dependent services and aim for generic usages. As shown in Figure 3, a business process can contain multiple Web services.

As shown in Figure 3, a service can be either an individual service or a composite service. An individual service refers to an atomic service that does not dependent on other services. A composite service refers to a service comprising multiple other services.

Service Component

A service component element refers to more low-level software components with clearly defined interfaces and can be used to build Web services. These service components can reside either in the Internet or Intranet. For example, a service component can be a wrapper over a legacy system. As shown in Figure 3, a Web service can contain multiple service components.

Backend Resource

A backend resource element refers to existing applications that can be used to build new business logic, including packaged applications, customer applications, and legacy systems. These backend resources can be wrapped into service components for higher-level constructions. Without the backed resources, new SOA solutions do not have to be built from scratch, saving significant man power and time to market. As shown in Figure 3, a service component can contain multiple backend resources.

Integration/QoS/Data Architecture/Governance

An integration element refers to the system facility that enables and formalizes component integration, routing, and interactions in a uniform manner. A

Quality of Service (QoS) element refers to the system facility that monitors, tracks, manages, and ensures solution-level quality of service requirements, including: reliability, availability, security, safety, maintainability, adaptability, and fault tolerance. A data architecture element refers to the system facility that enables solution-level smooth data structure and data interactions in a uniform manner. A governance element refers to the system facility that supervises and guides solution-level best practice and support.

IT System View Model

The IT system view model illustrates a high-level overview of the SOA-RA. As shown in Figure 4, from IT perspective, an SOA solution is divided into three tiers: front-end, middle-tire, and back-end. Firewalls are set up between the three tiers for security purposes. The presentation element serves as the front-end of the SOA solution; a firewall is set up between the front-end and the middle-tire; three elements (business processes, services, and service components) serve as the middle-tire of the SOA solution; another firewall is set up between the middle-tire and the backend; the backend resources serve as the backend of the solution. Meanwhile, as shown in Figure 4, the integration, the QoS, the data architecture, and the governance elements serve as the SOA-oriented platform to enable and facilitate SOA solutions on-top.

As shown in Figure 4, from system perspective, these elements are organized into logical software layers to enhance flexibility and extensibility of the system architecture. The detailed functionaliry of each layer can be found in S3 descriptions (Arsanjani, A., Zhang, L.-J., Ellis, M., Allam, A., & Channabasavaiah, K., 2007) .

Services View Model

The main goal of SOA-RA is to provide a proven re-usable framework to deliver SOA solutions. SOA-RA is designed in a way that each identified layer can be implemented and delivered as a

Figure 4. IT system view model

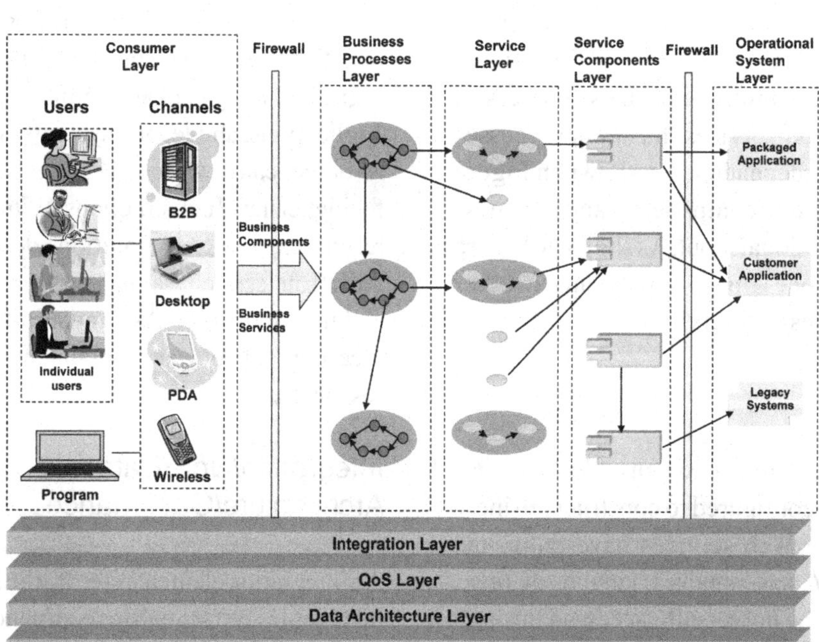

standalone SOA service, as well as being delivered as one of the layers in the final SOA solution, as shown in Figure 5. In other words, the entire SOA-RA framework can be delivered as an architectural model for an SOA solution, and each layer in the SOA-RA framework can be delivered as a layer-specific services. In yet another word, SOA-RA intends to deliver software as service, and deliver service as software.

SOA-RA delivers services into software. *Services as Software* refers to transforming the current consulting experiences into software products, which can be shared by others. We incorporate the SOA solution delivery experiences and knowledge of the professionals and experts into SOA-RA, and leverage the SOA-RA to help realize and manage a new SOA solution delivery. To certain degree, an SOA consulting process turns into a consulting service based upon SOA-RA. Furthermore, SOA-RA carries a library of software components encapsulating knowledge and expertise of business consultants. These software components (e.g., layers, ABBs, options, and architecture decision documents) can be reused and integrated together into new solutions. By rapidly constructing an SOA solution using the re-configurable and reusable SOA-RA elements, the consulting services can be greatly facilitated. In this way, we can transform the original labor-based SOA solution delivery into an asset-based service business.

SOA Services Enablement

SOA-RA delivers software into services. SOA-RA is designed in a way that each identified and implemented layer can be implemented and delivered as a standalone SOA service in addition to being one of the layers in the final SOA solution. In detail, SOA-RA intends to deliver a set of services: (1) presentation services, (2) SOA transformation services, (3) SOA design services, (4) SOA implementation services, (5) SOA integration services, (6) SOA management services, (7) SOA data transformation services, and (8) SOA governance services.

Figure 5. Services view model

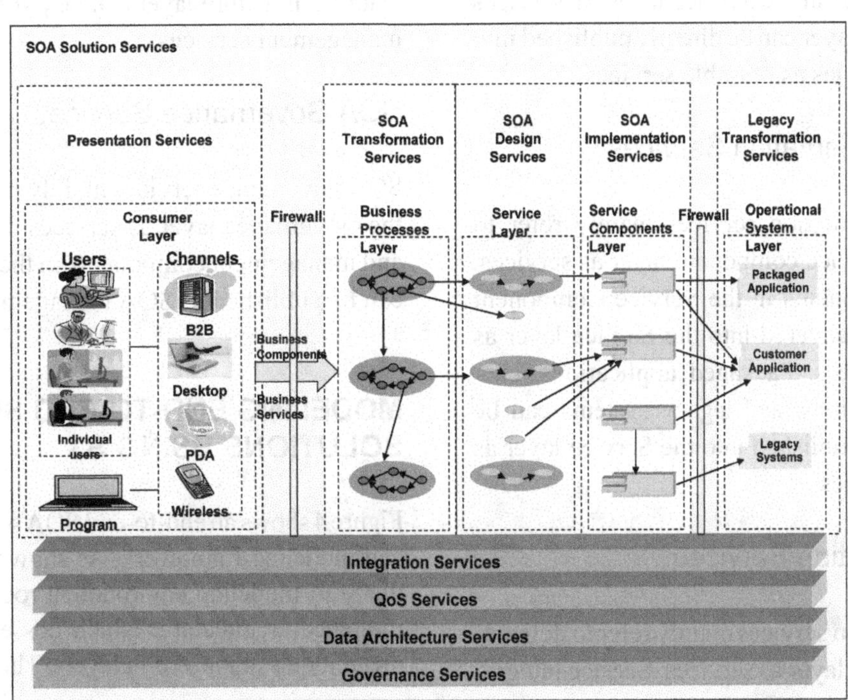

Presentation Services

Presentation services mainly refer to delivering the Consumer layer as services. Presentation management and navigation system in the Consumer layer can be delivered as front-end presentation delivery services. In more detail, such a presentation delivery service can be used to support the presentation of other applications to end users.

SOA Transformation Services

SOA transformation consulting services mainly refer to delivery business components as services.

SOA Design Services

SOA design services mainly refer to delivery business services, business processes, and IT services as services. Business services can be directly delivered to serve a specific business goal. Business processes in the Business Process layer can be delivered as reusable business services. In more detail, business processes formed in the Business Process layer can be published as a business service in the Service layer. IT services in the Service layer can be directly published into services registries as reusable services.

SOA Implementation Services

SOA implementation services mainly refer to deliver the service component layer as services. Service components in the Service Component layer can be delivered into the Service layer as business services. Packaged applications, customer applications, and legacy systems can be wrapped and published into the Service layer as business services.

SOA Integration Services

SOA integration services mainly refer to delivery the Integration layer as services. Service integration facility in the Integration layer can be published as integration services. In more detail, such an integration service provides access to other resources. It hides the complexities of integration from users of this service. Specially, such a service typically provides (1) brokering components providing routing, transformation, translation, and queuing facility, (2) coordinating components assembling required information from multiple resources, and (3) application adapters providing access to information to a specific resource or data source.

SOA Management Services

SOA management services mainly refer to delivery the QoS layer as services. QoS monitoring, tracking, and management facilities can be published as system-level QoS management services.

SOA Data Transformation Services

SOA data transformation services mainly refer to delivery the Data Architecture layer as services. Data handling and transformation facility in the Data Architecture layer can be published as data management services.

SOA Governance Services

SOA governance services mainly refer to deliver the Governance layer as services. Best practices and management components in the Governance can be published as SOA management services.

MODELING END-TO-END SOA SOLUTIONS USING S3

Figure 4 shows an end-to-end SOA solution design and modeling framework. As shown in Figure 6, the SOA modeling environment roots in an SOA reference architecture, which possesses a set of metamodels organized in layers. The metamodels

Figure 6. End-to-End SOA solution modeling

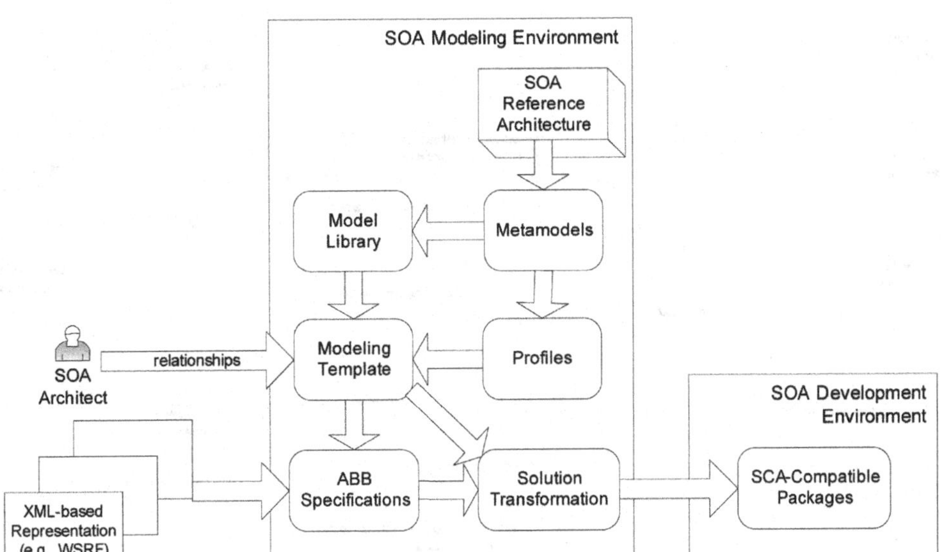

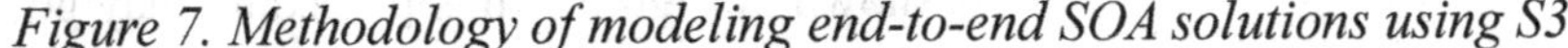

can generate model libraries that in turn generate modeling templates; the metamodels also generate profiles to guide and regulate user interactions with modeling templates.

In order to facilitate reusability and interoperability, an SOA solution comprising ABBs is represented in XML-based formats, for example, in WSRF to favor stateful ABBs. Since WSRF does not support relationships modeling between components, an SOA architect needs to interact with the SOA modeling environment to customize generated modeling template for the relationships between identified ABBs.

Customized SOA models comprising modeling templates and specifications are then executed

Figure 7. Methodology of modeling end-to-end SOA solutions using S3

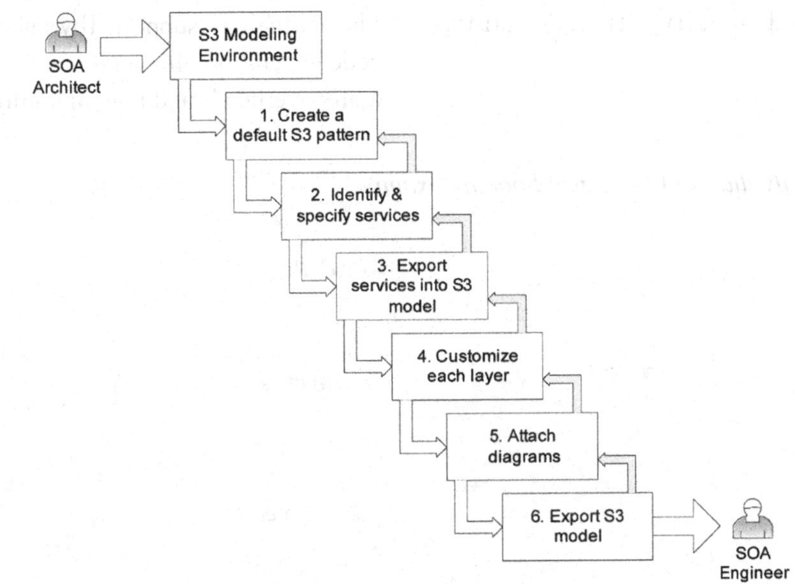

Figure 8. ABBs identified for the Business Process layer

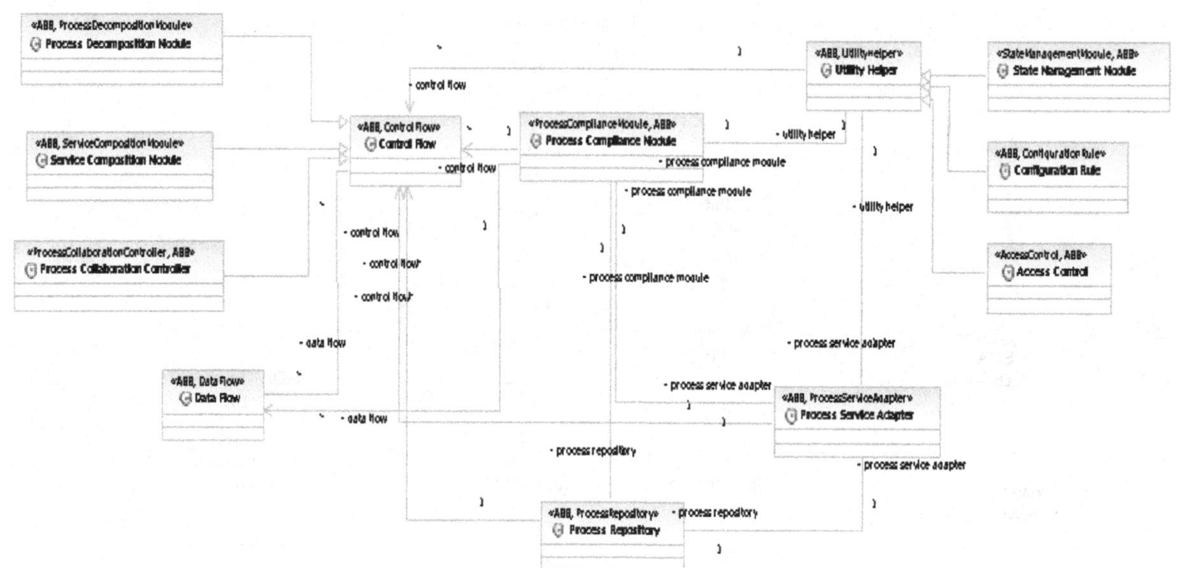

model-to-solution transformation. Resulting SCA-compatible code packages, which can be imported into SOA development platforms, such as IBM WebSphere Integration Developer (WID).

We can now summarize how to model an end-to-end SOA solution using the S3 model. Our methodology comprises a six-phase procedure, as shown in Figure 7:

1. Create a default S3 patterns;
2. Identify and specify services using techniques;
3. Export identified and specified services to the default S3 model;
4. Customize each layer;
5. Attach additional diagrams if necessary, and
6. Export customized S3 model into an SCA-compatible solution skeleton.

As shown in Figure 7, this procedure may go through many rounds of iterations between phases. Since each step is supported by automatic model and code generation, the iterations will not create too many overheads and potential information loss.

Figure 9. An activity diagram for travel booking example

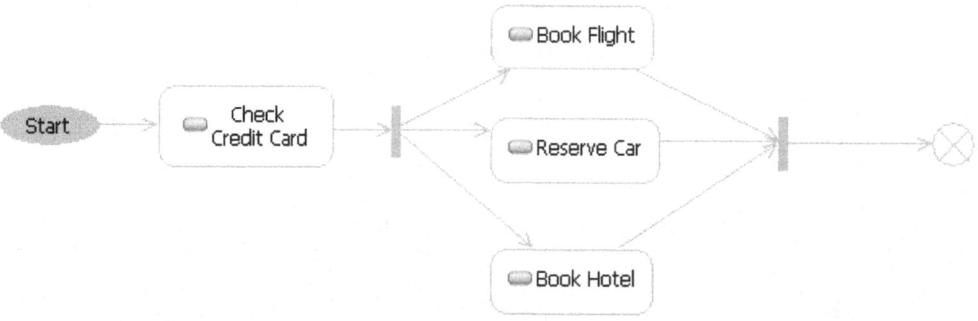

First, we create a UML project with a complete nine-layer S3 model comprising instances of all ABBs together with their relationships with each other. Second, we go through each layer and customize the default pattern using one of the aforementioned approaches, by either extending default ABBs with sub-ABBs or replacing default ABBs with customized ABBs. Third, we attach additional diagrams to some ABBs if it is necessary. In the Business Process layer, existing services are to be organized in a synergistic manner using business logic. The ABBs with their relationships of the Business Process layer is shown in Figure 8. An instance of the control flow ABB is responsible for carrying a specific business logic scenario, which can be used to guide process composition, decomposition, and collaboration.

Take the travel booking example again. The business logic to compose services in the example can be represented by a UML activity diagram as shown in Figure 9. It can be seen that the activity diagram illustrates the business logic described in Figure 9. A travel booking process starts from invoking the credit card checking sub-process. Then three sub-processes are invoked in parallel: flight reservation, car reservation, and hotel reservation. Afterwards all results are aggregated and finish the process.

It is natural to associate the activity diagram with the control flow ABB. This activity diagram can be used to generate process algorithms for later development, for example, a Business Process Execution Language (BPEL) file.

CONCLUSION

In this chapter, we provide an overview of the SOA reference architecure. We first give a brief overview of the S3 model, which defines a conceptual view of a service-oriented architecture in the context of solution design and delivery. We focus on the architectural style and metamodel of S3. The we provide a break-down view S3 solution model into an enterprise view model, an IT system view model, and a services view model. Finally, we describe an end-to-end SOA solution design and modeling framework and methodology.

REFERENCES

Arsanjani, A. (2005). Toward a Pattern Language for Service-Oriented Architecture and Integration. IBM developerWorks. Retrieved from http://www.ibm.com/developerworks/webservices/library/ws-soa-soi/

Arsanjani, A., Zhang, L.-J., Ellis, M., Allam, A., & Channabasavaiah, K. (2007). S3: A Service-Oriented Reference Architecture. *IT Professional*, *9*(3), 10–17. doi:10.1109/MITP.2007.53

Zhang, L.-J., Zhang, J., & Allam, A. (2008). A Method and Case Study of Designing Presentation Module in an SOA-based Solution Using Configurable Architectural Building Blocks (ABBs). In *Proceedings of the 2008 IEEE International Conference on Services Computing (SCC 2008)*, Jul. 8-11, 2008, Honolulu, HI, USA (pp. 459-467).

Chapter 2
WSMoD:
A Methodology for Qos-Based Web Services Design

M. Comerio
Università di Milano Bicocca, Milano, Italy

F. De Paoli
Università di Milano Bicocca, Milano, Italy

S. Grega
Università di Milano Bicocca, Milano, Italy

A. Maurino
Università di Milano Bicocca, Milano, Italy

C. Batini
Università di Milano Bicocca, Milano, Italy

ABSTRACT

Web services are increasingly used as an effective means to create and streamline processes and collaborations among governments, businesses, and citizens. As the number of available web services is steadily increasing, there is a growing interest in providing methodologies that address the design of web services according to specific qualities of service (QoS) rather than functional descriptions only. This chapter presents WSMoD (Web Services MOdeling Design), a methodology that explicitly addresses this issue. Furthermore, it exploits general knowledge available on services, expressed by ontologies describing services, their qualities, and the context of use, to help the designer in expressing service requirements in terms of design artifacts. Ontologies are used to acquire and specialize common knowledge among the entities involved in service design, and to check the consistency of the web service model with constraints defined by provider and customer requirements. To improve the effectiveness of the process, the authors propose a Platform Independent Model that includes the description of specific context of service provision, without considering implementation details. The discussion of a QoS-based web service design within a real case study bears evidence of the potentials of WSMoD.

DOI: 10.4018/978-1-61520-684-1.ch002

INTRODUCTION

Web services provide added value e-services over the Internet by overcoming the limitations of existing component models. Web services take advantages from the Universal Resource Identifier (URI) model to support open naming and addressing systems. They exploit XML features to supply rich descriptions of involved concepts, such as WSDL descriptions to service interfaces, UDDI to service lookup, SOAP to service interoperability, and Ws-BPEL to service orchestration.

Web services are the building blocks of the Service Oriented Architecture (SOA) a paradigm focused on the composition of loosely coupled systems. In this architecture, a service provider publishes its web services in a registry that can be searched by a consumer who can then access to a service, which has been found directly by means of XML-based messages. The increasing availability of web services offering similar functionalities (for example in bookselling or hotel reservation domains) creates new opportunities in discovery and selection activities. In fact, the selection of a web service can not only be related to what operations are offered, but also to how those operations are provided. Consequently, Quality of Services is becoming a crucial issue for the selection of web services that fulfill customer requests better.

In this novel scenario, business requirements support the discovery of web services and the development of new ones. In fact, web service design should start from business needs and business processes, instead of starting from application features as in traditional software design. Such business requirements should drive the identification of the needed features, potential suppliers, technological, organizational, and social constraints. Therefore, the development process requires a change in the overall approach.

In this paper we present WSMoD a Web Service Modeling Design methodology for quality of service (QoS)-based Web Services. The approach of the methodology consists in considering non-functional aspects derived from business requirements, as well as functional requirements, and incorporating and refining them throughout the design process. In this paper we use the term *functional*, to mean the operations that a service is expected to provide, and the term *non-functional* (or sometimes with the general term *quality*) to collect all the other characteristics associated with a service, related to QoS, user profiles, and delivery channels. The advantage of managing qualities, users and channels along the design process is twofold: achieving at the end of the process, a ready-to-implement specification, and reducing the risk of delivering unsatisfactory services. In fact, the knowledge of the technical, organizational and social characteristics of the environment in which the service will be deployed allows the designer to effectively evaluate and customize the design of the service.

WSMoD extends the Model Driven Architecture (MDA) proposed by (OMG, 2004), whose development process is divided into three steps: (i) first, a Platform Independent Model (PIM) is created, expressed in UML; this model describes business rules and functionalities of the application, and exhibits a high degree of platform independence; (ii) then, a Platform Specific Model (PSM) is produced, mapping the PIM into a specific platform; (iii) finally, the application is generated. The proposed extension is in two directions. The first one, according to the well-known software engineering principle "divide et impera", adds in the definition of the platform independent model a specific methodological step for the definition of the non-functional requirements. Users and channels, which support the interaction between web services and users, should be considered first-class concepts in the analysis and design of new services. The second extension concerns the platform independent model to represent quality aspects and the specific context related to user profile and channel constraints. This kind of context is still independent from a specific deployment platform, so that it can be adapted to different providers offering new web services. The goal of this extension of Platform Independent Model is to improve the design of software applications by avoiding modelling choices that are not deployable in real provisioning environments.

Ontologies have the role of providing a formal organization of knowledge that can be exploited to rationalize decision and evaluation processes. We use an ontology-based approach to understand, discover, classify and reason on qualities related to user constraints, user preferences, technological features (such as devices and networks), and domain peculiarities. Our final goal is to end up with a rich service description that includes service functionality and qualities, and a platform independent model of the service architecture that incorporates the quality constraints.

The WSMoD methodology has been developed within the MAIS project (Pernici, 2006), which is focused on the definition of models, tools and languages for Multichannel Adaptive Information Systems. WSMoD takes advantage of developed tools, in terms of models and techniques, in particular ontologies supporting the description of technological and user requirements and reflective architectures, which, on the base of the reflection principles (Capra, Emmerich et al., 2001) provides web services with context information on the actual channels and devices employed by the user. Even if the methodology has been conceived and tested in the context of MAIS. Its validity goes beyond MAIS since ontologies and reflective platforms are becoming popular in many research and industrial projects.

The paper is organized as follows. In the Related work Section we describe the state of the art of the ontology-based design of web services augmented with QoS. The next Section describes the ontologies we use in depth. Section WSMoD in a nutshell presents an overview of the WSMoD methodology and describes the phases. The case study Section introduces the real-life example that will be discussed throughout the paper. The following four sections present the methodological phases in more details and their application to the case study. In the final section we draw conclusions and discuss future works.

RELATED WORK

Lately the topics of web service design, quality of services, and ontology driven design frameworks have often been investigated as separate aspects instead of related issues of the same modeling and design problem.

Web Services Design Approaches

Different approaches for the design of Web services based on the MDA strategy have been proposed by many research and industrial projects.

OptimalJ, a development environment to fully implement a model-driven approach to Web service design and development, is presented in (Stephenson, 2003). The approach starts with the creation of a logical business model and automatically transforms this into a WSDL description. A different strategy is proposed in (Skogan, Groenmo et al., 2004). As in our methodology, a Platform Independent Model is produced, and then, WSDL and Ws-BPEL specifications are created by means of a translator tool. However these strategies do not provide Web service descriptions with QoS specifications and do not use ontologies to support designers. A different approach is shown in (Mylopoulos & Lau, 2004) where authors propose agent-oriented software development techniques to design web services. Such techniques support early and late requirements analysis, as well as architectural and detailed design, but do not offer ontology support for QoS description. Moreover, the framework does not drive the deployment of web services, since no automatic tool is available to generate WSDL descriptions.

Another model-driven approach for designing Web services has been presented in (Benatallah,

Sheng et al., 2003). Self-serv is a model-driven approach that facilitates the rapid and scalable composition of web services. It supports the declarative composition of new services from existing ones, the composition of web services with multi attribute dynamic selection, and the peer-to-peer orchestration of composite service executions. The mechanism for composing services in Self-serv is based on two major concepts: the composite service, and the service container. They support the composition of elementary services that aggregate several similar services providing a common functionality (i.e., the same set of operations). When a requester invokes the operations of a service container, the container is responsible for selecting the actual service that will execute the operation. Self-serv addresses QoS issues, defining a fixed web services quality model, composed of five different QoS dimensions, namely execution price, execution duration, reputation, reliability, and availability. However, Self-Serv focuses only on Web service composition and does not provide a complete environment for cooperative Web service design.

A new proposal for software development is the IBM Rational Software Development Platform (IBM, 2006). This proposal is a framework of integrated tools and best practices that supports a proven end-to-end process for all developer roles in the application development life cycle. It supports a complete set of software development capabilities (requirements and analysis, design and implementation, software quality, software configuration management, process and project management, and deployment management). It is composed of an integrated set of components that can be adopted to perform the development process. Regarding design and implementation capabilities, the IBM Rational Software Development Platform uses the WebSphere Application Server (IBM, 2008). WebSphere delivers a transaction engine that can be used to build, run, integrate and manage dynamic applications. However, WebSphere does not support specification and evaluation of non-functional requirements at design time.

Quality of Services

Quality of services is a key factor in the service-oriented literature (for example (Manasce, 2004), and (Papazoglou, Traverso et al., 2006)); the focus, however, is often in modeling issues rather than in the design process. The problem of evaluating QoS dimensions in composite web services is faced in several papers. Often, the evaluation is associated with workflow execution whose tasks are accomplished by Web Services. An example is the AgFlow framework that evaluates the QoS of composite services with an extensible multidimensional quality model (Zeng, Benatallah et al., 2004). Moreover, the selection of component services is made to optimize the QoS of the composite service starting from user requirements and candidate component services. Other examples of dynamic composition are in (Jaegger, Rojec-Goldmann et al., 2004) and (Ulbrich, Weis et al., 2003) that aims at defining composition rules to evaluate global values of QoS dimensions according to specific workflow patterns, but the problem of joint design of services and their qualities is not addressed.

Concerning papers addressing QoS issues in design processes (Buchmann & Bass, 2001) presents the ADD (Attribute-Drived Design) method, which is based on understanding the relationship between software qualities and the architectural mechanisms used to achieve these qualities. A drawback is the lack of a quality model that can help the designer to identify and relate qualities. Moreover, ADD is tailored for generic software development, without specific focus on SOA. Dealing with web services, (Cardoso, Sheth et al., 2004) presents a QoS model, addressing time, cost, and reliability dimensions. The model computes the quality of service for workflows automatically based on QoS attributes of an atomic task. This QoS model is then implemented on the top of the METEOR workflow system.

Finally, QoS is also considered in several papers (for example (Shuping, 2003), (Kritikos & Plexousakis, 2006) and (Comerio, De Paoli et al., 2007)) to improve the outcome of web services discovery.

Ontology and Design Frameworks

With the development of Semantic Web, ontologies have become widely used to capture the knowledge about concepts and their relationships defined in a domain for information exchange and knowledge sharing. Ontologies have been used in different ways. (Fensel & Bussler, 2002) use ontologies within WSMF (Web Services Modeling Framework) to define formal semantics for information. They describe real-world semantics, which make it possible to link machine-processable content with human-understandable meaning based on consensual terminologies and also to map different concepts allowing interoperability among web services. (Benatallah, Hacid et al., 2005) use ontologies to effectively discover services based on their capabilities, while (Klien, Einspanier et al., 2004) propose architecture for the ontology-based discovery and retrieval of geographic information.

Several papers address the QoS description by means of ontologies. In (Tsesmetzis, Roussaki et al., 2005) the authors provide a standard model to formally describe QoS parameters by means of an ontology where eleven QoS concepts involved in WS provisioning are described in depth. In a similar way, in (Afandi, Zhang et al., 2006) an integrated collection of reference frameworks to handle QoS features along the discovery, selection, composition and monitor of SWSs is proposed. The framework is based on a semantic QoS ontology model that defines the nature of associations between QoS concepts, QoS metrics, and the way they are measured and monitored. Another QoS ontology is shown in (Maximilien & Singh, 2004), and is used to let providers express QoS-based policies, and consumers express preferences. The proposed ontology is structured in three levels: upper, middle, and lower. The upper ontology captures the most generic quality concepts and defines the basic concepts associated with a quality, such as quality measurement and relationships. The middle ontology incorporates several quality aspects encountered in distributed systems. This ontology specifies domain independent quality concepts and is typically completed by a domain-specific lower ontology.

Ontology-driven design frameworks are mainly investigated in the context of Semantic Web. (Gomez-Perez, Gonzalez-Cabero et al., 2004), (Pahl & Casey, 2003) propose an MDA compliant, ontology-based framework; the use of ontologies is limited to functional descriptions and to the definition of axioms representing composition rules while it is not adopted to support the definition of QoS.

Open Issues

As discussed previously, several issues, which are still unresolved, are starting points for our research. MDA aims to improve the separation from the high-level platform independent design to low level platform dependent design. However, the application development process focuses on the software functional development, without considering the profile of the target users. As claimed in the user-oriented literature (Bolchini & Paolini, 2004), the end-users should be first-class citizens in software design. With regard to ontologies, notwithstanding their relevant representation power, few papers exploit their use at design time as a tool for designer support. In our approach, ontologies represent the way in which the existing knowledge about services, QoS, and architectural layers can be represented, used and retrieved in an integrated knowledge base. Finally, we aim to conceive a knowledge based "design for qualities" approach in which functional and non-functional requirements, the relevant requirements, their target values and priorities, have the same relevance, in order to determine at service design time, in a wide range of domain dependent and independent qualities.

THE ROLE OF ONTOLOGIES

To effectively support the cross enterprise use of web services, that is, to support service selection and adaptation, a clear and machine-processable definition is needed. In particular, a shared understanding of the non-functional requirements is important to let (i) the designer specify the characteristics of the developed service, (ii) the supplier specify the characteristics of the deployed service, and (iii) the client specify the characteristics of the required service. The role of ontologies is crucial to provide the rationale for making decisions at different levels of abstraction. In WSMoD, ontologies are exploited along three different perspectives:

1. Acquisition of common knowledge and mutual relations among entities;
2. Verification of the web service compliancy with ontology definitions;
3. Enrichment of ontologies by adding new services, qualities and relationships discovered during the development process.

As discussed in the Related work Section, several definitions have been proposed for ontologies. Among them, we have adopted OWL as reference ontology language. The level of acceptance among users, the availability of tools and the possibility of expressing new knowledge by means of description logic motivates the choice. Although any ontology that reflects domain specific characteristics and quality models can be suitable for WSMoD, we have exploited the MAIS ontologies to support the experimental evaluation of the methodology. These ontologies are:

- Service ontology (*OntoServ* in the following);
- Quality ontology (*OntoQoS*);
- Context ontology (*OntoContext*).

The three ontologies capture the relevant types of knowledge associated with services, together with semantic relationships among them. Figure 1 shows the top-level ontologies and the main relationships; further details about internal organization of ontologies and relationships will be presented throughout the paper when necessary.

OntoServ has the purpose of classifying and describing relevant properties of the different services according to domain characteristics. Among comprehensive services classifications we adopt the universal standard products and services classification, promoted by the Electronic Commerce Code Management Association (ECCMA) that classifies thousands of services in any domain. The OntoServ ontology augments these kinds of classifications, by adding relations to the other two ontologies with the goal of supporting integrated reasoning. Thus, for example, it is possible to identify a tax payment service and discover that associated qualities are, among others, security and accessibility. Moreover, it can be discovered that preferred delivery channels include PC devices with low bandwidth network connections.

OntoContext defines the context of a service. It deals with the definition of user profiles and channels. *UserProfile* is based on the user description proposed by (Graziani, Billi et al., 2003). It includes UserRole, UserActivity, representing a specific human activity (e.g. FreeTime, Lunch, Lesson, Meeting). UserPreference describes both domain independent and domain dependent references over objects (e.g. AirPreference, BookPreference), and UserDescription including mental, personal and physical data such as relational capabilities, expertise, and skills.

The concept of channel is often overloaded with different meanings, according to the technological

Figure 1. Top-Level ontologies and their relationships

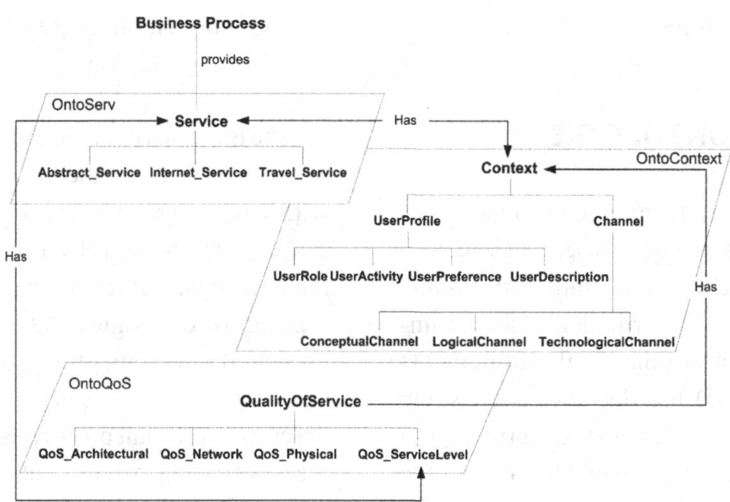

background of people. We adopt the *distribution channel model* defined in (Maurino, Pernici et al., 2003) that consider a channel at three different levels of abstraction, namely conceptual, logical and physical or technological: (i) a *conceptual channel* is the description, from a business point of view, of a medium enabling the access to a set of information and operational services, (ii) a *logical channel* is composed of a set of devices, network interfaces, networks and application protocols components that refine a conceptual channel, (iii) a *technological channel* represents concrete technological components. For example, the conceptual channel *mobile* can be refined, at the logical level, by the concepts of mobile devices (e.g., PDAs and cellular phones with certain characteristics) with transmission protocols, and, at the technological level, by actual manufactured devices, and concrete implementations of transmission protocols (e.g. GPRS and UMTS). By using relationships among ontologies, business experts can discover that mobile channels may support *localization* and the related quality *precision*, which are properties of the logical channel defined by technology experts. This information is included as a relationship between *OntoServ* and *OntoContext*.

OntoQoS is the result of a unique effort in classifying the qualities that can be associated with services. Currently *OntoQoS* includes the description of more than 200 domain independent QoS dimensions (Cappiello, Missier et al., 2004)). Top-level ontologies are *QoS_Architectural*, including QoS aspects of software and hardware architecture, e.g. screen resolution, *QoS_Network*, representing QoS related to network, e.g. bandwidth *QoS_Physical*, related to physical aspects of devices, e.g. power consumption, and *QoS_ServiceLevel*, describing QoS intrinsic to Service. QoS_ServiceLevel includes QoS dimensions that are independent from specific domains, such as price, privacy or usability. Moreover, according to specific application domain, OntoQoS can be augmented with domain dependent QoS dimensions. Domain experts have the task of settings relationships between OntoQoS and the other ontologies. Examples of relationship creation activities are given in the running case of the Service identification phase.

As results from the above discussion, and as will be further detailed in the case study, in WSMoD we exploit ontologies as a powerful repository of knowledge that design experts may use to guide the process in the generation of design artifacts and find a common agreement on concepts involved in service design. In a typical application scenario, graphical and knowledge-based tools that support browsing, navigation and selection can aid the designer in knowledge discovery and extraction. Thus, in this paper we use ontologies as an aid for the experts in the design process, while knowledge representation, processing issues, ontology evolution management, and the selection of formal ontology models to enact automatic or semiautomatic support are out of the scope of the paper.

WSMOD IN A NUTSHELL

The WSMoD methodology is composed of six main phases, as illustrated in Figure 2.

The *Service Identification* phase specifies, from a business point of view, *what* the service will offer with its operations, and *how* it will provide them. Inputs to the phase are the specification of conceptual channels and domain requirements, in terms of user roles and domain processes. The output of this phase is a complete, informal specification of functional and non-functional requirements for the web service to be developed. According to the relations described in Figure 1, a service specification has to fulfill the requirements of the business process(es). Business process experts define the features of the new service, in order to identify processes and contexts (user roles and channels). This phase, as all the others, will be examined in more detail in the second part of the paper.

The functional requirements and possible actual services to be re-designed (represented with natural language descriptions and UML diagrams) are the input of the *Service Modeling* phase, which has the goal to define the high-level model of the web service, in terms of data and operations diagrams. In this phase, the major design decisions deal with the identification of possible existing services that will be included as components of the new service, and the definition of high-level functional diagrams that describe the structure of the new service. This phase corresponds to the definition of an initial instance of the platform independent model in the MDA terminology.

The non-functional requirements, defined in the service identification phase, and the UML diagrams, defined in the service modeling phase, are inputs of the *High-Level Re-Design* phase, whose goal is to revise, and possibly change, the diagrams to include non-functional requirements, user requirements and specification of logical channels. In this phase the designer makes use of the three ontologies above described. This phase is a refinement of the initial definition of the platform independent model.

The next phase, *Customization*, further refines the current design specifications by evaluating the actual deployment scenario. Design decisions taken so far are compared with the different characteristics of users and providers to verify the adequacy of service qualities, user and channel profiles. The idea is that the design process should start with loose constraints that need to be verified and, if necessary, revised to meet real-world requirements. This process ensures that the delivered service will be effective from both technological and business perspectives. Note, anyway, that we are still dealing with high-level specifications. The result of the customization phase is an instance of the platform contextual model, which includes, functional, non-functional, and contextual aspects, but it is still independent from specific technological details.

At this stage of the design process, we need to transform diagrams into web services descriptions using standard languages. The *Web Service Description* phase will deliver the WSDL and WSOL (a language for quality descriptions proposed by Tosic, Kruti et al. 2002) documents. Final UML

Figure 2. The WSMoD methodology

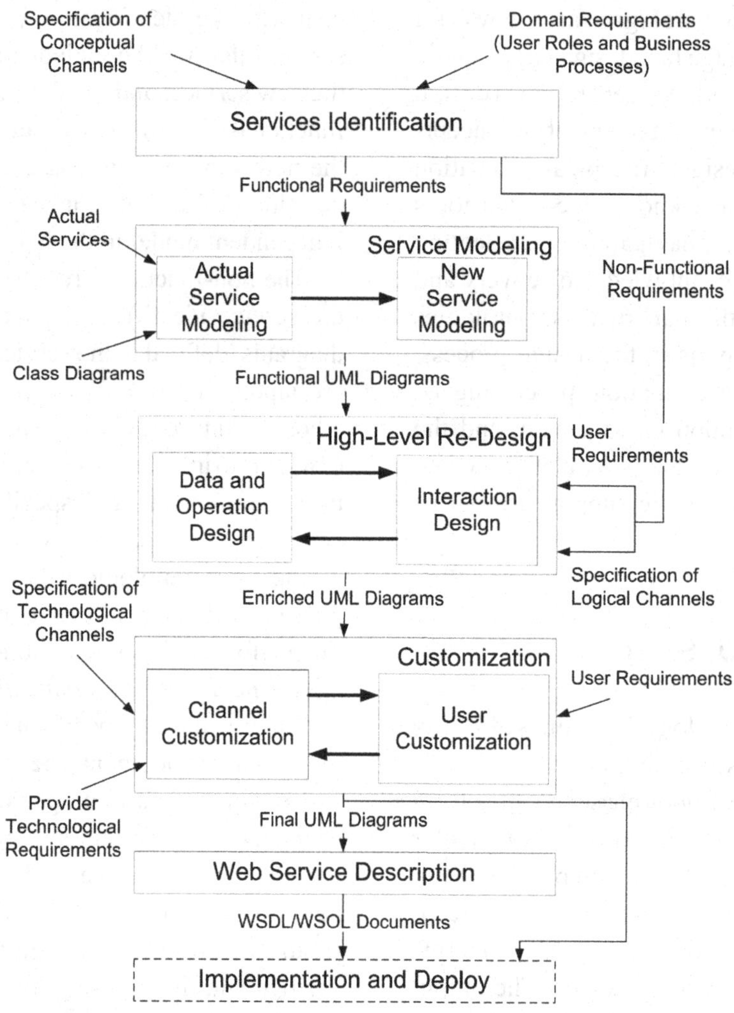

diagrams and description documents will be the input for the *Implementation and Deploy* phase that deals with the actual implementation technologies (e.g., .NET, Java) and application server (e.g. JBoss, WebSphere, etc). This a phase is out of the scope of this paper.

It is worth noting that, even if the different phases have been discussed as a sequence of activities, they are to be considered as part of a process, in which every step can be re-executed according to the well-known spiral development approach. Within each phase the activities, when not alternative as in the Service Modeling phase, have to be executed establishing reciprocal coherence and completeness checks. Further, from any phase, it is possible to go back to the previous ones to deal with new and unexpected problems. WSMoD can be adopted in agile development processes. In fact, the redesign capabilities of WSMoD can support the development through iterative life cycles with short cycles to support the evolution of rapidly changing requirements. Further, agile methodologies (e.g. eXtreme Programming, (Beck, 2000) provide for active participation of customers. WSMoD involves business experts and designers in joint discussions and definition of requirements as well as in the quantitative evaluation of qualities. Moreover, phase 3 (and in part phase 4) can be viewed as a sort of refactoring activity within the design process. Finally, the produced documentation is kept to the essence by defining only the necessary, but complete and coherent, information to move to an effective implementation and allow for the next evolution.

A key characteristic of WSMoD is to consider the specification of channels and users at three levels of refinement, as reported in Table 1. The different levels enforce the principle of taking decision at the right stage to ensure an effective refinement of the design process from conceptual modeling to more concrete modeling that is compliant to real environments. We assume that the minimum on specific technologies includes the widest range of devices and networks. Another element to consider is the role of the people involved throughout as the development process. In the highest phases the key role has to be assigned to business experts, who have the task of identifying the business processes, identifying services to support the processes, and defining high-level requirements, both functional and non-functional.

The identification and if needed, the enhancement of these ontologies is also part of the requirements definition phase. During the modeling phases, the role of software engineers becomes more important, since the business requirements need to be translated into technological requirements and implemented. Business experts play a supervision role as domain experts along the design phases. In particular, during the customization phase that requires an evaluation of the designing services, the decision makers validate, reject or change a service feature. All phases of the WSMoD methodology are powerfully supported by the three ontologies described in the previous section. Along the WSMoD phases, roles using ontologies are described in Table 2, where the aim for which each ontology is exploited it is also shown. Notice the strategic task of ontologies that capture and share knowledge among the actors. During the design process, ontologies can be enriched with respect to business or technological perspective.

In order to enhance interoperability and practical applications, we have provided the methodology with an integrated suite of widely used tools. In this way it is also possible to reduce the well-known learning-curve problem and resistance-to-change attitude. In the service identification phase we use Protègè, a popular free-software tool originally developed at Stanford University for knowledge acquisition (Noy, Fergerson et al., 2000) and (Noy, Sintek et al., 2001). Protègè allows for the editing of ontologies and building of knowledge bases with a user-friendly interface and interactive environment. Protègè supports OWL, RDF schema, XML files with a DTD, and XML schema files. WSMoD designers can navigate the ontologies and/or augment them to fulfill their requirements. Service modeling, high-level re-design and customization phases use the well-known design tools such as Rational Rose as the UML modeller tool and Protègè tool to exploit ontologies. In the customization phase

Table 1. Channel and user role in WSMoD

Phase	Channel	User
service identification	conceptual characteristics	user roles
high-level re-design	logical characteristics	user requirements
customization	technological characteristics	user profiles

Table 2. Ontology usage in WSMoD

Phase	Role	OntoServ	OntoContext	OntoQoS
Service Identification	Business expert	Identification of needed service category and insertion of new web service	Identification of roles and conceptual channels	Selection of business qualities
Service Modeling	Software designer	Selection of existing services (if any)	Selection of high level concepts	
High Level Redesign	Software designer	Discovery of additional properties	Definition of the context for the designing service	Identification of influencing and influenced Qualities
Customization	Software designer Business expert	Not exploited	Comparison of actual and reference contexts	Evaluation of design assumptions
Web Service Description	Software designer	Insertion of the new Web Service	Not exploited	Not exploited

we adopt Lp-solve (Lp-solve, 2005) as Integer Linear Programming (see the customization Section). In the web service descriptions, we have exploited UMT (UMT, 2005), a tool that provides for model transformation and code generation based on UML models in the form of XMI. XMI models are imported by the tool and converted to a simpler intermediate format, which is the basis for validation and generation towards different target platforms. The intermediate format is an XML format, which in UMT is called XMI Light. UMT transforms the XMI Light to the desired target technology using a transformer. In UMT, this is normally XSLT, but it may also be a Java-implementation. We have extended this tool by adding a XSLT stylesheet in order to perform the WSOL transformation. To support the automatic generation of web service descriptions and to provide a unique way to make use of ontologies in the design of UML diagrams we defined a specific UML profile to identify the core service elements, QoS dimensions and channel specifications. In Table 3 we report the stereotypes used during the design process.

RUNNING CASE

In the following sections, we discuss in more depth the WSMoD methodology, by making use of a realistic example, extracted from a project that aims to redesign services in the zootechnical domain. The general issue is to augment browser-based services with new features to exploit different distribution channels. Among others, the use of cellular phones and therefore, the capability to locate the user are considered a strategic objective in order to involve the totality of the users, namely cattle breeders. In fact, today only few stockbreeders own and use PCs, while most of

Table 3. WSMoD UML Profile

Stereotype Name	Description
<<BusinessService>>	Represents the component implementing the web service, the public methods of a <<BusinessService>> class represent interfaces of the web service
<<ComplexType>>	Represents a type of the WSDL
<<QoS level-agreement>>	Represents a QoS-constraint

them use cellular phones daily (for more details on the zootechnical domain, the reader can refer to (Comerio, De Paoli et al., 2004)).

Among others, our aim is to design an emergency service to let a stockbreeder contact a vet whenever an emergency (e.g. suspected bovine spongiform encephalopathy also know as mad cow disease, which is a chronic, degenerative disorder affecting the central nervous system of cattle) occurs in his/her herd. Today, there is no centralized service to keep a stockbreeder in touch with the nearest vet, possibly an expert on a specific subject. The new service will provide a reliable channel to contact a qualified and available vet in the shortest time, possible through the automatic selection of the most suitable channel (e.g., e-mail message, SMS, voice message). To support such a complex service, a multi-channel flexible notification service, *FlexSend*, has been developed to deliver messages over different channels according to the contexts pf specific receivers (preferences, device, and activity). The innovative aspect of FlexSend is the capability of selecting the delivery channel by considering different information such as QoS requested by the sender, location and available channels of the receiver, etc. FlexSend will be used as running case to illustrate the methodology. The functional requirements for the FlexSend service are quite simple. This is done intentionally, to allow us to concentrate on the non-functional requirements that represent the most innovative aspect in our methodology. They are described in the following.

Before sending a message, users need to *register* by inserting information such as name, surname, e-mail address and cellular phone number. Then they *set their preferences, use an address book* service to get an address, and finally *send* messages and *receive* notifications. The functionality of *sending* a message to register users can be further described by stating that the message is composed of one or more receivers, an optional subject, the body (considered as a text) and a set of attachments (considered as independent files). The system selects the delivery channels by considering the properties associated with the message, the QoS requested by the sender and the delivery preferences of the receiver. Non-functional requirements associated with a message are a set of attributes representing the level of priority, privacy, and the possibility to send messages without attachments, and other characteristics that will be discussed in the running case.

PHASE 1: SERVICE IDENTIFICATION

The goal of this phase is to identify the type of services that satisfy the user needs, according to social and business goals. In this phase the focus is on the definition of the high-level characteristics of the new service. Such characteristics will be refined along the design process.

Methodological Step

Inputs of the phase are the business processes that an organization needs to support, the roles of the involved users, and a set of candidate channels. At this stage, business experts are interested in defining high-level, abstract descriptions for the web service, identifying the operations to be supplied, the distribution channels to deliver the service, and the profiles of users (either humans or machines) that will access the service. The output of the phase is a set of functional and non-functional requirements, when informally describe the service at this stage.

The identification of the functional requirements is performed with standard techniques; domain and business experts define a list of high-level operations to support the business process. In this phase the focus is on the identification of the non-functional requirements, in which the use of ontologies plays a central role. Browsing the service ontology OntoServ, the business expert can progressively establish the existing service category where the new web service belongs to;

Figure 3. Use-Case diagram for FlexSend

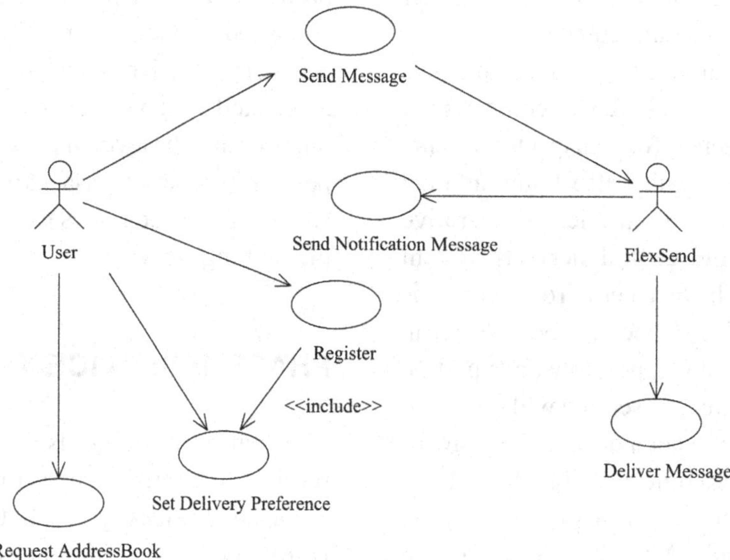

through service classification, the expert can state the characteristics of the web service and discover a first set of quality relationships with OntoQoS. In a similar way, experts can exploit OntoContext to identify the context dimensions (user and channel) relevant for the new service. The expert can then decide to stay with the specifications extracted from the ontologies, or to augment them by adding new properties and relationships. At the end of the phase, the list of non-functional requirements will reflect the concepts in the ontologies, so that the software engineers will clearly understand the semantics of the requirements.

Running Case

The FlexSend functionality can be illustrated by means of a use-case diagram, as in Figure 3. The *User* actor is either a stockbreeder or a vet in our scenario since the service has been designed as bi-directional. The other actor is the *FlexSend* service that is invoked to actually send a message. Moreover, FlexSend delivers the requested message and sends a notification message.

Table 4 summarizes the functional specifications of FlexSend, while Figure 4 shows a fragment of OntoServ and OntoQoS, with relationships defined between the two ontologies (dashed lines). According to the WSMoD methodology the business expert has to identify the category of the web service. As FlexSend is to be provided on the Internet and is a special sort of mail service, it is classified as a message delivery service. Consequently, FlexSend is added in the OntoServ ontology as shown in Figure 4; this means that it inherits all the properties of a generic delivery service. Hence, from the relationships with the QoS ontologies, the business expert identifies *availability* and other qualities as relevant for FlexSend. Moreover, new qualities can be associated with the new service, such as *usability*.

We have next to associate qualities with measurements and ranges of values. According to the type of quality, measurements can be expressed as: (i) sets of acceptable values, to be chosen and specified later in the contract between the user and the provider (see selected qualities and corresponding values in Table 5), and (ii) constraints,

Figure 4. A fragment of OntoServ and OntoQoS and their relationships

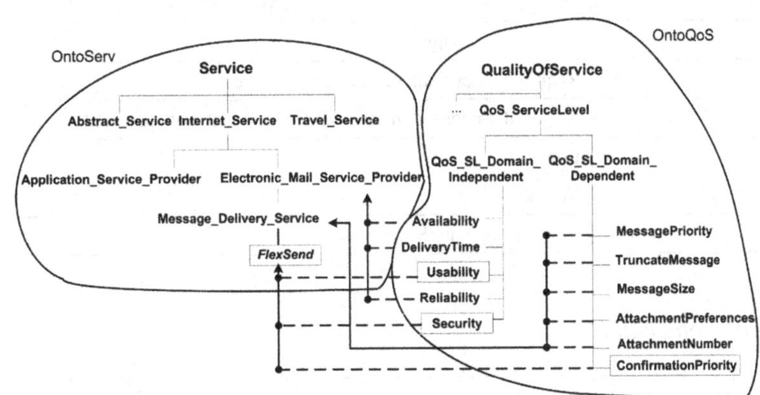

Table 4. FlexSend functional specifications

Operation	Description
Send	Sends a message (that is a text with zero or one subject, zero or more attachments) to a set of receivers with a set of constraints
Register	Allows a user to register with the FlexSend service. The user has to describe his/her contact information
Preference	Assigns the delivery preference about a message according to situation and address book
GetAddressBook	Returns a set of identification code(s)of person(s) to which the user wants to send a message

expressed by a minimum or maximum accepted level, (see corresponding qualities in Table 6).

In much a similar way, OntoContext can support the identification of meaningful information to define user profiles. Relevant elements of the ontology are:

- *UserRole*: states the role a user can assume. Possible roles are *sender* and *receiver*. Receivers can be further detailed as: a. *registered user*, characterized by a profile, or b. *anonymous user*, which is a non-registered user. In both cases, we assume he/she is a MAIS user so that it is possible to use the MAIS reflective platform.
- *UserActivity*: describes the typical activities that a user can realize during the day. In the zootechnical domain possible values are: break, exam, freetime and so on.
- *UserPreference*: states how a service should behave in particular situations. Preferences are selected by users from predefined combinations.
- *UserDescription*: profiles the user by job interests, physical and mental characteristics, etc.

The last non-functional requirement deals with the identification of conceptual characteristics of channels. At business level requirements, we need to identify critical success factors like that, besides the traditional support for desktop computers, mobile devices need to be supported, and that location capabilities of such devices and related technology are to be exploited. In the following we use the term *Situation* to couple *UserActivity* and *Location*. For example, the vet carries out an activity, exam, break, etc. in a specific location,

Table 5. Specification of business QoS

QoS Name	Acceptable Values
Message priority	Low, medium, high
Attachment preference	Required, important, recommended, optional
Confirmation priority	Required, important, recommended, optional, not requested
Usability	Low, medium, high
Truncate message	Yes, no
Security	Low, medium, high

Table 6. Business QoS constraints

QoS Name	Acceptable Values
Messge size	10MB at the most
Attachment number	5 at the most
Reliability	99% at the most
Usability	Medium at the least
Delivery time	5 sec at the most
Availability	90% at the least

examination room, cafeteria, etc. For the sake of simplicity, in this paper we consider locations and distribution channels as strictly related, even if the relationship is more complex in a real scenario. Hence, a user is requested to select from a list of predefined combinations.

PHASE 2: SERVICE MODELING

Methodological Step

This phase deals with either the creation of a new definition of the service or the new specification from an existing actual service, if a similar service is already provided. In both cases the goal is to identify and describe the domain objects involved in the service, according to the functional requirements of the new service. The designer has to decide, with a case-by-case approach, which domain elements correspond to functional elements and have to be represented at this stage. The first task for the designer is to evaluate the availability of services that are suitable for providing one or more operations as defined in the service identification phase. OntoServ can help the designer in this analysis, which can lead to two possible results: (i) no services exist or else (ii) exist services that partially or fully satisfy the requirements. In the first case the designer starts the new service modeling sub-phase (see below); in the second case the designer extracts the high level description of the service (actual service modeling sub-phase) from available documentation (Comerio, De Paoli et al., 2004) and then, if necessary integrates that description with the functional specifications the service does not support (new service modeling sub-phase).

Running Case

A check among existing services available in OntoServ lets us conclude that no existing services can be exploited in the design of FlexSend.

Therefore, for the *GetAddressBook operation* we may assume that FlexSend can take advantage of an existing LDAP repository that maintains information on both vets and stockbreeders. The repository is accessible as a web service; hence FlexSend users can acquire the needed information in a standard way. In this phase the designer can use sequence diagram to specify the needed interactions between a user and FlexSend to perform the delivery of a message.

Figure 5 shows the class diagram that provides an abstract description of the new service. In this phase we are not interested in specifying the channel as a technological component, but only as an abstract resource involved in sending a message. Thus, in the class diagram, we introduce a *Channel* class characterized by a generic *description* attribute and by the *send()* method. The abstract class *Message* is extended in terms of two classes: *Confirmation message* and *Requested message*, which represent the two kinds of messages the web service is requested to deliver. It is worth noting that stereotypes: BusinessServices, ComplexType, Actors and class Channel derive from the UML profile we proposed for the platform independent model.

PHASE 3: HIGH LEVEL RE-DESIGN

The goal of this phase is the re-design of the new service, in the light of non-functional requirements defined in the service identification phase. The re-design consists of two sub-phases: *data and operation design* and *interaction design*. The former sub-phase deals with the definition of a structure of the new service that fulfils the previously identified qualities (in their ranges of values). The latter sub-phase deals with the definition of the interaction protocols that will be exploited by the users. An important issue of this phase is a requirement-validation activity that allows for an early identification of inconsistencies and conflicts. It might be the case that some of the conflicts between requirements cannot be solved; in this case, the service-modeling phase is to be executed again to redefine the functional model. In this phase, OntoQoS, which can help in the refinement of business qualities, and OntoContext, which allows for the identification of constraints and dependencies on these qualities, support designers' activities.

Figure 5. FlexSend class diagram

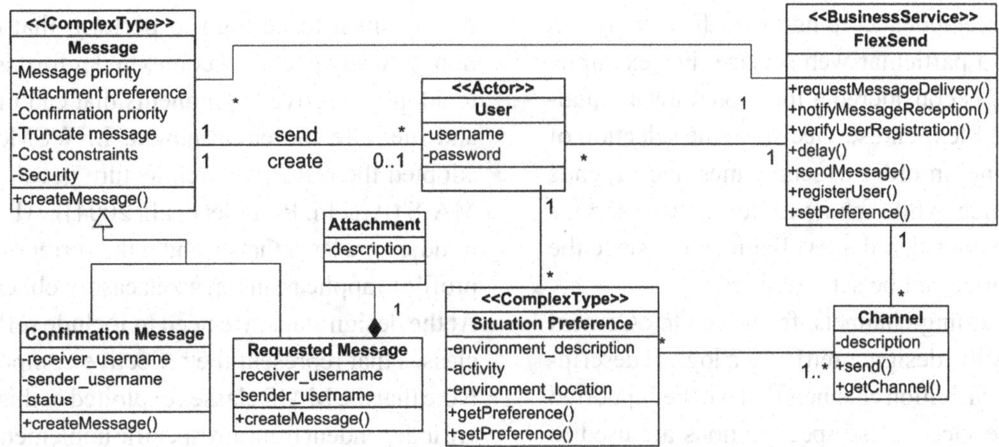

Data and Operation Design

In this sub-phase, the designer enriches the UML class-diagram of services with non-functional requirements including QoS, channel description and user profile. The selected QoS dimensions can be grouped into two categories:

- *functional-aware QoS*. This category includes all QoS dimensions that, in order to fulfill the requirements, have to be expressed in the functional service description. For example, for a notification service the choice of a secure channel implies the inclusion of encryption/decryption functionalities as part of the message processing. Notice that this is a domain-independent feature.
- *level-agreement QoS*, that does not influence the functional features of the web service and is involved in the formal or informal contract between the provider and the user. An example of domain-independent, level-agreement QoS dimension is the price for a weather forecast service, while an example of domain-dependent dimension is the maximum provisioning time in a notification service.

Notice that a QoS dimension could be considered either a functional-aware quality or a level-agreement according to the different role it plays in a particular web service. For example, the price is considered a functional-aware quality in the FlexSend service since the selection of the channel in order to send a message depends on the price, while for a weather forecast service it can be considered a level-agreement since the selling price can be set afterwards.

Concerning channels, from the OntoContext ontology the designer retrieves a logical description of distribution channels that will be supported by the service. These specifications are used to specialize the channel component defined in the service-modeling phase. The specialization includes: (i) the channel logical components (device, network interface, network, protocols) and their properties, and (ii) the range of values and constraints of logical components. The designer can now evaluate the service, as it has been designed in the previous phase to verify if it can be provided over a channel. In case of conflicts, the designer redesigns the UML diagrams to fulfill the new quality requirements imposed by channel characteristics.

The OntoContext ontology also helps the designer in the identification of features describing reference users. The designer selects non-functional requirements, and discovers other user characteristics that accomplish the requirements given in the service identification phase. For example, in a Web Service for package holiday selling, a typical user profile requirement is localization, which, among other characteristics deals with the language exploited in the conversation between users and services. In the OntoContext ontology this feature is related to *linguistic skills* that determines the level of comprehension of a foreign language. The inclusion of information such as mother tongue and skills in other languages provides a more precise description of the user.

A crucial aspect of this phase is the way the system is aware of the current context for a given user. Such information is mandatory to evaluate quality constraints (for example: "the level of battery must to be high to perform that operation"). A way to collect contextual information is to adopt reflective components that can monitor and measure the environment. In WSMoD we adopted the reflective architecture developed in MAIS (Arcelli, Raibulet et al., 2004)), which is a middleware layer that provides the current context profile to applications or, in our case, web services. At the design stage, we need to include reflective classes that represent the reflective components. Note that the MAIS classes exploited in this paper are independent from any specific implementation, thus preserving the Model Driven Architecture approach. Developers can make the choice of adopting the MAIS reflective architecture or replace it with another reflective mechanism (Adorni, Arcelli et al., 2005).

Interaction Design

The interaction design sub-phase deals with the enrichment of interaction diagrams (e.g. UML sequence diagrams) with user, channel and QoS requirements previously extracted from ontologies. In particular, the designer describes the behavior of software components defined in the previous sub-phase for each relevant interaction scenario. During this phase the designer evaluates the functionalities of the new service to verify if they satisfy the interaction scenarios. When necessary, the designer executes the data and operation design sub-phase again to add or change functionalities. For example, the designer may discover that, in order to address the mobile channel due to a different screen size, information has to be presented with a different format than in PCs. Therefore, since the logical behavior changes, different operations are needed and a new interface has to be conceived to support the new channel. Another example is an operation that translates an image from gif to jpg format since mobile devices do not support gif.

Running Case

In the data and operation design sub phase, we first have to identify functional-aware and level agreement qualities, among the qualities of Table 5 and Table 6. Functional-aware qualities, e.g. message priority, attachment preferences, truncate message, and so on, have to be evaluated in the diagrams as delivered by the previous phase. Moreover personal experience and knowledge supported by ontologies allow the designer to complete the requirements list by adding new items. In FlexSend we introduce *QoS_MessageConstraint* and *QoS_ServiceConstraint* classes to model qualities related to the Message and FlexSend classes. Then, these classes can be further refined according to OntoQoS relations. For example, the *Usability*, selected as a requirement by domain experts (see Table 5), can be refined according to the relations reported OntoQoS

A second activity concerns level-agreement qualities, for example privacy in message delivery. Privacy can be implemented by means of encrypt and decrypt messages and attachments. Moreover, different cryptographic algorithms can implement the privacy level. Such requirements lead to the modification of class and sequence diagrams to include a new class defining encryption/decryption features. The class diagram is also augmented with methods and attributes to complete the specification. For example, in the FlexSend class, methods related to QoS evaluation (*selectChannelQoS* and *verifyConstraint*) have been introduced as private operations. The updated version of the class diagram for FlexSend is augmented with functional-aware qualities that have been added as attributes of the message class.

A similar approach is used to model instances of the OntoServ, and OntoContext ontologies. User characteristics are modelled in the *UserInformation* class, an instance of OntoContext. This class refers to component classes modeling the user delivery preferences expressed by the requirements defined in the first phase of the methodology. In particular, the *R_User_Information* class includes meaningful information supplied by the MAIS Reflective Architecture (e.g. available channels and location). This information is automatically provided by devices (e.g. mobile phone) that are equipped with reflective middleware.

Another issue to be addressed is the definition of the logical channels that will be exploited by the actual users of the service. The class diagram is also modified to describe the FlexSend class and the structure of the delivery channels descriptions, according to OntoServ (Figure 4) and OntoContext. In Figure 6 the refined class diagram of FlexSend is reported; for the sake of readability we report only a one-level refinement for usability.

The actual configuration for the selected channels drives and constraints the design of the new service. In the case study, samples of chosen configurations extracted from OntoContext are:

- C1: notebook, any interface, Wi-Fi Network, SMTP protocol;
- C2: personal computer\notebook, any interface, any network, SMTP protocol;
- C3: Mobile phone, GSM\UMTS interface, GSM\UMTS, SMS\MMS protocol.

In the interaction design sub-phase the designer defines and models the interaction between users and service. In FlexSend, the sender issues a request to send a message. The service behavior depends on sender parameters and on receiver contexts. For example, if there are no available channels to deliver the message according to the requested QoS dimension, the service applies one of the predefined delivery policies.

Figure 6. A fragment of class diagram describing QoS refinements

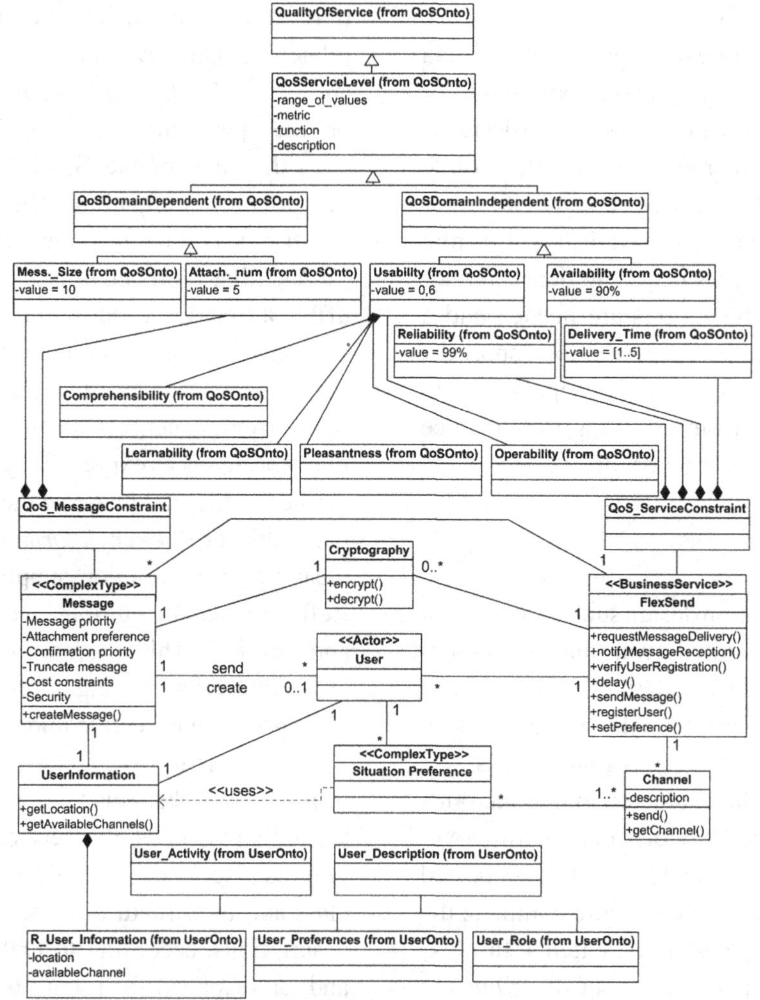

The interaction between a user and FlexSend is designed according to scenarios and use cases. UML activity diagrams are the suitable means to express such interactions. Actions performed by FlexSend are specified by means of UML sequence diagrams. Figure 7 shows an enriched version of the sequence diagram modeled in the previous phase to take into account the internal delivery algorithm and the activity diagram.

In the case study, the scenario for the emergency service described in the running case could be described as follows. The stockbreeder initiates the process by invoking the *emergency service* with info such as the message (e.g., request for examination) and the requested QoS. The service processes the request to find a vet candidate. FlexSend is then used to contact the vet and deliver the stockbreeder's message. As shown in Figure 7 the *emergency service* invokes the *requestMessageDelivery()* of FlexSend with the requested parameters. Note that this is an example of a non-human client for the FlexSend service; in fact, one of the key issues is to design services that supply and receive information in machine-processable formats and protocols. An example of QoS for an emergency request could be:

- *attachment_preference = optional*;
- *truncate_message = yes*;
- *confirmation_priority = not requested.*

After receiving a send request, and after the creation of a *Message* instance, FlexSend selects the actual delivery channels. For example, with the QoS given above the selected delivery channel is the configuration C3: Mobile phone, GSM\UMTS interface, GSM\UMTS, SMS\MMS protocol. The next actions performed by FlexSend are the control of the vet registration and the detection of his/her location and his/her available channels. Information on location and channel profile are supplied by the MAIS reflective architecture. The information about the position on the territory permits the identification of the situation where the vet is involved in the selection of the delivery preference of the receiver. This information is assumed to be the parameter of the *defineChannelsOrdering()* method. This method returns the definitive ordering of the delivery channels to let FlexSend send the requested message. A confirmation message is not requested, thus FlexSend ends.

Figure 7. Sequence diagram output of the High-level Re-Design phase

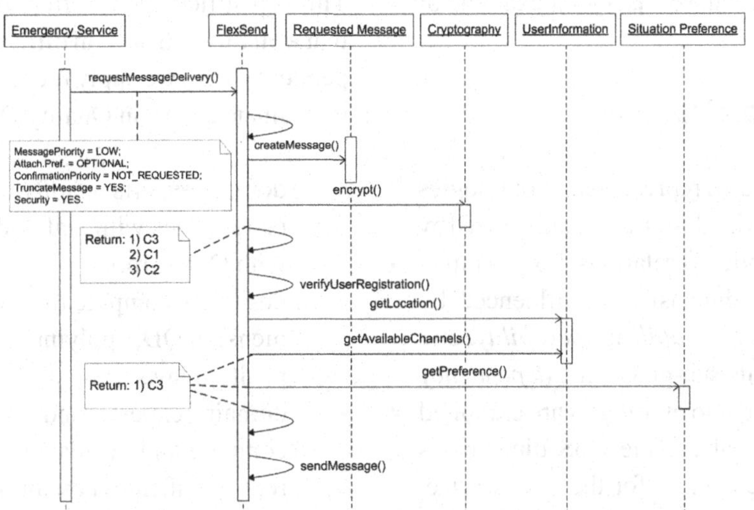

PHASE 4: CUSTOMIZATION

This phase is focused on the definition of an extended platform independent model that considers user profiles and channel profiles. These profiles are abstractions of real devices, network interfaces, networks and application protocols that providers can exploit for service provisioning.

The goal of this phase is to verify whether the design assumptions match the actual deployment scenario or if a revision process is necessary. It is worth noting that the separation between the high-level re-design phase, where the designer defines a technological independent solution, and the customization phase, where actual constraints are evaluated, improves the service re-use and the service evolution according to the MDA philosophy. In fact, if the actual deployment scenario changes, the service has to be adapted, but only this phase needs to be executed to identify changes.

The customization phase is split into two sub-phases: channel customization, which evaluates the UML diagrams defined up till now, with respect to the available technologies, and user customization that validates the service specification with respect to actual user profiles. The two types of customization require different strategies, and will be examined in two different sections. In the FlexSend running case, the achievement of the *usability* QoS is chosen as a joint example of customization.

Channel Customization

The different concepts represented in ontologies and involved in service design are characterized by a wide set of dependency relations. For example, the *usability* QoS dimension is influenced by *comprehensibility, learnability, operability*, and *pleasantness*. In this sub-phase, the *dependency relations* embedded into ontologies are exploited to quantitatively evaluate the QoS dimensions with respect to the context for the new service. Composition laws, which express how a quality value can be derived from given values of influencing qualities, characterize these relationships. Our approach (Ardagna, Comerio et al., 2005) to composition of qualities derives from the Simple Additive Weighting (SAW) technique, which is one of the most widely used techniques (Lum & Lau, 2003), (Zang, Benatallah et al., 2004) to handle dimensions having different units of measure. SAW basically consists in associating a weight with every influencing dimension to express the level of dependency in a composition. The score is obtained by summing the weighted values of the influencing dimensions. Weights are normalized, i.e. their sums equal to 1, so that the value of every node ranges from [0…1]. However, it is worth noting that the SAW method cannot be used for every dimension. In these cases, a proper composition law (i.e., a function or a table of values) has to be added by domain experts.

To accomplish the task of evaluating the dimensions involved in the design, the activity starts with the extraction from OntoQoS of *quality dependency graphs* to represent the dependency relations between qualities. Nodes of a graph represent ontology instances. A dependency graph is often a tree, or it can be transformed into a tree with a top-level quality as root and influencing qualities as children. The transformation consists in duplicating nodes with more then one father. This is justified by the different kind of influence that a quality can have in different cases. On a dependency tree, we apply the following procedure to evaluate a certain Quality Dimension (QD):

- domain experts or software engineers associate values with leaf nodes of the sub-tree with QD as root;
- designers compute the value of the root dimension QD, applying iteratively the composition laws;
- domain experts and software engineers compare and evaluate results with the current specification assumptions.

The output of this sub-phase could be, for example, the understanding that provisioning of a web service over a GPRS network would be inefficient due to slow transmission speed, or that screen size and pointing tools of cellular phones prevent from fulfill the desired usability requirements.

When the quality analysis leads to unsatisfactory results, the designer has three alternatives: (i) constraints associated with the involved dimensions can be relaxed; this computation task is a typical operation research problem that can be automated by means of Integer Linear Programming tools, such as Lp_Solve (Lp-solve, 2005)); (ii) another distribution channel to provide the service may be selected; (iii) the re-design phase can be executed again to change the shape of the service.

When the evaluation does not satisfy business requirements, QoS dimensions, which are controlled in depth by the designer, are considered. In fact, a QoS dimension can be further classified as dependent on the delivery channel, or dependent on the service-supplier profile. In particular it is:

- *delivery-based QoS*, representing the QoS dimensions offered by service provider (e.g. network speed). Such QoS dimensions are not directly controllable by the designer and often they represent constraints that he/she has to consider in the design of the web service.
- *service-based QoS*, representing the QoS dimensions that are not offered by the service provider. The designer is responsible for the setting of specific values to such instances

Running Case

Following the running case, we show the checking of the value of usability obtained is compliant with the business requirements. The top level QoS tree related to usability is reported in Figure 8. *Usability*, as we said, depends on *comprehensibility, learnability, operability and pleasantness*. Furthermore, *comprehensibility* depends on *screenQoS* and *soundQoS*. Finally, *screenQoS* depends on the quality attributes of the screen device (resolution, size, etc).

To evaluate a quality, on one hand we need to consider the requirements stated in the service identification phase, on the other hand a possible configuration for actual channels has to be selected. Moreover, to be able to compare and evaluate qualities expressed by scalar values, we convert them in normalized numeric values be-

Figure 8. SAW method

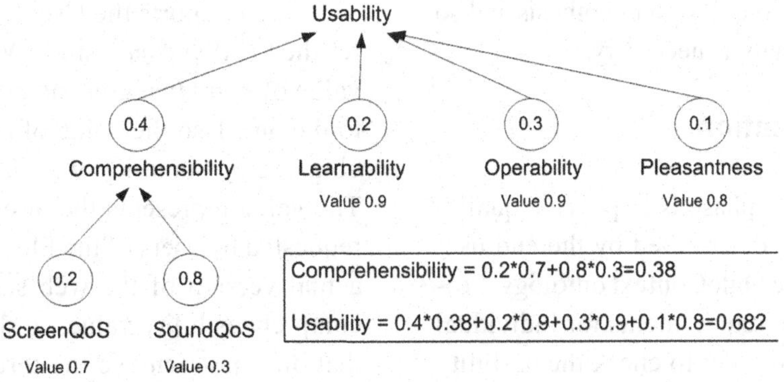

Table 7. Example of a channel configuration

Resolution	176×208
Size	2,0"
BitsForPixel	24
ColorCapable	Yes
ImageCapable	yes

tween 0 and 1. In our case, business experts have requested a *medium* level of usability (see Table 6). Hence, a *usability* value '*medium at least*' can be regarded as *usability>0.6*. At this point, the selection of one or more channel configurations is performed. In OntoContext the device component class is composed of hardware and software components. The hardware components are CPU, input system, display, sound system, memory, and power. Instead, the software components are the operative system, the browser and the Java virtual machine version that are available. Moreover each sub-component is described in terms of its technological characteristics.

In our case, we need to assign values to define the technical characteristics of the device display. An example of configuration is given in Table 7. As we did for usability requirements we assign a normalized value for *screenQoS* equal to *0.7*.

Figure 8 shows how to evaluate *usability* and *comprehensibility* when the device selected for the end user provides *screenQoS* = 0.7 and *soundQoS* = 0.3. In this case, we obtain that *comprehensibility* is equal to 0,38 and *usability* is equal to 0,682. This value satisfies our design hypothesis and so no any further activity is necessary.

User Customization

The aim of this sub-phase is to provide quality thresholds that are determined by the end user profile stored in the OntoContext ontology. Profiles define service requirements for individual and group users. In order to check the usability of the provided services, specific peculiarities of every user should be highlighted (Graziani, Billi et al., 2003). The dependency relationships are used to define a User profile/QoS matrix. The values of the matrix are weights, that is numeric values that represent the level of dependency between user profile and QoS dimensions. Such numeric values are domain dependent and therefore assigned by domain experts. Values are normalized so that the sum of weights of each column is equal to 1.

Running Case

The quality evaluation of an end user profile starts with the identification of the dependency relationships between the QoS computed in the channel customization phase and the user profile characteristics derived from the OntoContext ontology. In the proposed example, *body function* (physical and psychological condition of the user), *skills* (ability to perform a particular operation), *education, expertise* and *relational capabilities* (capacity to interact with the system) influence the usability dimension.

Table 8 reports the User Profile/QoS matrix for the FlexSend case study. We assume that the value of *body function* and *education* are equal to 0.6 and 1 so the value of *comprehensibility*, obtained by summing weighted values is 0,76. The value represents the threshold of usability requested by users of the FlexSend service. The actual version of the web service generates a comprehensibility value, as shown in Figure 8, that does not achieve the threshold and so the design assumptions have to be revised.

Table 8. User Profile -QoS values matrix

User Profile/ QoS	Comprehensibility	Learnability	Operability	Pleasantness
Skills		0,2	0,3	
Body function	0,6	0,4	0,3	
Expertise		0,3		
Education	0,4	0,1	0,1	
Relation capabilities			0,3	1

Analyzing the QoS tree (Figure 8), *comprehensibility* is related to channel device QoS (*screenQoS* and *soundQoS*) only. Qualities related to the actual version of FlexSend service do not influence this QoS. So, *comprehensibility* is classified as delivery-based QoS. Thus the designer must return to the previous phase, identify the most violated constraints and select new technical configuration. If this change does not satisfy the business constraints, the designer has to go back to the High-Level Re-Design phase and change UML diagrams describing the web service.

WEB SERVICE DESCRIPTION

According to the most accepted implementations of the SOA, each web service has to be described by a WSDL document. WSDL, however, lacks the description of some aspects such as QoS offered and the behavior of the web service (Shuping, 2003), and (Zang, Benatallah et al., 2004). Unfortunately there are no widely accepted standards to describe such relevant information. Consequently WSMoD directly supports the production of the WSDL and WSOL descriptions (Tosic, Kruti et al., 2002), but the designer is free to translate the results of previous phases in another web service description language. The choice of UML as a modeling language offers the possibility to describe diagrams in XMI (XML metadata Interchange). The designer, by means of the XSLT technology can translate a UML diagram described in XMI into another XML specification.

Methodological Step

Concerning the translation from UML to WSDL, in (Provost, 2003) a WSDL-oriented UML profile has been proposed. According to this profile, a web service should be modelled using the specified UML stereotypes and tagged values, resulting in a WSDL-dependent model. This model contains a number of WSDL details that are irrelevant for understanding the semantics of the web service. We chose an approach close to the one presented in (Groenmo, Skogan, et al. 2004) by providing a platform independent model of the functional description. Even if there is not a well-accepted way to transform a platform independent model into web services, OMG provides some guidelines in order to design a UML class diagram able to be translated into a WSDL description (Radhakrishnan & Wookey, 2004)). The class diagram modelled with the UML profile shown in the service modelling phase can be automatically translated into WSDL as shown in the running case. For example, the stereotype <<business service>> is used to specify the component implementing the web service. The public methods of this stereotyped class specify a WSDL *portType* and a WSDL *binding*. Moreover, other classes of the class diagram (e.g., message in the FlexSend example of Figure 6) are used to indicate a complexType for the type section of the WSDL document. These conversion rules are implemented in a XSLT stylesheet and executed in the UMT tool. In a similar way we developed a style sheet able to translate UML diagrams into a WSOL specification as shown below.

Running Case

In the following, we propose examples of WSDL sections that are generated using UMT tool and the class diagram produced in the customization phase. The Message class is translated as a ComplexType in the <type> section of the WSDL document (Figure 9). This ComplexType has the same name of the class and the composed part elements represent all the class attributes. Every attribute is shown with the same name and the same type of UML attributes (e.g String, Int, Boolean, etc.). The public methods of the class stereotyped as <<BusinessService>> are translated as both a WSDL portType and a WSDL binding. For example, the RequestMessageDelivery method is represented by the portType shown in Figure 10. Following this approach we generate the WSDL description of the FlexSend web service.

The same approach can be used to generate a WSOL document that describes non-functional aspects of the web service. The used UML profile and the proposed QoS classification allow the definition of the transformation rules implemented in our new XSLT stylesheet. We translate each <<QoS level-agreement>> class with a precondition WSOL constraint.

CONCLUSION AND FUTURE WORK

The QoS-based web service design process is one of the most relevant issues in service-oriented architectures. To support organizations in the design of quality-based web services, we have proposed WSMoD, a methodology that makes use of knowledge available in the organization related to services, context of use and the provided quality of service. Such knowledge is represented by ontologies, which are used to guide the design process by providing several heuristics in order to characterize services and their qualities. Furthermore, the use of ontologies allows the different players in the design process

Figure 9. ComplexType of FlexSend

```
<types>
  <xsd:complexType name="Message">
    <xsd:sequence>
      <xsd:element name="Message Priority" type="xsd1:String">
      <xsd:element name="Attachment_preference" type="xsd1:String">
      <xsd:element name="Confirmation priority" type="xsd1:String">
      <xsd:element name="Truncate message" type="xsd1:String">
      <xsd:element name="Cost constraints" type="xsd:int">
      <xsd:element name="Security" type="xsd1:String">
    </xsd:sequence>
  </xsd:complexType>
</types>
```

Figure 10. RequestMessageDelivery portType of FlexSend

```
<portType name="RequestMessageDelivery">
  <operation name="RequestMessageDelivery">
  <input message="xsd1:sendRequest"/>
  <output message="xsd1:sendResponse"/>
  </operation>
</portType>
```

to set up common understandings by sharing and capturing knowledge. The methodology enriches the Model Driven Architecture philosophy by extending the platform independent model with a contextual model, which aims to include context information related to users and distribution channels independent of technological details. In order to enhance interoperability and practical applications, we provided the methodology with an integrated suite of widely used tools. Finally, we have reported the results of the use of WSMoD in a real-life case study, concerning FlexSend, a flexible QoS-based web service for message notification.

Furthermore our work will proceed in several directions. We are investigating an extension of OntoServ to include domain dependent aspects in the current OWL definitions by means of OWL-S expressions. Currently, OWL-S is only exploited to describe the actual services; in the future OntoServ concepts might be enriched with service-specific notations. We aim to exploit the full power of ontologies, moving to a more supporting formal framework. We will also study how to automatically import/export to/from Protégé the UML diagrams defined in our methodology (this issue has been recently addressed in (Timm & Gannod, 2005)). Furthermore, WSMoD is presently suited to the design of elementary web services; our final goal is to extend the methodology to include the design of composite web services as orchestrations of existing (or new) QoS-enabled web services. In particular, the customization phase needs to be extended to address the different service composition rules (sequence, parallel, switch, etc.) that require the definition of related quality composition laws. The issue is to compose the quality dependency graphs of the composing elementary services to deliver a unified quality profile associated with the composite service. The work in that direction, which has already started, and preliminary results that extend the hybrid approach introduced in this paper have been achieved (Comerio, De Paoli et. al., 2006). Finally, we are working to integrate the different tools exploited in the methodology to ensure interoperability and support for the design process. In particular, the development of an integrated tool based on Eclipse is under development. The goal is to provide designers with the visual representation of ontologies to support navigation, advanced searching facilities to identify relevant concepts and relations, computational features associated with quality related ontologies to compute quantitative evaluation of qualities, management of UML diagrams and generation of service specification (WSDL and quality profiling).

ACKNOWLEGMENT

This work has been partially supported by the European IST project n. 27347 SEEMP - Single European Employment Market-Place and Italian FIRB project eG4M - eGovernment for Mediterranean countries.

REFERENCES

Adorni, M., Arcelli, F., Ardagna, D., Baresi, L., Batini, C., Cappiello, C., et al. (2005). The MAIS approach to web service design. In *EMMSAD '05: Proceeding of Tenth International Workshop on Exploring Modeling Methods in Systems Analysis and Design*, Porto, Portugal (pp. 387-398).

Afandi, R., Zhang, J., & Gunter, C. A. (2006). Ampol-q: Adaptive middleware policy to support qos. In *ICSOC '06: Proceeding of the 4th International Conference on Service-Oriented Computing*, Chicago, IL, USA (pp.165–178).

Arcelli, F., Raibulet, C., Tisato, F., & Adorni, M. (2004). Architectural Reflection in Adaptive Systems. In *SEKE '04: Proceeding of the International Conference on Software Engineering & Knowledge Engineering*, Banff, Canada (pp. 74-79).

Ardagna, D., Comerio, M., De Paoli, F., & Grega, S. (2005). An Hybrid Approach to QoS Evaluation. In *EMMSAD '05: Proceeding of the International Workshop on Exploring Modeling Methods in Systems Analysis and Design*, Porto, Portugal, (pp. 581-592).

Beck, K. (2000). *Extreme Programming Explained: Embrice Change*. Boston, MA: Addison-Wesley.

Benatallah, B., Hacid, M., Leger, A., Rey, C., & Toumani, F. (2005). On automating Web Services Discovery. *The VLDB Journal, 14*(1), 84–96. doi:10.1007/s00778-003-0117-x

Benatallah, B., Sheng, Q. Z., & Dumas, M. (2003). The Self-Serv Environment for Web Services Composition. *IEEE Internet Computing, 7*(1), 40–48. doi:10.1109/MIC.2003.1167338

Bolchini, D., Paolini, P. (2004). Goal-Driven Requirements Analysis for Hypermedia-intensive Web Applications. *Requirements Engineering Journal, RE03 Special Issue (9),* 85-103.

Buchmann, F., & Bass, L. (2001). Introduction to the attribute driven design method. In *ICSE '01: Proceeding of the 23rd international Conference on Software Engineering*, Toronto, Ontario, Canada.

Cappiello, C., Missier, P., Pernici, B., Plebani, P., & Batini, C. (2004). QoS in Multichannel IS: The MAIS Approach. In *ICWE Workshops '04: Proceeding of the International Conference on Web Engineering*, Munich, Germany (pp. 255-268).

Capra, L., Emmerich, W., & Mascolo, C. (2001). Reflective Middleware Solutions for Context-Aware Applications. In *REFLECTION '01: Proceeding of the Third International Conference on Metalevel Architectures and Separation of Crosscutting Concerns*, London, UK (pp. 126-133).

Cardoso, J., Miller, J., Sheth, A., & Arnold, J. (2004). Modeling Quality of Service for Workflows and Web Service Processes. *Web Semantics Journal, 1*(3), 281–308.

Comerio, M., De Paoli, F., & Grega, S. (2006). Quality Composition in Web-Service Design. In *ICDCSW '06: Proceeding of the International Conference on Distributed Computing Systems-Workshops*, Lisbon, Portugal.

Comerio, M., De Paoli, F., Grega, S., Batini, C., Di Francesco, C., & Di Pasquale, A. (2004). A Service Re-design Methodology for Multi-channel Adaptation. In *ICSOC '04: Proceeding of the International Conf. of Service Oriented Computing*, New York, NY, USA (pp.11-20).

Comerio, M., De Paoli, F., Maurino, A., & Palmonari, M. (2007). NFP-aware Semantic Web Services Selection. In *EDOC '07: Proceeding of the 11th IEEE International Enterprise Distributed Object Computing Conference*, Annapolis, Maryland, USA (pp. 70-78).

Fensel, D., & Bussler, C. (2002). The Web Service Modeling Framework WSMF. *Electronic Commerce Research and Applications, 1*(2), 113–137. doi:10.1016/S1567-4223(02)00015-7

Gomez-Perez, A., Gonzalez-Cabero, R., & Lama, M. (2004). A Framework for Design and Composition of Semantic Web Services. *IEEE Intelligent Systems, 19*(4), 24–31. doi:10.1109/MIS.2004.32

Graziani, P., Billi, R., Burzagli, L., Gabbanini, A., Palchetti, B., Bertini, E., Kimani, S., Sbattella, L., Barbieri, T., Bianchi, C., Batini, C. (2003). Definition of User Typologies. *MAIS internal report R 7.3.1.*

Groenmo, R., & Solheim, I. (2004). Towards Modelling Web Service Composition in UML. In *WSMAI '04: Proceeding of the International Workshop on Web Service Modeling, Architecture and Infrastructure*, Porto, Portugal (pp.72-86).

IBM. (2006). *IBM Rational Software Development Platform*. Retrieved August 17, 2007, from http://www.ibm.com/software/developmentplatform.

IBM. (2008). *WebSphere Application Server*. Retrieved March 20, 2008, from http://www-306.ibm.com/software/webservers/appserv/was/.

Jaeger, M. C., Rojec-Goldmann, G., & Muhl, G. (2004). QoS Aggregation for Web Service Composition using Workflow Patterns. In *EDOC '04: Proceeding of the Enterprise Distributed Object Computing Conference*, Washington, DC, USA, (pp. 149-159).

Klien, E., Einspanier, U., Lutz, M., & Hübner, S. (2004). An Architecture for Ontology-based Discovery and Retrieval of Geographic Information. In *AGILE '04: Proceeding of the 7th Conference on Geographic Information Science*, Heraklion, Greece (pp. 179-188).

Kritikos, K., & Plexousakis, D. (2006). Semantic QoS Metric Matching. In *ECOWS '06: Proceeding of the European Conference on Web Services*, Washington, DC, USA (pp. 265–274).

LP. (2005). *LP_SOLVE: Linear Programming Code*. Retrieved March 1, 2006, from http://www.cs.sunysb.edu/~algorith/implement/lpsolve/implement.shtml

Lum, W. Y., & Lau, F. C. M. (2003). User-Centric Content Negotiation for Effective Adaptation Service in Mobile Computing. *IEEE Transactions on Software Engineering, 29*(12), 1000–1111.

Manasce, D. (2004). Composing Web Service: A QoS View. *IEEE Internet Computing, 8*(6), 88–90. doi:10.1109/MIC.2004.57

Maurino, A., Pernici, B., & Schreiber, F. A. (2003). Adaptive channel behavior in financial information system. In *CAiSE '03: Proceeding of the Conference on Advanced Information System Engineering*, Klagenfurt/Velden, Austria (pp. 109-112).

Maximilien, E., & Singh, M. P. (2004). A framework and ontology for dynamic web services selection. *IEEE Internet Computing, 8*(5), 84–93. doi:10.1109/MIC.2004.27

Mylopoulos, J., & Lau, D. (2004). Designing Web Services with Tropos. In *ICWS '04: Proceeding of the IEEE International Conference on Web Services*, Washington, DC, USA (p. 306).

Noy, N. F., Fergerson, R. W., & Musen, M. A. (2000). The Knowledge Model of Protégé-2000: Combining Interoperability and Flexibility. In *EKAW '00: Proceeding of the 12th European Workshop on Knowledge Acquisition, Modeling and Management*, London, UK (pp. 17–32).

Noy, N. F., Sintek, M., Decker, S., Crubezy, M., Fergerson, R. W., & Musen, M. A. (2001). Creating semantic web contents with protege-2000. *IEEE Intelligent Systems, 16*, 60–71. doi:10.1109/5254.920601

OMG. (2004). *UML Profile for Modeling Quality of Service, Fault Tolerance Characteristics, Mechanisms*. Retrieved June 14, 2005, from http://www.omg.org/docs/ptc/04-06-01.pdf

Pahl, C., & Casey, M. (2003). Ontology support for web service processes. In ESEC/FSE-11: Proceeding of the 9th European software engineering conference held jointly with 11th ACM SIGSOFT international symposium on Foundations of software engineering, New York, NY, USA (pp. 208–216).

Papazoglou, M., Traverso, P., Dustdar, S., Leymann, F., & Krämer, B. (2006). Service-oriented computing: A research roadmap. In *Service Oriented Computing (SOC) Dagstuhl Seminar Proceeding*.

Pernici, B. (2006). *Mobile Information Systems – Infrastructure and Design for Adaptivity and Flexibility (the MAIS approach)*. Springer.

Provost., W. (2003). *UML for Web services*. Retrieved March 1, 2006, from http://www.xml.com/lpt/a/ws/2003/08/05/uml.html

Radhakrishnan, R., & Wookey, M. (2004). *Model driven Architecture enabling Service oriented architectures*. Retrieved March 3, 2005, from http://www.omg.org/news/whitepapers/mdasoa.pdf

Shuping, R. (2003). A Framework for Discovering Web Services with Desired Quality of Services Attributes. In *ICWS '03: Proceedings of the International Conference on Web Services*, Las Vegas, Nevada, USA (pp. 208-213).

Skogan, D., Groenmo, R., & Solheim, I. (2004). Web Service Composition in UML. In *EDOC '04: Proceeding of the IEEE Enterprise Distributed Object Computing,* Monterey, USA (pp. 47-57).

Stephenson, J. (2003). *Service Oriented Architecture, OptimalJ, CBDI Report*. Retrieved March 1, 2006, from http://www.omg.org/mda/mda_files/CBDI-SOAOptimalJ-US2003.pdf.

Timm, J. T. E., & Gannod, G. C. (2005). A Model-Driven Approach for Specifying Semantic Web Services. In *ICWS '05: Proceeding of the IEEE International Conference on Web Services*, Washington, DC, USA (pp. 313–320).

Tosic, V., Patel, K., & Pagurek, B. (2002). WSOL - Web Service Offerings Language. In *CAiSE '02/ WES '02: Revised Papers from the International Workshop on Web Services, E-Business, and the Semantic Web*, London, UK (pp. 57–67).

Tsesmetzis, D., Roussaki, I., Papaioannou, I., & Anagnostou, M. (2006). Qos awareness support in web-service semantics. In *AICT/ICIW '06: Proceeding of the Advanced International Conference on Telecommunications and International Conference on Internet and Web Applications and Services*, Guadeloupe, French Caribbean, (pp. 128–135).

Ulbrich, A., Weis, T., & Geihs, K. (2003). QoS Mechanism Composition at Design-Time and Runtime. In *ICDCSW '03: Proceeding of the 23rd International Conference on Distributed Computing Systems, Washington*, DC, USA (pp. 118-136).

UMT SINTEF. (2005). *UML Model Transformation Tool*. Retrieved March 1, 2006, from http://umt-qvt.sourceforge.net

WSMO. (2005). *Web Services Modeling Ontology*. Retrieved March 1, 2006, from http://www.wsmo.org/TR/d2/v1.2/

Zeng, L., Benatallah, B., Ngu, A., Dumas, M., Kalagnanam, J., & Chang, H. (2004). QoS-aware middleware for Web Service Composition. *IEEE Transactions on Software Engineering, 30*(5), 311–327. doi:10.1109/TSE.2004.11

Chapter 3
A Metamorphic Testing Methodology for Online SOA Application Testing

W. K. Chan[1]
City University of Hong Kong, Hong Kong

S. C. Cheung
Hong Kong University of Science and Technology, Hong Kong

Karl R. P. H. Leung
Hong Kong Institute of Vocational Education, Hong Kong

ABSTRACT

Testing the correctness of service integration is a step toward assurance of the quality of applications. These applications however may bind dynamically to their supportive services using the SOA pattern that share the same service interface, yet the latter services may behave differently. In addition, a service may implement a business strategy, such as best pricing, relative to the behaviors of its competitors and the dynamic market conditions. As such, defining a test oracle that specifies the absolute expected outcomes for individual test cases is hard. Many existing works ignore these issues to address the problem of identifying failures from test results. This chapter studies an approach to online testing. Service testing is divided into two steps. In the spirit of metamorphic testing, the offline step determines a set of successful test cases to construct their corresponding follow-up test cases for the online step. These test cases will be executed by metamorphic services that encapsulate the services as well as applicable metamorphic relations. Thus, any failure revealed by the approach will be a failure of the service under test.

INTRODUCTION

Service-oriented architecture (SOA) is a kind of architectural reference model (Bass et al., 2003) to support distributed computing. A notable example is Web services (W3C, 2002). It promises to alleviate the problems related to the integration of applications of heterogeneous technologies (Mukhi et al., 2004; Kreger et al., 2003). In this reference model, a SOA application consists of a set of self-contained, communicating components, known as *services*, in which each service should make little

DOI: 10.4018/978-1-61520-684-1.ch003

or no assumption about its collaborating services. This setting advocates the dynamic composition of services by using different configurations of supportive services.

Typical end-users of a decent SOA application, such as bank customers using an online foreign exchange trading service, may however expect consistent outcomes each time they use the service, probably except some upgrade of the services. For instance, the customers may compare the online foreign exchange service of a bank to similar services of other banks to judge whether the service is good in product quality. If a Business-to-Business (B2B) service provider is driven by a predefined business strategy, for example, to maintain its market share, then the criteria to define functional correctness of the service may vary according to the dynamic banking environment. As such, testers may not be provided with predefined expected test outcomes; and by the business nature, testers (technical professionals) may not know the decisions of business managers, and vice versa. Such a barrier in the application domain of the service under test makes the manual judgment on the test results by the testers ineffective and inefficient. This may lengthen the testing of services.

Services may be subject to both offline testing and online testing. Unlike the testing of conventional programs, services bind dynamically to other peer services when it is tested online. In some cases, the behaviors of these peer services are not known precisely in advance, and may evolve during testing. While the offline testing of services is analogous to the testing of conventional programs, the online testing of services needs to address new issues and difficulties.

In testing, testers should address both the test case selection problem and the test oracle problem (Beizer, 1990). As we have explained above, identifying failures from the test results is challenging in service testing. Therefore, we restrict our attention to the latter problem in this chapter.

A *test oracle* is a mechanism that reliably decides whether a test succeeds. In services computing, formal test oracle may be unavailable. Instead, the expected behavior of a service may evolve dynamically according to the environment. Such an expected behavior may be relative to the behaviors of competing services or other services. Tsai et al. (2004), for example, suggest using a progressive ranking of similar implementations of the same service interface to alleviate the test oracle problem. Their proposal is useful when all implementations should provide the same results on the same input. However, sometimes, the behaviors of different implementations of the same service (e.g., search engines) may vary. The test result of a particular group of implementations cannot be served reliably as the expected result of another group of implementations of the same service on the same test case. In addition, a typical SOA application may comprise collaborative services of multiple organizations. Knowing all the implementations of different organizations is hard (Ye et al., 2006). For example, a travel package consultant may bundle services of hotels, airlines and entertainment centers to personalize tour packages for a particular client. Without the implementation details, static analysis appears hard to be applied to assure the quality of the application. The black-box approach to checking the test results remains popular to assure the correctness of these applications.

Traditionally, the expected result of a program on a test case is defined in the *absolute* sense (Beizer, 1990). Having the program output for the test case, a tester compares the program output with the expected result. If they match, then no failure has been revealed. The test case is termed as a *successful test case*. On the other hand, if there is any mismatch, tester deems that the test case is *failure-causing*.

Metamorphic testing (MT) (Chan et al., 1998; Chen et al., 1998, 2002) is an approach to alleviating the test oracle problem in the *relative* sense. When the program output of the above test case is collected, the program output will not be directly compare to the expected results because of the test oracle problem. Instead, when the program outputs for some test cases have been collected, MT constructs more test cases from them, and collects their program outputs. Then, MT compares the program outputs of these entire test cases, with the aim to identify failures. The former kind of test cases is known as *source test case*, and those constructed by MT are called *follow-up test cases.*

The main contributions of the chapter include:

1. It applies the notion of metamorphic testing to services computing to alleviate the test oracle problem.
2. It proposes a metamorphic testing mechanism for services computing. It suggests encapsulating a service under test in a metamorphic service, which also executes test cases and cross-validates their test results. This strategy integrates seamlessly to existing popular SOA frameworks. It automates the construction of follow-up test cases and their test results checking.
3. It formulates a strategy to use successful test cases identified in the offline testing step as the source test cases for online testing step. When a service is tested offline, the testing environment could be controlled by the testers, test oracle is thus easier to be defined. When it is the case, any failure revealed by our metamorphic testing approach will be the failures in the online testing mode.
4. It evaluates the proposal in a controlled experiment. The experimental result indicates that our proposal is superior to a rival approach that the test results of source test cases have not been verified as in the conventional MT sense. The rival approach suffers from an extra 16% of effort to check test results and a 13% reduction of failure detection capability.

The content of this chapter is mainly taken from (Chan et al. 2007). The chapter further supplements the related work on the development of service testing. We also take this opportunity to clarify some concepts that have not been done satisfactorily.

The rest of the chapter is organized as follows. We first introduce the concepts of services, metamorphic testing and other preliminaries. Then, we describe our testing proposal through a running scenario, followed by an experiment on applying the proposal in a SOA application. Finally, we compare our approach to related work and discuss the lessons learnt.

PRELIMINARIES

In this section, we briefly introduce the notion of service, metamorphic relation, and metamorphic testing. We will also introduce the key terminologies and assumption of our model in relation to service testing used in this chapter.

Service

A *service* in SOA is a well-defined, self-contained application function, packaged as a reusable component, for the use in a business process (Colan, 2004). It can be described publicly so that other services may discover and locate the service. Services also use simple and self-contained messages with well-defined interfaces for communications. Those interfaces are neutral to different hardware or software platforms to support the execution of a service. Meta-models, such as XML Schema (W3C, 2001), are often used to govern the syntactic validity of the messages.

For example, the Web Services (Curbera, 2002; W3C, 2002) use the *web service definition language* or WSDL (W3C, 2005) to enable each service of an application define the syntactic and interoperability requirements. It also uses the *universal description, discovery and integration* or UDDI (OASIS, 2005) to offer applications a unified and systematic way to locate services from service registries. The *simple object access protocol* or SOAP (W3C, 2003) is then used to support XML[2]-based messaging between peer services.

In general, there are two types of service, namely *stateless* and *stateful*. They are analogue to conventional programs and object-oriented programs, respectively. Both types are popular in these days.[3] Intuitively, in terms of modeling, one may use a stateless service with self-addressing stateful messages to simulate a stateful service. We restrict ourselves to consider stateless services in this chapter.

Metamorphic Relation (MR)

As a service is a self-contained and function-oriented component, some functional properties of the service should be identifiable. One way to specify the functional properties of a service is to co-relate the service under different conditions. It is similar to specify a function using an implicit form in the sense of mathematics.

A *metamorphic relation*, or *MR* for short, is an existing or expected relation over a set of distinct inputs and their corresponding outputs for multiple executions of the target function (Chen et al., 1998, 2002, 2003). For example, consider a sorting program *Sort*() that re-arranges the input list of integers into a list of integers in the ascending order. The expected result of *Sort*(⟨*1,4,3*⟩) should be the same as that of *Sort*(⟨*1,3,4*⟩). Generalizing the above sorting instance, we may construct the following relation: *Sort*(*X*) = *Sort*(*Y*) *if Y* = *Permutation*(*X*), which means that the sorting program should give the same sorted list for different permutations of the same list of integers serving as inputs.

The above kind of permutation property seems not easy to quantify if testers insist on defining the expected results explicitly. Suppose that such quantification is not within the reach of testers to define them, testers may resolve to define the expected results of test cases explicitly and individually; intuitively, the test oracle will be more tedious. On the other hand, if a property can be easily to be defined either explicitly or implicitly, then testers may opt to use either one (or both) to quantify the expected results.

One may observe that the above metamorphic relation does not check whether the integers in the output are sorted in the ascending order. Testers may design some metamorphic relations to cover similar properties, which aim at checking the ordering of integers. For instance, testers may design the following metamorphic relations to serve the purpose: *last(Sort(Y^Z)* ≥ *last(Sort(X^Z)) if last(Sort(Y))* ≥ *last(Sort(X))*, where *X, Y, Z* are lists of integers, the *last*() returns the last element in the given list, and the operation "^" concatenates two lists. One may further strengthen the condition to require *X* should be a sublist of *Y*.

One can easily observe that in the above example, the expected output of the input ⟨*1,4,3*⟩ can only be induced implicitly. This relieves testers to predetermine the expected behavior of a test case in an absolute term.

Formally, a metamorphic relation can be described as follows:

Suppose that f is an implemented function under test. Given a relation r over n distinct inputs $x_1, x_2, \ldots, x_n$ the corresponding n computation outputs $f(x_1), f(x_2), \ldots, f(x_n)$ must induce a necessary property r_f.

A metamorphic relation MR_f of f over n inputs and n outputs can be defined as follows:

$$MR_f = \{(x_1, x_2, \ldots, x_n, f(x_1), f(x_2), \ldots, f(x_n)) \mid r(x_1, x_2, \ldots, x_n) \Rightarrow r_f(x_1, x_2, \ldots, x_n, f(x_1), f(x_2), \ldots, f(x_n))\}$$

We observe that, when a service is seen to be a function, and all input and output messages are self-contained, the notion of metamorphic relation readily applies to services. We will give a running example after the introduction of metamorphic testing in the following section.

Metamorphic Testing (MT)

Metamorphic testing or MT (Chen et al., 1998, 2002, 2004) is a program testing technique that employs the mathematical relations, namely metamorphic relations, to conduct testing. It has been applied to different types of applications such as numerical applications (Chan et al., 1998), and context-aware applications (Chan et al., 2005c, 2006).

MT uses successful test cases to alleviate the test oracle problem when a test oracle is unavailable or costly. Given a program, P of a target function f with input domain D. A set of test cases T, $\{t_1,\ldots,t_k\}$ ($\subset D$), can be selected according to a test case selection strategy. Executing the program P on T produces corresponding outputs $P(t_1),\ldots,$ $P(t_k)$. When they reveal any failure, testing may stop and debugging could be begun. On the other hand, when no failure is revealed, these test cases will be termed as *successful*. A set of successful test cases is called a successful test set.

Testers may apply the metamorphic testing approach to verifying whenever some necessary property of the target function f is satisfied by the implementation P. The metamorphic testing approach constructs the *follow-up* test set T', $\{t'_1,\ldots,t'_m\}$ ($\subset D$), automatically from the initial successful test set T, with the reference to some given metamorphic relation.

Let us give an example in the services computing setting. Suppose that S is an expected USD–HKD exchange service, which accepts deal orders in USD and returns deal orders in HKD; x and y are two deal orders; $g()$ is a function that accepts a deal order and returns its order amount. Further suppose that the following metamorphic relation is given, meaning that double the deal order in USD, would double the resultant amount in HKD:

$MR_a(x, y, S(x), S(y))$:

$$2g(S(y)) = g(S(x)) \text{ if } g(x) = 2g(y)$$

Consider a successful test case x_1 = "a deal order of US$20,000". The MT approach will construct automatically another test case y_1 = "a deal order of US$10,000" based on the condition $g(x) = 2g(y)$ of MR_a.

Suppose P is an implementation of S. If the comparison $2g(P(y_1)) = g(P(x_1))$ fails, the MT approach reveals a failure based on the pair of failure-causing inputs x_1 and y_1. As x_1 is successful in the first place, the test case y_1 should cause the failure.

x_1 is termed as a *source test case*, and y_1 is termed as a *follow-up test case*. By checking the results amongst multiple input-output pairs, MT bypasses the need to define the expected result explicitly to alleviate the test oracle problem. We refer readers to (Chen et al, 2002, 2003, 2004; Chan et al., 2005c, 2006; Tse et al., 2004) for more details about metamorphic testing.

In this chapter, we assume that all MRs are provided by testers. In practice, we recommend testers to define their MRs in a style so that they are coded straightforwardly. As such, the implementation of MRs is a second-class issue when testers use our methodology. When an implementation of MRs involves non-trivial programming, it may contain faults. We invite readers to the work (Liang, 2007) on the robustness of metamorphic testing for more details.

Assumptions and Terminologies

In this section, we list out a few major assumptions to establish our model for online testing of services.

We model a service to associate with a component view, and hence such a service could be wrapped by another service (wrapper). Our rationale is that services are loosely coupled amongst them, and they recognize one another through the common service registries. Adding a wrapper does not alter the messages for collaboration and the service interfaces kept in service registries. Indeed, we also assume that in the common service registries, the entries of wrapper services replace these original services for the testing purpose. This setting enables wrappers to query and catch messages for the original services. In our model, due to the component nature of a service, we use a message relevant to a service as a *test case* or *test result* of the service. Other researchers also adapt similar strategies (Tsai et al., 2004; Offutt and Xu, 2004). It enables a wrapper service to construct test cases and evaluate their test results.

Many services do not have prior knowledge about their target business partners to form service compositions. To allow services to be useful and reusable in different environments, we agree with other researchers that a major kind of services is self-contained and independent to the contexts of other services. It also outputs results on every input. When there is no output in between two consecutive inputs, the respective wrapper service should be able to detect the case. Hence, a consecutive sequence of inputs in between a pair of consecutive outputs can be considered as an input message to the service under test in our model.

We refer the term *online testing* to the testing of a service under the SOA environment, and the term *offline testing* to the testing of a service without interaction with other services relevant to the service under test. We also term *offline testing* and *testing in the offline mode* interchangeably, and *online testing* and *testing in the online mode* interchangeably.

AN ONLINE TESTING APPROACH

In this section, an online testing methodology will be presented. We propose to test a service in two distinct modes (steps), namely offline mode (step) and online mode (step). We use the test oracle available to an offline testing and make it also available to an online testing via metamorphic relations. In the Overview section below, we first introduce the two modes of testing. Next, in the Metamorphic Service section, we present the notion of metamorphic service, which serves as a surrogate of the services under test to relay messages; at the same time, it constructs follow-up test cases and evaluates results accordingly. We then summarize the methodology in the Testing in the Online Mode section.

Overview

The offline mode tests a service in the absence of interacting services. We view that it resembles to the convention techniques for the unit test of a conventional program. Many test data selection strategies, such as dataflow testing (Beizer, 1990; Zhu et al., 1997), and test oracle construction for the unit test of conventional programs have been researched for years. Alternatively, one may factor the XML aspect of services into testing activity (Mei et al., 2008). Since testers could control the offline environment (such as providing test drivers and stub services, and messages), intuitively, it is relatively easy to define test sets for a service, and validate the test results in this mode. Thus, whether a test case reveals a failure or not, for offline testing, could be determined through the checking of their test results against certain test oracle.

The above observation inspres us to apply the successful test cases of an offline test as the source test cases for subsequent online test. In the sequel, we restrict ourselves to discuss the online testing mode. We presume a set of successful test cases for the offline testing being given.

In online testing, as these source test cases are determined to be successful in advance in its preceding offline test, any violation of a corresponding metamorphic relation should be rooted by the follow-up test cases. Thus, our approach pinpoints the failure-causing inputs automatically even if the test oracle for online testing is

Figure 1. The Integration between offline and online testing

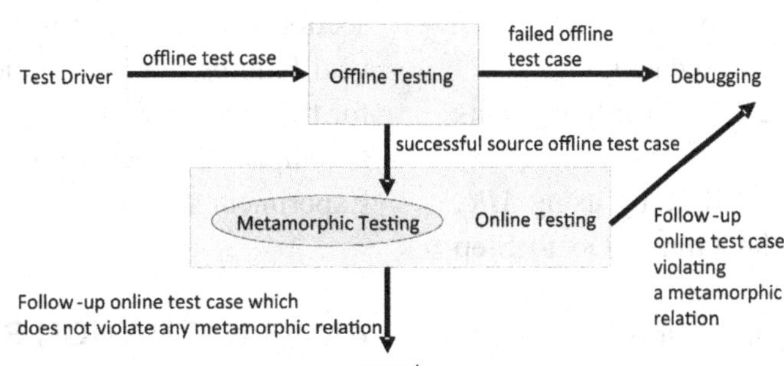

not directly available. Figure 1 depicts the relation between offline testing and our proposal for online testing.

Readers may compare the above strategy and the strategy that a source test case is unknown to be successful or not. In the latter strategy, when a violation of a metamorphic relation is detected, testers should further evaluate whether the violation is contributed by the source test case (no matter it is in the offline or online testing mode) or by the follow-up (online) test case. Intuitively, this alternative strategy may incur more overheads than our proposal. We will further study this issue in our empirical experiment in the Experiment section.

To ease our discussion, in the sequel, we use a metamorphic relation with two input-output pairs. The extension of the approach to higher dimensional input-output pairs is not hard. In the next section, we present notion of wrapper service.

Metamorphic Service (MS)

A *metamorphic service* is both (1) a service that has the characteristics of being an access wrapper (Mecella and Pernici, 2001; Umar, 1997) and (2) an agent to conduct metamorphic testing. In brief, a metamorphic service imitates all the data and application access paths of the service being encapsulated. It also implements necessary metamorphic relations to compute follow-up test cases based on an incoming (or outgoing) message, and evaluates test results according to the implemented metamorphic relations.

Since a metamorphic service is a service, it dynamically discovers a peer service to receive a follow-up test case. The result of the follow-up test case will send to the metamorphic service for the detection of failures. The metamorphic service checks the test results against other test cases generated by its metamorphic relations using the received and generated messages.

Testing in the Online Mode

The testing in the online mode validates whether a service interacts correctly with the other services. The following presents the self-explanatory methodological procedure for this mode.

(ON-1). For a service under test *S*, collect the set of service descriptions D_S that represents the services interacting with *S*.

(ON-2). Design a metamorphic relations MR_i applicable to test *S* in the online mode.

(ON-3). Implement MR_i in the metamorphic service *MS* of the service *S*.

(ON-4). Repeat Steps (ON-2) to (ON-3) until no additional metamorphic relation is required for online testing.

(ON-5). For each available successful offline test case t_o, do

i. *MS* uses applicable MR_i to construct the following-up test case t_f of t_o.
ii. *MS* invokes *S* to execute t_f.
iii. *MS* obtains the corresponding results of *S* on t_f
iv. If *MS* detect a failure by using MR_i, then reports the failure. Go to Step (ON-7).
v. Repeat Steps (On-5-i) to (On-5-iv) until no more applicable MR_i.

(ON-6). Report that no failure is found.
(ON-7). Exit

Step (ON-1) collects the service description that the service under test intends to collaborate. They facilitate testers to define and implement relevant metamorphic relations[4] in Steps (ON-2) and (ON-3) respectively.

If a tester does not identify additional metamorphic relation, Step ON-4 naturally stops. On the other hand, if a tester recognizes a metamorphic relation, but is inaccessible to implement such a relation for the service under test, the tester hardly uses MT approach to test services. It is akin to a tester who cannot implement assertions in program code (Beizer, 1990) to check individual program executions.

Step (ON-5) uses a source test case to construct a follow-up test case, applies it to the service under test and collects the respective test result. Next, it evaluates the results until all implemented and applicable metamorphic relations have been enumerated. When it detects a violation of any metamorphic relation, in Step (On-5-iv), it reports the detected failure and stops the testing procedure. Otherwise, the procedure iterates, using another source test case until all source test cases has been enumerated. If no failure could be detected by any test case, the methodology will report such a case in Step (ON-6) and stop at Step (ON-7). Alternatively, one may naturally use the newly generated set of follow-up test cases as another set of source test cases to conduct the testing procedure further.

After presenting our approach above, the next section will demonstrate a way to use MT to reveal failures relevant to the relative correctness for the testing of a service. We will then present an empirical experiment of our proposal in the Experiment section.

AN ILLUSTRATION SCENARIO

In this section, our proposal for online testing will be illustrated via an example. We first describe an application and its faults. Then, we illustrate how these faults can be revealed.

Figure 2 shows a foreign exchange dealing service application with five services (from FXDS1 to FXDS5). In particular, FXDS2 is embraced by a metamorphic service (*MS*). It has three metamorphic relations, namely MR1, MR2 and MR3. To ease our discussion, we focus our attention on discussing the deal order that converts the currency between US dollars and Renminbi.

A bank normally offers cross-currency rates inquiry services. A sample USD–RMB exchange rate is a pair of values such as 8.2796/8.2797. The first value and the second value in the pair refer to the *bid rate* and the *ask* rate, respectively. The difference between the two values in such a pair is known as the spread. We will use this rate for the following illustration, and assume these rates to be provided by the service FXDS4.

Suppose the expected behaviors of FXDS2 include:

(i) It provides a uniform exchange rate for any deal order.
(ii) It provides a better, or at least the same, exchange rate to its clients than its rivals (e.g. the service FXDS3).
(iii) It checks the exchange rates from central banks dynamically (e.g. the service FXDS4 for Central Bank of China, or FXDS5 for European Central Bank).

Figure 2. A foreign exchange services system

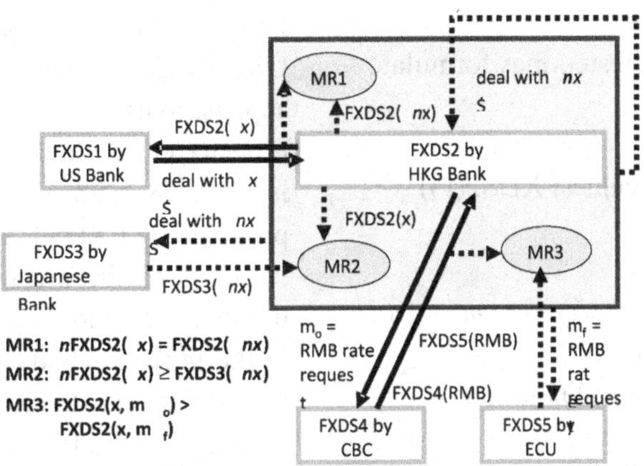

Further suppose that the implementation FXDS2 contains the following two faults:

(a) It uses the bid rate or the ask rate to process a deal order non-deterministically.
(b) It uses the minimum (that is, the worst rate) instead of the maximum (that is, the best rate) for its rate calculations.

To test the service FXDS2, testers can apply our testing methodology, which is illustrated as follows.

Testers first formulate metamorphic relations. For the requirement (*i*), testers can check whether the output amount of service FXSD2 for a deal order is proportional to the "size" of the deal order. It forms the first metamorphic relation:

MR1: nFXDS2(x) = FXDS2(nx).

Consider an original test message t_o: a deal order of x (= US\$100). FXDS2 correctly uses the above bid rate to output a message FXDS2(US\$100) = 827.96 = 8.2796 × 100 in the offline testing mode (with the help of test stubs if necessary). The metamorphic service *MS* constructs a follow-up test case t_f: a deal order of US\$200 = 2 × x. It then passes this message to FXDS2 to execute in the online testing mode. (This is shown as the top-right dotted arrow in Figure 2.)

Suppose, unfortunately, FXDS2 incorrectly uses the above ask rate and outputs 1655.94 (i.e, FXDS2(US\$200) = 1655.94 = 2× 827.97). Since both messages FXDS2(US\$100) and FXDS2(US\$200) can be checked by *MS* via MR1, we have, 2 × FXDS2(US\$100) = 1655.92 ≠ 1655.94 = FXDS2(US\$200). It violates MR1. Hence, a failure relevant to the fault (*a*) is revealed and reported by the metamorphic service.

Readers may be interested to know the results of other combinations of using bid and ask rates for either the original or the follow-up test cases. When the source test case and the follow-up test cases use the bid rate or the ask rate, MR1 will be ineffective to reveal any failure. However, when the source test case incorrectly uses the ask rate and the follow-up test case correctly uses the bid rate, MR1 will reveal a failure relevant to the fault (*a*).

Let us next describe the scenarios to reveal the fault (*b*). For the requirement (*ii*), testers may increase or decrease a deal order size by a multiplier. (In practice, a deal order size applicable to a global bank may be inapplicable to a small foreign exchange shop at a street corner.) Such a follow-up deal order will be forwarded to a competing service (e.g. FXDS3). *MS* may be used to determine whether the output of FXDS2 of the same order size is better than or equal to that provided by a rival service. This formulates the following metamorphic relation:

MR2: nFXDS2(x) ≥ FXDS3(n x).

For the requirement (*iii*), testers may formulate the metamorphic relation:

MR3: value(FXDS2(x)) > value(FXDS2(y))

if centralbank(FXDS2(x)) = m_o and centralbank(FXDS2(y)) = m_f

Alternatively, in a shorthand notation:

MR3: FXDS2(x, m_o) > FXDS2(x, m_f)

MR3 means that if the currency conversion is from USD to RMB, then the rate, provided by the Central Bank of China via the rate request m_o, should be strictly better than any other rate request m_f from other (central) banks. We note that we choose to show the outgoing messages that interact with other services as parameters in the metamorphic relation in the shorthand notation. To ease our presentation, we use a slightly modified notation (that is, m_o and m_f, instead of t_o and t_f) for outgoing messages that serve as test cases for the metamorphic testing.

According to MR2, a follow-up test case m_f can be formulated: a deal order of US$60 (i.e., = 0.3 × US$200). Suppose that an implementation of the service FXDS3 is discovered dynamically in online testing, and the latter correctly receives m_f and returns a message amounted 496.776 (i.e., FXDS3(US$60) = 60 × 8.2796 = 496.776) to *MS*. Both messages FXDS2(US$200) and FXDS3(US$60) are verified by the metamorphic service via MR2. We have, 0.3 × FXDS2(US$200) = 496.782 > 496.776 = FXDS3(US$60). It satisfies MR2. Hence, no failure will be reported by *MS* for this particular follow-up test case.

In the execution of a deal order, FXDS2 should communicate with services of central banks to collect relevant exchange rates. Thus, the source test case t_o includes an outgoing message m_o, a USD–RMB rate request, for such a purpose. Suppose that FXDS2 discovers both FXDS4 and FXDS5 to provide the quotes of exchange rates for USD–RMB. For the illustration purpose, further suppose that the exchange rate provided by the European Central Bank via FXDS5 for USD–RMB is 8.2795/8.2798. This spread is wider than that provided by FXDS4, and thus is poorer.

MS uses the metamorphic relation MR3 to produce the follow-up test case m_f of m_o. Owing to the faults (*a*) and (*b*), FSDS2 incorrectly selects the ask rate of the service FXDS4 to process the deal order. FSDS2 will output a message FXDS2(US$100) = 827.98 = 8.2798 × 100. We have, FXDS2(US$100, m_o) = 827.96 < 827.98 = FXDS2(US$100, m_f). It violates *MR*3, and *MS* reports a failure due to the combination of faults (*a*) and (*b*).

We have illustrated the usefulness of using a metamorphic service for the testing of services. In reality, there are domain-specific rounding practices compliant to the international accounting practice. Since rounding rules are a part of the application domain, it is natural for the designed metamorphic relations to take this type of rounding rules into account. This type of domain-specific rounding does not affect the metamorphic approach for services testing, albeit complicating it. It is worth mentioning that there could be implementation-specific rounding errors also. We refer readers to a previous work on metamorphic testing (Chen et al., 2003) for using a metamorphic approach to identifying failures in the presence of the implementation-specific rounding errors. In the next section, we report an experiment that applies our proposal and discuss observations therein.

EXPERIMENT

In this section, we would like to study the effectiveness of our proposal and the overhead when some of the source test cases are not successful. The latter simulates the situation that the test oracle in the offline mode is imperfect. This is to validate our proposal to use successful test cases applicable to offline testing as the source test cases for online testing. Our rationale is that if the overhead, on the contrary, is marginal; it is unnecessary to predetermine the successfulness of source test cases. This also helps reduce the testing effort for online testing of services.

The Subject Program

The subject service implements a service-oriented calculator of arithmetic expressions. It is developed in C++ on Microsoft Visual Studio for .NET 2003 as a set of web services. It consists of 16 classes with 2,480 lines of code.

Functionally, the calculator accepts an arithmetic expression consisting of constants of designated data type and arithmetic operators, and computes the result of the arithmetic expression. The set of supported operators are $\{+,-,\times,\div\}$, in which each operator is overloaded to enable every operand belonging to different data types. Five data types of operands are supported: integer, long integer, decimal, floating-point number, and floating-point number with double precision. Each operator is implemented as a supportive service of the subject service.

The subject service parses the inputted arithmetic expressions, locates the other services applicable to calculate the sub-expressions of an arithmetic expression, and composes the results from the results returned by its individual supportive services. When different data types can be associated with an operator (due to overloading) in a sub-expression, the subject service is responsible to resolve the appropriate data types and to pass the sub-expression to a selected supportive service. In the design of the application, we choose to allow at most three concurrent instances of the above logic in the subject service. It is mainly due to the physical resource constraint. These service instances together with an expression dispatcher instance compose our subject service. The expression dispatcher discovers the above supportive services of the subject service, and sends outgoing messages and receives incoming messages. The metamorphic service for the subject service is composed of the dispatcher and a program unit that implements a set of metamorphic relations, which will be explained in the next section.

A team of five developers (non-authors) develops all the above services. They have completed software engineering training and have at least one year of research-oriented and application software development experience to location-based systems, mobile positioning systems and common business applications.

Experimental Setup

In this section, we describe the setup configuration.

In the experiment, each instance of services is executed on a designated desk-top computer. In total, 14 desk-top computers (equipped with Pentium P4 3.2GHz processor, 512M memory and run Microsoft XP as the operating system) are used. All the machines to collect our data are located in the Compuware Software Testing Laboratory of the Hong Kong Institute of Vocational Education (Tsing Yi), Hong Kong.

The selection of the set of the source test cases is a black-box combinatorial testing approach. This allows the test cases to serve as the source test cases in both the offline testing mode and online mode. Consider an arithmetic expression of length three, where we mean to have an expression having three values and two operators (e.g., $13 + 0.45 - 7$). In our experiment, there are five types of data type and four types of operator. In total, there are 2,000, (that is, $5^3 \times 4^2$), combinations, even not counting the possible choices of value to initialize each variable. Since the length of an arithmetic expression could be ranged from zero to a large number, we choose to fix the length to three in this experiment. This minimizes the potential problem of using a very long expression to compare with a very short expression in our subsequent analysis. We also initialize test cases that do not cause integer value overflow, and the overflow of other data types alike. We are aware that we have implemented some design decisions in the test case selection process. We minimize these highlighted threats by designing our metamorphic relations *neutral* to these design decisions.

In ideal cases, a user would perceive every calculation as if it is derived analytically using mathematics. However, some expressions would incur rounding errors due to the limitation of programming or system configuration. Different orders of evaluations of an expression may thus produce inconsistent results. A good calculator would present consistent results to its users. For example, the arithmetic expression "(1 ÷ 3) × 3" would be evaluated as "(1 × 3) ÷ 3" by a good calculator.

We follow the above general "good calculator" guideline to formulate our metamorphic relations. We first describe how we determine and implement metamorphic relations. Next, we will describe the chosen metamorphic relations.

The arithmetic operators for the calculator application domain naturally define associative and commutative properties amongst arithmetic operators. We use these properties as the basis to design our metamorphic relations. This aligns with our objective to design such relations neutral to the selection of the source test cases. We experience a marginal effort to design associative and commutative relations and specify them as metamorphic relations. Furthermore, since the .NET framework for C++ directly supports the chosen operators, the effort to implement the metamorphic relations in our experiment is also marginal. This aligns with the common MT strategy that the implementation of MR should be of low cost.

The types of metamorphic relation used in the experiment are as follows. Suppose *A*, *B* and *C* are operands of some data type in the set {integer, long integer, floating point number, floating point number with double precision}, and θ_1 and θ_2 are overloaded operators in the set {+, −, ×, ÷}. Consider the expression "(A θ_1 B) θ_2 C". A commutative-property rule to generate the follow-up test cases is: "(A θ_1 B) θ_2 C" ⇒ "C θ_2 (A θ_1 B)". It derives the follow-up test case "C θ_2 (A θ_1 B)" based on the source test case "(A θ_1 B) θ_2 C".

Let us denote our subject service by *S*. The corresponding metamorphic relation of the above commutative rule would be: *S*("(A θ_1 B) θ_2 C") = *S*("C θ_2 (A θ_1 B)"). A metamorphic relation derived from an associative rule is *S* ("(A θ_1 B) θ_2 C") = *S*("A θ_1 (B θ_2 C)"). We manually enumerate all possible communicative and associative rules for all three-operand expressions to be the metamorphic relations in the experiment. The generation of test cases is implemented as simple codes (logics) in our program. We have inspected the codes to assure the correctness of these MR implementations.

After describing the metamorphic relations, we proceed to present the test cases aspect. Even a program is ideal, messages could still be lost or corrupted in a distributed environment. Our subject application does not implement a sophisticated fail-and-retry strategy to handle these anticipated scenarios. To compensate the lacking of this kind of strategy, we choose to abort the execution of a test case when a service returns no output after a timing threshold. After some trials-and-errors in our laboratory environment, we choose the threshold to be 50 seconds per execution of a pair of (original and follow-up) test cases. A typical test case will return the result in three seconds.

Based on the implementation of the subject application, we create additionally six consecutive faulty versions of the set of supportive services. Each version injects one additional mutation fault to its immediate ancestor. The six consecutive faults are created in the following order: changing a "+" operator to the operator "−"; changing a "−" operator to a "+" operator'; changing a "×" operator to a "−" operator; swapping the operand of a "÷" operator; changing a "−" operator to the "×" operator; and changing a "×" operator to a "+" operator. These faults support operands of the following data types respectively: floating-point number with double precision, integer, decimal, floating-point number with single precision, long integer, and floating-pointer number with single precision.

The following configurations were deployed for offline testing and online testing.

- The subject application (the subject service with the original version of the supportive services) simulates an offline testing environment. The original (non-faulty) versions of the supportive services serve as stub services for the offline testing, in the sense of conventional testing. Inexperienced developers implement the subject service and, thus, it naturally contains real faults. Some random test cases do reveal failures from our subject service. We however have assured that a set of test cases for the subject service for offline testing are successful. This set of test cases could be used as the source test cases for online testing according to our approach. We refer this set of test cases to as the set of source test cases in the experiment.
- A faulty application (the subject service with a faulty version of the supportive services) simulates an online testing environment. A faulty version of the supportive services is not identical in behavior to its original counterpart (the test stub used in the offline testing). The six faulty versions therefore facilitate us to re-use the above set of source test cases yet provide failed test results for some of them. This allows us to compare the effect of source test cases that may not be successfully. To avoid biases towards a particular faulty implementation, we put all source test cases and their results of the faulty versions in the same pool for analysis and do not distinguish them.

In total, we executed 22,503 follow-up test cases and 22,503 source test cases. These two values are the same because we use metamorphic relations with two input-output pairs in this experiment. For the original version, we execute 3,987 pairs of test cases, and for each faulty version, we execute 3,086 pairs of test cases. The numbers of pairs between the original version and the faulty version are not the same due to the above-mentioned message lost problem. To facilitate us to evaluate the effectiveness of test cases, in the experiment, we also mark every test case to be successful or failure-causing, according to the expected result of the arithmetic expression. The result will be presented in the next section.

Empirical Results

In this section, we will present the empirical results of the experiment and discuss our observations from the results. In summary, our experimental result shows that our approach uses 16% less effort to detect 13% more failures, compared to the control experiment having no prior confirmation of test results of source test cases.

We first analyze the overhead of including failure-causing source test cases for online testing. According to the above experimental setup, we have collected a pool of 18,516 (= 3,086 × 6) pairs of test cases from the six faulty versions. Some of the pairs contain failure-causing source test cases. We evenly partition the pool into 18 groups so that each group consists of around 1,000 test cases. For the i-th group (for $i = 1$ to 18), we use database queries to help us randomly draw around $5i$ percent of its elements having failure-causing source test cases and all elements having successful source test cases to calculate the overhead in terms of test result checking. The total numbers of elements drawn from each group at 10% interval are shown in Table 1. We note that in some group, the actual number of test cases drawn is not close to 1000; it is because when a pair of test cases that cause the original version of program to fail has been excluded in our analysis.

Table 1. No. of elements drawn from selected groups

Group	2	4	6	8	10
Percentages of failure-causing test cases drawn	10%	20%	30%	40%	50%
No. of elements drawn	767	791	809	839	885
Group	12	14	16	18	Total
Percentages of failure-causing test cases drawn	60%	70%	80%	90%	-
No. of elements drawn	904	945	973	997	7,910

The calculation of the *overhead* of a test pair is as follows.

- If no violation of the associated metamorphic relation is detected, then the overhead value is zero. It is because the test pair does not reveal any failure.
- If a violation of the associated metamorphic relation is detected, then the overhead value is equal to the number of actual failure-causing test case(s) in the test pair. In other words, if both test cases are failure-causing inputs, the overhead value will be two; otherwise, it will be one.

We further define that the number of additional test result checking to confirm the failure-causing inputs for a set of test pairs, denoted by Ω, is the sum of the overhead of every test pair in the set.

Figure 3 shows the value of Ω for 10%, 20% and up to 90% of the total number of the failure-causing source test cases of a group for the analysis. The mean value is 141 and the standard derivation is 29.4. (We are aware that there are inadequate numbers of data to calculate a good standard derivation statistically. We show the value just to give readers an impression about the skewness of data set.)

As expected, the value of Ω increases when the percentage increases. When more failure-causing source test cases are added to a set for the calculation of Ω, the chance to detect failures increases.

However, as we increase the number of test cases from 762 (for group 2) to 997 (for group 18), the change in Ω is moderate and is equal to 77 (= 173 – 96). When around 10% of failed source test cases are included, the value of Ω is 96. This initial value, 96, is even larger than the cumulated change, 77, in failure counts when the percentage of failure-causing test cases in a test set changes from 10% to 90%.

It shows that the inclusion of small percentages of failure-causing source test cases for the online testing of a service accounts for a major source of overhead in terms of additional test result checking. This substantiates our recommendation of using successful source test cases only for online testing to alleviate the test oracle problem.

We also observe that the overall percentage is not high. The mean is 15.9%. It suggests that even testers had to include inevitably some failure-causing source test cases; measures should be taken to minimize such an inclusion.

We further examine the chance that we would miss to detect a failure if some failure-causing source test cases are used for online testing. For a set of test pairs, we define ω as the number of test pairs that each pair consists of a failure-causing source test case and a follow-up test case (with unknown test verdicts) such that no applicable metamorphic relation detects any failure. The ω thus measures the missed opportunities to detect failures for online testing.

We also use the data sets reported in Table 1 to calculate ω for each group. The results are shown in Figure 4. The mean value is 118.7, that is, 13%

Figure 3. The overheads for different percentages of failure-causing source test cases

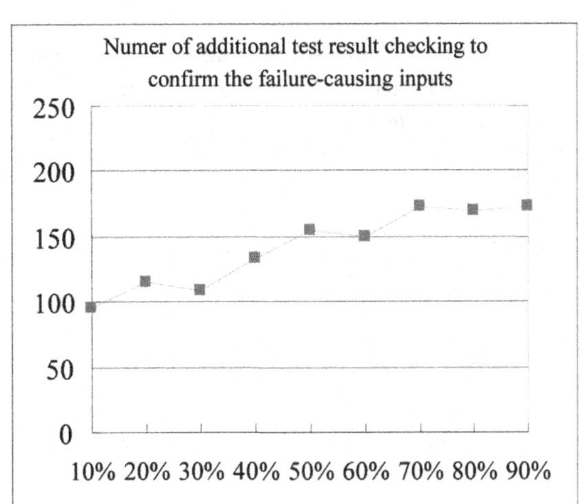

of all failure-causing test cases. The corresponding standard derivation is 64.2. The minimum is 25 for Group 2 (that is, the 10% group) and the maximum is 212 for Group 18 (that is, the 90% group).

The trend is that the missed detection of failures ω increases as the percentage of failure-causing source test cases included in a group increases. Moreover, the number of missed detection appears roughly proportional to the percentages of failure-causing source test cases in the data set. The implication of this proportion relation looks interesting and warrants more research.

In the rest of this section, we discuss the threats to validity of the experiment. The evaluation of using the metamorphic testing approach for services testing in the online mode is conducted in a small application. The application domain of the subject application is generic that it uses the basic computing functionality, namely a fundamental set of arithmetic operations and basic (communicative and associative) properties to define metamorphic relations. It is unknown about the impact on the results when certain domain-specific knowledge is taken into account to both define metamorphic relations and selections of test cases. We use a small number of faulty versions to conduct the experiment to discuss our findings. The co-relation between the program size, the number of faults used in an experiment is still not understood. The statistics may be different if other faulty versions are used.

Similarly, using different test sets as source test cases, and different metamorphic relations may produce different results. Obviously, when using more metamorphic relations, more follow-up test cases can be generated to look for program failures. On the other hand, it incurs more overheads to execute these test cases, in particular in an online mode, where services may not be owned by the organization.

Our subject program does contain real faults and hence some metamorphic relation instances are violated even if the original version is used. We believe that it is common for a typical testing of a newly coded software program. However, the assumption is not valid if other rigorous quality assurance techniques such as rigorous regressions, code inspections or formal methods have been applied to a software development project. We have evaluated our approach on the Microsoft .NET 2003 platform only. The present implementation of the subject program is not portable to other platforms because it directly uses the .NET feature to implement web services. There is a threat to interpret the empirical results in

Figure 4. The number of missed detection of failure-causing inputs

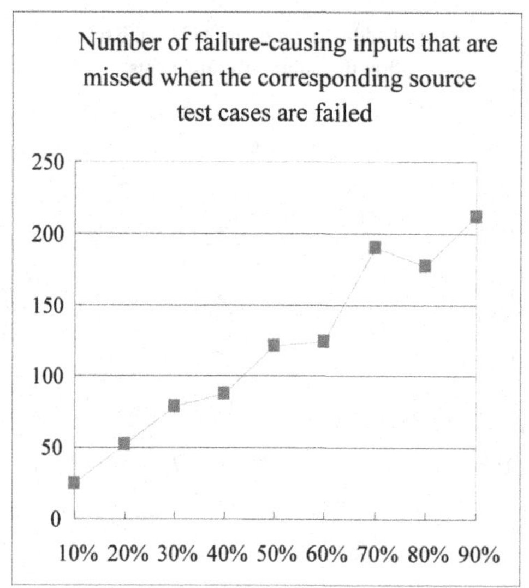

other configurations. We have reviewed the set test cases and the set follow-up test cases, and use a commercial spreadsheet to help us to check whether the target relation is maintained in the reviewed samples.

RELATED WORK

Works of literature on function testing research for SOA applications or Web services are still not plenty. Bloomberg (2002) presents an overview a few major types of testing activity for testing web services. We refer interested readers to the work of Bloomberg (2002) for the overview. In the rest of the section, we review selected related work on providing tools for testing, exception handling testing, generation of test cases and test result evaluation for service-oriented programs.

The use of testing tool is an indispensable part to automate testing activities. Dustar and Haslinger (2004) propose to develop an experimental testing tool prototype to conduct batch mode and online mode testing. Their tool is reported to expect to handle several types of testing such as functional test and reliability test. However, the recent development of their tool has not been reported in the literature. Deng et al. (2004) extend AGENDA, a database application testing tool that populates database instances as a part of a test case, to test web-based database applications. Rather than populating test database instances, SOATest (Parasoft, 2005) also reads data from different data sources to conduct testing. Zhu (2006) presents a plug-in approach to supporting services or test stubs to be hooked on the framework for web service testing.

To generate test cases, Offutt and Xu (2004) propose a set of mutation operators to perturb messages of web services. They also suggest three types of rule to develop test cases based on the XML schema of messages. Their initial result on a sample application shows that 78% of seeded faults can be revealed. These faults include communication faults in SOAP, faults in statements for database query languages and conventional faults. The mutated messages could be considered as a method to construct follow-up test cases in the sense of metamorphic testing. Their empirical study of their approach is valuable. Rather than injecting faults to messages, Looker and Xu (2003) inject faults in SOAP-based programs to test the programs for robustness. Martin et al. (2007) also use a similar approach, but they mutate WSDL files instead.

Apart from the mutation or fault-injection approach, there are other approaches to selecting or measuring test cases. García-Fanjul et al. (2006) use the BPEL codes in a workflow application to construct test cases to test the applications. Li et al. (2005) construct control-flow test cases to test BPEL programs, and their research group further extends the approach to construct test cases having concurrent paths (Yan et al., 2006). Mei et al. (2008) addresses the complexity of XPath in testing by identifying test cases using a data flow approach.

Chen et al. (2004a) aims at testing for robustness. They focus on testing the exception handling of Java web services through a data flow coverage approach. They propose to inject faults to system calls to trigger exception throws and require test cases to cover the exception-oriented def-use relations. Through their subject programs are Java-based web service program; their techniques are not specialized to services testing. Pentra et al. (2007) proposes an approach to regression testing of the QoS aspects of web services.

Tsai et al. (2004, 2005) propose to test web services having multiple implementations with the same intended functionality. They apply test cases to a set of implementations of the same intended functionality progressively. Their test results are ranked by a voting strategy to assign a winner as the test oracle. A small set of winning implementations is selected for the integration testing purpose. At an integration testing level, they follow the same approach except using a weighted version of the voting strategy instead. To deal with the test case selection problem, their research group (Tsai et al., 2002a) proposes to generate test cases based on WSDL. Although WSDL-based testing has been proposed for a few years and implemented in testing tools such as SOATest (Parasoft, 2005), their version of WSDL (Tsai et al., 2002b) extends the standardized WSDL (W3C, 2001) to include features to express semantics.

The advantages of semantics checking are also explored by other researchers. A handy example is our adaptation of metamorphic relation in this chapter. Keckel and Lohmann (2005), on the other hand, propose to apply the notion of *design by contract* to conduct testing for Web services. They suggest defining formal contracts to describe the behavior of functions and interactions of Web services. Based on the contracts, combinatorial testing is suggested to apply to conduct conformance testing against the contracts of intended services.

Our approach uses metamorphic relations to construct follow-up test cases. It is not a fault-based approach; whereas Looker and Xu (2003) suggest a fault-based approach to testing for program robustness. In addition, unlike the work of Offutt and Xu (2004) and Martin et al. (2007), these follow-up test cases in our approach are intentionally to allow automated test result evaluations. A follow-up test case triggers a service to produce an output. The output of a follow-up test case is allowed to be different from the output of the source test case. Hence, it can be applied to configurations when multiple implementations of the same functionality are too expensive to be used. This feature essentially distinguishes our work from Tsai et al. (2005). Our approach checks test results amongst them; whereas the work of Keckel and Lohmann (2005) checks the test results against some formal contract specifications. Their contract approach does not address the construction of follow-up test cases. Chen et al. (2004a) and Mei et al. (2008) are white-box approaches; whereas our proposal is a black-box approach. The tools (Parasoft, 2005; Dustar and Haslinger, 2004) appear to be developed as an integrated testing tool that includes a number of different testing modules. Their architectures are unclear to us at this moment. Our metamorphic service is an access wrapper to facilitate the integration of offline and online testing of a service. We are not aware of the other approaches having this type of idea. We aim at reducing the amount of non-core elements from our metamorphic service. In this way, when exposing the function to other services, we would like to develop the approach further so that it enjoys a good scalability.

CONCLUDING REMARKS

We have presented an approach to online testing and an experiment on a sample application to study metamorphic testing for services testing in this chapter. The approach is useful for the online testing of a service if testers have difficulties to obtain the expected results of individual test cases in a cost-effective manner. The test oracle problem has been identified for many years (see also (Beizer, 1990). In practice, many testers validate their software without a formal test oracle. Metamorphic testing is an approach towards solving the problem when a metamorphic relation exists and could be identified. We believe that this trend is promising in online testing of services.

Testing in a services computing environment needs to deal with a number of issues. They include: (*i*) the unknown communication partners until the service discovery; (*ii*) the imprecise black-box information of software components; (*iii*) the potential existence of non-identical implementations of the same service; and (*iv*) the expected behavior of a service potentially depending on the behavior of competing services.

We have presented a testing approach to the online testing of service-oriented applications. We formulate the notion of metamorphic service that is an access wrapper to encapsulate the access for the service under test and implements the metamorphic testing approach. We also propose to use the successful test case for offline testing as the source test case for online testing because a test oracle is more likely to be available in offline testing. Using our online testing methodology, testers builds a bridge between the test oracle available during the offline testing of a service and the test oracle problem encountered in the online testing of the service.

The services approach to conducting an online test alleviates the problem (*i*). It delays the binding of communication partners of the follow-up test cases after service discovery. Our implementation of the metamorphic testing approach alleviates the problems (*ii*), (*iii*) and (*iv*).

We have also conducted an experiment to evaluate the feasibility of our proposal. The experimental results encouragingly indicate that, on average, when the set of source test cases are unknown to be successful, an extra 16% effort to check test results and a 13% reduction of failure detection are obtained. This preliminary finding supports our proposal that source test cases can had better be successful, particularly when the checking is (much) less costly when it can be conducted in the offline testing mode.

There are quite a number of future research directions. We have not evaluated our proposal extensively. The way to control the chain reaction of the follow-up test cases generations due to interferences of multiple metamorphic services warrants more researches. Would using code coverage or fault coverage of the service under test useful? How to deal with the scenarios of a service being treated as malicious attacks from the perspective of the other services to support the online testing of the service? How do testers arrange test cases to minimize the number of remote service invocations? There are many issues relevant to online testing of services to be explored.

ACKNOWLEDGMENT

This research was partially supported by the Research Grants Council of Hong Kong under grant numbers CITYU 111107 and 123207, HKUST 612108, and National Science Foundation of China under grant number 60736015.

REFERENCES

W3C (2001). XML Schema. Retrieved from http://www.w3.org/xml/schema.

W3C (2002). Web Services Activity. Retrieved from http://www.w3.org/2002/ws.

W3C (2003). SOAP Version 1.2 Part 1: Messaging Framework. Retrieved from http://www.w3.org/tr/soap12-part1/

W3C (2004). Extensible Markup Language (XML) 1.0 (3rd ed.). Retrieved from http://www.w3.org/TR/2004/REC-xml-20040204/.

W3C (2005). Web Services Description Language (WSDL) version 2.0 Part 1: Core Language. Retrieved from http://www.w3.org/tr/wsdl20/

Bass, L., Clements, P., & Kazman, R. (2003). *Software Architecture in Practice* (2nd ed.). Addison Wesley.

Beizer, B. (1990). *Software Testing Techniques*. New York: Van Nostrand Reinhold.

Bloomberg, J. (2002). Testing Web services today and tomorrow. Retrieved from http://www-106.ibm.com/developerworks/rational/library/content/rationaledge/oct02/ webtesting_therationaledge_oct02.pdf.

Chan, F. T., Chen, T. Y., Cheung, S. C., Lau, M. F., & Yiu, S. M. (1998). Application of Metamorphic Testing in Numerical Analysis. In *Proceedings of IASTED International Conference on Software Engineering (SE 1998)* (pp. 191–197). Calgary. Canada: ACTA Press.

Chan, W. K., & Chen, T. Y. Lu, Heng, Tse, T. H., & Yau, S. S. (2005c). A metamorphic approach to integration testing of context-sensitive middleware-based applications. In *Proceedings of the Fifth Annual International Conference on Quality Software (QSIC 2005)* (pp. 241-249). Los Alamitos, California: IEEE Computer Society Press.

Chan, W. K., & Chen, T. Y., Lu, Heng, Tse, T. H., & Yau, S. S. (2006). Integration testing of context-sensitive middleware-based applications: a metamorphic approach. *International Journal of Software Engineering and Knowledge Engineering, 16*(5), 677–703. doi:10.1142/S0218194006002951

Chan, W. K., Cheung, S. C., & Leung, K. R. P. H. (2005a). Towards a Metamorphic Testing Methodology for Service-Oriented Software Applications. The First International Workshop on Services Engineering (SEIW 2005), in *Proceedings of the 5th Annual International Conference on Quality Software (QSIC 2005)* (pp. 470–476). Los Alamitos, California: IEEE Computer Society.

Chan, W. K., Cheung, S. C., & Leung, K. R. P. H. (2007). A Metamorphic Testing Approach for Online Testing of Service-Oriented Software Applications. *International Journal of Web Services Research, 4*(2), 60–80.

Chan, W. K., Cheung, S. C., & Tse, T. H. (2005b). Fault-based testing of database application programs with conceptual data model. In *Proceedings of the 5th Annual International Conference on Quality Software (QSIC 2005)* (pp. 187-196). Los Alamitos, California: IEEE Computer Society Press.

Chen, F., Ryder, B., Milanova, A., & Wannacott, D. (2004a). Testing of Java Web Services for Robustness. In *Proceedings of the International Symposium on Software Testing and Analysis (ISSTA 2004)* (pp. 23–34). New York: ACM Press.

Chen, T. Y., Cheung, S. C., & Yiu, S. M. (1998). *Metamorphic testing: a new approach for generating next test cases* (Technical Report HKUST-CS98-01). Hong Kong: Department of Computer Science, Hong Kong University of Science and Technology.

Chen, T. Y., Huang, D. H., Tse, T. H., & Zhou, Z. Q. (2004b). Case studies on the selection of useful relations in metamorphic testing, in *Proceedings of the 4th Ibero-American Symposium on Software Engineering and Knowledge Engineering (JIISIC 2004)* (pp. 569−583). Madrid, Spain: Polytechnic University of Madrid.

Chen, T. Y., Tse, T. H., & Zhou, Z. Q. (2002). Semi-proving: an integrated method based on global symbolic evaluation and metamorphic testing. In *Proceedings of the ACM SIGSOFT International Symposium on Software Testing and Analysis (ISSTA 2002)* (pp. 191−195). New York: ACM Press.

Chen, T. Y., Tse, T. H., & Zhou, Z. Q. (2003). Fault-based testing without the need of oracles. *Information and Software Technology, 45*(1), 1–9. doi:10.1016/S0950-5849(02)00129-5

Colan, M. (2004). Service-Oriented Architecture expands the vision of Web Services, Part 1: Characteristics of Service-Oriented Architecture. Retrieved from http://www-128.ibm.com/developerworks/webservices/library/ws-soaintro.html.

Curbera, F., Duftler, M., Khalaf, R., Nagy, W., Mukhi, N., & Weerawarana, S. (2002). Unraveling the Web services web: An introduction to SOAP, WSDL, and UDDI. [Los Alamitos, California: IEEE Computer Society Press.]. *IEEE Internet Computing, 6*(2), 86–93. doi:10.1109/4236.991449

Deng, Y., Frankl, P., & Wang, J. (2004). Testing web database applications. Workshop on testing, analysis and verification of web services (TAV-WEB), *SIGSOFT Software Engineering Notes, 29*(5), 1-10. New York: ACM Press.

Dustar, S., & Haslinger, S. (2004). Testing of Service-Oriented Architectures: A Practical Approach. In *Proceedings of the 5th Annual International Conference on Object-Oriented and Internet-Based Technologies, Concepts, and Applications for a Networked World (NODe 2004)* (LNCS 3263, pp. 97−112).

Frankl, P. G., & Weyuker, E. J. (1988). An Applicable Family of Data Flow Testing Criteria. *IEEE Transactions on Software Engineering, 14*(10), 1483–1498. doi:10.1109/32.6194

García-Fanjul, J., Tuya, J., & de la Riva, C. (2006). Generating Test Cases Specifications for BPEL Compositions of Web Services Using SPIN. In *International Workshop on Web Services Modeling and Testing* (*WS-MaTe 2006*) (pp. 83-94). Berlin: Springer-Verlag.

Kapfhammer, G. M., & Soffa, M. L. (2003). A family of test adequacy criteria for database-driven applications. In *Proceedings of the 9th European software engineering conference held jointly with 11th ACM SIGSOFT international symposium on Foundations of software engineering (ESEC/FSE 2003)* (pp. 98–107). New York: ACM Press.

Keckel, R., & Lohmann, M. (2005). Towards contract-based testing of Web services. *Electronic Notes in Theoretical Computer Science, 116*, 145–156. doi:10.1016/j.entcs.2004.02.073

Kreger, H. (2003). Fulfilling the web services promise. *Communications of the ACM, 46*(6), 29–34. doi:10.1145/777313.777334

Li, Z. Sun, W., Jiang, Z., & Zhang, X (2005). BPEL4WS unit testing: framework and implementation. In *Proceedings of Internatonal Conference on Web Services (ICWS 2005)* (pp. 103-110). Los Alamitos, California: IEEE Computer Society.

Liang, F. (2007). On the Robustness of Metamorphic Testing. MSc Thesis. Department of Computer Science, The University of Hong Kong.

Looker, N., & Xu, J. (2003). Assessing the Dependability of SOAP RPC based Web Services by Fault Injection. In *Proceedings of IEEE International Workshop on Object-Oriented, Real-Time and Dependable Systems* (pp 163-170). Los Alamitos, California: IEEE Computer Society Press.

Martin, E., Basu, S., & Xie, T. (2007). Automated Testing and Response Analysis of Web Services. In *Proceedings of 2007 IEEE International Conference on Web Services (ICWS 2007)* (pp. 647-654). Los Alamitos, California: IEEE Computer Society Press.

Mecella, M., & Pernici, B. (2003). Designing wrapper components for e-services in integrating heterogeneous systems. *The VLDB Journal, 10*(1), 2–15.

Mei, L., Chan, W. K., & Tse, T. H. (2008). Data flow testing of service-oriented workflow applications. In *Proceedings of the 30th International Conference on Software Engineering (ICSE 2008).* New York, NY, USA: ACM Press.

Mukhi, N. K., Konuru, R., & Curbera, F. (2004). Cooperative middleware specialization for service oriented architectures. In *Proceedings of the 13th international World Wide Web conference on Alternate track papers & posters (WWW 2004)* (pp.206–215). New York: ACM Press.

OASIS. (2005). Universal Description, Discovery and Integration (UDDI) version 3.0.2. Retrieved from http://uddi.org/pubs/uddi_v3.htm.

Offutt, J., & Xu, W. (2004). Generating test cases for Web services using data perturbation. Workshop on testing, analysis and verification of web services (TAV-WEB), *SIGSOFT Software Engineering Notes, 29*(5), 1-10.

Parasoft Corporation. (2005). SOATest. Available at http://www.parasoft.com/jsp/products/home.jsp?product=SOAP&itemId=101.

Penta, M., Bruno, M., & Esposito, G. V., Mazza, & Canfora, G. (2007). Test and Analysis of Web Services. In *Web Services Regression Testing* (pp. 205-234). Berlin: Springer.

Rajasekaran, P., Miller, J. A., Verma, K., & Sheth, A. P. (2004). Enhancing Web Services Description and Discovery to Facilitate Composition. In *Proceeding of The First International Workshop on Semantic Web Services and Web Process Composition (SWSWPC 2004)* (LNCS 3387, pp. 55-68).

Tsai, W. T., Chen, Y., & Cao, Z. Bai, X., Hung, H., & Paul, R. (2004). Testing Web services using progressive group testing. In *Proceedings of Advanced Workshop on Content Computing (AWCC 2004)*, (LNCS 3309, pp. 314–322).

Tsai, W. T., Chen, Y., Paul, R., Huang, H., Zhou, X., & Wei, X. (2005). Adaptive Testing, Oracle Generation, and Test Case Ranking for Web Services. In *Proceedings of the 29th Annual International Computer Software and Applications conference (COMPSAC 2005)* (pp. 101–106). Los Alamitos, California: IEEE Computer Society Press.

Tsai, W. T., Paul, R., Song, W., & Cao, Z. (2002b). Coyote: An XML-Based Framework for Web Services Testing. In *Proceedings of The 7th IEEE International Symposium on High-Assurance Systems Engineering (HASE 2002)* (pp. 173–176). Los Alamitos, California: IEEE Computer Society Press.

Tsai, W. T., Paul, R., Wang, Y., Fan, C., & Wang, D. (2002a). Extending WSDL to facilitate Web services testing. In *Proceedings of The 7th IEEE International Symposium on High-Assurance Systems Engineering (HASE 2002)* (pp. 171–172). Los Alamitos, California: IEEE Computer Society Press.

Tse, T. H., Yau, S. S., Chan, W. K., Lu, H., & Chen, T. Y. (2004), Testing context-sensitive middleware-based software applications, in *Proceedings of the 28th Annual International Computer Software and Applications Conference (COMPSAC 2004)*, pp. 458–466. Los Alamitos, California: IEEE Computer Society Press.

Umar, A. (1997). *Application Reengineering: Building Web-Based Applications and Dealing with Legacy*. Englewood, Cliffs, NJ: Prentice-Hall.

Yan, J., Li, Z., Yuan, Y., Sun, W., & Zhang, J. (2006). BPEL4WS Unit Testing: Test Case Generation Using a Concurrent Path Analysis Approach. In *Proceedings of the 17th International Symposium on Software Reliability Engineering* (ISSRE 2006) (pp. 75-84). Los Alamitos, California: IEEE Computer Society Press. Chunyang Ye, S.C. Cheung & W.K. Chan (2006). Publishing and composition of atomicity-equivalent services for B2B collaboration. In *Proceedings of the 28th International Conference on Software Engineering (ICSE 2006)* (pp. 351-360). Los Alamitos, California: IEEE Computer Society Press.

Zhu, H. (2006). A framework for service-oriented testing of Web services. In Proceedings of 30th *Annual International Computer Software and Applications Conference (COMPSAC 2006), Vol 2.* Los Alamitos, California: IEEE Computer Society Press.

Zhu, H., Hall, P. A. V., & May, J. H. R. (1997). Software unit test coverage and adequacy. *ACM Computing Surveys*, *29*(4), 366–427. doi:10.1145/267580.267590

ENDNOTES

1. All correspondence should be addressed to Dr. W. K. Chan at Department of Computer Science, City University of Hong Kong, Tat Chee Avenue, Kowloon, Hong Kong. Tel: (+852) 2788 9684. Fax: (+852) 2788 8614. Email: wkchan@cs.cityu.edu.hk
2. XML stands for Extensible Markup Language (W3C, 2004).
3. IBM also proposes to design stateless web services when it introduces service-oriented architecture (see http://www-128.ibm.com/developerworks/webservices/library/ws-soaintro.html .)
4. The design of metamorphic relations is not within the scope of this paper. We refer interested readers to a case study (Chen et al., 2004) on the selection of effective metamorphic relations for more details.

Chapter 4
Integrated Design of eBanking Architecture

Tony C. Shan
Keane Inc., USA

Winnie W. Hua
CTS Inc., USA

ABSTRACT

This chapter describes a service-oriented framework for integrated design of eBanking architecture (IDEA) in the financial services industry. A pragmatic approach is developed to help facilitate sustainable design practices in migrating conventional n-tier online systems to a service-oriented computing paradigm, composed of Service-Oriented Architecture (SOA), Integration (SOI), Process (SOP) and Management (SOM). This comprehensive model comprises 5 modules, namely, Hybrid Methodology, Architecture Baseline Model, Service Patterns, Enterprise Service Model, and Domain-specific Model. A hybrid methodology is designed to leverage the benefits of both top-down and bottom-up approaches, in which a converging layer is conceived to incorporate the latest technologies such as portal, mashup, RIA, process orchestration, service aggregations, collaborations, choreography, business rule engine, virtualization, cloud computing, Web 2.0/3.0, and so on. A multi-tier architecture baseline model is constructed to cope with the architecture complexity in a disciplined manner. E-business patterns are applied to categorize diverse banking services, which form the foundation for subsequent selection justifications of appropriate technologies, platforms, products, tools, and infrastructure. Furthermore, common business functionalities are built in the enterprise service model as shared services to be reused across lines of business as well as delivery channels, along with the sharable technical services and infrastructure services. A domain-specific model for the Internet Channel is defined by operationalizing the hybrid methodology in a particular portfolio. In addition, a holistic reusable application platform is introduced to address the key design considerations and concerns in the implementation of service-oriented solutions. Various challenges and best-practice recommendations are also articulated in the context.

DOI: 10.4018/978-1-61520-684-1.ch004

INTRODUCTION

Most financial institutions typically possess a heterogeneous information technology (IT) environment, resulting from a long history of mergers, acquisitions, and siloed builtouts with aging infrastructure, architecture, tools, and platforms. They are finding themselves ill-prepared to deliver timely enhancements or fast rollouts of new products and services as business grows. The required migration to a customer-centric view, coupled with the need for quicker turnaround time for systems improvements and releases, requires a more agile solution model and process as well as closer alignment with the business domain model. Banks must be able to tie together dynamic transactions occurring through different delivery channels and lines of business, which are usually supported by multiple systems and applications. Banking processes tend to converge on a platform that is scalable, flexible, reliable, responsive, and positioned for easy growth as well as one that supports multiple customer channels and customer-centric views.

The financial services provided by a bank are generally accessible through a variety of servicing channels – branch offices, automated teller machines (ATMs), telephony voice response unit (VRU), Call Centers, snail mails, fax, emails, messaging, and web browser, to just name a few. The online services accessed through web browsers have played an increasingly critical role in the overall customer relationship management (CRM). The Internet channel has become an integral part of the business operating model, as more and more customers have been using online services like online banking and billpay in their banking activities. The next level's goal is to present a holistic view of services and products to customers and prospects, and implement long-duration transactional processes with the session statefulness capability across the delivery channels.

A number of diversified IT systems have been built or acquired over the past years to support a variety of banking business processes. Through the evolution and maturing of various technologies and products, drastically different platforms, architectures, techniques, tools, and programming languages have been used, which led to a complicated mix of applications in legacy monolithic, client/server, n-tier thin client, n-tier rich client, message-oriented, pervasive computing, and distributed computing models. The demanding challenges are threefold: 1) how to change the mindset to build new applications in a service-oriented fashion; 2) how to migrate the existing systems to a service-oriented paradigm; and 3) how to converge the IT assets to provide holistic services to various delivery channels. Several prevailing architecture frameworks and process models have been evaluated. Zachman Framework (Zachman 2002) is largely data-driven and is well suited for planning and management rather than detailed technical designs of an individual system. Rational Unified Process (RUP) (Kruchten 2003) is a heavyweight process-oriented approach primarily for software development, lacking a broad coverage on inter-application integration, application/project portfolio, system engineering, and infrastructure aspects. Extended Enterprise Architecture Framework (E2AF) (IFEAD 2004) takes a similar approach in Zachman Framework by using a 2-D matrix with a focus on the architecture part. The Open Group Architectural Framework (TOGAF) (TOGAF 2003) has a fairly comprehensive scope on the major elements in the architecture design. It is mainly targeted to the enterprise architecture area. Model-Driven Architecture (MDA) (OMG 2002) emphasizes the platform-independent model in addition to the platform-specific model, but it is limited to the qualitative architecture description at the conceptual level. The Solution Architecture of N-Tier Applications (Shan, 2006) represents a multi-layer and multi-pillar reference architecture model for web-based applications.

Other related work has also been investigated and justified (Albin 2003; Bass et al 1998; Broemmer 2002; Carbone 2004; Dustdar et al 2004; Erl 2004; Fowler 2003; Frankel 2003; Giaglis 2001; Gronmo et al 2004; Gulzar et al 2003; Jorstad et al 2004; McGovern 2003; McGovern et al 2003; Schekkerman 2003; Sessions et al 2003; Shan et al 2004; and Zimmermann et al 2003). It turns out that most of these published works serve different purposes with different structures, and are based on different principles in different scopes. None of them can be directly applied to define a systematic approach for service-oriented ebanking solution design, in order to meet the growing business needs in the finance industry.

COMPREHENSIVE APPROACH

A comprehensive framework is designed in this chapter with pragmatic methods to facilitate the process changes and technology migrations for banking applications. The goal of this approach is to define the practical steps to analyze the business-domain requirements, design a realistic methodology, establish architecting practices and focuses in architecture designs, identify service patterns, construct a logical service model, build domain-specific models, and develop an implementation platform for service-oriented solutions. The characteristic attributes of *IDEA* are:

- ***Architecture abstraction***: The framework provides an effective mechanism to simplify the architecture complexity in a large organization, so that the total cost of ownership (TCO) of IT solutions can be reduced.
- ***Process standard***: The framework imposes a governance process to measure and monitor the IT development efforts, to assure the compliance of policies, standards and regulations.
- ***Cross-application framework***: The framework establishes a common foundation for sustainable application development practices and runtime environment infrastructure, to expedite the delivery and improve the quality of services.
- ***Portfolio engineering***: The framework enforces a software/service engineering discipline to generalize and optimize the technical architecture and methodology, to better equip IT assets with flexibility and agility in alignment with the business domain models.

As illustrated in Figure 1, this holistic framework for integrated design of eBanking architecture (IDEA) comprises the following key modules:

- ***Hybrid Methodology***: A combination of the top-down and bottom-up designs not only provides the forward-thinking direction, but also leverages the existing IT investments to the maximum extent.
- ***Architecture Baseline Model***: A multi-level architecture model effectively copes with the architecture complexity in diverse IT solutions across the lines of business in a large organization.
- ***Service Patterns***: Systems/applications are categorized into specific groups for efficient portfolio management and cross-application reusability.
- ***Enterprise Service Model***: The logical service model is built across the lines of business based on the service patterns identified, following the Hybrid Methodology defined.
- ***Domain-Specific Model***: The domain-specific model is a technical SOA blueprint for a particular delivery channel or portfolio.

The five modules of the *IDEA* framework may be chained in a sequential order to form the logi-

Figure 1. Integrated design of ebanking architecture framework

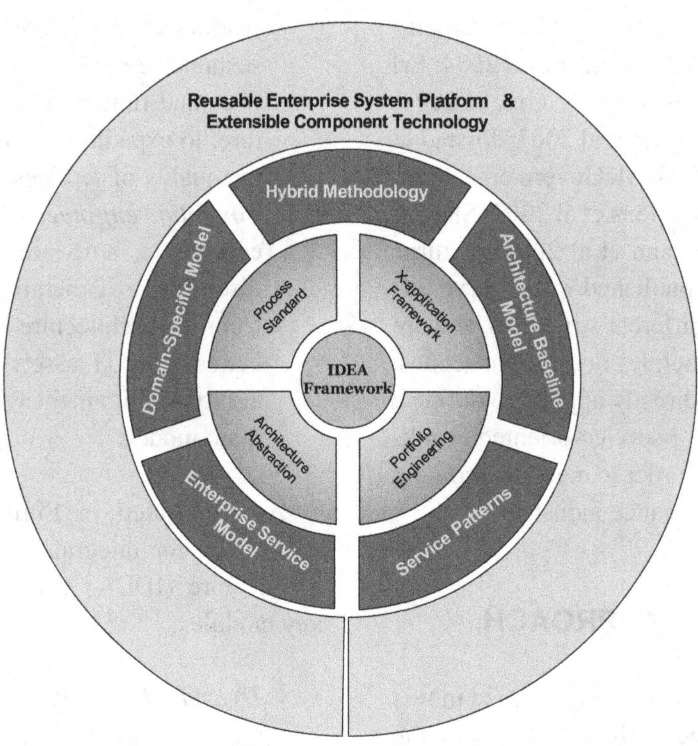

cal steps in designing service-oriented solutions in a forward-engineering fashion. However, these modules may also be used individually or in combination to analyze the application portfolio, craft migration plans, estimate work efforts, mitigate project risks, plan resources, and identify skillset gaps. In addition, an overarching platform, called Reusable Enterprise System Platform & Extensible Component Technology (RESPECT), is built to address the key design considerations, concerns, artifacts, and best practices in the lifecycle of service-oriented solution development.

In the next few sections we successively describe the features and designs of the constituents of the *IDEA* framework in detail. Afterwards the discussion of applying *IDEA* in system development is provided, followed by a section on the challenges in the service-oriented solution design, taking the SOA standards and technology convergence areas as two examples. Finally, the conclusions drawn in this framework design are presented in the last section.

HYBRID METHODOLOGY

The most common approach to designing a service-oriented computing solution is a top-down method. This is a natural forward-engineering way to compose a set of technical models, which is closely aligned with the long-term business process mission. Typically the technology team works with the business partners to identify the business requirements and directions, and then a comprehensive analysis of the business operations is conducted, which helps build the foundation of the overall architecture platform and construct a high-level technology blueprint. This method is particularly efficient in constructing technical models from ground up, and identifying brand-new services. Taking a similar approach in Model-Driven Architecture (MDA), we define a platform-independent technical model (PITM) from the analysis result of the business process model in the business domain. This is of paramount importance as this adaptive model gains

Figure 2. Hybrid Methodology

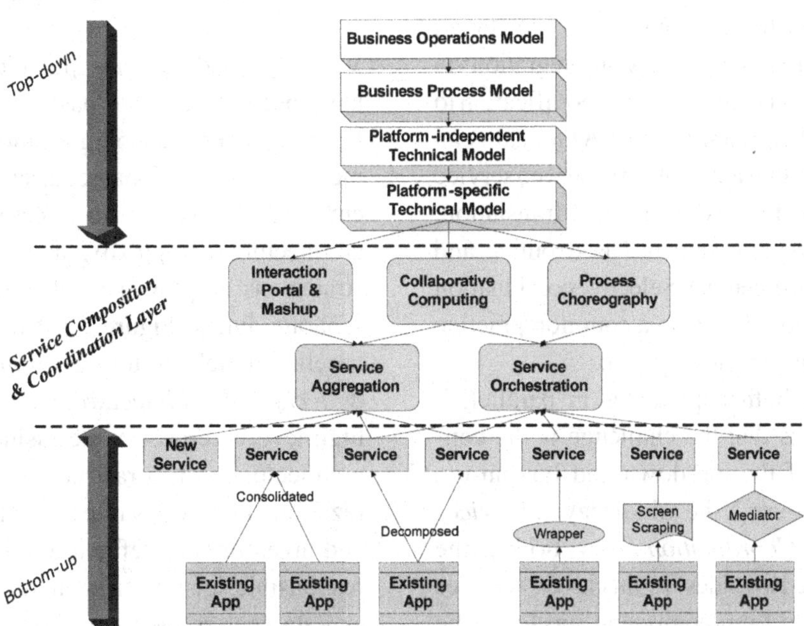

the maximum freedom for the future expansion in the long run, and avoids any lock-in to particular platforms or proprietary technologies, which may fade in uncertainty. Furthermore, the platform-specific technical model (PSTM) is defined based on the *PITM* to formulate tactical solutions for near-future implementations. The combinations of *PITM* and *PSTM* provide greater changeability, flexibility, and agility for steadfast strategic growth as well as short-term resolutions to meet immediate business needs. The top-down approach is illustrated in the upper part of Figure 2.

On the other hand, a complex set of legacy systems and diverse technologies have already been built in the past development, which cannot be directly mapped to a unified vision of the future. A bottom-up approach seeks to rebuild current systems into a new paradigm that supports a coherent future course, by maximizing the reuse of the existing investment. Depending on where an existing application stands in its lifecycle, it may be revamped by one of three approaches: *Refactoring*, *Reengineering*, and *Rearchitecting*. *Refactoring* is useful to improve an existing application without a drastic structural shakeup. It also helps reverse-engineer an application to rebuild the technical model, if not previously created in the forward engineering process. *Reengineering* is a valuable solution to migrate an application to the next-generation technologies with no fundamental restructuring in architecture. It is sometimes the most cost-effective way to deal with legacy systems. *Rearchitecting* becomes necessary when an aging application almost reaches the end of its lifecycle in terms of its technical model and architecture. *Replatforming* usually falls between the *Reengineering* and *Rearchitecting* stages.

In general, there are five methods that may be utilized to service-enable an existing application with minimal efforts: *consolidating*, *decomposing*, *wrapping*, *screen scraping*, and *mediating*. The consolidation method merges multiple applications or components to build services. The decomposition method breaks up a stove-piped application and transforms it into multiple services. A wrapper technology converts the legacy applications to become callable web-services disrupting the original state of the applications, so that the applications can continue to provide the same services through the existing APIs. The screen scarping method enables the session integration via terminal emulation with little or no modification to the internal application structures. A mediator can transform an existing application to be web service aware, with capabilities of protocol translation, data format conversion, content-based routing, and service policy enforcement. Selective combination of these five methods is also a common practice in dismantling a complex system.

As we take both approaches in parallel, it becomes obvious that the challenge is the converging point of the top-down and bottom-up. As charted in Figure 2, the middle layer, *Services Composition & Coordination Layer*, bridges the gap between the two sides. In this layer, services are augmented to form compound services. The *Service Orchestration* module facilitates the business workflow and long-lived transactional process with one-phase commit. The *Interaction Portal & Mashup* module provides delivery channels and content aggregation to different access devices. Collaborative services and computing are realized via Web 2.0/3.0 technologies, such as Wiki, Blog, tagging, social networking, SaaS, and the like. And the *Process Choreography* module forms the business processes constructed from choreography of web services in a multi-party collaboration with externally observable interactions between services.

The hybrid methodology that combines both top-down and bottom-up methods with the service augmentation layer has proved to be a practical approach strategically and tactically. It provides the forward-thinking and structural stability inherent in the top-down analysis, but allows the flexibility and reusability that come with a bottom-up approach. Most of common architectural models can be mapped directly to support this methodology. In the sections that follow, we will apply this methodology to create service-oriented models for financial services.

ARCHITECTURE BASELINE MODEL

Virtually hundreds of applications and systems have been built in the past few years, utilizing heterogeneous technologies and architectures to meet diverse functional requirements from different lines of business. To effectively manage the architecture complexity, a divide-and-conquer strategy is employed to abstract concerns and separate duties. Figure 3 shows an architecture baseline model. The top tier is *Enterprise Business & Technical Architecture*, which deals with the high-level enterprise-wide business and technical architecture and infrastructure across the organization. Policies, strategies, standards, assets, and inventory are defined in this layer. It is also responsible for all infrastructural services, such as data centers, network, hosting environment, monitoring and system management as well as security. A compliance certification and ratification process is imposed in the governance.

The middle tier is *Cross Channel/LOB Architecture*, which accounts for the core and common business functionalities sharable across delivery channels and lines of business. It describes a channel-agnostic and LOB-independent architecture that can be leveraged by multiple channel-delivery applications across business lines to improve the complete customer experience and reduce overall expenses. The current and target states are defined, and subsequently the gaps are identified, followed by a roadmapping exercise to craft a phased plan to address the gaps.

The bottom tier comprises domain-specific architectures for a particular portfolio or delivery channel. These service-oriented architecture models are tailored to the specific lines of business and delivery channels. As an implementation of the SOA in Internet Channel, The Reusable Enterprise System Platform & Extensible Component Technology (RESPECT) is illustrated in the diagram. Served as a foundational structure for all Internet applications, this platform addresses the majority of system-level concerns and operation services

Figure 3. Architecture Baseline Model

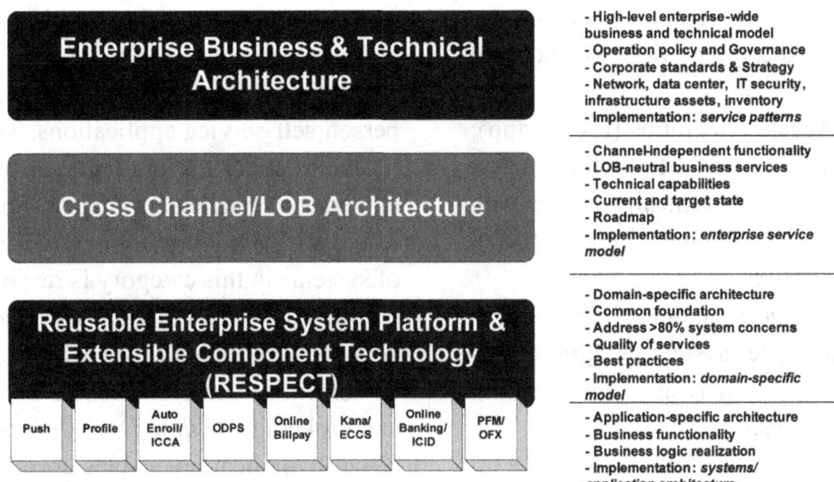

attributes, such as load balancing, scalability, high availability, capacity planning, storage, security, system monitoring and management, and so on.

The application specific architectures are built on top of the cross-application SOA model in a domain and the *RESPECT* platform. As illustrated at the bottom in the diagram, the architectures of individual applications adapt to the common platform in a plug-n-play mode, with a focus on the realization of business use cases and implementation of the business logic and rules. Vertical industry models and off-the-shelf solution packages can also be leveraged to be integrated with RESPECT.

SERVICE PATTERNS

A pattern-based method is leveraged to manage and organize different services in a large-scale enterprise computing environment. E-business patterns are high-level artifacts that are used to describe the principal business purpose of a solution. They identify the high-level participants who interact in the solution based on the primary objectives of the solutions, and define the nature of the interactions between the participants. They also specify the nature of the services from a usage perspective. The primary patterns are classified in the following list.

- B2P Self-Service (business to person): enable users to use the business functionalities via the graphical user interfaces of a thin client (web browsers), thick client (typically Windows GUI applications), and rich client (rich Internet applications) as well as other pervasive platforms like personal digital assistants (PDA) and mobile devices such as cell phones – e.g. money transfers between accounts, and bill payments.
- P2P Collaboration (person to person): enable users to communicate with other people like customer services representatives electronically – e.g. emails, text messaging, and web-based instant messaging.
- P2D Data Aggregation (person to data): enable users to access product information, service details, directory, branch/ATM locations, and data summary – e.g. check images, and interim account statements.
- B2B Enterprise (business to business): enable business partners to collaboratively

provide services with seamless navigations between sites – e.g. user account aggregations, and co-marketing with external vendors.

- Front-end Access Integration (user to app): enable the integration of front ends of servicing applications, typically at the web server tier – e.g. Single Sign-On (SSO), and portal services.
- Back-end Application Integration (app to app): enable inter-system integrations – e.g. asynchronous messaging middleware, and web services.

The major Internet applications in a financial institution are categorized to these six patterns, and summarized in Table 1.

The first category consists of business-to-person self-service applications. The user interfaces are either the predominant web browsers or personal financial manager applications like Microsoft *Money* and Intuit *Quicken*. One group of systems in this category is responsible for the enrollment process of various services and products. *Auto Enrollment* system allows users to sign up for online services such as banking, billpay and brokerage. *Online Deposit Product Services* (ODPS) application enables users to open a new

Table 1. Online Services Patterns and Exemplary Solutions

Pattern	Exemplary Solution	Characteristics
B2P Self-Service	- Auto Enrollment - Online Deposit Products Services - Yodlee service registration - Alerts subscription - MyProfile - Online Banking and Billpay - Internet Check Card Activation - Prepaid Debit Card - Personal Financial Manager (PFM)	- Enrollment process - E-sign - E-disclosure - Profile management - Alerts via email, pager, & cell phone - Banking & bill pay - PFM (Microsoft Money & Quicken) - External services
P2P Collaboration	- Kana - Secure Message Center - Alerts - ServiceProfile	- Email collaboration - Secure message box - Alerts delivery - Agent assistance
P2D Data Aggregation	- Internet Check Image Delivery - ServiceProfile - Reporting	- View cancelled checks - Aggregation for service agents - Centralized reporting services
B2B Enterprise	- Yodlee seamless router - Check Reorder (Harland) - Onestop shopping - Credit card (MBNA)	- B2B single sign-on solution - Supply chain integration for check orders - B2B partnership
Front-end Access Integration	- Online Services Homepage - SSO - Service representatives portals (ServiceProfile) - PFM	- Homepage for online services - Single sign-on - Portal for customization and personalization - PFM data integration
Back-end Application Integration	- MyProfile Web API - Protocol Translation Server - Push Messaging API & message queue - Kana API - DocCentral - Cimphony/Tibo/Integration Hub	- Synchronous HTTP - Asynchronous message queues - Mainframe access - Multi-channel adapter design - Web Services

checking or saving account online. Customers may register for the *Yodlee* account aggregation services and alerts services as well.

An integral part of the online enrollment process is the electronic signature and disclosures. As a user enrolls in a new service via a web browser remotely, current technology is unable to obtain a physical signature electronically from the user in an economic way. Instead, an e-sign page is presented to the user, who must click the accept button on the page, in lieu of a traditional physical signature. In the e-disclosure phase afterwards, legal terms associated with each specific service are sequentially displayed for the applicant to review and agree upon. An app-to-app integration pattern is used for the communications with a Content Management System (CMS), which is a central repository of all legal documents.

Another group in this category is composed of self-service management applications. All customers' personal profile information and other service-related data can be updated online via self-service. For instance, a user can go to the *MyProfile* system to change the email address, message format (html or text), solicitation flag, and newsletter subscription options (interest areas). Online Banking system is a heavily-used web-based application that allows users to check balances, view account activities, transfer funds between eligible accounts, order checks, stop payment on checks and view images of the posted checks securely. It also has links to other services such as enrolling in other online services, subscribing balance alerts, and sending and receiving secure messages with the Customer Services division.

The second category includes the person-to-person collaboration systems. *Kana* is a system for the personal service representatives (PSRs) to handle various issues sent by customers via regular emails or the *Secure Message Center*. It has collaborative case management features such as Forward & Track, and Follow-up. The *Secure Message Center* is a web-based mail inbox for every online customer, similar to the popular web mail accounts like Yahoo and Google Mail. The key difference is that users have to log in to the *Message Center* to read messages, and all communications are protected in a Secure Socket Layer (SSL) session. For the sake of security, the correspondences with sensitive data related to the customer accounts are only stored in the *Message Center* and an alert is dispatched to the customer's regular email address. Moreover, clients may also write secure messages to PSRs, after authenticated through a login process, if they do not feel comfortable sending the info through a regular plain-text mail system.

The third category comprises the person-to-data applications. The *Check Image* system enables users to search and view their cancelled checks online. Both sides of a check can be viewed with zoom in and out capability. *ServiceProfile* is a portal-like application to assist the PSRs to retrieve various audit logs from different systems via a web browser while communicating with customers over the phone. The system also allows the PSRs to modify the settings in the customer profile on behalf of a client in real time. Centralized reporting services allow users to create ad hoc reports and scheduled jobs in an easy way.

The fourth category is the business-to-business enterprise pattern, which involves interactions between the business partners. A seamless router application is built to enable a user to log on to the main website, and then visit the *Yodlee* account aggregation services during the session without the need of another login at the *Yodlee* site. Similarly, a customer can reorder checks online at the bank website, which subsequently dispatches the request to the business partner *Harland* behind the scene.

The fifth category is with regard to the front-end access integration. The *Online Services Homepage* serves as a portal to the diverse services offered. A consistent look & feel and navigation scheme are imposed in all systems involved. A custom-built single sign-on (SSO) solution is constructed, so that a user just needs to log on once, and subsequently navigate through different sub-systems in an active session. A similar mechanism is developed for the commercial customers and merchant accounts.

Lastly, the sixth category relates to back-end application integration for inter-system communications. This includes traditional enterprise application integration (EAI) for app-to-app integrations, the data integrations via a broker and hub mechanism, the business integration via a workflow and message broker, Extract-Transform-Load (ETL) for data warehousing, and the service choreography as well as a service bus. Diverse integration technologies are applied for the API-level access, asynchronous messaging, protocol-level translation, and web services.

Due to the space constraint, brief descriptions of the other applications are given in Table 1, but comprehensive elaborations are not provided in this context, whereas some applications will be discussed in further detail in the subsequent sections.

ENTERPRISE SERVICE MODEL

The overall logical enterprise service model across major lines of business and channels is illustrated in Figure 4. The design is in accordance with the hybrid methodology and architecture baseline model discussed in the foregoing sections. The core business services, common business services, and customer relationship services are defined at the bottom, based on the requirements from various business units. The primary services in this group are customer management, contact management, banking, payment processing, funds transfer, and business rules. The core and common cross-channel services are described in the middle layer, which contain access services, service grid bus, customer profile, bill payment, check image, and electronic statements. Channel-specific services are outlined at the top, for branch, ATM, VRU, Internet, and so on. All these services are primarily functional services from a business viewpoint. Additionally, the basic and advanced technical services are shared services used by other services across the layers in the technical implementations. The service infrastructure contains the foundation for operations, availability, security and versioning.

DOMAIN-SPECIFIC MODEL

Figure 5 depicts the service-oriented architecture for the Internet channel in this financial services organization. The access points are divided into the authenticated and non-authenticated space. In the non-authenticated space, a client does not need credentials to use the services. For example, a prospective client may research information on any particular products and services on the website. One may open a checking account online, or activate a recently-received ATM card. On the contrary, authenticated space requires customers to enter credentials to log in first. A Single Sign-On (SSO) solution is implemented, which intercepts all incoming Https requests at the web tier in the demilitarized zone (DMZ) for authentication. First time access is redirected by the Perimeter Authentication Plug-In (PAPI) on the web servers to the Login application, where a user must enter the user ID and password. Once authenticated, an encrypted cookie is embedded in the session, and the user traffic is routed to the target service system. All subsequent accesses are validated by the *PAPI* to assure that the session token is legitimate and unexpired.

By default, after successful login, a user is presented with the *Online Services Homepage*, which is a portal-like page with multiple links to various services. For convenience, a user may choose to set the service selection to jump to the banking, billpay or brokerage service page directly once the authentication is completed. Customization and personalization of themes and skins as well

Figure 4. Enterprise Service Model

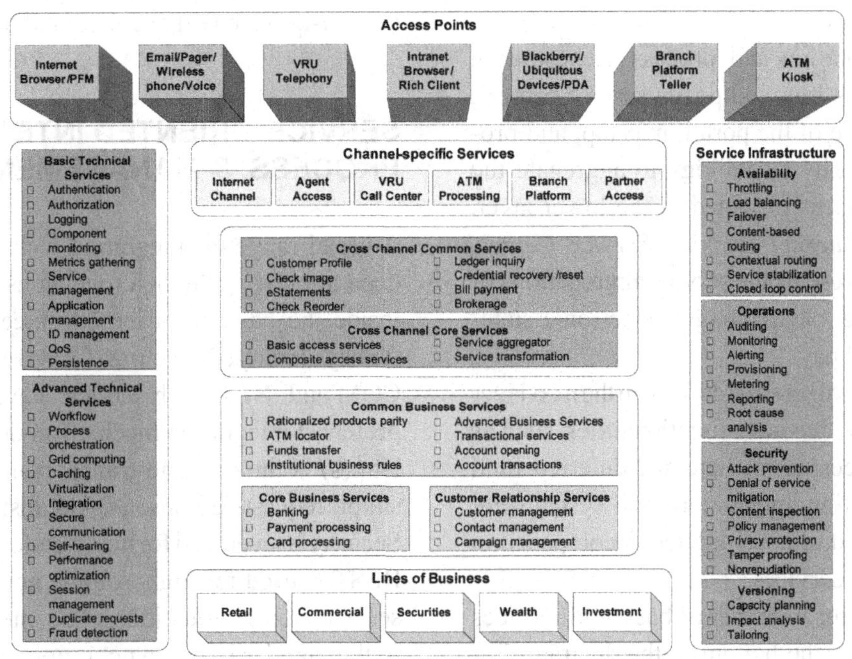

Figure 5. Service-Oriented Architecture for Internet Channel

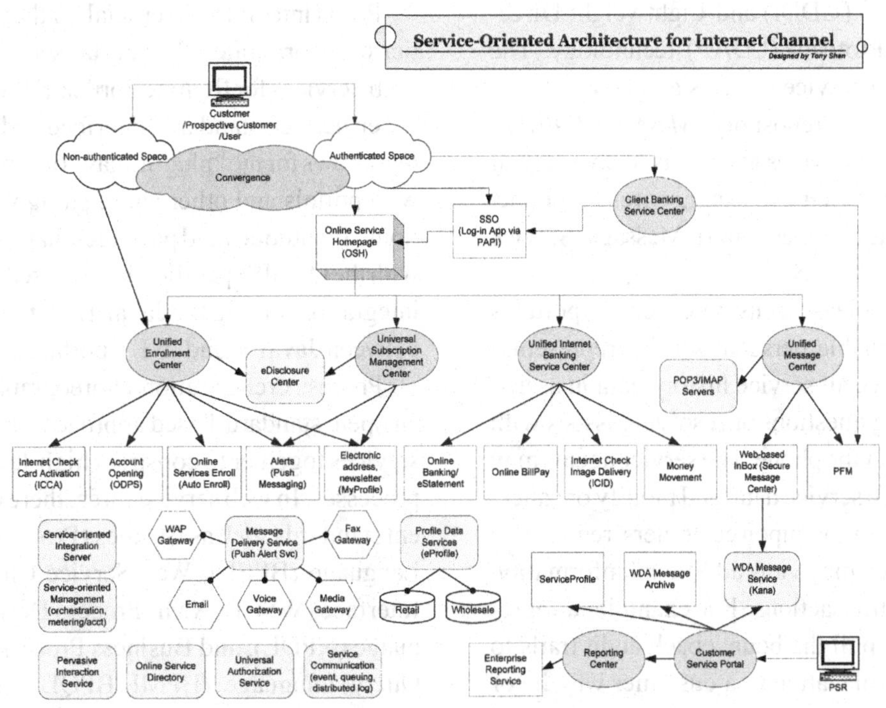

as contents order and layout are to be provided in the near future.

The presentation and process orchestration layer comprises four composite service centers, which make use of the portal, mashup, and process choreography technology to aggregate the individual services provided in the lower layer. The *Unified Internet Banking Service Center*, for example, presents the service aggregations of online banking, check images, electronic statements, and bill pay.

The individual services defined in the next layer provide specific business functionalities, such as account balances, immediate and deferred fund transfers. Existing applications and systems are either converted or consolidated/decomposed to establish these services.

What is more, a number of back-end services are illustrated at the bottom in the diagram. For example, the *Online Service Directory* is a meta-data repository to store all service-related information for service registration and lookup, using both Universal Description, Discovery and Integration (UDDI) and Lightweight Directory Access Protocol (LDAP) technology. The corresponding service policies and contracts are also stored in the repository. *Message Delivery Services* send messages and alerts to a variety of devices, such as email, pager, wireless phone, secure message center, Short Message Service (SMS), voice and fax.

Last but not least, a customer service portal is designed to enable personal service representatives to retrieve all service history data in assisting answering questions or resolving issues with customers over the phone. The service agents may also update the service data, and modify or cancel service subscriptions upon customers' requests. If necessary, they may view additional information about failed transactions. For example, a representative can pull the bounceback audit trails to provide an explanation to a customer why he or she has not received the expected message -- an incompatible message format (text vs. html) specified at signup, incorrect electronic address or over-quota email account, and the like.

SERVICE-ORIENTED INTEGRATION, PROCESS, & MANAGEMENT

A broad range of integration technologies have been applied in the heterogeneous environment inside the bank. Distributed object models are widely deployed, such as CORBA, RMI, EJB, COM and .NET. Web services have become the preferred integration mechanism down the road. Http(s) is the de facto transport mechanism for simple request-response SOAP calls, whereas WS-Security is leveraged for message-level protection. REST is used for high-volume non-confidential service communications. The message queue is the standard for asynchronous non-blocking invocations, such as SOAP over JMS. To ensure the interoperability across the organization, the WS-I Basic Profile and Basic Security Profile have been adopted.

Portal integration is crucial for the presentation tier to incorporate other portal services directly. Web Services for Remote Portlets (WSRP) defines a web service standard (interface and semantics) that allows for the "plug-n-play" of content sources with portals and other aggregating web applications. Techniques and packages that are compliant with the OASIS specification are used in the portal integration among the JavaEE portlets as well as between JavaEE and .NET portal servers.

Process orchestration/choreography provides an open, standard-based approach for connecting services together to construct high-level business processes. In web services area, there exist different standards such as Business Process Execution Language (BPEL), Web Service Choreography Interface (WSCI), XML Process Definition Language (XPDL), and Business Process Modeling/Query Language (BPML/BPQL). It turns out that BPEL tends to gain broader acceptance, and obtain more vendor supports. The leading web services vendors have been providing tools to ease the development. In addition, technologies are available for asynchronous business integration through a message broker, integration server, and process choreographer.

Service management primarily contains access mechanism (authentication, authorization, and audit), secure communications, web services provisioning (subscription, service-level objectives, licensing, contract management, monitoring, metering, and billing), service virtualization, workflow management, service metadata and repository, service maturity and lifecycle, documentation, quality of services, service continuity, policy enforcement, tools, event management, configuration management, and governance. Several commercial products have emerged, which provides similar functionalities that are available in the traditional system management suites for non-service oriented applications. Our service management capability is focused on the seamless integration of design-time, run-time, and change-time governance. Furthermore, the business activity monitoring (BAM) is the analysis, aggregation, and presentation of real time information about activities inside organizations and involving customers and partners. The metrics of key performance indicators (KPI) in BAM enable an organization to make better informed business decisions, quickly address problem areas, and reposition the company to take full advantage of emerging opportunities.

REUSABLE ENTERPRISE SYSTEM PLATFORM & EXTENSIBLE COMPONENT TECHNOLOGY

A service-oriented solution platform is a pragmatic model to implement service-oriented architecture, integration, process and management in electronic banking systems. The Reusable Enterprise System Platform & Extensible Component Technology (RESPECT) is composed of several blocks, as illustrated in Figure 6. *RESPECT* is a common baseline for all Internet application development projects. The key artifacts in the platform are architecture, hosting environment, application frameworks, components, tools, unit testing, build/deploy management, integration, methodology, system management, security, quality of services, and best practices.

The *Logical Architecture* block deals with the application partitioning through multiple layers/tiers using architectural patterns. The Model-View-Controller (MVC) pattern is a common practice for the overall structure at the application level. The *Physical Architecture* block covers the system topology, performance optimization through intelligent load balancing, scalability via horizontal and vertical scaling, high availability through different redundancy and fail-over mechanisms as well as clustering, disaster recovery, and network specifications.

The *Hardware Model* block includes the server brands and models, with CPU, memory and disk space specifications as well as networking and storage requirements. Hardware resources may be shared to host multiple applications in a server farm or via on-demand server virtualization. Public, private, and hybrid clouds can be leveraged for both computing and storage resources. The *Server Software* block contains software products installed on the web, application and database servers. Server plug-ins and clustering are defined. Communications or integration server requirements, if needed, are specified.

The *Application Framework* block categorizes application frameworks, which are the foundation of application micro-structures. Criteria are established for selection of appropriate frameworks in different business scenarios. The *Software Components* block comprises the packages and toolkits used in software development. A substantial number of open source libraries are available, such as Log4J for logging, Axis for SOAP invocations, JDOM for XML parsing, Quartz for job scheduling, JFreeChart for chart-

Figure 6. Reusable Enterprise System Platform & Extensible Component Technology

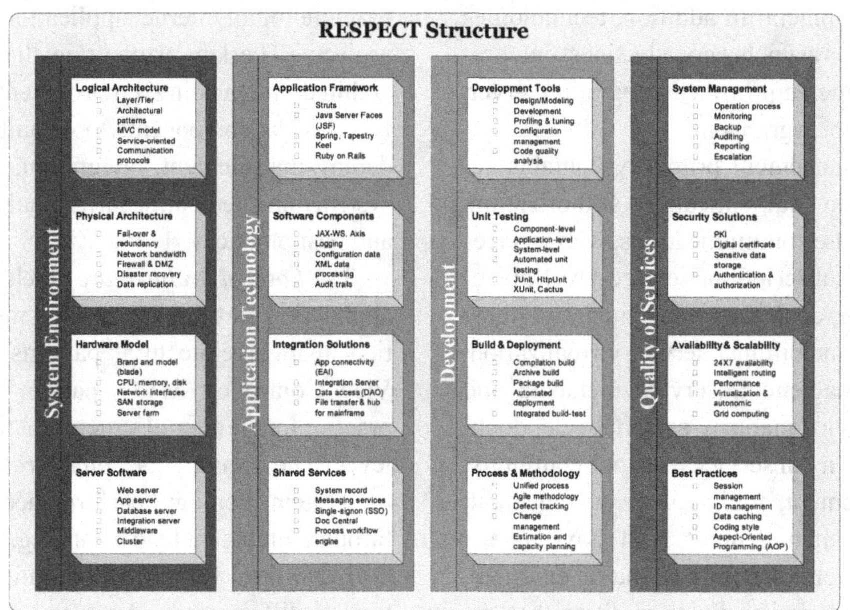

ing, iText/Jasper for PDF, OpenJMS/ActiveMQ for messaging, and Jakarta Commons for utility functions, to name a few.

The *Integration Solutions* block handles the data resource integration. Both synchronous and asynchronous mechanisms are defined for application-to-application integration and batch processing. Data access techniques are specified based on business scenarios, such as ODBC, JDBC, ADO.NET, JDO, SDO, Hibernate and EJB, with help of auto code generation tools like XDoclet and Middlegen. The *Shared Services* block contains common services sharable across channels and lines of business. Examples are system records of customer data, corporate messaging services, single sign-on (SSO), and the document central service, which prints hard copies of documents to be delivered to customers.

The *Development Tools* block is composed of tools used in modeling, development, profiling, defects tracking, configuration management, and code quality analysis. Seamless integration of modeling tools with IDEs enables instant round-trip engineering, and closes the gap between architects and developers. The *Unit Testing* block consists of standardized unit testings at the component, application, and system levels. The unit testing process is automated in both whitebox and blackbox approaches, by means of JUnit, HttpUnit, XUnit, NUnit, Cactus, and Cruise Control. The testing is automated via the seamless integration with tools like Maven.

The *Build & Deployment* block copes with the build process and deployment. Three levels of builds are defined for the JavaEE applications – compilation build, archive build, and package build. The *Process & Methodology* block takes advantage of the best-of-breed from both heavyweight unified process and agile methodologies. Effective defect tracking and change management are employed. Estimation and capacity planning are critical design aspects.

The *System Management* block handles the application- and server-level management. It includes capacity planning, health check, real-time performance monitoring, backup, auditing, self-healing, dashboard charting, issue management, escalation, and reporting. The *Security Solutions* block deals with security at the data, application, system, network, and data center levels. Standards are defined for the sensitive data stored in each application database, access privilege of credential data at the application level, penetration protection at system level, communications across the local network via SSL or IPSec, message-level data encryption, hardware hardening, ID management, and access control to the perimeter points via firewalls and DMZ.

The *Availability & Scalability* block addresses the high availability and service level agreement verification with regard to the performance requirements. Solutions can be scaled up or out with seamless interoperability and portability. The *Best Practices* block concentrates on industry proven effective solution patterns for common design concerns, such as session management and federated ID management. For example, data caching is a key aspect in the application design, and is frequently utilized for performance enhancement and session management. Careful deliberation must be made in choosing a right solution option, among the techniques like in-memory replication, database persistence, and clustering, to ensure data integrity and efficient data synchronization (Shan et al 2005).

APPLYING IDEA FRAMEWORK IN SYSTEM DEVELOPMENT

The *IDEA* framework described in the preceding sections provides a pragmatic method for the application development in Internet Banking space. The best-practice approach to constructing an individual IT solution based on *IDEA* is to apply the modules in the framework in a logical order sequentially. First, establish a sound methodology, based on which the design approach and technical options are formulated. Second, use the architecture baseline model to identify tasks, roles, and accountabilities to develop and contribute different artifacts, and assess what stakeholders need to be engaged in which activities. Third, classify the application in the project scope to one of the service patterns. Large projects may fall into a combination of multiple patterns, depending on the overall architecture complexity. Fourth, check the overall enterprise service blueprint and the cross-portfolio SOA model to specify detailed development aspects and necessary modifications/expansions. Finally, build the portfolio solution and individual services/systems using the domain-specific model.

The "traditional" methods in IT system development are tailored to the object-oriented and component-based models, typically resulting in stove-piped applications in a solo mode. Even though the majority of the eCommerce systems in our environment are based on multi-tier distributed computing architecture, they are becoming obsolete due to the non-service oriented nature. *IDEA* has been applied to systematically transform the existing applications to be service aware. For example, we use different techniques in *IDEA* such as the wrapper and decomposition to convert servlets in JavaEE applications to web services for application-to-application integrations. In this way, the proprietary message formats that were used before between the callers and callees via Http(s) are completely eliminated. The message parsing and construction as well as format/content validations are streamlined, taking advantage of the standard SOAP marshalling/unmarshalling and built-in mechanisms in some popular application frameworks. In addition, the inter-application authentication via web services leverages the standard specifications such as WS-Security in place of the previous ad-hoc approach by passing credentials or tokens in every service invocation inside the message payload, commonly used in Https API calls when client digital certificates are not utilized.

In contrast, the design philosophy in the new system development is entirely changed. Rather than thinking of the IT solutions at the standalone application and system platform levels, the top-down approach facilitates the forward-engineering design in the service-oriented paradigm. The solution architecture is partitioned in a new structure as the access interaction, process orchestration, service aggregation, service choreography, collaborations, services, integrations, data resources, and security. The development process follows the templates provided in *IDEA*, focusing on the progressive levels of the application block, method, object, component, service, integration, process, and user access. Moreover, the pattern-based analysis and design help refine the pattern classification and characterization of sub-categories, which in turn standardizes and commoditizes the complicated development process, and enhances the overall reusability. We have observed substantial progress towards the service-oriented goal and significant impact of the *IDEA* framework in our practices.

Further, the blocks in the Reusable Enterprise System Platform & Extensible Component Technology address the major, if not all, fault/weak points in the design and development of an IT application. The conventional way to deal with these key artifacts is usually in an isolated fashion. This RESPECT platform presents an overarching view of these aspects, and more importantly the correlations between these artifacts. The cross-cutting design concerns are treated as the aspects at the application level beyond the component level. Taking the logging as an example, the platform standardizes the entry format of log files, so that the records in different files on different servers at different servers in different geographical data centers can be correlated for a user session in a multi-layer web application. The standardized format of log entries is extremely useful in the troubleshooting of multiple systems collaboratively serving a user request. A standard logger utility is specified in the platform, providing various logging mechanisms, such as synchronous, asynchronous, caching, persistent to file system, persistent to database, and integration with event alert services, via an aspect component. A log analyzer is built to automate the examination of log files, and recognize patterns of faults and usage for a trend analysis in the log mining.

CHALLENGES

New technologies have been emerging at an unprecedented pace. Web services technology is a widespread implementation technique for service-oriented solutions. However, the standardization in the web services area is still immature and the artifacts keep changing all the time. There have been a plethora of recommendations, specifications, proposals, and standards with different commitments and supports from various vendors. To sort these out in a systematic way, a SOA standard and specification stack is complied, in which corresponding standard artifacts are cataloged in logical groups, as summarized in Figure 7. Competing and conflicting WS-* exist in most categories. This essentially prevents the end users from planning a realistic approach in this uncertain world in order to apply these technologies in the solution designs. A good strategy is twofold for both long term and short term. On the one hand, we need to firmly stay with an open platform baseline, which exclusively relies on open standards and matured specifications only. The key of this base model is the adaptability and expandability for future growth, while maintaining the architectural and infrastructural stability as much as possible. On the other hand, a tactical approach is formed to leverage solutions backed by the dominant vendors/groups to meet our immediate business needs. The technologies chosen in the short-term implementations are relatively established in the foreseeable future. The adapter pattern is extensively used in the system design, to enforce loose-coupling interfaces and plug-and-play in structure.

One of the biggest challenges becomes how to converge all the new technologies and implement them in the service-oriented platform without

Figure 7. SOA Standards and Specification Stack

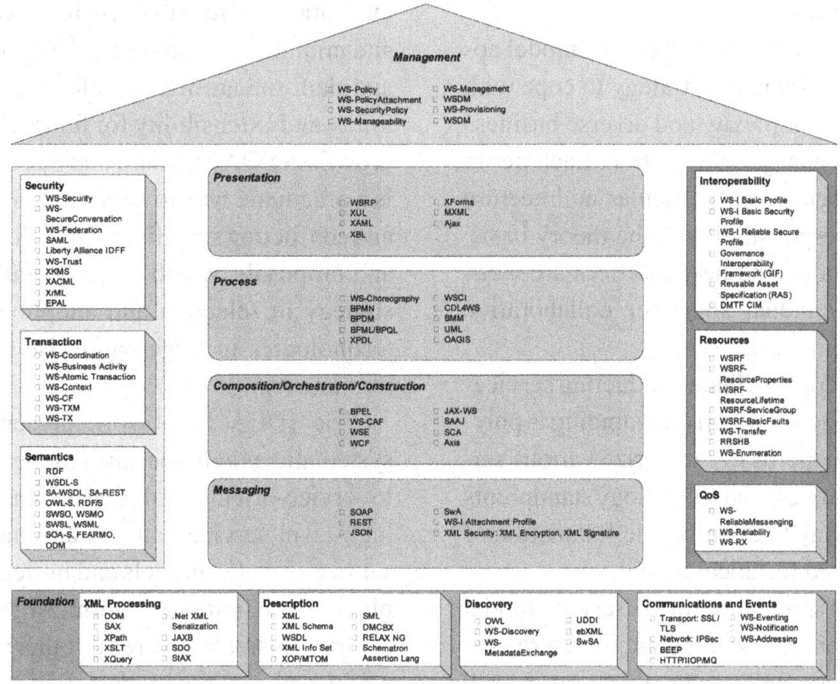

significant impacts on the business continuity. Consider the Business Intelligence (BI), which is the discipline of developing solutions that are conclusive, fact-based, and actionable. These solutions help the enterprise combine and analyze key insights and data points that can be used to make informed and intelligent business decisions, using techniques such as data mining and trend analysis. As an example, an online enrollment of new services typically has several web pages presented to a user to fill out sequentially. It is not uncommon that a fraction of users start the process by completing the first few pages, but stop the registration in the middle and never come back. Analysis of the abandonment rate with the assistance of the BI tools helps reveal the root causes and patterns of the problems, being ambiguity in the terms, lengthy process, unintuitive navigation, or usability issues (lack of needed help links at particular points in the process). This facilitates enhancing the service interfaces, and improving the effectiveness of the transaction process, and in turn the customers' satisfaction and loyalty.

CONCLUSION

The integrated design of eBanking architecture (IDEA) framework introduced in this Chapter is a comprehensive approach for architecture abstraction, process standard, cross-application framework and portfolio engineering in the service-oriented application development and migration. The key modules in this framework are *Hybrid Methodology*, *Architecture Baseline Model*, *Service Patterns*, *Enterprise Service Model*, and *Domain-Specific Model*.

A hybrid methodology of both top-down and bottom-up methods is an efficient method to take advantage of the benefits of both schemes. The *Services Composition & Coordination Layer* is an important bridge between the two methods. Depending on where an existing application stands in its lifecycle, it may be revamped by one of three approaches: *Refactoring*, *Reengineering*, and *Reachitecting*. In general, there are five practical methods that may be utilized to service-enable existing applications with minimal efforts:

consolidating, *decomposing*, *wrapping*, *screen scraping*, and *mediating*.

A multi-level architecture baseline model applies a divide-and-conquer strategy to cope with the architecture complexity and diverse business requirements in a large organization. Each tier in the model is focused on particular architecture functions and responsibilities. The theory basis, body of knowledge and best practices are well-captured in individual areas for collaborative system development.

Service patterns facilitate conducting service-oriented modeling in enterprise computing. Applying e-business patterns to categorize various services from the process and technology standpoints is an effective way to establish the foundation of a service-oriented technical model.

A service-oriented enterprise service model incorporates service-oriented architecture, integration, process and management. An overall logical service model across lines of business is recommended to be designed from top down, and must be platform-independent and adaptive to be aligned with the business domain model. A bottom-up method is preferred to define a domain-specific technical architecture for a particular portfolio or delivery channel, to leverage the existing systems and minimize the impact to existing service APIs. The synchronous and asynchronous app-to-app integration, portal integration, process orchestration for long-lived transactional choreography, and service management as well as security are important elements in the migration path to a service-oriented computing paradigm.

The Reusable Enterprise System Platform & Extensible Component Technology (RESPECT) is a reference implementation model addressing the common design considerations and concerns, which is comprised of architecture, technologies, frameworks, components, process, methodology, tools, hosting environment, security, unit testing, patterns, best practices, and so forth.

More challenges are expected in the convergence of new and emerging technologies, some of which are cutting-edge and immature. In-depth evaluation and research will help avoid the pitfalls and minimize the potential risks. Open standards and platforms are highly preferred, to provide flexibility and extensibility for future expansions and growth. A SOA Standard and Specification Stack is a pragmatic way to sort out various competing and conflicting specifications, recommendations, and proposals, which helps formulate a realistic strategy in selection and adoption of emerging technologies in large enterprise computing environments.

The IDEA framework presents a holistic, systematic, pragmatic, and engineering approach to service-oriented solution design, ranging from high-level service patterns and methodology to service-oriented models and in-depth application blocks in a common platform, which has not been comprehensively covered by other existing frameworks and process models. Part of this solution framework has been successfully implemented in the Internet application development and migrations in a large financial institution, which has significantly reduced the development time and runtime environment cost while delivering better quality solutions in compliance with standards and policies. Although this framework is designed specifically for the eBanking sector, the structure is highly adaptive and extensible to be utilized in other business domains and industry areas, with minor modifications or expansions.

REFERENCES

Albin, S. (2003). *The Art of Software Architecture: Design Methods and Techniques*. New York: John Wiley & Sons.

Bass, L., Clements, P., & Kazman, R. (1998). *Software Architecture in Practice*. Massachusetts: Addison Wesley.

Broemmer, D. (2002). *J2EE Best Practices: Java Design Patterns, Automation, and Performance*. Massachusetts: John Wiley & Sons.

Carbone, J. A. (2004). *IT Architecture Toolkit*. New Jersey: Prentice Hall PTR.

Dustdar, S., Gall, H., & Schmidt, R. (2004). Web Services for Groupware in Distributed and Mobile Collaboration. *12th IEEE Euromicro Conference on Parallel, Distributed and Network-Based Processing (PDP 2004)* (p. 241).

Erl, T. (2004). *Service-Oriented Architecture: A Field Guide to Integrating XML and Web Services*. New Jersey: Prentice Hall PTR.

Fowler, M. (2003). *Patterns of Enterprise Application Architecture*. Massachusetts: Addison Wesley.

Frankel, D. S. (2003). *Model Driven Architecture: Applying MDA to Enterprise Computing*. New York: John Wiley & Sons.

Giaglis, G. M. (2001). A Taxonomy of Business Process Modeling and Information Systems Modeling Techniques. *International Journal of Flexible Manufacturing Systems*, *13*(2), 209–228. doi:10.1023/A:1011139719773

Gronmo, R., & Solheim, I. (2004). Towards Modeling Web Service Composition in UML. In *Proceedings of the 2nd International Workshop on Web Services: Modeling, Architecture and Infrastructure* (WSMAI 2004) (pp. 72-86). Porto, Portugal, April 13-14, 2004.

Gulzar, M., & Ganeshan, K. (2003). *Practical J2EE Application Architecture*. California: McGraw-Hill Osborne Media.

IFEAD. The Institute for Enterprise Architecture Developments (2004). *Extended Enterprise Architecture Framework*. Retrieved February 8, 2008 from http://enterprise-architecture.info

Jorstad, I., Thanh, D. V., & Dustdar, S. (2004). An Analysis of Service Continuity in Mobile Services. In *Proceedings of the 2nd International Workshop on Distributed and Mobile Collaboration (DMC 2004)* (pp. 121-126). Modena, Italy, June 14-16, 2004.

Kruchten, P. (2003). *The Rational Unified Process: An Introduction* (3rd ed.). Massachusetts: Addison Wesley.

McGovern, J. (2003). *Java Web Services Architecture*. New York: Morgan Kaufmann.

McGovern, J., Ambler, S. W., Stevens, M. E., Linn, J., Sharan, V., & Jo, E. K. (2003). *A Practical Guide to Enterprise Architecture*. New Jersey: Prentice Hall PTR.

OMG. Object Management Group (2002). *Model Driven Architecture*. http://www.omg.org/mda. (February 8 2008).

Schekkerman, J. (2003). *How to Survive in the Jungle of Enterprise Architecture Framework: Creating or Choosing an Enterprise Architecture Framework*. North Carolina: Trafford Publishing.

Sessions, R., & Sickler, J. V. (2003). *Software Fortresses: Modeling Enterprise Architectures*. Massachusetts: Addison Wesley.

Shan, T. C., et al. (2004). *WebSphere MQ Solutions in a Microsoft. NET Environment*. New York: IBM Corporation.

Shan, T. C., et al. (2004). *Websphere Business Integration for SAP*. New York: IBM Corporation.

Shan, T. C., & Hua, W. W. (2005). High-performance Data Caching Mechanisms. 2005 *Web Information and System Application Conference (WISA 2005)*.

Shan, T. C., & Hua, W. W. (2006). Solution Architecture of N-Tier Applications. In *Proceedings of 3rd IEEE International Conference on Services Computing* (pp. 349-356). California: IEEE Computer Society.

TOGAF. The Open Group (2003). The Open Group Architecture Framework Version 9 ("Enterprise Edition"). Retrieved February 8, 2008 from http://www.opengroup.org/togaf

Zachman, J. (2002). *Zachman Framework*. Retrieved February 8, 2008 from http://www.zifa.com.

Zimmermann, O., Tomlinson, M., & Peuser, S. (2003). *Perspectives on Web Services*. Heidelberg: Springer.

Chapter 5
A Similarity Measure for Process Mining in Service Oriented Architecture

Joonsoo Bae
Chonbuk National Univ, South Korea

Ling Liu
Georgia Institute of Technology, USA

James Caverlee
Georgia Institute of Technology, USA

Liang-Jie Zhang
IBM T.J. Watson Research Center, USA

Hyerim Bae
Pusan National Univ, South Korea

ABSTRACT

Business processes continue to play an important role in today's service-oriented enterprise computing systems. Mining, discovering, and integrating process-oriented services has attracted growing attention in the recent years. This chapter presents a quantitative approach to modeling and capturing the similarity and dissimilarity between different process designs. The authors derive the similarity measures by analyzing the process dependency graphs of the participating workflow processes. They first convert each process dependency graph into a normalized process matrix. Then they calculate the metric space distance between the normalized matrices. This distance measure can be used as a quantitative and qualitative tool in process mining, process merging, and process clustering, and ultimately it can reduce or minimize the costs involved in design, analysis, and evolution of workflow systems.

DOI: 10.4018/978-1-61520-684-1.ch005

INTRODUCTION

With the increasing interest and wide deployment of web services, we see a growing demand for Service-Oriented Architectures (SOA) and technologies that support enterprise transformation. Effective enterprise transformation refers to strategic business agility in terms of how efficiently an enterprise can respond to its competitors and how timely an enterprise can anticipate new opportunities that may arise in the future. In the increasingly globalized economy, enterprises face complex challenges that can require rapid and possibly continual transformations. As a result, more and more enterprises are focused on the strategic management of fundamental changes with respect to markets, products, and services (Rouse, 2005). Such transformation typically has a direct impact on the business processes of an enterprise. Enterprise transformation may range from traditional business process improvement to wholesale changes to the processes supported by the enterprise – from performing current work in a new fashion to performing different work altogether. Each of these challenges may lead to a different degree of enterprise transformation.

Fundamental to enabling the transformation of an enterprise is the development of novel tools and techniques for transforming the business processes of an enterprise. In this paper, we present a critical component to the problem of process transformation from a web services point-of-view. In particular, we present a novel process difference analysis method using distance measures between process definitions of two transactional web services. The process difference analysis focuses on process activity dependencies and process structure to identify distance measures between processes.

The proposed difference analysis method achieves three distinct goals. First, by analyzing the attributes of process models, we present a quantitative process similarity metric to determine the relative distance between process models. This facilitates not only the comparison of existing process models with each other, but also provides the flexibility to adapt to changes in existing business processes. Second, the proposed method is quick and flexible, which reduces the cost of both the analysis and design phases of web service processes. Third, the proposed method enables the flexible deployment of process mining, discovery, and integration – all key features that are necessary for effective transformation of an enterprise.

SOA and Business Process Mining

Business environments are getting more complex and more dynamic, and information technology including networking is developing rapidly to support them. SOA plays a key role to associate them and thus accelerates deploying web services. Change of business environments requires many companies to transform all their business functions into serviceable elements, and the major functions are possessed in a format of business processes. Therefore, Business Process Management (BPM) and SOA are becoming two sides of the same coin, and the success of IT system is dependent on whether it can derive synergy of BPM and SOA or not. The relationships between BPM and SOA can be viewed from both sides, which are described below.

- **Business process as serviceable assets**: SOA helps BPM proliferate, helping it to be implemented through its loosely coupled and agile enabling infrastructure. Thus processes modeled by BPM tools can be rapidly implemented as services by SOA.
- **Orchestration and choreography of business services:** In muti-organizational environments such as supply chain and logistics, services should be organized and flowed over partners, which has to be supported by process management functions.

From the view points above, when combined together, enterprises are required to implement business processes as services and BPM tools as service-oriented composition of service flow. In order for service consumer to accept this situation seamless, SOA provides the architecture illustrated in Fig. 1.

Under the architecture of SOA, BPM makes services or applications easily reused and quickly changed. One of the most important things required from such settings is to find and discover proper processes for the right service. Even in an environment, where lots of companies or branches own a number of processes, the requirement of process discovery is more clarified. In a supply chain, to find a proper partner who can provide a right business service is prerequisite for supply chain optimization. Hereby, we need a method for representing similarity between process models, which are presented with network of activities, precedence relations among them, and attributes for process objects.

Web Service Process Reference Model

The web service process reference model consists of business process definitions and the specification of workflows among the processes with respect to data flow, control flow, and operational views (Rush, 1997; Schimm, 2004). We define a business process in terms of business activity patterns. An activity pattern consists of objects, messages, message exchange constraints, preconditions and postconditions (WfMC, 2005), and is designed to specify the service actions and execution dependencies of the business process. An activity pattern can be viewed as a web service process when it is executable as a web service. We consider two types of activity patterns – elementary activity patterns and composite activity patterns (Aalst, 2003a; Bae, 2004). An elementary activity pattern is an atomic unit. A composite activity pattern consists of a one or more elementary activity patterns or other composite activity patterns. The dependencies could capture complex interactions between activities.

We define a business process as a collection of business activities connected by data flow and control flow, where each represents a business process. A process definition can be seen as a web service (or a collection of web services). We use data flow among processes to define the data dependencies among processes within a given business process. We use control flow to capture the operational structure of the business process service, including the process execution ordering, the transactional semantics and dependencies of the process. A number of workflow specifications have gathered attention, including BPEL4WS

Figure 1. SOA and business processes

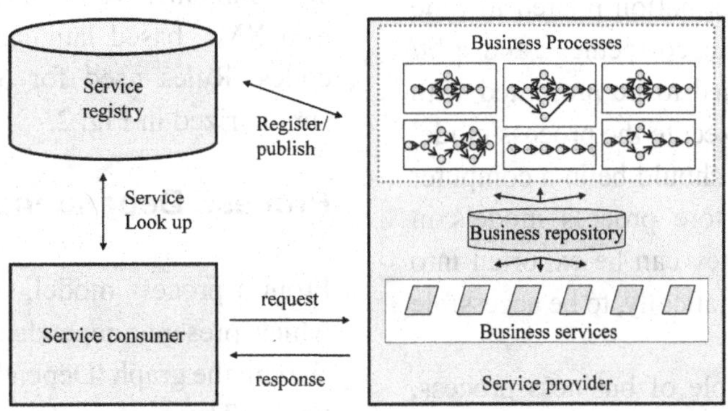

(BEA, IBM, Microsoft), WSFL (IBM), XLANG (Microsoft), and XPDL (WfMC) (WfMC, 2005). In our prototype development, we choose to use a variant of BPEL4WS.

Formally, each workflow service is specified in terms of process definitions. We can model each process definition as a process model using activities, precedence relation between activities, and their properties.

Definition 1 (Process Model, *PM*)

A process model *PM* consists of tasks, links, and attributes. That is, $PM= <A, L, Attr>$.

- A set of activities: $A = \{a_i \mid i= 1,..., I\}$, where, a_i represents *i*-th activity and *I* is the total number of tasks in a process.
- A set of links: $L=\{l_k=(a_i, a_j)|a_i,a_j \in A, i \neq j \}$, where, l_k represents a link between two activities, a_i and a_j. A link also represents a precedence relation. The link (a_i, a_j) indicates that a_i immediately precedes a_j.
- A set of attributes: *Attr* is a set of attributes ($attr_l$), whose element represents feature of objects such as process, activity and link. An attribute of an object is represented using common dot(.) notation. For example $a_i.attr_{Name}$ represents *name* attribute of activity a_i.

In our process model definition, structural information is specified using activities and links. All the other information related to time properties, business logic, correctness, and split/merge pattern is assumed to be presented with attributes. In order to execute the process model after being designed, it should be in a computer readable format. We store process models in an XML format, and they can be exported into BPEL4WS codes automatically, to be accessible via web services.

As a real-life example of business process, there are many PIPs (Partner Interface Processes) as defined by RosettaNet (RosettaNet). PIPs define business processes between trading partners. PIPs fit into seven Clusters, or groups of core business processes, that represent the backbone of the trading network. Each Cluster is broken down into Segments and within each Segment are individual PIPs. RosettaNet standards provide the infrastructure for integrating business processes with trading partners across the globe, delivering essential value to industries and proven real-world business results. Fig. 3 shows a standard process of procurement order by buyer, which is in Segment 3A (Quote and Order Entry) of Cluster 3 (Order Management). This example process has 13 activities, 22 links, and many attributes, which can be presented with our formal model in the following.

$A = \{a_1, a_2, a_3, ..., a_{13}\}$

$L = \{l_1, l_2, l_3, ..., l_{22}\} = \{(a_1, a_2), (a_1, a_3), (a_1, a_4), ..., (a_{12}, a_{13})\}$

$Attr = \{a_1.attr_{TaskName}$(= "Analyze ordering needs"), $a_2.attr_{TaskName}, ...,$

$a_1.attr_{ExpTime}, ..., l_1.attr_{TransCond}, ...\}$

Recent business environments impel enterprises to interface with each other, and SOA (Service Oriented Architecture) is considered as a natural tool for B2B (Business to Business) collaboration. For our model to be used in such computing environments, we transform our process model into XML based language, that is, BPEL4WS codes. Rules used for our transformation are summarized in Fig. 2.

Process Dependency Graph

From a process model, we can extract a graph which presents dependencies among activities. We call the graph 'Dependency Graph' in Definition 2. The process dependency graph captures

Figure 2. Rules for transforming process model into BPEL4WS codes

Pattern	Graph	(Structured) BPEL4WS
Sequence	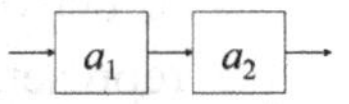 a_1 a_2	<sequence> <a_1> <a_2> </sequence>
Parallel Flow	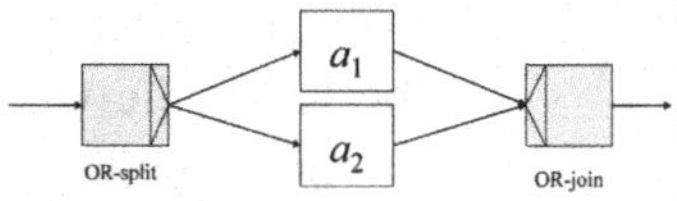 a_1 a_2 OR-split OR-join	<switch> <case condition="condition"><a_1></case> <case condition="condition"><a_2></case> </switch>
	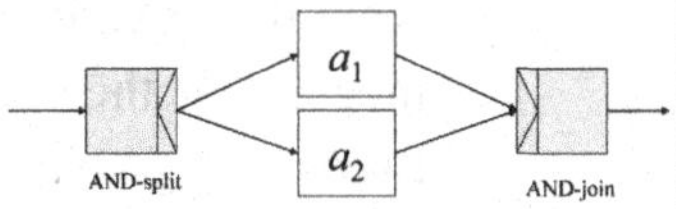 a_1 a_2 AND-split AND-join	<flow> <a_1> <a_2></flow>
Loop	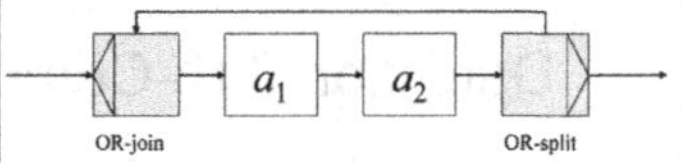 a_1 a_2 OR-join OR-split	<loop condition="condition"> <a_1> <a_2></loop>
Switch-sequence	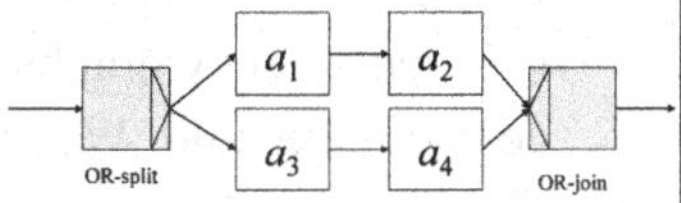 a_1 a_2 a_3 a_4 OR-split OR-join	<switch> <case condition="condition"> <sequence> <a_1><a_2></sequence> </case> <case condition="condition"> <sequence> <a_3><a_4></sequence></case> </switch>
Complex Flow	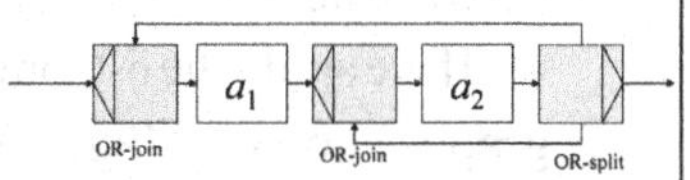 a_1 a_2 OR-join OR-join OR-split	<sequence><a_1><a_2></sequence> <loop> <switch> <case><a_1></case> </switch> <a_2> </loop>

Figure 3. A real-life example of business process

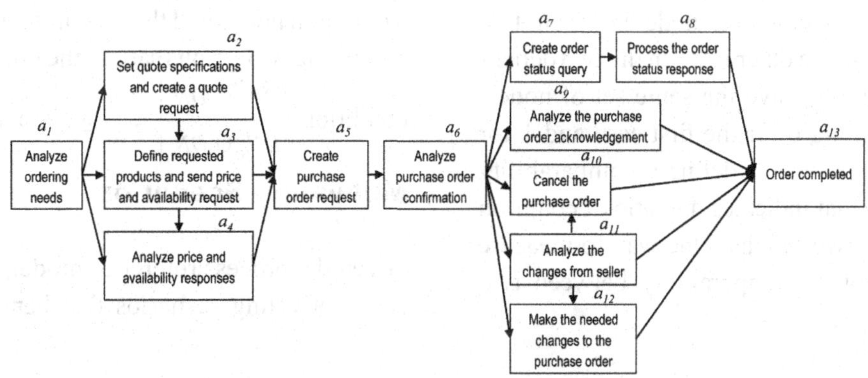

information about how activities share information and how data flows from one activity to another. Depending on whether the edges indicate execution dependencies or data flow dependencies, we have a process aggregation hierarchy, which captures the hierarchical execution ordering of activities.

Definition 2 (Dependency Graph, *DG*)

A dependency graph *DG* is defined by a binary tuple <*DN*, *DE*>, where

- $DN=\{nd_1,nd_2,\ldots,nd_n\}$ is a finite set of activity nodes where $n \geq 1$.
- $DE=\{e_1,e_2,\ldots,e_m\}$ is a set of edges, $m \geq 0$. Each edge is of the form $nd_i \rightarrow nd_j$.

Note that in the dependency graph formulation, self-edges are disallowed since edges are intended to denote data flow dependencies between different activities (nodes). Additionally, a dependency graph must be a connected graph. Unconnected nodes and isolated groups of nodes are disallowed in the graph, as isolated nodes or groups of nodes are considered a separate service process in our reference model.

- Given two processes and their respective dependency graphs, there are numerous ways these two graphs may differ. Typically, it makes more sense to compare only those graphs that have sufficient similarity in terms of their dependency graphs. Consider two extreme cases: one is when there is no common node between two graphs and the other is when the two dependency graphs have the same set of nodes. By assigning 0 for the first case and 1 for the latter case, we define a comparability measure that indicates the ratio of common nodes in two graphs. One way to measure the extent of comparability between two graphs is to use a user-controlled threshold, called δ-Comparability, which is set to be between 0 and 1. Because this value represents the ratio of common nodes over the union of all nodes in two graphs, the larger the value is, the greater degree of comparability between the two graphs. Note that δ value cannot be 0 since $\delta = 0$ means that there is no common node between two graphs, i.e., $DN_1 \cap DN_2 \neq \emptyset$.

Definition 3 (δ-Comparability of *DG*)

Let $DG_1=(DN_1,DE_1)$ and $DG_2=(DN_2,DE_2)$ be two dependency graphs, and δ be a user-defined control threshold. We say that DG_1 and DG_2 are *δ-comparable* if the condition $\frac{|DN_1 \cap DN_2|}{|DN_1 \cup DN_2|} \geq \delta$ holds, where $0 < \delta \leq 1$

If we apply the δ-Comparability to the example graphs shown in Fig. 4 with $\delta=0.5$, g^0 and f^2 are not comparable because the number of common nodes is only one but the number of total nodes is 7, that is $\frac{|DN_1 \cap DN_2|}{|DN_1 \cup DN_2|} = \frac{1}{7} < 0.5$. On the other hand, g^0 and g^2 are δ-comparable because there are 3 common nodes and the total number of nodes is 5, thus the two graphs satisfy the δ-comparability condition $\frac{|DN_1 \cap DN_2|}{|DN_1 \cup DN_2|} = \frac{3}{5} \geq 0.5$ and $\delta = 0.5$.

Motivating Scenarios

Given the process reference model, we consider two motivating scenarios that benefit from the

Figure 4. Examples of δ-Comparability

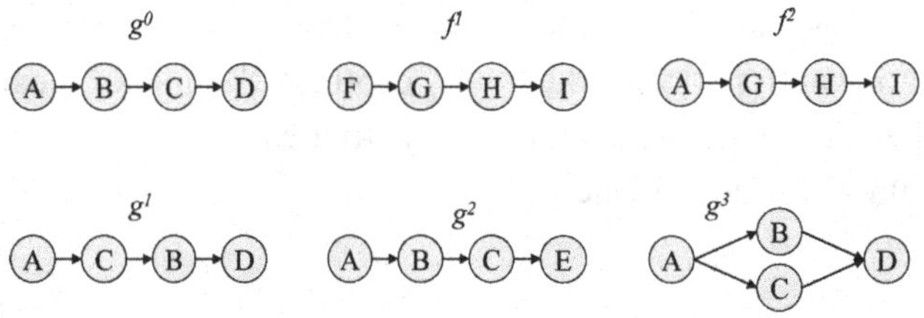

difference analysis methodology introduced in this paper. Consider a scenario where a company has maintained a warehouse of existing processes used in various business locations. *Process mining* (Aalst, 2003b; Aalst, 2004a; Aalst, 2004b, Jansen-Vullers, 2006; Medeiros, 2008) of the process warehouse can help the enterprise to discover interesting associations or classifications among business processes running at different locations or branches of the company.

In Fig. 5, we show a process warehouse that contains many types of processes (for example, g_1, g_2, g_3, g_4, g_5). A typical process mining scenario is the identification of the processes most similar to a query process template in the process warehouse. Given a query process and a comparability threshold δ-value, the process mining will identify (g_3) as the process that is most similar based on the comparability criterion. It is obvious that the concept of process similarity (or distance) is critical to the effectiveness of process mining.

Process Difference Analysis

In this section, we present the process difference analysis method for evaluating the distance between two processes. We first define the concept of a process matrix and introduce the concept of a normalized matrix. And then, we define the dependency distance measure by measuring the difference between the normalized matrices.

In order to show the proposed procedure, we use two derived processes that are variations of procurement order process in Fig. 3. These two processes have 10 activities respectively but have different activities with each other. The first process (g_{11}) has A_6 but does not have A_8, and the second process (g_{22}) has A_8 but does not have

Figure 5. Process mining example

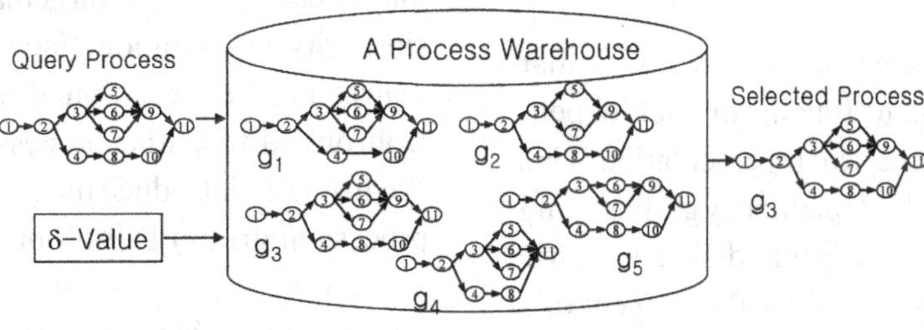

Figure 6. Flow chart of Difference Analysis

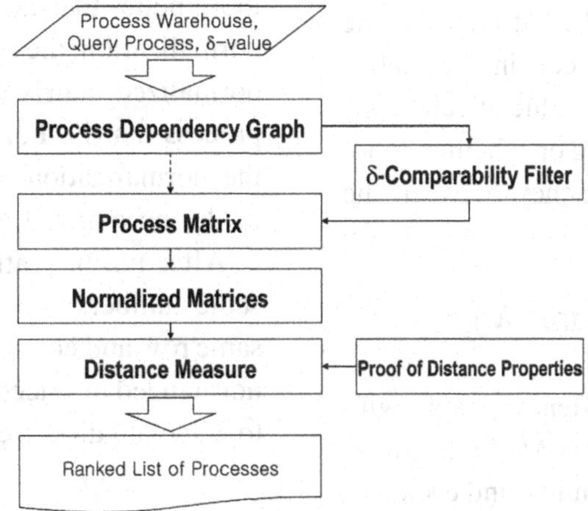

A_6. These two graphs satisfy δ-Comparability as $\frac{|DN_1 \cap DN_2|}{|DN_1 \cup DN_2|} = \frac{9}{11} \geq 0.5$ and $\delta = 0.5$.

Comparison Matrices

Two dependency graphs are said identical if the two graphs have the same set of nodes and the same set of edges. Formally we define identical dependency graphs as follows:

Definition 4 (Identical Dependency Graphs)

Let $DG_1=(DN_1,DE_1)$ and $DG_2=(DN_2,DE_2)$ be two dependency graphs. We say that DG_1 and DG_2 are identical if the two graphs have the same set of nodes and the same set of edges.

i) $DN_1 =_{set} DN_2$ ii) $DE_1 =_{set} DE_2$

One way to compare and rank a set of similar process definitions is to transform each dependency graph into a numerical representation. This allows us to compare the dependency graphs using similarity distance in Euclidian distance metric space. This leads us to introduce the concept of a process matrix. A process matrix *M* is established in order to describe the precedence dependencies between two activities (tasks). The size of *M* is determined by the number of nodes in the dependency graph and each cell in the matrix denotes an element of *M*. The value of cell *M(i,j)* is set either to 1 or 0 depending on whether or not there is a precedence dependency between the two nodes *i* and *j*.

Definition 5 (Process Matrix, *M*)

Let $g=(DN,DE)$be a dependency graph with $|DN|=n$ nodes. A process matrix *M* of *g* is *n*-by-*n* matrix with *n* rows and *n* columns, and each row is named after the node name. Let $M_g(i,j)$ denote the value of the ith row and the jth column in *M*, $1 \leq i,j \leq n$. We define $M_g(i,j)$ as follows:

$$M_g(i,j) = \begin{cases} 1 & \text{if } \exists\, nd_i, nd_j \in DN \text{ such that } (nd_i, nd_j) \in DE \\ 0 & \text{else} \end{cases}$$

Table 1 depicts the transformation of a process dependency graph g_{11} shown in Fig. 7 (a) into its process matrix *M*, a 10×10 matrix. Each element of *M* is determined according to whether or not the corresponding two activities have precedence dependency. An edge between nodes a_1 and a_2 shows that activity a_1 precedes activity a_2. Thus, $M_g(a_1, a_2)$ is set to a value of 1. There is no direct edge between nodes a_1 and a_3. Thus $M_g(a_1, a_3)$ is set to a value of 0.

In order to compare the two process dependency graphs g_{11} and g_{22}, we need to further normalize each process matrix that participates in the similarity computation. Each normalized process matrix includes the union of all sets of nodes, each from one participating process dependency graph. We formally introduce the concept of normalized process matrix in Definition 6 by extending the definition of a process matrix to include the entire union of nodes in the two graphs. The size of the normalized matrix is increased to the size of the union of the sets of nodes in both graphs. For those nodes that exist in a process matrix before normalization, the corresponding elements in the normalized matrix are the same as those in the process matrix. For those nodes added through the normalization, the corresponding elements in the normalized matrix are set to a value of 0. After normalization, both matrices have the same number of rows and columns, and share the same row and column names and sequences. The normalized matrices can then be used as an input to calculate distance.

Table 1. Process matrix of g_{11}

M_{11}	TO										
		a_1	a_2	a_3	a_4	a_5	a_6	a_7	a_9	a_{10}	a_{11}
	a_1	0	1	0	0	0	0	0	0	0	0
	a_2	0	0	1	1	0	0	0	0	0	0
	a_3	0	0	0	0	1	1	1	0	0	0
F	a_4	0	0	0	0	0	0	0	0	1	0
R	a_5	0	0	0	0	0	0	0	1	0	0
O	a_6	0	0	0	0	0	0	0	1	0	0
M	a_7	0	0	0	0	0	0	0	1	0	0
	a_9	0	0	0	0	0	0	0	0	0	1
	a_{10}	0	0	0	0	0	0	0	0	0	1
	a_{11}	0	0	0	0	0	0	0	0	0	0

Figure 7. Two extended examples of Fig. 3

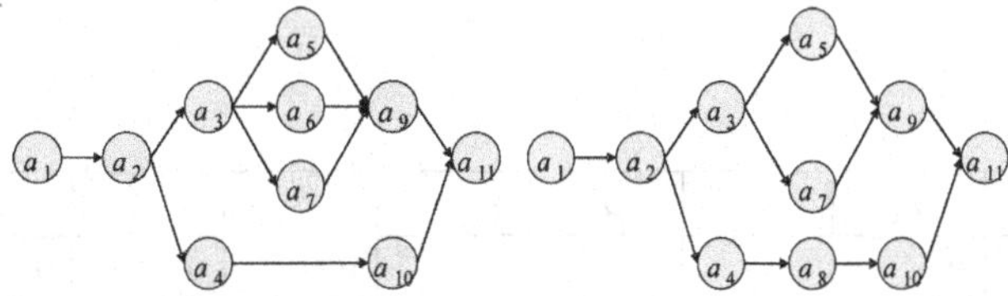

Definition 6 (Normalized Matrix, *NM*)

Let $DG_1=(DN_1,DE_1)$ and $DG_2=(DN_2,DE_2)$ be two dependency graphs. Let NM_1 and NM_2 denote the normalized matrices for DG_1 and DG_2 respectively. We generate NM_1 and NM_2 from DG_1 and DG_2 as follows.

i) The number of rows and columns are computed by $m=|DN_1 \cup DN_2|$
ii) Let $DN_1 \cup DN_2=\{a_1,a_2,\ldots,a_m\}$. Note that the row and column names of NM_1 and NM_2 are now normalized into the same node names $a_1,a_2,\ldots,a_m$ in the union of DN_1 and DN_2.
iii) Let $NM_1(i,j)$ denote the value of the ith row and the jth column in NM_1, and $NM_2(i,j)$ denote the value of the ith row and the jth column in NM_2

$$NM_1(i,j) = \begin{cases} 1 & \text{if } (a_i, a_j) \in DE_1 \\ 0 & \text{otherwise} \end{cases},$$

$$NM_2(i,j) = \begin{cases} 1 & \text{if } (a_i, a_j) \in DE_2 \\ 0 & \text{otherwise} \end{cases}$$

Consider processes in Fig. 7 as an example. By constructing normalized matrices for g_{11} and g_{22}, denoted by NM_{11} and NM_{22} respectively, the size of NM_{11} of g_{11} is increased to 11 because NM_{11} should include node a_8, which was not originally included in g_{11}. All the elements of the newly added column for node a_8 are set to a value of 0 because there is no dependency between any node of g_{11} and node a_8. Similarly, node a_6 is added in NM_{22}. Now NM_{11} and NM_{22} have the same row names and column names: a_1 through a_{11}. We can use NM_{11} and NM_{22} to compare g_{11} and g_{22}.

Table 2 An example of comparison matrices

NM_{11}	a_1	a_2	a_3	a_4	a_5	a_6	a_7	a_8	a_9	a_{10}	a_{11}
A_1	0	1	0	0	0	0	0	0	0	0	0
A_2	0	0	1	1	0	0	0	0	0	0	0
A_3	0	0	0	0	1	1	1	0	0	0	0
A_4	0	0	0	0	0	0	0	0	0	1	0
A_5	0	0	0	0	0	0	0	0	1	0	0
A_6	0	0	0	0	0	0	0	0	1	0	0
A_7	0	0	0	0	0	0	0	0	1	0	0
A_8	0	0	0	0	0	0	0	0	0	0	0
A_9	0	0	0	0	0	0	0	0	0	0	1
A_{10}	0	0	0	0	0	0	0	0	0	0	1
A_{11}	0	0	0	0	0	0	0	0	0	0	0
(a) NM_{11}											

Table 3. $NM_1 - NM_2 =$

	a_1	a_2	a_3	a_4	a_5	a_6	a_7	a_8	a_9	a_{10}	a_{11}
a_1	0	0	0	0	0	0	0	0	0	0	0
a_2	0	0	0	0	0	0	0	0	0	0	0
a_3	0	0	0	0	0	1	0	0	0	0	0
a_4	0	0	0	0	0	0	0	-1	0	1	0
a_5	0	0	0	0	0	0	0	0	0	0	0
a_6	0	0	0	0	0	0	0	0	1	0	0
a_7	0	0	0	0	0	0	0	0	0	0	0
a_8	0	0	0	0	0	0	0	0	0	-1	0
a_9	0	0	0	0	0	0	0	0	0	0	0
a_{10}	0	0	0	0	0	0	0	0	0	0	0
a_{11}	0	0	0	0	0	0	0	0	0	0	0

- The algorithm for construction of normalized process matrices consists of three steps. First, we must determine whether or not DG_1 and DG_2 are δ-comparable for the given δ value. Second, we compute the size of the normalized NM by $m=|DN_1 \cup DN_2|$ and label nodes in $\{DN_1 \cup DN_2\}$ as $\{a_1, a_2, \ldots, a_m\}$ using a uniform naming scheme. Third, we create the matrix data structures for DG_1 and DG_2: $NM_1(i,j)$ and $NM_2(i,j)$, where $i, j = 1, 2, \ldots, m$, and assign a value of 1 or 0 to each element in the two normalized matrices.

Distance-Based Process Similarity Measures

With the concept of a normalized matrix, we now transform the problem of comparing two processes into the problem of computing the distance-based similarity of the two normalized process matrices. One obvious idea is to compute the distance of two normalized matrices using matrix subtraction.

Consider the example processes g_{11} and g_{22} in Fig. 7. One way of computing the distance between g_{11} and g_{22} by matrix subtraction is to simply perform subtraction element by element. By subtracting NM_{22} from NM_{11}, we can see only five elements have values 1 and -1 respectively and the rest of the elements are 0. This means that five elements are unmatched between the two dependency graphs g_{11} and g_{22}.

A drawback of this approach is that both 1 and -1 values in the resulting matrix represent the fact that there are some discrepancies between two graphs g_{11} and g_{22} in five elements. But it does not tell the degree of such discrepancies in terms of concrete distance measure. Thus we need an efficient way to represent the total number of non-zero values in the resulting matrix.

One obvious way to capture the degree of the difference between NM_{11} and NM_{22} is to use the sum of the squares of elements in NM_1-NM_2 as shown below, which is $(1)^2+(-1)^2+(1)^2+(1)^2+(-1)^2=5$ because only five elements have non-zero values 1 and -1.

Interestingly, we can calculate the sum of the squares of elements in a matrix by the notion of trace in linear algebra. According to (Anton, 1994), the sum of diagonal elements in a matrix is defined as the trace of the matrix. The best way to calculate the sum of the squares of elements in a matrix is using the concept of inner products, which is defined by the trace concept.

Definition 7 (Dependency Difference Metric, *d*)

Let $DG_1=(DN_1,DE_1)$ and $DG_2=(DN_2,DE_2)$ be two dependency graphs. Let NM_1 and NM_2 be the normalized matrix of DG_1 and DG_2 respectively. We define the symmetric difference metric on graphs DG_1 and DG_2 by the trace of the difference matrix of NM_1 and NM_2 as follows:

$$D(DG_1,DG_2)=tr[(NM_1-NM_2)\times(NM_1-NM_2)^T]$$

- where $tr[\cdot]$ denotes the trace of a matrix, i.e., the sum of the diagonal elements.

This distance function counts the number of edge discrepancies between DG_1 and DG_2. Now, we want to show that the dependency difference metric *d* satisfies the distance measure properties. The function *d* is called a metric if and only if for all graphs g_1, g_2, g_3, the following conditions hold (Banks, 1994):

Table 4. $(NM_{11}-NM_{22})(NM_{11}-NM_{22})^T =$

	a_1	a_2	a_3	a_4	a_5	a_6	a_7	a_8	a_9	a_{10}	a_{11}
a_1	0	0	0	0	0	0	0	0	0	0	0
a_2	0	0	0	0	0	0	0	0	0	0	0
a_3	0	0	1	0	0	0	0	0	0	0	0
a_4	0	0	0	2	0	0	0	-1	0	0	0
a_5	0	0	0	0	0	0	0	0	0	0	0
a_6	0	0	0	0	0	1	0	0	0	0	0
a_7	0	0	0	0	0	0	0	0	0	0	0
a_8	0	0	0	-1	0	0	0	1	0	0	0
a_9	0	0	0	0	0	0	0	0	0	0	0
a_{10}	0	0	0	0	0	0	0	0	0	0	0
a_{11}	0	0	0	0	0	0	0	0	0	0	0

i) $d(g_1, g_2) = 0$ iff g_1 and g_2 are identical
ii) $d(g_1, g_2) = d(g_2, g_1)$
iii) $d(g_1, g_2) \leq d(g_1, g_3) + d(g_3, g_2)$.

Theorem 1. $d(DG_1, DG_2)$ Satisfies Distance Measure Properties

Proof:

Concretely, we want to prove that if $A = NM_1 - NM_2$ and $d(DG_1, DG_2) = \langle A, A^T \rangle = tr(A \times A^T) = \sum_{i=1}^{n}\sum_{j=1}^{n} a_{ij}^2$, then this distance $d(DG_1, DG_2)$ satisfies the three distance measure properties:

i) $d(DG_1, DG_2) = 0$ iff DG_1 and DG_2 are identical, because the matrix A becomes 0.
ii) $d(DG_1, DG_2) = d(DG_2, DG_1)$ by the d definition.
iii) $d(DG_1, DG_2) \leq d(DG_1, DG_3) + d(DG_3, DG_2)$

For any two nodes i, j, let

$$NM_k(i,j) = \begin{cases} 1 & \text{if } (a_i, a_j) \in DE_1 \\ 0 & \text{otherwise} \end{cases}$$

for k=1, 2, 3

Then we can show the property iii) holds.

$$\begin{aligned} d(DG_1, DG_2) &= tr[(NM_1 - NM_2) \times (NM_1 - NM_2)^T] \\ &= \sum_{i,j} \{NM_1(i,j) - NM_2(i,j)\}^2 \\ &= d(DG_2, DG_1) \end{aligned}$$

Now we show that the property iii) holds as well, because $NM_1(i,j)$-$NM_2(i,j)$ is either 0 or ±1, thus we have $d(DG_1, DG_2) = \sum_{i,j} |NM_1(i,j) - NM_2(i,j)|$.

$$\begin{aligned} & d(DG_1, DG_3) + d(DG_3, DG_2) \\ &= \sum_{i,j} |NM_1(i,j) - NM_3(i,j)| + \sum_{i,j} |NM_3(i,j) - NM_2(i,j)| \\ &= \sum_{i,j} \{|NM_1(i,j) - NM_3(i,j)| + |NM_3(i,j) - NM_2(i,j)|\} \\ &\geq \sum_{i,j} |NM_1(i,j) - NM_3(i,j) + NM_3(i,j) - NM_2(i,j)| \\ &= \sum_{i,j} |NM_1(i,j) - NM_2(i,j)| \\ &= d(DG_1, DG_2) \end{aligned}$$

So the new process distance measure is, in fact, a distance metric.

Since the dependency distance metric $d(g^1, g^2)$ counts the number of asymmetric arcs, it can reflect the difference of some characteristics between two processes, such as activity precedence, activity commonality, flow structure, etc. Activity precedence describes how the activities are linked and sequenced in terms of execution ordering. The dependency distance metric denotes the disparity of sequence between two activities and can be extended to represent the sequence disparities between all activities. In Fig. 8, the distance of two processes g^0 and g^1, denoted by $d(g^0, g^1)$, illustrates the difference of activity precedence. Activity commonality means how many activities are shared between two process models. This counts the different activities or new activities of two processes, as illustrated by processes g^0 and g^2 in Fig. 8. In addition, flow structure denotes the difference between serial and parallel flows. Two processes g^0 and g^3 show the difference measurement of flow structures, serial and parallel flows.

Figure 8. Examples of dependency distance

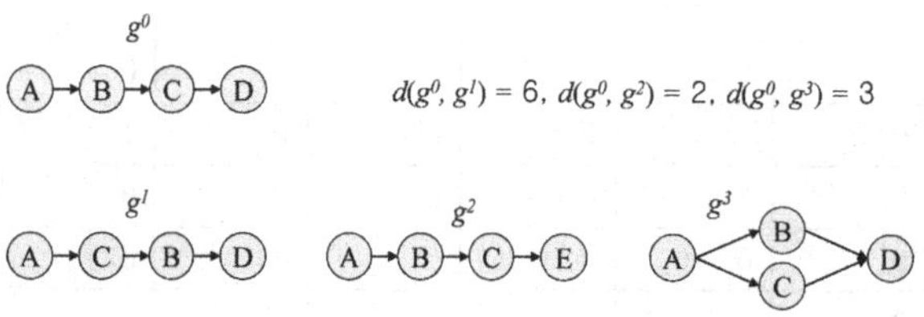

g^0: A → B → C → D

$d(g^0, g^1) = 6$, $d(g^0, g^2) = 2$, $d(g^0, g^3) = 3$

g^1: A → C → B → D

g^2: A → B → C → E

g^3: A → B, A → C, B → D, C → D

In Fig. 8, if we follow the previous procedure to calculate the dependency distance, all of the graphs are transformed to process network matrices and normalized process matrices. Then the distance of dependency between g^0 and g^1 is 6, the distance of g^0 and g^2 is 2, and the distance of g^0 and g^3 is 3. This means that g^0 and g^2 are the most similar, which is intuitively correct because the first three activities are in the same sequence but only the last activity is different. g^0 and g^1 are mostly different because the sequence of the activities in g^1 is quite different from g^0. In this dependency distance measure, the parallel execution in g^3 is not considered important and only the precedence relationships and common activities are considered important.

If we look into more extended examples in Fig. 7 again, each graph is transformed into process matrix, and then normalized matrix. These two normalized matrices are subtracted and squared. Finally we can get the proposed dependency distance 5 by obtaining the trace of it.

Prototype Implementation and Experiments

The presented concepts of this paper were implemented to analyze the similarity of processes in process warehouse. This system, called "BPSAT(Business Process Similarity Analysis Tool)", is developed by using Java language. This prototype system has three windows: process browser, graph editor, and execution log output window. We can select some processes in the left process browser, and the selected process is shown and modified in the right graph editor. All the execution log and analysis outputs are displayed in the bottom window. There are also necessary buttons in tool bar. The basic manipulation such as creating and editing of process graph can be done in this prototype system, and the functionality of similarity analysis methods proposed in this paper can be done in this system. Also other new similarity criteria can be added in this system. The current version of this system can be downloaded at http://it.chonbuk.ac.kr/~jsbae/BPMstuff/BPMstuff.html.

After we check the candidate processes to be compared, we select two processes to be compared,

Figure 9. Prototype system of BPSAT

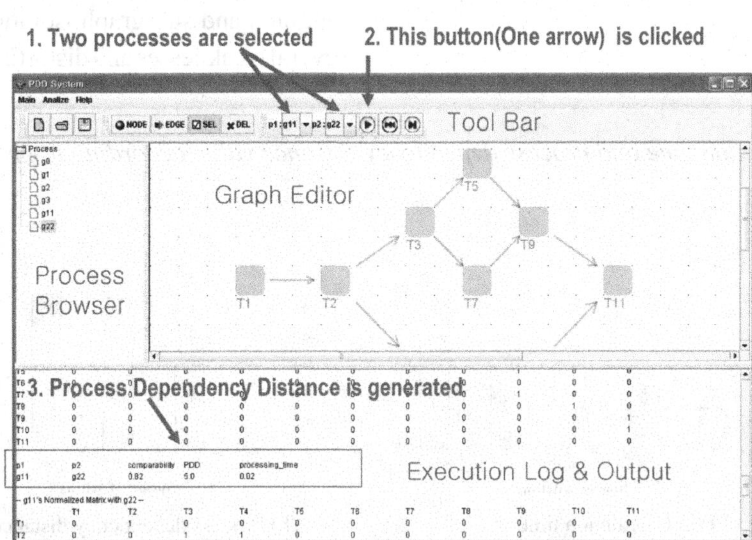

g_{11} and g_{22}. Then we can get the proposed process dependency distance is generated and shown in the output window.

Using the prototype system, we conducted experiments to analyze effectiveness of our method with variation of activity number. We did our experiments for processes including a number of activities. All the processes are generated using random process generator developed in (Ha, 2006). Ten pairs of different distances were calculated for processes with the same number of activities, and an average value was obtained for each number of activities.

First, we observed time required for calculating process dependency distance with increase of activity number. As we expected, more time is required as the number of activities increases, but the increase rate is not so high. The experimental result is presented in Fig. 10 (a).

Next, we examined how values of process dependency distance change as the number of activities increases, which is illustrated in Fig. 10 (b). Our result shows that absolute values of the distance in case of more activities are higher than those of fewer activities. This means that distance values among processes cannot be compared for an arbitrary number of activities, which we reserve as our future research work.

Related Work

Although business process management systems have been deployed in many industrial engineering fields, research on analysis, mining and integration of business processes are still in its infancy. One of the representative existing studies on process improvement is workflow mining, which investigates the traces and results of workflow execution, and determines significant information in order to improve the existing workflow processes (Aalst, 2003b; Aalst, 2004a; Aalst, 2004b; Agrawal, 1994; Cook, 1999; Jansen-Vullers, 2006; Medeiros, 2008; Schimm, 2004). However, most of the existing workflow mining research does not provide a quantitative measure to compare and capture the similarity of different workflow designs.

The graph theory in a traditional algorithm textbook is a useful means to analyze the process definitions. Graphs, or representative data structures, are used as an accepted effective tool to represent the problem in various fields, which include pattern matching and machine recognition, such as pattern recognition, web and XML document analysis, and schema integration (Bunke, 1998; Hammouda, 2004; Wombacher, 2004; Zhang, 1989). For example, research on similarities in graph structures can be divided into three categories. The first category of traditional similarity is based on graph and sub-graph isomorphism, which has several weaknesses and distortions in the input data

Figure 10. Calculation time and process dependency distance value according to process structure

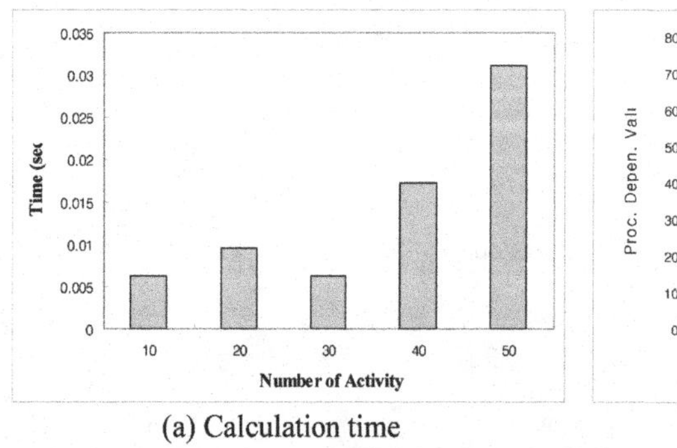

(a) Calculation time

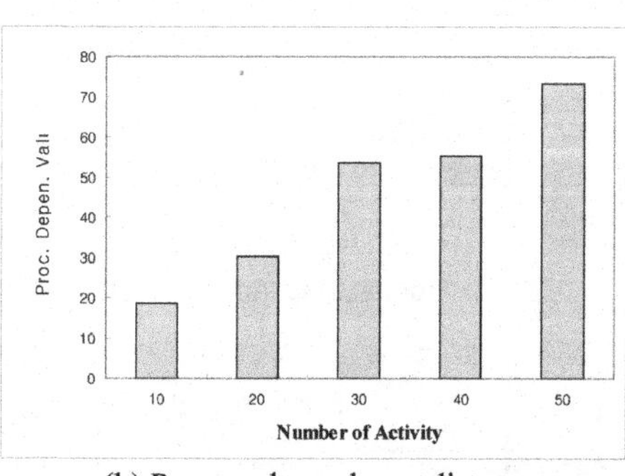

(b) Process dependency distance

and the models. In order to overcome these weaknesses, other graph similarity analysis techniques, such as the graph edit distance (GED) metric and maximal common sub-graph (MCS) have been introduced (Bunke, 1998; Zhang, 1989). It is also worth mentioning that Bunke (Bunke, 1998) has shown that with generic graphs, under certain assumptions concerning the edit-costs, determining the maximum common sub-graph is equivalent to computing the graph edit-distance. This MCS is a basic concept of workflow similarity that measures the common activities and transitions of workflow processes. In this paper we utilize the graph theory results to derive the metric space distance metric for measuring process similarity and difference.

Our research on workflow similarity measure is mainly inspired by the research results on document similarity analysis and graph similarity measures. A large number of document similarity measures are presented in existing literature for building document management systems, knowledge management systems, as well as search engines (Bunke, 1998; Hammouda, 2004; Lian, 2004).

In order to support web service composition, an infrastructure for searching and matchmaking of business processes is needed. One example is using annotated deterministic finite state automata (aDFA) to model the business processes (Wombacher, 2004). If a business process is specified as aDFA, the match between two aDFAs is determined by the intersection of their languages. When there is non-empty intersection, the two business processes are matched.

Recently process evaluation metrics research is proposed to evaluate the stability and validity of process model. Cardoso (Cardoso, 2005) proposed process model complexity metric, which computes the split and merge complexity in process model in order to reduce execution errors. Reijers & Vanderfeesten (Reijers, 2004) tried to generate a balanced process model in the sense of cohesion and integration metrics, which is the level of information coupling between process models.

CONCLUSION AND FUTURE WORK

We have presented a difference analysis methodology using distance measures between process definitions of web services. The proposed difference analysis method achieves three distinct goals. First, by analyzing the attributes of process models, we can present a quantitative process similarity metric to determine the relative distance between process models. This facilitates not only the comparison of existing process models with each other, but also provides the flexibility to adapt to changes in processes. Second, the proposed method is fast and flexible, which reduces the cost of both the analysis and design phases of complex web service processes. Third, the proposed method enables the flexible deployment of process mining, discovery, and integration – all desirable functionality that are critical for fully supporting the effective transformation of an enterprise.

Our research on process mining, discovering and integration through similarity analysis continues along several directions. First, we are interested in distance measures that can compare workflow designs with complex block structure and various execution constraints. Second, we are interested in developing a prototype system that provides efficient implementation of various similarity analysis methods, including the dependency distance metric presented in this paper. Furthermore we are interested in applying the method developed to concrete case studies of existing enterprise transformations and to evaluate and improve the similarity measures proposed in this paper.

ACKNOWLEDGMENT

The first author was supported by the Korea Research Foundation Grant (KRF-2005-214-D00192). The second author is partially supported by NSF grants under CSR, CyberTrust, SGER, ITR, a grant from AFOSR, and IBM SUR grant and a recent IBM faculty award.

REFERENCES

Agrawal, R. Gunopulos, D., Leymann, F. (1998). Mining Process Models from Work-flow Logs, *6th International Conference on Extending Database Technology* (pp. 469-483).

Anton, H., & Rorres, C. (1994). *Elementary Linear Algebra: Applications*. John Wiley & Sons.

Bae, J., Bae, H., Kang, S., & Kim, Y. (2004). Automatic control of workflow process using ECA rules. *IEEE Transactions on Knowledge and Data Engineering, 16*(8), 1010–1023. doi:10.1109/TKDE.2004.20

Banks, D., Carley, K. (1994). Metric inference for social networks, *Journal of classification, 11*(1), 121-149.

Bunke, H., & Shearer, K. (1998). A Graph Distance Metric based on the Maximal Common Subgraph. *Pattern Recognition Letters, 19*(3-4), 255–259. doi:10.1016/S0167-8655(97)00179-7

Cardoso, J. (2005). How to Measure the Control-flow Complexity of Web processes and Workflows. In L. Fischer (Ed.), *Workflow Handbook 2005* (pp. 199-212). Lighthouse Point, FL: WfMC.

Cook, J. E., & Wolf, A. L. (1999). Software Process Validation: Quantitatively Measuring the Correspondence of a Process to a Model. *ACM Transactions on Software Engineering and Methodology, 8*(2), 147–176. doi:10.1145/304399.304401

de Medeiros, A. K. A., van der Aalst, W. M. P., & Weijters, A. J. M. M. (2008). Quantifying process equivalence based on observed behavior. *Data & Knowledge Engineering, 64*(1), 55–74. doi:10.1016/j.datak.2007.06.010

Ha, B.-H., Reijers, H. A., Bae, J., Bae, H. (2006). An Approximate Analysis of Expected Cycle Time in Business Process Execution (LNCS 4103, pp. 65-74).

Hammouda, K. M., & Kamel, M. S. (2004). Efficient Phrase-Based Document Indexing for Web Document Clustering. *IEEE Transactions on Knowledge and Data Engineering, 16*(10), 1279–1296. doi:10.1109/TKDE.2004.58

Jansen-Vullers, M. H., van der Aalst, W. M. P., & Rosemann, M. (2006). Mining Configurable Enterprise Information Systems. *Data & Knowledge Engineering, 56*(3), 195–244. doi:10.1016/j.datak.2005.03.007

Leymann, F., & Roller, D. (2000). *Production workflow: concepts and techniques*. New Jersey: Prentice Hall PRT.

Lian, W., Cheung, W. W., Mamoulis, N., & Yiu, S. (2004). An Efficient and Scalable Algorithm for Clustering XML Documents by Structure. *IEEE Transactions on Knowledge and Data Engineering, 16*(1), 82–96. doi:10.1109/TKDE.2004.1264824

Reijers, H. A., & Vanderfeesten, I. T. P. (2004), Cohesion and Coupling Metrics for Workflow Process Design. In *Proc. 2nd Int. Conf. on Business Process Management* (pp. 290-305).

RosettaNet (n.d.). RosettaNet Standard (RosettaNet Partner Interface Processes). Retrieved from http://www.rosettanet.org

Rouse, W. B. (2005). A Theory of Enterprise Transformation. *Systems Engineering, 8*(4), 279–295. doi:10.1002/sys.20035

Rush, R., & Wallace, W. A. (1997). Elicitation of knowledge from multiple experts using network inference. *IEEE Transactions on Knowledge and Data Engineering, 9*(5), 688–698. doi:10.1109/69.634748

Schimm, G. (2004). Mining exact models of concurrent workflows. *Computers in Industry*, *53*(3), 265–281. doi:10.1016/j.compind.2003.10.003

van der Aalst, W. M. P., Hofstede, A.H.M., ter, , & Kiepuszewski, B. Barros, A.P. (2003a). Workflow Patterns. *Distributed and Parallel Databases*, *14*(3), 5–51. doi:10.1023/A:1022883727209

van der Aalst, W. M. P., van Dongen, B. F., Herbst, J., Maruster, L., Schimm, G., & Weijters, A. J. M. M. (2003b). Workflow Mining: A Survey of Issues and Approaches. *Data & Knowledge Engineering*, *47*(2), 237–267. doi:10.1016/S0169-023X(03)00066-1

van der Aalst, W. M. P., & Weijters, A. J. M. M. (2004a). Process Mining: a Research Agenda. *Computers in Industry*, *53*(3), 231–244. doi:10.1016/j.compind.2003.10.001

van der Aalst, W. M. P., Weijters, A. J. M. M., & Maruster, L. (2004b). Workflow Mining: Discovering Process Models from Event Logs. *IEEE Transactions on Knowledge and Data Engineering*, *16*(9), 1128–1142. doi:10.1109/TKDE.2004.47

WfMC (2005). Workflow Management Coalition Workflow Standard Process Definition Interface -- XML Process Definition Language, Document Number WFMC-TC-1025 Version 1.13.

Wombacher, A., Fankhauser, P., Mahleko, B., & Neuhold, E. (2004). Matchmaking for Business Processes Based on Choreographies. *International Journal of Web Services*, *1*(4), 14–32.

Zhang, K., & Shasha, D. (1989). Simple Fast Algorithms for the Editing Distance between Trees and Related Problems. *SIAM Journal on Computing*, *18*(6), 1245–1262. doi:10.1137/0218082

Chapter 6
Rapid Development of Adaptable Situation-Aware Service-Based Systems

S. S. Yau
Arizona State University, USA

S. Mukhopadhyay
Louisiana State University, USA

H. Davulcu
Arizona State University, USA

D. Huang
Arizona State University, USA

R. Bharadwaj
Naval Research Laboratory, USA

K. Shenai
University of Toledo, USA

ABSTRACT

Service-based systems have many applications, such as collaborative research and development, e-business, health care, military applications and homeland security. In these systems, it is necessary to provide users the capability of composing appropriate services into workflows offering higher-level functionality based on declaratively specified goals. In a large-scale and dynamic service-oriented computing environment, it is desirable that the service composition is automated and situation-aware so that robust and adaptive workflows can be generated. However, existing languages for web services are not expressive enough to model services with situation awareness (SAW) and side effects. This chapter presents an approach to rapid development of adaptable situation-aware service-based systems. This approach is based on the α-logic and α-calculus, and a declarative model for SAW. This approach consists of four major components: (1) analyzing SAW requirements using our declarative model for SAW, (2) translating the model representation to α-logic specifications and specifying a control flow graph

DOI: 10.4018/978-1-61520-684-1.ch006

in α-logic as the goal for situation-aware service composition., (3) automated synthesis of α-calculus terms that define situation-aware workflow agents for situation-aware service composition, and (4) compilation of α-calculus terms to executable components on an agent platform. An example of applying our framework in developing a distributed control system for intelligently and reliably managing a power grid is given.

INTRODUCTION

Nowadays, heterogeneous networked systems involving sensors, actuators, access points, and control stations connected through wired/wireless networks are being widely used in many mission-critical applications, such as healthcare, military, automobile and space applications. These systems often need to satisfy various requirements simultaneously, such as real-time, fault-tolerance, and security, and may need to be run in resource-poor environments with bandwidth limitations and shortage of memory space and/or other critical resources. Such systems often need to monitor physical and/or computational contexts, which are any instantaneous, detectable, and relevant properties of the environment, the system, or the users (Yau, Karim, Y. Wang, B. Wang, & Gupta, 2002; Yau, Wang & Karim, 2002), and react to situation changes in an autonomous and distributed manner. A *situation* is a set of contexts in a system over a period of time that affects future system behavior for specific applications (Yau, Karim, Y. Wang, B. Wang, & Gupta, 2002; Yau, Wang & Karim, 2002). Components of these systems can migrate from one physical/logical location to another in runtime. Hence, it is of utmost importance that such systems are adaptable and situation-aware so that they can provide services to users reliably and intelligently in accordance with the user goals in harsh and rapidly-changing environments.

One of the most promising architectures for developing such adaptable situation-aware systems is the Service-Oriented Architecture (SOA) (W3C, 2004b) due to the major advantage of enabling rapid composition of distributed applications from available services, regardless of the programming languages and platforms used in developing and running the applications. The systems based on SOA are called *service-based systems (SBS)*. In SBS, various capabilities are provided by different organizations as services, which are software/hardware entities with well-defined interfaces to provide certain functionality. These services can be used to compose higher-level functionality representing a certain *workflow*, which is a series of cooperating and coordinated activities achieving certain user goals. Hence, the development of an SBS can be viewed as a process involving the specification of user goals, the identification of suitable services, the composition of identified services into workflows satisfying the specified goals, and the implementation, testing and validation of the service composition.

A workflow can often be specified by a *control flow graph* (Hsu, 1993; Georgakopoulos, Hornick, & Sheth, 1995; WFMC, 1996), which is a common type of framework used in most workflow management systems for depicting the local execution dependencies among key activities in the workflow. A typical control flow graph specifies the initial and final activities in a workflow, the successor-activities for each activity in the graph, and branch selection or parallel execution of the successor-activities. However, dependencies among service invocations in a workflow in adaptable situation-aware SBS are often based on situation changes in highly dynamic environments, where users often have different requirements in various situations, or services cannot provide desirable QoS due to attacks, system failures or overload. Such dependencies can be effectively captured by *situational constraints*, which are the restrictions on what and how services should be invoked in various situations. Although it is possible to incorporate situational constraints in control flow graph specification, it is necessary to separate situational constraints from control flow graph specifications and specify situational constraints in a modular and reusable fashion so that a service composition system can discover appropriate services based on situations and users' goals, use the discovered services to compose a workflow achieving users' goals, and coordinate service execution adaptively based on situation changes. We consider such a process as *situation-aware service composition*. Since a large-scale SBS usually consists of thousands of services and may encounter many different situations in runtime, it is desirable that situation-aware service composition can be automated based on declaratively specified user goals.

So far, the most widely used specification language for web services is WSDL (WSDL, 2001), which is not expressive enough to specify these situational constraints. Other frameworks for modeling and executing workflows in web-service based systems, such as BPEL4WS (Andrews, et al., 2003) and OWL-S (W3C, 2004a), are not expressive enough to model services with side effects (i.e. services can change states of themselves or other services), and do not provide any facilities for automated service composition.

In this article, we will present an approach to the rapid development of adaptable situation-aware SBS, which is based on our α-logic, α-calculus, and declarative model for SAW (Yau, Huang, Gong, & Davulcu, 2005; Yau, et al., 2005) and provide an example to show how our approach can effectively be applied to real-world applications. In the following sections, we will first discuss the existing research related to our approach. Then we will summarize the key concepts and features of our SAW model, α-logic and calculus. We will show how to use our SAW model and α-logic to specify situational constraints and control flow graphs. We will present an algorithm for automated situation-aware service composition based on α-logic proof theory. We will also show how situation-aware workflow agents described in α-calculus terms are synthesized from the workflows generated using our service composition algorithm, and present a virtual-machine based environment, where these agents will be executed to monitor and coordinate the workflows. An accident response scenario will be used to illustrate our approach. We will also present a case study on applying our approach to intelligent management and optimization of power systems.

RELATED WORK

In this section, we will first review the existing work on developing adaptable and situation-aware networked systems for some real-world applications. Then, we will provide a summary of research in several areas related to our approach to rapid development of adaptable situation-aware SBS: planning and web service composition, web services and workflow specification languages, and situation awareness (SAW).

Applications

In this subsection, we will review the existing work for developing adaptable and situation-aware networked systems for applications like power system management. In (Hopkinson, et al., 2003), the authors have developed an agent-based framework for simulating power and communication systems. In (Gay, et al., 2003; Awan, Jagannathan, & Grama, 2007; Newton, Morrisett, & Welsh, 2007), the authors have developed techniques and languages for programming sensor networks. In (Birman, et al., 2005), the authors described the problems in monitoring and controlling large scale power systems and presented the Astrolabe framework (Renesse, Birman, & Vogels, 2003) for solving these problems. In (Amin, 2001), the author has presented an approach to using multi-agent systems for ameliorating the problem of power system failures. However, none of these works are concerned with the problem of using formal methods for building distributed adaptable situation-aware networked systems that provide provable guarantees of meeting their requirements. In the Case Study section, we will show how to apply our approach to developing such systems.

Planning and Web Service Composition

Substantial research has been done in the areas of planning and web service composition. Planning goals can be expressed as temporal formulas in TLPlanner (Bacchus & Kabanza, 1996). TLPlanner then generates plans using a forward chaining engine which generates finite linear sequences of actions. As these linear sequences are generated, the paths are incrementally checked against the temporal goals. The approach used in TLPlanner is sound and complete. However, this approach, in the worst case, performs an exhaustive search of the state space, which is often referred to as the *state-explosion problem*. A technique for semi-automatic service composition in the context of web services using semantic description of the services was presented in (Sirin, Hendler & Parsia, 2003). In this technique, non-functional properties are used to reduce the set of services satisfying service composition requirements. In (Rao, Kungas & Matskin, 2003), deduction in linear logic is used to compose web services, but no execution model is provided for the synthesized composition of web services. In (Ponnekanti & Fox, 2002), the first order logic is used to declaratively specify web-service-based systems, and deduction is used to synthesize service compositions from the declarative first order logic specifications. However, this approach cannot deal with SBS, because services often have side effects. In (Woodman, Palmer, Shrivastava, & Wheater, 2004), composition and verification of web services are specified using π-calculus (Milner, 1999), but the π-calculus terms from declarative specifications of the clients' requirements cannot be automatically synthesized. Besides, the π-calculus terms representing service compositions, which are manually generated by developers, cannot be reconfigured under changing environments and cannot be used to specify non-functional QoS goals, like SAW, deadlines, etc.

A problem closely related to service composition is the workflow scheduling problem. Existing workflow schedulers are passive. Passive schedulers receive sequences of events from an external source, such as a workflow or a services coordinator, and validate that these sequences satisfy all constraints, possibly after rejecting, suspending and reordering some events in the sequences. Several such schedulers for workflows, which are specified using *event-condition-action rules* (ECA rules) (Dayal, Hsu & Ladin, 1990), constraint languages, such as *intertask dependencies* (Attie, Singh, Sheth, & Rusinkiewicz, 1993) and *Event Algebra* (Singh, 1995), are described in (Singh, 1995; Attie, Singh, Sheth, & Rusinkiewicz, 1993; Gunthor, 1993). To validate a particular sequence of events, each of these schedulers takes at least quadratic time of the number of events. However, in these approaches, an unspecified external system is used to do the consistency checking to ensure the liveliness of the scheduling strategy, and to select the event sequences for execution. The complexity of the algorithms for these tasks is exponential in the worst case.

In contrast to passive scheduling, our approach is pro-active. In particular, we do not rely on any external system. Instead, we synthesize an explicit control flow graph of all allowed executions, i.e., executions that are known to satisfy all situational constraints. This representation can be used to enumerate all allowed executions at linear time per execution path (linear in the size of the path). In this way, at each stage in the execution of a workflow, the scheduler knows all the events that are eligible to start, and can initiate their execution. There is no need to validate the specified situational constraints at run time since the constraints are "compiled into" the synthesized control flow structure. Similarly, our approach detects inconsistency in workflow specifications during the static analysis and compilation phase.

Workflows tend to fail in real-world scenarios due to the uncertain/unreliable sensory information which sometimes needs to be updated during the execution of workflows. In a logic-based framework, these dynamic predicates that can be updated are called non-monotonic predicates (NMPs). During automated synthesis, we also focus on reducing the risk of a given workflow due to the NMPs in the workflow. The main idea is to synthesize a backup workflow by augmenting the main workflow without introducing new NMPs. The backup workflow is generated using expected values of NMPs if necessary instead of given values. The expected values are obtained from the execution history or provided by a domain expert.

(Hundal & Brown, 1991) is the seminal paper of non-monotonic planning. A theory of planning that uses non-monotonic reasoning on the modal quantification logic Z is developed. It does forward reasoning and backward planning to reach the goal. The proposed theory uses frame axioms and the modal quantification logic Z to propagate the facts from the current situation to the next situation. The method states the most obvious consequences of each action, and it can not use domain knowledge or history to handle failures due to the non-monotonic predicates.

The idea of confidence level and degree of belief goes back to the paper (Hawthorne, 1996). In (Hawthorne, 1996), Hawthorne described a range of non-monotonic conditionals that behave like conditional probability functions at various levels of probabilistic support. These conditionals were defined as semantic relations on an object language for sentential logic. When the evidence is uncertain, the resulting degrees of belief in Bayesian updating appear to be sensitive to the order in which the uncertain evidence is acquired, a rather un-Bayesian looking effect.

Web Services and Workflow Specification Languages

WSDL (WSDL, 2001), BPEL4WS (Andrews, et al., 2003) and OWL-S (W3C, 2004a) are the most widely used languages for specifying web services and business processes composed of web services. However, WSDL can only model services, and does not provide constructs for modeling processes. While BPEL4WS and OWL-S are suitable for describing, modeling and executing workflows corresponding to business processes in web service-based systems, it is difficult to use these languages to describe systems involving sensors and other physical devices with complex dynamic behavior for continuously accessing information, monitoring the environment and reacting to changes in systems. Both BPEL4WS and OWL-S lack a satisfactory programming model with formal operational semantics, which makes it difficult to understand, reason with and verify the behavior of systems described in such languages. BPEL4WS and OWL-S are not expressive enough to specify workflows with side effects. Furthermore, they do not provide facilities for automated service composition based on user requirements. Hence, processes in BPEL4WS or service models in OWL-S have to be specified manually by developers.

Situation Awareness (SAW)

SAW has been studied in artificial intelligence, human-computer interactions and data fusion community. Existing research on SAW may be classified into two categories. One focuses on modeling and reasoning SAW (McCarthy & Hayes, 1969; Pinto, 1994; McCarthy, 2001; Plaisted, 2003; Matheus, Kokar & Baclawski, 2003; Matheus, Kokar, Baclawski, & Letkowski, 2003), and the other on providing toolkit, framework or middleware for development and runtime support for SAW (Yau, Karim, Y. Wang, B. Wang, & Gupta, 2002; Yau, Wang & Karim, 2002; Yau, Huang, Gong, & Davulcu, 2005; Yau, et al., 2005; Yau, Gong, Huang, Gao, & Zhu, 2006; Dey & Abowd, 2001; Roman, et al., 2002; Ranganathan & Campbell, 2003; Chan & Chuang, 2003). In the first category, situation calculus and its extensions (McCarthy & Hayes, 1969; Pinto, 1994; McCarthy, 2001; Plaisted, 2003) were developed for describing and reasoning how actions and other events affecting the world. A situation is considered as a complete state of the world, which cannot be fully described and leads to the well-known frame problem and ramification problem (Pinto, 1994). A core SAW ontology (Matheus, Kokar & Baclawski, 2003; Matheus, Kokar, Baclawski, & Letkowski, 2003) refers a situation as a collection of situation objects, including objects, relations and other situations. However, it does not address how to verify the specification and perform situation analysis. In the second category, Context Toolkit (Dey & Abowd, 2001) provides architectural support for context-aware applications, but it does not provide analysis of complex situations. GAIA (Roman, et al., 2002; Ranganathan & Campbell, 2003) provides context service, space repository, security service and other QoS for managing and interacting with active spaces. MobiPADS (Chan & Chuang, 2003) is a reflective middleware designed to support dynamic adaptation of context-aware services based on which runtime reconfiguration of the application is achieved. Reconfigurable Context-Sensitive Middleware (Yau, Wang & Karim, 2002; Yau, et al., 2002) provides the capabilities of context data acquisition, situation analysis and situation-aware communication management, and a middleware-based situation-aware application software development framework. Recently, a declarative SAW model for analyzing and specifying SAW requirements, and algorithms for generating software agents for situation analysis from SAW requirements have been developed for SBS (Yau, Huang, Gong, & Davulcu, 2005; Yau, et al., 2005; Yau, Gong, Huang, Gao, & Zhu, 2006; Yau, Gong, Huang, Gao, & Zhu, 2008). The declarative SAW model will be used in our approach and discussed in the Background section.

BACKGROUND

As discussed in the Introduction section, our approach to automated situation-aware service composition is based on our α-logic, α-calculus, and declarative model for SAW (Yau, Huang, Gong, & Davulcu, 2005; Yau, et al., 2005). In this section, we will summarize the α-calculus, the α-logic, and our declarative model for SAW.

α-Calculus

Process calculi have been used as programming models for concurrent (May & Shepherd, 1984) and distributed systems (Caromel & Henrio, 2005). α-calculus is based on classical process calculus (Milner, 1999). It provides a formal programming model for SBS, which has well-defined operational semantics involving interactions of external actions and internal computations for assessing the current situation and reacting to it (Yau, et al., 2005). The external actions include communication between processes, logging in and out of groups/domains (Yau, et al., 2005). The internal computations involve invocation of services as well as internal control flow (Yau, et al., 2005).

For the sake of completeness, we summarize in Table 1 part of the syntax of α-calculus which will be used in this chapter. Similar to classical process calculus, a system in α-calculus can be the parallel composition of two other systems, or a recursive or non-recursive process. A recursive or non-recursive process can be an inactive process, a nominal identifying a process, a process performing external actions, a process performing internal computations, a service exporting a set of methods, or the parallel composition of two other processes. The methods are described by the preconditions and postconditions specifying the constraints on the inputs accepted and outputs provided by the methods, respectively. Continuation passing (Appel, 1992) is used to provide semantics of asynchronous service invocations. In Table 1, $I{:}l_i(y)\text{^}cont$ denotes the invocation of the method l_i exported by I with parameter y and continuation *cont*. External actions involve input and output actions on named channels with types as in the ambient calculus (Cardelli & Gordon, 2000). Internal computation involves beta reduction, conditional evaluation for logic control, and invocation of public methods exported by a named service or private methods exported by the process itself.

α-Logic

α-logic is a hybrid normal modal logic (Blackburn, deRijke & Venema, 2003), which has been used for specifying SBS (Yau, et al., 2005). The logic has both temporal modalities for expressing situation information as well as modalities for expressing communication, knowledge and service invocation. It provides atomic formulas for expressing relations among variables and nominals for identifying agents. The α-logic supports developers to declaratively specify SAW requirements. Models for the logic are (annotated) processes in the α-calculus. These processes provide constructive interpretations for the logic. Following a Curry-Howard style isomorphism (Sorensen & Urzyczyn, 2006), in which proofs are interpreted as processes, a novel proof system of α-logic can support the synthesis of α-calculus terms from declarative α-logic specifications.

Table 1. A partial syntax of α-calculus

(System) $S::=$ *fix* $I=P$ (recursive or non-recursive process) $S\|\|S$ (parallel composition of two systems)	$N::=$ x (name variable) n (name)
(Processes) $P::=$ 0 (inactive process) $P\|\|P$ (parallel composition) I (identifier) $E.P$ (external action) $C.P$ (internal computation) $P\{l_1(x_1),\dots l_k(x_k);\dots l_n(x_n)\}$ (method export) $l_1,\dots l_k$ are private methods that can be invoked by P itself only while $l_{k+1},\dots l_n$ are public methods that can be invoked by other processes.	**(External actions)** $E::=$ K (Communication actions) $K::=$ $Ch(x)$ (input) $Ch<Str>$ (output) $Ch::=$ N (named channel with type)
(Internal computations) $C::=$ *let* $x=D$ *instantiate* P (beta reduction) *if* $C(x)$ *then* P *else* P' (conditional evaluation) ρ (constraint) ε (no-computation) *tt* (constant true) *ff* (constant false) $D::=$ $I{:}l_i(y)\text{^}cont$ (method invocation) $I{:}l_i::=pre_i::post_i[y]$ (method definition)	$pre::=\sigma[y]\wedge\rho[y]$ $post::=(\sigma[x]\wedge\rho[x])\ x$ $\sigma::=$ b (base type) $\sigma\rightarrow\sigma$ (function type) $\rho::=$ $x\geq y+c$ $x>y+c$ $x\leq y+c$ $x<y+c$

Here, we will only summarize the parts of syntax, semantics and proof system of α-logic, which will be used in this chapter, and provide some intuitive explanations to the logic. Table 2 shows the part of the syntax of α-logic.

In the table, we assume that every variable x has a type. Intuitively, the nominals act as identifiers to processes. The knowledge formula intuitively states that after a process receives the item named u from another process, the process satisfies φ. Sensors such as voltmeters, ampere meters as well as observers can be modeled as services disseminating results in a "push" mode. On the other hand, components such as power system simulators and static VAR compensators can be modeled as services disseminating computation results in the "pull" mode. Table 2 shows a fragment of the syntax of α-logic. α-logic is a normal hybrid modal logic. It is hybrid in the sense that it allows terms, called nominals, denoting states to be used as formulas. We assume the set of nominals is finite. α-logic specifications can express QoS requirements such as context awareness and timeliness. The logic has a sometime/eventually modality for temporal evolution, and a somewhere modality for spatial location. There are atomic formulas with typed signatures for describing relations among variables. We provide a constructive/intuitionistic interpretation of the logic, i.e. classical negation is not allowed and for any formula φ, the formula $(\varphi \vee (\varphi \rightarrow \boldsymbol{F}))$ is not a tautology. Such interpretation of the logic is necessary for generating constructive proofs of formulas from which software agents will be synthesized.

We provide a brief explanation of important formulas of the logic as follows:

- The formula $serv(u; v; \varphi 1; I)$ describes the properties of a software/hardware service disseminating results in the pull mode declaratively. The formula states that (1) a service exported by the entity with nominal I can be invoked by a process that matches the pattern $\varphi 1$, and (2) the service, to which an object u is passed as the parameter, returns object v as the result. Note that the nominal I also indicates the location of the entity, and the patterns that can be used in the logic are limited to regular patterns.

Table 2. A partial syntax of α-logic

$\Phi 1, \varphi 2 ::=$ formula
$\boldsymbol{T}$ true
0 inactivity
U nominal
$pred(x_1, \ldots, x_n)$ atomic formula
$x \sim c$ atomic constraint // $\sim ::= > \mid < \mid \leq \mid \geq$, *c is a natural number*
$\varphi 1 \vee \varphi 2$ disjunction
$\neg \varphi$ negation
$E(\varphi 1 \boldsymbol{u} \varphi 2)$ until
$E(\varphi 1 \boldsymbol{s} \varphi 2)$ since
$\varphi 1 \mid\mid \varphi 2$ parallel composition
$K(u; \varphi)$ knowledge of u
$sense(u; \varphi; I)$ senses u through a push service
$serv(x; u; \sigma; \varphi)$ invocation of a pull service σ using input x by φ and returning u
$\exists t\ \varphi$ existential quantification on time
$<u>\ \varphi$ behavior after sending message
$\varphi 1 \wedge \varphi 2$ conjunction
$@T(I, \sigma)$ constraint σ becomes true
$@F(I, \sigma)$ constraint σ becomes false
$@C(I, x)$ variable x changes
$PREV(x)$ previous value of variable x
$INIT(x, u)$ initial value of x is u

- The formula *sense(u; φ; I)* states that the object *u* is sensed by a sensor, i.e. a service that disseminates its results in the push mode, and received by an agent that matches the pattern *φ*. The service is exported by an entity with nominal *I*.
- The formulas *@T(I, σ)*, *@F(I, σ)*, and *@C(I, x)* state that the entity with nominal *I* knows that the constraint *σ* has changed from false to true, the constraint *σ* has changed from true to false, and the value of variable *x* has changed, respectively.
- The formula *PREV(x)* (a term used as a formula since this is a hybrid logic) denotes the previous value of the variable *x*. The formula *INIT(x, u)* states that the initial value of *x* is *u*.
- The formula *<u>φ* describes the behavior of a process after sending out *u*.

The following modalities, which will be used in this chapter, can be defined in terms of the primitive connectives and modalities defined in Table 2:

$\Diamond\varphi := E(\mathbf{Tu}\varphi)$ eventually

$\varphi\, \pi\sigma := \Diamond(\varphi \wedge \Diamond\sigma)$ φ before σ

We do not describe the full semantics of the α-logic in this chapter, but illustrate only the following salient features with the α-logic formulas interpreted over systems or processes decorated with atomic formulas. The logic has a sound and complete proof system based on natural deduction. The proof rules involve introduction and elimination rules for the various logical constants.

$S \models I$ if S is the system *fix I=P*

$S \models \langle u\rangle\, \varphi$ if S is the system *fix I=P* and there exist processes *Q, R, S,* and *T,* such that $P \equiv \langle u\rangle Q$, $R \equiv (x).S$, $T \equiv P||R$ and $Q \models \varphi$

$S \models pred(u1,...,un)$ if *S* is decorated with *pred(u1,...,un)*

$P \models K(u;\varphi)$ if $P \equiv (x).Q$ and $Q[u/x] \models \varphi$

$P \models serv(x;u;I;\varphi)$ if $P \equiv$ *let* $y=I{:}l_i(x)$ *instantiate Q* for some method l_i exported by some process identified by *I* and $Q[u/y] \models \varphi$

The part of the proof system of α-logic used in this chapter consists of a set of axioms along with the following rules:

Modus Ponens (MP): $\vdash \varphi \wedge (\varphi \rightarrow \psi) \rightarrow \psi$

- Substitution: There are two substitution rules:

Substitution A: If φ is a valid formula and ψ is a subformula of φ, ψ is an atomic formula, and τ is a formula in the α-logic, then infer $\varphi[\tau/\psi]$.

Substitution B: If φ and τ are valid formulas and ψ is a subformula of φ, and $\neg\psi$ is not a formula of φ, then infer $\varphi[\tau/\psi]$.

- Generalization: There are two types of generalization rules for modalities and quantifiers respectively.

Generalization A: $\vdash\varphi \rightarrow \Box\varphi$ $\vdash\varphi \rightarrow \Theta\varphi$ $\vdash\varphi \rightarrow K(u, \varphi)$ for any u, $\vdash\varphi \rightarrow serv(x;u;\sigma;\varphi)$ for any x, u and σ

Generalization B: $\vdash\varphi \rightarrow \forall x\, \varphi$

The set of axioms includes all axioms of propositional normal modal logic along with the following self-duality axioms:

D1: $serv(x;u;\sigma;\varphi) \rightarrow \neg serv(x;u;\sigma;\neg\varphi)$

D2: $K(u;\, \varphi) \rightarrow \neg K(u;\, \neg\varphi)$

We also include axioms such as $@T(I, \varphi) \rightarrow @C(I, x)$ and $sense(x, I, J) \rightarrow \Diamond @T(I, \varphi)$, where φ is an expression involving the variable x.

An example specification in α-logic is shown below specifying a meter "met" sensing voltage:

□(meter(voltage,"met")→◊(Sense(voltage,S,"met"))

Note that instead of using material implication, we use Lewis style strict implication (Priest, 2001) to avoid vacuous truth; here □ is the dual of ◊. Furthermore, *S* is a nominal and not a constant. The specification states that if any entity *S* subscribes to the voltage variable published by "*met*", it will receive a sampled voltage every time "*met*" publishes it.t

Our Declarative SAW Model

In general, SAW requirements for a service composition include situations related to the goal of the composition, and relations among the situations and services in SBS. Developers need to analyze users' SAW requirements to capture the above information and record it precisely. Formal specifications are unambiguous and concise, but are often difficult to use. Hence, we have developed a declarative model for SAW as shown in Figure 1 to facilitate developers to analyze SAW requirements and rapidly model the requirements with the following constructs (Yau, Huang, Gong, & Davulcu, 2005; Yau, et al., 2005; Yau, Gong, Huang, Gao, & Zhu, 2006):

Figure 1. An ontology for SAW in service-based systems

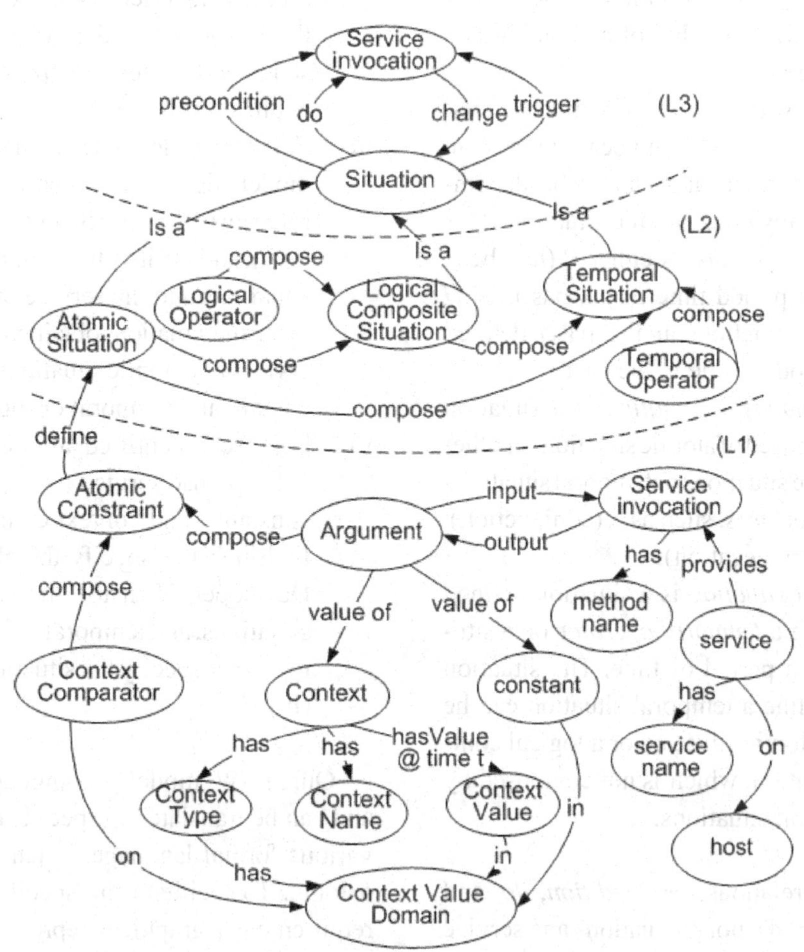

- A *context* has a unique *context name*, a *context type* and a *context value* at a time.
- A *context comparator* is a binary operator returning a Boolean value.
- A *service* has a unique *service name*, and is on a *host*.
- A *service invocation* is provided by a service, and has a unique *method name*, accepts inputs as arguments and returns outputs as context values.
- An *argument* can be a *constant* in the context value domain, or a *context variable* whose value is obtained through service invocations at runtime.
- An *atomic constraint* is used for comparing two arguments using a context comparator.
- A *situation* can be an *atomic situation*, a *logical composite situation* or a *temporal situation*. The value of a situation is a Boolean value.
- An *atomic situation* is a situation defined using a set of service invocations and an atomic constraint, and cannot be decomposed into any other atomic situations.
- A *temporal operator* is either *P* (had been true over a period time in the past), or *H* (was true sometime in the past) defined over a period of time in the past.

A *logical composite situation* is a situation recursively composed of atomic situations or other logical composite situations or temporal situations using *logical operators*, such as ∧ (conjunction), ∨ (disjunction), ¬ (negation).

- A *temporal situation* is a situation defined by applying a *temporal operator* on a situation over a period of time. The situation used to define a temporal situation can be either an atomic situation or a logical composite situation, which is not composed by any temporal situations.

Three basic relations, *precondition*, *do*, and *trigger*, are defined among situations and service invocations. Relation *precondition* describes a situation as a *precondition* of a service invocation. Relation *do* describes the effect of a service invocation. Relation *trigger* represents a reactive behavior of the system. In SBS, we assume that context data can be retrieved by invoking one or more services provided by the system platform or developed by various service providers.

Based on our SAW model, developers can analyze the SAW requirements of an application as follows:

i) Based on the functionality of the application required by users and the specifications of the services available in SBS, developers identify the services to be used in the application.
ii) Developers identify the contexts and all the methods (service invocations) provided by the services found in (i), as well as constants and context comparators used in the application.
iii) Following the basic relations in our SAW model, developers identify the situations relevant to the service invocations identified in (ii), and identify the relations among these situations and the service invocations.
iv) From the situations obtained in (iii), developers identify atomic situations if the situations contain any temporal or logical operators.
v) For each identified atomic situation, developers use service invocations, contexts, constants, and context comparators identified in (ii) to specify the atomic situation. Developers then use the specified atomic situations, and temporal or logical operators to further specify the situations identified in (iii).

Our SAW model is language-independent and can be translated to specifications written in various formal languages, such as F-Logic and α logic. To facilitate the specification of SAW requirements, graphical representations for the constructs in our SAW model and a GUI tool based on the graphical representations have been developed to facilitate developers to model SAW requirements visually. Later, we will discuss how to extract the situational constraints for service composition from users' SAW requirements and translate them to α-logic specifications.

OVERVIEW OF OUR APPROACH

Figure 2 depicts our approach to the rapid development of adaptable situation-aware SBS. Our approach consists of the following four major components:

(1) Use our declarative model for SAW to analyze and specify SAW requirements.
(2) Extract the situational constraints, which are the restrictions on what and how services should be invoked in various situations, from the specified SAW requirements, and specify a control flow graph in α-logic as the user's goal for the service composition.
(3) Conduct situation-aware service composition using the α-logic proof system, and

Figure 2. Our approach to rapid development of adaptable situation-aware SBS

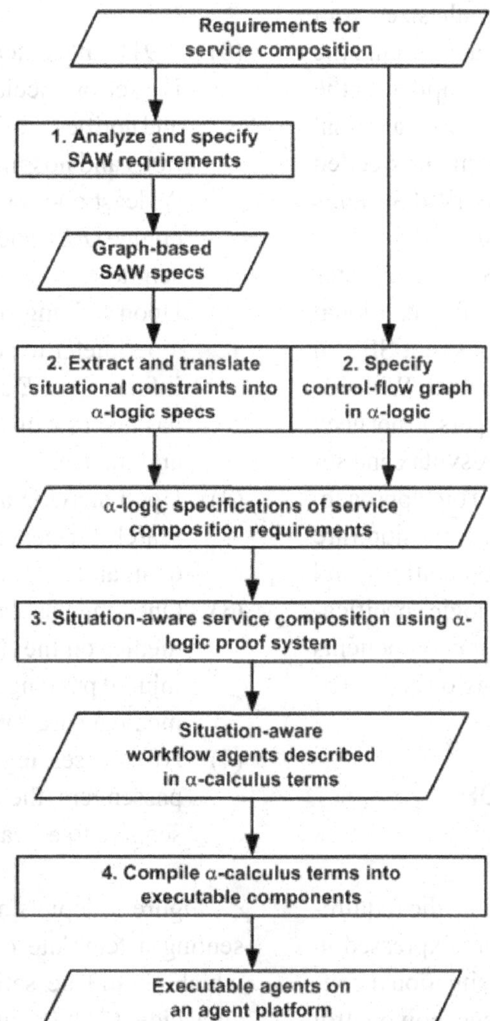

automated synthesis of situation-aware workflow agents described in α-calculus terms for runtime execution.

(4) Compile α-calculus terms to executable components on an agent platform.

α-logic and α-calculus provide the logical foundation of our approach. Automated situation-aware service composition is achieved by our approach with the construction of a proof for the user's service composition goal using the α-logic proof system. The constructed proof satisfies the given control flow and situational constraint specifications, and corresponds to a workflow that coordinates available services in the SBS to achieve the user's goal. Situation-aware workflow agents described in α-calculus terms are synthesized from the constructed proof to monitor and execute the workflow. We have constructed a compiler for the α-calculus terms to executable agents on a virtual machine-based agent platform, which extended the Secure Infrastructure for Networked Systems (SINS) platform (Bharadwaj, 2003).

The declarative model for SAW facilitates developers to analyze and specify situational constraints of service compositions in a SBS in a hierarchical and graph-based manner. With our declarative model for SAW, developers do not need to learn or understand the complex syntax and semantics of the logical foundation of our approach. Situational constraints for service composition are extracted from the graphical representations, and translated to the corresponding α-logic specifications. We will present the four major components of our approach in the following two sections.

SAW REQUIREMENTS FOR SERVICE COMPOSITION

As discussed in the previous section, the requirements of a service composition are expressed in a control flow graph and a set of situational constraints. In this section, we will discuss how control flow graphs and situational constraints are specified in α-logic, and how situational constraints are extracted from the user's SAW requirements using our graph-based SAW model.

For illustration purpose, let us consider an SBS that connects the 911 call center at the Police Department (*PD*), the Fire Department (*FD*), the hospitals with emergency services, and Ambulance Services (*AMS*) for coordinating various first responders (*PD*, *FD* and *AMS*) in handling serious traffic accident situations. *PD*, *FD* and *AMS* provide various capabilities as services in the system. The following simplified *accident response scenario* illustrates how an automatically generated workflow coordinates the field rescue operations:

(0) A 911 call center receives a report that there is a serious accident at location *L* on a road, and notifies nearby police patrol cars, fire stations and hospitals for emergency services. At least one police patrol car (*CAR*), a fire engine (*FE*), and an ambulance (*AMB*) were sent to *L*.

(1) Upon arriving at *L*, the police officers set up a perimeter to secure the accident site, and inform the *FE* and *AMB* that the perimeter has been set up, and ask for firefighters and ambulance.

(2) Upon arriving at *L*, the firefighters start to search for passengersinvolved in the accident, and rescue the passengers.

(3) Once the passengers are rescued, the paramedics on the *AMB* assess the status of the injured passengers to decide the appropriate medical care for them.

(4) After assessing the status of the injured passengers, the *AMB* takes the injured passengers to a nearby hospital.

Figure 3 depicts a control flow graph representing a template of the service composition, which should be satisfied when responding to an accident. The control flow graph depicts the

Figure 3. The overall goal for the accident response scenario service composition depicted as a control flow graph

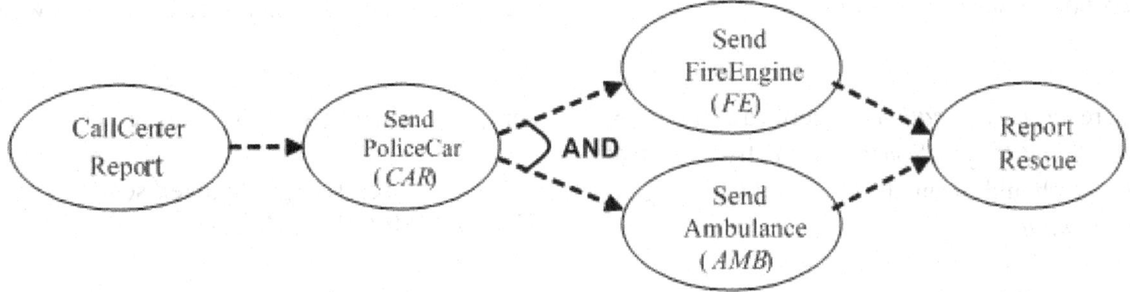

requirements that whenever the 911 call center receives an accident report, a *CAR* will be first sent to the accident site, and then a *FE* and an *AMB* will be sent to the accident site to rescue any injured passengers involved in an accident.

The following situational constraints need to be satisfied when the above workflow in the accident response scenario is executed:

- In a low visibility situation, upon arriving at the accident location, the police officers should set up a perimeter to secure the accident site, and then inform the *FE* and *AMB* that the perimeter has been set up.
- If the injured passengers are in critical conditions and it will take a relatively long time to the nearest hospital with emergency service, a helicopter *HELI* should be requested to take the critically injured passengers quickly to the hospital.

Specifying Control Flow Graphs

Since α-logic has connectives for service invocation (*serv*), eventuality (◊), parallel composition (||), and disjunction (∨) as well as atomic constraints, it is straightforward to specify control flow graphs using α-logic formulas. For example, the control flow graph in Figure 3 can be specified in α-logic as follows:

(◊serv(;L,T,'accident';U;911CallCenter) <
◊serv(L,T;'car_sent';X;911CallCenter) <

(◊serv(L,T;'fe_sent';Y;911CallCenter) ||
◊serv(L,T;'amb_sent';Y;911CallCenter)) <

◊serv(L,T;'rescued';Z;911CallCenter))

Specifying Situational Constraints

Similar to the coordination events in (Klein, 1991), we define the following five types of situational constraints for service composition:

a. *Allowance constraint*: A service can be invoked in a certain situation.
b. *Prohibition constraint*: A service cannot be invoked in a certain situation.
c. *Ordering constraint*: Service invocations should follow a specific order in a certain situation.
d. *Existential constraint:* In a certain situation, the invocation of a service causes another service to be invoked eventually.
e. *Set constraint*: In a certain situation, a set of services should be invoked together if they are concatenated by "∧", or one of them should be invoked if they are concatenated by "∨".

These situational constraints can be specified using α-logic as follows:

a. *Allowance constraint* is represented as

situation → service invocation,

where *service invocation* is described by modality *◊serv(Input;Output;Service;Agent)*. It denotes that *service* should eventually be invoked by *Agent* in *situation*.

b. *Prohibition constraint* is represented as

situation → ¬ service invocation.

Similar to allowance constraints, it denotes that *service* should not be invoked in *situation*.

c. *Ordering constraint* is represented as

situation → $service_1$ *invocation<*$service_2$ *invocation< … <*$service_m$ *invocation,*

where operator "<" means before. It describes that, in *situation*, $service_1$ should be invoked first, followed by $service_2$ to be invoked, until $service_m$ to be invoked.

d. *Existential constraint* is in the format

situation→ (service invocations → service invocation),

where *service invocations* are invocations of multiple services concatenated by conjunction (∧) and disjunction (∨). It states that in *situation*, *service invocations* cause *service* to be eventually invoked.

e. *Set constraint* is in the format

situation→ service invocations.

For example, our accident response scenario with the requirement, "If the injured passengers are in critical conditions, a helicopter HELI should be requested to bring them quickly to the hospital", can be expressed by the following situational constraint:

serv(L,T;'critical';AMB;911CallCenter)

→ ◊serv(L,T;'helicopter_sent', HeliID;AMB;911CallCenter),

where *serv(L,T;'critical';AMB;911CallCenter)* represents that the *911CallCenter* agent detects critically injured passengers in location *L* at time *T* by invoking a service provided by *AMB*.

Extracting Situational Constraints from SAW Requirements

The complex syntax and semantics of α-logic make them difficult for developers to specify situational constraints directly in α-logic. In addition, it would be time-consuming for developers to manually specify all situational constraints for service composition since dynamic SBS may consist of many services and its behavior may be affected by various situations. Hence, we have developed an algorithm to automatically extract all situational constraints from the users' SAW requirements. The situational constraint extraction algorithm involves the following three major steps:

- Step 1) translate the graphical representations of the users' SAW requirements to corresponding α-logic specifications,
- Step 2) partition the set of specified situations for distributed situation analysis, and
- Step 3) extract the situational constraints from the α-logic specifications obtained in Step 2).

The final output of the algorithm is the α-logic

Table 3. Specifying SAW requirements in AS^3 logic

Specification	Syntax
Service invocation	$m(a; b; \varphi; I) \rightarrow serv(x; u; \varphi; I)$
Atomic situation	$serv(x_1; u_1; \varphi_1; I) \wedge \ldots \wedge serv(x_n; u_n; \varphi_n; I) \wedge arg_1\ op_c\ arg_2$ $\rightarrow \Diamond(k([u_1, \ldots, u_n, s], I)$
Logical composite situation	$k([u_1, \ldots, u_k, s_1], I_1) \wedge k([u_{k+1}, \ldots, u_n, s_2], I_2) \mid k([u_1, \ldots, u_k, s_1], I_1) \vee k([u_{k+1}, \ldots, u_n, s_2], I_2) \mid$ $\neg k([u_1, \ldots, u_k, s_1], I_1)$ $\rightarrow \Diamond(k([u_1, \ldots, u_n, s], I)$
Temporal situation	$\forall\ t, now\text{-}\omega \leq t \leq now\text{-}\omega+\varepsilon, s' \mid$ $\exists\ t, now\text{-}\omega \leq t \leq now\text{-}\omega+\varepsilon, s'$ $\rightarrow \Diamond(k([u_1, \ldots, u_n, s], I))$
Relation among situations and service invocations	*trigger(m, s)* *precondition(m, s)* $do(m, s_1, s_2)$

specifications of situational constraints, which will be the input to our α-logic proof system for service composition.

Step 1) Translation from SAW Model to α-Logic Specifications

Step 1) of the algorithm is quite straightforward following a direct mapping from the constructs in our declarative SAW model to the formulas in α-logic as summarized in Table 3. Due to the limited space, we only briefly explain the α-logic formulas for atomic situation, and relations among situations and service invocations here. More details can be found in (Yau, et al., 2007; Yau, Gong, Huang, Gao, & Zhu, 2008).

- α-logic formula for atomic situation

In atomic situation specifications, each atomic situation *s* consists of a set of service invocations $serv(x_1; u_1; \varphi_1; I), \ldots, serv(x_n; u_n; \varphi_n; I)$ for collecting context values $u_1, \ldots u_n$ and an atomic constraint $arg_1\ op_c\ arg_2$ for comparing arguments arg_1 and arg_2 using context comparator op_c. Argument arg_1 is always a context variable, whose value is one of $u_1, \ldots u_n$. Argument arg_2 can either be one of $u_1, \ldots, u_n$ or be a constant in the context value domain. The atomic constraint determines the value of situation *s*. *I* denotes the agent that monitors situation *s*. However, developers do not need to manually specify *I* when specifying SAW requirements. In Step 2), a specified situation can be automatically assigned to an agent that is most suitable for monitoring this situation.

- α-logic formulas for relation specification

Relations among services and situations in our SAW model are specified using atomic formulas in α-logic. A *precondition* relation is specified as an atomic formula *precondition(m, s)*, which indicates that a situation *s* is the precondition of invoking service *m*. Similarly, an atomic formula $do(m, s_1, s_2)$ specifies a *do* relation, which indicates that the invocation of *m* under situation s_1 makes s_2 become true; and an atomic formula *trigger(m, s)* specifies a *trigger* relation, which indicates that the situation *s* should immediately lead to the invocation of *m*. The *precondition* and *do* relations are sufficient for specifying the conditions and possible effects of service invocations. The *trigger* relation is sufficient for specifying the reactive behaviors of an SBS in various situations.

By directly mapping the model constructs for services, situations and relations in our SAW model to the corresponding α-logic formulas, Step 1) of our situational constraint extraction algorithm translates the model representation of SAW requirements for a service composition to the α-logic specifications of these SAW requirements. From these α-logic specifications of SAW requirements, Step 2) of our situational constraint extraction algorithm will automatically partition the set of specified situations for distributed analysis.

Step 2) Automated Partitioning of Specified Situations

The analysis of a situation can be done by a single agent or multiple agents distributed on multiple hosts collaboratively. A host *h* is considered the *sink point* of a situation *s* if the final value of *s* is calculated on *h*. Due to various system capacities and network bandwidths among hosts, different selections of *sink points* for situations in SBS will have different impacts on the performance of situation analysis. Furthermore, reconfiguration of SAW requirements in runtime will require re-synthesis of affected agents. In particular, changes in the specification of a situation *s* most likely affect the situations used to define *s* or the situations defined using *s*. Hence, to reduce the effort of re-synthesizing agents, it is desirable to let an agent process as many related situations as possible. Hence, the purpose of our automated partition of the set of specified situations is to determine the appropriate *sink point* for each situation and group the related situations together for agents to perform situation analysis efficiently. Due to the limited space, we will only highlight the main ideas of our partitioning algorithm. Interested readers can refer to (Yau, JSS08) for more detailed information.

- System-specific knowledge and decision factors for automated partition of the set of specified situations

The automated partition requires system-specific knowledge of network topology and communication bandwidth between each pair of hosts in the system. The network topology specification describes which service is on which host. Generally, system-specific knowledge are provided by domain experts. Based on the SAW requirement specifications and system-specific knowledge specifications, the automated partition in our approach depends on the following two factors:

Factor 1) Communication Cost

The communication cost for analyzing situation *s* when host h_k is selected as the sink point is denoted as $cost(s, h_k)$, which is calculated using the following formula:

$$\mathrm{cost}(s, h_k) = \begin{cases} 0, \ \mathrm{H} = \{\mathrm{h_k}\} \\ \sum_{i=1,\, i\neq k}^{n} (num_x + num_y) \times \frac{1}{bw(h_k, h_i)}, \ \mathrm{n} > 1, \mathrm{s} \notin \mathrm{TS}, \mathrm{s} \not\bowtie \mathrm{TS} \\ \frac{1}{fr \times bw(h_k, h_{sys})} + \sum_{i=1,\, i\neq k}^{n} (num_x + num_y) \times \frac{1}{bw(h_k, h_i)}, \ \mathrm{n} > 1, \mathrm{s} \notin \mathrm{TS}, \mathrm{s} \not\bowtie \mathrm{TS} \\ \frac{1}{bw(h_k, h_{sys})} + \sum_{i=1, i\neq k}^{n} n_y \times \frac{1}{bw(h_k, h_i)}, \ \mathrm{n} > 1, \mathrm{s} \in \mathrm{TS} \end{cases}$$

where *H* denotes a set of unique hosts related to situation *s* by providing either the contextual or situational information for analyzing *s*, or the service invocations to be triggered under *s*; *TS* denotes a set of temporal situations for the system; h_{sys} is the host, where the system special service locates; $s \rhd TS$ denotes that *s* is used to define a temporal situation in *TS*; and $s \not\bowtie$ TS denotes that *s* is not used to define any temporal situation in *TS*. There are four cases for calculating the communication cost $cost(s, h_k)$:

1) *H* contains only one element, which is h_k. In this case, situation *s* will be assigned to h_k with no choice. Hence, $cost(s, h_k) = 0$.
2) $s \notin TS$ and $s \not\bowtie$ TS, i.e. *s* is not a temporal situation and not used to define any temporal situation. If *s* is an atomic situation, then num_x is the number of interactions between h_k and h_i for collecting context values for *s* from h_i. If *s* is a logical composite situation, then num_x is the number of interactions between h_k and h_i for collecting situational information for

s from h_i. Regardless of the type of s, num_y is the number of interactions between h_k and h_i for triggering service invocations, which are provided by services on h_i.

3) $s \notin TS$ and $s \rhd TS$, i.e. s is not a temporal situation, but is used to define a temporal situation. In this case, the communication cost for analyzing s is calculated in the same way as 2). In addition, the communication cost for recording the information of s in the system special service is $\frac{1}{fr \times bw(h_k, h_{sys})}$, where fr denotes the frequency of analyzing s, and h_{sys} is the host, where the system special service locates.

4) $s \in TS$. In this case, situation s is a temporal situation. The communication cost has two parts: a) $\frac{1}{bw(h_k, h_{sys})}$, the communication cost for retrieving situational information from the system special service, b) $\sum_{i=1, i \neq k}^{n} n_y \times \frac{1}{bw(h_k, h_i)}$, the communication cost for triggering service invocations for s_i.

To achieve efficient distributed situation analysis, the final selection of *sink point* for situation s should be the host that requires the minimum communication cost among all possible hosts.

Factor 2) Situation Composition Tree Representing Composition Relations of a Set of Situations

A *situation composition tree* is a tree that reflects the composition relation of a set of situations used in defining another situation. Leaf nodes correspond to atomic situations. The edge between a parent node and its child node represents the definition or composition relation. For a logical composite situation cs_i, its child nodes are the situations used to compose cs_i. For a temporal situation ts_i, its child node is the situation used to define ts_i. Every situation belongs to a situation composition tree. If the situation is the root of the tree, it means that the situation is not used to define any other situation. Otherwise, the situation is used to define other situations. Situations on the same tree are more likely to be affected by the SAW requirement reconfiguration in runtime. Hence, situations on the same tree should be grouped together as much as possible, in order to reduce the effort of re-synthesizing agents.

- Partitioning algorithm

Partitioning the set of specified situations is conducted in the following three steps: 1) find related hosts for each situation, 2) determine the *sink point* for each situation, and 3) generate the final partition of the set of specified situations. For a situation s, the related hosts are those where necessary context information or intermediate analysis results for analyzing s are available. The *sink point* for a situation s is determined by selecting the host that incurs the lowest cost (Factor 1) for analyzing s from all the related hosts for s. The final partition of the set of specified situations is generated by grouping the situations with the same sink points according to the situation composition trees (Factor 2), which can be easily constructed based on situation definitions. The detailed algorithm can be found in (Yau, JSS08).

Step 3) Automated Extraction of Situational Constraints

After Step 2), the complete specification of SAW requirements for service composition is generated. Due to the complexity of Step 3), we will first briefly describe the extraction of allowance and existential constraints using the following process, and then highlight the main ideas for extracting prohibition, ordering and set constraints:

0 **For** each *precondition*(S_x, *Method*)

Find *serv(Input; Output; Service; Agent)* for *Method* from service specification, and generate an *allowance constraint* $S_x \rightarrow \Diamond$*serv(Input; Output; Service; Agent)*

1 **If** S_x is an effect of the invocation of a service,
1a Find *do*(M_x, S_x) and *precondition(Situation,* M_x) from the relation specifications
1b Find *serv(Input*$_x$*; Output*$_x$*; Service*$_x$*; Agent*$_x$) for M_x from service specification
1c Generate an *existential constraint* as follows:

Situation → (*serv(Input*$_x$*; Output*$_x$*; Service*$_x$*; Agent*$_x$) → ◊*serv(Input; Output; Service; Agent)),*

where the left hand side of "→" is a service invocation for M_x, and the right hand side is a service invocation for *Method*

1d Go back to 0
2 **If** S_x is an effect of two or more service invocations,
2a Decompose S_x into a set of atomic situations *aSituSet*.
2b For each atomic situation *aSitu*$_i$ in *aSituSet*
2bi Find *do*(M_i, *aSitu*$_i$) and *precondition* (S_i, M_i) as described in 1a, put S_i in a set of situations *situSet*
2bii Find service invocation *serv*$_i$ for M_i as described in 1b, put *serv*$_i$ in a set of service invocations *servSet*.
2c Compose all situations in *situSet* into *Situation* and compose all service invocations in *servSet* into *service invocations*, in the way that is same as atomic situations in *aSituSet* compose S_x
2b Generate an *existential constraint* as follows:

Situation → (*service invocations* → ◊*serv(Input; Output; Service; Agent)),*

2c Go back to 0

The extraction of prohibition constraints from SAW requirements is based on the analysis of conflicting situations. If a situation $S_1 \rightarrow \neg S_2$, and *precondition*(S_2, *Method*) are defined, a prohibition constraint $S_1 \rightarrow \neg\, \Diamond$*Method* will be generated.

The extraction of ordering constraints from SAW requirements is based on the analysis of *trigger* relations. If *precondition*(S_0, M_1), *do*(M_1, S_1) and *trigger*(M_2, S_1) are defined, an ordering constraint $S_0 \rightarrow \Diamond(M_1 < M_2)$ will be generated.

Finally, a set of constraints will be generated when a situation S_0 triggers multiple service invocations (concatenated by "∧"), or appears in multiple allowance constraints.

AUTOMATED SYNTHESIS OF SITUATION-AWARE WORKFLOW AGENTS

Service Composition with α-Logic

Our service composition algorithm aims at the synthesis of non-iterative services compositions without loops, which means that we cannot automate the synthesis of workflows with repetitive invocations of certain services until a particular condition is satisfied. Fortunately, such behavior can be captured by defining the termination condition as a situation *S*, and the *trigger* relations that invoke certain services when *S* is not true. Hence, the implementation of such behavior can be automatically done using our technique presented in (Yau, Gong, Huang, Gao, & Zhu, 2006). However, further investigations are needed to properly integrate this technique with our service composition approach presented in this chapter.

Given an α-Logic formula *G* describing a control flow graph and a set of situational constraints *C*, we have developed an algorithm for synthesizing a workflow G_C, which is described by an α-logic formula, and represents the class of executions of G satisfying *C*, i.e. $(G \wedge C)$. Although $(G \wedge C)$ represents all the executions of *G* satisfying *C*, it is not an explicit set of instructions to the workflow scheduler for executing the workflow. In order for $(G \wedge C)$ to be executable, it must be a formula corresponding to an explicit workflow control flow specification. Hence, "synthesizing" $(G \wedge C)$ means that we need to obtain a formula G_C which does not contain conjunctions and satisfies $G_C \models (G \wedge C)$. The above service composition problem can be formulated as follows:

Given a control flow graph G and a set of situational constraints C, construct an executable control flow graph $G_C \models (G \wedge C)$.

Now, we will present our algorithm, called *Enforce*, which takes G and situational constraints C as inputs, and produces a conjunction-free control flow specification G_C through a series of transformations. Our algorithm includes a proof procedure based on forward-chaining natural deduction presented in detail in the Background section to enforce existential constraints, and aprocedure to enforce ordering and other constraints. In order to enforce situational constraints at design time, during each step of the forward chaining proof procedure, the left-hand side (or the body) of each situational constraint is evaluated using the current sequence of service composition. If the body of a constraint is evaluated to be true, the right-hand side (or the head) of the constraint is enforced using the following procedure:

The Enforce Procedure

Allowance constraint:

Enforce(◊serv(I;O;M;A), Goal) ≡ Goal || *◊serv(I;O;M;A)*, if *M* is new

Composite constraints:

Enforce(C1 ∧ C2, Goal) ≡ Enforce(C2, Enforce(C1, Goal))

Enforce(C1 ∨ C2, Goal) ≡ Enforce(C1, Goal) ∨ Enforce(C2, Goal)

Ordering constraint:

Enforce(◊(serv(I1;O1;M1;A1) < serv(I2;O2;M2;A2)), Goal)

≡ Synch(Enforce(◊serv(I2;O2;M2;A2), Enforce(◊serv(I1;O1;M1;A1), Goal))

where *Synch* replaces every occurrence of *◊serv(I1;O1;M1;A1)* with *◊serv(I1;O1;M1;A1).<ξ>* and every occurrence of *◊serv(I2;O2;M2;A2)* with *k(ξ ;A2). serv(I2;O2;M2;A2)* in the *Goal*.

Existential constraint:

Enforce(C1 → C2, Goal) ≡ Enforce(C1, Goal) ⊢ Enforce(C2, Goal)

Prohibition constraint:

Enforce(¬◊serv(I;O;M;A), Goal) ≡ Enforce(◊serv(I;O;M;A) →⊥, Goal)

To illustrate the above procedure, consider the service composition in our accident response scenario discussed before. In order to demonstrate the interactions between the control flow specification and situational constraints, let us consider the following simple control flow stating a sequential composition template made up of invocations of the Ambulance service (*AMB*) and the reporting of successful rescue operations to the *911CallCenter*:

(◊serv(L,T;'amb_sent';Y;911CallCenter)<◊serv(L,T;'rescued';Z;911CallCenter))

with the following situational constraints:

◊serv(L,T;'amb_sent';AMB;U) → ◊serv(L,T;Status;AMB;V)

◊serv(L,T;'critical';AMB;V) → ◊serv(L,T;'helicopter_sent';AMB;V)

The proof procedure uses the two steps of natural deduction with Modus Ponens (MP) (see the Background section) to discover the corresponding agents and the services composition plan.

◊ (serv(L,T;'amb_sent';Y;911CallCenter)<serv (L,T;'rescued';Z;911CallCenter))

The *Enforce* procedure synthesizes the following workflow goal, and natural deduction enables services discovery:

Hence, the body of the following existence constraint becomes true:

◊serv(L,T;'AMB_sent',AmbID;AMB;U) → ◊serv(L,T;Status;AMB;V),

which causes an insertion and leads to the following new workflow goal:

◊(serv(L,T;'AMB_sent',AmbID;Y;911CallCenter).<ξ>.◊serv(L,T;Status;AMB;V) ||

k(ξ).◊serv(L,T;'rescued';Z;911CallCenter))

Because *get_injury_status* is a method having non-deterministic results, the natural deduction over the specification of *get_injury_status* branches out to two distinct workflow goals is shown if Figure 4.

One of the sub-goals satisfies the body of another situational constraint:

serv(L,T;'critical';AMB;V) → ◊ serv(L,T;'helicopter_sent';AMB;V)

which causes another insertion into the control flow graph on the *critical* branch:

(◊(serv(L,T;'critical';AMB;V).◊serv(L,T;'helicopter_sent',HeliID;AMB;V)))

Successive applications of natural deduction will complete the control flow graph by finding and inserting all the necessary services and terminates the proof procedure.

A Risk Reduction Framework for Dynamic Workflows

When we consider real-world scenarios, such as the accident scenario above, workflows tend to fail due to uncertain or unreliable information mostly based on their sensing actions. For instance, during the search for passengers, it might be discovered that there are four injured passengers instead of two. In the original workflow since there is only one ambulance allocated, it would not be possible to rescue all injured passenger unless another available ambulance can be found and deployed to the accident location.

Figure 5 depicts an extended control flow graph containing a backup workflow. The extended control flow graph represents a template of the service composition, which should be satisfied when responding to an accident. The control flow graph depicts the requirements that whenever the call center receives an accident report, it should notify a CAR and a FE, and then an AMB to rescue any injured passengers involved in an accident. If the information is updated to be four injured passengers then the system can activate the backup workflow to send another AMB' to the accident location.

Figure 4.

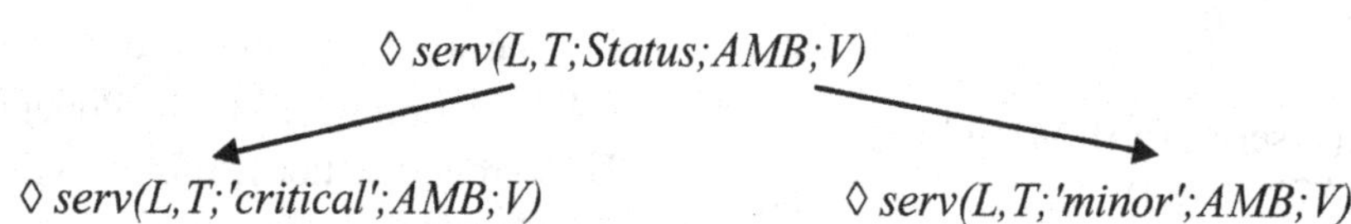

Figure 5. An extended control flow graph containing a backup workflow for the accident response scenario service composition

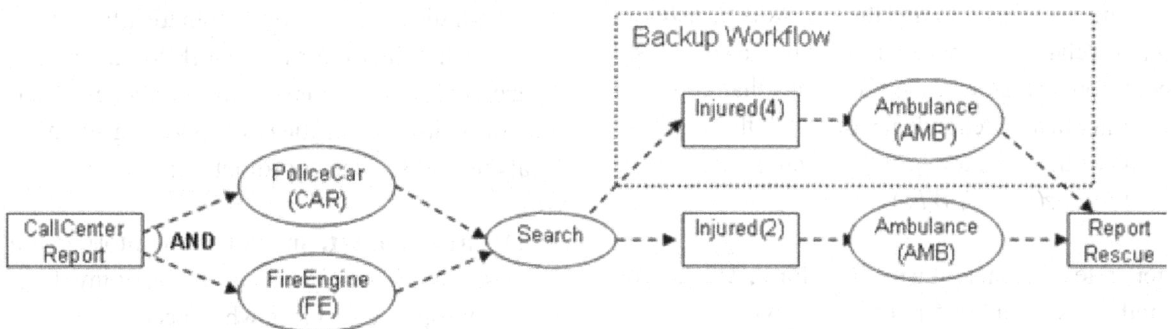

In this section, our focus will be on the non-monotonic predicates (NMPs) which might be updated during the execution of the workflow such as number of injured passengers (Singh, Gelgi, Davulcu, Yau, & Mukhopadhyay, 2008; Davulcu, Mukhopadhyay, Singh, & Yau, 2009). Updating NMPs is one of the major reasons for workflow failures.

Due to the unreliability of the non-monotonic predicates, a good idea is to generate an alternative workflow to backup the main workflow. Assuming that the execution history gives us enough statistics, we synthesize a backup workflow by using the expected values of all the non-monotonic uninstantiated predicates and the non-monotonic predicates that are below the confidence levels with their given values.

To keep the backup workflow consistent with the main workflow, the execution of the workflow is monitored. Whenever it is inconsistent with the backup workflow, the backup workflow is re-generated. Consider the previous accident response scenario in Figure 3 which assumes that the number of injured passengers is two. Suppose the expected number of injured passengers is four, then we can generate a backup workflow as follows,

Plan B: injured(4), send(Ambulance2), send(Ambulance1).

When the main workflow fails due to the number of injured passengers, we can switch to the backup workflow by just sending Ambulance2 to the accident location. The idea of backup workflow is to generate a workflow that is executable in parallel with the main workflow.

Backup Workflow Synthesis

Our algorithm utilizes the *Enforce* procedure as follows in order to synthesize a backup workflow for each NMP (Singh, Gelgi, Davulcu, Yau, & Mukhopadhyay, 2008; Davulcu, Mukhopadhyay, Singh, & Yau, 2009). Let *d* be a given NMP and *d'* is the NMP of *d* with its expected value. Let *Before* and *After* be functions that returns the set of predicates that precedes and succeeds *d* in the original workflow:

$Before(d, WF) \prec d'$

$D' \prec After(d, WF)$

We can then use the *Enforce* method presented earlier to synthesize the backup workflow. Here $\prec$ is a transitive relation, i.e, if $(a \prec b) \wedge (b \prec c) \rightarrow (a \prec c)$. In other words, upon its synthesis *d'* shouldn't violate any ordering constraints of *d*. Let *D* be the dependency set of the main workflow. Then the dependency set of backup workflow *D'* should augment the dependencies of the main workflow by inheriting the ordering dependencies of *d* for *d'*. That is,

$D' = D \cup \{x < d' \mid x < d \in D\} \cup \{d' < x \mid d < x \in D\}$

The next step is to find the sub-workflow *WFs* that is related to *d'* which has the root as the least common ancestor of the predicates that appears together in any dependency of *d'*. All the descendants of that root are in *WFs*. Then,

Enforce($d \wedge d'$, *WFs*)

generates the backup workflow for d. The given method is sound and reduces the overall risk of the original workflow by incorporating a new backup path for the expected values of each NMP. Also, the generated backup workflow is always consistent with the dependencies of the original workflow and it does not introduce any new NMPs into the workflow.

Cycle Detection and Simplification

The above transformation may yield a proof tree which may have sub-formulas, where the *send* and *receive* primitives introduced during the application of the Synch function cause a cyclic wait. The problem with such *cyclic blocks* is that, when they exist, the specification of the derived control flow graph may be inconsistent, and hence not executable. Fortunately, a variant of depth- first search procedure on the control flow graph generated from our *Enforce* algorithm can identify all executable cyclic blocks and remove all cyclic blocks in time $O(|G|^3)$. This procedure, called *unblock,* is shown below and yields a cyclic-block-free and executable service composition satisfying the original workflow goal made up from a conjunction of the control flow template and the situational constraints.

Representing Situation-Aware Workflow Agents Using α-calculus

To enable the automated synthesis of situation-aware workflow agents, we use α-calculus as the programming model for agents to develop a deductive technique to synthesize α-calculus terms defining situation-aware workflow agents from α-logic specification automatically.

Note that situation-aware workflow agents are distributed autonomous software entities and have the following capabilities of supporting situation analysis and service coordination:

(C1) **Participant t,** including monitoring the status of participant services, and invoking appropriate services when needed.

(C2) **Context acquisition and situation analysis**, including collecting contexts from its participant services and analyzing situations continuously based on its configuration.

(C3) **Communication among agents**, including communication with other agents to exchange context and situation information, service status, requests and responses for service invocation.

The above capabilities of situation-aware workflow agents can be represented using α-calculus as follows:

(C1) Management of participant services by situation-aware workflow agents is modeled by internal computations and external communications in α-calculus. In SBS, collecting information on the status of participant services is done by invoking certain methods provided by participant services. Such service invocation is represented by the method invocation in α-calculus. Similarly, invoking appropriate participant services is also represented by the method invocation in α-calculus. The condition that determines when a service should be invoked is represented by the conditional evaluation and constraint evaluation in α-calculus. For example, assume that we want to represent a Ticketing agent, which checks the Reservation service of an airline to find out the availability of tickets on the flight XYZ

Table 4.

procedure *unblock(G)* 1. for each $cycle_i$ in *G* do using *DFS* 2. for each input action $K(\xi_{ij};\sigma)$ in $cycle_i$ do //σ is an arbitrary process 3. $W_{ij} = remove(W, K(\xi_{ij};\sigma))$ 4. return $\vee W_{ij}$	procedure *remove(W, K(ξ;σ))* 1. $W' = (W \wedge \neg K(\xi;\sigma))$ 2. $S = S(W) - S(W')$ //$S(W)=\{<\xi> \mid <\xi>$ is an output action in $W\}$ 3. if $S \neq 0$ then 4. for each $<\xi>$ in *S* do 5. $W' = remove(W', K(\xi;\sigma))$ 6. else return *W'*

for a particular date, and reserves a ticket if there are still tickets left. Such an agent is represented using α-calculus as follows:

Fix Ticketing:=
let integer x = Reservation:checkAvailability (flightNo, date) instantiate
//collecting information from the participant service, "TicketingService"
if x > 0 //conditional evaluation
then Reservation:reserveTicket(flightNo, date, 1) //service invocation
else string ch<"This flight is booked full." >

(C2) Similarly, service invocation for context acquisition and processing context information by situation-aware workflow agents is represented by the method invocation in α-calculus. Situation analysis process in situation-aware workflow agents is represented by conditional evaluation, input and output actions in α-calculus.

(C3) Communication among agents can be represented by the input and output actions in α-calculus. One restriction imposed on communication between two agents is that the agents must run in parallel, i.e. if $Agent_1 = (u).T$, and $Agent_2 = <u>.T$, $Agent_1$ can receive *u* only when the calculus term $Agent_1 \,||\, Agent_2$ is satisfied in the system.

In addition, the recursive process, concatenation and parallel composition of processes, and conditional evaluation in α-calculus can be used to represent complex control structures, such as loops and conditional branches, for more complex behavior of situation-aware workflow agents.

Automated Synthesis of α-Calculus Terms Defining Situation-Aware Workflow Agents

From the proof generated using our algorithm for service composition based on α-logic, we can extract executable α-calculus terms in a straightforward way following the lines of (Waldinger, 2000). For example, from the proof process of the following workflow goal

◊(serv(L,T;'AMB_sent',AmbID;Y;911CallCenter) <serv(L,T;'rescued';Z;911CallCenter)),

which we have shown previously, the following 911CallCenter agent can be synthesized as follows:

fix 911CallCenter= (line 1)
integer ch1(l, t). (line 2)
let string r1=AMB:dispatch_amb(l, t)^c_dispatch instantiate (line 3)
let string status=AMB:get_injury_status(l, t)^c_get instantiate (line 4)
if status=='critical' then (line 5)
let string r2=AMB:dispatch_heli(l, t)^c_heli instantiate (line 6)
let string result=AMB:heli_send_hospital()^c_sendIf instantiate (line 7)
string o<string result> (line 8)
*else let string result=AMB:amb_send_*

hospital()^c_sendElse instantiate (line 9)
string o<string result> (line 10)

In the above calculus terms, *c_dispatch*, *c_get*, *c_heli*, *c_sendIf*, and *c_sendElse* are identifiers for continuation passing (see the Background section) of different service invocations.

The Agent Platform

The synthesized α-calculus terms encode a situation-aware workflow generated by the α-logic proof system. To deploy and execute the workflow, the synthesized α-calculus terms need to be compiled to executable components on an agent platform, such as the SINS (Bharadwaj, 2003) and Ajanta (Ajanta, 2002). We selected the SINS as the agent platform due to the following reasons:

(1) SINS platform comprises SINS Virtual Machines (SVM) which provide various support for agents running on SVMs, such as marshalling and de-marshalling data for service invocations, instantiating agents, and built-in data provenance mechanisms. Furthermore, it uses the Spread (Amir, Danilov, Miskin-Amir, Schultz, & Stanton, 2004) group communication tool from Johns Hopkins University as a transport layer to provide secure and reliable group communication among agents,
(2) Agents running on SINS are specified using Secure Operation Language (SOL), which is a platform-independent high-level synchronous programming language (Bharadwaj, 2002), and can be verified and compiled to other programming languages, such as Java. Hence, compiling α-calculus terms to SOL programs is easy because there is no need to handle any platform-dependent low-level details. The generated programs can be migrated to different systems supporting SINS. We have already developed a compiler from α-calculus to SOL.
(3) SVMs have a small footprint and can run on Java Kilobyte Virtual Machines (KVMs), thus allowing deployment on resource-constrained motes.
(4) Agents can be automatically and wirelessly deployed on SVMs running on different hosts in the network (base stations, motes) using specified deployment information. Xito (http://www.xito.org/) is used in SINS to provide the necessary functionality for deploying agents over the network.

To better support our approach to rapid development of adaptable situation-aware SBS, we have extended SINS to provide the following new capabilities:

- Parameterized initialization of agents, which subsequently enables runtime reconfiguration of agents.
- Invocation of functional services in SBS and system control services, such as system performance packages, network management and migration, to support workflow execution, monitoring and control in SBS.
- Event logging into a persistent data repository for recording workflow execution history.

Figure 6 shows a high-level architecture of our extension, which is called Workflow Virtual Machine (WVM). The composition of WF Controllers and WF Monitors for monitoring and adapting workflow execution have been presented in (Yau, Huang, & Zhu, 2007; Yau, Huang, Zhu, & Cai, 2007; Yau, Zhu, Huang, & Gong, 2007), and will not be discussed in this chapter due to space limitation. The WVM Core is mainly responsible for these new capabilities. The ServiceProxy in the WVM provides an interface for each functional service or system control service in SBS. When an agent (may be a WF agent, WF monitor or WF controller) evaluates its input data and makes a decision to invoke a certain service, the WVM handles the service invocation as follows:

i) The agent generates a service invocation request with the necessary information, such as the name of the service to be invoked and the identity of the user invoking this service if access control for the service is required. Specifically, the name of the input channel, where the agent expects to receive the result of this service invocation, is included in the service request.
ii) The agent puts the request into an output channel named *ServiceInvoke*.
iii) Instead of sending out the request in the *ServiceInvoke* channel, the WVM Core parses the service request, performs security checking, if necessary, and invokes the corresponding interface in the ServiceProxy.
iv) Once invoked, the corresponding interface in the ServiceProxy constructs an appropriate service request or API call, depending on the form of the service to be invoked. (For example, if the service to be invoked is in the form of Web Service, a SOAP message will be constructed.)
v) When the ServiceProxy receives the result of the service invocation, it puts the result into the input channel specified by the agent in (i).

The above service invocation process in the WVM not only provides agents the capability to make asynchronous service invocations and perform other tasks in parallel, but also provides richer information regarding service invocations, which will be very useful in our workflow execution monitoring approach. For example, service delay can be easily measured in the ServiceProxy to capture more semantics-rich events, not just the information on success or failure.

CASE STUDY

Intelligent Management and Optimization of Power Systems

In this section, we will present a case study to show an application of our approach to intelligent management and optimization of power systems.

Figure 6. Our virtual machine-based architecture for executing, monitoring and controlling workflows in SBS.

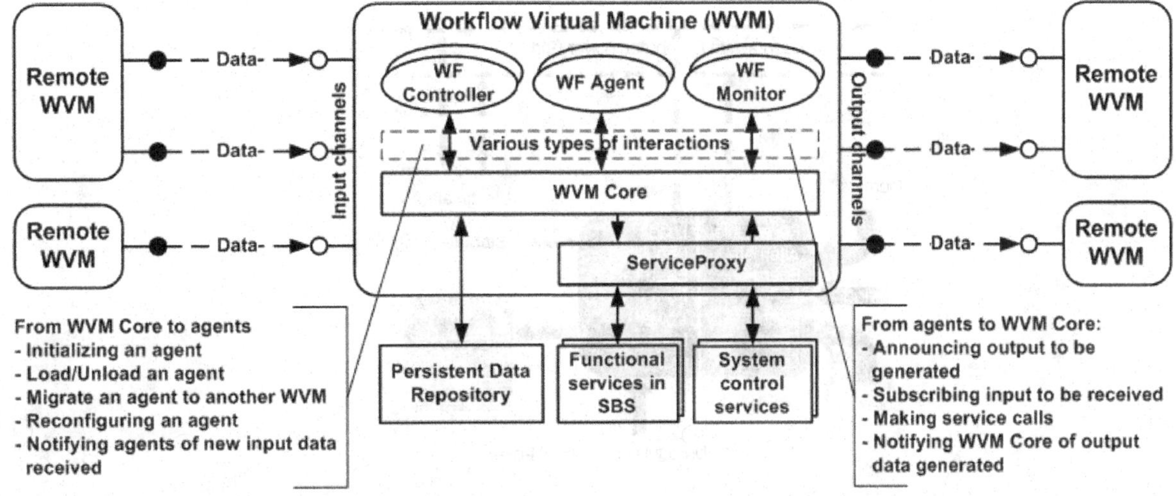

Over the last thirty years, neglect as well as lack of investment on power systems has resulted in the poor state of our infrastructure for generating and delivering power. Currently, over 60% of the equipment needs replacement (Global Environment Fund, 2005). Meanwhile, existing power systems as shown in Figure 7 become increasingly heterogeneous, which greatly increases the difficulty of managing the hybrid power grid in North America. Reliability has become a main concern in managing an expensive power system. With the proliferation of digital and analog devices being used in mission-critical environments, the need for delivery of high quality power becomes more critical. Furthermore, even with costly state-of-the-art equipments, such as power electronic-based transformers, the power systems are still inefficient due to the lack of intelligent management and optimization mechanisms. *Situation-aware power systems* can greatly improve the efficiency and reliability of power systems. A *situation-aware power system* is an electric power system, in which power generation, transmission, and distribution are managed intelligently and adaptively by smart distributed networked systems, which may consist of wireless or wired sensors (e.g., power factor meters and thermometers), actuators (e.g., static VAR compensators and variable voltage transformers), simulators, and other services orchestrated by a network software layer. Such systems are modulated by distributed closed loop control systems. Apart from transforming our obsolete power grid into an autonomous and survivable one, these control systems aim to optimize the operation of power systems with objectives including, but not limited to, minimization of line loss, voltage fluctuations, illegal usage, and peak time load imbalance.

In this case study, we will show how a novel adaptable situation-aware knowledge-based control system can be developed to intelligently and reliably manage the operation of large power systems. The development of such a control system uses our approach with the state-of-the-art distributed information integration and wireless sensor network technologies. The control system integrates intelligent sensor coordination and data fusion techniques to access, retrieve, process, and communicate with disparate wireless sensors in an ad-hoc manner to collect adequate information for making management decisions and delivering dynamic decisions. The control

Figure 7. Distributed Hybrid Power System

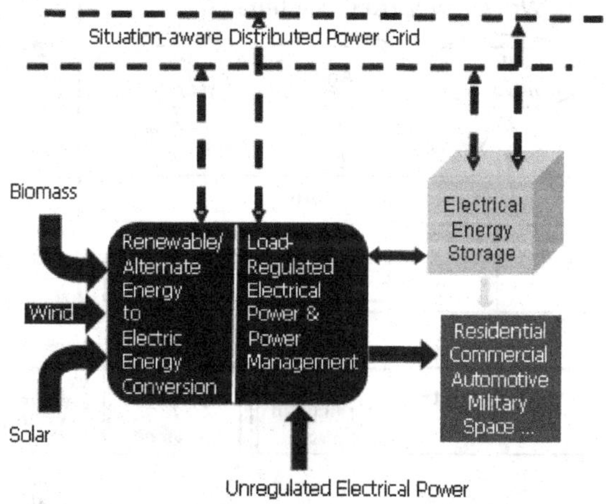

system is amenable to dynamic reconfiguration in response to changing requirements without incurring any system downtime. The control system is integrated with state-of-the-art provenance management techniques to prevent false triggers of actuating devices.

An Example Management Scenario

Let us consider a sample scenario for controlling the power factor and voltage fluctuation in a power grid. Low power factors can result in increased losses while voltage fluctuations can damage equipments. Low power factors are generally caused by inductive or capacitive loads, such as furnaces and fluorescent lamps. Today, energy companies impose penalty surcharges on customers (e.g., steel plants) that operate loads such as furnaces. This increases the electricity bills of manufacturing industries by millions of dollars per year. Given the current off-shoring trend of manufacturing industry, such penalty surcharges will not result in a business friendly atmosphere. Intelligent management of power systems and loads can alleviate the problem.

The voltage as well as the power factor across the power system is sampled by power factor meters and voltmeters distributed spatially at different loads. These meters locally report to motes running knowledge-based distributed intelligent software agents, which make intelligent control decisions based on the data. Motes can communicate among each other as well as with control stations. In case the power factor is significantly below unity in a particular area, the control action might be switching on a static VAR compensator (capacitive or inductive depending on whether the power factor is lagging or leading) to correct the power factor. This action is actuated through a driver. Switching on a static VAR compensator may result in voltage fluctuations (with voltage increasing for a capacitive compensator and decreasing for an inductive compensator). The software agents, in response to such data from the local voltmeters, will automatically switch on of a transformer (step up or step down) depending on the situation. Depending on the stability characteristics of the power system, the transient effects will wear down over time resulting in stabilization of voltage and power factor at the respective set points.

Developing an Intelligent Control System

Figure 8 depicts the conceptual framework of our control system. Figure 9 depicts an agent generation and deployment architecture for developing our control system based on our approach to the rapid development of adaptable situation-aware SBS. In our control system, data from different sources, such as reports from observers, voltmeters, ampere meters, energy meters, power factor meters, and power system simulators, are received by distributed intelligent software agents running in motes at different locations. Typically these motes will be physically located close to loads. For example, several such motes can be installed in a steel plant. Sensors such as voltmeters, ampere meters and observers can be viewed as services disseminating results in a "push" mode. On the other hand, power system simulators and actuators such as static VAR compensators are services disseminating computation results in the "pull" mode. Deployed software agents will provide naming, discovery, routing, identifying, and security for motes. Agents in different motes can communicate among themselves as well as with base stations and can interact with physical devices through drivers for actuation and receiving alerts.

The process of developing such a control system using the agent generation and deployment architecture shown in Figure 9 is as follows:

(1) Given a set of services and devices available in a network, including software services, different meters and sensors, base stations, and hardware services running on them, their interfaces are formally specified as

Figure 8. Conceptual framework of our control system

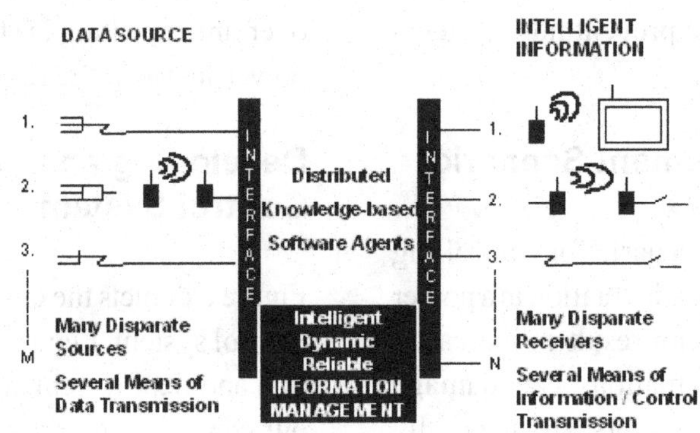

Figure 9. Agent Generation and Deployment Architecture

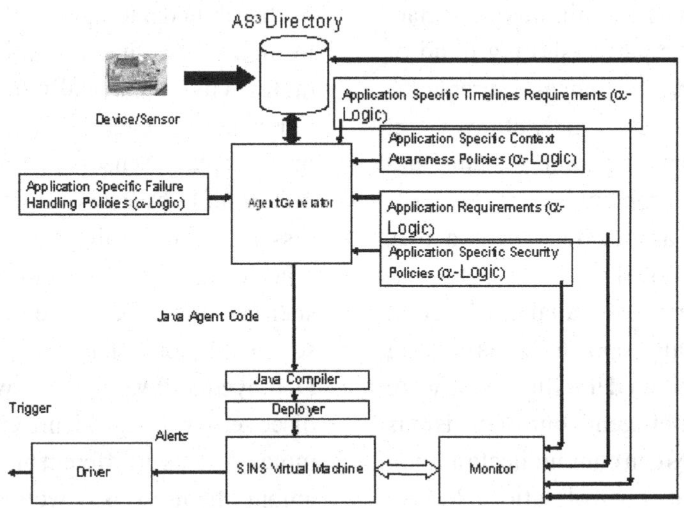

logical formulas in α-Logic and stored in a service and resource directory, which is a knowledge base providing necessary query and update interfaces. The α-Logic interface specifications of services and devices can be obtained by automatically compiling UPnP (UPnP, 2007) specifications (available as a UPnP database from the manufacturers) to α-Logic using a compiler. The service and resource directory is replicated for fault-tolerance with standard techniques used to maintain consistency.

(2) The agent generator (see Figure 9), which implements our natural deduction-based proof systems for the α-Logic, uses knowledge represented declaratively as

α-Logic sentences to automatically generate distributed intelligent software agents that are guaranteed to meet the application requirements. Inputs to the agent generator include application-specific requirements for security, SAW, failure handling (Yau, Mukhopadhyay, & Bharadwaj, 2005), and timeliness, the management objective of a customer, and interface specifications of services and devices stored in the service and resource directory. All the inputs to the agent generator are specified in α-Logic. The agent generator constructively proves the management objective of the customer using α-Logic formulas in the service and resource directory as axioms, and application-specific requirements as application constraints. The proof shows how data from different sources are integrated under the application constraints to make decisions for meeting the management objective.

(3) From the proof, distributed agents described in α-calculus are synthesized automatically using a Curry-Howard style correspondence (Barendregt, 1984).

(4) The synthesized agents are compiled to executable code to run on SINS platform.

During the development, in order to hide the formal logic from an untrained user, an SCR table-like (Heitmeyer, Jeffords, & Labaw, 1996) intuitive graphical user interface (GUI) is provided. The GUI can be readily assembled using Adobe's flex (www.adobe.com/products/ flex/). In runtime, the agent generator uses the inputs of the meters and the management policies of the customer to generate real-time control decisions for managing energy flow. The control decisions can either be delivered to appropriate personnel for manual intervention or directly actuated through wireless actuators. The agents can be deployed automatically on a distributed network involving meters tracking system parameters, actuators controlling devices, relays, breakers, and valves, and diverse computing and communication elements such as PDA. Our approach provides formal guarantees that the policies of the customer will be enforced and the Quality of Service (QoS) goals specified by them will be met even under changing environments, such as meters failing, actuators changing their configuration, and network nodes being compromised. Changing environments are handled by a dynamic reconfiguration of the agents by a monitoring agent. Reconfiguration may include substituting new services/devices for existing ones and can be used to provide new functionalities in response to changing requirements.

For sake of readability, instead of showing the entire specification for a voltage and power controller, the specification fragment for a simple voltage controller is given below:

Spec1)*Sense(voltage, VoltageController, I)* ∧ *(INIT(alert, off)* →

(PREV(alert)= off ∧ Sense(voltage, VoltageController, I)

→ (@T(VoltageController, voltage >= 1000)

→ High)

∧ (¬(@T(VoltageController, voltage >=1000)

→

PREV(alert))))

Spec1) indicates the voltage controllers action starts after sensing voltage and that alert should be initially off and thereafter if voltage is sensed and it has changed to 1000 or more then a High alert should be sent. Note that when we specify the *VoltageController*, we do not care where the sensed voltage comes from; we assume that it comes from an unknown entity denoted by the nominal *I*. From *sense(voltage, VoltageController, I)*, as well as the presence of the specification of the meter "*met*" in the service and resource directory that publishes the variable voltage (using the *sense* modality), the proof system will conclude that the *VoltageController* will subscribe to a variable *voltage* that is published by the meter *"met"*, i.e., it resolves I = *"met"* using a natural deduction of *sense(voltage, VoltageController, "met")*. This will allow the meter *"met"* (or the wrapper for *"met"*) – we use the Observer Pattern (Gamma, Helm, Johnson, & Vlissides, 1994) to generate the code for the wrapper – to know to which agents the *voltage* values should be sent, i.e., the set of observers for *voltage*. Hence, the agent generator will generate the following Java code fragment for the *VoltageController* for indicating that *voltage* is the variable that it monitors.

```
public HashMap<String, HashMap<String, Object>> getMonVars()
throws Exception {
HashMap<String, HashMap<String, Object>> ht = new HashMap<String, HashMap<String, Object>>();
HashMap<String, Object> prop = null;
prop = new HashMap<String, Object>();
prop.put("value", Voltage);
ht.put("Voltage", prop);
return ht;
}
```

The rest of the specification spec1 would be translated to the following Java code.

```
import java.util.*;
import sins.*;
public class VoltageController implements Deterministic, Reactive{
enum YAlert { Off,High };
int Voltage, PREV_Voltage;
YAlert Alert, PREV_Alert;
public void init(){
Alert=YAlert.Off;
}
public YAlert Alert(){
switch(PREV_Alert){
case Off:
if((Voltage>=1000) && !(PREV_Voltage>=1000)) return YAlert.High;
return PREV_Alert;
}
return YAlert.Off;
}
}
```

Software Engineering Experiences in the Case Study

Our approach has been used for developing significantly large mission-critical service-oriented applications. These include along with the situation-aware power management system discussed above, a distributed soil and water management system for agriculture, golf courses, and athletic fields, and a distributed food safety management system in restaurant chains (deployed in a real ice-cream store chain). Graduate students as well as professional programmers were involved in these projects. In some cases, the applications were directly specified using α-logic, whereas in others intuitive GUIs were provided. The requirements were first validated using the proof system of α-logic. One of the facts that we observed was the reluctance of professional programmers in using α-logic or its proof system due to its unusual syntax (compared to C++, Java). In order to gain industrial acceptance, we are currently trying to embed α-logic as a domain-specific extension of Java.

In all the case studies that we had conducted, our framework reduced the development and deployment time of the systems by 80~85%. The impact was more visible in cases where the requirements changed dynamically. Modified systems were automatically deployed through the network in a matter of hours. While reducing the development time, our framework significantly improved the reliability of the systems developed. So far no defects have been reported other than changes in requirements by users. The combination of SAW with SOA allows our framework to develop systems that are fault-tolerant, robust, and rapidly reconfigurable.

CONCLUSION AND FUTURE WORK

In this chapter, we have presented an approach to rapid development of adaptable situation-aware SBS. Our approach is based on α-logic and α-calculus, and a declarative model for SAW. An accident response scenario was given to illustrate how situational constraints for situation-aware service composition are specified, how the proof system of α-logic is used to compose a workflow using available services, and how to synthesize α-calculus terms representing situation-aware workflow agents that can monitor and execute the composed workflow. We have also presented a case study on using our approach to develop a novel adaptable situation-aware knowledge-based control system for intelligent management and optimization of power systems. To make this approach more useful, future research in this research will focus on developing a dynamic proof system to deal with various situations requiring workflow adaptation, and to incorporate security and real-time in the service composition.

ACKNOWLEDGMENT

The work reported here was based on the research supported by the DoD/ONR under the Multidisciplinary Research Program of the University Research Initiative under Contract No. N00014-04-1-0723. In addition, Dr. Mukhopadhyay is partially supported by the National Science Foundation under grant number CCF-0702600. Any opinions, findings, conclusions or recommendations expressed in this material are those of the authors and do not necessarily reflect the views of the National Science Foundation, DOD/ONR or the United States Government

REFERENCES

W3C. (2004a). *OWL Web Ontology Language: Overview.* Retrieved December 4, 2005, from http://www.w3.org/ TR/owl-features

W3C. (2004b). *Web services architecture*. Retrieved December 4, 2005, from http://www.w3.org/TR/2004/NOTE-ws-arch-20040211/

Ajanta. (2002). *Ajanta project website*. Retrieved December 4, 2005, from http://www.cs.umn.edu/Ajanta/

Amin, M. (2001). Towards Self-Healing Energy Infrastructure Systems. *IEEE Computer Applications in Power, 14*(1), 20–28. doi:10.1109/67.893351

Amir, Y., Danilov, C., Miskin-Amir, M., Schultz, J., & Stanton, J. (2004). *The Spread Toolkit: Architecture and Performance* (Technical Report CNDS-2004-1). Johns Hopkins University, April. Retrieved April 4, 2008, from http://www.cnds.jhu.edu/pub/papers/cnds-2004-1.pdf

Andrews, T., Curbera, F., Dholakia, H., Goland, Y., Klein, J., Leymann, F., et al. (2003). *Business Process Execution Language for Web Services Version 1.1.* Retrieved December 4, 2005, from ftp://www6.software.ibm.com/software/developer / library/ws-bpel.pdf.

Appel, A. W. (1992). *Compiling with continuations*. Cambridge University Press.

Attie, P., Singh, M. P., Sheth, A. P., & Rusinkiewicz, M. (1993). Specifying and enforcing intertask dependencies. In *Proceedings of the International Conference on Very Large Databases (VLDB)*, August (pp.134-145).

Awan, A., Jagannathan, S., & Grama, A. (2007) Macroprogramming Heterogeneous Sensor Networks using COSMOS. In *Proceedings of the 2007 EuroSys Conference,* March (pp. 159-172).

Bacchus, F., & Kabanza, F. (1996). Using temporal logic to control search in a forward chaining planner. In M. Ghallab & A. Milani (Eds.), *New Directions in Planning* (pp. 141-153). IOS Press.

Barendregt, H. P. (1984). *The Lambda Calculus, Its Syntax and Semantics*. North-Holland.

Bharadwaj, R. (2002). SOL: a verifiable synchronous language for reactive systems. In *Proceedings of Synchronous Languages, Applications, and Programming (SLAP '02)*. Retrieved December 4, 2005, from http://chacs.nrl.navy.mil/publications/CHACS/2002/2002bharadwaj-entcs.pdf

Bharadwaj, R. (2003). Secure middleware for situation-aware naval C^2 and combat systems. In *Proceedings of the 9th International Workshop on Future Trends of Distributed Computing System (FTDCS'03)*, 2003, May (pp. 233-240).

Birman, K. P., Chen, J., Hopkinson, E. M., Thomas, R. J., Thorp, J. S., & van Renesse, R. (2005). Overcoming Communications Challenges in Software for Monitoring and Controlling Power Systems. *Proceedings of the IEEE, 93*(5), 1028–1041. doi:10.1109/JPROC.2005.846339

Blackburn, P., deRijke, M., & Venema, Y. (2003). *Modal Logic*. Cambridge University Press.

Cardelli, L., & Gordon, A. D. (2000). Mobile ambients. *Theoretical Computer Science, 240*(1), 177–213. doi:10.1016/S0304-3975(99)00231-5

Caromel, D., & Henrio, L. (2005). *A Theory of Distributed Objects.* Springer Verlag.

Chan, A. T. S., & Chuang, S. N. (2003). MobiPADS: a reflective middleware for context-aware computing. *IEEE Transactions on Software Engineering, 29*(12), 1072–1085. doi:10.1109/TSE.2003.1265522

Davulcu, H., Mukhopadhyay, S., Singh, P., & Yau, S. S. (2009). Default α-Logic for Modeling Customizable Failure Semantics in Workflow Systems Using Dynamic Reconfiguration Constraints. In *Proceedings of International Conference on Grid and Distributed Computing (GDC)*, December (pp. 49-56).

Dayal, U., Hsu, M., & Ladin, R. (1990). Organizing long running activities with triggers and transactions. In *Proceedings of the 1990 ACM SIGMOD International Conference on Management of Data*, May (pp. 204-214).

Dey, A. K., & Abowd, G. D. (2001). A conceptual framework and a toolkit for supporting the rapid prototyping of context-aware applications. *Human-Computer Interaction (HCI). Journal, 16*(2-4), 97–166.

Gamma, E., Helm, R., Johnson, R., & Vlissides, J. M. (1994) *Design Patterns: Elements of Reusable Object-Oriented Software.* Addison-Wesley.

Gay, D., Philip, L., von Behren, R., Welsh, M., Brewer, E., & Culler, D. (2003). The nesC Language: A Holistic Approach to Networked Embedded Systems. In *Proceedings of ACM SIGPLAN 2003 Conference on Programming Language Design and Implementation*, June (pp. 1-11).

Gelgi. F. (2005). *Embedding AI planning techniques into single machine total weighted tardiness problem* (Technical Report), Arizona State University. Retrieved December 4, 2005, from http://www.public.asu. edu/~fgelgi/ai/atoc/smtwt-report.pdf

Georgakopoulos, D., Hornick, M., & Sheth, A. (1995). An overview of workflow management: from process modeling to workflow automation infrastructure. *Journal on Distributed and Parallel Databases, 3*(2), 119–153. doi:10.1007/BF01277643

Global Environment Fund. (2005). *The Emerging Smart Grid: Investment and Entrepreneurial Potential in the Electric Power Grid of the Future*, October. Retrieved from: http://www.globalenvironmentfund.com/GEF%20white%20paper_Electric%20Power%20Grid.pdf

Gunthor, R. (1993). Extended transaction processing based on dependency rules. *International Workshop on Research Issues in Data Engineering: Interoperability in Multidatabase Systems (RIDE-IMS'93)*, April (pp.207-214).

Hawthorne, J. (1996). On the Logic of Nonmonotonic Conditionals and Conditional Probabilities. *Journal of Philosophical Logic, 25*(2), 185–218. doi:10.1007/BF00247003

Heitmeyer, C. L., Jeffords, R. D., & Labaw, B. G. (1996). Automated Consistency Checking of Requirements Specifications. *ACM Transactions on Software Engineering and Methodology, 5*(3), 231–261. doi:10.1145/234426.234431

Hopkinson, K. M., Birman, K. P., Giovanini, R., Coury, D. V., Wang, X., & Thorp, J. S. (2003). EPOCHS: Integrated COTS Software For Agent-based Electric Power and Communication Simulation. In *Proceedings of 2003 Winter Simulation Conference*, December (pp. 1158-1166).

Hsu, M. (1993). Special issue on workflow and extended transaction systems. *Bulletin of the IEEE Technical Committee on Data Engineering, 16*(2).

Hundal, S. S., & Brown, F. M. (1991). A Theory of Nonmonotonic Planning. *Proceedings of the 19th Annual Conference on Computer Science*, March (pp. 247-254).

Klein, J. (1991). Advanced Rule-driven Transaction Management. In. *Proceedings of IEEE COMPCON, 1991*(February), 562–567.

Matheus, C. J., Kokar, M. M., & Baclawski, K. (2003). A core ontology for situation awareness. In *Proceedings of 6th International Conference on Information Fusion,* July (pp. 545-552).

Matheus, C. J., Kokar, M. M., Baclawski, K., & Letkowski, J. (2003). Constructing RuleML-based domain theories on top of OWL ontologies. In *Proceedings of 2nd International Workshop on Rules and Rule Markup Languages for the Semantic Web*, October (pp. 81-94).

May, D., & Shepherd, R. (1984). The transputer implementation of occam. In *Proceedings of the International Conference on Fifth, Generation Computer Systems, Tokyo,* 1984.

McCarthy, J. (2001). *Situation calculus with concurrent events and narrative*. Retrieved December 4, 2005, from http://www-formal.stanford.edu/jmc/narrative.html

McCarthy, J., & Hayes, P. J. (1969). Some philosophical problems from the standpoint of artificial intelligence. *Machine Intelligence, 4*, 463–502.

Milner, R. (1999). *Communicating and Mobile Systems: the π -Calculus*. Cambridge University Press.

Newton, R., Morrisett, G., & Welsh, M. (2007). The regiment macroprogramming system. In *Proceedings of the 6th International Conference on Information Processing in Sensor Networks (IPSN'07)*, April (pp. 489-498).

Pinto, J. A. (1994). *Temporal Reasoning in the Situation Calculus*. PhD Thesis, University of Toronto, Toronto.

Plaisted, D. (2003). *A hierarchical situation calculus*. Retrieved December 4, 2005, from http://arxiv.org/abs/cs/0309053

Ponnekanti, S., & Fox, A. (2002). Sword: A developer toolkit for web service composition. In *Proceedings of the 11th International World Wide Web Conference (WWW 2002).*

Priest, G. (2001). *An Introduction to Non-Classical Logic*. Cambridge University Press.

Ranganathan, A., & Campbell, R. H. (2003). A middleware for context-aware agents in ubiquitous computing environments. In *Proceedings of 5th ACM/IFIP/USENIX International Middleware Conference*, October (pp. 143-161).

Rao, J., Kungas, P., & Matskin, M. (2003). Application of linear logic to web service composition. In *Proceedings of the 1st International Conference on Web Services (ICWS'03)*, June (pp. 3-9).

Renesse, R., Birman, K. P., & Vogels, W. (2003). Astrolable: A Robust and Scalable Technology for Distributed System Monitoring, Management and Data Mining. *ACM Transactions on Computer Systems*, *21*(2), 164–206. doi:10.1145/762483.762485

Roman, M., Hess, C., Cerqueira, R., Ranganathan, A., Campbell, R. H., & Nahrstedt, K. (2002). A middleware infrastructure for active spaces. *IEEE Pervasive Computing / IEEE Computer Society [and] IEEE Communications Society*, *1*(4), 74–83. doi:10.1109/MPRV.2002.1158281

Singh, M. P. (1995). Semantical considerations on workflows: an algebra for intertask dependencies. In *Proceedings of the 5th International Workshop on Database Programming Languages (DBPL-5)*, September (pp. 5-19).

Singh, P., Gelgi, F., Davulcu, H., Yau, S. S., & Mukhopadhyay, S. (2008). A Risk Reduction Framework for Dynamic Workflows. In *Proceedings of 2008 IEEE International Conference on Services Computing*, July (pp. 381-388).

Sirin, E., Hendler, J. A., & Parsia, B. (2003). Semi-automatic composition of web services using semantic descriptions. In *Proceedings of the Web Services: Modeling, Architecture and Infrastructure (WSMAI) Workshop in conjunction with the 5th International Conference on Enterprise Information Systems (ICEIS 2003)*, April (pp. 17-24).

Sorensen, M. H., & Urzyczyn, P. (2006). *Lectures on the Curry-Howard Isomorphism,* Elsevier.

UPnP. (2007). *Universal Plug and Play Device Standards*, UPnP Forum, September. Retrieved April 4, 2008, from http://upnp.org/standardized-dcps/default.asp

Waldinger, R. J. (2000). Web agents cooperating deductively. In *Proceedings of the 1st International Workshop on Formal Approach to Agent-Based Systems*, April (pp. 250-262).

WFMC. (1996). *WorkFlow Management Coalition. Terminology and glossary*. Retrieved December 4, 2005, from http://www.wfmc.org/standards/docs/TC-1011_term_glossary_v3.pdf

Woodman, S. J., Palmer, D. J., Shrivastava, S. K., & Wheater, S. M. (2004). Notations for the specification and verification of composite web services. In *Proceedings of the 8th IEEE International Enterprise Distributed Object Computing Conference (EDOC'04)*, September (pp. 35-46).

WSDL. (2001). *Web services description language*. Retrieved December 4, 2005, from http://www.w3.org/TR/wsdl

Yau, S. S., Davulcu, H., Mukhopadhyay, S., Huang, D., Gong, H., & Singh, P. (2007). Automated situation-aware service composition in service-oriented computing. [IJWSR]. *International Journal of Web Services Research*, *4*(4), 59–82.

Yau, S. S., Gong, H., Huang, D., Gao, W., & Zhu, L. (2006) Automated agent synthesis for situation awareness in service-based systems. In *Proceedings of the 30th IEEE International Computer Software and Applications Conference (COMPSAC'06)*, September (pp. 503-510).

Yau, S. S., Gong, H., Huang, D., Gao, W., & Zhu, L. (2008). Specification, decomposition and agent synthesis for situation-aware service-based systems. *Journal of Systems and Software*, *81*(10), 1663–1680. doi:10.1016/j.jss.2008.02.035

Yau, S. S., Huang, D., Gong, H., & Davulcu, H. (2005) Situation-awareness for adaptable service coordination in service-based systems. In *Proceedings of the 29th Annual International Computer Software and Application Conference (COMPSAC'05),* July (pp.107-112).

Yau, S. S., Huang, D., & Zhu, L. (2007) An approach to adaptive distributed execution monitoring for workflows in service-based systems. In *Proceedings of the 4th IEEE International Workshop on Software Cybernetics (IWSC'07)*, July (pp. 211-216).

Yau, S. S., Huang, D., Zhu, L., & Cai, K.-Y. (2007) A software cybernetic approach to deploying and scheduling workflow applications in service-based systems. In *Proceedings of the 11th International Workshop on Future Trends of Distributed Computing Systems (FTDCS'07)*, March (pp. 149-156).

Yau, S. S., Karim, F., Wang, Y., Wang, B., & Gupta, S. K. S. (2002). Reconfigurable context-sensitive middleware for pervasive computing. *IEEE Pervasive Computing / IEEE Computer Society [and] IEEE Communications Society*, *1*(3), 33–40. doi:10.1109/MPRV.2002.1037720

Yau, S. S., Mukhopadhyay, S., & Bharadwaj, R. (2005) Specification, analysis and implementation of architectural patterns for dependable software systems. In *Proceedings of the 10th IEEE International Workshop on Object-oriented Real-time Dependable Systems (WORDS 2005)*, February (pp. 197-204).

Yau, S. S., Mukhopadhyay, S., Huang, D., Gong, H., Davulcu, H., & Zhu, L. (2005). Automated agent synthesis for situation-aware service coordination in service-based systems. Retrieved December 4, 2005, from http://dpse.eas.asu.edu /as3/papers/ASU-CSE-TR-05-009.pdf

Yau, S. S., Wang, Y., & Karim, F. (2002). Development of situation-aware application software for ubiquitous computing environments. In *Proceedings of the 26th IEEE International Computer Software and Applications Conference (COMPSAC'02)*, August (pp. 233-238).

Yau, S. S., Zhu, L., Huang, D., & Gong, H. (2007). An approach to automated agent deployment in service-based systems. In *Proceedings of the 10th IEEE Symposium on Object-oriented Real-time distributed Computing (ISORC'07),* May (pp. 257-264).

Chapter 7
Object-Oriented Architecture for Web Services Eventing

Krzysztof Ostrowski
Cornell University, USA

Ken Birman
Cornell University, USA

Danny Dolev
The Hebrew University of Jerusalem, Israel

ABSTRACT

Existing web service notification and eventing standards are useful in many applications, but they have serious limitations that make them ill-suited for large-scale deployments, or as a middleware or a component-integration technology in today's data centers. For example, it is not possible to use IP multicast, or for recipients to forward messages to others, scalable notification trees must be setup manually, and no end-to-end security, reliability, or QoS guarantees can be provided. This chapter proposes an architecture based on object-oriented design principles that is free of such limitations, extremely modular and extensible, and that can serve as a basis for extending and complementing the existing standards. The new approach emerges from the authors' work on Live Distributed Objects, a new programming model that brings object-orientation into the realm of distributed computing.

INTRODUCTION

Motivation

Notification is a valuable, widely used primitive for designing distributed systems. The growing popularity of RSS feeds and similar technologies shows that this is also true at the Internet scales. The WS-Notification (Graham et al., 2004) and WS-Eventing (Box et al., 2004) standards have been offered as a basis for interoperation of heterogeneous systems deployed across the Internet. Unlike RSS, they are subscription-based and hence free of the scalability problems of polling, and they support proxy nodes that could be used to build scalable notification trees. Nonetheless, they embody restrictions that make them unsuitable as a middleware technology in large-scale systems:

DOI: 10.4018/978-1-61520-684-1.ch007

- *No forwarding among recipients.* Many content distribution schemes build overlays within which content recipients participate in message delivery. In current web services notification standards, however, recipients are *passive*, limited to data reception. Given the tremendous success of peer-to-peer technologies such as BitTorrent for multicast file transfer, one could imagine a future event notification system that uses a BitTorrent-like protocol for tranferring multimedia content. But BitTorrent depends on direct peer-to-peer interactions by recipients.
- *Not self-organizing.* While both standards permit the construction of notification trees, such trees must be manually configured, and require the use of *proxies*, dedicated infrastructure nodes, to build forwarding trees. Our vision would require the ability to automatically setup such trees, either by means of a protocol running directly between the clients or by leveraging external naming and membership services, but the current standards preclude this possibility.
- *Weak reliability.* Reliability in the existing schemes is limited to per-link guarantees resulting from the use of TCP. Many applications, including our live distributed object model, require end-to-end guarantees, and sometimes of strong flavor, e.g. to support virtually synchronous, transactional or state-machine replication. Because receivers are assumed passive and cannot cache, forward messages or participate in multiparty protocols, even very weak end-to-end guarantees cannot be provided.
- *Difficult to manage.* It is hard to create and maintain an Internet-scale dissemination structure that would permit any node to serve as a publisher or as a subscriber, for this requires many parties to maintain a common infrastructure, agree on standards, topology and other factors. Any such large-scale infrastructure should respect local autonomy, whereby the owner of a portion of a network can set up policies for local routing, the availability of IP multicast etc.
- *Inability to use external multicast frameworks.* The standards leave it entirely to the recipients to prepare their communication endpoints for message delivery. This makes it impossible for a group of recipients to dynamically agree upon a shared IP multicast address, or to construct an overlay multicast within a segment of the network. Such techniques are key to achieving high performance and scalability, and could be used to provide QoS guarantees or to leverage emergent technologies, e.g. scalable peer-to-peer overlays for streaming multimedia content.

One could imagine extending WS-Notification or WS-Eventing with the ability to forward data or add explicit support for IP multicast, but ultimately, there is a limit to how much one can achieve with a uniform scheme enforced globally across a heterogeneous system, such as today's Internet. The path to high performance and scalability leads through a composable, modular architecture, one that respects the diversity and the democratic nature of the Internet and can leverage different, locally optimized protocols for different types of content, or within different parts of the network.

In this article, we propose a principled approach to web service notification in large-scale systems, free of the limitations listed above, modular, and highly extensible. The design presented here is a basis for Live Distributed Objects (Ostrowski, Birman & Dolev, 2008), a novel object-oriented programming model and development environment for large-scale distributed systems. While this architecture is inspired by our work on Live Distributed Objects, it is designed to be generic, and it is compatible, in general, with a wide range of existing protocols, interfaces, and standards.

Model

We employ the usual terminology, where events are associated with ***topics***, they are produced by ***publishers*** and delivered to ***subscribers***. The term "*group X*" refers to the set of nodes subscribed to topic "*X*". Multiple nodes may publish to a given topic. Prospective publishers and subscribers register with a ***subscription manager***, which can be independent of the publishers (Figure 1).

The manager may be replicated to tolerate failures, or hierarchical, to scale. A single manager may track the publishers and subscribers for many topics, and many independent managers may co-exist. Nodes may reside in many ***administrative domains*** (LANs, data centers etc.). Nodes in the same domain may be *jointly managed*. It is often convenient to define policies, such as for message forwarding or resource allocation, in a way that respects domain boundaries, e.g. for administrative reasons, or because communication within a domain is cheaper than across domains, as it is often related to network topology. Publishers and subscribers might be scattered across organizations. These need to cooperate in message dissemination, which often presents a logistic challenge (Figure 2).

Example

To facilitate discussion, the paper uses a running example. Obviously, the architecture is not limited to any particular application; the architecture is intended to be flexible enough to serve as a general, multi-purpose middleware component-integration technology, and to be used in settings such as large data centers, trading systems, military infrastructure, etc. However, the example helps us illustrate the architecture with specific scenarios that highlight the role of specific features.

Figure 1. Publishers and subscribers register for a topic with the subscription manager

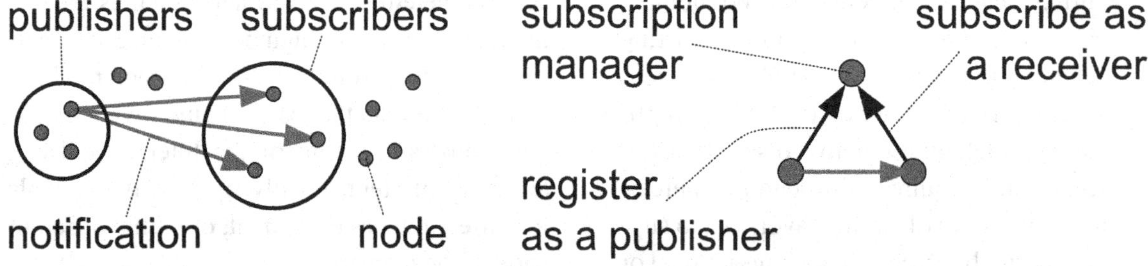

Figure 2. Nodes can be scattered across administrative domains hierarchically divided into sub-domains

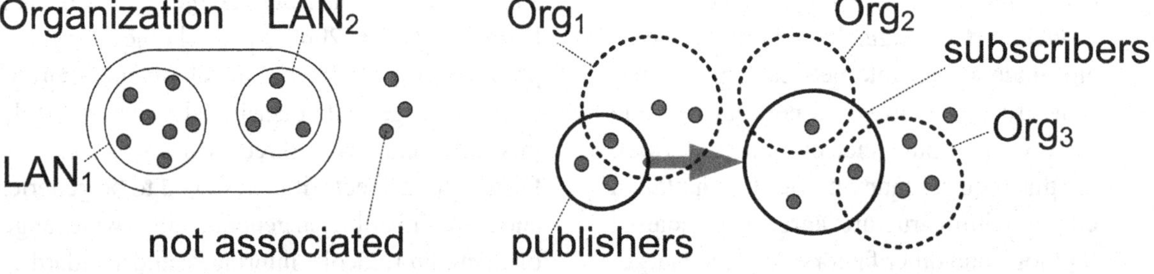

The example involves a possible vision for the future of the Internet. Even today, the Web is moving towards very dynamic and interactive content. Massively multiplayer online gaming and virtual realities, such as the World of Warcraft and Second Life, are becoming increasingly popular. However, current techniques are insufficient for massive-scale deployments. As of this writing, the latter platform is reported to host online 17,000 of a total of 2 million of its users, on a server farm of nearly 2600 dual-core Opteron machines. As the number of online users simultaneously browsing through such virtual realities will grow to tens and hundreds of millions, as users start to expect a smoother and more realistic experience, and they start transmitting high-resolution audio, video and animation streams, it will become very difficult to host entire virtual worlds in a centralized manner. Centralized systems are invariably costly and suffer from bottlenecks and high latencies. We believe that the most cost-effective (and perhaps ultimately the only feasible) way to implement such scenarios is for the virtual worlds to be decentralized, and for the users to interact directly, without any expensive servers in the middle.

Apart from the scalability aspect mentioned above, we also believe that the Internet community is unlikely to accept a situation where all content is controlled by a handful of providers. Instead, we envision that just as today users create web pages, they would eventually want to be able to create their own virtual rooms or landscapes, where participants could interact with one-another much as they do in online multiplayer games. A successful technology base of this sort could eventually transform the Web into a multi-verse, a federation of millions of inter-connected virtual places or entire worlds, created and hosted by the Internet community collaboratively, with a mixture of infrastructure services, services hosted on data centers, and services introduced and hosted by individual users.

A high-performance, scalable, and reliable variant of the *publish-subscribe* paradigm could be the enabling technology for such applications. To see this, think of each location in a virtual world as a separate publish-subscribe topic, and of the users that currently reside inside the location as subscribers (Figure 3).

The state of the room, e.g. its interior, user positions, actions in progress, all objects inside the room etc. is replicated among all the subscribers. The state is loaded by the users upon entering the room, and can be updated in a consistent manner by multicasting any updates (such as users speaking, moving, handing objects to each other etc.)

Figure 3. A virtual room in a virtual world, modeled as a "publish-subscribe" topic

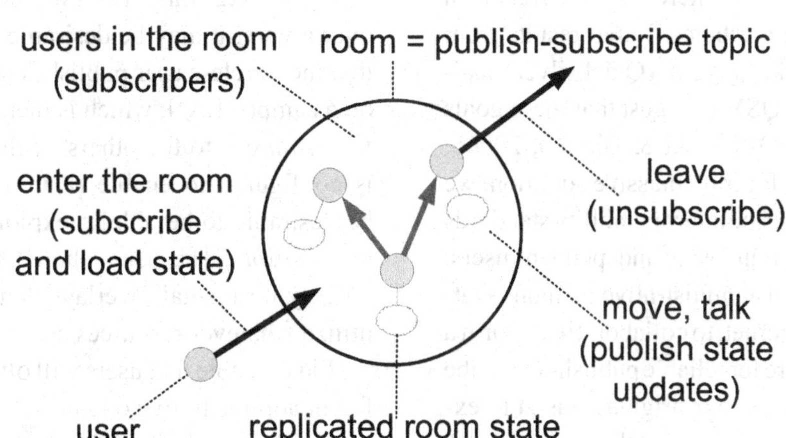

reliably to the set of all subscribers. The state can be retained while no visitors are in the room by a room *guardian*, a special entity that can either stay in the room at all times, or slip in only if the last "regular" user leaves, depending on how the room is setup. Unlike in the centralized approaches, here users interact directly with each other, with no server in between. Although this solution does require infrastructure components, e.g. to track subscriptions, inform users of each other's existence, control the "guard" etc., none of the required infrastructure sits on the "critical path" and acts as a proxy or intermediary. If one user speaks or projects a video clip to others, the data can be transmitted directly to participants, without the involvement of any such infrastructure. Infrastructure that controls a virtual location could thus be hosted even on a home machine of the user who created it. The network of user's home machines, hosting their virtual rooms connected by virtual corridors, can thus form a background *backbone* structure that controls the virtual reality in a way similar to how DNS serves as a backbone of the Internet.

To realize the vision outlined above, we need a publish-subscribe platform that can provide very high performance, scalability in multiple dimensions, such as the size of the system, the number of publish-subscribe topics, or data rates etc., end-to-end reliability guarantees, and a way to integrate with modern development platforms. In work reported elsewhere, we've created a system with these attributes. Initial results from experiments on the system (Quicksilver Scalable Multicast, or QSM) suggest that these goals can be achieved (Ostrowski & Birman, 2006b, 2006c). However, for truly massive adoption, we need publish-subscribe interoperability standards that allow a large number of independent users, residing in different administrative domains scattered across the Internet, to collaboratively form a single infrastructure for reliable publish-subscribe notification. This was our original reason to explore the architectural proposal that is the subject of this article.

Let's now revisit the problems listed in section "Motivation" in the context of our example. Consider a user sitting in a cafeteria with his laptop that enters a virtual room and starts interacting with friends in our 3-dimensional virtual reality. The user would act as one of several publishers and subscribers. Because such interactions would be ad-hoc, the technique that the users would use to disseminate data between them should be *self-organizing*, i.e. it should not rely on proxies, or other dedicated infrastructure.

A simple way to meet this requirement could be for each publisher to send updates directly to all subscribers over TCP, but this is not acceptable for several reasons. First, to ensure that all users see a consistent history of events, we'd need *reliability guarantees*, such as a global ordering of all updates published by different users (so that all of them see events occurring in the same order, or that two users don't pick up the same object), atomicity (so that if one user can see something happening, then so do all the others) etc. While solutions to such problems are well known from the literature, they need more than a plain point-to-point TCP-based dissemination scheme. Thus, the users would need to run a suite of special reliability protocols.

Secondly, the wireless link of the user in the cafeteria, or his laptop, may not be fast enough to simultaneously send updates to ten other people who may be in the virtual room. If other users are connected e.g. directly to the campus network, over a wire, it may be desirable to arrange it so that the wireless user publishes updates to a user on a campus LAN, which is then responsible for *forwarding* it to the others. If the campus LAN is configured to enable IP multicast, it would be desirable to be able to exploit such *external mechanisms*. The users should thus be able to quickly form small overlays that can efficiently utilize whatever resources are available.

Finally, note that users will often reside in different administrative domains, e.g. in a cafeteria wireless network, in different campus networks, on a cable LAN etc. The administrators of these domains may need to impose acceptable use policies that specify how dissemination should be performed internally in the domain they own. For example, one domain might disallow IP multicast, while another might permit IP multicast provided that various rules are respected. Policies could govern sharing of connections, what data rates are acceptable, what multicast protocol to use etc.

Different domains will often have distinct administrative policies. And yet, users residing in those domains would expect a smooth operation, as if the entire Internet formed a single, fully-connected administrative domain. Such *management* issues are a logistic headache, and require better *interoperability* standards. An update published by the user in the cafeteria should be disseminated in every campus network, or among wireless users, locally according to the local policies setup by the domain administrators, but all these domains need to cooperate with each other, ideally without reliance on costly *proxies*. Existing eventing standards have overlooked such issues, but they form the core of our proposal.

Design Principles

The limitations of the existing architectures, listed in section "Motivation", and our experience in designing scalable multicast systems, led us to the following design principles:

- *Programmable nodes*. Senders and recipients should not be limited to sending or receiving. They should be able to perform certain basic operations on data streams, such as forwarding or annotating data with information to be used by other peers, in support of local *forwarding policies*. The latter must be expressive enough to support protocols used in today's content delivery networks, such as overlay trees, rings, mesh structures, gossip, link multiplexing, or delivery along redundant paths.
- *External control*. Forwarding policies used by subscribers must be selected and updated in a consistent manner. A node cannot predict a-priori what policy to use, or which other nodes to peer with; it must thus permit an external trusted entity or an agreement protocol to control it: determine the protocol it follows, install rules for message forwarding or filtering etc.
- *Channel negotiation*. The creation of communication channels should permit a handshake. A recipient might be requested to e.g. join an IP multicast address, or subscribe to an external system. The recipient could also make configuration decisions on the basis of the information about the sender. For example, a LAN domain asked to create a communication endpoint for receiving could select a well-provisioned node as its entry point to handle the anticipated load.
- *Managed channels*. Communication channels should be modeled as *contracts* in which receivers have a degree of control over the way the senders are transmitting. In self-organizing systems, reconfiguration triggered by churn is common and communication channels often need to be reopened or updated to adapt to the changing topology, traffic patterns or capacities. For example, a channel that previously requested that a given source transmits messages to one node may notify the source that messages should now be transmitted to some two other nodes.
- *Hierarchical structure*. The principles listed above should apply to not just individual nodes, but also to entire administrative domains, such as LANs, data centers or corporate networks. This allows the definition and enforcement of Internet-scale forwarding policies, facilitating cooperation among organizations in maintaining the global infrastructure. The way messages are delivered to subscribers across

Figure 4. A hierarchical decomposition of the set of subscribers along the domain boundaries

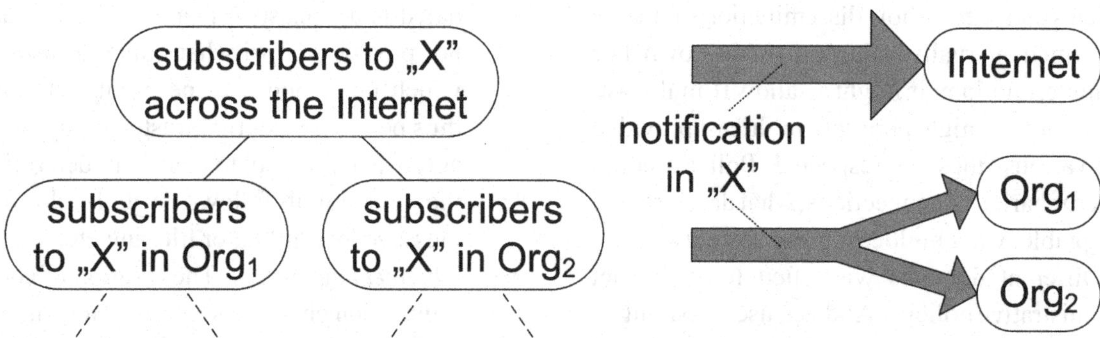

the Internet thus reflects policies defined at various levels (for example, policies "internal" to data centers, and a global policy "across" all data centers).

- *Isolation and local autonomy.* A degree of a local autonomy of the individual administrative domains should be preserved; such as how messages are forwarded internally, which nodes are used to receive incoming traffic or relay data to other domains etc. In essence, the internal structure of an administrative domain should be hidden from other domains it is peering with and from the higher layers. Likewise, the details of the subcomponents of a domain should be as opaque to it as possible.
- *Reusability.* It should be possible to specify a policy for message forwarding or loss recovery in a standard way and post it into an online library of such policies as a contribution to the community. Administrators willing to deploy a given policy within their administrative domain should be able to do so in a simple way, e.g. by drag-and-drop, within a suitable GUI.
- *Separation of concerns.* Motivated by the end-to-end principle, we separate implementation of loss recovery and other reliability properties from the unreliable dissemination of messages, as well as from message ordering, security, and subscription management. Accordingly, our design includes *reliability*, *dissemination*, *ordering*, *security*, and *management* frameworks: five independent, yet complementary structures. This decoupling gives our system an elegant structure and a degree of modularity and flexibility unseen in existing architectures.

Hierarchical View of the Network

A group X of subscribers for a given topic across the entire Internet can be divided into subsets Y_1, Y_2,.. ., Y_N of subscribers in N top-level administrative domains (Figure 4).

This may continue recursively, leading to a hierarchical perspective on the group X. Hierarchies of this sort have been previously exploited in scalable multicast protocols, e.g. in RMTP (Paul et al., 1997), or in the context of content-based filtering (Banavar et al, 1999). The underlying principle, implicit in many scalable protocols, is to exploit locality. Following this principle, sets of nodes, clustered based on proximity or interest, cooperate semi-autonomously in message routing and forwarding, loss recovery, managing membership and subscriptions, failure detection etc. Each such set is treated as a single cell within a larger infrastructure. A protocol running at a global level connects all cells into a single structure. Scalability arises as in the *divide-and-conquer* principle. Additionally, the cells can locally share workload and amortize dissemination or control overheads, e.g. buffer messages from different sources and locally disseminate such combined bundles etc.

In the architecture described here we go one step further. Following our principle of *isolation* and *local autonomy*, each administrative domain should manage the registration of its own publishers and subscribers internally, and it should be able to decide how to distribute messages among them or how to perform loss recovery according to its local policy. Unlike in most hierarchical systems, where hierarchy and protocol are inseparable, and hence the "sub-protocols" used at all levels of the hierarchy are identical, in our architecture we decouple the creation of the hierarchy from the specific "sub-protocols" used at different levels of the hierarchy and we allow the "sub-protocols" to differ. Thus for example, our architecture permits the creation of a single, global dissemination scheme for a topic that uses different mechanisms to distribute data in different organizations or data centers. Likewise, it permits the creation of a single Internet-scale loss recovery scheme that employs different recovery policies within different administrative domains. Previously, this has only been possible with proxies, which can be costly, and which introduce latency and bottleneck. In this paper, we propose a way to do this efficiently, and in a very generic, flexible manner. This novel hierarchical protocol "composition" approach, motivated by the principles of locality and local autonomy, is central to our architecture (Figure 5).

ARCHITECTURE

The Hierarchy of Scopes

Our architecture is organized around the following key concepts: *management scope, forwarding policy, channel, filter, session, recovery protocol, recovery domain,* and *agent.*

Figure 5. Multiple local multicast protocols combined into an Internet-wide structure. The local protocols disseminate data and perform loss recovery locally within the respective organizations, using different techniques and leveraging different types of hardware support, e.g. by organizing nodes into a token ring, a star topology, or by using IP multicast. A cross-organization protocol then coordinates the work performed by these local protocols, relays data and performs recovery across organizations, to ensure that every message is reliably disseminated across the Internet

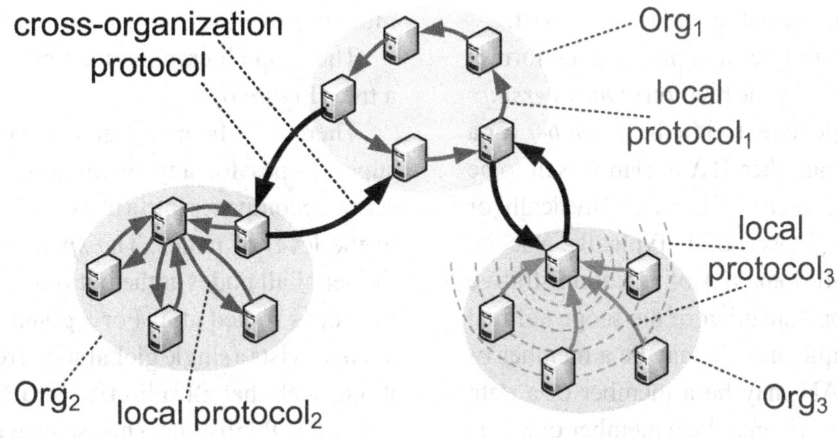

A ***management scope*** (or simply *scope*) represents a set of jointly managed nodes. It may include a single node, span over a set of nodes residing within a certain administrative domain, or include nodes clustered based on other criteria, such as common interest. In the extreme, a scope may span across the entire Internet. We do not assume a 1-to-1 correspondence between administrative domains and the scopes defined based on such domains, but that will often be the case. A LAN scope (or just a LAN) will refer to a scope spanning all nodes residing within a LAN. The reader might find it easier to understand our design with such examples in mind.

A scope is not just *any* group of nodes; the assumption that they are *jointly managed* is essential. The existence of a scope is dependent upon the existence of an infrastructure that maintains its membership and administers it. For a scope that corresponds to a LAN, this could be a server managing all local nodes. In a domain that spans several data centers in an organization, it could be a management infrastructure, with a server in the company headquarters indirectly managing the network via subordinate servers residing in every data center. No such global infrastructure or administrative authority exists for the Internet, but organizations could provide servers to control the Internet scope in support of their own publishers or to manage the distribution of messages in topics of importance to them. Many global scopes, independently managed, could thus co-exist.

Like administrative domains, scopes form a hierarchy, defined by the relation of *membership*: one scope may declare itself to be a *member* (or a "*sub-scope*") of another. If *X* declares itself to be a member of *Y*, it means *X* is either physically or logically a part (subset) of *Y*. Typically, a scope defined for a sub-domain *X* of an administrative domain *Y* will be a member of the scope defined for *Y*. For example, a node may be a member of a LAN. The LAN may be a member of a data center, which in turn may be a member of a corporate network. A node may also be a member of a scope of an overlay network. For a data center, two scopes may be defined, e.g. *monitoring* and *control* scopes, both covering the entire data center, with some LANs being a part of one scope, or the other, or both. The corporate scope may be a member of several Internet-wide scopes etc.

The generality in these definitions allows us to model various special cases, such as clustering of nodes based on interest or other factors. Such clusters, formed e.g. by a server managing a LAN and based on node subscription patterns, could also be treated as (virtual) scopes, all managed by the same server. Nodes would thus be members of clusters, and clusters (not nodes) would be members of the LAN. As we shall explain below, every such cluster, as a separate scope, could be locally and independently managed. For example, suppose that we are building an event notification system that needs to disseminate events reliably, and is implemented by an unreliable multicast mechanism coupled to a reliability layer that recovers lost packets. In the proposed architecture, different clusters could run different multicast or loss recovery protocols; this technique is used in the QSM platform (Ostrowski & Birman, 2006b, 2006c). Thus, if one cluster happens to reside within a LAN that permits the use of IP multicast, it could use that technology, while a different cluster on a network that prohibits IP multicast, or consisting of a large number of nodes across the Internet, could instead form an end-to-end multicast overlay.

The scope hierarchy need not necessarily be a tree (Figure 6).

There may be many global scopes, or many super-scopes for any given scope. However, a scope decomposes into a tree of sub-scopes, down to the level of nodes. The *span of a scope X* is the set of all nodes at the bottom of the hierarchy of scopes rooted at *X*. For a given topic *X*, there always exists a single global scope responsible for it, i.e. such that all subscribers to *X* reside in the span of *X*. Publishing a message to a topic is thus always equivalent to delivering it to all subscribers

Figure 6. An example hierarchy of management scopes in a game

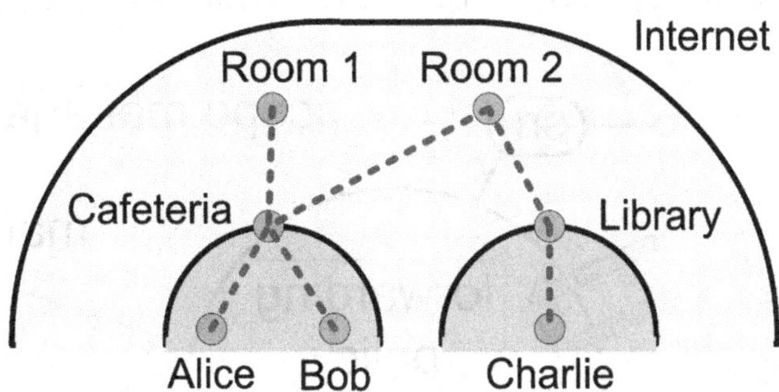

in the span of some global scope, which may be further recursively decomposed into the sets of subscribers in the spans of its sub-scopes.

Suppose that Alice and Bob are sitting with their laptops in a cafeteria, while Charlie is in a library. Both the cafeteria's wireless network and the local network in the library are separately managed administrative domains, and they define their own *management scopes*. Alice's and Bob's laptops are also *scopes*, both of which become members of the cafeteria's scope. Now suppose that Alice opens her virtual realities browser and enters a virtual place "Room1" in the virtual reality, while Bob and Charlie enter "Room2". Each of the virtual rooms defines a global, internet-wide scope that could be thought of as "the scope of all users in this room, wherever they are". If the networking support for Alice and Bob is still provided by the cafeteria and library wireless networks respectively, when the students enter the rooms, the cafeteria's and library's scopes become *members* of these global scopes (Figure 6).

The Anatomy of a Scope

The infrastructure component administering a scope is referred to as a ***scope manager*** (SM). A single SM may control multiple scopes. It may be hosted on a single node, or distributed over a set of nodes, and it may reside outside of the scope it controls. It exposes a *control interface*, a web service hosted at a well-known address, to dispatch control requests (e.g. "subscribe") directed to the scopes it controls (Figure 7).

A scope maintains ***communication channels*** for use by other scopes. A *channel* is a mechanism through which a message can be delivered to all those nodes in the span of this scope that subscribed to any of a certain set of topics. In a scope spanning a single node, a channel may be just an address/protocol pair; creating it would mean arranging for a local process to open a socket. In a distributed scope, a channel could be an IP multicast address; creating it would require all local nodes to listen at this address. It could also be a list of addresses, if messages are to be delivered to all of them, or if addresses are to be used in a random or a round-robin fashion. In an overlay network, for example, a channel could lead to a small set of nodes that forward messages across the entire overlay. In general, a scope that spans a set of nodes can thus be governed by a ***forwarding policy*** that determines how messages originating within the scope, or arriving through some communication channel, are disseminated internally, within the local scope.

Continuing our example, the cafeteria and the library would host the managers of their scopes on dedicated servers, and each of the student laptops would run a local service that serves as a scope manager for the local machine. The library's SM may be on a campus network with IP multicast enabled. When the cafeteria's SM requests a channel from the library's SM, the latter might

Figure 7. A scope is controlled by a scope manager, which exposes a standardized control interface, and may create a number of incoming data channels, to serve as "entry points" for the scope

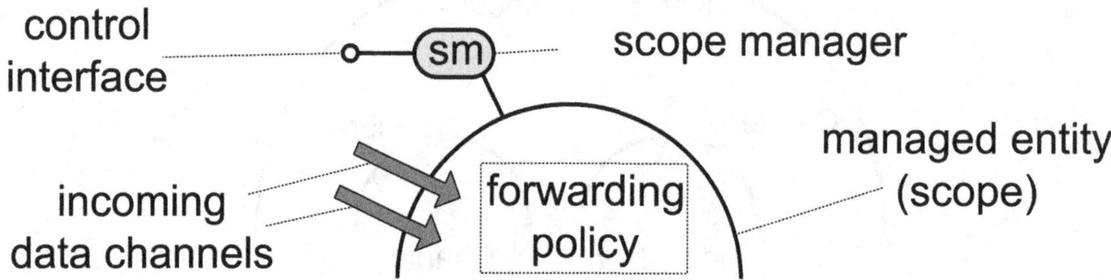

e.g. dedicate some machine as the entry point for all messages coming from the cafeteria, instruct it to retransmit these messages to the IP multicast address, and instruct all other laptops to join the IP multicast address. Similarly, the cafeteria's SM might setup a local forwarding tree. In most settings, a scope manager would live on a dedicated server. It is also conceivable to offload, in certain scenarios, parts of the SM's functionality to nodes currently in the scope (e.g. to Alice's and Bob's laptops), but a single "point of contact" for the scope would still need to exist.

The control interfaces "exposed" by scopes (interfaces exposed by their scope managers) are "accessed" by other scopes (i.e. by their SMs). When interacting, scopes can play one of a few standard roles, corresponding to the three principal interaction patterns: *member-owner*, *sender-receiver*, and *client-host* (Figure 8, left).

A *member* registers with an *owner* to establish a relation of *membership*, i.e. to "declare" itself as a sub-scope of the owner (Figure 8, right). After such a relationship has been established, the member may then register with the owner as a publisher or subscriber in one or more topics. Depending on the topics for which the member has registered and its role in these topics, it may be requested by the owner to perform relevant actions, e.g. by forwarding messages or participating in the construction of an overlay structure. At the same time, the owner is responsible for tracking the health of its members, and in particular for detecting failures and performing local reconfiguration.

The *client-host* relationship is similar to *member-owner*, in that a *client* can register with a *host* as a publisher or as a subscriber (Figure 9, right). However, unlike the *member-owner* relationship, which involves a mutual commit-

Figure 8. When interacting, scopes follow one of three standardized relationship patterns, in which they can play one of the standard roles. One of these includes a member-owner relationship

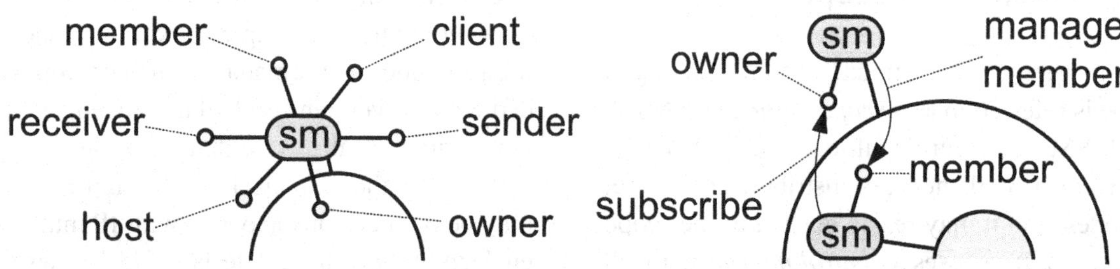

ment, the *client-host* relationship is more casual, in the sense that the host cannot rely on the client to perform any tasks for the system, or even to notify the host when it leaves, and similarly, the client cannot rely on the host to provide it with the same quality of service and reliability properties as the regular members. Thus for example, while a member can form a part of a forwarding tree, a client will not; the latter will also typically get weaker reliability guarantees, because the protocols run by the scope members will not be prevented from making progress when transient clients are unreachable. The same applies to publishers. A long-term publisher that forms a part of a corporate infrastructure will register as a member, but handheld devices roaming on a wireless network will usually register as clients.

The *sender-receiver* relationship is similar to a publisher registering as a client or member, in that the *sender* registers with the *receiver* to send data (Figure 9, left). However, whereas a *member* registers with its *owner* to publish to the set of all subscribers in a topic, including nodes inside as well as nodes outside of the *owner*, a *sender* will register with a *receiver* to establish a communication channel between the two to disseminate messages only within the scope of the receiver. When a publisher registers as a member with an owner scope that is not the global scope for the given topic, the owner may itself be forced to subscribe with its super-scope. The sender-receiver relationship is horizontal; no cascading subscriptions take place. On the other hand, while a member scope never exchanges data with the owner (instead, it is "told" by the owner to form part of a dissemination structure that the owner controls), the sender-receiver relationship serves exactly this purpose; the two parties involved in the latter will negotiate protocols, addresses, transmission rates etc.

The reader should recognize in our construction the design principles we articulated earlier. Scopes, whether individual nodes, LANs or overlays, are *externally controlled* using the control interfaces exposed by SMs, may be *programmed* with policies that govern the way messages are distributed internally, forwarded to other scopes etc., and transmit messages via *managed* communication channels, established through a dialogue between a pair of SMs, and dynamically reconfigured.

Hierarchical Composition of Policies

Following our design principles, we propose to solve the issue of a large-scale global cooperation in message delivery between independently managed administrative domains by introducing a hierarchical structure, in which forwarding policies defined at various levels are merged into a single dissemination scheme. Each scope is configured with a policy dictating, on a per-topic (and perhaps a per-sender) basis, how messages are forwarded among its members. For example, a policy governing a global scope might determine

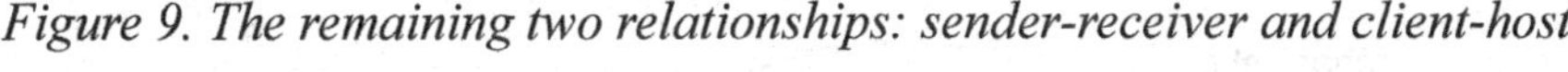
Figure 9. The remaining two relationships: sender-receiver and client-host

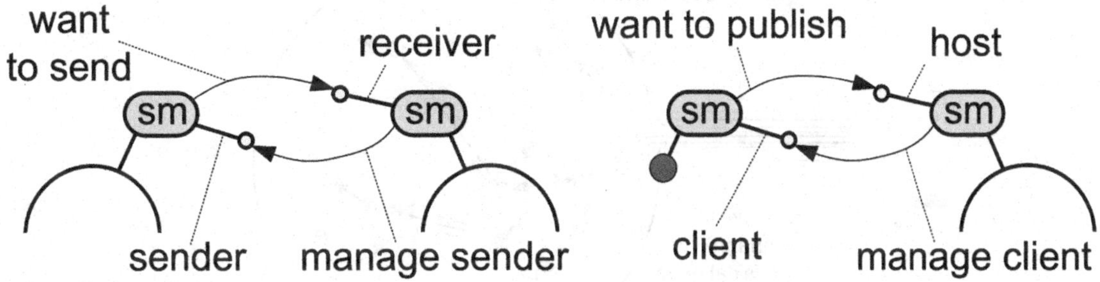

how messages in topic *T*, originating in a corporate network *X*, are forwarded between the various organizations. A policy of a scope of the given organization's network might determine how to forward messages among its data centers, and so forth. A policy defined for a particular scope *X* is always defined at the granularity of *X*'s members (not individual nodes). The way a given sub-scope *Y* of *X* delivers messages internally is a decision made autonomously by *Y*. Similarly, *X*'s policy may specify that *Y* should forward messages to *Z*, but it is up to *Y*'s policy to determine how to perform this task.

Accordingly, a global policy may request that organization *X* forward messages in topic *T* to organizations *Y* and *Z*. A policy governing *X* may then determine that to distribute messages in *X*, they must be sent to LAN_1, which will forward them to LAN_2. The same policy might also specify which LANs within *X* should forward to *Y* and *Z*, and finally, the policies of these LANs will delegate these forwarding tasks to individual nodes they own. When all the policies defined at all the involved scopes are combined together, they yield a global *forwarding structure* that completely determines the way messages are disseminated (Figure 10).

In the examples above, the forwarding policies are simply graphs of connections: each message is always forwarded along every channel. In general, however, a channel could be constrained with a ***filter*** that decides, on a per-message basis, whether to forward or not, and may optionally tag the message with custom attributes (more details are in section "Communication Channels"). This allows us to express many popular techniques, e.g. using redundant paths, multiplexing between dissemination trees etc.

Every scope manager maintains a mapping from topics to their forwarding policies. A ***forwarding policy*** is defined as an object that lives in an *abstract context*, and that exposes a fixed set of *events* to which members must be prepared to react, and the *operations* and *attributes*. A scope manager might be thought of as a *container* for objects representing *policies*. The interfaces that the container and the policies expose to each other and interact with are standardized, and may include, for example, an event informing the policy that a new member has been added to the set of members locally subscribed to the topic, or an operation exposed by the container that allows the policy to request a member to establish a channel to another member and instantiate a given type of filter (Figure 11).

A scope manger thus provides a *runtime environment* in which policies can be hosted. This allows policies to be defined in a standard way, independent not only of the platform, but also of the type of the administrative domain. For example, one can imagine a policy that uses some sort of a novel mesh-like forwarding structure

Figure 10. Channels created in support of forwarding policies defined at different levels

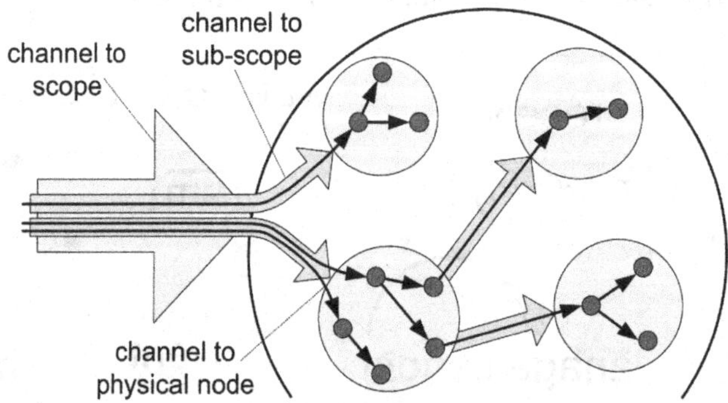

Figure 11. A forwarding policy as a code snippet

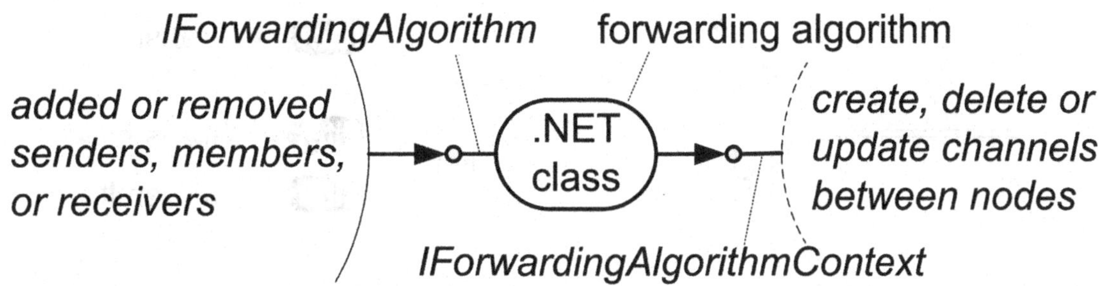

with a sophisticated adaptive flow and rate control algorithm. Our architecture would allow that policy to be deployed, without any modifications, in the context of a LAN, data center, corporate network, or a global scope. In effect we've separated the policy from the details of how it should be implemented in a particular domain. Policies may be implemented in any language, expose and consume web service APIs, stored online in *protocol libraries*, downloaded as needed, and executed in a secure manner.

Graphs of connections for different topics, generated by their respective policies, are superimposed (Figure 12).

The SM of the scope maintains an aggregate structure of channels and filters, and issues requests to the SMs of its members to create channels, instantiate filters etc. If multiple policies request channels between the same pair of nodes, the SM will not create multiple channels, but rather a single channel, for multiple topics. To avoid the situation where every member talks to every other member, the SM may use a single forwarding policy for multiple topics, to ensure that channels created for different topics overlap.

Communication Channels

Consider a node *X*, which is a member of a scope *Y* that, based on a forwarding policy at *Y*, has been requested to create a communication channel to scope *Z* to forward messages in topic *T*. Following the protocol, *X* asks the SM of *Z* for the specification of the channel to *Z* that should be used for messages in topic *T*. The SM of *Z* might respond with an address/protocol pair that *X* should use to send over this channel. Alternatively, a forwarding policy defined for *T* at scope *Z* may dictate that, in order to send to *Z* in topic *T*, scope *X* should establish channels to members *A* and *B* of *Z*, constrained with filters α and β. After *X* learns this from the SM of *Z*, it contacts SMs of *A* and *B* for further details. Notice that the channel to *Z* decomposes into sub-channels to *A*

Figure 12. Forwarding graphs for different topics are superimposed. Two members may be linked by multiple channels, each with a different filter

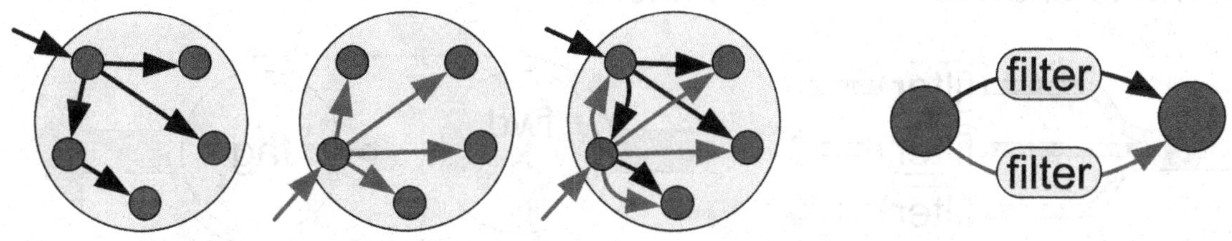

Figure 13. A channel split into sub-channels and a possible filter tree corresponding to it

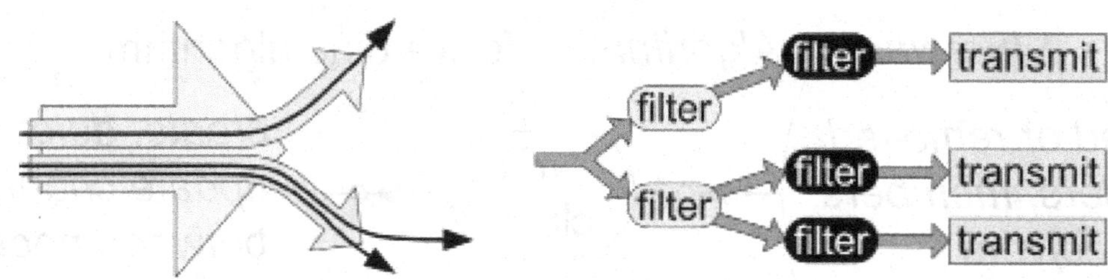

and B through a policy at a target scope Z. This procedure will continue hierarchically, until the point when X is left with a tree with filters in the internal nodes and address and protocol pairs at the leaves (Figure 13).

Now, to send a message along a channel constructed in this way, X executes filters, starting from the root, to determine recursively which sub-channels to use, proceeding until it is left with just a list of address / protocol pairs, and then transmits the message. Filters will usually be simple, such as modulo-n; hence X can perform this procedure very efficiently. Indeed, with network cards becoming increasingly powerful and easily programmable (Weinsberg et al., 2006), such functionality might even be offloaded to hardware.

Accordingly, to support the hierarchical composition of policies described in the preceding section, we define a **channel** as one of the following: an address/protocol pair, a reference to an external multicast mechanism, or a set of sub-channels accompanied by filters. In the latter

Figure 14. A channel may be an address / protocol pair (left), or it may consist of sub-channels, with an algorithm deciding what goes where (right)

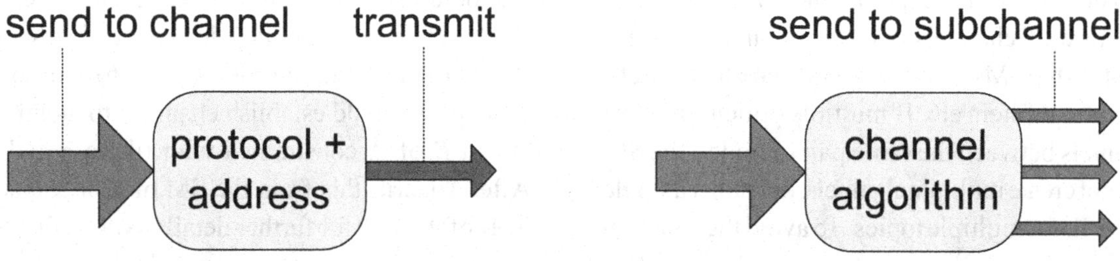

Figure 15. Channel algorithms are realized as sets of filters, one per subchannel, deciding whether to forward, and optionally adding custom tags

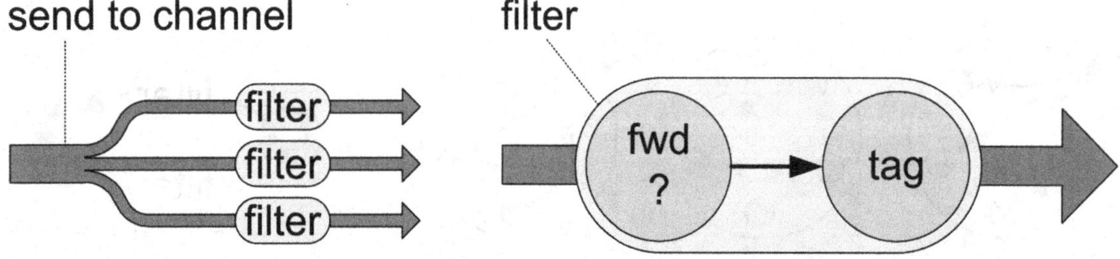

case, the filters jointly implement a multiplexing scheme that determines which sub-channels to use for sending, on a per-message basis (Figure 14, Figure 15).

Consider now the situation where scope *X*, spanning a set of nodes, has been requested to create a channel to scope *Y*. Through a dialogue with *Y* and its sub-scopes, *X* can obtain a detailed channel definition, but unlike in prior examples, *X* now spans a *set of nodes*, and as such, it cannot *execute* filters or *send* messages. To address this issue, we now propose two simple, generic techniques: *delegation* and *replication* (Figure 16).

Both of them rely on the fact that if *X* receives messages in a topic *T*, then some of its members, *Z*, must also receive them (for otherwise *X* would not declare itself as a subscriber and it would not be made part of the forwarding structure for topic *T* by *X*'s super-scope). In case of *delegation*, *X* requests such a sub-scope *Z* to create the channel on behalf of *X*, essentially "delegating" the entire channel to its member. The problem can be recursively delegated, down to the level where a single physical node is requested to create the channel, and to forward messages it receives along the channel. A more sophisticated use of delegation would be for *X* to delegate sub-channels. In such case, *X* would first contact *Y* to obtain the list of sub-channels and the corresponding filters, and for each of these sub-channels, delegate it to its sub-scopes. In any case, *X* delegates the responsibility for forwarding over a channel to its sub-scopes.

Our approach is flexible enough to support even more sophisticated policies. An example of one such policy is a *replication* strategy, outlined here. In this scheme, scope *X* could request that *n* of its sub-scopes create the needed channel, constraining each with a modulo-*n* filter based on a message sequence number. Hence, while each of the sub-scopes would create the same channel on behalf of its parent scope (hence the name "replication"), sub-scope *k* would only forward messages with numbers *m* such that *m* mod *n* equals *k*. By doing this, *X* effectively implements a round-robin policy of the sort proposed in protocols such as MIT's SplitStream. Although all sub-scopes would create the same channel, the round-robin filtering policy would ensure that every message is forwarded only by one of them. This technique could be useful e.g. in the cases where the volume of data in a topic is so high that delegation to a single sub-scope is simply not feasible.

Our point is not that this particular way of decomposing functionality should be required of all protocols, but rather that for an architecture to be powerful enough and flexible enough to be used with today's cutting-edge protocols and to support state-of-the-art technologies, it needs to be flexible enough to accommodate even these kinds of "fancy" behaviors. Our proposed architecture can do so. The existing standards proposals, in

Figure 16. A distributed scope may delegate a channel or some of its sub-channels to its members, or it may replicate the channel among members, with filters that jointly implement a round-robin policy etc

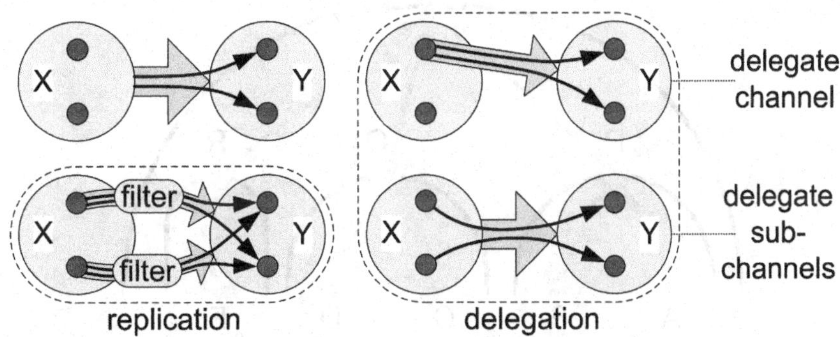

contrast, are incredibly constraining. Each only accommodates a single rather narrowly conceived style of event notification system.

Constructing the Dissemination Structure

A detailed discussion of how forwarding policies can be defined and translated to filter networks is beyond the scope of this paper. We describe here just one simple, yet fairly expressive scheme.

Suppose that the forwarding policies in all scopes define forwarding trees on a per-topic basis and possibly also depending on the location at which the message locally originated. By saying that a message *locally originated from* a member *X* of scope *Y*, we mean that either the message was created by *X* (if *X* is itself a node) or a member of *X*, or that the message was created outside of *Y*, but *X* is (or contains) the first node in all of *Y* to which the message was forwarded. The technique described here implicitly assumes that messages do not arrive along redundant paths, i.e. that the forwarding policy at each level is a tree, not a mesh. This scheme may be extended to cover the more general case with redundant paths and randomized policies, but we omit it here, for it would unnecessarily complicate our example. A comprehensive treatment of dissemination policies is beyond the scope of this paper.

A scope manager thus maintains a graph, in which the scope members are linked by edges, labeled with constraints such as β:*X*, μ:*Y*, ..., meaning that a message is forwarded along the edge if it was sent in topic β and locally originates at *X*, or if it was sent in topic μ and locally originates at *Y*, and so on. We shall now describe, using a simple example, how a structure of channels is established based on scope policies, and how filters are instantiated. We shall then explain how messages are routed.

Consider the structure of scopes depicted on Figure 17.

Here *A*, *B*, *C*, *D*, and *E* are student laptops. *P*, *Q*, and *R* are three departments on a campus, with independent networks, hence they are separate scopes. *X* represents the entire campus. All students subscribe to topic *T*. Topic *T* is local to the campus, and *X* serves as its root. The scopes first register with each other. Then, the laptops send requests to subscribe for topics to *P*, *Q* and *R*. Laptop *A* requests the publisher role, all others request to be subscribers. None of *P*, *Q* or *R* are roots for the topic, hence they themselves subscribe for topic *T* with *X*, in a cascading manner. Now, all scopes involved create objects that represent local forwarding policies for topic *T*, and feed these objects with the "new member" events. The policy at *P* for messages in *T* originating at *A* creates a channel from *A* to *B*. Similarly, the policy at *X* for

Figure 17. An example hierarchy of scopes with cascading subscriptions

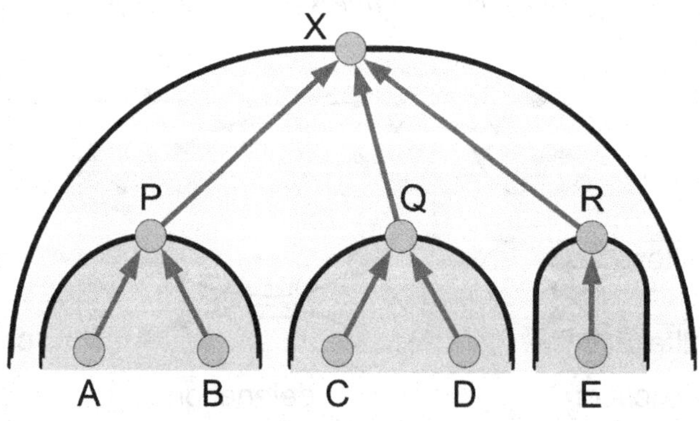

messages in *T* originating at *P* creates channels *P* to *Q* and *Q* to *R* (Figure 18).

Each channel has a label of the form "*X-Y, T:Z*", meaning that it is a channel from *X* to *Y,* for messages in *T* originating at *Z.* Note that no channels have been created in scope *Q*. Until now, *Q* is not aware of any message sources because neither *C* nor *D* is a publisher, and because no other scope has so far requested a channel to *Q*, hence there is no need to forward anything. Channels are now delegated to individual nodes, as described in section "Communication Channels". *P* delegates its channel to *B,* and *Q* delegates to *D* (Figure 19).

Channel labels are extended to reflect the fact that they have been delegated, e.g. *P-Q* becomes *P:B-Q*, which means that *P* has delegated its source endpoint to its member *B,* etc. At this point, *B* and *D* contact the destinations *Q* and R, and request the channels to be created. *Q* and *R* select *C* and *E* as their *entry points* for these channels. Now *Q* also has a local source of messages (node *C,* the entry point), so now it also creates an instance of a forwarding policy, which determines that messages in *T,* locally originating at *C,* are forwarded to *D* (Figure 20).

The entire forwarding structure is complete. A message in transit is a tuple of the form (*T, k, r*),

Figure 18. Channels created by the policies based on subscriptions

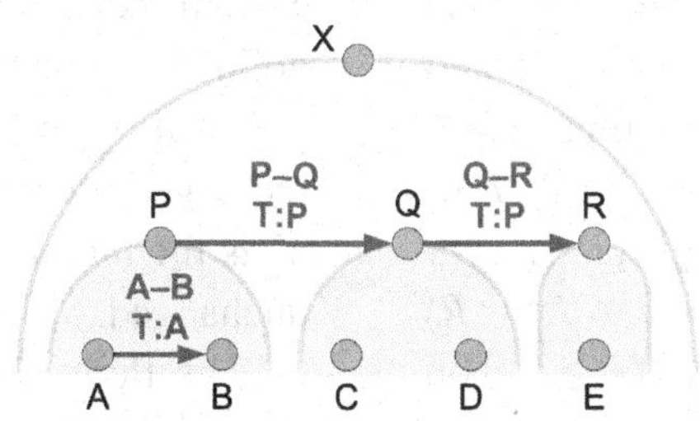

Figure 19. Channels are delegated

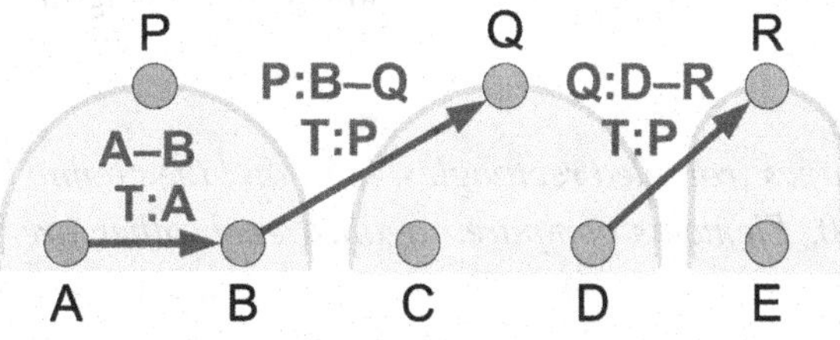

Figure 20. ***B*** *and D contact Q and R to create channels. Q and R select C and E as entry points. Q now has a local message source and creates its own local channel, from C do D*

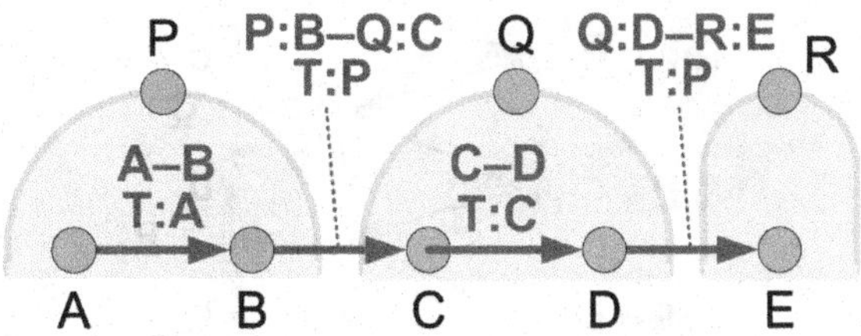

where T is the topic, k is the identifier that may include the source name, one or more sequence numbers etc., and R is a *routing record*. The routing record is an object of the form $((X_K–Y_K), (X_{(K-1)}–Y_{(K-1)}), \ldots, (X_1–Y_1))$, in which every pair of elements (X_i, Y_i) represents the state of dissemination in one scope; X_i is the member of the scope that the message locally originated from and Y_i is the member of the scope that the message is moving inside of or that it is entering. Pair (X_1, Y_1) represents individual nodes, and for each i, scopes X_i and Y_i are a level below X_{i+1} and Y_{i+1}, respectively, and Y_i is always a member of Y_{i+1}. This list of entries does not need to "extend" all the way up to the root. If entries at a certain level are missing, they will be filled up when the message jumps across scopes, as it is explained below.

When a message arrives at a node, the node iterates over all of its outgoing channels, and matches channel filters against the routing record. Message $(T, k, ((X_K–Y_K), (X_{(K-1)}–Y_{(K-1)}), \ldots, (X_1–Y_1)))$ matches channel $(P_L{:}P_{L-1}{:}\ldots{:}P_1 – Q_L{:}Q_{L-1}{:}\ldots{:}Q_1, T{:}R)$ when $(K \geq L \wedge X_L = R \vee K < L \wedge P_L = R)$ holds. This condition has two parts. If $K \geq L$, then in the scope in which the channel endpoints P_L, Q_L and R are members, the message originated at X_L and is currently at Y_L. According to our rules, the message should be forwarded iff $X_L = R$ (and $Y_L = P_L$, but this is always true). If $K < L$, then the routing record does not carry any state for the scope at which P_L, Q_L and R are members. This means the message must have originated in this scope (the recovery record is filled up when the message is forwarded, as explained below), hence the condition $P_L = R$. Note that there might be several channels originating at the node; the message is forwarded across each one it matches. Now, when the message is forwarded, its routing record is modified as follows. First, the record is extended. If $K < L$, then for each i such that $i > K$ and $i \leq L$, we set $X_i = P_i$ and $Y_i = P_i$. Then, the details internal to the scope that the channel is leaving are replaced with the details internal to the scope the channel is entering, so for each i such that $i < L$, we set $X_i = Q_i$ and $Y_i = Q_i$. Finally, the current scope at the level at which the channel is defined is updated, we set $Y_L = Q_L$. The original value of X_L, once set, is not changed until the message is forwarded out of the scope of which X_L is the member. Entries for $i > L$ also remain unchanged.

The flow of messages and matching in the example of Figure 20 is shown on Figure 21.

When created on the publisher A, the message initially has a routing record $A–A$, since we know that it originated locally at A and that it is

Figure 21. The flow of messages (rounded rectangles, left), and the channels (square rectangles, right) in the scenario of Figure 20. Elements compared against each other are shown as black, bold, and underlined

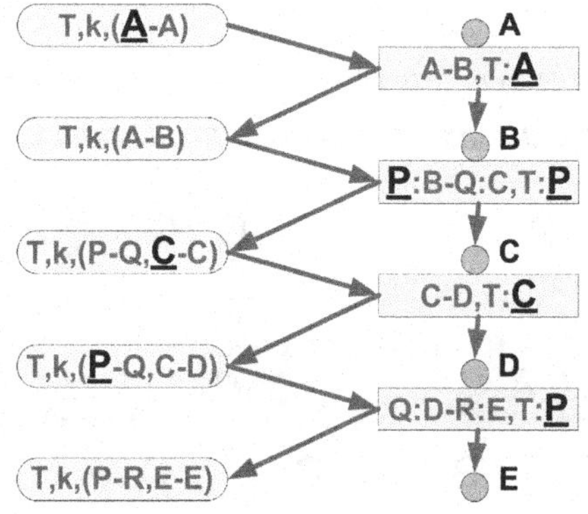

still at *A*. No entries are included at this point for routing in the scopes above *A*. There is no need for doing so since no routing has been done so far at those higher levels, so there is no state to maintain. Now the routing record is compared against channel *A-B, T:A*. The local origin *A* does match the channel's constraint *A*, so the message is forwarded along *A-B*, with a new record *A-B* to reflect the fact that it is now entering *B*. While matching this record to channel *P:B–Q:C* at *B*, we find that the record lacks routing information for the scope at which this channel is defined. This means that the message must have originated at the channel's source endpoint (which we know is *P* from the channel's description). We find that the channel's constraint *P* is the same as the channel's source endpoint *P*, so we again forward the message. While doing so, we extend its routing record with a new entry *P-Q* to record the fact that we made progress at this higher level. We also replace information local to *P* (the entry *A-B*) with new information local to *Q* (the new entry *C-C*). Forwarding at *C* and *D* works similarly to how it worked on *A* and *B*.

The Local Architecture of a Dissemination Scope

So far we focused in our description on peer-to-peer aspects of the dissemination framework, but we have not described how applications use this infrastructure, and how leaf scopes are internally organized. Of a number of possible architectures of the leaf scopes, the most general one involves the following components: ***scope manager***, *local controller*, and *controlled element* (Figure 22).

The *controlled element* is a very thin layer that resides in the application process. Its purpose is to serve as a hookup to the application process that allows for controlling the way the application communicates over the network. As such, it serves two principal purposes: (a) passing to the local controller requests to subscribe/unsubscribe, and (b) opening send and receive sockets in the process per request from the controller. The controlled element does not forward messages, nor does it include any other peer-to-peer functionality, and it is not a part of the management network. This simplicity allows it to be easily incorporated into legacy applications. It can be implemented in any way, for as long as it exposes a *control endpoint*,

Figure 22. The architecture of a leaf scope in the most general scenario, with a local scope manager, a thin controlled element linked to the application, and with a local controller to handle peer-to-peer aspects, e.g. forwarding

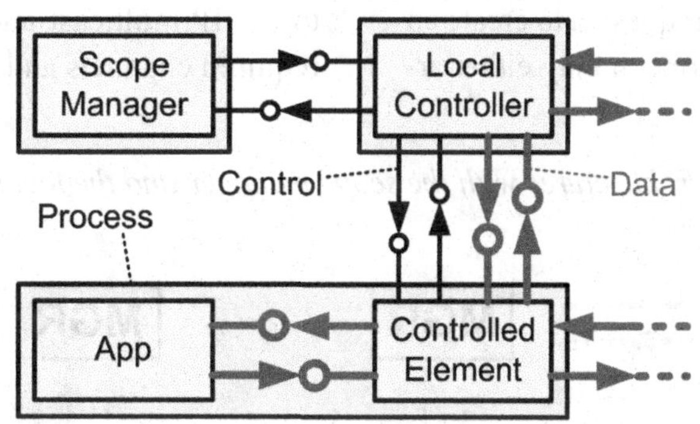

a standardized web service interface, and as long as it can create *communication endpoints* (thick, red) to receive or connect to remote endpoints to send. The local controller implements all the peer-to-peer functionality such as forwarding etc., and hosts such elements as channels or filters. It may also create communication endpoints, and may send data to or receive it from the controlled element. The controller is not a part of the management network, and it does not interact with any scope mangers besides the local one. These interactions are the job of the local SM, which, on the other hand, never sends or receives itself any messages.

In general, the three components can live in separate processes, or even physically on different machines, and may communicate over local sockets or over the network. However, in the typical scenario, the scope manager and local controllers are located in a single process ("manager"). The manager runs as a system service and may control multiple applications, either local or running on subordinate devices managed by the local node, through the control elements embedded in these applications. Within this scenario, we can distinguish three basic sub-scenarios, or three patterns of usage (Figure 23), depending on whether applications participate in sending or receiving directly, or only through the manager.

In the first scenario, the applications only receive data, directly from the network (Figure 23, left). When the manager is requested to create an incoming channel to the scope, it may either arrange for all applications to open the same socket to receive messages directly from the network (if the applications are all hosted one the same machine), or it may make them all subscribe to the same IP multicast address (if they are running on multiple subordinate devices), or it may have them create multiple endpoints, in which case the definition of the local channel endpoint will include a set of addresses rather than just one. The manager does not sit on the critical path; hence we avoid bottleneck and latency. If the local scope is required to forward data to other scopes, the manager also creates an endpoint (opens the same socket, or extends the receive channel endpoint definition to include its own address), to receive the data that needs to be forwarded.

In our example, the library's server might act as a leaf scope, and students' laptops might act as subordinate devices that do not host their own local scope managers and do not forward messages. Applications on the laptops would have the embedded controlled elements that communicate with the local controller on the library server via a standard web interface. When students subscribe to a local topic, such as an online lecture transmitted by another department, the server chooses an IP multicast address and has all the laptops subscribe to it. The data arriving on the local network is received by all devices without any intermediary. If the library needs to forward messages, the server also subscribes to the IP multicast address and creates all the required channels and filters.

Figure 23. Three example architectures with the scope manager and the local controller merged into a single local system "daemon"

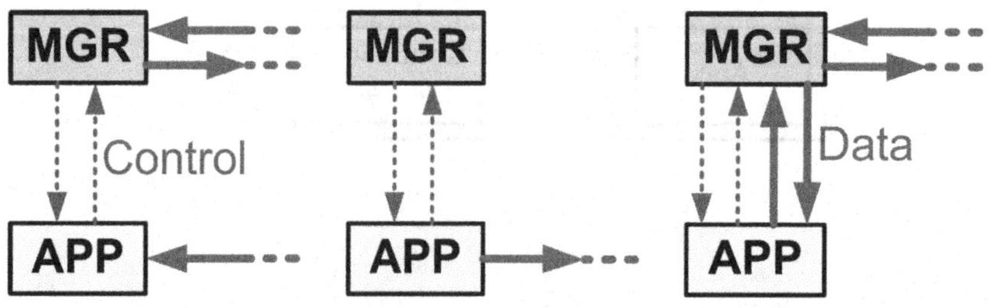

In the second scenario, the applications act as publishers (Figure 23, center). There is no need to forward data, hence the manager does not create any send or receive channels. In order to support this scenario, the controlled element must allow transmitting data to multiple IP addresses; embed various headers provided by the local controller etc. There can be different "classes" of controlled elements, depending on what functionality they provide; this scenario might be feasible only for some such classes. This scenario avoids proxies, thus it could be useful e.g. in streaming systems.

In the third scenario, the applications communicate only with the local controller, which acts as a proxy (Figure 23, right). Unlike in the first two scenarios, this introduces a bottleneck, but since the controlled elements do not need to support any external protocols or to be able to embed or strip any external headers, this scenario is always feasible. This scenario could also be used to interoperate with other eventing standards, such as WS-Eventing or WS-Notification. Here, the manager could act as the publisher or a proxy from the point of view of the application, and provide or consume messages in the format defined by all those other standards, while using our general infrastructure "under the hood". And similarly, for high-performance applications that reside on the server, an efficient implementation is possible using shared memory as a communication channel between the manager and the applications, and permitting applications to deserialize the received data directly from the manager's receive buffers, without requiring extra copy or marshaling across domains.

Sessions

We now shift focus to consider architectural implications of reliability protocols. Protocols that provide stronger reliability guarantees traditionally express them in terms of what we shall call *epochs*, corresponding to what in group communication systems are called *membership views*. In group communication systems, the lifetime of a topic (also referred to as a *group*) is divided into a sequence of *views*. Whenever the set of topic subscribers changes after a "subscribe" or an "unsubscribe" request, or a failure, a new view is created. In group communication systems, the corresponding event initiates a new epoch. Subscribers are notified of the beginnings or endings of epochs, and of the membership of the topic for each epoch. One then defines consistency in terms of which messages can be delivered to which subscribers and at what time relative to epoch boundaries. The set of subscribers during a given epoch is always fixed.

Whereas group communication views are often defined using fairly elaborate models (such as virtual synchrony, a model used in some of our past research, or consensus, the model used in Lamport's Paxos protocol suite), the architectural standard proposed here needs to be flexible enough to cover a range of reliability protocols, include many that have very weak notions of views. For example, simple protocols, such as SRM or RMTP, do not provide any guarantees of consistent membership views for topics.

In developing our architectural proposal, we found that even for protocols such as these two, in which properties are not defined in terms of epochs, epochs can still be a very useful, if not a universal, necessary concept. In a dynamic system, configuration changes, especially those resulting from crashes, usually require reconfiguration or cleanup, e.g. to rebuild distributed structures, release resources, or cancel activities that are no longer necessary. Most simple protocols lack the notion of an epoch because they do not take such factors into account and do not support reconfiguration. Others do address some of these kinds of issues, but without treating them in a systematic manner. By reformulating such mechanisms in terms of epochs, we can standardize a whole family of behaviors, making it easier to talk about different protocols using common language, to compare protocols, and to design applications that can potentially run over any of a number of protocols, with the actual binding made on the basis of runtime information, policy, or other considerations.

Our design includes two epoch-like concepts: *sessions*, which are global to the entire topic, across the Internet, are shared by different frameworks (reliability, ordering, etc.), and which we discuss in this section, and *local views*, which are local to scopes, and which are discussed in section "Building the Hierarchy of Recovery Domains".

A ***session*** is a generalization of an epoch. In our system, sessions are used primarily as means of reconfiguring the topic to alter its security or reliability properties, or for other administrative changes that must be performed online, while the system is running.

The lifetime of any given topic is always divided into a sequence of sessions. However, session changes may be unrelated to membership changes of the topic. Since introducing a new session involves a global reconfiguration, as described further, it is infeasible for an Internet-scale system to introduce a new session, and disseminate membership views, every time a node joins or leaves. Instead, such events are handled locally, in the scopes in which they occur, and without introducing a new, global, Internet-wide epoch.

Session numbers are assigned globally, for consistency. As explained before, for a given topic, a single global scope ("root") always exists such that all subscribers to that topic reside within its span. Although, as we shall explain, dissemination, reliability and other frameworks may use different scope hierarchies, the root scope is always the same and all the dissemination, reliability, and other aspects of it are normally managed by a single scope manager. This top-level scope manager maintains the topic's metadata; it is also responsible for assigning and updating session numbers. Note that local topics, e.g. internal to an organization, may be rooted locally, e.g. in the headquarters, and managed by a local SM, much in a way local newsgroups are managed locally. Accordingly, for such topics, sessions are managed by a local server (internal to the organization).

To conclude, we explain how sessions impact the behavior of publishers and subscribers. After registering, a publisher waits for the SM to notify it of the session number to use for a particular topic. A publisher is also notified of changes to the session number for topics it registered with. All published messages are tagged with the most recent session number, so that whenever a new session is started for a topic, within a short period of time no further messages will be sent in the previous session. Old sessions eventually quiesce as receivers deliver messages and the system completes flushing, cleanup and other reliability mechanisms used by the particular protocol. Similarly, after subscribing to a topic, a node does not process messages tagged as committed to session k until it is explicitly notified that it should receive messages in that session. Later, after session $k+1$ starts, all subscribers are notified that session k is entering a *flushing* phase (this term originates in *virtual synchrony* protocols, but similar mechanisms are common in many reliable protocols; a protocol lacking a flush mechanism simply ignores such notifications). Eventually, subscribers report that they have completed flushing and a global decision is made to cease any activity and *cleanup* all resources pertaining to session k, thus completing the transition.

Incorporating Reliability, Ordering, and Security

As mentioned earlier, we rooted our design in the principle of *separation of concerns*, and we implement tasks such as reliability, ordering, security or scope management independently from dissemination. In section "The Local Architecture of a Dissemination Scope", we explained how the management and the dissemination infrastructures interact in our system. The remaining frameworks, reliability, security and ordering, are decomposed in a similar manner, and they also include three base components: (a) the *controlled element* that lives in the application processes and implements only base functionality, related to sending or receiving from the applications, but none of the peer-to-peer or management aspects; (b) the *local controller* that may live outside of the application process, and where all the peer-to-peer aspects are implemented; and (c) the *scope manager* that implements the interactions with other scope managers, but that is not involved in any activities related to the data flows, such as forwarding, calculating recovery state, managing encryption keys, assigning message order etc.

In general, each of the *dissemination*, *reliability*, *security* and *ordering* frameworks has a separate hierarchy of scopes, and a separate network of scope managers. For example, reliability scopes isolate and encapsulate the local aspects related to reliability, such as loss recovery etc., and hide their internal details from other scopes, just like dissemination scopes manage local dissemination and hide the local aspects of message delivery. In some cases, the different scopes would overlap. This will be normally the case, for example, with the four "flavors" of scopes (ordering, security, reliability, and dissemination) local to a node. In such cases, a single local service would act as a scope manager for all the scopes of all four flavors. The same would typically be the case for the servers that control administrative domains, such as a departmental LAN, a wireless network in a cafeteria, a data center, a corporate network etc. Scopes of all flavors would again overlap, and they would be managed by a single server.

Irrespective of whether components of the four different frameworks overlap, or are physically hosted on the same machine or in the same process, the frameworks always logically converge in the application (Figure 24).

The complete local architecture includes a *multiplexer* (*MUX*), which serves as the entry point for messages from the application, and assigns messages to sessions, and a separate protocol stack for each session (rows on Figure 24).

Elements of the per-session stacks are subcomponents owned by the four "controlled elements" (columns on Figure 24): *security* (*SEC*), *dissemination* (*DISS*), *reliability* (*REL*), and *ordering* (*ORD*), each of which exposes the standard web interface required for interaction with its corresponding local controller. Now, when the application sends a message, it is first assigned to a session by the multiplexer, and assigned a local sequence number within the session. It is then passed to the appropriate per-session protocol stack, simultaneously to the sub-components that handle security and ordering. Each of these two sub-components processes the message independently and concurrently; the security component may encrypt and sign it, if necessary, and then passes it further to the dissemination component for transmission, and independently, to the reliability component to place it in a local cache for the purpose of retransmission, forwarding etc., and to update the local structures to record the fact that the message was created. At the same time,

Figure 24. Internal architecture of the application process

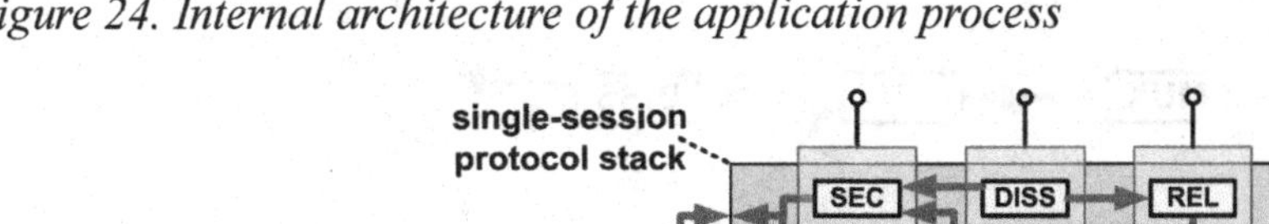

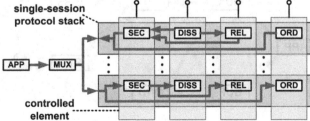

the ordering component, also working in parallel with the dissemination and reliability components, records the presence of the message in its own structures, which are used later by the ordering infrastructure to generate *ordering requests*, to be submitted to the orderer (for details, see section "Ordering").

On the receive path, the process would look similar (Figure 25).

Messages may arrive either through the dissemination framework, in the normal case, or via the reliability framework if they were initially lost, and have been later recovered. Messages that arrive from the dissemination framework are routed via the reliability sub-component, so that they are registered, can be cached, or so that delivery can be suppressed. When ordering arrives from the ordering framework, messages can be decrypted, placed in a buffer (*BUF*), and delivered in the appropriate order to the application.

The exact manner in which the subtasks performed by the four sub-components are synchronized may vary. On the send path, messages may not be transmitted until the entire protocol stack for a given session can be assembled, i.e. if the dissemination framework learned of a new session, but the reliability framework has not, the transmission might be postponed until the information about the new session propagates across the reliability framework as well, to avoid problems stemming from such misalignments. On the receive path, the decryption of the message might be postponed until the ordering is known, to avoid maintaining two copies of the message in memory, one for the purpose of loss recovery (encrypted) and one for delivering to the application (decrypted) etc.

Hierarchical Approach to Reliability

Our approach to reliability resembles our hierarchical approach to dissemination. Just as channels are decomposed into sub-channels, in the reliability framework we decompose the task of loss repair and providing other reliability goals. Recovering messages in a given scope is modeled as recovering within each of its sub-scopes, concurrently and independently, then recovering across all the sub-scopes (Figure 26).

For example, suppose that scope X has members Y_1, Y_2, ..., Y_K. A simple reliability property $P(X)$ requiring that "if some node X in the span of scope X receives a message m, then for as long as either X or some other node keeps a copy of it, every other node Y in the span of X will also eventually get m", can be decomposed as follows. First, we ensure $P(Y_i)$ for every Y_i, i.e. we ensure that in each sub-scope Y_i of scope X, if one node has the message, then so eventually do the others. The protocols that lead to this goal can run in all these sub-scopes independently and concurrently. Then, we run a protocol across sub-scopes Y_1, Y_2, ..., Y_K, to ensure that if any of them has in its span a node X that received message m, then each of the other Y_i also eventually has a node that received m. When these tasks, i.e. recovery

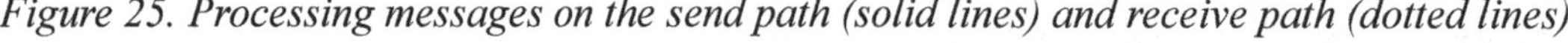
Figure 25. Processing messages on the send path (solid lines) and receive path (dotted lines)

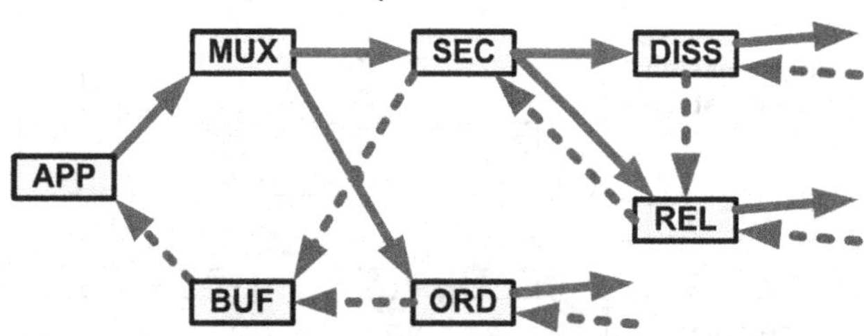

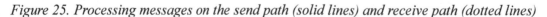

Figure 26. The similarities between hierarchical dissemination (left) and recovery (right)

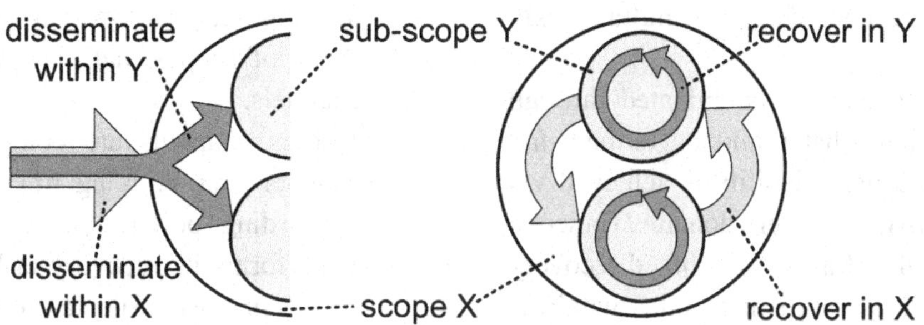

in each Y_i plus the extra recovery across all Y_i, are all performed for sufficiently long, $P(X)$ is eventually established.

Coming back to our example, assume that students with their laptops sit in university departments, each of which is a scope. Suppose that some, but not all of the students received a message with a homework problem set from their professor sitting in a cafeteria. We would like to ensure that the problem set gets reliably delivered to all students. In our architecture, this would be achieved by a combination of protocols: a protocol running in each department would ensure that internally, for every pair *X*, *Y* of students, if *X* got the message then so eventually does *Y*, and likewise a protocol running across the departments ensures that for each pair of departments *X*, *Y*, if some students in *X* got the message, so eventually do some students in *Y*. In the end, this yields the desired outcome.

Just like recovery among individual nodes, recovery among LANs might also involve comparing their "state" (such as aggregated ACK/NAK information for the entire LAN) or forwarding lost messages between them. We give an example of this in section "Recovery Agents". As mentioned earlier, in our architecture, different recovery schemes may be used in different scopes, to reflect differences in the network topologies, node or communication link capacities, the availability of IP multicast and other local infrastructure, the way subscribers are distributed (e.g. clustered or scattered) etc.

For example, in one department, the machines of the students subscribed to topic *T* could form a spanning tree. The property we mentioned above could be guaranteed by making neighbors in the tree compare their state, and upon discovering that one of them has a message *m* that the other is missing, forwarding *m* between the two of them. The same approach may also be used across the departments, i.e. departments would form a tree, the departments "neighboring" on that tree could compare what their students got, and perhaps arrange for messages to be forwarded between them. For the latter to be possible, the departments need a way to calculate "what their students got", which is an example of an aggregated, "department-wide" state. Finally, some departments could use a different approach. For example, a department enamored of gossip protocols might require that student machines randomly gossip about messages they got; a department that has had bad experiences with IP multicast and with gossip might favor a reliability protocol that runs on a token ring instead of a tree, and a department with a site-license for a protocol such as SRM (which runs on IP multicast) might favors its use, where the option is available. In each department, a different protocol could be used locally. As long as each protocol produces the desired outcome (satisfies the reliability property inside of the department), and as long as the department has a way to calculate aggregate "department-wide" state needed for inter-department recovery, these very different policies can be simultaneously accommodated.

Just as messages are disseminated through channels, forming what might be termed *dissemination domains*, reliability is achieved via ***recovery domains***. A recovery domain *D* in scope *X* may be thought of as a "distributed recovery protocol running among some nodes within *X* that performs recovery-related tasks for a certain set of topics".

For example, when some of the students sitting in a library subscribe to topic *T*, the library might create a "local recovery domain for topic *T*". This domain could be "realized" e.g. as a spanning tree connecting the laptops of the subscribed students and running a recovery protocol between them. The library could internally create many domains, e.g. many such trees of student's laptops.

The concept of a **recovery domain** is dual to the notion of a channel; here we present the analogy.

- Just like a channel is created to disseminate messages for some topics T_1, T_2, ... T_k in scope *X*, a recovery domain is created to handle loss recovery and other reliability tasks, again for a specific set of topics, and in a specific scope. Just like there could exist multiple channels to a scope, e.g. for different sets of topics, there could also exist multiple recovery domains within a single reliability scope, each ensuring reliability for different sets of topics.
- Just as channels may be composed of sub-channels, a recovery domain *D* defined at a scope *X* may be composed of *sub-domains* D_1, D_2, ... D_n defined at sub-scopes of *X* (we will call them the *members* of *D*). Each such sub-domain D_i handles recovery for a set of subscribers in the respective sub-scope, while *D* handles recovery across the sub-domains. The hierarchy of recovery domains reflects the hierarchy of scopes that have created them, just as channels are decomposed in ways that reflect the hierarchy of scopes that have exposed those channels.
- Just as channels are composed of sub-channels via applying filters assigned by forwarding policies, a recovery domain *D* performs its recovery tasks using a ***recovery protocol***. Such a protocol, assigned to *D*, specifies how to combine recovery mechanisms in the sub-domains of *D* into a mechanism for all of *D*. Recovery protocols are defined in terms of how the sub-domains "interact" with each other. We explain how this is done in more detail in section "Hierarchical Approach to Reliability".
- Just like a single channel may be used to disseminate messages in multiple topics, a recovery domain may run a single protocol to perform recovery simultaneously for a set of topics. In both cases, reusing a single mechanism (a channel, a token ring, a tree etc.) may significantly improve performance due to the reduction in the total number of control messages and other such optimizations. Indeed, we implemented and evaluated this idea in QSM (Ostrowski & Birman, 2006b, 2006c).

Each individual node is a recovery domain on its own. In a distributed scope such as a LAN, such as the library in our example, on the other hand, many cases are possible. In one extreme, a single domain may cover the entire LAN. All internal nodes could thus form a token ring, or gossip randomly to exchange ACKs for messages in all topics simultaneously, and use this to arrange for local repairs. In the other extreme, separate domains could be created for every individual topic; subscribers to the different topics could thus form separate structures, such as separate rings and trees, and run separate protocol instances in each of them, exchanging state and the lost messages.

In our system, recovery domains actually handle recovery for specific *sessions*, not just specific topics. Each of the recovery domains created internally by a scope performs recovery for some set of sessions, and these sets are such that for each session in which this scope has subscribers, there is a recovery domain in this scope that performs recovery for this session.

A recovery domain *D* of a data center could have as its members recovery domains created by the LANs in that data center (by the SMs of these LANs). Note that in this case, members of *D* would themselves be distributed domains, i.e. sets of nodes. A recovery protocol running in *D* would specify how all these different sets of nodes should exchange state and forward lost messages to one another. Note the similarity to a forwarding policy in a data center, which would also specify how messages are forwarded among sets of nodes. As explained in section "Recovery Agents" and section "Implementing Recovery Domains with Agents", recovery protocols are implemented through delegation, just like forwarding. A concept of a *recovery protocol* is, to some extent, dual, symmetric to the notion of a *forwarding policy*.

Building the Hierarchy of Recovery Domains

Before we show how the hierarchical recovery scheme can be implemented, we need to explain how domains created at different scopes are related to each other. As explained in the preceding section, domains are organized by the relation of membership: domains in super-scopes can be thought of as containing domains in sub-scopes as members. Just as was the case for scopes, a given domain can have many parents, and there may be multiple global domains, but for a given topic, all domains involved in recovery for that topic always form a tree. Domains know their *members* (sub-domains) and *owners* (super-domains), and through a mechanism described below, also their *peers* (other domains that have the same parent). This knowledge of *membership* allows the scopes that create those domains to establish distributed structures in an efficient way.

A consistent view of membership is the basis for many reliable protocols, and could benefit many others that don't assume it. Knowing the members of a topic helps to determine which nodes have crashed or disconnected. In existing group communication systems, this is usually achieved by a Global Membership Service (GMS) that monitors failures and membership changes for all nodes, decides when to "install" new membership views for topics, and notifies the affected members of these new views, including the lists of topic members. Nodes then use those membership views to determine e.g. what other nodes should be their neighbors in a tree, who should act as a leader etc.

In our framework, the manager of the root scope for a given topic is responsible for creating the top-level recovery domain, announcing when sessions for that topic begin or end, and so forth. However, if the root SM, which in case of an Internet-wide scope would "manage" the entire Internet, had to process all subscriptions, and respond to every failure across the Internet, it would lead to a non-scalable design: beyond a certain point the system would be constantly in the state of reconfiguration, trying to change membership or install new sessions, and hence unable to make useful progress. It would also violate the principle of isolation: the higher-level scopes would process information that should be local, e.g. a corporate network would have to know which nodes in data centers are subscribers, whereas according to our architectural principles, the administrator of a corporate network, and the policies defined at this level, should treat the entire data centers as black boxes.

To avoid the problem just mentioned, rather than collecting all information about membership in a topic *T* and processing it centrally, we distribute this information across all scope managers in the hierarchy of scopes for topic *T* (recall this hierarchy defined in section "The Hierarchy of Scopes"). Each SM thus has only a partial membership view for each topic and session. This scheme is outlined below.

In the reliability framework, if a scope *X* subscribes to a topic *T*, it first selects or creates a local recovery domain *D* that will handle the recovery for topic *T* locally in *X*, and then sends a request to one of its parent scopes, some *Y*, asking to subscribe this specific domain, to topic *T*. At this point, it is not significant which of its parent scopes *X* directs the request to. *X* may be manually setup by an administrator with the list of parent scopes, and to send requests in all topics that have names matching a certain pattern to a given parent, or it could use an automated, or a semi-automated scheme to discover the parent scopes that it should subscribe with. Exactly how such a discovery scheme can be most efficiently constructed is beyond the scope of this paper, but we do hope to explore the issue in a future work.

The super-scope *Y* processes the *X*'s subscription request jointly with requests from other of its sub-scopes, e.g. batching them together for efficiency. It then either joins *X* and other sub-scopes to an existing recovery domain or creates a new one, some *D'*. When joining an existing recovery domain, *Y* follows a special protocol, some details of which are given in section "Reconfiguration". In any case, scope *Y* informs all scopes of the new membership of domain *D'*. So for each recovery domain *D"* that is a member of *D'*, the sub-scope of *Y* that owns this domain will be notified by *Y* that domain *D'* changed membership, and will be given the list of all sub-domains of *D'*, together with the names of the scopes that own those sub-domains. Finally, if domain *D'* has just been created, and scope *Y* is not the root scope for the topic, *Y* itself sends a request to one of its parent scopes, asking to subscribe domain *D'* to the topic. Topic subscriptions thus travel all the way to the root scope for the topic, in a cascading manner, creating a tree of recovery domains in a bottom-up fashion.

In our example, when a student *A* sitting in a library *L* enters a virtual room *T*, *A*'s laptop creates a local recovery domain D_A, and sends a request to the library server. Suppose that there are other students in the library that are already subscribed to *T*, so the library server already has a recovery domain D_L that performs recovery in topic *T*. In this case all that is left to do for the library server is to update the membership of D_L, and to inform student *A*'s laptop, as well as the laptops of the other students subscribed to *T*, of the new membership of D_L, so that the laptops can update the distributed recovery structure, and build a new distributed structure. For example, if laptops used a spanning tree, or a token ring, to compare the sets of messages they have received and exchange messages between neighbors, the spanning tree or the ring may be updated to include the new laptop. On the other hand, suppose that student *A* is the first in the library to subscribe to *T*. In this case, the library server creates a new recovery domain D_L, with D_A as its only member, and sends its own request, in a cascading manner, to a campus server *C*, asking to subscribe D_L to topic *T*, and so on.

The above procedure effectively constructs a hierarchy of sub-domains, with the property that for each topic *T*, the recovery domains subscribed to *T* form a tree. At the same time, a membership hierarchy is built in a distributed manner. Specifically, for each domain μ in some scope *S*, *S* will maintain a list of the form $\{ X_1{:}\beta_1, X_2{:}\beta_2, ..., X_K{:}\beta_K \}$, in which $\beta_1, \beta_2, ..., \beta_K$ are the *members*, i.e. sub-domains of domain μ, and $X_1, X_2, ..., X_K$ are the names of the scopes that own those sub-domains (i.e. that created them). In the process of establishing this structure, each of the scopes X_i receives the list, along with any future updates to it. This information is not "pushed" all the way down to the leaf nodes. Instead, every scope maintains the membership of the domains it created (so, for example, scope *S* maintains the list mentioned above), plus a copy of the membership of all super-domains of the domains it created (so, for example, each X_i has a copy of the list above), but not the membership of any domains created below it (so, for example, S would not track the membership of any of the domains $\beta_1, \beta_2, ..., \beta_K$), more than one level above it (so, for example, while scope S would know what are the peers of its own domain μ, scopes $X_1, X_2, ..., X_K$ would not know those peers, because this information is, logically, two levels "above"), or any internal details of its peers (so, for example, while all of $X_1, X_2, ..., X_K$ would know the membership of μ, i.e. the entire list $\{ X_1{:}\beta_1, X_2{:}\beta_2, ..., X_K{:}\beta_K \}$, they would not know the membership of any of the domains $\beta_1, \beta_2, ..., \beta_K$ besides their own; they only know the names of their peer domains).

Figure 27 and Figure 28 show an example of the structure the system would construct in a scenario similar to the one above.

Laptop A creates a new domain α, which may have a version number, like any other domain, say α_1. Then, A directs a request subscribe $A{:}\alpha$ to T to the library L. Note that the version number of α was not included in the request to L. This is a detail internal to A that L does not need to know about. Now, the library creates a new domain μ, and gives it a version number, say μ_1, and directs subscribe $L{:}\mu$ to T to the campus C (omitting the version number). Concurrently, L notifies A that $A{:}\alpha$ is now a member of μ_1. This means that a domain μ has been created at L, and version (view) number 1 of μ has just a single member $A{:}\alpha$. Similarly, C creates a new domain ε with initial version ε_1 that includes a single member $L{:}\mu$ and notifies L. Later, another laptop B in the library L also joins topic T. This time, no request is sent to campus C. The library handles the request internally. A new version (view) μ_2 of domain μ is created, with two members $A{:}\alpha$ and $B{:}\beta$, and both A and B are notified of this new view. A and B undergo a special protocol to "transition" from recovery domain μ_1 to recovery domain μ_2 in a

Figure 27. Node A subscribes to topic T with the library L. Library L subscribes with campus C. Membership information and view numbers are passed one level down (never up) the hierarchy

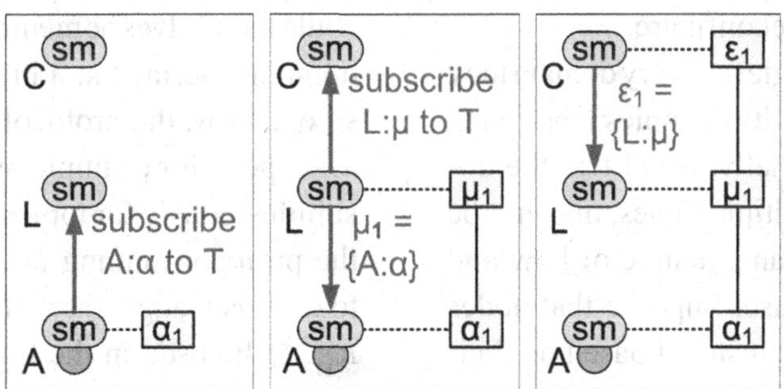

Figure 28. A continuation of the example from Figure 27

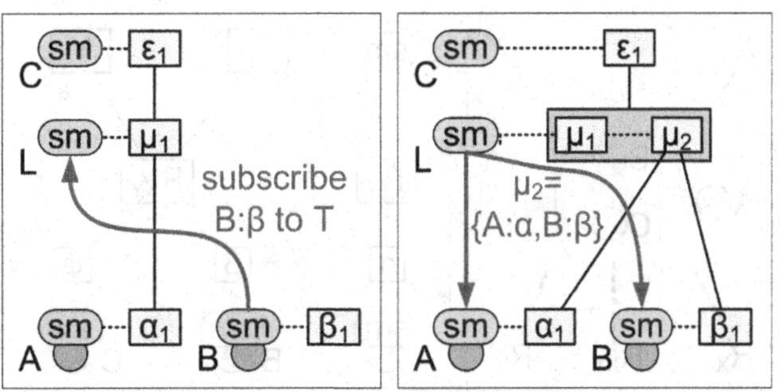

reliable manner, and the protocol running for μ_1 eventually quiesces. The protocols that run at higher levels are unaffected. Domain ε_1 still has only a single member $L{:}\mu$, and the view change that occurred internally in domain μ is transparent to C, and to the protocols that run at this level, and handled internally in the library L, between nodes A and B.

By keeping the information about the hierarchy of domains distributed, and by limiting the way in which this information is propagated to only one level below, we remain faithful to the principles of isolation and local autonomy laid out earlier. At the same time, this enables significant scalability and performance benefits. Because parent domains are oblivious to the membership of their sub-domains, and reconfiguration can often be handled internally, as in the example above, churn and failures in lower layers of the hierarchy do not translate to churn and failures in higher layers. A failure of a node, or a mobile user with a laptop joining or leaving the system, does not need to cause the Internet-wide structure of recovery domains, potentially spanning across tens of thousands of nodes, to fluctuate and reconfigure.

As stated earlier, a single recovery domain may perform recovery for multiple topics (sessions), simultaneously. Additionally, recall that the domain hierarchy, with multiple topics, may not be a tree. We now present an example of how and why this could be the case. Suppose that nodes in a certain scope L are clustered based on their interest. Nodes A and B would be in the same cluster if A and B subscribed to the same topics. Clusters are thus defined by sets of topic names, e.g. cluster R_{XY} would include nodes that have subscribed to topics X and Y, and that have not subscribed to any other topics besides these two. The set of nodes subscribed to each topic would thus include nodes in a certain set of clusters. We might even think of as topics "including" clusters, and the clusters including the individual nodes (Figure 29).

Accordingly, a scope manager in L might create a separate recovery domain for each cluster, and then a separate recovery domain for each topic. If node A subscribes to topic X, and nodes B and C subscribe to topic Y, then L could create a recovery domain R_X for cluster R_X and a recovery domain R_{XY} for cluster R_{XY}. Domain R_X would have a single member $A{:}\alpha$, while R_{XY} would have two members, $B{:}\beta$ and $C{:}\varphi$. Scope L would also create a local domain $L{:}X$ for topic X and $L{:}Y$ for topic Y. Domain $L{:}X$ would have members $L{:}R_X$ and $L{:}R_{XY}$ while domain $L{:}Y$ would have a single member $L{:}R_{XY}$. Domains $L{:}X$ and $L{:}Y$ defined at scope L could themselves be members of some higher-level domains, defined at a higher-level scope C, and so on. Now, the protocol running in domain R_{XY} at scope L, for example, would perform recovery simultaneously for topics X and Y. As said earlier, the protocol running in R_{XY} would also be used to calculate aggregate information about domain R_{XY}, to be used in the higher-level protocols. In

Figure 29. A hierarchy of recovery domains in a system that clusters nodes based on interest

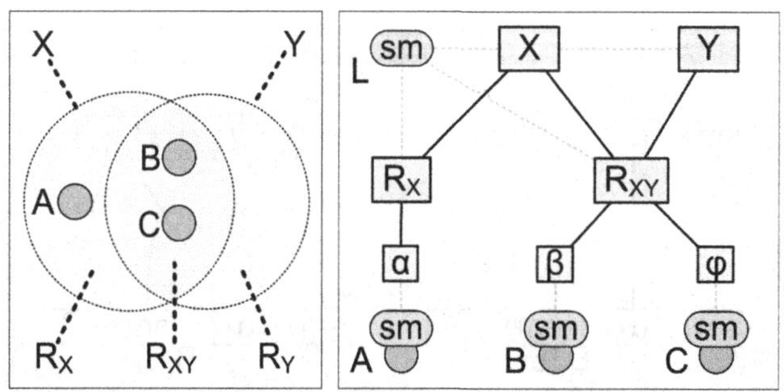

our example, the information collected by the protocol running in $L{:}R_{XY}$ would be used by two such protocols, a protocol running in domain $L{:}X$ and a protocol running in $L{:}Y$.

While the structure just described may seem complex, the ability to perform recovery in multiple topics simultaneously is important in systems like our virtual worlds, where the number of topics (virtual rooms) may be very large. QSM, mentioned previously, uses the architecture just presented, and is able to scale to thousands of publish-subscribe topics.

To complete the discussion of recovery hierarchy, we now turn to sessions. As explained earlier, in our architecture recovery is always performed in the context of individual sessions, not topics, because whenever a session changes, so can the reliability properties of the topic. The creation of the domain hierarchy, outlined above, is mostly independent of the creation of sessions. The only case when these two processes are synchronized arises when the last member, across the entire Internet, leaves the topic, or when the first member rejoins the topic after a period when no members existed, for in such cases, it is impossible to handle the event via a local reconfiguration between members (such as transferring the state from some existing member to the newly joining member, or "flushing" any changes from the departing member to some of the existing members). Such an event will force an existing session to be flushed or a new session to be created.

In any case, sessions for a topic *T* are created by the scope that serves as the root for *T*. The root maintains topic metadata and the information about sessions in persistent storage. It assigns new session number whenever a new session is created, and then *installs* the new session and *flushes* the existing session in the top-level recovery domain that it created to perform recovery in topic *T*. More on how the *installing* and *flushing* of a session are realized will be explained in section "Implementing Recovery Domains with Agents". Now, concurrently with installing of a new session and flushing of the old session in the top-level recovery domain, the scope manager passes the session change event further, to the sub-domains that are members of this global recovery domain, by communicating with the scope managers that created those sub-domains. This notification travels down the hierarchy of recovery domains in a cascading manner, until the session change events are disseminated across the entire structure.

Recovery Agents

The reader will have noticed by now that the structure of recovery domains we've just described "exists" only virtually, inside the scope managers. These recovery domains are "implemented" by physical protocols running directly between physical nodes, the publishers and subscribers, in a manner similar to how we implemented channels between scopes, by *delegating* the tasks that the recovery domains are responsible for to physical nodes. Just as channels between scopes are "implemented" by physical connections between nodes that can be constrained with filter chains and that are "installed" in the physical nodes by their super-scopes, in the reliability framework recovery domains are "implemented" by ***agents***. Similarly to filters, these agents are also small, "downloadable" components, which are installed on physical nodes by their super-scopes. Before going into details of how precisely this is done, however, we first explain how existing recovery protocols can be modeled in a hierarchical manner that is compatible with our architecture.

Modeling Recovery Protocols

The *reliability framework* is based on an abstract model of a scalable distributed protocol dealing with loss recovery and other reliability properties. In this model, a protocol such as SRM, RMTP, virtual synchrony, or atomic commit, is defined in terms of a group of cooperating *peers* that exchange control messages and can forward lost packets to each other, and that may perhaps interact with a distinguished node, such as a sender or some node higher in a hierarchy, which we will refer to as a *controller* (Figure 30).

The controller does not have to be a separate node; this function could be served by one of the peers. The distinction between the peers and the controller may be purely functional. The point is that the group of peers, as a whole, may be asked to perform a certain action, or calculate a value, for some higher-level entity, such as a sender, a higher-level protocol, or a layer in a hierarchical structure. Examples of such actions include retransmitting or requesting a retransmission for all peers, reporting which messages were successfully delivered to all peers, which messages have been missed by all peers etc. Irrespectively of how exactly the interaction with the controller is realized, it is present in this form or another in almost every protocol run by a set of receivers. We shall refer to the possible interactions between the peers and the controller as the *upper interface*. Notice that some reliability protocols aren't traditionally thought of as hierarchical; we would view them as supporting only a one-level hierarchy. The benefit of doing so is that those protocols can then be treated side by side with protocols such as SRM and RMTP, in which hierarchy plays a central role.

Each peer inspects and controls its *local state*. Such state could include e.g. a list of messages received, and perhaps copies of those that are cached (for loss recovery), the list and the order of messages delivered etc. Operations that a peer may issue to change the local state could include retrieving or purging messages from cache, marking messages as deliverable, delivering some of the previously missed message to the application etc. We refer to such operations, used to view or control the local state of a peer, as a *bottom interface*.

In protocols offering strong guarantees, peers are typically given the membership of their group, received as a part of the initialization process, and subsequently updated via *membership change* events. Peers send control messages to each other to share state or to request actions, such as forwarding messages. Sometimes, as in SRM, a multicast channel to the entire peer group exists.

To summarize, in most reliable protocols, a peer could be modeled as a component that runs in a simple environment that provides the following interface: a *membership view* of its peer group, *channels* to all other peers, and sometimes to the entire group, a *bottom interface* to inspect or control local state, and an *upper interface*, to interact with the sender or the higher levels in the hierarchy concerning the aggregate state of the peer group (Figure 31).

In some protocols, certain parts of this interface might be unavailable, e.g. in SRM peers might not know other peers. The bottom and upper interfaces also would vary.

This model is flexible enough to capture the key ideas and features of a wide class of protocols, including virtual synchrony. However, because in our framework protocols must be reusable in different scopes, they may need to be expressed in a slightly different way, as explained below.

Figure 30. A group of peers in a reliable protocol

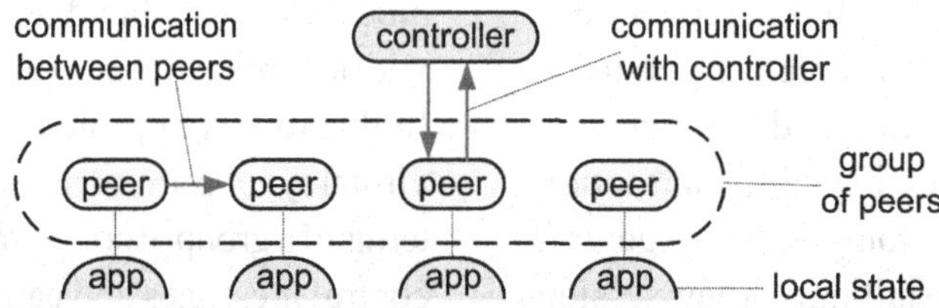

Figure 31. A peer modeled as a component living in abstract environment (events, interfaces etc.)

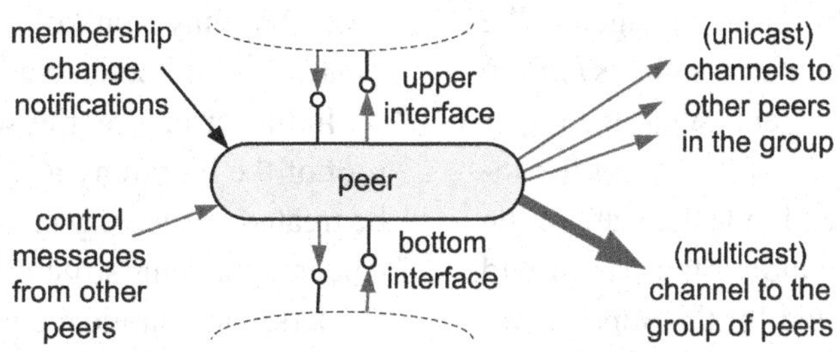

In RMTP, the sender and the receivers for a topic form a tree. Within this tree, every subset of nodes consisting of a parent and its child nodes represents a separate local recovery group. The child nodes in every such group send their local ACK/NAK information to the parent node, which arranges for a local recovery within the recovery group. The parent itself is either a child node in another recovery group, or it is a sender, at the root of the tree. Packet losses in this scheme are recovered on a hop-by-hop basis, either top-down or bottom-up, one level at a time. This scheme distributes the burden of processing the individual ACKs/NAKs, and of retransmissions, which is normally the responsibility of the sender. This improves scalability and prevents ACK implosion.

There are two ways to express RMTP in our model. One approach is to view each recovery group consisting of a parent node and its child nodes as a separate group of peers (Figure 32).

Since internal nodes in the RMTP tree simultaneously play two roles, a "parent" node in one recovery group and a "child" node in another, we could think of each node as running two "agents", each representing a different "half" of the node, and serving as a peer in a separate peer group. In this perspective it would be not the nodes, but their "halves" that would represent peers. Every group of peers, in this perspective, would include the "bottom agent" of the parent node, and the "upper agents" of its child nodes. When a node sends messages to its child nodes as a result of receiving a message from its parent, of vice versa, we may think of those two "agents" as interacting with each other through a certain interface that one of them views as upper, and the other as bottom. These two types of agents play different roles in the protocol, as explained below.

The bottom agent of each node interacts via its *bottom interface* with the local state of the node. It also serves as a distinguished peer in the peer group, composed of itself and the upper agents of the child nodes. A protocol running in this peer group is used to exchange ACKs between child nodes and the parent node and arrange for message forwarding between peers, but also to calculate collective ACKs for the peer group, i.e. which messages were not recoverable in the

Figure 32. RMTP expressed in our model. A node hosts "agents" playing different roles

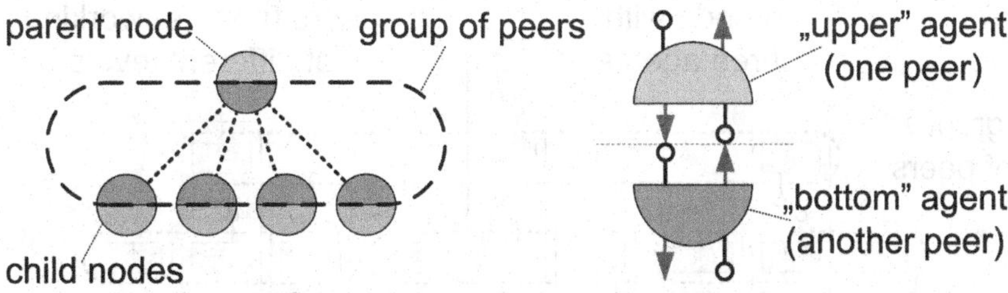

group. This is communicated by the bottom agent, via its *upper interface*, to the upper agent. The upper agent of every node interacts via its *bottom interface* with the bottom agent. What the upper agent considers as its "local state" is not the local state of the node. Instead, it is the state of the entire recovery group, including the parent and child nodes, that is collected for the upper agent by the bottom agent though the protocol that the bottom agent runs with the upper agents in child nodes. Such interactions, between a component that is logically a part of a "higher layer" ("upper agent") with components that reside in a "lower layer" ("bottom agent"), both components co-located on the same physical node, and connected via their upper and bottom interfaces, are the key element in our architecture.

At the top of this hierarchy is the sender, the root of the tree. The bottom agent of the sender node collects for the upper agent the state of the top-level recovery group, which subsumes the state of the entire tree, and passes it to the upper agent through its upper interface. The upper agent of the sender can thus be thought of as "controlling" through its *bottom interface* the entire receiver tree.

The second way to model RMTP, which builds on the concepts we just introduced, captures the very essence of our approach to combining protocols. It is similar to the first model, but instead of the "upper" and "bottom" agents, each node can now host multiple agents, again connected to each other through their "bottom" and "upper" interfaces. Each of these agents works at a different level. We may think of every node as hosting a "stack" of interconnected **agents** (Figure 33).

In this structure, the sender would not be the root of the hierarchy any more. Rather, it would be treated in the very same way as any of the receivers. The same structure could feature multiple senders, and a single recovery protocol would run for all of them simultaneously.

Focusing for a moment on a concrete example, assume that nodes reside in three LANs, which are part of a single data center (Figure 33). Each of these administrative domains is a scope. Each node hosts, in its "agent stack", a "node agent" (bottom level, Figure 33). The "local state" of the node agent, accessed by the node agent through its bottom interface, is the state of the node, such as the messages that the node received or missed etc. Now, in each LAN, the node agents of all nodes in that LAN form a peer group and communicate with each other to compare their local state, or to arrange for forwarding messages between them. One of these node agents in each LAN serves as a leader (or "parent"), and the others serve as subordinates (or "children"). The leader collects the aggregate ACK/NAK information about the LAN from the entire peer group. The node that hosts the leader also runs anther, higher-level component that we shall call a "LAN agent" (middle level, Figure 33). The LAN agent accesses, through its bottom interface, the aggregated state of the LAN that the "leader" node agent, co-located with it on the same "leader" node, calculated. The LAN

Figure 33. Another way to express RMTP. Each node hosts multiple "agents" that act as peers at different levels of the RMTP hierarchy

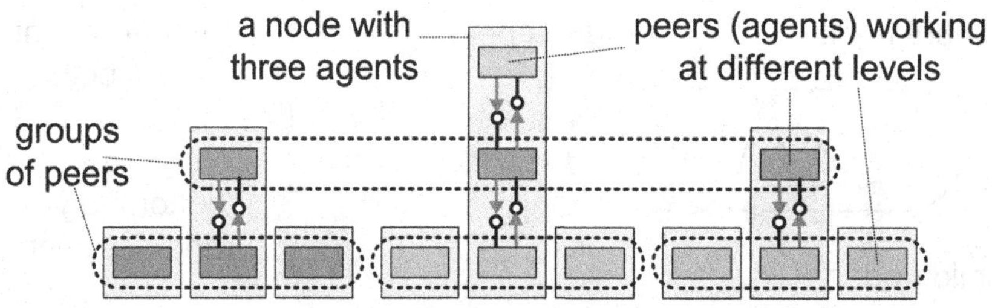

agent can therefore be thought of as controlling, through its bottom interface, the entire LAN, just like a node agent was controlling the local node. Now, all the LAN agents in the data center again form a peer group, compare their state (which are aggregate states of their LANs), arrange for forwarding (between the LANs), and calculate aggregate ACK/NAK information about the data center. Finally, one of the nodes that host the LAN agents hosts an even higher-level component, a "data center agent" (top level, Figure 33). The aggregate state of the data center, collected by the peer group of LAN agents, is communicated through the upper interface of the "leader" LAN agent to the data center agent; the latter can now be thought as controlling, through its bottom interface, the entire data center. In a larger system, the hierarchy could be deeper, and the scheme could continue recursively.

Note the symmetry between the different categories of agents. In essence, for every entity, be it a single node, a LAN, or a data center, there exists exactly one agent that collects, via lower-level agents, the state of the entity it represents, and that acts on behalf of this entity in a protocol that runs in its peer group. The agent that represents a distributed scope is always hosted together with one of the agents that represent sub-scopes. By now, the reader should appreciate that this structure corresponds to the hierarchy of recovery domains we introduced in section "Building the Hierarchy of Recovery Domains". In our design, every recovery domain is represented, as a part of some higher-level domain, by an agent that collects the state of the domain, which it represents, and acts on behalf of it in a protocol that runs among the agents representing other recovery domains that have the same parent (Figure 34).

In order to be able to do their job, these agents are updated whenever a relevant event occurs. For example, they receive a membership change notification, with the list of their peer agents, when a new recovery domain is created. To this end, each agent maintains a bi-directional channel from the scope that created the recovery domain represented by this agent, down to the node that hosts the agent, along what we call an agent "delegation chain".

Note also that as long as the interfaces used by agents to communicate with one-another are standardized, each group of agents could run an entirely different protocol, because the only way the different peer groups are connected with each other is through the bottom and upper interfaces of their agents. For example, in smaller peer groups with small interconnect latency agents could use a token ring protocol, whereas in very large groups over a wide area network, with frequent joins and leaves and frequent configuration changes agents might use randomized gossip protocol.

Figure 34. A hierarchy of recovery domains and agents implementing them

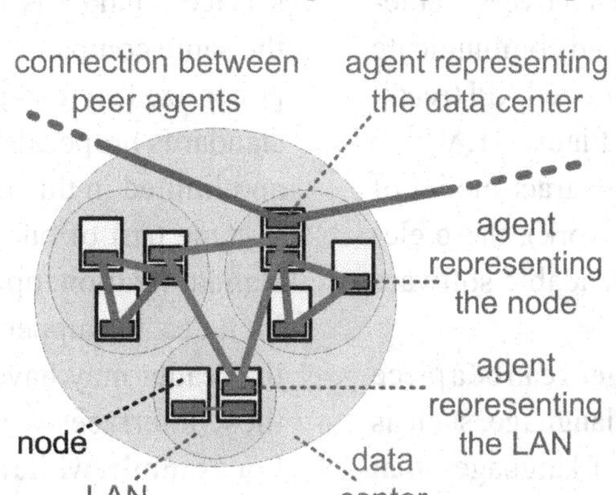

This flexibility could be extremely useful in settings where local administrators control policies governing, for example, use of IP multicast, and hence where different groups may need to adhere to different rules. It also allows for local optimizations. Protocols used in different parts of the network could be adjusted so as to match the local network topology, node capacities, throughput or latency, the present of firewalls, security policies etc. Indeed, we believe that the best approach to building high-performance systems on the Internet scale is not through a uniform approach that forces the use of the same protocol in every part of the network, but by the sorts of modularity our architecture enables, because it can leverage the creativity and specific domain expertise of a very large class of users, who can tune their local protocols to match their very specific needs.

The flexibility enabled by our architecture also brings a new perspective on a node in a publish-subscribe system. A node subscribing to the same topics in different portions of the Internet, joining an already established infrastructure (existing recovery domains and agents implementing them running among existing subscribers) may be forced to follow a different protocol, potentially not known in advance. Indeed, if we exploit the full power of modern runtime platforms, a node might be asked to use a protocol that must first be downloaded and installed, in plug-and-play fashion. Because in our architecture, elements "installed" in nodes by the forwarding framework (filters and channels) and by the recovery framework (agents) are very simple, and communicate with the node via a small, standardized API (recall the abstract model of a peer on Figure 31, which can also be interpreted as the abstract model of an agent in the recovery framework), these elements can be viewed as downloadable software components.

Thus, a filter or a **recovery agent** can be a piece of code, written in any popular language, such as Java or one of the family of .NET languages, that exposes (to the node hosting it, or to agents above and below in the agent stack) and consumes a standardized interface, e.g. described in WSDL. Such components could be stored in online repositories, and downloaded as needed, much as a Windows XP user who tries to open a file in the new Vista XPS format will be prompted to download and install an XPS driver, or a visitor to a web page that uses some special ActiveX control will be given an opportunity to download and install that control. In this perspective, the subscribers and publishers that join a publish-subscribe infrastructure, rather than being applications compiled and linked with a specific library that implements a specific protocol, and thus very tightly coupled with the specific publish-subscribe engine, can now be thought of as "empty containers" that provide a standard set of hookups to host different sorts of agents (Figure 35).

Nodes using a publish-subscribe system are thus runtime platforms, programmable "devices", elements of a large, flexible, programmable, dynamically reconfigurable runtime environment, offering the sort of flexibility and expressive power unseen in prior architectures.

We believe that in light of the huge success of extensible, component-oriented programming environments, standards for distributed eventing must incorporate the analogous forms of flexibility. To do otherwise is to resist the commercial, off-the-shelf (COTS) trends, and history teaches that COTS solutions almost always dominate in the end. It is curious to realize that although web services standards were formulated by some of the same companies that are leaders in this componentized style of programming, they arrived at standards proposals that turn out to be both rigid and limited in this respect.

One part of our architecture, for which API standardization options may not be obvious, includes the upper and bottom interfaces. As the reader may have realized, the exact form of these interfaces would depend on the protocol. For example, while a simple protocol implementing the "last copy recall" semantics of the sort

Figure 35. A node as a "container" for agents

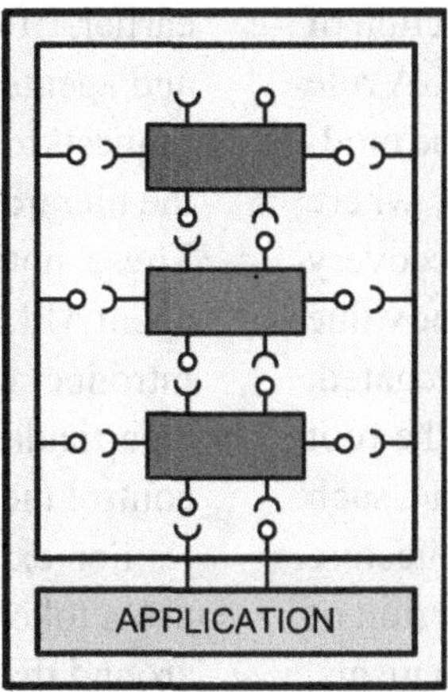

we used in some of our examples require agents to be able to exchange a simple ACK/NAK information, more complex protocols may need to determine if messages have been persisted to stable storage, to be able to temporarily suppress the delivery of messages to the application, control purging messages from cache, decide on whether to commit a message (or an operation represented by it) or abort it etc. The "state" of recovery domain and the set of actions that can be "requested" from a recovery domain may vary significantly.

As it turns out, however, defining the upper and bottom interfaces in a standard way is possible for a wide range of protocols. In our technical report (Ostrowski, Birman & Dolev, 2006d), we have outlined elements of a novel architecture being developed by the three authors of this article, called the "QuickSilver Properties Framework", and based on the very architecture presented here, that achieves precisely this form of standardization. Moreover, the properties framework allows a large class of protocols, including such protocols as virtually synchronous multicast and multicast with transaction semantics etc., to be implemented in a declarative manner, using a special, domain-specific rule-based language, without requiring that the developer worry about performance and scalability aspects.

The key idea behind this approach is based on the observation that the state of most distributed protocols can be accurately described by a set of "properties". Properties are essentially variables that can be associated with various distributed entities (the reader might think of these entities as recovery domains, which they would indeed be, were the system described there to be implemented within the architecture described here). An example of a property is *Received*(x), parameterized by an entity name X. The value of this variable would be the set of identifiers of all messages that have been received by at least one node that is still in X. Other examples, values of all of which would again be sets of message identifiers, include *Cached*(x) – the messages cached at some nodes in X, *Cleaned*(x) – the messages received, but no longer cached in X, *Stable*(x) – messages received by all nodes in X, and so on.

In (Ostrowski, Birman & Dolev, 2006d), we argue that the logic of most protocols could be modeled as a set of rules that determine how the values of such properties are created and propagated. For example, some properties are aggregated. For a distributed entity X, *Received*(x) can be defined as the set sum of *Received*(y) for all Y that are members of X. If this rule is applied recursively to a distributed entity, it will yield the set of messages that are received by any node in the span of that entity, as requested. Similarly, *Stable*(x) can be defined as the set intersection of *Stable*(y) for all Y that are members of X. A rule that implements message cleanup could be modeled as *CanClean*(*root*) ← *Stable*(*root*), where root is the top-level entity (the top-level recovery domain), and *CanClean*(x) is a property, the value of which is disseminated rather than aggregated, i.e. passed in a top-down fashion, from the root down to the individual nodes. As it turns out, such rules can be implemented on top of the architecture outlined in this paper, using a special version of an agent that supports a few simple mechanisms, such as different flavors of property aggregation or dissemination, and the ability to produce a property based on a value of a certain expression, either periodically, or in response to events, such as receiving a message etc.

We believe that even without using the properties framework, a *set of properties*, expressed in a standard manner, including their "types", is a good candidate for the upper or bottom interface. Agents could still be implemented in an imperative manner, explicitly use the messaging API and the membership notifications from the scopes controlling them, but using the "properties" API to interact with other agents in the agent stack. The details of how exactly such interface could be defined is, however, beyond the scope of this paper. Moreover, other similarly expressive schemes may exist. Indeed, it is conceivable that agents co-located on the stack could be able to "negotiate" the manner in which they interact, and download appropriate "converter" components if necessary to ensure that their upper and bottom interfaces match against each other.

To conclude this section, we now turn to recovery in many topics at once. Throughout this section, the discussion focused on a single topic, or a single session, but as mentioned before, the recovery domains created by the reliability framework, and hence the sets of agents that are instantiated to "implement" those recovery domains, may be requested to perform recovery in multiple sessions at once, for reasons of scalability. As mentioned earlier, after recovery domains are established, and agents instantiated, the root scope may issue requests to install or flush a session, passed along the hierarchy of domains, in a top-down fashion. These notifications are a part of the standard agent API. Agents respond to the notifications by introducing or eliminating information related to a particular session in the state they maintain or control messages they exchange.

For example, agents in a peer group could use a token ring protocol and tokens circulating around that ring could carry a separate recovery record for each session. After a new session would get installed, the token would start to include the recovery record for that session. When a flushing request would arrive for a session, the session would eventually quiesce, and the recovery record related to that session would be eliminated from the tokens, and from the state kept by the agents. The exact manner in which introducing a new session and flushing are expressed would depend on how the agent implements it. The available agent implementation might not support parallel recovery in many sessions at once; in this case, the scope manager could simply create a separate recovery domain for each topic, or even for each session, so that separate agents are used for each.

If an agent performs recovery for many sessions simultaneously, its "upper" and "bottom" interfaces would be essentially arrays of interfaces, one for each session. Likewise, agent stacks might no longer be vertical. The stacks for a scenario of Figure 29 are shown on Figure 36.

Here, agents on node *B* form a tree. Two parts of the upper interface of one agent that correspond to two different sessions that the agent is performing recovery for, are connected with two bottom interfaces of two independent higher-level agents. At this point, the structure depicted in this example may seem confusing. In section "Implementing Recovery Domains with Agents", we come back to this scenario, and we explain how such structures are built.

Figure 36. Agents stacks that are not simply vertical that may be created on nodes in the scenario from Figure 29. Agents are shown as gray boxes, with the parts of their upper or bottom interfaces corresponding to particular sessions as small yellow boxes. On node B, the bottom-level agent connects the two parts of its upper interface to two different higher-level agents, one to each of them. The peer groups are circled with thick dotted red lines

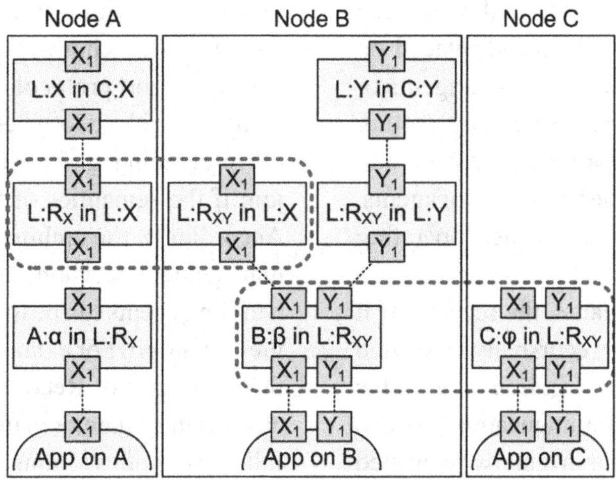

Implementing Recovery Domains with Agents

In section "Building the Hierarchy of Recovery Domains" we've explained how a hierarchy of recovery domains is built, such that for each session, there is a tree of domains performing recovery for that session. In section "Recovery Agents" we indicated that the recovery domains are "implemented" with agents, and in section "Modeling Recovery Protocols" we explained how recovery protocols can be expressed in a hierarchical manner, by a hierarchy of agents that represent recovery domains. We now explain how agents are created.

A distributed recovery domain D in our framework (i.e. a domain different than a node, not a leaf in the domain hierarchy) will correspond to a peer group. When D is created at some scope X, the latter selects a protocol to run in D, and then every sub-domain $Y_k{:}D_k$ of D is requested to create an agent that acts as a "peer $Y_k{:}D_k$ within peer group $X{:}D$". We will refer to an agent defined in this manner as "$Y_k{:}D_k$ in $X{:}D$". Note how the membership algorithm provides membership view at one level "above", i.e. the scope that owns a particular domain would learn about domains in all the sibling scopes. This is precisely what is required for each peer $Y_k{:}D_k$ in a peer group $X{:}D$ to learn the membership of its group. Hence, the scopes Y_k that own the different domains D_k will learn of the existence of domain $X{:}D$, each of them will realize that they need to create an agent "$Y_k{:}D_k$ in $X{:}D$", and each of them will receive from X all the membership change events it needs to keep its agent with an up to date list of its peers.

For example, on Figure 29, domains $B{:}\beta$ and $C{:}\varphi$ are shown as members of $L{:}R_{XY}$, so according to our rules, agents "$B{:}\beta$ in $L{:}R_{XY}$" and "$C{:}\varphi$ in $L{:}R_{XY}$" should be created to implement $L{:}R_{XY}$. Indeed, the reader will find those agents on Figure 36, in the protocol stacks on nodes B and C.

When the manager of a scope Y discovers that an agent should be created for one of its recovery domains D_k that is a member of some $X{:}D$, two things may happen. If X manages a single node, the agent is created locally. Otherwise, Y delegates the task to one of its sub-scopes. As a result, the agents that serve as peers at the various levels of the hierarchy are eventually delegated to individual nodes, their definitions downloaded from an online repository if needed, placed on the agent stack and connected to other agents or to the applications. We thus arrive at a structure just like on Figure 33, Figure 34, Figure 35, and Figure 36, where every node has a stack of agents, linked to one another, with each of them operating at a different level.

While agents are delegated, the records of it are kept by the scopes that recursively delegated the agent, thus forming a *delegation chain*. This chain serves as a means of communication between the agent and the scope that originally requested it to be created. The scope and the agent can thus send messages to one another. This is the way membership changes or requests to install or flush sessions can be delivered to agents.

When the node hosting a delegated agent crashes, the node to which that agent is delegated changes. That is, some other node is assigned the role of running this agent, and will instantiate a new version of it to take over the failed agents responsibilities. Here, we again rely on the delegation chain. When the manager of the super-scope of the crashed node (e.g. a LAN scope manager) detects the crash, it can determine that an agent was delegated to the crashed node, and it can request the agent to be re-delegated elsewhere. Since our framework would transparently recreate channels between agents, it would look to other peers agents as if the agent lost its cached state (not permanently, for it can still query its bottom interface and talk to its peers). On the one part, this frees the agent developer from worrying about fault-tolerance. On the other part, this requires that agent protocols be defined in a way that allows peers to crash and "resume" with some of their state "erased". Based on our experience, for a wide class of protocols this is not hard to achieve.

Reconfiguration

Many large systems struggle with costs triggered when nodes join and leave. As a configuration scales up, the frequency of join and leave events increases, resulting in a phenomenon researchers refer to as "churn". A goal in our architecture was to support protocols that handle such events completely close to where they occur, but without precluding global reactions to a failure or join if the semantics of the protocol demand it. Accordingly, the architecture is designed so that management decisions and the responsibility for handling events can be isolated in the scope where they occurred. For example, in section "Building the Hierarchy of Recovery Domains" we saw a case in which membership changes resulting from failures or nodes joining or leaving were isolated in this manner. The broad principle is to enable solutions where the global infrastructure is able to ignore these kinds of events, leaving the local infrastructure to handle them, without precluding protocols in which certain events do trigger a global reconfiguration.

An example will illustrate some of the tradeoffs that arise. Consider a group of agents implementing some recovery domain D that has determined that a certain message m is locally cached, and reported it as such to a higher-level protocol. But now suppose that a node crashed and that it happens to have been the (only) one on which m was cached. To some extent, we can hide the consequences of the crash: D can reconfigure its peer group to drop the dead node and reconstruct associated data structures. Yet m is no longer cached in D and this may have consequences outside of D: so long as D cached m, higher level scopes could assume that m would eventually be delivered reliably in D; clearly, this is no longer the case. Thinking back to the properties framework, the example illustrates the risk that a property such as *Cached*(x), defined earlier, might not grow monotonically: here, *Cached*(x) has lost an item as a consequence of the crash.

This is not the setting for an extended discussion of the ways that protocols handle failures. Instead, we limit ourselves to the observations already made: a typical protocol will want to conceal some aspects of failure handling and reconfiguration, by handling them locally. Other aspects (here, the fact that *m* is no longer available in scope *D*) may have global consequences and hence some failure events need to be visible in some ways outside the scope. Our architecture offers the developer precisely this flexibility: events that he wishes to hide are hidden, and aspects of events that he wishes to propagate to higher-level scopes can do so.

Joining presents a different set of challenges. In some protocols, there is little notion of state and a node can join without much fuss. But there are many protocols in which a joining node must be brought up to date and the associated synchronization is a traditional source of complexity. In our own experience, protocols implementing reconfiguration (especially joins) can be greatly facilitated if members of the recovery domains can be assigned certain "roles". In particular, we found it useful to distinguish between "regular" members, which are already "up to date" and are part of an ongoing run of a protocol, and "light" members, which have just been added, but are still being brought up to date.

When a new member joins a domain, its status is initially "light" (unless this is the first membership view ever created for this domain). The job of the "light" members, and their corresponding agents, is to get up-to-date with the rest of their peer group. At some point, presumably when the light members are more or less synchronized with the active ones, the "regular" agents may agree to briefly suspend the protocol and request some of these "light" peers to be promoted to the "regular" status.

The ability to mark members as "light" or "regular" is a fairly powerful tool. It provides agents with the ability to implement certain forms of agreement, or consensus protocols that would otherwise be hard to support. In particular, this feature turns out to be sufficient to allow our architecture to support virtually synchronous, consensus-like, or transactional semantics.

Ordering

As mentioned in section "Incorporating Reliability, Ordering, and Security", ordering is implemented independently of dissemination. When a publisher submits a message to the dissemination framework, it simultaneously submits an *ordering request* into the ordering framework. An ordering request is a small object that lists the sender identifier, message topic and a sequence number. In response to the ordering requests, the ordering framework produces *orderings*. Orderings are small objects assigning indexes to batches of messages, perhaps coming from different publishers. These orderings are then delivered to the interested subscribers (Figure 37).

Because the ordering framework is designed to process requests from different publishers together, it is possible to e.g. totally order messages in each topic, or even totally order messages across different topics.

Messages transmitted by publishers may be marked as *ordered*, as a hint for subscribers that these messages should not be delivered until an ordering for these messages arrives through the ordering framework. The subscribers that do not care about ordering will simply not subscribe to the ordering framework, and will ignore such markings.

The ordering framework consists of two components: a component that collects ordering requests from multiple sources and produces orderings in response to these requests, and a component that delivers these orderings to subscribers. The first of these components is essentially an aggregation mechanism, and the second is similar to the dissemination framework.

Like every other element of our architecture, ordering is performed in a hierarchical manner

Figure 37. For all messages for which ordering across multiple senders is required, publishers create ordering requests and submit these in batches to the ordering framework. The latter produces orderings in response to the ordering requests, and delivers these orderings to the subscribers

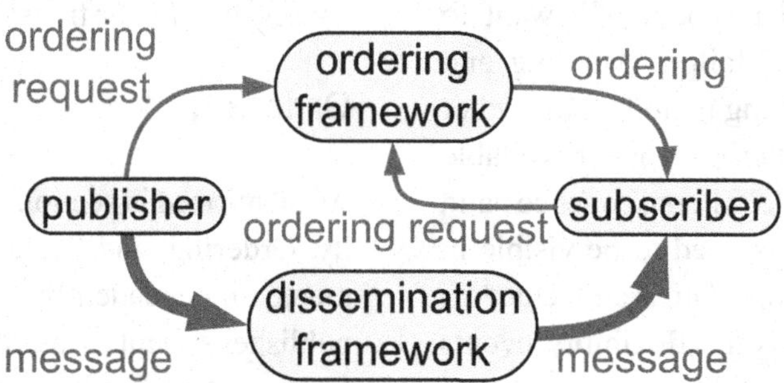

that respects isolation and local autonomy of administrative domains. Thus, the ordering framework also relies on the concept of *management scopes*, in this case the *ordering scopes*, which may or may not overlap with the other flavors of scopes. Each scope can define its own policies that govern the way ordering is performed: how ordering requests are collected, which member of the scope should serve as the *orderer* (collect these requests and produce orderings), and how these orderings should be disseminated to subscribers. The resulting architecture is a product of policies defined at various levels, just as it was the case for dissemination and reliability.

To prevent the article from becoming excessively long, we shall omit the details of the ordering framework. The design shares common elements and ideas with the dissemination and reliability frameworks, and will be covered comprehensively in the first author's Ph.D. thesis.

Other Possible Frameworks

Up to now, we've focused on the dissemination, recovery, and ordering frameworks within our overall architecture. However, the same structure can also support additional frameworks, which exist as logical "siblings" to the ones already presented. These include:

- *Flow and rate control.* Architectural mechanisms in support of flow and congestion control handling, negotiating rates, managing leases on bandwidth etc.
- *Security.* Architectural support for integrating security (managing keys, granting or revoking access, managing certificates etc.) into scalable eventing systems.
- *Auditing.* Self-verification, detection of inconsistencies (e.g. partitions, invalid routing etc.).
- *Failure detection and health monitoring.* Scalable detection of faulty or underperforming machines.

CONCLUSION

We have argued that new and more flexible event notification standards are going to be needed if the web services community is to gain the benefits of architectural standardization while also exploiting the full power of component architectures and integration platforms. The proposal presented here draws heavily from our experience building Quicksilver, a new and extremely scalable eventing infrastructure that scales in multiple dimensions, integrates seamlessly with modern component-style platforms, and has the flexibility to support a wide range of reliability models including best-effort, virtual synchrony, consensus and transactional ones. In contrast, our experience trying to express Quicksilver within the existing web services options was discouraging; we found them to be narrowly conceived and incapable of offering needed flexibility and scalability.

ACKNOWLEDGMENT

Our research was supported by AFRL/Cornell Information Assurance Institute. We acknowledge Mahesh Balakrishnan, Lars Brenna, Yejin Choi, Maya Haridasan, Tudor Marian, Ingrid Jansch-Porto, Robert van Renesse, Yee Jiun Song, Einar Vollset, and Hakim Weatherspoon for their feedback.

REFERENCES

Banavar, G., Chandra, T., Mukherjee, B., Nagarajarao, J., Strom, R., & Sturman, D. (1999). An Efficient Multicast Protocol for Content-Based Publish-Subscribe Systems. In *Proceedings of the 19th IEEE international Conference on Distributed Computing Systems* (May 31 - June 04, 1999) (p. 262). ICDCS. IEEE Computer Society.

Box, D., Cabrera, L. F., Critchley, C., Curbera, D., Ferguson, D., Geller, A., et al. (2004). Web Services Eventing (WS-Eventing). Retrieved December 9, 2006, from http://www.ibm.com/developerworks/webservices/library/specification/ws-eventing/

Floyd, S., Jacobson, V., Liu, *C.*, McCanne, S., & Zhang, L. (1996). A Reliable Multicast Framework for Light-weight Sessions and Application Level Framing. *IEEE/ACM Transactions on Networking, 5*(6), 784-803.

Graham, S., Niblett, P., Chappell, D., Lewis, A., Nagaratnam, N., Parikh, J., et al. (2004). Web Services Brokered Notification (WS-Brokered-Notification). Retrieved December 9, 2006, from http://www.ibm.com/developerworks/library/specification/ws-notification/

Keidar, I., & Dolev, D. (1995). Increasing the Resilience of Atomic Commit, at No Additional Cost. In *Proceedings of the Fourteenth ACM SIGACT-SIGMOD-SIGART Symposium on Principles of Database Systems* (San Jose, California, United States, May 22 - 25, 1995). PODS '95 (pp. 245-254). New York: ACM Press.

Keidar, I., Sussman, J., Marzullo, K., & Dolev, D. (2002). Moshe: A group membership service for WANs. *ACM Transactions on Computer Systems, 20*(3), 191–238. doi:10.1145/566340.566341

Ostrowski, K., & Birman, K. P. (2006a). Extensible Web Services Architecture for Notification in Large-Scale Systems. In *Proceedings of the IEEE international Conference on Web Services (ICWS'06) - Volume 00* (September 18 - 22, 2006). ICWS (pp. 383-392). IEEE Computer Society.

Ostrowski, K., & Birman, K. P. (2006b). Scalable Group Communication System for Scalable Trust. In *Proceedings of the First ACM Workshop on Scalable Trusted Computing* (Alexandria, Virginia, USA, November 3, 2006). STC '06 (pp. 3-6). New York: ACM Press.

Ostrowski, K., & Birman, K. P. (2006c). *Scalable Publish-Subscribe in a Managed Framework.* Cornell University Technical Report.

Ostrowski, K., Birman, K. P., & Dolev, D. (2006d). *Properties Framework and Typed Endpoints for Scalable Group Communication.* Cornell University Technical Report.

Ostrowski, K., Birman, K. P., Dolev, D., & Ahnn, J.-H. (2008). *Programming with Live Distributed Objects*. Submitted to the European Conference on Object-Oriented Programming (ECOOP'08).

Paul, S., Sabnani, K. K., Lin, J. C.-H., & Bhattacharyya, S. (1997). Reliable Multicast Transport Protocol. *IEEE Journal on Selected Areas in Communications*, *15*(3), 407–421. doi:10.1109/49.564138

Weinsberg, Y., Dolev, D., Anker, T., & Wyckoff, P. (2006). Hydra: A Novel Framework for Making High-Performance Computing Offload Capable. In *Proceedings of the 31st IEEE Conference on Local Computer Networks (LCN 2006)*. Tampa, November 2006.

Chapter 8
Composing and Coordinating Transactional Web Services

Frederic Montagut
SAP Schweiz AG, Switzerland, and Institut Eurecom, France

Refik Molva
Institut Eurecom, France

Silvan Tecumseh Golega
Hasso-Plattner-Institut, Germany

ABSTRACT

Composite applications leveraging the functionalities offered by Web services are today the underpinnings of enterprise computing. However, current Web services composition systems make only use of functional requirements in the selection process of component Web services while transactional consistency is a crucial parameter of most business applications. The transactional challenges raised by the composition of Web services are twofold: integrating relaxed atomicity constraints at both design and composition time and coping with the dynamicity introduced by the service oriented computing paradigm. This chapter proposes a new process to automate the design of transactional composite Web services. This solution for Web services composition does not take into account functional requirements only but also transactional ones based on the Acceptable Termination States model. The resulting composite Web service is compliant with the consistency requirements expressed by business application designers and its execution can easily be coordinated using the coordination rules provided as an outcome of the authors' approach. An implementation of these theoretical results augmenting an OWL-S matchmaker is further detailed as a proof of concept.

INTRODUCTION

Web services composition has been gaining momentum over the last years as a means of leveraging the capabilities of simple operations to offer value-added services. Complex services such as airline booking systems can be designed as the aggregation of Web services offered by different organizations. As for all cross-organizational collaborative systems, the execution of composite services requires transactional properties so that the overall consistency of data modified during

DOI: 10.4018/978-1-61520-684-1.ch008

the process is ensured. Yet, existing Web services composition systems appear to be limited when it comes to integrating at the composition phase, the consistency requirements defined by designers in addition to functional matchmaking. Composite Web services indeed require different transactional approaches than the ones developed for usual database systems (Elmagarmid, 1992), (Greenfield, Fekete et al. 2003). The transactional challenges raised by the composition of Web services are twofold. First, like classical workflow systems, composite services raise less stringent requirements for atomicity in that intermediate results produced by some components may be kept without rollback despite the failure to complete the overall execution of a composite service. Second, composite services are dynamic in that their components can be automatically selected at run-time based on specific requests. Existing approaches only offer means to validate transactional requirements once a composite Web service has been created (Bhiri, Perrin et al. 2005) and do not address the integration of these requirements into the composite application building process.

In this chapter, we propose a systematic procedure to automate the design of transactional composite Web services. Given an abstract representation of a process wherein instances of services are not yet assigned to component functional tasks, our solution enables the selection of Web services not only according to functional needs but also based on transactional requirements. In this approach, transactional requirements are specified by designers using the Acceptable Termination States *(ATS)* model. The resulting composite Web service is compliant with the defined consistency requirements and its execution can be easily coordinated as our algorithm also provides coordination rules that can be integrated into a transactional coordination protocol. Besides, the theoretical results developed in our approach have been implemented as a proof of concept and integrated into an OWL-S (OWL Services Coalition, 2003) functional matchmaker providing it with transactional matchmaking capabilities.

The remainder of the chapter is organized as follows. Section 2 and 3 introduce the methodology of our approach and a motivating example, respectively. In section 4, the transactional model underpinning this work is outlined. In section 5 we provide details on the termination states of a composite Web service then in section 6 we describe how transactional requirements are formed based on the properties of the termination states. The transaction-aware composition process through which transactional composite Web services are designed is detailed in section 7 while the implementation of our results in an OWL-S based framework is presented in section 8. Finally, section 9 discusses related work and section 10 presents the conclusion.

PRELIMINARY DEFINITIONS AND METHODOLOGY

Consistency is a crucial aspect of composite services execution. In order to meet consistency requirements at early stages of the service composition process, we need to consider transactional requirements a concrete parameter determining the choice of the component Web services. In this section we present a high level definition of the consistency requirements and a methodology taking into account these requirements during the composition of Web services.

Consistent Composite Web Services

A composite Web service W_s consists of a set of n Web services $W_s = (s_a)_{a \in [1,n]}$ whose execution is managed according to a workflow W which defines the execution order of a set of n tasks $W = (t_a)_{a \in [1,n]}$ performed by these services (for the sake of simplicity, we consider in our approach that a given service executes only one task). The assignment of services to tasks is performed by means of composition engines based on functional requirements. Yet, the execution of a composite service may have to meet transactional requirements aiming at the overall assurance of consistency. Our goal is to design a service assignment procedure that takes into account the transactional requirements associated with W in order to obtain a consistent instance W_s of W whose execution can be supported by a transactional protocol defined using these transactional requirements as depicted in Figure 1. We consider that each Web service component might fulfill a different set of transactional properties. For instance a service can have the capability to compensate the effects of a given operation or to re-execute the operation after failure whereas some other service does not have any of these capabilities. It is thus necessary to select the appropriate service to execute a task whose execution may be compensated if required. These transactional properties can be advertised by services in the fashion of their functional capabilities as part of their WSDL (W3C, 2002) interface or OWL-S profile. The assignment procedure based on transactional requirements follows the same strategy as the one based on functional requirements. It is a matchmaking procedure between the transactional properties offered by services and the transactional requirements associated to each task. Once assigned, the services $\left(s_a\right)_{a\in[1,n]}$ are coordinated with respect to the transactional requirements during the process execution. The coordination protocol is indeed based on rules deduced from the transactional requirements. These rules specify the final states of execution or termination states each service has to reach so that the overall process reaches a consistent termination state. Two phase-commit (ISO, n.d.) the famous coordination protocol enforces for instance the simple rule: all tasks performed by different services have to be compensated if one of them fails. The challenges of the transactional approach are therefore twofold.

- specify a Web service assignment procedure that creates consistent instances of W according to defined transactional requirements
- specify the coordination rules that can be integrated into a coordination protocol managing the execution of consistent composite services

Methodology

In our approach, the candidate services for the execution of W_s are selected based on their transactional properties by means of a matchmaking procedure. We therefore need first to specify the semantic associated with the transactional properties advertised by transactional services. The matchmaking procedure is indeed based on this semantic. This semantic is also to be used in order to define a tool allowing workflow designers to specify their transactional requirements for a given workflow. Using these transactional requirements,

Figure 1. Principles

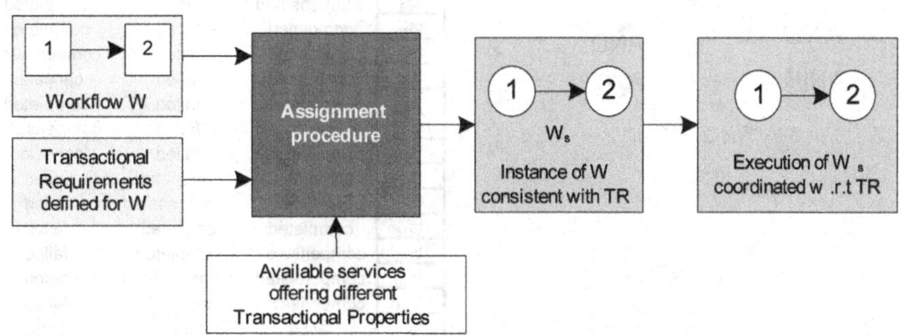

we are able to assign services to workflow tasks based on rules which are detailed later on. Once the composite service is defined, we are able to specify the coordination rules that can be used to support the execution of the composite application according to the transactional requirements specified at the workflow design phase.

Motivating Example

In this section we introduce a motivating example that will be used throughout the chapter to illustrate the presented methodology. We consider the simple process W_1 of a manufacturing firm involving four steps as depicted in Figure 2. A first service, order handling service is in charge of receiving orders from clients. These orders are then handled by the production line (step 2) and in the meantime an invoice is forwarded to a payment platform (step 3). Once the ordered item has been manufactured and the payment validated, the item is finally delivered to the client (step 4). Of course in this simple scenario, a transactional approach is required to support the process execution so that it can reach consistent outcomes as for instance the manufacturing firm would like to have the opportunity to stop the production of an item is the payment platform used by a customer is not a reliable one. On the other hand, it may no longer be required to care about canceling the production if the payment platform claims it is reliable and not prone to transaction errors. Likewise, customers may expect that their payment platform offer refunding options in case the delivery of the item they ordered is not successful.

Those possible outcomes mostly define the transactional requirements for the execution of this simple process and also specify what actions need to be taken to make sure that the final state of the process execution is deemed consistent by the involved parties. This example although simple perfectly meets our illustration needs within this chapter as it demonstrates the fact that based on the specified transactional requirements a clever selection of the business process participants has to be performed prior to the process instantiation since for instance the selection of both a payment platform that do not offer any refunding options and an unreliable delivery means may result in a disappointed customer. It should be noted that the

Figure 2. Production line process

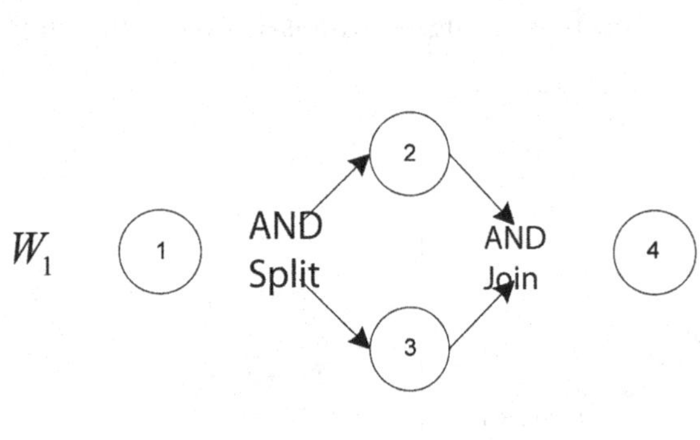

$TS(W_1)$	Task 1	Task 2	Task 3	Task 4
ts_1	completed	completed	completed	completed
ts_2	completed	completed	completed	failed
ts_3	completed	compensated	completed	failed
ts_4	completed	compensated	compensated	failed
ts_5	completed	completed	compensated	failed
ts_6	compensated	compensated	compensated	failed
ts_7	compensated	completed	compensated	failed
ts_8	compensated	completed	completed	failed
ts_9	compensated	compensated	completed	failed
ts_{10}	completed	failed	completed	aborted
ts_{11}	completed	failed	compensated	aborted
ts_{12}	completed	failed	canceled	aborted
ts_{13}	compensated	failed	completed	aborted
ts_{14}	compensated	failed	compensated	aborted
ts_{15}	compensated	failed	canceled	aborted
ts_{16}	completed	completed	failed	aborted
ts_{17}	completed	compensated	failed	aborted
ts_{18}	completed	canceled	failed	aborted
ts_{19}	compensated	completed	failed	aborted
ts_{20}	compensated	compensated	failed	aborted
ts_{21}	compensated	canceled	failed	aborted
ts_{22}	failed	aborted	aborted	aborted

focus of this example is not the trust relationship between the different entities and we therefore assume the trustworthiness of each of them yet we are rather interested in the transactional characteristics offered by each participant.

TRANSACTIONAL MODEL

In this section, we define the semantic specifying the transactional properties offered by services before specifying the consistency evaluation tool associated to this semantic. Our semantic model is based on the "transactional Web service description" defined in (Bhiri, Perrin et al. 2005).

Transactional Properties of Services

In (Bhiri, Perrin et al. 2005) a model specifying semantically the transactional properties of Web services is presented. This model is based on the classification of computational tasks made in (Mehrotra, Rastogi et al. 1992), (Schuldt, Alonso et al. 1999) which considers three different types of transactional properties. An operation and by extension a Web service executing this task can be:

- compensatable: the results produced by the task can be rolled back
- retriable: the task is sure to complete successfully after a finite number of tries
- pivot: the task is neither compensatable nor retriable

These transactional properties allow us to define four types of transactional services: retriable *(r)*, compensatable *(c)*, retriable and compensatable *(rc)* and pivot *(p)*. In order to properly understand this transactional model and the defined transactional properties, we can map the state diagram of transactional services with the state of data during the execution of computational tasks performed by these transactional services. This mapping is depicted in Figure 3. Basically, data can be in three different states: *initial* (0), *unknown* (x), *completed* (1). In the state (0), either the task execution has not yet started *initial*, the execution has been stopped, *aborted* before starting, or the execution has been properly completed and the modifications have been rolled back, *compensated*. In state (1) the task execution has been properly completed. In state (x) either the task execution is not yet finished *active*, the execution has been stopped, *canceled* before completion, or the execution has *failed*. Particularly, the states *aborted*, *compensated*, *completed*, *canceled*, and *failed* are the possible final states of execution of these tasks. Figure 4 details the transition diagram for the four types of transactional services. We distinguish within this model:

- the *inherent* termination states: *failed* and *completed* which result from the normal course of a task execution
- the *forced* termination states: *compensated*, *aborted* and *canceled* which result from a coordination message received during a coordination protocol instance and forcing a task execution to either stop or rollback

In the state diagrams of Figure 3 and Figure 4 plain and dashed lines represent the *inherent* transitions leading to *inherent* states and the *forced* transitions leading to *forced* states, respectively. In this model, the transactional properties of services are only differentiated by the states *failed* and *compensated* which indeed respectively specify the retriability and compesatability properties.

Definition 4-1: We have for a service *s*:

- *failed* is not a termination state of *s* ⇔ *s* is retriable
- *compensated* is a termination state of *s* ⇔ *s* is compensatable

From the state transition diagram, we can also derive some simple rules:

Figure 3. Service state diagram

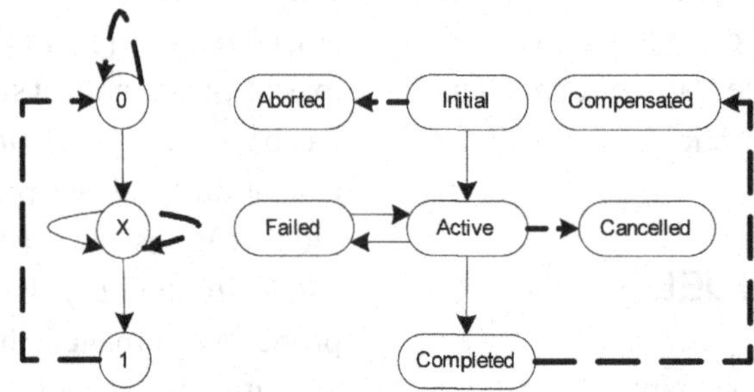

Figure 4. Transactional properties of services

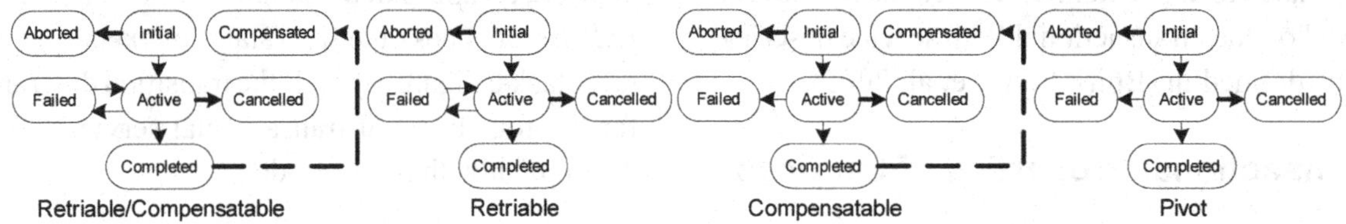

- The states *failed*, *completed* and *canceled* can only be reached if the service is in the state *active*.
- The state *compensated* can only be reached if the service is in the state *completed.* The state *aborted* can only be reached if the service is in the state *initial.*

Termination States

The crucial point of the transactional model specifying the transactional properties of services is the analysis of their possible termination states. The ultimate goal is indeed to be able to define consistent termination states for a workflow i.e. determining for each component service executing a workflow task which termination states it is allowed to reach.

Definition 4-2: We define the operator termination state *ts(x)* which specifies the possible termination states of the element *x*. This element *x* can be:

- a service *s* and $ts(x) \in \{aborted, canceled, failed, completed, compensated\}$
- a workflow task *t* and $ts(t) \in \{aborted, canceled, failed, completed, compensated\}$
- a workflow composed of *n* tasks $W = (t_a)_{a \in [1,n]}$ and $ts(W_s) = (ts(t_1), ts(t_2), \ldots, ts(t_n))$
- a composite service W_s of W composed of *n* services $W_s = (s_a)_{a \in [1,n]}$ and $ts(W_s) = (ts(s_1), ts(s_2), \ldots, ts(s_n))$

The operator *TS(x)* represents the finite set of all possible termination states of the element *x*, $TS(x) = (ts_k(x))_{k \in [1,j]}$. We have especially, $TS(W_s) \in TS(W)$since the set $TS(W_s)$ represents the actual termination states that can be reached by W_s according to the transactional properties of the services assigned to workflow tasks. We also define for *x* workflow or composite service and $a \in [1,n]$:

- $ts(x,t_a)$: the value of $ts(t_a)$ in $ts(x)$
  $tscomp(x)$: the termination state of x such that $\forall a \in [1,n]$ $ts(x,t_a)$=*completed*

For the remainder of the chapter, $W = \left(t_a\right)_{a\in[1,n]}$ represents a workflow of *n* tasks and $W_s = \left(s_a\right)_{a\in[1,n]}$ a composite service of *W*.

Transactional Consistency Tool

We use the Acceptable Termination States (*ATS*) (Rusinkiewicz and Sheth 1995) model as the consistency evaluation tool for our workflow. *ATS* defines the termination states a workflow is allowed to reach so that its execution is deemed consistent.

Definition 4-3: *ATS(W)* is the subset of *TS(W)* whose elements are deemed consistent by workflow designers. A consistent termination state of *W* is called an acceptable termination state $ats_k(W)$ and we note $ATS(W) = \left(ats_k(W)\right)_{k\in[1,i]}$ the set of Acceptable Termination States of *W* i.e. the transactional requirements of *W*.

ATS(W) and *TS(W)* can be represented by a table which defines for each termination state the tuple of termination states reached by the workflow task as depicted in Figure 4 and Figure 5. As mentioned in the definition, the specification of the set *ATS(W)* is done at the workflow designing phase. *ATS(W)* is mainly used as a decision table for a coordination protocol so that W_s can reach an acceptable termination state knowing the termination state of a set of tasks. The role of a coordination protocol indeed consists in sending messages to component services in order to reach a consistent termination state given the current state of the workflow execution. The coordination decision, i.e. the termination state that has to be reached, made given a state of the workflow execution has to be unique; this is the main characteristic of a coordination protocol. In order to cope with this requirement, *ATS(W)* which is used as input for the coordination decision-making process has therefore to verify some properties that we detail later on.

ANALYSIS OF *TS(W)*

Since $ATS(W) \subseteq TS(W)$, *ATS(W)* inherits the characteristics of *TS(W)* and we logically need to analyze *TS(W)* first. In this section, we first make precise some basic properties of *TS(W)* derived from inherent execution rules of a workflow *W* before examining *TS(W)* from a coordination perspective.

Inherent Properties of *TS(W)*

We state here some basic properties relevant to the elements of *TS(W)* and derived from the transactional model presented above. *TS(W)* is the set of all possible termination states of *W* based

Figure 5. Acceptable termination states of W_1 and available services

$ATS_1(W_1)$		Task 1	Task 2	Task 3	Task 4
ats_1	ts_1	completed	completed	completed	completed
ats_2	ts_6	compensated	compensated	compensated	failed
ats_3	ts_{14}	compensated	failed	compensated	aborted
ats_4	ts_{15}	compensated	failed	canceled	aborted
ats_5	ts_{20}	compensated	compensated	failed	aborted
ats_6	ts_{21}	compensated	canceled	failed	aborted

$ATS_2(W_1)$		Task 1	Task 2	Task 3	Task 4
ats_1	ts_1	completed	completed	completed	completed
ats_2	ts_{17}	completed	compensated	failed	aborted
ats_3	ts_{11}	completed	failed	compensated	aborted
ats_4	ts_5	completed	completed	compensated	failed
ats_5	ts_{18}	completed	canceled	failed	aborted
ats_6	ts_{12}	completed	failed	canceled	aborted

Available Services		Retriable	Compensatable
Task 1	s_{11}	yes	no
	s_{12}	no	yes
	s_{13}	yes	yes
Task 2	s_{21}	yes	no
	s_{22}	no	yes
Task 3	s_{31}	yes	no
	s_{32}	no	yes
Task 4	s_{41}	no	no

on the termination states model we chose for services. Yet, within a composite service execution, it is not possible to reach all the combinations represented by a n-tuple $(ts(t_1),ts(t_2),\ldots,ts(t_n))$ assuming $\forall a\in[1,n]$ $ts(t_a)\in\{aborted, canceled, failed, completed, compensated\}$. The first restriction is introduced by the sequential aspect of a workflow:

(P1) A task becomes *activated* ⇔ all the tasks executed beforehand according to the execution plan of W have reached the state *completed*

(P1) simply states that to start the execution of a workflow task, it is required to have properly *completed* all the workflow tasks required to be executed beforehand. Second, we consider in our model that only one single task can fail at a time and that the states *aborted, compensated* and *canceled* can only be reached by a task in a given $ts_k(W)$ if one of the services executing a task of W has failed. This means that the coordination protocol is allowed to force the abortion, the compensation or the cancellation only in case of failure of a service. We get *(P2)*:

(P2) if $\exists\ a,k\ \in[1,n]\times[1,j]$ such that $ts_k(W,t_a)\in\{aborted, canceled, compensated\}\Rightarrow$

$\exists! l\in[1,n]$ such that $ts_k(W,t_l)=failed$

Classification Within *TS(W)*

As we explained above the unicity of the coordination decision during the execution of a coordination protocol is a major requirement. We try here to identify the elements of *TS(W)* that correspond to different coordination decisions given the same state of a workflow execution. The goal is to use this classification to specify rules to build *ATS(W)*. Using the properties *(P1)* and *(P2)*, a simple analysis of the state transition model reveals that there are two situations whereby a coordination protocol can make different coordination decisions given the state of a workflow task. Let $a,b\in[1,n]$ and assume that the task t_b has failed:

- the task t_a is in the state *completed* and either it remains in this state or it is *compensated*
- the task t_a is in the state *active* and either it is *canceled* or the coordinator lets it reach the state *completed*

From those two statements, we define the incompatibility from a coordination perspective and the flexibility notions.

Definition 5-1: Let $k,l\in[1,j]$. $ts_k(W)$ and $ts_l(W)$ are said to be incompatible from a coordination perspective $\Leftrightarrow\exists a,b\in[1,n]$ *such that* $ts_k(W,t_a)=completed$, $ts_k(W,t_b)=ts_l(W,t_b)=failed$ and $ts_l(W,t_a)=compensated$. Otherwise, $ts_k(W)$ and $ts_l(W)$ are said compatible from a coordination perspective. The value in $\{completed, compensated\}$ reached by a task t_a in a termination state $ts_k(W)$ whereby $ts_k(W,t_b)=failed$ is called recovery strategy of t_a against t_b in $ts_k(W)$. By extension, we can consider the recovery strategy of a set of tasks against a given task.

If two termination states are compatible, they correspond to the same recovery strategy against a given task. In fact, we have two cases for the compatibility of two termination states $ts_k(W)$ and $ts_l(W)$. Given two tasks t_a and t_b such that $ts_k(W,t_b)=ts_l(W,t_b)=failed$:

- $ts_k(W,t_a)=ts_l(W,t_a)$
- $ts_k(W,t_a)\in\{compensated, completed\}$ and $ts_l(W,t_a)\in\{aborted, canceled\}$

The second case is only possible to reach if t_a is executed in parallel with t_b. Intuitively, the failure of the service assigned to t_b occurs at different instants in $ts_k(W)$ and $ts_l(W)$.

Definition 5-2: Let $a,b\in[1,n]$. A task t_a is said to be flexible against t_b $\exists k\in[1,j]$ *such that* $ts_k(W,t_b)=failed$ and $ts_k(W,t_a)=canceled$. Such a termination state is said to be flexible to t_a against t_b. The set of termination states of W flexible to t_a against t_b is denoted $FTS(t_a, t_b)$.

This definition simply means that a task which is flexible against another can be canceled when the latter fails.

From these definitions, we now examine the termination states of W according to the compatibility and flexibility criteria in order to identify the termination states that follow a common strategy of coordination.

Definition 5-3: Let $a \in [1,n]$. A termination state of W $ts_k(W)$ is called generator of $t_a \Leftrightarrow ts_k(W,t_a)$=*failed* and $\forall b \in [1,n]$such that t_b is executed before or in parallel with t_a, $ts_k(W,t_b) \in \{$*compensated, completed*$\}$. The set of termination states of W compatible with $ts_k(W)$ generator of t_a is denoted $CTS(ts_k(W), t_a)$.

A termination state generator of a task t_a is thus a termination state wherein t_a is in the state failed while other tasks are in the state *compensated* or *completed* if executed prior or in parallel with t_a, in the state *aborted* otherwise.

The set $CTS(ts_k(W),t_a)$ specifies all the termination states of W that follow the same recovery strategy as $ts_k(W)$ against t_a.

Definition 5-4: Let $ts_k(W) \in TS(W)$ be a generator of t_a. Coordinating an instance W_s of W in case of the failure of t_a consists in choosing the recovery strategy of each task of W against t_a and the $z_a < n$ tasks $(t_{a_i})_{i \in [1,z_a]}$ flexible to t_a whose execution is not *canceled* when t_a fails. We call coordination strategy of W_s against t_a the set:

$$CS(W_s, ts_k(W), (t_{a_i})_{i\in[1,z_a]}, t_a) = CTS(ts_k(W), t_a) - \bigcup_{i=1}^{z_a} FTS(t_{a_i}, t_a)$$

If the service s_a assigned to t_a is retriable then $CS(W_s, ts_k(W), (t_{a_i})_{i\in[1,z_a]}, t_a) = \varnothing$ W_s is said to be coordinated according to $CS(W_s, ts_k(W), (t_{a_i})_{i\in[1,z_a]}, t_a)$ if in case of the failure of t_a, W_s reaches a termination state in $CS(W_s, ts_k(W), (t_{a_i})_{i\in[1,z_a]}, t_a)$. Of course, it assumes that the transactional properties of W_s are sufficient to reach $ts_k(W)$. The coordination strategy only specifies the set of termination states that should be reached by a composite service when the latter is coordinated by means of a transactional protocol.

From these definitions, we can deduce a set of theorems.

Theorem 5-5: W_s can only be coordinated according to a unique coordination strategy at a time.

Proof: Let $a \in [1,n]$. Two termination states $ts_k(W)$ and $ts_l(W)$ both generator of t_a are incompatible.

Theorem 5-6: Let $a,k \in [1,n]\times[1,j]$ such that $ts_k(W,t_a)$=*failed* but not generator of t_a. If $ts_k(W) \in TS(W_s) \Rightarrow \exists l \in [1,j]$ such that $ts_l(W) \in TS(W_s)$ is a generator of t_a compatible with $ts_k(W)$. This theorem states that if a composite service is able to reach a given termination state wherein a task t_a fails, it is also able to reach a termination state generator compatible with the latter.

Proof: We define $ts_l(W)$ by: $ts_l(W,t_a)$=*failed*, $\forall i \in [1,n]-\{a\}$ $ts_l(W,t_i)=ts_k(W,t_i)$ if $ts_k(W,t_i) \in \{$*completed, compensated, aborted*$\}$, $ts_l(W,t_i)$=*completed* otherwise.

Given a task t_a the idea is to classify the elements of $TS(W)$ using the sets of termination states compatible with the generators of t_a. Using this approach, we can identify the different recovery strategies and the coordination strategies associated with the failure of t_a as we decide which tasks can be *canceled*.

FORMING *ATS(W)*

Defining $ATS(W)$ is deciding at design time the termination states of W that are consistent. $ATS(W)$ is to be input to a coordination protocol in order to provide it with a set of rules which leads to a unique coordination decision in any cases. According to the definitions and properties we introduce above, we can now make explicit some rules on $ATS(W)$ so that the unicity requirement of coordination decisions is respected.

Definition 6-1: Let $a,k \in [1,n]\times[1,j]$ such that $ts_k(W,t_a)$=*failed* and $ts_k(W) \in ATS(W)$.

ATS(W) is valid ⇔ $\exists! l \in [1,j]$ such that $ts_l(W)$ generator of t_a compatible with $ts_k(W)$ and $CTS(ts_l(W),t_a) - \bigcup_{i=1}^{z_a} FTS(t_{a_i},t_a) \subset ATS(W)$ for a set of tasks $(t_{a_i})_{i\in[1,z_a]}$ flexible to t_a.

The unicity of the termination state generator of a given task comes from the incompatibility definition and the unicity of the coordination strategy. A valid *ATS(W)* therefore contains for all $ts_k(W)$ in which a task fails a unique coordination strategy associated with this failure and the termination states contained in this coordination strategy are compatible with $ts_k(W)$. In Figure 5, an example of possible *ATS* is presented for the simple workflow W_1 of the motivating example. It just consists of selecting the termination states of the table $TS(W_1)$ that we consider consistent and respect the validity rule for the created $ATS(W_1)$. Of course for the same workflow it is possible to build different sets of acceptable termination states depending on the transactional requirements of the business application. For instance in $ATS_1(W_1)$ designers specify that the production task performed at step 2 has to be *compensated* intuitively meaning that the manufactured products have to be reprocessed whenever the delivery task fails while in $ATS_2(W_1)$ they allow these same products to remain intact.

Deriving Composite Services From *ATS*

In this section, we introduce a new type of service assignment procedure: the transaction-aware service assignment procedure which aims at assigning *n* services to the *n* tasks t_a in order to create an instance of *W* acceptable with respect to a valid *ATS(W)*. The goal of this procedure is to integrate within the instantiation process of workflows a systematic method ensuring the transactional consistency of the obtained composite service. We first define a validity criteria for the instance W_s of *W* with respect to *ATS(W)*, the service assignment algorithm is then detailed. Finally, we specify the coordination strategy associated to the instance created from our assignment scheme and discuss the complexity of our approach.

7.1. Acceptability of Ws with respect to *ATS(W)*

Definition 7-1: W_s is an acceptable instance of *W* with respect to *ATS(W)* ⇔ $TS(W_s) \subseteq ATS(W)$.

Now we express the condition $TS(W_s) \subseteq ATS(W)$ in terms of coordination strategies. The termination state generator of t_a present in *ATS(W)* is noted $ts_{k_a}(W)$. The set of tasks whose execution is not *canceled* when t_a fails is noted $(t_{a_i})_{i\in[1,z_a]}$.

Theorem 7-2:

$$TS(W_s) \subseteq ATS(W) \Leftrightarrow \forall a \in [1,n] \quad CS(W_s, ts_{k_a}(W), (t_{a_i})_{i\in[1,z_a]}, t_a) \subset ATS(W)$$

Proof: straightforward derivation from 5-6 and 6-1.

An instance W_s of *W* is therefore an acceptable one ⇔ it is coordinated according to a set of *n* coordination strategies contained in *ATS(W)*. It should be noted that if $failed \notin ATS(W,t_a)$ where $ATS(W,t_a)$ represents the acceptable termination states of the task t_a in *ATS(W)* then $CS(W_s, ts_{k_a}(W), (t_{a_i})_{i\in[1,z_a]}, t_a) = \varnothing$. From 5-6 and 7-1, we can derive the existence condition of an acceptable instance of *W* with respect to a valid *ATS(W)*.

Theorem 7-3: Let $a,k \in [1,n]\times[1,j]$ such that $ts_k(W,t_a)=failed$ and $ts_k(W) \in ATS(W)$. $\exists W_s$ acceptable instance of *W* with respect to *ATS(W)* such that $ts_k(W) \in TS(W_s)$ ⇔ $\exists! l \in [1,j]$ such that $ts_l(W) \in TS(W_s)$ is a generator of t_a compatible with $ts_k(W)$ in *ATS(W)*.

This theorem only states that an *ATS(W)* allowing the failure of a given task can be used to coordinate a composite service also allowing the failure of the same task ⇔ *ATS(W)* contains a complete coordination strategy associated to this task, i.e. it is valid.

Transaction-Aware Assignment Procedure

In this section, we present the procedure that is used to assign services to tasks based on transactional requirements. This algorithm uses *ATS(W)* as a set of requirements during the service assignment procedure and thus identifies from a pool of available services those whose transactional properties match the transactional requirements associated to workflow tasks defined in *ATS(W)* in terms of acceptable termination states. The assignment procedure is an iterative process, services are assigned to tasks one after the other. The assignment procedure therefore creates at each step *i* a partial instance of *W* noted W_s^i. We can define as well the set $TS(W_s^i)$ which represents the termination states of *W* that the transactional properties of the *i* services already assigned allow to reach. Intuitively the acceptable termination states refer to the degree of flexibility offered when choosing the services with respect to the different coordination strategies verified in *ATS(W)*. This degree of flexibility is influenced by two parameters:

- The list of acceptable termination states for each workflow task. This list can be determined using *ATS(W)*. This is a direct requirement which specifies the termination states allowed for each task and therefore introduces requirements on the service's transactional properties to be assigned to a given task: this service can only reach the states defined in *ATS(W)* for the considered task.
- The assignment process is iterative and therefore, as we assign new services to tasks, $TS(W_s^i)$ changes and the transactional properties required to the assignment of further services too. For instance, we are sure to no longer reach the termination states $CTS(ts_k(W),t_a)$ allowing the failure of the task t_a in *ATS(W)* when we assign a service *(r)* to t_a. In this specific case, we no longer care about the states reached by other tasks in $CTS(ts_k(W),t_a)$ and therefore there is no transactional requirements introduced for the tasks to which services have not already been assigned.

We therefore need to define first the transactional requirements for the assignment of a service after *i* steps in the assignment procedure.

Extraction of Transactional Requirements

From the two requirements above, we define for a task t_a:

- $ATS(W,t_a)$: Set of acceptable termination states of t_a which is derived from *ATS(W)*
- $DIS(t_a, W_s^i)$: This is the set of transactional requirements that the service assigned to t_a must meet based on the previous assignments. This set is determined based on the following reasoning:
- (DIS_1): the service must be compensatable $\Leftrightarrow$ $compensated \in DIS(t_a, W_s^i)$
- (DIS_2): the service must be retriable $\Leftrightarrow$ $failed \notin DIS(t_a, W_s^i)$

Using these two sets, we are able to compute $MIN_{TP}(s_a, t_a, W_s^i) = ATS(W, t_a) \cap DIS(t_a, W_s^i)$ which defines the transactional properties a service s_a has at least to comply with in order to be assigned to the task t_a at the *i+1* assignment step. We simply check the retriability and compensatability properties for the set $MIN_{TP}(s_a, t_a, W_s^i)$:

- $failed \notin MIN_{TP}(s_a, t_a, W_s^i) \Leftrightarrow s_a$ has to verify the retriability property
- $compensated \in MIN_{TP}(s_a, t_a, W_s^i) \Leftrightarrow$ s_a has to verify the compensatability property

The set $ATS(W,t_a)$ is easily derived from $ATS(W)$. We need now to compute $DIS(t_a, W_s^i)$. We assume that we are at the $i+1$ step of an assignment procedure, i.e. the current partial instance of W is W_s^i. Computing $DIS(t_a, W_s^i)$ means determining if (DIS_1) and (DIS_2) are true. From these two statements we can derive three properties:

1. (DIS_1) implies that state *compensated* can definitely be reached by t_a
2. (DIS_2) implies that t_a cannot *fail*
3. (DIS_2) implies that t_a cannot be *canceled*

The two first properties can be directly derived from (DIS_1) and (DIS_2). The third one is derived from the fact that if a task cannot be *canceled* when a task fails, then it has to finish its execution and reach at least the state *completed*. In this case, if a service cannot be *canceled* then it cannot *fail*, which is the third property. In order to verify whether 1., 2. and 3. are true, we introduce the set of theorems 7-4, 7-5 and 7-6.

Theorem 7-4: Let $a \in [1,n]$. The state *compensated* can definitely be reached by $t_a \Leftrightarrow \exists b \in [1,n]-\{a\}$ verifying *(7-4b)*: s_b not retriable is assigned to t_b and $\exists ts_k(W) \in ATS(W)$ generator of t_b such that $ts_k(W,t_a)$=*compensated*.

Proof: $\Leftarrow$: Since the service s_b is not retriable, it can *fail* and $ts_k(W) \in ATS(W)$ generator of t_b such that $ts_k(W,t_a)$=*compensated* is in $TS(W_s)$.

$\Rightarrow$: Derived from *(P2)* and 5-6.

This theorem states that the execution of a composite service may lead a task t_a to the state *compensated* if:

- there exists a termination state part of $ATS(W)$ wherein a task t_b fails and t_a is compensated and
- t_b has been assigned to a service that is not retriable.

The two following theorems are proved similarly:

Theorem 7-5: Let $a \in [1,n]$. t_a cannot *fail* $\Leftrightarrow \exists b \in [1,n]-\{a\}$ verifying *(7-5b)*: (s_b not compensatable is assigned to t_b and $\exists ts_k(W) \in ATS(W)$ generator of t_a such that $ts_k(W,t_b)$=*compensated*) or (t_b is flexible to t_a and s_b not retriable is assigned to t_b and $\forall ts_k(W) \in ATS(W)$ such that $ts_k(W,t_a)$=*failed*, $ts_k(W,t_b) \neq$*canceled*).

Theorem 7-6: Let $a, b \in [1,n]$ such that t_a is flexible to t_b. t_a is not *canceled* when t_b *fails* $\Leftrightarrow$ *(7-6b)*: s_b not retriable is assigned to t_b and $\forall ts_k(W) \in ATS(W)$ such that $ts_k(W,t_b)$=*failed*, $ts_k(W,t_a) \neq$*canceled*.

According to the theorems 7-4, 7-5 and 7-6, in order to compute $DIS(t_a, W_s^i)$, we have to compare t_a with each of the i tasks $t_b \in W-\{t_a\}$ to which a service s_b has been already assigned. This is an iterative procedure and at the initialization phase, since no task has been yet compared to t_a, s_a can be of type *(p)*: $DIS(t_a, W_s^i) = \{failed\}$.

1. if t_b verifies *(7-4b)* $\Rightarrow$ $compensated \in DIS(t_a, W_s^i)$
2. if t_b verifies *(7-5b)* $\Rightarrow$ $failed \notin DIS(t_a, W_s^i)$
3. if t_b is flexible to t_a and verifies *(7-6b)* $\Rightarrow$ $failed \notin DIS(t_a, W_s^i)$

The verification stops if $failed \notin DIS(t_a, W_s^i)$ and $compensated \in DIS(t_a, W_s^i)$. With $MIN_{TP}(s_a, t_a, W_s^i)$, we are able to select the appropriate service to be assigned to a given task according to transactional requirements.

Service Assignment Process

Services are assigned to each workflow task based on an iterative process. Depending on the transactional requirements and the transactional properties of the services available for each task, different scenarios can occur:

(i) services of type *(rc)* are available for the task. It is not necessary to compute transactional requirements as such services match all transactional requirements.
(ii) only one service is available for the task. We need to compute the transactional requirements associated to the task and either the only available service is sufficient or there is no solution.
(iii) services of types *(r)* and *(c)* but none of type *(rc)* are available for the task. We need to compute the transactional requirements associated to the task and we have three cases. First, (retriability and compensatability) is required in which case there is no solution. Second, retriability (resp. compensatability) is required and we assign a service of type *(r)* (resp. *(c)*) to the task. Third, there is no requirement.

The idea is therefore to assign first services to the tasks verifying *(i)* and *(ii)* since there is no flexibility in the choice of the service. Tasks verifying *(iii)* are finally analyzed. Based on the transactional requirements raised by the remaining tasks, we first assign services to tasks with a non-empty transactional requirement. We then handle the assignment for tasks with an empty transactional requirement. Note that the transactional requirements of all the tasks to which services are not yet assigned are also affected (updated) as a result of the current service assignment. If no task has transactional requirements then we assign the services of type *(r)* to assure the completion of the remaining tasks' execution.

Theorem 7-7: The service assignment procedure creates an instance of W that is acceptable with respect to a valid *ATS(W)*.

Proof: Let W_s be an instance of W resulting from the service assignment procedure and a service s_a assigned to a task t_a in W_s. The definition 7-1 has to be verified and we therefore consider *(A)* and *(B)* (keeping the notations of theorem 7-2):

$$\forall\ a \in [1,n],\ failed \in ATS(W,t_a) \Rightarrow$$
(A) $$CS(W_s, ts_{k_a}(W), (t_{a_i})_{i\in[1,z_a]}, t_a) \subset ATS(W)$$

$$\forall\ a \in [1,n],\ failed \notin ATS(W,t_a) \Rightarrow$$
(B) $$CS(W_s, ts_{k_a}(W), (t_{a_i})_{i\in[1,z_a]}, t_a) \subset ATS(W)$$

(A): We suppose that $failed \in ATS(W,t_a)$ then we have two possibilities:

- s_a is retriable and

$$CS(W_s, ts_{k_a}(W), (t_{a_i})_{i\in[1,z_a]}, t_a) = \varnothing \subset ATS(W)$$

- s_a can *fail* and with 1., 2. and 3. we get $ts_{k_a}(W) \in TS(W_s)$ and therefore $CS(W_s, ts_{k_a}(W), (t_{a_i})_{i\in[1,z_a]}, t_a) \subset ATS(W)$ since *ATS(W)* is valid.

(B): We suppose that $failed \notin ATS(W,t_a)$ then $failed \notin MIN_{TP}(s_a, t_a, W_s^i)$ and s_a is retriable. Therefore, $CS(W_s, ts_{k_a}(W), (t_{a_i})_{i\in[1,z_a]}, t_a) = \varnothing \subset ATS(W)$.

Finally, we get $CS(W_s, ts_{k_a}(W), (t_{a_i})_{i\in[1,z_a]}, t_a) \subset ATS(W)$ and W_s is an acceptable instance of W with respect to *ATS(W)*.

Coordination of W_s

Now, using *(A)* and *(B)* defined in the proof of 7-7 and keeping the same notations, we are able to specify the coordination strategy of W_s against each workflow task. We get indeed the following theorem.

Theorem 7-8: Let W_s be an acceptable instance of W with respect to *ATS(W)*. We note $(t_{a_i})_{i\in[1,n_r]}$ the set of tasks to which no retriable services have been assigned. We get:

$$TS(W_s) = \{tscomp(W_s)\} \cup \bigcup_{i=1}^{n_r} \left(CTS(ts_{k_{a_i}}(W), t_{a_i}) - \bigcup_{j=1}^{z_a} FTS(t_{a_{i_j}}, t_{a_i}) \right)$$

Having computed $TS(W_s)$, we obtain the list of the possible termination states that can be reached by the instance W_s and thus that defines the coordination rules associated with the execution of W_s. $TS(W_s)$ is indeed derived from $ATS(W)$ which contains for all tasks at most a single coordination strategy as specified in 6-1. As a result, whenever the failure of a task t_a is detected, a transactional protocol in charge of coordinating an instance W_s resulting from our approach reacts as follows. The coordination strategy $CS(W_s, ts_{k_a}(W), (t_{a_i})_{i\in[1,z_a]}, t_a)$ corresponding to t_a is identified and a unique termination state belonging to $CS(W_s, ts_{k_a}(W), (t_{a_i})_{i\in[1,z_a]}, t_a)$ can be reached given the current state of the workflow execution.

Discussion

The operations that are relevant from the complexity point of view are twofold: the definition of transactional requirements by means of the acceptable termination states model and the execution of the transaction-aware service assignment procedure.

One can argue that building an *ATS* table specifying the transactional requirements of a business process *W* consists of computing the whole *TS(W)* table, yet this is not the case. Building a *ATS(W)* set in fact only requires for designers to identify the tasks of *W* that they allow to fail as part of the process execution and to select the termination state generator associated with each of those tasks that meet their requirements in terms of failure atomicity. Once this phase is complete, designers only need to select the tasks whose execution can be canceled when the former tasks may fail and complete the associated coordination strategy.

The second aspect concerns the complexity of the transaction aware assignment procedure that we presented in section 6 and 7.

Theorem 7-9: Let $W = (t_a)_{a\in[1,n]}$ a workflow. The complexity of the transaction-aware assignment procedure is $O(n^3)$.

Proof: We can show that the number of operations necessary to compute the step *i* of the assignment procedure for a task t_a is bounded by $4\times n\times i$. Computing the step *i* indeed consists of verifying the theorems 7-4, 7-5 and 7-6 and determining $ATS(W,t_a)$. On the one hand, performing the operations part of theorems 7-4 (one comparison), 7-5 (two comparisons) and 7-6 (one comparison) requires at most 4 comparisons. On the other hand, building $ATS(W,t_a)$ requires at most *n* operations (there is at most *n* generators in a *ATS(W)* set). Therefore, we can derive that the number of operations that needs to be performed in order to compute the *n* steps of the assignment procedure for a workflow composed of *n* tasks is bounded by $4\times n\times\left(\sum_{j=1}^{n} j\right)$ which is equivalent to n^3 as $n\to\infty$.

Example

Back to our motivating example, we consider the workflow W_1 of Figure 2. Designers have defined $ATS_2(W_1)$ as the transactional requirements for the considered business application and the set of available services for each task of W_1 is specified in Figure 5. The goal is to assign services to workflow tasks so that the instance of W_1 is valid with respect to $ATS_2(W_1)$ and we apply the assignment procedure presented in section 7.2. We first start to assign the services of type *(rc)* for which it is not necessary to compute any transactional requirements. s_{13} which is available for task 1 is therefore assigned without any computation. We then consider the tasks for which only one service is available. This is the case for task 4 for which only one service of type *(p)* is available. We therefore verify whether s_{41} can be assigned to task 4. We compute $MIN_{TP}(s_a, t_4, W_{1s}^1) = ATS_2(W_1, t_4) \cap DIS(t_4, W_{1s}^1)$. $ATS_2(W_1, t_4) = \{completed,\ failed\}$ and $DIS(t_4, W_{1s}^1) = \{failed\}$ as s_{13} the only service already assigned is of type *(rc)* and the theorems 7-4, 7-5 and 7-6 are not verified, none the conditions required within these theorems are indeed verified by the service s_{13}. Thus

$MIN_{TP}(s_a, t_4, W_{1s}^1) = \{failed\}$ and s_{41} can be assigned to task 4 as it matches the transactional requirements. Now we compute the transactional requirements of task 2 for which services of type *(r)* and *(c)* are available and we get $MIN_{TP}(s_a, t_2, W_{1s}^2) = \{failed\}$. As described in the assignment procedure we do not assign any service to this task as it does not introduce at this step of the procedure any transactional requirements to make a decision on the candidate service to choose. We therefore compute the transactional requirements of task 3 and we get $MIN_{TP}(s_a, t_3, W_{1s}^2) = \{failed, compensated\}$ as theorem 7-4 is verified with the service s_{41} that is indeed not retriable. The service s_{32} which is of type *(c)* can thus be assigned to task 3 as it matches the computed transactional requirements. We come back now to task 2 and compute the transactional requirements once again and we get $MIN_{TP}(s_a, t_2, W_{1s}^3) = \{failed, compensated\}$ as theorem 7-4 is now verified with the service s_{32} which is indeed not retriable. It should be noted that at this step, the transactional requirements associated to task 2 have been modified because of the assignment of the service s_{32} to task 3. As the device s_{22} matches the transactional requirements it can be assigned to the task.

IMPLEMENTATION

To implement the above presented work we augmented an existing functional OWL-S matchmaker (Tang, Liebetruth et al. 2003), with transactional matchmaking capabilities. In order to achieve our goal, the matchmaking procedure has been split into two phases. First, the functional matchmaking based on OWL-S semantic matching is performed in order to identify subsets of the available services that meet the functional requirements for each workflow task. Second, the implementation of the transaction-aware service assignment procedure is run against the selected sets of services in order to build an acceptable instance fulfilling defined transactional requirements.

The structure of the matchmaker consists of several components whose dependencies are displayed in Figure 6. The composition manager manages the process of matchmaking and provides a Java API that can be invoked to start the composition. It gets as input an abstract process description specifying the functional requirements for the candidate services and a table of acceptable termination states. The registry stores OWL-S profiles of services that are available. Those OWL-S profiles have been augmented with the transactional properties offered by services. This has been done by adding to the non-functional information of the OWL-S profiles a new element called *transactionalproperties* that specifies two Booleans attributes *retriable* and *compensatable* as shown in the sample listing below:

```
<tp:transactionalproperties
retriable="true"
compensatable="true"/>
```

In the first phase of the composition procedure, the service manager is invoked with a set of OWL-S profiles that specify the functional requirements for each workflow task. The service manager gets access to the registry where all published profiles are available and to the functional matchmaker provided by (Tang, Liebetruth et al. 2003) and that is used to match the available profiles against the functional requirements specified in the workflow. For each workflow task, the service manager then returns a set of functionally matching profiles along with their transactional properties. The composition manager then initiates the second phase, passing these sets along with the process description, and the table of acceptable termination states to the transactional composer. The transactional composer starts the transaction-aware service assignment procedure using the transactional matchmaker by classifying first those sets into five groups:

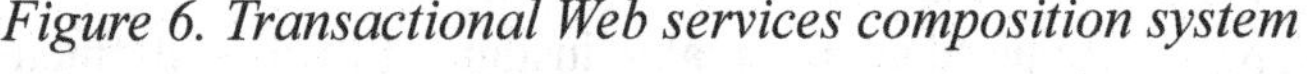

Figure 6. Transactional Web services composition system

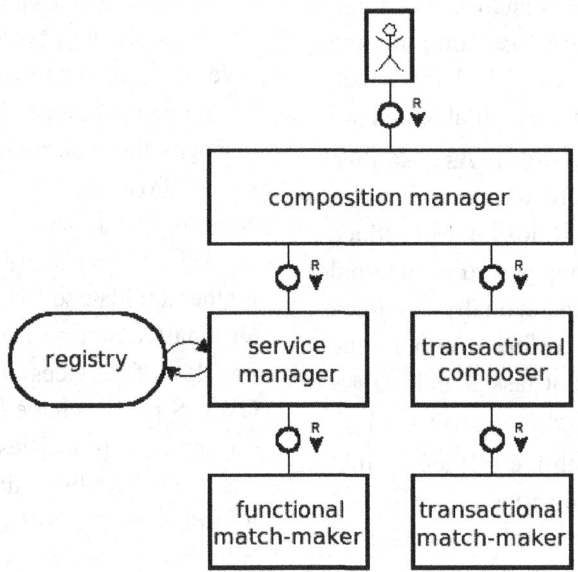

- sets including only services of type *(p)*
- sets including only services of type *(r)*
- sets including only services of type *(c)*
- sets including services of types *(r)* and *(c)*
- sets including services of type *(rc)*

Once those sets are formed, the iterative transactional composition process is performed as specified above based on the table of acceptable termination states defined for the process. Of course depending on the set of available services and the specified acceptable termination states, the algorithm execution may end without yielding a solution. The implementation work we have performed reveals that the execution overhead introduced by our transaction-aware assignment procedure within the complete service composition procedure is in fact negligible with respect to the time required to parse OWL-S documents and execute the functional match-making procedure.

COORDINATION

In this section we suggest a coordination framework for transactional composite applications, based on Web services technologies. To illustrate the latter, we introduce a scenario featuring the transactional coordination of a cross-organizational composite application that is built based on our transaction-aware assignment procedure. To that respect, the business partners involved in the composite application share their services and communicate through local workflow engines that help them manage the overall collaboration in a distributed manner. The system architecture is depicted in Figure 7. In order to support the execution of cross-organizational composite applications, we designed in the fashion of the WS-Coordination initiative (Langworthy, 2005) a transactional stack composed of the following components:

Figure 7. Transactional Architecture

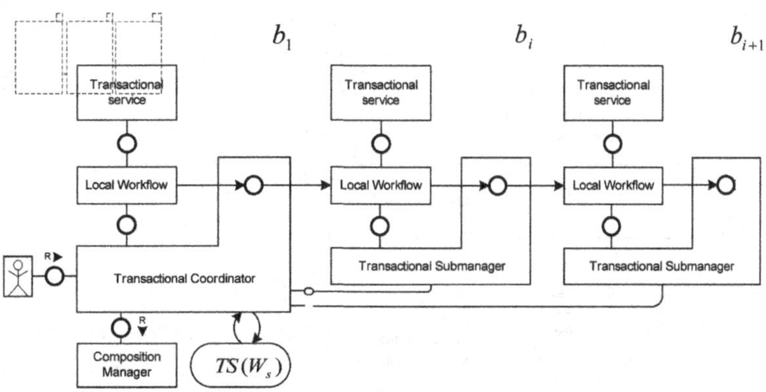

- **Transactional coordinator**: this component is supported by the composite application initiator. On the one hand it implements the transaction-aware business partner assignment procedure as part of the composition manager module and on the other hand it is in charge of assuring the coordinator role relying on the set *TS(Ws)* outcome of the assignment procedure.
- **Transactional submanager**: this component is deployed on the other partners and is in charge of forwarding coordination messages from the local workflow to the coordinator and conversely.

In the infrastructure that is deployed on each business partner to implement the coordination framework presented in this section, the transactional coordinator plays the role of interface between the business process and the other business partners when it comes to managing the notification messages exchanged based on the coordination rules extracted from *TS(Ws)*. Some of these messages received by the transactional coordinator should be forwarded to the local business process to take appropriate actions while some others are only relevant to the local transactional (sub)coordinator. The business process may also require to issue a notification to its local transactional (sub)coordinator when a failure occurs. The messages exchanged between these three layers are derived from the state model depicted in Figure 3. The infrastructure deployed on a given business partner basically consists of three layers:

- **The transactional service layer** representing the business partner's available operations,
- **The local workflow layer** corresponding to the local workflow engine,
- **The coordination layer** implementing the local (sub)coordinator module.

The message exchanges that can take place on a given business partner between these three layer are depicted in Figure 8 and specified as follows.

- **Activate**: The activate message is basically issued by the local workflow engine to the local workflow engine of the next business partner involved in the workflow. In fact this message instantiates the process execution on the business partner side.
- **Compensate, Cancel**: The compensate and cancel messages are received at the coordination layer and forwarded to the local workflow layer that forwards them in a second time to the transactional service layer to perform to corresponding

Figure 8. Infrastructure internal communications

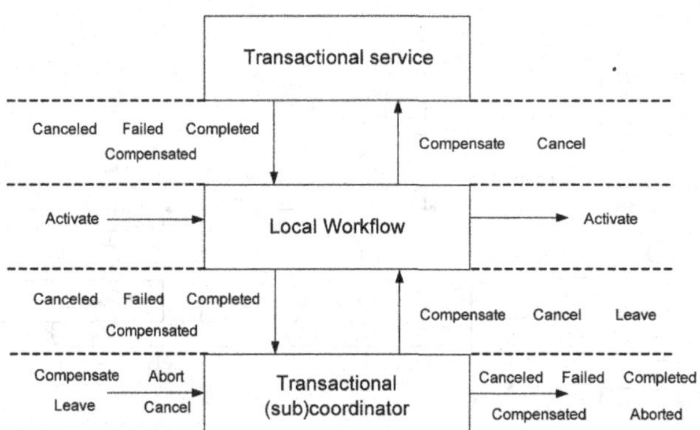

functions i.e. compensation or cancellation of an operation.

- **Compensated, Cancelled, Completed**: These messages simply notify that the corresponding events have occurred: compensation, cancellation, or completion of an operation. Issued at the transactional service layer, they are forwarded to the coordination layer in order to be dispatched to the composite application coordinator.
- **Failed**: Issued at the transactional service layer, the failed message is forwarded to the coordination layer in order to be dispatched to the composite application coordinator. If the operation performed at the transactional service layer is retriable, no failed message is forwarded to the local workflow layer as we consider that the retry primitive is inherent to any retriable operation.
- **Abort, Aborted**: The abortion message is received at the coordination layer and acknowledged with an aborted message. Upon receipt of this message, the business simply leaves the composite application execution; no message is forwarded to the other layers since the local workflow has not yet been instantiated.

RELATED WORK

Transactional consistency of workflows and database systems has been an active research topic over the last 15 years yet it is still an open issue in the area of Web services (Curbera, Khalaf et al. 2003), (Gudgin, 2004), (Little, 2003) and especially composite Web services. Composite Web services indeed introduce new requirements for transactional systems such as dynamicity, semantic description and relaxed atomicity. Existing transactional models for advanced applications (Elmagarmid, 1992) lack flexibility to integrate these requirements (Alonso, Agrawal et al. 1996) as for instance they are not designed to support the execution of dynamically generated composite services. Our solution allows the specification of transactional requirements supporting relaxed atomicity for an abstract workflow specification and the selection of a semantically described service set meeting the transactional requirements defined at the workflow design stage.

Our work is based on (Bhiri, Perrin et al. 2005) which presents the first approach specifying relaxed atomicity requirements for composite Web services based on the ATS tool and a transactional semantic. Despite a solid contribution, this work appears to be limited if we consider the possible integration into automatic Web services composition systems. It indeed only details transactional rules to validate a given composite service with respect to defined transactional requirements. In this approach, transactional requirements do not play any role in the component services selection process which may result in several attempts for designers to determine a valid composition of services. On the contrary, our solution provides a systematic procedure enabling the automatic design of transactional composite Web services. Besides, our contribution also defines the mathematical foundations to specify valid *ATS* for workflows based on the concept of coordination strategy.

Finally, our solution can be used to augment recent standardization efforts in the area of transactional coordination of Web services (Abbott, 2005), (Langworthy, 2005). Our approach indeed provides adaptive coordination specifications based on the transactional properties of the component services instantiating a given workflow. Existing Web services coordination specifications (Langworthy, 2005) are indeed not flexible enough as they do not neither allow workflow designers to specify their transactional requirements nor take into account the transactional properties offered by Web services.

CONCLUSION

We presented a systematic procedure to automate the design of transactional composite Web services. Our solution enables the selection of component Web services not only according to functional requirements but also to transactional ones. Transactional requirements are defined by designers and serve as an input to define both reliable composite Web services and coordination protocols used to ensure the consistency of their execution. On the one hand this service assignment approach can be used to augment existing Web services composition systems (Agarwal, Dasgupta, et al. 2005) as it can be fully integrated in existing functional matchmaking procedures. On the other hand, our approach defines adaptive coordination rules that can be deployed on Web services coordination specifications (Langworthy, 2005) in order to increase their flexibility. Besides, the theoretical results presented in this chapter have been integrated into an OWL-S matchmaker as a proof of concept.

ACKNOWLEGMENT

This work has been partially sponsored by EU IST Directorate General as a part of FP6 IST projects MOSQUITO and R4eGov and by SAP Labs France S.A.S.

REFERENCES

W3C. (2002). *Web Services Description Language (WSDL)*.

Abbott, M. (2005). *Business transaction protocol*.

Agarwal, V., Dasgupta, K., Karnik, N., Kumar, A., Kundu, A., Mittal, S., & Srivastava, B. (2005), A service creation environment based on end to end composition of web services. In *Proceedings of the WWW conference* (pp. 128-137). Chiba, Japan

Alonso, G., Agrawal, D., Abbadi, A. E., Kamath, M., Gnthr, R., & Mohan, C. (1996). Advanced transaction models in workflow contexts. In *Proceedings of the 12th International Conference on Data Engineering*, New Orleans (pp. 574-581).

Bhiri, S., Perrin, O., & Godart, C. (2005). Ensuring required failure atomicity of composite web services, *Proceedings of the WWW conference* (pp. 138-147). Chiba, Japan.

Curbera, F., Khalaf, R., Mukhi, N., Tai, S., & Weerawarana, S. (2003). The next step in web services. *Communications of the ACM, 46*(10), 29–34. doi:10.1145/944217.944234

Elmagarmid, A. K. (1992). *Database Transaction Models for Advanced Applications*. Morgan Kaufmann.

Greenfield, P., Fekete, A., Jang, J., & Kuo, D. (2003), Compensation is not enough. In *Proceedings of the 7th International Enterprise Distributed Object Computing Conference (EDOC'03)*, 232. Brisbane, Australia.

Gudgin, M. (2004), Secure, reliable, transacted; innovation in web services architecture, In*Proceedings of the ACM International Conference on Management of Data* (pp. 879-880).

ISO. (n.d.). *Open System Interconnection- Distributed Transaction Processing (OSI-TP) Model, ISO IS 100261.*

Langworthy, D. (2005). *WS-AtomicTransaction.*

Langworthy, D. (2005). *WS-BusinessActivity.*

Langworthy, D. (2005). *WS-Coordination.*

Little, M. (2003). Transactions and web services. *Communications*, *46*(10), 49–54.

Mehrotra, S., Rastogi, R., Silberschatz, A., & Korth, H. (1992), A transaction model for multidatabase systems. In *Proceedings of the 12th IEEE International Conference on Distributed Computing Systems (ICDCS92)* (pp. 56-63). Yokohama, Japan.

OWL Services Coalition. (2003). *OWL-S: Semantic Markup for Web Services.*

Rusinkiewicz, M., & Sheth, A. (1995). Specification and execution of transactional workflows. *Modern database systems: the object model, interoperability, and beyond* (pp. 592–620).

Schuldt, H., Alonso, G., & Schek, H. (1999) Concurrency control and recovery in transactional process management. In *Proceedings of the Conference on Principles of Database Systems* (pp. 316-326). Philadelphia, Pennsylvania.

Tang, S. Liebetruth, C., & Jaeger, M. C. (2003) The OWL-S matcher software. Retrieved from http://flp.cs.tu-berlin.de/

Thatte, S. (2003). *Business Process Execution Language for Web Services Version 1.1 (BPEL).*

Chapter 9
Security Personalization for Internet and Web Services

George O.M. Yee
National Research Council Canada, Canada

Larry Korba
National Research Council Canada, Canada

ABSTRACT

The growth of the Internet has been accompanied by the growth of Internet services (e.g., e-commerce, e-health). This proliferation of services and the increasing attacks on them by malicious individuals have highlighted the need for service security. The security requirements of an Internet or Web service may be specified in a security policy. The provider of the service is then responsible for implementing the security measures contained in the policy. However, a service customer or consumer may have security preferences that are not reflected in the provider's security policy. In order for service providers to attract and retain customers, as well as reach a wider market, a way of personalizing a security policy to a particular customer is needed. We derive the content of an Internet or Web service security policy and propose a flexible security personalization approach that will allow an Internet or Web service provider and customer to negotiate to an agreed-upon personalized security policy. In addition, we present two application examples of security policy personalization, and overview the design of our security personalization prototype.

INTRODUCTION

The term "Internet service" is used here to mean any electronic service that is accessed using the Internet, for example electronic banking. In the following, we use "Internet service" to refer to all electronic services that are available through the Internet, including Web services that are based on the service oriented architecture. We use "Web service" when we wish to indicate that we are treating Web services in particular.

A large number of Internet services targeting consumers have accompanied the rapid growth of the Internet. Internet services are available for banking, shopping, learning, healthcare, and the government online, to name a few. However, these services are subject to malicious attack in one form or another. This leads to concerns over their security (Joshi, Aref, Ghafoor, & Spafford, 2001).

In order for Internet services to be successful, they must be secured from malicious individuals who constantly try to compromise them. An effective and flexible way of managing security for these services is to make use of security policies. An Internet service security policy is a specification of what security measures will be used to protect the service from security attacks. A security policy by itself does not guarantee that its stated security measures will be put in place or be complied with. That is an area of policy compliance that is outside the scope of this article.

An Internet service provider makes use of a security policy to specify the security measures that it has put or will put in place to protect its services. However, this security policy may not match up with the security preferences of a customer or consumer (we use "user," "customer," and "consumer" interchangeably) of the services. For example, suppose the security measure is user authentication via password. This authentication approach is known to be insecure. A security-sensitive consumer such as a defense contractor, may wish to add biometric authentication. Unless the user authentication is changed to include biometrics, the defense contractor would not be able to make use of the service. As another example, suppose the security measure is access control. The provider's security policy may provide access to five features of a service, whereas a particular customer may need access to only three features. In this case, the customer may be reluctant to make use of this provider's service, especially if the customer can find another provider that only offers the features needed and at a lower price. One solution to these mismatches of a provider's security policy with a customer's security preferences is to allow the customer to personalize the security policy by negotiating with the provider regarding the security measures that are in the provider's security policy. We call this negotiation process *security policy personalization*, that is, the provider's security policy becomes personalized to a particular customer through negotiation.

This article extends Yee & Korba (2005b) by: (a) providing new details on the "scheme for online help in making offers" during the negotiation process, (b) providing new details on how the approach can be implemented for Web Services, (c) giving a more complete description of the prototype, (d) adding example applications, (e) enlarging the section on related works, (f) including an evaluation of the proposed approach for security policy personalization, and (g) improving the clarity of the writing in all sections.

The objectives and contributions of this article are to: (a) introduce the need for personalization of provider service security policies, (b) derive a security policy template suitable for use with Internet services, (c) present an approach for consumer-provider negotiation that accomplishes this personalization, including a novel method of providing help during negotiation, (d) show how security policy personalization can be implemented for Web services, (e) give example applications of security policy personalization, (f) describe our prototype for security policy negotiation, and (g) evaluate this work and discuss related works.

Note that our security policy template is only an example template, since it may change depending on future security requirements as well as available security technology.

The remainder of this article is organized as follows. The next section defines Internet services and derives requirements for security policies and their negotiation. Section "Security policy negotiation," derives an Internet service security policy template, presents our approach for Internet services security policy personalization using negotiation, and shows how this approach can be implemented for Web services. Section "Application Examples," describes two example applications of security policy personalization. Section "Prototype for Security Policy Negotiation," gives an overview of our prototype. Section "Related Work," examines the literature for related work. Section "Evaluation," discusses the applicability and effectiveness of our personalization approach. We end with conclusions and future research.

INTERNET SERVICES, REQUIREMENTS FOR SECURITY POLICIES AND THEIR NEGOTIATION

In this section, we begin by defining an Internet service. We then describe requirements for security policies and security policy negotiation.

Internet Services

An Internet service, for the purposes of this article, is characterized by the following attributes:

- The service is performed by application software (service software) that is owned by a provider (usually a company); the service is accessible across the Internet.
- The provider's service software can make use of the service software of other providers in order to perform its service.
- The provider has a security policy that specifies what security measures it will use to secure the service.
- The service may require the use of the consumer's private information, in which case it should also have a privacy policy that states what private information it requires and how it will make use of the private information.
- The service is consumed by a person or another application accessing the service across the Internet.
- The consumer has security and privacy preferences for the service that may not be reflected in the provider's security and privacy policies respectively.
- There is usually a fee that the consumer pays the provider for use of the service.

Thus, an Internet service includes all electronic services that are accessible via the Internet, including Web services. These services may differ in the way they are implemented but our approach applies to all of them. Two classes of Internet services that differ in implementation are: (a) client-server type services where consumers (clients) access a service Website (server) with the service software running at the backend, and (b) Web services that are based on the service oriented architecture (O'Neill et al., 2003) and use protocols based on XML (World Wide Web Consortium, n.d.). Examples of current Internet services are Amazon.com (online retailer), optionsxpress.com (online stockbroker), and WebMD.com (health information and technology solutions provider).

Security Policy Requirements

Requirements for Internet services security policies address what security measures should be covered in the policy. Since Internet services fall under the category of open systems, we begin by looking at requirements prescribed by ISO 7498-2, the reference model for security architectures by the International Organization for Standardization (International Organization for Standardization, n.d.).

This standard identifies five main categories of security services, as follows:

1. Authentication
2. Access Control
3. Data Confidentiality
4. Data Integrity
5. Non-repudiation

The International Telecommunication Union Telecommunication Standardization Sector (ITU-T) provides Recommendation X.800, Security Architecture for OSI (open systems interconnection) (ITU-T) that lists the same five main categories of security services mentioned previously. We propose that these five categories of security services be covered in an Internet security policy since they are part of standards. We would add the following security services:

6. Secure Logging—of user transactions by the provider
7. Certification—user or provider would use some certifying authority to certify credentials
8. Malware Detection—user or provider would use some anti-malware software to detect and eliminate malware from their computing platforms
9. Application Monitoring—user platform monitoring for licensed, verified, and permitted applications (results only reported to the user)

Security services 6 through 9 are added to enhance security required in the Internet services environment. Secure logs assist in the verification of policy compliance. Certification is required for credentials such as certificates exchanged across the Internet. Malware detection is a definite requirement in today's Internet-connected computing platforms that are open to all sorts of virus and Trojan horse attacks. Application monitoring protects the user from the inadvertent use of unlicensed, illegal, or malicious programs, which may be loaded onto the user's platform via the Internet by attackers. We thus have 9 security services that should be specified in an Internet service security policy. Figure 1 identifies where these security services are typically applied using an Internet service network view. In Figure 1, the certification authority is typically a certificate authority as used for public key infrastructure (PKI). The double arrows represent two-way

Figure 1. Application of security services (numbers correspond to security services listed above)

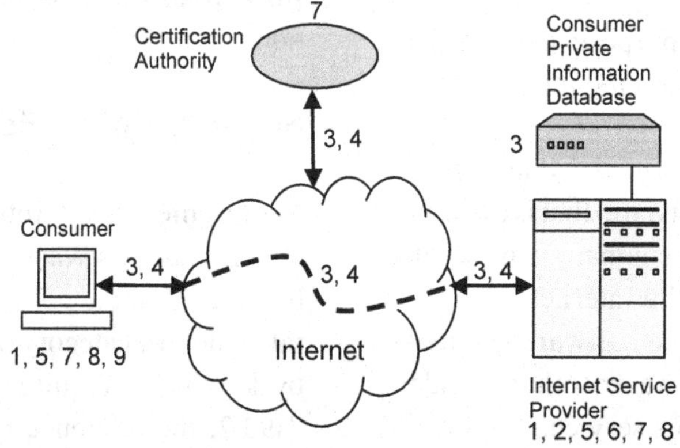

communication channels, and the dashed line represents logical traversal of the Internet, that is the actual traversal, possibly using diverse physical links, is not shown. The storage of the consumer's private information is identified explicitly as requiring confidentiality. The provider may make use of other service providers in the provision of its service but this aspect is not shown.

These standards also list specific security services under the main security service categories. As an example, non-repudiation has the specific services (with the obvious meanings): "Non-repudiation, Origin" and "Non-repudiation, Destination." As well, security mechanisms (e.g., digital signature) are used to support or implement security services. We will employ specific services and security mechanisms to formulate our Internet services security policy template in the next section.

Security Policy Negotiation Requirements

Based on the Internet service environment (i.e., providers providing services to consumers across the Internet), and negotiation processes in general, we propose the following requirements for Internet services security policy negotiation:

1. The security services and mechanisms to be negotiated must be clear and understandable.
2. The consumer may negotiate any subset of security services and mechanisms in the policy.
3. There needs to be some form of trusted online help for the consumer in cases where it is difficult to know what choice to make in a particular step in the negotiation.
4. The consumer normally initiates negotiation after finding the service that she (note: we use "she" and "her" to stand for both sexes) wants to use. However, when a provider changes its service and requires new security levels, it may initiate a new security policy negotiation with the consumer.
5. Negotiation may be terminated by either the consumer or the provider, at any step in the negotiation prior to a successful outcome. If so terminated, the associated service may not proceed.
6. The user interface for the negotiation must be easy to use, intuitive, and trustable (i.e., give the user a sense of ease that everything is working as stated or planned).

Requirement 3 is needed in order that the negotiation is not blocked simply due to the fact that the consumer does not know what security choice to make. This can occur quite easily where the consumer is not knowledgeable about security resources. We will propose a way for achieving this requirement in the next section.

SECURITY POLICY NEGOTIATION

In this section, we first discuss the goals of security policy negotiation. We then define an Internet service security policy template according to the above security policy requirements. Finally, we present an approach for security policy negotiation that satisfies the above negotiation requirements.

Goals of Security Policy Negotiation

The consumer's objectives or goals for security policy negotiation differ from the provider's goals for such negotiation. In the absence of security policy personalization, the provider is concerned with protecting its systems (e.g., servers) and ensuring that there is just sufficient security to comply with laws and what is needed for the general working of the service (e.g., authentication,

Table 1. Internet service security policy template

Policy Use: **E-learning**	***Owner:*** **Learners Online, Inc.**	***Valid:*** **unlimited**
CONSUMER PROVISIONS	**PROVIDER PROVISIONS**	**PROVIDER PROVISIONS**
Consumer Authentication *Implement:* yes (default) *Mechanism:* password *Mechanism:* V+F biometrics	**Provider Authentication** *Implement:* yes (default) *Mechanism:* security token *Mechanism:* digital signature	**Communication Confidentiality** *Implement:* yes (default) *Mechanism:* SSL
Consumer Non-Repudiation *Implement:* yes (default) *Mechanism:* digital signature	**Provider Non-Repudiation** *Implement:* yes (default) *Mechanism:* digital signature	**Communication Integrity** *Implement:* yes (default) *Mechanism:* MD5 Hash
Consumer Certification *Implement:* yes (default) *Mechanism:* certificate	**Provider Certification** *Implement:* yes (default) *Mechanism:* certificate	**Secure Logging** *What:* order transactions *Mechanism:* 3DES encrypt *What:* user input *Mechanism:* 3DES encrypt
Consumer Malware Detect *Implement:* yes (default) *Mechanism:* Norton	**Provider Malware Detect** *Implement:* yes (default) *Mechanism:* Norton	**Access Control** *User Role:* Secretary *Resource:* scheduling module *Resource:* admin module *User Role:* President *Resource:* admin module *Resource:* salary module
Application Monitoring *Implement:* yes (default) *Mechanism:* IIT-ISG	**Data Store Confidentiality** *Implement:* yes (default) *Mechanism:* 3DES encrypt	

secure communication channel). Providing extra security beyond this level would take away from profitability, so the provider in all likelihood will not do so. However, in the presence of security policy negotiation, the provider must additionally comply with the customer's security requirements or face losing the customer to another provider. This does not necessarily mean that the provider's security costs will be higher since the consumer may require less security for special situations (e.g., consumer trades off security for performance where the service is supplied through a mobile device of limited power and where the lower security level is still adequate for the application). The consumer's goals for negotiation are to have the provider put in place the security measures that the consumer requires for her *personal* use of the service. These requirements may depend on the following aspects of the consumer's use of the service: service device (e.g., mobile or connected to physical lines), how the service is used (e.g., e-learning with highly sensitive information or e-learning with public information), and even environment (e.g., consumer's neighborhood has hackers that delight in breaking into Wi-Fi networks). Our application examples of security policy personalization will illustrate some of these consumer goals.

Internet Service Security Policy

Based on the requirements of the subsection title "Security Policy Requirements," and using example values and security mechanisms, we propose the Internet service security policy template shown in Table 1.

In Table 1, the top shaded portion is the policy header. The header contains the following administrative fields: *policy use* identifies for which service the policy is provided, *owner* identifies the name of the provider of the service, and *valid* specifies the end date after which the policy is no longer valid, or "initial/continuing" which indicates whether or not the security policy is enforced only initially or continuously. The figure also shows that some security services can have multiple mechanisms (e.g., consumer authentication using password and biometrics). In such cases, the additional mechanisms can simply be listed under the security service. Similarly, secure logging and access control can have additional items (e.g., access control can have additional resources under each role). Note that for most services, security policy negotiation would involve the selection of a particular mechanism. However, consumers can also select a set of mechanisms where the consumer either cannot decide or it does not matter to her which mechanism from the set will be implemented. In that case, the provider chooses which mechanism from the set to implement. The security policy outcome of a negotiation that chooses sets of security mechanisms instead of single mechanisms would look like Table 1.

Security Policy Negotiation

We propose that security policy negotiation be the first of two stages of negotiation, the second stage being privacy policy negotiation. Privacy policy negotiation is fully described in Yee & Korba (2003a) and Yee & Korba (2003b); it is outside the scope of this paper. Security policy negotiation is entered once the consumer has determined which service she wants to use. Privacy policy negotiation is entered only if security policy negotiation is successful. The service can only be activated if both stages of negotiation are successful. Where negotiation is not needed due to a match found between the provider's policy and the consumer's preferences, this result still signals a successful negotiation. Where a negotiation is unsuccessful, the consumer needs to look for another Internet service to try (or find ways to match the security requirements of the service but it is probably easier to just find another service). Figure 2 gives a flowchart of this process, where each box is only carried out if all the boxes above it are successful. Otherwise, the control flow returns to "start."

In this work, (see Figure 3), a non-autonomous software agent acts on behalf of the consumer to receive/send negotiation messages from/to the

Figure 2. Negotiation Stages prior to service execution

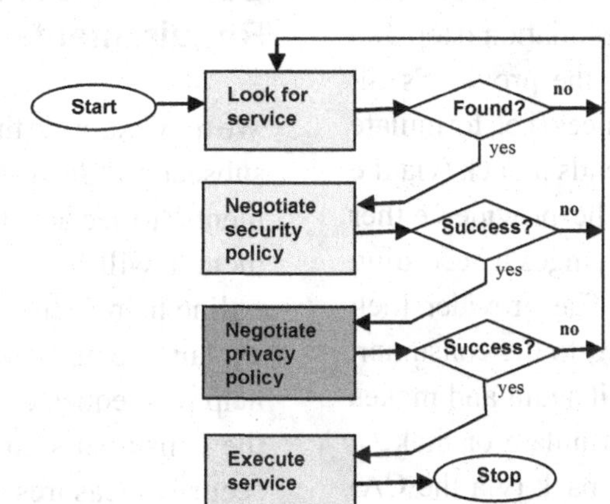

Figure 3. Security policy negotiation entities

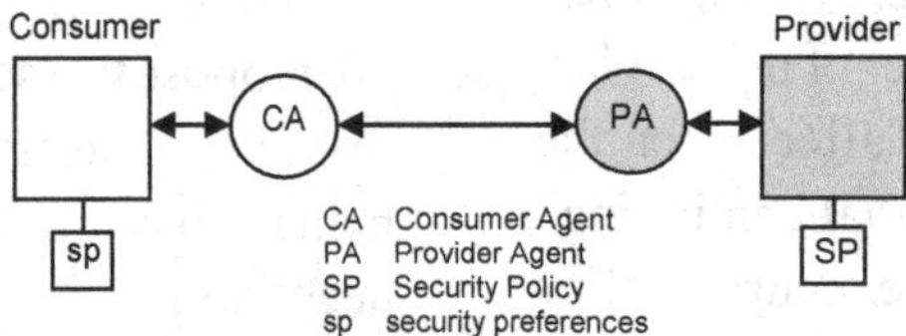

provider. Another non-autonomous agent serves the provider in the same way. These agents also perform validation checks on the information to be sent. It is probably feasible to use autonomous agents to automate our form of security policy negotiation, but this is for future work.

Once the consumer has determined the service she wants to use, the security policy negotiation proceeds as follows (assuming a consumer-initiated negotiation):

1. The consumer requests the provider's security policy from the PA.
2. The consumer compares the provider's SP with her own security preferences to see if there is a "match." A "match" can occur for either a single security mechanism or for a set of security mechanisms and means that the consumer's preferred security mechanism(s) is (are) identical to the mechanism(s) in the provider's SP. If there is a match, the CA signals a "successful negotiation" and the processing proceeds to privacy negotiation. If there is no match, consumer and provider begin security policy negotiation (step 3).
3. The consumer changes the provider's SP according to her preferences (i.e., formulate or make an offer) and sends it back (via the CA) to the provider. The provider either accepts the new SP or changes it according to what it can accept. The provider then sends it back (via the PA) to the consumer. The consumer looks at it again and makes further changes (i.e. formulate or make a new offer) and sends it back (via the CA) to the provider. This negotiation process continues back and forth until a) both sides agree and the negotiation is successful or b) one side terminates the negotiation (after concluding that no progress can be made) and the negotiation is unsuccessful. If the negotiation is unsuccessful, the consumer searches for another service to try (or tries to satisfy the provider's security requirements).

Figure 4 illustrates these steps using a message sequence chart for a consumer initiated negotiation (a provider initiated one would replace the top two arrows with one arrow from provider to consumer representing a request for negotiation together with the provider's SP). In Figure 4, SP1 is the consumer's first offer, SP2 is the provider's counter-offer, SP3 is the consumer's counter-counter offer and so on. After n steps the negotiation is successful, since the provider returns SPn, the consumer's last offer, unchanged.

Satisfying the Negotiation Requirements

We now examine the negotiation requirements of subsection "Security Policy Negotiation Requirements" to see how they can be fulfilled. Requirement 1 will be fulfilled in our prototype using online help in the form of pop-up windows that explain the particular security service for which help was requested. Requirement 2 is fulfilled by the consumer's ability to change any subset of security measures in the policy. Requirement 3 is

Figure 4. Security policy negotiation steps

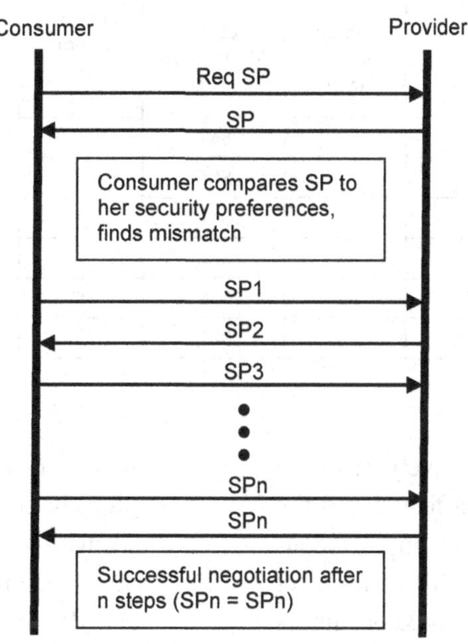

addressed in the following paragraphs. Requirements 4 and 5 are already part of our negotiation procedure. Requirement 6 will be fulfilled in our prototype by an appropriate interface design. We will describe this interface in Section four, "Prototype for security policy negotiation."

Scheme for Online Help in Making Offers

Negotiation requirement 3, the provision of trusted online help for the consumer to formulate a particular offer (i.e., change the provider's policy to reflect her security preferences) is fulfilled using the knowledge of what others selected under the same circumstances. This knowledge is acquired through the following steps:

1. Each provider stores the security policies that have been used with its services, identifying the services for which they were used and the dates they were used but not identifying the consumers with whom they were used (to preserve privacy). A services authority (SA) periodically collects these security policies from all providers, along with the types of Internet services to which they were applied, the dates they were applied, and the name of the provider that applied them.
2. Over a moving period *P* of the last *p* months (e.g., *p=12*), the SA constructs the following Security Score Table (Table 2), using the security services and mechanisms from each security policy within *P*, together with security violation and impact data (from providers, discussed below) corresponding to these security services and mechanisms. Providers are asked or required (through legislation, for example in some jurisdictions, hospitals are required to report patients that have been shot to police) to report the number and nature of security violations over period *P*, along with the number of consumers affected by each violation to the SA. The latter then assigns an impact number to each violation using a scale of 1 to 5, corresponding to low-

Table 2. Security score table

Pro-vider	Internet Service (S)	Security Policy (SP)	Security Service (SS)	Security Mecha-nism (SM)	No. of Security Violations *(k)*	Average Impact per Violation *(v)*	Security Score *(s = kv)*
P_1	S_1	SP_1	SS_1	SM_1	2	3	6
P_1	S_1	SP_1	SS_1	SM_2	3	1	3
P_1	S_1	SP_1	SS_1	SM_3	2	2	4
P_1	S_1	SP_2	SS_1	SM_1	1	4	4
P_1	S_1	SP_2	SS_1	SM_4	8	2	16
P_1	S_1	SP_2	SS_1	SM_5	5	2	10

est and highest impact respectively, based on the number of consumers affected and the nature of the violation. For example, a consumer failure to use Norton software to detect malware (see Table 1) involving 3 consumers may be assigned a low impact score (e.g., 2). On the other hand, a consumer authentication violation arising from password abuse involving 200 consumers may be assigned a high impact score (e.g., 4).

3. In the course of a security policy negotiation, a consumer who needs help in making a security choice (e.g., a security service or a security mechanism) can request from the SA the security services and mechanisms matching the service, the provider, and a security score below a certain threshold (clearly, the lower the security score, the more effective the corresponding security mechanism and security service). This information can be displayed as the number of security policies making use of the qualifying security mechanisms and associated security services. For example, from the above table, for P_1, S_1, threshold 7, the qualifying mechanisms are SM_1, SM_2, and SM_3 for SS_1 in SP_1 as well as SM_1 for SS_1 in SP_2. This information can be displayed as $SS_1(2)$, $SM_1(2)$, $SM_2(1)$, $SM_3(1)$ signifying that for P_1, S_1, threshold 7: (a) SS_1 has mechanisms below the threshold and was used in 2 security policies, (b) SM_1 of SS_1 is below the threshold and was used in 2 security policies, (c) SM_2 of SS_1 is below the threshold and was used in 1 security policy, and (d) SM_3 of SS_1 is below the threshold and was used in 1 security policy. The consumer would then use this frequency of utilization information to guide her choice of security services and mechanisms during negotiation. We will illustrate this step further in describing our prototype below.

Figure 5 illustrates this scheme. In Figure 5, providers provide the SA with the inputs mentioned above. The SA then computes the security score tables and stores them in a database. The consumer can then use standard database queries to retrieve the assistance needed.

Implementation for Web Services

Web services operate within a service-oriented architecture (SOA) which uses XML, UDDI, SOAP, and WSDL to publish a service, find a service, and bind to a service (O'Neill et al., 2003). In this scenario, a consumer wishing to execute a particular service would first find details of the provider and the services offered by the provider in the UDDI Web services directory. (Providers would have previously populated the UDDI directory with their names and details of the services

Figure 5. Scheme for online help in making offers in security policy negotiation

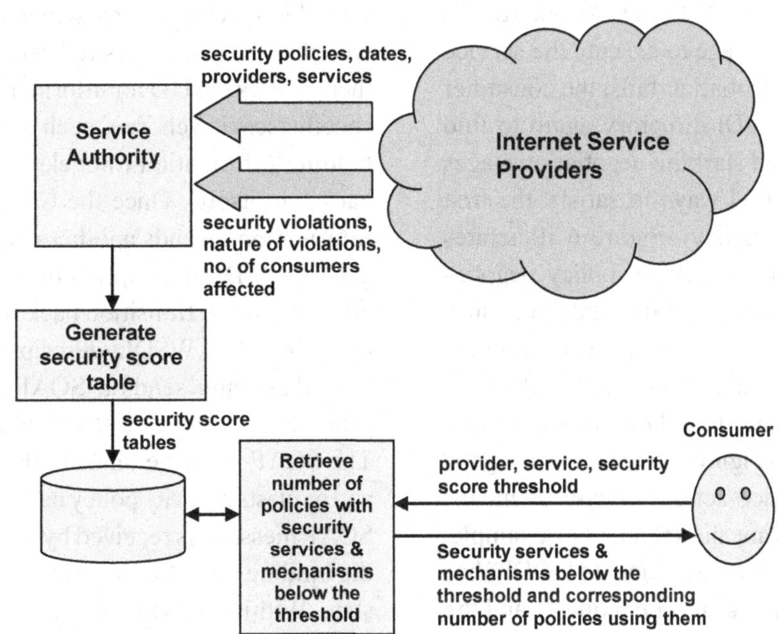

Figure 6. Implementation of security policy negotiation for Web Services

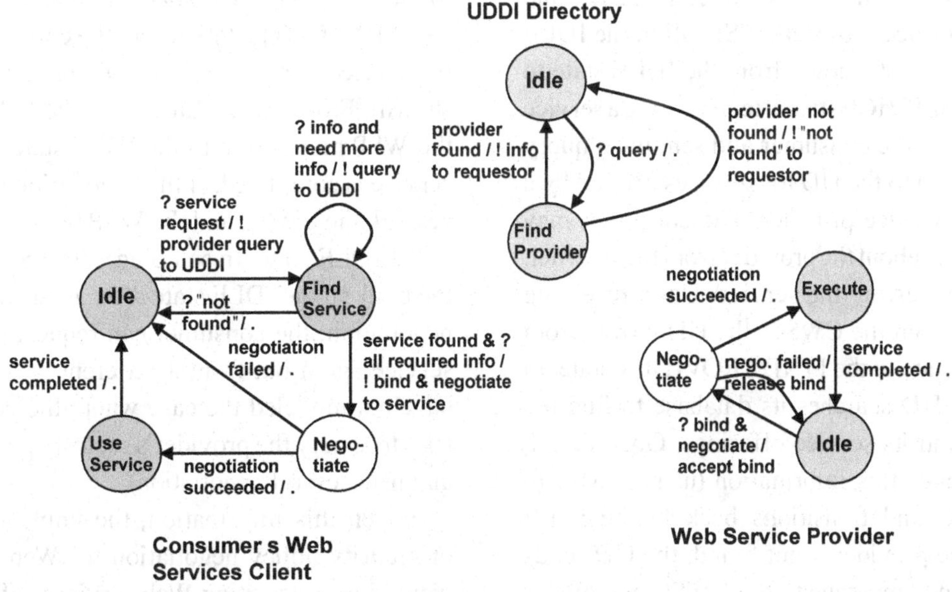

they offer.) Once the consumer has sufficient information about the service, including service key and binding information, the consumer formulates a SOAP message to send to the provider to execute the service. It is here where our negotiation stages can be inserted. The initial SOAP message to the provider would not be to execute the service but to request the provider's security policy to begin the negotiation sequence. Only after the privacy policy negotiation is successful (with the negotiation stages described above in subsection "Security Policy Negotiation") would the SOAP message to execute the service be sent. Where a negotiation fails, the consumer could access the UDDI directory again to find another provider and start the negotiation stages all over again (or find ways to satisfy the first provider's security policy). Figure 6 illustrates the implementation of security policy negotiation for Web services using three state machines representing the consumer's Web services client (running on the consumer's computer), the Web service provider, and the UDDI directory. The transition arrows in Figure 6 are labeled using the convention "condition/action" where "?" means "received" and "!" means "send." For example, "? service request/! provider query to UDDI," has the condition "received service request" and the action "send provider query to UDDI."

We explain Figure 6 by describing the execution flow, starting with the consumer's Web services client (CWSC), the UDDI directory (UD), and the Web service provider (WSP) all in the IDLE state. The CWSC moves from the IDLE state to the FIND SERVICE state after receiving a service request from the consumer and sending a query (using XML) to the UD for services offered by a particular service provider. The consumer may have learned about the provider from the Internet, prior to requesting the service. Upon receiving the query from the CWSC, the UD moves from the IDLE state to the FIND PROVIDER state, in which the UD searches its database to find the provider and its service offerings. Once found, the UD sends this information (using XML) to the CWSC and transitions back to the IDLE state. If the provider is not found, the UD sends a "not found" message to the CWSC and moves back to the IDLE state. While in the FIND SERVICE state, if the CWSC receives a "not found" message from the UD, it transitions back to the IDLE state where the consumer would need to request the service from another provider and the CWSC would start again. If the CWSC receives the requested provider's service offerings, the available services are presented to the consumer who then chooses a desired service. The CWSC then queries the UD for information related to the specific service chosen, such as service key and binding information (modeled by the transition back into itself). Once the CWSC receives this information it sends another query to the UD to get the WSDL description of the service (again modeled by the transition back into itself). Upon receiving this WSDL description, the CWSC formulates and sends a SOAP message to the provider and moves to the NEGOTIATE state. The SOAP message binds to the desired service and requests security policy negotiation. Once this SOAP message is received by the WSP, it accepts the binding and also moves to the NEGOTIATE state. Within the NEGOTIATE state, the CWSC and the WSP carry out security policy negotiation as described above (see Figure 4). If this negotiation is successful, the CWSC transitions to the USE SERVICE state and the WSP moves to the EXECUTE state where the consumer uses the service (any service specific parameters not shown). From these states, both the CWSC and the WSP move back to the IDLE state once the service is completed. If the negotiation is unsuccessful, the CWSC and the WSP both move back to the IDLE state. In so doing, the WSP releases the bind. In the IDLE state after an unsuccessful negotiation, the consumer can request the same service again but from a different provider (we have not modeled the case where the consumer tries to satisfy the provider's security policy after an unsuccessful negotiation).

Given this information, the implementation of security policy negotiation for Web services would involve writing Web services software to implement the NEGOTIATE state in Figure 6 (i.e., implementing Figure 4) with appropriate user interfaces as well as interfaces to the adjacent states, since Web services software for the rest of the states and state machines already exist. In addition, XML-based policy languages would be needed to express security policies so that they may be machine processed, for policy creation, editing, and compliance checking. We examine this aspect next.

Web services already possess XML-based language specifications to implement security policies. These specifications are generally worked on by a consortium of companies and then submitted to OASIS (organization for the advancement of structured information standards) for standardization. We may use WS-Policy (Bajaj et al., 2006a) and WS-SecurityPolicy (Della-Libera et al., 2005) to express Web service security policies. WS-Policy may be applied to express security requirements for web services in general. WS-SecurityPolicy contains the policy elements (security assertions) applicable to WS-Security (OASIS, 2006). WS-Security provides security enhancements for SOAP messaging to ensure message integrity and confidentiality. In addition, we would need WS-PolicyAttachment (Bajaj et al., 2006b) to define how policies are discovered or attached to a Web service. WS-PolicyAttachment specifies mechanisms for associating a policy with arbitrary XML elements, WSDL artifacts, and UDDI elements. At the time of this writing, WS-Policy, WS-SecurityPolicy, and WS-PolicyAttachment are all draft specifications from a number of companies, including IBM and Microsoft, that are waiting to be standardized. WS-Security became an OASIS standard in February 2006.

WS-Policy, also known as the Web services policy framework, provides a general purpose model with corresponding syntax to specify the policies of a Web service. It does this by defining a basic set of constructs that can be used and extended by other Web services specifications to specify a broad range of requirements and capabilities for services. Web services specifications (WS*) are in fact designed to be intercomposable. WS-Policy is often composed with WS-SecurityPolicy. In addition, WS-Policy should be regarded as a building block that can be used together with other Web services and application specific protocols (such as the one defined by Figure 4) to provide a negotiation solution for Web

Listing 1. Example WS-Policy specification of authentication

```
<wsp:Policy
  xmlns:sp="http://schemas.xmlsoap.org/ws/2005/07/securitypolicy"
  xmlns:wsp="http://schemas.xmlsoap.org/ws/2004/09/policy" >
        <sp:ConsumerAuthentication>
              <wsp:Policy>
                    <wsp:ExactlyOne>
                          <sp:password />
                          <sp:V+F_biometrics />
                    </wsp:ExactlyOne>
              </wsp:Policy>
        </sp:ConsumerAuthentication>
        <sp:ProviderAuthentication>
              <wsp:Policy>
                    <wsp:ExactlyOne>
                          <sp:securitytoken />
                          <sp:digital_signature />
                    </wsp:ExactlyOne>
              </wsp:Policy>
        </sp:ProviderAuthentication>
</wsp:Policy>
```

services. An example of this building block aspect is the use of WS-Policy in conjunction with WS-PolicyAttachment as previously mentioned.

WS-Policy specifies a policy as a collection of policy alternatives, where each policy alternative is a set of policy assertions. Listing 1 gives an example WS-Policy specification of the authentication portion of the security policy template in Table 1. This example uses WS-SecurityPolicy to define consumer authentication (lines 04-11) and provider authentication (lines 12-19) where it is assumed that the alternatives (lines 07-08 and lines 15-16) are assertions defined in WS-SecurityPolicy (assumed for illustrative purposes only, this is not currently the case). Note that the "ExactlyOne" operator requires that only one of the encapsulated alternatives (e.g., lines 07-08) can be implemented. A valid interpretation of Listing 1 is that an invocation of the Web service to which this policy corresponds requires that one and only one of the alternatives in lines 07-08 be implemented for consumer authentication, and one and only one of the alternatives in lines 15-16 be implemented for provider authentication.

APPLICATION EXAMPLES

In this section, we present two example applications of security policy personalization. The first example concerns a customer using a mobile device to access a stock quotation and order entry service called Stocks Unlimited. The second example describes an e-learning service called Easy Learn that targets a wide range of clients with different security preferences. The first example applies security personalization to accommodate personal preferences and the operational environment. The second example looks at personalization to accommodate personal security preferences. These two examples show that security personalization is a good solution to meeting diverse security needs that can arise from today's technological society.

Stocks Unlimited

Stocks Unlimited is an Internet service accessible using a mobile device such as a cell phone or wireless PDA. Figure 7 shows a network view of this service. In this figure, the mobile ISP (Internet Service Provider) provides mobile wireless

Figure 7. Network view of the Stocks Unlimited service

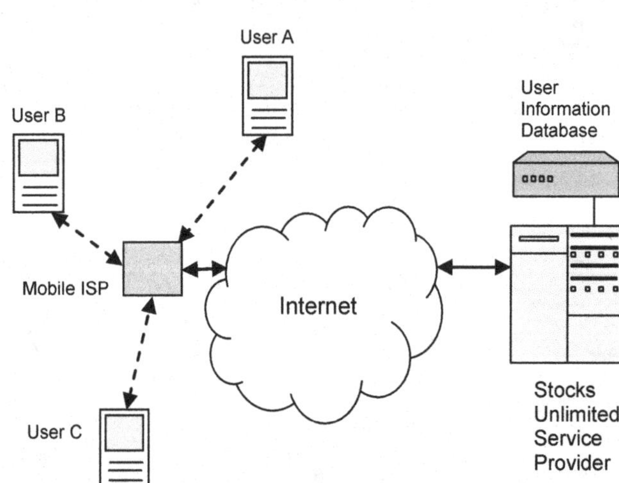

Table 3. Example negotiated security policy for Stocks Unlimited

Policy Use: stock trading	*Owner:* Stocks Unlimited	*Valid:* unlimited
CONSUMER PROVISIONS	**PROVIDER PROVISIONS**	**PROVIDER PROVISIONS**
Consumer Authentication *Implement:* yes (default) *P1: Mechanism:* password *P2: Mechanism:* V+F biometrics	**Provider Authentication** *Implement:* yes (default) *P1: Mechanism:* security token *P2: Mechanism:* digital signature	**Data Store Confidentiality** *Implement:* yes (default) *Mechanism:* 3DES encrypt
Consumer Non-Repudiation *Implement:* yes (default) *Mechanism:* digital signature	**Provider Non-Repudiation** *Implement:* yes (default) *Mechanism:* digital signature	**Communication Confidentiality** *Implement:* yes (default) *P1: Mechanism:* SSL *P2: Mechanism:* VPN
Consumer Certification *Implement:* yes (default) *Mechanism:* certificate	**Provider Certification** *Implement:* yes (default) *Mechanism:* certificate	**Communication Integrity** *Implement:* yes (default) *Mechanism:* MD5 Hash
Consumer Malware Detect *Implement:* yes (default) *Mechanism:* Norton	**Provider Malware Detect** *Implement:* yes (default) *Mechanism:* Norton	**Secure Logging** *What:* order transactions *Mechanism:* 3DES encrypt *What:* user input *Mechanism:* 3DES encrypt

access to the Internet. Stocks Unlimited provides the actual service.

Stocks Unlimited makes use of a security policy to specify the security measures that it will use to protect its service. However, this security policy may not match up with the security preferences of the service user as we have seen above in the introduction section. In addition, this security policy may not match up with the computational power of the user's mobile platform, or with security requirements imposed by the location of the mobile platform. To illustrate this, suppose the security policy of Stocks Unlimited calls for encrypting the communication channel using AES (advanced encryption standard). However, the user's cell phone has insufficient computing power to compute AES with reasonable performance, possibly leading to a security breach. Again, suppose there is an area of a large city that is notorious for man-in-the-middle attacks against mobile Internet services. Service users try to avoid this area but occasionally they have to traverse it in order to get to their destination, resulting again in a possible security breach. Our approach of security policy personalization can be applied to remedy these situations by having the consumer negotiate a suitable security policy with Stocks Unlimited, containing the desired sets of security mechanisms, and then using a software agent to select particular mechanisms on-the-fly. The agent would initiate the best available security mechanisms from among the negotiated choices, depending on the user's security preferences for the service, the computational power of the user's mobile platform, and the location of the user's mobile platform. We refer to this combination of user preferences, power, and location as "UPL."

Let us assume that the user negotiates with the provider to personalize the security policy following the procedure described above for negotiating sets of mechanisms, starting from the security policy template in Table 1. She then obtains, for example, the security policy in Table 3, where alternative mechanisms have been labeled with "P1" and "P2" for selection by the software agent.

We call the software agent in this example a *context-aware security policy agent (CASPA)*. A

Figure 8. Behaviour of CASPA

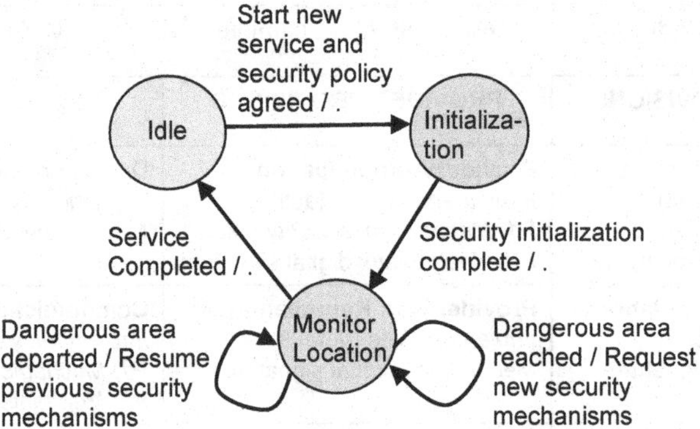

CASPA is an intelligent software agent that resides in a mobile device and is responsible for selecting security services and mechanisms from the provider's security policy for a particular service, according to the values of UPL. The behaviour of a CASPA is described by the state machine in Figure 8, where the arrow labels are in the form "condition / action."

In Figure 8, the *Idle* state is exited once the service is ready to begin (i.e., the service has been found and the security policy agreed to between consumer and provider). In the *Initialization* state, the CASPA accounts for the U and P of UPL (i.e., reflects the user's security preferences and the computational power of the device) by setting the options in the negotiated provider's security policy to implement appropriate security services and mechanisms (see Table 3). For example, suppose the user has several mobile devices that she uses with the same security policy, including a PDA and a less powerful cell phone. CASPA would set security services and mechanisms that both reflect the consumer's security preferences and be appropriate to the computing power of each device. It would be straight forward to program a CASPA to perform this task. In the *Monitor Location* state, the agent is monitoring the device's location using GPS. Note that this location is only used by the CASPA and is not reported to either the mobile ISP or the provider of the service so that there should be no privacy concerns. An alternative way of determining the consumer's location is the use of signaling analysis by the mobile ISP. However, the latter would then learn the consumer's location leading to privacy concerns. When a dangerous area (i.e., an area with a high number of attackers) is entered, the agent messages the service provider to initiate a more powerful security mechanism for communication to defend against the attackers. Of course, this more powerful mechanism consumes more computing resources and should only be used when necessary. When the dangerous area is exited, the agent messages the provider that the normal security mechanism for communication may be resumed. The CASPA executes concurrently with the service. However, the service does not begin until the CASPA has completed the initialization. This example has been adapted from Yee & Korba (2005c), which may be consulted for further details including how the above dangerous area can be known, the secure communication protocols needed between the CASPA and the provider, certain operational requirements, and a discussion on location privacy.

This example application of security policy personalization calls for the use of a context-aware security policy agent to further personalize the security services according to UPL. This can be termed double personalization. The first personalization using security policy negotiation determines the sets of security mechanisms and corresponding security services required by the consumer. The second agent-based personalization dynamically accounts for the user's specific security preferences, the mobile device's available computing power, and the user's movement into a dangerous area with a higher number of attackers, where more powerful security mechanisms are needed. Security policy personalization is a form of service personalization that studies have shown is attractive to consumers (Ho & Kwok, 2003).

Easy Learn

Easy Learn is an Internet-based e-learning service provider whose services consist of the delivery of online courses on numerous subjects, ranging from courses for the general public (e.g., "Finding Reliable Information on the Internet") to courses that are highly technical and of interest only to specific groups (e.g., "Maintenance Requirements for Next Generation M-5000 Tanks" for the military). Easy Learn has a security policy that it uses for all its e-learning courses, mainly focusing on user authentication and communications security. Suppose that user authentication is implemented using the familiar USERID/ password combination and secure communications is achieved using SSL. This security policy may suffice for someone taking the finding information course since the course content is probably not of a secretive or classified nature. However, the tank maintenance course is quite the opposite, since maintenance information could reveal vulnerabilities that can be taken advantaged of by adversaries. Thus, the military would want to negotiate the security policy, perhaps requiring two-factor biometrics authentication in addition to USERID/password, and the use of AES encryption for the course content while in transit.

PROTOTYPE FOR SECURITY POLICY NEGOTIATION

We have extended a prototype that we had developed for privacy policy negotiation (Yee & Korba, 2003a; Yee & Korba, 2003b) so that it can be used for security policy negotiation. The prototype is based on a peer-to-peer architecture programmed in JADE (Java agent development framework) (Telecom Italia Lab). The prototype allows a consumer and a provider to contact each other across the Internet, initiate, and carry on a negotiation session.

The high-level functionality of the prototype is described by Figure 9. In Figure 9, a consumer-provider negotiation is considered a partner-partner negotiation, so for such a negotiation, the consumer's partner is the service provider and vice versa. Also, "topic of interest" refers to the type of service, and "consult with peers" means obtain help for negotiation using the scheme for online help in making offers.

Only minor changes were needed to the prototype for security policy negotiation. The changes primarily involved: (a) provision of a pop-up window help facility for consumers who need to learn about a particular security service or mechanism (to satisfy requirement 1 of subsection "Security Policy Negotiation Requirements"), and (b) enhancing the user selection mechanism to allow for selection of multiple choices needed for some security services such as authentication and for negotiating sets of security mechanisms.

For security policy negotiation, the main component of the user interface consists of a table (see Figure 10) that has columns for security service, implement (Y/N), and security mechanism. Figure 10 only shows 3 security services for ease of explanation. A consumer can change the "Y" (default) to "N" to delete the associated security service. If the "Y" is left alone, the consumer

Figure 9. High-level functionality of the security policy negotiation prototype

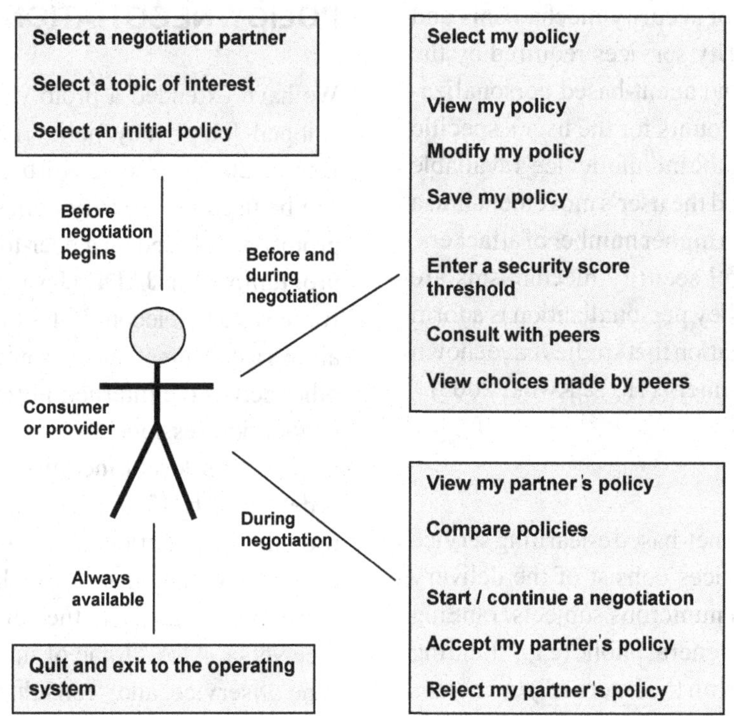

Figure 10. Tabular interface of security policy negotiation prototype

Security Service	Y/N	Security Mechanism
Consumer Authentication	Y	V+F Biometrics Certificate
Provider Authentication	Y	Certificate
Communication Confidentiality	Y	SSL VPN

can then select one or more of the corresponding security mechanisms.

For consumers who need help regarding what security choice to make during a negotiation session, we implemented the help scheme described above. The user interface provides this help by showing the number of previously used security policies (corresponding to the same service and provider, with security scores below the threshold) that implemented each previously used choice by appending the number next to the choice (see Figure 11). Of course, the consumer must have previously requested help (via a button) and entered a security score threshold. For example, Figure 11 shows that "consumer authentication" having mechanisms below the threshold was used in 15 policies. In addition, mechanism "V+F Biometrics" of consumer authentication is below the threshold and used in 5 policies. Mechanism "certificate" of consumer authentication is also

Figure 11. Frequency of security services and mechanisms

Security Service	Y/N	Security Mechanism
Consumer Authentication (15)	Y	V+F Biometrics (5) Certificate (10)
Provider Authentication (7)	Y	Certificate (7)
Communication Confidentiality (13)	Y	SSL (10) VPN (3)

below the threshold and used in 10 policies. This advises the consumer that consumer authentication is "a good security service to have" relative to the other two services. This does not mean that the consumer will only select consumer authentication, as the choices also depend on the needs of the consumer and the service. However, this information does guide the consumer in making a selection by letting her know what security measures have been used previously and how often they were used. Within consumer authentication, the certificate mechanism is more popular than the biometrics mechanism. This may guide the consumer into choosing certificate over biometrics, assuming the negotiation is for single mechanisms. Although some of these choices (e.g., consumer authentication) may seem obvious to security knowledgeable people, we point out that we are targeting the general public with our approach and there are people in this group who are not familiar with the choices. We have not yet trialed this prototype on the public to evaluate validity and usability. We plan to do this next and report the results in a subsequent paper.

RELATED WORK

Work related to the topic of this article generally fall under three categories: (i) the specification and use of security policies, (ii) the negotiation of trust, and (iii) the personalization of security policies. One work (Ryutov et al., 2005) straddles (ii) and (iii). Of these three, category (i) has the most number of papers, followed by category (ii) with fewer but still many papers, followed by category (iii) with only a handful of papers. The latter category not only has the smallest number of papers, but the works they describe do not deal with personalization using *personal* negotiation between a service consumer and a service provider. Rather, they concern automatic negotiation for networking resources or other forms of automatic adaptation of privacy or security policies. Thus our work on personal security policy negotiation is unique as far as we can tell. We provide a summary of each related work below.

Category (i): The Specification and Use of Security Policies. Security policies have traditionally been used to specify security requirements for networks and distributed systems (Varadharajan, 1990). Bertino, Ferrari and Squicciarini (2001) present a XML-based language for specifying credentials and security policies for Web documents. More recently, security policies have been applied to manage security for distributed multimedia services (Duflos, 2002) and for very large, dynamically changing groups of participants in, for example, joint command of armed forces for some time period (Dinsmore et al., 2000). Ventuneac, Coffey and Salomie (2003) describe a policy-based security framework for web-enabled applications, focusing on role-based security policies and mechanisms. Scott and

Sharp (2003) present a structuring technique for abstracting security policies from large Web applications. The abstracted policy is expressed in a machine-processable policy language and used to program an application level firewall. This firewall then dynamically analyzes and transforms HTTP requests/responses to enforce the policy. They claim that such a high-level technique is needed to overcome the problem of too many security holes in Web applications to fix individually. More recently, Bhargavan et al. (2005) describe a rule-based advisor tool that detects typical errors in Web services configuration and security policy files. The tool generates a security report after checking for over thirty syntactic conditions corresponding to errors found during security reviews. Faheem (2005) presents a multi-agent based system for managing security policies, with the goal of making it easier to configure and implement a given security policy under dynamically changing threat conditions. Tan et al. (2004) describe the use of meta-level architectures for managing and discerning policy-based security specifics. They discuss how such use can detect and resolve policy conflicts as well as lead to a security reconfiguration if warranted by a change in the environment. Finally, Yau et al. (2005) present an adaptable security framework for large scale service-based systems. Their framework includes a core ontology, together with a security specification language, for specifying dynamic security policies, policy conflict detection and resolution, and tools for deploying agents to enforce security policies. They claim that their framework allows security policies of large scale service-based systems to be rapidly specified, updated, verified, and enforced for various threat situations.

Category (ii): The Negotiation of Trust. Trust negotiation is applied to situations where peers need to interact across a network (such as the Internet) and the peers are complete strangers to one another. Trust negotiation is used to establish trust between such peers by iteratively exchanging certified digital credentials. Trust negotiation differs from security policy negotiation as described in this work in that the purpose of trust negotiation is to establish trust between interacting parties who do not trust one another, so that further online processing can proceed. It does not usually negotiate all the security mechanisms to be used for an electronic service where there is already some trust for the service provider. Examples of typical papers on trust negotiation are Bertino, Ferrari and Squicciarini (2004), Winslett et al. (2002), and Winsborough, and Li (2004). More recently, Lee et al. (2006) present a third party authorization service that leverages the power of existing prototype trust negotiation systems by acting as an authorization broker. Their system issues resource access tokens in an open system after the interacting parties use trust negotiation to satisfy the appropriate resource access policies. For this work we view trust negotiation as complementary but not needed in most cases of provider-consumer relationship. This is because providers of Internet services have ways of making themselves known to consumers (e.g., advertising) and readily conduct business with strangers (with appropriate safeguards).

Category (iii): The Personalization of Security Policies. The available papers largely describe security policy negotiation across Internet domains needed to manage cross domain network security (e.g., Barrere, Benzekri, Grasset et al.,2003; Park & Chung 2003;Yang, Fu & Wu, 2003), negotiated resource sharing agreements between members of coalitions (Khurana, Gavrilal, Bobba et al., 2003), security policy mediation between heterogeneous information systems (Hale, Galiasso, Papa, & Shenoi, 1999) for secure interoperation, and negotiation of security parameters within protocols such as SSL (Chou, 2002). Additional examples of security mediation or adaptation follow. Rannenberg (2001) discusses multilateral security in which security policies of different parties may conflict and gives some examples and solutions to resolve the conflicts. In considering that different interests must be respected,

Rannenberg (2001) confirms our ideas that: (a) different parties may have different (or personal) security goals, (b) these parties can specify their own interests or security goals, and (c) conflicts may be negotiated. Torrellas and Vargas (2003) propose the use of multi-agent security systems to react to a changing threat environment due to new virus attacks, active intrusions, and new attack technologies. They emphasize the need for flexible security, which again supports our contention that "one size does not fit all." Finally, Ryutov et al. (2005) (can also be classified under Category (ii)) propose a framework for adaptive trust negotiation that targets security attacks where the participants interact across security domains. Their framework adapts the associated security policies according to the sensitivity of the access request and a suspicion level assigned to the information requester.

It is interesting to note that some of the above works refer to changes in security policy necessitated by changes in the environment. This idea is also at the heart of this work. For us, a user is part of the environment and changes in security preferences among users mean changes to the environment that necessitate personalization of (changes to) security policies. Note that we only provide brief summaries of the above works, believing that more detail is not justified since these works relate to this work only in a minor way.

EVALUATION

We have presented a negotiations approach for Internet services security policy personalization, including a scheme for providing online help to consumers who are not sure of what security choices to make. Some strengths of our personalization approach are: (a) straightforward and easy to use with appropriate interfaces as previously mentioned for our prototype, (b) achieves its principal goal of meeting the personal security requirements of each user, and (c) provides online help for the user in making security choices during negotiation. Some potential weaknesses of our approach are: (a) in order for the approach to be used, users need to be somewhat Internet and security literate, (b) the scheme for online help may be vulnerable to malicious biasing of security services and mechanisms through purposeful selection of weak security for a particular Internet service over some time period, and (c) the scheme for online help may not be scalable with the number of users.

Regarding the potential weakness that users need to be Internet and security literate, we can say that users will become more literate in these areas over time. We have only to point to the large number of people using e-commerce and banking services over the Internet today, something that required higher levels of online literacy just a few years ago. In addition, the frequent lapses in electronic security that are headlined in the media also result in improved knowledge of security in the general population. In terms of the malicious biasing vulnerability, one simple solution would be for the SA to reject security policies that employ outlandishly weak security so that such policies would not enter into the security score table. Another solution would be to have the provider simply not accept a security choice if it is deemed too weak. As for the potential scalability weakness, we need to research this possibility further.

The scheme for online help clearly increases the workload of providers, but perhaps they would not mind the extra work if they can advertise that they are doing this to help consumers, and thereby gain more business. The scheme works for the negotiation of both single security mechanisms or sets of security mechanisms. For sets, the consumer would simply select a set from the better mechanisms (those having lower security scores) for a selected security service during negotiation. There would be a need for the SA to make sure the security score tables are kept up-to-date. In addition, the consumer's database retrievals need to occur in real-time so that the provider is not kept waiting unduly for the consumer to respond during negotiation. Both of these requirements can be easily fulfilled. The SA may be a government department or an extended role for a certification authority currently part of public key infrastructure. The authority can recover its costs by charging consumers a small subscription rate for the use of its security consultation service (step 3 in the scheme for online help).

The use of the UDDI web services directory brings up an interesting possibility. Providers could store their security policies, in addition to details of their service offerings, in this directory. Consumers could then use the UDDI directory to select only those services with security policies that match (or come close to matching) their security preferences. This could lessen the need for negotiation (but not get rid of it entirely, as there may not be services with security policies that match completely). This can result in faster service invocation. However, the UDDI directory would need appropriate security protection, since successful attacks on this directory would be disastrous.

CONCLUSION AND FUTURE RESEARCH

Users of Internet services, including Web services, have differing security requirements when invoking the services. The approach presented in this work for security policy personalization is a good way to fulfill these requirements that can lead to more widespread use of such services, with accompanying economic benefits. While some challenges remain before the approach can be widely adopted (see above evaluation section), we feel that these challenges can be overcome and the full benefits of the approach realized.

The novel contributions of this work include: (a) a security policy personalization approach for consumers of Internet services, (b) a scheme for online help in making security policy offers during negotiation, and (c) an interface for (b) that easily and intuitively conveys the help needed. In addition, we have purposely kept our approach for (a) simple, primarily so that the average consumer who is not a computer expert can understand how to use it.

Future research includes the following areas: (a) performance and scalability of the scheme for providing online help to consumers for making security choices, (b) alternative methods for ranking the security mechanisms in this scheme, (c) the use of autonomous agents to automate the security policy negotiation process, (d) the use of the UDDI directory to store provider security policies, (e) further details on implementing security policy negotiation for Web services—we have only indicated how it can be done at a high level, and (f) security mechanisms required for the security policies and the negotiations themselves.

ACKNOWLEDGMENT

The authors gratefully acknowledge the support of the National Research Council Canada for this work. In addition, the authors would like to thank colleagues Chris McDonald and Andrew Patrick for contributing to the design of the prototype's user interface.

REFERENCES

Bajaj, S., Box, D., Chappell, D., Curbera, F., Daniels, G., Hallam-Baker, P. et al. (2006a). *Web Services Policy Framework (WS-Policy)*. Version, 1.2, March. Retrieved March 28, 2006 from: http://download.boulder.ibm.com/ibmdl/pub/software/dw/specs/ws-polfram/ws-policy-2006-03-01.pdf

Bajaj, S., Box, D., Chappell, D., Curbera, F., Daniels, G., Hallam-Baker, P. et al. (2006b). *Web Services Policy Attachment (WS-PolicyAttachment)*. Version, 1.2, March. Retrieved March 28,

2006 from: http://download.boulder.ibm.com/ibmdl/pub/software/dw/specs/ws-polatt/ws-polat-2006-03-01.pdf

Barrere, F., Benzekri, A., Grasset, F., Laborde, R., & Nasser, B. (2003). Inter-Domains Policy Negotiation. In *Proceedings of the 4th International Workshop on Policies for Distributed Systems and Networks (POLICY'03),* (pp. 239-242), Lake Como, Italy.

Bertino, E., Castano, S., & Ferrari, E. (2001). On Specifying Security Policies for Web Documents with an XML-Based Language. In *Proceedings of the Sixth ACM Symposium on Access Control Models and Technologies,* (pp. 57-65), Chantilly, Virginia.

Bertino, E., Ferrari, E., & Squicciarini, A. (2004). Trust negotiation: Concepts, systems, and languages. *Computing in Science and Engineering, July/August,* 27-34.

Bhargavan, K., Fournet, C., Gordon, A., & O'Shea, G. (2005). An Advisor for Web Services Security Policies. In *Proceedings of the 2005 Workshop on Secure Web Services (SWS '05),* (pp. 1-9), Fairfax, Virginia, USA.

Chou, W. (2002, July-August). Inside SSL: The secure sockets layer protocol. *IT Pro*, 47-52.

Della-Libera, G., Gudgin, M., Hallam-Baker, P., Hondo, M., Granqvist, H., Kaler, C. et al. (2005). *Web Services Security Policy Language (WS-SecurityPolicy)*. Version 1.1, July. Retrieved July 28, 2006 from: ftp://www6.software.ibm.com/software/developer/library/ws-secpol.pdf

Dinsmore, P., Balenson, D., Heyman, M., Kruus, P., Scace, C., & Sherman, A. (2000). Policy-Based Security Management for Large Dynamic Groups: An Overview of the DCCM Project. In *Proceedings, DARPA Information Survivability Conference and Exposition (DISCEX'00),* Vol. 1, (pp. 64-73). Hilton Head, South Carolina.

Duflos, S. (2002). An Architecture for Policy-Based Security Management for Distributed Multimedia Services.In *Proceedings of the 10th ACM International Conference on Multimedia,* (pp. 653-655), Juan-les-Pins, France.

Faheem, H. (2005). A Multiagent-Based Approach for Managing Security Policy. In *Proceedings of the 2nd IFIP International Conference on Wireless and Optical Communications Networks (WOCN 2005),* (pp. 351-356), Dubai, UAE.

Hale, J., Galiasso, P., Papa, M., & Shenoi, S. (1999). Security Policy Coordination for Heterogeneous Information Systems. In *Proceedings of the 15th Annual Computer Security Applications Conference (ACSAC '99)*, (pp. 219-228), Scottsdale, Arizona.

Ho, S., & Kwok, S. (2003). The attraction of personalized service for users in mobile commerce: An empirical study. *ACM SIGecom Exchanges, 3*(4),10-18,.

International Organization for Standardization. (n.d.). IS0 7498-2, *Information Processing Systems – Open Systems Interconnection – Basic Reference Model – Part 2: Security Architecture*. Retrieved Feb. 11, 2004 from http://www.iso.org/

ITU-T. (n.d.). *Recommendation X.800, Security Architecture for OSI.* Retrieved Feb. 11, 2004 from: http://www.itu.int/rec/recommendation.asp?type=items&lang=e&parent=T-REC-X.800-199103-I

Joshi, J., Aref, W., Ghafoor, A., & Spafford, E. (2001). Security models for Web-based applications. *Communications of the ACM, 44*(2), 38-44.

Khurana, H., Gavrilal, S., Bobba, R., Koleva, R., Sonalker, A., Dinu, E., Gligor, V., & Baras, J. (2003). Integrated Security Services for Dynamic Coalitions. In *Proceedings of the DARPA Information Survivability Conference and Exposition (DISCEX'03),* Vol. 2, (pp. 38-40), Washington D.C..

Lee, A.J., Winslett, M., Basney, J., & Welch, V. (2006). Traust: A Trust Negotiation-Based Authorization Service for Open Systems. In *Proceedings of the 11th ACM Symposium on Access Control Models and Technologies,* (pp. 39-48), Lake Tahoe, California.

OASIS (2006). *Web Services Security: SOAP Message Security 1.1 (WS-Security 2004)*. OASIS Standard Specification, February 1. Retrieved March 28, 2006 from http://www.oasis-open.org/committees/download.php/16790/wss-v1.1-spec-os-SOAPMessageSecurity.pdf

O'Neill, M., Hallam-Baker, P., Cann, S.M., Sherma, M., Simon, E., Watters, P.A. & White, A. (2003). *Web Services Security*. McGraw-Hill/Osborne.

Park, J., & Chung, J. (2003). Design of SPS Model Using Mobile Agent System. In *Proceedings of the IEEE 37th Annual 2003 International Carnahan Conference on Security Technology*, (pp. 38-42), Taipei, Taiwan.

Rannenberg, K. (2001). Multilateral Security a Concept and Examples for Balanced Security. In *Proceedings of the 2000 Workshop on New Security Paradigms*, (pp. 151-162), Ballycotton, County Cork, Ireland.

Ryutov, T., Zhou, L., Neuman, C., Leithead, T., & Seamons, K.E. (2005). Adaptive Trust Negotiation and Access Control. In *Proceedings of the 10 ACM Symposium on Access Control Models and Technologies*, (pp. 139-146), Stockholm, Sweden.

Scott, D. & Sharp, R. (2003). Specifying and enforcing application-level Web security policies. *IEEE Transactions on Knowledge and Data Engineering, 15*(4), 771-783.

Tan, J.J., Poslad, S., & Xi, Y. (2004). Policy Driven Systems for Dynamic Security Reconfiguration. *Proceedings of the 3rd International Joint Conference on Autonomous Agents and Multiagent Systems,* Vol. 3, (pp. 1274-1275), New York, New York.

Telecom Italia Lab. (n.d.). *JADE (Java Agent Development Framework)*. Retrieved Feb. 14, 2005 from http://jade.tilab.com/

Torrellas, G.A.S. & Vargas, L.A.V. (2003). Modelling a Flexible Network Security Systems Using Multi-Agents Systems: Security Assessment Considerations. In *Proceedings of the 1st International Symposium on Information and Communication Technologies (ISICT 03)*, pp. 365-371, Dublin, Ireland.

Varadharajan, V. (1990). A Multilevel Security Policy Model for Networks. In *Proceedings of the 9th Annual Joint Conference of the IEEE Computer and Communication Societies (INFOCOM 90),* Vol. 2, (pp. 710-718), San Francisco, California.

Ventuneac, M., Coffey, T., & Salomie, I. (2003). A Policy-Based Security Framework for Web-Enabled Applications. In *Proceedings 1st International Symposium on Information and Communication Technologies,* (pp. 487-492), Dublin, Ireland.

Winsborough, W., & Li, N. (2004). Safety in Automated Trust Negotiation. In *Proceedings, 2004 IEEE Symposium on Security and Privacy (S&P '04),* (pp. 147-160), Oakland, California.

Winslett, M., Yu, T., Seamons, K., Hess, A., Jacobson, J., Jarvis, R. et al. (2002). Negotiating trust on the web. *IEEE Internet Computing, November/December*, 30-37,.

World Wide Web Consortium (W3C) (n.d.). *Extensible Markup Language (XML)*. Retrieved March 18, 2006 at http://www.w3.org/XML/

Yang, Y., Fu, Z., & Wu, S. (2003). Bands: An Inter-Domain Internet Security Policy Management System for IPSEC/VPN. In *Proceedings of the IFIP/IEEE 8th International Symposium on Integrated Network Management,* (pp. 231-244), Colorado Springs, Colorado.

Yau, S., Yao, Y., Chen, Z., & Zhu, L. (2005). An Adaptable Security Framework for Service-based Systems. In *Proceedings 10th IEEE International*

Workshop on Object-Oriented Real-Time Dependable Systems (WORDS 2005), (pp. 28-35), Sedona, Arizona.

Yee, G., & Korba, L. (2003a). Bilateral E-services Negotiation Under Uncertainty. In *Proceedings of the 2003 International Symposium on Applications and the Internet (SAINT2003),* (pp. 352-355), Orlando, Florida.

Yee, G., & Korba, L. (2003b). The Negotiation of Privacy Policies in Distance Education. In *Proceedings of the 14th IRMA International Conference*, (pp. 702-705), Philadelphia, Pennsylvania.

Yee, G., & Korba, L. (2005a). Semi-automatic derivation and use of personal privacy policies in e-business. *International Journal of E-Business Research, 1*(1), 54-69.

Yee, G., & Korba, L. (2005b). Negotiated Security Policies for E-Services and Web Services. In *Proceedings of the 2005 IEEE International Conference on Web Services (ICWS 2005),* Vol. 2, (pp. 605-612), Orlando, Florida.

Yee, G., & Korba, L. (2005c). Context-Aware Security Policy Agent for Mobile Internet Services. In *Proceedings of the 2005 IFIP International Conference on Intelligence in Communication Systems (INTELLCOMM 2005)*, (pp. 249-259), Montreal, Quebec, Canada.

ENDNOTE

1 NRC Paper No.: NRC 49358

This work was previously published in the International Journal of Web Services Research Volume 5, Issue 1, edited by L. Zhang, pp. 1-23, copyright 2008 by IGI Publishing (an imprint of IGI Global).

Chapter 10
XML Security with Binary XML for Mobile Web Services

Jaakko Kangasharju
Helsinki Institute for Information Technology, Finland

Tancred Lindholm
Helsinki Institute for Information Technology, Finland

Sasu Tarkoma
Helsinki Institute for Information Technology, Finland

ABSTRACT

In the wireless world, there has recently been much interest in alternate serialization formats for XML data, mostly driven by the weak capabilities of both devices and networks. However, it is difficult to make an alternate serialization format compatible with XML security features such as encryption and signing. We consider here ways to integrate an alternate format with security, and present a solution that we see as a viable alternative. In addition to this, we present extensive performance measurements, including ones on a mobile phone on the effect of an alternate format when using XML-based security. These measurements indicate that, in the wireless world, reducing message sizes is the most pressing concern, and that processing efficiency gains of an alternate format are a much smaller concern. We also make specific recommendations on security usage based on our measurements.

INTRODUCTION

In recent years, two developments in the computing landscape appear to be having a significant impact on the future. One of these is the rising popularity of XML (extensible markup language), which is now being used also for machine-to-machine messaging, most notably in the form of SOAP (World Wide Web Consortium [W3C], 2003a, 2003b). The other is the increasing number of available mobile devices with sophisticated networking capabilities, potentially heralding an age of truly pervasive, or ubiquitous computing (Satyanarayanan, 2001; Weiser, 1993).

In a pervasive computing situation, a person carries a small computing device, such as a smart phone or a PDA (personal digital assistant). These kinds of devices have much less processing power available than typical personal computers. They are normally battery powered, meaning that the available energy should not be squandered, especially as battery capabilities tend to increase very slowly over time. Finally, their connection to other computers, including to the Internet, will often be on a low-bandwidth, high-latency wireless link, though in some places more powerful devices can take advantage of wireless LAN (local area network) hotspots that provide much better network connectivity.

There has been concern that XML is not suitable for use on mobile devices due to its verbosity and processing requirements. Because of this, there have been proposals to replace XML with an alternate binary XML format, which would be compatible with XML on some level but is purported to be more compact and more efficient to process. When communicating with existing systems on a fixed network, gateways can convert between this binary format and XML to permit piecewise introduction of the new format. A well-known gateway-based solution is the wireless application protocol (WAP; WAP Forum, 2001a) that includes one of the earliest binary formats for XML (W3C, 1999).

However, compatibility achieved through gateways breaks down in the case of security features such as encryption and digital signatures. If serialized content is encrypted, a gateway cannot convert it, so the ultimate recipient needs to be able to understand the used format. In the case of signatures, the signature will be computed over the serialized form, so again the recipient will need to be able to regenerate that version.

In this article, we explore the effect of a binary format in the context of XML security, in particular to determine what benefits, if any, such a format could bring. We focus on communication between a mobile device using a wireless link and a server in a fixed network. While direct peer-to-peer communication between mobile devices is also an important topic, the issues of compatibility arise more strongly in the client-server case due to the number of existing deployed systems.

The main contributions of this article are a review of options for achieving compatibility between different formats and a comparison. We present extensive measurements, of both time and energy consumption, that were performed with real mobile devices over real networks. Finally, drawing on our measurements, we make recommendations for new features in XML security specifications that would support mobile devices better than is currently achievable.

We begin the article with usage scenarios supporting fine-grained XML security and an overview of the relevant specifications. We continue by presenting three different compatibility options to allow use of a binary format, and then show measurements using our proposed option. Next, we review related work, and finally conclude the article with specific recommendations and some view of the future.

XML SECURITY

There are several existing ways to secure network traffic, many of which can be deployed immediately without needing to worry about interoperability at the application layer. On the network layer, it is possible to use IP (Internet protocol) security (Kent & Atkinson, 1998) for authentication and encryption. Transport-layer connections can be secured with SSL (secure sockets layer; Freier, Karlton, & Kocher, 1996), which provides authentication and a secure communication channel. The problems with these are that they only secure network traffic, so stored data need to be reencrypted and re-signed, and they lack the granularity to support some use cases that require multiple transport-layer connections.

Figure 1. Message flow and content with different kinds of security

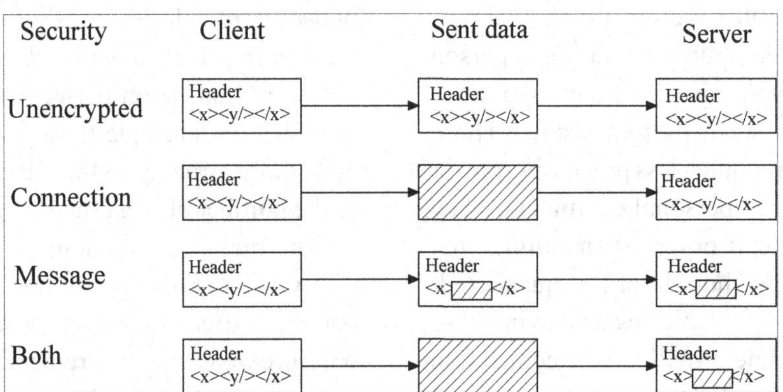

The differences between connection-level security and message-level security are illustrated in Figure 1. Here we assume a message to consist of a protocol header and an XML document, and at the client end, we show the unencrypted form of the message in all cases. When connection-level security is used, the full message is encrypted in transit, and when message-level security is used, a part of the XML document is encrypted. The main difference in message-level security is that the message, as received by the server, still has the sensitive parts of the XML document encrypted. We continue by considering scenarios where this feature is an advantage to the overall system.

Usage Scenarios

We first consider the case of a user wishing to place an order with an online retailer. The order will include the user's identification, identification of the ordered goods, and payment information (such as a credit card number). The user will want to keep private, that is, encrypt, the payment information. The retailer wishes to authenticate the user to make sure no fraudulent orders are placed, which requires a digital signature. Authenticating the retailer to the user is better handled at the messaging protocol level and not at the message level.

Figure 2 shows a simple example of this scenario where the client (C) sends an order to the retailer's outward-facing system (S). S then further sends the payment information to its payment processor (P), and the list of ordered goods to its order processor (O). O also needs to confirm from P that the payment succeeded. Both O and P are located inside the retailer's secure internal network, and only S is accessible from outside.

With communication-level security, the decryption of the payment information and authentication of C both need to happen at S. In contrast, with message-level security, S only needs to extract the relevant pieces of information from C's order and send them on to P and O. Therefore, S can be a simpler system, and

Figure 2. The online retailer scenario

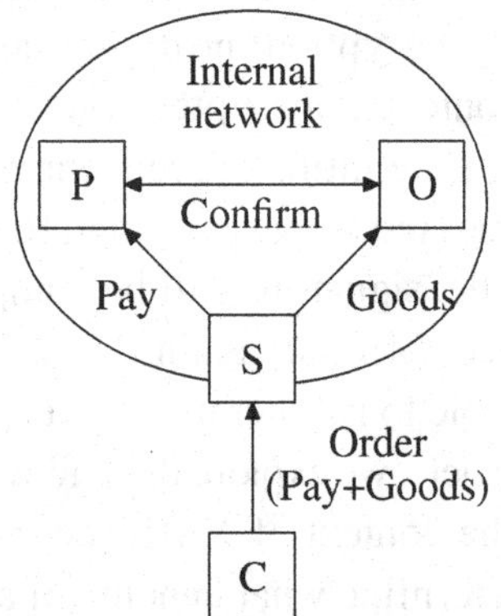

since it does not perform security processing on the messages, compromising S is not sufficient for an external attacker to alter the orders or extract payment information. Furthermore, the message-level model is less coupled as payment information decryption and client authentication are separated into different components, P and O, respectively.

Workflow systems in business processing are another application area for fine-grained security. A workflow system consists of a number of message processors and communication channels between pairs of processors so that each message flows through certain processors. Typically, each processor is only interested in looking at specific parts of each message and not at the whole message. The combined actions of the processors then form the processing that is performed on a message.

An example of a simple workflow system is shown in Figure 3, where there are three processors, A, B, and C, and an XML message (shown in tree form) is passed through the system. In the example, A needs to touch only Nodes 3 and 5, B only the subtree rooted at Node 2, and C only Node 8. In a fully XML-based system, such processing could be accomplished with XSLT (extensible stylesheet language transformations; W3C, 2007d) or XQuery (W3C, 2007c).

If this system were secured with connection-level security, each processor would have to decrypt, encrypt, verify, and sign the whole message. If the message were large, this could be a prohibitive additional cost. On the other hand, with message-level security, only the parts that are touched by each processor need to be processed, which should increase efficiency. Furthermore, the system is better compartmentalized as each encryption and signature can be targeted only to those processors that need it. Finally, each signature naturally retains the identity of its creator instead of that of the previous processor in the chain, which happens in connection-level security. This security processing can even be integrated with fully XML-based processing using XSLT (Chang & Hwang, 2004).

One way to provide fine-grained message-level security would be to use S/MIME (secure/multipurpose Internet mail extensions; Internet Engineering Task Force [IETF], 2004) by splitting the message into multiple parts, with each component to encrypt or sign being its own part, as is done with e-mail. Since much communication is moving toward XML, there would therefore need to be a way to represent XML documents as multipart MIME messages, as is done in XOP (W3C, 2005) to split Base64-encoded content out of an XML document to be transmitted in binary.

However, a solution for security based on S/MIME would require a subpart in the message for each piece of XML that is to be signed or encrypted, obscuring the content on the wire and increasing the message size due to the required MIME headers. Furthermore, due to potential security processing inside encrypted XML, this multipart solution would need to be integrated into XML processing, essentially forcing the integra-

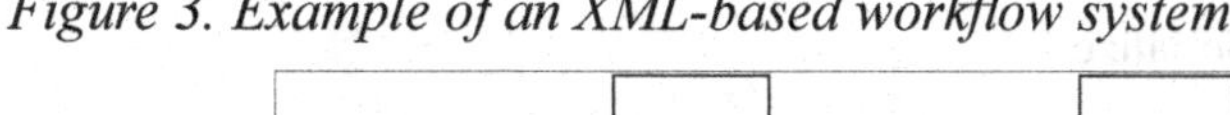
Figure 3. Example of an XML-based workflow system

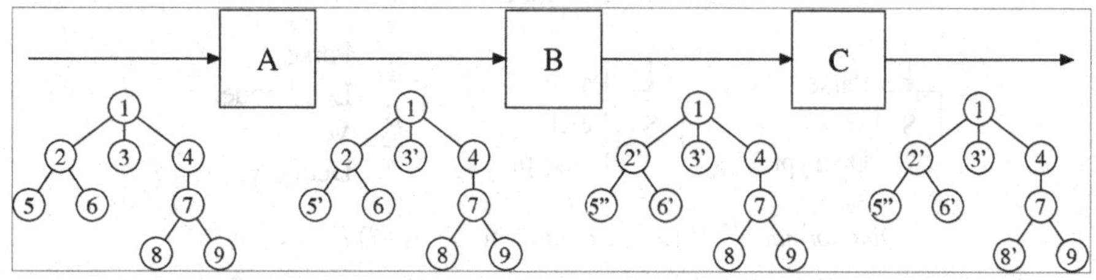

tion of MIME into XML. Therefore, S/MIME is not very suitable for fine-grained XML security, and an XML-based solution is needed.

XML Security Standards

To solve the issue of fine-grained XML document security, W3C has produced specifications for XML signatures (W3C, 2002b) and XML encryption (W3C, 2002a). XML signatures are complemented by canonical XML (W3C, 2001), which specifies an algorithm to serialize an XML document so that equivalent XML documents produce the same byte sequence. This is necessary so that an XML document passed through processing can still have its signature verified.

In XML signatures, the content to be signed is marked with a reference. This reference also includes transformation methods, which are applied to the signed content to get the bytes to digest. These references are collected inside a single XML element, which is then canonicalized using canonical XML or the like; the resulting bytes are digested, and this digest is signed. If the signed data are in XML, one of the transformations applied to it will normally be a canonicalization.

The use of XML encryption results in an element that replaces the encrypted content. Such an element contains minimally an element containing the encrypted bytes. These bytes can be either embedded in the document or given as a URI (uniform resource identifier) reference. The encrypted element will also contain a type, which denotes, for example, that the encrypted content is an XML element. XML encryption also permits transformations to be applied, but these are performed only on referenced URIs to produce the actual encrypted bytes for the decrypter and not on decrypted data.

The Web services security specification from the Organization for the Advancement of Structured Information Standards (OASIS, 2004) defines how XML encryption and signatures are used to secure SOAP messages. It defines a SOAP header that contains an XML signature element if the message contains signed content and an encrypted key if the message contains encrypted content. This latter element consists of a symmetric key encrypted with the recipient's public key and references to the XML content encrypted with that key.

Figure 4. The processing by the client, gateway, and server in each compatibility model

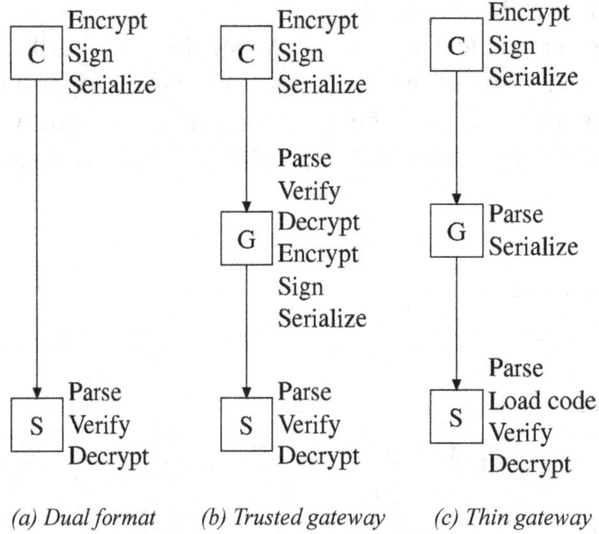

COMPATIBILITY OPTIONS

For the purposes of this article, we assume that a Web service client resides on a mobile device and a server resides somewhere in a fixed network. The situation will be such that the server supports XML but potentially not any other formats. We also assume that the mobile user would prefer to use a binary format for its presumed compactness and processing efficiency. We consider three different ways to allow the mobile client and the server to communicate within these constraints, illustrated in Figure 4.

Dual Format

The simplest of these is the dual-format (Figure 4a) case when either the server also supports the client's binary format or the client also supports XML. In this case, the client will simply sign and encrypt according to the specifications, and the server understands this. However, when the client wishes to use a binary format that the server does not understand, this solution cannot be used.

Trusted Gateway

Currently it is possible for the mobile device to use a binary format if a gateway on the network side translates between this format and XML. Various gateways have been used for mobile device access in IP (Perkins, 1996), CORBA (common object request broker architecture; Object Management Group [OMG], 2005), and WAP (WAP Forum, 2001a). Of these, WAP is the only one that rewrites the actual messages, converting them between XML and the WAP binary format (W3C, 1999). The WAP gateway also includes the WTLS (wireless transport layer security) protocol (WAP Forum, 2001b), where the gateway reencrypts and re-signs all content passing between the mobile client and the network.

The WTLS solution can obviously be extended to handle XML security. Since the gateway already needs to handle translating between XML and the binary format, it can easily handle reencrypting and re-signing any element content as well. We call this model the trusted gateway (Figure 4b) because it requires the gateway to possess the private keys of the client and to sign and encrypt messages on its behalf. In essence, the communication path is split into two separate individually trusted paths with the gateway in between and no end-to-end security between the client and server.

The trusted-gateway model can be optimized by establishing a secure tunnel, for example, with SSL, between the client and the gateway. Then, the client will not need to actually perform XML encryption and signatures, but it will be enough to indicate which parts of the message are to be signed or encrypted by the trusted gateway. This is significant savings in processing time for the client since the secure tunnel, after establishment, requires only symmetric cryptography and not the more computationally intensive asymmetric cryptography.

Thin Gateway

Since the trusted-gateway model lacks true end-to-end security, we propose a model that we call the thin gateway (Figure 4c). In this model, the gateway is only responsible for conversions between XML and the binary format and will not do any security processing. This permits, among other things, a much larger selection of potential gateways for clients since there is no additional trust involved.

The client behavior in the thin-gateway model is exactly the same as if it were communicating with a binary-aware server. Specifically, the canonicalization and transformation algorithms, as well as encrypted content types, are specified to be in the binary format. The gateway will only convert between the XML and binary formats and will not touch these values. Naturally, as the gateway does not possess the decryption keys, it can convert only the unencrypted data and has to pass the encrypted data along as the same byte sequence they were received.

On the server side, modifications are required only to the XML security processing. The XML security implementation needs to recognize the algorithms for the binary format and have these available (denoted by "Load code" in Figure 4c to indicate these algorithms may not always be integrated into the security implementation itself). This limits the recognition of the binary format to a single piece of code, which may even be provided by a separate entity, instead of requiring the binary format to be integrated into XML parsing and serializing.

The signature processing on the server side is essentially the same as with normal XML signatures. The only difference is that the final canonicalization algorithm that is applied to convert from the abstract infoset representation to bytes will produce the binary format. Similarly, any decrypted plaintext will be in the binary format, so the server will need to use a binary format parser to produce the SAX (simple application programming interface for XML) events or DOM (document object model) tree, or whichever application-level representation is expected.

Discussion

At the moment, the dual-format solution is only applicable by requiring the client to support XML since there is no widely accepted binary format. Therefore, this solution may not be acceptable to the mobile world, which does not consider XML's verbosity and processing requirements to be suitable. Even if agreement is reached on a binary format, support for it in the dual-format model will need to be implemented at the XML parser level, which may take some time. Therefore, gateway-based solutions will need to be at least considered.

Even if the server does not support a binary format, gateways still allow clients to use it for the unencrypted parts of a message. However, XML must be used for the encrypted contents as well as for computing the signature digests, but if the signed content is sent unencrypted, it can be serialized in binary up to the gateway. Since most traffic will likely be unencrypted even in the future, a simple gateway suffices for many applications. However, we specifically consider the security case here, so a simple gateway is not sufficient.

The obvious drawback of the trusted-gateway model is the requirement of trust. While, for example, the current mobile phone networks require placing some trust in the operator, it is still possible to engage in secure communication by performing security operations at the ends. The trusted-gateway model would effectively make the gateway owner a proxy for any secure communication initiated by the mobile client. Considering that more and more can be done through these kinds of systems, this appears unacceptable from the point of view of privacy and trust.

The main benefits of the thin-gateway model are that it does not require complete adoption of a binary format, that it permits a more flexible convergence in the binary format landscape, and that it does not require trusting the gateway. This last point is important as it means that the number of usable gateways can be significantly larger than with the trusted-gateway model.

A downside of the thin-gateway model compared to the trusted-gateway model is obviously that it requires modification to the server side. However, as only the XML security implementation needs to be modified, the impact on the server code is smaller than if binary format support were required at the parsing level. Also, the security implementation will already need to process canonicalization and transformations generically, so adding this code is less of a burden than it would be to support an alternate message serialization format.

Still, there is the question of which binary formats are supported by the security implementation. If there is no standard, the expectation could be that implementations would be provided by third parties. Since the code in this context is security related, it would need to be carefully vetted and certified by a trusted entity. Furthermore, such a third-party implementation would need to be provided for several different Web service platforms. We do not consider this to be likely for generic binary formats, but rather expect at most one format to be widely supported.

We consider the thin-gateway model to be a reasonable alternative, especially because the same canonicalization and transformation algorithm specifications will need to be utilized with full binary support on the server, too. However, it does not seem feasible to support arbitrary binary formats. Rather, if a binary format is standardized, the thin-gateway model can be used as a stepping-stone toward full support of this format on the server.

EXPERIMENTATION RESULTS

We performed several experiments on XML security performance in the context of Web services security. Our measurements were intended to discover the effect of using a binary format instead of XML, especially with mobile phones. Furthermore, as battery life is a significant concern on mobile devices, we also measured battery consumption and show it broken down to its components so that we can determine the most fruitful avenues for improvements.

Experimentation Setup

Our experimentation platform consisted of three components: the client, gateway, and server. The server and the gateway were running on the same machine, which has a 1.5 GHz AMD Athlon XP processor, 512 MB of main memory, and the Debian GNU/Linux 3.1 operating system. For the client, we measured on two different machines. One was a desktop system with a 3 GHz Intel Pentium 4 processor, 1 GB of main memory, and Debian GNU/Linux 3.1. The other was a regular Nokia 7610 mobile phone that supports the second-generation GSM (global system for mobile communication) and GPRS (general packet radio service) networks. The desktop systems run Java 5.0 from Sun Microsystems, and the mobile phone supports Mobile Information Device Profile (MIDP) 2.0.

We used Axis, XML-Security, and WSS4J, all from the Apache project (http://www.apache.org), for the SOAP server and its Web Services security implementation. We implemented our thin-gateway model by extending XML-Security to recognize Java scheme URIs to indicate that the correct algorithm to use is the class given by the URI. We recognize that this is not the correct solution as allowing arbitrary Java classes to be loaded to perform security processing is an obvious weakness. However, if we wish to experiment with several alternate formats, this is a more extensible solution than hard-coding the binary processor classes. We also note that the thin-gateway model was extremely straightforward to implement, requiring only approximately 50 lines of new or changed code in four classes, which serves as partial validation of the feasibility of this model.

The client-side system was a simple one written by us, both to make it easy to switch XML serialization formats and to run the same system on both clients. The cryptographic algorithms we used were 3DES for symmetric encryption, 1,024-bit RSA for asymmetric encryption, and SHA-1 for digests. On the server side, the implementations were the default ones shipped with Java, and on the client side, they were provided by the Bouncy Castle library (http://www.bouncycastle.org). We pregenerated the RSA keys for both the client and the server and hard-coded them on the client-side applications.

Table 1. Formats used in the experiments

Format	Description
Xml	XML, security processing
Xebu	Xebu, security processing
Xmlunsec	XML, no security processing
Xebuunsec	Xebu, no security processing
Xmlssl	XML, no security processing, over SSL
Xebussl	Xebu, no security processing, over SSL

For the desktop client, we used a fixed two-hop network route with ICMP (ping) latency of approximately 0.25 ms, and for the phone client, a regular GPRS connection from a major provider with a 12-hop route and ICMP latency ranging between 600 ms and 1.3 s. (The latter figures were measured from a laptop computer using the same GPRS provider as in the actual experiments.) Both the magnitude and variation of the GPRS latency are what is expected in mobile phone networks. The maximum data rates of these networks were measured to be 100 Mbps for the fixed network and 32 Kbps for GPRS, but these are less important as the small data sizes mean that the TCP (transmission-control protocol) connections do not have time to achieve their steady-state behavior.

Experiments were performed with various formats, all described in Table 1. Xebu is our binary format (Kangasharju, Tarkoma, & Lindholm, 2005), which gives similar final sizes compared to other general-purpose binary formats. Our previous measurements indicate that the results reported below for the size and processing time are typical and not specific to this particular test data.

The actual scenario was a simple Web service invocation over HTTP (hypertext transfer protocol) containing a number of card elements, each containing four subelements (these elements are credit card descriptions, but their actual content is less relevant to the measurements than their size, which is approximately 140 bytes in XML and 70 bytes in Xebu). The measurements reported below are all plotted against the number of card elements contained in a message and averaged for a single invocation. The sequence of elements was encrypted, and after this, the SOAP body was signed. The server responded with a similar message, that is, one containing the same elements with the same encryption and signing.

In the measurement application, a SOAP message is represented as an object that knows how to serialize itself as XML through a generic XML serialization API (application programming interface) that can support both normal XML and a binary format. The Web services security header is represented similarly as a component in the SOAP message object. The SOAP body is essentially an in-memory list of the SAX events constituting the body. The content to be encrypted or signed is indicated by qualified name, as is also the case with WS-Security.

We measured three different components of the total time. First, the system serializes the SOAP message into memory as bytes, including all security processing. The second component is opening an HTTP connection to the server, sending the message, and reading the response into memory. The server and gateway both measure the time they take in processing and include this in the response so that we can compute the time spent on communication alone. The third is parsing the server's response message, including decryp-

Table 2. Description of the experiments

Experiment	Description
Desktop	Messages with 20-200 elements at 20-element increments, 100 invocations, 20 replications
Phone	Messages with 2-20 elements at two-element increments, 10 invocations, 10 replications
Battery	Message with 10 elements, enough replications to completely drain the phone battery, measure number of invocations

Table 3. Message sizes in bytes, per element and constant overhead

	Request		Response	
Format	Elem	Over	Elem	Over
Xml	218	4743	163	6419
Xebu	69	1580	69	2598
Xmlunsec	151	676	121	386
Xebuunsec	69	49	70	43

Table 4. Encrypted and signed sizes in bytes, per element and constant overhead

Measurement	Encrypt	Decrypt	Sign	Verify
Xml elem	161	121	218	163
Xebu elem	69	69	69	69
Xml over	128	273	715	1502
Xebu over	15	16	111	257

tion and signature verification. We also measured individual times for each security operation.

We summarize the experiments that we ran and their parameter variations in Table 2. In both the desktop and phone experiments, we began with some unmeasured invocations to eliminate any incidental startup costs. The required number of these was determined experimentally by increasing the number and observing when the measurements stabilized. The battery experiment was performed to determine the amount of energy consumed by computation and communication in this context.

Message Sizes

We first show the sizes of the messages and their relevant components. Table 3 shows the sizes of the request and response messages in bytes by giving the size of one element and the additional constant overhead in each message; that is, if a message contains n elements, its size is approximately $Over + n\times Elem$. Table 4 gives, in similar format, the number of bytes that were actually encrypted or digested.

Table 3 shows that a secured Xebu message is between one third and two fifths of the corresponding XML message in size per element. The size of a secured Xebu message quickly becomes smaller than that of an unsecured XML message. The large overhead of the secured messages is due to the Web services security SOAP header. Finally, we note that since XML requires binary data (such as encrypted content) to be Base64 encoded, the signed content in Table 4 is one third larger than encrypted content, whereas with Xebu there is no difference.

Timing Measurements

Figure 5 shows the measured times for processing on the client, and on the gateway and server, and for communication from bottom to top. Error lines are marked at one standard deviation. Note that both figures have three lines marking processing times. However, in the phone experiment case, the time taken for remote processing at the gateway and the server is such a negligible part of the whole that its line is indistinguishable from the line drawn for local processing.

Figure 5. Total times taken in the experiment for secured and unsecured formats (divisions are client, remote, network, from bottom to top)

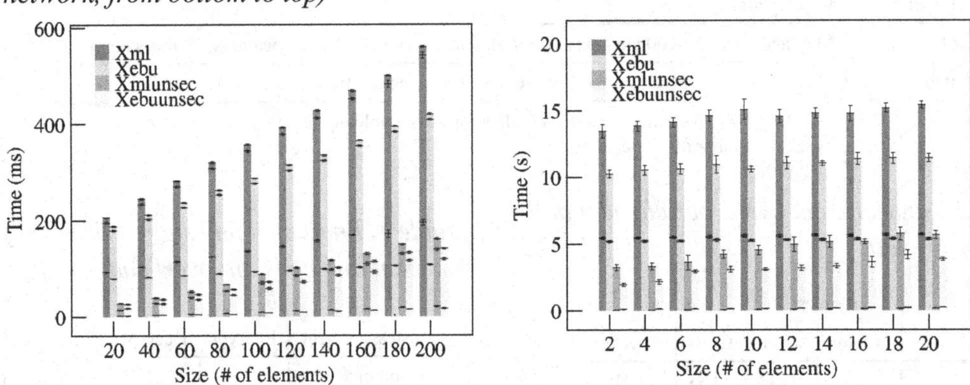

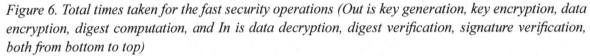

Figure 6. Total times taken for the fast security operations (Out is key generation, key encryption, data encryption, digest computation, and In is data decryption, digest verification, signature verification, both from bottom to top)

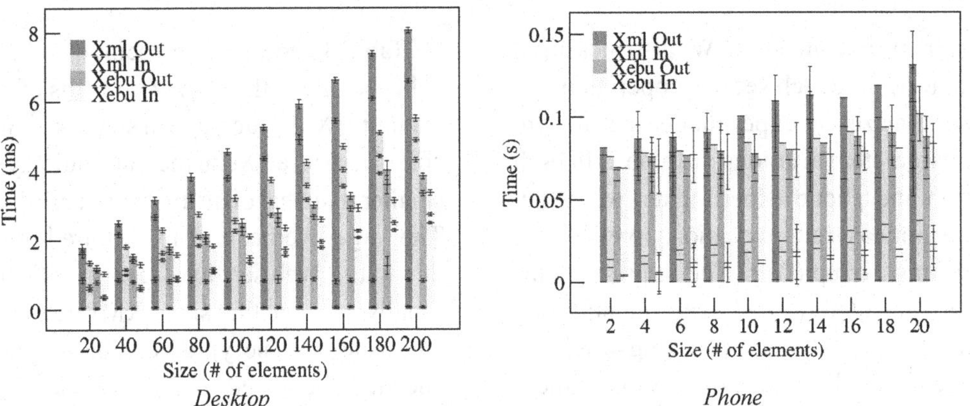

We can also see that the time taken for communication in the phone case is much higher for the security-enabled formats. By examining network packet dumps, we can see that the messages are sent in TCP segments of maximum size 1,348 bytes. Since the sizes of the messages with security processing are so much larger, this generates additional round trips. With the aforementioned latency of the GPRS network, and recalling the slow-start algorithm of TCP, this becomes clearly visible in the timings.

As with the size measurements, we also take a more detailed look into the security-enabled messages. Figure 6 shows the times taken processing encrypted data and message digests, excluding the expensive RSA private-key operations. The output bar shows symmetric key generation, key encryption, data encryption, and digest computation. The input bar shows data decryption, digest verification, and signature verification. Both of these sequences are from bottom to top.

For large messages, the dominant output component is data encryption because its processing requirements grow with message size. For the smaller messages of the phone experiment, the constant-time RSA public-key operation of

Table 5. RSA private-key operation sizes and times

Measurement	Size (B)	
Signing size	35	
Keydec size	128	
	Desktop (ms)	Phone (s)
Xml Signing	35.70±0.01	2.19±0.01
Xml Keydec	35.52±0.04	2.26±0.00
Xebu Signing	35.71±0.03	2.20±0.01
Xebu Keydec	35.34±0.03	2.23±0.00

symmetric key encryption dominates. For input processing, the most expensive one is again data decryption with the RSA public-key operation of signature verification dominating for smaller sizes.

There is much variation in many of the timings on the phone, which is due to the coarse granularity of the phone's internal clock. The actual measurement numbers show that the phone is capable of measuring time only in 15- or 16-ms increments. Since many of the operations only take a few such increments, we see both no variation and high variation, but very little low variation.

From the gathered data, we can estimate that for the same processing time as a single key encryption, we can encrypt symmetrically approximately 3.5 Kb of data on the desktop and 4.2 Kb on the phone. Similar numbers hold for the verification and data decryption pair of operations.

Finally, we show the time taken by RSA private-key operations, that is, signature computation and key decryption, in Table 5. These times do not depend on the message size at all. As we can see when comparing to Figure 6, these two operations consume several times the time spent on all other security-related processing. Extrapolating from Figure 6, we see that in the same time as one of these operations, we could potentially encrypt at least 250 Kb on the desktop.

Furthermore, we note that for the smallest messages on the phone, these operations consume up to 85% of the processing time on the client and almost 50% of the total invocation time. Therefore, it seems prudent to attempt to avoid repeated RSA private-key operations. However, there is no reason to avoid RSA public-key operations: As we saw earlier, the requirements of these are quite comparable to other processing.

Comparison with SSL

While SSL is not appropriate for all use cases, it is a widely deployed security solution and very suitable for many other cases. For this reason, we also ran our measurements using HTTP over SSL without XML-level security. This was done by replacing the HTTP URLs in Java's standard connection opening with HTTPS URLs. The algorithms used in SSL were forced to be the same as those with XML security, namely, 3DES, 1,024-bit RSA, and SHA-1.

We show the results of comparing SSL with our security-enabled formats in Figure 7 in the same way as the comparison with completely unsecured formats in Figure 5. To reiterate, each bar shows the time taken for local processing on the client, the time taken for processing at the gateway and the server, and the time taken for communication from bottom to top in this order.

Comparing to the regular HTTP case on the phone, we note that SSL adds approximately 2 s of processing to the invocation time. A network packet dump reveals this to be the SSL handshake cost, which takes two network round trips. Otherwise, the measurements remain the same. However, we also note that the first SSL handshake takes 6 s due to the key exchange; on later invocations, the session is reused, so the only overhead consists of the two network round trips of the abbreviated SSL handshake.

We noted when discussing the online retailer scenario that server authentication may be better handled at the transport level, so using both XML security and SSL is likely. In this case, we would expect the overhead of SSL to be essentially the

Figure 7. Total times taken in the experiment for secured XML and XML over SSL (divisions are client, remote, network, from bottom to top)

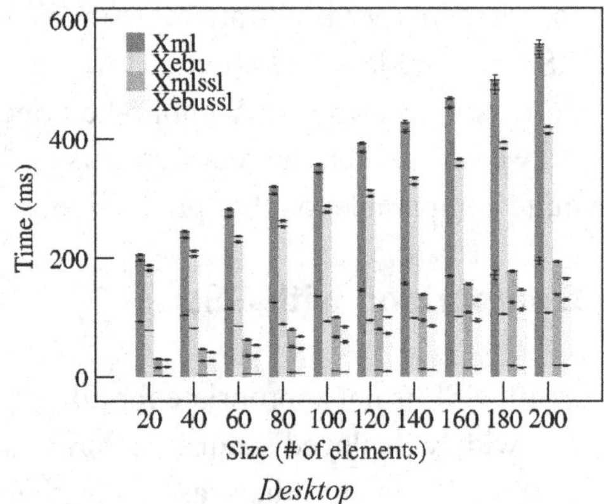

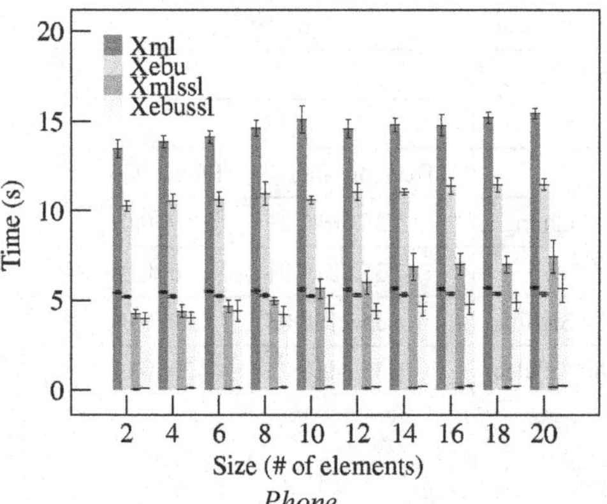

same as with unsecured XML. The only addition would be for the larger messages, which require more processing when encrypted in SSL, but this is all symmetric cryptography, and as our timing measurements show, symmetric encryption is sufficiently low in processing costs that the overhead probably would not change significantly.

One thing to note is that the SSL experiment was somewhat problematic on the phone. An observation that we made concerned the unreliability of the connection: How many invocations are received by the gateway and not returned correctly to the client? For the regular HTTP case, this rate remained at a few tenths of a percent of the number of total invocations, but with SSL, we observed a rate of 6 to 7% of such dropped connections. The most probable cause is a too-stringent network time-out somewhere, but based on our past experience with phones, we cannot rule out the possibility of an unreliable SSL implementation on the mobile phone.

Battery Consumption Measurements

Our final experiment was the repeated invocation of a 10-element message from the phone until its battery ran out. The measurement in this case was the number of invocations performed at the server. We devised a method to use this number of invocations to determine the ratio of energy consumption between communication and computation. To eliminate measurement errors as much as possible, we used only the WS-Security-based XML and Xebu formats to get measurements that were heavy on both communication and computation.

In addition to the Nokia 7610 that we used for the other experiments, we also repeated this experiment with a Nokia 9500 communicator. The 9500 is a much higher end device than the 7610: It has a slightly faster processor, more memory, a more capacious battery, and a more sophisticated Java virtual machine. Therefore, we would expect it to provide an interesting comparison. We used the GPRS network on the 9500 as well.

As a first step in computing the energy consumption ratio, let m be the amount of energy required to communicate 1 byte of data and let p be the amount of energy required to run 1 ms on the processor. If E is the total amount of energy on the phone, we get the formula:

$$E = i \cdot (s \cdot m + t \cdot p), \quad (1)$$

where s is the amount of data per invocation, t is the time spent in local processing of one invocation, and i is the total number of invocations achieved with a full battery.

By taking two measurements for the two different formats—s_1 and s_2 for size, t_1 and t_2 for processing time, and i_1 and i_2 for the number of invocations—and inserting them into Equation 1, we get a pair of linear equations that we can solve for m and p to get

$$m = E \cdot \frac{i_1 \cdot t_1 - i_2 \cdot t_2}{i_1 \cdot i_2 \cdot (s_2 \cdot t_1 - s_1 \cdot t_2)} \quad (2)$$

and

$$p = E \cdot \frac{i_1 \cdot s_1 - i_2 \cdot s_2}{i_1 \cdot i_2 \cdot (t_2 \cdot s_1 - t_1 \cdot s_2)}. \quad (3)$$

As E is here unknown to us, we can only compute the ratio between m and p. In Equations 2 and 3, the denominator is the determinant of the equation pair's matrix, so it cancels; we therefore get

$$r = \frac{m}{p} = \frac{i_2 \cdot t_2 - i_1 \cdot t_1}{i_1 \cdot s_1 - i_2 \cdot s_2}. \quad (4)$$

The numbers to insert into this equation are given in Table 6. The number of invocations is given as an interval between the minimum and maximum of our measurements. The sizes were measured from a network packet dump at the gateway so they are larger in proportion to the ones in Table 3. The times are the total processing times (i.e., total time minus communication time) of single invocations.

With these numbers, we can calculate r values for both devices from Equation 4, taking several different (i_1, i_2) pairs. The values, in the order of minimum, 25th percentile, median, 75th percentile, and maximum, are

0.47, 1.06, 1.44, 2.86, and 28.76
for the 7610, and
0.15, 0.15, 0.17, 0.19, and 0.21
for the 9500.

Table 6. Numbers of invocations and per-message communicated sizes and processing times in the battery experiment

Format	Invocations	Size (B)	Time (ms)
7610			
Xml	[842,979]	17385	5591.40±21.87
Xebu	[1444,1666]	8703	5225.04±8.72
9500			
Xml	[3084,3181]	17385	4481.30±35.72
Xebu	[4079,4153]	8703	4228.39±8.76

The calculated numbers for r give the number of milliseconds that the processor can run with the amount of energy it takes to communicate 1 byte. The Nokia 7610 has a 123 MHz ARM processor, and the Nokia 9500 a 150 MHz ARM processor. Therefore, taking the median value for both, the 7610 can run the processor for 177,000 cycles and the 9500 for 26,000 cycles.

One conclusion that we can draw from this is that the ratio of energy consumption for communication and computation is highly dependent on the device, and for different devices, even the order of magnitude can be different. Therefore, it is not possible to make general statements of how much computation the transmission of 1 byte is worth. However, we do note that the equivalent of 1 byte is in both cases best measured in milliseconds instead of seconds or microseconds, so we might assume that to be true for a larger class of devices as well.

We note that there is a large variation in the measured values for the 7610 and hardly any variation for the 9500. We believe this to be an effect of the network conditions. Since we used a real network, the daily variation will affect the results, but the measurement on the 9500 took long enough that these variations happen for all measurement runs, whereas for the 7610, the time when a measurement run was performed may have a significant effect.

We believe, however, that it is useful to run measurements in real conditions, especially in cell-based networking where there is contention for the base stations. A private base station would give results for transmission that could never be achieved in actual conditions. Furthermore, by running measurements at a variety of times, we can get a better estimate of the range of possible network behaviors.

The method that we selected for measuring energy consumption is not very sophisticated, nor does it always produce very accurate results. Furthermore, it is not possible to measure absolute energy consumption, but only relative numbers for different types of energy-consuming operations. Finally, a single run will take a long time: On the 7610, draining the battery took 3 to 4 hours, and on the 9500, it took 8 to 9 hours.

However, our measurement method is much simpler than the proper alternative and does not require any additional equipment. Furthermore, as is evident from the measurements on the 9500, it can produce good accuracy in some cases. Therefore, we believe that in cases where absolute values do not matter, this technique may be useful.

RELATED WORK

Existing work on binary formats for XML data (Sandoz, Triglia, & Pericas-Geertsen, 2004; Schneider, 2003) led W3C to begin standardization in its Efficient XML Interchange (EXI) Working Group (http://www.w3.org/XML/EXI). As the measurements above indicate, the most pressing concern in wireless communication is reduction in size. The potential future format, now in working-draft stage (W3C, 2007a), can often achieve a size reduction of at least 50% for small messages, and well over 90% when a good schema is available (W3C, 2007b).

Gateway architectures have been very popular for adding support for mobile devices (OMG, 2005; Perkins, 1996), and protocol conversions have also been used to improve the performance of, for example, TCP (Kojo, Raatikainen, Liljeberg, Kiiskinen, & Alanko, 1997) and CORBA (DOLMEN, 1997). However, these architectures only consider underlying layers and do not address either the needs of content-based routing or the requirement for end-to-end security. As we noted, security is considered by WAP with the WTLS protocol (WAP Forum, 2001b), which is essentially our trusted-gateway model for SSL.

The other security solutions that we mentioned, namely, IP security, SSL, and S/MIME, have been the targets of prior performance measurements on handheld devices as well (Argyroudis, Verma, Tewari, & O'Mahony, 2004). The processing requirement results of Argyroudis et al. appear to be in line with ours, but due to the use of wireless LAN and no mention of network latencies, total communication times are not directly comparable. This work also includes energy consumption measurements performed similarly to ours, but it does not consider how consumed energy is split between computing and communication.

The measurements that we performed were intended to reflect a single message exchange. For a longer term exchange of messages, it is beneficial to establish a security context, such as IP's security association or SSL's secure tunnel (we saw partial effects of this with the SSL session reuse). At the Web service level, such an establishment method is defined by WS-SecureConversation (IM, 2005).

The use of SSL in wireless communication was evaluated by Gupta and Gupta (2001), especially in contrast to the WTLS solution of WAP. The conclusion is that SSL can be implemented efficiently enough to be usable on mobile devices. Our measurements on SSL processing times essentially agree with this analysis.

The SSL protocol has been subjected to extensive measurements on energy consumption (Potlapally, Ravi, Raghunathan, & Jha, 2006). The tests of Potlapally et al. were performed on a PDA using wireless LAN. One of the findings is that the noncryptographic parts of the protocol, that is, mostly data transmission, consume 40 to 45% of the total energy, and for small data transmission, the cryptographic part is dominated by the asymmetric algorithms.

Comparing these figures on SSL to our results, we note that our messages were small enough that the asymmetric algorithms dominate. Estimating from our computed energy consumption ratios, we see that on the 7610, nearly 80% of the energy is spent on data transmission with XML and nearly 70% with Xebu. The 9500 is closer to a PDA in functionality than the 7610, and with it the amount spent on data transmission is 40% with XML and 25% with Xebu, which are closer to the values measured by Potlapally et al. (2006).

We note that existing detailed measurements of XML signatures (Shirasuna, Slominski, Fang, & Gannon, 2004) indicate that most of the time spent on signature processing is actually spent on canonicalization. As our experimental system was designed so that it wrote and read everything directly in canonical form, this effect is not visible in our timing measurements, but we could observe some of it on the server while running the experiments.

Shirasuna et al. (2004) also compare XML-based security solutions with SSL and note that SSL should be used if message-level security is not needed, a conclusion that agrees with ours. Also notable is the evaluation of WS-SecureConversation; the authors note that it provides a two-fold improvement for repeated messages and only a small overhead for single messages. This indicates that WS-SecureConversation is definitely a technology that is worth keeping in mind, but in the wireless communication context, the added overhead in message size may prove to be prohibitive.

An architecture for secure Web-services-based communication for pervasive computing is defined by Helander and Xiong (2005). This system uses Web services security for its security needs, and the authors' conclusion is that security interoperability is possible even with low-cost devices. Unlike the off-the-shelf components used in our measurements, this system's Web service implementation is a special-purpose one, written especially for the embedded devices they are targeting. Energy consumption is briefly considered and requirements for processing calculated, but there is no breakdown of costs.

RECOMMENDATIONS

The measurements shown in this article lead us to the bottlenecks in a secure Web services system for mobile devices. Based on these bottlenecks, we can note some recommendations on avoiding them. Some of these recommendations are usable even today with the existing standards, but others require modifications to existing practice.

First of all, we note that in our measurements, most of the processing time went to RSA private-key operations. In comparison, the time taken by RSA public-key operations is on par with the symmetric encryption of even a modest-sized message. The reason for this is that the public exponent of RSA is usually selected to be small (we used the common choice of $65537 = 2^{16}+1$), so the modular exponentiation does not take much time. In contrast, the private exponent, being the inverse of the public exponent, usually is of the same size as the modulus itself.

This property of RSA, of one operation being much faster than its opposite, is in contrast with other common asymmetric algorithms, DSA and Elgamal. In many cases, for example, in certificate verification, only RSA public-key operations are needed so we conclude that RSA is often the best algorithm to use despite its somewhat slower operation in its slower direction than the other algorithms.

Next, we move to extensions of existing standards. In light of our energy consumption measurements, we note that reducing the amount of data transmitted over the network can be worth a significant amount of computation. Therefore, it does not seem that in this specific case the purported processing efficiency gains of a binary format should matter much compared to compressed XML, especially if the latter produces smaller messages.

As an example, our previous measurements on the effectiveness of binary XML (Kangasharju et al., 2005) indicate that gzip on top of XML gives, for 3-Kb messages, a 75% reduction in size. These measurements were made on a desktop computer, so the additional time consumed cannot be directly translated, but based on the characteristics of the devices and other measurements, we estimate the additional processing to be between 10 and 100 ms on the 7610. In light of the ratios we computed for energy consumption, this is a massive benefit.

However, existing compression solutions are applied at the protocol level to the complete message. This means that compression is applied to the Base64-encoded form of the encrypted bytes, and should not be able to compress more than by the Base64 overhead of one fourth. This problem is naturally not specific to XML, and the common recommendation is to always compress messages before encryption (Schneier, 1990).

At the moment, XML encryption does not offer a method to encrypt compressed XML and have it be recognized as such by the receiver. This can be worked around by a simple extension to the EncryptedData element. Currently, it indicates with its Type attribute what kind of XML content has been encrypted. In our opinion, the simplest method to extend this to recognize compressed XML would be to add another attribute, perhaps ContentEncoding, that would work similarly to the Content-Encoding header of HTTP (Fielding et al., 1999), but would indicate how the XML fragment indicated by the Type attribute was encoded (compressed) before encryption. Our recent results (Kangasharju, 2007) demonstrate that large gains are possible with this simple extension.

Our final recommendation is a modification of the protocol itself and is specifically designed for the situation where the processing capabilities of the client and the server differ greatly. We assume that RSA is used per our earlier recommendation. In this case, there are two operations that require the expensive private-key use: signing a computed digest and decrypting a symmetric key received from the server.

To remove processing from signing, we suggest replacing the signature with HMAC (Bellare, Canetti, & Krawczyk, 1996). This requires a shared secret between the client and the server, which can be established by the client with a securely generated random number encrypted for the server and signed by the client in the first message.

For decrypting the symmetric key, it is possible to use a similar method, that is, the client including an encrypted and signed random number in the message. Then, the server will use this number as the encryption key for the response message, and, as usual, include it encrypted with the client's public key. Now the client can simply encrypt the proposed key with its own public key and compare the encrypted keys for a match, thus replacing a private-key operation with a public-key one, which is much faster.

These suggestions have the drawbacks that the keys used in the operations will still need to be generated and signed by the client, and that the amount of traffic over the network is increased by the keys that are sent. For the former issue, we note that these keys can be generated beforehand when energy consumption is not an issue and stored securely on the client. Furthermore, the same keys can be used with the same server (but note that using the same key for two different servers is insecure).

For the latter, we note from our measurements that eliminating a single public-key operation saves 2.2 s on the 7610, which is equivalent to 1.5 Kb of data. However, on the 9500, the savings are 1.8 s, which is equivalent to only 300 bytes of data. In both cases, this is more than the 128-byte result of RSA, so our scheme is still more energy efficient than the standard. The results from the

9500 indicate that this is not necessarily true for all devices, but on the other hand, the large savings on the 7610 are definitely worth considering.

CONCLUSION

Summarizing our findings, we make the following main conclusions and recommendations:

- XML-level security is still a heavyweight operation and should only be used if the required security semantics demand it.
- SSL overhead is sufficiently small to make it fully usable in the wireless world.
- The compression of XML messages is vital for mobile devices, and specifications like XML encryption should be extended to integrate compression better.
- A characteristic of mobile Web services is a clear asymmetry in processing capabilities between clients and servers, and protocols may need to take this into account.

Based on our experience in the area, we believe that the adoption of an alternate serialization format for XML in the wireless world is very likely in the near future, especially if the W3C EXI effort makes progress. Since security is vitally important in the modern networked world, it must not be compromised or lessened. In our view, the thin-gateway model is a valid method for the initial inclusion of XML-based security in the case where an alternate format is adopted. Independently of that, however, we see the processing requirements of cryptography and energy requirements of large messages to be the major issues in this field.

ACKNOWLEDGMENT

The authors would like to thank the anonymous reviewers for helpful comments. This research was performed in the Fuego Core research project, funded by the National Technology Agency of Finland, Nokia, and TeliaSonera.

REFERENCES

Argyroudis, P. G., Verma, R., Tewari, H., & O'Mahony, D. (2004). Performance analysis of cryptographic protocols on handheld devices. In *Third IEEE International Symposium on Network Computing and Applications* (pp. 169-174).

Bellare, M., Canetti, R., & Krawczyk, H. (1996). Keying hash functions for message authentication. In *Advances in Cryptology: CRYPTO 1996* (LNCS 1109, pp. 1-15). Santa Barbara, CA: Springer-Verlag.

Chang, T.-K., & Hwang, G.-H. (2004). Using the extension function of XSLT and DSL to secure XML documents. In *18th International Conference on Advanced Information Networking and Applications* (pp. 556-561).

DOLMEN. (1997). *Bridging and wireless access for terminal mobility in CORBA* (Rep. No. LK-OMG01). Paper presented at the DOLMEN Consortium.

Fielding, R., Gettys, J., Mogul, J., Nielsen, H. F., Masinter, L., Leach, P., et al. (1999). *RFC 2616: Hypertext transfer protocol: HTTP/1.1.* Internet Engineering Task Force.

Freier, A. O., Karlton, P., & Kocher, P. C. (1996). *The SSL protocol version 3.0.* Netscape Communications.

Gupta, V., & Gupta, S. (2001). Securing the wireless Internet. *IEEE Communications Magazine, 39*(12), 68-74.

Helander, J., & Xiong, Y. (2005). Secure Web services for low-cost devices. In *Eighth IEEE International Symposium on Object-Oriented Real-Time Distributed Computing* (pp. 130-139).

IM. (2005). *Web services secure conversation language (WS-SecureConversation)*. IBM, Microsoft, et al.

Internet Engineering Task Force (IETF). (2004). *RFC 3851: Secure/multipurpose Internet mail extensions (S/MIME) version 3.1 message specification*. Author.

Kangasharju, J. (2007). Efficient implementation of XML security for mobile devices. In *IEEE International Conference on Web Services* (pp. 134-141). Salt Lake City, UT: Institute of Electrical and Electronic Engineers.

Kangasharju, J., Tarkoma, S., & Lindholm, T. (2005). Xebu: A binary format with schema-based optimizations for XML data. In A. H. H. Ngu, M. Kitsuregawa, E. Neuhold, J.-Y. Chung, & Q. Z. Sheng (Eds.), *Sixth International Conference on Web Information Systems Engineering* (LNCS 3806, pp. 528-535). New York: Springer-Verlag.

Kent, S., & Atkinson, R. (1998). *RFC 2401: Security architecture for the Internet protocol*. Internet Engineering Task Force.

Kojo, M., Raatikainen, K., Liljeberg, M., Kiiskinen, J., & Alanko, T. (1997). An efficient transport service for slow wireless telephone links. *IEEE Journal on Selected Areas in Communication, 15*(7), 1337-1348.

Organization for the Advancement of Structured Information Standards (OASIS). (2004). *Web services security: SOAP message security 1.0*. Billerica, MA: Author.

Object Management Group (OMG). (2005). *Wireless access and terminal mobility in CORBA, version 1.2*. Needham, MA: Author.

Perkins, C. (1996). *RFC 2002: IP mobility support*. Internet Engineering Task Force.

Potlapally, N. R., Ravi, S., Raghunathan, A., & Jha, N. K. (2006). A study of the energy consumption characteristics of cryptographic algorithms and security protocols. *IEEE Transactions on Mobile Computing, 5*(2), 128-143.

Sandoz, P., Triglia, A., & Pericas-Geertsen, S. (2004). Fast infoset. *Sun Developer Network*.

Satyanarayanan, M. (2001). Pervasive computing: Vision and challenges. *IEEE Personal Communications, 8*(4), 10-17.

Schneider, J. (2003). Theory, benefits and requirements for efficient encoding of XML documents. In *W3C Workshop on Binary Interchange of XML Information Item Sets*. World Wide Web Consortium.

Schneier, B. (1990). *Applied cryptography* (2nd ed.). New York: John Wiley & Sons.

Shirasuna, S., Slominski, A., Fang, L., & Gannon, D. (2004). Performance comparison of security mechanisms for grid services. In R. Buyya (Ed.), *Fifth IEEE/ACM International Workshop on Grid Computing* (pp. 360-364).

WAP Forum. (2001a). *Wireless application protocol: Architecture specification*.

WAP Forum. (2001b). *Wireless transport layer security specification*.

World Wide Web Consortium (W3C). (1999). *WAP binary XML content format*. Cambridge, MA: Author.

World Wide Web Consortium (W3C). (2001). *Canonical XML version 1.0*. Cambridge, MA: Author.

World Wide Web Consortium (W3C). (2002a). *XML Encryption Syntax and Processing*. Cambridge, MA: Author.

World Wide Web Consortium (W3C). (2002b). *XML signature syntax and processing*. Cambridge, MA: Author.

World Wide Web Consortium (W3C). (2003a). *SOAP version 1.2 part 1: Messaging framework*. Cambridge, MA: Author.

World Wide Web Consortium (W3C). (2003b). *SOAP version 1.2 part 2: Adjuncts.* Cambridge, MA: Author.

World Wide Web Consortium (W3C). (2005). *XML-binary optimized packaging.* Cambridge, MA: Author.

World Wide Web Consortium (W3C). (2007a). *Efficient XML interchange (EXI) format 1.0.* Cambridge, MA: Author.

World Wide Web Consortium (W3C). (2007b). *Efficient XML interchange measurements note.* Cambridge, MA: Author.

World Wide Web Consortium (W3C). (2007c). *XQuery 1.0: An XML query language.* Cambridge, MA: Author.

World Wide Web Consortium (W3C). (2007d). *XSL transformations (XSLT) version 2.0.* Cambridge, MA: Author.

Weiser, M. (1993). Some computer science issues in ubiquitous computing. *Communications of the ACM, 36*(7), 75-84.

This work was previously published in the International Journal of Web Services Research, Volume 5, Issue 3, edited by L. Zhang, pp. 1-19, copyright 2008 by IGI Publishing (an imprint of IGI Global).

Chapter 11
Efficient and Effective XML Encoding

Christian Werner
University of Lübeck, Germany

Carsten Buschmann
University of Lübeck, Germany

Ylva Brandt
University of Lübeck, Germany

Stefan Fischer
University of Lübeck, Germany

ABSTRACT

Compared to other middleware approaches like CORBA or Java RMI the protocol overhead of SOAP is very high. This fact is not only disadvantageous for several performance-critical applications, but especially in environments with limited network bandwidth or resource-constrained computing devices. Although recent research work concentrated on more compact, binary representations of XML data only very few approaches account for the special characteristics of SOAP communication. This chapter will discuss the most relevant state-of-the-art technologies for compressing XML data. Furthermore, it will present a novel solution for compacting SOAP messages. In order to achieve significantly better compression rates than current approaches, the compressor described in this chapter utilizes structure information from an XML Schema or WSDL document. With this additional knowledge on the "grammar" of the exchanged messages, this compressor generates a single custom pushdown automaton, which can be used as a highly efficient validating parser as well as a highly effective compressor. The main idea is to tag the transitions of the automaton with short binary identifiers that are then used to encode the path through the automaton during parsing. The authors' approach leads to extremely compact data representations and is also usable in environments with very limited CPU and memory resources.

DOI: 10.4018/978-1-61520-684-1.ch011

INTRODUCTION

The text-oriented data encoding of XML is the reason for SOAP messages causing significantly more overhead than the binary message formats of Java RMI and CORBA. In an earlier work we compared different approaches for realizing Remote Procedure Calls (RPC) and showed that SOAP over HTTP causes significantly more traffic than similar technologies. Using SOAP the data volume is about three times higher than with Java RMI or CORBA (Werner et al., 2007).

Fortunately, most of today's wired networks are fast enough to provide sufficient bandwidth for all applications. However, there are still some application domains with tight bandwidth limits: For example, in cellular phone networks it is still common to charge the customer according to the transmitted data volumes. Another very common example is a dial-up connection over older technologies like modem or ISDN links. Although their bandwidth is very limited they are still in use in many enterprise networks. Additional limitations are imposed by foreseen application domains of web services such as Ubiquitous Computing. In such energy-constrained environments the radio interface is usually a main power consumer and therefore tight restrictions apply to the transmitted data volumes on mobile devices.

In order to address the problem of excessive XML message sizes in these domains a lot of research effort went into the development of binary (and therefore more compact) representations of XML data.

In order to preserve the universal compatibility of binary encoded XML, standardization is a very important issue: The W3C founded the W3C XML Binary Characterization Working Group in March 2004. Its members analyzed various application scenarios and created a survey of the existing approaches in this field (W3C, 2005a). Furthermore, this working group has specified a set of requirements that are important for binary XML representations. The most requested features are compactness, the possibility of directly reading and writing the binary format, independence of a certain transport mechanisms, and processing efficiency.

Another major outcome of this working group was a set of 18 typical use cases for binary XML representations with a detailed analysis of their individual requirements. In all use cases the property "compactness", which is in the focus of this article, was of major importance or has been rated as a nice-to-have feature. In ten of 18 cases it was even rated as mandatory.

The W3C XML Binary Characterization Working Group has finished its work and its successor, the Efficient XML Interchange Working Group (W3C, 2005b), has taken up work in December 2005. It focuses on interoperability aspects of binary XML and has published its current working draft in September 2008. It describes the Efficient XML Interchange (EXI) Format (W3C, 2008) which we discuss in the section on related work.

In this article we elaborate on how to encode SOAP messages efficiently. We exploit the fact that web service messages are described by an XML grammar that is known to both the sender and the receiver (usually in form of a WSDL file). A large part of the information contained in a message can be inferred from this grammar. This "a priory" known part can therefore be omitted during transmission; this leads to very promising compression results.

Although the idea of creating web service-specific compressors from WSDL descriptions is not new and has already been presented by the authors in a previous publication in this book series (Werner et al., 2007), considerable advances are presented here: The original idea was to create a set of "empty" web service messages, called skeletons, containing all XML constructs that reoccur in subsequent service calls. When a service is called only the differences between the message and the corresponding skeleton is transmitted over the network. We could show that this differential encoding leads to very promising results in terms of message size. However, calculating the difference between two XML documents is a task with high computational complexity. This slows down web service communication and degrades the applicability of this approach in practice. In the following we will present a novel encoding technique that is extremely efficient and, as we will show, can be implemented even on devices with very limited resources. With this technique it is possible to implement SOAP-based web services on tiny embedded systems.

Please note that XML message compression is not an all-embracing solution to the problem of web services overhead. Furthermore, the used transport binding may introduce a significant amount of additional overhead. Therefore, it is advisable to combine message compression with an optimized transport binding in order to get the best results in real-world environments. We have comprehensively studied the influence of the transport binding in a previous contribution (Werner et al., 2006).

The remainder of this article is structured as follows: At first, we conduct a survey on state-of-the-art compression methods for SOAP and XML. We focus on techniques that make use of the availability of grammar descriptions. We then present the results of an extensive evaluation measuring the compression effectiveness of the different algorithms. After this we present our new approach to SOAP compression and evaluate its effectiveness. In the subsequent section we show an exemplary implementation of our approach on an embedded device. Finally, we draw a conclusion and give an outlook on promising topics for future work.

RELATED WORK

Because XML documents are usually represented as text, the approach of applying well-known general purpose text compressors such as gzip is obvious. Unfortunately, typical web service messages are rather small and this fact heavily degrades the compression effectiveness of such compressors (Werner et al., 2007). Therefore, the subsequent section takes into account only approaches that specialize on XML data.

Overview

In the past years many XML-aware concepts have been invented. A very common approach is to separate the markup from the character data and compress both independently with different algorithms. *XMill* (Liefke and Suciu, 2000) and *xmlppm* (Cheney, 2001) are two compressors that are based on this technique.

Another promising idea is to exploit the XML syntax rules: When compressing well-formed documents, the name of any end tag can be inferred from the name of the corresponding opening tag. Hence, the name of an end tag does not have to be encoded. The *Fast Infoset* (Sandoz et al., 2004) compressor uses this technique and produces a binary serialization that is optimized for high-speed XML processing. A recent approach in the field of XML compression that does not rely on Schema information is *Exalt* (Toman, 2004). It analyzes typical tag sequences in the input data and stores this information by generating a set of finite state automata. Using these, Exalt predicts the next tag at a certain stage of compression and encodes only the difference between the read value and the prediction.

A different way of efficiently compacting XML data is to build a compressor that is custom-tailored to a certain XML language. If the vocabulary and the grammar of an XML language is known in advance, specialized compressors can be built that map the markup-structures of this particular language to shorter binary tokens. A very common approach for implementing this is to use fixed coding tables that are integrated into the compression engine. *WBXML* (https://libwbxml.opensync.org/) and *Millau* (Girardot and Sundaresan, 2000) are two examples of such compressors. Both support various languages in the field of mobile devices like WML or SyncML. A similar technique is used by the *Binary Format for MPEG-7 Metadata (BiM)* compressor (Niedermeier et al., 2002) which is specialized in processing MPEG-7 Metadata.

While these highly optimized Schema-based XML compressors feature very impressive compression results (Werner et al., 2007), their practical value is limited. Their main disadvantage is that they do not support the extensibility XML has been designed for. The SOAP format is a typical example: The SOAP body can carry arbitrary application specific data. Hence, a compression algorithm that relies on fixed coding tables is obviously not optimal in this case.

XML Compressors Supporting Dynamic Schema Processing

The idea of combining the high compression performance of language-specific compressors with the flexibility of general purpose compressors was the driver for developing compressors with dynamic Schema support, i.e. compression algorithms that can be customized to application specific XML grammars at runtime.

Information on the document structure, typically available through an XML grammar description like XML Schema or DTD, enables two new compression strategies. The first is to infer optimized binary content encodings from the data type definitions in the XML grammar. Thus numeric values in the XML document can be represented as binary encoded integer numbers instead of using the default representation as strings. Second, improvements of the compression effectiveness are possible because the XML grammar provides information on how valid instance documents are structured. Therefore, large parts of the structure information are redundant and can be omitted in the compressed document. Of course, the reconstruction of the original document during decompression also requires the Schema information to be present in order to avoid information loss.

An example of a compressor that can dynamically process Schema information is *XGrind* (Tolani and Haritsa, 2002). It employs a so called "context-free" compression strategy, i.e. it generates a data format that is capable of processing XML queries efficiently without decompressing the whole content. Therefore, XGrind can neither omit tags that can be inferred from the grammar nor use efficient binary encodings for numeric content like xsd:int. Instead, it represents the text values of tag and attribute names by mapping them to shorter identifiers: It uses the grammar (in DTD format) to identify all possible tag names, which are then assigned to compact 8 bit identifiers in the binary format. Additionally, XGrid omits the names of closing tags, because these can be inferred from the name of the corresponding opening tag in well-formed XML documents. Furthermore, XGrind represents the values of enumeration types using binary block codes. The remaining XML content is Huffman encoded. In order to minimize the codeword lengths a separate Huffman table is maintained for each tag name in the document. With these techniques XGrind is able to generate quite compact data representations even under the constraint of context-free compression.

Another compressor that supports dynamic grammar processing is *Xebu* (Kangasharju et al., 2005). It uses a general purpose SAX parser to prepare the input data and encodes the resulting sequence of events in a compact binary fashion: During compression all tag names are indexed on their first appearance and on repetition only the index ID (a byte value) is encoded. Unlike XGrind, the Xebu encoder also detects numeric data and encodes it in an efficient binary format. These two compression features are always available even if no grammar is present.

To further improve the effectiveness of the Xebu compressor, so called omission automata can be generated from a Relax NG grammar (Clark and Makoto, 2001). The basic idea here is to omit the encoding of SAX events that can be inferred from the grammar. For example, if the grammar prescribes a sequence of elements with each element occurring exactly once, we do not have to encode any structure information because there is only one correct tag sequence, which can be unambiguously inferred from the grammar. Unfortunately, the paper does not provide an algorithm for constructing these omission automata.

Another feature of Xebu is called pre-caching. The idea is to pre-fill the index ID tables with initial values extracted from the Schema. This is possible because the XML grammar usually contains detailed information on the possible element and attribute names in the document. Pre-caching leads to significantly better compression results especially on short input files, because strings in the document can be replaced by shorter IDs throughout the whole document and not only on repetition.

The current specification of the *EXI Format* (W3C, 2008) represents the markup of an XML document as a sequence of event codes. These are either provided by fixed, predefined rules (so called Built-in XML Grammars) representing the general XML syntax rules or by optional, dynamic rules (so called Schema-informed Grammars) representing the structure information of a certain XML language. Pieces of simple content, so called values, are attached to their corresponding event codes. Both event codes and the attached values are then grouped into so called channels which can then be serialized either uncompressed or by employing the *deflate* compression method defined in RFC 1951.

The *Differential Encoding* approach (Werner et al., 2007) targets the special requirements of SOAP communication and also belongs to the category of compressors with dynamic schema support. The authors apply the well-known method of differential encoding to generate more compact SOAP message representations. The compression process works as follows: Instead of transmitting the whole SOAP message, only the difference between the message and a so called "skeleton" message is sent over the network. Skeletons can be automatically generated from WSDL service descriptions. The difference information can be expressed using various data formats. Practical experiments showed that the Document Update Language (DUL) in combination with the xmlppm compressor performs very well. This approach yields very high compression rates (even with files smaller than 10 kBytes, which is typical for SOAP communication). Unfortunately, the Differential Encoding approach is afflicted with a very high algorithmic complexity due to the problem of calculating the differences between two XML documents. Hence, on devices with limited memory and CPU resources this approach can only be used with small input documents.

Evaluation Setup

In order to compare the compression performance of the different schemes, we generated a consistent test bed that was used to evaluate all available compressors.

To obtain representative results, we chose to use two different benchmark web services that are typical for nowadays SOAP applications. These were used to evaluate the compression efficiency of the aforementioned schemes.

The first service represents a class of applications transmitting only little payload. A stock quote service may serve as an example for this kind of web service. Its request might contain a short string that identifies the stock of interest, the so-called ticker symbol. The service answers with a response containing nothing but the current stock price encoded as an integer value. It is rather difficult to compress such messages, because any static overhead imposed by the compressor (such as coding tables) quickly becomes as big as or even bigger than the original message. As a result, not all schemes that yield promising compression ratios on long messages also work equally well on small messages. An additional characteristic of such services is that the XML Schema that describes the message format is usually very restraining. This means that little or no message structure variation is possible.

To represent this kind of service, we constructed a benchmark web service implementing a calculator. It features four different operations that exchange messages with different payload lengths. While void doNothing() does not respond anything, int increment(int i1) replies with a message that contains the call parameter plus one. Both int add(int i1, int i1) and int add6ints(int i1, int i2, int i3, int i4, int i5, int i6) return the sum of their input parameters. The calculator was implemented as a literal-style web service using the Microsoft .NET framework. We then called the different operations with random values and saved the resulting SOAP requests and responses into files. These were then fed into the different compressors for evaluating their compression performance.

The second class of services transmits significantly more data, particularly string data, resulting in large messages. Here the amount of payload clearly dominates the enveloping SOAP protocol overhead. The Amazon E-Commerce Service (http://webservices.amazon.com/AWSECommerceService/AWSECommerceService.wsdl) is as an example of this type. Its message format is defined by a complex XML Schema that makes heavy use of attributes for content structuring.

This service was used for our performance evaluation as the second benchmark. The underlying API provides an *ItemSearch* operation with a *ResponseGroup* parameter that controls the response message verbosity. We started three calls with the search keyword "web service". While we set the ResponseGroup parameter to "small" for the first call, we chose "medium" and "large" for the other two requests. The according request and response messages were again saved into files. For analytical reasons we recorded the fraction of xsd:string data in the response messages: 47% (small), 35% (medium) and 37% (large).

For evaluating XML Schema aware compressors, we needed to obtain the Schemas for both benchmark web services. These consist of an application-specific part (that can be extracted from the corresponding WSDL file) and an application-independent part for the enveloping SOAP 1.1 markup (available at: http://schemas.xmlsoap.org/soap/envelope/). In order to be able to include Xebu into our evaluation, we had to convert the schemas to the Relax NG language because Xebu does not support XML Schema. We used the tools *Sun Relax NG Converter* (http://www.xml.com/pub/r/1265) and *Trang* (http://www.thaiopensource.com/relaxng/trang.html) for this conversion.

Compression Performance

We used the SOAP data generated by the previously described benchmark web services to evaluate the compression effectiveness of the different approaches. We applied all compressors in their default settings, i.e. we did not use any additional command line parameters. Because Xebu is not a ready-to-use command line tool but a set of Java classes providing an API, we implemented a minimal wrapper application that uses omission automata as well as pre-caching.

For the results achieved by the different compressors we state not only the resulting file sizes S but also λ, the so-called compression ratio which is the quotient $S_{compressed}/S_{uncompressed}$. Besides the values for every single operation request and response, we also state the sum of all file sizes $\sum$. The results are shown in Table 1.

For the sake of readability we omitted the individual values of λ. Instead, we specify only the best, worst and average values here. Since the average compression value is not weighted by file size, it differs from $\sum_{compressed}/\sum_{uncompressed}$.

Because WBXML, Millau and BiM cannot be applied to SOAP data, we could not include them into our evaluation. We also excluded XMLXpress because there is no publicly available implementa-

Table 1. Compression results for the SOAP data from both web services. All file sizes are specified in bytes

	uncompr.	gzip	XMill	xmlppm	Fast Infoset	EXI (w/o Schema)	EXI (w/ Schema)	Xebu	Diff. Enc.
doNothing (Request)	336	224	338	167	210	99	3	103	21
doNothing (Response)	344	229	352	173	210	107	3	103	21
increment (Request)	381	236	334	177	246	112	9	127	52
increment (Response)	425	249	351	187	246	134	9	127	52
add (Request)	401	239	360	181	269	114	14	135	106
add (Response)	401	238	361	180	246	122	9	127	95
add6ints (Request)	559	307	436	242	397	189	35	217	155
add6ints (Response)	429	255	378	195	254	134	9	135	104
Amazon "small" (Request)	680	371	519	319	455	259	70	-	255
Amazon "small" (Response)	9,144	1,625	2,072	1,576	7,446	4,724	4,441	-	2,366
Amazon "medium" (Request)	681	373	518	321	456	260	71	-	257
Amazon "medium" (Resp.)	60,319	8,795	8,298	7,190	46,283	19,503	18,934	-	16,096
Amazon "large" (Request)	680	371	520	319	455	259	70	-	255
Amazon "large" (Response)	229,619	31,977	31,977	32,171	236,349	97,349	99,376	-	88,103
Σ	374,399	59,353	46,814	43,398	293,522	123,365	123,053	-	107,938
λ_{best}	1.00	0.15	0.11	0.11	0.58	0.28	0.01	0.30	0.06
λ_{worst}	1.00	0.67	1.02	0.50	0.81	0.52	0.49	0.39	0.38
$\lambda_{average}$	1.00	0.50	0.71	0.39	0.67	0.34	0.12	0.32	0.24

tion. Unfortunately, the implementation of XGrind from July 19, 2002 (which is available online at http://sourceforge.net/projects/xgrind/) did not work properly. When decompressing, XGrind yielded invalid SOAP messages and thus was excluded from our evaluation, too. Because Xebu failed to process the Relax NG translation of the Amazon web service grammar, we omitted the according test cases for this compressor. The EXI Format was produced using the open source implementation Exificient (available at http://exificient.sourceforge.net/). For our measurements we used the included test application that generates two sets of output files – one with and the other one without considering Schema information.

The best average compression ratios are achieved by EXI with Schema information. It performs especially well with the small messages originating from the calculator web service. These can hardly be compressed by gzip and XMill because they have to embed extra encoding rules in addition to the actual data. Also if EXI is used without Schema information it shows the best performance out of the other non-schema-aware approaches. An exception to that rule is the compression of the Amazon response messages that contain a lot of string data. Here, approaches performing particularly well on text compression yield the most compact representations.

While none of the available compressors achieved good compression ratios for all kinds of files and file sizes, it becomes obvious that schema-aware compression seems to be the most promising way to arrive at compact SOAP message encodings.

PUSHDOWN AUTOMATA APPROACH

XML compression tools with dynamic Schema support are either using very expensive computations (differential encoding) or dynamically growing data structures like coding tables (Xebu). Both strategies are disadvantageous, especially in the domain of resource-constrained devices. For this reason, it was our major concern to develop an approach with excellent compression ratios that features a low computational complexity and requires only small amounts of memory.

Existing XML compressors like Exalt, BiM and Xebu suggest that using automata for representing structure information of XML data is a promising way to achieve these goals. However, since the languages described by a DTD or XML Schema do not necessarily belong to the class of regular languages, a plain finite-state automaton (FSA) as used by Exalt, BiM and Xebu is not sufficient to represent the described grammars. Therefore, only parts of the XML tree, like the direct children of a node, can be processed by a single FSA. Segoufin and Vianu discuss this problem in detail (Segoufin and Vianu, 2002). Consequently, BiM and Exalt have to employ multiple automata and an additional mechanism that organizes the compression process by deciding when to use which of them. In Xebu, the implemented FSA does not fully represent the Relax NG grammar, either. Instead, it only extends the compression algorithm in order to improve the compression results.

Hence, more powerful automata concepts like tree or pushdown automata are required for expressing XML grammars entirely (Murata et al., 2001).

Architecture

The commonly available WSDL description of a web service provides an XML Schema definition. Our approach is based on a single deterministic pushdown automaton (PDA) that is derived from this specific grammar. Both, the sender as well as the receiver generate this PDA as a first step. Before sending a SOAP message the sender traverses the PDA according to the message structure. The markup structure of the message is thus represented by the path taken through the automaton. The states passed (markup) as well as the values of the leaf elements (simple types) are encoded and sent to the receiver. Finally, the receiver reconstructs the original document following the encoded path through the automaton.

For DTD grammars Segoufin and Vianu show that improved speed of parsing can be achieved by using deterministic pushdown automata. Since DTD grammars are outdated by now, we adopted the concept of using PDAs for XML processing and extended it for the use with XML Schema.

In the following, we introduce an algorithm that constructs a single PDA representing an entire XML Schema. It is the nature of this approach, that the PDA provides two important features. On the one hand, it is a highly efficient parser and on the other hand it can also be used for data compression, as we will show.

The input of our algorithm is an arbitrary XML Schema document that defines the structure of the documents to be exchanged. Table 2 shows an example that will be used to demonstrate our approach. Common SOAP applications use more complex Schema documents, of course, and import

Table 2. Recursive XML Schema description

```
<xsd:schema xmlns:xsd="http://www.w3.org/2001/XMLSchema">
<xsd:element name="a" type="A"/>
<xsd:complexType name="A">
<xsd:choice>
<xsd:element name="b" minOccurs="0">
<xsd:complexType>
<xsd:choice>
<xsd:element ref="a" minOccurs="2" maxOccurs="2"/>
<xsd:element name="c" type="xsd:int"/>
</xsd:choice>
</xsd:complexType>
</xsd:element>
</xsd:choice>
</xsd:complexType>
</xsd:schema>
```

other XML Schema documents for processing different namespaces.

First of all, the XML Schema document has to be converted into a Regular Tree Grammar (RTG) *G*. An RTG is defined as a 4-tupel consisting of a set of non-terminal symbols *N*, a set of terminal symbols *T*, a set of production rules *P* and a set of start symbols $S \subseteq N$. Murata et al. describe the conversion of an XML Schema document into an RTG in detail (Murata et al., 2001).

The RTG for our example looks as follows:

$G = (N, T, P, S) = (\{A, B, C, \text{xsd:int}\}, \{a, b, c\}, P, \{A\})$ with

$P = \{$

$A \rightarrow a\,(B + \varepsilon),$

$B \rightarrow b\,(AA + C),$

$C \rightarrow c\,(\text{xsd:int})$

$\}$

Every simple and complex data type used is converted into a non-terminal symbol (written in capital letters or prefixed with xsd:). Element names result in terminal symbols (small letters). Each non-terminal symbol that represents an element that is declared on the top-level of the XML Schema document belongs to the set of start symbols.

The structure of valid documents is defined by the production rules. The non-terminal symbols on the left-hand side are subsequently replaced by the terminal symbol and the regular expression on the right hand side. The regular expression describes the content model of the terminal symbol. Since the non-terminal symbols of the content model will also be replaced by terminal symbols matching the rules, the content model defines which child elements an XML element may have. The rules in this example can be read as follows: an element *a* contains an element *b* or (+) nothing (ε), while *b* contains either two *a* elements or a *c* element, which contains an integer value. Therefore, *G* is equivalent to the Schema in Table 2.

In a second step, an FSA is constructed for each content model, i.e. for each regular expression (see Figure 1). Aho et al. describe the underlying conversion algorithm in detail (Aho et al., 1988). For each element of the grammar the FSAs define the sequences of direct child elements that are allowed to follow.

Finally, the PDA is constructed. It accepts input words by emptying the stack. Thus it stops when a special start symbol *Z* that is initially put on the stack is popped and not pushed again immediately. The states of the PDA consist of a special start

Figure 1. Set of finite state automata generated from the regular tree grammar

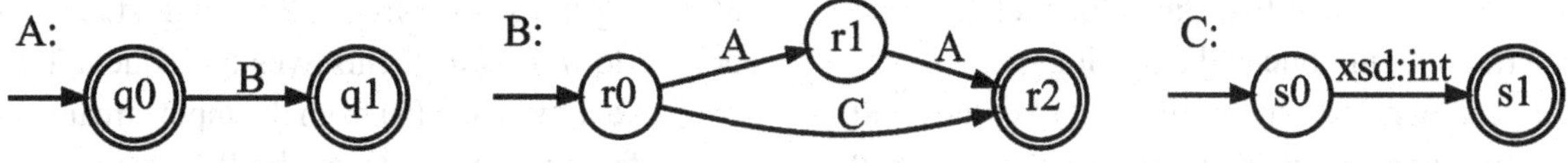

Table 3. Constructing the PDA transitions from a set of FSAs

```
for all fsa ∈ FSAs do
  for all state ∈ fsa.states do

    for all t_in ∈ state.transitions_incoming do
      for all t_out ∈ state.transitions_outgoing do
        label = (
          t_out.type.tag_open,
          state,
          (FSAs.getFSA(t_out.type).startState, t_out.destState));
        createPDATransition(
          PDAStates_close.get(t_in.type),
          PDAStates_open.get(t_out.type),
          label);
      end for
    end for

   if state ∈ fsa.finalStates then
      for all t ∈ state.transitions_incoming do
        label = (fsa.type.tag_close, state, null);
        createPDATransition(
          PDAStates_close.get(t.type),
          PDAStates_close.get(fsa.type),
          label);
      end for
    end if

    if state = fsa.startState then
      for all t ∈ state.outgoingTransitions do
        label = (
          t.type.tag_open,
          state,
          (FSAs.getFSA(t.type).startState, t.destState));
        createPDATransition(
          PDAStates_open.get(fsa.type),
          PDAStates_open.get(t.type),
          label);
      end for
    end if

    if state □ ({fsa.startState} ∩ fsa.finalStates) then
      label = (fsa.type.tag_close, state, null);
      createPDATransition(
        PDAStates_open.get(fsa.type),
        PDAStates_close.get(fsa.type),
        label);
    end if

  end for
end for
```

state, one state for each simple type (like xsd:int, xsd:string, etc.) and two states for each complex type (an opening one and a closing one).

Creating the transitions of the PDA comes next. Each transition consists of a 3-tupel (*read,pop,push*), where *read* represents the tag to be read from the input. The value *pop* indicates the top stack symbol. Both have to be matched by the current input stream and stack for the transition to be executed. The *push* value announces the symbols that will be written onto the stack. It can consist of zero, one or more symbols. Note that *push* values consisting of multiple symbols are specified in inverse order.

There need to be transitions from the start state to each opening state of a non-terminal symbol n_i that belongs to the set of start symbols ($n_i \in S$). Each transition consists of the opening tag that belongs to the destination state (*read*), the stack start symbol Z (*pop*), that will be pushed onto the stack again and is followed by the start state of the FSA belonging to the destination state type (*push*). Matching transitions from all closing states that belong to $n_i \in S$ to themselves are added. They read an empty string (#) from the input stream and pop Z from the stack. Thus, the PDA terminates. Table 3 shows the algorithm that describes how to create all other transitions.

A graphical representation of the resulting PDA is given in Figure 2. The basic idea behind this type of automaton is to simulate the processing of the FSAs by stack operations. In this way, the PDA checks if the number and sequence of child elements is correct for each element.

At this stage the automaton is ready for parsing. Finally, we augment the PDA with the core feature that additionally allows data compression: Each transition that originates in a state with more than one outgoing path is tagged with a unique binary identifier (depicted as circled values in Figure 2).

Figure 2. Pushdown automaton constructed form the XML grammar

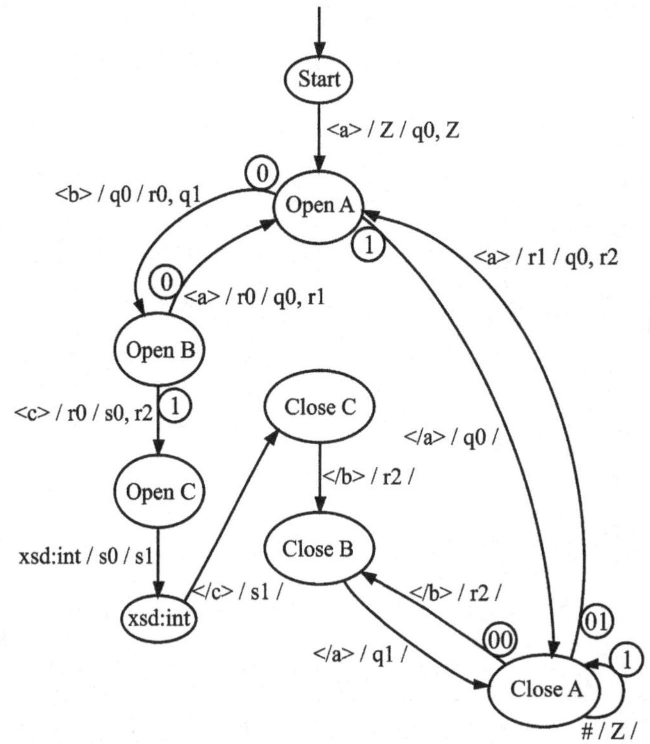

The basic idea of our compression method is to represent a document by the sequence of transitions that were passed when processing the document with the PDA. It is an essential premise, of course, to ensure an unambiguous decoding of the code words used for tagging the transitions. A suitable and beneficial algorithm for generating such codes is the Huffman algorithm (Huffman, 1952). Our implementation creates a Huffman table for every state that maps code words to outgoing transitions. Currently, we apply equal probabilities for each transition. In future implementations one could, however, deduce appropriate heuristics about transition traversal probabilities from the Schema.

While the Huffman algorithm is used to encode the path through the PDA, i.e. the markup of the document, another method is needed to encode the simple type values efficiently. Our compressor provides the functionality of encoding, decoding and validating for all simple types considered by XML Schema. For each simple type an appropriate binary encoding is used, e.g. a 32-bit integer value for xsd:int. Whenever the PDA executes a transition labeled with a simple type, it appends the binary encoded value to the output bit stream. Since this data format does not require any data to be buffered during compression or decompression, it is ideal for XML streaming. This is a principal advantage compared to container-based approaches like XMill.

Figure 3 illustrates the encoding generated by the automaton in Figure 2 for an exemplary document matching the grammar in Table 2. The markup is encoded as the path of transitions through the PDA (using zero bits for unambiguous transitions). Compact binary representations are used to inline encode the simple types.

The decompression process works vice versa: The receiver seeks its path through its instance of the PDA according to the instructions of the bit stream generated during compression. Whenever a transition is executed, the matching XML tag is written into the output document. Transitions labeled with simple types are processed as follows: Either the PDA reads a fixed number of bits from the bit stream (e.g., 32 bits for xsd:int) or it reads an arbitrary number of bytes until it encounters a stop byte sequence (this is done for all character encoded data types like xsd:string).

In order to keep our example simple and compact, it does not provide any information about the handling of attributes and namespaces. Both features are supported, though. Attributes are

Figure 3. Example XML document before and after compression

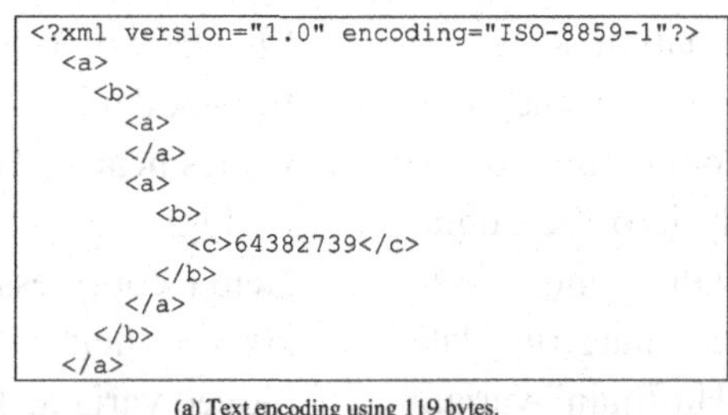

```
<?xml version="1.0" encoding="ISO-8859-1"?>
  <a>
    <b>
      <a>
      </a>
      <a>
        <b>
          <c>64382739</c>
        </b>
      </a>
    </b>
  </a>
```

(a) Text encoding using 119 bytes.

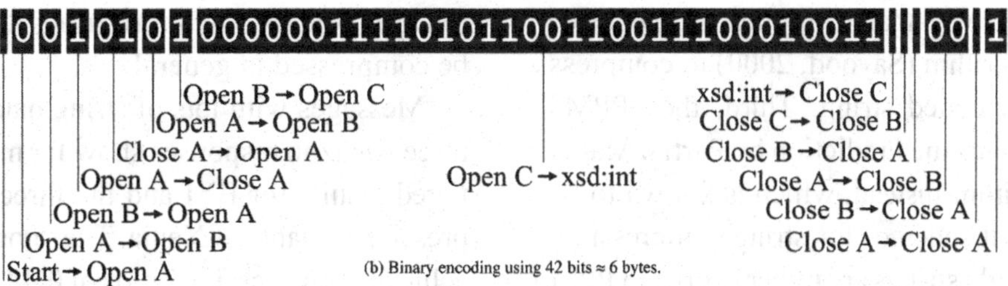

(b) Binary encoding using 42 bits ≈ 6 bytes.

handled in the same way as elements. However, they are marked with a special flag to avoid naming ambiguities. For instance <a b="c">d</a> is treated like <a><b$_{att}$>c</b$_{att}$>d</a>. The entire namespace information provided by an XML Schema document is also adopted and incorporated into the PDA, i.e. each transition label holds information about the namespace of the tag to be processed. Since the namespace prefixes of the input document are not encoded, this information is lost during compression. Therefore, the decompression step includes the generation of new generic namespace prefixes.

Our approach addresses the main requirements annunciated by the W3C. If an application uses an API like SAX and interacts with the automaton instead of working with the XML text representation, the binary representation can be written (or read) directly. Furthermore, the generated encoding is independent of transport mechanisms in any case and can be processed very efficiently. In the following section we will evaluate the compactness achieved by our approach.

Performance Comparison

As the first step to evaluation, we implemented our approach in Java. The resulting program, called Xenia, was used to compress the recorded messages of the two benchmark web services described in the above section on the evaluation setup.

Three different settings for string encoding were tested. The "none" encoding places the UTF-8 encoded strings directly into the output stream and marks their ends with a unique byte sequence. This in particular means that string data is not compressed at all. The "Huffman" variant differs in the way that it applies the adaptive Huffman algorithm (Sayood, 2000) to compress the UTF-8 encoded string. Third, the "PPM" encoding applies the Prediction by Partial Match (PPM) algorithm instead, which is known to be one of the best schemes for string compression. However, single strings are rather short and PPM needs a few hundred bytes of data to achieve its maximum performance. Hence, we gathered all string data occurring in the input stream in a so called string container. In the output stream the string is replaced by a reference to the location of the string in this container. The string container is then compressed using PPM and appended to the output stream, as described by Liefke (Liefke, 2000). Note, that this appending of the container prevents direct stream processing because the original data cannot be restored until the end of the stream (and thus the container) has been decompressed. However, this is just an implementation issue. This disadvantage can be avoided by splitting up the PPM output and multiplexing it with the markup stream. Thus, the streaming option is preserved (Cheney, 2001).

Compression results for the messages yielded by the calculator web service are shown in Figure 4. Because no strings are exchanged here, all three Xenia variants produce the same results. Hence, variants are not differentiated here. Xenia and EXI (with Schema) outperform all other compressors clearly in this benchmark. However, on average Xenia produces files that are more than 20% smaller than those resulting from EXI.

The results for the messages of the Amazon web service are depicted in Figure 5. We chose to show the compression ratio λ instead of file sizes. The reason is that the size of the uncompressed files varies between 680 and 229.619 bytes. Hence, file size depiction would have rendered small byte values nearly invisible.

Figure 5 shows that EXI (with Schema) and Xenia compress all requests to approximately 10% of their original size regardless of the employed variant. This is hardly surprising because requests contain only short strings that can hardly be compressed in general.

Messages with lots of string data such as the three Amazon responses show far more differentiated results for EXI and the three string compression variants of Xenia. The "none" encoding achieves compression ratios of 0.48 (small), 0.37

Figure 4. Compression results for the calculator web service

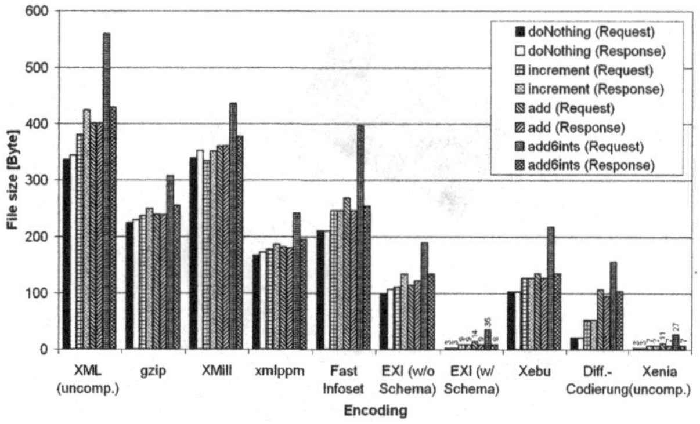

Figure 5. Compression results for the Amazon web service

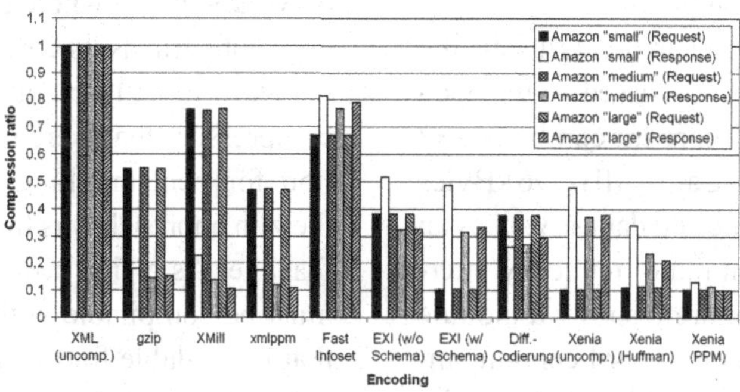

(medium) and 0.38 (large) for the three responses. These results are comparable with the performance of EXI. Note that this implies that the markup is nearly compressed to zero, as the fraction of text that remains uncompressed here was 47%, 35% and 37% (c.f. section "Evaluation Setup" above). However, significant further improvements can be achieved by employing the string compression variants of Xenia: the compression ratio for the large response improves to approximately 0.2 (Huffman) and 0.1 (PPM). Obviously in these cases the overall compression performance is dominated by the employed string compression method. Hence, we also evaluated the optional *deflate* compression available for EXI. As expected, this results in smaller file sizes for cases with a large fraction of string content. However, this comes at the cost of a slightly degraded compression effectiveness in most other cases due to the incompatibility of this feature with bit-packed encoding.

IMPLEMENTATION ON RESOURCE-CONSTRAINED DEVICES

In the introduction we pointed out that a very important application domain of SOAP compression is the field of mobile and embedded computing. The devices predominating here are typically battery powered. Furthermore, they have only limited computing power and memory resources at their disposal. We evaluated our approach with regard to code size and processing time in order to show that our solution is viable for such devices. As a basis for our measurements we implemented a

Figure 6. Coin-sized embedded controller module

code generation module for Xenia which is capable of outputting C code embodying the constructed Schema specific XML compressor.

We conducted our measurements using the Jennic JN5121 controller. It is based on the open source "OpenRISC 1000" core and combines a 32 bit microcontroller running at 16 MHz, 96 kBytes of shared memory for code and data as well as an IEEE 802.15.4 compliant radio frequency interface on a single chip. Figure 6 shows a module bearing the controller, an on-board ceramic antenna, a crystal and a non-volatile memory chip. All it needs to make such a stamp sized board operational is a battery attached to it. An adapted version of the GNU C-Compiler (gcc) is available for this platform.

We confined our evaluation to the calculator web service and omitted the Amazon web service because Amazon's uncompressed SOAP response messages are too large to be held in the microcontroller's memory. In addition, a web service returning large amounts of text appeared not to be a typical use case for embedded SOAP processing.

As a benchmark for code size and processing performance of Xenia we used the "zlib" compression library (http://www.zlib.net/). It is the basis of the well-known gzip compressor, which was also used for benchmarking in the previous section. The gzip compressor directly uses the algorithms implemented in zlib and adds a command line user interface as well as file-based input and output operations. Since both of these features are not useful on our embedded device, we decided not to work with the whole gzip implementation but only with zlib as its core-component.

We originally planned to include the other compressors that were used in the previous section for benchmarking, too, but unfortunately the zlib approach was the only one that rendered feasible: As a first requirement the compressor must be compilable with the GNU C-Compiler that is available for the target platform and, as a second restriction, the code must not exceed a size of 96 kBytes.

Since the Differential Encoding approach has been implemented in Java and Python instead of C, it was not usable on our target platform. The same holds for the Fast Infoset and EXI implementations, which are written in Java. XMill and xmlppm are written in C++, which is generally supposed to compile. Unfortunately, both projects exceeded the available memory size, which made the linking process fail. It is impossible to name the exact code sizes for our target platform, because these are determined by the linking process. However, in order to roughly estimate the sizes of their memory footprints we compiled and linked both projects successfully on an Intel 32-Bit system. This resulted in the following code size for the statically linked binaries: 829.404 bytes (XMill compressor), 828.508 bytes (XMill decompressor), 643.416 bytes (xmlppm compressor), and 647.512 bytes (xmlppm decompressor). Although these code sizes are generally not transferable to our target device (because they where measured for a different architecture), these values show clearly that it is certainly impossible to build these projects with a memory limit of 96 kBytes. Therefore, we use zlib as the only benchmark for Xenia in this section.

One difficulty in conducting runtime measurements is to isolate different sources of execution time and memory demand from each other. In order to consider the compression step only, we parsed the XML input files offline and then fed the resulting sequences of SAX events into the Xenia compression engine running on the microcontroller. In a real application scenario, these SAX events would have been generated by the application. For zlib we used the plain XML strings, since this is the most natural way of using a general purpose compressor. In order to eliminate input/output times as far as possible, we included all input data into our binaries instead of using the serial port or radio the interface of our device. In consequence, we could continuously measure in-memory compression and decompression performance.

The Xenia pushdown automaton for compressing the SOAP messages of the calculator web service has 59 states and 83 transitions. In the generated C file it is implemented through a number of cascaded switch-case statements for transiting the automaton from the current state to the next one. This stepping is triggered by the reception of a SAX event for the compression case or the reception of the corresponding bit sequence for the decompression case.

In order to use zlib on our device we had to isolate all relevant parts for doing gzip compatible compression and decompression, because the full-featured zlib library was also to big to fit into the device memory. Then we implemented a short wrapper program (minimal "in-memory" gzip/gunzip) for invoking these routines in their default settings.

Table 4 gives an overview of the resulting code sizes for the calculator web service. The values in the "Xenia" row include the code sizes of the automaton, the stack and a number of helper functions. The "zlib" row shows the code sizes of all functionalities needed for executing gzip-compatible compression and decompression. We have listed the code sizes for compression and decompression separately, as well as for the case where both functions are included. For Xenia the code for compression is slightly bigger than for decompression. This mainly results from the fact that the compression PDA contains a number of string constants that incoming SAX tokens must be compared to. In addition, the stack is not required for decompression and can thus be omitted there. If both automata are included the resulting code is slightly smaller than the sum of compression and decompression because they share a certain amount of functionality that is not duplicated. Even though the PDAs for compression and decompression are basically the same – except for switching input and output – we currently generate two stand-alone automata for the sake of simplicity. However, if both functionalities are required, a shared automaton could be realized that is hardly bigger than one of the two separate

Table 4. Code sizes for compressing and decompressing calculator web service messages using "Xenia" and the general purpose compression library "zlib"

	Compression	Decompression	Both
Code size "Xenia" [bytes]	22,328	20,228	39,556
Code size "zlib" [bytes]	39,420	39,504	51,608

ones. Like this, even smaller implementations are possible. The results clearly show that Xenia has a significantly smaller memory footprint than the general purpose compression and decompression routines of zlib. This is true for compression, decompression and the combination of both.

Anyhow, it is important to stress that the measured code sizes of Xenia do not include code for transforming the string representation of a SOAP message into a sequence of SAX events. If this functionality is required an additional SAX tokenizer must be implemented on the device. A suitable solution is available from Unicoi Systems, Inc. which roughly adds 15 kB of code (http://www.unicoi.com/fusion_web/fusion_xml_sax_microparser.htm). Anyhow, most applications in this field will fire these events directly, bypassing the string representation of SOAP messages.

To measure the execution time we subtracted the time when the first piece of input data was fed into the (de-)compressor from the time when the last output piece left it. The measurement resolution (the so called tick time) was 0.25 ms. That means that if, e.g. an execution time of 3 ms was measured, the execution actually took between 3.0 and 3.25 ms. In order to compensate for this systematic error we added the average underestimation of 0.125 ms (half a tick time) to the measured time intervals. Table 5 shows the resulting execution times of compression and decompression for the eight different SOAP messages. As a benchmark, the performance of the zlib routines is also shown in the table. We repeated the experiment ten times but did not notice any differences in execution time.

The performance result of Xenia can be interpreted as follows: It is notable, that in most cases decompression works faster than compression. We found two reasons for that. One is that the strings attached to the transitions must be compared with those in the sax events in order to trigger the automaton for the compression case. This inherently slow operation is not required for decompression. The other reason is that the stack of the pushdown automaton does not have to be considered during decompression. Despite this, the decompression of the add6ints request is slower than the corresponding compression. This is due to an implementation issue: The conversion of numeric values into strings is currently implemented rather inefficiently. This becomes especially noticeable for this request because it contains six integer values. Comparing the processing times of the different SOAP documents shows that the duration of both compression and decompression correlates with the number of XML elements contained in the input files. This is hardly surprising because each element causes

Table 5. Execution time of compression and decompression for different messages of the calculator web service

	Xenia		zlib	
	Compression [ms]	**Decompression [ms]**	**Compression [ms]**	**Decompression [ms]**
doNothing (Request)	1.875	0.875	27.125	14.375
doNothing (Response)	1.875	0.875	27.875	14.625
increment (Request)	2.875	1.875	29.125	15.375
increment (Response)	2.875	2.125	30.625	16.625
add (Request)	3.375	3.125	31.125	16.375
add (Response)	2.875	2.125	30.875	16.375
add6ints (Request)	6.625	11.125	42.625	24.375
add6ints (Response)	3.125	2.875	32.625	17.625

a number of state transitions in the PDA that in turn dominate the execution time. As the binary Xenia encodings of the SOAP messages hold the contained information in a very compact fashion, the execution time correlates closely with the size of the binary encodings of the corresponding messages (c.f. the rightmost column of Figure 4).

The zlib compression and decompression routines work significantly slower than Xenia – with factors ranging between 2 and 15. Unlike Xenia, the execution time obviously does not correlate linearly with the input data sizes. Comparing the results in the different rows we can clearly see a temporal offset: roughly 20 ms for compression and 10 ms for decompression. This dates back to certain initialization tasks that have to be executed each time before starting a new compression or decompression task. Similarly to Xenia, the zlib decompression works nearly two times faster than the zlib compression. This effect is caused by the runtime profile of the Lempel-Ziv-Storer-Szymanski algorithm (Storer & Szymanski, 1982), which has to carry out a text pattern search for compression. Decompression on the other hand is basically done by performing an index lookup, which is a significantly faster operation.

All in all these results show that Xenia achieves very promising compression results – with respect to compression effectiveness, to code size, as well as to runtime performance. Although the current Xenia implementation in C definitely leaves room for further performance optimizations it already outperforms the general purpose compression routines of zlib in terms of speed and memory-efficiency.

CONCLUSION AND FUTURE WORK

The verbose nature of the XML text representation has bred several efforts in research and standardization groups aiming at more compact serializations. In this article we contribute a Schema-aware XML binary encoding algorithm that complies to the recommendations of the W3C Binary XML Working Group.

We outlined how a push-down automaton (PDA) can be derived from an XML Schema document. In addition to XML parsing and validation, such an automaton can be used for XML compression. This is done by encoding the path through the automaton while parsing the input document instead of encoding the document directly. Most simple types can inherently be serialized very efficiently with their optimal binary representations because the PDA also incorporates type information. In addition, three different encodings for string data were proposed and evaluated.

We conducted an extensive performance analysis that compared our PDA compressor implementation, called Xenia, with other XML compression approaches. We showed that Xenia compresses markup nearly to zero. The only approach that shows a comparable compression effectiveness is EXI.

A key advantage of our compression approach is that it economizes on resources. Hence, it is predestinated for SOAP processing on embedded devices. We implemented a code generator module for Xenia which is capable of exporting a schema specific (de-)compressor in C. In our evaluation we showed that this approach leads to encoders that are fast and memory-saving at the same time. To the knowledge of the athors there are currently no EXI Implementations written in C. If such an implementation becomes available we will conduct a memory footprint and message throughput comparison between EXI and Xenia.

Furthermore, we will extend the idea of exporting source code from our Java implementation to application specific XML compression *hardware*: To reach this goal future work might include code generation for hardware description languages like VHDL or Verilog.

While web service technology promised to overcome heterogeneity problems in distributed systems, it so far failed to penetrate the field of ubiquitous computing, which is considered to be one of the major developments of the last years. From our perspective, one of the key inhibitors for XML gaining ground here is its resource demanding nature. Thus, the rise of techniques for efficient XML handling will boost the coalescence of two of the most exiting fields in computer science.

REFERENCES

W3C (2005a). Working group note: XML binary characterization. Retrieved March 17, 2009, from http://www.w3.org/TR/xbc-characterization/

W3C (2005b). Charter of the efficient XML interchange working group. Retrieved March 17, 2009, from http://www.w3.org/2005/09/exi-charter-final.html

W3C (2008). Working Draft: Efficient XML Interchange (EXI) Format 1.0. Retrieved March 17, 2009, from http://www.w3.org/TR/2008/WD-exi-20080919/

Aho, A. V., Sethi, R., & Ullman, J. D. (1988). *Compilers: Principles, Techniques and Tools*. New York: Addison-Wesley.

Cheney, J. (2001). Compressing XML with multiplexed hierarchical PPM models. In *Data Compression Conference, Snowbird, USA* (pp. 163–172).

Clark, J., & Murata, M. (2001). Definitive specification for RELAX NG using the XML syntax. Retrieved March 17, 2009, from http://www.relaxng.org/spec-20011203.html

Girardot, M., & Sundaresan, N. (2000). Millau: An encoding format for effcient representation and exchange of XML over the web. In *9th International World Wide Web Conference, May 2000, Amsterdam, Netherlands* (pp. 747–765).

Huffman, D. A. (1952). A method for the construction of minimum-redundancy codes. *Proceedings of the Institute of Radio Engineers, 40*(9), 1098–1101.

Kangasharju, J., Tarkoma, S., & Lindholm, T. (2005). Xebu: A binary format with schema-based optimizations for xml data. In *Proceedings of the International Conference on Web Information Systems Engeneering, November 2005, New York City, USA*, (pp. 528–535).

Liefke, H., & Suciu, D. (2000). XMill: an efficient compressor for XML data. In *Proceedings of the 2000 ACM SIGMOD International Conference on Management of Data, Dallas, USA* (pp. 153–164).

Murata, M., Lee, D., & Mani, M. (2001). Taxonomy of XML schema languages using formal language theory. In *Proceedings of Extreme Markup Languages, August 2001, Montreal, Canada* (pp. 153-166).

Niedermeier, U., Heuer, J., Hutter, A., Stechele, W., & Kaup, A. (2002). An MPEG-7 tool for compression and streaming of XML data. In *Proceedings of the IEEE International Conference on Multimedia and Expo, August 2002, Lausanne, Switzerland* (pp. 521–524).

Sandoz, P., Triglia, A., & Pericas-Geertsen, S. (2004). Fast infoset. Retrieved March 17, 2009, from http://java.sun.com/developer/technicalArticles/xml/fastinfoset/

Sayood, K. (2000). *Introduction to data compression* (2nd ed.). San Francisco: Morgan Kaufmann Publishers Inc.

Segoufin, L., & Vianu, V. (2002). Validating streaming xml documents. In *Proceedings of the 21st ACM SIGMOD-SIGACT-SIGART symposium on Principles of database systems, New York, USA* (pp. 53–64).

Storer, J., & Szymanski, T. (1982). Data compression via textural substitution. *Journal of the ACM*, *29*(4), 928–951. doi:10.1145/322344.322346

Tolani, P., & Haritsa, J. R. (2002). XGRIND: A query-friendly XML compressor. In *Proceedings of the International Conference on Data Engineering, February 2000, San Jose, USA*, (pp. 225–234).

Toman, V. (2004). Syntactical compression of XML data. In *Proceedings of the International Conference on Advanced Information Systems Engineering, June 2004, Riga, Latvia,* (pp. 273–282).

Werner, C., Buschmann, C., & Fischer, S. (2007). Advanced Data Compression Techniques for SOAP Web Services. In L.-J. Zhang (Ed.), *Modern Technologies in Web Services Research* (pp. 76–97). Hershey: IGI Publishing.

Werner, C., Buschmann, C., Jäcker, T., & Fischer, S. (2006). Bandwidth and Latency Considerations for Efficient SOAP Messaging. *International Journal of Web Services Research*, *3*(1), 49–67.

Chapter 12
Data Mining in Web Services Discovery and Monitoring

Richi Nayak
Queensland University of Technology, Australia

ABSTRACT

The business needs, the availability of huge volumes of data and the continuous evolution in Web services functions derive the need of application of data mining in the Web service domain. This article recommends several data mining applications that can leverage problems concerned with the discovery and monitoring of Web services. This article then presents a case study on applying the clustering data mining technique to the Web service usage data to improve the Web service discovery process. This article also discusses the challenges that arise when applying data mining to Web services usage data and abstract information.

INTRODUCTION

Simplicity and ubiquity are factors that brought upon the success of the Web. Once solely a repository that provides access to information for human interpretation and use, the Web has evolved to become a repository of software components (Alesco & Smith, 2004; Clark 2002; Newcomer, 2002). These service-oriented components, or Web services, are emerging as the key enabling technology for today's e-commerce and business-to-business applications, and are transforming the Web into a distributed computation and application framework. The implication of this transformation is that the volume of data generated on the Web is increasing exponentially. Whilst human users have generated huge volumes of data from using the Web and warranted a myriad of research in the data mining community (Kosala & Blockeel, 2000), the volume of data generated by machines using and providing Web services would certainly make the former dwarf in size. Since Web servers store the access request information in Web server access logs, all interactions between Web services are recorded, similar to the human-server interactions that are prevalent on the Web now. Web server access logs recording site accesses have been a rich source for discovering the browsing behavior of site visitors in Web mining. In a similar manner, logs that record the Web services accesses can be mined for Web services usage patterns by organizations. With the huge volume of accesses, the amounts of logs that can be collected make a feasible source for data mining. Data mining (DM) methods search for distinct patterns and trends that exist in data but are 'hidden' among the vast amount of data (Han & Kamber, 2001).

Since Web service is a relatively new technology, there are a lot of areas where improvements can be made to complement the current state of the art. Not only these improvements enhance the technical workings of Web services, they can also generate new business opportunities. As will be shown in this article, some of these improvements can be made possible through data mining. For example, as the number of Web services increases, it becomes increasingly important to provide a scalable infrastructure of registries that allows both developers and end-users to perform service discovery.

Given the competitiveness of the current business market place, the need to exploit sources of data for business intelligence is greater than ever before. The ability for a business to obtain previously unknown knowledge about itself and its customers is a valuable asset. Business needs, the availability of huge volumes of data, and in particular, the possible Web services improvement areas form the premises for the application of data mining using the Web services data. The goal of this article is thus to present how Web services data can be utilized in data mining and the kinds of benefits that can be gained from such operations.

This article discusses the Web services in the context of data mining. It first discusses the basics of data mining, and then recommends a set of data mining applications that can leverage problems concerned with the discovery and monitoring of Web services. A case study is presented that demonstrates the improvement in the Web discovery with a proposed clustering data mining method on using the Web query logs. Some of the challenges that arise while mining Web services data are also presented. In the end, this article looks at the current technologies in use for Web service discovery and log mining.

DATA MINING AND ITS OPEARTIONS

Data mining is the search for distinct patterns and trends that exist in datasets but are 'hidden' among the vast amount of data. A data mining task includes problem identification, data pre-processing, data modeling and pattern evaluation. With the high costs associated with data mining operations, it is essential for businesses to know whether their investments are worthwhile. This requires the analyst to have an understanding of the application domain, the relevant prior knowledge, the data that is available for mining, and the goals of the end user. Once the objective of data mining task is identified, the next step is to prepare the data for mining. This pre-processing step involves basic operations such as the removal of noise or outliers, handling inconsistencies and missing values to ensure the quality of the data set, and transforming it into data structures specific to the data mining task. Traditionally used for extracting information from data within databases, recent researches in data mining are geared towards Web data, including Web server logs (Cooley, Mobasher, & Srivastava, 1997; Nayak, 2002; Nayak & Seow, 2004; Wang, Huang, Wu, & Zhang, 1999). The preprocessing step is particularly relevant to this study as its assists to determine how the Web services data can be mined. Data modeling is next used to infer rules from the pre-processed data or build model that fits best on this data set. The data modeling step refers to the application of a DM technique or a combination of techniques for identifying patterns from the derived data set. The kinds of patterns that can be mined depend on the data mining operation as listed in Table 1.

Predictive modeling solves a problem by looking at the past experiences with known answers, and then projecting to new cases based on essential characteristics about the data. This process enables the prediction of the unknown value of a variable given known values of other variables. The classification predictive modeling is used to predict discrete nominal values, whereas value prediction, or regression, is used to predict continuous values. Clustering or segmentation solves a problem by identifying objects with similar characteristics in a data set, and thus forming the groups of similar objects. The link analysis operation establishes association among objects by finding items that imply the presence of other items in the given data set. A specialization of link analysis is a similar time sequence discovery that identifies similar occurrences, or similar sequences of occurrences, in sets of time-series data. This analysis explores the temporal relationship between sets of time-series data by matching all data sequences that a similar to a given sequence, or by matching all sequences that are similar to one another. Deviation analysis is concerned with identifying anomalies, unusual activities or events within a data set, which are indicated by the presence of outliers.

The final step involves the interpretation of derived models or rules. Operations such as filtering, restructuring, and data visualization are utilized to represent the extracted knowledge in a meaningful and easily understandable manner to users.

APPLICATION OF DATA MINING IN WEB SERVICES

The benefits of the data mining applications can be seen as falling into two broad categories—those that deliver business value and those that have technical value (Nayak & Tong, 2004). Applications with business value are those that can be used by management to assist in making strategic decisions or by human resource in maximizing staffing levels while minimizing costs. Applications with technical value are those that can be used by technical staff in devising new services or in services that their organization can use.

Business Applications

The development in business analytics using data mining has accelerated tremendously over the past few years. With the availability of operational data stored in transactional systems, coupled with advances in efficient data mining algorithms and increased power in processors, data mining operations have become viable solutions for de-

Table 1. Various DM operations and approaches

Mining Operation	Goal	Approaches
Predictive Modeling (Classification, Value prediction)	To predict future needs based on previous data	Decision tree, Neural networks, Bayesian, linear and non-linear regression
Clustering or Segmentation	To partition data into segments	Demographic, Neural networks
Link Analysis (Association, Sequential, Similar time discovery)	To establish association among items	Counting occurrences of items such as Apriori Algorithms
Deviation Analysis	To detect any anomalies, unusual activities	Statistics and visualization techniques

riving business intelligence. Data mining can be used to provide insights on the planning of Web services deployment via "Web services cost and savings prediction," and on how costs on staffing for the monitoring of services can be optimized via "performance monitoring."

Web Services Cost and Savings Prediction

Chen (2003) performed an analysis on factors that are affecting the adoption of Web services. Financial considerations were identified as major cause. The enabling technologies of Web services are only concerned with the technicalities and do not have any provision for the planning of costs and savings. Unless businesses have an idea of how much they should spend on Web services, and on the foreseeable savings, they will be indecisive on the adoption of Web services. A possible solution is the cost and performance model for Web services investment (Larsen & Bloniarz, 2000). The model helps businesses to assess the costs in terms of the functionalities required and to increase in target performance. For each assessment area, three levels of service (modest, moderate, and elaborate) are defined in order to identify the most profitable option. The model, however, does not take into consideration that many businesses may not have any experience in Web services and thus find the estimation difficult in the first place. Furthermore, it does not provide measures on the effectiveness at which a business can deploy Web services. For example, if a business can find out that other similar projects cost less but yield the same returns, then it may consider outsourcing the project.

Businesses can learn from the experiences of similar organizations and get a good approximation of these values from the data collected by research firms such as Nemertes (Johnson, 2003). If *predictive mining* models representing Web services deployment costs can be built considering the previous data, then businesses intending to adopt Web services can make use of these models both for estimating the cost of their deployment, as well as deciding whether outsourcing them is more feasible than developing them in-house. *Value prediction* is suitable in this instance to model the investment versus return functions for the prediction of figures for costs and savings. *Regression techniques* (Han & Kamber, 2001) derive the predicted continuous values obtained from functions that best fit the case. For predicting the costs, the input data required consists of, for each deployment, the number of staff member involved, the time it took, and the complexity of the deployment. The complexity of the deployment can be quantified in terms of the lines of code used in the programs, and the annual revenue from the operations that the deployment oversees. The costs of the proposed deployment can be predicted based on these parameters. Once the costs are known, prospective savings can be predicted. Using inputs such as the cost of the deployment, and the original and new cost of the operation, savings can be determined. Having determined the costs and the savings that can be gained, businesses can identify the size of Web services deployment that is best suited for them and turn the discovered insights into action.

Performance Monitoring

Strategic placement of human resource plays a crucial role in the effective monitoring of performance and handling of events. In today's business environment where resources are stretched to minimize costs, adequate resources especially personnel with the required expertise may not be available to handle all reported incidents. This leads to the need to prioritize tasks. A service being used by many clients at the time when a problem occurs should have a higher priority than a service being used by few clients at the same time. By knowing the usage pattern of services, training programs on groups of services with *similar usage patterns* can be developed. This allows staff monitoring the services at certain times to have a more in depth knowledge of particular services. As an example, if a Web service uses an Oracle database to support its back-end operations, then presence of the Oracle database administrator at times when the service is at peak usage would be desirable. Such knowledge is especially valuable to companies that do not need permanent staff with some specialist knowledge, but whose service is required only under certain circumstances.

To identify Web services with similar usage patterns, similar time sequence analysis can be used (Peng, Wang, Zhang et al., 2000). The input for such an operation is time-series data recording the number of clients using a particular service at any moment in time. Although such data is not normally collected explicitly, it is implicitly recorded in the Web server access logs. The steps in generating this time-series data from Web server logs are as follows:

1. Select from the Web server log all entries related to the offered Web services by extracting all entries containing the Web service's URL in the URL field.
2. Group the entries by Web services and client IP addresses, and then order the entries by time. This gives a set of a client's interaction with a Web service.
3. Calculate the time between each interaction to determine separate client sessions with the Web service. A client session is one 'use' of the Web service. The duration of a client session for different services varies depending on the nature of the service. Setting the threshold of session boundaries thus requires the knowledge about the individual services.
4. For each service, count the number of clients using it at specified time intervals. This can then be used to construct the time-series graph for each service.

Algorithms for approximate subsequence matching in time-series now can be applied to find Web services that have similar usage patterns. These patterns can then be used to help in the design of roster schedules that optimize staffing levels and skill requirements while minimizing the number of employees that need to be present.

Technical Applications

This section discusses applications which are more technically oriented. Although the applications will ultimately produce business benefits in some way, the immediate analysis of the results are targeted towards technical staff that implement Web services.

Service Innovation

The Web services market has gathered much momentum, however, the number and choice of services that are on offer is limited, a fact that spawned the creation of the Web site WebServicesIdea.com, which is tied to the renowned Web services broker Salcentral.com. For businesses, this lack of innovation in Web services represents business opportunities. For technical staff, this limits their ability to take advantage of the reusability concept that is central to the Web services architecture. It is important for service providers to establish themselves in the market by offering a range of quality services. The set of queries used by potential clients to find suitable Web services is a rich source for finding clues about what the clients want. If an unusual search term is used with other common search terms in the queries, and the search terms are all related, then it is a good indication that there is a demand for a new service. The unusual search term may represent a new concept, or a specialization of a general service currently being offered. For example, SMS (short message service) sends text messages to mobile phones while a more recent technology MMS (multimedia message service) sends multimedia messages. SMS is a frequently used search term but MMS is not. As the technology becomes more prevalent, demand for MMS Web services will emerge and the appearance of MMS in query data will be evidence of this.

The simplest approach in discovering uncommon search terms is by *deviation analysis* (Devore, 1995). Having counted the frequencies of the search terms appearing, simple measures such as median, quartiles and inter-quartile range (IQR) can be calculated. Then using the common heuristic that outliers fall at least 1.5 * IQR above the third quartile or below the first quartile, the unusual search terms can be identified. An alternative measure is the use of support to count the number of times the term appeared in total terms. If a search term has very low support, then it can be classified as an outlier. Given that the demand for different services varies, applying these measures to the raw frequency count will produce biased results towards less popular services, producing many false positives. This is best illustrated using the following example. A popular service is searched 1,000 times using a common search term Q_1 and 10 times using an uncommon search term Q_2. A very specific service aimed at a niche market is searched seven times using Q_3 and 3 times using Q_4, both of which are common for the service. When search terms for all the services are taken into account, and statistics is applied to the data, Q_2, Q_3 and Q_4 will be identified as uncommon search terms. However, Q_3 and Q_4 are false positives because they represent 70 percent and 30 percent of searches for the service. On the other hand, although Q_2 has 10 occurrences, it is only 1 percent of all searches for the popular service. Clearly, Q_2 is the outlier that should be identified in this case.

The solution to this is to group searches into search areas and then find the outliers for each search area. This can be done by:

1. Grouping the queries into search sessions
2. Joining all search sessions that are similar to form search areas
3. Form search term pools for each search area.
4. Within each search term pool, apply statistics to find the uncommon search terms that suggest demands for a new Web service.

Service Recommendation

Recommender systems have been studied extensively in data mining (Mobasher, 2005). By analyzing the behavior and preferences of past and current customers, businesses are able to predict the characteristics and needs of new customers. In e-business cases, the goods or services recommended are typically consumable and the cost of a replacement in case of a wrong choice by the customer is small. The same principle can be applied in Web services for recommending services that may be of interest to Web service clients. With the current Web service framework, providers and requesters must choose the names and description of services very precisely when using the UDDI. For example, a service named "SMS" may not be returned from the query "mobile messaging service" submitted by a user. The user while performing the search may not be aware of this other search term, and thus will fail to retrieve the service.

With the expected increase of Web service use, it is beneficial for the UDDI or Web services framework to be able to provide recommendations of appropriate Web services of interest. However, the situation is quite different in recommending Web services. Firstly, the selection of a Web service that a business will use as part of its business process cannot just be based on preference. The suitability of a service also depends on various resources required by the service such as the interfaces, functionality and security offered by the service, as well as the cost. A service fitting the aims is a matter of whether it satisfies the list of strict criteria. Secondly, the role of the chosen service in the business can also be important. If not chosen carefully, the cost of replacing the service is not limited only to searching for a new service, but also the cost of reconfiguring the systems and the loss in staff productivity due to the system downtime that incur.

Web services providers can recommend services to clients based on the services that other similar clients have used in the past. This is because similar clients are likely to have similar service needs. A systematic use of a single data mining operation or in combinations can achieve this. The following case study details a proposed method of improved Web service discovery with the use of clustering data mining approach.

A CASE STUDY: IMPROVED WEB SERVICE DISCOVERY

Searching for Web services using Web services search engines, such as Salcentral and the UDDI, is limited to keyword matching on names, locations, business, buildings, and tModels (unique identifiers for reusable concepts). A user wishing to locate a particular service can do so by specifying a partial service name. With the UDDI, the user can also search by service provider name or browse the registry by the various taxonomic schemes it supports, such as NAICS and UNSPSC (UDDI.org). However, since users are usually interested in the functionalities of services, they would typically begin searching by service name. The other attributes, such as the provider, will only be secondary for discriminating services.

The matching of a query to a set of services is based on the names of the services. If the query does not contain at least one exact word as the service name, the service is not returned. Since Web service names are generally very short consisting of no more than five words, it is essential that search terms are precise and contain the words in the desired service's name. The implication of matching services at the string level only is that synonymous queries do not return the same set of services, even though the services have similar functionality. Queries that are different at the string level, but are similar semantically, retrieve result sets that are disjoints. This is a major drawback when searching for Web services because the users are ultimately concerned with the functionality of the services. The keyword-based method of service discovery suffers from low recall, where results containing synonyms or concepts at a higher or lower level of abstraction to describe the same service are not returned. For example, a service named "car" may not be returned from the query "automobile" submitted by a user, even they are obviously the same at the conceptual level.

This problem can be approached in two ways, either by returning an expanded set of results to the user, or by suggesting the user with other relevant search terms. The Web search engines make use of ontology to return an expanded set including subclasses, superclasses, and "sibling" classes of the concept entered by the user (Lim, Song, & Lee, 2004). Although this approach improves recall by returning a very large result set that are related to the search term, it introduces the poor precision problem where many entries are of no interest to the user. Many researchers in the information retrieval field have also proposed different approaches of enhancing semantic similarly for expanding query terms with synonyms, hyponyms, hypernyms, latent semantic space (Varelas et al., 2005; Voorhees, 1995). They showed only some minor improvements for short queries and no improvement (even the degradation) for long queries. The lack of semantics has led to the development of OWL-S and DAML-based languages for service description in WSDL, where service capability matching is based on the inputs, outputs, preconditions and effects, and ontology are used to encode relationship between concepts (McIlraith, Son, & Zeng, 2001; Paolucci, Kawamura, Payne et al., 2002). However, with the current state of Web services, we are still a long way from automatic service matching. For now, the manual discovery of services will have to suffice and effort is needed to improve its efficiency.

This proposed method of improved Web service discovery (summarized as in Table 2) employs the second approach that is to suggest the user with other related search terms based on what other users had used in similar queries by using the clustering technique. Whilst previous Web search engine approaches capture the intra-query relationships by clustering queries on a per query basis (Beeferman et al., 2000; Wen et al., 2002), they omit the inter-query relationships that exist between queries submitted by a user in one search session. When a user cannot find a Web service with the required functionality, the user will submit other search terms that are synonymous to the initial query. This is based on the assumption that a user's need of a service does not change even when it cannot be satisfied by any service from the set of results. Therefore, the set of search terms used consecutively in a search session form a query trail and represent a user's service need. *Clustering* based on search sessions instead of individual queries can leverage the problem by taking advantage of user judgment implied in the query and Web server logs to provide the semantic links between keywords. If queries are clustered independent of other queries used in the same search session, the resulting clusters will have search terms that are highly similar at the string level and so will not be very useful. On the other hand, if grouping is performed based on search sessions, then query terms such as "SMS" and "mobile messaging service" or "cars" and "automobile" would likely to be clustered together.

Step 1: Data Pre-Processing

The data required for clustering the session queries come from both the user query log and the Web server log. The query log contains the search terms together with some identification of the queries submitted, such as the IP address of the client and the timestamp. The entries required from the Web server log are those that correspond to the entries in the query log, as well as the service description pages that follow each query. The data from these two sources require to be consolidated for *query—service descriptions matching.* Each entry in the query log forms a one-to-many relationship with entries in the Web server log. These relationships can be captured by matching the query recorded in the query log with the subsequent service descriptions viewed by the user recorded in the Web server log. The resulting structure is: query {service descriptions} where query is the search term used, and the set of service descriptions correspond to those the user viewed and is a subset of the results returned from the query.

The next step is to group the above structure into *search sessions* (an example is shown in Table 3). A search session is defined as a set of

Table 2. The proposed method of improved web service discovery

Step 1: Perform data Pre-processing
- **1.1** Extract the related entries from the user query log and the Web server log.
- **1.2** Generate the query-service descriptions matching by consolidating entries in both logs.
- **1.3** Form the search session by grouping the entries by clients IP addresses and Web services.

Step 2: Perform search session similarity
- **2.1** Calculate the Jaccard similarity coefficient independently for search terms and service descriptions between each pair of Web services
- **2.2** Form a similarity matrix by aggregating the similarity coefficients for both components.

Step 3: Perform clustering
- **3.1** Apply hierarchal clustering to form the groups from this similarity matrix.
- **3.2** Store these clusters in the UDDI register to allow the improved search.

Table 3. Queries grouped into search sessions

Search session	IP address	Query	Service Descriptions
1	123.456.789 123.456.789	q1 q2	ID001, ID003 ID007, ID012, ID005
2	234.567.890 234.567.890 234.567.890	q1 q3 q4	ID002, ID003 ID007 ID008, ID012
3	345.678.901 345.678.901 345.678.901	q4 q5 q6	ID008 ID020, ID025 ID028, ID030

queries submitted in sequence by a user to locate a particular service. It is similar to a transaction or server session in Web mining (Cooley et al., 1997; Srivastava et al., 2000), and thus its identification is done using the same approach. A set of queries are identified by using the IP address recorded in the Web server log together with the timestamps. The IP address identifies the user, while the timestamp differentiates multiple search sessions by the same user. Entries with the same IP address are grouped together and then sorted by time to obtain all searches performed by the same user. A threshold on the amount of time between query submissions is then be set to distinguish the different sessions.

Step 2: Search Session Similarity

Similarity, between a pair of search sessions is an indication of their mutual relevance. For example, search sessions containing many of the same keywords and same service descriptions would presumably be relevant to each other. Search session similarity can be calculated based on the similarity of the set of search terms used and the set of service descriptions viewed between two search sessions. The similarity between two different search sessions X and Y is defined as:

$$\text{similarity}\ (X,Y) = \text{similarity}_{\text{search term}}\ (X, Y) + \text{similarity}_{\text{service descriptions}} (X, Y)$$

The Jaccard coefficient (Han & Kamber, 2001) is used to calculate the similarity using the search terms and service descriptions sets between X and Y. This measure calculates similarity based on the attributes that are present in both data instances being compared. Attributes that do not describe either of the data instances are regarded as unimportant. The Jaccard coefficient suits well in this situation as it is only practical to compare search sessions based on their contents and not all the possible keywords and service descriptions that exist in the entire search engine. Keywords and service descriptions that are absent in search sessions being compared are therefore insignificant. Each search session is first transformed into two binary vectors, with one representing the queries and the other the service descriptions viewed. The value 1 shows the presence of a keyword or service description. The length of these vectors corresponds to the total number of distinct queries and the total number of distinct descriptions viewed in the search session respectively. The search term similarity and service description viewed similarity are therefore given as:

$$\text{similarity}_{\text{search term}} (X, Y) = (T_{XY}) / (T_X + T_Y + T_{XY})$$

$$\text{similarity}_{\text{service descriptions}} (X, Y) = (D_{XY}) / (D_X + D_Y + D_{XY})$$

T_{XY} is the number of common search terms used in X and Y, T_X is the number of search terms used in X only, and T_Y is the number of search

Box 1.

Query vector	q1 q2 q3 q4	
	X = 1 1 0 0	
	Y = 1 0 1 1	

Service description vector		ID001	ID002	ID003	ID005	ID007	ID008	ID012
	X =	1	0	1	1	1	0	1
	Y =	0	1	1	0	1	1	1

$similarity_{search\ term}(X, Y) = 0.25$

$similarity_{service\ descriptions}(X, Y) = 0.429$

similarity (123.456.789, 234.567.890) = 0.679

terms used in Y only. $D_{XY,}$ D_X and D_{XY} have the same meaning for the second equation but in terms of the service descriptions viewed. As an example, consider a comparison of the first two search sessions in Table 3, with X and Y representing the IP addresses 123.456.789 and 234.567.890 respectively see Box 1.

Having obtained the similarity measure between the search sessions, a *similarity* matrix is constructed for use as input for clustering. A clustering algorithm usually requires a similarity matrix to determine the groups within the search sessions. A similarity matrix is an *m* by *m* matrix containing all the pair wise similarities between the search sessions being considered. If *xi* and *xj* are the *ith* and *jth* search sessions, respectively, then the entry at the *ith* row and *jth* column of the similarity matrix is the similarity value, *similarityij*, between *xi* and *xj* (Jain et al., 1999). Table 4 shows a similarity matrix for the search sessions listed in table 3, where X, Y and Z are distinct search sessions.

Step 3: Clustering of Search Sessions

The hierarchical agglomerative clustering method, which is often used in information retrieval for grouping similar documents (Kosala & Blockeel, 2000) is used. This method uses a bottom-up strategy that starts by placing each data instance in its own cluster, and then successively merge clusters together until a stopping criterion is satisfied (Karypis, Han, & Kumar, 1999). The reasons to use this method are manyfold. Firstly, similarity of search sessions is based on the number of common queries and service descriptions they share. This means that search sessions are assigned to the same cluster if they have many queries and service descriptions common. The type of clusters desired is therefore globular in nature. This algorithm has been proven powerful at discovering arbitrarily shaped clusters. Secondly, the algorithm must be resistant to noise and outliers. Since users can submit any arbitrary query in a search session that may not be related to other queries in the same session, outliers may be

Table 4. A similarity matrix for search sessions in Table 3

	X	Y	Z
X	1.000	0.679	0.000
Y	0.679	1.000	0.311
Z	0.000	0.311	1.000

present. The algorithm uses a k-nearest neighbor graph in the partitioning phase that ensures to reduce the effects of noise and outliers. Thirdly, because the volume of query data can be very large, the algorithm should be scalable.

After the clusters are formed, the support for each of the search terms in each cluster is counted and then assigned weights. The weights are used to predict a user's service need by suggesting search terms from the cluster with the largest weight for the user's search term. Depending on the size and number of search terms that make up the clusters, the suggested terms can either be all search terms within the cluster, or be limited to those from the most similar search sessions.

Experimental Evaluation

This experiment demonstrates the effectiveness of the search session clustering based on cross-referencing between the queries submitted and the service descriptions viewed. In order to facilitate the evaluation of the similarity measure, the synthetic data represent disjoint clusters among the queries and among the descriptions. The data is generated based on three clusters of queries and three clusters of service descriptions. This was done to mimic the real data where similar queries lead to similar service descriptions viewed. Table 5 shows a sample (sub-set) data set containing the processed search sessions. The keyword and

Table 5. Sample of the input dataset

IP address	Query	Service Description Viewed			
123.456.789	AB	53	54		
123.456.789	AC	52	55	56	
138.256.980	AI	53	55	56	
138.256.980	BB	67	68	69	74
140.214.100	BC	68	70	76	
146.210.012	CD	81	82		

Table 6. Similarity based on keywords, service descriptions viewed and combining both

Cluster		Keyword only	Service description only	Combining Keyword and service descriptions
0	Avg. Internal Similarity	0.211	0.281	0.675
	Avg. External Similarity	0.111	0.050	0.013
1	Avg. Internal Similarity	0.637	0.772	0.838
	Avg. External Similarity	0.127	0.156	0.100
2	Avg. Internal Similarity	0.182	0.256	0.535
	Avg. External Similarity	0.088	0.126	0.064

Table 7. Web services discovery improvement by using the similar query terms

User	Query Term	Web Services Returned	Matching Cluster	Expanded Query Terms	Web services Returned (with expanded set)
A	q1	1, 100	Cluster 1	q1, q5, q7, q9, q23	1, 3, 5, 100
B	q2, q4	2, 56, 67	Cluster 2	q2, q4, q8, q11, q12, q19	2, 15, 25, 56, 67
C	q3, q6	4, 9, 13	Cluster 3	q3, q6, q10, q15, q13, q18	4, 9, 13, 69, 84, 97
D	q14	89	N/A	N/A	N/A

service description vectors were clustered separately, and then the combined similarity matrix was clustered. The three clustering solutions are then compared. The results (Table 6) imply that the search sessions clustered using the combined measure are more compact than those of the single similarity measures. Higher internal similarity of a cluster shows that the search terms within the cluster share a closer affinity. Lower external similarity of a cluster shows that the search terms with other clusters share a lesser affinity. This is essential in the suggestion of search terms as users are interested in suggestions that are highly similar to those submitted.

Upon the generation of clusters, each term in the cluster is weighted according to their support in the cluster and ranked. Now, when a user inserts a query term, the terms in the cluster that are found in higher ranking are returned as the expended set of queries in order to improve the service discovery. A test was conducted for evaluating the effect of recommending the similar query search terms according to the session similarity in locating a particular service. Table 7 presents a subset of results with and without the use of expanded query terms. Initially the Web services were located using the original query term (s). The query term set was then expanded if matched with a cluster. In this experiment, we used the clusters generated by combining both keywords and service descriptions similarity to match a term(s) in the query. Results show that the proposed Web service discovery method was successful in locating more relevant Web services by expending the search terms with similar terms according to the session similarity. The last row of the Table 7 shows that the 'q14' query term does not exist in any cluster. Based on the analysis of several (25) queries we conclude that the expanded query terms set returned the results with higher recall than with the original query terms. The recall measures the degree of how well a returned Web service satisfy the need requested by a query. It is the percentage of relevant Web services returned with respect to the total number of relevant Web services to a query. For example, the search program created for testing purposes returns one match for the term "cars." However if the search term is changed to "automobile" or "vehicle," no match is found without including the recommended terms with clustering results, it is a general knowledge that "cars" is also known as "automobile" or "vehicle." This problem is solved by using the terms appearing in the same clusters. Recall of the search results is increased by 47 percent but the precision is reduced by 10 percent. This is due to the fact that results included irrelevant results due to the wide coverage with similar terms in clusters. However, this overall precision figure (reduction by 10 percent) is better than the precision achieved when the simple ontology methods (such as synonyms, etc.) (reduction by 23 percent) are used for improving the search results. Overall, the expansion of query terms with the terms as found in the best matched clusters improves the total number of relevant Web services returned by making the search wider.

This approach utilizes clustering to improve Web service discovery. However, other data mining methods or combinations of methods could also be used in improved Web service discovery. The predictive mining techniques can be used to build rules on service subscriptions based on the usage of services by the clients. Service providers have information such as the line of business, size of business and what services their clients use, they can use these as inputs for predictive modeling. Inputs such as the interfaces, functionality, and security offered by the service, as well as the cost, and other resources required by the service can also be considered to improve the result. Classification techniques such as *decision trees* (Quinlan, 1999) can be used to build rules on service subscriptions. Since the only information service providers have about clients are those for billing purposes, the number of attributes available is small. Consequently, the structure of the resulting decision tree will be relatively simple and easily comprehensible to a human analyst. To further enhance the success rate of recommendations, service providers can find dissociations among the services they offer. Dissociations (Teng, 2002) capture negative relationships between services with rules such as the use of service X and Y implies that it is unlikely service Z will also be used, even though service X and Z are often used. That is, $X \Rightarrow Z$; $X \wedge Y \Rightarrow \neg Z$. By incorporating these dissociations in the recommendation process, specific recommendations can be made.

Association mining can also be used to analyze the Web server access logs that record all interactions between Web services and users. With the huge volume of Web services accesses, these logs can be used for identifying Web services with similar usage patterns. The tasks would be: the selection of all entries related to the offered Web services from the Web server log; extracting a set of a client's interaction with a Web service; calculating client sessions with the Web service, application of the *link analysis algorithm* (Agrawal & Srikant; 1994) to find Web services with similar usage patterns, associate the new client with a usage pattern, and finally, recommend a set of similar services after being identified with a usage patterns.

CHALLENGES IN PERFORMING DATA MINING TO WEB SERVICES DATA

Data Fusion and Data Collection

The extraction-transform-load (ETL) process that precedes data mining operations is typically complex and costly (Han & Kamber, 2001). With businesses spanning their operations across the entire globe, as well as having multiple servers that provide mirrored services, the Web server access logs from Web servers located at different sites must be consolidated to facilitate data mining. Therefore there is a need for controlled and reliable data collection. Because of the huge volume of data that have to be consolidated, a scheme must be in place to co-ordinate the transfer and storage of the data, while keeping the associated costs down. The scheme should minimize network traffic so that it does not interfere with the normal operations of the service provider. By compressing the data before transport, and scheduling transfers during off-peak hours, the impact of data transfer and the volume that need to be transported can be greatly reduced.

Additionally, with the growing popularity of Web services, services are not just being used in performing simple functions, such as accepting registration. Web services are increasingly being used as the automated solution generation enabling integration of various tasks. To accomplish a task, a Web service needs to consolidate many operations and manage interactions between systems. Consequently, the abstract information of Web services in communicating various operations such as service interfaces, operations, messages, service/bindings elements and process instance execution logs containing event traces about transaction services during their execution are required to be considered along with the Web service usage logs and Web query logs at the user request level. For example, to find some useful information about a Web service on tour operation, many other services (or system to system interactions) such as money payment, location finder etc are required to be coupled with the process of mining. The Web service usage logs should solemnly be used as sole input data to improve the process of Web service discovery or other suggested applications in this article. The challenge lies in the integration of data in various forms but representing the information leading to achieve the same goal.

Moreover, research has shown that the use of non functional attributes, such as quality of service (QoS) and cost of service (CoS) descriptors improve the Web service discovery, ranking and matching (Hung & Li, 2003). As the QoS characteristics of a Web service may comprise of service availability, efficiency, accessibility, reliability, performance, scalability, and security. Due to the dynamic nature of such QoS and CoS descriptors, however, the current technologies for publishing and finding Web services (WSDL and UDDI) lack support for these. New frameworks, such as OWL-S and WSMO should be used to collect information for these non functional attributes.

Computing Resources

A data mining task is usually resources-consuming. At the same time, Web services are often large-scale distributed applications. Asynchronous operations of data mining and Web clients request should be considered, otherwise, a client application may be undesirably blocked until the service results are returned. With the data mining functionality, the Web services should be flexible enough to run on any server reliably and accurately appropriate to client volumes.

Analysis Results Interpretation

Results from DM operations often require specialist domain knowledge to obtain the full benefits of the discovered knowledge. To maximize the end user's understanding, the outputs of data mining must be translated to a language or visualization appropriate for the user's need. For example, in the search term suggestion application, the end users are service requesters trying to locate a particular service. Instead of graphical clusters showing which queries are similar, the terms present in the clusters should be shown to them. On the other hand, in the performance monitoring application, the users would find it useful to see the similar sub-sequences in the time-series represented graphically when determining services with similar usage patterns. Furthermore, the results should be easy to comprehend and display only the details that are relevant. One approach is to show only the important attributes so that users are not distracted by the less important details (Kohavi, Mason, Parekh et al., 2005). By removing the complexity, users can focus their efforts on gaining insight from the result.

Data Reliability

Mining for Web services usage from Web server logs may not produce accurate results reflecting the real usage. This is due to wrong reflection of service usage in the collected data. For example, implementations of firewalls often involve the masking of internal IP addresses by substituting this with the IP address of the server that connects the network to the Internet. When a Web service client accesses a Web service, the Web server of the Web service provider logs the communication from the service client. If a firewall is used at the client side, then multiple accesses to the same service from different clients within the network may be recorded as one client—that of the server. This in effect masks the service usage in terms of number of clients using the service. Additionally, Web services execution is a stateless operation. This makes the recording of the event in the Web service usage log a difficult task. Appropriate solutions should be used to deal with this issue such as simulating a stateful session by including a session ID in the Web services strings.

Proprietary Nature of Data

Data is a valuable asset for businesses and so is not normally released into the public domain. Many data mining tasks require data to be collected from multiple sources such as query logs collected by Web services search engines and the cost of Web services deployments. Unless there are mutual agreements between the parties, obtaining the data, and in sufficient volume, may be a problem. The quality of the input data is a key factor in determining the quality of the final model. Reputable research companies such as IDC may provide an answer to this. With the resources to arrange the necessary legal agreements, these research firms can perform data mining on data collected from multiple businesses to discover knowledge that cannot be gained from other ways. This will be beneficial to all parties while preserving the privacy of the businesses involved, as it is the nature of data mining to produce results that are generalizations of the input data.

Privacy and Security

Although, as previously mentioned that data mining produces generalizations of data, it does have the problem that some sensitive information can be inferred. This is called the inference problem and arises when users submit queries and deduces sensitive information from the legitimate response they receive (Thuraisingham, 2005). This can be a hindrance when collecting data from many businesses, as well as a problem when mining Web server access logs that record the services used by certain clients. Data integrity and confidentiality could be compromised. Therefore, even if data can be collected, measures must be in place to ensure that businesses contributing to data mining such as the service recommendation application are not disadvantaged.

EXISTING WORK

We do not know of any work that has investigated the detailed use of data mining in Web services as us. There are some researchers who have applied the concepts of data mining into service discovery and Web service log mining. Some of them are discussed here.

Web Service Discovery

Researchers have worked in the direction of addressing the shortcoming of UDDI by finding relationships between search terms and service descriptions, and of WSDL to represent semantics while describing service. Sajjanhar, Jingyu and Yanchun (2004) apply the regression function called singular value decomposition to discover semantic relationships on services for matching best services. Their preliminary results show a significant increase in correct matching between service descriptions and the search terms after application of their algorithm with IBM UDDI. The matched results are not merely based on the number of matched keywords within the service descriptions. The algorithm evaluates the keyword global weights within the SVD procedure and aggregates services containing the highest global weight words to find semantic matched services.

Wang and Stroulia (2003) developed a method for assigning a value of similarity to WSDL documents. They use vector-space and WordNet to analyze the semantic of the identifiers of the WSDL documents in order to compare the structures of their operations, messages and types, and determine the similarity among two WSDL documents. This helps to support an automatic process to localize Web services by distinguishing among the services that can potentially be used and that are irrelevant to a given situation. Dong et al. (2004) build a Web service search engine (Woogle) to support the similarity search for Web services along with keyword searching with utilizing clustering and association mining. Starting with a keyword search, a user can drill down to a particular Web service operation. However, when unsatisfied, instead of modifying the keywords, user can query for Web service operations according to the most similar and semantically associated keywords suggested by the engine using the data mining techniques.

Some preliminary works have also been conducted to employ semantic languages and techniques in the description of Web services resources. Web ontology language for services (OWL-S) and DARPA agent semantic markup language for Web services (DAML-S) are high-level ontology at the application level meant to answer the 'what' and 'why' questions about a Web Service (Alesso & Smith 2004). Ontology-based semantic Web describes its properties and capabilities so that: (1) software can automatically determine its purpose thus automating service discovery; and (2) software can verify and monitor service properties thus automating service monitoring. As the future of Web services greatly depends on their ability to automatically identify the Web resources and execute them for achieving the intended goals of user, OWL-S and DAML-S can achieve what UDDI cannot.

Gruninger, Hull and McIlraith (2005) propose the process models to be described as first order ontology, and then automate the searching and composition of Web services. Mandell and MacIlraith (2003) present a technology for the customized and dynamic localization of Web services using the business process language for Web service (BPWS4J) with the semantic discovery service. It provides semantic translation of services to match the user requirements. Soyaden and Singh (2004) develop a repository of Web services that extends the UDDI current search model. The repository in the form of ontology of attributes (based on DAML) provides a wide variety of operations such as the publication of services, costs of services and services selection based on their functionality. Li, Yang and Wu (2005) propose an approach of DAML based ontology use in e-commerce service search. The ontology positioning above WSDL relates service description of a WSDL document to descriptions of other WSDL documents. Benatallah et al. (2005) propose a matching algorithm that takes as input the requirements to be met by the Web services and an ontology of services based on logic descriptions, and recommends the services that best comply with the given requirements.

Web Service Log Mining

Gombotz, Halevy, Madhavan et al. (2006) apply "WSIM—Web Services Interaction Mining" to analyze the log data (interactions between Web service consumers and providers). They identify three levels of abstraction with respect to WSIM: the operation level, the interaction level and the workflow level. On the Web service operation level, only one single Web service and its internal behavior is examined by analyzing a given log output of the Web service. On the Web services interaction level, one Web service and its "direct neighbors" Web services (that the examined service interacts with) are examined. This analysis reveals interesting facts about a Web service's interaction partners, such as critical dependencies. On the Web service workflow level, the large-scale interactions and collaborations of Web services which together form an entire workflow is examined. This details the execution of the entire process, for example what is the general sequence of execution of various operations.

Malek and Haramantzis (2004) show the impact of data mining in detecting security attacks which could cripple Web services or compromise confidential information. They determine the relevance of different log records and define the attack signature with the use of sequential pattern mining. Then they discover the highly compact decision rules from the intrusion patterns for pattern searching that helps to describe some safeguard against the attacks.

CONCLUSION

Recent advances in storage technology make data collection a very cheap exercise. Often data is collected for recording indicating that a transaction has taken place. Beyond that there is little use for the data. This is especially the case in Web services, where the generation and collection of transaction data is an automated process. However, hidden in these data are patterns and trends that are unknown to its keeper and may provide insights about the current situation. For businesses, these can represent new opportunities to provide better services to customers and to improve the operations of the business. For other fields, they may represent unknown facts whose discovery prompts for investigations for the reasons behind them, and as a result build on the body of knowledge in the field. Data mining has the capability to take advantage of the collected data and extract previously unknown knowledge from them.

Driven by factors such as the availability of huge volume of data, and the increasing need for businesses to obtain intelligence on their customers and internal operations, data mining technologies have found successful applications in many areas. Since Web services data are generated and collected automatically as well as being in digital form, the quality of the data is good compared to those collected manually. The amount of data generated by Web activity and collected automatically by servers enable businesses to extract strategic insights about the activity on their sites, as well as about the characteristics of their customers. With the emergence of Web services, the next step in the mining of electronic commerce data will naturally turn from Web sites to Web services.

In this research, a number of data mining applications that make use of Web services data have been proposed. In particular, they focus on applications that would directly facilitate and improve the use of Web services. The usage range from delivering business value that can be used by management for strategic decision making, to providing technical benefits that target specialist end users. In particular, we focus on the use of data mining techniques in Web services discovery. The proposed search term suggestion for improved Web service discovery is based on the idea of finding search sessions that are similar to the one by a user to locate a particular service, and then suggest words used in those sessions. The usage data at the user request level is only being considered, the process instance execution logs and abstract information of Web services are not being utilized in this process. The experimental results on a data set reveal that the search sessions clustered using the combined measure of keywords and search session viewed are more compact than those of the single similarity measures. This indicates that the suggestion of search terms to users is more relevant when given on the basis of considering query sessions instead of considering one single query.

Recent work on conceptualizing Web services with data mining techniques is also included emphasizing that the data mining techniques will play an important role in Web service discovery and monitoring. Each suggested application requires performing further testing for validation and usability. We also plan to improve the search term suggestion method by combining the clustering based on session similarity with the query term expansion based on ontology (such as synonyms, hyponym, etc.). In the future work, we will study whether the method combining these two methods outperforms the individual ones. As data mining applications built on Web services become more popular, there will be a growing need for further research to develop data mining algorithms which can scale the large, distributed data sets as well as deal with the concurrent, synchronous and real-time responses delivered for user requests. Most importantly, the data mining benefits should result in cost-saving to the businesses rather than incurring an extra cost to deploy data mining resources.

ACKNOWLEDGMENT

Sincere thanks go to Cindy Tong for conducting experiments and analysis, also to students in ITB239, 2005 semester 1 who conducted a survey on Web services and data mining usage.

REFERENCES

Agrawal, R., & Srikant, R. (1994). *Fast Algorithms for Mining Association Rules*. IBM Research Report RJ9839, IBM Almaden Research Center.

Alesso, P. & Smith, C. (2004). *Developing the next generation web services — semantic web services.* A K Peters Ltd.

Beeferman, D., & Berger, A. (2000). *Agglomerative clustering of a search engine query log.* Paper presented at the Sixth ACM SIGKDD, Boston, (pp. 407-416).

Benatallah, B., Hacid, M., Leger, Alain., Rey, C., & Toumani, F. (2005). On automating web service discovery. *VLDB Journal, 14*(1) 84-96.

Chen, M. (2003). Factors affecting the adoption and diffusion of XML and web services standards for e-business systems. *Int. J. of Human-Computer Studies, 58*, 259-279.

Clark, D. (2002). Next-generation web services. *IEEE Internet Computing, 6*(2), 12-14.

Cooley, R., Mobasher, B., & Srivastava, J. (1997). *Web mining: Information and pattern discovery on the World Wide Web.* Paper presented at the 9th IEEE International Conference on Tools with Artificial Intelligence (ICTAI '97), Newport Beach, California.

DAML-S http://www.daml.org/services/

Devore, J. L. (1995). Probability and statistics for engineering and sciences, Duxbury Press.

Dong, X, Halevy, J., Madhavan, E., Nemes, & Zhang. (2004). Similarity Search for Web Services. In *Proceedings of the 13th International Conference on Very Large Data Bases VLDB,* Toronto, Canada, August 31 - September 3, 2004

Gombotz, R., & Dustdar, S. (2006). *On Web services workflow mining.* BPI Workshop, co-located at BPM, Nancy, France, Springer (LNCS 3812, pp. 216–228).

Gruninger, M., Hull, R., McIlraith, S. (2005). *A first – order ontology for semantic Web services.* W3C Workshop on Frameworks for Semantics in Web Services, June 2005, Innsbruck

Han, J., & Kamber, M. (2001). *Data mining: Concepts and techniques*. San Francisco: Morgan Kaufmann.

Hung, P., & Li, H. (2003). Web services discovery based on the trade-off between quality and cost of service: a token-based approach, *ACM SIGecom Exchanges*, 4(2), 21-31.

Jain, A. K., Murty, M. N., & Flynn, P. J. (1999). Data clustering: A review. *ACM Computing Surveys (CSUR), 31*(3), 264-323.

Johnson, J. T. (2003). *State of the Web services world.* Retrieved April 17, 2003, from the http://www.computerworld.com.au/index.php?secid=1398720840&id=622609517

Karypis, G., Han, E. H., & Kumar, V. (1999). Chameleon: A hierarchical clustering algorithm using dynamic modeling. *Computer, 32*(8), 68-75.

Kohavi, R., Mason, L., Parekh, R., & Zheng, Z. (2005). Lessons and challenges from mining retail e-commerce data. *Machine Learning, 57*(1-2), 83 -113.

Kosala, R.& Blockeel, H. (2000). Web mining research: A survey. *ACM SIGKDD Explorations, 2*(1),1-15.

Larsen, K. R. T., & Bloniarz, P. A. (2000). A cost and performance model for web service investment. *Communications of the ACM, 43,* 109-116.

Li, L., Yang, Y., & Wu, B. (2005). Ontology-Based Matchmaking in e-Marketplace with Web Services. In *Proceedings of APWeb 2005: Web Technologies Research and Development 7th Asia-Pacific Web Conference*, Shanghai, (pp. 620-631) March 29 - April 1, 2005.

Lim, S.-Y., Song, M,-H, & Lee, S,-J. (2004). *The construction of domain ontology and its application to document retrieval.* ADVIS 2004, (LNCS 3261, pp. 117-127), 2004.

Malek, M., & Haramantzis, F. (2004). Data mining techniques for security of Web services. In *Proceedings of the International Conference on E-Business and Telecommunication Networks (ICETE-2004),* August 25-28, 2004, Setubal, Portugal

Mandell, D., & McIlraith, S. (2003). A Bottom Up Approach to Automating Web Services Discovery, Customization, and Semantic Translation. In *Proceedings of the 12th International World Wide Web Conference Workshop on E-Services and the Semantic Web (ESSW '03).* Budapest, 2003.

McIlraith, S. A., Son, T. C., & Zeng, H. (2001). Semantic web services. *IEEE Intelligent Systems, 16*(2), 46-53.

Mobasher, B. (2005). Web usage mining and personalization. In Munindar P. Singh (Ed.), *Practical handbook of internet computing/* CRC Press.

Nayak, R. (2002). Data mining for web-enabled electronic business applications. In S. Nanshi (Ed.), *Architectural issues of web-enabled electronic business* (pp. 128-139). Hershey, PA: IGI Publishers.

Nayak, R., & Seow, L. (2004). Knowledge discovery in mobile business data. In S. Nanshi (Ed.), *Wireless communication and mobile commerce*(pp 117-139). Heshey, PA: IGI Publishers.

Nayak, R., & Tong, C. (2004). Applications of Data Mining in web services. In *Proceedings of the 5th International Conferences on Web Information Systems* (pp. 199-205), Brisbane, Australia, 22- 26 Nov.

Newcomer, E. (2002). *Understanding web services: XML, WSDL, SOAP, and UDDI.* Boston: Addison-Wesley.

OWL-S http://www.w3.org/Submission/OWL-S

Paolucci, M., Kawamura, T., Payne, T. R., & Sycara, K. (2002). Semantic Matching of Web Services Capabilities. In I. Horrocks and J. Handler (Eds.), *1st Int. Semantic Web Conference (ISWC),* (pp. 333-347), Sardinia, Italy:Springer Verlag.

Peng, C. S., Wang, H., Zhang, S. R.& Patker, D. S. (2000). Landmarks: A new model for similarity-based patterns querying in time-series databases. In *Proceedings of the 16 International Conference of Data Engineering (ICDE),* (pp 33-42). San Diego, CA, February.

Quinlan, R. (1999). Simplifying decision trees. *Int. J. Hum.-Comput. Stud. 51*(2), 497-510

Sajjanhar, A, Jingyu, H., & Yanchun, Z. (2004). High Availability with clusters of Web Services. *APWeb* 2004, (LNCS 3007, pp. 644–653).

Soydan, A. & Singh, M. (2004). *A DAML – Based repository for QoS – aware semantic Web service selection*. Paper presented at teh IEEE International Conference on Web Services. (2004)

Srivastava, J., Cooley, R., Deshpande, M., & Tan, P.-N. (2000). Web usage mining: Discovery and applications of usage patterns from web data. *SIGKDD Explorations, 1*(2), 12-23.

Teng, C. M. (2002). Learning from Dissociations. In *Proceedings of the 4th International Conference on Data Warehousing and Knowledge Discovery DaWaK* 2002, Aix-en-Provence, France.

Thuraisingham, B. (2005). Privacy-preserving data mining: Developments and directions, *Journal of Database Management, 16*(1), 75 - 87.

Varelas, G., Voutsakis, V.. Raftopoulou, P., Petrakis, E. G., & Milios, E. E. (2005). Semantic similarity methods in wordnet and their application to information retrieval on the web. In *WIDM '05: Proceedings of the 7th annual ACM international workshop on Web information and data management*, (pp. 10-16), NY. ACM Press.

Voorhees, E. M. (1994). Query expansion using lexical-semantic relations. In *Proceedings of the 17th annual international ACM SIGIR conference on Research and development in information retrieval*, (pp. 61-69). Springer-Verlag New York, Inc., Dublin, Ireland, 1994.

Wang, J., Huang, Y., Wu, G., & Zhang, F. (1999). *Web mining: Knowledge discovery on the Web*. Paper presented at the IEEE International Conference on Systems, Man, and Cybernaetics 1999, Tokyo.

Wang, Y., & Stroulia, E. (2003) Semantic structure matching for assessing Web – Service similarity. *First International Conference on Service Oriented Computing*. (LNCS 2910, pp. 194-207). Springer, 2003.

Wen, J.-R., Nie, J.-Y., & Zhang, H.-J. (2002). Query clustering using user logs. *ACM Transactions on Information Systems (TOIS), 20*(1), 59-81.

This work was previously published in the International Journal of Web Services Research, Volume. 5, Issue 1, edited by L. Zhang, pp. 63-81, copyright 2008 by IGI Publishing (an imprint of IGI Global).t

Chapter 13
A Reengineering Approach for Ensuring Transactional Reliability of Composite Services

Sami Bhiri
National University of Ireland, and Galway Digital Enterprise Research Institute IDA Business Park, Ireland

Walid Gaaloul
TELECOM & Management SudParis, France

Claude Godart
LORIA-INRIA, France

ABSTRACT

Different from traditional software applications, Web services are defined independently from any execution context. Their consequent inherent autonomy and heterogeneity fostered by a continuous evolution in business context and requirements make ensuring the execution of a composite service as intended a challenging task. This chapter presents a reengineering approach to ensure transactional reliability of composite services. Contrary to previous approaches which check correctness properties based on the composition model, the authors start from executions' log to improve services' recovery mechanisms. Basically, the chapter proposes a set of mining techniques to discover the transactional behavior from an event based log. Then, based on this mining step, the authors use a set of rules in order to improve services' reliability.

INTRODUCTION

Nowadays, enterprises are able to outsource their internal business processes as services and make them accessible via the Web. Then, they can dynamically combine individual services to provide new added-value composite services (CS for short). Due to the inherent autonomy and heterogeneity of Web services, a fundamental problem concerns the guarantee of correct executions of a CS. An execution is correct if it reaches its objectives or fails (properly) according to the designers requirements.

DOI: 10.4018/978-1-61520-684-1.ch013

Figure 1. A composite Web service for Online Travel Arrangement (OTA for short)

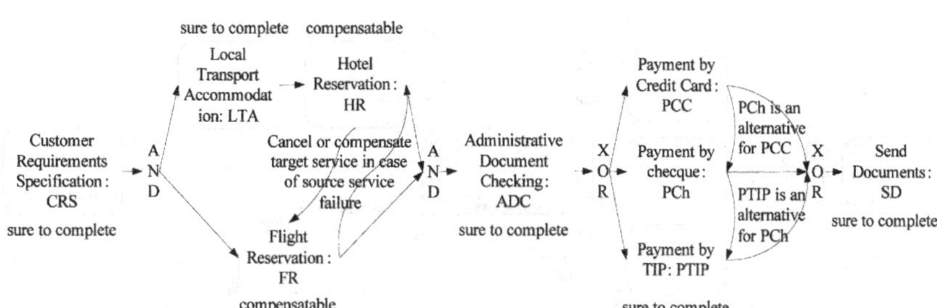

Motivating example Let us consider an application for Online Travel Arrangement (OTA for short) carried out by a composite service as illustrated in Figure 1. The customer specifies its requirements in terms of destination and hotel through the *CRS* service. The application launches in parallel flight and hotel reservation (*FR* and *HR* respectively) (after a study of the local transport accommodations (*LTA*)). The *ADC* service disposes administrative documents. Then, the customer is requested to pay by credit card (*PCC*), by check (*PCh*), or by TIP (*PTIP*). The Send Documents (*SD*) service ensures the delivery of documents to the customer. To deal with exceptions, designers specify additional mechanisms for failure handling and recovery. First, they specify that the hotel reservation can be compensated (by cancellation for instance) when the service *FR* fails to book a flight, and reciprocally. Second, in order to ensure the payment they specify that the service *PCh* is a payment alternative to the service *PCC*. Similarly, they specify that the service *PTIP* is a payment alternative to the service *PCh* with the assumption that the service *PTIP* always succeeds. Finally, designers specify that *CRS, LTA, ADC* and *SD* services are sure to complete. The main problem at this stage is how to ensure that the specified composition model guaranties reliable executions.

Generally, previous approaches develop based on their modeling formalisms a set of techniques to analyze the composition model and check "correctness" properties. Although powerful, these approaches may fail in some cases to ensure reliable executions even if they validate the composition model formally. This is because properties specified in the studied composition model remains assumptions that may not coincide with reality.

Back to our example, let us suppose for instance that in reality (by observation of sufficient execution cases) *FR* and *PCh* services never fail and the service *PTIP* is not sure to complete. That means, among others, (i) there is no need for the service *HR* to support compensation policies (which can be costly), and (ii) the payment can fail while the hotel and flight reservations are maintained. Formal approaches cannot deal with such anomalies.

Mining the effective transactional behavior enables to detect these gaps and thereafter improve the application reliability. For instance, mining the transactional behavior enables to improve the OTA service composition model by specifying the service *PCh* as a payment alternative to the service *PTIP* (since we notice that *PCh* is sure to complete).

Overview of our approach As explained in section 2, we distinguish between the control flow and the transactional flow of a composite service. The former specifies a partial ordering between the executions of component services. The latter defines the recovery mechanisms. In this paper we present an approach to improve CS recovery mechanisms based on the analysis of their execution history. Figure 2 gives an overview of the main steps of our approach:

Figure 2. Overview of our approach

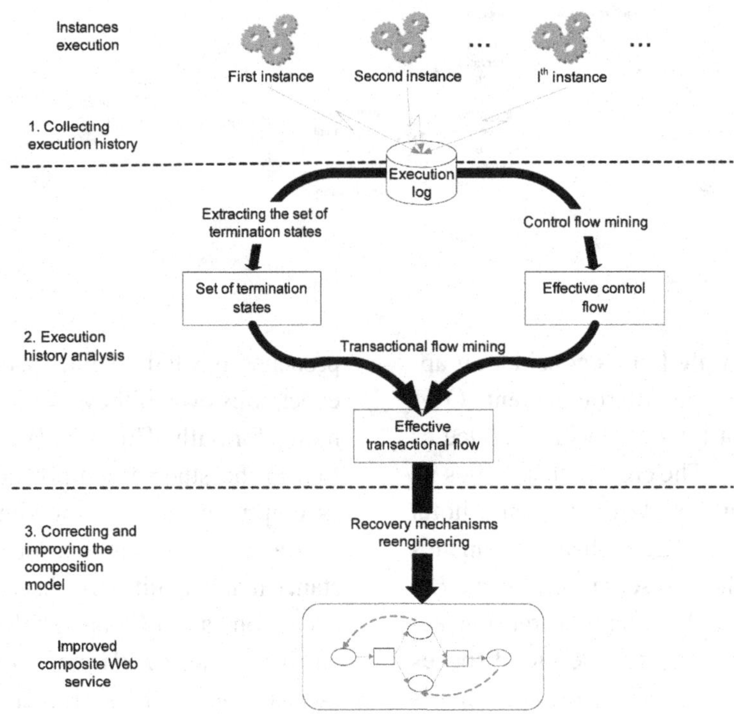

1. Collecting execution history: the purpose of this phase is to keep track of the composite service execution by capturing the relevant generated events.
2. Analyzing the execution history: the purpose of this phase is to mine the effective transactional flow of a composite service. For that we need first to mine its effective control flow and extract its set of termination states.
3. Improving the composition model: based on the execution history analysis we use a set of rules to improve the composite service recovery mechanisms.

The remainder of this chapter is organized as follows. In section 2 we introduce our transactional service model. Section 3 illustrates how we model a composite service according to the model presented in section 2. Section 4 discusses Web services logging and shows how we can capture composite service execution history. Section 5 and Section 6 present respectively our control flow and transactional flow mining techniques. In section 7 we show how we proceed to improve CS recovery mechanisms. Section 8 discusses some related work. Section 9 concludes our paper.

TRANSACTIONAL WEB SERVICE MODEL

In this section, we introduce our service composition model. We introduce the concept of a transactional Web service (TWS for short). Then we show how we combine a set TWS to define a new added-value service.

Transactional Web Service: TWS

In this paper, by Web service we mean a self-contained modular program that can be discovered and invoked across the Internet. A transactional Web service is a Web service of which the behavior manifests transactional properties.

The main transactional properties we are considering are *retriable, compensatable and pivot* (Mehrotra, Rastogi et al. 1992). A service *s* is said to be ***retriable*** if it is sure to complete after several finite activations. *s* is said to be ***compensatable*** if it offers compensation policies to semantically undo its effects. Then, *s* is said to be ***pivot*** if once it successfully completes, its effects remains forever and cannot be semantically undone. Naturally, a service can combine properties, and the set of all possible combinations is {∅; *retriable; compensatable; pivot; (retriable, compensatable); (retriable, pivot)*}.

The rational for using these properties is that they enable to characterize two properties relevant for reliability namely the failure im/possibility of a service and its compensation capacity.

Every service can be associated to a life cycle state chart that models the possible states through which its instances can go, and the possible transitions between these states. The set of states and transitions depend on the service transactional properties. Each service has a minimal set of states (*initial, active, cancelled, failed, completed*) and a minimal set of transitions (*activate(), cancel(), fail(), complete()*). The *activate()* transition creates a new instance that becomes *active*. Once it is *active*, the instance can continue its execution normally or it can be *cancelled* during its execution. In the first case, an instance can achieve its objective and *completes* successfully or it can *fail*. A compensatable service has in addition, a state *compensated* and a transition *compensate()*. A retriable service has a state *to-be-retried* instead of the state *failed*. In addition it has a transition *retry()* that activates it again.

Within a transactional service, we distinguish between external and internal transitions. External transitions are fired by external entities. Typically they allow a service to interact with the outside and to specify service orchestrations (see next section). The external transitions we are considering are *activate(), cancel(),* and *compensate()*. Internal transitions are fired by the service itself (the service agent). Internal transitions we are considering are *complete(), fail()*, and *retry()*. We note *TWS* the set of transactional Web services.

In accordance with Web service coordination specifications (Newcomer, Robinson, Feingold, & Jeyaraman, 2007), we suppose that each transactional service has a transactional coordinator that exposes its external transitions as operations, thus enabling to activate an instance, cancel or compensate it.

Transactional Composite Web Service: TCS

A transactional composite (Web) service (TCS for short) is a composite Web service of which the component services are TWS. Such a service leverages its component services' transactional properties to specify failure handling and recovery mechanisms. We note *TCS* the set of transactional composite Web services.

Composition of Transactional Web Services

A TCS defines a set of preconditions on each component service's external transition in order to define the orchestration schema (a.k.a composition model). These preconditions specify for each component service when it is activated, canceled, or compensated. For example, the service OTA specifies that *ADC* is activated after the completion of *HR* and *FR*. This means that the precondition of the transition *activate()* of *ADC* is the completion of *HR* and the completion of *FR*. Thus, a TCS can be defined as the set of its component services and the set of the preconditions defined on their external transitions. More formally we define a TCS as following.

Definition 1: A transactional composite Web service *tcs* is a couple *tcs* = $(ES \in TWS, Prec)$

where *ES* is the set of its component Web services and *Prec* is a function that defines for each component service's external transition a set of preconditions for its firing.

Thus, we distinguish for each component service, s, a set of **exclusive** preconditions for each of its external transition, *activate()*, *cancel()*, and *compensate()*. For instance, the service OTA specifies that *PCh* is activated either after the completion of *ADC* (exclusively) or after the failure of *PCC*. This means that $Prec(PCh.activate()) = \{(ADC.completed \wedge PCh$ chosen for delivery), $PCC.failed\}$.

Preconditions express at a higher abstract level relations (successions, alternatives, etc) between component services in form of dependencies. These dependencies express how services are coupled and how the behavior of certain component service(s) influences the behavior of other service(s). For example the precondition on the transition *activate()* of the service *PCh* expresses (i) a succession relation (or dependency) between the service *ADC* and the service *PCh* and (ii) an alternative relation (or dependency) between the service *PCC* and the service *PCh.*

Definition 2 Let *cs* be a TCS, s_1 and s_2 two component services of *cs*, $s_1.t_1()$ a transition of s_1, and $s_2.t_2()$ an external transition of s_2, a dependency from $s_1.t_1()$ to $s_2.t_2()$, denoted $dep(s_1.t_1(), s_2.t_2())$, exists if the completion of $s_1.t_1()$ may trigger off $s_2.t_2()$.

In our approach, we consider *activation*, *alternative*, *compensation* and *cancellation* dependencies which we detail in the following.

Activation dependency and activation condition: An activation dependency expresses a succession relation between two services. An activation dependency from s_1 to s_2 exists *iff* the completion of s_1 may fire the activation of s_2. Such dependency is defined according to the activation condition of s_2 $ActCond(s_2)$. $ActCond(s)$ specifies when *s* is activated (as a successor for other(s) service(s)).

For example, the service OTA shown in figure 1 defines an activation dependency from *HR* to *ADC*, and from *FR* to *ADC* such that *ADC* is activated after the completion of *HR* and *FR*. This means that $ActCond(ADC)=\{HR.completed \wedge FR.completed\}$.

Alternative dependency and alternative condition: Alternative dependencies allow defining execution alternatives as forward recovery mechanisms. An alternative dependency from s_1 to s_2 exists *iff* the failure of s_1 may fire the activation of s_2. Such dependency is defined according to the alternative condition of s_2 $AltCond(s_2)$. $AltCond(s)$ specifies when *s* is activated as an alternative to other(s) service(s).

For instance the service OTA shown in figure 1 defines an alternative dependency from *PCC* to *PCh* such that *PCh* is activated when *PCC* fails. This means that $AltCond(PCh) = \{PCC.failed\}$.

Compensation dependency and compensation condition: A compensation dependency allows defining a backward recovery mechanism by compensation. A compensation dependency from s_1 to s_2 exists *iff* the failure or the compensation of s_1 may fire the compensation of s_2. Such dependency is defined according to the compensation condition of s_2 $CpsCond(s_2)$. $CpsCond(s)$ specifies when *s* is compensated after the failure or the compensation of other(s) service(s).

The service OTA described in Figure 1 defines a compensation dependency from *HR* to *FR* such that *FR* is compensated when *HR* fails. This means that $CpsCond(FR) = \{HR.failed\}$.

Cancellation dependency and cancellation condition: A cancellation dependency allows signaling a service instance failure to other service instance(s) being carried out in parallel by canceling their execution if necessary. A cancellation dependency from s_1 to s_2 exists *iff* the failure of s_1 may fire the cancellation of s_2. Such dependency is defined according to the cancellation condition of s_2 $CnlCond(s)$. $CnlCond(s)$ specifies when *s* is canceled after the failure of other(s) service(s).

Control and Transactional Flow of a TCS

We call the compensation, cancellation and alternative dependencies transactional dependencies. Activation and transactional dependencies express at a higher abstract level respectively the control flow and the transactional flow of a TCS.

Control flow The control flow of a TCS specifies a partial ordering between component services' activations. Intuitively the control flow of a TCS is defined by the set of its activation dependencies. Formally, we define a control flow as a TCS where its dependencies are only activation dependencies.

Definition 3 A control flow is a TCS, $cf = (ES, Prec)$ such that $\forall s \in ES\ AltCond(s) = \perp$; $CpsCond(s) = \perp$; and $CnlCond(s) = \perp$.

We note *CFlow* the set of all control flows. We define the function *getCFlow* that returns the control flow of a given TCS.

Definition 4 We define the function *getCFlow* that returns the control flow of a TCS.

$getCFlow: TCS \longrightarrow CFlow$

$sc = (ES, Prec) \longmapsto cf = (ES', Prec')$

such that $ES' = ES$ and $\forall s \in ES\ Prec'(s.activate()) = ActCond(s)$; $Prec'(s.cancel()) = \perp$; $Prec'(s.compensate()) = \perp$.

Transactional flow The transactional flow of a TCS specifies the recovery mechanisms. Intuitively, a transactional flow of a TCS is defined by its component services transactional properties and its set of transactional dependencies. Formally we define a transactional flow as a TCS where its dependencies are only transactional dependencies.

Definition 5 A transactional flow is a TCS, $tf = (ES, Prec)$ such that $\forall s \in ES\ ActCond(s) = \perp$.

We note *TFlow* the set of all transactional flows. We define the function *getTFlow* that returns the transactional flow of a given TCS.

Definition 6 We define the function *getTFlow* that returns the transactional flow of a TCS. $getTFlow: TCS \longrightarrow TFlow$

$sc = (ES, Prec) \longmapsto tf = (ES', Prec')$

such that $ES' = ES$ and $\forall s \in ES\ Prec'(s.activate()) = AltCond(s)$.

A TCS *cs* can be defined as the union of its control flow *getCFlow(cs)* and its transactional flow *getTFlow(cs)*. In general, the union of two TCS cs_1 and cs_2 is a TCS where (i) the set of its component services is the union of cs_1's and cs_2's component services (ii) the precondition of an external transition of a component service *s* is the one defined by cs_1 if *s* belongs only to cs_1, the one defined by cs_2 if *s* belongs only to cs_2, or the union of the preconditions defined by cs_1 and cs_2 if *s* belongs to both of them.

Definition 7 Let cs_1 and cs_2 be two TCS: $cs_1 = (ES_1, Prec_1)$ and $cs_2 = (ES_2, Prec_2)$. The union of cs_1 and cs_2 is the TCS defined as follows: $cs = cs_1 \cup cs_2 = (ES, Prec)$ where

- $ES = ES_1 \cup ES_2$

- $\forall s \in ES$

$$Prec(s) = \begin{cases} Prec_1(s) \text{ if } s \in ES_1 \wedge s \notin ES_2 \\ Prec_2(s) \text{ if } s \in ES_1 \wedge s \in ES_2 \\ Prec_1(s) \cup Prec_2(s) \text{ if } s \in ES_1 \wedge s \in ES_2 \end{cases}$$

Relation between the Control Flow and the Transactional Flow of a TCS

A TCS transactional flow is tightly related to its control Flow. Indeed, the recovery mechanisms (defined by the transactional flow) depend on the execution process logic (defined by the control flow). For example, regarding the composite service OTA it is possible to define the service *PCh* as an alternative to the service *PCC* because (according to the XOR control flow operator) they are defined on exclusive branches.

More generally, a control flow implicitly tailors all possible recovery mechanisms. We call a potential transactional flow of a given TCS the transactional flow including all possible transactional dependencies (i.e. recovery mechanisms) that can be defined w.r.t to its control flow. More formally each component service *s* has according to the TCS control flow:

- *ptCpsCond(s)*: its potential compensation condition that specifies when it may eventually be compensated.
- *ptAltCond(s)*: its potential alternative condition that specifies when it may eventually be activated as an alternative.
- *ptCnlCond(s)*: its potential cancellation condition that specifies when it may eventually be canceled.

Back to our example, according to the service OTA control flow *FR* may eventually be compensated (i) either after the failure of *ADC*, (ii) or after the compensation of *ADC* (ii) or after the failure of *HR*. This means that the potential compensation conditions of *FR* are the failure of *ADC*, the compensation of *ADC*, or the failure of *HR*: *ptCpsCond(FR)* = *{ADC.failed, ADC.compensated, HR.f ailed}*.

Many TCS can be specified according to the same control flow *cf*. Each one of them extends *cf* with a transactional flow included in its (*cf*) potential transactional flow, *potential(cf)*. More formally:

∀TCS *cs* defined according to a control flow *cf*

cs = *getCFlow(cs)* ∪ *getTFlow(cs)* such that

getCFlow(cs) = *cf and getTFlow(cs)* ⊆ *potential(cf)*.

Figure 10 illustrates two TCS defined according to the same control flow. Each of these TCS extends the control flow shown in Figure 3 by a transactional flow included in its potential transactional flow defined in Figure 4.

TCS Set of Termination States

Many executions can be instantiated according to the same TCS model. The state at a specific time of a TCS instance composed of *n* services can be represented by the tuple (s_1, *s2*,.. .s_n), where s_i is the state of the service instance x_i at this time. The set of termination states of a TCS is the set off all possible termination states of all its instances.

We distinguish two kinds of termination state. The first one corresponds to the termination states reached after normal executions (without unexpected failures according to the control flow). We call a termination state of this first type a termination state without failure. The set of termination states without failures of a TCS is defined by its control flow.

The second kind of termination state corresponds to the ones reached in case of failure(s) of certain component service(s) (according to the transactional flow). We call a termination state of this second type a termination state with failure. The set of termination states with failure of a TCS is defined by its transactional flow. We define the function $computeTS_{withFailure}$ that returns the set of termination states with failure of a given TCS (more precisely given its transactional flow).

PATTERN BASED MODELING

In the previous section, we presented our transactional Web service model that enables to capture the control and the transactional flow of a TCS. In this section, we show how we model a TCS. We adopt an approach based on workflow patterns (van der Aalst, ter Hostede et al. 2003). We extend them in order to specify, in addition to the control flow they are considering by default, the transactional flow.

Figure 3. The control flow of the service OTA is defined as a union of pattern instances

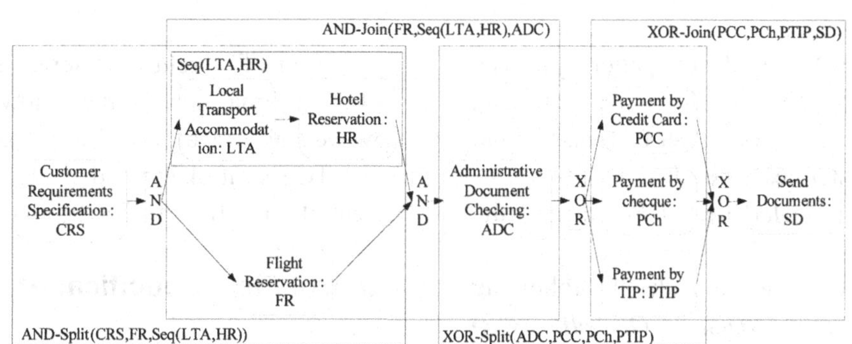

Pattern based modeling is interesting for many reasons. Patterns are relatively simple (compared to workflow language) thanks to the abstraction they ensure. Patterns are practical since they are deduced from the practice. In addition they enhance reusability and comprehension between designers. Pattern based modeling also allows modular and local processing. In the following, section 3.1 introduces the composition patterns. Section 3.2 shows how we make use of them in order to specify TCS.

Composition Patterns

In the following, we present the workflow patterns from the perspective of our model. Then we show how a given workflow pattern implicitly tailors a set of possible transactional flows.

Workflow Patterns

As defined in (Gamma, Helm et al. 1995), a pattern "is the abstraction from a concrete form which keeps recurring in specific non arbitrary contexts". Regarding that, a workflow pattern (van der Aalst, ter Hostede et al. 2003) can be seen as an abstract description of a recurrent class of interactions. For example, the AND-join pattern (see Figure 3) describes a class of interactions between services as follows: *a service is activated after the completion of several other services*.

With respect to our TCS model, the basic workflow patterns consider only the control flow side. Thus, they can be considered as control flow patterns. Formally, we define a control flow

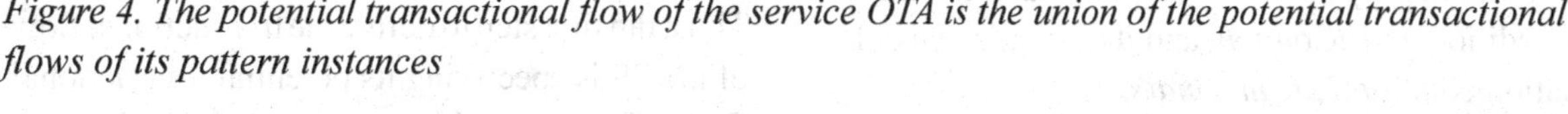
Figure 4. The potential transactional flow of the service OTA is the union of the potential transactional flows of its pattern instances

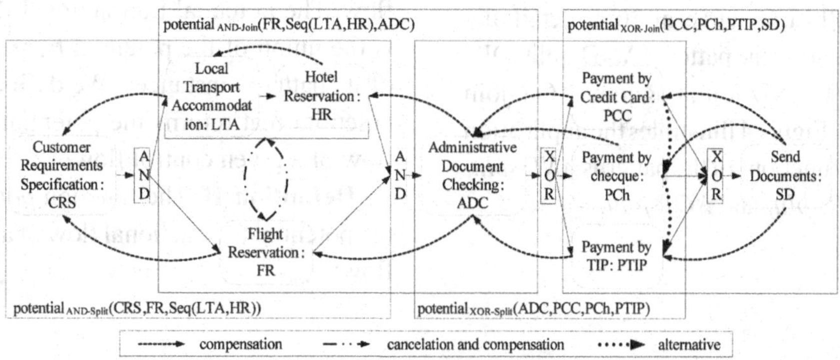

pattern as a function that returns a control flow given a set of services.

Definition 8 A control flow pattern, *pat*, is a function *pat*: $P(TWS) \longrightarrow CFlow$, that returns a control flow *pat(S)* given a set of transactional services *S*. *pat* defines for each service $s \in S$, its activation condition *ActCond(s)*. *P(S)* denotes the set of subsets of a set *S*.

In our approach, we consider the following patterns: *sequence, AND-split, OR-split, XOR-split, AND-join, OR-join, XOR-join and m-out-of-n* (van der Aalst, ter Hostede et al. 2003). Our paper (Bhiri, Godart et al. 2006) details how we define each of these patterns according to the definition 8. Figure 3 illustrates the application of the patterns *AND-split, AND-join, XOR-split,* and *XOR-join*.

Patterns Transactional Potential

A workflow pattern *pat* defines a control flow *pat(S)* given a set of services. As all control flows, *pat(S)* possesses a potential transactional flow. We define for each workflow pattern, *pat*, a function, $potential_{pat}$, that returns given a set of services *S* the potential transactional flow of *pat(S)*.

Definition 9 Let *pat* a pattern. The function $potential_{pat}$: $P(TWS) \longrightarrow TFlow$, returns given a set of services *S*, the potential transactional flow of the control flow *pat(S)*. $potential_{pat}$ defines for each service $s \in S$ its potential compensation condition, *ptCpsCond(s)*, its potential alternative condition, *ptAltCond(s)*, and its potential cancellation condition *ptCnlCond(s)*.

Our paper (Bhiri, Godart et al. 2006) details the potential functions of the patterns AND-split, OR-split, XOR-split, AND-join, OR-join, XOR-join and m-out-of-n. Figure 4 illustrates the application of the potential functions of the patterns *AND split, AND join, XOR split,* and *XOR join*.

TCS Specification

Specifying a TCS returns to define its control and its transactional flow. In the following we show how we make use of (i) workflow patterns for defining TCS' control flow and (ii) their transactional potential for defining TCS' transactional flow.

Control Flow Specification

We call pattern instance, the control flow resulting from the application of a pattern to a set of services. Let *pat* be a pattern and *S* a set of services, *pat(S)* is an instance of *pat*. We use pattern instances as the basic bricks for specifying TCS' control flow (Bhiri, Godart et al. 2006). Indeed, in our approach a control flow is defined as the union of pattern instances. More formally:

$\forall$TCS $cs = (ES, Prec)$ $\exists$ a set of patterns $\{P_1, \ldots, P_n\}$ and a partition *S* of *ES*: $S = \{S_1, \ldots S_n\}$ (with $ES = \cup_{1 \leq i \leq n} (S_i) \mid getFControl(cs) = \cup_{1 \leq i \leq n} P_i(S_i)$.

Figure 3 shows how we define the control flow of the service OTA as a union of pattern instances.

Transactional Flow Specification

The transactional flow of a TCS is included in the potential transactional flow of its control flow. Thus, the first step to define the transactional flow of a TCS is specifying its potential transactional flow. The potential transactional flow of a TCS is the union of the potential transactional flows of its patterns instances. We define the function potential that returns the potential transactional flow of a given control flow.

Definition 10 The function *potential* returns the potential transactional flow of a given control flow:

$$CFlow \longrightarrow TFlow$$

$$Cf = \cup_i pat_i(S_i) \longmapsto ptf = \cup_i \text{potential}_{pati}(S_i)$$

Figure 4 displays the transactional potential flow of the control flow defined in figure 3. It illustrates how it is the union of the potential transactional flow of the control flow pattern instances.

WEB SERVICE LOGGING

Following a common requirement in the areas of business process and service management, we expect that the executions of composite services are traceable, meaning that the system should in one way or another keep track of ongoing and past executions. Several research projects deal with the technical facilities necessary for the collecting and the logging of Web services' execution logs (Sahai, Machiraju et al. 2001; Fauvet, Dunas et al. 2002 ; Rouached, Gaaloul et al. 2006). In the following, we examine and formalize the logging possibilities in service oriented architectures.

Web Service Collecting Solutions

The first step in the Web Service mining process consists of gathering relevant Web data which will be analyzed afterwards. We discuss how these log records could be obtained by using existing tools or by specifying additional solutions. Then, we show that the mining abilities are tightly related to the information provided in web service log and depend strongly on its richness.

Existing logging solutions provide a set of tools to capture web service interactions' logs. These solutions remain quite "poor" to mine advanced web service behaviors. That is why **advanced logging solutions** are required in order to record the needed information and thereafter mine more advanced behavior.

Existing Logging Solutions

Web data logs can be collected from two locations Web server side and client side. Existing techniques are commonly achieved by enabling Web server's logging facilities. There already exist many investigations and proposals on Web server log collecting and associated analysis techniques. Works about Web Usage Mining (Punin, Krishnamoorthy et al. 2001) describe the most well-known means of web log collection. Basically, server logs are either stored in the *Common Log Format* or the more recent *Combined Log Format*. Most of the Web servers support by default the *Common Log Format* which is a fairly basic form of Web server logging.

However, the emerging paradigm of Web services requires richer information in order to fully capture business interactions and customer electronic behavior. Since Web server logs are derived from users' requests to retrieve and navigate Web pages, it is not possible to capture information related to service choreographies and orchestrations. That is why, we propose in the following a set of advanced logging techniques that enables to record additional information in order to mine more advanced behaviors.

Advanced Logging Solutions

Identifying Web Service Composition Instances

Effective mining of advanced Web service models requires tracking of information related to choreographies and orchestrations of Web services. Such information is not available in conventional Web server logs. Advanced logging solutions must provide an identifier for both choreography and orchestration models and a case identifier for each instance.

A known method for debugging is to insert logging statements into the source code of each service every time it calls another service or component. However, this solution has a main disadvantage: we do not have ownership over third parties code and we cannot guarantee they are willing to change it on someone else behalf. Furthermore, modifying existing applications may be time consuming and error prone.

Since all interactions between Web Services happen through the exchange of SOAP messages (over HTTP), another alternative is to use SOAP headers to include additional information concerning **choreography**. Basically we modify SOAP headers to include and gather the required information that captures **choreography** details. These data are stored in the element <WSHeaders>. This node encapsulates sub elements like: choreographyprotocol, choreographyname, choreographycase and any other tag inserted by the service to record optional information. For instance, the <soapenv:choreographyprotocol> element can be used to track that the service was invoked by *WS−CDL* choreography protocol. Table 1 shows how a modified SOAP message header looks like.

We use then SOAP intermediaries (Anbazhagan and Arun 2002) to extract and gather such data. SOAP intermediaries are applications located between a client and a service provider. These intermediaries are capable of both receiving and forwarding SOAP messages. They can intercept SOAP requests and capture SOAP responses. The implementation of data collection on the client side requires user co-operation, either in enabling the functionality of the remote agent, or to voluntarily use and process the modified SOAP headers but without changing the Web service implementation itself.

Concerning **orchestration** log collecting, we can extend WSBPEL engines with a sniffer that captures information and events related to instance executions such as the process-ID and instance-ID. This solution is centralized but less constrained than the previous one which collects choreography information.

Collecting Web Service Composition Instance

The focus of this section is on collecting and analyzing a **single** composite service instance. The issue of identifying and differentiating between several instances has been discussed in the previous section. The exact structure of web logs or the event collector depends on the used execution engine. In our experiments, we have used the engine bpws4j that uses log4j to generate logging events. Log4j is an Open Source logging API

Table 1. The SOAP message header

```
< soapenv: Header >
< soapenv: choreographyprotocol
soapenv: mustUnderstand = ”0”
xsi: type = ”xsd: string” >WS−CDL
< /soapenv: choreographyprotocol >
< soapenv: choreographyname
soapenv: mustUnderstand = ”0”
xsi: type = ”xsd: string” > OTA
< /soapenv: choreographyname >
< soapenv: choreographycase
soapenv: mustUnderstand = ”0”
xsi: type = ”xsd: int” > 123
< /soapenv: choreographycase >
< /soapenv: Header >
```

Table 2. Example of log4j 'logging event'

```
2006-03-13 10:40:39,634 [Thread-35] INFO bpws.runtime – Outgoing
response: [WSIFResponse:serviceID =
'{http://tempuri.org/services/CRS}CustomerRegServicefb0b0-fbc5965758--8000'operationName
= 'completed'
isFault = 'false' outgoingMessage = 'org.apache.wsif.base.WSIFDefaultMessage@
1df3d59 name:null parts[0]:[JROMBoolean:: true]'
faultMessage = 'null' contextMessage = 'null']
2006-03-13 10:40:39,634 [Thread-35] DEBUG bpws.runtime.bus -
Response
for external invoke is[WSIFResponse:serviceID='{http://tempuri.org/services
/CCRS}CustomerRegServicefb0b0-fbc5965758--8000'
operationName = 'authenticate' isFault = 'false' outgoingMessage =
org.apache.wsif.base.WSIFDefaultMessage@1df3d59 name:null parts[0]:
[JROMBoolean:: true]'faultMessage = 'null' contextMessage = 'null']
2006-03-13 10:40:39,634 [Thread-35] DEBUG bpws.runtime.bus -
Waiting
for request
```

developed within the Jakarta Apache project. It provides a robust, reliable, fully configurable, easily extensible, and easy to implement framework for logging Java applications for debugging and monitoring purposes. The event collector (which is implemented as a remote log4j server) sets some log4j properties of the bpws4j engine to specify the level of event reporting (INFO, DEBUG etc.), and the destination details of the logged events. At runtime bpws4j generates events according to the log4j properties set by the event collector. Table 2 shows some example of log4j 'logging event' generated by bpws4j engine. The event extractor captures a logging event and converts it to a unique TCS log format. This format is described in the next section.

Web Mining Log Structure

The UML class diagram of a TCS log structure is given in Figure 5. This log structure represents syntheses through a unique format of the information captured by log4j. The conversion from log4j to this format is given in more details in our paper (Rouached, Gaaloul et al. 2006).

As shown, a TCSLog (see Definition 11) is composed of a set of EventStreams. Each EventStream traces the execution of one case (instance). It consists of a set of Events that capture the life cycle of component services performed in a particular instance. An Event is described by the service identifier that it concerns, the current service state (*failed, cancelled, completed and compensated*) and the time when it occurs (TimeStamp).

Definition 11 A TCSLog is considered as a set of EventStreams. Each EventStream represents the execution of one case. More formally, an EventStream is defined as a quadruplet ***EventStream***: (*beginTime, endTime, sequenceLog, SOccurence*) where:

- (*beginTime: TimeStamp*) and (*endTime: TimeStamp*) are the moment of log beginning and end,
- *sequenceLog*: Event* is an ordered Event set belonging to one TCS case,
- (*SOccurence:int*) is the instance number.

So, ***TCSLog***: (*TCSID*, {$ServiceStream_i$: ***EventStream***; $0 \leq i \leq$ number of TCS instantiations}) is a TCS log where $ServiceStream_i$ is the EventStream of the ith TCS execution case.

An example of an **EventStream** extracted from our TCS model example is given below:

EventStream(5, 20, [**Event**(*CRS*, 5, completed), **Event**(*LTA*, 6, completed), Event(*FR*, 8, com-

Figure 5. Structure of a TCS log

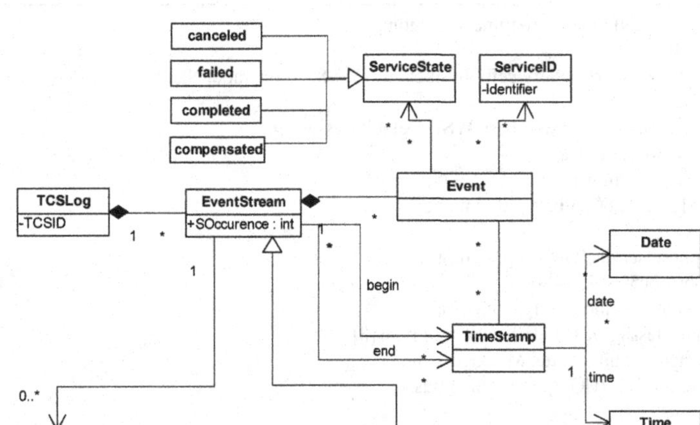

pleted), **Event**(*HR*, 9, completed), Event(*ADC*, 12, completed), **Event**(*PCC*, 13, failed), **Event**(*PCh*, 15, completed), **Event**(*SD*, 20, completed)], 1)

CONTROL FLOW MINING

In this section, we are interested in discovering "elementary" control flow patterns: Sequence, AND-split, OR-split, XOR-split, AND-join, OR-join, and M-out-of-N Join patterns (van der Aalst, ter Hostede et al. 2003). We proceed in three steps: (i) the construction of statistical dependency table SDT, (ii) the statistical specifications of patterns' sequential, conditional and concurrent behaviors, and (iii) the mining of control flow patterns using a set of rules that build on the aforementioned statistical specifications.

Construction of the Statistical Dependency Table SDT

We use statistical calculus to extract activation dependencies between services executed without "exceptions" (*i.e.* they reached successfully their state *completed*). There is no need to use other EventStreams related to failed executions (containing *failed*, *compensated*, or *canceled* states). That is why we need to filter execution logs and take only EventStreams of instances executed without failures. We denote by $TCSLog_{completed}$ this TCS log selection

Thus, the minimal condition to discover control flow patterns is to have TCS logs containing at least *completed* event states. This feature allows us to mine control flow from "poor" logs which contain only *completed* event state. Any information system using transactional systems offer this information in some form (van der Aalst, Weijters et al. 2003).

From $TCSLog_{completed}$ we extract for each service *A* the following information in the statistical dependency table (SDT): (i) the overall frequency of this service (denoted *#A*) and (ii) the activation dependencies to previous services B_i (denoted $P(A/B_i)$). The size of SDT is N*N, where N is the number of component services. The *(m,n)* table entry (notation *P(m/n)*) denotes the frequency of cases where the nth service **immediately precedes** the mth service. Table 3 represents a fraction of the SDT of our motivating example. For instance, *P(HR/LTA)*=0.69 expresses that *LTA* occurs immediately before *HR* in 69% of cases in the TCS log.

As it is computed, the initial SDT presents some problems to express correctly dependencies between services especially for those related to concurrent and parallel behavior. In the following, we detail these issues and propose solutions to correct them.

Erroneous Dependencies

If we assume that each EventStream from TCSLog comes from a sequential (i.e. no concurrent behavior) control flow, a zero entry in SDT represents a causal independence and a non-zero entry means a causal dependency (*i.e.* sequential or conditional relations). But in case of concurrent behavior, EventStreams may contain interleaved event sequences from concurrent threads. As a consequence, some entries in the initial SDT can indicate non-zero entries while they do not actually correspond to dependencies. For example the EventStream given in section 4 "suggests" erroneous activation dependencies between *LTA* and *FR* on one side and between *FR* and *HR* on the other side. Indeed, it induces that *LTA* comes just before *FR* and *FR* comes immediately before *HR* which is not true. These erroneous entries are reported by *P(FR/LTA)* and *P(HR/FR)* in SDT which are different from zero. These entries are erroneous because there are no activation dependencies between these services. Underlined values in SDT report this behavior for other similar cases.

Formally, two services *A* and *B* are in concurrence *iff P(A/B)* and *P(B/A)* entries in SDT are different from zero. Based on this definition, we propose an algorithm (Gaaloul, Baina et al. 2008) to discover concurrent behavior and then mark the erroneous entries in SDT. This algorithm scans the initial SDT and marks concurrent service dependencies by changing their values to (−1). Through this marking, we can eliminate the confusion caused by concurrent behaviors that produce these erroneous non-zero entries.

Undetectable Dependencies

For concurrency reasons, a service might not depend on its immediate predecessor in the EventStream, but it might depend on another preceding service. As an example of this behavior, *FR* is logged between *LTA* and *HR* in the EventStream given in section 4. As consequence, *LTA* does not always appear immediately before *HR* in TCSLog. Thus we have *P(HR/LTA)=0.66* which is an under evaluated dependency frequency. In fact, the right value is 1 because the execution of *HR* depends exclusively on *LTA*. Values in bold in SDT report this behavior for other cases.

In order to discover these indirect dependencies, we introduce the notion of service concurrent window (Definition 12). A concurrent window (CW) of a service *S* is a fraction of an EventStream where its last event corresponds to the completion of *S* and which covers its directly and indirectly

Table 3. Fraction of Statistical Dependencies Table SDT (P(x,y)) and Services Frequencies (#)

P(x,y)	*CRS*	*LTA*	*HR*	*FR*	*ADC*
CRS	0	0	0	0	0
LTA	**0.54**	0	0	<u>0.46</u>	0
HR	0	**0.69**	0	<u>0.31</u>	0
FR	**0.46**	<u>0.31</u>	<u>0.23</u>	0	0
ADC	0	0	**0.77**	**0.23**	0
#P=#*CRS*=#*LTA*=#*HR*=#*FR*=#*ADC*=#ST=100 #*PCC*=#*PCh*=#*PTIP*=35					

preceding services. Initially, the width of a CW (i.e. the number of services within it) is equal to 2. Every time the corresponding service is in concurrence with another service we add 1 to the CW width. If this service is not in concurrence with other services and has preceding concurrent services, then we add their number to its CW width. For example *FR* is in concurrence with *LTA* and *HR*, the width of its CW is equal to 4. Based on this we give an algorithm (Gaaloul, Baina et al. 2008) that calculates the CW width for each service and regroups them in a CW table. This algorithm scans the "marked" **SDT** and updates the CW table in consequence.

Definition 12 A Window (see Figure 5) defines a log slide over an EventStream S:***EventStream*** (*bStream, eStream, sLog, TCSocc*). Formally, we define a log window as a triplet ***window***(*wLog, bWin, eWin*):

- (*bWin*: TimeStamp) and (*eWin*: TimeStamp) are the moment of the window beginning and end (with $bStream \leq bWin$ and $eWin \leq eStream$),
- $wLog \subset sLog$ and ∀ e: **event** ∈ *S.sLog* where $bWin \leq e.TimeStamp \leq eWin) \Rightarrow e \in wLog$.

After that, we proceed through an EventStream partition (Definition 13) that builds a set of partially overlapping Windows over the EventStream using the CW table. Finally, we use an algorithm (Gaaloul, Baina et al. 2005) to compute the final SDT. For each CW, it computes for its last service the frequencies of its preceding services. The final SDT is computed by dividing each row entry by the frequency of its service.

Definition 13 A Partition (see Figure 5) builds a set of partially overlapping Windows partition over an EventStream. *Partition*: TCSLog → (Window)*

S: *EventStream*(*bStream, eStream, sLog, TCSocc*) → $\{w_i$:Window; $1 \leq i \leq n\}$:

- $w_1.bWin = bStream$ and $w_n.eWin = eStream$,
- ∀*w*: *window* ∈ *Partition*, *e*:Event = the last event in *w*, *width(w)= CW[e.serviceID]*,
- $\forall\ 0 \leq i \leq n$; $w_{i+1}.wLog$ - {the last *e*:Event in $w_{i+1}.wLog\} \subset w_i.wLog$ and $w_{i+1}.wLog \neq w_i.wLog$.

By applying aforementioned algorithms, we have computed the final SDT (Table 4) which is used to discover control flow patterns. Note that, our approach adjusts **dynamically**, through the CW width, the process calculating service dependencies. Indeed, this width is sensible to concurrent behavior: it increases in case of concurrence and is "neutral" in case of non concurrent behavior.

Statistical Specifications of Sequential, Conditional and Concurrent Properties

We have identified three kinds of statistical properties (sequential, conditional and concurrent) which describe the main behaviors of control flow patterns. We specify these properties using SDT's statistics. We use these properties to identify separate TCS patterns from execution log. Then using a dynamic algorithm we build global solution (i.e. global WS composition model) based on local solutions (i.e. TCS patterns) iteratively. We begin with the statistical exclusive dependency property (property 1) which characterizes the sequence pattern.

Property 1 Mutual exclusive dependency property (P1 for short**):** A ***mutual*** exclusive dependency relation between a service S_i and a service S_j specifies that the enactment of the service S_i depends only on the completion of the service S_j and the completion of S_j enacts only the execution of S_i. It is expressed in terms of:

- service frequencies: $\#S_i = \#S_j$
- service dependencies: $P(S_i/S_j) = 1 \wedge 0 \leq k,$

$l < n; k \neq j; P(S_i/S_k) = 0 \wedge \forall l \neq i; P(S_l/S_j) = 0.$

The next two statistic properties: concurrency property (Property 2) and choice property (Property 3) are used to insulate pattern behaviors in terms of concurrence and choice after a "fork" or before a "join" point.

Property 2 Concurrency property (P2 for short**):** A ***concurrency*** relation between a set of services $\{S_i, 0 \leq i \leq n\}$ specifies how, in terms of concurrency, the enactment of these services is performed. This set of services is commonly found after a "fork" operator or before a "join" operator. We distinguish between three concurrency behaviors:

- ***P2.1: Global concurrency*** where in the same instantiation all services are performed simultaneously: $\forall 0 \leq i \neq j < n; \#S_i = \#S_j \wedge P(S_i/S_j) = -1$
- **P2.2:** ***Partial concurrency*** where in the same instantiation we have at least a partial concurrent execution of services: $(\exists\, 0 \leq i \neq j < n; P(S_i/S_j) = -1)$
- **P2.3:** ***No concurrency*** where there is no concurrency between services: $\forall(0 \leq i \neq j < n; \wedge P(S_i/S_j) \neq -1)$

Property 3 Choice property (P3 for short**):** A ***choice*** property characterizes the relation between a service S before a "fork" operator and the following set of services $S_c=\{S_i, 0 \leq i < n\}$ on one hand and the relation between this set of services S_c and the service after the "join" operator. We distinguish between three choice behaviors:

- **P3.1:** ***Free choice*** where some services of S_c are chosen. We have in terms of service frequencies $(\#S \leq \sum_{i=0}^{n-1} (\#S_i)) \wedge (\#S_i \leq \#S)$. In terms of service dependencies we have:
- Regarding the "fork" operator (S_i occurs certainly after S occurrence): $\forall 0 \leq i < n; P(S_i/S) = 1$
  - Regarding the "join" operator (S occurs certainly after some S_i occurrences "1 <", but not always after all S_i "< n"): $1 < \sum_{i=0}^{n-1} P(S/S_i) < n$
- **P3.2:** ***Single choice*** where only one service is chosen from S_c. We have in terms of service frequencies $(\#S = \sum_{i=0}^{n-1} (\#S_i))$. In terms of service dependencies we have:
- Regarding the "fork" operator (S_i occurs certainly after S occurrence): $\forall 0 \leq i < n; P(S_i/S) = 1$
  - Regarding the "join" operator (S occurs certainly after only one of S_i occurrences): $\sum_{i=0}^{n-1} P(S/S_i) = 1$
- **P3.3:** ***No choice*** where all services in S_c are executed. We have in terms of service frequencies $\forall 0 \leq i < n, \#S = \#S_i$ and in terms of service dependencies we have:
- Regarding the "fork" operator (S_i occurs certainly after S occurrence): $\forall 0 \leq i < n; P(S_i/S) = 1$
- Regarding the "join" operator (S occurs certainly after all S_i occurrences): $\forall 0 \leq i < n; P(S/S_i) = 1$

Patterns Mining

Using statistical specifications of sequential, conditional and concurrent behaviors we define a set of rules that identify control flow patterns. Indeed, each pattern has its own statistical features which abstract its activation dependencies statistically

Table 4. Fraction of new calculated SDT

P(x,y)	*CRS*	*LTA*	*HR*	*FR*	*ADC*
CRS	0	0	0	0	0
LTA	**1**	0	0	-1	0
HR	0	**1**	0	-1	0
FR	**1**	-1	-1	0	0
ADC	0	0	**1**	**1**	0

and represent its unique identifier.

Our control flow mining rules are characterized by "local" discovery. These rules proceed through a **local log analysis** that allows us to **recover partial results.** In fact, in order to discover a particular control flow pattern we need only events relating to that pattern's elements. Thus, even using only fractions of TCS logs, we can discover corresponding TCS patterns correctly (which their events belong to these fractions).

We divide control flow patterns in three categories: sequence, fork and join patterns. Note that the rule formulas noted by: (P1) refers to the statistical mutual exclusive property, (P2) refers to the statistical concurrency property and (P3) refers to the statistical choice property.

Sequence pattern: In this category, we find only the sequence pattern (Figure 6). In this pattern, the enactment of the service *B* depends only on the completion of the service *A*. We use the statistical exclusive dependency property to describe this relation between *B* and *A*.

Fork patterns: The three patterns of this category (Figure 7) have a "fork" point where a single thread of control splits into multiple threads of control which can be, according to the used pattern, executed or not. The AND-split and OR-split patterns differentiate themselves through the no choice and free choice properties. Effectively, only a part of services are executed in the OR-split pattern after a "fork" point, while all the B_i services are executed in the And-split pattern. The non-parallelism between B_i in the XOR-split pattern are ensured by the no concurrency property while the partial and the global parallelism in OR-split and AND-split is identified through the application of the statistical partial and global concurrency properties.

Join patterns: The three patterns of this category (Figure 8) have a "join" point where multiple threads of control merge in a single thread of control. The number of the necessary incoming branches for the activation of the service *B* after the "join" point depends on the used pattern. The single choice and the no concurrency properties are used to identify the XOR-join pattern where two or more alternative branches come together without synchronization and none of the alternative branches is ever executed in parallel. As for the AND-join pattern where multiple parallel services converge into one single thread of control, the no choice and the global concurrency are both used

Figure 6. Rules of sequence TCS pattern

Rules	**TCS patterns**
(P1) (#B = #A)	Sequence Pattern
(P1) (P(B/A) = 1)	A → B

to discover this pattern. In contrary, in the M-out-of-N-Join pattern we need only the termination of M out of the N incoming concurrent services to enact the service *B*, the concurrency between A_i would be partial and the choice is free.

Transactional Flow Mining

In this section, we show how we proceed in order to discover a TCS transactional flow given its control flow and its set of termination states. Back to our motivating example, we suppose that the two previous mining steps lead to discover the TCS control flow initially defined by the designers and the TCS set of termination states shown in Table 5.

Key Idea

A termination state with failure keeps track of the occurred failure(s) and the applied recovery mechanisms. For instance, the termination state with failure ts_4 (see Table 5) is reached following *HR* failure. In addition, the applied recovery mechanism consists in compensating *FR*.

For the following, we argue that the control flow *cf* is known and fixed. Let $STS_{withFailure}$ a set of termination states with failure of a composite service *cs* (of which we know only its control flow *cf*). The transactional flow induced by $STS_{withFailure}$ is the transactional flow (defined according to *cf*) leading to $STS_{withFailure}$ as a set of termination states with failure. It is defined by the reverse function of $computeTS_{withFailure}$: $computeTS^{-1}_{withFailure}$. This

Figure 7. Rules of fork TCS patterns

Rules	TCS patterns
(P3) ($\sum_{i=1}^{n}$ (#B$_i$)= #A) (P3) ($\forall$ 1 $\leq$ i $\leq$ n; P(B$_i$/A) = 1) $\wedge$ (P2)($\forall$ 1 $\leq$ i, j $\leq$ n; P(B$_i$/B$_j$) = 0)	XOR-split Pattern 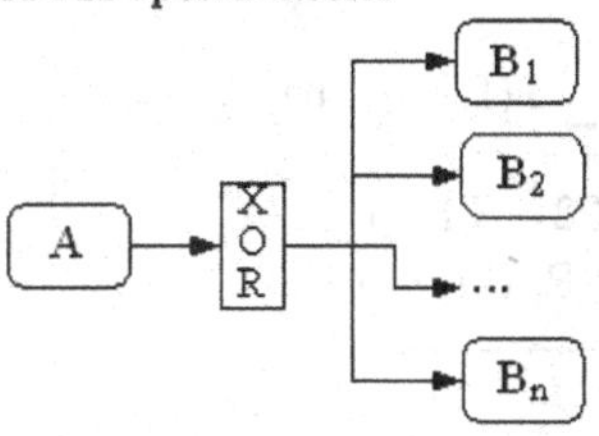 A, XOR, B$_1$, B$_2$, …, B$_n$
(P3) ($\forall$ 1 $\leq$ i $\leq$ n; #B$_i$ = #A (P3) ($\forall$ 1 $\leq$ i $\leq$ n; P(B$_i$/A) = 1) $\wedge$ (P2)($\forall$ 1 $\leq$ i, j $\leq$ n; P(B$_i$/B$_j$) $\neq$ 0)	AND-split Pattern 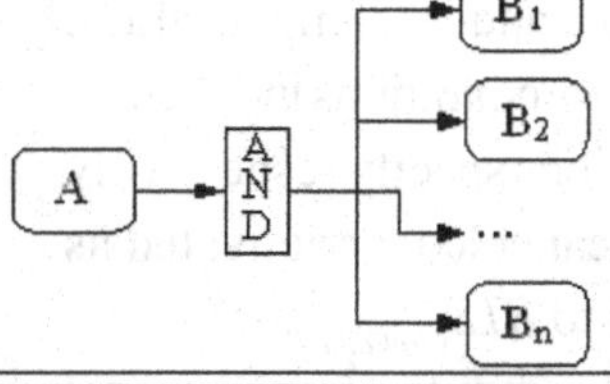 A, AND, B$_1$, B$_2$, …, B$_n$
(P3) (#A $\leq$ $\sum_{i=1}^{n}$ (#B$_i$)) ($\forall$ 1 $\leq$ i $\leq$ n; #B$_i$ $\leq$ #A) (P3) ($\forall$ 1 $\leq$ i $\leq$ n; P(B$_i$/A) = 1) $\wedge$ (P2)($\exists$ 1 $\leq$ i, j $\leq$ n; P(B$_i$/B$_j$) $\neq$ 0)	OR-split Pattern 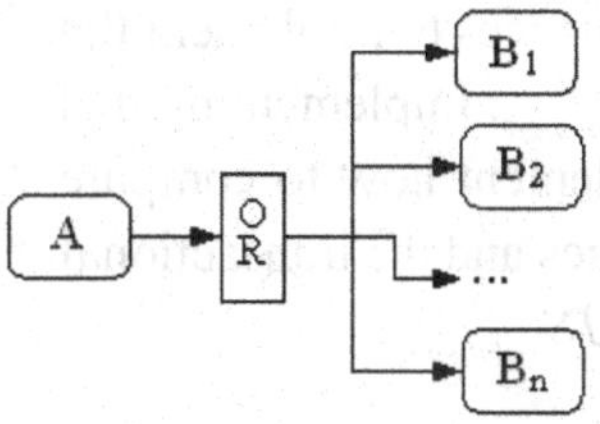 A, OR, B$_1$, B$_2$, …, B$_n$

Figure 8. Rules of join TCS patterns

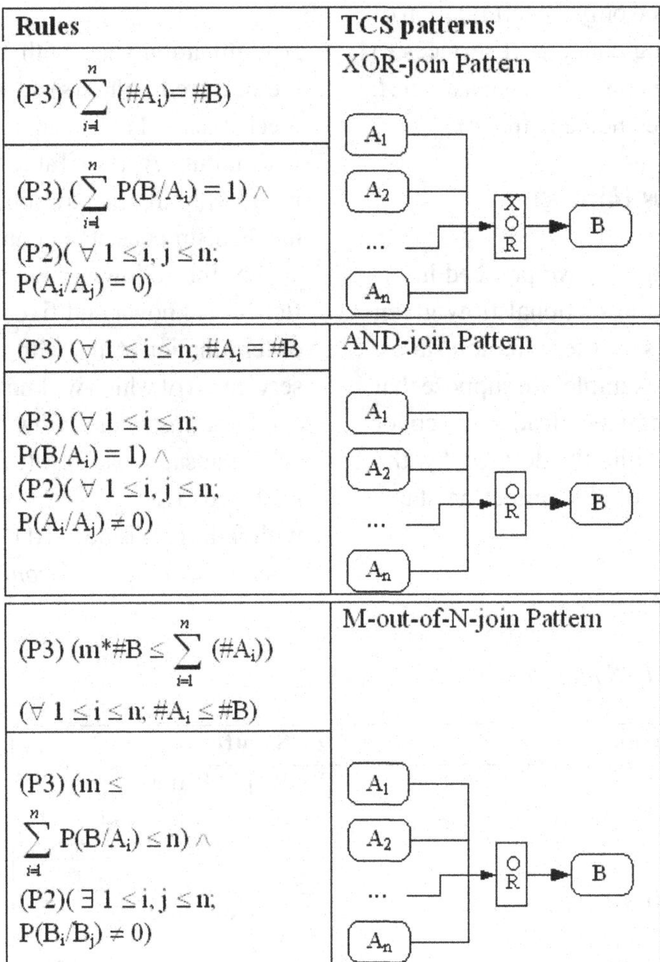

Rules	TCS patterns
(P3) $(\sum_{i=1}^{n} (\#A_i) = \#B)$	XOR-join Pattern
(P3) $(\sum_{i=1}^{n} P(B/A_i) = 1) \wedge$ (P2)($\forall\, 1 \le i, j \le n;$ $P(A_i/A_j) = 0)$	
(P3) $(\forall\, 1 \le i \le n; \#A_i = \#B$	AND-join Pattern
(P3) $(\forall\, 1 \le i \le n;$ $P(B/A_i) = 1) \wedge$ (P2)($\forall\, 1 \le i, j \le n;$ $P(A_i/A_j) \ne 0)$	
(P3) $(m{*}\#B \le \sum_{i=1}^{n} (\#A_i))$ $(\forall\, 1 \le i \le n; \#A_i \le \#B)$	M-out-of-N-join Pattern
(P3) $(m \le \sum_{i=1}^{n} P(B/A_i) \le n) \wedge$ (P2)($\exists\, 1 \le i, j \le n;$ $P(B_i/B_j) \ne 0)$	

function defines for each component service *s*: its transactional properties and its compensation, cancellation, and alternative conditions induced by $STS_{withFailure}$. These conditions specify respectively when s is compensated, canceled, or activated as an alternative according to $STS_{withFailure}$.

Thereafter in order to compute a transactional flow of a TCS given its control flow and its set of termination states it suffices to implement the function $computeTS^{-1}_{withFailure}$. Implementing this function returns to implement how to compute the transactional properties and the transactional conditions induced by $STS_{withFailure}$.

Computing Service Transactional Properties Induced by $STS_{withFailure}$

Given the set of termination states of a composite service we can easily deduce the set of termination states *STS(s)* of each component service *s*. For example, given the set of termination states of the service OTA (given in Table 5) we can deduce that the set of termination states of *FR* is *STS(FR)={completed, compensated, cancelled}*. We use the following rules to compute the transactional properties of a component service. ∀ component service, *s*

Table 5. The extracted set of termination states of the OTA service

	CRS	*LTA*	*HR*	*FR*	*ADC*	*PCC*	*PCh*	*PTIP*	*SD*
ts_1	completed	completed	completed	completed	completed	completed	initial	initial	completed
ts_2	completed	completed	completed	completed	completed	initial	completed	initial	completed
ts_3	completed	completed	completed	completed	completed	initial	initial	completed	completed
ts_4	completed	completed	failed	compensated	initial	initial	initial	initial	initial
ts_5	completed	completed	completed	completed	failed	initial	initial	initial	initial
ts_6	completed	completed	failed	canceled	initial	initial	initial	initial	initial
ts_7	completed	completed	completed	completed	completed	failed	completed	initial	completed
ts_8	completed	completed	completed	completed	completed	initial	initial	failed	initial

1. By default *s* is retriable and not compensatable,
2. if *s.failed* ∈ *STS(s)* then *s* is not retriable,
3. if *s.compensated* ∈ *STS(s)* then *s* is compensatable.

The first and second rules enable to deduce if a service is retriable or not. The first and third rules enable to deduce if a service is compensatable or not. By applying these rules we can deduce, among others, that *FR* is retriable and compensatable. Figure 10.a summarizes the computed transactional properties of component services. Bold properties are the ones that do not match with the initial model.

Computing Transactional Conditions Induced by STSwithFailure

In the following we show how we proceed to compute the compensation condition of a given component service *s* induced by $STS_{withFailure}$. We proceed similarly to compute the cancellation and alternative conditions. Figure 9 allows computing the compensation condition of *s* induced by $STS_{withFailure}$: $CpsCondSTS_{withFailure}(s)$. The principle is: a potential compensation condition of *s* becomes induced by $STS_{withFailure}$ if it occurs in a termination state (with failure) where *s* is compensated.

Thus, the algorithm goes through the set of termination states (line 4 to line 14). For each termination state where *s* is compensated (line 5), the algorithm looks for the potential compensation condition of *s* that holds in this state (line 6 to line 13). Line 7 and line 13 allows going through the potential compensation conditions of *s*. The Boolean variable "satisfied" (line 6 and line 11) enables to mark if the current potential compensation condition holds or not in the current termination state (variable *ts*). A potential compensation condition that holds in *ts* is considered as induced by $STS_{withFailure}$ (line 10). This condition is retrieved from the set of potential compensation condition of *s* in order to not to examine it again in other termination states (line 12).

For example, the potential compensation condition of *FR*, *HR.failed*, becomes induced by $STS_{withFailure}$ (Table 5) because it is satisfied in ts_4 (in which the state of *FR* is compensated). Figure 10.a illustrates the discovered TCS after the control flow and transactional flow mining.

Improving TCS Recovery Mechanisms

To improve recovery mechanisms, we introduce the concept of intuitively valid transactional flow. An intuitively valid transactional flow is, as its name stands, a transactional flow that respects the following properties of well transactional behavior:

- P_1: following a service failure, it tries first to execute an alternative if it exists,
- P_2: otherwise (in case of a fatal failure causing the overall composite service failure) it compensates the work already done and
- P_3: cancel all running executions in parallel.

For example, the discovered transactional flow shown in Figure 10.a is not intuitively valid since it does not respect, among others, the property P_1 for the service *PTIP* and the property P_2 for the service *ADC*.

To improve recovery mechanisms, we propose a set of rules that generate suggestions to designers in order to define an intuitively valid transactional flow (given the computed transactional properties). We suppose that ◇F means F is eventually true: ∀ component service, *s*

1. $\forall ptAltCond_i(s) \in AltCond(s), \diamond(ptAltCond_i(s)) \wedge ptAltCond_i(s) \notin AltCond(s) \Rightarrow$ *suggest that* $AltCond(s) = AltCond(s) \cup ptAltCond_i(s)$.
2. $\forall\ ptCpsCond_i(s) \in ptCpsCond(s), \diamond(ptCpsCond_i(s)) \wedge ptCpsCond_i(s) \notin CpsCond(s) \Rightarrow$ *suggest that*
   a. s must be compensatable and
   b. $CpsCond(s) = CpsCond(s) \cup ptCpsCond_i(s)$.
3. $\forall\ ptCnlCond_i(s) \in ptCnlCond(s), \diamond(ptCnlCond_i(s)) \wedge ptCnlCond_i(s) \notin CnlCond(s) \Rightarrow$ *suggest that* $CnlCond(s) = CnlCond(s) \cup ptCnlCond_i(s)$.

The first rule aims at ensuring the above property P_1. It postulates that each potential alternative condition of *s*, $ptAltCond_i(s)$, eventually true must be considered as an alternative condition of *s*. For example, the potential alternative condition of *PCh* (and *PCC*), *PTIP.failed* is eventually true

Figure 9. Extracting the compensation condition of a service s induced by $STS_{withFailure}$

Input: *STS*: the TCS set of termination states
PtCpsCond(s): The potential compensation condition of s defined by the control flow
Output: $CpsCond_{STSwithFailure}(s)$: the compensation condition of s induced by *STSwithFailure*
Data: *ts*: the current termination state in *STS*
$PtCpsCond_i(s)$: a potential compensation condition of s
satisfied: a Boolean variable set to true when $PtCpsCond_i(s)$ is satisfied in *ts*

```
begin
  CpsCondSTS_withFailure(s) ← ∅
  ts ← the next ts in STS
  while ts ≠ null do
     if the state of s in ts is compensated then
        satisfied ← false
        PtCpsCond_i(s) ← the next PtCpsCond_i(s) in PtCpsCond(s)
        while none satisfied and PtCpsCond_i(s) ≠ null
           if PtCpsCond_i(s) is satisfied in ts then
              CpsCondSTSwithFailure(s) ← CpsCondSTSwithFailure(s) ∪ PtCpsCond_i(s)
              satisfied ← true
              PtCpsCond(s) ← PtCpsCond(s) - PtCpsCond_i(s)
           PtCpsCond_i(s) ← the next PtCpsCond_i(s) in PtCpsCond(s)
     ts ← the next ts in STS
end
```

Figure 10. Discovering and improving the OTA service

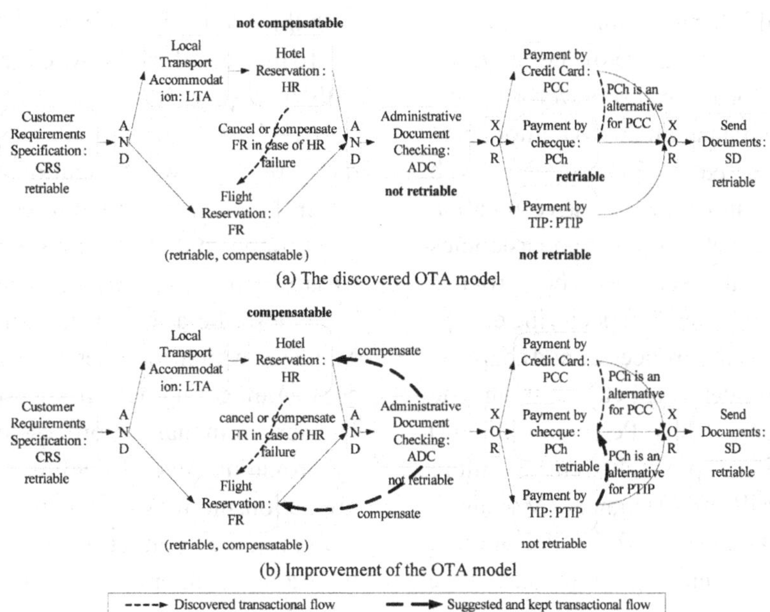

(since *PTIP* is not retriable) and is not considered as one of its alternative conditions. By applying this rule we generate the following suggestion: S_1: add an alternative dependency from *PTIP* to *PCh* and S_2: add an alternative dependency from *PTIP* to *PCC*.

The second rule aims at ensuring the property P_2. It postulates that each potential compensation condition of *s*, *ptCpsCond$_i$(s)*, eventually true must be considered as a compensation condition of *s*. For instance, the potential compensation condition of *HR* (and *FR*), *ADC.failed*, is eventually true (since *ADC* is not retriable) and is not considered as one of its compensation condition. By applying this rule we generate the suggestion S_3: add two compensation dependencies from *ADC* to *FR* and from *ADC* to *HR*. Similarly by applying this rule we generate the suggestion S_4: add a compensation dependency from *HR* to *LTA*. The third rule aims at ensuring the property P_3. It postulates that each potential cancellation condition of *s*, *ptCnlCondi(s)*, eventually true must be considered as a cancellation condition of *s*.

It is worthwhile noting that the designers have the final decision about which suggestions consider and which refuse. For instance, designers may reject suggestions S_2 and S_4 because *PCC* is not retriable and *LTA* is without effect. Doing so, our approach allows taking into account designers specific needs that may violate the well behavior properties introduced above. Figure 10.b illustrates the OTA service after improvement.

RELATED WORK

Several works have been interested in ensuring correct executions of composite services. However to the best of our knowledge none of them, but our previous work (Bhiri, Gaaloul et al. 2008), tackled such problem from a reengineering perspective.

Some previous approaches analyze composition models and check correctness properties a priori. (Bultan, Fu et al. 2003) propose a formal framework for modeling, specifying and analyzing the global behavior of Web service compositions. This approach models web services using mealy machines (finite state machines with input an output). Based on this formal framework, authors illustrate the unexpected nature of the interplay between local and global composite Web services. In (Hamadi, Benatallah et al. 2008) authors propose Petri net-based algebra for composing Web services. This formal model allows the verification of properties and the detection of inconsistencies both between and within services. They propose an extended Petri net model for specifying exceptional behavior in business processes and adapt the mechanisms of the underlying Petri net at run time to handle exceptions. (Bhiri, Perrin et al. 2005) propose a transactional approach to ensure failure atomicity as required by the designers. (Montagut, Molva et al. 2008) builds on (Bhiri, Perrin et al. 2005) to define a procedure for automatic service composition that takes into account designers' transactional requirements. (Li, Liu et al. 2007) present an approach that computes the transactional properties of a composite Web service and check if it is schedulable or not.

Emerged standards such as WS-TXM (Acid, BP, LRA) (Doug, Martin et al. 2003), WS-AtomicTransaction (Little and Wilkinson 2007) and WS-Business-Activity (Freund and Litlle 2007) define transaction protocols between composed services. These approaches rely on advanced transactional models (Elmagarmid 1992). (Limthanmaphon and Zhang 2004) present a transaction management model based on the tentative hold and compensation concepts. (Ray and Xin 2006) investigate how to correctly specify dependencies in advanced transactions. The authors classify transactional dependencies in two categories: event ordering and event enforcement dependencies. Then they describe different types of conflicts that can arise due to the presence of multiple dependencies and describe how one can detect such conflicts.

Although powerful, the above approaches may fail in some cases to ensure reliable executions even if they validate their composition models formally. This is because properties specified in the studied composition models may not coincide with the reality (i.e. effective CS executions).

To the best of our knowledge, there are practically no approaches to correct transactional web services based on event-based logs, and in general there are very few contributions in this area. Prior art in this field is limited to estimating deadline expirations and exceptions prediction (Sayal, Casati et al. 2002; Grigori, Casati et al. 2004). They describe a tool set on top of HPs Process Manager which includes a so-called "BPI Process Mining Engine". It supports business and IT users in managing process execution quality by providing several features, such as analysis, prediction, monitoring, control, and optimization. However, they neither discuss the correctness of transactional interactions nor address the issue of failures handling and recovery. Indeed, our approach differs from the above: we discover and prevent transactional anomalies and also propose solutions to enhance the CS model. We start from a CS log and analyze it in order to reengineer the CS model.

A number of research efforts in the area of workflow management have been directed for mining workflows models. This issue is close to that we propose in terms of discovery. There are practically no approaches to transactional behavior mining except in (Gaaloul, Bhiri et al. 2004a; Gaaloul, Bhiri et al. 2004b). Indeed, previous works in workflow discovery focus mainly on control flow mining. The idea of applying process mining in the context of workflow management was first introduced in (Agrawal, Gunopulos et al. 1998). This work proposes methods for automatically deriving a formal model of a process from a log of events related to its executions and is based on workflow graphs, which are inspired by workflow products such as IBM MQSeries workflow (formerly known as Flowmark) and InConcert. Cook and Wolf (Cook and Wolf 1998a) investigated similar issues in the context of software engineering processes. These works are limited to sequential processes.

Cook and Wolf extended their work, in (Cook and Wolf 1998b), to concurrent processes. Herbst et al. (Herbest, 2000a; Herbest, 2000b) present an inductive learning component used to support the acquisition and adaptation of sequential process models, generalizing execution traces from different workflow instances to a workflow model covering all traces. Starting from the same kind of process logs, van der Aalst et al. (van der Aalst, Weijters et al. 2003) explore also the area of workflow process mining. They propose techniques to discover workflow models expressed in their own desired workflow modeling notation, which is based on Petri nets. (van der Aalst, Dumas et al. 2008) check and quantify how much the actual behavior of a process, as recorded in execution logs, conforms to the expected behavior as specified in a process model. (Rozinat and van der Aalst 2005) use log analysis techniques to measure process alignments, i.e. to compare the execution behavior with the intended behavior. However, this work does not describe how to use the results of this process alignment to improve or correct the process model. (de Medeiros, Weijters et al 2007) propose genetic algorithms to tackle log noise problem or non-trivial constructs using a global search technique.

Compared to these works our control flow mining approach focuses on concurrent behavior. Indeed, we give better specification of concurrency behavior through the discovery of control flow patterns. In addition, we propose a set of control flow mining rules that are characterized by "local" patterns discovery. These rules are context-free, they proceed through a local log analysis enabling us to recover partial results correctly even if we have only fractions of executions' log. Moreover, our approach discovers an M-out-of-N-Join pattern which can be seen as a generalisation of the Discriminator pattern, a non free-choice construct which is considered a difficult pattern to mine.

CONCLUSION

In this chapter we presented an original approach for ensuring reliable Web service compositions. Different from previous works, our approach starts from a composite service (CS for short) executions log and uses a set of mining techniques to discover its control flow and its transactional flow. Then, based on this mining step, we use a set of rules to improve its recovery mechanisms according to designers' specific needs.

Our composition model distinguishes explicitly between the control flow and the transactional flow. We show the relation between them. This composition model integrates efficiently workflow ability for defining complex control structure and transactional models reliability. We also discussed the existing Web logging solutions and gave advanced solutions in order to track CS execution and build the corresponding logs.

Compared to other techniques, our process mining approach distinguishes itself by using a set of control flow mining rules that are characterized by a "local" pattern discovery enabling partial results to be discovered from log fractions. In addition, our approach discovers more behavioral complex features with a better specification of "fork" point and "join" point. Moreover, it deals better with concurrency through the introduction of the "*concurrent window*" that proceeds dynamically with concurrency. Indeed, the size of the "*concurrent window*" is not static or fixed, but variable according to the activity's concurrent behaviour without increasing the computing complexity.

However, the work described in this paper represents an initial investigation. In our future works, we hope to discover more complex patterns by using more metrics (e.g. entropy, periodicity, etc.) and by enriching the TCS log. We are also interested in the modeling and the discovery of more complex transactional characteristics of cooperative TCSs.

ACKNOWLEDGMENT

This material is based upon works jointly supported by the Science Foundation Ireland under Grant No. SFI/08/CE/I1380 and the EU funding under the SUPER project (FP6-026850).

REFERENCES

Agrawal, R., Gunopulos, D., & Leymann, F. (1998). Mining Process Models from Workflow Logs. In *Proceedings of the 6th International Conference on Extending Database Technology* (pp. 469-498). Valencia, Spain.

Anbazhagan, M., & Arun, N. (2002). Use SOAP-based intermediaries to build chains of Web service functionality. Retrieved September 1, 2002 from http://www.ibm.com/developerworks/java/library/ws-soapbase/?loc=dwmain.

Bhiri, S., Gaaloul, W., & Godart, C. (2008). Mining and Improving Composite Web Services Recovery Mechanisms. *International Journal of Web Services Research, 5*(2), 23–48.

Bhiri, S., Godart, C., & Perrin, O. (2006). Transactional patterns for reliable web services compositions, In *Proceedings of the 6th international conference on Web engineering* (pp. 137-144). Palo Alto.

Bhiri, S., Perrin, O., & Godart, C. (2005). Ensuring required failure atomicity of composite Web services, In *Proceedings of the 14th International World Wide Web Conference* (pp. 138-147). Chiba, Japan.

Bultan, T., Fu, X., Hull, R., & Su, J. (2003). Conversation specification: a new approach to design and analysis of e-service composition. In *Proceedings of the 12th International World Wide Web Conference* (pp. 403-410). Budapest, Hungary.

Cook, J. E., & Wolf, A. L. (1998a). Discovering models of software processes from event-based data. [TOSEM]. *ACM Transactions on Software Engineering and Methodology, 7*(3), 215–249. doi:10.1145/287000.287001

Cook, J. E., & Wolf, A. L. (1998b). Event-based detection of concurrency. In *Proceedings of 6th ACM SIGSOFT FSE conference* (pp. 35-45). Florida, USA.

de Medeiros, A. K. A., Weijters, A. J. M. M., & van der Aalst, W. M. P. (2007). Genetic process mining: an experimental evaluation. *Data Mining and Knowledge Discovery, 14*(2), 245–304. doi:10.1007/s10618-006-0061-7

Doug, B., Martin, C., Oisin, H., Mark, L., Jeff, M., Eric, N., et al. (2003). Web Services Composite Application Framework (WS-CAF). Retrieved July 28, 2003 from http://www.arjuna.com/standards/ws-caf/

Elmagarmid, A. K. (Ed.). (1992). *Database transaction models for advanced applications*. San Francisco: Morgan Kaufmann Publishers Inc.

Fauvet, M.-C., Dumas, M., & Benatallah, B. (2002). Collecting and Querying Distributed Traces of Composite Service Executions. In *Proceedings of the 14th International Conference on Cooperative Information Systems* (pp. 373-390). California.

Freund, T., & Little, M. (Eds.). (2007). *Web Service Business Activity Version 1.1*. Retrieved April 16, 2007 from http://docs.oasis-open.org/ws-tx/wstx-wsba-1.1-spec-os.pdf

Gaaloul, W., Baïna, K., & Godart, C. (2008). Log-based mining techniques applied to Web service composition reengineering. [SOCA]. *Service Oriented Computing and Applications, 2*(2-3), 93–110. doi:10.1007/s11761-008-0023-6

Gaaloul, W., Bhiri, S., & Godart, C. (2004a). Discovering Workflow Patterns from Timed Logs. In *Proceedings of Informationssysteme im E-Business und E-Government, Beiträge des Workshops derGI-Fachgruppe EMISA* (pp. 84-94). LNI, Luxemburg.

Gaaloul, W., Bhiri, S., & Godart, C. (2004b). Discovering Workflow Transactional Behavior from Event based Log. In *Proceedings of the 12th International Conference on Cooperative Information Systems*, Cyprus, October 2004, 25-29.

Gamma, E., Helm, R., Johnson, R., & Vlisside, J. (1995). *Design Patterns: Elements of Reusable Object-Oriented Software*. Reading, MA: Addison-Wesley.

Grigori, D., Casati, F., Castellanos, M., Dayal, U., Sayal, M., & Shan, M.-C. (2004). Business process intelligence. *Computers in Industry, 53*(3), 321–343. doi:10.1016/j.compind.2003.10.007

Hamadi, R., & Benatallah, B. (2003). A Petri net-based model for web service composition. In *Proceedings of the Australasian Database Conference* (pp. 191-200). Adelaide, Australia.

Herbest, J. (2000a). A Machine Learning Approach to Workflow Management. In *Proceedings of the 11th European Conference on Machine Learning* (pp. 183-194). Barcelona, Spain.

Herbest, J. (2000b). Dealing with Concurrency in Workflow Induction. In *Proceedings of the European Concurrent Engineering Conference*, Leicester, United Kingdom.

Li, L., Liu, C., & Wang, J. (2005). Deriving Transactional Properties of CompositeWeb Services. In *Proceedings of IEEE International Conference on Web Services* (pp. 631-638). Salt Lake City, USA.

Limthanmaphon, B., & Zhang, Y. (2004). Web service composition transaction management. In *Proceedings of the 15th Australasian Database Conference* (pp. 171-179). Dunedin, New Zealand.

Little, M., & Wilkinson, A. (Eds.). (2007). Web ServiceAtomic Transaction Version 1.1. Retrieved April 16, 2007 from http://docs.oasis-open.org/ws-tx/wstx-wsat-1.1-spec-os.pdf.

Mehrotra, S., Rastogi, R., Korth, H. F., & Silberschatz, A. (1992). A Transaction Model for Multidatabase Systems. In *Proceedings of International Conference on Distributed Computing Systems* (pp. 56-63). Yokohama, Japan.

Montagut, F., Molva, R., & Golega, S. T. (2008). Automating the Composition of transactional Web Services. *International Journal of Web Services Research, 5*(1), 24–41.

Punin, J., Krishnamoorthy, M., & Zaki, M. (2001). Web Usage Mining: Languages and Algorithms. In *Proceedings of Studies in Classification, Data Analysis, and Knowledge Organization*. Springer-Verlag.

Ray, I., & Xin, T. (2006). Analysis of dependencies in advanced transaction models. *Distributed and Parallel Databases, 20*(1), 5–27. doi:10.1007/s10619-006-8593-9

Rouached, M., Gaaloul, W., van der Aalst, W. M. P., Bhiri, S., & Godart, C. (2006). Web Service Mining and verification of Properties: An approach based on Event Calculus. In *Proceedings of the International Cooperative Information Systems* (pp. 408-425). Montpellier, France.

Rozinat, A., & van der Aalst, W. M. P. (2005). Conformance testing: measuring the fit and appropriateness of event logs and process models. In *Proceedings* of *Business Process Management Workshops* (pp. 163–176). Nancy, France.

Sahai, A., Machiraju, V., Ouyang, J., & Wurster, K. (2001). *Message tracking in SOAP-based Web services* (Tech Rep HPL-2001-199). Retrieved 2001 from http://www.hpl.hp.com/techreports/2001/HPL-2001-199.html.

Sayal, M., Casati, F., Shan, M., & Dayal, U. (2002). Business Process Cockpit. In *Proceedings of 28th International Conference on Very Large Data Bases* (pp. 880-883). Hong Kong, China.

van der Aalst, W. M. P., Dumas, M., Ouyang, C., Rozinat, A., & Verbeek, H. M. W. (2008). Conformance checking of service behaviour. [TOIT]. *ACM Transactions on Internet Technology*, *8*(3), 13.

van der Aalst, W. M. P., ter Hofstede, A. H. M., Kiepuszewski, B., & Barros, A. P. (2003). Workflow Patterns. *Distributed and Parallel Databases*, *14*(1), 5–51. doi:10.1023/A:1022883727209

van der Aalst, W. M. P., Weijters, T., & Maruster, L. (2004). Workflow Mining: Discovering Process Models from Event Logs. *IEEE Transactions on Knowledge and Data Engineering*, *16*(9), 1128–1142. doi:10.1109/TKDE.2004.47

Chapter 14
Karma2:
Provenance Management for Data-Driven Workflows[1]

Yogesh L. Simmhan
Microsoft Research, USA

Beth Plale
Indiana University, USA

Dennis Gannon
Indiana University, USA

ABSTRACT

The increasing ability for the sciences to sense the world around us is resulting in a growing need for data-driven e-Science applications that are under the control of workflows composed of services on the Grid. The focus of our work is on provenance collection for these workflows that are necessary to validate the workflow and to determine quality of generated data products. The challenge we address is to record uniform and usable provenance metadata that meets the domain needs while minimizing the modification burden on the service authors and the performance overhead on the workflow engine and the services. The framework is based on generating discrete provenance activities during the lifecycle of a workflow execution that can be aggregated to form complex data and process provenance graphs that can span across workflows. The implementation uses a loosely coupled publish-subscribe architecture for propagating these activities, and the capabilities of the system satisfy the needs of detailed provenance collection. A performance evaluation of a prototype finds a minimal performance overhead (in the range of 1% for an eight-service workflow using 271 data products).

INTRODUCTION

The need to access and share large-scale computational and data resources to support dynamic computational science and agile enterprises is driving the growth of Grids (Foster, Kesselman, Nick & Tuecke, 2002). In the realm of e-Science, *science gateways* are archetypes for accessing, managing, and sharing virtualized resources to solve large collaboratory challenges (Catlett, 2002; Gannon et al., 2005). Science gateways are built as a *service-oriented architecture* with Grid resources virtualized as services. These resources—including physical resources such as sensors, computational clusters, and mass storage devices, and software resources such as scientific tasks and models—are available as services that provide an abstraction to access the resources through well-defined interfaces.

A significant constituent of applications that make use of the science gateways is *data-driven applications* (Simmhan, Pallickara, Vijayakumar & Plale, 2006a). The proliferation of wireless networking and inexpensive sensor technology is allowing the sciences an increasing ability to sense the world around us (West, 2005). This is specifically resulting in a growing need for data-driven applications; that is, applications that can be computation-intense and are usually either dataflow applications in which data flows from one process to another, or demand-driven in which computations are triggered in response to events occurring in the world around us. Data-driven scientific experiments are designed as workflows composed of services on the Grid, and data flow from one service to another, being transformed, filtered, fused, and used in complex models. These workflows capture the invocation logic for the scientific investigation and may be composed of hundreds of services connected as complex graphs. Data-driven workflow executions also see the participation of thousands of data products that reach terabytes in size. At this scale of processing, users need the ability to automatically track the execution of their experiments and the multitude of data products created and consumed by the services in the workflow. Provenance collection and management, also called process mining, workflow tracing, or lineage collection, is a new line of research on the execution of workflows, and the derivation and usage trail of data products that are involved in the workflows (Bose & Frew, 2005; Moreau & Ludascher, 2007; Simmhan, Plale & Gannon, 2005).

Provenance collected about the tasks of a workflow describes the workflow's service invocations during its execution (Simmhan et al., 2005). This helps track service and resource usage patterns, and forms metadata for service and workflow discovery. In data-driven applications, however, it is provenance about the data that is central to understanding and recreating earlier runs. In *data-driven workflows*, data products are first-class parameters to services that consume and transform the input data to generate derived data products. These derived data products are ingested by other services in the same or a different workflow, forming a data derivation and data usage trail. *Data provenance* provides this derivation history of data that includes information about services and input data that contributed to the creation of a data product. This kind of information is extremely valuable, not only for diagnosing problems and understanding performance of a particular workflow run, but also to determine the origin and quality of a particular piece of derived information (Goble, 2002; Simmhan, Plale & Gannon, 2006b).

Current methods of collecting provenance are from workflow engine logs (IBM, 2005) or by instrumenting the services (Bose & Frew, 2004; Zhao, Wroe, Goble, Stevens, Quan & Greenwood, 2004). In the former case, the logs from the workflow engine are at the message level and insufficient for deciphering provenance about the data products, while instrumenting services introduce a burden on the service author to modify their service to generate provenance metadata. They also tend to be specific to the workflow framework and are not interoperable with heterogeneous workflow models that are likely to be present in a Grid environment. Work is also emerging on more general information models for provenance collection (Moreau & Ludascher, 2007).

The challenge we address in our work is to record uniform and usable provenance metadata independent of the workflow or service framework used, while minimizing the modification burden on the service authors and the performance overhead on the workflow engine and the services. The Karma provenance framework we describe collects two forms of provenance: *process provenance*, also known as workflow trace (Simmhan et al., 2005), which is metadata describing the workflow's execution and associated service invocations; and *data provenance,* which provides complementary metadata about the derivation history of the data product, including services used and input data sources transformed to generate it. These forms of provenance allow scientists to monitor workflow progress at runtime (Gannon et al., 2005) and, post-execution, mine the provenance to locate sources of errors, determine data quality (Simmhan et al., 2006b), and validate the results through repetition or simulated replay of the workflow execution (Szomszor & Moreau, 2003). It also assists resource providers to review resource usage for purposes of auditing (Greenwood et al., 2003) and provisioning (Churches et al., 2006).

This article details the Karma provenance framework for collecting and managing provenance for data-driven workflows. The current Karma system, which we describe in this article, builds upon previous exploratory work we undertook on provenance management; hence the allusion to the present Karma version 2, or Karma2. The remainder of the article is organized as follows. In Section 2, we motivate the need for provenance collection with an example from mesoscale meteorology, which is an exemplar domain for data-driven applications. In Section 3, we define a generalized data-driven workflow model for which the provenance is collected. In section 4, we discuss provenance activities that occur during the lifetime of the workflow that go toward building provenance. Section 5 describes the provenance model of Karma and the various forms of provenance that are available. Section 6 grounds the provenance model in an implementation of the framework that we discuss. Section 7 presents details on performance evaluation of provenance collection and querying. Related work appears in Section 8 and future work in Section 9.

MOTIVATION

Scientific workflows (Yu & Buyya, 2005) often use a *service-oriented architecture* to solve advanced scientific problems in a Grid environment (Gannon et al., 2005). Workflows are composed from services that provide a well-defined functionality with open interfaces to access them. Workflows model the interactions between the services as directed graphs whose edges represent dependencies and dataflows, and incorporate decision-making logic for runtime selection of execution paths (BEA, 2003). There are different models for workflow execution. Orchestration can be done by a central workflow engine that interprets the workflow document and invokes the services according to the dependencies, ensuring dataflow between connected services. Execution may also be handled in a distributed manner by the services themselves.

In the Linked Environments for Atmospheric Discovery (LEAD) (Droegemeier et al., 2005) project, regional-scale numerical weather forecasting is done using dynamically adaptive workflows, as shown in Figure 1, that run end-to-end forecast models. These computationally intense workflows may be launched on demand in response to a severe weather event and may ingest new data products at any point during execution directly

Figure 1. Sample LEAD weather forecasting workflow

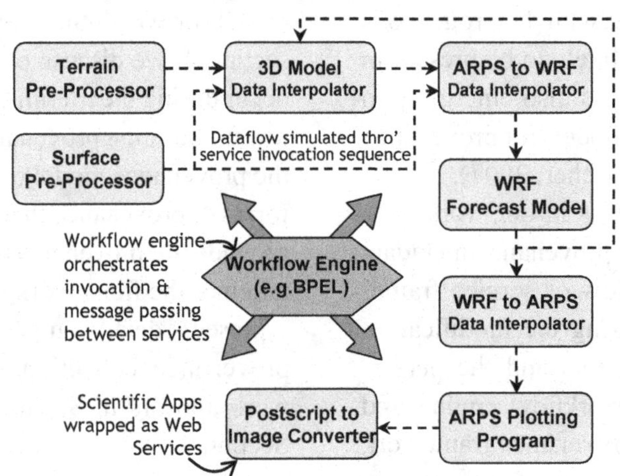

from real-time observational sources. The model data products generated by the services may be reused in the same or in a different workflow, forming a data processing pipeline (Liu, Franklin, Garlick & Abdulla, 2005; Ludäscher et al., 2006). The *dynamic* nature of the workflows means that the workflow execution path is not static and can change at runtime due to external events, while *adaptability* implies the ability to bind to an appropriate and available service instance at the time of workflow execution.

A typical meteorological experiment shown in Figure 1 is a weather prediction workflow using the Weather Research and Forecasting (WRF) Model. Pre-processing, interpolation, post-processing, and visualization are done by the Advanced Regional Prediction System (ARPS) Model. The workflow is composed using the Business Process Execution Language (BPEL) and orchestrated by a central BPEL engine (Slominski, 2006). The workflow can be broadly divided into pre-processing and grid interpolation stage (Services 1–4, Figure 1, starting with Surface Pre-Processor and moving clockwise), numerical weather prediction stage (Service 5), and post-processing and visualization stage (Services 6–8). Each of these services produces and consumes between 4 and 100 data products in the form of files, transparently referenced through URIs (Plale, 2005). This workflow applied to data from Hurricane Katrina's landfall on the Gulf Coast in 2005 is used for the performance evaluation in Section 7. More complex workflows with high degrees of parallelism and complex conditional logic are also seen in LEAD when running ensemble simulations (Droegemeier et al., 2005).

Provenance is collected from such workflows in order to verify that a simulation run was successful and to validate its results. This may be through visual inspection of the provenance graphs or through automated processes. This is important, given the dynamic and adaptive nature of the workflows, to determine what really happened. Data provenance also helps to keep track of data products used by and generated from the experiments and discover them for reuse at a later time. This can even avoid running the workflow if an identical run made by another user has generated the required output data and the workflow is deterministic. Data quality models have been developed to mine historic provenance information for patterns of service execution that can assist in making quality predictions about data products generated by services as a function of their input data and parameters (Simmhan et al., 2006b).

WORKFLOW MODEL

An abstract workflow model, for which provenance is collected, is necessary to ensure that the provenance model is independent of the workflow implementation or design. This generalized data-driven workflow model is based on a service-oriented architecture, with four principal components: *workflows, services, service clients*, and *data products* that are produced and consumed within the workflow. Services are black-box tasks accessed through a well-defined interface. They frequently are, but not limited to Web services by the model. The workflow is a *directed graph* of services, with the services forming nodes in the graph and its edges constituting dataflow between services or applications wrapped by the service. The graph can have cycles such as iterative loops. Workflows themselves are considered services, allowing them to participate in other workflows. This allows for a hierarchical pattern of constructing workflows by reusing existing workflows and services.

Data products, often logical or physical files, are passed as inputs to and generated as outputs from a service invocation. The data products are identified by a globally unique ID in the request and response messages, and they are said to be *consumed* by that service invocation if used as input, while those newly created by that invocation are said to be *produced* by it. Every service invocation in a data-driven workflow consumes or produces data products, and these form their own dataflow graph, which is captured as part of the provenance.

Paradigms for Workflow Execution and Service Invocation

There are several invocation paradigms for running workflows (Yu & Buyya, 2005). In a *centralized model*, such as used by BPEL, a central workflow engine that has the workflow dependency logic invokes the services in the workflow in succession, passing messages between the services and acting as their client. As a variation, the control could be distributed, with different engines being aware of a portion of the workflow graph (e.g., one engine for each workflow in a nested workflow) and acting as clients at different times of the workflow lifecycle. In a *component model* (Armstrong et al., 1999; OMG, 2006), each service in the workflow would be aware of the subsequent service(s) "connected" to it and invoke the next service(s) once its invocation completes, thus acting as a client to the next service(s).

An invocation of a service by a client, be it a workflow engine, another service, or just a stand-alone client, can either be *synchronous* or *asynchronous*. In the former, the invocation request message is sent to the service and the client blocks until the response message, which may be a successful result or a fault, is returned by the service. In the latter, a request by the client returns an acknowledgement message synchronously (if the request was received successfully; otherwise, an exception), while the actual response from for the invocation arrives at a later time (i.e., in the form of a callback to the client).

All these paradigms are possible in the generalized workflow model we consider, and hence, the provenance model we describe is compatible to these, too. In the interest of space, we restrict our examples in this article to a *centralized workflow engine* that acts as an *asynchronous client* to the services, which we have found is a common use case.

Resource Naming and Unique IDs

One fundamental requirement of provenance is the ability to uniquely identify the data products whose provenance is being described, as well as the services that use or generate these data products. This is driven by the fact that the service and the data products are distributed across organizational and geographical boundaries, and also by the fact that the provenance needs to be preserved for a period longer than the lifetime of the services or the workflows themselves. All resources that participate on our workflow model, including running or completed workflow instances, service instances, and data products, are assigned a globally unique identifier (GUID). These are referred to as *Workflow ID*, *Service ID*, and *Data Product ID*, respectively. It is possible to transparently map from these logical IDs to the actual physical resources, which may be an endpoint reference or a data URL, through a naming service. Use of such logical handles to resources instead of physical addresses makes the provenance independent of the data product representation since they are identified by just an ID, which could equally well point to a remote file, a database tuple, or a virtual collection. The format of the GUID does not matter as long as its uniqueness is guaranteed. Another identifier that is assigned to services in the context of a composed workflow is the *Workflow Node ID*. This ID is distinct for every service (node) in an abstract workflow. It differs from the Service ID in that late binding of workflows allows them to use different service instances for the same node when invoked in different iterations.

PROVENANCE ACTIVITIES

Provenance is collected during the lifecycle of the generalized workflow model in the form of discrete activities that are expressed using an *activity* object. These activity objects are generated by the services and clients that participate in the workflow during a service invocation, and are distributed over *time*, *space*, *depth*, and *type of operation*. Some of these activities define the boundaries of the invocation, while others describe the operation being performed. These provenance activity objects sufficiently describe the workflow execution and the dataflow to enable reconstruction of the workflow and data provenance graph exclusively from this runtime information without requiring access to the original workflow graph that was composed.

Activity Dimensions

The workflow model executes as a series of invocations over time that results in devolvement of control to different depths in the workflow execution, and within each invocation context, operations defined in the service implementation are performed. Activity objects can be distributed over several dimensions in the activity space, and certain attributes present in the activity object will help place the activity at the exact point in this space. This allows the activities to identify the invocation state and the operations that take place as part of the invocation unambiguously.

Starting with a client that initiates the workflow, control passes to the services in the workflow, and deeper still into nested workflows that these services may represent. The dimension of *depth* gives the distance of a service invocation from the root of the workflow graph, and holds for all activities generated by that service invocation. The depth comes out through the parent-child relationship between the workflow and the invoked service that is part of that workflow. The activity object contains the globally unique *Workflow ID* for the workflow that this service invocation is part of as well as the *Service ID* for the service. If this service invoked is itself another child workflow, the service invocations it performs would contain the Workflow ID of the child workflow as well as the service IDs of services invoked. These Workflow ID–Service ID pairs make it possible to determine the depth of an invocation in the workflow graph in a recursive manner.

Activities take place as discrete events ordered over time, and the logical time forms an additional dimension to distinguish between activities. A *logical timestamp* attribute present in the activity helps with temporal ordering of the activities, in addition to causal ordering that may be implicit. For example, during an invocation, the invocation started activity would have to appear before the invocation finished activity, and hence can be implicitly ordered, while activities that described several data products being generated by the invocation may have appeared in any order unless explicitly sequenced using a logical timestamp. Logical time is also necessary to order across service invocations, if there is no causality between them in the form of a dataflow from one to another. While a dataflow between all services is the norm in data-driven workflows, we presuppose a globally synchronized logical time to support non-dataflow workflows too.

The services and clients are distributed in *space*, and the workflow execution takes places across different services. The ability to identify the service instance through a globally unique ID helps distinguish between instances in space. Finally, the various *operations* that take place as part of the invocation, including dataflow operations that produce or consume a data product, are a separate dimension of the activity object. Depending on the type of operation, there may be additional attributes to fully describe them.

Activity Types

Bounding activities describe the interaction between two entities: the client invoking a service and the service being invoked. These activities are generated at the boundaries of the invocation, when an invocation request or response is being exchanged between the service and the client. For each request and response message, three activities are generated: two by the initiator of the message before and after sending it, and one by the receiver of the message upon receiving it. In the case of an invocation request message from the client to service, this includes the InvokingService activity before sending the request message to the service and the ServiceInvoked activity after the request message has been sent to the service. The service generates one ServiceInvoked activity upon receiving the request message. Similarly for the response sent by the service to the client, three activities are generated as shown in Table 1.

The activity objects that are generated contain several attributes that describe the activity's dimensions and uniquely identify the entities that participate in the interaction. The state of the client and service entities at the time of invocation is given by a set of attributes collectively referred to as the *entity ID*, which is a complex key consisting of {*<u>Service ID</u>*, *Workflow ID*, *Workflow Node ID*, *Logical Timestamp*}. The entity ID for a service requires the Service ID. If this service invocation is part of a workflow run, the entity ID additionally has the Workflow ID of that workflow, the Workflow Node ID of this service in that workflow, and logical timestamp of this invocation. If the client were itself another service, then it would have a similar entity ID that reflects its own state when initiating the invocation. Otherwise, the client would just identify itself through the Service ID attribute. Having both the client and service entity IDs present in the bounding activities serves two purposes: (1) it allows the client and service to present their individual views of the invocation information so that any conflicting views can be detected; and (2) in the absence of activities generated by either the client or the service, it provides the minimum, although one-sided, information required to reconstruct the invocation chain.

Operation activities describe the tasks that take place within a service invocation and occur between the bounding activities. The operations that take place depend on the type of service. However, for a data-driven workflow, two operations that are guaranteed to take place and are of interest to provenance are the consumption and production of data products. When a service uses a data product in an invocation, the service is said to have consumed the data product, and it generates a DataConsumed activity. When a service creates a new data product during the course of an invocation, it generates a DataProduced activity. These consumed and produced data products may or may

Table 1. List of provenance activities, the source of the activity, and the attributes present in each. The activities are listed in the order in which they are typically generated. Attributes that are underlined are required. Those in italics are complex attributes composed of those in curly braces. A '+' after an attribute represents an array, while a choice is denoted by a '|'.

Activity	Generated By	Attributes NOTE: Timestamp, Description, and Annotation are common to all activities
ServiceInitialized	Service	Service ID, is Workflow
ServiceTerminated	Service	Service ID
InvokingService	Client	*Client Entity ID* {Service ID, Workflow ID, Workflow Node ID, Logical Timestamp}, *Service Entity ID* {Service ID, Workflow ID, Workflow Node ID, Logical Timestamp}, Request Message
ServiceInvoked	Service	*Service Entity ID* {Service ID, Workflow ID, Workflow Node ID, Logical Timestamp}, *Client Entity ID* {Service ID, Workflow ID, Workflow Node ID, Logical Timestamp}, Request Message
InvokingService [Succeeded | Failed]	Client	*Client Entity ID* {Service ID, Workflow ID, Workflow Node ID, Logical Timestamp}, *Service Entity ID* {Service ID, Workflow ID, Workflow Node ID, Logical Timestamp}, [— | Failure Trace]
DataTransfer	Service	*Service Entity ID* {Service ID, Workflow ID, Workflow Node ID, Logical Timestamp}, Data ID, Source URL, Target URL, Size, Duration
Computation	Service	*Service Entity ID* {Service ID, Workflow ID, Workflow Node ID, Logical Timestamp}, Application, Duration
DataProduced	Service	*Service Entity ID* {Service ID, Workflow ID, Workflow Node ID, Logical Timestamp}, *Data Product*+ {Data ID, URL+, Size, Timestamp}
DataConsumed	Service	*Service Entity ID* {Service ID, Workflow ID, Workflow Node ID, Logical Timestamp}, *Data Product*+ {Data ID, URL+, Size, Timestamp}
SendingResponse	Service	*Service Entity ID* {Service ID, Workflow ID, Workflow Node ID, Logical Timestamp}, *Client Entity ID* {Service ID, Workflow ID, Workflow Node ID, Logical Timestamp}, Response Message {Result | Fault}
ReceivedResponse	Client	*Client Entity ID* {Service ID, Workflow ID, Workflow Node ID, Logical Timestamp}, *Service Entity ID* {Service ID, Workflow ID, Workflow Node ID, Logical Timestamp}, Response Message {Result | Fault}
SendingResponse [Succeeded | Failed]	Service	*Service Entity ID* {Service ID, Workflow ID, Workflow Node ID, Logical Timestamp}, *Client Entity ID* {Service ID, Workflow ID, Workflow Node ID, Logical Timestamp}, [— | Failure Trace]

not have been passed as parameters in the request or response messages sent to/from the service. Other than the entity ID of the service and client, these activities contain the Data Product ID of the data that were produced or consumed as attribute. In addition to these *dataflow* operations, two other operations that usually take place in scientific workflows are data transfer and computation. We define these two additional activities given the nature of the e-Science project for which Karma was designed. The operation activities and their attributes are listed in Table 1.

Example

The set of activities generated by a service invocation or a workflow changes with the pattern of execution. For example, a service could be invoked synchronously or asynchronously, and a workflow can be invoked by a workflow engine or enact as components in a dataflow. We present two examples of service and workflow execution with corresponding provenance activities generated for them plotted as a sequence diagram.

Figure 2(a) shows a client invoking a service, passing data product D1 as input and receiving D2 as output. This invocation can take place synchronously or asynchronously, and the sequence diagram for each of these styles of execution is shown in Figure 2(b) and 2(c), respectively. The diagrams show the transfer of control from the client to the service at different points in the invocation over *time*, shown in the Y Axis. The activities produced at each state are marked with a red circle, and the type of activity is in the left column. The center column shows the distribution of the client and service entities over *space* and their *depth*. Since this case has just two levels of depth—the client and the service—the depth shown on the top X axis moves from the solid line to the dotted line. The spatial location of the entity, shown on the lower X axis, varies with each unique entity. The vertical lines in the right column represent various *operations* the service performs during its invocation.

Figure 2a. Client invoking a service, passing data product D1 as input and receiving D2 as output

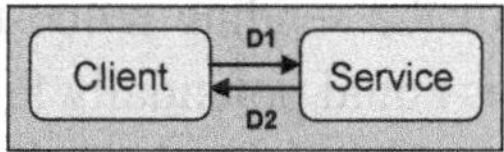

Figure 2b. Sequence diagram of a synchronous invocation of Figure 2a

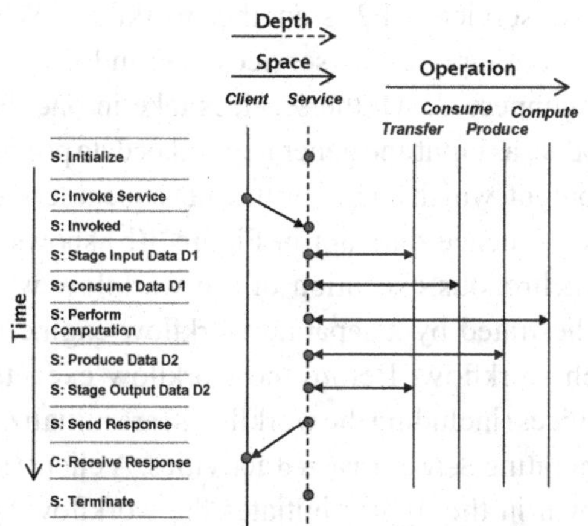

Figure 2c. Sequence diagram of an asynchronous invocation of Figure 2a

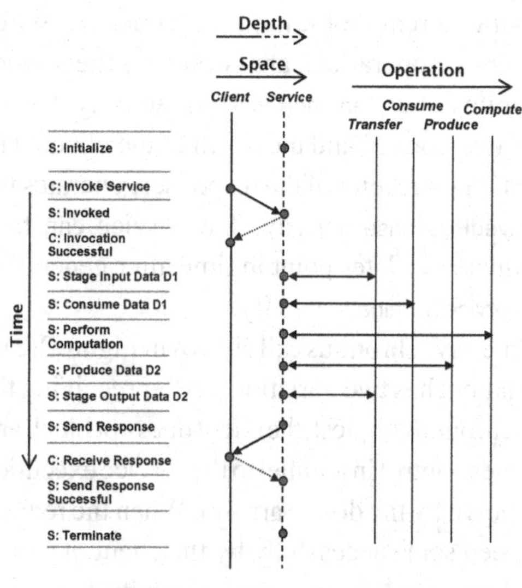

Figure 3a. Nested workflow. The root workflow WF1 contains two services—S1 and WF2—where the latter is another workflow that is nested. WF2, in turn, has two services—S2 and S3. All services and workflows produce and consume one data product each.

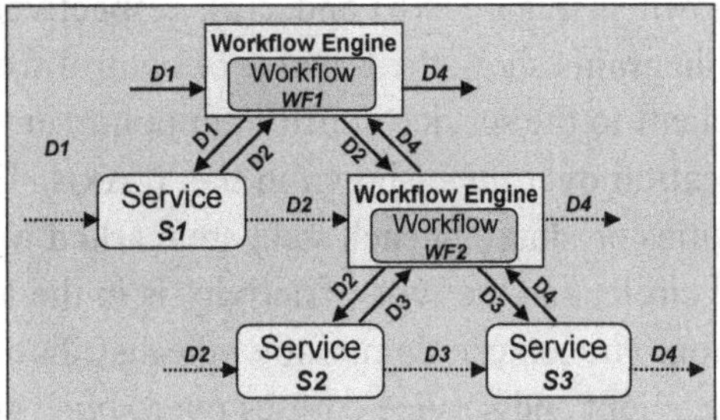

Figure 3b. Sequence diagram for nested workflow in Figure 3a

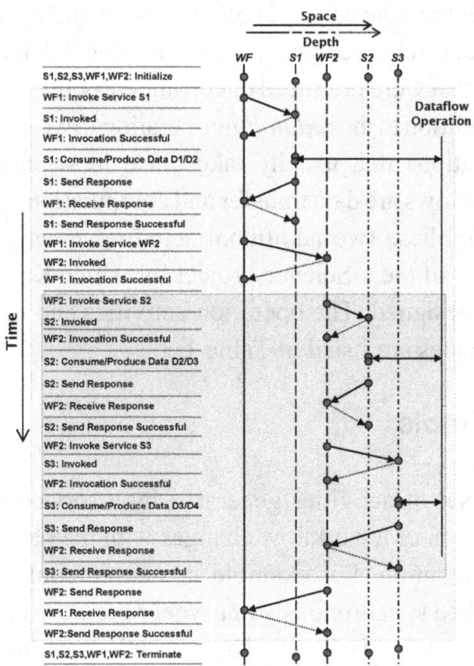

In the synchronous invocation shown in Figure 2(b), once the service is started and generates the ServiceInitialized activity, the client invokes the service. The client generates an InvokeService activity and then calls the service, and control passes to the service. The service generates the ServiceInvoked activity and starts the execution. This involves transferring the input data D1 (DataTransfer), using the data product (DataConsumed) in a computation or application (Computation), producing the output data product D2 (DataProduced), and staging the output to a remote location (DataTransfer). When the service operations are complete, the service generates the SendingResponse activity before returning control and the result to the client. The client, upon receipt of the response, generates the ReceivedResponse activity. The service can then terminate at a later point in time after generating the ServiceTerminate activity.

The asynchronous call shown in Figure 2(c) is similar but has two variations. After receiving the asynchronous request, the client does not block and receives control in parallel to the service execution (as shown by the dotted arrow). When the request has been sent successfully by the client, it generates the InvokingServiceSucceeded activity. Likewise, after the service returns the response to the client, it gets back control in parallel to the client and generates a SendingResponseSuccess activity. This three-phase protocol is necessary in order to track the fact that the invocation cycle was successful, since either of the sending request or receiving response steps could potentially fail.

A more complex scenario is shown in Figure 3(a), where a nested workflow executes. Workflow WF1 consists of two services—S1 and WF2—where service WF2 is another workflow. WF2, in turn, comprises two services—S2 and S3—that are connected. All the services take in one data product as input and generate another data product as output, which is used by the subsequent service. The sequence diagram in Figure 3(b) shows an asynchronous execution of the workflow when orchestrated by a separate workflow engine for each workflow. Before the workflow executes, services (including the workflows) are initialized, generating ServiceInitialized activities. A client (not shown in the figure) initiates the workflow and control passed to the workflow (engine) WF1. The sequence diagram starts from this stage. The workflow WF1 starts executing by invoking the first service in the workflow, S1, with input parameter data product D1. Since WF1 acts as the client to S1, it generates InvokingService and InvokingServiceSuccess activities before and after calling S1. Service S1 generates ServiceInvoked activity after being invoked by WF1. The service performs operations such as consuming and producing data products (DataConsumed and DataProduced), computation and file transfers (not shown). When execution completes, S1 asynchronously returns the response message to the workflow WF1, in the process generating SendingResponse and SendingResponseSuccess activities. WF1 receives the response for the invocation and generates the ReceivedResponse activity.

WF1 then invokes service WF2, which is next in the workflow sequence. Although WF2 is actually a workflow, WF1 interacts with it just as with any other service, generating the same activities as a service client; namely, InvokingService, InvokingServiceSuccess, and ReceivedResponse. WF2, upon receiving the invocation, executes the workflow as if it received an invocation from a client, and proceeds to invoke services S2 and S3. These generate the usual activities as seen before. When these services return, the final response from S3 is returned by workflow WF2 to workflow WF1, its client. Workflow WF1 then continues to completion.

PROVENANCE MODEL

The provenance model describes the structure of the provenance metadata exposed by Karma (Simmhan, Plale & Gannon, 2007). It is an aggregation of the various facets portrayed by the provenance activities, and this information model forms the basis for querying over and exporting of provenance. The model describes two primary types of provenance: one centered on service invocations, called *process provenance*; and the other relating to data usage and generation, termed *data provenance*. These two concepts are complementary in that process provenance describes service invocations and makes a reference to the input and output data products to the invocation, while data provenance describes the data product and makes references to services that use it and the invocation that created it. They provide two different views over the global provenance information available from the activities.

Process Provenance

Process provenance describes the execution of a single process, which translates to an invocation

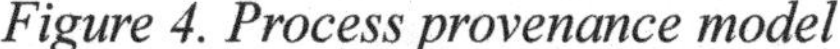
Figure 4. Process provenance model

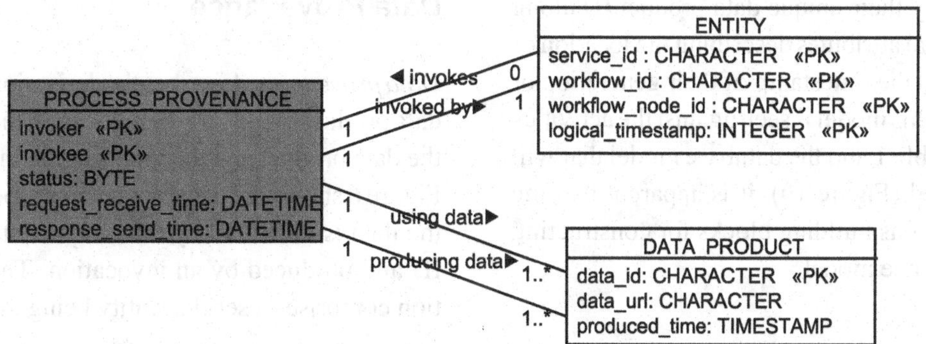

Figure 5. Workflow trace model

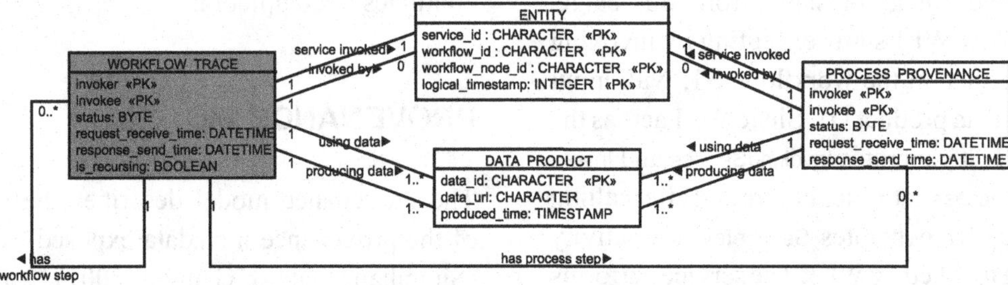

Figure 6. Data provenance model

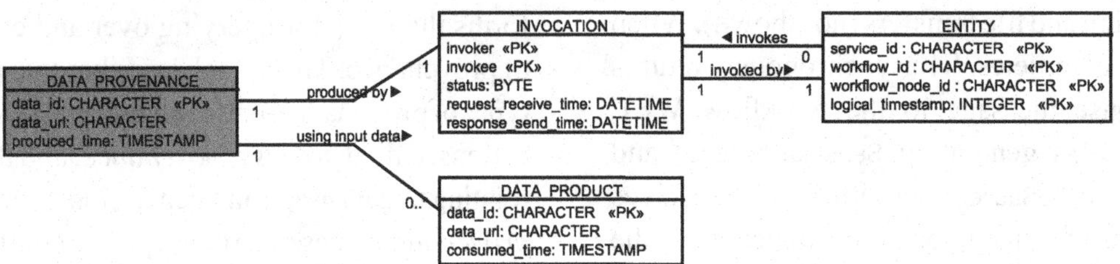

of a service instance by a client. The process provenance information model, shown in Figure 4, identifies the service that was invoked and the client that invoked the service using the entity IDs described in the activities. These comprise the relevant attributes from Service ID, the Workflow ID, Workflow Node ID, and the Logical Timestamp of the service and the client at the time of invocation. It also contains attributes such as the actual timestamp of the invocation, the status of the invocation, and optionally, the messages that were exchanged by the entities. The process provenance also references the data products that were used by the invocation and that the invocation created. The data products are identified by their unique data product ID along with optional attributes describing the location of the data and the timestamp of their generation or use. When this model is seen against the activities listed in Table 1 and the database model that will be described (Figure 10), it is apparent that the activities act as building blocks for constructing the provenance model.

While process provenance describes a single service invocation, the complete workflow run is captured by the *workflow trace* shown in Figure 5. The workflow trace is a coarser degree of abstraction of the provenance and includes zero or more records of process provenance relating to service invocations that were part of the workflow execution. In addition to the service invocation steps, workflow traces can also recursively refer to other workflow traces in the case of hierarchically composed workflows. The depth of recursion is configurable, allowing an arbitrary level of granularity at which process provenance can be viewed.

Data Provenance

Data provenance describes the derivation path of a data product as the service invocation that created the data product and the inputs to the invocation. Figure 6 shows the data provenance model where the data is identified by the unique data product ID and produced by an invocation. The invocation comprises a service entity being invoked by

Figure 7. Recursive data provenance model

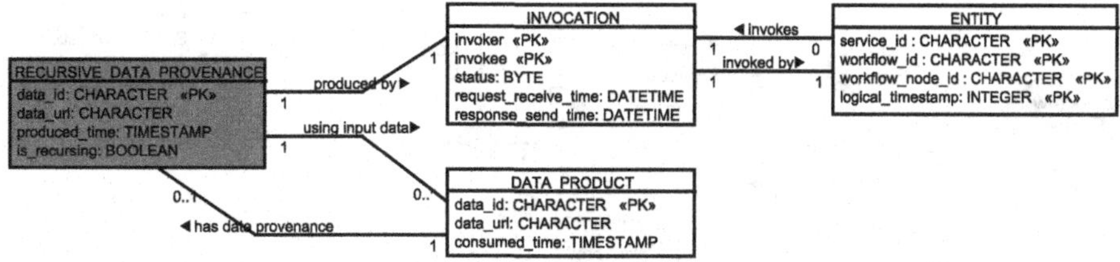

Figure 8. Data usage model

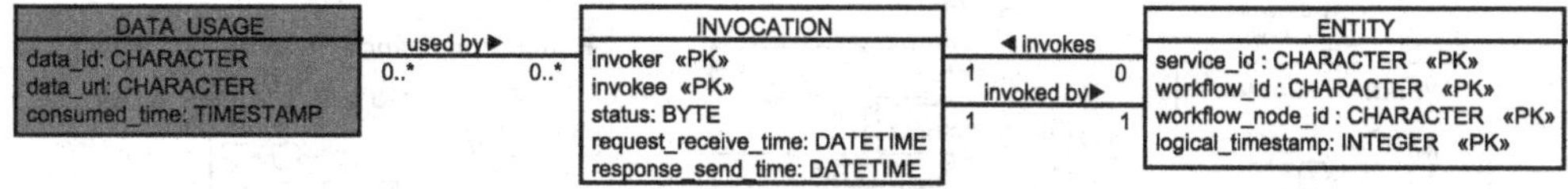

a client entity using zero or more data products as inputs to the data. The invocation attributes are similar to those for the process provenance record seen earlier; likewise the attributes for the data products.

Data provenance is, by default, the immediate data derivation history—the service invocation that directly created this data. A recursive form of data provenance, analogous to the workflow trace, is the deep or *recursive data provenance* (Cohen-Boulakia, Cohen & Davidson, 2007) shown in Figure 7. Deep data provenance recursively tracks the data provenance for the inputs to the invocation up to an arbitrary depth. This can be used to build the complete historical record of the ancestral data and invocations that caused this data to be derived.

Data provenance looks back in time on the derivation chain. A similar model can be constructed when moving forward in time and tracking the usage of a data product in various invocations. The *data usage* model, shown in Figure 8, describes the service invocations that use a certain data product as their input. The invocations are described by the service invoked and its client, while the data are identified by the data product ID and optional locations and timestamp of when it was used.

The various forms of process and data provenance are graph structures. The workflow trace consists of service invocation nodes and data product edges, with the process provenance records forming an edge-node-edge subgraph. Similarly, the data provenance and data usage have data products as nodes and service invocations as edges.

IMPLEMENTATION

The *Karma framework* implementation in the above provenance model consists of a focal Web service to collect provenance activities and query over the provenance model, client libraries to generate the provenance activities, and graphical interfaces to visualize the provenance graphs and monitor workflow execution (Figure 9). Provenance activities are modeled as XML documents whose schema maps to activity attributes. The clients and services participating in a service or workflow execution can use the provided *workflow tracking* client library to generate the provenance activity documents shown in Table 1. The Java library maintains the state information for the service or client during the invocation and fills in the relevant entity ID fields for all activities once

Figure 9. Interaction between karma provenance service and workflow

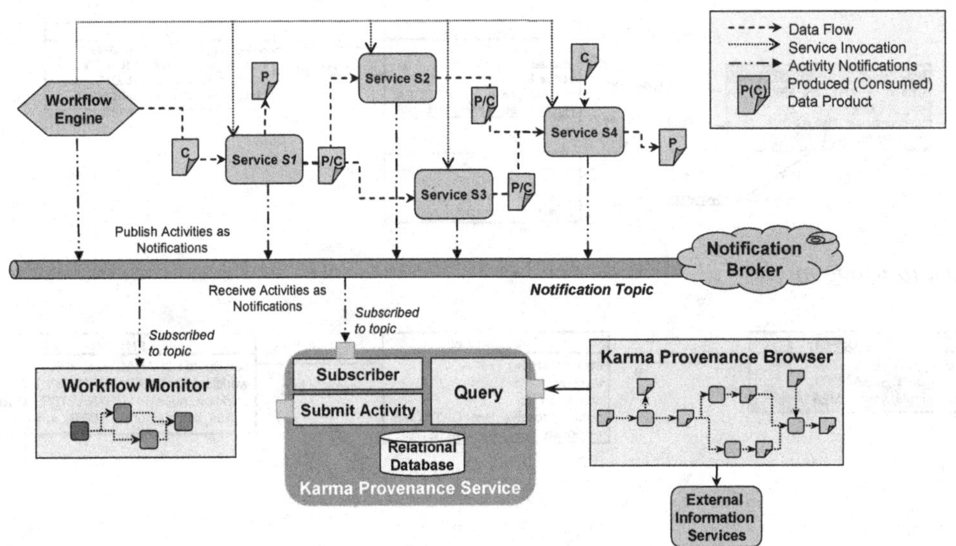

Figure 10. Relational Database model for storing provenance (Simmhan, 2007)

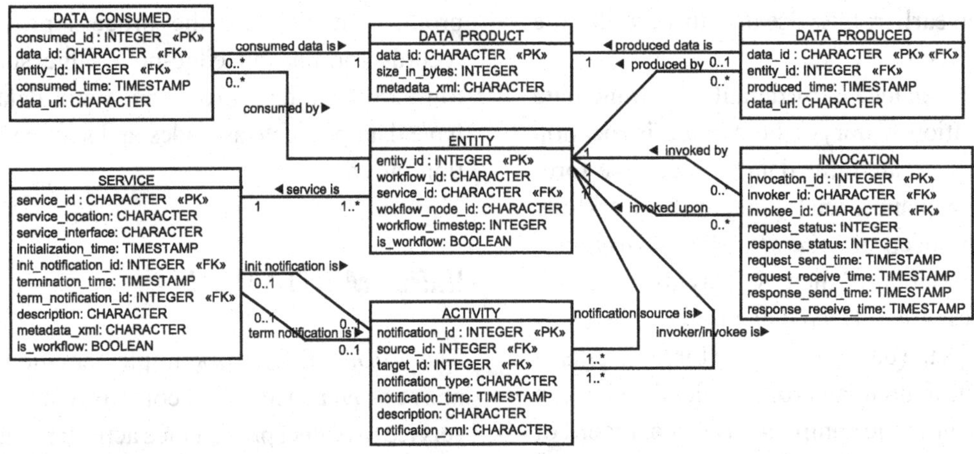

they are initially specified. It provides a simple API, akin to logging tools, for clients and services to populate the activity attributes for the bounding and operation activities. When the services being executed are Web services, Karma also provides a SOAP library that can encode the entity ID information of the client and service in the SOAP header of the request and response messages, to allow transparent exchange of client and service state information that each need in order to fill in the activities they produce. This allows existing Web services to generate provenance activities without having to change the WSDL definition for the Web service.

The provenance service provides a Web service interface for services and clients in the workflow in order to submit the provenance activities they generate. In addition to a synchronous submission of the activities, the implementation also allows an asynchronous publishing of activities as notifications that the provenance service subscribes to. The provenance service shreds the XML provenance activities and stores them in a relational database. This then can be queried through the Web service API that provides methods to retrieve each of the five provenance models described earlier through their IDs.

Publishing Activities as Notifications

A *Publish-Subscribe* (or Pub-Sub) notification protocol is a unidirectional, asynchronous communication between publishers and consumers that communicates by means of "channels" or "topics." Consumers, *decoupled in space* from the publisher, receive events by subscribing to one or more topics (Eugster, Felber, Guerraoui & Kermarrec, 2003).

A notification protocol is a good choice for publishing provenance activities from the workflows, services, and clients, since provenance gathering can be done without perturbing the publishers and can be collected independent of the provenance service location. *Time decoupling* (Eugster et al., 2003), whereby the listeners need not be active when the notification is published, puts less stringent requirements on the availability of the provenance service. Archival or message-box facilities present in many notification brokers remove the onus from workflow components in ensuring reliable delivery of activity messages. Since provenance is more often used for mining and analysis post workflow execution than for runtime monitoring of the workflow, users are tolerant to delayed receipt of activities at the provenance service. Pub-sub is a mature field with several open-source and commercial implementations, and many open standards such as JMS and WS-Eventing (Box et al., 2004), which aid interoperability when collecting provenance across different domains, as is common in Grid systems.

A representative notification service is *WS-Messenger* (Huang, Slominski, Herath & Gannon, 2006), which uses a topic-based, publish-subscribe system based on the WS-Eventing standard (Box et al., 2004). WS-Messenger contains four main components relevant to Karma: the *notification publisher*, the *notification consumer*, the *notification broker*, and the *message box*. The notification publisher generates notifications that are published to a topic at the notification broker. The broker, a Web service, provides a topic-based subscription interface and routes notifications published to a certain topic to the registered listeners. Notifications consumers are Web services that subscribe with the broker for notifications and receive them via a standard Web service interface they implement. For listeners that lie behind a firewall or that would like to have notifications buffered for them, a message box service can act as a proxy and subscribe to the broker on the listener's behalf. The listeners periodically retrieve the notification from the message box, which provides a means to persist the notification for reliable delivery.

For each workflow execution, a unique notification topic is created with the notification broker. All components in the workflow and its clients use the same broker and topic to publish their notifications. This allows listeners interested in only notifications from a certain workflow execution, such as a workflow monitor, to listen to just that topic. The broker allows wildcard or "*" subscriptions, and the provenance service uses this feature to subscribe to all provenance activity notifications that are generated from all workflows that use that broker.

Database Model

The Karma provenance service uses a relational database to store the activities it receives for a workflow execution as notifications or directly submitted through the Web service API. The database schema is shown in Figure 10 (Simmhan et al., 2007). As XML activities arrive, the provenance service extracts the relevant attributes from them and creates or updates the tables in the database. The tables closely resemble the provenance data model with entities described in the *entity table* and the *invocation table* referencing client and service entity pairs along with the state of the invocation. Data products present in the *data product table* are consumed and produced by the invocations as captured by the *data produced* and *consumed tables* that relate the two. A separate *service table* is present to record information about the service instances, such as their initialization and termination times, and possibly their WSDL in the case of Web services. An additional *activity table* keeps a log of all activities that were used to populate the tables. This forms a provenance or audit trail about the provenance itself in case the provenance needs to be verified in the future. It should also be noted that provenance is immutable and is only appended to over time as new activities take place (e.g., when a service invocation changes from an invoked state to invocation complete state). Once all activities relating to an invocation have been received, its process provenance and the data provenance for data products created by the invocation are static.

Mapping the provenance model to a relational database helps to keep the implementation compatible with a different representation of the activities or of the provenance graphs. Any other transport mechanism or metadata representation besides XML can be used to gather the activities, as long as all attributes for each activity are present. These will require simple conversions from the activity's format to the database/provenance model. Similarly, the provenance graphs can be exported in formats other than the present XML schema, as may be required by visualization applications (Brandes, Eiglsperger, Herman, Himsolt & Marshall, 2002). Efforts are emerging to standardize provenance representation (Moreau & Ludascher, 2007); our approach allows us to interoperate with any future provenance standard that follows the broad principles of provenance being recorded as a causal graph. The availability of mature relational databases also allows for an efficient implementation of the provenance service, which gives superior performance for activity updates and provenance queries as is further described in the following section.

Provenance Queries

The Karma provenance service provides APIs to query over the provenance model and returns the various provenance graphs using an XML representation. The XML schema for each of the five types of provenance graphs maps to the information model for each provenance graph, as shown in Figures 4–8. The query API has a method for each of the five provenance graphs; namely, process provenance, workflow trace, data provenance, recursive data provenance, and data usage. In order to retrieve the process provenance or workflow trace, the entity ID (i.e., the set of Service ID, Workflow ID, Workflow Node ID, Logical Timestamp) of the client invoking the service or workflow, along with the entity ID of the service or workflow being invoked, is passed as parameter. In the case of workflow trace, an additional parameter is specified on how deep the workflow trace should recurse in case the workflow contains nested workflows. The methods return the process provenance and workflow trace graphs as XML documents. The immediate and deep data provenance and data usage methods take a data product ID as input parameter. The recursive data provenance also takes the depth into which the ancestral provenance needs to be recursed. The immediate data provenance is equivalent to invoking the recursive data provenance with the recursion factor set to 0. These return the data provenance and usage graphs as XML documents. These basic query APIs can be used as building blocks to construct and perform more complex queries, as was shown in our entry at the First Provenance Workshop (Moreau & Ludascher, 2007).

In Karma, the provenance graph is constructed natively in the service, unlike other provenance collection approaches that require external means for doing so (Groth, Luck & Moreau, 2004). The algorithm for constructing the provenance graphs from a series of provenance activities is similar to an algorithm used to construct a graph, given the set of node-edge pairs that comprise the graph. For example, in the case of process provenance, the *entity table* is looked up for the client and the service entity IDs that correspond to the provided Service ID, Workflow ID, Workflow Node ID, and Logical Timestamp for the client and the service. From these two entity IDs, the invocation in the *invocation table* is identified. The invocation ID also leads to the data produced and consumed by that invocation, available through the *data produced* and *consumed tables*. Further details about the data products are retrieved from the *data product table*, while further information about the service is present in the *service table*. These fields are sufficient to populate the process provenance model in the result. In the case of workflow trace, this step is repeated for all service invocations whose Workflow IDs match the workflow. In the case of data provenance or data usage, the procedure is similar, but the starting point is the *data produced* or *consumed tables* instead of the *entity table*. The immutability property of provenance also can be used to cache the results of building the provenance graph and reuse it, provided additional activities have not been appended to the provenance document since its construction.

Provenance Dissemination

The *Karma* provenance service's query interface can be invoked by any Web service client in order to retrieve data and workflow provenance in XML. The *Karma Provenance Browser* is a graphical tool that uses the provenance service API to integrate provenance metadata with additional metadata on the services, workflows, and data products available from external information catalogs such as service registries or metadata catalogs found in the LEAD Project (Simmhan et al., 2006a). Provenance acts as a glue to relate the services with the data products but does not include complete metadata describing the service or the data product. The browser can retrieve and visualize the provenance graph for, say, a given Workflow ID, and users can select services and data products within that workflow and retrieve metadata about them from the external catalogs. The browser also allows seamless navigation from a workflow graph to a data provenance graph or data usage graph for data products in that workflow, allowing users to jump across provenances from different workflow executions or view the graph from data or service perspectives.

The XBaya workflow monitor GUI (Shirasuna & Gannon, 2006) is another tool that allows users with access to the original workflow document to monitor the progress of the workflow execution by listening to the provenance activities sent as notifications. The monitor supports BPEL workflows and also acts as a workflow composer interface. So users can compose a workflow visually using XBaya, launch the workflow, and later use the same workflow graph to monitor it within XBaya at runtime. The workflow monitor subscribes to the notification topic for that workflow and updates the status of the different components in the composed workflow graph as it receives the provenance activity. Since activities are directly delivered as notifications to the monitor by the notification broker, this obviates the need to access the provenance service for the workflow status and makes the monitoring more realtime. We are additionally exploring the use of workflow provenance available from the provenance service to perform visual replays of the workflow execution in the workflow monitor GUI.

PERFORMANCE EVALUATION

Provenance collection incurs a cost. We quantify the overhead using the sample weather forecasting workflow given in Section 2, a workflow that exemplifies the data-driven applications in LEAD. More detailed experiments on the provenance system, both for collecting provenance as well as to query the provenance records, have been performed and are available through a separate publication (Simmhan, Plale, Gannon & Marru, 2006c). The workflow of Section 2 performs weather prediction for a 183x163 spatial domain with 53 vertical levels and 9-km grid spacing around the center at 28.5°N and –87.0°E. The experiment is initialized with observational data at 1200 Hours UTC on August 28, 2005, and simulates the weather for the next 37 hours, tracking Hurricane Katrina's landfall on the Gulf Coast. The output of the simulation model is analyzed and visualized by generating animations.

The eight services in the workflow are invoked sequentially to collect execution times for each application invocation. The service's execution time includes staging times for input and output files, the wall clock time of the computation, and the provenance overhead. The first four preprocessing and interpolation applications, and the last two postprocessing and visualization applications are executed on a Linux workstation with dual-Xeon 3 GHz processors, 2GB memory, and a Gbps Ethernet network. The WRF forecasting model and WRF2ARPS postprocessor are executed using 32 and 8 processors, respectively, on an Itanium2 1.3GHz Linux cluster with 6GB memory linked by Myrinet network and connected to a 10GB external network. The WS-Messenger notification broker runs on a Solaris workstation with dual-Sparc 1.2GHz processor, 4GB memory, and a 1Gbps Ethernet network. The Karma provenance service runs on a Windows XP workstation with P4 2GHz processor, 1.5GB memory, and 100Mbps Ethernet.

The bar graph in Figure 11 shows the cumulative time taken by the services in the workflow, with and without generating provenance notifications. As seen from the bars on the far right, the time taken for the entire workflow to finish is 2,834 secs when the services generate provenance notifications, and 2,809 secs when they do not. This translates to a total overhead of about 0.8% of execution time for the forecasting workflow, which is a very small overhead. Currently, the overhead percentage depends upon the number of

Figure 11. (a) [Bar Graph, Left Y Axis] Cumulative execution time, with and without provenance, for applications in workflow; (b) [Line Graph, Right Y Axis] Provenance overhead for individual applications in workflow. Σ(script provenance overhead) = 26s ≅ (total time w/ provenance – total time w/o provenance)=25s

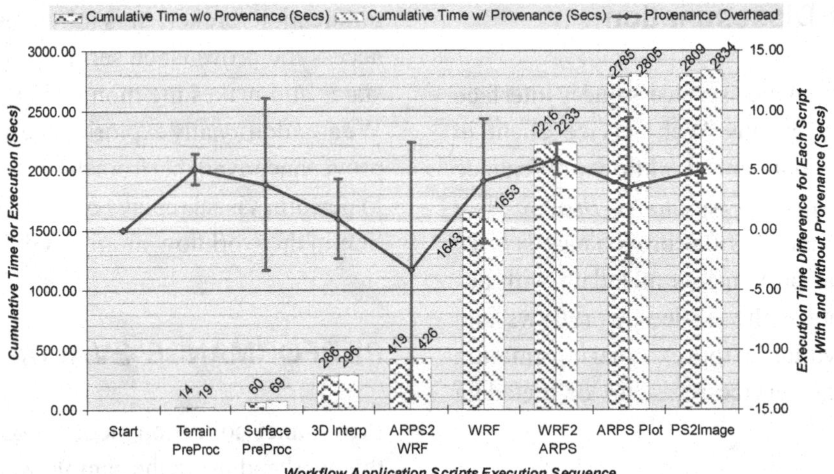

activities generated in each script. Since the number of bounding activities for a service invocation is constant, the number of activities generated is closely tied to the number of operation activities; in particular, the number of data produced, and consumed activities are generated since those are liable to number higher. We have initial results from batching data –produced and –consumed activities in the XML activity representation that circumvent this problem to achieve near constant time overhead. Each of the applications produces and consumes between 11 and 61 files each, ranging in size from 55MB to 3.5GB, for a total of 147 files consumed and 124 files produced. This corresponds to a total of 271 dataflow activities, the small number of bounding activities from the workflow, and services. These figures are typical of data-driven scientific workflows in the meteorology domain, and the provenance overhead is bound to be similarly small.

The line graph on the right Y axis in Figure 11 shows the additional time taken by each application due to publishing provenance notifications. The vertical lines mark the standard error of the mean time at each data point due to variations in the measurement caused by I/O wait times and system processes. Ignoring data points with large standard errors, we see that the overhead time for each application is in the range of 1 to 6 seconds. This is quite low, considering the normal execution time for LEAD applications is between 10s of seconds to several hours.

A separate and more detailed study (Simmhan et al., 2006c) has shown comparable results. A simulated ensemble workflow with nine services, which included a four-way parallel service invocation that iterated 10 times, has an overhead of about 70 seconds for collecting the provenance activities. That workflow has 63 service invocations and involved 2,400 data products; a real execution of the workflow would have taken several hours to complete. Hence, the relative overhead of provenance collection is minor. Those tests also show that the provenance system scaled with the number of parallel workflows, taking linear or sublinear time as the number of simultaneous workflows increase. The response time for querying provenance was equally low in that study, taking less than one second for querying individual provenance graphs and showing linear increase in query response time as the query selectivity or the number of parallel clients increases.

RELATED WORK

A synthesis of requirements for an effective and usable provenance system for scientific workflows should, in broad terms, require it to (1) provide an open and interoperable interface to collect provenance, (2) track workflow and data provenance within a virtual organization independent of workflow models and data formats, and (3) minimize performance overheads and modifications required of workflow components. While systems and techniques to collect provenance in scientific workflows exist, they fall short of these needs. Workflow environments such as the Virtual Data Grid (Foster, Vöckler, Wilde & Zhao, 2003), myGrid (Zhao et al., 2004), and GridDB (Liu et al., 2005) provide the capability to record provenance but are tightly integrated with their workflow execution environment and do not provide interoperable means for collecting and using provenance. Earth System Sciences Workbench (ESSW) (Bose & Frew, 2004) collects lineage as simple parent-child links between services and files, but recording provenance is tightly coupled to its lineage database, and lack of support for logical data products hinders tracking data across the virtual organization. Provenance Aware Service Oriented Architecture (PASOA) (Groth et al., 2004; Groth, Miles, Fang, Wong, Zauner & Moreau, 2005) defines an open protocol for recording provenance through a set of messages exchanged between service invocation actors and a provenance server. While recording the in-wire service requests and responses allows PASOA to track workflow provenance in a nonrepudiable manner, users have to extend the provided schema in order to track data products used in the invocations, and native support to build provenance graphs is absent. Workflow tracing tools such as IBM Data Collector (IBM, 2005) log request-response messages for Web service calls that can be can be correlated and visualized, but this is limited to workflow provenance and not data provenance. Distributed logging tools like Net Logger (Gunter, Tierney, Jackson, Lee & Stoufer, 2002) that provide generic logging support for distributed applications lack the higher level abstractions necessary for a service-oriented architecture. Instrumentation and performance analysis systems like svPablo (de Rose & Reed, 1999) and AutoPilot (Ribler, Vetter, Simitci & Reed, 1998) are oriented toward realtime monitoring of distributed applications in order to tune application performance and optimize resource allocation, but they do not help with holistic tracking of the dataflow and workflow execution.

Surveys on provenance systems include a metamodel for a systems architecture for lineage retrieval (Bose & Frew, 2005), present a taxonomy of approaches taken toward building provenance systems (Simmhan et al., 2005), and exemplify use cases for a provenance system in biology (Miles, Groth, Branco & Moreau, 2005). Several workshops on this topic (Bose, Foster & Moreau, 2006; Moreau & Foster, 2006), including a recent provenance challenge workshop (Moreau & Ludascher, 2007), have shown an active interest emerging in this field in the e-Science domain.

CONCLUSION AND FUTURE WORK

In this article, we have identified challenges involved in collecting provenance—both data and workflow provenance—for data-driven applications. The Karma provenance framework we propose provides a generic solution for collecting provenance for heterogeneous workflow environments and independent of the workflow orchestration model or service invocation style. Indeed, it is not specific to Web service-based workflows alone, and we have examples of it being used by workflows composed of Jython scripts. The activity model is compatible with a publish-subscribe paradigm that provides a ubiquitous means for interoperable collection of provenance; we leverage this to implement provenance collection with low perturbation. Use of the WS–Eventing standard allows the choice of the most suitable pub-sub implementation for the domain. In addition, users also have the capability to directly submit provenance activities without the requirement to publish them as notifications. The user involvement is limited to instrumenting the workflow components to generate the provenance notifications. This is similar to logging information that workflows usually generate for debugging, and the libraries we provide alleviate the burden on the service providers. We also have toolkits to automatically create services from an XML description of an application that already comes instrumented to collect provenance, completely doing away with user overhead (Kandaswamy, Fang, Huang, Shirasuna, Marru & Gannon, 2006). This toolkit is widely used in the LEAD project. Our evaluation of the framework implementation also shows that provenance collection can be done with minimal performance overhead on the workflow, on the order of 1% of the execution time for 271 files used. More comprehensive tests support these numbers and provide equally favorable performance figures for querying for provenance (Simmhan et al., 2006c).

The framework described here is the basis for our ongoing research in the use of provenance to automatically determine data product quality based on user-guided metrics and through collaborative feedback on the products and services participating in the data provenance (Simmhan et al., 2006b). Long-running workflows increase the probability of incomplete provenance. Using this information effectively is an area under investigation, as is handling missing activities and undelivered notifications, possibly using WS-Reliable Messaging (Pallickara, Fox, Yildiz, Pallickara, Patel & Yemme, 2005). Also of interest are data products that appear in collections that are themselves data products. Provenance for the collection data products and for individual data products within them needs to be tracked without breaking the transparency offered by uniform naming. Provenance collected over time serves as a promising resource for mining and detecting patterns that can assist in anything from workflow completion tools to automated resource scheduling.

ACKNOWLEDGMENT

This work is supported in part by NSF cooperative agreement ATM-0331480 and NSF grant EIA-0202048. The authors would like to thank the members of the LEAD project for their active support in this work; in particular, Marcus Christie, Yi Huang, Suresh Marru, Srinath Perera, Satoshi Shirasuna, and Aleksander Slominski.

REFERENCES

Armstrong, R., et al. (1999). Toward a common component architecture for high-performance scientific computing. *HPDC*.

BEA Systems, IBM Corporation, Microsoft Corporation, SAP AG, & Siebel Systems (2003). Business process execution language for Web services (BPEL 1.1). *Technical Report*.

Bose, R., & Frew, J. (2004). Composing lineage metadata with XML for custom satellite-derived data products. *SSDBM*.

Bose, R., & Frew, J. (2005). Lineage retrieval for scientific data processing: A survey. *ACM Computing Surveys*, *37*, 1–28.

Bose, R., Foster, I., & Moreau. L. (2006). Report on the international provenance and annotation workshop. *SIGMOD Record*, *35*(3), 51–53.

Box, D., et al. (2004). Web services eventing (WS-eventing). *Technical Report*.

Brandes, U., Eiglsperger, M., Herman, I., Himsolt, M., & Marshall, M.S. (2002). GraphML progress report: Structural layer proposal. *LNCS*, *2265*, 501–512.

Catlett, C. (2002). The TeraGrid: A primer. Retrieved from www.teragrid.org

Churches, D., et al. (2006). Programming scientific and distributed workflow with Triana Services. *Concurrency and Computation: Practice and Experience*, *18*(10), 1021–1037.

Cohen-Boulakia, S., Cohen, S., & Davidson, S. (2007). Addressing the provenance challenge using zoom. *Concurrency and Control: Practice and Experience*.

de Rose, L.A., & Reed, D.A. (1999). SvPablo: A multi-language architecture-independent performance analysis system. *ICPP*.

Droegemeier, K.K., et al. (2005). Service-oriented environments for dynamically interacting with mesoscale weather. *Computing in Science and Engineering*, *7*(6), 12–29.

Eugster, P.T., Felber, P.A., Guerraoui, R., & Kermarrec, A.M. (2003). The many faces of publish/subscribe. *ACM Computing Surveys*, *35*, 114–131.

Foster, I., Kesselman, C., Nick, J., & Tuecke S. (2002). The physiology of the grid: An open grid services architecture for distributed systems integration. *Global Grid Forum*.

Foster, I.T., Vöckler, J., Wilde, M., & Zhao, Y. (2003). The virtual data grid: A new model and architecture for data-intensive collaboration. *CIDR*.

Gannon, D., et al. (2005). Service oriented architectures for science gateways on grid systems. *ICSOC*.

Goble, C. (2002). Position statement: Musings on provenance, workflow and (semantic Web) annotations for bioinformatics. *Workshop on Data Derivation and Provenance*.

Greenwood, M., et al. (2003). Provenance of e-science experiments—experience from Bioinformatics. *UK OST e-Science 2nd AHM*.

Groth, P., Luck, M., & Moreau, L. (2004). A protocol for recording provenance in service-oriented grids. *OPODIS*.

Groth, P., Miles, S., Fang, W., Wong, S.C., Zauner, K.-P., & Moreau, L. (2005). Recording and using provenance in a protein compressibility experiment. *HPDC*.

Gunter, D., Tierney, B., Jackson, K., Lee, J., & Stoufer, M. (2002). Dynamic monitoring of high-performance distributed applications. *HPDC*.

Huang, Y., Slominski, A., Herath, C., & Gannon, D. (2006). WS-Messenger: A Web services based messaging system for service-oriented grid computing. *CCGrid*.

IBM (2005). Web services data collector. Retrieved from www.alphaworks.ibm.com/tech/wsdatacollector

Kandaswamy, G., Fang, L., Huang, Y., Shirasuna, S., Marru, S., & Gannon, D. (2006). Building Web services for scientific grid applications. *IBM Journal of Research and Development*, *50*(2/3), 249–260.

Liu, D.T., Franklin, M.J., Garlick, J., & Abdulla, G.M. (2005). Scaling up data-centric middleware on a cluster computer. *Technical Report, Lawrence Livermore National Laboratory*.

Ludäscher, B., et al. (2006). Scientific workflow management and the Kepler system. *Concurrency and Computation: Practice and Experience*, *18*(10), 1039–1065.

Miles, S., Groth, P., Branco, M., & Moreau, L. (2005). The requirements of recording and using provenance in e-science experiments. *Technical Report, Electronics and Computer Science, University of Southampton*.

Moreau, L., & Foster, I. (2006). *Provenance and annotation of data*. Proceedings of the International Provenance and Annotation Workshop, *LNCS* 4145.

Moreau, L., & Ludascher, B. (2007). The first provenance challenge. *Concurrency and Control: Practice and Experience*.

OMG (2006). CORBA component model v4.0. *Technical Report, OMG*.

Pallickara, S., Fox, G., Yildiz, B., Pallickara, S.L., Patel, S., & Yemme, D. (2005). On the costs for reliable messaging in Web/grid service environments. *e-Science*.

Plale, B. (2005). Resource requirements study for LEAD storage repository. *Technical Report 001, Linked Environments for Atmospheric Discovery*.

Ribler, R.L., Vetter, J.S., Simitci, H., & Reed, D.A. (1998). Autopilot: Adaptive control of distributed applications. *HPDC*.

Shirasuna, S., & Gannon, D. (2006). XBaya: A graphical workflow composer for the Web services architecture. *Technical Report 004, Linked Environments for Atmospheric Discovery*.

Simmhan, Y., Plale, B., & Gannon, D. (2005). A survey of data provenance in e-science. *SIGMOD Record*, *34*(3), 31–36.

Simmhan, Y.L., Pallickara, S.L., Vijayakumar, N.N., & Plale, B. (2006a). *Data management in dynamic environment-driven computational science*. Proceedings of the IFIP Working Conference on Grid-Based Problem Solving Environments (WoCo9).

Simmhan, Y.L., Plale, B., & Gannon, D. (2006b). *Towards a quality model for effective data selection in collaboratories*. Proceedings of the IEEE Workflow and Data Flow for Scientific Applications (SciFlow) Workshop.

Simmhan, Y.L., Plale, B., & Gannon, D. (2007). Query capabilities of the Karma provenance framework. *Concurrency and Control: Practice and Experience*.

Simmhan, Y.L., Plale, B., Gannon, D., & Marru, S. (2006c). Performance evaluation of the Karma provenance framework for scientific workflows. *IPAW* and *LNCS* 4145.

Slominski, A. (2006). Adapting BPEL to scientific workflows. *Workflows for e-Science*.

Szomszor, M., & Moreau, L. (2003). Recording and reasoning over data provenance in Web and grid services. *ODBASE*.

West, K. (2005). Scoping out the planet. *Scientific American*.

Yu, J., & Buyya, R. (2005). A taxonomy of scientific workflow systems for grid computing. *SIGMOD Record, 34*(3), 44–49.

Zhao, J., Wroe, C., Goble, C.A., Stevens, R., Quan, D., & Greenwood, R.M. (2004). Using semantic Web technologies for representing e-science provenance. *ISWC*.

ENDNOTE

1 Based on work done at Indiana Univesity, USA.

This work was previously published in International Journal of Web Services Research, Voluem 5, Issue 2, edited by L. Zhang, pp. 1-22, copyright 2008 by IGI Publishing (an imprint of IGI Global).t

Chapter 15
Result Refinement in Web Services Retrieval Based on Multiple Instances Learning

Yanzhen Zou
Peking University, China

Lu Zhang
Peking University, China

Yan Li
Peking University, China

Bing Xie
Peking University, China

Hong Mei
Peking University, China

ABSTRACT

Web services retrieval is a critical step for reusing existing services in the SOA paradigm. In the UDDI registry, traditional category-based approaches have been used to locate candidate services. However, these approaches usually achieve relatively low precision because some candidate Web Services in the result set cannot provide actually suitable operations for users. In this article, we present a new approach to improve this kind of category-based Web Services retrieval process that can refine the coarse matching results step by step. The refinement is based on the idea that operation specification is very important to service reuse. Therefore, a Web Service is investigated via multiple instances view in our approach, which indicates that a service is labeled as positive if and only if at least one operation provided by this service is usable to the user. Otherwise, it is labeled as negative. Experimental results demonstrate that our approach can increase the retrieval precision to a certain extent after one or two rounds of refinement.

INTRODUCTION

Faced with limited time-to-market and volatile requirements, software development currently relies on reusing of existing software components more and more. As the foundation of Services-Oriented Architecture (SOA), Web Services technologies aim at facilitating and improving the quality of component-based applications on the Web (Wang & Stroulia, 2003). Web Services has gained a lot of support in both the academic and industrial fields. Many corresponding tools and specifications have been developed. A Web Service is described through the Web-Services Definition Language (WSDL), and it can be advertised, discovered, and integrated via the Universal Description, Discovery, and Integration (UDDI), or be invoked at run time by the Simple Object Access Protocol (SOAP). As a result, application developers usually wrap existing software components as Web Services and build a new system by leveraging existing Web Services.

To facilitate discovering and reusing existing Web Services, UDDI provides directory services for Web Services offered by businesses (Colgrave, Akkiraju & Goodwin, 2004). In UDDI registry, Web Services are organized according to some categories of business activities. Service providers could advertise their services by classifying a service to the appropriate UDDI directory category. Thus, to discover the potentially relevant services, service requestors (e.g., software developers) can submit a query leveraging some category information to UDDI registry for discovering an appropriate service. Here we treat this kind of approach as category-based retrieval (Prieto-Diaz & Freeman, 1987; Ostertag, Hendler, Prieto-Diaz & Braun, 1992; Mili, Mili & Mittermeier, 1997), because they are actually performed by matching the user's requirement against each Web Service's category information.

Currently, UDDI is limited in its retrieval mechanism by its inability to extend the simple keyword-based matches and category-based matches. It is pointed out that the precision of the retrieval mechanism in UDDI registry is not satisfying (Wang et al., 2003; Li, Pan, Zhang, Xie & Sun, 2006) In a typical retrieval process, a service registry will acquire a query generated by the service requestor and match the query against each Web Service's category information. Thus, they return all functionally relevant Web Services in a category as candidates, which can achieve relatively high recall. However, the precision of these approaches is quite low, partially because some Web Services with relevant semantic descriptions in the candidate set may not provide actually suitable operations for users. Subsequently, the service requestor has to browse and comprehend those candidate services in order to identify the appropriate ones. Thus, the process of identifying appropriate services will become much more tedious and time-consuming when the candidate services set is quite large.

In this article, we present a novel approach to refine the coarse-matching results in the category-based Web Services retrieval mechanism. The basic idea of our approach is to exploit category matching as the first step whose target is to gain coarse candidate services with the required functionality description. Secondly, the retrieval results are refined based on a multiple instances learning technique (Dietterich & Lathrop, 1997; Zhou, Jiang & Li, 2005). In this refinement step, a retrieval mechanism collects some browsed services in the retrieval process as training examples to refine the coarse retrieval results. The browsed services are fed back as user interested (positive) or user uninterested (negative) and stored in a log for learning the interface requirements of the user-required service in order to achieve better retrieval performances. The refinement iterates until the matching result is refined enough for the service requestor to select. Based on our approach, we have built a prototype service retrieval system, which is composed of three parts: a category matching based retriever, a log collector, and a refinement tool based on multiple instances learning. Experimental results demonstrate that our approach can increase the retrieval precision to a certain extent after one or two rounds of refinement.

The rest of this article is organized as follows: Section 2 presents the motivation for refining coarse services set. Section 3 explains the technology background of multiple instances learning (MIL). Section 4 describes an improved Web Services retrieval process integrated into our refinement mechanism. Section 5 proposes our refinement tool for Web Services retrieval using MIL. Section 6 shows a case study, and Section 7 presents our experiments for evaluating our refinement. Section 8 discusses related works. Finally, we conclude this article and present our future work in Section 9.

MOTIVATION

The Need to Refine Traditional Web Services Retrieval Results

To help users discover Web Services efficiently, services are organized according to some categories in a UDDI registry. A typical Web Services retrieval process is summarized in Figure 1. In the first step, a service requestor (here named Alice) submits her requirement with a query to a UDDI registry. Then the UDDI registry invokes the matching algorithm and returns a matched Web Services results list. In the next step, Alice has to browse the services in the results list to identify the appropriate ones. However, for a service registry containing a very large number of services, a typical candidate set of services for

Figure 1. Traditional Web Services retrieval process

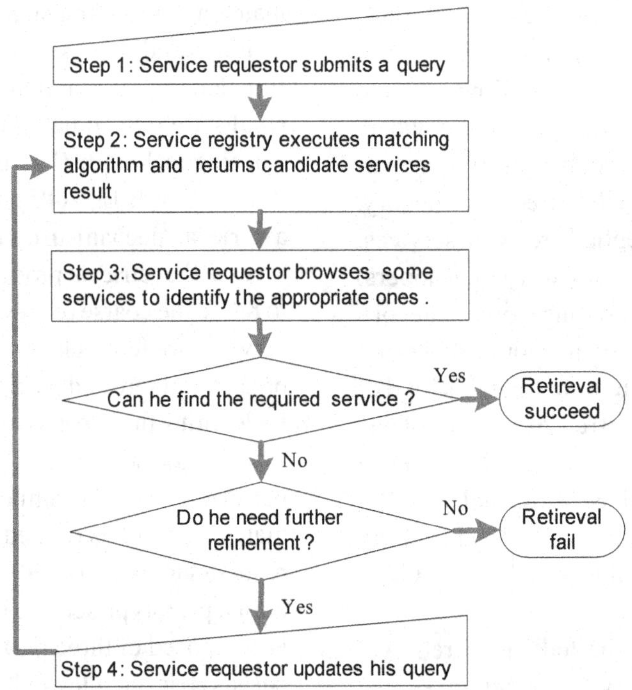

a category query may become so large that usually the precision of the result is not satisfying. Thus, the process of identifying appropriate services will become much more tedious and time-consuming for service requestors.

Obviously, Alice may update her current query and repeat the previous retrieval process. However, this method certainly may not lead to better matching results. There are two reasons to explain this circumstance. First, the number of services displayed in some "leaf" category attributes can be so large that the situation could not be alleviated by this category-based retrieval process unless new category attributes are added to the taxonomy in the service registry. Second, there is information loss in service description and service matching process. Alice may not be sure whether her query could match well the concepts of category attributes if she is not quite familiar with the UDDI registry. Besides, Alice may have no idea about which category in which the candidate services have been published, so she may submit a "fault" category as misled by some other publishers. As a result, the iterative query may not refine the result as she expected.

From the previous analysis, we can see that the category-based Web Services retrieval process usually involves more than one time of defining query and matching results. The service requestor has to update his or her query step by step in order to discover the appropriate services. Additionally, the number of services in a registry can be quite large, which may exacerbate the situation. Therefore, to accelerate the retrieval process, assistant approaches that can refine the coarse matching results automatically are essential to a service registry.

Why Operations are Important in Refinement

When searching for a service based on a particular application requirement, requestors will be very specific about a service's operations they are looking for (Ravichandran, 2003). Web Services is a kind of black-box component, and its implementation logics are not visible to any user. This indicates that the constraints of a service's operation are essentially important to cooperative applications. This feature of Web Services motivates service requestors to pay more attention to the operation specifications in services identification and selection. However, some services returned by a category query may not provide required operation, or their operations may not hold user-required preconditions and parameters specification, although they are classified in the same function category attribute. Therefore, candidate services should be refined according to their required operation specifications acting as contracts for composition.

On the other hand, a service may not be reused entirely, although it is described as a whole in UDDI registry. Actually, a service sometimes can provide a large number of operations. However, a particular application system may need only a part of operations in binding and reusing this service. For example, eBay has provided eBaySvcl Web Service for the authenticated eBay users to support interaction through software applications. There are more than 100 operations in this service, such as "AddOrder" and "GetCategories." However, for someone who wants to get category information of interested items, he or she may care only about whether the eBaySyc Web Service contains a "GetCategories" operation.

Bearing these issues in mind, we can get two points of conclusion: (1) automatic assistant approach is needed to accelerate the retrieval process; and (2) the assistant approach should make the retrieval system shift its focus of attention to those required operations in Web Services retrieval.

BACKGROUND

To investigate the problem of drug activity prediction, Dietterich, et al. (1997) proposed the notion of Multiple Instances Learning (MIL). The goal was to endow learning systems with the ability to predict whether a new molecule was qualified to make some drugs through analyzing a collection of known molecules (Zhou, 2005).

In drug activity prediction problem, a pre-condition is that most drugs are small molecules working by binding to larger protein molecules such as enzymes and cell-surface receptors. For molecules qualified to make a drug, one of its low-energy shapes could bind tightly to the target protein molecule. On the contrary, for molecules unqualified to make a drug, none of its low-energy shapes could bind tightly to the target protein molecule. The main difficulty of drug activity prediction is that each molecule may have many alternative low-energy shapes, but biochemists only know whether a molecule is qualified to make a drug or not, instead of knowing which low-energy shape responses there are for the qualification (Zhou et al., 2005). Therefore, Dietterich (1997) formulated the Multiple Instances Learning process, which treats every training example (molecule) as a bag that contains many instances (low-energy shapes). A bag is positively labeled if it contains at least one positive instance. Otherwise, it is labeled as a negative bag. The task is to learn some concept from the training set for correctly labeling unseen molecules.

The learn ability of multiple Instances Learning has been studied by many researchers. Recently, Multiple Instance Learning has been regarded as a new learning framework (Zhou et al., 2005), and many learning algorithms have been proposed. A kind of representative practical multiple instances learning algorithm is extended k-nearest neighbor algorithms, including Bayesian-kNN and Citation-kNN presented by Wang and Zucker (2000), and Diverse Density proposed by Maron and Lozano-Pérez (1998). Intuitively, diverse density at a point in the feature space is defined as a measure of how many positive bags have instances near that point, and how far the negative instances are from that point. Thus, the task of multi-instance learning is transformed to search for a point in the feature space with the maximum diverse density.

At present, extended k-nearest neighbor algorithms of MIL have been applied to several applications, including content-based image retrieval (CBIR) (Zhang, Chen & Shyu, 2004; Zhang &

Figure 2. Refining matching results in Web Services retrieval

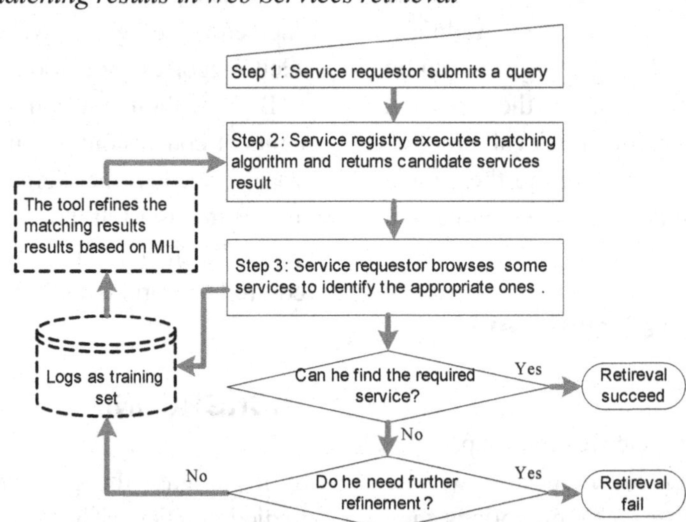

Chen, 2005), stock selection (Maron & Ratan, 1998), natural scene classification (Maron & Lozano-Pérez, 1998), and Web page recommendation (Ming, Xiao-Bing & Zhou, 2004; Zhou et al., 2005). The representative is the content-based image retrieval mechanism proposed by Zhang, which incorporates Multiple Instances Learning into the user relevance feedback in a seamless way to discover where the user's most interested regions lie and how to map the local features of that region(s) to users' high-level concepts.

Process of Refining Web Services Retrieval

Based on the traditional Web Services retrieval process, we propose an improved process that integrates an assistant tool to refine coarse services matching results. As shown in Figure 2, when a service requestor gains coarse retrieval results by category matching, he or she may only browse the top 3 to 5 services in order to identify favorite ones by judging whether a service has provided the required operations. However, the retrieval process usually cannot end at this step, as the precision of the matching result is not satisfying. In our approach, the retrieval mechanism will record the browsing information of the service requestor in a database as logs. In detail, a log includes the browsed service's ID and a label used to present the service requestor's judgment. In the next step, a refinement tool is used to train a model by leveraging these labeled services and updating a service query to get a better candidate matching result set automatically. The refinement process iterates until the service requestor gains a satisfying matching result and an appropriate service is identified.

As already depicted, the refinement mechanism in Web Services retrieval is divided into two parts: a log collector and a refinement tool. In the log collector, the browsed services by the service requestor are stored. Here the difficulty is that because a Web Service with hosts of operations is entirely described in the UDDI registry, a user only can specify whether he or she is interested in a service, instead of specifying the particular operations in which he or she is really interested. As a result, a Web Service is positively labeled if it contains at least one operation that interests the service requestor; otherwise, it is labeled as negative. Therefore, we have to learn the most general operation specifications that the user required from his or her log information in the refinement tool. In the refinement step, the labeled services are used as a training set, and the Multiple Instances Learning technique is chosen to train a matching model that makes the retrieval system shift its focus from the entire services to those useful operations. In the following sections, we will introduce in detail the Multi-Instance Learning algorithm for Web Services retrieval used in this article.

The proposed service retrieval process is a variation of the relevance feedback (RF), a popular retrieval process typically used in text retrieval fields. Relevance feedback is an interactive process in which the user judges the quality of the retrieval results for giving an improved query. We describe how this process can be adapted for users' browsing information collection in Web Services retrieval. When users browse a service's WSDL document, they are required to feedback by giving a label on whether the service has provided at least one user-interested operation. Finally, we store the feedback information and convert it into training examples so they can be applied in the refinement algorithm.

Results Refinement Based on MIL

The functional requirements of Web Services such as in a particular service composition scenario motivate the discovery of Web Services focusing the operation specifications in service's description (such as WSDL document). However, a Web Service with lots of operations is described in the service registry now as a whole; then users only can record whether a service is useful, but not the required operations in the Web Services retrieval process. This is a big challenge for our refining mechanism. Fortunately, if we regard each Web Service as a bag, while each of its operations is regarded as an instance in the bag, then we can solve this Web Services filtering problem with the Multiple Instances Learning technique.

In order to apply the Multiple Instances Learning method to the refining mechanism of Web Services retrieval, we must address the following issues:

- **Comparable service description:** This means that structural and complex WSDL documents must be converted to an interested and comparable description for a service. In this article, every operation in a Web Service is described by a feature vector. For example, *Oa* is one operation in Service *Sa*, and the input message of *Oa* includes 2 parameters: *InPara1* and *InPara2*, the output message of *Oa* includes 1 parameter: *OutPara1*; then we could define *Oa* as [*Oa*: *InPara1*, *InPara2*; *OutPara1*]^T. This feature vector is gained through exploiting the WSDL document. We will introduce this work in detail in the next subsection.
- **A training example set.** Training examples are the base of a learning algorithm. Here we can collect the logs of a service requestor's feedback on services. In the training set, every service has been labeled, so it can be described by a services name or ID, multiple operation feature vectors, and a label of positive or negative.
- **A learning algorithm**. The learning algorithm is used to measure the similarity between the examples and the candidate services for refining a candidate services set. Obviously, the learning algorithm is the key factor of our work. It could learn the most general operations from those feedback services and get a new result set against the general operations' signatures.

The learning algorithm is built based on Multiple Instances Learning.

Extracting Operation's Features Vector

WSDL documents can be used to register service in the UDDI registry. There are two types of documents with respect to registering a service: Service Interface Document and Service Implementation Document (Brittenham, Cubrera, Ehnevuske & Graham, 2001). Service Interface Document defines XML tags of <types>, <message>, <portType>, and <binding>; it gives the input and output attributes for each service operation and

Figure 3. WSDL specification of operation getData

```
… …
<types>
 <schema>
<complexType name="POType">
<all>
<element name="id" type="string"/>
<element name="name" type="string"/>
<element name="items">
<complexType>
</all>
</complexType>
</schema>
 </types>

<complexType name="Item">
<all>
<element name="quantity" type="int"/>
<element name="product" type="string"/>
</all>
</complexType>
… …
<message name="getDataRequest">
<part name="id" type="string"/>
</message>
<message name="getDataResponse">
<part name="data" type="POType"/>
</message>
<portType name="Data_PortType">
<operation name="getData">
<input message="tns:getDataRequest"/>
<output message="getDataResponse"/>
</operation>
… …
</portType>
… …
```

omits implementation details (defined in Service Implementation Document) such as port address, communication protocol, and so forth. For our retrieval approach, operation's parameter vector is drawn out from Service Interface Document or a complete WSDL document.

WSDL is an XML-based hierarchical interface-definition language. The <types> tag lies at the lowest level of the hierarchy. The <message> tag is defined one layer above <types>, and the next layer specifies the service operations under <portType>, which are composed of messages. Finally, the whole service is defined as the composition of its data types and operations.

In our experiments, an operation's feature vector is gained through exploiting the hierarchical structure of a WSDL document. Compared with a parameter's name, its XML data types are more important to end users. Therefore, we represent every operation as [*(Cons), OperName: InparaList; OutParaList*]^T. The input/output parameters are separated by a dot, and input parameters list and out parameters list are separated by a semicolon. *Cons* is an optional item used to present some constraint to this operation. If the parameter's XML data type is a complex type, it should be presented by its subtypes. For example, the specification of operation "getData" in a Web Service described in Figure 3 would be converted to a feature vector as [*getData: id:sring; data: POType* [*id:sting, name:string, Item:*[*quantity:int, product:string*]]]^T. Therefore, a service should be described as its services name (or ID), multiple feature vectors of its operations, and a state tag used to identify positive or negative. If a service has not been labeled, its state is presented as unknown.

We designed and implemented a parser to exploit the hierarchical structure of a WSDL document to capture the operations' feature vectors of a service. Every feature vector describes a function delivered by the service in terms of operations. The hypothesis underlying our matching algorithm is that if two services are conceptually similar, they are more likely also to contain a structurally similar operations set than others (Wang & Stroulia, 2003). Therefore, the learning algorithm involves the comparison of the operations' feature vector, which is based on the comparison of the structures of the operations' input and output messages. As a result, the overall process roots in comparing the data types involved in the two WSDL documents.

Learning Algorithm Based on MIL: SigO-kNN

In order to adapt Multiple Instances Learning to the service discovery problem, we proposed a new distance equation for operation's feature vector and types matching. This distance equation is used as similarity metrics between training examples and candidate services (test examples) in a multiple instances learning algorithm.

The k-nearest neighbor algorithm (kNN) is one of the most widely used algorithms in multi-instance problem, which marks an unknown case with the label holding by the majority of its k-nearest neighboring training examples. Typically, Wang and Zucker (2000) employed modified Hausdorff distance to measure the neighboring distances between numerical objects. By definition, two bags—A and B—are within Hausdorff distance *d* if and only if every object of A is within distance *d* with at least one object of B, and vice versa. Since the standard Hausdorff distance is very sensitive to outliers, they defined the Minimal Hausdorff distance as Equation 1, where ||a-b|| is the Euclidean distance between a and b.

$$minH(A,B) = \min_{\substack{1\le i\le m \\ 1\le j\le n}}(Dist(a_i - b_j)) = \min_{\substack{a\in A \\ b\in B}}\|a-b\| \quad (1)$$

Some representative multiple instances problems can be resolved using the method described previously. However, for the services retrieval problem presented in this article, instances (operations) are not described by numerical attributes. For each operation, the WSDL document has provided a description of the input and output message and their substructure. It indicates that two operations have the least distance if and only if they have the most compatible name and message parameters. Therefore, the Minimal Hausdorff distance from Web Service A to B would be defined as Equation 2.

$$\text{SigO-H}(A,B) = \min_{\substack{1\le i\le m\\ 1\le j\le n}}(Dist(a_i - b_j)) = \max_{\substack{a\in A\\ b\in B}}(Dist(a,b)) \quad (2)$$

Here, *Dist(a, b)* presents the distance from operation a to operation b. It is measured by the similarity of the operation's feature vector. This feature vector is used to identify the signature information in an operation, such as name and parameter types. Formally, given two Web Services A and B, *Oa* is one operation in A, and *Ob* is one operation in B. We could define the feature vector of *Oa* as [*Oa*: $InPara_{a1}$, $InPara_{a2}$, $InPara_{am}$; $OutPara_{a1}$, ..., $OutPara_{ak}$]^T , and define the feature vector of *Ob* as [*Ob*: $InPara_{b1}$, $InPara_{b2}$, $InPara_{bm}$; $OutPara_{b1}$,..., $OutPara_{bk}$]^T. As a result, the distance from a to b can be defined as Equation 3.

$$Dist(a,b) = 1 - \frac{\alpha}{m}\sum_{i=1}^{m} Sim(InPara_{ai}, InPara_{bi}) * \frac{\beta}{k}\sum_{j=1}^{k} Sim(OutPara_{aj}, OutPara_{bj}) \quad (3)$$

Here, m is defined as m= min{am, bm}, k=min{ak, bk}, m or k is regarded as 1 if there are not any input or output parameters. α and βcan be used to describe the weight, and α+β=1. *Sim(Pa, Pb)* gives similarity of the two parameters *pa* and *pb*.

The data types used in a Web Service could potentially have highly complex structures. In this article, if two data types have the same name and they are imported from the same namespace, they are identical. Otherwise, they are compared according to their substructures repeatedly until it ends with simple type such as "*int*". The result of comparing two simple types is decided by a measure matrix that contains similarity values of all pair-wise combinations of source data type and target data type. For illustration, Table 1 gives an example of basic data type matching values. In this matrix, the source types are listed at the left, and the target types are listed on the top row. The similarity of two parameters is computed by identifying the correspondence matching scores of the individual parameter pairs. Obviously, the measure matrix is asymmetrical. For example, if a service requestor requires an operation with input parameter of type "*int*", then not only the type of "*int*" but also the type of "*float*" in a candidate service's operation can gain a high similarity matching score. However, when a service

Table 1. Basic data types matching scores

	int	**String**	**float**	**Boolean**	**short**	**long**	**double**	**decimal**
int	*1*	*0.5*	*1*	*0.8*	*0.5*	*1*	*1*	*0.5*
String	*0.5*	*1*	*0.5*	*0.5*	*0.5*	*0.5*	*0.5*	*0.5*
float	*0.8*	*0.5*	*1*	*0.5*	*0.8*	*1*	*1*	*0.5*
Boolean	*0.8*	*0.5*	*0.5*	*1*	*0.5*	*0.5*	*0.5*	*0.5*
short	*0.8*	*0.5*	*0.5*	*0.5*	*1*	*0.8*	*1*	*0.5*
long	*1*	*0.5*	*1*	*0.5*	*1*	*1*	*0.8*	*0.5*
double	*0.8*	*0.5*	*0.8*	*0.5*	*0.8*	*0.8*	*1*	*0.5*
decimal	*0.5*	*0.5*	*0.5*	*0.5*	*0.5*	*0.5*	*0.5*	*1*

requestor need inputs a parameter of "*float*", the candidate type "*int*" only gains *0.8* score, because there will be data information loss if we map data from type "*float*" to "*int*".

Finally, the determinant expression for Web Services refinement is defined as Equation 4. Here, *Sc* stands for a candidate Web Service in the coarse result set. *kNNS* is the k-nearest neighbors set of *Sc* that have been labeled by the users, where *Ap* is positive labeled and *An* is negative labeled. Then *Sc* is labeled as positive when the positive similarity sum is larger than the negative similarity sum; otherwise, it is labeled as negative.

$$L(Sc)=\begin{cases}1 & \text{if } \sum_{\substack{Ap\in kNNS\\ Sc\in TS}} \text{SigO-H}(Ap,Sc) > \sum_{\substack{An\in kNNS\\ Sc\in TS}} \text{SigO-H}(An,Sc)\\ 0 & \text{Otherwise}\end{cases} \quad (4)$$

CASE STUDY

This work is based on requirements from a real-world case study on Web Services retrieval in Jade Bird Software Component Library (JBCL) system, which is implemented by the institute of software of Peking University (Zou, Zhang, Zhang, Xie & Mei, 2006). JBCL is an extension of UDDI registry, and it supports both traditional code component management and Web Services management. Thus, to facilitate users finding their required services efficiently, JBCL published some taxonomies to classify these services and provided category-based matching method in its retrieval mechanism.

Bob, a user of JBCL, wants to discover some geography information search Web Services now. Then Bob submits a query with simple key words of "geo" and a leaf category attribute of "geography"; the JBCL retrieval mechanism returns a service matching result set with 35 candidate services. However, only 14 services in this candidate set have provided Bob the required operations. The precision is 40%. As shown in Table 2, to simplify description, we enumerate all theses candidate services with natural numbers. Therefore, our refining tool is expected to refine this candidate set to improve the precision of Web Services retrieval.

The refinement is based on the fact that Bob will browse some services among the 35 candidates. In order to identify an appropriate service, Bob

Table 2. Bob browses some services, and the matching results is refined

	Log Collection as training set		Matching results (not including services in training set)		
Feedback times	Positively labeled	Negatively labeled	Result set	Right Num	Sum
0	{}	{}	{s1, s2, s4, s9, s10, s11, s5, s6 s7, s12 s30, s20, s19, s21, s14, s13, s15, s17, s29, s3, s31, s22, s28, s26, s8, s16, s39, s41, s42, s24, s34, s43, s35, s36, s18 }	14	21
1	{s1, s2, s4}	{s9, s10, s11}	{s6, s12, s30, s3, s20, s5, s7, s15, s29, s14, s31, s8, s42, s36 }	9	14
2	{s1, s2, s4, s5, s6 }	{s9, s10, s11, s7, s12}	{s30, s3, s20, s29, s31, s19, s8, s36, s41, s42, s43, s35 }	9	12
3	{s1, s2, s4, s5, s6, s30, s20}	{s9, s10, s11, s7, s12, s19, s21}	{s29, s3, s31, s8, s41, s42, s43, s35}	7	8
Expect			*{s1, s2, s4, s5, s6, s30, s20 ,s29, s3, s31, s8, s41, s42, s43}*	*14*	*14*

usually browses some candidate services to see whether it has provided the required operations. If a service has provided Bob's required operations, it is labeled as positive; otherwise, it is labeled as negative. In the first feedback, Bob may only click and browse six services in the candidate services set, three of which are positive and the other three negative. These labeled services are stored to be used as a training set. In the following, JBCL retrieval mechanism invokes the refinement tool, and 14 services are returned at this time. On line 2 in Table 3, nine services are right recommended (matched and returned as new candidates). The precision reaches 64%. Therefore, compared with the initial matching results, Bob could select from a more confined scope, and the retrieval process can be accelerated.

As shown on line 3 of Table 2, when 10 services are labeled in feedback 2, the refinement tool has returned 12 candidate services, of which nine services are rightly recommended. The precision arrives at 75%. In Feedback 3, the precision reaches 87.5%. Therefore, the precision of a learning algorithm will increase more quickly as more services are fed back. This will confirm a scalable retrieval process as Bob browses and gives feedback on new services every time.

It can also be found that not only the sum of labeled services, but also the ratio between the number of services positively labeled and the number of services negatively labeled will affect the refining efficiency. For a certain amount of training set, if more negatives are labeled, the precision will be much higher. Therefore, we will give the number of positive training instances and the number of negative training instances separately in the following experiments.

EXPERIMENTS AND RESULTS

Experiment Setup

For experiments, we selected 275 Web Services from three sources: 18 Web Services were selected from seven big practice projects in a graduate course named "Web Services Technology & .NET Framework." This course required every student group (about three or four students) to develop a particular Web application system, such as "online bookstore management system," and the application should be composed by some Web Services they have developed by themselves or discovered from others. In the second part, 192 Web Services were selected from our JBCL system. In the third part, 65 WSDL-specific documents were downloaded from XMethods (xmethods.com). On average, each Web Service (bag) contained 5.04 operations (instances).

All these Web Services can be classified into eight categories according to their function. We named these categories from D_1 to D_8. It could be found that in each category, just a part of the services is useful, because only these services can provide operations required by particular applications. For example, D_1 includes all services that

Table 3. The experiment Web services categories

Categories	Positive Number	Negative Number	Sum
D_1	9	11	20
D_2	7	21	28
D_3	12	25	37
D_4	15	30	45
D_5	11	20	31
D_6	*14*	*21*	*35*
D_7	12	21	33
D_8	17	29	46
Sum	*97*	*178*	*275*

can be used to sort data. If a user wants to sort a list of student records, it requires inputting a parameter of "*float.*" However, only nine services in this category can provide this required operation. Therefore, the precision of category-based retrieval approaches is only 45%. As the SigO-kNN algorithm described, these nine services that have provided required operations for the service requestor are positive from a multiple instances view. On the contrary, the other 14 services are negative. Table 3 shows the number of positive and negative services in each category. Thus, we expect that the refinement tool would refine the candidate services set of D_1 from 20 services to new matching results only including those positive nine services for the service requestor selecting. This will accelerate the services retrieval process efficiently.

To evaluate our refinement algorithm, the recall and precision of the algorithm is measured. Suppose there are a total of P positive Web Services and N negative Web Services in the category. After once refining, Pa positive services and Na negative services are recommended. On the other hand, Pr positive services and Nr negative services are rejected by the refinement algorithm. It is obvious that $P = Pa + Pr, N = Na + Nr$. Then, the accuracy, recall, and precision are defined as Equations 5 to 7, respectively. They reflect the correctness of the refine algorithm.

$$\text{Accuaracy} = (\text{Pa}+\text{Nr})/(\text{P}+\text{N}) \tag{5}$$

$$\text{Precision} = \text{Pa} / (\text{Pa}+\text{Na}) \tag{6}$$

$$\text{Recall} = \text{Pa} / \text{P} \tag{7}$$

Average Performance Analysis

In this section, we illustrate average performance of our refining algorithm based on the eight services set. For each category, an average of 3.5 Web Services are randomly selected as positive training services, and four services are labeled as negative training services. That is, we assume that if a browser labels three Web Services every time, and he or she needs only two or three times of feedback, it is acceptable to a common browser. In fact, we find that more than 93% of users (coming from statistical data of JBCL) are glad to give a label in his or her browsing time when he or she is not satisfied with the matching results. This information will help us carry out the next round of refining. Therefore, the number of services in the training examples used in our experiments is reasonable.

Table 4. SigO-kNN performance analysis

Categories	Feedbacks Sum		Performance		
	Positive	Negative	Accuracy	Recall	Precision
D_1	2	4	0.7	0.6	0.75
D_2	4	6	0.93	0.86	1
D_3	4	5	0.85	1	0.77
D_4	3	5	0.84	1	0.71
D_5	5	5	0.87	1	0.79
D_6	3	3	0.76	0.82	0.64
D_7	3	3	0.79	0.82	0.65
D_8	4	4	0.89	1	0.81
Avg	3.5	4.375	0.82875	0.8875	0.765

Figure 4. Average performance after feedback

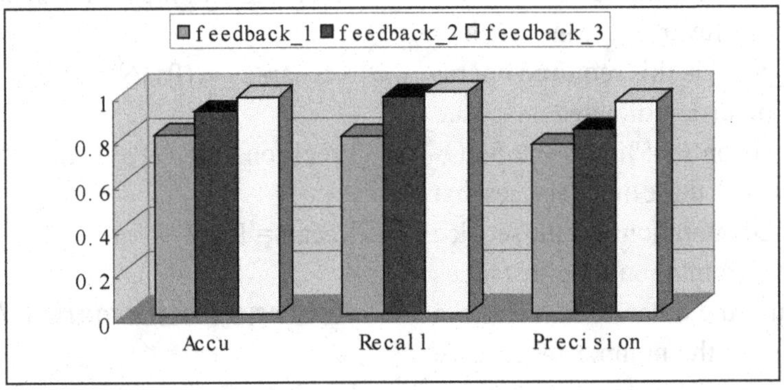

Table 4 shows the experimental matching results after refinement. The distance between services (bags) is measured by Equation2 and Equation3, and we set k=3 in the k-nearest neighbor algorithm of Sigo-kNN. For category D_1, it could be found that the performance of Sigo-kNN based matcher is 70% accuracy, 60% recall, and 75% precision, which is not as good as the performance applied in category 2 (93% accuracy with 86% recall and 100% precision), while the fourth category gets 84% accuracy with 100% recall and 71% precision. On average, 82.8% refinement is correct, and the retrieval precision can be improved to 76.5%.

Figure 4 gives the accuracy, recall, and precision on average after every refinement in Web Services retrieval. Here, about five, eight, and 11 services are labeled as positive or negative, and they are used as training examples in the next refinement process. In general, Feedback_1 (the first feedback) gives two positive labeled examples and three negative examples at random. Then the second time (i.e., feedback_2), another three services are labeled again. Similarly, three services are labeled at feedback_3. Seen from the histogram, Sigo-kNN presents a scalable retrieval performance after every feedback. For example, the precision is 83% on average after two times of feedback, and it reaches 96% when another three services are labeled after the third feedback. On the other hand, when the number of training examples is very small, some services are mistakenly recommended (they do not provide any user interested operations), because

Figure 5.1. Recall comparison.

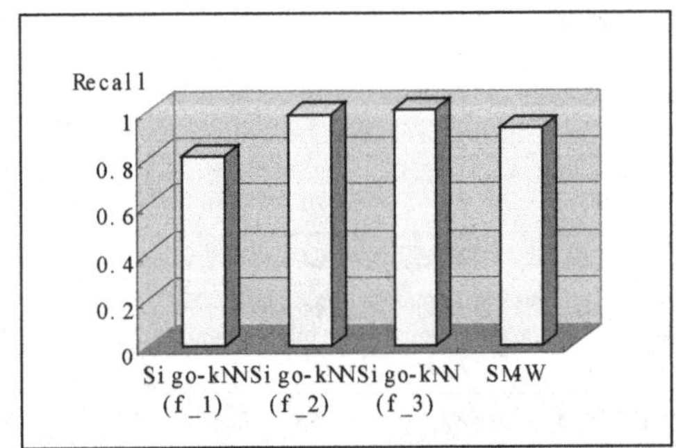

Figure 5.2. Precision comparison

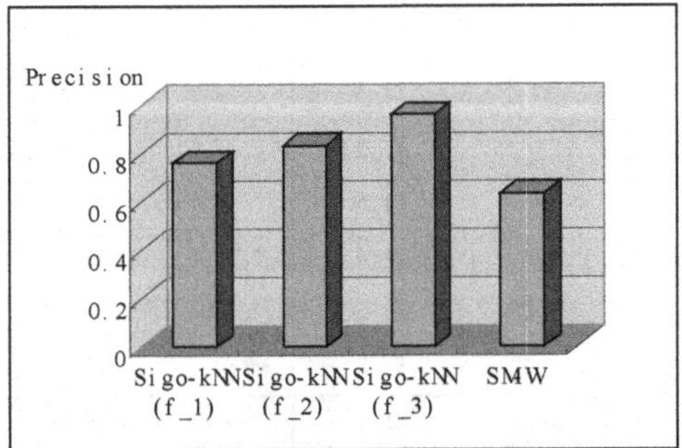

the user uninterested operations in some positive labeled service may affect the distance measure in MIL. However, with the number of training examples increasing, this effect will disappear very quickly.

In order to further verify the validity of our learning algorithm, we also implement the Structure Matching service discovery algorithm (shown as SM-W in Figure 5) proposed by Wang and Stroulia (2003) and test this algorithm with the data sets shown in Table 3. The main idea of SM-W is to match two services utilizing the structure information of WSDL document; it requires users to input a (potentially partial) specification of the desired WSDL specification and returns the similar Web Services from a set of WSDL specification available. In Figure 5.1 and Figure 5.2, we illustrate the comparison of performance of our Sigo-kNN algorithm and SM-W algorithm. Here, the Sigo-kNN(f_i) indicates the recall and the precision of Sigo-kNN after the i (i = 1,2,3) times of feedback.

Shown as Figure 5.1, the average recall of SM-W is about 92%. However, the recall Sigo-kNN after the second feedback reaches 98%, although it only gains 80% candidate services at first refinement. In Figure 5.2, it indicates that Sigo-kNN algorithm gains 76% precision after one feedback, which is better than 63.3% precision of SM-W algorithm. From the comparison, we can conclude that our Sigo-kNN algorithm can reach the same discovery performance after one or two feedbacks. At the same time, our algorithm does not need the retrieval users to input any new discovery terms; it accelerates the retrieval process and helps users find their interested service more quickly.

RELATED WORK

Since the problem of Web Services retrieval is an instance of the more general problem of component retrieval, researches in the components retrieval area are directly relevant. Mili, Valtchev, Di Sciullo, and Gabrini (2001) classify the existing component retrieval approaches into four categories: simple keyword and string search (Maarek, Berry & Kaiser, 1991), faceted classification and retrieval (Prieto-Diaz & Freeman, 1987; Ostertag & Hendler, 1992; Mili et al., 1997), signature matching (Zaremski & Wing, 1995; Wang & Stroulia, 2003; Degwekar, Su & Lam, 2004), and behavioral matching (Zaremski & Wing, 1997). The majority of retrieval mechanisms uses simple keyword searching, as it can be highly automated with a low operational cost. When using the keyword matching method to acquire the desired components, the user can specify his or her query in the form of a set of keywords. Then the retrieval mechanism filters out components by calculating the similarity between the query and the description of components. Unfortunately, in most circumstances, it is unavoidable that the descriptions of components may contain improper or even noisy information, which results in low recall and precision. The faceted classification approaches try to classify the objects from several orthogonal aspects. For each facet, a keyword set is given by the domain experts. Components are described and retrieved using the keyword set. However, sometimes it is hard to define the proper keyword set under each facet. Signature matching focuses on the name and the parameter types of arguments defined for components. Methods belonging to this category help users retrieve components by comparing the type of arguments in the signature. Our refining mechanism is based on this kind of approach. The behavior matching approaches leverage the executable property of the component. The candidate components are selected according to the comparison between the execution results and the expected outputs in the query. However, these approaches are rather restrictive because the overheads of executing components are quite high. Besides, the execution of components may cause unexpected results; for example, deleting records in the database.

In recent years, researchers also paid attention to how to better rank the component retrieval results, as well as how to retrieve components from multi-repositories simultaneously. To help users identify their desired components from results quickly and conveniently, Inoue, Yokomori, Yamamoto, Matsushita, and Kusumoto (2005) used an algorithm to rank the retrieval results according to the relationship among components. Li, et al. (2006) further improved Inoue's work by taking the user preference information into consideration. Pan, Wang, Zhang, Xie, and Yang (2004) proposed an approach to support retrieving components from several repositories via a single interface based on the Bayesian network.

With the rapid development of Web Services technology, many research efforts have been devoted to the Web Services discovery field. These service discovery approaches can be divided into four categories: text-based methods, signature-based methods, specification-based methods, and ontology-based methods. Text-based methods utilize the text description information to find proper services, and it can be used as the basis for many other approaches.

Signature-based methods are widely used in Web Services retrieval. Wang and Stroulia (2003) proposed a service discovery method that compares two services utilizing the structure information of the WSDL documents. The similarity is calculated according to the iterative signature matching of the elements in the WSDL file, including data types, messages, and operations. However, sometimes it may be too constraining for a Web Service to match a query exactly. Furthermore, it is usually very time-consuming to formulate a good signature query in the form of XML-based specification (Wang & Stroulia, 2003). We differentiate their work by the signature requirements that are formed automatically instead of manually. In some sense, our improved Web Services retrieval process can be seen as an integration of category-based matching and signature-based matching. The category-based matching returns all services in some category as candidate results in a lower precision in the first step. In the following step, the refining algorithm based on the MIL technique is used to optimize the retrieval results. Because we utilize specifications of labeled services in logs to form a better query, the refining mechanism thus can be seen as a kind of signature-based matching.

Degwekar, et al. (2004) and ShaikhAli and Rana (2003) extended WSDL to include constraint specifications in service descriptions and requests. So the discovery methods can find matching between a service's capabilities and a user's requirements by comparing the specification information. These specification-based methods also can be used as the base in our work. However, in most circumstances, service providers are unwilling to provide the specification for services. Also, it is hard for users to give an exact query by using specification.

Paolucci and Kamwamura (2002) and Akkiraju and Goodwin (2003) import the Semantic Web technology to the Web Services discovery process, which forms the base for ontology-based discovery methods. In these methods (Paolucci & Kamwamura, 2002), the Web Services are described using ontology language such as DAML-S, OWL-S. Then the retrieval mechanism returns the qualified Web Services according to the query by using ontological reasoning. These discovery approaches all rely on the domain information and ontology. However, it is usually very difficult to establish a perfect ontology. Besides, currently, the overhead of giving semantic description for Web Services based on the ontology language is quite high.

CONCLUSION

In Web Services retrieval process, traditional category-based approaches have been used to match candidate services against their function description. These approaches usually can achieve high recall but low precision, because some Web Services with semantic relevant descriptions may not provide suitable interfaces. In this article, we present a new approach to increase the precision of category-based matching results step by step. In this approach, a service is investigated from a multiple instances view because users cannot record whether an operation in a candidate service is useful as a service is entirely described in UDDI registry. In order to adapt a Multiple Instances Learning technique to the service retrieval process, we proposed a new distance equation for matching the operation feature vectors. At the same time, we collected the service requestor's feedback information from his or her browsing history. Experimental results show that our approach can improve the effect in Web Services retrieval process.

The key contribution of this approach is that it could learn from user's browsing information and tell the matching mechanism to shift its focus to those useful operations. Our approach can increase the precision of the matching results, and the service requestor thus can select a target in a smaller scope. However, we do not take the service's QoS or reputation information into consideration currently, which is also very important in the service reuse scenario. Therefore, we believe it will be crucial to expand this approach through much richer log information so that we can gain higher precision and recall in matching.

ACKNOWLEDGMENT

We would like to thank Liangjie Zhang for his valuable work on the implementation of our early version of the service refinement tool. This research was sponsored by the National Science Foundation (SN: 60473059, SN: 90412011, SN: 90612011), the National Grand Fundamental Research Program (973 Program) of China (SN: 2005CB321805), the National Key Technology R&D Program (No.2006BAH02A02), and 863 Program (SN: 2005AA112030) in China.

REFERENCES

Akkiraju, R., & Goodwin, R. (2003). *A method for semantically enhancing the service discovery capabilities of UDDI*. Proceedings of the Workshop on Information Integration on the Web, IJCAI 2003, Acapulco, Mexico, 87–92.

Brittenham, P., Cubrera, F., Ehnevuske, D., & Graham, S. (2001). Understanding WSDL in a UDDI Registry. Retrieved from http://www-106.ibm.com/developerworks/webservices/library/ws-wsdl/ .

Colgrave, J., Akkiraju, R., & Goodwin, R. (2004). *External Matching in UDDI*. Proceedings of the International Conference on Web Services, 2004.

Degwekar, S., Su, S.Y.W., & Lam, H. (2004). *Constraint specification and processing in Web services publication and discovery*. Proceedings of the IEEE International Conference on Web Services (ICWS 04), 210–217.

Dietterich, T.G., & Lathrop, R.H. (1997). Solving the multiple-instance problem with axis-parallel rectangles. *Artificial Intelligence, 89*(1-2), 31–71.

Inoue, K., Yokomori, R., Yamamoto, T., Matsushita, M., & Kusumoto, S. (2005). Ranking significance of software components based on use relations. *IEEE Transactions on Software Engineering, 31*(3), 213–225.

Li, Y., Pan, Y., Zhang, L., Xie, B., & Sun, J.S. (2006). *Ranking component retrieval results by leveraging user history information*. Proceedings of the 18th International Conference on Software Engineering and Knowledge Engineering (SEKE), 284–289.

Maarek, Y.S., Berry, D.M., & Kaiser, G.E. (1991). An information retrieval approach for automatically constructing software libraries. *IEEE Transactions on Software Engineering, 17*(8), 800–813.

Maron, O, & Lozano-Pérez, T. (1998). A framework for multiple-instance learning. *Advances in Neural Information Processing Systems 10*, 570–576.

Maron, O., & Ratan, A.L. (1998). *Multiple-instance learning for natural scene classification*. Proceedings of the 15th International Conference on Machine Learning, Madison, WI, 341–349.

Mili, A., Mili, R., & Mittermeier, R. (1997). Storing and retrieving software components: A refinement-based system. *IEEE Transactions on Software Engineering, 23*(7), 445–460.

Mili, H., Valtchev, P., Di Sciullo, A.-M., & Gabrini, P. (2001). *Automating the indexing and retrieval of reusable software components*. Proceedings of the 6th International Workshop (NLDB 01), Madrid, Spain, 75–86.

Ming, L., Xiao-Bing, X., & Zhou, Z. (2004). Chinese Web index page recommendation based on multi-instance learning. *Journal of Software, 15*(9), 1328–1335.

Ostertag, E., Hendler, J., Prieto-Diaz, R., & Braun, C. (1992). Computing similarity in a reuse library system: An AI-based approach. *ACM Transactions on Software Engineering and Methodology, 1*(3), 205–228.

Pan, Y., Wang, L., Zhang, L., Xie, B., & Yang, F.Q. (2004). *Relevancy based semantic interoperation of reuse repositories*. Proceedings of the 12th ACM SIGSOFT Symposium on Foundations of Software Engineering (FSE), 211–220.

Paolucci, M., & Kawamura, T. (2002). *Importing the Semantic Web in UDDI*. Proceedings of the E-Services Semantic Web Workshop (ESSW 2002), 225–236.

Paolucci, M., Kawamura, T., Payne, T.R., & Sycara, K. (2002). *Semantic matching of Web services capabilities*. Proceedings of the First International Semantic Web Conference (ISWC), Sardinia, Italy, 333–347.

Prieto-Diaz, R., & Freeman, P. (1987). Classifying software for reuse. *IEEE Software, 4*(1), 6–16.

Ravichandran, T. (2003). Special issue on component-based software development. *The DATA BASE for Advances in Information Systems, 34*(4), 45–46.

ShaikhAli, A., & Rana, O.F. (2003). *UDDIe: An extended registry for Web services*. Proceedings of the 2003 Symposium on Applications and the Internet Workshops, 85–89.

UDDI Technical Committee. About UDDI. OASIS UDDI Member Section. Retrieved from http://www.uddi.org/about.html .

Wang, J., & Zucker, J.-D. (2000). *Solving the multiple-instance problem: A lazy learning approach*. Proceedings of the 17th International Conference on Machine Learning, San Francisco, California, 1119–1125.

Wang, Y.Q., & Stroulia, E. (2003). Flex*ible interface matching for Web Services discovery*. Proceedings of the Fourth International Conference on Web Information Systems Engineering (WISE 03), 147–156.

XMethods. http://www.xmethods.com/

Zaremski, A.M., & Wing, J.M. (1995). Signature matching: A tool for using software libraries. *ACM Transactions on Software Engineering and Methodology, 4*(2), 146–170.

Zaremski, A.M., & Wing, J.M. (1997). Specification matching of software components. *ACM Transactions on Software Engineering and Methodology,* 333–369.

Zhang, C., & Chen, X. (2005). *A multiple instance learning approach for content based image retrieval using one-class support vector machine*. Proceedings of the IEEE International Conference on Multimedia and Expo (ICME 2005), 1142–1145.

Zhang, C., Chen, S.-C., & Shyu, M.-L. (2004). *Multiple object retrieval for image databases using multiple instance learning and relevance feedback*. Proceedings of the 2004 IEEE International Conference on Multimedia and Expo (ICME), Taipei, Taiwan, 775–778.

Zhou, Z.-H., Jiang, K., & Li, M. (2005). Multi-instance learning based web mining. *Applied Intelligence, 22*(2), 135–147.

Zou, Y.Z., Zhang, L.J., Zhang, L., Xie, B., & Mei, H. (2006). *User feedback-based refinement for Web services retrieval using multiple instance learning*. Proceedings of the International Conference on Web Services, Chicago, 18–22.

ENDNOTE

1 http://developer.ebay.com/webservices/latest/eBaySvc.wsdl

This work was previously published in the International Journal of Web Services Research, Volume 5, Issue 2, edited by L. Zhang, pp. 77-93, copyright 2008 by IGI Publishing (an imprint of IGI Global).

Chapter 16
A Model-Driven Development Framework for Non-Functional Aspects in Service Oriented Architecture

Hiroshi Wada
University of Massachusetts - Boston, USA

Junichi Suzuki
University of Massachusetts - Boston, USA

Katsuya Oba
OGIS International, Inc., USA

ABSTRACT

Service oriented architecture (SOA) is an emerging style of software architectures to reuse and integrate existing systems for designing new applications. Each application is designed in an implementation independent manner using two major abstract concepts: services and connections between services. In SOA, non-functional aspects (e.g., security and fault tolerance) of services and connections should be described separately from their functional aspects (i.e., business logic) because different applications use services and connections in different non-functional contexts. This paper proposes a model-driven development (MDD) framework for non-functional aspects in SOA. The proposed MDD framework consists of (1) a Unified Modeling Language (UML) profile to model non-functional aspects in SOA, and (2) an MDD tool that transforms a UML model defined with the proposed profile to application code. Empirical evaluation results show that the proposed MDD framework improves the reusability and maintainability of service-oriented applications by hiding low-level implementation technologies in SOA.

INTRODUCTION

A key challenge in large-scale distributed systems is to reuse and integrate existing systems to build new applications in a cost effective manner (Vinoski, 2003; Zhang, 2004). Service Oriented Architecture (SOA) addresses this challenge by improving the reusability and maintainability of distributed systems (Arsanjani, Zhang, Ellis, Allam, & Channabasavaiah, 2007; Bichler & Lin, 2006; Endrei, Ang, Arsanjani, Chua, Comte, Krogdahl, Luo, & Newling, 2004; Foster, 2005; Lewis, Morris, Brien, Smith, & Wrage, 2005; Papazoglou, 2003). It is an emerging style of software architectures to design applications in an implementation independent manner using two major abstract concepts: *services* and *connections* between services. Each service encapsulates the function of a subsystem in an existing system. Each connection defines how services are connected with each other and how messages are exchanged through the connection. SOA hides the implementation details of services and connections (e.g., programming languages and remoting middleware) from application developers. They can reuse and combine services to build their applications without knowing the implementation details of services and connections.

In order to make this vision of SOA a reality, this article focuses on a research issue of increasing the reusability of services and connections and addresses this issue by separating non-functional aspects (e.g., security and fault tolerance) of services and connections from their functional aspects. The separation of functional and non-functional aspects can improve the reusability of services and connections because it allows different applications to use services and connections in different non-functional contexts. For example, an application may unicast messages to a service and another may manycast messages to multiple replicas of the service to improve fault tolerance. Also, an application may send signed and encrypted messages to a service, when the messages travel to the service through third-party intermediaries, in order to prevent the intermediaries from maliciously sniffing or altering the messages. Another application may send plain messages to the service via unsecured connection when the service is hosted in-house. The separation of functional and non-functional aspects can also improve the ease of understanding application design and enable the two different aspects to evolve independently. This results in higher maintainability of applications.

This article describes a model-driven development (MDD) framework for non-functional aspects in SOA. The MDD framework consists of (1) a Unified Modeling Language (UML) profile to model non-functional aspects in SOA, and (2) an MDD tool that accepts a UML model defined with the proposed profile and transforms it to application code (e.g., program code and deployment descriptors). The proposed UML profile allows application developers to graphically describe and maintain non-functional aspects in SOA as UML diagrams (composite structure diagrams and class diagrams). Using the proposed UML profile, non-functional aspects can be modeled without depending on any particular implementation technologies. The proposed MDD tool, called Ark, transforms implementation independent UML models into implementation specific application code.

This article describes design details of the proposed UML profile and demonstrates how Ark transforms an input UML model to application code that runs with certain implementation technologies such as Enterprise Service Buses (ESBs) (Chappell, 2004), secure file transfer protocols and grid computing platforms. Empirical evaluation results show that the proposed MDD framework improves the reusability and maintainability of service-oriented applications by hiding implementation technologies in UML models.

CONTRIBUTIONS

This article offers the following three contributions to the design space of service-oriented applications.

- **Modeling support for non-functional aspects in SOA**: This work is the first attempt to investigate a UML profile to consistently model a wide range of non-functional aspects in SOA, although there exist several UML profiles for specific aspects (e.g., functional aspects and service discovery) in SOA. (See the Related Work section for more details.) The proposed UML profile covers the following four areas of non-functional aspects.
  1. **Service deployment semantics:** Service redundancy.
  2. **Message transmission semantics:** Messaging synchrony, message delivery assurance, message queuing, multicast, manycast, anycast, message routing, message prioritization, messaging timeout, message logging, and message retention.
  3. **Message processing semantics:** Message conversion, message split, message aggregation, message validation, and message filtering.
  4. **Security semantics:** Transport-level encryption, message-level encryption (entire/partial message encryption), message signature, message access control, and service access control.
- **Modeling support for regulatory compliance**: As regulatory compliance has been becoming an important factor in software development and maintenance, regulatory mandates (e.g., the Sarbanes-Oxley Act and HIPPA) dramatically increase the number of non-functional aspects that application developers need to consider (O'Grady, 2004). This work is the first attempt to investigate a visual modeling language to describe non-functional aspects derived from regulatory mandates. The proposed UML profile allows application developers (or compliance management staffs) to graphically specify and verify how their applications meet regulatory mandates. Currently, the proposed UML profile addresses data retention, data/process validation (e.g., consistency validation among an order, invoice, and payment) and security (e.g., access control and data integrity).
- **MDD support for service-oriented applications**: Non-functional requirements change during application lifecycle more often than functional aspects (Bieberstein, Bose, Fiammante, Jones, & Shah, 2005). It can be expensive to manage frequent changes in non-functional requirements. This results in escalating maintenance cost, in turn total cost of owning. When a non-functional requirement (e.g., security policy) changes in an application, the proposed MDD framework allows application developers to make the change in a UML model specifying the application's non-functional aspects and keep its functional part intact. The proposed MDD tool (Ark) generates non-functional code from the updated UML model and combines the generated code with existing functional code. Ark makes application's functional aspects reusable across the changes in non-functional requirements, thereby improving the productivity of application development and maintenance.

BACKGROUND AND A MOTIVATING EXAMPLE

UML is a modeling language to describe application designs as graphical diagrams. It specifies the syntax (or notation) and semantics of every model element that appears in diagrams (e.g., class, interface and association). The syntax and semantics are defined in the UML metamodel

(Object Management Group, 2004), which is the grammar specification for standard (default) model elements in UML.

In addition to standard model elements, UML provides extension mechanisms (e.g., stereotypes and tagged-values) to specialize them to precisely describe domain or application specific concepts (Fuentes & Vallecillo, 2004). A stereotype is applied to a standard model element and specializes its semantics to a particular domain or application. Each stereotyped model element can have data fields, called tagged-values, specific to the stereotype. Each tagged-value consists of a name and value. A particular set of stereotypes and tagged-values is called a UML profile.

For example, a UML profile for Enterprise Java Beans (EJB) (Java Community Process, 2001) defines the stereotype <<EJBEntityBean>>, which extends Class in the UML metamodel. This means the stereotype can be applied to classes. Thus, a UML class stereotyped with <<EJBEntityBean>> indicates that the class is designed as an EJB entity bean. The stereotype <<EJBEntityBean>> has a tagged-value, called EJBPersisitenceType, to specify who provides persistence to an entity bean. The tagged-value can have a value Bean or Container. Bean indicates an individual entity bean is responsible for its own persistence, and Container indicates an EJB container takes care of persistence.

Figure 1 shows an overview of an example purchasing system across buyers, retailers, suppliers, and inventory managers. All example models in this article focus on and define several particular parts of this system. In this example system, a Buyer purchases a product from a Supplier via Retailer. A Supervisor authorizes each order that a Buyer places. An Accountant performs accounting tasks for a Retailer. An InventoryManager manages a Retailer's inventory.

Figure 1. The structural architecture of an example purchasing system

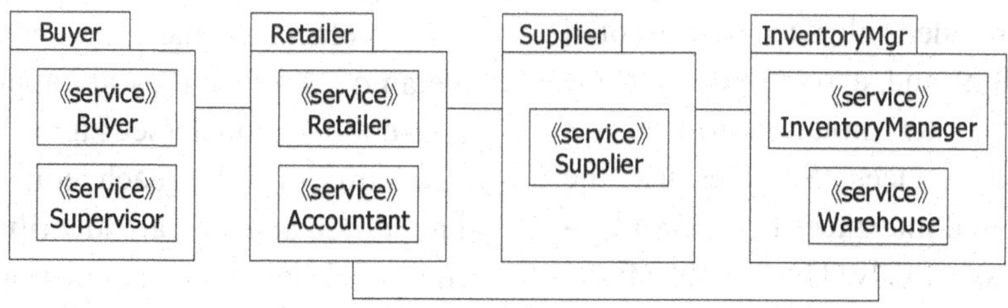

Figure 2. An example UML model

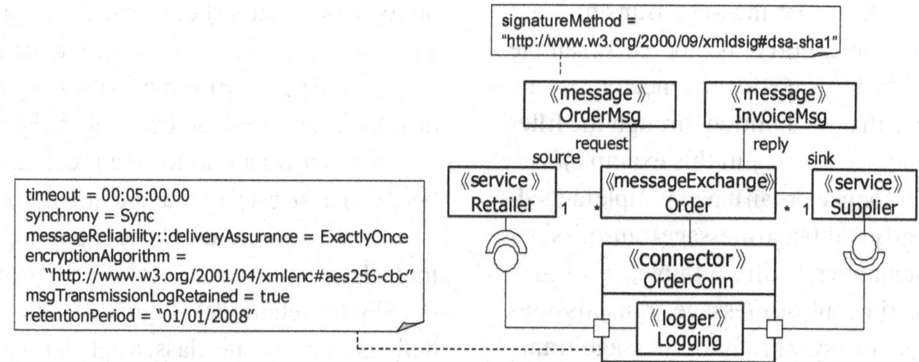

Figure 2 shows an example model built with the proposed UML profile. This model focuses on an interaction between a `Retailer` and `Supplier` in Figure 1, and defines an order processing scenario in which a `Retailer` places an order and a `Supplier` issues an invoice. In this example, two services (`Retailer` and `Supplier`) exchange messages. Each service is represented by a class stereotyped with `<<service>>`. These services exchange two types of messages (`OrderMsg` and `InvoiceMsg`), each of which is stereotyped with `<<message>>`. Each message can have multiple tagged-values to specify additional message transmission/processing semantics. In this example, the tagged-value `signatureMethod` specifies that an `OrderMsg` carries a digital signature created with DSA (Digital Signature Algorithm). Each pair of a request and reply messages is represented by a class stereotyped with `<<messageExchange>>`.

`<<connector>>` represents a connection that transmits messages between services. In this example, messages are delivered through a connector called `OrderConn`. Every message exchange is bound with a connector in order to specify which connector is used to deliver messages. A connector has a provided interface (represented as a "ball" notation) and a required interface (represented as a "socket" notation) to transmit messages between services. Services use the provided and required interfaces to send and receive messages, respectively. The two interfaces are intended to show how services use (connect with) a connector.

Each connector can have multiple filters inside. They are used to define message transmission/processing semantics in a connector. This example uses a `Logger` in the `OrderConn` connector. `Logger` logs messages that transmitted through the filter (`OrderMsg` and `InvoiceMsg` in this example).

Also, each connector can have multiple tagged-values to specify additional message transmission/processing semantics. In this example, `OrderConn` specifies the timeout of message transmissions (five minutes), the synchrony of message transmissions (synchronous), the assurance level of message delivery (exactly once) and the message encryption algorithm (Advanced Encryption Standard). Also, through the use of tagged-values `msgTransmissionLogRetained` and `retentionPeriod`, `OrderConn` specifies to retain the logs of message transmissions until a certain date.

As shown above, the proposed UML profile provides a visual and intuitive abstraction to model the architectures and non-functional aspects of service-oriented applications.

DESIGN OF THE PROPOSED UML PROFILE

The proposed UML profile provides key model elements to specify service-oriented applications: *service*, *message exchange*, *message*, *connector*, and *filter*, each of which is defined as stereotypes (Table 1). Figure 3 shows how the proposed profile defines these stereotypes by extending the UML metamodel. Each stereotype is defined as a metaclass stereotyped with `<<stereotype>>`[1]. Except `Connector`, four stereotypes inherit the `Class` metaclass in the `Kernel` package of the UML metamodel. Thus, they are applied to classes in user-defined models (see Figure 2). A `Service` can be a source or sink of each request/reply message. The source and sink are identified with `source` and `sink`, roles on two associations between a `MessageExchange` and `Services` (Figure 2). Each `MessageExchange` may have multiple reply messages per request message (Figure 3). Using multiplicity on two associations between a `MessageExchange` and `Services`, `MessageExchange` can indicate one-to-one (unicast) and one-to-many (multicast or manycast) message exchanges. For example, Figure 2 shows a one-to-one message exchange between a `Retailer` and a `Supplier`.

`Connector` is a stereotype extending the `Class` metaclass in the `InternalStructures` package of the UML metamodel (Figure 3). This metaclass defines a composite class, a special type of class,

Table 1. Key model elements (stereotypes) in the proposed UML profile

Stereotype	Description
<<service>>	Represents a service.
<<messageExchange>>	Represents a pair of a request and reply messages. Specifies which services send and receive the messages.
<<message>>	Represents a (request or reply) message.
<<connector>>	Represents a connection between services (i.e., message source and destination). Defines the semantics of message transmission and processing. Specifies which messages (message exchange) to transmit.
<<filter>>	Customizes the semantics of message transmission and message processing in a connector.

Figure 3. Definition of stereotypes

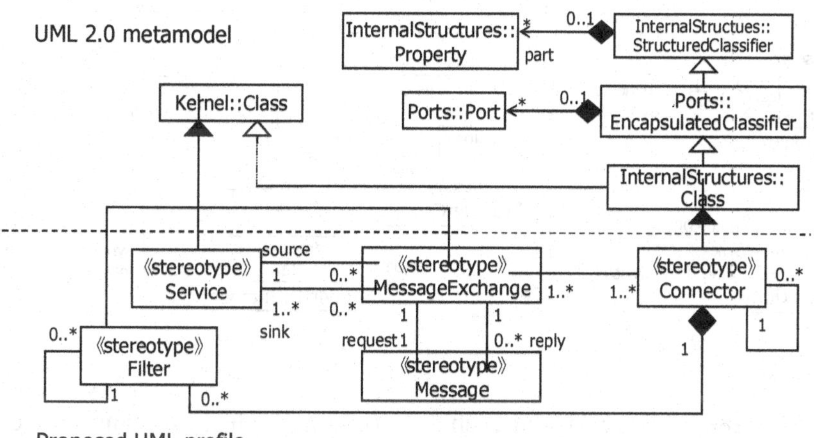

which can contain other model elements (e.g., inner classes)[2] and have `Ports` to specify how internal model elements interact with external elements. In the proposed UML profile, a `Connector` can contain `Filters` to specify the semantics of message transmission and message processing. The `Ports` connected with a `Connector` identify the `Messages` it receives and sends out, using association roles `input` and `output`. For example, Figure 2 shows the `OrderConn` connector , which contains a filter (a `Logger`). This filter receives, records message's log, and sends out `OrderMsg` or `InvoiceMsg` messages.

Connector

`Connector` has 10 tagged-values (Figure 4). `timeout` is a mandatory tagged-value to specify the timeout period (in millisecond) in which a connector needs to deliver each message. If a message is not delivered to its destination (sink) within the timeout period, a connector discards the message. In Figure 2, the timeout period of the connector `OrderConn` is specified as five minutes.

`synchrony` is a mandatory tagged-value to specify the synchrony semantics of message transmissions between a message source and destination. Synchronous, asynchronous and oneway non-blocking semantics are defined as an

Figure 4. Tagged-values of connector

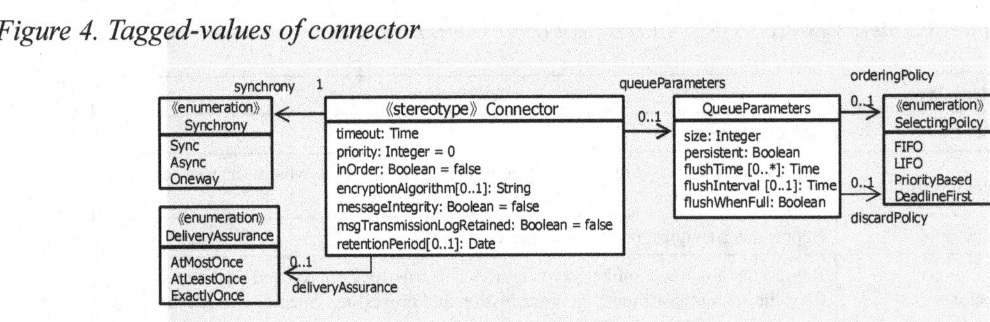

Figure 5. An example of inorder and delivery assurance

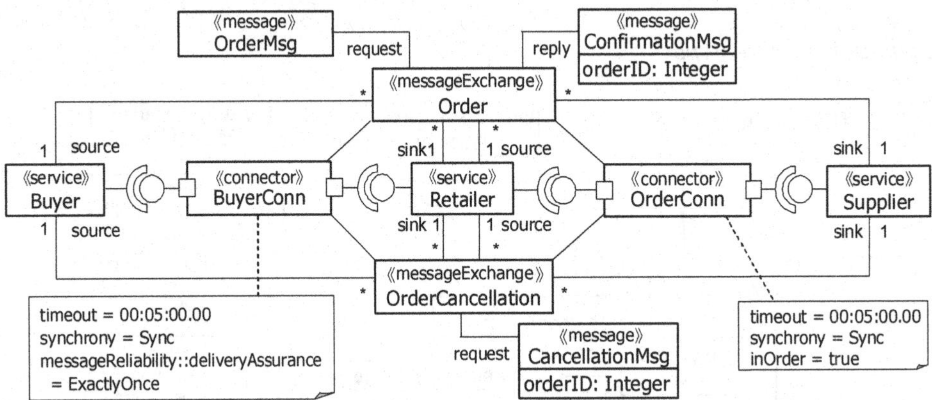

enumeration in `Synchrony` (Figure 4), and each connector chooses one of them. In Figure 2, a `Retailer` and a `Supplier` exchange `OrderMsg` and `InvoiceMsg` messages synchronously.

`priority` is a mandatory tagged-value to specify the priority of each message that a connector delivers. The range of `priority` is from 0 to 255 (0 is the lowest and 255 is the highest), and the default value is 0 (Figure 4).

`inOrder` is a mandatory tagged-value to specify whether the order of messages that a service (message destination) receives is same as the order of messages that the other service (message source) sends out. The default value of `inOrder` is false.

`deliveryAssurance` is an optional tagged-value to specify the assurance level of message delivery. Three different semantics are defined as an enumeration in `DeliveryAssurance` (Figure 4), and each `Connector` chooses one of them at a time. `AtLeastOnce` means that a connector retries delivering a message until its destination receives the message. (A message retransmission is triggered with the `timeout` tagged-value.) However, the message may be delivered to its destination more than once. `AtMostOnce` means that a connector discards a message if the message has already been delivered to its destination; however, there is no guarantee of message delivery. `ExactlyOnce` satisfies the requirements of the above both semantics. It guarantees that a connector delivers a message to its destination without duplications. When `inOrder` is true, `ExactlyOnce` is implicitly (automatically) set to `deliveryAssurance` because duplicated or missing messages violate the `inOrder` semantics.

Figure 5 shows an example model using `inOrder` and `deliveryAssurance`. This example illustrates an extension to an order processing application in Figure 2. In this example, a Buyer transmits an OrderMsg to a Supplier via Retailer (see also Figure 1). After a Retailer forwards an OrderMsg from a Buyer to a Supplier, the Buyer can cancel the order by transmitting a CancellationMsg to the Retailer, and in turn, to the Supplier. In this example, the order of message transmissions is important between Retailer and Supplier because an order must be delivered to a Supplier before a corresponding order cancellation. Therefore, the inOrder semantics is assigned to the OrderConn connector. This semantics implicitly assigns ExactlyOnce to the deliveryAssuarance semantics in the OrderConn connector.

encryptionAlgorithm is an optional tagged-value used for transport-level encryption in a connector. This tagged-value defines an algorithm to secure a connection upon which request and response messages are transmitted. (See Figure 2 for an example.) The encryption algorithm is specified as a URI defined in the XML Encryption specification (World Wide Web Consortium, 2002). For example Triple DES is represented with http://www.w3.org/2001/04/xmlenc#tripledes-cbc, and AES-256 (Advanced Encryption Standard) is represented with http://www.w3.org/2001/04/xmlenc#aes256-cbc.

queueParameters is an optional tagged-value to deploy a message queue between services (i.e., message source and destination) and specify the semantics of message queuing between them. size specifies the maximum number of queued messages. flushWhenFull specifies whether queued messages are flushed from a queue to their destinations when the queue overflows. When flushWhenFull is false, the overflowing queue discards a message according to discardPolicy (Figure 4); discarding the oldest message (First-In-First-Out), the newest message (Last-In-First-Out), the lowest priority message or the closest deadline message. These four policies are defined as an enumeration in SelectionPolicy (Figure 4). flushTime and flushInterval specify when and how often a queue flushes messages, respectively. orderingPolicy specifies how to order messages in a queue: FIFO, LIFO, highest-priority-first or earliest-deadline-first. persistent specifies whether a queue stores messages in a storage (e.g., a file or database) so that the queue can recover them when it crashes unexpectedly.

Figure 6 shows an example using queueParameters. It illustrates an inventory management

Figure 6. An example of queue

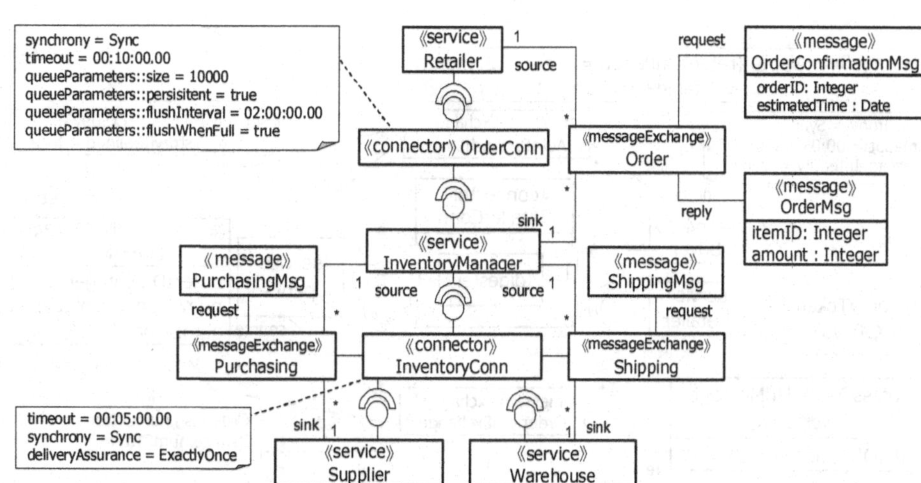

application for retailers (see also Figure 1). Each Retailer transmits an OrderMsg to an InventoryManager when it has no or few products in stock. The InventoryManager receives OrderMsgs from multiple Retailers every two hours in a batch manner. The OrderConn connector implements a synchronous queue that stores and forwards OrderMsgs. The InventoryManager schedules which warehouses deliver which products to which retail stores (every two hours), and based on the shipping schedule, sends ShippingMsgs to Warehouses. If a warehouse has a small inventory of a particular product, the InventoryManager orders the product by sending a PurchasingMsg to a Supplier.

msgTransmissionLogRetained is a mandatory tagged-value to specify whether to retain logs on message transmissions (see Figure 2 for an example). Regulatory mandates require applications to retain the logs and make them auditable for the third party organizations in the future. A connector with this tagged-value records (1) which messages are transmitted, (2) message source and destination (services), and (3) when the messages are transmitted. If msgTransmissionLogRetained is true, retentionPeriod must be specified to define the period to retain each message transmission log. The default value of msgTransmissionLogRetained is false. If it is false, retentionPeriod is ignored.

messageIntegrity is a mandatory tagged-value to specify whether to ensure the message integrity. The default value of messageIntegrity is false. A connector with this tagged-value checks whether messages are changed during their transmission.

Figure 7 illustrates an order processing application in which a Buyer places an order and a Retailer receives it via authorization by a Supervisor. By assigning a signature to the authSignature data field of an OrderMsg, Supervisor authorizes the message (order). Services are connected through a connector with the messageIntegrity semantics. This semantics ensures that OrderMsg messages are not altered during their transmission, and eliminates the possibility of malicious alteration.

A package stereotyped with <<messageRetention>> specifies that contained connectors have the msgTransmissionLogRetained semantics implicitly if the connectors omit it (Figure 7). Each connector follows the retentionPeriod specified in the package. When a connector specifies msgTransmissionLogRetained and retentionPeriod explicitly, they override the retentionPeriod specified in a package. Also, a

Figure 7. An example model for regulatory compliance

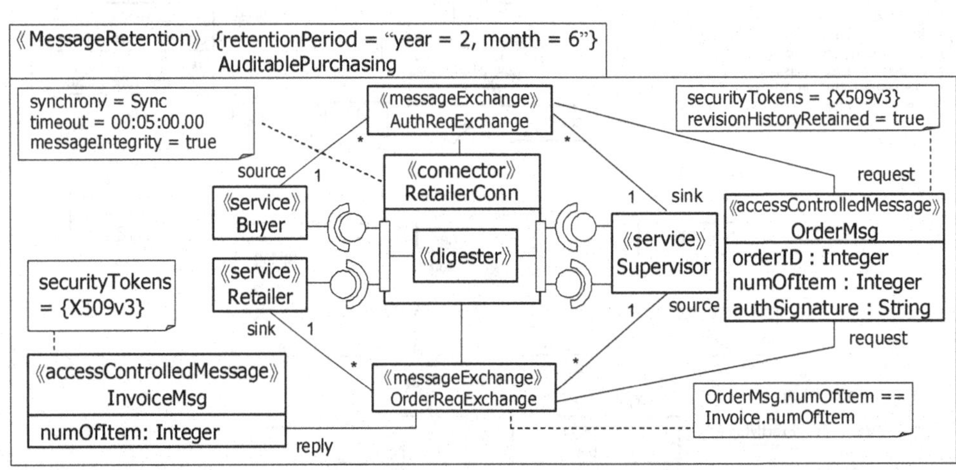

package stereotyped with <<messageRetention>> enforces contained services and messages to log their message transmissions. Connectors, services, and messages retain their logs independently, and the third party organizations can discover fraud activities by checking the inconsistencies between their logs.

Application developers can specify constraints using the Object Constraint Language (OCL). Constraints are used to ensure the consistency among application data and check whether services work correctly. For example, in Figure 7, `OrderReqExchange` has a constraint that ensures the number of items in an order (`OrderMsg`) and a corresponding invoice (`InvoiceMsg`) are always equal. When this constraint is violated, fraud activities could be committed.

Filter

This article describes eight of the filters that the proposed UML profile defines. Filters are defined as stereotypes extending the `Filter` stereotype (Figure 8). New filters can be defined as its subclasses. This section shows six filters to specify message transmission semantics and two filters to specify message processing semantics.

The stereotypes `Multicast`, `Manycast`, `Anycast`, `Router`, `Logger`, and `Digester` are used to define the message transmission semantics in a connector. A `Multicast` filter receives a request message from its source and transmits it to multiple destinations (services) simultaneously (one-to-many message exchange). A group of destinations can contain different types of services. When the `Multicast` filter receives reply messages from the destinations, it sends them back to the source of the request message. `Multicast` is used to improve the efficiency of message transmissions.

Figure 9 shows an example that models an application for wholesale price notification using `Multicast`. A `Retailer` subscribes for the price changes of a particular supply, and a `Supplier` notifies (or publishes) any price changes to the `Retailer`. A `Retailer` transmits a `Subscription` message to a `Supplier` in a synchronous and exactly-once manner. A `Supplier` multicasts a `PriceNotificationMsg` message, which contains a supply's GTIN (Global Trade Item Number)[3] and price, to multiple `Retailers` in asynchronous and at-most-once semantics.

`Manycast` is used to improve fault tolerance by forwarding a request message to a group of replicated destinations (i.e., to the same type of services). The tagged-value `groupSize` specifies how many services are deployed as a group. `standby` specifies the operation of replicated services: *hot standby, warm standby,* or *cold standby.* In hot standby, all services in a group remain active to receive request messages. A `Manycast` filter sends a message to all services in a group. `Manycast` returns only one reply message to the source of a request message, out of multiple replies from services. `backtracking` defines two policies to

Figure 8. Tagged-values of filters

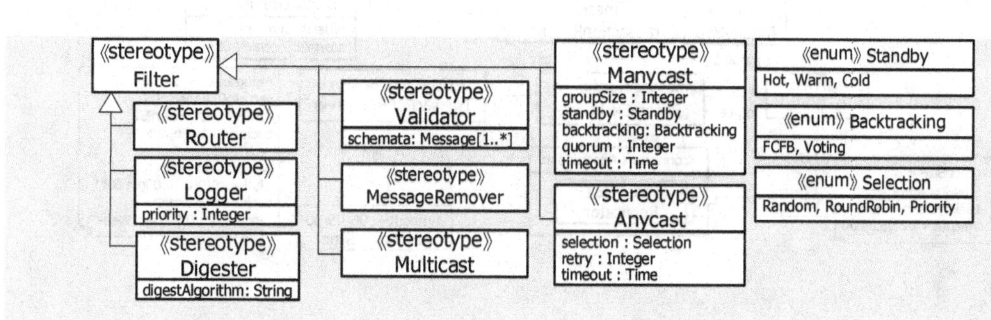

decide which reply message to be returned. When `FCFB` (first-come-first-backtracked) is selected, a `Manycast` filter returns the first reply that it receives from destination services. When `Voting` is selected, the `Manycast` filter performs a voting process. It counts the number of reply messages and inspects their contents. If the number of replies that have the same content reaches `quorum`, the `Manycast` filter returns one of the replies. If the number does not reach `quorum` within `timeout`, the `Manycast` filter returns the reply that generates the highest voting count.

In warm standby, all services in a group remain active to receive request messages. A `Manycast` filter sends a message to all services in a group, but only one service returns a reply. In this case, `backtracking` is not used. In cold standby, only one service in a group is active, and a `Manycast` filter sends a message to the service. If the service does not respond within `timeout`, the filter activates another service in the group and sends a message to the service. In cold standby, `backtracking` is not used.

In an example model shown in Figure 10, a supplier sends an inquiry to a cluster of transaction record servers to obtain a transaction record containing a set of orders. A manycast filter, `Replicator`, is used in the connection `RecordConn`. The filter intercepts each `Inquiry` (request) message and sends it to three replicated instances of `TransactionRecServer`, which is maintained with the hot standby policy. `Replicator` returns a `TransactionRecordMsg` (reply message) to a `Supplier` on FCFB basis.

Figure 9. An example of multicast

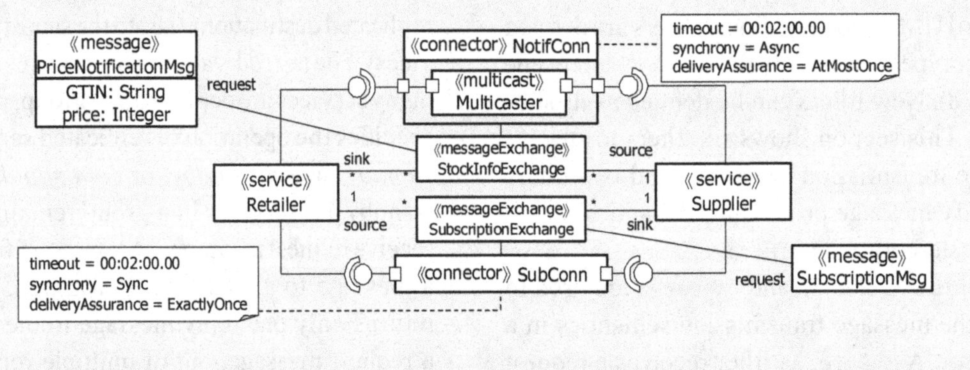

Figure 10. An example of manycast

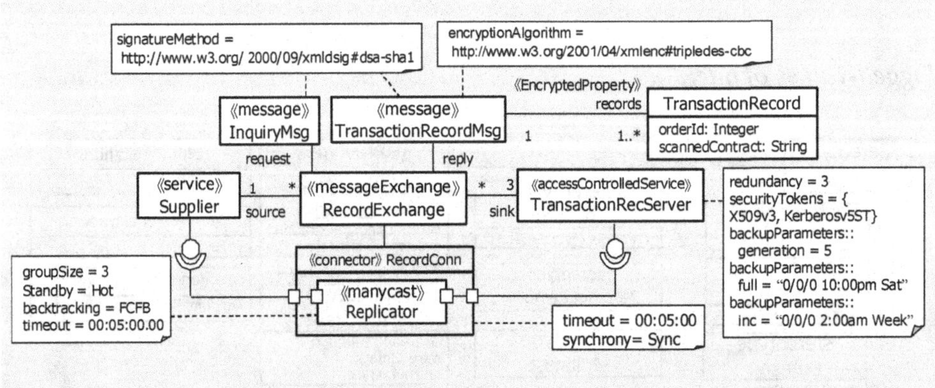

`Anycast` is a variation of the hot standby policy in `Manycast`. It forwards a request message to only one destination in a group of replicated services. This filter is used to balance workload placed on services. `selection` defines how to choose a destination from multiple services; randomly, on round robin or on destination's priority basis (the service with the highest priority in a group is selected). If an `Anycast` filter fails to deliver a request message within `timeout`, it retries to forward the request message. `retry` specifies the maximum number of retries. If the `Anycast` filter fails the maximum number of retries, it returns an error message to the source of the request message.

Figure 11 shows an example model describing a content delivery system, for example, for delivering contents among supplier's online catalogs of their supplies. (For simplicity, tagged-values of the connector `RedirectionConn` and `CacheUpdateConn` are omitted, but both have the synchronous semantics and their timeout is five minutes.) A user agent (`UserAgent`) sends a request (`ContentReqMsg`) to a content server (`OriginServer`) through a connector (`ContentDeliveryConn`). To balance workload, the content server redirects the request to a surrogate server (`SurrogateServer`). This model has a cluster of surrogate servers which consists of 10 replica servers. An `Anycast` filter in the connector `RedirectionConn` selects one of servers on their priority basis and redirects a request to it. (tagged-values of the `Anycast` filter is described on the upper left corner.) If a surrogate server does not have data to process a request, it sends a request (`CacheReqMsg`) to a content server to obtain cache data (`CacheMsg`). After processing a request, a surrogate server returns content (`ContentMsg`) to a user agent.

`Router` routes an incoming message to one or more destinations with certain criteria. Since UML does not provide a means to define rules, the proposed profile has no facility to specify routing rules at design time. Supporting tools transform a `Router` to a skeleton source code (e.g., in Java) or a rule description (e.g., in XPath) that performs message routing. Developers are expected to complete the skeleton code/description.

`Logger` records the transmission of each message whose priority value is higher than `priority`. When `priority` is omitted, all message transmissions are recorded.

`Digester` records digest values of all messages. This filter can be used to check whether a message is altered after its transmission. The digest algorithm is specified as a URI defined in the XML Encryption specification (The World Wide Web Consortium, 2002a). For example, `http://www.w3.org/2000/09/xmldsig#sha1` specifies SHA-1.

In addition to the stereotypes for message transmission semantics, the proposed UML profile provides two other stereotypes to define

Figure 11. An example of anycast

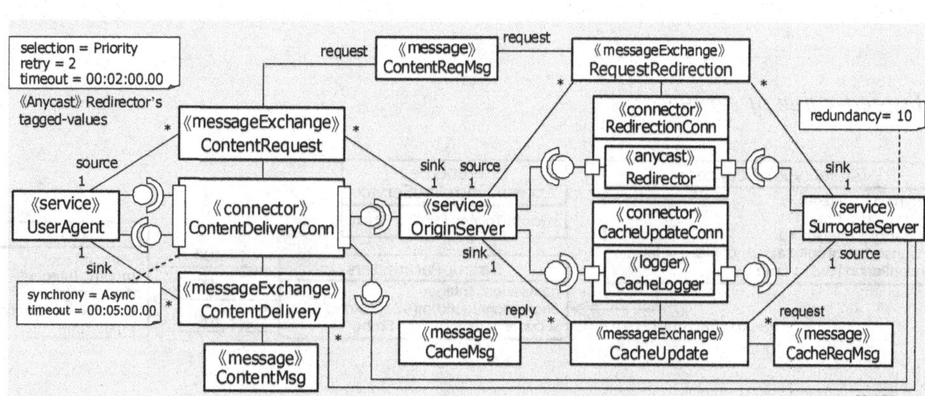

the message processing semantics in each connector: Validator and MessageRemover (Figure 8). Validator and MessageRemover validate incoming messages against the message schema specified in its tagged-value schemaURI and a given criteria (e.g., rules specifying valid data ranges) respectively, and transmit only validated messages. Since UML does not provide a means to define rules, the proposed profile has no facility to specify message filtering rules for MessageRemover at design time. Supporting tools transform a Validator and MessageRemover to a skeleton source code (e.g., in Java) or a rule description (e.g., in XPath) that performs message filtering. Developers are expected to complete the skeleton code/description. When a connector is encrypted with encryptionParameter, Validator and MessageRemover in the connector cannot validate messages (all messages are transmitted to their destinations.)

Service

Service has six tagged-values (Figure 12). timeout is an optional tagged-value to specify the timeout period (in millisecond) of each message that a service issues. If a message is not delivered to its destination within this time period, a connector discards the message.

priority is an optional tagged-value to specify the priority of each message that a service issues. Anycast filter uses priority to select its destinations. Also, it is used to order messages in a message queue when a connector has queueParameters.

Each service is expected to have data fields corresponding to the priority and timeout tagged-values. Usually, class instances cannot read and write tagged-values because tagged-values are defined in a metamodel (see Figure 3) and used in a model. The data fields allow different class instances to have different tagged-values, and tagged-values specified in a model behave as default values of corresponding data fields.

redundancy is an optional tagged-value to specify the number of runtime instances of a service. This tagged-value must be specified when a service is accessed by Manycast or Anycast filters. In Figure 10, three instances of TransactionRecServer are used for fault tolerance with the manycast filter Replicator.

Same as a connector, a service with msgTransmissionLogRetained and retentionPeriod records information on its message transmissions. A package stereotyped with <<messageRetention>> specifies that enclosed services have the msgTransmissionLogRetained semantics implicitly if the services omit it (Figure 7). When a service specifies msgTransmissionLogRetained and retentionPeriod explicitly, they can overrides package's ones.

backupParameters is an optional tagged-value to specify service's backup policy. full, diff, and inc specify the time when full, differential, and incremental backups is performed respectively. The class Calendar can specify a specific time

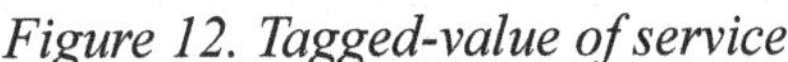
Figure 12. Tagged-value of service

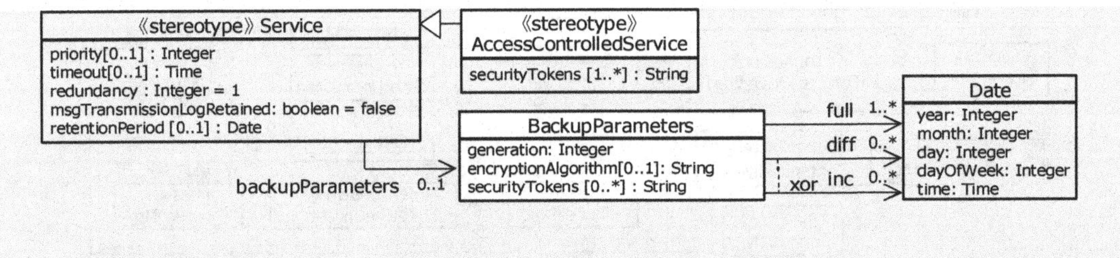

in point and a repetition time. For example, when `year` is omitted (value zero means omission), the backup is performed every year (the date and time to perform a backup is specified by other data fields in `Calendar`). Full backup stores all data in a service, differential backup stores all data which have been modified since the last full backup, and incremental backup stores all data which have been modified since the last full or incremental backup. Differential backup requires much amount of storage and longer time to perform than incremental backup, but it can restore data faster. Also, data redundancy in differential backup reduces the risk of data loss. Differential and incremental backups must be used with full backup, and full backup must be performed at least once before differential or incremental backups are performed. One backup policy can have either differential or incremental backup at a time (xor). If `diff` and `inc` are omitted, only full backup is performed. `generation` specifies the number of full backups retained in a storage. `encryptionAlgorithm` specifies an algorithm to secure backup data. `encryptionAlgorithm` specifies an algorithm to secure backup data. `securityTokens` specifies security tokens for the purpose of authentication (see below). In Figure 10, the service `TransactionRecServer` has a backup policy. The backup policy specifies the generation (five), the time when full and incremental backup are performed (10:00pm on every Saturday and 2:00am on week days respectively).

`AccessControlledService` is a stereotype extending the stereotype `Service` (Figure 12). It is a special type of service that enforces an access control policy. The tagged-value `securityTokens` is mandatory to specify security tokens (or certificates). The security tokens are used to authenticate entities (e.g., services) that access a message. This tagged-value can contain multiple values in order of precedence. The values use the names defined in the WS-SecurityPolicy specification (Organization for the Advancement of Structured Information Standards, 2005). In Figure 10, `TransactionRecServers` control accesses from `Suppliers` using X.509 certificates or Kerberos tickets. Since UML does not provide a good means to describe policies (or rules), the proposed UML profile does not define how to specify access control policies. `<<accessControlledService>>` is used only for indicating a service implements a certain access policy. A supporting tool transforms an `AccessControlledService` to a skeleton program code or an access control description in accordance with an implementation technology that an application designer chooses. Application developers are required to complete implementing access control policies.

In addition to the general type of service, the proposed UML profile provides three special types of services, `MessageConverter`, `MessageSplitter`, `MessageAggregator`, to define the message processing semantics. They inherit the `Service` stereotype.

`MessageConverter` converts an incoming message with a given rule. Similar to `Router`, supporting tools transform a `MessageConverter` to a skeleton source code or rule description (e.g., in XSLT) that performs message conversions, and developers complete the skeleton code/description.

`MessageSplitter` divides an incoming message into multiple fragments with a certain rule. Similar to `MessageConverter`, supporting tools transform a `MessageSplitter` to a skeleton code or rule description that performs message split, and developers complete the skeleton. In an example model shown in Figure 13, a `Retailer` sends an order message (`OrderMsg`) to a `MessageSplitter`, and the splitter divides the message into two fragments (`PurchasingMsg` and `AccountingMsg`), and sends them to different destinations (`Supplier` and `Accountant`). The destinations directly returns reply messages (`PurchasingConf` and `AccountingConf`) to the `Retailer`. The connector `OrderConn` encrypts all messages with Triple DES. Also, the message `OrderMsg` retains routing information,

Figure 13. An example of messagesplitter

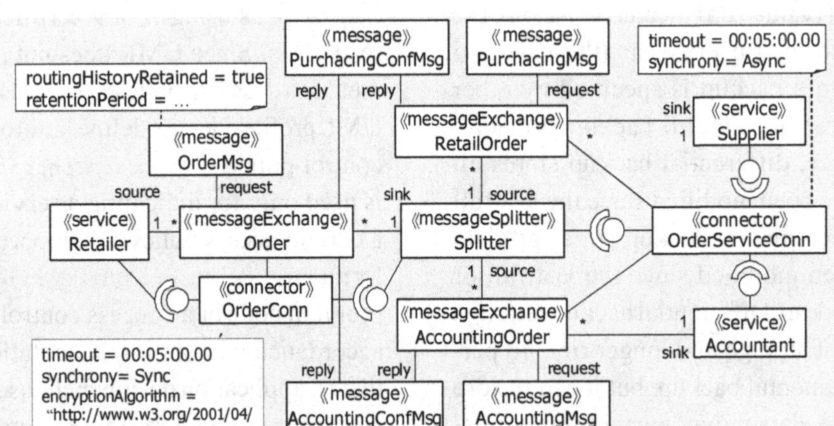

Figure 14. An example of messageaggregator

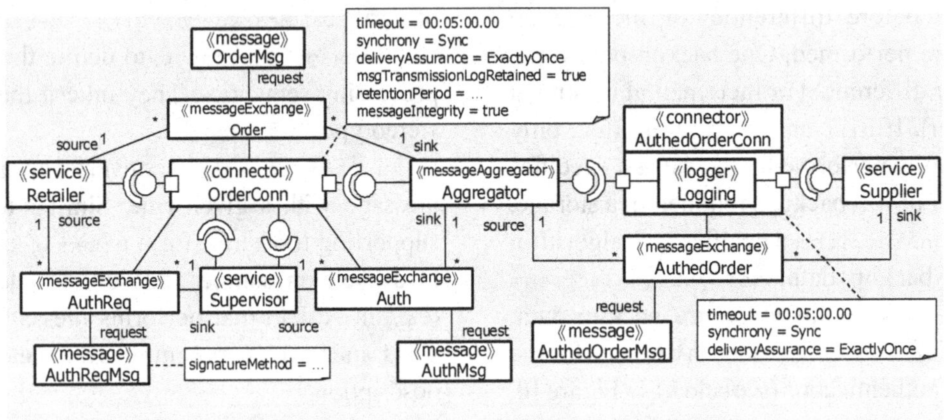

which includes source of a message. (i.e., it is auditable which customer sends which message.)

`MessageAggregator` combines multiple incoming messages. Figure 14 shows an example extending the model in Figure 2. In addition to `OrderMsg`, `Retailer` sends a message `AuthReqMsg` to ask the service `Supervisor` to authorize the order. `Aggregator` synchronizes and combines `OrderMsg` and `AuthMsg` (an authorization message from `Supervisors`), and it sends new message `AuthedOrderMsg` to `Supplier`. The connector `OrderConn` retains logs on message exchanges between `Buyer`, `Supervisor`, and `Aggregator`. It makes logs on order and authorization process auditable. Also, `OrderConn` ensure the integrity of messages.

Message

`Message` has seven tagged-values (Figure 15). `schemaURI` is a mandatory tagged-value to identify the schema of a message. The default value of `schemaURI` is message's qualified name (a combination of a package name and message's name).

`priority` and `timeout` are optional tagged-values to specify the priority and timeout period of messages. `Connector` has `timeout`, and `Service`

Figure 15. Tagged-values of message

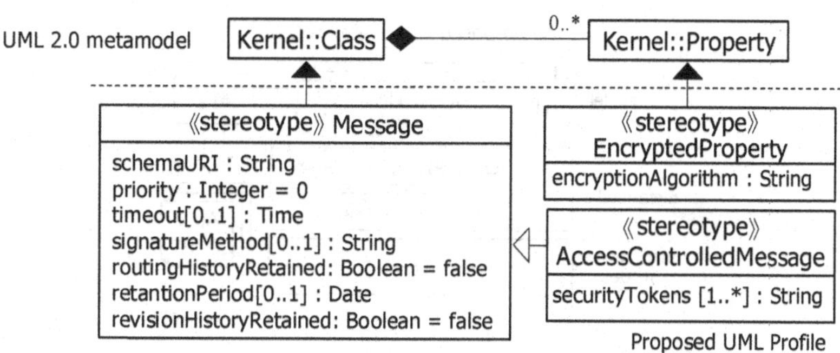

also has those two tagged-values. The precedence is that `Message`'s tagged-values override `Service`'s ones, and `Service`'s tagged-values override `Connector`'s ones. Same as `Service`, each message is expected to have data fields corresponding to the `priority` and `timeout` tagged-values, and different message instance can have different `priority` and `timeout`.

`signatureMethod` is used an optional tagged-value to ensure the integrity of a message. It specifies an algorithm for generating the message's digital signature. The algorithm is represented with a URI defined in the XML Signature specification (The World Wide Web Consortium, 2002b). For example, DSA (Digital Signature Algorithm) is represented with `http://www.w3.org/2000/09/xmldsig#dsa-sha1`. In Figure 10, each `Inquiry` and `TransactionRecord` message is signed with DSA. When `signatureMethod` is specified, each message is expected to maintain its signature in a data field called `signature`.

Same as a connector, a message with `routingHistoryRetained` and `retentionPeriod` records information on its message transmissions. A package stereotyped with `<<messageRetention>>` specifies that enclosed messages have the `routingHistoryRetained` semantics implicitly if the services omit it (Figure 7). When a message specifies `routingHistoryRetained` and `retentionPeriod` explicitly, they can overrides package ones.

`revisionHistoryRetained` is an optional tagged-value to specify whether to retain message's revision history (Figure 7). It makes the revision history to auditable in the future. A message with this semantics records 1) which data fields are revised, 2) how they revised (i.e., newly created, replaced, or deleted), 3) when they revised, and 4) who revised them. The tagged-value `retentionPeriod` is used to specify the period to retain the history. A package stereotyped with `<<messageRetention>>` specifies that enclosed messages have the `revisionHistoryRetained` semantics implicitly

The stereotype `EncryptedProperty` is used for message-level (end-to-end) encryption. It is defined as a stereotype extending `Property` in the UML metamodel (Figure 15). This stereotype is attached to data fields to be encrypted in a message. `EncryptedProperty` has a tagged-value, `encryptionAlgorithm`, to specify an algorithm used to encrypt a message. The semantics of this tagged-value is same as that of `encryptionAlgorithm` in `Connector`. An encryption algorithm is specified as a URI that the XML Encryption specification defines (World Wide Web Consortium, 2002a). Different data fields in a message can be encrypted with different encryption algorithms. In Figure 10, `orders` in `TransactionRecordMsg` are encrypted with Triple DES, which is represented with `http://www.w3.org/2001/04/xmlenc#tripledes-cbc`.

`AccessControlledMessage` is a stereotype extending `Message` (Figure 15). Similar to `Ac-`

Figure 16. The Architecture of Ark

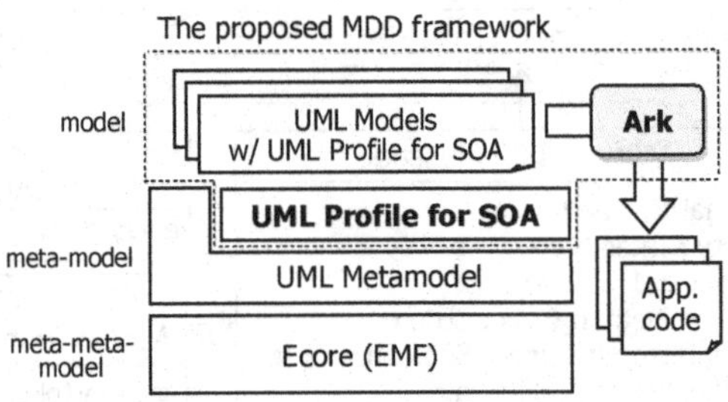

cessControlledService it is a special type of message that enforces an access control policy. It removes the possibility of unauthorized accesses (i.e., altering messages by unauthorized users) and accidental altering (i.e. altering messages mistakenly by authorized users). The tagged-value securityTokens must be specified in AccessControlledMessage for the purpose of authentication. Since UML does not provide a good means to describe policies (or rules), the proposed UML profile does not define how to specify access control policies. AccessControlledMessage is used to indicate a message implements a certain access policy. A supporting tool transforms an AccessControlledMessage to a skeleton program code or an access control description in accordance with an implementation technology that an application developer chooses. Application developers are required to complete implementing access control policies.

APPLICATION DEVELOPMENT WITH THE PROPOSED MDD FRAMEWORK

This section describes a model-driven development (MDD) tool, called Ark, which accepts a UML model designed with the proposed UML profile and transforms the model into a skeleton of application code (program code and deployment descriptor). Currently, Ark implements transformations between the proposed UML profile and three middleware technologies: Mule ESB[4], ServiceMix ESB[5] and GridFTP[6] (Figure 16). UML models in this work are maintained with the metameta model of the Eclipse Modeling Framework (EMF; http://www.eclipse.org/emf/). The proposed UML profile is defined as an extension to the UML metamodel. Each application designer gives his/her UML model to Ark, and instructs Ark which transformation to use for generating skeleton application code.

Figure 17 shows the development process using Ark. (This figure assumes that generated application code uses Mule ESB.) Application designers define application models using the proposed UML profile (e.g., an example model in Figures 2). Ark Transformer, one of the components in Ark, takes the application models in the format of XML Metadata Interchange (XMI) and transforms the input models into application code compliant with Mule ESB.

Ark has been tested with MagicDraw[7], a visual UML modeling tool that can serialize UML models to XMI (Figure 18). Ark Transformer is implemented based on openArchitectureWare[8], a model transformation engine. Each input UML model (XMI file) is validated against the UML standard metamodel and the proposed profile's metamodel (see Figure 3), and transformed to application code for Mule ESB (Java programs and

Figure 17. Application development with Ark

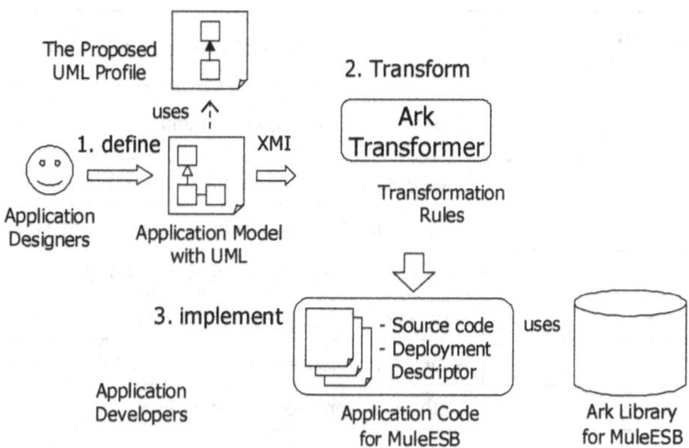

Figure 18. A UML model in magicdraw

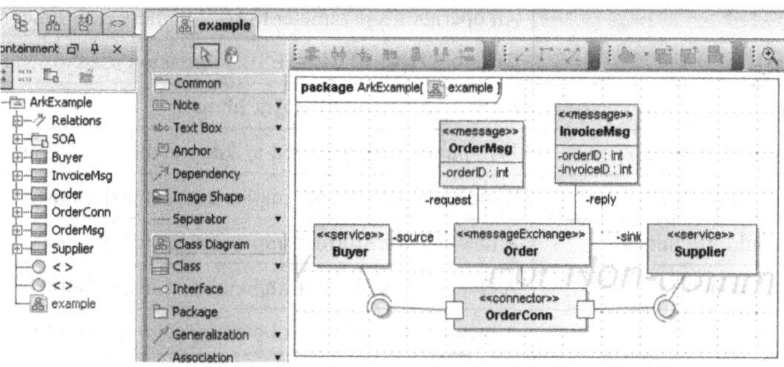

Figure 19. Generated code for mule ESB

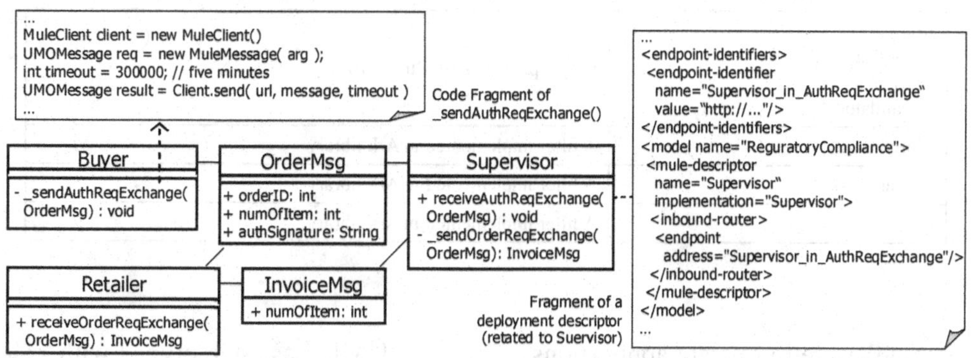

deployment descriptors in XML). A transformation rule between UML models and application code is implemented as a set of transformation templates, which define how to transform UML model elements to program elements in application code.

Transformation Rules for ESB Applications

Figure 19 shows some of the Java classes and deployment descriptors that Ark generates from the UML model in Figure 7 when Mule ESB is

Table 2. Transformation between the proposed UML profile and mule ESB

Model Element in the Proposed UML Profile	Program Element in Mule ESB
<<service>> <<accessControlledService>>	A Java class with the same name.
securityTokens	A security filter implemented in Ark library
<<message>>	A Java class implementing Serializable interface
signatureMethod	A security filter implemented in Ark library
<<encryptedProperty>>	A property in a corresponding Java class
encryptionAlgorithm	A message transformer implemented in Ark library
<<messageExchange>>	Methods to send/receive messages
sink (Service's role)	Service's operations sending messages.
source (Service's role)	Service's operations receiving messages.
<<connector>>	A set of entities in a deployment descriptor
timeout	An operation's parameter to specify message's timeout period
synchrony	Different types of Mule ESB's operation used to send a message.
deliveryAssurance	A filter implemented in Ark library
queueParameters	JMS parameters specified in a deployment descriptor
encryptionAlgorithm	A message transformer implemented in Ark library
msgTransmissionLogRetained	A message transformer implemented in Ark library
routingHistoryRetained	A message transformer implemented in Ark library
messageIntegrity	A message transformer implemented in Ark library
<<messageAggregator>>	A class implementing AbstractEventAggregator in Mule ESB
<<messageConverter>>	A class implementing DefaultTransformer in Mule ESB
<<messageSplitter>>	A class implementing AbstractMessageSplitter in Mule ESB
<<logger>> <<messageFilter>> <<router>> <<validator>>	Filters provided by Mule ESB
<<multicast>>	A filter implemented in Ark library
<<manycast>>	A filter implemented in Ark library
<<anycast>>	A filter implemented in Ark library

selected as middleware to operate applications. Table 2 shows the transformation between model elements in the proposed UML profile and program elements in Mule ESB. Ark transforms a UML class stereotyped with <<message>> to a Java class that has the same class name and the same data fields. The Java class implements the interface Serializable. This is required to implement messages exchanged with Mule ESB.

A UML class stereotyped with <<service>> is transformed to a Java class that has the same class name and the same data fields. Ark inserts several operations to the Java class, depending on whether its association role is source or sink against a message exchange. The operations are used to send and receive messages: _sendX() to send messages where X references the name of a message exchange, and receiveX() to receive messages. For example, in Figure 19, `Supervisor` has `_sendOrderReqExchange()` and `receiveAuthReqExchange()` to send and receive `OrderMsg` messages to `Supplier` and from `Retailer` respectively. `_sendX()` is supposed to be invoked by methods in the same service class. (This is why its visibility is private.) `receiveX()` is called by source services that have messages to deliver. A fragment of a deployment descriptor in Figure 19 specifies the URL of `Supervisor`. `<endpoint-identifier>` specifies a name of an end point (`name`) and its URL (`value`), e.g., when a service is deployed to be accessed via HTTP, `value` is `http://....` `<mule-descriptor>` specifies the implementation (`implementation`) of a service (`name`), and `<inbound-router>` specifies the URL of a service by referencing an end point.

A template fragment of this transformation rule is shown below. `<<service.name>>` in the template represents the name of a UML class stereotyped with `<<service>>`. (Note that the variables and keywords in a transformation rule are embraced with << and >>.) `<<messageExchange.name>>` references the name of an UML class stereotyped with `<<messageExchange>>`. `<<requestMessage.name>>` and `<<replyMessage.name>>` represent the names a request and reply messages, respectively. Ark replaces each variable in a transformation template with the name of a UML model element (e.g., class name), and generates Java code. When a service transmits multiple pairs of request and reply messages, Ark generates corresponding sets of `_sendX()` and `receiveX()`. `<<sinkID>>` represents the logical name of a destination service. Each pair of a logical service name and its access point is specified in a deployment descriptor. For example, if a service is deployed to be accessed via HTTP, its access point starts with `http://`.

```
public class <<service.name>> {
  private void
   _send<<messageExchange.name>>(
     <<requestMessage.name>> request){
     MuleClient muleClient =
        new MuleClient();
     String endpointName =
     <<sinkID>>;
     UMOEndpoint url =
       MuleManager.
        getInstance().
        lookupEndpoint(
            endpointName );
     int timeout =
     <<connector.timeout>>000;
     <<IF connector.synchrony
        == Sync>>
     UMOMessage result =
        muleClient.send(
        url, message, timeout );
   <<ELSEIF connector.synchrony
            == Oneway>>
     // generating code for
     //an oneway call
     <<ELSE>>
     // generating code for
     //an asynchronous call
     <<ENDIF>>
     }

     public void
     receive<<messageExchange.name>>(
        <<replyMessage.name>>reply){
     }
}
```

UML classes stereotyped with `<<messageExchange>>` and `<<connector>>` are not transformed to particular Java classes. The message transmission/processing semantics specified in a UML model is implemented in Java classes of message sender and destination. For example, in Figure 7, a `Buyer` sends an `OrderMsg` message to a `Supervisor` synchronously. Therefore, Ark generates a Java code to send the message synchronously using Mule ESB's API[9], and embeds the code in `_sendAuthReqExchange()` of `Buyer`.

<<connector.synchrony>> in the above transformation template references the synchrony of a connector, and Ark interprets it to generate Java code to send messages to a destination service. (<<IF>>, <<ELSEIF>> and <<ENDIF>> are the reserved keywords for branching statements.) Ark also generates Java code to handle timeout using Mule ESB's API (<<connector.timeout>> references the timeout period specified in a UML model.), and embeds the code in `_sendAuthReqExchange()` of `Buyer` (see also Figure 19).

As Figure 7 shows, a connector has the `messageIntegrity` semantics. To support this semantics, Ark provides a pair of message transformers to generate and verify a message's hash value. (These transformers are implemented as a part of Ark Library; see Figure 19.) In Mule ESB, each service can have an arbitrary number of message transformers as the classes implementing the interface `org.mule.transformer.UMOTransformer`. Message transformers are invoked (or hooked) when a service sends/receives a message. At a message source, a transformer (`edu.umb.cs.MessageIntegrityGenerator`) generates a message's hash value and embeds it into the message's header. At a message sink, a transformer (`edu.umb.cs.MessageIntegrityVerifier`) verifies the message's integrity using the hash value. Ark Library also implements the `msgTrasmissionLogRetained` and `routingHistoryRetained` semantics as message transformers `edu.cs.umb.TransmissionLogger` and `edu.cs.umb.RoutingHistoryLogger`).

When a UML model specifies a connector as a message queue, Ark generates application code that uses Java Message Service (JMS) because Mule ESB supports message queues through the use of JMS. For example, in Figure 6, `OrderConn` is specified as a message queue. Ark generates a corresponding deployment descriptor to configure and establish JMS connector that exchanges `OrderMsg` and `OrderConfirmationMsg` between `Retailer` and `InventoryManager`.

When a UML model uses the `MessageSplitter` or `MessageAggregator` filter (e.g., Figures 14 and 15), Ark generates application code that uses corresponding class in Ark Library. Corresponding to `MessageSplitter`, Ark generates a class implementing the interface `org.mule.routing.outbound.AbstractMessageSplitter`. In Mule ESB, the implementation class can be attached to arbitrary services in order to split an outgoing message into fragments and route them to different services. When Ark transforms a UML model in Figure 14, the implementation class is attached to a `Retailer` for intercepting an `OrderMsg` message from the `Retailer` and spliting it to a `PurchasingMsg` and `AccountingMsg`.

Similarly, corresponding to `MessageAggregator`, Ark generates a class implementing the interface `org.mule.routing.outbound.AbstractEventAggregator`. The implementation class can be attached to arbitrary services to aggregate an incoming message into a single message. In order to transform a UML model in Figure 15, Ark attaches the implementation class to a `Supplier` to aggregate a `OrderMsg` and a `AuthMsg` to a `AuthedOrderMsg` and pass the aggregated message to the `Supplier`.

The `Logger`, `MessageFilter`, `Router`, and `Validator` filters are transformed to and implemented with corresponding classes built in Mule ESB. Those classes are attached to services to perform message loging, filtering, routing, and validation functionalities as specified in an input UML model.

Transformation Rules for Secure and Broadband File Transfer Applications

When an application designer chooses GridFTP to operate his/her application, the application is deployed on Mule ESB and configured to use GridFTP as a message transport. Figure 20 shows some of the Java classes and deployment

Figure 20. Generated code for mule esb and gridFTP

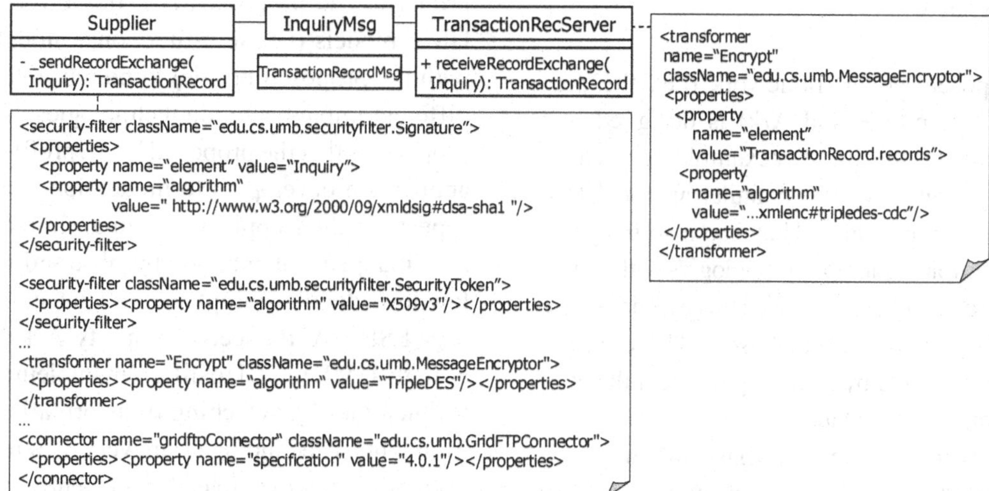

descriptors that Ark generates from a UML model in Figure 10.

As Figure 10 shows, the data field `records` is encrypted in `TransactionRecordMsg`. Since Mule ESB does not support message-level encryption, Ark Library provides a pair of message transformers to encrypt and decrypt data fields in messages (`edu.cs.umb.MessageEncryptor` and `edu.cs.umb.MessageDecryptor`). Ark generates a deployment descriptor to configure services so that they use those encryption/decryption transformers when they send/receive messages. Figure 20 shows a fragment of generated deployment descriptor for `TransactionRecServer`. It configures `TransactionRecServer` to use a message encryption transformer (`edu.cs.umb.MessageEncryption`) to encrypt the data field `records` in `TransactionRecordMsg` using Triple DES.

As Figure 10 shows, each `InquiryMsg` and `TransactionRecordMsg` message is signed with DSA, and `TransactionRecServer` performs authentication with X.509 or Kerberos. Since Mule ESB does not support DSA signatures and X.509/Kerberos security tokens, Ark Library provides a set of security filters to write/read signatures and security tokens by implementing the interface `org.mule.umo.security.UMOEndpointSecurityFilter`. Similar to message transformers, security filters are invoked when a service sends/receives a message. Ark generates a deployment descriptor that configures services to use the security filters Ark provides. Figure 20 shows a fragment of generated deployment descriptor for `Supplier`. It configures `Supplier` to include a DSA signature and an X.509 security token in each `Inquiry` message using two filters (`edu.cs.umb.securityfilter.Signature` and `edu.cs.umb.securityfilter.SecurityToken`).

In Figure 10, a `TransactionRecordMsg` is expected to contain a huge amount of data (e.g., scanned contract). When this example application uses GridFTP as a message transport to improve its throughput, Ark generates a deployment descriptor that configures `Supplier` and `TransactionRecordServer` to use GridFTP to transmit `InquiryMsg` and `TransactionRecordMsg` messages (Figure 20). Although Mule ESB does not support GridFTP, it provides a plug-in mechanism to implement arbitrary message transports. Ark Library implements a plug-in for GridFTP (`edu.cs.umb.GridFTPConnector`) so that services can use it in Mule ESB.

Extensibility of the Proposed MDD Framework

The proposed MDD framework (i.e., the proposed UML profile and Ark) is designed and implemented extensible. For example, application developers can change the default transformation rules that Ark provides. They can also integrate arbitrary implementation technologies with Ark in addition to currently-supposed three middleware (e.g., other ESBs and databases). These extensions can be made by changing the default set of transformation templates.

Moreover, the proposed MDD framework allows application developers to introduce arbitrary non-functional aspects that it does not support currently. Since the proposed UML profile is built on the UML standard metamodel with the standard extension mechanism (i.e., stereotypes and tagged-values), application developers can add new stereotypes and tagged-values representing their own non-functional aspects. This extension can be made by defining a set of transformation rules for new stereotypes and tagged-values. These newly-defined stereotypes/tagged-values and transformation rules have no effects on existing UML models and Ark itself (e.g., existing transformation rules, Ark Transformer and Ark Library).

Another type of extensibility of the proposed MDD framework is the ability to support arbitrary UML modeling tools. As described earlier, MagicDraw has been used as the default UML modeling tool; however, Ark can accept UML models from any modeling tools that serialize them in XMI. Choices of modeling tools have no effects on existing models and Ark.

EVALUATION

This section evaluates how the proposed MDD framework (i.e., the proposed UML profile and Ark) improves the reusability and maintainability of service-oriented applications. Given its two properties, the proposed MDD framework allows UML models (i.e., non-functional models built with the proposed profile) to be reusable across different implementation technologies. The first property is that the proposed UML profile allows application developers to model non-functional aspects in their applications in an implementation independent manner by abstracting away low-level details of implementation technologies (e.g., ESBs). As the second property, Ark can map a single UML model to different implementation technologies by switching transformation rules, even if those technologies are very different with each other. For example, Ark currently supports very different ESBs as implementation technologies: Mule ESB and ServiceMix ESB; their APIs and deployment descriptor schemata have no compatibility. The following code fragments are Java classes that Ark generates from the `Supervisor` class in Figure 7 to Mule ESB and ServiceMix ESB. In Mule ESB, a service can be implemented as a simple Java class.

```
public class Supervisor {

public void
receiveAuthReqExchange(
 OrderMsg reply){
  //...
 }

private void
_ sendOrderReqExchange(
OrderMsg request){
MuleClient muleClient =
 new MuleClient();
String endpointName = …
UMOEndpoint url = …
Int timeout = …
FutureMessageResult result =
 muleClient.sendAsync(
    url, request, timeout );
}}
```

On the other hand, in ServiceMix ESB, a service is implemented as a class that extends the `ComponentSupport` class and implements the `MessageExchangeListener` interface. Messages are received through the `onMessageExchange` method.

```
public class Supervisor
extends ComponentSupport
implements MessageExchangeLis
 tener {
public void
onMessageExchange(
 MessageExchange exchange)
     throws MessagingException {
     if (exchange.getRole() ==
     Role.CONSUMER) {
   ServiceEndpoint ep =
 exchange.getEndpoint();
   if (ep.getServiceName()
 .getLocalPart()
 .equals(RETAILER)) {
receiveAuthReqExchange(exchange}}}
private void
receiveAuthReqExchange(
 MessageExchange exchange)
     throws MessagingException {
   // ...
 }

 private void
_ sendOrderReqExchange(
OrderMsg orderMsg){
InOut inout =
 createInOutExchange(
 SUPPLIER, null, null);
  NormalizedMessage msg =
 inout.createMessage();
 // ...
 inout.setInMessage(msg);
 sendSync(inout);
}}
```

By making UML models (i.e., non-functional models) reusable across different implementation technologies, the proposed MDD framework allows application developers to reuse or repurpose services without knowing the details of implementation technologies.

Table 3 shows the program elements (Java code and/or deployment descriptors: DD) that Ark generates for Mule ESB and ServiceMix ESB from a single UML model element. Table 3 also shows the lines of code (LOC) of each generated program element. (LOC is shown in parentheses.) As this figure illustrates, a single model element represents multiple program elements in the proposed MDD framework. For example, `queueParamters` represents 34 LOC in Mule ESB and 33 LOC in ServiceMix ESB. This contributes to improve the maintainability of service-oriented applications by freeing application developers from manually and carefully dealing with many lower-level program elements in a consistent manner.

RELATED WORK

This article is a set of extensions to the authors' prior work (Wada, Suzuki, & Oba, 2006a, 2006b, 2006c). As one of the extensions, this work investigates new non-functional aspects for regulatory compliance, which were beyond of the scope of the prior work. Another extension is that Ark currently supports a wider range of implementation technologies. As a result, the proposed MDD framework now allows application developers to model SOA's non-functional aspects through hiding the implementation differences across two of the most major ESBs (Mule ESB and ServiceMix ESB). Given these extensions, this article fully discusses the updated details in the design and implementation of the proposed MDD framework. Moreover, unlike the prior work, this work empirically evaluates how the proposed MDD framework

Table 3. Generated program elements and their LOC

Model Elements in the Proposed UML Profile	Program Elements and their LOC in Mule ESB	Program Elements and their LOC in ServiceMix ESB
<<service>> <<accessControlledService>>	A Java class (8) An endpoint identifier in DD (1) A service entry in DD (7)	A Java class (9) A service entry in DD (6)
securityTokens	An in-bound filter in DD (3)	An in-bound filter in DD (3)
<<message>>	A Java class (2)	A Java class (2)
signatureMethod	In-bound and out-bound filters in DD (6)	In-bound and out-bound filters in DD (6)
<<encryptedProperty>>	An attribute in a Java class (1)	An attribute in a Java class (1)
encryptionAlgorithm	In-bound and out-bound filters in DD (6)	In-bound and out-bound filters in DD (10)
<<messageExchange>>	In-bound and out-bound routers in DD (6)	A routing conf. in DD (14)
sink (Service's role)	A method to send in Java (10)	A method to send in Java (10)
source (Service's role)	A method to receive in Java (2)	A method to receive in Java (12)
<<connector>>	No code generated (0)	No code generated (0)
synchrony	Java code in Mule ESB API (1)	Java code in ServiceMIX API (1)
deliveryAssurance	A configuration entry in DD (3)	A configuration entry in DD (6)
queueParameters	A configuration entry in DD (14) A JMS configuration file (20)	A configuration entry in DD (6) JNDI configuration in DD (7) A JMS configuration File (20)
encryptionAlgorithm	In-bound and out-bound filters in DD (6)	In-bound and out-bound filters in DD (10)
msgTransmissionLogRetained	In-bound and out-bound filters in DD (6)	In-bound and out-bound filters in DD (6)
routingHistoryRetained	In-bound and out-bound filters in DD (6)	In-bound and out-bound filters in DD (6)
messageIntegrity	In-bound and out-bound filters in DD (6)	In-bound and out-bound filters in DD (6)
<<messageAggregator>>	A Java class (4) An In-bound filter in DD (3)	A Java class (4) An endpoint conf. in DD (2)
<<messageConverter>>	A Java class (4) An out-bound filter in DD (3)	A Java class (4) An endpoint conf. in DD (2)
<<messageSplitter>>	A Java class (4) An out-bound filter in DD (3)	A Java class (4) An endpoint conf. in DD (2)
<<logger>>	An out-bound filter in DD (3)	An out-bound filter in DD (3)
<<messageFilter>>	An out-bound filter in DD (3)	A filter conf. in DD (7)
<<router>>	An out-bound filter in DD (3)	A routing conf. in DD (7)
<<validator>>	An out-bound filter in DD (3)	An out-bound filter in DD (3)
<<multicast>>	An out-bound filter in DD (3)	A routing conf. in DD (7)
<<manycast>>	An out-bound filter in DD (3)	A routing conf. in DD (7)
<<anycast>>	An out-bound filter in DD (3)	A routing conf. in DD (7)

contributes to the reusability and maintainability of service-oriented applications.

There are several UML profiles proposed for SOA. Marcos, Castro, and Vela (2003) and Amsden, Gardner, Griffin, and Iyengar (2005) propose UML profiles to specify functional aspects in SOA. Both profiles are designed based on the XML schema of Web Service Description Language (WSDL). Each profile provides a set of stereotypes and tagged-values that correspond to the elements in WSDL, such as `Service`, `Port`, `Messages` and `Binding`[10]. Since WSDL is designed to define only functional aspects of web services, non-functional aspects are beyond of the scope of Marcos et al. (2003) and Amsden et al. (2005). Ermagan and Krüger (2007) propose and Object Management Group (2006b) standardizes UML profiles for functional aspects in SOA. Unlike the above profiles, the proposed profile focuses on specifying non-functional aspects in SOA.

Amir and Zeid (2005) propose a UML profile to describe both functional and non-functional aspects in SOA. This profile is generic enough to specify a wide range of non-functional aspects. For example, the stereotypes for non-functional aspects include `<<policy>>` and `<<permission>>`. However, their semantics tend to be ambiguous. This profile does not precisely define what non-functional aspects developers can (or are supposed to) specify and how to represent them with tagged values in accordance with given stereotypes. Ortiz and Hernández (2006) also propose a generic UML profile to describe various non-functional aspects (called extra-functional properties). Arbitrary non-functional aspects can be defined as stereotypes extending the `<<Extra-Functional Property>>` stereotype. However, it is ambiguous how to define particular non-functional aspects with user-defined stereotypes and tagged-values. The World Wide Web Consortium (2006) standardizes the WS-Policy specification, a generic XML format to specify arbitrary non-functional aspects of web services. No explicit principles and guidelines are available on how to define particular non-functional aspects with XML document elements. Unlike the above three schemes, the proposed UML profile carefully and precisely defines a variety of stereotypes and tagged-values for non-functional aspects in SOA so that the proposed MDD tool (Ark) can interpret and transform models to code in an unambiguous manner.

Vokäc (2005) proposes a UML profile for data integration in SOA. It provides data structures to specify messages. Application developers can use the data structures for building dictionaries that maintain message data used in existing systems and new applications. This profile separates data integration as a non-functional aspect from functional aspects, and enables specifying data integration in an implementation independent manner. This UML profile and the proposed profile focus on different issues in SOA. Data integration is beyond of the scope of the proposed profile, and Vokäc (2005) does not consider non-functional aspects in message transmission, message processing, security and service deployment.

Heckel, Lohmann, and Thöne (2003) propose a UML profile for dynamic service discovery in SOA. This profile provides a set of stereotypes (e.g., `<<uses>>`, `<<requires>>` and `<<satisfies>>`) to specify relationships among service interfaces, service implementations and functional requirements. For examples, a relationship can specify that a service *uses* other services, and another relationship can specify that a service *requires* other services that *satisfy* certain functional requirements. These relationships are intended to aid dynamic discovery of services. Rather than service discovery, the proposed UML profile focuses on non-functional semantics in message transmission, message processing, security, and service deployment.

Object Management Group (2007) standardizes a UML profile for Data Distribution Service (DDS). DDS is a standard specification for publish/subscribe middleware, and it supports several non-functional aspects in real-time messaging. OMG's UML profile for DDS allows

UML models to specify these non-functional aspects. In contrast, the proposed profile is not limited to real-time messaging, but supports a wider range of non-functional aspects. Moreover, OMG's profile is designed to be mapped into only DDS implementations. In contrast, the proposed profile is designed in an implementation independent manner; it can be mapped to arbitrary implementation technologies.

Gardner (2003), List and Korherr (2005), Johnston (2004) and Object Management Group (2005a) define UML profiles to specify service orchestration and map it to Business Process Execution Language (BPEL) (Organization for the Advancement of Structured Information Standards, 2003). These profiles provide a limited support of non-functional aspects in message transmission, such as messaging synchrony. The proposed profile does not focus on service orchestration, but a comprehensive support of non-functional aspects in message transmission, message processing, security and service deployment.

Lodderstedt, Basin, and Doser (2002) propose a UML profile, called SecureUML, to define role-based access control for network applications. SecureUML provides stereotypes to assign roles (`<<security.role>>`) and access control permissions (`<<security.constraint>>`) to applications (e.g., UML interfaces and classes). SecureUML uses Object Constraint Language (OCL) to define access control. Jürjens (2002) propose another UML profile, called UMLsec, to define data encryption (`<<data security>>`) and secure network links (`<<encrypted>>`). Wang and Lee (2005) and Nakamura, Tatsubori, Imamura, and Ono (2005) also propose UML profiles to define security aspects. In addition to security aspects, Soler, Villarroel, Trujillo, Medina, and Piattini (2006) propose a UML profile extending the Common Warehouse Metamodel (Object Management Group, 2003) in order to define regulatory audit policies in data warehouses. For example, the profile provides stereotypes to specify whether a data warehouse retains logs to access data sources. Gönczy and Varró (2006) propose a formal definition of reliable messaging mechanisms as a metamodel. These profiles/metamodels are parallel to the proposed UML profile in terms of the ability to describe security aspects, audit policies, and reliable messaging in network applications. However, the proposed UML profile covers not only security, auditing or reliable messaging aspects but also many other non-functional aspects in SOA (e.g., message queuing, message validation/filtering, and message.

Zhu and Gorton (2007) and Zou and Pavlovski (2006) propose UML profiles to visually define non-functional requirements such as desirable response time and throughput. However, they do not consider model transformation to map non-functional requirements to certain implementation technologies. In contrast, the proposed profile is designed to consider model transformation, although non-functional requirements are beyond of the scope of the proposed profile.

There are several specifications and research efforts to investigate implementation techniques for non-functional aspects in SOA (Baligand & Monfort, 2004; Mukhi, Konuru, & Curbera, 2004; Organization for the Advancement of Structured Information Standards, 2003, 2004a, 2004b; Wang, Chen, Wang, Fung, & Uczekaj, 2004). Each specification and technique provides a means to implement non-functional requirements in, for example, performance, reliability, and security and to enforce services to follow the requirements. Rather than investigating specific implementations of non-functional aspects in SOA, the proposed MDD framework is intended to provide a means for application developers to model and maintain non-functional aspects in an implementation independent manner so that they can be mapped on different specifications or implementation technologies.

CONCLUSION

This article proposes a model-driven development (MDD) framework for non-functional aspects in SOA. The proposed MDD framework consists of (1) a UML profile to graphically specify and maintain SOA non-functional aspects in an implementation independent manner and (2) an MDD tool that accepts a UML model defined with the proposed profile and transforms it to application code (program code and deployment descriptors). This article presents design details of the proposed UML profile and describes how the proposed MDD tool uses the profile to develop service-oriented applications that can run with different implementation technologies such as Mule ESB, ServiceMix and GridFTP. Empirical evaluation results show that the proposed MDD framework contributes to improve the reusability and maintainability of service-oriented applications by hiding the details of implementation technologies.

Several extensions to the proposed MDD framework are planned as future work. As described in the Related Work section, there are several other UML profiles for SOA. The proposed profile will be co-used or integrated with some of them (e.g., Oba, Hashimoto, Fujikura, & Munehira, 2005; Object Management Group, 2005b) in order to investigate a more comprehensive development framework for SOA.

Another extension is to integrate the proposed UML profile with a modeling language for business processes such as Business Process Modeling Notation (Object Management Group, 2006a). The proposed profile is designed to specify applications from a structural point of view; it does not consider a viewpoint of processes or workflows. Therefore, as the size of a model (application) increases, it becomes harder to understand how messages are exchanged among services and define non-functional aspects along with message flows. For example, in order to specify secure messaging for a certain business process (e.g., order processing process), it can be time-consuming and error-prone to find all the services associated with the process and define a security aspect for the connections among those services. The integration with a business process modeling language can make non-functional modeling more intuitive by providing both structural and process viewpoints.

The proposed MDD framework will be evaluated in several different application domains[11]. One of them is service-oriented system integration in a natural gas utility company. The proposed UML profile and Ark are planned to be used in a system integration project, and their design and implementation will be enhanced through the project experience. Another application domain is eco-informatics. The proposed framework has been used to design and maintain ecological observation systems (Wada & Suzuki, 2006d). Ecological observation systems monitor ecosystems, record various observation data (e.g., a niche of a particular species and weather in the niche), and help ecologists understand and predict the observation of ecosystems. Currently, ecological observation systems are often implemented monolithic; their extensibility and customizability are limited. SOA is expected to overcome this issue by decomposing an observation system into multiple services, implementing the system as a combination of services, and extending/customizing it through a recombination of services (Bermudez, Bogden, Bridger, Creager, Forrest, & Graybeal, 2006). The proposed MDD framework has been used to separate functional and non-functional aspects in an ecological observation system and model/implement non-functional aspects in the system. Through this practice, the proposed MDD framework will be enhanced to improve its generality.

ACKNOWLEDGMENT

This work is supported in part by OGIS International, Inc.

REFERENCES

Allcock, W., Bresnahan, J., Kettimuthu, R., Link, M., Dumitrescu, C., Raicu, I., & Foster, I. (2005). The Globus striped GridFTP framework and server. *ACM Super Computing.*

Amir, R., & Zeid, A. (2004). A UML profile for service oriented architectures. *ACM Object-Oriented Programming, Systems, Languages, and Applications Poster session.*

Amsden, J., Gardner, T., Griffin C., & Iyengar, S. (2005). UML 2.0 profile for software services. IBM developerWorks.

Arsanjani A., Zhang L., Ellis M., Allam A., & Channabasavaiah K. (2007) S3: A service-oriented reference architecture. *IT Professional, 9*(3).

Baligand, F., & Monfort, V. (2004). A concrete solution for web services adaptability using policies and aspects. *Proceedings of UNITN/Springer International Conference on Service Oriented Computing.*

Bermudez, L., Bogden, P., Bridger, E., Creager, G., Forrest, D., & Graybeal, J. (2006). Toward an ocean observing system of systems. *MTS/IEEE Oceans.*

Bichler, M., & Lin, K. (2006). Service-oriented computing. *IEEE Computer, 39*(6).

Bieberstein N., Bose S., Fiammante M., Jones K., & Shah R. (2005). *Service-oriented architecture (SOA) compass: Business value, planning, and enterprise roadmap.* IBM Press.

Chappell, D. (2004). *Enterprise service bus.* O'Reilly.

Endrei, M., Ang, J., Arsanjani, A., Chua, S., Comte, P., Krogdahl, P., et al., (2004). *Patterns: Service-oriented architecture and Web services.* IBM Red Books.

Ermagan, V., & Krüger, H. (2007). A UML2 profile for service modeling. *Proceedings of ACM/IEEE International Conference on Model Driven Engineering Languages and Systems.*

Foster, I. (2005). Service-oriented computing. *Science, 308*(5723).

Fuentes, L., & Vallecillo, A. (2004). An introduction to UML profiles. *The European Journal for the Informatics Professional, 5*(2).

Gardner, T. (2003). UML modeling of automated business processes with a mapping to BPEL4WS. *Proceedings of European Conference on Object-Oriented Programming Workshop on Object Orientation and Web Services.*

Gönczy, L., & Varró, D. (2006). Modeling of reliable messaging in service oriented architecture. *Proceedings of Telcert International Workshop on Web Services Modeling and Testing.*

Heckel, R., Lohmann, M., & Thöne, S. (2003). Towards a UML profile for service-oriented architectures. *Proceedings of Workshop on Model Driven Architecture: Foundations and Applications.*

Java Community Process. (2001). UML profile for Enterprise Java Beans.

Johnston, S. (2004). UML 1.4 profile for software services with a mapping to BPEL 1.0. *IBM developerWorks.*

Jürjens, J. (2002). UMLsec: Extending UML for secure systems development. *Proceedings of ACM/IEEE International Conference on Unified Modeling Language.*

Lewis, G., Morris, E., Brien, L., Smith, D., & Wrage, L. (2005). *Smart: The service-oriented migration and reuse technique.* Technical report, Software Engineering Institute, Carnegie Mellon University.

List, B., & Korherr, B. (2005). A UML 2 profile for business process modelling. *Proceedings of ACM International Conference on Conceptual Modeling Workshop on Best Practices of UML at the International Conference on Conceptual Modeling.*

Lodderstedt, T., Basin, D., & Doser, J. (2002). SecureUML: A UML-based modeling language for model-driven security. *Proceedings of ACM/IEEE International Conference on Unified Modeling Language.*

Marcos, E., Castro, V., & Vela, B. (2003). Representing Web services with UML: A case study. *Proceedings of UNITN/Springer International Conference on Service Oriented Computing.*

Mukhi, N., Konuru, R., & Curbera, F. (2004). Cooperative middleware specialization for service oriented architectures. *Proceedings of ACM International World Wide Web Conference.*

Nakamura, Y., Tatsubori, M., Imamura, T., & Ono, K. (2005). Model-driven security based on a Web services security architecture. *Proceedings of IEEE International Conference on Services Computing.*

Oba, K., Hashimoto, M., Fujikura, S., & Munehira, T. (2005). The status quo and challenges of service-oriented architecture based application design. *Proceedings of IPSJ Workshop on Software Engineering.*

Object Management Group. (2003). Common warehouse metamodel, version 1.1.

Object Management Group. (2004). UML 2.0 super structure specification.

Object Management Group. (2005a). Business process definition metamodel.

Object Management Group. (2005b). UML profile for modeling quality of service and fault tolerance characteristics and mechanisms.

Object Management Group. (2006a). Business process modeling notation, version 1.0.

Object Management Group. (2006b). UML profile and metamodel for services, request for proposal.

Object Management Group. (2006c) UML profile for data distribution service, request for proposal.

Object Management Group. (2007) Data Distribution Service for Real-time Systems, version 1.2.

O'Grady, S. (2004). *SOA meets compliance: compliance oriented architecture.* White paper, RedMonk.

Organization for the Advancement of Structured Information Standards. (2003). Web services business process execution language.

Organization for the Advancement of Structured Information Standards. (2004a). Web service reliability 1.1.

Organization for the Advancement of Structured Information Standards. (2004b). Web service reliable messaging.

Organization for the Advancement of Structured Information Standards. (2005). Web services security policy language.

Ortiz, G., & Hernández, J. (2006). Toward UML profiles for Web services and their extra-functional properties. *Proceedings of IEEE International Conference on Web Services.*

Papazoglou, M. (2003). Service-oriented computing: concepts, characteristics and directions. *Proceedings of IEEE International Conference on Web Information Systems Engineering.*

Roberts, D., & Johnson, R. (1997). *Evolving frameworks: A pattern language for developing object-oriented frameworks.* Pattern Languages of Program Design 3, Chapter 26. Addison Wesley.

Soler, E., Villarroel, R., Trujillo, J., Medina, E., & Piattini, M. (2006). Representing security and audit rules for data warehouses at the logical level by using the common warehouse metamodel.

Proceedings of IEEE International Conference on Availability, Reliability and Security.

Vinoski, S. (2003). Integration with Web services. *IEEE Internet Computing, 7*(6).

Vokäc, M. (2005). Using a domain-specific language and custom tools to model a multi-tier service-oriented application: Experiences and challenges. *Proceedings of ACM/IEEE International Conference on Model Driven Engineering Languages and Systems.*

Wada, H. & Suzuki, J. (2006). *Designing ecological observation systems using service oriented architecture.* Elsevier/ISEI International Conference on Ecological Informatics, poster paper.

Wada, H., Suzuki, J., & Oba K. (2006a). A model-driven development framework for non-functional aspects in service oriented grids. *Proceedings of IEEE International Conference on Autonomic and Autonomous Systems.*

Wada, H., Suzuki, J., & Oba K. (2006b). Modeling non-functional aspects in service oriented architecture. *Proceedings of IEEE International Conference on Services Computing..*

Wada, H., Suzuki, J., & Oba K. (2006c). A service-oriented design framework for secure network applications. *Proceedings of IEEE International Conference on Computer Software and Applications Conference.*

Wang, G., Chen, A., Wang, C., Fung, C., & Uczekaj, S. (2004). Integrated quality of service (QoS) management in service-oriented enterprise architectures. *Proceedings of IEEE Enterprise Distributed Object Computing Conference.*

Wang, L., & Lee, L. (2005). *UML-based modeling of Web services security.* IEEE European Conference on Web Services, poster paper.

World Wide Web Consortium. (2002a). XML encryption syntax and processing.

World Wide Web Consortium. (2002b). XML signature syntax and processing.

World Wide Web Consortium. (2006). Web services policy framework.

Zhang, Z., & Yang, H. (2004). Incubating services in legacy systems for architectural migration. *Proceedings of IPSJ/IEEE Asia-Pacific Software Engineering Conference.*

Zhu, L., & Gorton, I. (2007). UML profiles for design decisions and non-functional requirements. *Proceedings of ACM/IEEE International Conference on Software Engineering Workshop on Sharing and Reusing Architectural Knowledge - Architecture, Rationale, and Design Intent.*

Zou, J., & Pavlovski, C. (2006). Modeling architectural non functional requirements: From use case to control case. *Proceedings of IEEE International Conference on e-Business Engineering.*

ENDNOTES

1. According to the UML specification, the first letter of a stereotype's name is capitalized when the stereotype is defined (Figure 3). However, it is not capitalized when the stereotype is used in UML models (Figure 2).
2. Precisely, a composite class can contain any *classifiers*, defined in the UML metamodel.
3. http://www.gtin.info/
4. http://mule.mulesource.org/
5. http://servicemix.apache.org/
6. An extension to FTP for transmitting files of large size (Allcock, Bresnahan, Kettimuthu, Link, Dumitrescu, Raicu, & Foster, 2005)
7. http://www.magicdraw.com/
8. http://www.openarchitectureware.org/

9 Mule ESB provides three different APIs to send messages in synchronous, asynchronous and oneway (non-blocking) manners.

10 In WSDL, a `Service` defines an interface of a web service. A `Port` specifies an operation in a `Service`, and `Messages` defines parameters for a `Port`. A `Binding` specifies communication protocols used by `Ports`.

11 A software engineering discipline suggests investigating at least three applications on a framework in order to examine the framework's generality and reusability. (Roberts & Johnson, 1997)

This work was previously published in the International Journal of Web Services Research, Vol. 5, Issue 4, edited by L. J. Zhang, pp. 1-31, copyright 2008 by IGI Publishing (an imprint of IGI Global).

Chapter 17
Interoperability Among Heterogeneous Services:
The Case of Integration of P2P Services with Web Services

Aphrodite Tsalgatidou
National and Kapodistrian University of Athens, Greece

George Athanasopoulos
National and Kapodistrian University of Athens, Greece

Michael Pantazoglou
National and Kapodistrian University of Athens, Greece

ABSTRACT

Service-oriented computing (SOC) has been marked as the technology trend that caters for interoperability among the components of a distributed system. However, the emergence of various incompatible instantiations of the SOC paradigm, e.g. Web or peer-to-peer services (P2P), and the divergences encountered within each of these instantiations state clearly that interoperability is still an open issue, mainly due to its multi-dimensional nature. In this paper we address the interoperability problem by first presenting its multiple dimensions and then by describing a conceptual model called generic service model (GeSMO), which can be used as a basis for the development of languages, tools and mechanisms that support interoperability. We then illustrate how GeSMO has been utilized for the provision of a P2P service description language and a P2P invocation mechanism which leverages interoperability between heterogeneous P2P services and between P2P services and Web services.

INTRODUCTION

The software community has been confronted with the issue of interoperability between software components during the last couple of decades. Various approaches such as object and component based approaches tackle this problem in various ways. However, they have not yet managed to provide a widespread solution that enables the interoperation of diverse components developed by different providers, in multi-vendor platforms (Medvidovic, 1999). Service oriented computing (SOC) emerged as an evolutionary step of object and component based approaches, with the promise to support the loose coupling of system parts thus providing agility, flexibility and cost savings via reusability and interoperability. However, the existence of many heterogeneous types of services and the vast amount of existing and emerging standards still constitutes a major obstacle towards interoperability, as it will become apparent in the following.

The most well-known instantiations of the service-oriented computing paradigm are Web services (Christensen, 2001) and Grid services (Czajkowski, 2004). However, other types of services such as Peer-to-Peer (P2P) services, see for example the JXTA services (Gong, 2001), are currently gaining momentum. All these types of services are usually built on top of XML standards (Bray, 2004) and other proven communication protocols such as HTTP (Fielding, 1999) and TCP/IP (Tanenbaum, 2003). The establishment of a set of common characteristics for these service types including properties such as self-description, internet accessibility and message-oriented communication has been one of the main research topics in this area and existing results comprise models such as the ones that have been specified by W3C in (Booth, 2004), by Werner Vogels in (2003), and by Karl Czajkowski, et al. in (2004). These features along with the use of XML standards (Bray, 2004) provide an infrastructure that promises to leverage interoperability among the components of a service-oriented system.

Nonetheless, although existing SOC instantiations, provide for a basic infrastructure that tackles interoperability, they still do not fully address it. This is mainly due to the multidimensional nature of interoperability, as it has also been noted in (Fang, 2004; Burstein 2005). Furthermore, the multiplicity of continuously emerging service types, see for example Sensor services (Gibbons, 2003) or UPnP services (Newmarch, 2005), is further aggravating the problem, as, albeit these service types share some common characteristics, they adhere to incompatible models and standards and rely on distinct platforms and middleware to perform their basic activities. It is worth noting here that, the interoperability problem exists, not only between services of different types, but also between services of the same type. See for example the area of P2P services, where there are no common standards or reference models; existing P2P platforms, e.g. JXTA (Gong, 2001), Gnutella (Ivkovic, 2001) or Edutella (Nejdl, 2001), use proprietary advertising, discovery and invocation mechanisms, thus hindering interoperability between these P2P services. Another example is the area of Web services, where, despite the use of standard protocols, there are still interoperability problems between Web services. Efforts such as those undertaken by WS-I (Ballinger, 2004) try to tackle the latter problem; specifically, WS-I has provided a basic interoperability profile for addressing some of the interoperability problems encountered between Web services; such an effort foregrounds the need for addressing the problem in various dimensions. However, there are still a lot of open issues which remain to be solved.

This article provides a solution on Interoperability between P2P and Web services. The provided solution is based on a generic framework which provides for interoperability between any type of service. This generic framework has been developed in the SODIUM project[1], which employs a unified approach towards the interoperability of heterogeneous service types. One of the advantages of this unified interoperability approach is that it allows the various service types to retain their own traits and characteristics. In this article we present: (i) the foundation of the SODIUM work which comprises a generic service model (GeSMO) that constitutes the underlying basis for the development of appropriate software for supporting service interoperability and, (ii) a specific solution that has been provided for the integration of P2P services with Web services which has been utilized in the SODIUM and SeCSE[2] projects.

The provided interoperability solution between Web and P2P services is described in detail in the rest of the article which we have structured as follows: We first present a motivating scenario which demonstrates the need for interoperability of heterogeneous services. Then, we examine interoperability among heterogeneous types of services from different dimensions, with an emphasis on Web and P2P services (see *section* "INTEROPERABILITY DIMENSIONS"); the issues that need to be addressed in order to facilitate the integration of heterogeneous services are identified in the *subsection* "Interoperability Concerns for Heterogeneous Services". In the sequel, we present a generic service model (GeSMO) that takes into account the identified interoperability issues. In particular the provided constructs catering for the description of P2P services are presented in the subsection "GeSMO Extensions for Peer-to-Peer Services". Then, in section "A Peer-to-peer Service Description Language" we describe how GeSMO and its extensions for P2P services have been utilized for the provision of the Peer-to-peer service description language (PSDL), which is an extension of WSDL (Christensen, 2001) and supports the description, discovery and invocation of P2P services. An example of a PSDL description document for the instant messaging service that is used in the motivating scenario is presented in the subsection "A PSDL Example". Then, section "JXTA Service Invocation Mechanism" illustrates the mechanism that has been built to support the invocation of JXTA P2P services. This mechanism utilizes JXTA service descriptions in PSDL so as to facilitate their seamless invocation. Next, in section "Application Case Study", we exemplify how P2P services providing location information have been integrated with Web services providing map information, for the implementation of a part of the motivating scenario. Finally, we compare our work with some other related approaches and we conclude this article with a discussion on open issues and on our future work plans.

MOTIVATING SCENARIO

Our motivating scenario is in the area of Crisis Management. This scenario was provided by LOCUS (www.locus.no), a leading supplier of mobile and other types of applications in the Scandinavian markets for transportation, emergency, security and the military. Actually, this motivating scenario was used in one of the SODIUM pilot applications which demonstrated the feasibility and usefulness of the provided solutions.

In the crisis management area a common task of paramount importance is determining how to get to a crisis location as fast as possible, as time is a critical factor. For example, in case of an accident where people are critically injured, it is imperative to reach these persons with the appropriate equipment within minutes, as if the injury causes lack of oxygen to the brain for 3-5 minutes, brain cells will start to die and after approximately 15 minutes there will be permanent damages. Therefore, it is vital that properly equipped ambulances and other rescue units are within a 15-minutes range at all times and places. In most cases this requirement is difficult to be satisfied due to the vast set of parameters such as accident/injury probability, population density and composition, accessibility, time of day/week/month/year, weather conditions, hospital locations and many others, which need to be considered.

It is thus vital that a crisis management system interoperates with various types of heterogeneous systems in order to incorporate the required information. LOCUS decided to use a service-oriented approach for the integration of all these types of systems, since there are a lot of available heterogeneous services which offer information useful to this crisis management application. Such services are:

- **Web services:** providing weather information such as temperature and precipitation, traffic conditions from roadside speed sensors and video surveillance cameras,
- **P2P services:** providing information about the locations and status of emergency vehicles or messaging facilities to the emergency vehicles with reposition message commands.
- **Other types of services** such as grid services providing driving route calculations, historical incident information and "response range" calculations based on current positions and conditions.

Figure 1 presents an example of a workflow based on this scenario, the tasks of which can be satisfied by various types of services[3]. As it can be seen in this figure, first we need to get information about the person who is calling and identify the accident location; see tasks *GetCallerInfo* and *GetCallerPosition*. Then, we need to identify the closest to the accident location, properly equipped ambulance; see task *GetBestSuitedAmbulance*. Subsequently, we need to calculate the shortest route to the accident location and to draw the route from the ambulance's current location to the accident location on a map (see related tasks *DetermineShortestRoute* and *GetMap*) which needs to be sent to the ambulance (see task *InformAmbulance*).

The services satisfying these tasks, do not need to be developed from scratch; instead the LOCUS company would like to utilize existing services (mentioned before) which have either

Figure 1. Composition example for crisis management scenario

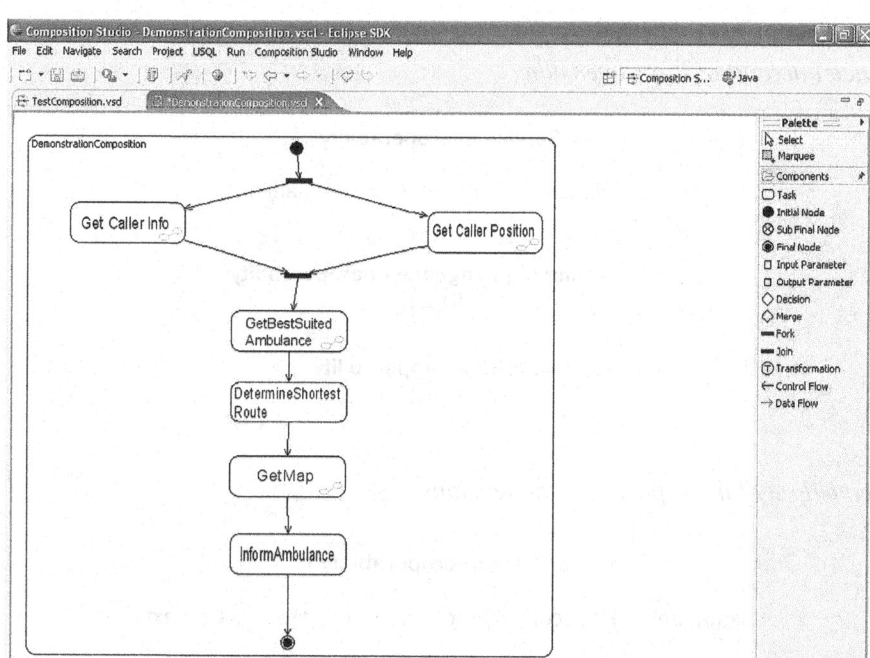

been developed in-house or are provided by trusted partners. For example, a Web service can be used to determine which ambulance is closest to the place of the accident, while a P2P instant messaging service can be used to satisfy the last task of the workflow which requires to send a map to the ambulance with the appropriate route information.

Therefore, the integration of heterogeneous services is of paramount importance, in order to satisfy the needs of service-oriented applications such as the above.

INTEROPERABILITY DIMENSIONS

In this section we briefly recap the results of current research on service interoperability and then we present our approach. Thus, according to the majority of the proposed interoperability models (Fang, 2004; Vallecillo, 2000; Murer, 1996), service interoperability has been divided into the signature, protocol and semantic levels. A classification scheme for interoperability that considers the evolution of distributed computing from the emergence of RPC or component models, such as DCOM (Microsoft, 1996) and EJBs (DeMichiel, 2006), to CORBA (Siegel, 1996), has been proposed in (Vallecillo, 2000) and it is presented in Figure 2. As we can see in this figure, the problem of interoperability is divided into three levels: service level, programming language level and platform level. The service level in particular is further decomposed in three interoperability dimensions i.e. *signature*, *protocol* and *semantic* dimensions.

Extensions to these three dimensions of the service interoperability level have been been provided in (Strang and Linnhoff-Popien, 2003) and in (Ruiz et al, 2000). In particular, Strang and Linnhoff-Popien added a context dimension to service interoperability which is of high importance to context-aware applications, where Ruiz et al proposed the addition of the *quality* dimension; see Figure 3.

Each of these dimensions describes specific interoperability concerns to be tackled when integrating two service-oriented systems. These concerns are briefly presented below:

Figure 2. Service interoperability dimensions

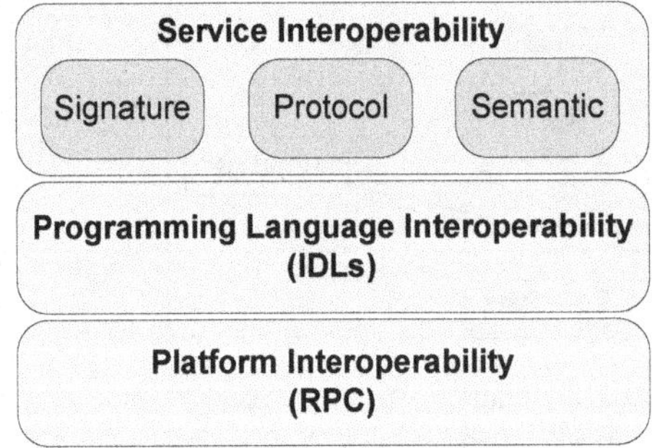

Figure 3. Extended set of interoperability dimensions

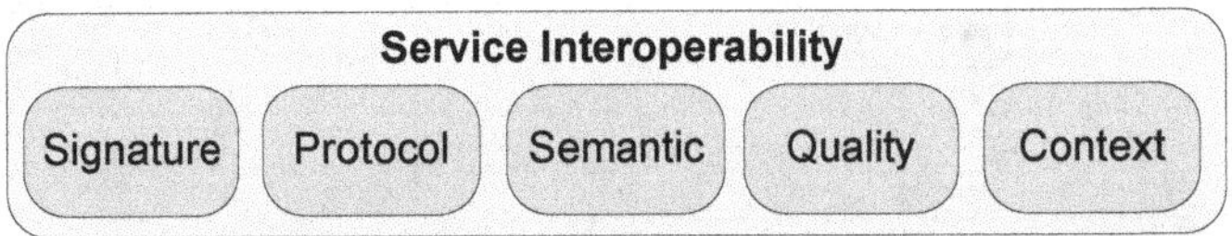

- The *signature* dimension addresses the interface definition conformance. This includes the operations, types and order of parameters of a service interface as well as standards such as the interface definition languages (IDL).
- The *protocol* dimension addresses the order in which the methods of a service are invoked. The Web Service Choreography Description Language (WS-CDL) (Kavantzas, 2005) can be seen as an effort to resolve this interoperability problem.
- The *semantic* dimension addresses the problem of common understanding between service providers and service consumers. This problem can be tackled through ontologies and semantic service description frameworks such as OWL-S (Martin, 2004), WSMO (Bruijn, 2005), SAWSDL (Farrell, 2006) or WSDL-S (Akkiraju, 2005).
- The *quality* dimension addresses the conformance of the quality requirements of a service consumer and the quality properties offered by the service provider. Solutions to this issue can be provided by description frameworks such as WS-QoS (Gramm, 2004), or WS-Policy (Bajaj, 2006).
- The *context* dimension refers to the conformance between the context representations used by service providers and the context representations requested by service clients. Context-level interoperability is important when employing services in ubiquitous computing environments. This problem could be tackled through the use of common ontologies and ontology frameworks e.g. RDF (Beckett, 2004), OWL (McGuinness, 2004) or via the use of context description frameworks such as ConteXtML (Ryan, 2005)

The aforementioned service interoperability dimensions (Figure 3) are the most commonly used. We argue that an additional set of interoperability dimensions needs to be defined at the service interoperability level, orthogonal to the aforementioned dimensions, in order to address interoperability from a global perspective (see Figure 4), providing in this way a more complete view of service interoperability.

The introduced orthogonal dimensions of service interoperability are: the business domain, the application and the platform dimensions. These dimensions have been layered in a top-down manner, starting from the most abstract system concepts related to business domain down to implementation specific concepts such as platform specific ones. Specifically, the introduced dimensions are as follows:

- **Business Domain:** Interoperability at this dimension represents the ability of two business systems to interoperate. This includes sharing of common domain concepts and processes which could be described using various standards and protocols such as RDF (Beckett, 2004), OWL (McGuinness, 2004), OWL-S (Martin, 2004), WS-CDL (Kavantzas, 2005), and ebXML BPSS (Dubray, 2006).
- **Application:** Applications are specific implementations of parts of business domains. Thus, application interoperability represents the ability of two specific business system

Figure 4. Additional service interoperability dimensions

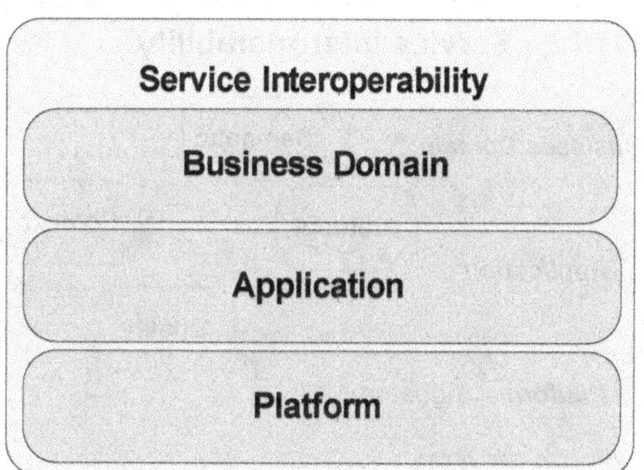

implementations to interoperate. This includes the use of compatible data structures, functionality and orchestrations that may be described using standards such as WSDL (Christensen, 2001) and WS-BPEL (Alves, 2006).

- **Platform:** Platform interoperability represents the ability of the middleware underlying two or more applications to interoperate. This includes features such as the use of compatible data type representations (e.g. real numbers having the same accuracy and same format), interface specification mechanisms (e.g. interface definition languages) or architectural styles (e.g. use of message-oriented communication styles). As it can be seen, this dimension differs from the platform interoperability layer appearing at the bottom part of Figure 2 in that it addresses both programming language and platform interoperability dimensions.

We believe that the utilization of a multi-viewpoint approach facilitates the clearer assessment of system interoperability. Thus, the dimensions depicted in Figure 3 take an internal look on the aspects that need to be considered when dealing with the integration of two systems, whereas the dimensions in Figure 4, which are orthogonal to the former ones, represent a system architect's 'coarse' point of view on the levels affected by the integration. Thus, we can integrate these two sets of dimensions into a single framework. Figure 5 illustrates this integrated view of service interoperability dimensions along with the associations between the concepts of the two individual frameworks. Such an integrated view facilitates the classification of the interoperability concerns for service interoperability from two distinct points of view.

Figure 5. An integrated view of service interoperability dimensions

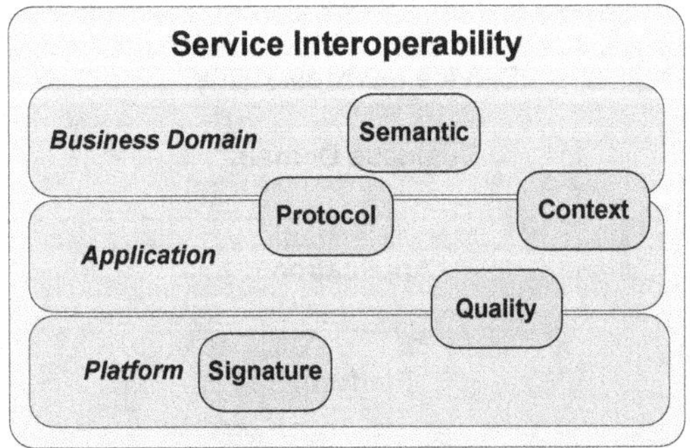

As it can be seen in Figure 5, the *semantic* and *signature* interoperability dimensions are clearly mapped to the orthogonal dimensions of Business Domain and Platform respectively; the *protocol and context* dimensions are shared between the dimensions of Business Domain and Application and Platform, while the *quality* dimension is shared among the Application and Platform dimensions. In order to better explain these mappings, let us consider the potential interoperability problem when integrating two systems that implement two incompatible processes (i.e. processes with incompatible choreographies). Such an incompatibility is at the *protocol* level. This problem may exist either due to the fact that the two systems support different and thus incompatible business processes (in which case we have an interoperability problem at the Business Domain level), or because their developers have selected different algorithms for their implementation (in which case we have an interoperability problem at the Application level). Similar arguments may be provided for the rest of interoperability dimensions.

There are also other frameworks such as the one presented in (Nezhad, 2006) focusing on Web service related interoperability. This framework leverages a different point of view for classifying Web service interoperability problems and hence, incorporates a different set of dimensions compared to the ones presented in Figure 5. Although this classification framework has been constructed to support the categorization of Web service related interoperability issues, it can also be used for the classification of interoperability issues of other types of services as well. Thus, its dimensions can easily extend the ones of our integrated framework without introducing any inconsistencies, since they have been conceived from a different point of view. However, we believe that there is no need to extend the dimensions of our framework in Figure 5, since these are generic enough to cater for the identification of all interoperability concerns that are also addressed in (Nezhad, 2006).

In the following, we present how the integrated service interoperability framework depicted in Figure 5 can be used for the classification of interoperability problems which arise when integrating heterogeneous services.

Interoperability Concerns for Heterogeneous Services

As it has been mentioned in the introduction, contemporary instantiations of the SOC paradigm, such as Web and P2P services, are ruled by different models, protocols and standards. The range of discrepancies and diversities among services spans across all of their aspects, such as description and discovery mechanisms, quality characteristics or service provision platforms. Based on the results of a thorough investigation on existing types of services that was undertaken for the purposes of the SODIUM project, we came up with a set of incompatibilities. The service types that we have investigated are that of Web, Grid and P2P services. In this article we focus on the incompatibilities between Web and P2P services which are the following:

- **Supported Models:** Web services and P2P services adhere to different models of operation; specifically Web services follow the stateless service model, although recently the concept of stateful Web services has arisen (Czajkowski, 2004) whereas P2P services are leaning towards the stateful service model, though some stateless implementations also exist (Nejdl, 2001).
- **Targeted Clients:** Although there might be specific security constraints dictating a different case, Web services in general may be invoked by any client with internet access, provided that the client has the necessary infrastructure (e.g. a SOAP engine) to exchange messages (e.g. SOAP messages) with the service provider. When it comes to P2P services, the respective client must be either a member of the P2P network or have access to the network through another peer (proxy peer).
- **Syntactic Features:** The different models supported by the investigated types of services result in a set of syntactic diversities as well. Briefly, while Web services adhere to the WSDL defined service model (i.e. a service comprises a set of distinct operations) and utilize the SOAP message format, P2P services adhere to a suppressed service model where each service comprises a single operation, and employ proprietary message formats (see for example JXTA Org, 2006). Furthermore, for the description of P2P services it is necessary to use concepts denoting the P2P network topology (e.g. peer, peer group, etc).
- **QoS Properties:** The origins of Web services are in business-oriented systems, whereas P2P services, such as instant messaging or file sharing systems, have been derived from community-oriented systems. Albeit there are certain implementations that do not adhere to the following claim, we may argue that the origins of each of these service types have dictated specific quality properties for each of them respectively. Thus, P2P services in general do not have to be reliable, secure and of high performance, whereas Web services should be.

All these incompatibilities and differences among the investigated types of services lead to a number of interoperability concerns that can be classified according to the previously identified interoperability dimensions (illustrated in Figure 5). These concerns are summarized below:

- **The incompatibility of the supported models has an impact on all interoperability dimensions but quality and context.**

The stateful service model that is accommodated by P2P services and stateful Web services, necessitates the use of additional features and processes e.g. resource lifetime properties and lifetime management mechanisms or processes supporting the discovery of resources. These additions have several ramifications on the platforms that are leveraged for the provision and invocation of stateful services, on the steps that need to be followed for the integration of such services, as well as on the semantics used for their description.

- **The difference on the targeted clients has an impact on the signature and protocol dimensions as well as on the platform and application dimensions.**

As it has been mentioned before, the invocation of P2P services can only be performed by peers of the P2P network using the API, mechanisms and protocols supported by the network. It henceforth, becomes apparent that interoperability among services which have different targeted clients e.g. Web and P2P services, should take into account the APIs, mechanisms and protocols supported by each service type.

- **The incompatibility of the syntactic features has an effect on the signature and platform dimensions.**

The use of incompatible structures and elements for the description of service syntactic characteristics has an effect on the languages used for their descriptions as well as on the middleware used for the provision and usage of such services. Therefore, in order to facilitate the integration of services with incompatible syntactic features, specific middleware needs to be provided, accommodating mappings of the features of one service type to the features of another service type.

- **The incompatibility of QoS properties has an effect on the quality dimensions as well as on the platform and application dimensions.**

Considering for example the issues of security, billing or availability, appropriate middleware and processes need to be used so as to cater for the provision, monitoring or management of such quality properties. Thus, the integration of services which are either demanding or providing incompatible quality characteristics has to be supported by appropriate middleware as well as by the use of specific process steps within an application.

Based on the results of our analysis that is illustrated in Table 1, the *signature* and *protocol* interoperability dimensions as well as the *platform* and *application* interoperability dimensions are the ones that seem to be highly affected by the integration of heterogeneous services. Thus, a solution for the integration of heterogeneous services should pay special attention on these dimensions.

We would like also to mention that, as it can be noticed, none of the identified discrepancies among P2P and Web services resulted in interoperability concerns for the context dimension. This is due to the fact that our investigation was focused on the interoperability problems that emerge when integrating heterogeneous services in general, regardless of their context.

Table 1. Effect of service differences on interoperability dimensions

		Differences Between Web, Grid and P2P Services			
		Supported Models	**Targeted Clients**	**Syntactic Features**	**QoS Properties**
Interoperability Dimensions	**Business Domain**	X			
	Application	X	X		X
	Platform	X	X	X	X
	Semantic	X			
	Protocol	X	X		
	Context				
	Quality				X
	Signature	X	X	X	

In the following section we present our approach in addressing the aforementioned interoperability dimensions which emerged by the differences between the investigated service types.

GENERIC SERVICE MODEL

Based on the findings of the previous section we developed a generic service model (GeSMO) which addresses service interoperability. GeSMO provides the basis for the development of appropriate middleware, languages and tools, which facilitate the interoperation of heterogeneous services. Its current version focuses on the syntactic aspects of a service; thus, it mainly addresses the signature and platform service interoperability dimensions. This was deemed necessary for the quick provision of input that would consequently be used in the development of the rest of the SODIUM project results i.e. tools and languages. However, as it will become apparent in the following, GeSMO is open and extensible, so it can easily support any other required interoperability dimensions.

As we have mentioned before, GeSMO was based on a thorough investigation of the current state of the art on contemporary types of services. Specifically with respect to P2P services, GeSMO has been primarily influenced by the work in JXTA (JXTA Org, 2006) as the latter is one of the very few P2P networks that inherently support the notion of a service. As regards Grid services, GeSMO was influenced by the WSRF specification (Czajkowski, et al. 2004). However, the following characteristics render GeSMO an ideal basis for supporting other types of services. Specifically, the model exhibits the following properties:

- **Generality:** The model is generic enough, as it provides a core part which contains concepts common to all investigated service types. On the other hand, it provides specific characteristics for each supported service type that are accommodated in the various modules of its extension layer. Modeling of service types beyond the Web, grid and P2P services that are currently supported, such as sensor services or UPnP services can be easily accommodated by adding extra modules in the GeSMO extension layer containing the specific characteristics of the new service types.
- **Abstraction:** The core part of the model incorporates abstractions of all common concepts of the addressed types of services,

e.g. the model contains concepts such as "service" and "message" which are part of all types of services; these abstract concepts can then be instantiated to the concepts supported by each specific type of service.

- **Extensibility:** The model can be easily extended with new features and properties, as well as with new service types. There are two ways of extending the model: a) by specialization of existing concepts; b) by appending new concepts in case there are no appropriate existing ones to be used as a basis for specialization. For example, the introduction of elements for the modeling of grid services has been achieved through the utilization of these mechanisms; in particular, elements for modeling the notion of "resource" were appended to the model whereas the notion of "grid service" was introduced as a specialization of the "Web Service" concept.
- **Modularity:** GeSMO has been structured in a modular manner; thus, information elements derived from specific viewpoints have been encapsulated within specific packages; for example, concepts related to the description of a service are contained within a description viewpoint package as it has been shown above. Such a modular structure allows for the easy modification and/or extension of the various parts.
- **Expressiveness:** The model is expressive enough to accommodate several service primal activities such as description, discovery, invocation, and composition. In addition, appropriate extension points were defined so as to accommodate additional features such as Semantics and QoS descriptions, etc. This expressiveness facilitated the development of tools & mechanisms which, based on the model, were able to support the unified discovery, composition and execution of Web, Grid and P2P services (Tsalgatidou, et al. 2006)
- **Simplicity:** The model is simple enough to be easily used by a variety of users and tools. For example, within the context of the SODIUM project the model was exploited in two ways: (a) it served as the basis for the development of service modeling, service discovery, service composition and service execution languages and tools; (b) it facilitated the communication among the project stakeholders.

The architecture selected for the development of the generic service model (GeSMO) is a layered one, consisting of the following layers which are depicted in Figure 6:

- The **core service concepts** layer which models concepts that are common to all investigated types of services, i.e. Web, Grid and P2P services;
- The **extended service concept** layer, on top of the core layer, which provides for the distinct features of each service type;
- A number of layers orthogonal to the core layer and its extensions, which provide appropriate extension points for modeling features related to *semantics, quality, trust, security* and *management*; these features can be applied to all concepts of the core layer and of its extensions; this approach renders GeSMO flexible enough with respect to the

Figure 6. GeSMO's layered architecture

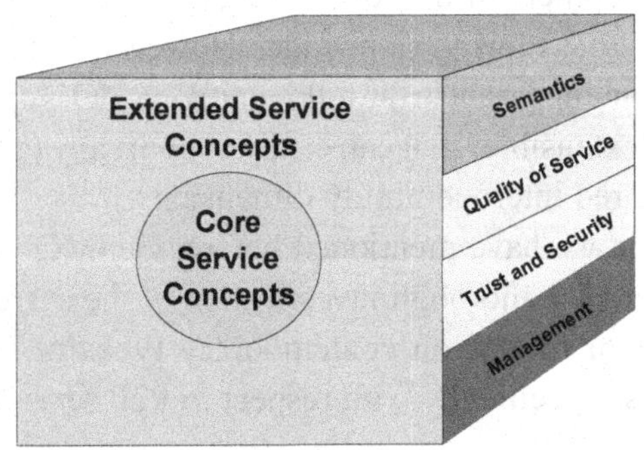

adoption of constructs for the representation of all these cross-cutting aspects in which currently there are no prevailing protocols or models.

The concepts of the core part of GeSMO are presented next, followed by the extensions that we have developed for P2P services.

The Core Part of GeSMO

The notion of service is the fundamental element in the core part of GeSMO model and it is modeled through various points of view. Figure 7 depicts the service concept along with the viewpoints that were used for its refinement.

As we can see in Figure 7, the viewpoints that were used for refining the concept of service are: the abstract point of view, the basic point of view, the description point of view, the structural point of view and the semantic and QoS point of view. These views are further detailed in the following figures.

Figure 8 depicts a service from an abstract view as a software system which has a set of functional and non-functional characteristics and exhibits a specific behavior. Its behavioral, functional and non-functional properties may have a semantic

Figure 7. Generic service model viewpoints

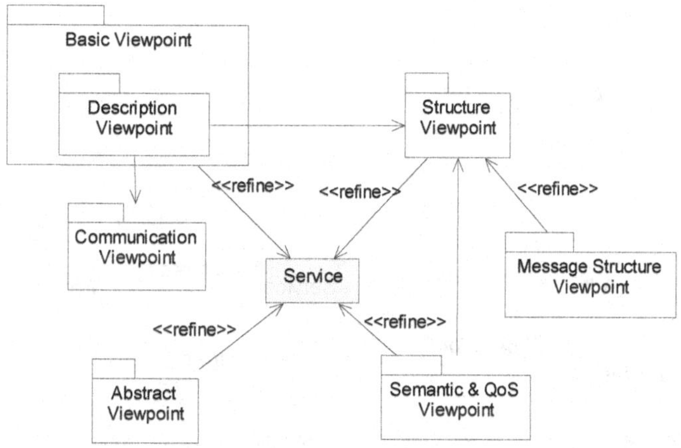

Figure 8. A service from an abstract point of view

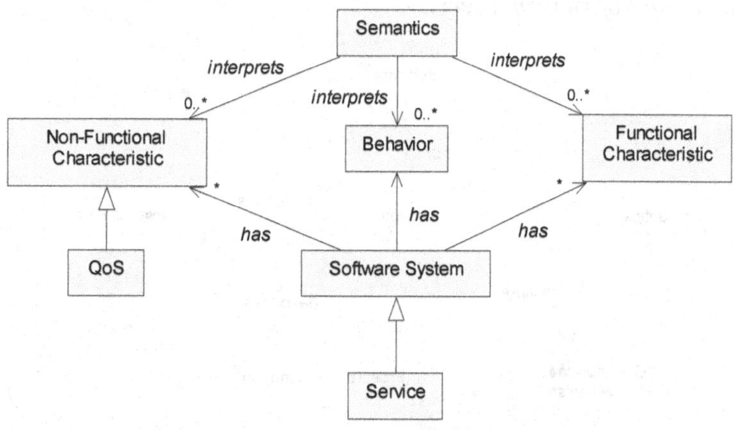

interpretation, whilst some of its non-functional properties can be considered as QoS properties.

Figure 9 depicts the basic service model where a service is a self-described software system that resides at a network address, is offered by a service provider and exchanges messages which are defined in its description.

The description of a service conveys a lot of important information, therefore we have developed a distinct description point of view which is presented in Figure 10. As we see in this figure, a service description may convey information about the behavioral, semantic and quality features of a service. In addition, it provides information about the communication mechanisms that may be used for accessing the service.

As regards the syntactic elements of a service, more information is provided by the structural point of view, which is depicted in Figure 11. According to this view, a service provides one or more interfaces consisting of operations that group a set of messages. Each message comprises a set of elements which adhere to specific data types. Messages are used for the communication between a service and its respective clients.

An additional point of view provided by the core part of GeSMO for a service is the semantic and quality-of-service (QoS) point of view depicted in Figure 12. As it can be seen, a service, its operations and the exchanged messages may have semantic interpretation. In addition, a service and its operations may also be associated with specific QoS properties.

Figure 9. Basic service model

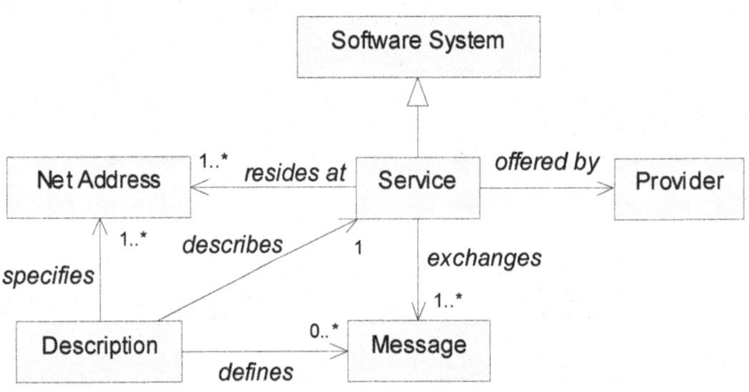

Figure 10. Description point of view of a service

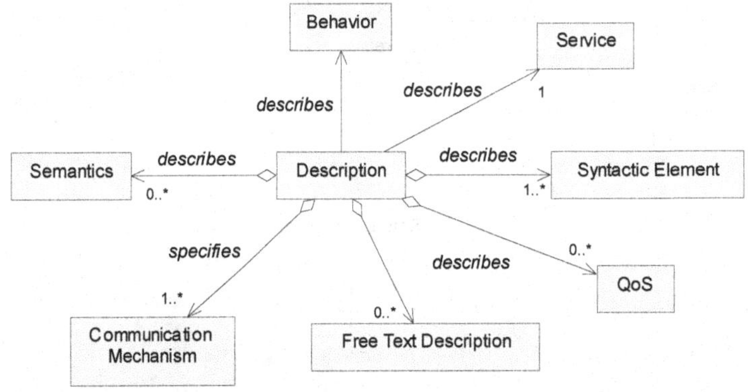

Figure 11. Structural point of view of a service

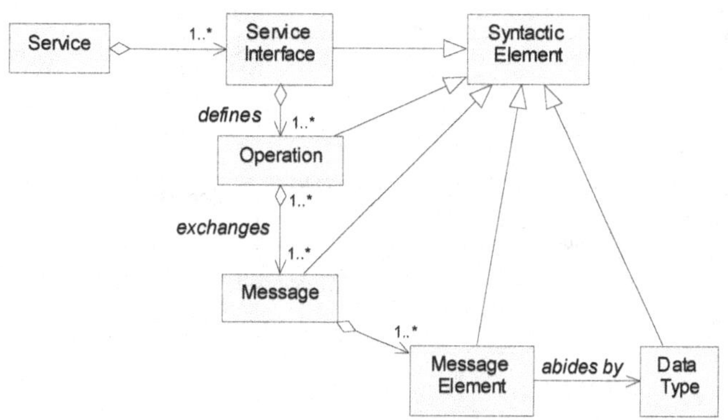

Figure 12. Semantic and QoS point of view for a service

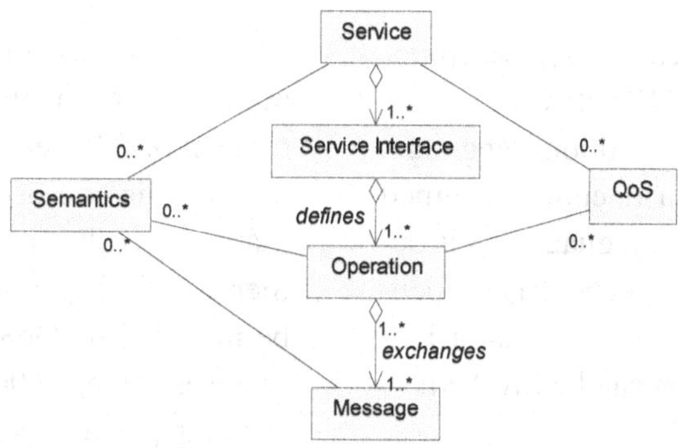

As we mentioned in the beginning of this section, the aforementioned concepts along with the additional ones which have been defined in (Tsalgatidou, 2005) establish the core part of the GeSMO model. In the following paragraphs, we present how these concepts were extended in order to support the rendering of P2P services in general as well as the description of JXTA P2P services offered by the JXTA platform. These concepts served as the basis for the specification of a language used for the description of P2P and JXTA services, as well as for the development of a P2P service invocation mechanism. Both the language and mechanism are described later on in this article.

GeSMO Extensions for Peer-to-Peer Services

The GeSMO peer-to-peer service model extends the GeSMO core concepts with additional elements needed for the description of P2P services. As it can be seen in Figure 13, the additional concepts catering for the description of P2P services are:

- **P2P service** which represents a service provided by a peer or a group of peers in a P2P network
- **Peer** which represents a node in a P2P network, capable of communicating with other peers and provide them with services

Figure 13. P2P service model

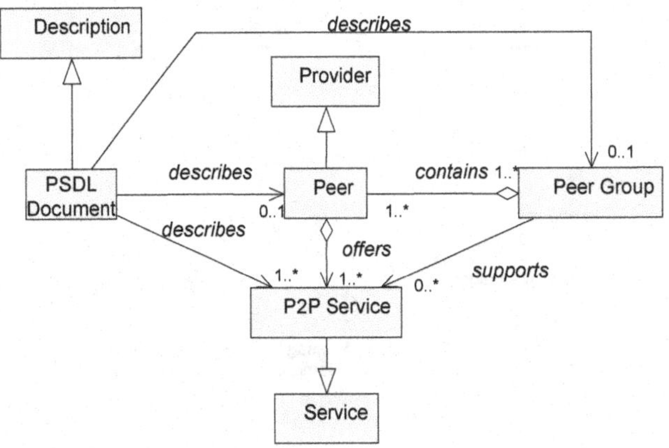

- **Peer group** that represents the logical grouping of peers within a P2P network
- **PSDL** (P2P Service Definition Language) description which is a document defined according to the PSDL language that is described in the following section. This document conveys information on what a P2P service does and how it can be invoked.

The PSDL concept was specifically added in order to facilitate the description of P2P services with additional information elements. Hence, a PSDL document does not aim at replacing the existing description constructs provided by the underlying P2P platform, but rather to enhance them with information that these constructs lack. Furthermore, PSDL descriptions provide the basis upon which mechanisms and middleware can be built so as to facilitate the more efficient discovery and utilization of P2P services.

The aforementioned concepts represent a basic set of elements that may be used for the description of any kind of P2P service. However, when it comes to modeling P2P services offered by specific platforms such as JXTA (JXTA Org, 2006) or Edutella (Nejdl, 2001), additional elements or specializations of the aforementioned ones might be needed.

JXTA is one of the most well known and mature platforms that can be used for the development of P2P services. Also, as we mentioned before, it is one of the very few P2P platforms that inherently support the notion of service, therefore it is the most prominent candidate to be modeled by GeSMO. With respect to JXTA services (Gong, 2001), JXTA offers constructs such as pipes, module specification advertisements and pipe advertisements. Pipes are communication mechanisms used for handling the exchange of messages among peers, thus facilitating the interactions between service requestors and service providers. Pipe advertisements and module specification advertisements are specializations of the advertisement construct and are used for publishing information about pipes and services, respectively.

Figure 14 illustrates the specializations of the P2P service model, which are provided by GeSMO for the representation of the aforementioned JXTA concepts. An extended PSDL description for the JXTA platform describes the pipes that can be used for exchanging messages with a service and provides references to their respective Pipe Advertisements. A P2P service module specification advertisement provides a reference to the PSDL description document of that service. This association is accomplished through the use of an extension element (i.e. SURI element (Duigou, 2003, pp. 23-24)) that is inherently supported by the JXTA Module Specification Advertisement.

The specification of the PSDL language which utilizes the aforementioned GeSMO extensions for the description of P2P service is presented next.

A PEER-TO-PEER SERVICE DESCRIPTION LANGUAGE

The *peer-to-peer service description language (PSDL)* was introduced as a mechanism that leverages interoperability between P2P services as well as between P2P and other types of services. Specifically, it incorporates a set of extensions upon the WSDL specification (Christensen, 2001) which were developed with the goal to support the description, discovery and invocation of P2P services. The design of PSDL was influenced by:

- the concepts and properties of the P2P service model as they have been perceived in GeSMO,
- the existing mechanisms (i.e. middleware, languages and tools) supporting the description, discovery and invocation of services, and
- the need to be extensible and customizable so as to enable the description of P2P services offered by various types of P2P platforms.

Instead of developing PSDL from scratch, we decided to develop it as an extension to WSDL. The main reason for this decision was our intention to reuse existing standards rather than introducting another totally new language and thus complicate further the interoperability problems. Thus, the intrinsic similarities between the concepts and the structure that were required to be supported by the PSDL and those of the WSDL language (i.e. the use of the syntactic elements modeled in the core layer of GeSMO (see Figure 11)), the availability of ample tools and middleware supporting the construction and utilization of WSDL documents and the WSDL support for extensibility, led us to use WSDL as a basis for the development of PSDL.

Although W3C (www.w3c.org) has lately released the specification of WSDL 2.0 (Chinnici, 2006) most of the existing tools and middleware have not yet completely adopted this new version of the specification. Therefore, the version of WSDL that we used as a basis for the development of the PSDL language is the WSDL 1.1 (Christensen, 2001).

As far as the elements of WSDL 1.1 (Christensen, 2001) are concerned, the ones catering for the description of a Web service abstract interface (e.g. PortType, Operation, Message and Types elements) can be reused in the description of a P2P service abstract interface as well, since both PSDL and WSDL utilize the same concepts. However, with respect to the concrete information part of a service, the elements provided by WSDL can not cater for the description of the concrete details of a P2P service. Thus, in order to render PSDL able to deliver its intended functionality, i.e. description, discovery and invocation of P2P services, we had to introduce appropriate extensions which are presented in the following.

According to (Christensen, 2001), WSDL provides the necessary extension points which can easily accommodate our requirements. The binding and port elements of the WSDL language provide the basis upon which P2P related concepts can be constructed. The introduced elements were devised in a way that enables the description of various types of communication/interaction patterns between a P2P service provider and its respective clients. Moreover, these elements were defined with extensibility and customizability in mind, in order to easily provide for the properties and characteristics of various P2P service provision platforms.

Apart from the PSDL language which facilitates the description of P2P services, one may argue that extensions and modification might be needed in other widespread protocols and standards of service oriented computing such as for example SOAP in order to further support interoperability among service types. There are projects striving towards the adoption of the SOAP protocol for exchanging messages among peers of a P2P network (e.g. http://soap.dev.java.net/), however, we decided not to ensue such an approach because our intention was to retain the autonomy of the existing P2P platforms and middleware without affecting their primal features, such as their communication mechanisms. Therefore, we focused on the provision of the PSDL language.

In the following, we will illustrate and elaborate on the extensions that we have developed, to support the representation of P2P services and their customizations for the description of JXTA services. Subsequently, we are going to exemplify how the PSDL language is used for the description of an Instant Messaging service.

The namespaces that were used as the basis for the development of appropriate extensions along with their associated prefixes are presented in Table 2.

The namespaces and assigned prefixes of the introduced elements are presented in Table 3.

The notation and the conventions that will be used hereafter for the description of the provided extensions are as follows:

- The name of each element is going to be preceded by its associated prefix that is specified in the tables above. Moreover the names of the WSDL elements that are going to be used in the following are in italics.
- The definition of each of the introduced elements (i.e. elements whose prefix is going to be 'gesmo' or 'jxta') adheres to an informal XML grammar, which uses the same notational conventions as the ones specified in (Christensen, 2001, section 1.2). In addition to the specified notational conventions the '|' character is used as separator among a list of optional values that can be assigned to an attribute or as a separator among a list of sub-elements that may be assigned to a specific element.
- The elements whose names start with a capital letter are abstract elements[4] whilst the elements whose name doesn't start with a capital letter can be instantiated within a document.

PSDL Language Elements

Since PSDL is based on the WSDL 1.1 specification (Christensen, 2001), it inherits and retains the structure of the WSDL elements. In addition, it extends WSDL with the information components that have been presented above. We need to stress here that only some of the elements of WSDL 1.1 are extended in PSDL, whilst the rest of the

Table 2. Imported Namespaces and associated prefixes

xsd	http://www.w3.org/2001/XMLSchema
wsdl	http://schemas.xmlsoap.org/wsdl/

Table 3. Namespaces for introduced concepts

gesmo	http://metis.di.uoa.gr/Sodium/gesmo/services/P2P/
jxta	http://metis.di.uoa.gr/Sodium/gesmo/services/P2P/jxta/

WSDL concepts, elements and mechanisms (e.g. the import and include WSDL mechanisms) are reused without any modification. An illustration of the WSDL information components that have been utilized to accommodate the concepts of the PSDL language and the provided extensions are presented in Figure 15. Please note that the provided extensions appear in the colored boxes, while the WSDL elements are white.

More details on those elements along with their definitions are presented in the following. First we present some general concepts that can be used in the description of various P2P services and then we illustrate the concepts that can be used in the description of JXTA services.

General P2P Service Related PSDL Elements

The gesmo:P2PBinding and the gesmo:P2PService components are abstract constructs that provide the foundation for the development of P2P platform related elements. These elements serve as placeholders where concrete information supporting the binding and invocation of P2P services may be conveyed.

Specifically, the gesmo:P2PBinding component is an extension of the *wsdl:binding* component, which provides information related to i) the interaction patterns supported by a service, ii) the operations associated with these patterns, and iii) the protocols used for the message exchange. On the other hand, the gesmo:P2PService component is an extension of the wsdl:service element, which conveys information related to i) the *wsdl:ports* where a service resides and ii) the *wsdl:bindings* that one may use to access each *wsdl:port.*

The formal definition of those elements is presented next.

gesmo:P2PBinding: This element denotes that the underlying communication mechanisms and the associated protocols will be related to P2P technology. An illustration of the attributes and sub-elements of this element is presented in Figure 16. According to this description, the P2PBinding element has a name and an interface attribute. The name attribute is used for the element identification and the interface attribute holds a reference to the associated interface (i.e. related wsdl:portType element) element. A P2PBinding element may include a documentation sub-element

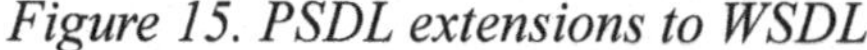

Figure 15. PSDL extensions to WSDL

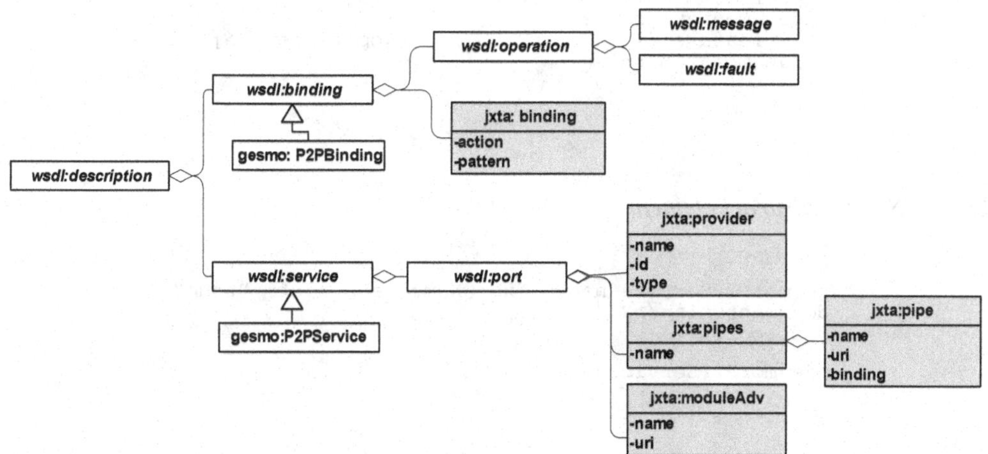

as well as a set of feature, property or operation sub-elements.

Please note that, the P2PBinding element is abstract, thus it can't be instantiated and included in a P2P service description document. Appropriate extensions of this element need to be created in order to convey information related to specific P2P service provision platforms.

gesmo:P2PService: The gesmo:P2PService element contains information about the endpoints where the service resides. Each P2PService element should have a name which uniquely identifies this element within a service description document. An illustration of the structure of this element is presented in Figure 17. As it can be seen, a P2PService element may contain additional documentation information as well as a set of *wsdl:ports* that its clients should use in order to access the service.

Note that, the P2PService element is also abstract, therefore appropriate extensions need to be provided in order to convey additional information related to specific P2P service provision platforms.

We would like to note here again that the gesmo:P2PBinding and the gesmo:P2PService abstract elements were introduced so as to serve as placeholders for future extensions of the PSDL language catering for specific types of P2P services e.g. Gnutella P2P services. Thus, these elements merely stand as boundary holders that support the structure of the PSDL language.

JXTA Specific PSDL Elements

JXTA provides a set of protocols and tools which leverage the development of P2P services and applications. According to (Sun Microsystems, 2005), JXTA services may be provided to their clients via various mechanisms, i.e. through pipes directly or via proxy modules which have to be installed by clients prior to accessing a service. In the work presented here, we describe the support that we have provided for JXTA services accessible through pipes.

Although our model can be extended to support JXTA services accessible through proxy modules, we have chosen not to address such services, mainly due to the following reasons:

Figure 16. P2PBinding abstract element

```
<gesmo:P2PBinding name= "xs:NCName"
interface="xs:QName" abstract= "true">
<documentation />?
  [<feature /> | <property /> | <operation />]*
</gesmo:P2PBinding>
```

Figure 17. P2PService abstract element

```
<gesmo:P2PService name= "xs:QName" abstract= "true">
<documentation/>?
<wsdl:port/>*
</gesmo:P2PService>
```

the first one being the deviation from the service model (Vogels,2003) that this approach would introduce, i.e. the resulting model would resemble more to a distributed component model rather than a service model; and the second reason being the complexity and source of inconsistencies that this would result in, e.g. the discovery and invocation of such services would also involve the discovery and invocation of appropriate proxy components.

The elements that have been introduced for the description of a JXTA service are the jxta:binding, jxta:provider, jxta:pipes, jxta:pipe and jxta:moduleAdv, as it can be seen in Figure 15. More details on each of these elements are presented next.

jxta:binding: In order to provide for the specification of JXTA binding schemes that may be used by a JXTA service, we have introduced the jxta:binding concept. This element is used for extending the *wsdl:binding* element in order to declare that this is a JXTA binding and in order to specify the action and the communication pattern that will be supported by this binding.

As it is illustrated in Figure 18, an element of this type has two optional attributes; the "action" attribute which is used for the specification of the type of actions that are supported i.e. send-receive, send or receive, and the "pattern" attribute which is used for the specification of the interaction type, i.e. synchronous or asynchronous.

The type of binding that is supported by a P2P service depends on the type of the pipe that will be used for communicating with that service. Hence, if a service uses a bi-directional pipe for receiving and replying to messages this service supports send-receive actions. Depending on if this is a blocking or a non-blocking communication the interaction pattern for this binding could be either synchronous or asynchronous.

jxta:provider: The jxta:provider element has been introduced to support the specification of the JXTA service provider and the type of the service. The PSDL specification dictates that only one instance of this element must be present within an enclosing port element and its properties should correspond to the ones of the service at hand.

The attributes of this element, which can be seen in Figure 19, provide for the distinction among the types of services that may be provided in a JXTA network (i.e. either Peer or Group services according to (Sun Microsystems, 2005)) and for the specification of the name of the service provider. Therefore the "name" attribute is used for describing the name of either the peer or the group which offers a specific service and the "type" attribute specifies whether this is a peer or a group service (see (Sun Microsystems, 2005).

jxta:pipes: The jxta:pipes element provides for the description of the list of pipes that are supported by a specific endpoint in order for someone to able to exchange messages with a service. Specifically the jxta:pipes element con-

Figure 18. Binding type declaration

```
<jxta:binding action= "send|receive|sendreceive"?
pattern= "synchronous|asynchronous"?/>
```

Figure 19. Provider element

```
<jxta:provider name= "xs:NCName" type= "Peer|Group"/>
```

veys a listing of the pipe advertisements that one should use in order to establish pipe connections with a JXTA service.

As it can be seen in Figure 20, a jxta:pipes element should contain at least one "pipeAd" element. Although, in most of the cases the use of a single pipe is adequate for the establishment of a communication channel among a JXTA service and its respective client the jxta:pipes element may contain additional jxta:pipeAd elements in order to be able to support more complex communication schemes - which are not excluded by the JXTA framework (Sun Microsystems, 2005) - that require the use of more than one pipes for the same endpoint. Furthermore, the jxta:pipes element may have a "name" that is used for referring to that element within a specific *wsdl:port.*

jxta:pipeAdv: The jxta:pipeAdv element is used for providing information regarding the pipe advertisement that a client may use in order to open a message exchange channel with a service. In addition, a jxta:pipeAd element provides information related to the types of interactions that are supported via the respective pipe.

As it is illustrated in Figure 21 each instantiation of the pipeAdv element should have a "name" which uniquely identifies this element within the list of pipeAdv elements that may be contained in an enclosing jxta:pipes element. Furthermore, an instantiation of the jxta:pipeAdv element should have a reference to the pipe advertisement file (by using the "uri" attribute) that a client should use in order to establish a pipe connection with the service. Finally, an instantiation of this element could have a description of the binding that this pipe supports. In case this is omitted, the binding of the enclosing Port element is used instead.

jxta:moduleAdv: The jxta:moduleAdv element was introduced so as to cater for the specification of the module specification advertisement that a JXTA service is using for its description (see Figure 22). A module specification advertisement is an advertisement document that is leveraged by the JXTA network so as to provide for the specification of JXTA services. More details on the Module Specification Advertisement can be found at (Duigou, 2006).

Figure 20. Pipes element

```
<jxta:pipes name="xs:NCName"? >
 <jxta:pipeAd/>+
</jxta:pipes>
```

Figure 21. PipeAdv element

```
<jxta:pipeAdv name= "xs:NCName" uri= "xs:URI"
binding="xs:QName"?/>
```

Figure 22. ModuleAdv element

```
<jxta:moduleAdv name= "xs:NCName" uri= "xs:URI"/>
```

An instantiation of this element (see Figure 22) has a "name" and a "uri" attribute. The "name" attribute is used for the identification of the moduleAdv element within the enclosing wsdl:port element. The "uri" attribute on the other hand provides for the specification of a reference to the module advertisement file of the service at hand.

This concludes the definition of PSDL and the description of its elements.

A PSDL Example

The elements of the PSDL language can be used to describe any JXTA service that adheres to the language constraints, as they were specified above. Taking for example an Instant Messaging (IM) service that reliably exchanges messages with its clients through a bi-directional pipe (Sun Microsystems, 2005, pp 14-17), its service description document will be as the one illustrated in Figure 23. The service described is a JXTA peer service called *"IMService"*, which comprises a single operation called *"sendReliableMessage"*. This method accepts messages of type *"IMessage"* and returns messages of type *"IMResponse"*. As it can be easily seen, the description of the abstract part of the *"IMService"* service is the same as that of a Web service. The elements that have been introduced for the specification of a JXTA service can be identified within the binding and service WSDL elements.

The jxta:binding element included in the *"JxtaBidiBind"* element denotes that the *"IM-*

Figure 23. Instant messaging service description in PSDL

```
<message name="IMessage">
  <part name="MessageContent" type="xsd:string"/>
  <part name="MessageSender" type="xsd:string"/>
</message>
<message name="IMResponse">
  <part name="MessageAknow" type="xsd:string"/>
</message>
<portType name="IMServiceIF">
  <operation name="sendReliableMessage" parameterOrder="MessageContent Mes-
sageSender">
    <input name="msg" message="tns:IMessage"/>
    <output name="resp" message="tns:IMResponse"/>
  </operation>
</portType>
<binding name="JxtaBidiBind" type="tns:IMServiceIF">
   <jxta:binding action="sendreceive"/>
   <operation name="sendReliableMessage">
     <input/>
     <output/>
   </operation>
</binding>
<service name="IMService">
   <port name="JxtaBidiPort" binding="tns:JxtaBidiBind">
     <jxta:provider name="Jemini" type="Peer"/>
     <jxta:pipes name="IMServicePipes">
     <jxta:pipeAd name="BidiPipe" uri="http://metis.di.uoa.gr/.../IMS_BidiPipeAd.xml" />
     </jxta:pipes>
<jxta:moduleAdv name="IMServiceModuleAd" uri="http://metis.di.uoa.gr/.../IMSpec-
Adxml"/>
   </port>
</service>
```

ServiceIF" port type, that is referenced by the binding's type attribute, is an interface of a JXTA service. This binding supports send-receive message exchanges using the default synchronous communication pattern. According to the information that is conveyed in the *"JXTABidiPort"* element, we can see that the *"IMService"* service, which adheres to the *"IMServiceIF"* port type, is a peer service. This service provided by a peer of a JXTA network whose name is *"Jemini"*. Clients of that service may use the *"BidiPipe"* pipe advertisement in order to access this service, whilst its module specification advertisement that is called *"IMServiceModuleAd"* can be retrieved at a specific location that is specified by the uri attribute of the jxta:moduleAdv element.

This PSDL description document can be fed as input to the JXTA service invocation mechanism that is described next, so as to facilitate the flexible invocation of the described service, without the developer caring for the underlying JXTA network details.

JXTA SERVICE INVOCATION MECHANISM

Based on (Sun Microsystems, 2005), a JXTA service, that is made available to its clients through pipes, can be invoked via messages that are a priori known to the service and its clients. The service advertisement mechanism provided by the JXTA framework does not convey appropriate information elements that could facilitate the documentation of the exchanged messages. Thus, the description as well as the interpretation of messages is normally embedded within the service and the client code.

Therefore, for someone to utilize JXTA P2P services in the same way as other types of services, e.g. Web services, and to compose them with other services, appropriate invocation mechanisms need to be put in place. These mechanisms should enable the dynamic invocation of JXTA P2P services based on annotated service description documents. Such a mechanism was developed by the authors of this article so as to enable the invocation of JXTA P2P services via the SODIUM execution engine based on the use of PSDL description documents.

The architecture of the provided JXTA P2P service invocation mechanism has been based on the use of the web service invocation framework (WSIF) (Duftler, 2001). This design decision was driven by the similarities of the PSDL and the WSDL languages and by the fact that WSIF is offered as open source.

WSIF accommodates the necessary programming abstractions that enable the invocation of WSDL compliant services over various communication protocols and message formats. It enables either the dynamic or the static (i.e. via appropriate stubs that are created at design time) invocation of services irrespectively of the protocol bindings and the implementation details that they use. In order to facilitate the invocation of any type of code that may be available at the network, the framework provides appropriate extension points that can be utilized by developers so as to accommodate the peculiarities of specific implementations and communication protocols.

Currently, the WSIF framework provides extensions that enable the utilization of implementations such as Java code, EJBs and J2EE Connectors in a service-oriented manner. Nonetheless, developers are able to create 'WSIF Providers' (i.e. extensions to the WSIF framework) along with appropriate extensions to the WSDL[5] language that enable the utilization of additional types of services. Such a 'WSIF Provider' was developed by the authors of this article in order to support the invocation of JXTA services in a more flexible and service-oriented way. An illustration of the provided component and its placement within the JXTA reference architecture is presented in Figure 24.

The provided mechanism (*'WSIF Invocation Service'* component illustrated in Figure 24) is an extension to the JXTA platform reference architecture (Gong, 2001) that leverages other JXTA supported services and core components so as to enable the flexible invocation of JXTA services. Specifically the *'WSIF Invocation Service'* component utilizes the PeerGroup component and the pipe service to support the establishment of pipe connections between a service and a client. Consequently the *'WSIF Invocation Service'* component can be utilized by other JXTA applications so as to facilitate the dynamic invocation of JXTA services that are described using the PSDL language.

As it can be seen in Figure 24, the components that have been added to the WSIF Platform in order to support the invocation of JXTA services are the *"JXTA WSDL4J Extensions"* and the *"JXTA WSIF Extensions"*. The *"JXTA WSDL4J Extensions"* contains all the necessary extensions to support the parsing of a PSDL description document and its mapping to in-memory objects, whereas the "JXTA WSIF Extensions" comprises the extensions that are mandated by the WSIF framework (WSIF Org, 2006) to enable the dynamic invocation of JXTA services. The "JXTA Pipe Connection Handler" on the other hand leverages services and components of the JXTA platform so as to enable the establishment of pipe channels and the exchange of messages.

Although JXTA supports the exchange of either XML or Binary messages (Sun Microsystems, 2005), our current implementation of the *'WSIF invocation service'* facilitates only the exchange of XML formatted messages. This decision was influenced by our need to have a clear mapping between the message representation conveyed in a PSDL description document and the message that is exchanged through a pipe connection. Nonetheless, the invocation mechanism may be extended in order to facilitate the transformation of messages to a Binary format that will be used over a pipe connection between a service and

Figure 24. "WSIF Invocation Service" component integration with the JXTA Reference Architecture

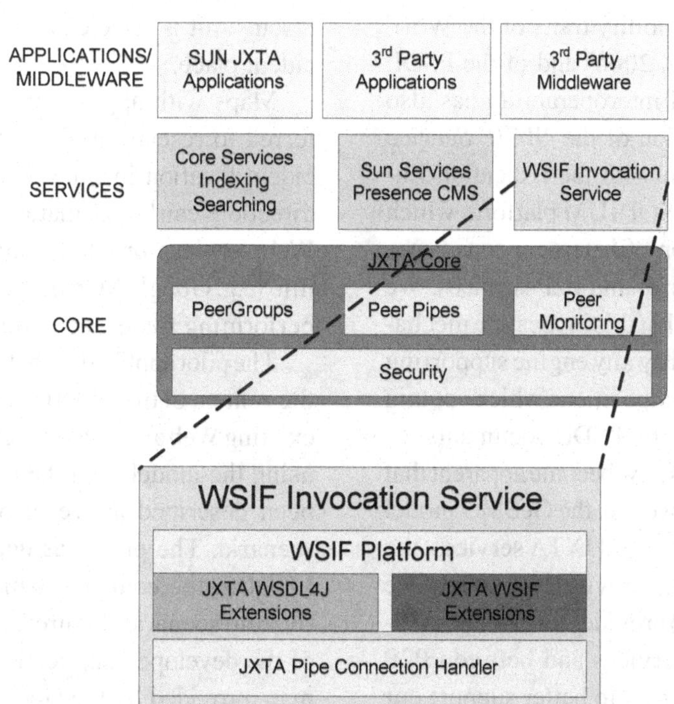

its clients. However, the description of such a transformation mechanism falls outside the scope of this article.

In spite of the placement of the *"WSIF Invocation Service"* component within the JXTA Reference Architecture (Sun Microsystems, 2005) (see Figure 24) we do not imply a tight bond between the JXTA platform and the service invocation mechanism. Provided that appropriate extensions are developed for the PSDL language as well as for the *'WSIF Invocation Service'* so as to cater for the description and invocation of other types of P2P services e.g. Gnutella services (www.gnutella.org) or Edutella services (Nejdl, 2001), this mechanism can be easily plugged in to those platforms so as to facilitate the interoperation of their respective services. This is possible because, service consumers may invoke any type of service via the WSIF framework in a way that is independent of the underlying bindings and protocols. Thus, a client which might be a node of a Gnutella network is able to invoke services provided by peers of a JXTA network and vice-versa.

The level of interoperability that is achieved by the *'WSIF Service Invocation'* component is sustained by the extensibility traits of the WSIF framework (WSIF Org, 2006) and of the PSDL language. This level of interoperability has also facilitated the integration of the *'WSIF Service Invocation'* mechanism with the Execution Engine component of the SODIUM platform which supports the integration of heterogeneous types of services i.e. Web, grid, and P2P services. We would like also to note that this invocation mechanism can be easily used by any engine supporting execution of service compositions which contain P2P services described by PSDL documents.

We believe that it has now become apparent that the work described above (i.e. the GeSMO model and its extensions for P2P and JXTA services, the PSDL Language and the provided JXTA service invocation mechanism) provides for the interoperability between P2P services and between P2P and Web services. In order to better support our argument we illustrate next an example from an application which leverages P2P and Web services for the implementation of the motivating scenario that was presented in the beginning.

APPLICATION CASE STUDY

An important part of the motivating scenario described earlier in this article is related to the identification of the location of an accident, the identification of the nearest rescue unit and the calculation of the shortest route between them. According to this scenario, when someone calls to report an accident, his/her location can be easily spotted either if he/she is calling from a fixed-line or from a mobile phone. Appropriate Web services providing the location of the caller already exist and can be used for this task.

Rescue units on the other hand are already equipped with communication devices which leverage P2P services in order to exchange location or other types of information (e.g. commands and other types of messages). Based on the caller location the closest and most properly equipped rescue unit is selected and dispatched to the accident place.

Maps with appropriate directions are transferred to rescue units in order to reach the accident location in time. Such maps and routing directions can be calculated using already existing Web services providing map and other related info (e.g. Google Maps) along with other services performing route calculations.

The pilot application that was developed within the context of the SODIUM project integrates the existing Web and P2P services (mentioned before) using the models and the mechanisms that have been described above in order to support this scenario. The pilot was deployed in Norway at LOCUS, the company which provided the motivating scenario. Figure 25 depicts the outcome of the developed application which is a satellite map, provided by the Google Map service, with

Figure 25. Rescue route calculation

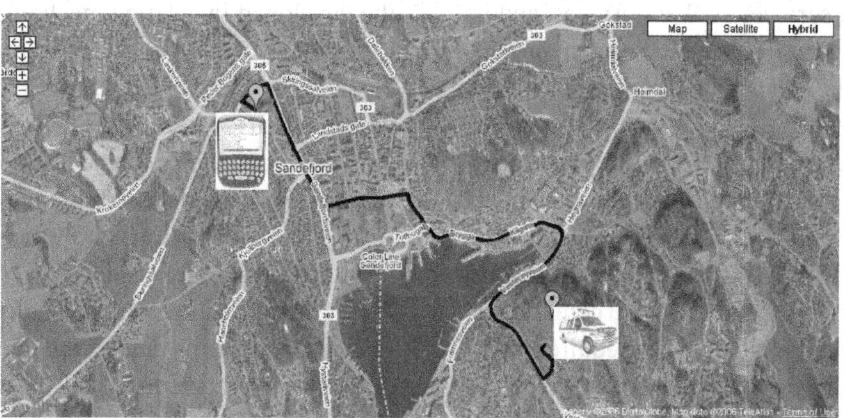

the calculated route drawn upon it. This map along with the calculated route is sent to the ambulance that is closest to the accident with the use of a P2P service; all ambulances are peers of the same p2p network.

We believe that through this case study, it becomes apparent that the integration of P2P services with Web services is of great importance and facilitates a lot the development of service-oriented applications which need to integrate such heterogeneous services.

RELATED WORK

The main contribution of this article is in service interoperability and service modeling in general, via the proposed interoperability framework and the generic service model (GeSMO), and in the interoperability among P2P services and between P2P and Web services in particular, via the P2P service description language (PSDL) and the JXTA service invocation mechanism. Therefore, the related work that follows refers to any of these results.

The convergence of Web service and P2P computing models is an issue that has been tackled by many researchers (Papazoglou et al, 2004; Benatallah et al, 2003). A plethora of approaches have been proposed on how this can be achieved. In (Papazoglou et al 2004) a P2P architecture is used for the organization of federated UDDI registries. The introduced federated model enables the formation of syndicates where services of the same domain can be advertised. This approach departs from the one that we have presented within this article as we are considering P2P services as another service-oriented computing paradigm that can be utilized in the same way as Web services. Regarding the P2P service publication and discovery, we reuse the mechanisms supported by the underlying P2P network infrastructures.

The SELF-SERV platform that is proposed by (Benatallah et al, 2003) is also using a P2P infrastructure as the enabling technology which leverages the utilization of Web services, i.e. the discovery and composition of Web services, in a P2P organized manner. This approach also does not regard P2P services as another instantiation of the service-oriented computing paradigm, as we do. Therefore our approach is different from the one followed within the SELF-SERV platform.

Integration of the P2P and Web services worlds was also attempted in (Qu, 2004), by means of two interaction scenarios: i) exposing the existing Edutella/JXTA services as Web services, and ii) integrating Web service-enabled content providers into Edutella/JXTA. The ultimate goal of the proposed approach was to establish integration of Web and P2P services at the service layer through the use of proxies. Although sharing some common ideas, our approach is distinguished by the fact that the P2P and Web service technologies retain their autonomy. No additional components or infrastructure modifications are required in our approach, besides the description of P2P services with the use of PSDL, or some other WSDL-based language.

P2P service description and invocation was also tackled in (Oriol, 2002). Therein, a number of alternative, distributed implementation infrastructures were proposed, which served the purpose of automating service discovery and invocation. Still, the approach was described from a different point of view than ours, addressing service description and invocation from a relatively higher level. In fact, our P2P service description language along with the WSIF-based invocation mechanism could be used complementary with respect to that approach. Combining our results with other similar efforts is one of our future research plans.

In (Elenius, 2004), a framework named Oden was proposed, which utilizes the OWL-S specification to annotate JXTA service descriptions with semantics. The results of this effort included automated P2P service discovery and invocation. However, the issue of P2P and Web services integration and interoperability goes beyond the scope of the Oden framework. As opposed to that, in our approach, we mainly focus on establishing a unified manner of describing and invoking heterogeneous services, and here we describe how this unified solution has been applied in the integration between Web and P2P services. To this end, we would like to note that, PSDL descriptions could be further annotated with semantic and QoS properties, so as to facilitate P2P service discovery without affecting the developed invocation mechanism.

Triana (Churches, 2006) is a platform that enables the distributed execution of scientific workflows. It leverages GAT (Allen, 2003) to support the provision of the necessary abstractions that facilitate the distribution and monitoring of workflows which is based on the Triana Group unit concept. GAT acts as an overlay above the JXTA infrastructure which enables the distribution of Group units among the peers of a JXTA network. GAT leverages the underlying JXTA Pipe and ID mechanisms to support the coordination and communication among the distributed Group units. Although, there are certain similarities between our service invocation mechanism and the GAT toolkit, our approach is different in that it has a direct support for the notion of JXTA service whilst GAT utilizes underlying JXTA communication and naming mechanisms to support the exchange of information among Triana's Group units.

CONCLUSION

Service oriented computing (SOC) has emerged as the computing paradigm for developing large-scale, distributed applications, by integrating existing pieces of software exposed as services. Although the primary objective of SOC was to leverage interoperability among the various heterogeneous software platforms and systems, its various diverse instantiations (e.g. Web and P2P services) introduced new interoperability issues. Thus, despite that the integration of the various heterogeneous types of services has been called for in many vital application domains, the incompatible underlying models, protocols and standards of such heterogeneous services render this an arduous task. Given this situation along with the absence of a set of common, widely-accepted standards governing all these service-oriented technologies, we argue that interoperability can be supported through the establishment of a unified approach in terms of models, languages and tools which are based on a common set of conceptual primitives.

In this article, we went through the foundations of our unified approach towards the integration and interoperability of heterogeneous services, and exemplified how such an approach was applied for the integration of Web and P2P services. In summary, we presented the dimensions influencing interoperability among the various service-oriented technologies and presented an integrated classification scheme for these dimensions. Then, we examined the impact of the discrepancies among the investigated types of services on the identified interoperability dimensions. The generic service model (GeSMO), which was developed in order to address some these interoperability dimensions was then described. Finally, we focused on the description of the extensions provided in GeSMO for P2P services, and specialized in the case of JXTA services.

As it was discussed in this article, the layered architecture of GeSMO renders it extensible and independent from the various service types and their related standards, thus, a perfect basis for the development of unified languages and tools. We defended this argument by presenting PSDL, a WSDL-based language which uses appropriate GeSMO concepts and is used for the description, discovery and invocation of P2P services, enabling in this way P2P services to be integrated and interoperate with Web services. Along with PSDL, we presented an effective mechanism for the invocation of JXTA P2P services. We believe that the combination of this invocation mechanism (being based on the WSIF framework) with the PSDL language (being based on WSDL) provides a novel solution for the integration of Web and P2P services.

It should be noted that the extensibility of the approach presented in this article was exemplified by the extensions of GeSMO within the context of the SODIUM project, so as to address grid services as well. Therefore, all SODIUM tools and languages support Grid services, too, via appropriate extensions on GeSMO; hence they provide a platform which supports the unified discovery, composition and execution of Web, grid and P2P services. Furthermore, the presented solution was integrated with the results of another European project, namely SeCSE, which supports the development of service-oriented applications. We would like also to note that GeSMO and its extensions have been included in a proposal submitted to OMG as a response to a Request for Proposal for a UML Profile and Metamodel for Services[6] .

Finally, we would like to mention that, GeSMO served as a basis for handling interoperability at the signature or platform level, therefore it needs to be further extended in order to fully address the interoperability problem. In this regard, issues related to other interoperability dimensions such as protocol, quality or application, as well as semantic or business domain are going to be addressed in our future work. Furthermore, future plans regarding GeSMO include the provision of extensions to accommodate other types of services, such as sensor services, and the incorporation of additional P2P networks and platforms that provide for other P2P services, besides the JXTA platform.

ACKNOWLEDGMENT

This work has been partially supported by the Special Account of Research Funds of the National and Kapodistrian University of Athens under contract 70/4/5829 and by the European Commission (under contract IST-FP6 004559 for the SODIUM project and IST-FP6 511680 for the SeCSE project). Finally, the authors would like to thank all the SODIUM partners which contributed in this work and in particular LOCUS for their input in the motivating scenario and in the case study.

REFERENCES

Akkiraju, R., Farrell, J., Miller, J., Nagarajan, M., Schmidt, M.-T., Sheth, A., Verma, K., (2005) Web Service Semantics, WSDL-S, W3C Submission, http://www.w3.org/Submission/WSDL-S/

Allen, G., Davis, K., Dolkas, K., Doulamis, N., Goodale, T., Kielmann, T., Merzky, A., Nabrzyski, J., Pukacki, J., Radke, T., Russell, M., Seidel, E., Shalf, J., and Taylor, I., (2003), Enabling Applications on the Grid: A GridLab Overview, International Journal of High Performance Computing Applications: Special issue on Grid Computing: Infrastructure and Applications, August 2003

Alves, A., Arkin, A., Askary, A., Bloch, B., Curbera, F., Ford, M., Goland, Y., Guízar, A., Kartha, N., Liu, C. K., Khalaf, R., König, D., Marin, M., Mehta, V., Thatte, S., Rijn, D., Yendluri, P., Yiu, A., (2006), Web Services Business Process Execution Language Version 2.0 Public Review Draft, 23rd August 2006, available at http://docs.oasis-open.org/wsbpel/2.0/

Bajaj, S., Box, D., Chappell, D., Curbera, F., Daniels, G., Hallam-Baker, P., Hondo, M., Kaler, C., Langworthy, D., Nadalin, A., Nagaratnam, N., Prafullchandra, H., Riegen, C., Roth, D., Schlimmer, J., Sharp, C., Shewchuk, J., Vedamuthu, A., Yalçinalp, Ü., Orchard, D., (2006), Web Services Policy 1.2 - Framework (WS-Policy), W3C Member Submission April 2006, available at http://www.w3.org/Submission/2006/SUBM-WS-Policy-20060425/

Ballinger, K., Ehnebuske, D., Ferris, C., Gudgin, M., Nottingham, M., Yendluri, P., (2004) Basic Profile Version 1.1, WS-I specification, 8 August 2004, http://www.ws-i.org/Profiles/BasicProfile-1.1-2004-07-21.html

Beckett, D., McBride, B., (2004), RDF/XML Syntax Specification (Revised), W3C Recommendation, February 2004, available at: http://www.w3.org/TR/rdf-syntax-grammar/

Benatallah, B., Dumas, M., and Sheng, Q. Z.,(2003), The SELF-SERV Environment for Web Services Composition, IEEE Internet Computing Jan/Feb Issue, Vol. 7 (1). IEEE Society 2003

Bray, T., Paoli, J., Sperberg-McQueen, C. M., Maler, E., Yergeau, F., (2004), Extensible Markup Language (XML) 1.0 (Third Edition), W3C Recommendation 04 February 2004, http://www.w3.org/TR/2004/REC-xml-20040204/

Burstein, M., Bussler, C., Zaremba, M., Finin, T., Huhns, N. M., Paolucci, M., Sheth, P. A., Williams, S., (2005), A semantic web service architecture, In IEEE Internet Computing, vol 9 issue 5, Sept.-Oct. 2005, 72-81

Booth, D., Haas, H., McCabe, F., Newcomer, E., Champion, M., Ferris, C., Orchard, D., (2004), Web Services Architecture, W3C Working Group Note, February 2004, available at http://www.w3.org/TR/ws-arch/

Bruijn, J., Bussler, C., Domingue, J., Fensel, D., Kifer, M., Kopecky, J., Lara, R., Oren, E., Polleres, A., Stollberg, M., (2005), Web Service Modeling Ontology (WSMO), WSMO Final Draft February 2005, available at http://www.wsmo.org/TR/d2/v1.1/

Christensen, E., Curbera, F., Meredith, G., Weerawarana, S., (2001) Web Services Description Language (WSDL) 1.1 W3C Note 15 March 2001, available at: http://www.w3.org/TR/wsdl

Chinnici, R., Gudgin, M., Moreau, J.-J., Weerawarana, S., (2003), Web Services Description Language (WSDL) Version 2.0 Part 1: Core Language, W3C Candidate Recommendation, 27 March 2006, available at http://www.w3.org/TR/wsdl20/

Churches, D., Gombas, G., Harrison, A., Maassen, J., Robinson, C., Shields, M., Taylor, I., Wang, I., (2006), Programming Scientific and Distributed Workflow with Triana Services, Concurrency and Computation: Practice and Experience Special

Issue: Workflow in Grid Systems 2006, V(18) n(10), 1021-1037

Czajkowski, K., Ferguson. D., Foster, I., Frey, J., Graham, S., Maguire, T., Snelling, D., Tuecke, S., (2004), From Open Grid Services Infrastructure to WS-Resource Framework: Refactoring & Evolution, Version 1.0, Whitepaper, February 2004.

DeMichiel, L., Keith, M., (2006), Enterprise Java Beans, Version 3.0: EJB Core Contracts and Requirements, Release 8 May 2006, available at http://java.sun.com/

Dubray, J. J., Amand, S., Martin, J. M., (2006), ebXML Business Process Specification Schema Technical Specification v2.0.4, Committee Specification, 13 October 2006, available at http://www.oasis-open.org/committees/documents.php?wg_abbrev=ebxml-bp

Duftler, J. M., Mukhi, K. N., Slominski, A., Weerawarana, S., (2001), Web Services Invocation Framework (WSIF), OOPSLA 2001 Workshop on Object-Oriented Web Services: Supporting the Development, Deployment and Evolution of Web Services, October 2001 - Tampa, Florida, USA

Duigou, M., (2006), JXTA v2.0 Protocols Specification, IETF Working Group Draft Specification, August 2006

Elenius, D. and Ingmarsson, M. 2004. Ontology-based service discovery in p2p networks. In Proceedings of the First International Workshop on Peer-to-Peer Knowledge Management, Boston, Massachusetts, USA, August 2004, CEUR-WS, August 2004, Vol. 108.

Fang, J., Hu, S., Han Y., (2004), A Service Interoperability Assessment Model for Service Composition, In Proceedings of the 2004 IEEE International Conference on Services Computing (SCC'04), Sept. 2004, Shanghai, China

Farrell, J., Lausen, H., (2006), Semantic Annotations for WSDL, W3C Working Draft 28, Sept. 2006

Fielding, R., Gettys, J., Mogul, J., Frystyk, H., Masinter, L., Leach, P., Berners-Lee, T., (1999), Hypertext Transfer Protocol - HTTP/1.1, IETF, June 1999

Ivkovic, I., (2001), Improving Gnutella Protocol: Protocol Analysis and Research Proposals, LimeWire Gnutella Research Contest, September 2001

Gibbons, P., Karp, B., Ke, Y., Nath, S., Seshan, S., (2003), IrisNet: An Architecture for a World-Wide Sensor Web, IEEE Pervasive Computing, V(2), N(4), October-December 2003

Gong, L., (2001). JXTA: a network programming environment, IEEE Internet Computing, May/Jun 2001, Vol. 5 (3), pp. 88-95.

Gramm, M., Ritter, A., Schiller, J. H., (2004). Efficient selection and monitoring of QoS-aware web services with the WS-QoS framework. In Proceedings of 2004 IEEE/WIC/ACM International Conference on Web Intelligence, Beijing, China, September 2004, 152-158.

Hoff, H., Gronmo, R., Skogan, D., Strand, A., (2005), D7 Specification of the Visual Composition Language (VSCL), SODIUM (IST-FP6-004559) Project's Deliverable, June 2005

JXTA Org, (2006) Project JXTA, available at http://www.jxta.org/, accessed 21 December 2006

Kavantzas, N., Burdett, D., Ritzinger, G., Fletcher, T., Lafon, Y.,Barreto, C., (2005), Web Service Choreography Description Language (WS-CDL) ver 1.0, Nov 2005, http://www.w3.org/TR/ws-cdl-10/

Martin, D., Burstein, M., Hobbs, J., Lassila, O., McDermott, D., McIlraith, S., Narayanan, S., Paolucci, M., Parsia, B., Payne, T., Sirin, E., Srinivasan, N., Sycara, K., (2004) OWL-S: Semantic Markup for Web Services, W3C submission, Nov. 2004 http://www.w3.org/Submission/OWL-S/

McGuinness, D., Harmelen, F.,(2004), OWL Web Ontology Language Overview, W3C Recommendation, February 2004, available at http://www.w3.org/TR/owl-features/

Medvidovic, N., Rosenblum, D., Gamble, R., (1999), Bridging Heterogeneous Software Interoperability Platforms, Technical Report, USC-CSE-99-529, Center for Software Engineering, USC, November 1999

Microsoft Corporation (1996), Distributed Component Object Model Protocol-DCOM/1.0, draft, November 1996, available at http://www.microsoft.com/Com/resources/comdocs.asp

Murer, T., Scherer, D., Wuertz, A., (1996), Improving component interoperability information, Proceedings of Workshop on Component-Oriented Programming (WCOP'96) at 10th European Conference on Object-Oriented Programming (ECOOP'96), pp. 150–158, dpunkt, July 1996

Nejdl, W., Wolf, B., Qu, C., Decker, S., Sintek, M., Naeve, A., Nilsson, M., Palmer, M., Risch, T., (2001), EDUTELLA: A P2P Networking Infrastructure Based on RDF, Edutella White Paper, November 2001, available at http://edutella.jxta.org/reports/edutella-whitepaper.pdf

Nezhad, H.R. M., Benatallah, B., Casati, F., Toumani, F., (2006), Web service interoperability specifications, IEEE Computer, vol. 39 no. 5, May 2006, pp 24-32

Newmarch, J. (2005) UPnP services and Jini clients. In Proceedings of the 2005 Conference on Information Systems: Next Generations, ISNG 2005, Las Vegas, Nevada, USA.

Oriol, M. (2002) Peer Services: From Description to Invocation. In Proceedings of the 2002 International Workshop on Agents and Peer-to-Peer Computing, July 2002, Bologna, Italy, Springer Berlin / Heidelberg, LNCS 2530/2003, 21-32

Pantazoglou, M., Tsalgatidou, A., and Athanasopoulos, G. (2006), Discovering Web Services and JXTA Peer-to-Peer Services in a Unified Manner, In Proceedings of the 4th International Conference on Service Oriented Computing, December 2006, Chicago, USA, Eds. A. Dan and W. Lamersdorf, 104-115

Papazoglou, M., Krämer, B., Yang, J., (2004), Leveraging Web Services and Peer-to-Peer Networks, Book Chapter in Advanced Information Systems, Feb 2004, Springer Berlin / Heidelberg 2681/2003, 485-501

Pautasso, C., Alonso, G., (2004) "From Web Service Composition to Megaprogramming" In Proceedings of the 5th VLDB Workshop on Technologies for E-Services (TES-04), Toronto, Canada, August 29-30, 2004

Qu, C., and Nejdl, W. (2004) Interacting the Edutella/JXTA Peer-to-Peer Network with Web Services. In Proceedings of the 2004 Symposium on Applications and the Internet, IEEE Computer Society.

Ryan, N., (2005), Smart Environments for Cultural Heritage, In Proceedings of 24th International Symposium on Reading the Historical Spatial Information in the World, pp 17-33, Kyoto, Japan, February 2005

Ruiz, A., Corchuelo, R., Martín,O., Durán, A., Toro, M., (2000), Addressing Interoperability in Multi-Organisational Web-Based Systems, Proceedings of the 2nd ECOOP Workshop on Object Interoperability (WOI'2000), Sophia Antipolis, France, June 12, 2000

Siegel, J., (1996), CORBA Fundamentals and Programming, Wiley, 1996

Strang, T., Linnhoff-Popien, C. (2003), Service Interoperability in Ubiquitous Computing Environments, Proceedings of International Conference on Advances in Infrastructure for Electronic Business, Education, Science, Medicine, and Mobile Technologies on the Internet (SSGRR2003w), L'Aquila, Italy, January,2003

Sun Microsystems, (2005), "JXTA v2.3.x: Java Programmers Guide", available at: http://www.jxta.org, April 2005

Tanenbaum, A. S., (2003), Computer Networks, Prentice Hall, fourth edition, 2003, ISBN: 0-13-066102-3

Tsalgatidou, A. Athanasopoulos, G., Pantazoglou, M., Pautasso, C., Heinis, T., Gronmo, R., Hoff, H., Berre, A-J., Glittum, M., Topouzidou, S. (2006) Developing Scientific Workflows from Heterogeneous Services, ACM SIGMOD-RECORD v(35) n(2) 22-28, June 2006

Tsalgatidou, A., Athanasopoulos, G., Pantazoglou, M., (2005), Generic Service Model Specification, Technical Report, available at: http://www.di.uoa.gr/~gathanas/TR/gesmo-1.0-report.pdf

Vallecillo, A., Hernandez, J., Troya J., (2000), Woi'00: New issues in object interoperability, LNCS (1964): ECOOP'2000 Workshop Reader, pp. 256–269, Springer

Vogels, W., (2003), Web Services Are Not Distributed Objects, IEEE Internet Computing, Nov.-Dec. 2003

WSIF Org, (2006), Web Service Invocation Framework, accessed at 21 December 2006, available at http://ws.apache.org/wsif/

ENDNOTES

1. Sodium project http://www.atc.gr/sodium/
2. SeCSE project http://secse.eng.it/
3. The visual language used in this example is the Visual Service Composition Language developed in the SODIUM project (Hoff, 2005).
4. More details on the abstract XML elements and attributes can be found at (Fallside, 2004)
5. WSIF leverages WSDL4J to support the parsing and the in-memory representation of WSDL information elements. However, WSDL4J supports only WSDL 1.1 descriptions. Furthermore according to WSDL 1.1 extensions may be provided only to the Service, Port and Binding elements.
6. The OMG UML Profile and Metamodel for Services (UPMS) RFP document can be retrieved from the following link: http://www.omg.org/cgi-bin/doc?soa/06-09-09.pdf

This work was previously published in the International Journal of Web Services Research, Vol. 5, Issue 4, edited by L. J. Zhang, pp. 79-110, copyright 2008 by IGI Publishing (an imprint of IGI Global).

Chapter 18

Service-Oriented Architecture for Migrating Legacy Home Appliances to Home Network System:

Principle and Applications

Masahide Nakamura
Graduate School of Engineering, Kobe University, Japan

Hiroshi Igaki
Graduate School of Engineering, Kobe University, Japan

Akihiro Tanaka
Graduate School of Information Science, Nara Institute of Science and Technology, Japan

Haruaki Tamada
Graduate School of Information Science, Nara Institute of Science and Technology, Japan

Ken-ichi Matsumoto
Graduate School of Information Science, Nara Institute of Science and Technology, Japan

ABSTRACT

This chapter presents a practical framework that adapts the conventional home electric appliances with the infrared remote controls (legacy appliances) to the emerging home network system (HNS). The proposed method extensively uses the concept of service-oriented architecture to improve programmatic interoperability among multi-vendor appliances. The authors first prepare APIs that assist a PC to send infrared signals to the appliances. Then the APIs are aggregated within self-contained service components, so that each of the components achieves a logical feature independent of device/vendor-specific operations. The service components are finally exhibited to the HNS as Web services. As a result, the legacy appliances can be used as distributed components with open interfaces. To demonstrate the effectiveness, the authors implement an actual HNS and integrated services with multi-vendor legacy appliances. The authors also show practical applications implemented on the developed HNS.

DOI: 10.4018/978-1-61520-684-1.ch018

INTRODUCTION

Research and development of **home network systems** (HNS, for short) are recently a hot topic in the area of ubiquitous/pervasive computing. In the HNS, general household appliances such as TVs, DVD players, lights, air-conditioners, refrigerators, ventilators, curtains and sensors, are connected to a network at home. These **networked appliances** are controlled, monitored, and even orchestrated via the network, to provide sophisticated applications and value-added services for home users (Kolberg, 2003). Several HNS products are already on the market (e.g., LG, 2008; Panasonic, 2008; Toshiba 2008).

The HNS provides many applications and services. The applications typically take advantage of wide-range control and monitoring of appliances inside and outside the home. Moreover, integrating different appliances via network yields more value-added and powerful services (Kolberg, 2003), which we call **HNS integrated services**. For instance, integrating a TV, a DVD player, speakers, lights and a curtain would implement a HNS integrated service, say, DVD theater service. When a user requests the service, the lights become dark, the curtain is closed, the 5.1ch speakers are selected, the sound volume is adjusted, and the contents are played with the DVD player. Thus, the user can watch movies in a theater-like atmosphere within just a single operation.

In general, each networked appliance is equipped with smart embedded devices, including a network interface, a processor and storage, in order to provide and execute the appliance features required for various HNS applications and services. As the embedded devices become more down-sized, cheaper, and more energy-saving, it is expected in the near future that every object will be networked (Geer, 2006).

However, transition to the networked appliances is gradual. Most people are still using **legacy appliances**, which are the conventional non-networked home appliances. Although it is usual to see a network and PCs at home, the networked appliances are not widely spread yet.

There are several reasons why the networked appliances are not spread yet. Firstly, the networked appliances are yet quite expensive. Secondly, types of available appliances are limited (audio/visual appliances have been being networked recently, but many others are not yet). Also, due to the lack of programmatic interoperability (Smith, 2005), the integration of appliances is strictly limited; especially in the **multi-vendor environment** the integration is quite a challenging problem. Finally, there is a major requirement that the users want to keep using the legacy appliances that they are accustomed to use. Considering the above reasons, it is not easy for the general home users to renew immediately all the existing legacy appliances with the networked ones.

To cope with both the emerging HNS and the legacy appliances, this paper presents a new framework that adapts the legacy appliances to the HNS. Specifically, for the legacy appliances with the conventional infrared remote controllers (denoted by IrRC), we propose a way to implement a smart adapter on a PC that connects the legacy appliances to the HNS. For this, we exploit the concept of the **service-oriented architecture** (SOA) (Loke, 2003; Papazoglou, 2003), extensively.

The adaptor is based on a three-layered architecture: **IR device layer**, **service layer** and **Web service layer**. In the IR device layer, we develop a set of APIs, called Ir-APIs, by which the PC can send any infrared signals to appliances. Note that the infrared signals are specific to devices and vendors. Also, executing a feature of an appliance requires the user **vendor-specific** operations of the IrRC. Thus, it is inconvenient for external HNS applications to use the Ir-APIs directly. Therefore, the service layer then aggregates multiple Ir-API calls within self-contained services, so that each of the service achieves a logical feature independent of the vendor (or device)-specific issues. Finally, the services are deployed in the HNS as Web services (W3C, 2002) in the Web service layer. Thus,

Figure 1. An Example of Home Network System

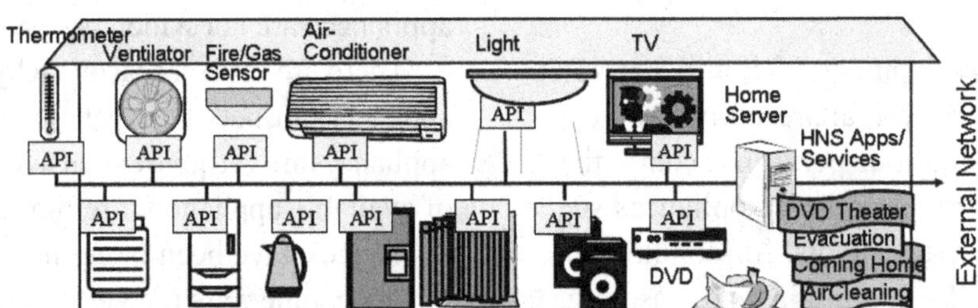

every legacy appliance becomes a distributed component with an open interface, which can be used by various kinds of HNS applications. The users can build their own integrated services and HNS applications with the legacy appliances.

To demonstrate the effectiveness, we have implemented an actual HNS and several integrated services. As a result, it was shown that the proposed framework is well applicable to multi-vendor legacy appliances, and that practical integrated services can be created as relatively small client applications.

The original version of this article was published as a journal paper in JWSR (Nakamura, 2008). To reflect the latest findings we have found since 2008, we added a new section of "Latest Application Development". There we discuss various user interfaces, a service creation environment for end-users, a mechanism of dynamic service binding, and an integration of appliances and information resources. We believe that these new findings make the proposed service-oriented framework more complete and reliable, and show the future perspective of the HNS.

PRELIMINARIES

Home Network System (HNS)

A HNS consists of one or more networked appliances connected to LAN at home. Each networked appliance has a set of control APIs, so that the user or software agents can control the appliance via the network. To process the API calls, each appliance generally has embedded devices including a processor and storage.

Figure 1 shows an example of HNS, which consists of various networked appliances and a home server. The home server typically plays a role of gateway to the external network. It also works as an application server, where the HNS applications are installed. As seen in Figure 1, every HNS integrated service is implemented as a software application that invokes the APIs according to a certain control flow. The services are supposed to be installed in the home server.

Communications among the appliances are performed based on the underlying network protocol. Currently, many standard protocols are being standardized for the networked appliances. Major protocols include DLNA (DLNA, 2006) for digital audio/video appliances and ECHONET (ECHONET, 2006) for white goods (e.g., refrigerator, air-conditioners and laundry machines). However, these standard protocols mainly prescribe a set of network-layer agreements of the appliance, such as address setup and message formats. The programmatic interoperability (Smith, 2005) at the application layer or higher is beyond the scope of the protocols.

To minimize the interoperability issue, most of the current HNS (e.g., LG, 2008; Panasonic 2008; Toshiba 2008) are comprised of the single-vendor appliances. Applications on the HNS are limited to the proprietary ones provided by the same vendor.

Figure 2. Architecture of Networked Appliance Based on SOA

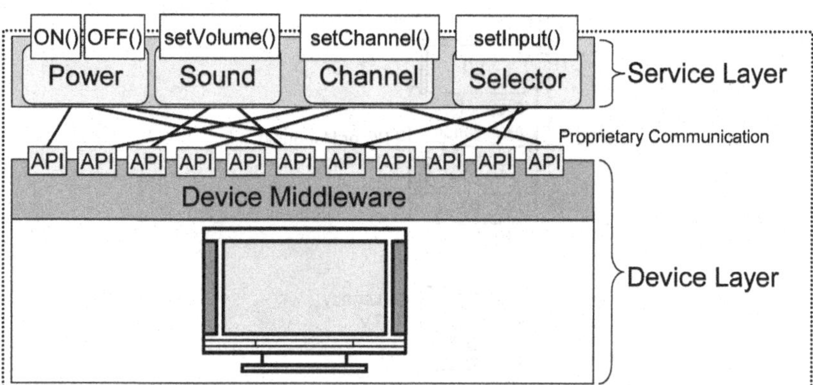

Types of appliances that can be integrated are limited, too. The next challenge for the industries is to establish standards at the application layer, which allows any combination of multi-vendor appliances over different protocols.

Service-Oriented Framework for HNS (Igaki, 2005)

Service-oriented architecture (SOA) is a system architecture that facilitates integration of distributed heterogeneous systems (Loke, 2003; Papazoglou, 2003). In SOA, primary features of each system are aggregated as a set of services. More sophisticated systems are basically constructed by integrating the existing services. SOA has been extensively studied and adopted in the domain of enterprise systems, since SOA-based systems are quite resilient for changes and integration of business processes. Web services (W3C, 2002) are known as a primary means to implement SOA-based systems.

To improve the programmatic interoperability discussed above, we have presented a service-oriented framework for HNS in our previous work (Igaki, 2005), which applies the concept of SOA to the networked appliances. Figure 2 depicts an example of a networked TV, illustrating the key idea of the framework. In this framework, each networked appliance is designed based on a two-layered architecture: a device layer and a service layer. The device layer represents the hardware and the control APIs (including the middle-ware) of the networked appliance. In the figure, the APIs denote the control APIs of the networked TV. They can be invoked by external entities in accordance with the HNS protocol conformed by the TV.

On the other hand, the service layer aggregates the control APIs according to the logical features of the TV. Then, the layer exports the features to the network as the self-contained services with open interface (i.e., methods). The communication among the device and service layer is supposed to be based on the device-proprietary procedure. Thus, the proprietary API calls at the device layer are hidden from the service user. The service layer is implemented as an application, and is supposed to be installed in the storage of the networked appliance.

As seen in Figure 2, features like power, sound and channel are quite generic features that every vendor's TV is supposed to have. Thus, in this example these features are considered to be TV services. The methods like ON(),OFF(), setVolume(), setChannel() are open and **vendor-neutral** interfaces for the TV service. Invocation of these methods does not require any knowledge specific to the underlying implementation or protocol of the device layer. Unless the interface definition is changed, any modification in the service and

Figure 3. Soft-Controller for a Legacy TV

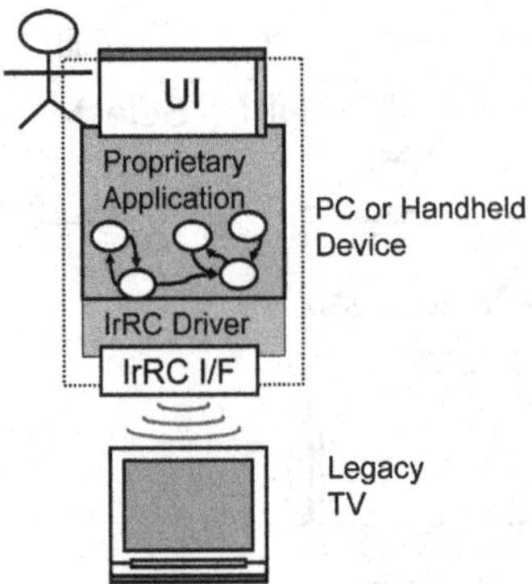

device layers does not give impact to the service users. Also, the service users can easily develop their own integrated services, by combining the method invocations of different appliances. As a result, we are able to achieve a HNS that copes with both system evolution and appliance interoperability.

Note however that this framework presented in (Igaki, 2005) assumes the networked appliances only. The legacy appliances without the processor or the storage are beyond the scope. Also, the framework is not yet fully evaluated or implemented with the actual networked appliances.

Software Controller for Legacy Appliances

There have been several software applications with which the user can control **legacy appliances** from a PC or a handheld device such as handy phones (Kaden 2006; NANO 2005). We here call such applications soft-controllers.

Figure 3 shows a typical example of the soft-controllers, which is for a legacy TV with the conventional **infrared remote controller for home appliances** (denoted by *IrRC*). The user first selects and executes a control command through the user interface (UI). Then, the application sends the corresponding infrared signals to the appliance through the driver (IrRC driver) and the interface (IrRC I/F)[1].

The soft-controllers basically assume a use case that a human user controls a single appliance at a time. They are not supposed to be invoked by other applications, or to be orchestrated by other appliances via the network. Also, since the appliance and the application are tightly coupled, the same controller cannot be used directly for other appliances. Therefore, it is difficult to apply the soft-controllers directly for the purpose of adaptation of legacy appliances to the HNS.

ADAPTING LEGACY HOME APPLIANCES TO HNS

Requirements

Our goal is to adapt the **legacy appliances** with the IrRC to the HNS. More specifically, we try to propose a framework to implement an adapter for the legacy appliances, satisfying the following requirements.

Requirement R1: The framework must achieve easy creation of HNS integrated services with arbitrary combinations of the legacy appliances.

Requirement R2: The framework must be implemented using generic PCs and IrRC devices without special hardware.

Requirement R3: The framework must be applicable to a wide range of types and vendors of the appliances.

Figure 4. Proposed Architecture for Adapting Legacy Appliances

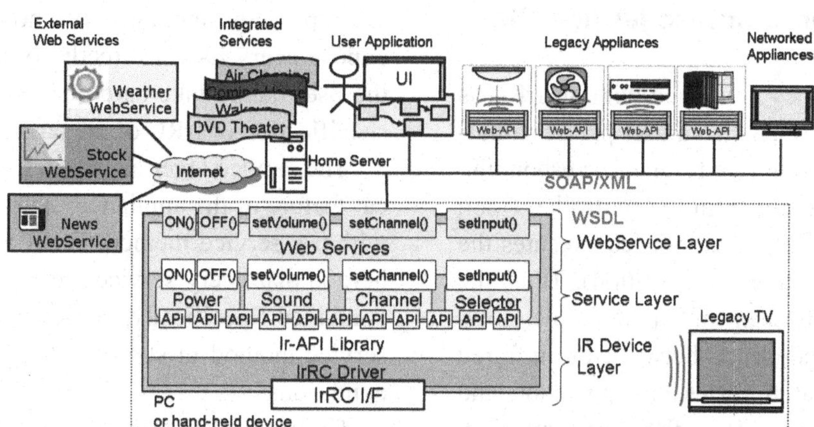

The current HNS products do not assume integration of the legacy appliances with the HNS. Also, they have yet problems in Requirements R1 and R3. Our previous framework in (Igaki, 2005) takes Requirements R1 and R3 into account, but it cannot satisfy Requirement R2. The soft-controllers are for legacy appliances, but cannot satisfy Requirement R1. Thus, the existing methods cannot be used directly to achieve our goal.

Proposed Architecture

To satisfy Requirements R1 through R3, we here propose a new architecture depicted in Figure 4. As an example, we explain the architecture of an adapter for a legacy TV in the figure. The proposed architecture replaces the device layer of our former architecture (see Figure 2) with the **IR device layer** consisting of IrRC devices and the legacy appliance. Also, it puts a Web service layer on top of the service layer.

To implement the adapter, we first prepare a PC (or handheld device) and an IrRC device that can be connected to the PC. On the PC, we implement a set of APIs called Ir-APIs with which applications can send any infrared signals to the appliance. Next, for a given legacy appliance, we develop a set of services of the appliance, each of which encapsulates several Ir-API calls to achieve a self-contained and **vendor-neutral** feature. Finally, we export these services as Web services and deploy them in the HNS. We call the methods of the Web services Web-APIs.

The integrated services and any user applications are implemented as client applications that invoke the Web-APIs. For this, the implementation of IrRC, which often varies among appliance types and/or vendors, is hidden within the **service layer**. The service users can execute various features of the appliance without device-specific knowledge. The same framework is applied to other legacy appliances. Then, the integrated service can be created by assembling Web-APIs provided multiple appliances, according to a desired control flow (i.e., workflow).

Taking full advantage of Web services, the proposed architecture also aims the integration of the legacy home appliances with the external Web services for the future extension (see left-side of Figure 4). Once every legacy appliance is adapted as a Web service, it is quite easy to implement services that mash up the appliances and various existing services available in the Internet. This fact implies that the proposed architecture has the great extendibility of HNS services.

IR Device Layer: Providing APIs for Infrared Remote Controller (Ir-APIs)

In general, a legacy appliance with an IrRC is operated as follows. When a user presses a button of the IrRC, an infrared signal corresponding to the button is issued from the controller. Upon receiving the signal, the appliance executes the corresponding feature (or operation). Thus, the communication mechanism is quite simple. However, the correspondence between the infrared signal and the feature varies among vendors and types of the appliance. Therefore, it is convenient to have all-purpose wrappers for the IrRC, with which the applications in the upper layer can flexibly switch and manage such vendor (and device)-specific signals.

For this purpose, we implement Ir-APIs on the top of the Ir-RC driver. The Ir-APIs provide a set of generic interfaces with which the applications can send any infrared signals to arbitrary types of legacy appliances. The Ir-APIs are relatively low-level but generic APIs, which should be commonly used by all types of appliances. Therefore, typical Ir-APIs must include; initialize IrRC, set signal type, send signal, start sending burst signal, stop sending burst signal, sleep.

Service Layer: Aggregating Features as Vendor-Neutral Services

The granularity of Ir-APIs is so fine that one Ir-API does not necessarily correspond to a single logical feature of the target appliance. Also, each IrRC operation heavily depends on the vendor and type of the appliance. It is not a good idea to expose every Ir-API directly to the HNS, since the user has to take care of the device-specific specification of IrRC of the target appliance.

The service layer aggregates, for every logical feature of the appliance, several Ir-API calls within a service method. What most important here is that every service method must be self-contained. Specifically, we recommend that every service method m should satisfy the following conditions:

Condition S1: m is always executable by itself, independent of the context of other services or appliances.

Condition S2: m achieves by itself a consistent logical feature of the appliance.

For instance, let us consider a TV manufactured by a vendor A, denoted by TV_A. Suppose that TV_A has the following restriction on its implementation: "Once turned on, it does not accept any infrared signals during 2 seconds until the hardware becomes fully operational". Then, the service method ON() for TV_A should be implemented as in the Java-like pseudo code in Figure 5. The first four statements are for achieving a logical feature "turn on TV_A", satisfying Condition S2. The last statement sleep(2) is for the subsequent method invocations to achieve the above Condition S1. The sleep statement consumes the 2-seconds wait, so that any methods executed after ON()should not be influenced by the device-specific restriction of TV_A.

Figure 5. Service Method ON() for TV_A

```
public void ON(void) {
 IrControler con = new IrController();  /*Controller and */
 IrSignal sig = new IrSignal();      /*signal objects of Ir-API*/
 sig.setSignalType(ON, TV_A);        /*set signal ON for TV_A*/
 con.sendSignal(sig);                /*send the signal*/

 sleep(2);                           /*Sleep during 2 seconds*/
}
```

Figure 6. Service Method setVolume() for TV_A

```
public void setVolume(unsigned int x) {
  IrControler con = new IrController();  /*Controller and */
  IrSignal sig = new IrSignal();         /*signal objects of Ir-API*/

  if (Power==OFF) ON(); /*Turn on when TV_A is off*/

  sig.setSignalType(VOLDOWN, TV_A); /*Volume down signal*/
  for (repeat_enough_times) {        /*Minimize the sound level*/
    con.sendSignal(sig);
  }

  sig.setSignalType(VOLUP, TV_A);    /*Volume up signal*/
  for (;x>0;x--) {                   /*Issue volume up x times*/
    con.sendSignal(sig);
  }
}
```

When a feature requires a sequence of multiple Ir-APIs, these APIs should be encapsulated within a service method. The pseudo code in Figure 6 is to set the sound volume of TV_A to a given level x. In general, the volume level is adjusted by a human user with a relative scale considering the current volume level. However, here the application needs to do the task. Hence, the method setVolume() first minimizes the sound volume by repeatedly sending the signal of volume-down, and then sends the signal of volume-up for x times. Moreover, the sound adjustment feature depends on the power feature, since it works only when TV_A is ON. Therefore, setVolume() contains an invocation of ON() in case the power is off. Thus, the service method becomes self-contained.

Supplementary Service: Getting Status

Some HNS applications may get the current status of an appliance, and then perform an appropriate action based on the status. A typical example is an energy-saving service, which stops a DVD player when a TV is turned off.

However, the communication among a user and a legacy appliance is basically one-way from the IrRC to the appliance. Hence, it is impossible for the external application to obtain the current status directly from the legacy appliance.

To cope with the problem, we implement, in the service layer, a supplementary feature that stores the current state of the appliance according to the history of service execution. Specifically, for every appliance, we prepare a database, called state DB, for storing the current values of primary properties the appliance. When a service method is executed, the values of the corresponding properties are updated in the state DB. We then deploy a service method getStatus()which returns the current state (i.e., the tuple of the property values) upon the request from the external applications.

Web Service Layer: Exporting Service Methods as Web-APIs

For every service method implemented in the service layer, we export the method to the HNS as a Web-API. In this paper, we adopt the Web services (W3C, 2002), which is a standard SOA framework, for the service exportation. The interface definition of each service method is strictly typed by an XML-based language, called WSDL. An external application first interprets the interface definition, and then invokes a Web-API via network with appropriate parameters.

HNS Integrated Services

Once features of every legacy appliance are exported as Web-APIs, the legacy appliances can be used as distributed components. By combining these components, the user can assemble various **integrated services**. Specifically, an integrated service can be implemented as a client application consisting of invocations of the Web-APIs and a control flow among the APIs. Note that the user can invoke Web-APIs with an arbitrary control flow, since every Web-API should be self-contained. For instance, let us consider the DVD theater service mentioned in Section INTRODUCTION. Figure 7 represents a sequence of Web-API invocations that can implement of the service.

The client application is installed on a remote PC or a handheld device owned by the user. It is also possible to install the integrated service on the home server. Then, the integrated service can be executed even from outside home. Also, the integrated service can be deployed as a new Web service to be reused for more sophisticated services.

IMPLEMENTATION: NAIST-HNS

Based on the proposed framework, we have implemented an actual HNS with the legacy appliances. The developed HNS is called NAIST-HNS.

Legacy Appliances Used

The following legacy appliances have been used in NAIST-HNS. Note that our system is composed of multi-vendor appliances.

Plasma display: NEC PX-50XM2

DVD/HDD recorder: Toshiba RF-XS46

Wireless LCD TV: Sony KLV-17WS1

Ceiling light: Panasonic HHFZ5310

Curtains with actuator: NAVIO Power-track

Air cleaner: Hitachi EP-V12

Air circulator: MORITA MCF-257NR

Power plug with IrRC: HORIBA IS-100

Climate monitor (sensor): IT Watchdogs WxGoos-1

Implementation of Legacy Adapter

Figure 8 depicts the overview of the developed legacy adapter for NAIST-HNS. In this implementation, we installed services for all appliances within a single PC. Note that this is just for convenience of the experiment. The services can be distributed among multiple PCs if necessary (see Section EVALUATION for more details).

Technologies used for the system components are summarized as follows.

PC: Celeron M360J, 512MB, 80GB, WinXP Pro

IrRC I/F: Sugiyama Electron -- Crossam2+USB

Figure 7. Integrated Service (DVD Theater)

```
TV.setInput(DVD);              /*Set input mode for DVD*/
Light.setBrightness(1);        /*Minimize brightness*/
Curtain.Close();               /*Close curtain*/
Speaker.setInput(DVD);         /*Set input mode for DVD*/
Speaker.setChannel(5.1);       /*Set channel to 5.1ch*/
Speaker.setVolume(25);         /*Set volume level to 25*/
DVD.play();                    /*Play DVD*/
```

Figure 8. Overview of the HNS Implementation

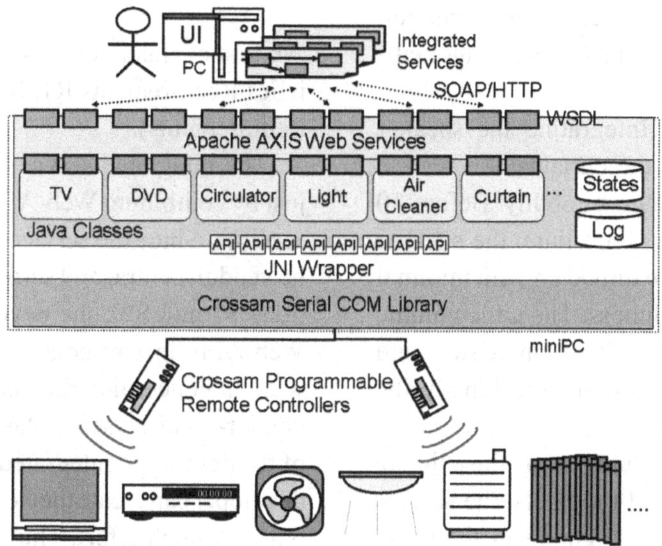

IrRC Driver: Serial COM library for Crossam2+USB

Ir-API: Java Native Interface (JNI) Wrapper

Service Layer: J2SE 5.0

Web Service Layer: Apache AXIS 1.3

The Crossam2+USB (Crossam, for short) adopted for IrRC I/F is a programmable infrared remote controller, which can be connected to a PC. Crossam can memory infrared signals of various legacy appliances, and can dispatch a signal in each button. The customization of Crossam is quite simple, and thus we can easily correspond to addition or replacement of legacy appliances.

Also, Crossam has a bundled serial port library written in C++. Using the library, the external program can send low-level commands, such as press a button, start and stop signal, to Crossam. Hence, we have used the bundle for IrRC Driver.

Next, we implemented Ir-APIs that can be invoked from Java programs by wrapping the Crossam library with Java Native Interface (JNI). The usage of JNI is due to consideration of the portability of Web services. The JNI wrapper comprised 130 lines of Java code.

The service layer was implemented in Java. For each appliance we constructed a Java class, where features of the appliance correspond to service methods. We constructed total 12 classes (4 for the climate monitor and 8 for other appliances) with 132 methods, comprising 1196 lines of code. Finally, the Java classes were deployed as Web services using Apache AXIS.

NAIST-HNS Integrated Services

We have implemented the following integrated services as client programs using Perl's SOAP::Lite module (Kulchenko, 2004).[2] Although the service scenarios seem to be sophisticated, they could be implemented in quite small programs, each of which comprises about 20-30 lines of code.

DVD Theater: Integrating the TV, the DVD player, the speaker, the lights and the curtains, the service automatically sets up the living room in a theater configuration. Upon a user's request, the TV is turned on with the DVD input, the curtains are closed, brightness of the lights are minimized, the speakers are configured for 5.1ch mode, and finally the DVD player plays the contents.

Air Cleaning: Integrating the smoke sensor of the climate monitor, the air cleaner, the circulator, the service cleans dirty air in the room, automatically and efficiently.

Wakeup Support: Integrating the speaker system, the lights, and the curtains, the service assists the user to wake up smoothly. Before 10 minutes of the given wakeup time, the speaker system and the lights are turned on with minimal sound volume and brightness. Then, the volume and the brightness are gradually increased, and set to the optimal at the wakeup time. Finally, the curtains are opened.

Auto illumination: Integrating the climate monitor, the curtains, and the lights, the service always keeps the optimal lighting in the room regardless of time and weather.

Figure 9 shows a picture of our experimental room, where a user is trying to activate the DVD theater service using a user interface (discussed in the following section).

EVALUATION

In this section, we evaluate the proposed framework from several viewpoints.

Achievements of Requirements

We first evaluate if the proposed framework satisfies Requirements R1, R2 and R3 (see Section Requirements).

The integrated services can be implemented just by combining Web-APIs deployed with Web services. Since the service layer was designed to be vendor-neutral and self-contained (see Conditions S1 and S2), the developer can invoke the Web-APIs in any combinations and any order, without concerning the underlying IR signals or vendor-specific issues. Also, as the lines of code of the developed integrated services indicate, the developer can create their own integrated services without much effort. Thus, R1 is achieved.

Requirement R2 is surely satisfied as we demonstrated it with NAIST-HNS. We have built up the whole NAIST-HNS by generic PCs and commercial universal remote controllers.

The proposed framework applies to a variety of legacy appliances, as long as the appliance has an infrared remote controller (IrRC), and its signals are compatible to the proposed legacy adapter. Thus, Requirement R3 is satisfied. As for appliances that do not have the IrRC, we can use a power relay device with IrRC (HORIBA,

Figure 9. HNS Experimental Room

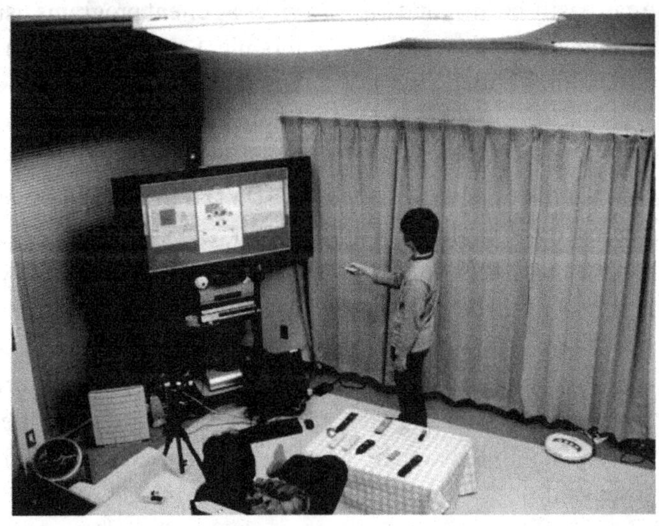

Table 1. Response Time of Integrated Services

	DVD Theater	Air Cleaning	Wakeup	Illumination
SRT (msec)	3,563	2,613	4,905	676
DRT (msec)	39,350	3,000	19,600	1,250
Total (msec)	42,913	5,613	24,505	1,926
# of Web-APIs executed	6	4	16	3

2000) for providing simple services like power on/off.

Performance

One of major concerns in any SOA-based system is performance. We have measured response time of each integrated service developed in Section IMPLEMENTATION, in order to clarify the overhead posed by the proposed framework. There are two kinds of response time: device response time (DRT) and service response time (SRT). The DRT is the time physically taken for the legacy appliances to execute features required in the service. For instance, turning on our DVD/HDD recorder required DRT about 30 seconds for initializing the system. On the other hand, the SRT is the time purely devoted for processing the service layer with Web services, which is interesting for us here.

Table 1 shows the result. Each row represents the corresponding response time in milliseconds. [3] The last row represents the number of Web-APIs executed in each integrated service.

It can be seen in the table that the total response time varies from service to service. This is because the different services use different sets of legacy appliances. However, SRT has a strong correlation with the number of Web-APIs executed, regardless of the features executed by the Web-APIs. This is because the time taken for the middleware to process Web service messages became a dominant factor for SRT. SRT for each Web-API invocation varied from 0.22 seconds to 0.65 seconds. Hence, it can be said that the proposed framework suffers from quite a little overhead. Hence, we should count the overhead carefully when developing services that require time-sensitive or real-time transactions.

However, we are optimistic for the overhead in the service layer. The overhead is basically due to performance of the current WSDL implementations in marshalling XML data to and from messages. This problem will likely be alleviated by future WSDL implementations as the technology matures.

Productivity

In the proposed architecture, vendor (or device)-specific operations of legacy appliances are completely encapsulated within the service layer, whereas vendor-neutral features can be accessed as Web services. Currently, many programming languages support SOAP and WSDL libraries invoking Web services. Therefore, what required for the application/service developer is just to know the location of the Web service definition (i.e., WSDL), and the names and parameters of desired Web-APIs.

After that, for each invocation of an appliance feature, the developer writes code just for two operations: (1) instantiate Web service, and (2) invoke the service object. In case of Perl, these operations can be written just within two lines. As for Java, the IDE (Integrated Development Environment), such as Eclipse or NetBeans, typically has a feature that automatically generates related skeleton code for Web service invocations. The developer just adds a few lines to the skeleton code. Thus, our idea of exploiting Web services significantly contributes to the high productivity of new services and applications using the legacy appliances.

Using the Web service integration framework such as BPEL4WS (Weerawarana, 2002) may enable more efficient service creation. The further discussion of the applicability of BPEL4WS to HNS applications/services is left to our future work.

Extendibility

The proposed architecture is not strictly bound with the legacy appliances only. The same architecture can also be applied to the emerging networked appliances. This is done by replacing the IR device layer in Figure 4 with a certain HNS protocol stack and control APIs of the networked appliances. The point is to deploy the service and Web service layers on top of the proprietary device implementation. Since different appliances can be uniformly managed as Web services, it is easy to add new appliances and new services.

Another merit in extendibility is that one can integrate legacy appliances with the external Web services in the Internet. That is, it is no more necessary to distinguish the home appliances from the conventional information services and resources in the Internet. This is a great benefit in creating more intelligent and sophisticated HNS services. The followings are interesting examples which integrate legacy appliances using news and stock Web services in the Internet:

News flash: As soon as important news arrives, turn on the TV with the selected channel.

Stock alarm: When a stock price rises, notify it of users by ringing chimes in the house.

Development of more sophisticated services is left to future work.

Portability

Since all features of legacy appliances are wrapped within Web services, applications using the legacy appliances can be ported to various platforms and languages. As seen in the previous section, the service layer of all appliances in NAIST-HNS was implemented in Java on the Windows platform. However, this fact does not require client applications or integrated services to use specific language and platform (e.g., Java and Windows). Indeed, we have implemented client applications and integrated services in Windows, Linux, and Sun Solaris platforms. They worked as expected. We have also tested various languages for implementing the integrated services. The languages tested include Perl, PHP, Java, C# .Net, VB, Delphi (Pascal). Thus, we were able to achieve the programmatic interoperability taking the full advantage of Web services. This characteristic is quite unique compared with other standards for home network systems and networked appliances.

Maintainability

The service layer of the proposed framework plays an important role, which achieves a loose-coupling between the HNS applications (as service consumers) and the appliances (as service providers). As long as the interface definition of the service is not changed, one can change, replace or update the appliances without influencing the service consumers. Therefore, the HNS based on the proposed framework is quite resilient for the system modification and evolution.

Limitations

A technical limitation of the proposed framework is in the reliability of the physical channel between

IrRC/IF and the appliance. As discussed in Section Supplementary Service, the communication from the PC to a legacy appliance is basically one-way. Hence, it is not easy to confirm whether or not an infrared signal is successfully received by the appliance. If the signal is lost, inconsistency between the state DB and the actual status of the appliance occurs, which may lead the integrated service to malfunction. Therefore, we need to guarantee the reliability of the physical channel at all cost.

Fortunately in our framework, the service layer can be distributed within multiple PCs. Hence, in an extreme case, we can assign a PC for every appliance so that the IrRC is close enough to the appliance. A smarter approach is to assign a PC for each group of neighbor appliances. The user has to choose a reasonable layout considering reliability requirement, cost for PCs, a floor plan and objects in the room.

User authentication and security management are beyond the scope of this paper, but are important issues in practical usage of the HNS. We conduct these problems in our future work.

LATEST APPLICATION DEVELOPMENT

In this section, we introduce the latest applications developed on the NAIST-HNS by our research team. Some of these applications have been published in conference paper or technical reports. Therefore, we here briefly review each application.

User Interfaces

Developing intuitive and user-friendly interface is an important issue to make full use of the HNS. We have implemented various graphical user interfaces (GUIs) for human users to operate NAIST-HNS. Figure 10 shows four kinds of the developed interfaces.

Figure 10 (a) shows a fancy interface written in Flash. This user interface displays a service menu on a TV in the room. Using a small remote controller, the user can choose an integrated service from the menu. Then, the user can activate and deactivate the service. By using this interface, it is no more necessary for the user to handle too

Figure 10. User Interfaces for NAIST HNS

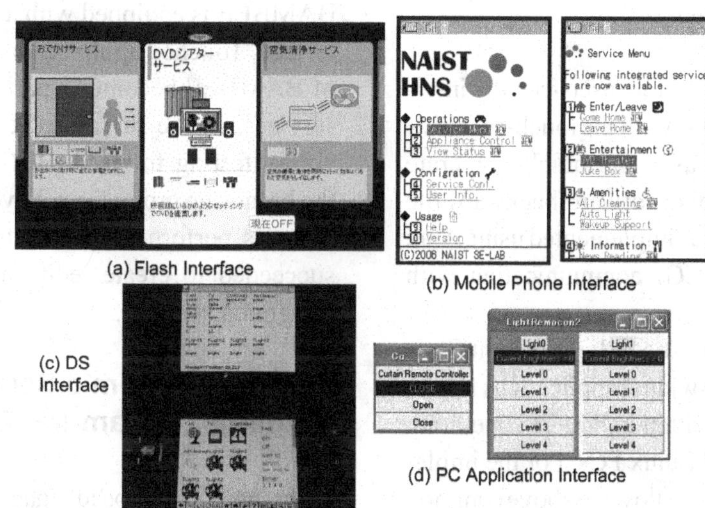

(a) Flash Interface

(b) Mobile Phone Interface

(c) DS Interface

(d) PC Application Interface

many remote controllers for multiple appliances (see controllers on the table in Figure 9).

Figure 10(b) shows a GUI designated for mobile phones. The interface has been implemented as a Perl-CGI Web application. Using the mini browser in the mobile phone, the user can control appliances and services even outside home. Thanking to the service and Web service layers of the proposed architecture, it was possible to implement the Web Application quite efficiently based on a typical MVC (Model-View-Controller) approach. That is, Web services, HTML templates, and the perl-CGI scripts correspond to the model, view and controller, respectively. Specifically, every CGI script was implemented so as to perform the following common steps.

- **Step 1:** On receiving an HTTP request, parse the request and obtain the user inputs.
- **Step 2:** Based on the inputs, activate Web services of appropriate legacy appliances.
- **Step 3:** Get the current state of the appliances through getStatus() Web-API.
- **Step 4:** Generate a status message from the current state and responses of the Web services.
- **Step 5:** Embed the message in the prepared HTML template, and output the HTML text as a HTTP Response.

Figure 10(c) shows a more user-friendly interface using Nintendo DS. With the touch-sensitive interface of DS, the user can quickly operate appliances without going forward/backward the pages. The interface was implemented using Ajax technology and Perl-CGI communicating with the Web-APIs.

Finally, Figure 10(d) shows light-weight GUIs developed as standard widget applications for the PC. The GUIs were written in Perl/Tk, operating on both Windows and Linux PCs. For the implementation, we basically follow the above common steps (Steps 2, 3, and 4). As a result, the size of application became quite small. For instance, the number of statements of CurtainRemocon.pl (left of Figure 10(d)) was as small as 28.

End-User Service Creation Environment: BAMBEE(Sekimoto, 2008)

Currently, the integrated services are developed by service providers as proprietary applications, and end-users execute provided services. However, personal tastes and life styles of end-users might vary from family to family. Therefore, it is natural that every end-user thinks to create their customized services suited for their specific HNS environment.

Conventionally, there are two ways for an end-user to create integrated services. One is end-user programming, and another is making use of learning remote controller with macro feature. These methods require some kinds of special knowledge for programming or cumbersome procedure to end-users.

BAMBEE is a visual programming environment for end-users aiming at assistance to create HNS integrated services easily. With using BAMBEE, end-users can create, edit, delete, and test the integrated services. Figure 11 shows a HNS integrated service created with BAMBEE. BAMBEE is equipped with a touch-sensitive interface. Touched appliance icon on the right side of BAMBEE becomes a part of HNS integrated services. In the literature(Sekimoto, 2008), usability testing for BAMBEE by 28 subjects in the broad age group from 22 years old to 72 years old was performed. In the testing, all subjects succeeded to create, edit and delete the HNS integrated services.

Verbena: Dynamic Service Bindings (Nakamura, 2008)

Although the proposed legacy adapter enables to realize multi-vendor HNS environment, it does not assume that appliances in HNS are changed

Figure 11. BAMBEE

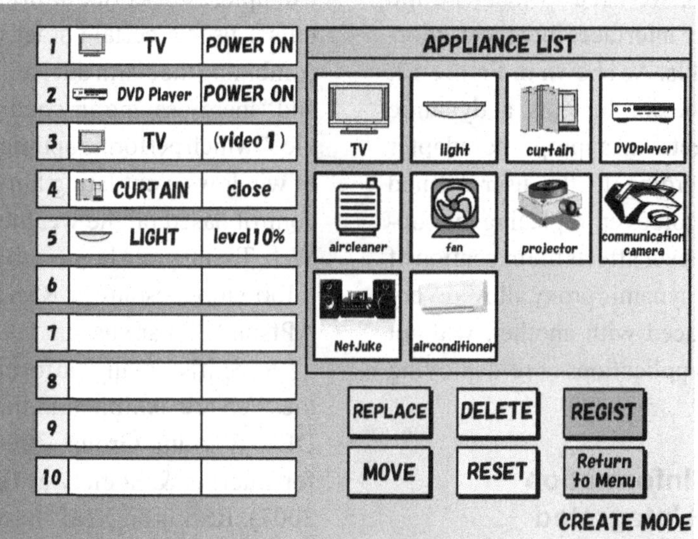

Figure 12. A HNS Architecture with Verbena Framework

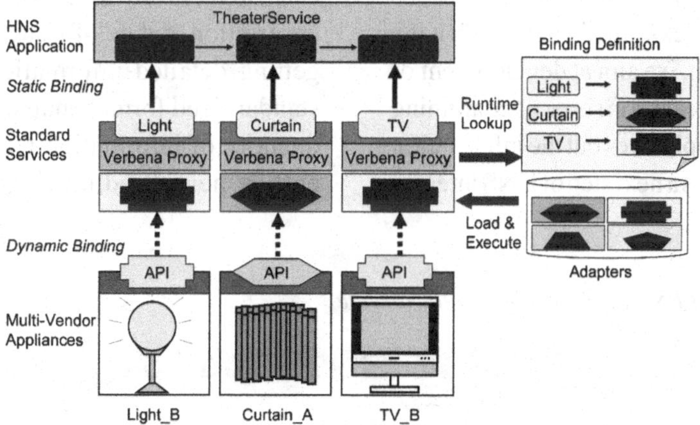

or replaced dynamically. The applications and the appliance features are statically bound via Web-APIs. As a result, if any appliance is replaced, added or removed during run-time, the applications have to be modified accordingly.

Verbena is a framework to achieve a loose coupling between Web-APIs and concrete appliance features that dynamically binds them during run-time. Figure 12 shows a HNS architecture example with Verbena framework. Generally, specifications of appliance APIs vary from vendor to vendor. To accept a wide range of multi-vendor appliances for such heterogeneous APIs, every standard service should provide a vendor-neutral service interface for the HNS applications, with encapsulating the underlying vendor-specific APIs. In the figure, standard services of Light, Curtain and TV exhibit their vendor-neutral service interfaces.

Since every standard service is an abstract model of an appliance, we then have to bind the service to the concrete appliance actually deployed in the HNS. For this, we need to translate the vendor-neutral service interfaces into the vendor-specific appliance APIs. As shown in Figure 12, each standard service implements a dynamic proxy, which interprets an appropriate adapter during runtime, according to the user-defined binding definition. Moreover, replacing any appliance with another never affects the execution of the applications. This dynamic proxy allows every appliance to be replaced with another, without reconstructing HNS applications or re-deploying HNS platforms.

Integration with Information Resources: RSS Integrated Service (Sakamoto, 2008)

As Web 2.0 technology spreads, mashup services with higher added value combining the various information resources exhibited on the Web have become popular. Then, we aim at development of more sophisticated integration services combining with not only home appliances but the information resources on the Web as a next step of HNS integration services with "RSS Integrated Service". For example, "stock price information service" which tells a user a certain stock price fluctuation by combining the alarm device and stock information, and "energy-saving air-conditioner ventilation service" which performs optimal opening and closing of windows, ventilating fans, and air-conditioner control based on the weather information on the Web. To integrate home network system and Web information resources, RSS documents and Web-APIs in HNS are used.

Recently, many information resources on the Web are exhibited in the form of RSS(RSS-DEV Working Group, 2000) (Berkman Center for Internet & Society at Harvard Law School, 2007). RSS is an XML-based document format for the syndication of web content so that it can be republished on other sites or downloaded periodically and presented to users. Typically, each item in an RSS document has a title, a description, a date of issue, and a hyperlink for getting detailed information of the item. This standardized format enables us to access a huge quantity of information resources such as blog entries, news headlines or podcasts, with using

Figure 13. Converted RSS by RSS Integrated Service

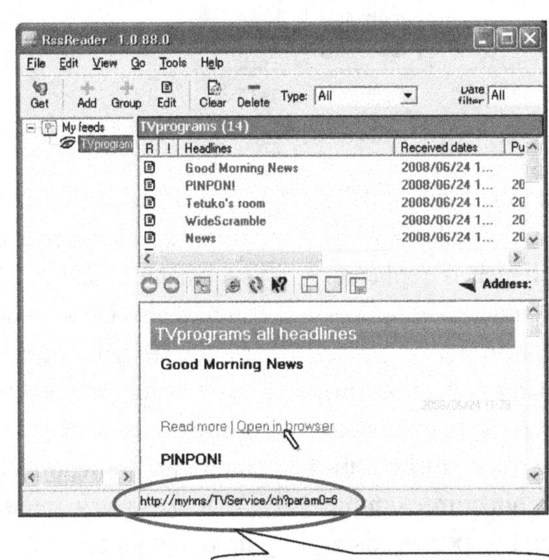

RSS reader (News On Feeds, 2008) or other applications.

The RSS Integrated Service combines web information resources (RSS documents) and HNS to provide users with high added value. In the service, the hyperlink of each item in an RSS document is replaced to a Web-API of home appliance control.

Figure 13 shows replaced RSS document on a RSS reader. In the RSS document, each item indicates a TV program. In this example, "Good Morning News" means a news program on channel 6, and hyperlink of the item is replaced into a Web-API "http://myhns/TVService/ch?param0=6" by the RSS Integrated Service. The Web-API means a TV is set to channel 6 in HNS.

In the conventional HNS environment, various kinds of information resources and appliance services are used separately. RSS Integrated Service integrates an RSS document as the information resources, and home appliance services. So, if only a user clicks a hyperlink of the item on an RSS reader, he/she can invoke the specified Web-API.

RELATED WORK

Loke (Loke, 2003) firstly modeled networked appliances as Web services, and proposed a workflow engine, called Decoflow, which prescribes integrated services using BPEL4WS. However, the method regards each networked appliance just as a black box with an open interface. Also, it does not mention the legacy appliances. The proposed framework can complement the method, which would allow efficient creation and management of the integrated services.

SOA with Web services is expected as a powerful means to achieve legacy migration. For instance, Lewis et al. (2005) presented a framework called SMART, which assists organizations in analyzing legacy capabilities for use as services in SOA. Zhang et al. (2004) proposed a method based on a code analysis, which facilitates legacy code extraction for Web service construction. However, most existing techniques including the above are addressing the legacy migration of enterprise systems. We believe that our original contribution was to show a concrete framework for legacy migration in the new domain, i.e., home network system, exploiting the essence of SOA with Web services.

Another interesting issue is the feature interaction problem (Kolberg, 2003; Wilson, 2008; Metzger, 2004; Weiss 2006), which is the functional conflicts among multiple HNS services on the appliances or environmental factors. Nakamura et al. (2005) formalized the feature interaction problem and presented a conflict detection method in the context of the HNS. We are currently implementing the method on the developed system.

CONCLUSION

This paper presented a framework that adapts the legacy home appliances to the emerging home network system. The proposed framework extensively adopted the concept of SOA. Features of the legacy appliances are exposed as self-contained Web-APIs with Web services. We also implemented the actual HNS with multi-vendor legacy appliances, as well as several integrated services.

Our future work includes the security issues and the feature interaction management. We also plan to investigate a method that supports non-expert users in creating integrated services easily.

ACKNOWLEDGMENT

This research was partially supported by: [the Japan Ministry of Education, Science, Sports, and Culture, Grant-in-Aid for Young Scientists (B) (No.18700062, No.20700027)], [JSPS and MAE under the Japan-France Integrated Action Program (SAKURA)].

REFERENCES

W3C (2002). *Web Service Activity*. Retrieved from http://www.w3.org/2002/ws/

Berkman Center for Internet & Society at Harvard Law School. (2007). *Rss2.0*. Retrieved from http://blogs.law.harvard.edu/tech/rss

DLNA. (2006). Digital Living Network Alliance. Retrieved from http://www.dlna.org

ECHONET. (2006). ECHONET Consortium. Retrieved from http://www.echonet.gr.jp/

Electronics, L. G. (2008). LGE Home Network. Retrieved from http://www.lge.com/products/homenetwork/html/lge_homenetwork.jsp

Geer, D. (2006). Nanotechnology: The Growing Impact of Shrinking Computers. *IEEE Pervasive Computing / IEEE Computer Society [and] IEEE Communications Society*, *5*(1), 7–11. doi:10.1109/MPRV.2006.10

HORIBA. (2000). Tsuichau-mon – Light Right. Retrieved from http://www.jp.horiba.com/products_e/hip08/ hip08_04.htm#6

Igaki, H., Nakamura, M., & Matsumoto, K. (2005). A Service-Oriented Framework for Networked Appliances to Achieve Appliance Interoperability and Evolution in Home Network System (short paper). In *Proc. of International Workshop on Principles of Software Evolution (IWPSE 2005)* (pp. 61-64).

Kaden Control Lab. (2006). AVT Series. Retrieved from http://d-purasu.hp.infoseek.co.jp/

Kolberg, M., Magill, E. H., & Wilson, M. (2003). Compatibility Issues between Services Supporting Networked Appliances. *IEEE Communications Magazine*, *41*(11), 136–147. doi:10.1109/MCOM.2003.1244934

Kulchenko, P. Reese. B. (2004). SOAP:Lite - Client and server side SOAP implementation. Retrieved from http://www.soaplite.com/

Lewis, G., Morris, E., O'Brien, L., Smith, D., & Wrage, L. (2005). *SMART: The Service-Oriented Migration and Reuse Technique* (Tech Rep CMU/SEI-2005-TN-029). Software Engineering Institute.

Loke, S. W. (2003). Service-Oriented Device Echology Workflows. In *Proc. of 1st Int'l Conf. on Service-Oriented Computing (ICSOC2003)* (LNCS 2910, pp. 559-574).

Metzger, A. (2004). Feature Interactions in Embedded Control Systems. *Computer Networks, 45*(5), Special Issue on Directions in Feature Interaction Research, 625-644.

Nakamura, M., Fukuoka, Y., Igaki, H., & Matsumoto, M. (2008). Implementing Multi-Vendor Home Network System with Vendor-Neutral Services and Dynamic Service Binding. In *IEEE International Conference on Services Computing (SCC 2008)* (pp. 275-282).

Nakamura, M., Igaki, H., & Matsumoto, K. (2005). Feature Interactions in Integrated Services of Networked Home Appliances -An Object-Oriented Approach-. In *Proc. of Int'l. Conf. on Feature Interactions in Telecommunication Networks and Distributed Systems (ICFI'05)* (pp. 236-251).

Nakamura, M., Tanaka, A., Igaki, H., Tamada, T., & Matsumoto, K. (2008). Constructing Home Network Systems and Integrated Services Using Legacy Home Appliances and Web Services. [JWSR]. *International Journal of Web Services Research*, *5*(1), 82–98.

NANO Media Inc. (2005). App-rimo-con. Retrieved from http://www.nanomedia.jp/english/service/s02.html

News On Feeds. (2008). List of news aggregators. Retrieved from http://www.newsonfeeds.com/faq/aggregators

Panasonic Electric Works, Ltd. (2008). Lifinity. Retrieved from http://denko.panasonic.biz/Ebox/kahs/index.html (in Japanese)

Papazoglou, M. P., & Georgakopoulos, D. (2003). Service-Oriented Computing. *Communications of the ACM*, *46*(10), 25–28. doi:10.1145/944217.944233

RSS-DEV Working Group. (2000). Rss1.0. Retrieved from http://web.resource.org/rss/1.0/

Sakamoto, H., Igaki, H., & Nakamura, M. (2008). Integrating Networked Home Appliances and Information Resources on the Internet Using RSS. ([in Japanese]. *Tech Rep, IEICE*, *108*(136), 47–52.

Sekimoto, J., Nakamura, M., Igaki, H., & Matsumoto, K. (2008). *Supporting End-Users for Creating Integrated Services in Home Network System* (Technical Report of IEICE, Volume 107, Number 525, 289-294) (in Japanese)

Smith, D. J., & Meyers, B. C. (2005). *Exploiting Programmatic Interoperability: Army Future Force Workshop* (Tech Rep CMU/SEI-2005-TN-042). Software Engineering Institute.

Toshiba (2008). *Toshiba home network – Feminity*. Retrieved from http://feminity.toshiba.co.jp/feminity/feminity_eng/index.html

Weerawarana, S., & Curbera, F. (2002). Business process with BPEL4WS: Understanding BPEL4WS, Part1. Retrieved from http://www-106.ibm.com/developerworks/webservices/\\library/ws-bpelcol1

Weiss, M., & Esfandiari, B. (2005). On Feature Interactions Among Web Services. *International Journal of Web Services Research*, *2*(4), 22–47.

Wilson, M., Kolberg, M., & Magill, E. H. (2008). Considering Side Effects in Service Interactions in Home Automation – an Online Approach. In *Proc. of Int'l. Conf. on Feature Interactions in Software and Communication Systems (ICFI'08)* (pp. 172-187).

Zhang, Z., & Yang, H. (2004), "Incubating Services in Legacy Systems for Architectural Migration. In *Proc. of 11th Asia-Pacific Software Engineering Conference (APSEC'04)* (pp. 196-203).

ENDNOTES

1. The IrDA, which is often used for exchanging data among PCs and handheld devices, is completely different from the IrRC, although both protocols use the infrared for the physical layer.
2. We did not use BPEL4WS for implementing the integrated services, since BPEL4WS was somehow exaggerated for our current HNS implementation. Further investigation of its applicability is left for our future work.
3. The time taken for each Perl client to prepare SOAP stubs from the corresponding WSDLs had been excluded from the data.

Chapter 19
Broadening JAIN-SLEE with a Service Description Language and Asynchronous Web Services

Paolo Falcarin
Politecnico di Torino, Italy

Claudio Venezia
Telecom Italia, Italy

José Felipe Mejia Bernal
Politecnico di Torino, Italy

ABSTRACT

Meshing up telecommunication and IT resources seems to be the real challenge for supporting the evolution towards the next generation of Web Services. In the telecom world, JAIN-SLEE (JAIN Service Logic Execution Environment) is an emerging standard specification for Java service platforms targeted to host value added services, composed of telecom and IT services. This chapter describes the StarSLEE platform which extends JAIN-SLEE in order to compose JAIN-SLEE services with Web Services and the StarSCE service creation environment which allows exporting value added services as communication Web Services. It analyzes open issues that must be addressed to introduce Web Services in new telecom service platforms.

INTRODUCTION

Nowadays telecom service providers are seeking new paradigms of service creation and execution to reduce new services' time to market and increase profitability. Furthermore, convergence of networks, services and content is taking place at an increasing speed. Convergence is increasingly speeding up the introduction of new and converged services.

DOI: 10.4018/978-1-61520-684-1.ch019

New market opportunities like integration of voice, video and data services are emerging from this trend; as a consequence, the main goal of telecom service providers is the development of Value Added Services, or next generation services (Licciardi, 2003) that leverage both on the Internet and on telephony networks, i.e. the convergence and integration of services offered by IT providers with telecom operators ones.

The creation of appealing value added services seems to be a key feature to avoid an operator being reduced to a "transport only" provider. The attractiveness of the service assortment offered seems to be the key to attract customers, and to increase revenues (Schülke, 2006).

The reuse and integration of existing IT services in value added ones is even made difficult both by the increasing software systems complexity and the different middleware standards used for communication.

To overcome these constraints the current vertically integrated networks are actually migrating to horizontally layered structures offering open and standard interfaces, i.e. a service platform, based on shared services and network enablers, which can be easily composed in a loosely coupled manner (Pollet, 2006).

Therefore, these goals pose new requirements on the software development process, on the platforms hosting these services, and on the middleware enabling communication among services.

JAIN-SLEE (JAIN - Service Logic Execution Environment) standard specification (JSR-240, 2008) is emerging as a new event-based service platform targeted to telecom domain, aiming at overcoming the performance limitations of J2EE-like application server, mainly designed for enterprise services, based on typical request-response interaction style.

In fact, communication services have strong real-time requirements (e.g. high throughput, low latency time), support mainly asynchronous interactions (e.g., voice-mail, call forwarding), and leverage efficiently on native protocol capabilities.

Web Services standards are emerging as a new middleware standard for providing, composing and integrating IT services (Chung, 2003), but their introduction in the telecom domain means facing up with some open issues.

Generalizing telecom functionalities to more abstract standard interfaces, like Web Services interfaces (WSDL, 2007), is often necessary to allow IT developers to reuse telecom services without mastering all technical issues related to telecom protocols; thus exposing telecom resources as Web Services means losing some of the technical details of the underlying proprietary interface.

Based on the former ideas, a Communication Application Server (named StarSLEE) inspired to the JAIN-SLEE specification has been developed, together with a graphical Service Creation Environment (StarSCE) for helping IT-developers in creating Value Added Services and Communication Web Services (Venezia, 2006).

The service lifecycle process is sped up by means of a Service Creation Environment (SCE) that supports as much as possible the reuse and the composition of pre-existing consolidated components deployed in the telecom platforms, and third-party Web Services.

A SCE must offer an intuitive interface enabling graphical composition and easy configuration of value added services, and it must automatically deploy value added services in the shape of service description languages which can be used to orchestrate and execute services running in a service execution environment.

This paper aims at analyzing the current challenges encountered during a prototyping activity carried on to provide an effective composition and integration of Web Services and Value Added Services deployed on a JAIN-SLEE platform.

In the following sections we describe the JAIN-SLEE standard architecture, the issues regarding the integration of Web Services in JAIN-SLEE, the problems of exporting a JAIN-SLEE value-added service as a communication Web Service, and the current issues for moving such telecom platform towards telecom service oriented architecture.

VALUE ADDED SERVICES IN JAIN-SLEE

A value added service aims at encompassing either communication or enterprise service components (Glitho, 2003).

The following is an example of a simple information retrieval target service:

1. The user invokes the service using his/her mobile phone by sending an SMS (Short Message Service) whose body contains the information needed to retrieve the closest merchant of a particular category (e.g. restaurant, bar or cinema).
2. The service localizes the user, retrieves the information requested and replies with a SMS containing the information retrieved.
3. Afterwards the user can send another SMS to be connected with the found merchant via an audio call.

The former service combines a communication service (SMS) with an enterprise service, i.e. the information retrieval services (Yellow Pages Web Service).

As communication services have particular performance and availability requirements, it is difficult to realize such service integration using a typical application server, which architecture has been mainly designed for enterprise services.

In fact, enterprise services aim at business processes, which are typically transactional and potentially long running.

Instead, communication services have strong real-time requirements and are based on asynchronous interactions. Voice mail, call forwarding and ring back tone are typical examples belonging to this service category.

Moreover while enterprise services are typically synchronous remote procedure calls (RPC) characterized by coarse-grained events with low frequency, communication services are typically asynchronous and characterized by fine-grained events with high frequency.

Within the communication domain, at the control layer, Session Initiation Protocol (Rosenberg, 2002) is considered the converging protocol for call and message signaling. Either fixed or mobile networks will leverage on SIP for providing integrated capabilities. SIP will improve the ability to build new services and will play the role that Web Services are playing in the IT world (the universal glue).

Although they play a similar role in the respective realms, SIP and SOAP are profoundly different.

For example, a SIP based communication platform (Rosenberg, 2002) is made up of a set of systems which interact through a service bus allowing information push based on a publish/subscribe model.

This platform relies on a SIP Registry which collects relevant information from a SIP network, stores and distributes it. This information regards both service and network elements descriptions. The SIP Registry is available both for network resources (where services are running), service managers (watching services behavior) and service users (interested in invoking services).

In contrast, next generation service platforms aim at realizing an effective coexistence between enterprise and communication services.

In next sections we evaluate if Web Service technology can help reaching this objective.

JAIN-SLEE Architecture

JAIN SLEE (also known as JSLEE) aims at defining a new kind of application server designed for hosting value added services. In particular, a JSLEE container is designed for hosting communication applications while typical application servers have been designed for enterprise applications: such applications typically invoke one another synchronously (e.g. via Remote Procedure Call or Remote Method Invocation) and they usually do not consider high-availability and performance concerns.

Instead, the JAIN-SLEE specification has been designed for communication applications, and a JSLEE container relies on an event based model, with asynchronous interactions among components.

Figure 1. StarSLEE communication server

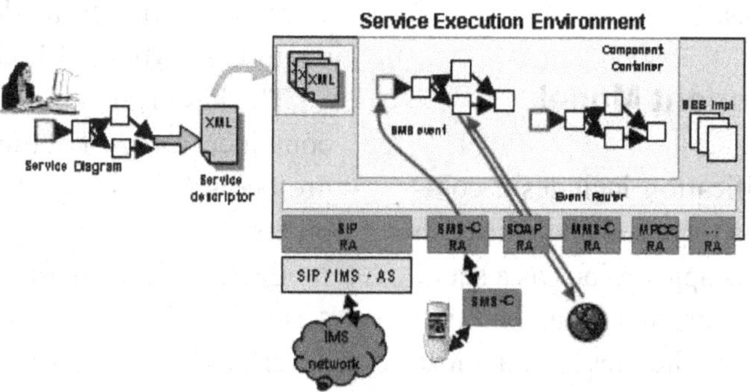

The design of a JSLEE container must meet the requirements of a telecommunication services, e.g. handling different kind of events with low latency, supporting lightweight transactions. Furthermore, a service deployed on a JSLEE container has to be composed of lightweight components with a short lifetime, which can be rapidly created, deleted and updated.

Another important feature of a JSLEE service is the ability of accessing multiple data sources with high independence of network protocols elements.

Therefore, it must be possible to deploy applications in the SLEE application environment that use diverse network resources and signaling protocols.

The integration of a new type of network element, or external system is satisfied by a Resource Adaptor Framework that supports integration of network resources; for example, a SIP server for voice-over-IP calls and instant messaging, a SMS (Short Message Service) gateway for communicating with mobile phones.

JAIN-SLEE specification requires that each telecom network resource is wrapped by a standard Resource Adaptor interface, in order to be connected to the event bus of the JAIN-SLEE container.

Figure 1 depicts the StarSLEE platform architecture, and a possible example scenario: the SIP resource adaptor may trigger the platform with events originating from the underlying SIP network; an event router dispatches these events to existing or new service instances; then a service instance is composed by various components which interact by means of events.

JAIN SLEE provides a standard programming model that can be used by the Java developer community. The programming model has been designed to simplify application development, promoting software reuse, and ensure that robust services can be developed rapidly with minimum configuration effort.

A standard JAIN-SLEE container should be able to clone application components between processing nodes in the system as particular processes and nodes may fail; it has to manage concurrent execution of application components, and allow application components to be dynamically upgraded. JAIN SLEE defines its own component model, which specifies how service logic has to be built, packaged, and executed, and how it interacts with external resources.

The last version of the JAIN SLEE specification (JSR-240, 2008) defines the contract between the SLEE and Resource Adaptors thereby providing a standard API for the connection of external resources to the SLEE environment. An example resource can be any protocol stack or other event based resource. This version also enhances some of the commonly used functions such as profile update, transaction boundaries, connection to synchronous external resources and facilities management capabilities.

JAIN-SLEE Component Model

The JAIN-SLEE specification includes a component model for structuring the application logic of communications applications as a set of object-oriented components, and for assembling these components into higher level and more complex services.

The SLEE architecture also defines how these components interact and the container that will host these components at run-time. The SLEE specification defines requirements of availability and scalability of a SLEE platform, even if it does not suggest any particular implementation strategy.

Applications may be written once, and then deployed on any application environment that implements the SLEE specification. The system administrator of a JAIN SLEE controls the life-cycle (including deployment, un-deployment and on-line upgrade) of a service.

The atomic element defined by JAIN SLEE is the Service Building Block (SBB). An SBB is a software component that sends and receives events and performs computations based on the receipt of events and its current state.

Every SBB subscribes to a given type of event. Whenever such an event is triggered by the network, or internally by some other SBB, StarSLEE container creates SBB instances, able to manage those events by means of specific handlers.

The event router, specified by JAIN-SLEE specification, is the engine which routes event, either created by action performed on SBB, or coming from Resource Adaptor (RA).

The RA architecture provides a standard way for enabling events on different networks to be received and transmitted from the event processing engine that is the Service Logic Execution Environment. The goal of the RA architecture is to allow Resource Adaptor implementations that use and fulfill contracts defined in the JAIN-SLEE 1.1 specification to be deployed and run in any compliant JAIN-SLEE application server.

The RA layer is useful to decouple the SLEE container from rest of the world in terms of other protocols (i.e. SIP protocol, SOAP protocol or others).

Each SBB is defined by its own SBB-descriptor, an XML file including information that describes it (e.g. its name, vendor and version), the list of events it can fire and receive, and the names of Java classes implementing the logic of the SBB itself.

In addition, StarSLEE the SBB descriptor contains:

- The list of SBB properties, e.g. the input action parameters;
- The list of SBB variables, e.g. the output set in the Activity Context;
- The list of SBB handlers, e.g. the events managed by SBB;
- The list of actions performed by SBB.

While SBB properties are input parameters for actions/operations performed by SBB, SBB variables are the results of those operations. Actions are triggered by events, SBB properties can be valued by SBB variables belonging to an Activity Context (AC), which is a portion of memory shared by all SBB instances running in a service instance, and that is used to read and write properties and variables of all SBB instances involved in the same service instance.

SBBs are stateful components since they can remember the results of previous computations and those results can be applied in additional computations. SBBs perform logic based on events received.

An event represents an occurrence that may require application processing. It contains information that describes the occurrence, such as the source of the event. An event may asynchronously originate from a number of different sources, for example an external resource such as a communications protocol stack, from the SLEE itself, or from application components within the SLEE.

Resources are external entities that interact with other systems outside of the SLEE, such as network elements (i.e. Messaging Server, SIP Server). A Resource Adaptor wraps the particular interfaces of a resource into the interfaces required by the JAIN SLEE specification.

JAIN-SLEE specification does not define any particular service description language to be used for composing different SBB instance.

Therefore, we defined StarSDL, a specific service description language for StarSLEE used for describing an event-oriented service scenario, which well suits the telecommunication service domain; in particular, the StarSDL must allow asynchronous activation of the service, and the service session is typically open-ended and with long-duration, because it often involves different services, and, of course, users.

The language specification aims at satisfying the abovementioned requirements; hence it allows developers to model asynchronous interactions to the service both for service activation and for other actors' involvement, through the event router contained in the StarSLEE execution environment.

As a set of SBB is available, the service developer can build service without worrying about single SBB programming, only considering service composition, once he knows each SBB interface, in terms of handlers, actions and properties.

Service Composition with StarSCE

The approach to service creation in telecom domain with Web Services infrastructure is driven by the constraint of being able to address heterogeneous target execution environments, where the technologies range from general Information Technology (IT) where, for example, Web Services are one of the leading technology in Service Oriented Architectures (Baravaglio, 2005), to very specific telecommunications ones, where an overabundance of protocols and standards are available (e.g. SIP, IMS). What seems to be clear in telecom services is the need to integrate many resources over different protocols and to be able to represent a set of interactions that are not limited to the classic request/response paradigm. In such a heterogeneous environment, the approaches to service creation should be as general as possible, supporting a stepwise approach that drives the developer from abstract to concrete definitions targeting a specific service execution environment.

Looking at the main challenges of the service creation process, the most important requirements are:

- A service description language that allows the specification of a telecom/IT integrated services;
- Tools that support the graphical composition services and their deployment to a target Service Execution Environment;
- A Service Execution Environment that allows combining effectively different technologies.

In order to provide Value Added Services (VAS), the service platform must be enhanced with a graphical service composition engine, i.e. a service creation environment which easily allows building new services by means of a collection of internal components or third-party Web Services. StarSCE allows the developer to choose the SBBs (Service Building Block) and link them in a graph structure which is a graphical representation of the service. A Service Building Block is either an External IT Web Service wrapper or a signaling network functionality provider.In JAIN-SLEE component model variables and properties can be set for each SBB: StarSCE allows to visually composing those SBBs in a service description diagram which can be translated in StarSDL repre-

Figure 2. Example of graphical Service description

sentation, which describes the service control flow and the usage of these variables and properties.

In particular, starting from the WSDL interface of a Web Service, StarSCE consents to automatically create the correspondent SOAP client wrapped in a new SBB.

The following figure (realized using the StarSCE graphical service creation environment) shows an example of a simple service which can be deployed on the StarSLEE service platform. Moreover given a set of Web Services wrapper SBB, StarSLEE can actually behave as a Web Service orchestration engine.

Once a service is graphically composed and the SBBs have been configured, StarSCE generates an XML file, called service descriptor.

A service descriptor represents the control-flow graph of the service composed of different SBBs, each one defined by its own SBB descriptor.

A service is made up of loosely coupled components, and it may provide different starting points, i.e. different SBB instances, each one triggered by a different kind of event, coming from the resource adaptors pool.

Each service instance is then made up of different SBB instances and one activity context holding shareable attributes that SBB instances want to share.

Therefore the state of a service instance can be represented by attributes stored in an activity context.

Using StarSCE it is possible to manage the automatic configuration, dynamic deployment, and publication of a Value Added Service in a JAIN-SLEE container.

Figure 3 shows main entities of StarSLEE container: an XML service descriptor is sent through the Service Bus to the Application Server Deployer, which creates the corresponding service instance (e.g. TimerService). This service is then running and listening on the event router, waiting for events coming from networks underlying the resource adaptors (e.g. HTTP, SIP).

StarSCE helps the developer in creating complex compositions of SBBs to be executed in a JAIN-SLEE container, which use Resource Adaptors to abstract interfaces of telecom networks resources, and it is not bounded abstracts and to represent the orchestration of such resources our approach aims at extending JAIN-SLEE platform and related SCE in two directions:

1. To compose both JAIN-SLEE service building blocks and Web Services.
2. To export JAIN-SLEE service as an asynchronous Web Service compliant to the WS-Notification specification.

COMMUNICATION WEB SERVICES

Traditional communication services are usually triggered by signaling messages like a SIP message (Rosenberg, 2002) or an instant message (IMS, 2006); instead Communication Web Services (Baravaglio, 2005) are usually Web Service interfaces of common telecom functionalities which

Figure 3. Service deployment on StarSLEE

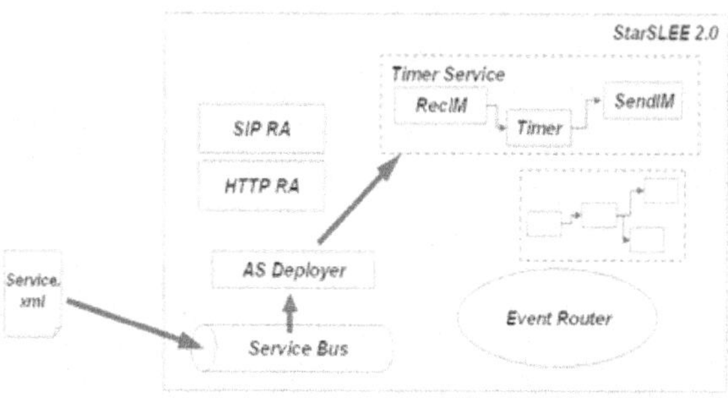

are triggered by a SOAP message. They can also exploit different network resources within the telecom domain and be published and used on the Internet.

For example, here is a list of telecom services which can be exposed as Communication Web Services:

- Third party call: provides the capability to initiate a call between two actors generated and managed by a third party.
- Multi media conference: provides the capability to initiate an audio/video conference with two or more actors within a session.
- Messaging: a set of Web Services which provide the capability to send Instant Messages, SMS and MMS
- Presence: provides the capability to retrieve user availability information in a network domain.
- Users' provisioning: provides the capability to interact with a Data Provisioning DB System by means of retrieving and storing user profiles information supporting various communication protocols and devices.

Using standard Web Services to abstract telecom network capabilities, service providers can offer to IT developers outside of the telecom industry, new possibilities for building innovative services.

Web Services standards enable telecom operators to provide third parties with controlled, reliable access to telecom network capabilities such as presence and call control.

Different international consortia have proposed standards for using Web Services in telecommunications domain:

- Parlay X Standards (ETSI, 2002) are a set of simplified telecom APIs based on Web services published by the Parlay Group and the European telecommunications Standards Institute (ETSI); Parlay-X has been standardizing WSDL interfaces for the most common signaling services, like Third Party Call, Call Notification, SMS, MMS, etc.
- Open Mobile Alliance (OMA, 2007) has proposed the OMA Web Services Enabler to define the means by which OMA applications can be exposed, discovered and consumed using Web Services technologies, and it specifies how mobile terminal can interact with Web Services.
- W3C (W3C, 2007) is providing WS-Addressing specification (WS-Addressing, 2004), which provides transport-neutral mechanisms to address Web Services and messages. Specifically, this specification defines XML elements and namespaces to identify Web Service endpoints and to

Figure 4. Extended JAIN-SLEE architecture

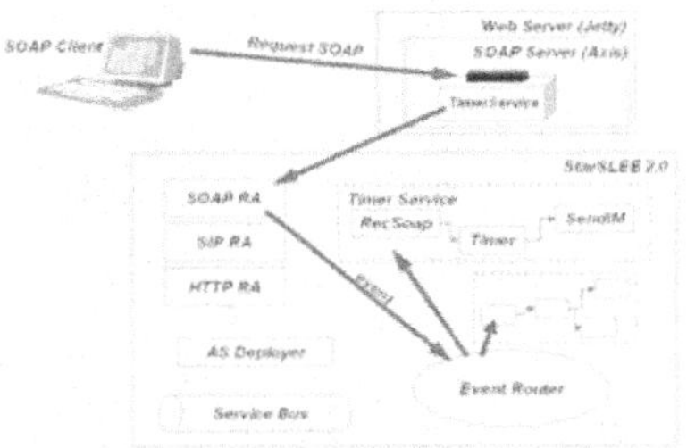

secure end-to-end endpoint identification in messages. This specification enables messaging systems to support message transmission through networks that include processing nodes such as brokers, firewalls, and gateways in a transport-neutral manner.

- OASIS consortium has defined a set of specifications like WS-Notification (WSN, 2007), WS-ResourceFramework, and WS-ReliableMessaging (WS-ReliableMessaging, 2007) which are important basis for developing communication Web Services.

In the following section we describe how StarSCE helps developers in transforming a JAIN-SLEE value added service in a communication Web Service.

From Value Added Service to Communication Web Service

Transforming a Value Added Service (in this context a JSLEE service) in a Communication Web Service requires some enhancements to the JAIN-SLEE architecture.

First of all a Web Server must be added for hosting a SOAP Server (Apache Axis, 2006). Then, for any service to be exposed, a Web Service implementation with related WSDL is provided and it has to interact with the actual service deployed in the SLEE container.

Therefore, the JAIN-SLEE architecture must be extended adding a SOAP Resource Adaptor (SOAP-RA), which acts as a communication bridge between a SLEE service and its correspondent Web Service implementation.

An alternative design may be based on adding a service-specific resource adaptor for each service to be exported as a Web Service, but this solution is not viable: in fact in JAIN-SLEE architecture a resource adaptor is a wrapper of an external network entity, and it is designed to be service-independent, because it must be unaware of which kind of services are deployed in the SLEE container.

Once defined the new extended architecture (see Figure 4), we can consider two different strategies to export a SLEE service in a Web Service: a wrapping strategy and a reengineering strategy.

Using the wrapping approach means considering the service as a single "black-box" entity which receives and sends events, while the reengineering approach consists in automatically modifying some parts of the service in order to be exported as a Web Service.

Following the wrapping strategy implies that the SOAP-RA should be able to send events the service is listening to; for example if the target service must be triggered by means of a SMS, the SOAP-RA should be able to send this event. Under these assumptions, this kind of SOAP-RA could send whichever kind of SLEE events, but this is in opposition to JAIN-SLEE design, where each ResourceAdaptor must only exchange events related to

Figure 5. ReceiveSOAP SBB

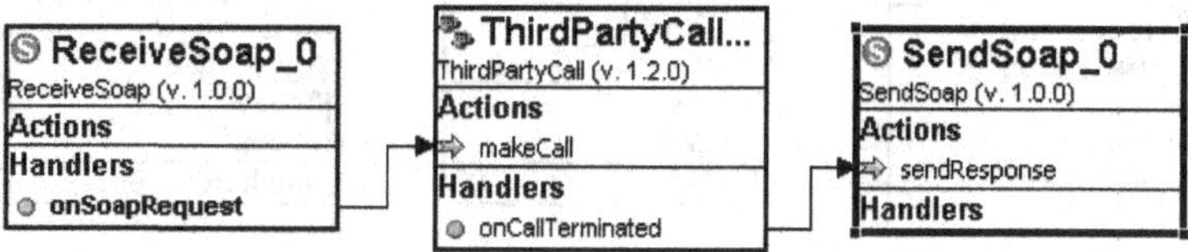

its own underlying network element. The SOAP-RA can only send events related to its own underlying network protocol, thus a SOAP-Event has been introduced to represent information coming from whichever Web Service implementation.

As a consequence, our approach is based on reengineering the value added service in order to automatically obtain its new Web Service version. Every service requires a root SBB which represents the service entry point (e.g. the SBB on the left side in Figure 5). Only when a root SBB is triggered a new service instance is created.

As the Value Added Service has been previously designed for listening to a particular event type, adding a new root SBB becomes necessary, i.e. the ReceiveSOAP SBB. The SOAP request is received from the SOAP-client through the Web Service Implementation and forwarded by the SOAP RA to a root SBB by means of a SOAP event.

The new root SBB (ReceiveSOAP) is then the service entry point which extracts data from the SOAP-Request and put them in the activity context.

The introduction of a new ReceiveSOAP SBB in place of the former root is not enough. In fact, reengineering a service by adding a new SBB requires a deeper analysis of service structure to find out dependencies among SBBs, both at the control-flow level and at the data-flow one.

For example, looking at the service in figure 2, we can identify different types of SBBs. The TPCC (Third-Party Call-Control) is a type of SBB representing the actual service logic implementation (we can call it "core SBB") and other SBBs whose main activity is the communication with external entities, that we call "connector SBBs". Among these ones we can further distinguish SBB receiving data (i.e. the RecvSMS which receive an SMS coming from the SMS-resource adaptor) from other ones sending out data (i.e. the SendSMS which sends an SMS to the SMS-resource adaptor): the ones receiving data can be labeled "service heads", because they are typically performed at the beginning of service execution, while the others sending data can be labeled "service tails", because they are typically performed at the end of service execution.

A service can be described by a direct cyclic graph, where a node corresponds to a SBB instance, and there is an arc from node A to node B only if the same type of event is sent by A and received by B.

Thus "service heads" are nodes with no incoming arcs, while "service tails" are nodes with no outgoing arcs.

For example in the service of figure 6 there are three service heads (ReceiveIM_0, ReceiveIM_1, and ReceiveIM_2) and two service tails (SendIM_0, and Echo_0).

On the other hand, the data-flow of a service instance can be deduced analyzing which attributes are read from (or written in) the activity context. The content of the activity context instance represents the state of the service instance at a particular time.

The attributes stored in the activity context by each SBB instance can be obtained from the XML service descriptor file.

Figure 6. Service heads and service tails

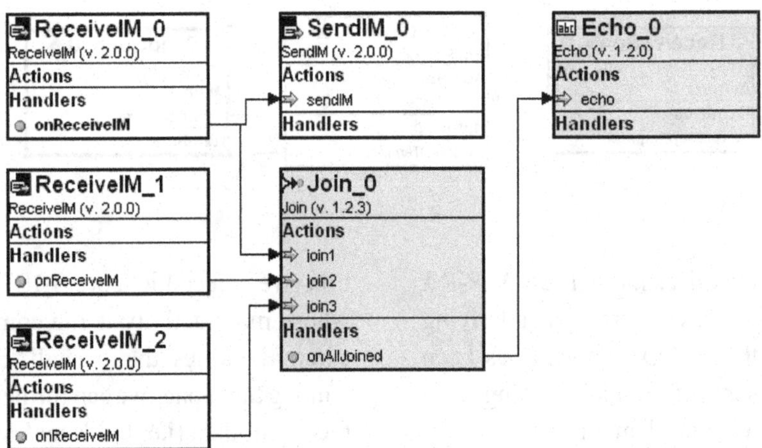

In practice, reengineering the service to be transformed in a Web Service means making some design decisions:

1. Which service heads must be replaced by a ReceiveSOAP SBB.
2. Which service attributes in the activity context must be mapped to parameters of Web Service operations.
3. Which interaction style to use between SOAP clients and the Communication Web Service.
4. Which service attributes in the activity context must be considered as a result to be sent back to SOAP clients.
5. Depending on the chosen interaction style, how service results should be transferred to the SOAP clients.

Once the developer makes these decisions, StarSCE can automatically generate the corresponding WSDL interface, the Web Service Implementation Java code to be deployed on the Web container, and the code of the ReceiveSOAP SBB.

Once a Communication Web Service has been deployed, it is provided with as many operations as the number of the available service heads. Invoking an operation mapped to a root service head means activating an instance of the corresponding service. The user can then interact with the service instance by means of invoking operations mapped on any of the other service heads.

For example, in figure 7 the original service of figure 6 has been reengineered, applying the following changes: the root SBB has been replaced by the SBB ReceiveSOAP_1, the other service head ReceiveIM_1 has been replaced by another ReceiveSOAP SBB instance, the two service tails have been substituted two SendSOAP SBBs.

A SendSOAP SBB is used to send service results back to the SOAP-RA sending a SOAP event containing attributes in the activity context, previously selected as service result.

Figure 8 shows how a Communication Service is accessed via SOAP:

1. The SOAP client request reaches the Web Service implementation of the SLEE Service;
2. The Web Service collects the parameters and delivers them to the SOAP RA;
3. The SOAP RA in turn identifies the corresponding reengineered SLEE Service and triggers it by generating the proper SOAP event, containing the service name and the

Figure 7. New Service heads and tails

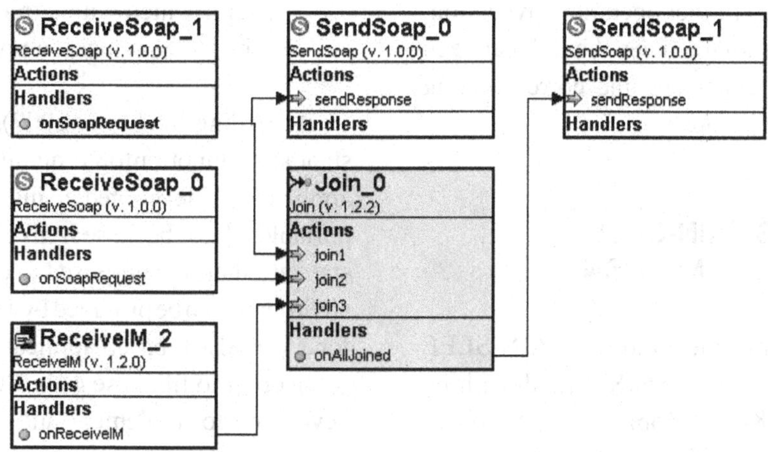

Figure 8. Web Service Request and SLEE Dispatching

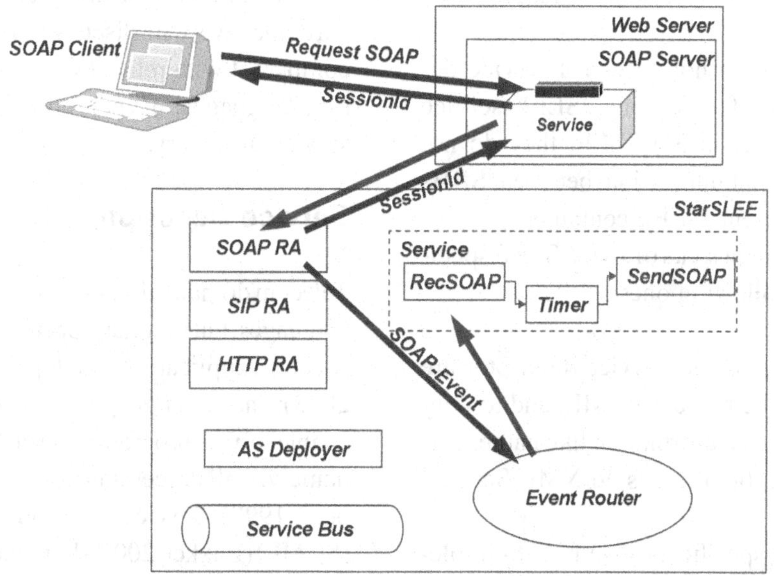

parameters of the invoked Web Service operation;

4. The root SBB (ReceiveSOAP) receives the SOAP event, creates the service instance, and then it copies the operation's parameters in the service activity context;
5. The service is executed and results are sent to the SOAP-RA with a SOAP event.

At this point, using a synchronous interaction style implies that SOAP-RA has to provide two more operations: getStatus and getResult. Invoking the former operation, while a service instance is running, allows SOAP clients to gain information on the state of its execution, polling on the latter returns service results whenever available.

Another important feature of SOAP RA is keeping a service session. In fact a session-ID is created and delivered to the SOAP client and it has to provide it for any further operation invocation. This session-ID is used to keep the link between the Web Service client and the corresponding StarSLEE service instance.

BROADENING JAIN-SLEE WITH STARSDL AND WSN

There are other implementations of JAIN-SLEE specification along with StarSLEE: the Rhino (OpenCloud, 2008) and MobiCents open source project (MobiCents, 2007). While they both provide a rich set of resource adaptors compliant to recent JAIN-SLEE specification, they do not implement a SOAP Resource Adaptor, like in StarSLEE.

Moreover they do not specify a service description language for defining JSLEE service descriptor, and, like in StarSLEE, they do not face with inter-communication between SBBs deployed on different JSLEE containers.

In particular, main lacks of JAIN-SLEE specification are the following ones:

- SBB descriptor and Service descriptor are required to be based on XML, and to contain some basic information like name, version, owner, but there is no XML-Schema to refer to.
- There is no specification on how to implement the event bus, neither how to define events namespaces, nor how this event bus can enable communications between SBBs deployed in different JAIN-SLEE containers.
- There is no specification on how to define services whose SBBs are running on different JAIN-SLEE containers, and how (i.e. with which middleware or protocol) these containers have to communicate.
- The JAIN-SLEE specification does not specify a service description language but it just suggest that SBB work-flow could be represented with a tree-structure, which limits the composition possibilities.

According to (Long, 2007), the JAIN SLEE standard cannot enforce quality or enforce that applications developed using JAIN SLEE are portable. This is because JAIN SLEE is a technical standard that was proposed to define the runtime environment to be provided by JAIN SLEE servers for JAIN SLEE based applications.

In order to fill these gaps, StarSLEE has been developed to implement and extend the JAIN-SLEE specification.

In this section we discuss important issues to be solved in order to obtain a smooth integration between JAIN-SLEE and Web Services world. In particular we will discuss our approach and we compare it with related work on service description languages, asynchronous interactions, and service discovery.

Service Description Languages

Telecom domain offers several service description languages, but they have been designed for domain specific applications and protocols (Licciardi, 2003); many languages have been proposed to enable service programming on telecom networks, namely: Call Processing Language (CPL) (Rosenberg, 1999), Service Creation Markup Language (SCML) (Bakker, 2002), Language for End System Services in Internet Telephony (LESS) (Wu, 2003), CCXML (CCXML, 2007), Session Processing Language (SPL) (Burgy, 2006), XTML (eXtensible Telephone Markup Language) (Pactolus, 2001), SPATEL (Belaunde, 2008).

The expressiveness of LESS and CPL have been intentionally limited to make them accessible to end-users without programming expertise, while SCML and CCXML require more technical knowledge and thus they target expert users: in particular CCXML offers interaction with VoiceXML capabilities.

SPL is a language which aims at raising the level of abstraction by introducing domain-specific constructs, such as sessions and branches. SPL hides SIP protocol complexity into appropriate language abstractions, and it makes programming telephony services accessible to more programmers, but it is bound to SIP-based services, it does not foresee integration with Web Services, and it still lacks a related service creation environment, able to automatically generate code and configuration files.

Both LESS and SPL use program analysis to check particular properties on the designed service: LESS use it to detect feature interactions, SPL to check for safety and robustness properties exploiting the high-level domain-specific constructs of the language.

Most of existing scripting languages for programming telephony services are tightened to a specific telecom network protocol, like SIP. Only recent versions of CPL and SPL specifications have introduced typical programming constructs like variables and loops.

SPATEL language (Belaunde, 2008) is based on OMG's Model Driven Architecture approach for describing IT-Telecom services. It is defined with a formal meta-model and it is enriched by semantic annotations used to ease service composition, but it is currently used to generate service orchestrations via BPEL (on server side) or python scripts (Python, 2009) to be run on smart-phones, thus its possible reuse and adaptation to JAIN-SLEE is not easy to obtain.

Using a network-independent service platform like JAIN-SLEE requires the definition of a service description language not coupled to the underlying network.

With respect to the service description and creation facets, JAIN-SLEE does not specify a language to describe services. As a consequence the new StarSDL language for StarSLEE platform has been defined to enable description of value added services less coupled to the underlying network resources, thanks to JAIN-SLEE event-based architecture.

StarSDL is inspired to a well known standard language in IT world to define service orchestrations, such as Business Process Execution Language (BPEL, 2003) for WS.

Several BPEL4WS implementations (ActiveBPEL, 2007) consist in environments which allow creating, deploying, executing and monitoring BPEL4WS services. Although these solutions encompass almost all the functional requirements for creating communication Web Services, they still cannot fulfill essential telecom services requirements like low latency and high throughput which implies that they do not easily scale for telecommunication Services environments.

Even if BPEL4WS language offers several workflow features, like Sequence, Parallel Split, Synchronization, Exclusive Choice, Simple Merge, Multi Choice, Synchronizing Merge, and Implicit Termination, it does not allow to define interactions based on publish-subscribe pattern: as a consequence, it is not possible to activate several process instances with the same event notification. In particular, StarSLEE execution environment requires to express and enact critical workflow patterns, like arbitrary cycles and multi-merges, not supported by BPEL language and related engines (Wohed, 2003).

Same limitations are observable in XPDL (XPDL, 2007), the standard language defined for easing interchange among business process languages in the Workflow Management domain. The goal of XPDL is more oriented to store and exchange the process diagram, in order to allow one tool to model a process diagram, another to read and edit the diagram, and another to run the process model on an XPDL-compliant engine.

The Web Services Choreography Description Language (WS-CDL, 2005) is an XML-based language that describes collaborations among different Web Services by defining, from a global viewpoint, their overall behavior, in order to achieve a common business goal.

While WS-BPEL represent the workflow orchestrated by a dominating entity (the BPEL engine running the BPEL script), WS-CDL defines the same workflow as a protocol between services which are independent peers working together to realize a collaboration: WS-CDL definition can be decomposed in different BPEL scripts, each one executed by a peer in the collaboration.

Recently, two other languages have been proposed: SOAP Service Description Language (Parastatidis, 2006) which enables contract specification on WSDL 2.0 and it is better suited to precisely specify a Web Service interface than representing an orchestration language; Taverna (Wolstencroft, 2005) is a data-centric workflow language which uses data dependencies to describe a workflow of GRID processes.

Any of these XML-based languages is not so useful without a related service creation environment, used to generate such languages from a high-level, possibly graphical representation.

Regarding the service creation environment, WebSphere Studio Application Developer (IBM, 2007) and RapidFLEX Application Server (Pactolus, 2001) provide a graphical SCE easing the service creation process of value added services.

The former strongly relies only on those telecom network resources exposed as Web Services compliant to the Parlay-X specification.

The latter allows creating workflows of elements representing telecom resources exposing their native interfaces or Java code snippets; such workflows are then represented with XTML files which are executed by the proprietary application server. In this platform Web Service invocations might be inserted manually in Java code snippets.

More specifically to JAIN-SLEE, Eclipslee (Eclipslee, 2007) is also available as a SCE for MobiCents services, but it does not support any Web Service facilities, as its underlying platform does not offer any SOAP Resource Adaptor.

Facing with asynchronous interactions

The aim of overcoming the limitations of SOAP toolkits in addressing asynchronous interactions with Web Services it is not just a Telecom Operator prerogative. Recent standard specification like WS-Notification (WSN, 2007) defines how to apply publish-subscribe interaction pattern among Web Services for implementing publish-subscribe interaction style among loosely coupled services, relying on standard SOAP protocol.

Apache Muse project (Muse, 2007) is a Java-based implementation of OASIS standard specifications, like Web Services Resource Framework (WSRF, 2007), Web Services Notification (WSN, 2007) and Web Services Distributed Management (WSDM, 2006).

Muse is a framework upon which developers can build Web Service interfaces for manageable resources. It hides the complexity of dealing with the specifications cited above. Furthermore the applications built with Muse can be deployed both in Apache Axis2 web services container (Apache Axis2, 2008) and in OSGi (OSGi, 2007) environments. Axis2 supports standards like OASIS WS-ReliableMessaging (WS-ReliableMessaging, 2007) and W3C WS-Addressing for providing asynchronous Web Services.

Apollo (Apollo, 2005) is an implementation of the Web Services Resource Framework specifications characterized by exposure of resource properties and property change notifications for a Web Service, code generation from WSRF compliant to WSDL and runtime support for Web Service implementations of WSRF specification.

The main requirement of a Communication Web Service Platform is to manage asynchronous interactions with clients by means of a fully asynchronous WS management system. Along with the synchronous SOAP solution described in the former section, we have implemented a full asynchronous management of client-server interactions.

This was obtained implementing an enhanced version of the SOAP resource adaptor in accordance with WSN family of specifications. WSN defines a set of specifications that standardize the way Web Services can interact using the Notification pattern, which specify a way for consumers to subscribe to a producer for notifications whenever a particular event occurs.

WS-Notification defines interfaces and behavior of five possible roles:

1. *Notification Producer* receives subscription requests from notification consumers;
2. *Notification Consumer*;
3. *Subscriber*;
4. *Subscription Manager* has to dispatch subscription requests, coming from event consumers, to event producers;
5. *Notification Broker*, if present, can both handle subscriptions and notifications transmissions.

Each subscription contains *Topic* (on which the subscription has been made), the *Id* of the Notification Consumer interested to events related to the specified topics and *Optional information* (whose semantics is not specified in the specification).

If a broker is not present, the Notification Producer must maintain the subscriptions list and handling notification dispatching. A producer can delegate the subscriptions list handling to the Subscription Manager.

The set of WS-Notification specifications includes WS-Base Notification (WSN, 2007), WS-Brokered Notification (WS-Brokered Notification, 2006), and WS-Topics (WS-Topics, 2006). The *WS-BaseNotification* specification defines the Web Services interfaces for notification producers and notification consumers. *WS-BrokeredNotification* (WS-Brokered Notification, 2006) defines the Web Services interfaces for notification brokers, when message broker is present among notification producers and consumers. The *WS-Topics* (WS-Topics, 2006) defines a mechanism to organize and categorize items of interest for subscription known as topics. This specification presents an XML description of topics and associated meta data.

Topics are a mechanism for organizing notification messages and can be organized hierarchically.

In case of WS-BaseNotification, the subscriber checks the topics hierarchy and makes a subscription request to the producer (once found some topic). In the other hand, the producer updates the subscriptions list and must send to all subscribed consumers the notification messages. Event consumer will receive the events and it may modify the resource state, according to the related subscription manager.

In case of brokered notification, the Notification Producer is responsible for specifying the list of topics to which users can subscribe, and topics can be added or deleted dynamically. The sequence for the publish-subscribe model is as follows:

1. The Notification Producer communicates to the broker the topics to which the subscribers can subscribe;
2. The subscriber registers its own callback to the broker;
3. The Notification Producer creates a message related to a topic and sends it to the broker;
4. The broker delivers the message to the appropriate subscribers.

Once all the subscribers have been notified and each subscriber has acknowledged the receiving of a message, the integration broker removes the message from the topic.

The WS-Notification specifications can be compared to some publish/subscribe mechanisms, like CORBA Event Service (Filho, 2003) and the

CORBA Notification Service (Gruber, 2001).

In (De Labey, 2008), authors have noticed that WSN still lacks support for advanced features concerning implicit service interactions that are currently available in CORBA-based systems.

In order to increase the expressiveness of the WSN event notification system, they have suggested to improve the WSN broker by supporting event correlation and ECA rules, which can be activated or deactivated based on events.

Web Services can act asynchronously as long as they make their own state persistent. This goal can be fulfilled by implementing the Web Service Resource Framework family of specifications (WSRF, 2007). The WS-Resource framework (WS-Resource Framework, 2004) is inspired by the work of the Global Grid Forum's Open Grid Services Infrastructure (OGSI) Working Group.

WSRF defines a generic and open framework for modeling and accessing stateful resources using Web Services. It provides mechanisms to describe views on the state, to support management of the state through properties associated with the Web Service, and to describe how these mechanisms are extensible to groups of Web services. WS-Resource framework provides building blocks for representing and structuring notifications; these are used and extended by WS-Notification specifications in order to allow requestors to ask to be asynchronously notified of changes occurred to particular resource property values.

In StarSLEE we extended JAIN-SLEE in order to implement the publish-subscribe interaction style, by adding a SOAP server which redirects inbound messages to the said SOAP resource adaptor which in turn creates:

- A SOAP service context;
- A client formal subscription to further outbound messages and
- A SOAP event to be dispatched by means of the event router.

On the other hand, whenever a service needs to contact back the client, it triggers an event to the SOAP RA which calls back the client.

In the following figure is shown what happens when a service instance in the SLEE container terminates its execution: before the service instance is released it notifies the router with an End of Service event, which is forwarded to the SOAP RA. Then the SOAP RA looks for the related SOAP service context, and the corresponding Web Service implementation is notified. At this point the Web Service provider notifies the Service Requestor with a SOAP message, containing the Web Service response.

Service Discovery

Service discovery and advertising are key facets in a telecom environment: for example, a SIP network leverages on its native publish-subscribe model to "push" new services information to clients belonging to a given network domain.

A communication service platform aiming at composing and integrating Web Services is fully concerned with static and dynamic discovery of Web Services. Furthermore the discovery process has to sort candidate services that fulfils given functionality and quality parameters, and can be combined in order to realize value added services.

Therefore, new processes, methods, and tools need to be provided to extend current software development practices to support these requirements. Discovering Web Services dynamically consists in identifying alternative services to replace services already participating in a given composition that may become unavailable or fail to meet specific functional or quality requirements during service execution. It is a challenging activity since it requires efficient discovery of alternative services that precisely match the functional and quality requirements needed and replacement of these services during run-time execution in an efficient and non-intrusive way.

Figure 9. Web Service Response: SOAP Notification

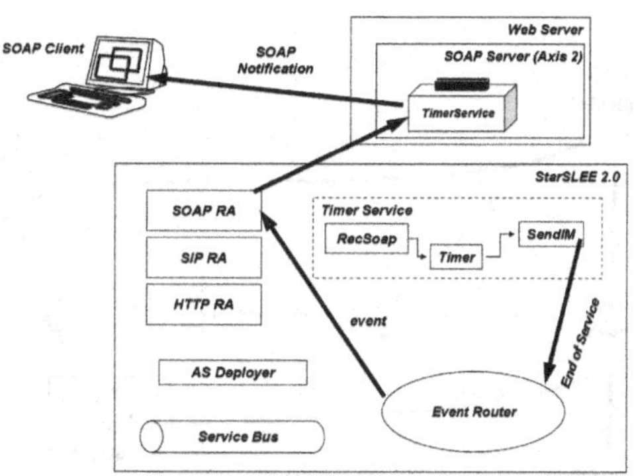

At its foundation, Universal Description Discovery and Integration (UDDI, 2007) is a group of specifications that lets Web Service providers publish information about their Web Services on a public UDDI registry and it lets Web Service discoverers or requesters search that information to find a Web Service and run it.

UDDI specification is then focused on the information model that enables a suitable categorization of the published services, but it does not address the following important requirements in telecom domain:

- Late binding: since service references are published as static data, Web Services are forced to be up and running continuously on a given URL. No dynamic instantiation of services and references is therefore possible.
- Personalization: UDDI does not support any form of personalization, i.e. the result of a specific query is the same for any requestor.
- Authorization: there is no mechanism in UDDI that allows defining and enforcing complex authorization policies for service requestors when inquiring the registry and retrieving the details of the services.
- Reference validity: UDDI does not guarantee that the service reference returned to the application (in response to a Get Service operation) really points to a Web Service.

In order to meet these requirements a "UDDI proxy" has been prototyped (see Figure 10). The proxy routes queries from a client application to the UDDI registry and provides additional and personalized capabilities, mediating the access to the actual UDDI registry.

The proxy can control the access to the information contained in the UDDI Registry allowing/denying the access, basing on a Service Requestor's Authorization Profile. The UDDI proxy is also able to dynamically create the Web Services instances, guaranteeing the existence of the Web Service, and to personalize the Web Service instances based on the Service Requestor identity.

The proxy exposes standard UDDI interfaces to the applications, so that the interactions with it are right the same as the ones with ordinary UDDI registry (i.e. UDDI clients use the same UDDI API). The solution has minimal impact on the pre-existing architecture since it does not require modifying the existing elements. In fact it only implies to add a separate node (the proxy), reconfiguring the applications by providing the reference to the new node and by configuring the UDDI registry to accept inquiries from the proxy.

Figure 10. UDDI proxy architecture

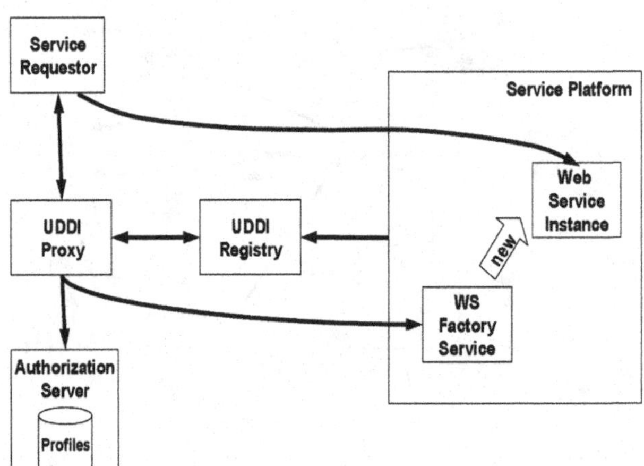

CONCLUSIONS AND FUTURE WORK

There is an increasing interest in introducing Web Service technology in telecom service platforms. On one hand it is an opportunity to enable new business models and reach new markets, nevertheless it points out that to get to a successful applicability to telecom domain many weaknesses have still to be overcome. A communication Web Service platform would be more familiar for Internet application developers, but it could imply some limitation in the usage of the network capabilities in terms of provided features.

The process of integrating Web Services in telecom platforms and services has shown that the Web Service orchestration approach has some limitations: the critical requirement for publish-subscribe interaction model is not supported, even if recent standards like WS-Notification (WSN, 2007) and recent W3C submissions like SOAP over JMS (SOAP-JMS, 2008) are improving Web Service applicability to telecom platforms.

Meanwhile emerging event based containers (such as JAIN-SLEE) are designed for telecom environment but may be extended to be capable of integrating Web Services.

Our work shows both benefits and drawbacks in supplying a telecom application server (inspired to JAIN-SLEE) with Web Services facilities to enable Value Added Services composition and execution. We defined StarSDL, a new service description language to cover the lacks of JAIN-SLEE specification and we developed a SOAP resource adaptor (which is essential for exposing JAIN-SLEE service as Web Services) able to forward SOAP requests both in the typical request-response interaction style and in the emerging asynchronous one, based on the recent implementation of WSN provided by Axis 2.

At the service creation level we defined in StarSCE service creation environment a semi-automated way for generating SOAP-related SBBs, and for modifying automatically all service descriptors, in order to interact with the SOAP resource adaptor.

The SCE, together with the StarSDL language, and JAIN-SLEE will ease IT and telecom service integration, thanks to a new way of reusing components and Web Services to provide advanced value added services which can also be exported as communication Web Services. This will ease the service creation process reducing time-to-market for the new services.

Current work is focused on extending current limitations of JAIN-SLEE implementations like the execution of services running on a single network node. We aim at using WSN as an inter-communication standard among different JAIN-SLEE containers running on distributed nodes, in order to deploy services which orchestrate many SBBs running on different JAIN-SLEE containers: by mapping events coming from resource adaptors to WSN events and vice versa, an event router of the JAIN-SLEE container can behave like a WSN Broker.

ACKNOWLEDGMENT

The authors want to thank Gianpiero Fici, Carlo Alberto Licciardi, Anna Picarella, Alessia Salmeri, and Massimo Valla for their valuable contribution to this work. which has been partially funded by the European Commission, under contract IST-2002-2.3.2.3, project SeCSE (Service Centric Systems Engineering).

REFERENCES

W3C (2007). World Wide Web Consortium. Retrieved December 5, 2007, from http://www.w3.org

Active, B. P. E. L. (2007). ActiveBPEL project website. Retrieved November 30, 2007, from http://www.active-endpoints.com/active-bpel-engine-overview.htm

Apache Axis2 (2008). Apache AXIS2 project website. Retrieved February 23, 2009, from http://ws.apache.org/axis2/

Apache Axis. (2006). Apache AXIS project website. Retrieved February 23, 2009, from http://ws.apache.org/axis/

Apollo (2005). Apache Apollo project website. Retrieved February 24, 2009, from http://incubator.apache.org/projects/apollo.html

Bakker, J. L., & Jain, R. (2002, April). Next generation service creation using XML scripting language. In *Proceedings of the IEEE International Conference on Communications (ICC2002), New York, USA* (pp. 2001-2007). Washington: IEEE Computer Society.

Baravaglio, A., Licciardi, C. A., & Venezia, C. (2005, August). Web Service Applicability in telecommunications Service Platforms. In *Proceedings of the International Conference on Next Generation Web Services Practices (NWeSP), Seoul, Korea* (pp. 39-44). Washington: IEEE Computer Society.

Belaunde, M., & Falcarin, P. (2008, June). Realizing an MDA and SOA Marriage for the Development of Mobile Services. In *4th European Conference on Model Driven Architecture (ECMDA-2008), Berlin, Germany* (pp. 393-405). Springer-Verlag.

BPEL. (2003). *Business Process Execution Language for Web Services (Version 1.1)*. Retrieved December 5, 2007, from http://www.ibm.com/developerworks/library/specification/ws-bpel/

Burgy, L., Consel, C., Latry, F., Lawall, J., Palix, N., & Reveillere, L. (2006, June). Language Technology for Internet-Telephony Service Creation. In *Proceedings of the IEEE International Conference on Communications (ICC2006), vol. 4, Istanbul, Turkey* (pp. 1795–1800). Washington: IEEE Computer Society.

CCXML. (2007). *W3C, Voice Browser Call Control: CCXML version 1.0 specification*. Retrieved December 5, 2007, from http://www.w3.org/TR/ccxml/

Chung, J.-Y., Lin, K.-J., & Mathieu, R. G. (2003). Web Services Computing: Advancing Software Interoperability. *IEEE Computer, 36*(10), 35–37.

De Labey, S., & Steegmans, E. (2008, Sept.). Extending WS-Notification with an Expressive Event Notification Broker. In *IEEE International conference on Web Services (ICWS'08), Beijing, China* (pp. 312-319). IEEE Computer Society.

Eclipslee (2007). Eclipslee project website. Retrieved December 30, 2007, from, https://eclipslee.dev.java.net/

ETSI. (2002). *The ETSI OSA Parlay-X 3.0 Specifications*. Retrieved December 5, 2007, from http://portal.etsi.org/docbox/TISPAN/Open/OSA/ParlayX30.html.

Filho, R. S. S., de Souza, C. R. B., & Redmiles, D. F. (2003, June). The design of a configurable, extensible and dynamic notification service. In *Proceedings of the 2nd international workshop on Distributed event-based systems* (pp. 1-8). San Diego, USA.

Glitho, R. H., Khendek, F., & De Marco, A. (2003). Creating Value Added Services in Internet Telephony: An Overview and a Case Study on a High-Level Service Creation Environment. *IEEE Transactions on Systems, Man and Cybernetics. Part C, Applications and Reviews, 33*(4), 446–457. doi:10.1109/TSMCC.2003.818499

Gruber, R. E., Krishnamurthy, B., & Panagos, E. (2001), Corba notification service: Design challenges and scalable solutions. In *Proceedings of the 17th International Conference on Data Engineering,*(pp. 13–20), *Washington, DC, USA*. IEEE Computer Society.

IBM. (2007). *WebSphere Telecom Web Services Server*. Retrieved December 5, 2007, from http://www-306.ibm.com/software/pervasive/serviceserver/.

IMS. (2006). *3GPP TS 23.228: IP multimedia subsystem (Stage 2) standard specification*. Retrieved December 5, 2007, from http://www.3gpp.org/ftp/Specs/html-info/23228.htm

JSR-240. (2008). *JAIN™ SLEE API Specification*. Retrieved March 19, 2009, from http://jcp.org/aboutJava/communityprocess/final/jsr240/index.html.

Licciardi, C. A., & Falcarin, P. (2003). Analysis of NGN Service Creation Technologies. In *IEC Annual Review of Communications, 56* (pp. 537-551). Chicago: IEC (International Engineering Consortium).

Long, D. T., & Page, D. C. (2007). Supporting Portable Applications with JAIN SLEE. In Telecommunications Networks and Applications Conference (pp. 454-459). Australasian: ATNAC.

MobiCents Project. (2007). *MobiCents: The Open Source VoIP Middleware Platform*. Retrieved December 5, 2007, from https://mobicents.dev.java.net/

Muse (2007). Apache Muse project website. Retrieved February 23, 2009, from http://ws.apache.org/muse/

OMA. (2007). *Open Mobile Alliance*. Retrieved December 5, 2007, from http://www.openmobilealliance.org

OpenCloud. (2008). *Rhino 2.0 Developer Preview Release*. Retrieved December 5, 2007, from http://www.opencloud.com/products/rhino-kit/dp1/docs/index.html

OSGi. (2007). OSGi™ - The Dynamic Module System for Java. Retrieved February 23, 2009, from http://www.osgi.org/

Pactolus (2001). RapidFLEX™ Service Creation Environment. Retrieved December 5, 2007, from http://www.pactolus.com/

Parastatidis, S., Woodman, S., Webber, J., Kuo, D., & Greenfield, P. (2006). Asynchronous messaging between Web services using SSDL. *IEEE Internet Computing, 10*(1), 26–39. doi:10.1109/MIC.2006.3

Pollet, T., Maas, G., Marien, J., & Wambecq, A. (2006, April). Telecom services delivery in a SOA. In *Proceedings of 20th International Conference on Advanced Information Networking and Applications (AINA 2006), 2* (pp. 529-533). Los Alamitos: IEEE Computer Society.

Python (2009). Python language's official website. Retrieved March 2 from http://www.python.org/

Rosenberg, J., Lennox, J., & Schulzrinne, H. (1999). Programming Internet telephony services. *IEEE Network, 13*(3), 42–49. doi:10.1109/65.767138

Rosenberg, J., Schulzrinne, H., Camarillo, G., Johnston, A., Peterson, J., Sparks, R., et al. (2002). *SIP: Session Initiation Protocol, RFC 3261*. Retrieved November 21, 2007, from http://www.ietf.org/rfc/rfc3261.txt.

Schülke, A., Abbadessa, D., & Winkler, F. (2006, April). Service Delivery Platform: Critical Enabler to Service Providers' New Revenue Streams. In *Proceedings of World Telecommunications Congress (WTC 2006), Budapest, Hungary.*

SOAP-JMS. (2008). *Simple Object Access Protocol, version 1.2*. Retrieved February 23, 2009, from http://www.w3.org/TR/2008/WD-soapjms-20081121/

UDDI. (2007). *UDDI Specification version 3.0.2*. Retrieved December 5, 2007, from http://uddi.xml.org/specification

Venezia, C., & Falcarin, P. (2006, September). Communication Web Services Composition and Integration. In *Proceedings of International Conference on Web Services (ICWS-06), Chicago, USA* (pp. 523-530). IEEE Press.

Wohed, P., van der Aalst, W. M. P., Dumas, M., & ter Hofstede, A. H. M. (2003, October). Analysis of Web Services Composition Languages: The Case of BPEL4WS. In *Proceedings of the 22nd International Conference on Conceptual Modeling (ER), Chicago, USA* (LNCS 2813, pp. 200-215).

Wolstencroft, K., Oinn, T., Goble, C., Ferris, J., Wroe, C., Lord, P., et al. (2005, December). Panoply of utilities in Taverna. In *First International Conference on e-Science and Grid Computing (e-science), Melbourne, Australia,* (pp. 156-162). Washington: IEEE Computer Society.

WS-Addressing. (2004). *W3C WS-Addressing specification*. Retrieved February 23, 2009, from http://www.w3.org/Submission/ws-addressing/

WS-Brokered Notification. (2006). *OASIS WS-Brokered Notification version 1.3 specification*. Retrieved February 23, 2009, from http://docs.oasis-open.org/wsn/wsn-ws_brokered_notification-1.3-spec-os.pdf

WS-CDL. (2005). *Web Services Choreography Description Language Version 1.0*. Retrieved December 5, 2007, from http://www.w3.org/TR/ws-cdl-10/

WS-ReliableMessaging. (2007). *OASIS WS-Reliable Messaging version 1.1 standard*. Retrieved February 23, 2009, from http://docs.oasis-open.org/ws-rx/wsrm/200702/wsrm-1.1-spec-os-01.pdf

WS-Resource Framework. (2004). Globus Alliance website. Retrieved February 25, 2009, from http://www.globus.org/wsrf/specs/ws-wsrf.pdf

WS-Topics. (2006). *OASIS Web Services Topics version 1.3 specification*. Retrieved February 23, 2009, from http://docs.oasis-open.org/wsn/wsn-ws_topics-1.3-spec-os.pdf

WSDL. (2007). *Web Service Description Language version 1.1 specification*. Retrieved December 5, 2007, from http://www.w3.org/TR/wsdl

WSDM. (2006). *OASIS Web Services Distributed Management standard specification.* Retrieved February 23, 2009, from http://www.oasis-open.org/committees/wsdm/

WSN. (2007). *OASIS Web Service Notification specifications version 1.3.* Retrieved February 23, 2009, from http://www.oasis-open.org/committees/wsn

WSRF. (2007). *OASIS Web Service Resource Framework standard specification.* Retrieved February 23, 2009, from http://www.oasis-open.org/committees/wsrf

Wu, X., & Schulzrinne, H. (2003, May). Programmable end system services using SIP. In *Proceedings of The IEEE International Conference on Communications (ICC 2003), Anchorage, Alaska, USA* (pp. 789-793). IEEE Press.

XPDL. (2007). Workflow Management Coalition: XML Process Description Language, version 2.0 standard. Retrieved December 5, 2007, from http://www.wfmc.org/standards/xpdl.htm

Chapter 20
Workflow Discovery:
Requirements from E-Science and a Graph-Based Solution

Antoon Goderis
University of Manchester, UK

Peter Li
University of Manchester, UK

Carole Goble
University of Manchester, UK

ABSTRACT

Much has been written on the promise of Web service discovery and (semi-) automated composition. In this discussion, the value to practitioners of discovering and reusing existing service compositions, captured in workflows, is mostly ignored. We present the case for workflows and workflow discovery in science and develop one discovery solution. Through a survey with 21 scientists and developers from the myGrid/Taverna workflow environment, workflow discovery requirements are elicited. Through a user experiment with 13 scientists, an attempt is made to build a benchmark for workflow ranking. Through the design and implementation of a workflow discovery tool, a mechanism for ranking workflow fragments is provided based on graph sub-isomorphism detection. The tool evaluation, drawing on a corpus of 89 public workflows and the results of the user experiment, finds that, for a simple showcase, the average human ranking can largely be reproduced.

INTRODUCTION

Problem Statement

As more scientific resources become available on the World Wide Web, scientists increasingly rely on Web and Grid services for performing in silico (i.e., computerised) experiments. Bioinformatics, for example, has seen a spectacular rise in the availability of distributed services—the myGrid/ Taverna workbench[1] offers access to over 3000 of these. A popular example of a bioinformatics Web service is BLAST (Basic Local Alignment Search Tool), a service for finding regions of genome sequence similarity.[2]

Distributed service composition is difficult, be it manual or automatic. In this light, and to promote cross-disciplinary scientific collaborations, research councils worldwide are building a supporting infrastructure under the banner of e-Science. Exemplar initiatives include the Open Middleware Infrastructure Institute in the United Kingdom,[3] D-Grid in Germany,[4] and the Kepler project in the USA.[5]

Workflow technology has been widely adopted in e-Science as the mechanism for orchestrating both distributed and local resources from within one environment. It potentially allows the e-Scientist to describe and enact her experimental processes in a structured, repeatable and verifiable way. Figure 1a displays a simple bioinformatics workflow loaded up in the myGrid/Taverna workbench (Oinn, Greenwood, Addis, Alpdemir, Ferris, Glover, Goble, Goderis, Hull, Marvin, Li, Lord, Pocock, Senger, Stevens, Wipat, & Wroe, 2006) on the left hand side, while a list of available services and workflows is shown on the right.

With the adoption of workflow environments by scientists comes a boom in the number of freely available scientific workflows. This motivates the problem of workflow discovery. Much has been written on the promise of Web service discovery and (semi-) automated composition. In this discussion, the value to practitioners of discovering and reusing existing service compositions, captured in workflows, is mostly ignored. Scientists have a need for finding workflows, either to draw from previous work investigating hypotheses similar to theirs or to discover fixes for broken workflows.

Article Contribution and Structure

Based on a case study from bioinformatics, the article (i) motivates the use of workflows in science, (ii) gathers requirements for workflow discovery, (iii) attempts building a benchmark to evaluate workflow discovery, (iii) develops a discovery technique and (iv) evaluates the technique. We expand on the work described in Goderis, Li, and Goble (2006) by presenting the case for workflows in bioinformatics, the role of the BPEL language, workflow discovery across workflow systems, and by covering related work in more detail.

In the next section we present the case for workflows in science. The following section contrasts Web service reuse with workflow reuse. Next, we consider why BPEL is not the workflow language of choice in e-science and present open issues for workflow discovery across systems. The subsequent section presents workflow discovery use cases, leading to workflow discovery requirements collected from 21 scientists and developers from the myGrid/Taverna workflow environment. Through a user experiment with 13 scientists, the next section attempts to build a benchmark for evaluating workflow rankings, with mixed results. Then, through the design and implementation of a workflow discovery tool, a mechanism for ranking workflow fragments is provided based on graph sub-isomorphism detection. The tool evaluation of the following section draws on a corpus of 89 public workflows to combine the results of the next two sections. It finds that, for a simple showcase, the average human ranking can largely be reproduced. We relate our work to the literature in the following section and the final section concludes.

Figure 1a. The AffyidToBlastxPDB.xml workflow loaded in the myGrid/Taverna workbench. The Available services pane provides access to both services and workflows.

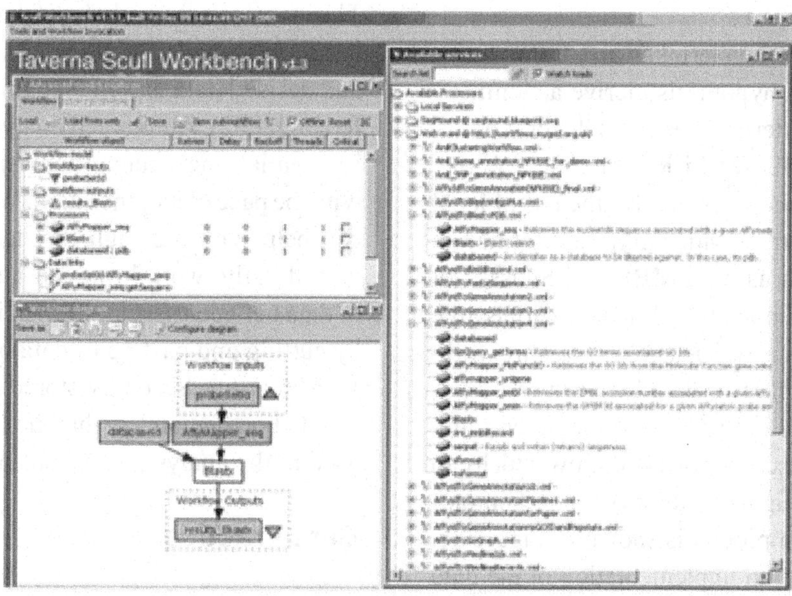

Figure 1b. Screenshot showing the Junger et al., (2003) workflow for the identification of homologous proteins between organisms. The workflow uses NCBI Blast, the EBI instance of the Sequence Retrieval System and two EMBOSS programs, Emma and Pretty Plot, which have all been wrapped as Soaplab style Web services.

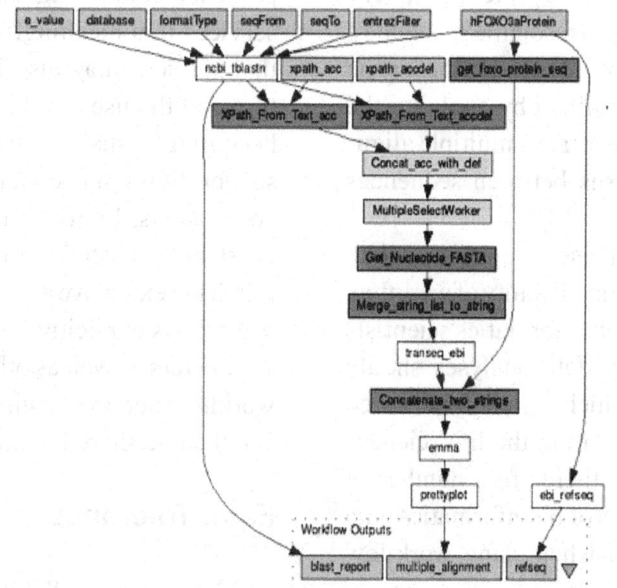

WORKFLOWS IN E-SCIENCE: A CASE STUDY

Analyses of data are undertaken in bioinformatics in order to test a hypothesis, derive a summary or search for patterns (Stevens, Glover, Greenhalgh, Jennings, Pearce, Li, Radenkovic, &Wipat, 2003). These procedures involve the use of local and remote resources which may be information repositories such as the EMBL and Swiss-Prot databases, or computational analysis tools like BLAST and ClustalW. Such procedures are workflows where the flow of data between resources has been directed in a pre-defined manner (Oinn et al., 2005). An example of a workflow which can be used to investigate to identify genes homologous to a given a protein is shown in Figure 1b. This workflow is an implementation of the data analysis described by Junger, Rintelen, Stocker, Wasserman, Végh, Radimerski, Greenberg, and Hafen (2003) which involved identifying proteins in the fruit fly, Drosophila melanogaster, which are homologous to the human protein FOXO3. The workflow begins by performing a BLAST search using the human FOXO3 protein as a query sequence to return similar Drosophila sequences. The evolutionary relationships between these gene sequences are then determined by applying the ClustalW algorithm to generate a multiple alignment showing the patterns between sequences (Figure 1b).

The accessibility of these resources as Web Services in addition to the availability of workflow technology has enabled bioinformatics scientists to explicitly define how data analyses should be executed as scripts which can then be stored for later use and shared within the life sciences community. In addition, there are a number of advantages in the analysis of bioinformatics data which can be addressed when using workflow technology:

Automation

The increase in the volume of data year upon year due to the continuous generation of new primary and derived data is well recognised (Hey & Trefethen, 2002). Automated analyses of these data is essential since manual analysis cannot keep up with the pace of its generation. Workflow systems can help with the high throughput analysis of data. Firstly, workflows can automate the flow of data between services which is done manually by cutting and pasting of data between forms in Web browsers. Secondly, stored workflows can be enacted on demand so that the latest data can be used in the analysis as well as new input data.

Best Practice

Workflows can be complex especially if many services are used in the analysis pipeline. The construction of such complex workflows requires substantial intellectual effort since intimate knowledge of the services used in the workflows is required from a syntactic and semantic standpoint for connecting the flow of data between services in a meaningful manner. With the fact that services may also be asynchronous in nature and the use of APIs, workflow systems are becoming visual programming languages and so workflows may contain data and control flow components. In addition, analysis tools such as Blast and ClustalW are sophisticated services requiring extensive parameterization in their use. Workflows explicitly capture the values of these parameters as well as other metadata used by the workflow author showing its best practice which can then be shared within the community.

Fault Tolerance

Issues with the reliability of services are particularly prevalent in the area of bioinformatics (Li, Chen, & Romanovsky, 2006). Academic and non-commercial organisations deploy Web Services for public use by scientists in the life sciences community without any prior service level agreements. Despite this fact, such services are used by scientists knowing of their unreliability despite the fact that they may not always be available for the reasons outlined above (Stevens, Tipney, Wroe, Oinn, Senger, Lord, Goble, Brass, & Tassabehji, 2004). It is therefore essential that such e-Science workflows are executed using the most reliable of services especially if workflows are long lived during their execution. Workflow systems like Taverna allow alternate services which are used if the initial service fails in the workflow (Oinn et al., 2005).

Recording of Provenance

The building of reliable workflows is reliant upon data in the form of performance metrics about services (Li et al., 2006) which may be captured during the enactment of workflows. This information is provenance which identifies the source and processing of data by recording the metadata and intermediate results associated with the workflow. This type of information provides a useful audit trail since its analysis can determine the origin of erroneous or unexpected results which can sometimes be produced by workflow processes.

WORKFLOW REUSE VERSUS WEB SERVICE REUSE

Now that we have established that there are multiple advantages to using workflows for online science, it is useful to compare workflows with Web services. Workflows and Web services are different yet similar, and this has an impact on their reuse potential. Both Web services and workflows in essence describe processes. Many different workflow languages exist, such as BPEL (the Business Process Execution Language), MOML (MOdeling Markup Language) of the Kepler workflow system (Ludaescher, Altintas, Berkley, Higgins, Jaeger, Jones, Lee, Tao, & Zhao, 2005) or Scufl (the Simple conceptual unified flow language) of Taverna (Oinn et al., 2005). Web services on the other hand are typically standardised over SOAP and WSDL interfaces. Online workflows typically orchestrate Web services in conjunction with other kinds of services: local components, different types of distributed services (Taverna, for instance, accesses eight different types [Lord, Alper, Wroe, & Goble, 2005]), even humans can be modelled as part of the process. Workflows are not executable without a workflow enactor. When combined with an enactor, they can be published as a Web service, and in turn possibly incorporated by another workflow.

Given their different nature, there is a difference in the reuse potential of workflows and Web services. Workflow reuse can be seen as the reuse of editable processes, whereas Web service reuse is reuse of encapsulated processes. It is the difference between being able to repurpose other people's work by editing it versus incorporating other people's work. Workflows allow a change of the process's data and control flow.

TO BPEL OR NOT TO BPEL, IS THAT THE QUESTION?

For workflow reuse to be possible, one needs a big set of workflows to reuse from. Standardizing on one workflow language would give e-science a head start in creating a freely available worldwide pool. Given its current status as a de facto standard in the business world, one might expect the Business Process Execution Language (BPEL) to be the language of choice in the e-science world, too, and hence the language to focus on for any work on workflow discovery. BPEL, however, has not seen wide adoption in scientific workflows. In a recent survey of six e-science middleware projects, we found that only one project was using the language (Goderis, Sattler, Lord, & Goble, 2005).

A different sample by Yu and Buyya shows the same phenomenon (Yu & Buyya, 2005).

What is the explanation for this? There are a number of factors that influence the adoption of a workflow language by e-scientists. They include: (i) workflow language expressivity in tune with the modeling problem, (ii) language abstractions reflecting user skills, (iii) data and provenance management, (iv) user interaction, (v) the availability of a scientist's favorite service and (vi) the prospect of a community sharing workflows and best practice in workflow design. It turns out the current BPEL specification and environments are unsatisfactory on most counts.

In terms of language expressivity, scientific problems often involve manipulation of datasets or simulations, e.g. gene annotation pipelines (Stevens et al. 2004) or Lattice-Boltzmann simulations in fluid dynamics (Haines, Mckeown, Pickles, Pinning, Porter, & Riding, 2005). Scientific workflow environments have favored models of computation that clearly reflect the scientific problems. The models of computation in use are primarily styles of functional programming for dataflow problems (e.g., a lambda calculus with a list monad for Taverna's Scufl language (Turi, Missier, De Roure, Goble, & Oinn, 2007) and time-based computation for simulations (e.g., the use of Continuous Time [Brooks, Lee, Liu, Neuendorffer, Zhao, & Zheng, 2005] in Kepler). Some environments allow the heterogeneous composition of these models of computation within one workflow (notably Kepler; see Goderis, Brooks, Altintas, Lee, & Goble, 2007). In contrast, BPEL semantics have long suffered from ambiguity, primarily due to BPEL's origin as the merger between Microsoft's XLANG semantics based on pi-calculus, and IBM's Web Service Flow Language (WSFL) based on a Petri Net operational semantics (Narayanan & McIlraith, 2003).

When it comes to language abstractions, typical BPEL environments expect users to program in terms of service messaging or handling state. In contrast, scientific environments often introduce abstractions allowing scientists to concentrate on higher levels of functionality, for instance the notion of a Processor in Taverna, an Actor in Kepler, or a Service in DiscoveryNet (Al Sairaf, Emmanouil, Ghanem, Giannadakis, Guo, Kalaitzopoulos, Osmond, Rowe, Syed, & Wendel, 2003). In the case of Taverna, IBM's WSFL language constructs were originally adopted but abandoned again in favour of a simpler language (Scufl) after none of the targeted users (bioinformaticians) were able to write such specifications based on them..

BPEL was not built with scientific datasets in mind. As Chappell notes (Chappell, 2005), everything is fine as long as a BPEL-defined process uses only XML data and communicates with other software only through Web services. In reality, a host of data sources, ranging from flat files to relational data, are used by scientists in conjunction with different types of distributed services. This is closely related to the importance of capturing scientific data provenance, that is, the origin of data, enabling scientists to verify and reproduce earlier results. Provenance support is mostly lacking in BPEL workflow systems. Providing support for capturing the intermediate and end data results of workflow enactments is the focus of many e-science systems. The scientific workflow community has recently explored different approaches based on a joint Provenance Challenge[6] and has scheduled provenance and workflow interoperability as the second challenge.

Similarly, the BPEL specification does not provide support for workflows requiring stepwise interactions with scientists, or, as mentioned, for accessing different types of services other than Web services (Chappell, 2005). Again, these are key requirements for scientific workflows. Among others, Taverna, Kepler and DiscoveryNet have built in functionality to cater for non-Web services and user interaction.

Finally, a scientist is more likely to adopt a given workflow language when there exists a large number of prior examples from which to draw.

The prospect of a community sharing workflows and best practice has led the Taverna environment for example to launch the myExperiment.org sharing and collaboration portal. We are not aware of similar repositories of BPEL workflows.

Some of the points could be addressed easily by changing the BPEL specification or by customizing BPEL environments. The current situation, however, driven by widely differing user requirements, has lead to the proliferation of workflow languages and systems in e-Science. They are likely to stay and are indicators that a worldwide pool of workflows will be created, with interoperability at differing levels.

This article focuses on workflow discovery in the context of a single workflow environment only—the Taverna workbench. Given the lack of a standardized language and a desire to maximize workflow reuse potential, a workflow sharing and collaboration platform would need to cater for workflows from different environments. With this comes the question of workflow discovery across environments. The following issues arise in this context, all of which are currently open.

1. *What can be meaningfully discovered across workflow systems?* Suppose I find a workflow created in an environment that is not my own—what can I meaningfully do with it? One option would be to integrate it in my workflow while executing it based on its original workflow engine. Examples of such integration exist between the Taverna and the VL-e environments.[7] In case I would like to make changes to it, however, could I import it as is into my environment, or import only parts of it, or only its data products?
2. *What is the impact of workflow language expressivity on discovery tools?* How much knowledge does a discovery tool need in terms of the data flow (e.g. list transformations performed, semantic descriptions of data) and control flow (e.g. state transitions or events) of a workflow in order to adequately solve discovery tasks? Different queries require different kinds of information. Which queries are common between systems? For example, one view is that workflow developers will be interested in finding prior examples of implemented complex control flow patterns (Goderis et al., 2005). It seems unlikely that that same detailed control flow description is needed to understand the overall scientific task of a workflow, which is the topic of discovery at a higher, domain specific level.
3. *Is a universal representation for workflow discovery feasible?* Work in the Workflow Management Coalition (WfMC)[8] has lead to XPDL, a process design format for storing the visual diagram and process syntax of business process models, as well as extended product attributes. XPDL was designed to support interoperability, not discovery. Recent initiatives like the second Provenance Challenge or, likewise, the VL-e workflow interoperability bus (Zhao et al., 2006) have a similar focus. Early examples of work on a semantic representation specifically for workflow discovery (based on the Web Ontology Language OWL) and not just service discovery can be found in Hull, Zolin, Bovykin, Horrocks, Sattler, and Stevens (2006) and in Goderis, Sattler, Lord, and Goble (2005b). None of these proposals have been evaluated for a range of workflow discovery tasks and across environments yet.

WORKFLOW DISCOVERY USE CASES

In specific scientific domains, collections of workflows are now starting to pile up. To give an example, to date in myGrid/Taverna some 500 workflows have been built, of a size ranging from five to 50 distributed services and covering biological topics like gene annotation (Stevens et al., 2004), protein structure prediction, microarray analysis (Li, Hayward, Jennings, et al., 2004), and systems biology.

Workflow by Example

In biology, users are often not an expert with computers, and therefore have a strong incentive to reuse as much of the existing workflow engineering as possible. As more of these workflows are released, we are indeed witnessing that bioinformaticians start to share, discover, reuse, and repurpose stand-alone compositions of services, or workflow fragments. Researchers repurpose an existing workflow or workflow fragment by first discovering one that is close enough to be the basis of a new workflow for a different purpose, and then making small changes to it. For example, consider the workflow AffyidToBlastxPDB.xml in Figure 2. It performs a BLAST search over some genes pulled out from a microarray experiment. This workflow sensibly could be adapted to incorporate retrieval of protein pathway annotation, perform protein structure prediction, and multiple researchers have done so in the past. In effect, such an approach represents a workflow by example style to building workflows, standing on the shoulders of colleagues in order to devise new workflows. In an earlier survey across middleware projects (Goderis et al., 2005), we found that workflow reuse and repurposing is also happening within research groups and projects in ecology, chemoinformatics, and engineering, treating experiments as commodities and "knowhow" in their own right.

The workflow by example approach complements the popular view in the Web services literature that online processes will be composed (semi-) automatically from scratch. Workflows hold within them successful examples of working service compositions which can help future compositions. In fact, the amalgamated collection of these workflows de facto provides the closest we currently have to a worldwide "Web of Services" (as opposed to a Web of pages) because workflows document which sets of real world services fit well together.

Use Cases for Workflow Discovery

In Wroe, Goble, Goderis, Lord, Miles, Papay, Alper, and Moreau (2007), a workflow lifecycle is presented that extends beyond execution in Taverna to include the discovery of previous relevant workflow designs, the reuse of those designs and their subsequent publication. Workflow reuse is expected to take place in e-Science in the following ways: personal reuse, reuse by collaborators and reuse by third parties who the workflow author

Figure 2. The exemplar workflow AffyidToBlastx-PDB.xml in more detail. From a workflow input (accompanied by a triangle), the workflow accesses the AffyMapper and BlastX Web services (the middle boxes) and yields an output (indicated by an upside down triangle).

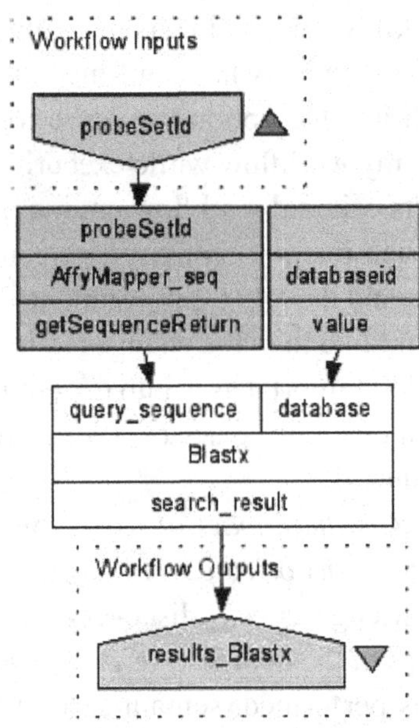

never met (Goderis et al. 2005). We provide new use cases here, specific to workflow discovery and based on a bioinformatics workflow repository. The repository is publicly available at www.myExperiment.org. In general, few workflow repositories have been made publicly available, and even fewer have similar workflows in them. The closest to our repository is that of the Kepler project (Ludaescher et al., 2005), which to date offers some 20 workflows covering different sciences.

1. **Personal discovery:** Building large workflows can be a lengthy process, and in some cases can take over a year. The handling of workflow versioning and evolution are pressing issues in e-Science because the development of scientific workflows yields many versions. Manually keeping track of the relationships is a challenging task as the workflows become more complex, so versioning support is required. Versioning can be seen as a case of "personal reuse." For example, bioinformatician Peter working on the myGrid project has been building microarray workflows to research Graves' disease for over a year now, and managed to produce 66 related workflows. One day he comes to work, only to discover he cannot quite remember how workflow

AffyidToGeneAnnotation2.xml, shown in Figure 3, differs from workflow AffyidToGeneAnnotation4.xml, shown in Figure 4, or from the version that lies in between. Unfortunately any documentation is missing. Can one provide support for Peter to quickly discover how his workflows differ?

2. **Discovery by collaborators:** Scientists are typically part of a research group and various research projects, inside of which they exchange knowledge. For example, Paul, a fresh PhD student eager to build microarray workflows, has heard news from his group leader that Peter did a lot of work with microarray services a while back. Unfortunately, Peter has since moved universities and on to another project. All that remains of his work is a public directory of

Figure 3. Workflow 1, AffyidToGeneAnnotation2.xml.

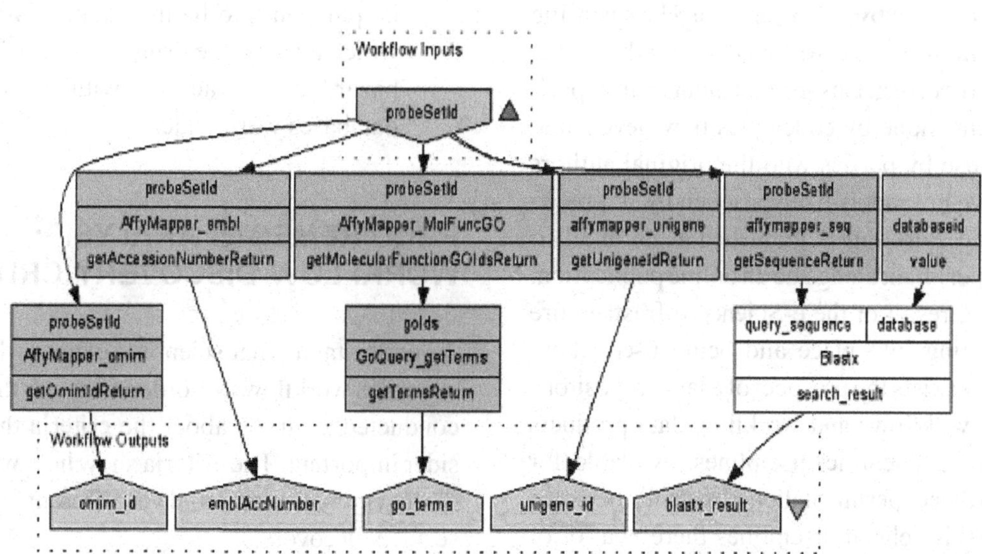

Figure 4. Workflow 2, AffyidToGeneAnnotation4.xml.

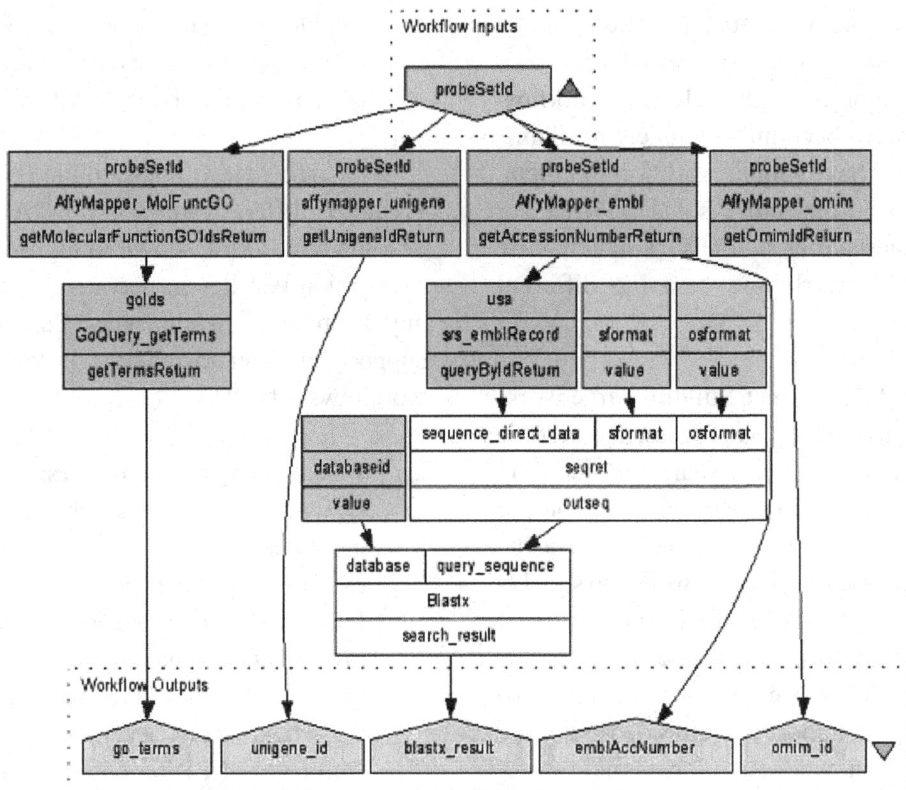

workflows at www.myexperiment.org. How can one best support Paul in making sense of the workflows?

3. **Discovery by third parties:** The scientific community is distributed across the globe, and people get insight and input from experiments done by colleagues they never met. Reuse by parties who the original authors have not met is likely, especially if a packaged workflow is published as an in silico experiment alongside an online publication. As a result of the e-Science infrastructure coming into place and being used, there now exists the prospect of a large repository of workflows and workflow data products across scientific disciplines, available for further experimentation. Especially between closely related disciplines there is a lot of potential for overlap and collaboration. For example, chemoinformatics workflows producing candidates for drug development can be plugged into bioinformatics workflows which retrieve the drug candidates' known hazardous interactions within cells from databases worldwide.

REQUIREMENTS ANALYSIS: WORKFLOW DISCOVERY CRITERIA

To understand what scientists expect when discovering workflows in order to reuse them, we conducted a survey about the criteria they consider important. The criteria show how workflow discovery is similar to and yet different from Web service discovery.

Participants

During two ^{my}Grid/Taverna User Day events (May 5-6 and November 15, 2005), 21 out of a total of 45 participants completed a questionnaire, of which 15 were bioinformaticians and six software developers.

Materials

A questionnaire was designed which asked users to indicate the importance of various criteria for doing workflow discovery. The questions were based on the capabilities offered by the ^{my}Grid/Taverna environment, with which the participants were familiar. The questions also probed for users' general attitude towards workflow reuse. The survey and the survey data are available online.[9] This survey complements an earlier one with interviews of core developers of six e-Science middleware projects, which is reported on in Goderis et al. (2005) and identifies seven bottlenecks for workflow reuse and repurposing.

Procedure

Participants were handed out a questionnaire during the User Days. Users were asked to rate the relevance of various search criteria, with values ranging from 1 (unimportant) to 5 (highly relevant).

Results

It took participants 15 minutes on average to complete the questions. The following answers were obtained.

1. **Sharing attitude:** All subjects indicated they wanted to share. Some were more nuanced and would share workflows but not their data inputs or outputs.
2. **Discovery based on workflow signature:** Four participants wrote they would search for workflows in the same way as they do for services. The question of workflow discovery then becomes one of discovery of a Web service based on its signature. We asked users how important various service search criteria were to them. All came out as relevant. The criteria, in order of decreasing relevance to participants, were: Task, Input, Output, Online documentation, Service Provider, Underlying Resource used (e.g. a particular database), and Algorithm used (e.g. a particular clustering algorithm). For details we refer to the online survey data. In an optional Other: field, users could enter additional criteria. A few users entered Quality of Service parameters here, in particular performance and reliability measures.
3. **Discovery based on workflow structure:** Five participants indicated they would not only rely on using a workflow's signature during workflow discovery. They expected to be using structural information, such as the services contained in a workflow, the specific subtasks addressed by the workflow or to start from existing template workflows. This suggests a type of discovery based more on the shape or structure of a workflow, using a more behavioural type of information.

We then asked users to rate the following criteria which also rely on structural information. The criteria are presented here in decreasing order of relevance as assigned by users.

- Data flow. Given a set of data points, have these been connected up in an existing base of workflows? Data flow queries came out as very important.
- Service flow. Given a set of services, have these been connected up in an existing base of workflows? Service flow queries also came out as very important.
- Workflow similarity. The use of similarity to identify relevant workflows came out as important.

- Use of specific control flow constructs. Queries based on specific control flow constructs, such as the appearance of looping and conditionals in a workflow, were not considered unimportant. This was against our expectations and indicates that users should be enabled to query specifically for such constructs.

Again, in an optional Other: field, users could also enter additional criteria, but no one did.

REQUIREMENTS ANALYSIS FOR A WORKFLOW DISCOVERY TOOL

Based on the survey, we have established that users consider discovery based on workflow structure to be a valuable part of the workflow discovery process. To support such discovery effectively with an automated tool, we have several questions left to answer:

- A benchmark. How do people rank workflows? Can we replicate this behaviour with a tool, based on a benchmark created by people? An alternative issue, which we do not explore, is the performance of discovery components in terms of response time or scalability.
- Predictive power of criteria. Which criteria are direct predictors of workflow (dis-) similarity?
- The link between task and structure. What can structural similarity of workflows tell us about task similarity?

By means of a follow-on survey we aimed specifically to create a benchmark for a workflow discovery tool. Our setup explores only one scientific domain—whether a tool does well in other domains would be subject to similar benchmarks in those domains. In this section we report on the data gathered during the follow-on survey and its statistical interpretation. Given the weak results of our statistical analysis afterwards, we are only able to provide a partial answer to the above questions.

Participants

During a myGrid/Taverna User Day event (February 6, 2005), 13 out of a total of 18 users completed an exercise to rate the similarity between an exemplar workflow (shown in Figure 2) and other workflows. Nine users were bioinformaticians and four were software developers.

Materials

The user experiment included the use of an online survey, a corpus of similar online workflows and the rendition of those workflows. All are made available online, see Footnote 9.

1. **An online survey:** An online survey was created containing three main sections.[10] The first section gathered basic information on the subject and established whether they understood the biology behind the exemplar workflow. The second part asked users to rate the workflows and their confidence in doing so. The final part asked which additional information would be helpful in making similarity assessments and whether they found the exercise difficult.

2. **A corpus of public workflows:** We used a corpus of 89 Taverna workflows as the basis for the exercise. The majority of workflows in the corpus (66) were created by one of the authors in support of research on Graves disease (Li et al., 2004) and, as a result, are highly related and form a good basis for a workflow similarity experiment. The biological goal of this set of workflows is to discover genes involved in the disease based on microarray data and to prepare the geno-

typing of single nucleotide polymorphisms (SNPs) which are nucleotide variations that occur in those genes. We made the workflows available online and rendered them as icons and diagrams. The workflows can be accessed from within Taverna, as shown in Figure 1a. Five workflows were selected from the corpus as comparison material for the exemplar workflow of Figure 2. The comparison workflows are shown in Figures 3 -7. They differ on dimensions such as size, node orderings, and differences in the scope of the biological task.

Procedure

The survey was presented as an exercise that was an integral part of the training at the User Day. The stated goal of the exercise was to allow a user to study and try to understand some more complex workflow diagrams, while allowing the [my]Grid team to understand how similarity between workflows is perceived. Users first were shown an overview of all available workflows, to give them an impression of the complexity involved in the manual discovery task. They were then explained the concept of a benchmark. Five workflows were presented for comparison, pre-selected from the corpus.

For each workflow, users were presented with five questions to judge how similar it was to the exemplar workflow. To indicate the similarity between a pair of workflows, users selected a bullet from nine options (see Figure 8).

Each bullet corresponds to a value: 1 corresponds to Identical, 5 to Similar, and 9 to Not similar at all. Users also provided a measure of confidence in their similarity assessment, ranging over: High--Medium--Low, with High having value 1 and Low being equal to 5. Finally, they had to rate how useful they found six factors for estimating similarity, with usefulness defined as: Very useful--Useful--Only a bit useful--Not useful at all, with Very useful equal to 1 and Not useful equal to 4. The factors users were asked to rate were the following.

Figure 5. Workflow 3, BlastNagainstDDBJatDDBJ.xml

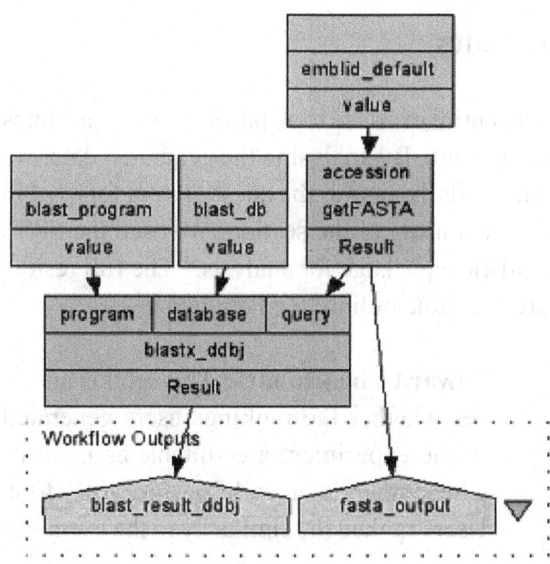

Figure 6. Workflow 4, AffyidToFastaSequence.xml

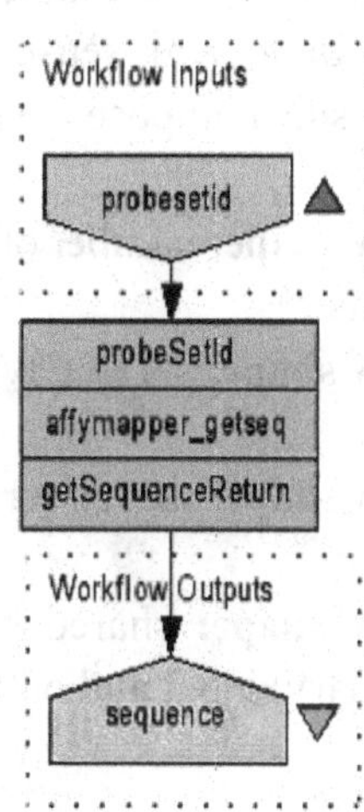

Figure 7. Workflow 5, williams-partA-paper.xml

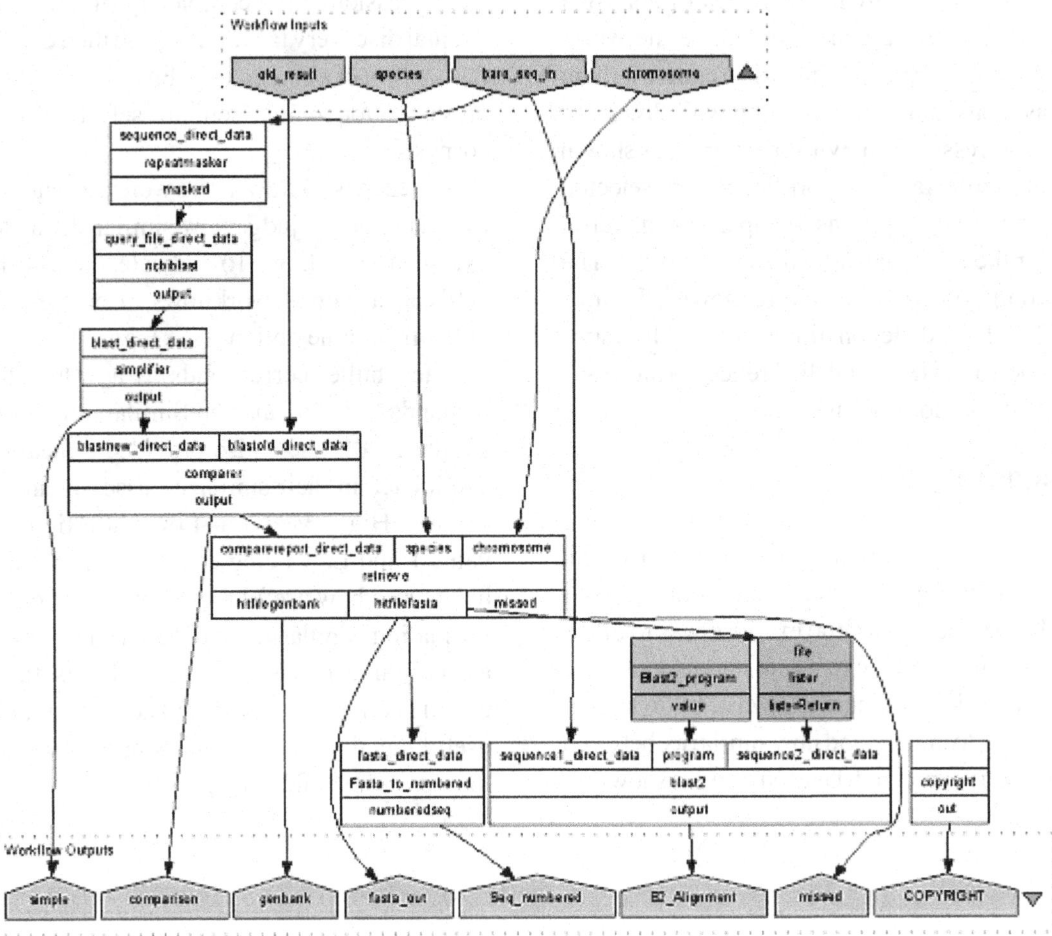

1. It makes biological sense to have this workflow as a part of the example workflow
2. It makes biological sense to have this workflow super imposed on the example workflow
3. **Workflow shape:** number of shared inputs and outputs
4. **Workflow shape:** service type correspondence
5. **Workflow shape:** shared service compositions
6. **Workflow shape:** shared paths between (intermediary) input and output

Results

The entire exercise took participants 30 minutes on average. By analysing the generated data, we can partially answer the questions put forward in the beginning of the section. We used the SPSS statistical package for analysis.[11] The full results are available online, see Footnote 9.

1. **Toward a benchmark:** This section analyses whether the rankings users generated in the experiment are suitable as input as a benchmark to a workflow discovery tool. Users ranked the similarity of the exemplar

Figure 8. The form for entering workflow similarity values

	Identical		Very similar		Similar		Marginally similar		Not similar at all
Biological functionality									
Overall shape									

Table 1. Similarity (1 = Identical, 9 = No Similarity) of five workflows with respect to the input workflow

Number	Biological similarity	Shape similarity	Confidence
1	4.5 (2.0)	5.0 (1.5)	3.0 (1.1)
2	5.8 (1.9)	6.8 (1.4)	2.9 (1.0)
3	7.0 (1.7)	6.8 (2.0)	3.3 (0.8)
4	6.2 (1.9)	5.0 (2.4)	2.9 (1.4)
5	8.0 (1.6)	8.4 (1.3)	3.2 (1.4)

workflow vis-a-vis the comparison workflows as indicated in Table 1.

The table shows the mean of values entered by all respondents per workflow. The standard deviation is given inside the brackets (two standard deviations away from the mean account for roughly 95 percent of the people). The respondents reported medium confidence overall in their own judgment.

Of all respondents, 66.7 percent found estimating the similarity of biological functionality very difficult to difficult. The estimation of the similarity of shape similarity on the other hand was a difficult task for only 25 percent of respondents. To establish whether there was consistency in the rankings produced between respondents, we need to know whether a correlation between these rankings exists. To confirm whether this is the case, we performed the following calculations.

The user similarity values of Table 1 were transformed for all participants to reflect the order in which each individual had ranked the workflows (in order of decreasing similarity). We then built a correlation matrix (not shown due to its size; available online) based on Spearman's correlation test and the transformed data. Spearman's correlation test is a measure of association between rank orders. With respect to the data, for biological functionality similarity, we only used data from people with a biological background (nine respondents and five workflows, no missing values), whilst taking into account data from all 13 respondents for shape similarity.

The data show the following. For rankings based on biological functionality, only for six out of 36 possible participant pairs (e.g., between participant 2 and participant 5) were the results correlated (at a 5 percent significance level). This means that participants in general disagreed on how to order the workflows according to their biological similarity and therefore lacked consistency in their rankings. A similar result was found in the correlation matrix for rankings based on shape: based on the 13 users, only 16 out of 77 pairs showed correlation (at a 5 percent significance level). As it stands, the current data set cannot serve as a general benchmark.

The overall message is that the task as presented to users is too difficult. This leads to inconsistent results. With respect to future experiments, this issue can be addressed by:

- Providing subjects with a clearer task definition, for example, practical reuse tasks such as finding extensions to current workflows.
- Providing subjects with more information about the workflow, say to include semantic annotation of the constituent services.
- Recruiting subjects with more experience with the workflow environment such as contributors to the myExperiment.org workflow portal.
- Recruiting subjects with more familiarity with the workflow corpus topic, for instance the original workflow authors.

2. **Predictive power of criteria:** One way to explain the diversity in behaviour during ranking we described above is to investigate whether different users use different criteria for establishing workflow (dis-) similarity. Users ranked the usefulness of the factors for establishing workflow similarity as indicated in Table 2. We are interested to find the effects of the six factors on the similarity, whilst the factors may be interacting (e.g., once people looked at how many services are shared, they might not care any more whether any inputs and outputs are shared). A common statistical way to establish such findings is through a Between-Subject Analysis of variance (ANOVA).[12] Analysis of variance assumes that the groups come from populations with equal variances. To test this assumption, we used Levene's homogeneity-of-variance test, only to find that the assumption was violated in all cases. As a result, little can be said on how particular factors impact the similarity measures based on ANOVA.

One explanation for the inconsistencies is that different people might be using different metrics, some of which not included in the list of six factors. One participant for instance indicated that the total number of services (i.e., the difference in size of workflows) played a role in the assessment of shape. One logical step in future experiments would be to fix the (combination of) criteria people can use, and see what similarity values across participants this generates. Another possibility to only ask participants to establish whether there is or there is no similarity relationship present, without probing for the underlying heuristics used.

3. **The link between task and structure:** From the data, a strong correlation was observed between the biological similarity and the shape similarity (see Table 3).

Table 2. Usefulness (1 = best, 4 = worst) of six factors for estimating similarity of five workflows with respect to the input workflow

Number	Subtask	Supertask	Input/output	Type	Services	Input/output paths
1	2.4 (1.0)	2.0 (0.9)	2.5 (0.9)	2.2 (0.8)	2.1 (0.5)	2.0 (0.6)
2	3.0 (0.8)	2.6 (0.9)	2.9 (1.1)	2.1 (0.9)	2.2 (0.8)	2.1 (0.9)
3	3.0 (0.8)	3.3 (0.8)	2.6 (0.8)	2.2 (0.8)	2.5 (0.5)	2.3 (0.7)
4	2.3 (0.9)	3.0 (0.8)	2.4 (0.9)	2.1 (0.8)	2.3 (0.7)	2.3 (0.5)
5	3.6 (0.7)	3.3 (1.2)	2.5 (1.1)	2.5 (1.1)	2.5 (1.1)	2.5 (1.1)

This suggests that having only the workflow specifications themselves available could be sufficient to reliably rank workflows, as opposed to workflows with semantic annotation. This fact does not remove the need for workflow documentation or annotation though: a user is primarily interested in those bits of the retrieved workflows that are different to hers, and without documentation on what these do, rankings will not be useful.

A WORKFLOW DISCOVERY TOOL

To address the requirements collected in the previous sections, we have developed a workflow discovery component. Given the breadth of the requirements, we gave priority to some requirements over others. We motivate our choice in this section. We also discuss the benefits and drawbacks of the adopted matching technology and give a tool overview.

Determining the Scope in Terms of Workflow Discovery Requirements

In the earlier mentioned survey of middleware projects (Goderis et al., 2005), all projects offer a search mechanism to look for available services; none however allow for the possibility to discover and compare workflow descriptions based on their behaviour or structure. Previously, we confirmed that some users would indeed find good use for such a mechanism. Such a component should be seen as complementary to other approaches retrieving a workflow by its signature description. The latter case could be addressed by adapting existing service discovery mechanisms to regard a workflow as just another service. We report here on the development of a workflow discovery component meant to work specifically over the structure or shape of a workflow.

In terms of the earlier posited requirements, the presented tool supports *service flow queries for personal discovery (versioning)*. The choice was driven by practical user needs, limitations in the corpus and limitations in the matching technology used:

- We aim to support and evaluate queries of direct relevance to users and personal discovery fits that requirement. Every user typically builds multiple workflows over a period of time and often loses track of their relationships.
- The corpus used is limited to similar workflows created by a small number of authors.[13] The workflow descriptions in the corpus are service centric, as opposed to data centric.
- We chose a graph as the data structure for capturing the structure of a workflow. The graph matching technology used, explained below, has no lexical component, which leaves the matching process vulnerable to differences in terminology. Such heterogeneity is a common characteristic of corpora created by multiple authors and also lead us to consider personal discovery first.

Choosing the Matching Technology

Which representation a matching component adopts to represent workflows depends on the queries to be answered, the expressivity of the

Table 3. Spearman test correlation for biological functionality and shape similarity, at a 1 percent significance level

	Shape similarity
Biological similarity	0.816 (N=45)

workflow language and the expressivity of the matching component. We chose a graph as the data structure and an algorithm for graph sub-isomorphism detection as the basis of the matching algorithm.

Our choice of a graph as the data structure for capturing a workflow is motivated as follows. Firstly, multiple scientific workflow environments have adopted a graphical representation to present workflows to end users. For these environments, the choice of a graph as the vehicle for matchmaking potentially makes explaining the discovery process and its results more intuitive. Taverna workflows, too, are visualized as graphs. Taverna's graphs are directed and acyclic—this follows from the semantics of Taverna's Scufl language, which correspond to a lambda calculus with a list monad (Turi et al., 2007). Secondly, a graph is a very expressive data structure. The benefits and drawbacks of different exact and inexact graph retrieval algorithms and heuristics are well understood. Finally, graphs provide a theoretical underpinning for the Resource Description Framework (RDF), a W3C recommendation for describing semantic information on the Web.[14] This means that any technique we adopt for workflow diagrams based on graphs potentially extends to RDF graphs describing workflows. Currently, over 500 biological Web services are annotated in RDF [15] and the transition path to workflows appears natural.

For the basis of the matching algorithm, we resorted to a technique for graph sub-isomorphism detection ("subgraph matching"), optimised to work over a repository of graphs. The technique was developed and implemented by Messmer and Bunke (2000). Standard methods for sub-isomorphism detection usually work on only two graphs at a time. However, when comparing workflows, there is more than one graph in the repository that must be matched with the input graph. Consequently, it is necessary to apply the subgraph isomorphism algorithm to each pair of repository graph – input graph, resulting in a computation time that is linearly dependent on the size of the repository. Messmer and Bunke's approach is based on a compact representation of the repository graphs that is computed off-line. The representation is created by decomposing the repository graphs into a set of subgraphs, where common subgraphs of different graphs are represented only once. During online matching, they are matched exactly once with the input graph, yielding a technique that is only sub-linearly dependent on the number of the graphs in the repository (Messmer & Bunke, 2000). As explained below, the optimisation is currently unavailable in our tool, but remains of interest.

The data structure and graph matching algorithm in itself are not sufficient to create a workflow discovery component. The translation of a workflow into a graph and the way results are ranked and presented have a great impact on results. These issues are discussed in the following section.

Tool Overview

The tool was designed and implemented as a component for the Taverna workbench. It takes in an input workflow and repository workflows and returns matching results. The results are rendered as a ranked list of workflows in an HTML document. An architecture diagram is given in Figure 9.

From the Taverna workbench, a user imports Web directories containing workflows into the Available services pane (see Figure 1). All workflows in the selected Web directories are translated by the Parser from the Scufl specification into a form and format the Graph Matcher understands. The user's current working directory and its subdirectories are also scanned for workflows. Put together, these workflows form the corpus against which to match the input workflow. The input workflow equals whatever the status of the workflow the user is currently working on. Again, the Parser reads in the input workflow by trans-

Figure 9. Workflow discovery component architecture

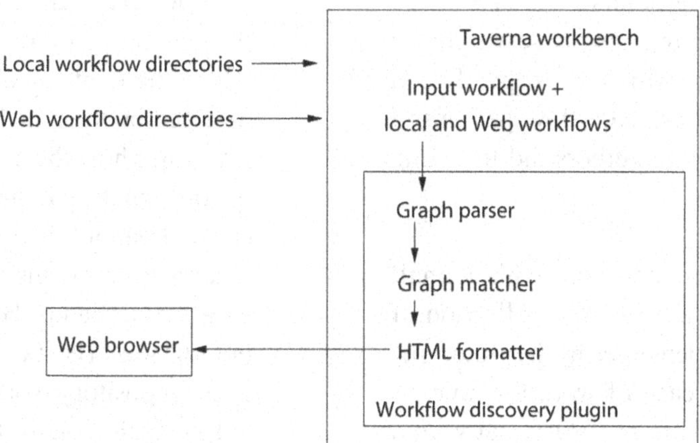

lating it to a form and format the Graph Matcher understands. The Graph Matcher detects which workflows are similar to the input and returns the results to the Formatter. The Formatter renders the results as an HTML page and launches the user's Web browser.

1. Graph Parser
   The Parser translates the Scufl specification of all workflows in a form and format suitable for the graph matcher.[16] Our chosen graph matcher is rather inexpressive and only accepts attribute-less graphs of nodes and (directed or undirected) attribute-less edges. The contents of a graph impact the outcome of the graph matching process, typically as a trade-off between accuracy and performance.

The following steps occur in our translation from a Scufl workflow to a graph:

1. The workflow's overall inputs and outputs are included as named nodes in the graph.
2. The intermediate nodes are instantiated with the names of the services connecting the workflow's input and output, while ignoring all information about intermediary inputs and outputs.
3. The graph's edges are defined as the connections between the services.

Therefore, the information that is captured roughly mirrors the type of information available in the workflow diagram in Figure 1a, as opposed to the rendition of the same workflow in Figure 2. The colouring which indicates service type has been lost in translation, though. We also lost the distinction between overall inputs, overall outputs, and services and conflated them into nodes.

Other parsing strategies are possible, for example based on including intermediary input and output names. The inexpressivity of the graph matcher means we cannot straightforwardly combine intermediary inputs and outputs with information about the service's name. Judging from our corpus, relying solely on intermediary input and output names would seem careless, given that they often consist of generic terms such as "value" or "query."

2. *Graph Matcher*
   With the workflows turned into graphs, Messmer and Bunke's (2000) graph matcher can be put to use. The implementation supports efficient matching of a large input graph to a collection of smaller graphs in

the repository. In the context of workflow retrieval, this corresponds to the case where users would want to retrieve those workflows in the repository which correspond to a fragment in the user's workflow, perhaps to find out which other authors did the same analysis.

The case where one starts out with a small input graph and matches this to a collection of larger graphs is not implemented by the prototype. Unfortunately, in the case of workflow matching, the latter case, where one starts out with a small exemplar workflow and one would like to compare it against a repository of large, finished workflows, seems of more practical relevance. Re-implementing the graph matching algorithm to cater for this scenario is non-trivial, however, and beyond the scope of this article. Instead, we resorted to inverting the matching process by sequentially treating each of the (large) repository graphs as an input graph to the matcher, and treating the (small) exemplar workflow as the whole repository. This work around destroys the graph repository optimisation since it treats the prototype as a standard subgraph matching package which is invoked as many times as there are workflows in the repository.

In terms of ranking the graphs retrieved by the graph matcher, we have experimented with three factors: the similarity in terms of overall input, overall output and internal services shared between workflows (i.e., nodes shared between graphs), the difference in workflow size (number of nodes) and a simple lexical transformation (uncapitalization on the nodes).

3. HTML Formatter
   The results from the Graph Matcher are rendered into an HTML page, which specifies how many nodes are shared between workflows and what their size difference is.[17] It also contains links to the workflow specifications (see Figure 10). Furthermore, we highlight the differences between the input workflow (AffyidToBlastxPDB.xml) and the retrieved ones. Figure 11 shows the example where the joint use of the Blastx service is detected by the matcher. The example also illustrates how the graph matcher conflates overall inputs and outputs and services because it cannot deal with typed nodes. As it cannot not distinguish between "Blastx" as a service and "Blastx" as a workflow output, the "Blastx" output is highlighted in the repository workflow, even though no output with exactly the string "Blastx" is present in the input workflow.

EVALUATION

Given the lack of a robust benchmark, no generic claims can be made as to how useful the tool is for end users. As a simple showcase, instead we aim to replicate the average workflow ranking of Table 1. The average ranking, in order of decreasing similarity with respect to the exemplar workflow AffyidToBlastxPDB.xml is: (i) Workflow 1; (ii) Workflow 4; (iii) Workflow 3; (iv) Workflow 2; and (v) Workflow 5.

Running the Parser on the 89 workflows available from www.myexperiment.org takes about ten seconds on a PentiumIV/512MB RAM/WindowsXP machine. The matching process itself takes about five seconds. The graph size ranged from three nodes to 36 nodes.

Different ranking strategies can be adopted. We show the impact of three different strategies.

1. **Shared nodes, string matching:** The Graph Matcher always returns the biggest subgraph found during matching with the input. We use the size of this subgraph as a measure to rank the collection of matched workflows. Without manipulating the names of the nodes (workflow input, output and services), this

Figure 10. Output for ranking strategy 3 with respect to the exemplar workflow. Workflows 3 and 5 are missing.

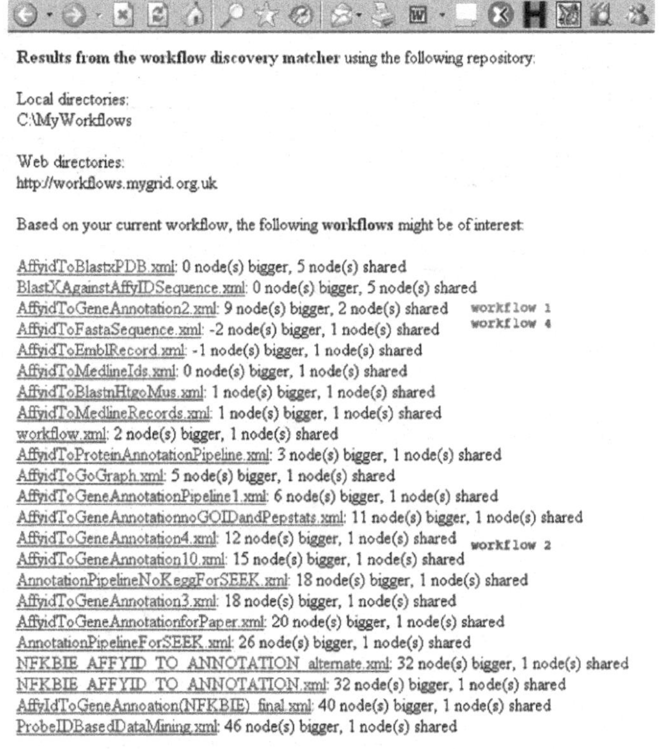

matching strategy returns 9 results, and of the list to be ranked contains workflows 1 and 2 (listings are provided online).

2. **Shared nodes, lowercase string matching:** When adapting the above strategy to make all node name assignments lower case during the Parser process, another 14 workflows show up in the matching results, including workflow 4. The list now includes workflows 1, 2 and 4, but wrongly ordered.
3. **Shared nodes, lowercase string matching, size:** Introducing a measure that compares the size of the exemplar workflow to the comparison workflow ranks workflows 1, 2 and 4 in the right way. We show the results of this strategy in Figure 10. Workflows are ordered in the first instance by the number of nodes they share with the exemplar, and, in those cases where two workflows in the list have the same number, they are ordered by the size of the difference between the two workflows.

Strategy 3 still fails to retrieve workflows 3 and 5. Upon closer inspection, it becomes clear that inexact string matching of the service names, or information retrieval techniques in general, could offer a solution for these cases. Another solution would be matching based on classes of similar services, which opens up the door for semantic annotation. The use of techniques for inexact graph matching also appears sensible. We plan on exploring the three approaches in future.

The tool developed here was built with personal discovery in mind. Addressing discovery by collaborators and discovery by third parties remains an important challenge for the future. As mentioned earlier, when corpora are authored

Figure 11. Visualization of overlap between the input workflow and one in the repository

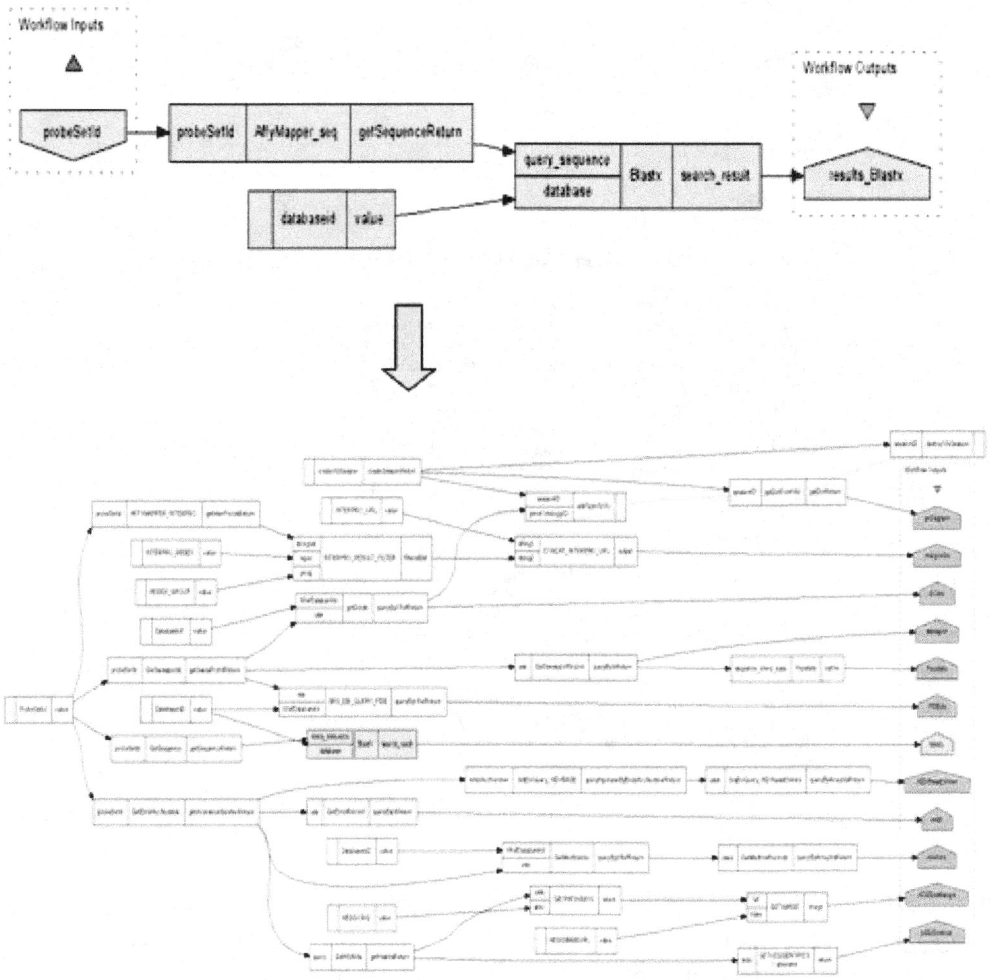

by different scientists, one can expect the exact graph matcher to have difficulty to establish links between them. In this case, the difference in use of terminology and naming conventions is likely to hurt the performance of the graph matcher even further. Different techniques, therefore, are likely to be effective on different discovery tasks. A lot of work remains on establishing which technique is best for which discovery task.

RELATED WORK

To our knowledge, no authors have tackled the discovery of online workflows through the combination of eliciting workflow discovery requirements with end users, building a benchmark and designing a tool specifically to rank the structural part of workflow descriptions.

Elicitation of Workflow Discovery Requirements and Building a Benchmark

In the workflow literature, we are unaware of work on requirements gathering for workflow discovery. Several authors focus on uncovering the particular metrics used for establishing workflow similarity. This is akin to our trying to establish predictive criteria. Bernstein and colleagues (Bernstein,

Kaufmann, Burki, & Klein, 2005) look for the best semantic similarity measures to rank business processes from the MIT Process Handbook, based on a process ontology. The processes are non-executable workflows hence no reuse of workflows in a Web services context is envisioned. Wombacher (2006) seeks to elicit the similarity metrics used by workflow researchers when performing the task of comparing the control flow complexity of workflows described by Finite State Machines (FSMs). He uses RosettaNet Partner Interface Processes as a corpus. Wombacher also investigates which metrics, known from workflow mining and FSM techniques, are able to reproduce the human rankings from this task.

In the service discovery literature, most of the articles focus on techniques and their technical evaluation, where it is demonstrated how expressive a technique is, or how scalable. One exception is the work by Dong and colleagues (Dong, Halevy, Madhavan, Nemes, & Zhang, 2004) who built a small test bench based on real Web services to test the performance of the Woogle tool. We know of two community initiatives to compare Web service discovery techniques: the Semantic Web Services Challenge and the Web Service Challenge.[18] Both initiatives have limited involvement from users. In the former, a challenging scenario is put forward involving fully automated discovery and invocation. In the latter, techniques are evaluated by a subjective score issued by the organizers on the system design as well as performance and accuracy. A third initiative is currently in the making in the context of the DIP project[19] which promises the involvement of end users to build a benchmark for semantic Web service discovery.

Tools for Ranking the Structural Part of Workflows

In the service discovery literature, in recent years many authors have focussed on formal techniques for the discovery of processes which are published as Web or Grid services or as software components, where the process's signature—what the process does—is the main source of information used, for example, based on semantic annotation (Lord et al., 2005). Process discovery nevertheless is also possible based on the process contents—how the process works, based on data flow and control flow (Berardi, De Giacomo, Lenzerini, Mecella, & Calvanese, 2004). Moreover, processes can be discovered based on the intermediate and final results generated from running them—their provenance (Zhao et al., 2006). All three kinds of process discovery can be applied to workflow discovery. During workflow discovery, one can choose either the workflow's signature as the discovery basis, the entire workflow definition specifying data flow and control flow or the results from running the workflow.

We focus here on discovery based on the data flow and control flow. In the e-science literature, a vision and tool for reuse of scientific workflows is described in Medeiros, Perez-Alcazar, Digiampietri, Pastorello Jr, Santanche, Torres, Madeira, and Bacarin, (2005) for a closed-world system. The article does not consider the problems associated with building or ranking online workflows. More generally, in the mentioned survey of scientific workflow middleware, no discovery techniques were found which use data or control flow for matching. Similarly, a wide survey of commercial business process management systems did not mention the existence of such techniques (Miers, Harmon, & Hall, 2006).

In the workflow research literature, techniques are rare and apparently limited to research prototypes such as Wroe, Stevens, Goble, Roberts, and Greenwood (2003); Wombacher, Fankhauser, Mahleko, and Neuhold (2004); and Grigori, Corrales, and Bouzeghoub (2006). In Wroe et al. (2003), an extensive and rich ontology is built that allows one to look for containing services of workflows. No ordering between the services is encoded, and matching is done through Description Logic subsumption matching without rankings. In Wombacher et al. (2004), the authors consider discovery of BPEL workflows based the messaging behaviour exhibited by a workflow's services, based on an n-gram representation of a workflow. The work of Grigori et al. (2006) introduces inexact graph matching to perform workflow retrieval.

One conclusion for the relative lack of workflow-specific discovery techniques is that they are not wanted by users. This is at odds with requirements expressed by the scientists in Section VI's user survey, who wanted to use the detailed contents of the workflow (e.g., to specify constituent services or the data flow) as input to the matching process. One explanation for the current situation with content-based workflow discovery techniques could be that large collections of workflows are not common yet, and hence there is no immediate need for fine-grained techniques. The situation is certainly changing in science where online collections are on the rise at places like myExperiment.org and one should anticipate the situation. An alternative explanation could be that existing techniques are deemed unsuitable. Either explanation provides a motivation to continue formally evaluating techniques for workflow discovery in the future.

CONCLUSION

Based on a case study from bioinformatics, this article started by motivating the use of workflows in science and considering the role of the BPEL workflow language. It then gathered requirements for workflow discovery and attempted to build a benchmark for evaluating workflow discovery. To generate workflow rankings, a workflow tool was developed based on graph matching and then tested within a workflow environment on a real corpus. The tool largely replicates the average of human rankings for a simple showcase but work remains on (i) creating a robust human benchmark, (ii) re-evaluating the tool on a new benchmark and (iii) developing new discovery techniques addressing the various discovery use cases. We anticipate that a range of discovery techniques will be needed to match the variety in discovery tasks.

ACKNOWLEDGMENT

The authors thank the participants in the survey for their time and helpful comments. Thanks to R. Mark Greenwood for discussions and to Bruno Messmer for making the graph matcher source code available. This work is supported by the UK e-Science programme EPSRC GR/R67743.

REFERENCES

Al Sairaf, S., Emmanouil, F. S., Ghanem, M., Giannadakis, N., Guo, Y., Kalaitzopoulos D., Osmond M., Rowe, A., Syed, J., Wendel, P. (2003). The design of discovery net: Towards open grid services for knowledge discovery. *International Journal of High Performance Computing Applications.*

Berardi, D., De Giacomo, G., Lenzerini, M., Mecella, M., & Calvanese. D. (2004). Synthesis of underspecified composite e-services based on automated reasoning. *Proceedings of the 2nd International Conference on Service Oriented Computing (ICSOC)*, pp. 105–114.

Bernstein, A., Kaufmann, E., Burki, C., & Klein M. (2005). How similar is it? Towards personalized similarity measures in ontologies. In *7. Tag. Wirt. Informatik*

Brooks, C., Lee, E. A., Liu, X., Neuendorffer, S., Zhao, Y., & Zheng, H. (2005). Heterogeneous Concurrent Modeling and Design in Java, Volume 3: Ptolemy II Domains. *Tech. Report UCB/ERL M05/21, University of California, Berkeley.* July 15.

Chappell, D. (2005) The case against BPEL: Why the language is less important than you think. *Opinari Blog*, Number 14, October 2005. Last accessed December 15, 2006 from http://www.davidchappell.com/HTML_email/Opinari_No14_10_05.html

Dong, X., Halevy, A., Madhavan, J., Nemes, E., & Zhang. J. (2004). Similarity search for Web services. *Proceedings of the 30th VLDB Conference*, Toronto, Canada

Goderis, A., Brooks, C., Altintas, I., Lee, E.A., & Goble, C.A. (2007). Composing different models of computation in Kepler and Ptolemy II. *Proceedings of the International Conference on Computational Science (ICCS) 2007*, Beijing, China, May 27-30.

Goderis, A., Li, P., & Goble, C.A. (2006). Workflow discovery: The problem, a case study from escience and a graph-based solution. *Proceedings of the IEEE International Conference on Web Services (ICWS)*, Chicago, USA, September 18-22.

Goderis, A., Sattler, U., Lord, P., & Goble, C. (2005). Seven bottlenecks to workflow reuse and repurposing. *Proceedings of the 4th International Semantic Web Conference (ISWC 2005)*, LNCS volume 3792, pages 323–337, Galway, Ireland.

Goderis, A., Sattler, U., Lord P., & Goble C. (2005b). Applying DLs to workflow reuse and repurposing. *International Description Logics workshop*, Edinburgh, Scotland, July 24-26.

Grigori, D., Corrales, J., & Bouzeghoub, M. (2006). Behavioral matchmaking for service retrieval. *Proceedings of the IEEE International Conference on Web Services (ICWS)*, Chicago, USA, September 18-22.

Haines, R., Mckeown, M., Pickles, S. M., Pinning, R. L., Porter A. R., & Riding, M. (2005). The service architecture of the TeraGyroid experiment, *Phil. Trans. R. Soc., 363*, 1743–1755

Hey, T., & Trefethen, A. (2002). The UKe-Science core program and the Grid. *International Conference on Computational Science, 1*(3), 21.

Hull, D., Zolin, E., Bovykin, A., Horrocks, I., Sattler, U., & Stevens, R. (2006). Deciding semantic matching of stateless services. *Proceedings of the 21st National Conference on Artificial Intelligence AAAI*

Jünger, M.A., Rintelen, F., Stocker, H., Wasserman, J.D., Végh, M., Radimerski, T., Greenberg, M.E., Hafen, E. (2003). The Drosophila forkhead transcription factor FOXO mediates the reduction in cell number associated with reduced insulin signaling. *Journal Biol., 2*(3), 20.

Kahn, G. & MacQueen, D. B. (1977). Coroutines and Networks of Parallel Processes, *Information Processing* 77, B. Gilchrist, editor, North-Holland Publishing Co.

Li P., Chen Y., & Romanovsky A. (2006). Measuring the dependability of Web services for use in e-Science experiments. *Proceedings of 3rd International Service Availability Symposium*, Helsinki, Finland, May 15-16.

Li, P., Hayward, K., Jennings, C. et al. (2004). Association of variations in I kappa b-epsilon with Graves' disease using classical methodologies and myGrid methodologies. In *UK e-Science All Hands Meeting.*

Lord, P., Alper, P., Wroe, C., & Goble C. (2005). Feta: A lightweight architecture for user oriented semantic service discovery. *Proceedings of the European Semantic Web Conference (ESWC).*

Ludäscher, B., Altintas, I., Berkley, C., Higgins, D., Jaeger, E., Jones, M., Lee, E. A., Tao, J., & Zhao, Y. (2005). Scientific workflow management and the KEPLER system. *Concurrency & Computation: Practice & Experience, Special issue on scientific workflows.*

Medeiros, C. B., Perez-Alcazar, J., Digiampietri, L., Pastorello Jr, G. Z., Santanche, A., Torres, R.

S., Madeira, E., & Bacarin, E. (2005). WOODSS and the Web: Annotating and reusing scientific workflows. *SIGMOD Record Special Issue on Scientific Workflows, 34*(3), September.

Messmer, B.T., & Bunke, H. (2000). Efficient subgraph isomorphism detection: A decomposition approach. *IEEE Transaction on Knowledge and Data Engineering, 12*(2), 307–323.

Miers, D., Harmon, P., & Hall., C. (2006). The 2006 BPM suites report, September. Retrieved from http://www.bptrends.com

Narayanan, S, & McIlraith, S. (2003). Analysis and Simulation of Web Services. *Computer Networks, 42*(5), 675-693.

Oinn, T., Greenwood, M., Addis, M,. Alpdemir, M., Ferris, J., Glover, K., et al. (2005). Taverna: Lessons in creating a workflow environment for the life sciences. *Concurrency and Computation: Practice and Experience Special issue on Scientific Workflows.*

Stevens,R., Glover,K., Greenhalgh,C., Jennings,C., Pearce,S., Li,P., et al. (2003). Performing in silico experiments on the Grid: A users perspective. *Proceedings of UK e-Science All Hands Meeting*, 43-50.

Stevens, R., Tipney, H., Wroe, C., Oinn T., Senger, M., Lord, P., et al. (2004). Exploring Williams-Beuren Syndrome Using myGrid. *Bioinformatics, 20*(i), 303–i310.

Turi, D., Missier, P., De Roure, D., Goble C., & Oinn, T. (2007). Taverna workflows: Syntax and semantics. *Proceedings of the 3rd e-Science conference*, Bangalore, India, December.

Wombacher, A. (2006). Evaluation of technical measures for workflow similarity based on a pilot study. *Proceedings of CoopIS*, Montpellier, France, November 1-3.

Wombacher, A., Fankhauser, A, Mahleko, P., & Neuhold, B. (2004). Matchmaking for business processes based on choreographies. *International Journal of Web Services, 1*(4).

Wroe, C., Goble, C., Goderis, A., Lord, P., Miles, S., Papay, J., et al. (2007). Recycling workflows and services through discovery and reuse. *Concurrency and Computation: Practice and Experience, 19*(2), 181-194.

Wroe, C., Stevens, R., Goble, C., Roberts, A., & Greenwood, M. (2003). A suite of DAML+OIL ontologies to describe bioinformatics Web services and data. *International Journal of Cooperative Information Systems, 12*(2), 197–224.

Yu, J., & Buyya, R. (2005). A taxonomy of scientific workflow systems for Grid computing. *SIGMOD Rec., 34*(3), 44-49.

Zhao, Y., Wilde, M., & Foster. I. (2006). Applying the virtual data provenance model. *Proceedings of the International Provenance and Annotation Workshop (IPAW)*, Chicago, USA, May 3-5.

Zhao, Z, Booms, S., Belloum, A., de Laat, C, & Hertzberger, B. (2006). VLE-WVBus: A scientific workflow bus for multi e-Science domains. *Proceedings of the 2nd IEEE Iint.Conference on E-Science and Grid Computing (e-Science 2006)* Amsterdam, Netherlands.

ENDNOTES

1. Web site: http://www.mygrid.org.uk/Taverna
2. Web site: http://www.ebi.ac.uk/Tools/webservices
3. Web site: http://www.omii.ac.uk
4. Web site: http://www.d-grid.de
5. Web site: http://www.kepler-project.org
6. Web site: http://twiki.ipaw.info/bin/view/Challenge
7. Web site: http://www.vl-e.nl

8 Web site: http://www.wfmc.org
9 Web site: http://wiki.myexperiment.org/index.php/Publications/JWSR
10 Created with the Keysurvey Web software; Web site: http://www.keysurvey.com
11 Web site: http://www.spss.com
12 For a good introduction, see http://davidmlane.com/hyperstat
13 With the launch of myExperiment.org beginning of August 2007, the number of authors publishing freely available workflows has increased, and cross-author discovery has become a real requirement.
14 Web site: http://www.w3.org/RDF
15 Web site: http://www.mygrid.org.uk/feta/mygrid/descriptions
16 The Parser's source code has been made available through the SimPack distribution. Web site: http://www.ifi.unizh.ch/ddis/simpack.html
17 Alternative views, based on the degrees of similarity of Section VII, would be possible and useful.
18 Web sites: http://ws-challenge.org and http://sws-challenge.org
19 Web site: http://dip.semanticweb.org

This work was previously published in the International Journal of Web Services Research, Vol. 5, Issue 4, edited by L. Zhang, pp. 32-58, copyright 2008 by IGI Publishing (an imprint of IGI Global).

Chapter 21
An Access Control Framework for WS-BPEL Processes

Federica Paci
Università degli Studi di Trento, Italy

Elisa Bertino
Purdue University, USA

Jason Crampton
University of London, UK

ABSTRACT

Business processes –the next generation workflows- have attracted considerable research interest in the last fifteen years. More recently, several XML-based languages have been proposed for specifying and orchestrating business processes, resulting in the WS-BPEL language. Even if WS-BPEL has been developed to specify automated business processes that orchestrate activities of multiple Web services, there are many applications and situations requiring that people be considered as additional participants that can influence the execution of a process. Significant omissions from WS-BPEL are the specification of activities that require interactions with humans to be completed, called human activities, and the specification of authorization information associating users with human activities in a WS-BPEL business process and authorization constraints, such as separation of duty, on the execution of human activities. In this chapter, we address these deficiencies by introducing a new type of WS-BPEL activity to model human activities and by developing RBAC-WS-BPEL, a role based access control model for WS-BPEL and BPCL, a language to specify authorization constraints.

INTRODUCTION

Business Process Management systems (BPM) have gained a lot of attention due to the pressing need of integrating **business processes** of different organizations. Research efforts have been devoted to improve current workflow technologies in order to support collaborative business processes. BPM systems can be considered as an extension of classical workflow management (WFM) systems. Older, proprietary workflow systems managed document-based processes where people executed the workflow steps of the processes. Today's BPM systems manage processes that include person-to-

DOI: 10.4018/978-1-61520-684-1.ch021

person work steps, system-to-system communications or combinations of both. In addition, BPM systems include integrated features such as enhanced (and portable) process modeling, simulation, code generation, process execution and process monitoring. All those functions and features have resulted in an increased interest in BPM suites because they enhance business processes flexibility while at the same time reducing risks and costs. Therefore, BPM suites are a way to build, execute and monitor automated processes that may go across organizational boundaries - a kind of next-generation workflows.

Recently, Web services have provided the basis for the development and execution of business processes that are distributed over the network and available via standard interfaces and protocols. Business processes or workflows can be built by combining Web services through the use of a process specification language. Such languages basically allow one to specify which tasks have to be executed and the order in which those tasks should be executed. Because of their importance, process specification languages have been widely investigated and a number of languages have been developed. One such language is WS-BPEL 2.0 (Web Services Business Process Execution Language), an XML-based workflow process language, which provides a syntax for specifying business processes in terms of Web services (Jordan, Evdemon, 2006). WS-BPEL resulted from the combination of two different workflow languages, WSFL (Leymann, 2001) and XLANG (Thatte, 2001), and adopts the best features of these language. WS-BPEL is layered on top of several XML standards, including WSDL 1.1 (Christensen, Curbera, Meredith, Weerawarana, 2001), XML Schema 1.0 (Peterson, Biron, Malhotra, 2004) and XPath 1.0 (Clarkand, DeRose, 1999), but of these, WSDL has had the most influence on WS-BPEL.

However, despite those significant progresses towards the development of an expressive language for business processes, significant challenges still need to be addressed before we see the widespread use of business processes management systems in distributed computer systems and Web services. WS-BPEL has been developed to specify automated business processes that orchestrate activities of multiple Web services. There are, however, cases in which people must be considered as additional participants to the execution of a process. Therefore, it is important to extend WS-BPEL to include the specification of activities that must be fully or partially performed by humans. The inclusion of humans, in turn, requires solutions for verifying the identity of users who request the execution of **human activities** and for the specification and enforcement of **authorizations** to users for the execution of human activities while enforcing **authorization constraints**, such as separation of duty, on the execution of those activities.

Therefore, in this chapter, we propose RBAC-WS-BPEL, a **role-based** access control model for WS-BPEL business processes that addresses the outlined requirements.

The chapter is organized as follows. In the next section we present an overview of WS-BPEL and we introduce an example that we will use throughout the chapter for illustrative purposes. In Section 3 we define the components of RBAC-WS-BPEL, including authorization policies and authorization constraints. In the subsequent section we provide an example of an RBAC policy for a purchase order WS-BPEL business process, specified in XACML (Moses, 2005). In Section 5 we describe our language to specify authorization constraints called Business Process Constraint Language (BPCL). In Section 6, we illustrate the specification of human activities and authorization information and constraints in the purchase order WS-BPEL business process. In Section 7 we present an algorithm to evaluate if a request by a user to execute an activity in a WS-BPEL process can be granted. In Section 8 we discuss a possible implementation of our model. Finally, we conclude with related work and future research directions.

INTRODUCTION TO WS-BPEL

WS-BPEL is an XML-based language to specify business processes that orchestrate the operations of several Web services. The top level element in the specification is <process>. It has a number of attributes, which specify the process name, the namespaces being referred to, and whether the process is an abstract process or an executable process. An executable process describes the internal implementation of the process, while an abstract process specifies the external behavior of a process. The <partnerLinks> element is used to identify the external Web services invoked from within the process. The <variables> element defines the data that flows within the process. The <correlationSets> element is used to bind a set of operations to a service instance. The <faultHandlers> element is used to handle exceptions. The <compensationHandlers> element is used to implement specify actions to be taken in the case of transaction rollback. The <eventHandlers>are used to specify actions in response to external events.

The actual business logic is represented as a group of activities, which are executed in a structured way. Activities are executed by invoking Web services' operations. The business logic includes basic control structures: the <sequence> activity contains one or more activities that are performed sequentially; the <if> activity is used to specify conditional branching execution; the <while> activity supports iterative execution of an activity; the <pick> activity is used to trigger an activity following a specified event; the <repeatUntil> activity provides for repeated execution of a contained activity; the <forEach> activity iterates the execution of an enclosed <scope> activity for a fixed number of times; the <flow> activity is used to specify one or more activities to be performed concurrently. <links> elements can be used within a <flow> activity to define explicit control dependencies between nested child activities: a <link> specifies that the activity the contains its <source> element must be executed before the one that includes the link's <target> element. These activities, in turn, may contain basic activities: the <invoke> activity, that allows the business process to invoke a one-way or request-response operation on a communications channel offered by a partner; the <receive> activity that allows the business process to wait in a blocking mode for a matching message to arrive; the <reply> activity that allows the business process to send a message in reply to a message that was received via a <receive> activity. The <scope> activity defines a sub-process with its own variables, partner links, message exchanges, correlation sets, event handlers, fault handlers, a compensation handler, and a termination handler.

The creation of a business process instance in WS-BPEL is always implicit; activities that receive messages (that is, <receive> activities and <pick> activities) can be annotated to indicate that the occurrence of that activity results in a new instance of the business process to be created. When a message is received by such an activity, an instance of the business process is created if it does not already exist. A business process instance is terminated when one of the following conditions hold: the last activity in the process terminates; a fault occurs, and it is not handled appropriately; or a process is terminated explicitly by a terminate activity.

To provide concrete examples of the proposed extensions to the WS-BPEL language, we introduce, as a running example, a purchase ordering process being part of a purchase ordering and financial system.

Example 1. *There are six activities involved in ordering and paying for goods:*

- *the creation of a purchase order requesting goods from a supplier (crtPO);*
- *the approval of the purchase order prior to dispatch to the supplier (apprPO);*
- *the acknowledgement of delivery of the goods by signing a goods received note (signGRN);*

Figure 1. A purchase order process specification

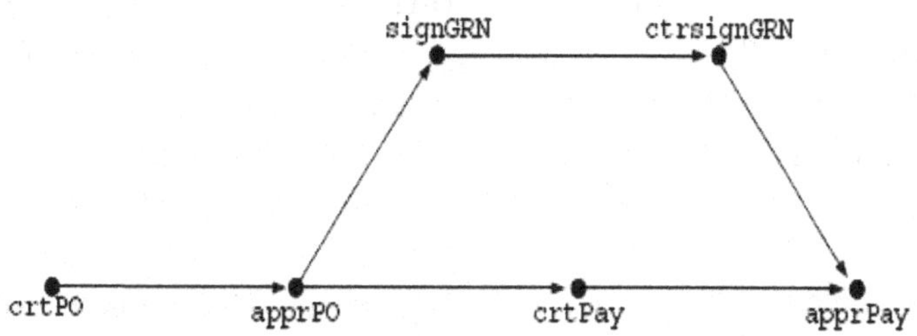

- *the acknowledgement of delivery by countersigning the goods received note (ctrsignGRN);*
- *the creation of a payment file on receipt of the supplier's invoice for the goods (crtPay);*
- *the approval of the payment to the supplier (subject to receipt of goods) (apprPay).*

An informal specification of the process is shown in Figure 1: an arc from one activity to another means that the former activity must be executed before the latter. Hence, the execution of the crtPO activity must precede that of the apprPO activity, while the signGRN and crtPay activities can be executed in parallel because no execution order is specified. Algorithm 1 shows how the purchase order process is expressed in WS-BPEL. The process orchestrates the operations of four Web services: a Web services that provides the operation "crtPay" to create the payment file; a Web service providing the operation "apprPO", to approve the order and to send it to the supplier; a Web service that provides the operation "signGRN" that allows the signature of the good request note; and a Web service that offers the operation "apprPay" to approve the payment for the order. The <process> element is the root element and represents the whole business process specification. The structure of the main processing section is defined by the outer <sequence> element, which states that the contained activities are to be sequentially executed.

Algorithm 1. The purchase order process expressed in WS-BPEL

```
<process
name="purchaseOrderProcess"
   targetNamespace="http://acme.
com/ws-bp/purchase"
   xmlns="http://schemas.xml-
soap.org/ws/2003/03/business-
process/"
   xmlns="http://manufacturing.
org/wsdl/purchase"/>
<partnerLinks>
<partnerLink name="customer"
    partnerLinkType="PurchaseOrd
erPartnerLT"

myRole="PurchaseOrderService" />
<partnerLink name="approverPO"

partnerLinkType="ApproverPOLT"
      partnerRole="approverPO"
/>
<partnerLink
name="approverPOPayment"
      partnerLinkType="ApproverP
OPaymentLT"

partnerRole="approverPOPayment"
/>
                        <part-
nerLink name="creator"
  partnerLinkType="creatorLT"
```

```
  partnerRole="creator" />
                      <part-
nerLink name="signerGRN"
  partnerLinkType="signerGNRLT"
  partnerRole=" signerGNR" />
</partnerLinks>
<variables>
    <variable name="PO"
messageType="POMessage"/>
    <variable name="GRN"
messageType="GRNMessage"/>
    <variable name="PF"
messageType="PFMessage"/>
</variables>
<sequence>
    <receive
partnerLink="customer
" portType="crtPOPT"
operation="crtPO" variable="PO"
name="Create Purchase Order "
createInstance="yes">
    </receive>
           <invoke
partnerLink="approverPO
" portType="approvePOPT"
operation="apprPO"
inputVariable="PO" "
name="Approve Purchase Order " >
           </invoke>
    <flow>
      <links>
        <link name="signGRN-to-
ctrsignGRN"/>
      </links>
   <invoke
partnerLink="signerGNR" p
ortType="signGRNPT"
operation="signGRN"
inputVariable="GRN"  name="Sign
GRN" >
        <source
linkName="signGRN-to-ctrsign-
GRN"/>
      </invoke>
        <invoke
partnerLink="signerGNR"
portType="ctrsignGRNPT"
operation="ctrsignGRN"
inputVariable="GRN"
name="CounterSign GRN" >
         <target
linkName="signGRN-to-ctrsign-
GRN"/>
      </invoke>
   <invoke partnerLink="creator"
portType="ctrPayPT"
operation="ctrPay"
outputVariable="PF" "
name="Create Payment File" >
     </invoke>
   </flow>
     <invoke
partnerLink="ApproverPOPayment"
portType="apprPayPT"
operation="apprPay"
inputVariable="PF" name="Approve
Payment" >
    </invoke>
   </sequence>
</process>
```

The <sequence> element contains, in the following order: a "Create Purchase Order" <receive> activity representing the receipt of an order from a customer and the creation of the purchase order document, an "Approve Purchase Order" <invoke> activity, representing the invocation of operation "apprPO"; a <flow> activity modeling the concurrent execution of "Sign GRN", "CounterSign GNR" and "Create Payment File" <invoke> activities, and another "Approve Payment" <invoke> activity representing the execution of operation "apprPay". The <invoke> activities in the <flow> activity are concurrently executed, except for "Sign GRN" and "CounterSign GNR" since the execution of Sign GRN" must precede the one of "CounterSign GNR". The execution dependency between the "Sign GRN" and "CounterSign GNR" <invoke> activities is expressed using a <link> element: "Sign GRN" <invoke> activity is the source activity of the link "signGRN-to-ctrsignGRN", while "CounterSign GNR" <invoke> is the target activity.

Note that all <invoke> activities in the purchase order process require interactions with humans. In Section 8 we show how the execution of these activities is handled.

RBAC-WS-BPEL: AN AUTHORIZATION MODEL FOR WS-BPEL

A WS-BPEL process is a representation of a business process and is typically specified as a set of activities and a set of dependencies between the activities. The dependencies fall into two broad categories: those determined by the application logic of the process such as the order of execution of the activities (Rusinkiewicz, Sheth, 1995), and those determined by security requirements. WS-BPEL supports only the first of those dependency categories.

In this chapter we deal with the second category and focus on developing a role based authorization model for WS-BPEL. The model, referred to as *RBAC-WS-BPEL*, inherits all the components of traditional RBAC models: users, roles, **permissions, role hierarchies**, user-role assignment and role-permission assignment relations. Users are assigned to roles and roles are assigned to permissions. An *RBAC-WS-BPEL permission* represents the ability to execute an activity of a WS-BPEL business process. A user acquires the permission to execute a business process' activity only if he is assigned to a role that has the permission to perform that activity. *RBAC-WS-BPEL roles* are structured in a *hierarchy* that reflects the different responsibilities associated with a business process and defines a permissions inheritance relation among the roles. Moreover, RBAC-WS-BPEL allows one to specify *authorization constraints* like separation of duty requirements that place restrictions on the potential inheritance of permissions from opposing roles.

The main difference with respect to traditional RBAC models is that WS-BPEL business processes coordinates the operations of Web services provided by different organizations. Therefore, roles do not represent job functions within a single organization like in traditional RBAC models and potential users of the business process are not the employees of an organization performing job functions identified by roles. Then, business process' users may not be known a priori and there is a need for a mechanism to identify users and to assign them to roles. In RBAC-WS-BPEL users are thus identified by means of **digital credentials**. A credential contains a set of **attributes** characterizing the owner specified via (name, value) pairs. An *RBAC-WS-BPEL role* identifies a set of conditions on users' attributes. A user is assigned to a role if the user's credentials match the user's attribute conditions associated with the role.

Figure 2 illustrates the relations among the various RBAC-WS-BPEL components that are defined in what follows.

Definition 1 (RBAC-WS-BPEL permission). Let BP be a WS-BPEL business process. An RBAC-WS-BPEL permission is a tuple (A_i, Action) where A_i is the identifier of an activity in BP and Action identifies the type of action can be performed on activity A_i.

To render our specification open to future extensions, we do not specify the types of action that can be performed on an activity. In the following examples, we will consider the type of action *execute*, allowing a subject to carry out an activity of the business process.

Definition 2 (RBAC-WS-BPEL role). An *RBAC-WS-BPEL role* r is a set of attribute conditions $r = \{ac_i \mid ac_i \equiv \text{AttrName}_i \text{ op AttrValue}_i\}$, where AttrName_i identifies a user attribute name, op is a comparison or a set operator and AttrValue_i is a value, a set or a range of attribute values.

Two roles *r* and *r'* can be identified by the same

Figure 2. RBAC-WS-BPEL components representation

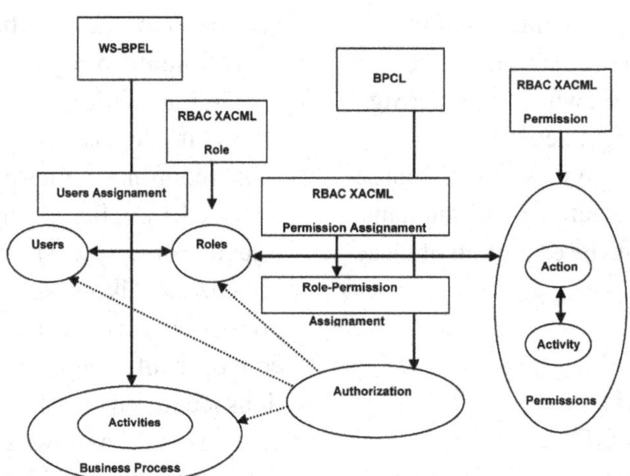

set of attributes names. However, it is required that at least one of the values that the attributes of *r* and *r'* assume must be different. Since we assume that a set of attribute conditions univocally identify a role, a user can be assigned only to one role, while two users identified by the same attributes with the same values are assigned to the same role.

Definition 3 (RBAC-WS-BPEL role hierarchy). Let R be a partially ordered set of roles. A *role hierarchy* defined over R is the graph of the partial order relation between the roles in R. If $r, r_0 \in R$ and $r < r_0$, then we say r_0 *dominates* r.

Example 3. *Figure 3 illustrates the RBAC-WS-BPEL role hierarchy for the purchase order business process. It consists of five different roles. The most senior role is Manager, which dominates the roles FinAdmin and POAdmin; FinAdmin and POAdmin, in turn, dominate, respectively, roles FinClerk and POClerk. For example, a user that wants to be assigned to the Manager role must provide digital credentials containing an Employment attribute equal to Manager, a Company attribute equal to Electronics&CO and an Age attribute equal to 45.*

Definition 4 (RBAC-WS-BPEL user-role assignment relation). Let U be the set of all potential users, R a partially ordered set of roles and CredSet(*u*) be the set of digital credentials associated with a user *u*. The *RBAC-WS-BPEL user-role assignment relation* is the set of tuples UA = $\{ (u, r) \in U \times R \mid \forall\, ac_i \equiv AttrName_i$ op $AttrValue_i \in r, \exists\, attr_j \in CredSet(u) \mid attr_j = AttrName_i \wedge ac_i$ is evaluated true according to the value of $attr_j \}$.

Definition 5 (RBAC-WS-BPEL authorization schema). Let BP be a WS-BPEL business process. A *RBAC-WS-BPEL authorization schema* for BP is a tuple (R, P, RA, UA) where R is a partially ordered set of roles associated with BP, P is the set of permissions defined for the activities in BP, $RA \subseteq R \times P$ is a role-permission assignment relation and UA is the user-role assignment relation.

One advantage of the role-based paradigm is that more senior roles inherit permissions assigned to more junior roles. This significantly reduces the number of permission-role assignments.

Example 4. *Figure 4(a)illustrates the set of permissions associated with the purchase order process comprising the ability to execute each of the activities in the purchase order.Figure 4(b) illustrates a typical permission-role assignment relation. Note that no permissions are explicitly assigned to the Manager role, although the role*

Figure 3. RBAC-WS-BPEL role hierarchy for the purchase order process

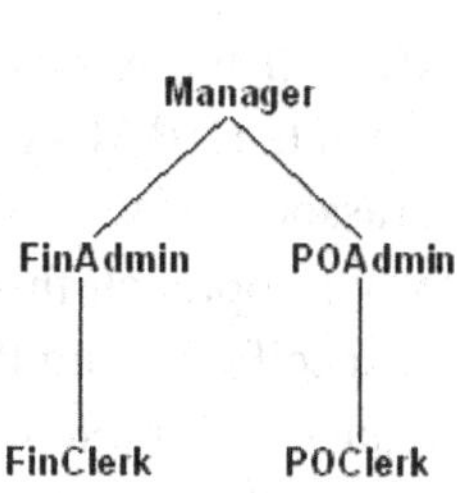

R	
Manager	{Employment = Manager, Company = Electronics&C O, Age = 45}
F inAdmin	{Bank = Chase, Employment = Branch Director}
F inC ler ck	{Bank = Chase, Employment = Employee}
POAdmin	{Employment = Administrator, Company = Electronics&CO, Age = 45}
POClerk	{Employment = Employee, Company = Electronics&C O}

Figure 4. RBAC-WS-BPEL permissions and role-permission assignment relation for the purchase order process

P	
P_1	(Approve Purchase Order, *execute*)
P_2	(Sign GNR, *execute*)
P_3	(Counter Sign GNR, *execute*)
P_4	(Create Payment File, *execute*)
P_5	(Approve Payment, *execute*)

a)

RA	
FinClerk	P_4
FinAdmin	P_5
POClerck	P_3
POAdmin	P_1

b)

does implicitly have the rights to execute all activities in the process. Similarly, the FinAdmin role has the permission to execute the Approve Payment <invoke> activity.

The above authorization model is complemented by a language supporting the specification of constraints. In particular, RBAC-WS-BPEL allows the specification of two different types of authorization constraints: *role authorization constraints* and *user authorization constraints*. We now formally introduce these two types of constraint.

Definition 6 (RBAC-WS-BPEL authorization constraints). Let U be a set of users and let be R a partially ordered set of roles. A *role authorization constraint* is a tuple $(D, (A_1, A_2), \rho)$, where $D \subseteq R$ is the domain of the constraint and $\rho \subseteq R \times R$. A *user authorization constraint* is a tuple $(D, (A_1, A_2), \rho)$, where $D \subseteq U$ is the *domain* of the constraint and $\rho \subseteq U \times U$. A constraint $(D, (A_1, A_2), \rho)$ is *satisfied* if, whenever $x \in D$ performs A_1 and y performs A_2, $(x, y) \in \rho$. Given a constraint $C \equiv (D,(A_1, A_2), \rho)$, we say that C *applies* to A_2.

An authorization constraint places some restrictions on the users/roles who can perform A_2 (the *consequent activity*) given that the user $u \in D$ or the role $r \in D$ has executed A_1 (the *antecedent activity*). We will use the notation $(D, (A_1, A_2), \neq)$ to denote a separation of duty constraint and $(D, (A_1,A_2), =)$ to denote a binding of duty constraint. Moreover, we can specify constraints that restrict the execution of two activities by users or roles, where that restriction can be expressed as a binary relation on the set of users or roles. Such relations could include "belongs-to-same-department-as" or "is-line-manager-of".

Example 5. *Finally, Figure 5 shows how the authorization constraints associated with the purchase order process are represented according to Definition 6. C_1, C_2 and C_3 are separation of duty constraints. C_1 and C_2 state, respectively, that the user that executes <invoke> activity "Approve Purchase Order" must be different from the user that performs <invoke> activity "Sign GNR" and the <invoke> activity "CounterSign GNR". C_3 imposes that the user that performs <invoke> activity "Sign GNR" must be different from the user that executes the <invoke> activity "CounterSign GNR". Finally, C_4 is a seniority constraint: it states that the role that performs <invoke> activity "Create Payment File" must be more senior than the role that performs <invoke> activity "Approve Payment".*

We can now formally introduce the notion of RBAC-WS-BPEL authorization specification combining all the previous notions.

Definition 7 (RBAC-WS-BPEL authorization specification). A RBAC-WS-BPEL *authorization specification* is a tuple (BP, AS, AC) where BP is a WS-BPEL business process, AS is the authorization schema defined for BP and AC is the set of authorization constraints that apply to the activities in BP.

RBAC-XACML-AUTHORIZATION SCHEMA

The first extension we propose to WS-BPEL is the specification of the RBAC-WS-BPEL authorization schema associated with a WS-BPEL business process. In our approach this component of the language is specified using the RBAC XACML policy language (Crampton 2005) proposed as an alternative to the RBAC profile for XACML (Anderson, 2004).

Algorithm 2. RBAC-WS-BPEL authorization schema expressed in pseudo-XACML

```
<!-- Role set -->
  <PolicySet
…….PolicySetId="set:roles" …….>
    <PolicySet
…….PolicySetId="role:Manager"
…….>
      <Target>…….Any user with
Employment attribute = "Manager"
and
      Company attribute
="Electronics&CO" and Age attri-
bute > " 45" …….
                    </Target>
      <PolicySetIdReference>perm
issions:Manager</PolicySetIdRef-
erence>
      <PolicySetIdReference>role
:FinAdmin</PolicySetIdReference>
      <PolicySetIdReference>role
```

Figure 5. RBAC-WS-BPEL authorization constraints for the purchase order process

AC	
C_1	(U, Approve Purchase Order, Sign GNR, $\neq$)
C_2	(U, Approve Purchase Order, CounterSign GNR, $\neq$)
C_3	(U, Sign GNR, CounterSign GNR, $\neq$)
C_4	(R, Create Payment File, Approve Payment, $<$)

```
:POAdmin</PolicySetIdReference>
    </PolicySet>
    <PolicySet
…….PolicySetId="role:FinAdmin"
…….>
      <Target> ……. Any user with
Employment attribute = "Branch
Director" and
                     Company at-
tribute ="Electronics&CO"…….
    </Target>
      <PolicySetIdReference>per
missions:FinAdmin</PolicySetI-
dReference>
      <PolicySetIdReference>role
:FinClerk</PolicySetIdReference>
    </PolicySet>
    <PolicySet
…….PolicySetId="role:FinClerk"
…….>
                     <Target>
…….Any user with Employment at-
tribute  = "Employee" and
     Bank  attribute   =
"Chase"…….
       </Target>
      <PolicySetIdReference>per
missions:FinClerk</PolicySetI-
dReference>
    </PolicySet>
    …….
  </PolicySet>
  <!-- Role-permission assign-
ment relation -->
  <PolicySet
…….PolicySetId="relation:ra"
…….>
    <PolicySet …….PolicySetId="p
ermissions:FinAdmin" …….>
      <PolicySetIdReference>perm
ission:pay:approve</PolicySetI-
dReference>
      <PolicySetIdReference>perm
ission:sign:grn</PolicySetIdRef-
erence>
   </PolicySet>
  <PolicySet …….PolicySetId="perm
issions:POClerk" …….>
      <PolicySetIdReference>per
mission:create:po</PolicySetI-
dReference>
      <PolicySetIdReference>perm
ission:sign:grn</PolicySetIdRef-
erence>
    </PolicySet>
  </PolicySet>
  <!-- Permission set -->
  <PolicySet …….PolicySetId="set
:permissions" …….>
    <Target> …….Any subject, any
resource, any action …….</Tar-
get>
    <Policy …….PolicyId="permiss
ion:po:approve" …….>
      <Rule …….>
        <Target> …….Approve pur-
chase order <invoke> activity
…….execute
        </Target>
      </Rule>
    </Policy>
    <Policy …….PolicyId="permiss
ion:pay:approve" …….>
      <Rule …….>
        <Target> …….Approve Pay-
ment <invoke> activity …….ex-
ecute </Target>
      </Rule>
    </Policy>
  </PolicySet>
```

Algorithm 2 shows how the RBAC-WS-BPEL authorization schema reported in Figures 4 and 5 can be encoded in XACML. The authorization policy uses three different kinds of XACML policies, each one represented by a <PolicySet> element. The set P of permissions associated with a WS-BPEL business process is represented by a

Permission <PolicySet> containing a Permission <Policy> element for each permission in P. The RA role-permission assignment relation is represented by a PermissionAssignment <PolicySet> element: it includes a <PolicySet> subelement for each role to which the relation RA assigns a permission. Each <PolicySet> subelement contains a <PolicySetIdReference> child node for each permission assigned to the role. <PolicySetIdReference> refers to the Permission <Policy> element that represents the permission. Finally, a Role <PolicySet> element represents a role in the hierarchy. For example, the Manager role is represented by the Role <PolicySet> element having <PolicySetId> attribute equal to role:Manager. The <Target> subelement limits the applicability of the Role <PolicySet> to users satisfying the specified attribute conditions. The <Target> subelement of Role <PolicySet> representing the Manager role has two <Subject> subelements that specify the attributes' conditions that a users has to satisfy to be assigned to Manager role: only the directors working for the "Electronic&CO" company older then 45 years can be assigned to Manger role. <PolicySetIdReference> subelements are used to refer to the PermissionAssignment <PolicySet> element containing the set of permissions associated with the Manager role. In addition, they are used to represent the role hierarchy, by referencing immediate junior roles. The Manager role, for example, references the Role <PolicySet> elements for roles FinAdmin and POAdmin.

Algorithm 3. BCPL representation of the constraints in Figure 5

```
<AuthorizationConstraints>
    <Constraint Id="C1">
      <Domain>
        <Type>User</Type>
        <Subject/>
      </Domain>
      <Activities>
       <AntecedentActivityRef-
erence xlink:type="simple"
xlink:href="purchase_order_wsb-
pelspec.xml#xpointer(//*[@
name="Approve Payment "])"/>
       <ConsequentActivityRef-
erence xlink:type="simple"
xlink:href="purchase_order_wsb-
pelspec.xml#xpointer(//*[@
name="Sign GRN"])"/>
      </Activities>
      <Predicate>not equal</
Predicate>
    </Constraint>
    <Constraint Id="C4">
      <Domain>
        <Type>Role</Type>
        <Subject/>
      </Domain>
      <Activities>
       <AntecedentActivityRef-
erence xlink:type="simple"
xlink:href="purchase_order_wsb-
pelspec.xml#xpointer(//*[@
name="Create Payment File"])"/>
      <ConsequentActivityRef-
erence xlink:type="simple"
xlink:href="purchase_order_wsb-
pelspec.xml#xpointer(//*[@
name="Approval Payment"])"/>
      </Activities>
      <Predicate>seniority</
Predicate>
    </Constraint>
  </AuthorizationConstraints>
```

BCPL-BUSINESS PROCESS CONSTRAINT LANGUAGE

We now introduce an XML-based language for the specification of authorization constraints such as separation of duty and binding of duty. We call this language BPCL (Business Process Constraint

Language). BPCL provides an XML Schema template for specifying authorization constraints, reported in Appendix A.

According to the proposed XML Schema, an <AuthorizationConstraints> element contains all the authorization constraints that apply to the activities in a WS-BPEL business process. Each constraint $C \equiv (D, (A_1, A_2), \rho)$ is represented by a <Constraint> element having an Id attribute by which it is referenced. The <Constraint> element has three subelements: <Domain>, <Activities> and <Predicate>. The <Domain> element represents the domain D of the constraint C. It has two child elements, <Type> and <Subject>. The data content of the <Type> element specifies the type of the constraint C: it contains the value "role" if C is a role authorization constraint and the value "user" if C is a user authorization constraint. The content of <Subject> element is either a set of roles or a set of users and depends on the contents of the <Type> element.

The <Activities> element specifies the two activities A_1 and A_2 to which the constraint C applies. In particular, <Activities> has two child nodes, <AntecedentActivityReference> and <ConsequentActivityReference>, containing, respectively, an XLink reference to the XML element representing activities A_1 and A_2 in the WS-BPEL specification. Finally, the <Predicate> element data content identifies the relation ρ in C: for example the string "equal" identifies the relation =, while the string "not equal" identifies the relation $\neq$.

Algorithm 3 illustrates the use of BPCL in defining the authorization constraints associated with the purchase order process. For example, the constraint (U, (Approve Payment, Sign GRN),$\neq$) is represented by the <Constraint> element with Id attribute "C_1". Notice that the content of the <Subject> element can be empty, as in both C_1 and C_4, in which case all elements in the appropriate domain are considered. In C_4, the <AntecedentActivityReference> and <ConsequentActivityReference> elements, respectively, refer to the "Create Payment File" and "Approval Payment" activities (in the purchase order WS-BPEL specification) to which the constraint is applied. The relation < is represented by the string "seniority" in the <Predicate> element data content. Further, since (R, (Create Payment File, Approve Payment),<) is a role authorization constraint, the <Type> data content element is equal to "role".

RBAC-WS-BPEL AUTHORIZATION SPECIFICATION

In this section we illustrate how our extensions are incorporated into the purchase order process WS-BPEL specification introduced in Section 2. WS-BPEL has been designed to be extensible. Extensions to WS-BPEL could include anything ranging from new attributes to new elements, to extended assign operations and activities, to enable restrictions or extensions of run time behaviour and so on. The <process> element contains an <extensions> element having an <extension> child element that is used to declare namespaces of WS-BPEL extension attributes/elements and indicate whether they carry semantics that must be understood by a WS-BPEL processor. WS-BPEL allows, also, the definition of new type of activities by placing them inside the <extensionActivity> element. The contents of an <extensionActivity> element must be a single element qualified with a namespace different from WS-BPEL namespace. We have applied the WS-BPEL extension rules to specify which activities requires the interaction with users and to specify the authorization information and the authorization constraints applied to these activities.

First, we have declared into the process specification an <extension> element specifying the namespace "http://www.example.org/ rbac-ws-bpel" that identifies our extensions. Then, we have introduced a new type of WS-BPEL activity called <HumanActivity> to specify the activities that must be performed by humans:

<HumanActivity> contains the activity that to be performed requires the interaction with a user. Finally, we have added two new child elements to the <process> element: <authorization_schema> and <authorization_constraints> to include the references to the authorization information necessary to state which roles or users are allowed to execute the business process' activities, and the authorization constraints that apply to the activities in the process. <authorization_schema> and <authorization_constraints> elements has a "ref" attribute of type URI respectively pointing, to the XML document defining the RBAC policy and to the BPCL representation of the authorization constraints.

As we can see from the RBAC-WS-BPEL specification of the purchase order, our approach for associating authorization information and authorization constraints with a business process' human activities is characterized by some interesting features. First, the specification of authorization information and authorization constraints in the WS-BPEL specification does not require a significant modification to the syntax of the language. We simply require the inclusion of two new XML elements in the WS-BPEL syntax, which refer to the authorization information and the authorization constraints. Hence, the specification of a WS-BPEL business process that includes authorization information and authorization constraints is modular. Furthermore, with this approach it is easy to modify the authorization information and authorization constraints associated with the business process since only the references to them need to be modified. Second, the language we have proposed for the specification of authorization constraints is very expressive. It supports the specification of binding of duty constraints, separation of duty constraints and constraints that restrict the execution of two activities by users or roles, whereby such restriction can be expressed as a binary relation on the set of users and roles.

Algorithm 4. Extended WS-BPEL purchase order business process

```
 <process
name="purchaseOrderProcess" tar-
getNamespace = " http://acme.
com/ws-bp/purchase" ....... "/>
<bpel:extensions>
   <bpel:extension  namespace= "
http://www.example.org/ rbac-ws-
bpel " mustUnderstand = "yes"/>
  </bpel:extensions>
  <rbac-ws-bpel: authoriza-
tion_schema    ref ="http://www.
example.org/rolehierachy.xml"/>
  <rbac-ws-bpel: authorization_
constraints  ref = " http://www.
example.org/authorization_con-
straints.xml"/>
<partnerLinks>
 </partnerLinks>
 <variables>
  </variables>
  <sequence>
    <receive
partnerLink="customer
" portType="crtPOPT"
operation="crtPO" variable="PO"
name="Create Purchase Order "
createInstance="yes">
    </receive>
     <extensionActivity>
        <rbac-ws-bpel: HumanAc-
tivity>
           <invoke
partnerLink="approverPO
" portType="approvePOPT"
operation="apprPO"
inputVariable="PO"
            name="Approve Pur-
chase Order " >
         </invoke>
       </HumanActivity>
```

```
  <extensionActivity>
 </sequence>
  </process>
```

RBAC-WS-BPEL ENFORCEMENT

In the previous sections we have presented the main components of RBAC-WS-BPEL, the access control model we have proposed for WS-BPEL. In this section we describe the algorithm we use to determine if a user request to execute an activity A_i in a WS-BPEL process can be satisfied or not.

When a user u issues a request to perform an activity A_i of a WS-BPEL process, the enforcement system evaluates the identity of the requester, assigns him to a role and checks the permissions he has. Further, it has to verify that the execution of the activity A_i by u does not violate any authorization constraints and does not prevent some other subsequent activities from completing because certain constraints are violated. Hence, for a given instance of WS-BPEL process, when the enforcement system receives a request to perform an activity A_i by a user u it has to verify that:

- u is authorized to perform A_i;
- all the constraints in which A_i is the consequent activity are satisfied;
- the WS-BPEL process instance can complete if u performs A_i.

In what follows, we present an algorithm to evaluate whether a request to execute an activity by a user can be granted or not. Our algorithm verifies whether the WS-BPEL process instance will complete and that no authorization constraints be violated. The algorithm is performed before executing any request (u, r, i, A_k) to check if the execution of the request does not prevent the WS-BPEL process instance from completing. To guarantee completeness, before granting a request, the authorization schema associated with the WS-BPEL process is updated with the fact that the user u under role r has executed activity A_k. Then, the algorithm computes for each activity in the WS-BPEL process the set of roles and users that are entitled to perform them. If one of these sets is empty the request cannot be granted. After each request is granted, the authorization schema AS is updated with the fact that the user u under role r has executed activity A_k to ensure that the fact that a particular user and role has executed a particular activity is considered in enforcing constraints that apply to subsequent activities.

In what follows, we denote with $((A_i, A_j), \rho)$, both role and user authorization constraints.

The algorithm receives as input an RBAC-WS-BPEL authorization specification (BP, AS, AC), an instance i of the WS-BPEL process BP and a request *(u, r, i, A_k)* by a user u to execute activity A_k in BP under the role r. When the request *(u, r, i, A_k)* is received, the algorithm first adds to the authorization schema the "fact" that the role r of user u is executing the activity A_k. To represent this, we have added a function I_R that associates with each activity A_i in BP the role that has executed A_i. This step is important to guarantee the completeness of the instance i (line 1).

Then, for each pairs of activities A_i and A_j, the algorithm builds $V_R(A_i, A_j)$ where $V_R(A_i, A_j)$ is the set of roles that can execute A_i and A_j (in that order) given the authorization schema AS and the role authorization constraints in AC. The basic strategy to compute $V_R(A_i, A_j)$ is to initialize each $V_R(A_i)$ to the set of roles that are authorized to perform A_i (line 3) and to apply all possible role constraints defined for each pair of activities, including those derived from authorization information (lines 5–6). If for some A_i and A_j, $V_R(A_i, A_j)$ is empty, then the algorithm terminates (line 07), since no a pair of authorized roles exist that comply with the role authorization constraints, and therefore no valid execution assignment exists for the instance i. Otherwise, for each task activity A_i we (re-)compute the set of roles that can perform A_i (lines 10–11). The same steps (lines 12-22) are repeated to compute for each activity

A_i the set $V_U(A_i)$ of users authorized to perform A_i. If the role *r* played by *u* belongs to $V_R(A_k)$, the set of roles authorized to execute the activity A_k and *u* belongs to $V_U(A_k)$, the set of users that are authorized to perform A_k, the request *(u, r, i,* A_k*)* can be granted.

Algorithm 5. An algorithm to evaluate a user request to perform an activity in a WS-BPEL process

```
INPUT:
A RBAC-WS-BPEL authorization specification (BP, AS, AC)
An instance i of BP
A request (u, r, i, A_k) by a user u to execute activity A_k in BP under the role r
OUTPUT:
Request (u, r, i, A_k) granted or denied
1) AS = AS ∩ I_R(A_k)
2) For each A_i in BP
3)    V_R (A_i) ={ r_i ∈ R | (r_i, P_Ai) ∈ RA }
4) For each possible couple of activities A_i and A_j in BP
5)    If ((A_i, A_j), ρ) ∈ AC
6)        V_R (A_i, A_j) = (V_R (A_i) x V_R (A_j)) ∩ ρ
7)        If V_R (A_i, A_j) = ∅
8)            (u, r, i, A_k) is denied
9)        Else
10)               V_R (A_i) = set of roles in first position of V_R (A_i, A_j)
11)               V_R (A_j) = set of roles in second position of V_R (A_i, A_j)
12)   AS = AS ∩ I_u(A_k)
13)   For each A_i in BP
14)       V_U (A_i) ={ set of user authorized to perform A_i }
15)       For each possible couple of activities A_i and A_j in BP
16)           If ((A_i, A_j), ρ) ∈ AC
17)               V_U (A_i, A_j) = (V_U (A_i) x V_U (A_j)) ∩ ρ
18)               If V_U(A_i, A_j) = ∅
19)                   (u, r, i, A_k) is denied
20)               Else
21)                   V_U (A_i) = set of users in first position of V_U (A_i, A_j)
22)                   V_U (A_j) = set of users in second position of V_U (A_i, A_j)
23)      If r ∈V_R (A_k) ∧ u ∈V_U (A_k)
24)          (u, r, i, A_k) is granted
```

RBAC-WS-BPEL SYSTEM ARCHITECTURE

In this section, we describe a possible implementation for the proposed RBAC-WS-BPEL access control model on top of a WS-BPEL engine. Figure 6 represents the architecture that implements the access control enforcement described in Section 7. The main components are: a WS-BPEL engine, a Web service called *RBAC-WS-BPEL Enforcement Service*, that is the core of the architecture, and three repositories: XACML Policy Store, BPCL constraints Store and the History Store. The WS-BPEL engine is responsible for scheduling and synchronizing the various activities within the business process, according to the specified activity dependencies, and for invoking Web service operations associated with activities. The RBAC-WS-BPEL Enforcement Service has two tasks. First, it manages the execution of business process's <HumanActivity> activity.

It is important to notice that our Enforcement Service is able to manage such execution without requiring any extensions to legacy WS-BPEL engines. Second, it acts as a reference monitor: when a user claims a <HumanActivity> activity, it verifies that the user is authorized to perform it according to the authorization schema and authorization constraints.

The RBAC-WS-BPEL Enforcement Service offers two WSDL interfaces: the first interface provides the operations to start and complete the execution of a human activity. This interface provides two operations "initiateActivity" and "onActivityResult". "initiateActivity" is a one-way operation that is invoked within a WS-BPEL process to start the execution of a <HumanActivity> activity. The invocation message of "initiateActivity" contains a set of information about the activity, the business process and references to authorization schema and authorization constraints. Algorithm 6 illustrates the content of "initiateActivity" invocation message for <HumanActivity> representing the execution of "Approve Purchase Order" <invoke> activity. The "onActivityResult" callback operation is performed to notify to WS-BPEL engine that the execution of a <HumanActivity> activity is completed. The message received by the WS-BPEL process contains the business process variables modified by the <HumanActivity>.

The second interface of the RBAC-WS-BPEL Enforcement service allows users to display the activities they can claim, and to claim and execute them. This interface offers two operations "listActivity" and, "claimActivity". The "listActivity" operation returns the list of the activities a user can claim. To claim an activity in the list, a user invokes the "claimActivity" operation. When this activity is executed, the RBAC-WS-BPEL Enforcement Services selects all possible BCPL constraints and the information in XACML authorization schema and runs Algorithm 5 to determine if the user request can be granted or not. If the user is authorized, the WSDL operation providing the interface of the <HumanActivity> activity that is specified in the invocation message of the "initiateActivity" operation is invoked.

XACML Policy Store contains the RBAC-WS-BPEL authorization schema associated with the business process, while BPCL constraints Store stores the authorization constraints. The History Store is used to record the past executions of each human activity: the user who has performed it and if the execution of the activity was successful or

Figure 6. RBAC-WS-BPEL Architecture

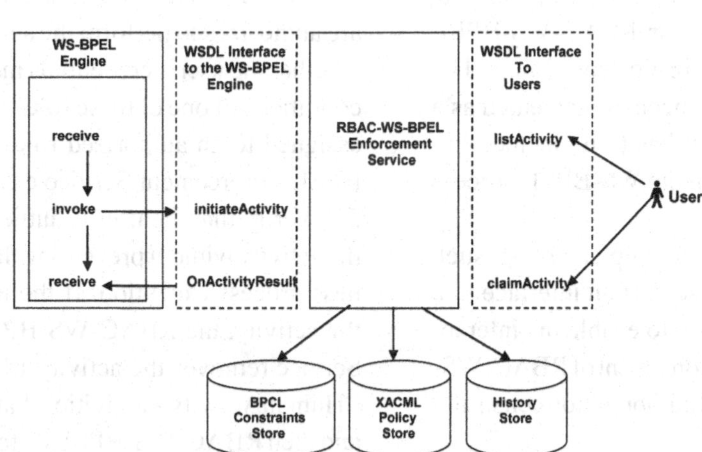

not. The history information is used to enforce authorization constraints.

Algorithm 6. Example of initiate Activity invocation message

```
<initiateActivityInputMsg>
            !--WS-BPEL Business
process variables  the task has
to manipulate--!
         <variables>
               <variable name =
"PO" > value<variable>
        </variables>
        <HumanActivityInter-
face portType="approvePOPT"
operation="apprPO"
inputVariable="PO"
                    name="Approve
Purchase Order " >
       </HumanActivityInterface>
       <rbac-ws-bpel: authoriza-
tion_schema
```

HANDLING <HUMANACTIVITY> ACTIVITY EXECUTION AND RBAC-WS-BPEL ENFORCEMENT

A prototype of the architecture which supports the execution of <HumanActivity> activities has been implemented choosing ODE as WS-BPEL engine and Oracle 10g to store for RBAC-WS-BPEL authorizations and authorization constraints. The Enforcement Service has been implemented as a JAVA Web service which has to be included to the <partnerLinks> list in the WS-BPEL process specification.

The main challenge in implementing such architecture is how to associate an interface to a <HumanActivity> activity to enable the interaction with a user and the enforcement of RBAC-WS-BPEL authorizations and authorization constraint on such activity.

First, it is necessary to configure the Enforcement Service to work with a specific instance of the WS-BPEL process which requires the execution of <HumanActivity> activities. Through a configuration wizard, the WS-BPEL process administrator has to specify the name of the WS-BPEL process, the URL of the process, the variables in the process that represent the correlation set used to identify an instance of the process, and the order on which the activities are executed. Moreover, for each <HumanActivity> activity, the WS-BPEL process administrator has to specify the name of the activity, the Web service operation that is associated with the execution of the activity, the operation portType, the template of the SOAP input message for the operation, and a jsp that is the interface for the user who has to perform the \xmlelement{HumanActivity} activity.

The execution of a <HumanActivity> activity starts when the WS-BPEL process invokes the ``initiateActivity'' operation of the Enforcement Service. The process then waits to be called back by the RBAC-WS-BPEL Enforcement Service. The RBAC-WS-BPEL Enforcement Service adds the name of the activity contained in the invocation message to the list of <HumanActivity> activities that can be claimed. When a user requests the <HumanActivity> activity by invoking the ``claimActivity'' operation it includes in the invocation message a set of digital credentials that are encoded as SAML assertions. Then, the RBAC-WS-BPEL Enforcement Service queries the XACML Policy store to determine the roles that are authorized to perform the activity and verifies whether the user's credentials match the attribute conditions of one of these roles. If the user can be assigned to an authorized role, the RBAC-WS-BPEL Enforcement Service executes Algorithm 5 to verify that the user is authorized to perform the activity without preventing the end of the business process execution. If the user can perform the activity, the RBAC-WS-BPEL Enforcement Service removes the activity from the list of the <HumanActivity> activities that can be claimed, and then RBAC-WS-BPEL Enforcement Service instantiates a JAVA class Action. Such class retrieves the information for the <HumanActivity>

activity set up by the WS-BPEL process administrator during the configuration of the RBAC-WS-BPEL Enforcement Service, and prompts the jsp interface to the user. Once the user has input the data necessary to perform the <HumanActivity> } activity, the RBAC-WS-BPEL Enforcement Service populates the SOAP invocation message of the operation associated with the execution of the <HumanActivity> activity, with the data inserted by the user and then invokes the operation. If the execution of the operation completes successfully, the RBAC-WS-BPEL Enforcement Service calls back the WS-BPEL process performing passing the output message of the operation. Finally, the RBAC-WS-BPEL Enforcement Service updates the History Store recording, the name of the user who performs the activity and whether the execution was successfully or not.

RELATED WORKS

The problem of associating an authorization model with a workflow has been widely investigated. Atluri et al. (Atluri, 1996) have proposed a workflow authorization model (WTA) that supports the specification of authorizations is such a way that subjects gain access to required objects only during the execution of a task, thus synchronizing the authorization flow with the workflow. To achieve such synchronization, their approach associates an Authorization Template (AT) with each task in the workflow, which allows appropriate authorizations to be granted only when the task starts and to revoke them when the tasks finishes. They have proposed an implementation of WAT using Petri nets in order to be able to perform safety analysis because the safety problem in WAT is equivalent to the reachability problem in Petri nets.

Compared with the work of Atluri et al., RBAC-WS-BPEL does not allow the specification of temporal authorizations that have a validity only within the expected duration of a certain task or activity, while both the model supports the specification of role based authorizations and separation of duties constraints. In both the models the assignment of authorized users to activities is done during the execution of the business process.

Arguably, the most sophisticated approach to the problem of authorizing users to execute tasks within a workflow, while enforcing constraints, is the one by Bertino et al. (Bertino, 1999). According to such approach a workflow is a list of task-role specifications. A task-role specification identifies a task, specifies the roles authorized to perform the task, and the maximum number of activations of the task that are permitted in an instance of the workflow. The model, however, supports only a sequential task execution. As part of such approach, a language for defining constraints on role assignment and user assignment to tasks in a workflow has been developed. Such constraint language supports, among other functions, both static and dynamic separation of duty constraints. The authors, also, have shown how such constraints can be formally expressed as clauses in a logic program; such reduction makes it possible to exploit results from logic programming and deductive databases. A further contribution of such approach is the development of algorithms for planning role and user assignments to the various tasks. The goal of algorithms is to precompute all the possible role-task assignments and users-tasks assignment, so that all constraints stated as part of the authorization specification are satisfied. A drawback of this approach is that the algorithms for roles and user assignment to tasks run in a time exponential in the number of tasks in the workflow.

Both the model of Bertino et al. and RBAC-WS-BPEL are role based authorization models and allow the definition of authorization constraints restricting the set of users and of roles that can execute an activity. Unlike the model of Bertino et al., in RBAC-WS-BPEL a role represents a set of user attributes conditions a user has to satisfy in order to be assigned to the role. Moreover, RBAC-WS-BPEL supports sequential, concurrent, conditional and iterative execution of activities, while the model of Bertino et al. supports only sequential execution. Finally, the model of Bertino et al. determines all the possible assignments of user and roles to activities before the execution of a workflow is started, while in RBAC-WS-BPEL the assignment is done at runtime when a user claims the execution of an activity.

Another interesting work is by Crampton (Crampton, 2005). He has proposed an expressive method for specifying authorization constraints in workflow systems. In particular, his model allows the specification of separation of duty constraints, weak separation of duty constraints, binding of duty constraints, constraints on the relative seniority of users who perform different tasks, and constraints determined by contextual user-based information. All the constraints are expressed as binary relations on the set of users. The model has the advantage of being independent from any computational model or access control mechanism. As part of such an approach, an algorithm has been proposed for the assignment of authorized users to tasks in a workflow that guarantees that the workflow instance completes. The algorithm runs in a time polynomial in the number of users and tasks, unlike the equivalent procedure in the model proposed by Bertino et al.

Unlike the work of Crampton, RBAC-WS-BPEL assumes a role based access control enforcement. Both models specify authorization constraints as a binary relation on the set of users. Unlike the model of Crampton, RBAC-WS-BPEL allows also the definition of authorization constraints on the set of roles. Moreover, in the models the assignment of authorized users to activities in a business process is performed at runtime in a way that guarantees that the business process instance completes.

Casati et al. (Casati, 2001) have proposed an authorization framework for the assignment of tasks to roles, organizational levels, and agents. Roles and organizational levels are structured into hierarchies to facilitate the assignment of tasks to agents. Authorizations for agents to play roles/levels and for roles/levels to execute tasks can be specified for all instances of a given workflow process, independently of time and workflow execution history. Then, the framework enables the definition of instance dependent, time-dependent, and history-dependent authorizations in the form of constraints: authorizations can be modified depending on the state or history of a workflow instance, on the time, or on the content of process data. Authorization constraints are enforced as Event-Condition-Action (ECA) rules, where the event part denotes when an authorization may need to be modified, and the condition part verifies that the occurred event actually requires modifications of authorizations, and determines the involved agents, roles, tasks, and processes, while the action part enforces authorizations and prohibitions. Active rules are also exploited for managing authorization inheritance along the role and level hierarchies of the framework. Active database technology has been adopted for the implementation of the framework; it has been used in particular, to support the definition and execution of ECA rules. Finally, they have presented the implementation of the authorization framework within the WIDE workflow management system.

RBAC-WS-BPEL and the model of Casati et al. are a role based access control model. In the model of Casati et al. authorization constraints also model time and history-dependent authorizations; RBAC-WS-BPEL supports only the specification of history-dependent authorization constraints. In both approaches authorization and authorization constraints are evaluated at runtime during the execution of a business process.

With the widespread adoption of Web services to implement complex business process and of WS-BPEL as the standard language to specify business processes based on Web services, the problem of how to associate authorized users with the activities of a WS-BPEL process is gaining attention. The RBAC-WS-BPEL authorization model that has been introduced in this chapter is one of the few approaches that address this problem. Another similar approach is the one of Koshutanski et al. (Koshutanski, 2003). They propose an authorization model for business processes based on Web services. In this approach, the authorization logic is decoupled from the application logic of the business process. Access control enforcement is based on two types of policies: access control policies and release policies. Both types of policy are expressed as logic rules specifying conditions on the credentials a user must submit to invoke business process activities. Access control policies are used to decide if a user request can be granted or not. A request is granted if is a logical consequence of an access control policy and of the credentials submitted by the user with the request. Release policies are used, when a user request is denied, to determine the additional credentials that a user has to provide for the request to be granted. The enforcement process involves different components. A Policy Evaluator is associated with each Web services the activities of which are orchestrated in a business process: it takes local authorization decisions. A Policy Orchestrator defines an authorization business process that orchestrates the authorization processes performed by the Policy Evaluators of the Web services invoked to fulfill a user's request. The authorization business process is executed by a third component called Authorization Server that returns the result of the execution to the user. If the user request is denied, the user receives a business process that defines the further actions that he has to execute in order to see its request accepted.

Both the model of Koshutanski et al. and RBAC-WS-BPEL assume a role based access control model. Both models support the specification of authorizations to roles and to users by assigning a user to a role and the specification of authorizations constraints on the set of users and roles.

In both models the assignment of users to roles is attribute based.

Authorizations in the model of Koshutanski et al. grant the execution of a Web service to a user or role, while in RBAC-WS-BPEL authorizations grant the execution of a Web service's operation.

In the model of Koshutanski et al. authorizations and authorization constraints are both expressed using logic rules, while in RBAC-WS-BPEL RBAC-XACML is used to model authorizations and BPCL to specify authorization constraints. Moreover, the model of Koshutanski et al. supports the specification of release policies to determine the additional credentials that a user has to provide to be granted a previously denied request. RBAC-WS-BPEL does not allow the specification of release policies: if a user cannot be assigned to a role on the basis of the credentials he submits, his request to perform an activity is denied.

Another interesting proposal is BPEL4People, recently proposed by IBM and SAP. BPEL4People includes extensions to WS-BPEL that are required in order to support user interactions. BPEL4People is comprised of the two following specifications:

- WS-BPEL Extension for People (Agrawal et al., 2007) layers features on top of WS-BPEL to describe human tasks as activities that may be incorporated as first class components in WS-BPEL process definitions.
- Web services Human Task (WS-HumanTask) (Agrawal et al., 2007) introduces the definition of standalone human tasks, including their properties, behavior, and operations used to manipulate them. Capabilities provided by WS-HumanTask may be utilized by Web services based applications beyond WS-BPEL processes.

WS-BPEL Extension for People introduces a new basic WS-BPEL activity called <people activity> which uses human tasks as an implementation, and allows specifying tasks local to a process or user tasks defined outside of the process definition. The definition of standalone human tasks is given in WS-HumanTask specification. A local task can be a) an inline task declared within the people activity, b) an inline task declared within either the scope containing the <people activity> or the process scope or c) a standalone task identified using a QName. The element <task> is used to define an inline task within a <people activity>. The elements <localtask> and <remotetask> are used to specify, respectively, standalone tasks that do not offer a callable Web service interface and those that offer a callable Web service interface. The users entitled to perform a <people activity> are specified by a <peopleAssignment> element that associates to the activity a query on an organizational directory.

Both RBAC-WS-BPEL and BPEL4People introduce a new type of WS-BPEL activity to handle human interactions in a WS-BPEL and specify how the execution of this activity is performed.

In RBAC-WS-BPEL human activities have always a callable Web service interface, while BPEL4People supports also human activities without a callable Web service interface. Moreover.

BPEL4People does not allow the specification and the enforcement of authorizations and authorizations constraints on human activities, while RBAC-WS-BPEL does.

Xiangpeng et al. (Xiapeng et al., 2006) propose an RBAC access control model for WS-BPEL business process. Roles correspond to <partnerRole> elements in the WS-BPEL specification and are organized in a hierarchy. Permissions corresponds to the execution of the basic activities in the process specification. In addition, it is possible to specify in linear temporal logic (LTL) separation of duty constraints and to verify that a business process is completable under these constraints. The verification is performed using SAL model checker. RBAC-BPEL and the model of Xiangpeng et al. apply RBAC model to WS-BPEL business processes and allow the specification of authorization constraints. RBAC-BPEL's BCPL constraints language allows to express a broader range of authorizations constraints than the model of Xiangpeng et al. Moreover, both the models propose an approach to verify that a business process terminates without violating any authorization constraints.

CONCLUSION

In this chapter we have proposed two extensions to WS-BPEL. The first extension is the introduction of a new type of WS-BPEL activity to specify those activities that are not automatically executed but require the interaction with a user to be completed. The second extension is RBAC-WS-BPEL, a role based access control model for WS-BPEL language that supports the specification of authorization information necessary to state if a role or a user is allowed to execute human activities composing the processes. The authorization information comprises a role hierarchy reflecting the organizational structure, a permission-role assignment relation and a set of permissions which represent the ability to execute activities. The authorization information is encoded using XACML. We have also defined a schema for BPCL, a new XML-based language for describing authorization constraints. Such constraints place restrictions on the roles and users that can perform the activities in the business process. Furthermore, we have illustrated how these components can be included in the business process specification. We have proposed an algorithm to evaluate if a request by a user to perform an activity in a WS-BPEL process can be granted or not. The algorithm verifies whether the execution of a WS-BPEL process will complete without violation to the authorization constraints. Finally, we have proposed an implementation of the access control enforcement on WS-BPEL engine that does not require any modification to existing engines.

One of the advantages of our approach is that the resulting specification, including a WS-BPEL business process specification, authorization information and authorization constraints, is modular. It is thus possible for the same business process specification to have different authorization information: different organizations may define different roles and different assignment of activities to roles. Moreover, different organizations may have different access control policies, which require the specification of different authorization constraints. A further advantage is the expressiveness of the BPCL language, which enables us to support specification constraints that go beyond basic separation and binding of duty constraints.

We are currently extending this work in several directions. The first extension deals with the introduction of a new type of authorization constraints. Currently, in the constraint (D, (A_1, A_2), ρ) the execution of activity A_2 is constrained by the execution of a single antecedent activity A_1. We plan to extend our language so that the execution of A_2 may be dependent from the execution of several antecedent activities. We want also to extend the BPCL to support both positive and negative authorizations. Another direction on which we will focus is the development of more sophisticated algorithms for the assignment of users and roles to the activities that satisfies authorization constraints. A final possibility for future work is to consider the use of BPCL as a general authorization constraint language and investigate how it could interoperate with XML-based authorization languages such as XACML.

REFERENCES

Agrawal, A., et al. (2007). Web Services Human Task (WS-HumanTask), Version 1.0. Retrieved from http://www.adobe.com/devnet/livecycle/pdfs/ws_humantask_spec.pdf

Agrawal, A., et al. (2007). WS-BPEL Extension for People (BPEL4People), Version 1.0. Retrieved from http://www.adobe.com/devnet/livecycle/pdfs/bpel4people_spec.pdf

Ahn, G.-J., Sandhu, R., Kang, M. H., & Park, J. S. (2000). Injecting RBAC to secure a web-based workflow system. In *Proceedings of the 5th ACM Workshop on Role-Based Access Contro* (pp. 1-10). Berlin, Germany. Retrieved from http://portal.acm.org/citation.cfm?doid=344287.344295

Anderson, A. (2005). Core and Hierarchical Role Based Access Control (RBAC) Profile of XACML, Version 2.0. OASIS Standard. Retrieved from http://docs.oasis-open.org/xacml/2.0/access_control-xacml-2.0-rbac-profile1-spec-os.pdf

Atluri, V., & Huang, W. (1996). An authorization model for workflows. In *Proceedings of the 4th European Symposium on Research in Computer Security* (LNCS 1146, pp. 4-64).

Bertino, E., Ferrari, E., & Atluri, V. (1999). The specification and enforcement of authorization constraints in workflow management systems. *ACM Transactions on Information and System Security*, *2*(1), 65–104. doi:10.1145/300830.300837

Biron, P., & Malhotra, A. (2004). XML Schema Part 2: Datatypes, W3C Recommendation. Retrieved from http://www.w3.org/TR/xmlschema-2/

Botha, R. A., & Elofi, J. H. P. (2001). Separation of duties for access control enforcement in workflow environments. *IBM Systems Journal*, *40*(3), 666–682.

Casati, F., Castano, S., & Fugini, M. (2001). Managing workflow authorization constraints through active database technology. *Information Systems Frontiers*, *3*(3), 319–338. doi:10.1023/A:1011461409620

Christensen, E., Curbera, F., Meredith, G., & Weerawarana, S. (2001). Web Services Description Language (WSDL) Version 1.1, W3C Note. Retrieved from http://www.w3.org/TR/2001/NOTE-wsdl-20010315.

Clark, J., & DeRose, S. (1999). XML Path Language (XPath) Version 1.0, W3C Recommendation. Retrieved from http://www.w3.org/TR/1999/REC-xpath-19991116.

Crampton, J. (2005). A reference monitor for workflow systems with constrained task execution. In *Proceedings of the 10th ACM Symposium on Access Control Models and Technologies,* Stockholm, Sweden (pp. 38-47).

Crampton, J. (2005). XACML and role-based access control. Presentation at *DIMACS Workshop on Security of Web Services and e-Commerce, DIMACS Center, CoRE Building, Rutgers University, Piscataway, NJ.*

Jordan, D., & Evdemon, J. (2007). Web Services Business Process Execution Language, Version 2.0, OASIS Standard. Retrieved from http://docs.oasis-open.org/wsbpel/2.0/OS/wsbpel-v2.0-OS.pdf.

Koshutanski, H., & Massacci, F. (2003). An Access Control Framework for Business Processes for Web Services. In *Proceedings of ACM Workshop on XML Security* (pp. 15-24). George W. Johnson Center at George Mason University, Fairfax, Va, USA.

Leymann, F. (2001). Web services flow language (WSFL 1.0). IBM Software Group. Retrieved from http://www-306.ibm.com/software/solutions/webservices/pdf/WSFL.pdf

Moses, T. (2005). Extensible Access Control Markup Language (XACML), Version 2.0, OASIS Standard, 2005. Retrieved from http://docs.oasis-open.org/xacml/2.0/access_control-xacml-2.0-core-spec-os.pdf

Rusinkiewicz, M., & Sheth, A. P. (1995). Specification and execution of transactional workflows. In *Modern Database Systems: The Object Model, Interoperability, and Beyond* (pp. 592-620). Addison-Wesley.

Thatte, S. (2001). XLANG Web Services for Business Process Design. Microsoft Corporation. Retrieved from http://www.gotdotnet.com/team/xml wsspecs/xlang-c/default.htm

Thompson, H. S., Beech, D., Maloney, M., & Mendelsohn, N. (2004). XML Schema Part 1: Structures, W3C Recommendation. Retrieved from http://www.w3.org/TR/xmlschema-1/

Wainer, J., Barthelmess, P., & Kumar, A. (2005). W-RBAC A workflow security model incorporating controlled overriding of constraints. *International Journal of Cooperative Information Systems, 12*(4), 455–486. doi:10.1142/S0218843003000814

Xiangpeng, Z., Cerone, A., & Krishnan, P. (2006). Verifying BPEL Workflows Under Authorisation Constraints. In *Proceedings of Fourth International Conference on Business Process Management* (BPM 2006), Vienna, Austria, September.

APPENDIX A

Here we report the XML Schema for the authorization constraints introduced in Section 5.

```
<xsd:schema xmlns:xsd= "http://www.w3.org/2001/XMLSchema">
    <xsd:element name="AuthorizationConstraints" type="Auth_
constrType"/>
    <xsd:complex Type name="Auth_ConstrType">
      <xsd:element name="Constraint" type="ConstrType" minOccurs="1"
maxOccurs="unbounded/>
    </xsd:complexType>
    <xsd:complexType name="ConstrType">
      <xsd:sequence>
        <xsd:element name="Domain" type="DomainType"/>
        <xsd:element name="Activities" type="ActivitiesType"/>
        <xsd:element name="Predicate" type="xsd:string"/>
      </xsd:sequence>
      <xsd:attribute name="Id" type="xsd:ID"/>
    </xsd:complexType>
    <xsd:complexType name="DomainType">
      <xsd:sequence>
       <xsd:element name="Type"    type="xsd:string"/>
       <xsd:element name="Subject" type="xsd:string"/>
      </xsd:sequence>
    </xsd:complexType>
    <xsd:complexType name="ActivitiesType">
      <xsd:element name="AntecedentActivityReference">
        <xsd:complexType>
           <xsd:attribute name="xlink:type" fixed="simple"
type="xsd:string"/>
           <xsd:attribute name="xlink:href" type="xsd:anyURI"/>
        </xsd:complexType>
     </xsd:element>
      <xsd:element name="ConsequentActivityReference">
        <xsd:complexType>
          <xsd:attribute name="xlink:type" fixed="simple"
type="xsd:string"/>
          <xsd:attribute name="xlink:href" type="xsd:anyURI"/>
        </xsd:complexType>
      </xsd:element>
    </xsd:complexType>
  </xsd:schema>
```

Chapter 22
Business Process Control-Flow Complexity:
Metric, Evaluation, and Validation

Jorge Cardoso
University of Madeira, Portugal and SAP AG Research, Germany

ABSTRACT

Deliberate exploitation of natural resources and excessive use of environmentally abhorrent materials have resulted in environmental disruptions threatening the life support systems. A human centric approach of development has already damaged nature to a large extent. This has attracted the attention of environmental specialists and policy makers. It has also led to discussions at various national and international conventions. The objective of protecting natural resources cannot be achieved without the involvement of professionals from multidisciplinary areas. This chapter recommends a model for the creation of knowledge-based systems for natural resources management. Further, it describes making use of unique capabilities of remote sensing satellites for conserving natural resources and managing natural disasters. It is exclusively for the people who are not familiar with the technology and who are given the task of framing policies.

INTRODUCTION

Business process management systems (BPMS) (Smith & Fingar, 2003) provide a fundamental infrastructure to define and manage business processes. BPMS, such as Workflow Management Systems (WfMS) (Cardoso, Bostrom & Sheth, 2004), have become a serious competitive factor for many organizations that are increasingly faced with the challenge of managing e-business applications, workflows, Web services, and Web processes. Business processes, such as Web processes (WS-BEPL, 2005) promise to ease several current infrastructure challenges, such as data, application, and process integration. With the emergence of Web services, a workflow management system becomes essential to support, manage, and enact processes, both among enterprises and within the enterprise (Sheth, van der Aalst & Arpinar, 1999).

A vast amount of work done so far in the business process field has targeted the development of WfMS, including models (e.g., Petri nets), modeling languages (BPML, 2004; BPMN, 2005; Leymann, 2001; Menzel, Mayer, & Edwards, 1994; Singh, 1995; van der Aalst, 1998; van der Aalst & Hofstede, 2003), and execution environments (Alonso, Mohan, Guenthoer, Agrawal, El Abbadi, & Kamath, 1994; Canós, Penadés, & Carsí, 1999; Jablonski, 1994; Kochut, Sheth, & Miller, 1999; Miller, Palaniswami, Sheth, Kochut, & Singh, 1998; Wodtke, Weissenfels, Weikum, & Dittrich, 1996). Work has also been carried out to develop methods to analyze processes in order to verify their correctness, testing the existence of livelocks and deadlocks (van der Aalst, 1998).

Recently, a new field of research for processes has emerged. This new field—termed process measurement—presents a set of approaches to the quantification of specific properties of processes. Important properties to analyze include the estimation of complexity, defects, process size, effort of testing, effort of maintenance, understandability, time, resources, and quality of service. Process measurement is still in its infancy, and much work has yet to be undertaken.

The effective management of any process requires modeling, measurement, and quantification. Process measurement is concerned with deriving a numeric value for attributes of processes. Measures, such as Quality of Service measures (Cardoso, Miller, Sheth, Arnold, & Kochut, 2004), can be used to improve process productivity and quality.

Designing and improving processes is a key aspect in order for businesses to stay competitive in today's marketplace. Organizations have been forced to improve their business processes because customers are demanding better products and services. When an organization adopts a process management philosophy, process improvement can take place. Independently of the approach taken, which can be a continuous process improvement (Harrington, 1993), a Business Process Redesign (Wastell, White, & Kawalek, 1994), or a Business Process Reengineering (Ould, 1995) approach, methods need to be available to analyze the processes undergoing improvements. To achieve an effective management, one fundamental area of research that needs to be explored is the complexity analysis of processes.

A business process is composed of a set of activities, tasks, or services put together to achieve a final goal. As the complexity of a process increases, it can lead to poor quality and be difficult to reengineer. High complexity in a process may result in limited understandability and more errors, defects, and exceptions, leading processes to need more time to develop, test, and maintain. For example, in software engineering, it has been found that program modules with high-complexity indices have a higher frequency of failures (Lanning & Khoshgoftaar, 1994). Therefore, excessive complexity should be avoided. For instance, critical processes in which failure can result in the loss of human life require a unique approach to development, implementation, and management. For these types of processes, typically found in healthcare applications (Anyanwu, Sheth, Cardoso, Miller, & Kochut, 2003), the consequences of failure are severe. The ability to produce processes of higher quality and less complexity is a matter of endurance.

Surprisingly, in spite of the fact that there is a vast amount of literature on software measurement of complexity (Zuse, 1997), no significant research on process measurement of complexity has yet been carried out. Analyzing the complexity at all stages of process design and development helps avoid the drawbacks associated with high-complexity processes. Currently, organizations have not adopted complexity metrics as part of their process management projects. As a result, simple processes may be designed in a complex way.

This article integrates and expands our previous work (Cardoso, 2005c; 2005d; 2005f) and discusses the complexity of processes. In the first main section, we present the Control-Flow Complexity (CFC) metric (Cardoso, 2005d) in order to measure the degree of complexity of business processes from a control-flow perspective. As Lord William Thomson Kelvin (1824–1907) said, "If you cannot measure it, you cannot improve it." The use of the CFC metric allows designers to improve processes, thus reducing the time spent reading and understanding processes in order to remove faults or adapt them to changed requirements. The CFC metric can be used to analyze the complexity of business processes, as well as workflows and Web processes. In the second main section, we evaluate the Control-Flow Complexity metric in terms of Weyuker's properties (Weyuker, 1988). Weyuker's properties give an important basis to classify a complexity measure in order to determine if it can be categorized as good, structured, and comprehensive (Cardoso, 2005c). Finally, the last main section describes the experiment that we have carried out for empirically validating the proposed metric (Cardoso, 2006). Such an experiment plays a fundamental role in our work, since the experimentation is a crucial part of the evaluation of new metrics and is critical for the success of any measurement activity (Zelkowitz & Wallace, 1998). Through empirical validation, we demonstrate with real evidence that the measure we proposed serves the purpose for which it was defined.

MOTIVATION

In this section, we describe a scenario in order to explain and illustrate the need for Control-Flow Complexity (CFC) analysis during the design and aging of a process. A major bank has realized that in order to be competitive and efficient, it must adopt a new, modern information system infrastructure. Therefore, a first step was taken in that direction with the adoption of a workflow management system to support its business processes. Since the bank supplies several services to its customers, the adoption of a WfMS has enabled the logic of bank processes to be captured in schema. As a result, part of the services available to customers is stored and executed under the supervision of the workflow system. One of the services supplied by the bank is the loan process depicted in Figure 1.

This very simple process is composed of only four activities. The Fill Loan Request activity allows clients to request a loan from the bank. In this step, the client is asked to fill out an electronic form with personal information and data describing the loan being requested. The second activity, Check Educational Loan, determines if the loan request should be accepted or rejected. When the result of a loan application is known, it is e-mailed to the client using the Notify Educational Loan Client activity. Finally, the Archive Application activity creates a report and stores the loan application data in a database record. A complete description of this process is described in Cardoso (2005e).

This first workflow application gains acceptance within the bank since it improves service to customers at several levels, allows significant cost savings, and improves communication among employees; the managers of the bank decide to add more services to be supported by the loan process. It was decided to support not only educational loans but also home and car loans.

Before making any changes to the process, a control-flow complexity analysis is carried out. The outcome of the analysis indicates that the

Figure 1. The loan process (version 1)

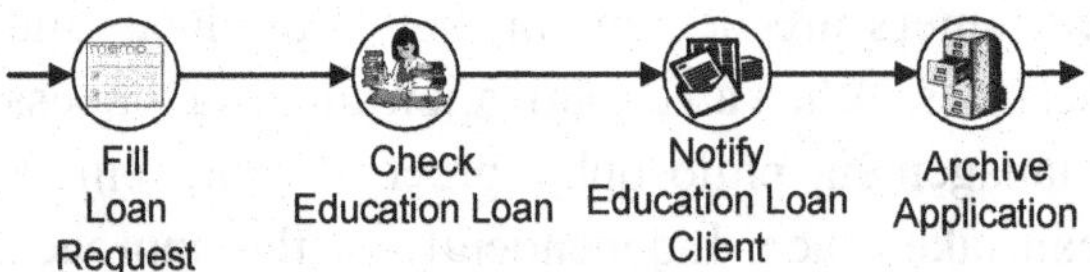

process has a very low complexity. Processes with a low complexity have the capability to quickly change to accommodate new products or services in order to meet the changing needs of customers and business partners. Based on the complexity analysis results, the process was changed, having now the structure illustrated in Figure 2.

The new process (version 2) is composed of nine activities. Because complexity was a concern during the development of the new process, it still maintains a complexity that is within an acceptable range.

For the twelve months that followed the design and implementation of the second version of the process, several small changes were introduced to the process. Unfortunately, since the changes were done incrementally and each one had a small impact on the structure of the process, complexity analysis was not carried out during the process redesign. As a result, the process structure is the following (Figure 3).

The process has evolved over time by modification and may have become fragile with age. Therefore, it is necessary to use techniques such as complexity analysis to assess the system's condition. A high complexity may be the sign of a brittle, nonflexible, or high-risk process. If high complexity is identified, the process may need to be redesigned to reduce its complexity. Redesign may involve breaking the process into subprocesses or simplifying the way the business process is carried out.

Let us consider again the process from Figure 3. Imagine that the designers are studying alternatives to extend the process to handle exceptions. The designers have identified three ways to implement an exception-handling mechanism, and they are undecided about which one to select. In such a scenario, the CFC measure can be effectively used to help the designers in their decision. A "what-if analysis" can be carried out. For each alternative, the CFC can be analyzed, and the alternative that entails a lower complexity for the process can be selected and implemented.

Analyzing the complexity at all stages of process design and development helps avoid the drawbacks associated with high-complexity processes. Currently, organizations have not implemented complexity limits as part of their business process management projects. The use of complexity analysis will aid in constructing and deploying processes and workflows that are more simple, reliable, and robust.

Processes are not static applications. They are constantly undergoing revision, adaptation, change, and modification to meet end users'

Figure 2. The loan process (version 2)

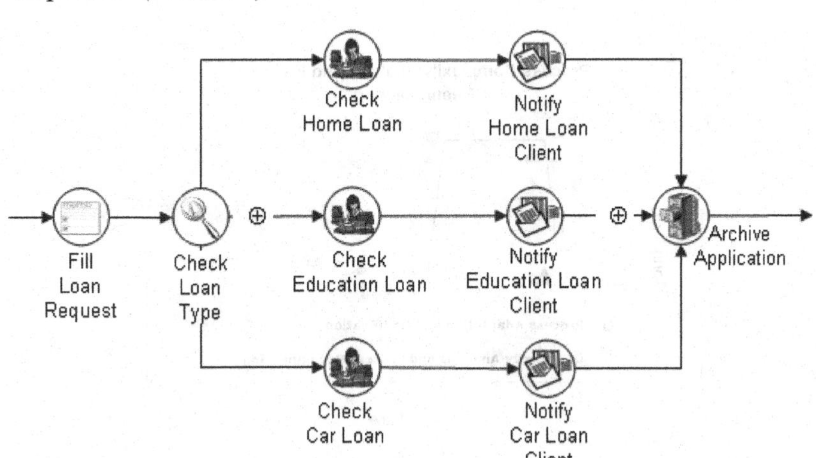

needs. The complexity of these processes and their continuous evolution make it very difficult to assure their stability and reliability. In-depth analysis is required for fixing defects in portions of processes of high complexity (Figure 4).

PROCESS COMPLEXITY

Several definitions have been given to describe the meaning of software complexity. For example, Curtis (1980) states that complexity is a characteristic of the software interface that influences the resources another system will expend or commit while interacting with the software. Card and Agresti (1988) define relative system complexity as the sum of structural complexity and data complexity divided by the number of modules changed. Fenton (1991) defines complexity as the amount of resources required for a problem's solution.

Figure 3. The loan process (version 3)

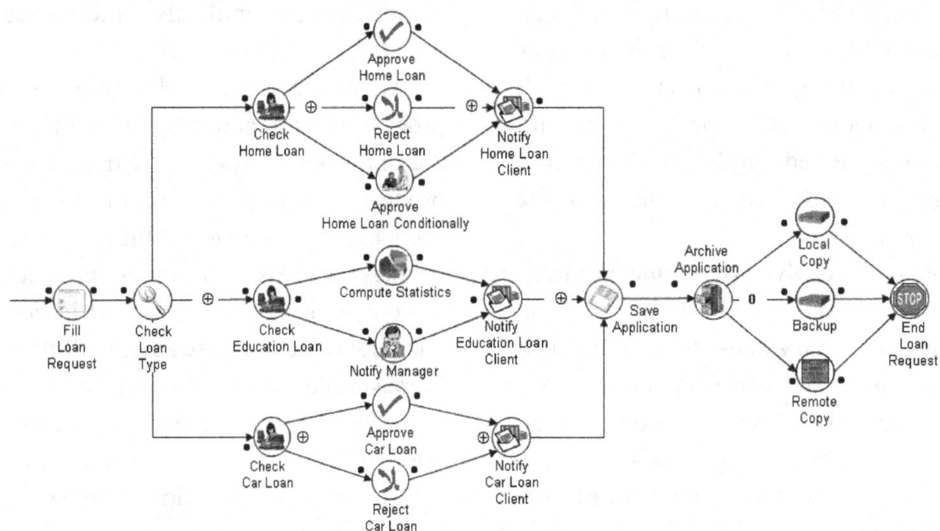

Figure 4. Process complexity analysis and process reengineering

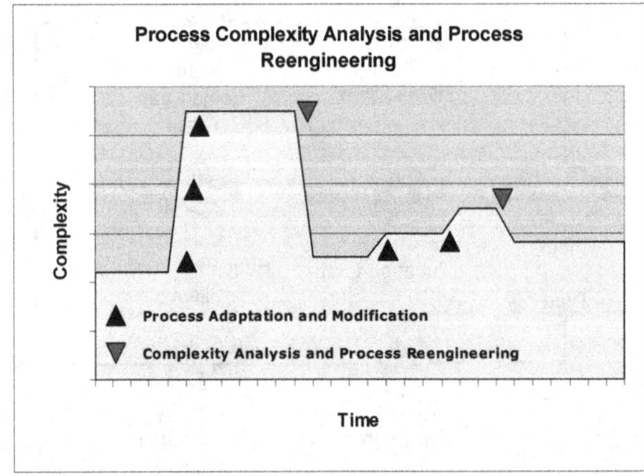

After analyzing the characteristics and specific aspects of business processes and workflows, we believe that the definition that is better suited to describe processes complexity can be derived from IEEE (1992). Therefore, we define process complexity as *the degree to which a process is difficult to analyze, understand, or explain. It may be characterized by the number and intricacy of activity interfaces, transitions, conditional and parallel branches, the existence of loops, roles, activity categories, the types of data structures, and other process characteristics.*

Process Complexity Measurement Requirements

The development of a model and theory to calculate the complexity associated with a process or workflow needs to conform to a set of basic but important properties. The metric should be easy to learn, computable, consistent, and objective. Additionally, the following properties are highly desirable (Tsai, Lopex, Rodriguez, & Volovik, 1986; Zuse, 1990):

- **Simplicity.** The metric should be easily understood by its end users (i.e., process analysts and designers).
- **Consistency.** The metric should always yield the same value when two independent users apply the measurement to the same process (i.e., they should arrive at the same result).
- **Automation.** It must be possible to automate the measurement of processes.
- **Measures must be additive.** If two independent structures are put into sequence, then the total complexity of the combined structures is at least the sum of the complexities of the independent structures.
- **Measures must be interoperable.** Due to the large number of existing specification languages both in academia and industry, the measurements should be independent of the process specification language. A particular complexity value should mean the same thing whether it was calculated from a process written in BPEL (BPEL4WS, 2002), WSFL (Leymann, 2001), BPML (BPML, 2004), YAWL (van der Aalst & Hofstede, 2003), or some other specification language. The objective is to be able to set complexity standards and interpret the resultant numbers uniformly across specification languages.

Perspectives on Process Complexity

There is no single metric that can be used to measure the complexity of a process. Four main complexity perspectives can be identified (Figure 5): activity complexity, control-flow complexity, data-flow complexity, and resource complexity. While in this article we will focus on control-flow complexity, we present the main ideas behind each complexity perspective.

Activity complexity. This view on complexity simply calculates the number of activities a process has. While this complexity metric is very simple, it is very important to complement other forms of complexity. The control-flow complexity of a process can be very low, while its activity complexity can be very high. For example, a sequential process that has a thousand activities has a control-flow complexity of 0, whereas its activity complexity is 100. This metric was inspired by lines-of-code (LOC) metric used with a significant success rate in software engineering (Jones, 1986).

Control-flow complexity. The control-flow behavior of a process is affected by constructs such as splits, joins, loops, and ending and starting points (Cardoso, 2005d). Splits allow defining the possible control paths that exist in a process. Joins have a different role; they express the type of synchronization that should be made at a specific point in the process. A control-flow complexity model needs to take into account the existence

Figure 5. Types of complexity analyses

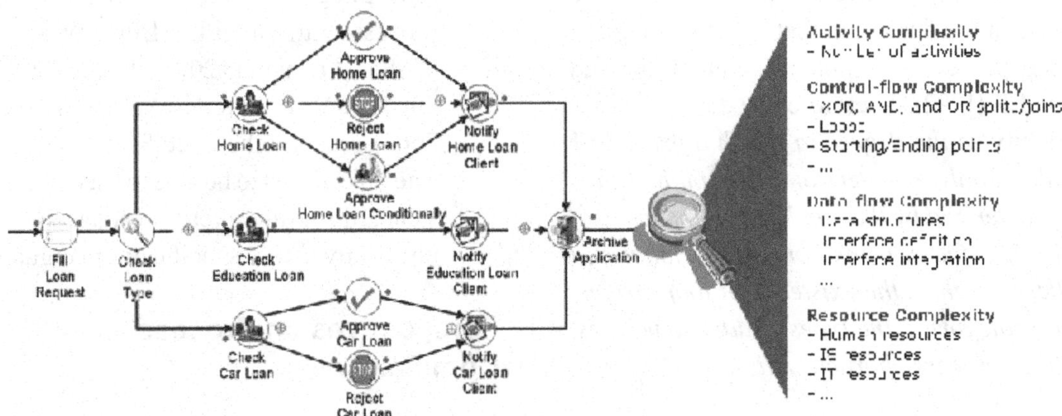

of XOR-split/join, OR-split/join, AND-split/join, loops, and so forth.

Data-flow complexity. The data-flow complexity of a process increases with the complexity of its data structures, the number of formal parameters of activities, and the mappings between activities' data (Reijers & Vanderfeesten, 2004). A data-flow complexity metric can be composed of several submetrics, which include: data complexity, interface complexity, and interface integration complexity (Cardoso, 2005b). While the first two submetrics are related to static data aspects (data declaration), the third metric is more dynamic in nature and focuses on data dependencies between the various activities of a process.

Resource complexity. Activities in a process need to access resources during their executions. A resource is defined as any entity (e.g., human resources, IS resources, IT resources) required by an activity for its execution, such as a document, a database, a printer, an external application, or role (Du, Davis, Huang, & Shan, 1999; zur Mühlen, 1999). Resources such as actors and roles can be structured into the context of an organization. The structure that is used to shape the various types of resources can be analyzed to determine its complexity. This analysis can help managers lower administrative costs and better optimize resource utilization.

BUSINESS PROCESS CONTROL-FLOW COMPLEXITY METRIC

The graphical representation of most process specification languages provides the user with the capability to recognize complex areas of processes. Thus, it is important to develop methods and measurements to automatically identify complex processes and complex areas of processes. Afterward, these processes can be redesigned to reduce the complexity of related activities. One key to the redesign is the availability of a metric that characterizes complexity and provides guidance for restructuring processes.

Overview of McCabe's Cyclomatic Complexity

Our work borrows some techniques from the branch of software engineering known as software metrics; namely, McCabe's cyclomatic complexity (MCC) (McCabe, 1976). A judicious adaptation and usage of this metric during development and maintenance of process applications can result in a better quality and maintainability. Based on MCC, we propose a control-flow complexity metric to be used during the design of processes. Process control-flow complexity is a design-time metric.

Since our work to evaluate process complexity borrows some ideas from MCC (McCabe, 1976) in order to analyze software complexity, we start by describing the importance of MCC and illustrate its usage. This metric was chosen for its reliability as a complexity indicator and its suitability for our research.

Since its development, MCC has been one of the most widely accepted software metrics and has been applied to tens of millions of lines of code in both the Department of Defense (DoD) and commercial applications. The resulting base of empirical knowledge has allowed software developers to calibrate measurements of their own software and arrive at some understanding of its complexity.

Software metrics often are used to give a quantitative indication of a program's complexity. However, it is not to be confused with algorithmic complexity measures (e.g., Big-Oh "O"-Notation), whose aim is to compare the performance of algorithms. Software metrics have been found to be useful in reducing software maintenance costs by assigning a numeric value to reflect the ease or difficulty with which a program module may be understood.

MCC is a measure of the number of linearly independent paths in a program. It is intended to be independent of language and language format (McCabe & Watson, 1994). MCC is an indication of a program module's control flow complexity. Derived from a module's control graph representation, MCC has been found to be a reliable indicator of complexity in large software projects (Ward, 1989). This metric is based on the assumption that a program's complexity is related to the number of control paths through the program. For example, a 10-line program with 10 assignment statements is easier to understand than a 10-line program with 10 if-then statements.

MCC is defined for each module as $e - n + 2$, where e and n are the number of edges and nodes in the control flow graph, respectively. Control flow graphs describe the logic structure of software modules. The nodes represent computational statements or expressions, and the edges represent transfer of control between nodes. Each possible execution path of a software module has a corresponding path from the entry to the exit node of the module's control flow graph. For example, in Figure 6, the MCC of the control flow graph for the Java code described is 14-11+2=5.

Figure 6. Example of a Java program and its corresponding flow graph

Node	Statement
(1)	`while(x<100){`
(2)	`  if (a[x] % 2 == 0) {`
(3)	`      parity =  0;`
	`    }`
	`    else {`
(4)	`      parity =  1;`
(5)	`    }`
(6)	`    switch(parity){`
	`      case 0:`
(7)	`        println( "a[" + i + "] is even");`
	`      case 1:`
(8)	`        println( "a[" + i + "] is odd");`
	`      default:`
(9)	`        println( "Unexpected error");`
	`    }`
(10)	`    x++;`
	`}`
(11)	`p = true;`

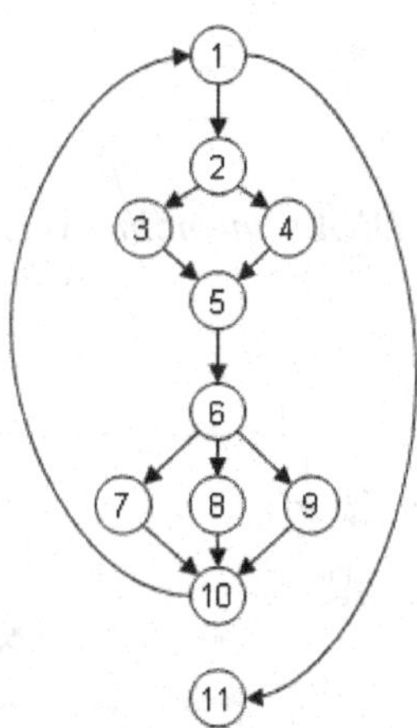

Our major objective is to develop a metric that could be used in the same way as the MCC metric, but to evaluate process complexity. One of the first important observations that can be made from an MCC control flow graph (Figure 6) is that this graph is extremely similar to processes and workflows. One major difference is that the nodes of an MCC control flow graph have identical semantics, while process nodes (i.e., activities, tasks, Web services) can have different semantics (e.g., AND-splits, XOR-splits, OR-joins, etc.).

Our approach uses the idea introduced by McCabe and tackles the semantic difference of nodes. Numerous studies and experience in software projects have shown that the MCC measure correlates very closely with errors in software modules. The more complex a module is, the more likely it is to contain errors. Our goal is to adapt McCabe's cyclomatic complexity to be applied to processes.

Control-Flow Graphs

Control flow graphs can be used to describe the logic structure of processes. A process is composed of activities and transitions. Activities are represented using circles, and transitions are represented using arrows. Transitions express dependencies between activities. An activity with more than one outgoing transition can be classified as an AND-split, OR-split, or XOR-split. Control flow graphs with activities that can have three types of output logic are called tri-logic workflows (Cardoso & Cravo, 2006). AND-split activities enable all their outgoing transitions after completing their execution. OR-split activities enable one or more outgoing transitions after completing their execution. XOR-split activities enable only one outgoing transition after completing their execution. AND-split activities are represented with a '•', OR-split with an 'O', and XOR-split activities with a '⊕'. An activity with more than one incoming transition can be classified as an AND-join, OR-join, or XOR-join. AND-join activities start their execution when all their incoming transitions are enabled. OR-join activities start their execution when a subset of their incoming transitions is enabled. XOR-join activities are executed as soon as one of the incoming transitions is enabled. As with AND-split, OR-split, and XOR-split activities, AND-join, OR-join, and XOR-join activities are represented with the symbols '•', 'O', and '⊕', respectively. Van der Aalst, Hofstede, Kiepuszewski, and Barros (2003) show that most workflow patterns can be constructed using the basic building blocks AND-split, OR-split, and XOR-split. Only OR and XOR-splits introduce nondeterminism. On the other hand, AND-splits and joins are deterministic.

An example of a process is shown in Figure 7. The process has been developed by the Fungal Genome Resource (FGR) laboratory in an effort to

Figure 7. The DNA sequencing workflow

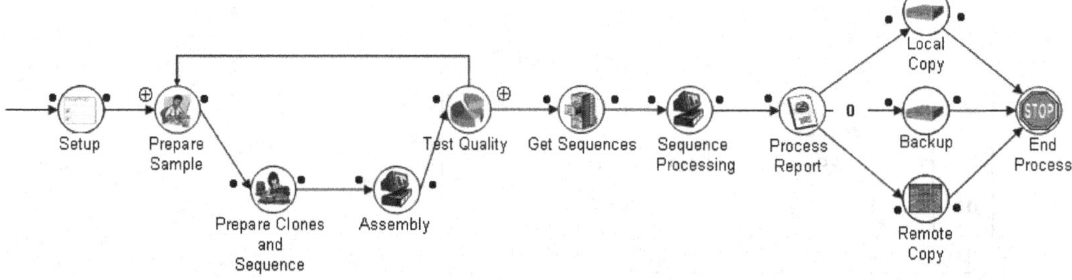

improve the efficiency of their processes (Cardoso, Miller, Sheth, Arnold, & Kochut, 2004). One of the reengineered processes was the DNA sequencing workflow, since it was considered to be beneficial for the laboratory's daily activities.

Definition and Measurement of Control-Flow Complexity

The control-flow behavior of a process is affected by constructs such as splits and joins. Splits allow defining the possible control paths that exist through the process. Joins have a different role; they express the type of synchronization that should be made at a specific point in the process.

Since we are interested in calculating the complexity of processes' control-flow, the formulae that we will present evaluate the complexity of XOR-split, OR-split, and AND-split constructs. We call this measurement of complexity Control-flow Complexity (CFC). Each formula computes the number of states that can be reached from one of the three split constructs. The measure is based on the relationships between mental discriminations needed to understand a split construct and its effects. This type of complexity has been referred to as psychological complexity. Therefore, the more possible states follow a split, the more difficulty the designer or business process engineer has to understand the section of a processes and, thus, the process itself.

In processes, the MCC cannot be used successfully since the metric ignores the semantics associated with nodes of the graph. While the nodes (i.e., activities) of processes have distinct semantics associated, the nodes of a program's flow graph are undifferentiated.

We now introduce several definitions that will constitute the basis for CFC measurement.

Definition 1 (Process): *A process is a collection of activities that takes one or more kinds of input and creates an output that is of value to the customer (Hammer & Champy, 1993). A process is a specific ordering of activities across time and place, with a beginning, an end, and clearly identified inputs and outputs (Davenport, 1993).*

Definition 2 (Process Property): *A property is a feature, characteristic, or attribute of a process such as complexity, maintainability, cost, reliability, and so forth. Process properties can be evaluated and quantified using suitable models, methods, and algorithms.*

Definition 3 (Process Measure): *A process measure is an empirical assignment of numbers (or symbols) to processes in order to characterize a specific property. Let P be a set of processes. Let N be a set of formal objects, such as numbers. A measure m is defined to be a mapping, m: P→N. This guarantees that every process has a measure, and every process has only one measure. However, it does not require that every number (in set N) be the measure of some process in set P.*

Definition 4 (Process Metric): *Process metric is any type of measurement related to a process. Process metrics allows attributes of processes to be quantified.*

Definition 5 (Activity Fan-out): *Fan-out is the number of transitions going out of an activity. The fan-out is computed using function fan-out(a), where a is an activity.*

Definition 6 (Control-flow-induced Mental State): *A mental state is a state that has to be considered when a designer is developing a process. Splits introduce the notion of mental states in processes. When a split (XOR, OR, or AND) is introduced in a process, the business process designer has to mentally create a map or structure that accounts for the number of states that can be reached from the split.*

The notion of mental state is important since there are certain theories (Miller, 1956) that prove that complexity beyond a certain point defeats the human mind's ability to perform accurate symbolic manipulations and, hence, results in error.

Definition 7 (XOR-split Control-flow Complexity): *XOR-split control-flow complexity is determined by the number of mental states that are introduced with this type of split. The function* $CFC_{XOR\text{-}split}(a)$*, where a is an activity, computes the control-flow complexity of the XOR-split a. For XOR-splits, the control-flow complexity is simply the fan-out of the split.*

$CFC_{XOR\text{-}split}(a) = \text{fan-out}(a)$

In this particular case, the complexity is directly proportional to the number of activities that follow an XOR-split and that a process designer needs to consider, analyze, and assimilate. The idea is to associate the complexity of an XOR-split with the number of states (e.g., activities, tasks, Web services) that follow the split. This rationale is illustrated in Figure 8. Please note that in this first case, the computation and result bear a strong similarity to the MCC.

Definition 8 (OR-split Control-flow Complexity): *OR-split control-flow complexity is also determined by the number of mental states that are introduced with the split. For OR-splits, the control-flow complexity is* 2^n-1*, where n is the fan-out of the split. This rationale is illustrated in* ***Figure 9***.

$CFC_{OR\text{-}split}(a) = 2^{\text{fan-out}(a)}-1$

This means that when a designer is constructing a process, he or she needs to consider and analyze 2^n-1 states that may arise from the execution of an OR-split construct.

Mathematically, it would appear more obvious that 2^n states can be reached after the execution of an OR-split. But since a process that has started its execution has to finish, it cannot be the case where, after the execution of an OR-split, no transition is activated (i.e., no Web service or workflow task is executed. Therefore, this situation or state cannot happen.

Definition 9 (AND-split Control-flow Complexity): *For an AND-split, the complexity is simply 1.*

$CFC_{AND\text{-}split}(a) = 1$

Figure 8. XOR-split control-flow complexity

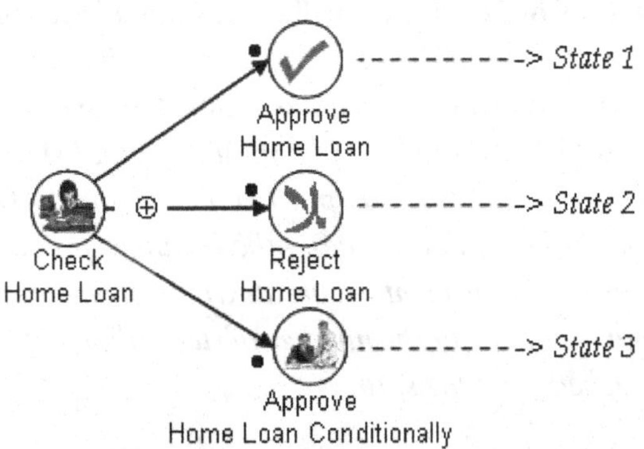

Figure 9. OR-split control-flow complexity

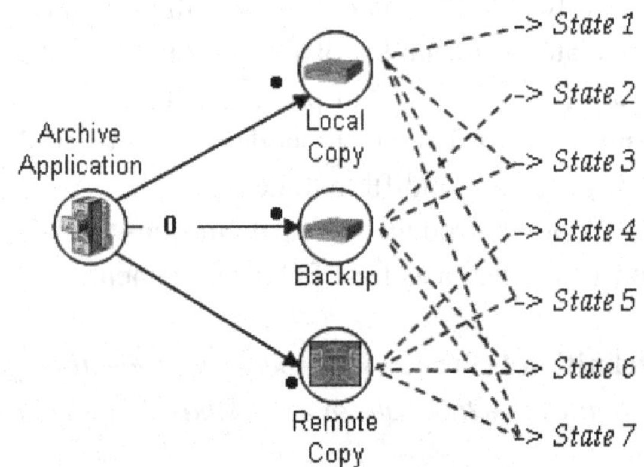

The designer constructing a process needs only to consider and analyze one state that may arise from the execution of an AND-split construct, since it is assumed that all the outgoing transitions are selected and followed. This rationale is illustrated in ***Figure 10***.

The higher the value of $CFC_{XOR\text{-}split}(a)$, $CFC_{OR\text{-}split}(a)$, and $CFC_{AND\text{-}split}(a)$, the more complex is a process's design, since developers have to handle all the states between control-flow constructs (splits) and their associated outgoing transitions and activities. Each formula to calculate the complexity of a split construct is based on the number of states that follow the construct.

Control-Flow Complexity of Business Processes

Mathematically, control-flow complexity metric is additive. Thus, it is very easy to calculate the complexity of a process simply by adding the CFC of all split constructs. The absolute control-flow complexity is calculated as follows, where P is a business process.

$$CFC_{abs}(P) = \Big(\sum_{i \in (\text{XOR-splits of P})} CFC_{XOR-split}\ i\Big) + \Big(\sum_{j \in (\text{OR-splits of P})} CFC_{OR-split}\ j\Big) + \Big(\sum_{k \in (\text{AND-splits of P})} CFC_{AND-split}\ k\Big) +$$

The relative control-flow complexity for process P is calculated as follows, where |P| is the number of activities of process P (see Box 1).

The greater the value of the $CFC_{abs}(P)$ and $CFC_{rel}(P)$, the greater the overall architectural complexity of a process. CFC analysis seeks to evaluate complexity without direct execution of processes. The function of CFC is computed based on the individual control-flow complexity of XOR, OR, and AND –splits. Unless otherwise stated, CFC(P) denotes the absolute control-flow complexity.

Example of CFC Calculation

As an example, let us take the process shown in Figure 3 and calculate its CFC. The process is composed of 21 activities, 29 transitions, three

Figure 10. AND-split control-flow complexity

Box 1.

$$CFC_{rel}(P) = \frac{CFC_{abs}(P)}{|\{\text{XOR-splits of p}\} \cup \{\text{OR-splits of p}\} \cup \{\text{AND-splits of p}\}|}$$

Figure 11. The loan application process

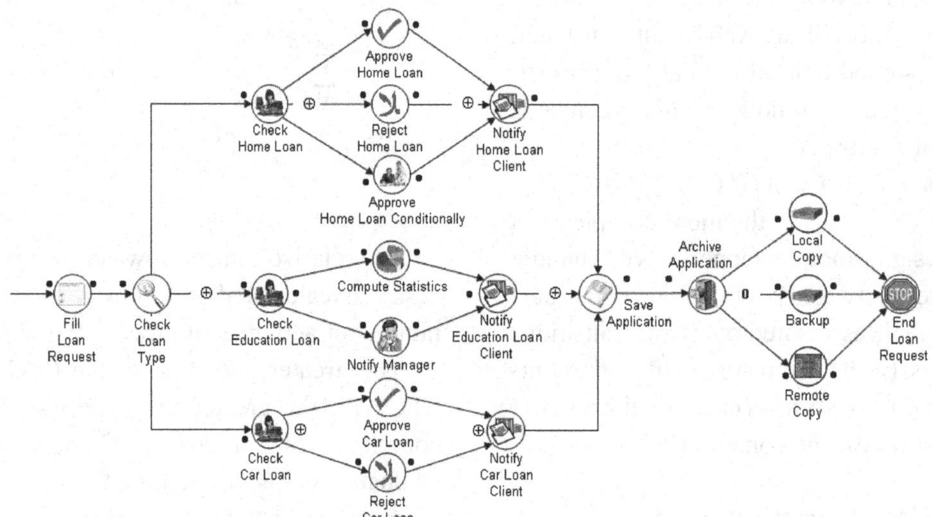

Table 2. CFC metrics for the process from Figure 3

Split	CFC
$CFC_{XOR\text{-}split}$(Check Loan Type)	3
$CFC_{XOR\text{-}split}$(Check Home Loan)	3
$CFC_{XOR\text{-}split}$(Check Car Loan)	2
$CFC_{OR\text{-}split}$(Archive Application)	2^3-1
$CFC_{AND\text{-}split}$(Check Education Loan)	1
CFC_{abs}(Loan Application)	=16
CFC_{rel}(Loan Application)	=3,2

XOR-splits (Check Loan Type, Check Home Loan, Check Car Loan), one OR-split (Archive Application), and one AND-split (Check Education Loan).

It was decided that before placing the process in a production environment, a process complexity analysis was required to evaluate the risk involved with the reengineering effort. The results of the control-flow complexity analysis carried out are shown in Table 1.

From these values, the control-flow complexity can be calculated easily. It is sufficient to mathematically add the CFC of each split. Thus, the resulting absolute CFC value is 16 (i.e., $3+3+2+2^3-1+1$). The relative CFC is 16/5=3,2.

Since the results of the CFC analysis gave a value considered to be low, it was determined that the process has a low complexity, and therefore, its implementation presented a low risk for the bank. Therefore, the process was deployed and implemented in a production environment. As further research is conducted in this area, it will become clear that in many cases, it is necessary to limit CFC of process applications.

It should be noticed that in order to correctly analyze the complexity of a business process, the CFC metric should not be used in isolation. A useful and simple metric that can be used in conjunction with the CFC metric is the activity complexity metric. This is because the CFC metric only analyzes a process from the control-flow point of view. As a result, it may happen that two processes with a different number of activities have the same control-flow structure and, therefore, the same CFC. The use of the activity complexity metric allows deriving additional information about the complexity of a process.

One important question that needs to be investigated and answered is what are both the meaning of a given metric (e.g., what is the significance of the CFC of 16 and 3,2 obtained in our example) and the precise number to use as a CFC limit in a process development. This answer will be given from empirical results only when organizations have successfully implemented complexity limits as part of their process development projects. For example, when using McCabe complexity metrics, the original limit of 10 indicates a simple program without much risk; a complexity metric between 11 and 20 designates a more complex program with moderate risk, and a metric between 21 and 50 denotes a complex program with high risk. Finally, a complexity metric greater than 50 denotes an untestable program with a very high risk. We expect that limits for CFC will be obtained and set in the same way, using empirical and practical results from research and from real-world implementation.

CONTROL-FLOW COMPLEXITY AND WEYUKER'S PROPERTIES

In the area of software measurement, the methods and theory developed have had a reduced industrial acceptance. According to some research, one reason is that there is a lack of serious validation of proposed metrics and, thus, a lack of confidence in the measurements. To overcome this difficulty, we will study nine desirable properties (necessary but not sufficient) suggested by Weyuker (1988) that should be satisfied by any good "complexity measure."

Weyuker properties have been applied to software engineering and have been seriously discussed in the literature (Fenton, 1994; Kitchenham, Pfleeger, & Fenton, 1996; Morasca, Briand, Weyuker, & Zelkowitz, 1997; Zuse, 1997) Although these properties also have been criticized (Cherniavsky & Smith, 1991), currently they are still subject to debate and refinement. Nevertheless, Weyuker properties are a widely known formal analytical approach and were therefore chosen for our analysis since they do provide a basis for some validation of complexity metrics. As shown by Weyuker, with such properties, it is possible to filter out measurements with undesirable properties.

The majority of these properties are formulated in a clear way. This is an advantage because we are able to discuss them. We will concentrate and study each property individually.

Summary of Weyuker's Properties

Weyuker's first property states that a metric cannot measure all software programs as being equally complex. The second property states that there is only a finite number of programs of the same complexity. The third property states that each program may be complex. The fourth property states that the complexity of a program depends on its implementation and that even if two programs solve the same problem, they can have different complexities. Weyuker's fifth property states that the complexity of two programs joined together is greater than the complexity of either program considered separately. The sixth property states that a program of a given complexity when joined to two other programs does not necessarily mean the resulting program will be of equal complexity, even if the two added programs are of equal complexity. Weyuker's seventh property states that a permuted version of a program can have a different complexity, so the order of statements matters. The eighth property states that if a program is a straight renaming of another program, its complexity should be the same as the original program. The final property states the complexity of two programs joined together may be greater than the sum of their individual complexities. The properties are summarized in Table 3.

Table 3. Weyuker's properties

Property	Description
1	A metric cannot measure all software programs as being equally complex.
2	There is only a finite number of programs of the same complexity.
3	Each program may be complex.
4	If two programs solve the same problem, they can have different complexities.
5	The complexity of two programs joined together is greater than the complexity of either program considered separately.
6	A program of a given complexity when joined to two other programs does not necessarily mean the resulting program will be of equal complexity, even if the two added programs are of equal complexity.
7	A permuted version of a program can have a different complexity.
8	If a program is a renaming of another program, its complexity should be the same.
9	The complexity of two programs joined together may be greater than the sum of their individual complexities.

Concatenation Operations on Processes

Weyuker introduces the concatenation operation (P1;P2) of program blocks. Weyuker defines the concatenation operation in the following way: a program can be uniquely decomposed into a set of disjointed blocks of ordered statements having the property whenever the first statement in the block is executed; the other statements are executed in the given order.

In our approach and since we are dealing with processes, four concatenation operations exist. Processes can be concatenated either sequentially using an AND, an OR, or an XOR. These last three concatenation operations use splits and joins. Every AND/OR/XOR split has also a corresponding AND/OR/XOR join, and the different splits do not overlap each other. We have decided to only allow the construction of well-structured processes (van der Aalst, 1998) that are based on a set of predefined building blocks. This protects users from designing invalid processes. Van der Aalst (1998) has shown that processes that are not well-structured contain design errors, such as nontermination, deadlocks, and splitting of instances. We use Weyuker's properties to evaluate the CFC metric, assuming that the processes are well-structured for simplicity reasons. The CFC metric can be applied to well-structured and unstructured processes.

In the list of following properties, P, Q, and R represent processes, and the complexity of P computed by our complexity measure CFC(P) is represented by |P|.

1. When process P is concatenated sequentially with process Q, we depict the resulting process as P-Q. This type of concatenation is illustrated in Figure 12.
2. When process P is concatenated with process Q using an AND-split and an AND-join, we depict the resulting process as P•Q. This type of concatenation is illustrated in Figure 13.
3. When process P is concatenated with process Q using an OR-split and an OR-join, we depict the resulting process as PoQ. This type of concatenation has the same illustration as the one in Figure 13, except that the AND-split and the AND-join shown are replaced with an OR-split and an OR-join, respectively.

Figure 12. Sequential concatenation

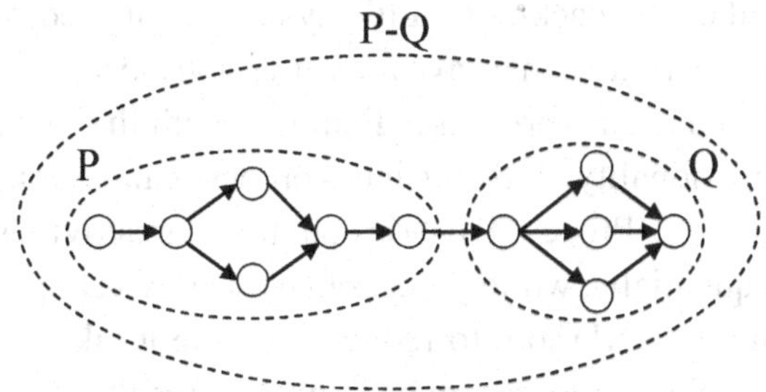

Figure 13. AND concatenation

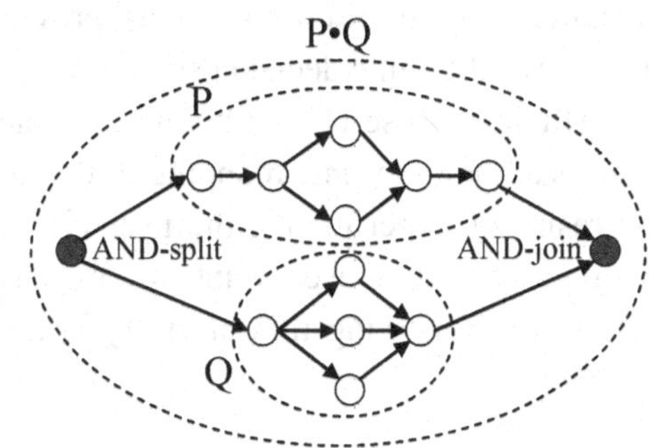

4. When process P is concatenated with process Q using a XOR-split and a XOR-join, we depict the resulting process as P⊕Q. This type of concatenation has also the same illustration as the one in Figure 13, except that the AND-split and the AND-join shown are replaced with an XOR-split and an XOR-join, respectively.

Evaluating the CFC Metric

The nine criteria proposed by Weyuker give a framework to evaluate software metrics' properties using a formal theoretical basis. The properties are intended to evaluate complexity measures on source code metrics. Since there is a strong similarity of source code flow graphs and processes (Cardoso, 2005d), we will use Weyuker's properties to validate our CFC measure. This widely used criterion will be presented, adapted, and applied to processes in the following paragraphs.

Property 1: *There are processes P and Q such that the complexity of P is not equal to the complexity of Q. The property requires that a measure should not produce the same complexity value for every process.*

$(\exists P)(\exists Q)(|P| \neq |Q|)$.

This property is an essential requirement for measures and process measurement. It says that a measure should distinguish between at least two processes. The property stresses that a measure in which all processes are equally complex is not really a measure.

With our measure, we can always come up with two processes with two different control-flow complexity values. We can always design a process P that has the same number of split types but with a higher fan-out from those in process Q. As another example, let us take two processes, P and Q, containing only XOR splits. Let us assume that P=Q (the processes are exactly equal). Let us replace the XOR splits of process P with OR splits. For correctness reasons (van der Aalst, 2000), let us also replace the XOR joins with OR joins). Since $CFC_{XOR\text{-}split}(a)$= fan-out(a) and $CFC_{OR\text{-}split}(a)= 2^{fan\text{-}out(a)}-1$, where a is an activity, then |P|>|Q|. Therefore, Property 1 is satisfied.

Property 2: *A measure has to be sufficiently sensitive. A measure is not sensitive enough if it divides all processes into just a few complexity classes.*

Let c be a nonnegative number. Then there are only finite processes for which $|P| = c$.

Our CFC measure does not follow this property. Therefore, it makes no provision for distinguishing between processes that have a small number of activities (possibly performing very little computation) and those that have a large number of activities (possibly performing a substantial amount of computation), provided that they have the same decision structure.

Nevertheless, Zuse (1997) points out that a measure is a homomorphic mapping. It depends on the result of experiments, the user-view, or the viewpoint that a user wants to measure. Therefore, not following this property is not a disadvantage.

Property 3: *We have processes that have different degrees of perceived complexity but map into the same complexity measurement value.*

There are distinct processes P and Q such that $|P|=|Q|$.

A measure that assigns a distinct value to every process is not much of a measure. It would go against the principle of measurements, which requires that the number of objects that can be measured be greater than the range of the values of the measure.

Our measure clearly satisfies this property. Let us take two processes, P and Q. Let us assume that P has an AND-split at activity *a* with a fan-out(a) of two. Let us construct process Q exactly in the same way as process P, but with a fan-out(a) of four at the AND-split activity *a*. Since $CFC_{AND\text{-}split}(a)=1$, the complexity of P is equal to the complexity of Q (i.e., |P|=|Q|), but the processes are distinct.

Property 4:

There exist processes P and Q such that P is equivalent to Q, but the complexity of P is not equal to the complexity of Q.

$$(\exists P)(\exists Q)(P \equiv Q|P| \neq |Q|).$$

Even though two processes may have the same functionality, it is the details of the design that determine the process's complexity. There are different process designs for the same functionality. For example, let us take a business process that makes the backup of a file system composed of four activities that save files at various locations. Two designs (processes P and Q) with the same functionality of the business process can be constructed. Process P carries out the four activities sequentially, while process Q uses an AND-split and an AND-join to reduce the time it takes to complete a file system backup. As a result, |P|=0, and |Q| =1 (i.e., |P|≠|Q|). Therefore, this property is satisfied by our metric.

Property 5:

For any processes P and Q, the complexity of P*Q, $* \in \{-, \circ, \bullet, \oplus\}$, is greater than or equal to the original complexity of P (weak positivity).

Case 1 (-):

$$(\forall P)(\forall Q)(|P - Q| \geq |P|)$$

For the concatenation operation '–', the weak positivity holds. For any two processes P and Q, |P-Q|=|P|+|Q|, thus |P-Q| ≥ |P|.

Case 2 (o):

$$(\forall P)(\forall Q)(|P \circ Q| > |P|)$$

For the concatenation operation '∘', the weak positivity holds. For any two processes P and Q, $|P \circ Q|=|P|+|Q|+2^2-1$, thus |P∘Q| ≥ |P|. Furthermore, for the concatenation operation '∘', the positivity also holds since |P∘Q| > |P|.

Case 3 (•):

$$(\forall P)(\forall Q)(|P \bullet Q| > |P|)$$

For the concatenation operation '•', the weak positivity holds. For any two processes P and Q, |P•Q|=|P|+|Q|+1, thus |P•Q| ≥ |P|. Furthermore, for the concatenation operation '•', the positivity also holds since |P•Q| > |P|.

Case 4 (⊕):

$(\forall P)(\forall Q)(|P \oplus Q| > |P|)$

For the concatenation operation '⊕', the weak positivity holds. For any two processes P and Q, |P⊕Q|=|P|+|Q|+2, thus |P⊕Q| ≥ |P|. Furthermore, for the concatenation operation '⊕', the positivity also holds since |P⊕Q| > |P|.

Property 6:

There exist processes P, Q, and R, such that |P|=|Q| and |P*R|≠|Q*R|, where *∈{–, ∘, •, ⊕}.

$$(\exists P)(\exists Q)(\exists R)\begin{pmatrix}|P| = |Q| \text{ and } |P * R| \neq |Q * R| \\ \text{and } * \in \{-, \circ, \bullet, \oplus\}\end{pmatrix}$$

As with property 5, this property has four distinct cases.

Case 1 (–): |P–R|=|P|+|R| and |Q–R|=|Q|+|R|, since |P|=|Q|, it holds that |P–R|= |Q|+|R|, thus |P–R| = |Q–R|.

Case 2 (∘): |P∘R|=|P|+|R|+2^2-1 and |Q∘R|=|Q|+|R|+2^2-1, since |P|=|Q|, it holds that |P∘R|= |Q|+|R|+2^2-1, thus |P∘R| = |Q∘R|.

Case 3 (•): |P•R|=|P|+|R|+1 and |Q•R|=|Q|+|R|+1, since |P|=|Q|, it holds that |P•R|= |Q|+|R|+1, thus |P•R| = |Q•R|.

Case 4 (⊕): |P⊕R|=|P|+|R|+2 and |Q⊕R|=|Q|+|R|+2, since |P|=|Q|, it holds that |P⊕R|= |Q|+|R|+2, thus |P⊕R| = |Q⊕R|.

As a result, it is clear that our measurement does not follow Weyuker's property 6 in any of the cases presented.

Property 7: *There are processes P and Q such that Q is formed by permuting the order of the activities of P, and |P| is not equal to |Q|.*

$(\exists P)(\exists Q)$ *If Q is formed by permuting the order of the activities of P, then* $|P| \neq |Q|$.

This property requires that permutation of elements within a process change the metric value. The intent is to ensure that the possibility exists for metric values to change due to permutation of process activities.

Let us assume that we have a process P that contains an AND-split and an OR-split for the activities a_1 and a_2, respectively. Each split has a different fan-out. Activity a_1 has a fan-out of two, while activity a_2 has a fan-out of three. Therefore,

$$|P| = CFC_{AND-split}(a_1) + CFC_{OR-split}(a_2) = 1 + 2^3 - 1 = 8$$

Let us assume that Q is a permutation of the activities of process P. More precisely, the activities a_1 and a_2 are exchanged. As a result, activity a_1 has now a fan-out of three, while activity a_2 has a fan-out of two. The complexity of Q becomes

$$|Q| = CFC_{AND-split}(a_1) + CFC_{OR-split}(a_2) = 1 + 2^2 - 1 = 4$$

Since |P| ≠ |Q| (i.e. 8 ≠ 4), it happens that our measurement follows this property.

Property 8: *This property states that uniformly changing activity names should not affect a process complexity.*

If P is a renaming of Q, then |P| = |Q|.

This property requires that when the name of the activities or processes changes, the metric should remain unchanged. As the metric being considered in this research does not depend on the name of activities or processes, it satisfies this property.

Property 9: *The complexity of a process formed by concatenating two processes can be greater than the sum of their individual complexities (wholeness property). This property states that the whole must be at least as great as the sum of the parts. The idea behind wholeness is that the whole is more complex than the sum of its components.*

$(\exists P)(\exists Q)(|P{*}Q|>|P|+|Q|$, and $* \in \{-, \circ, \bullet, \oplus\})$

This property states that, at least in some cases, the complexity of a process formed by concatenating two processes is greater than the sum of their complexities. This reflects the fact that there may be interactions between the concatenated processes.

As with previous properties, this property has four distinct cases.

Case 1 (-): $|P\text{-}Q|=|P|+|Q|$, thus $|P\text{-}Q| \geq |P|+|Q|$.

Case 2 (o): $|PoQ|=|P|+|Q|+2^2-1$, thus $|PoQ| > |P|+|Q|$.

Case 3 (•): $|P{\bullet}Q|=|P|+|Q|+1$, thus $|P{\bullet}Q| > |P|+|Q|$.

Case 4 (⊕): $|P{\oplus}Q|=|P|+|Q|+2$, thus $|P{\oplus}Q| > |P|+|Q|$.

As a result, our measurement follows property 9 for case 2, 3, and 4. Case 1 follows a variation of the wholeness property, called the weak wholeness property.

$(\exists P)(\exists Q)(|P - Q| \geq | P |+|Q|)$

Interoperability Property

Due to the large number of existing specification languages both in academia and industry, the measurements should be independent of the process specification language. A particular complexity value should mean the same thing whether it was calculated from a process written in BPEL (BPEL4WS, 2002), BPML (BPML, 2004), YAWL (van der Aalst & Hofstede, 2003), or some other specification language. The objective is to be able to set complexity standards and interpret the resultant numbers uniformly across specification languages.

This new property that we propose is not part of the properties proposed by Weyuker. Nevertheless, in the area of business processes and process modeling, we believe that it has an applicable importance.

Property 10: *Measures must be interoperable (i.e., independent of the process specification language).*

If $P=Q$, possibly specified with different languages (i.e., $P \in L_p$ and $Q \in L_q$, where L_p and L_q are process modeling languages), then $|P| = |Q|$.

As our metric only requires the existence of AND, OR, or XOR splits, and since most specification languages include these constructs, we conclude that our metric satisfies this property for a broad spectrum of modeling languages.

At first glance, it may seem that properties 8 and 10 have some relationship, since the naming of an activity (property 8) can be understood as a representation in a process modeling language that differs, although the underlying process is the same. However, the interoperability property considers the expressiveness of a process modeling language. For example, a modeling language L_p may be able to express only AND and XOR splits, while another language, L_q, also may be able to express OR splits. In this case, control-flow complexity metrics that only allow to express AND and XOR splits is not interoperable with language L_q since OR splits cannot be represented. On the other hand, if a metric considers the complexity based on AND and XOR splits, then it is interoperable across language L_p and L_q.

Conclusion

Since our CFC measure happens to fully satisfy seven of the Weyuker's nine properties and partially satisfies one property, it can be considered to have passed a significant part of the theoretically validation process. Therefore, it can be categorized as good, structured, and comprehensive.

METRIC VALIDATION

In this section, we describe the experiment we have carried out for empirically validating the CFC metric. This empirical study is an experiment that compares what we believe with what we observe. Such an experiment plays a fundamental role in our work. Zelkowitz and Wallace (1998) stress the importance of using experimental models for validating metrics. The authors suggest experimentation as a crucial part of the evaluation of new metrics.

For the experiment to be successful, it needs to be wisely constructed and executed. Therefore, we have followed some suggestions provided by Perry, Porter & Votta (2000) about the structure and the components of a suitable empirical study. To perform an experiment, several steps have to be taken in a certain order. An experiment can be divided into the following main activities (Perry et al., 2000): research context, hypotheses, experimental design, threats to validity, data analysis and presentation, results and conclusions.

In the remainder of this section, we explain how we have performed each of the activities described previously.

Research Context

In this section, the terminology is explained, the problem is defined, and a brief research review is undertaken to provide the historical context surrounding the problem.

Terminology and problem definition. Process complexity can be defined as the degree to which a business process is difficult to analyze, understand, or explain. The control-flow complexity refers to the degree of complexity of a process from a control-flow perspective.

The CFC metric can be used to automatically measure the control-flow complexity of a process based on its structure. It allows designers to create less complex processes, thus reducing the time spent reading and understanding processes in order to remove faults or adapt the process to changed requirements.

Our goal is to analyze the CFC metric for the purpose of evaluating and validating the proposed metric. For a set of processes, we wish to determine the correlation between the output of the CFC metric and the perceived control-flow complexity from the point of view of process designers. In our experiments, process designers (subjects) were Master students from the Department of Mathematics and Engineering at the University of Madeira (Portugal).

Research Review. In Cardoso (2005d), we have presented the CFC metric to analyze the degree of complexity of business processes. Nowadays, complexity analysis has an increased importance since the emergence of processes that span both between and within enterprises (Sheth, van der Aalst, & Arpinar, 1999) have an inherent complexity. Therefore, methods should be used to support the design, improvement, and redesign of processes to reduce their complexity. The CFC can be used to analyze the complexity of business processes, as well as workflow and processes.

Hypotheses Formulation

An important aspect of experiments is to know and state in a clear and formal way what we intend to evaluate. Hypotheses are essential, as they state the research questions we are asking. We present two hypotheses: an abstract and a concrete hypothesis.

Figure 14. Example of an object rated by the subjects

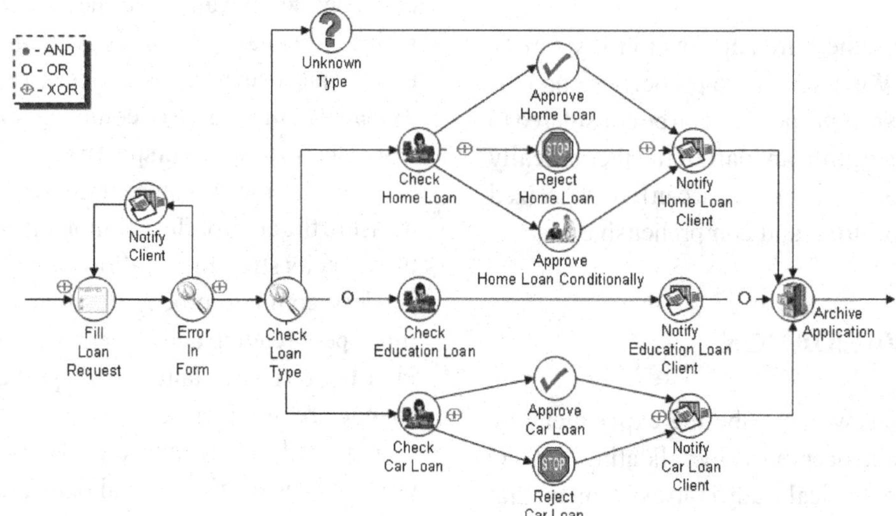

Abstract Hypothesis. "The CFC metric is a good and accurate metric to evaluate and establish the control-flow complexity of processes."

Concrete Hypothesis. "There is a significant correlation between the CFC metric and the subject's rating of the control-flow complexity of processes."

Study Design

After the research context and the hypotheses formulation, the design of the study took place. A study's design is a detailed plan for collecting the data that will be used to test the hypotheses. This phase also explains how the experiment was conducted and has several components.

Variable selection. One component is a set of variables that links causes and effects. Typically, there are two kinds of variables: dependent and independent.

The independent variable is the control-flow structure of processes.

The dependent variable is the control-flow complexity of processes, which varies when the control-flow structure of processes changes.

Subjects selection. Our subjects were students of the Department of Mathematics and Engineering enrolled in the first year of a Master's program in Computer Science at the University of Madeira, Portugal. Nineteen subjects were selected. Most of the students had industrial experience in several areas, but none had experience with business process management systems and methodologies. By the time the experiment was done, all the students had taken a 50-hour course in Business Process Management (BPM) and, therefore, gained experience in the design and development of business processes.

Experiment design. The objects to be rated were business processes graphically designed with the process language used by METEOR workflow management system (Kochut, 1999). An example of the processes analyzed and rated by the subjects is illustrated in Fig. 14. The independent variable was measured using the CFC metric. The dependent variable was measured according to a subject's ratings. All the tests were solved by the same group of subjects.

We prepared the material to give to the subjects. The material consisted of 22 professionally designed, error-free, processes (objects) of the same universe of discourse related to bank loan applications. The subjects were told how to carry out the experiment. Each subject carried out the experiment alone in class and could use unlimited time to solve it. We collected all the data, including subjects' ratings and the measurements automatically calculated by means of the CFC metric. All tests were considered valid because all of the subjects had at least medium experience in designing and analyzing business processes.

Threats to Validity

Threats to validity are influences that may limit our ability to interpret or draw conclusions from the study's data. We will discuss the empirical study's various threats to validity (construct, internal, and external validity) and the way we attempted to alleviate them.

Construct validity. All the measurements of the dependent variable were subjective and based on the perception of the subjects. As the subjects involved in this experiment had medium experience in BPM design, we think their ratings can be considered significant. The independent variable that measures the control-flow complexity of processes also can be considered constructively valid, because from a complexity theory point of view, a system is called complex if it is composed of many different types of elements.

Internal validity. We have considered the different aspects that could threaten the internal validity of the study, such as differences among subjects, precision of subjects' ratings, learning effects, fatigue effects, and subject incentive. Subjects were knowledgeable concerning the evaluation issues. Analyzing the results of the experiment, we can empirically observe the existence of a correlation between the independent and the dependent variable.

External validity. One threat to external validity has been identified: subject selection. This threat can limit the ability to generalize the results to settings outside the study. The subjects were Master students that had recently taken a 50-hour course on BPM, gaining an in-depth experience in the design and development of business processes. In order to extract a final conclusion that can be generalized, it is necessary to replicate this experiment with a more diversified number of subjects, including practitioners and designers with less experience.

Data Analysis and Presentation

Two main approaches to presenting and analyzing data can be chosen: quantitative and qualitative analysis. Since our subjects rated processes using a numerical scale from 0 to 100, we have selected a quantitative analysis to draw conclusions from our data. The qualitative analysis was done in conjunction with a statistical analysis.

As we have said previously, our goal is to determine if any correlation exists between subjects' ratings and the CFC metric proposed in Cardoso (2005d) and briefly described in Section 3. Since the data collected in the experiment is distribution-free, the Spearman Rank-Difference Correlation Coefficient (Siegel & Castellan, 1988), r_S, was used to determine the correlation of the data collected in the experiment. The Spearman r_S is a non-parametric statistic used to show the relationship between two variables that are expressed as ranks (the ordinal level of measurement). The correlation coefficient is a measure of the ability of one variable to predict the value of another variable. Using Spearman's correlation coefficient, the CFC metric was correlated separately to the different subject's rates of control-flow complexity. In our experiment, the null hypothesis was:

H_0: "there is no correlation between the CFC metric and the subject's rating of control-flow complexity."

The probability that the null hypothesis would be erroneously rejected was controlled with two confidence levels: α_1=0.005 and α_2=0.05. The decision rules for rejecting the null hypothesis were:

For α_1: reject H_0 if $r_S >= 0.586$; For α_2: reject H_0 if $r_S >= 0.425$

Results and Conclusion

The analysis performed on the collected data led to some interesting results. shows summary statistics describing the Spearman rank-difference correlation coefficient between subjects' ratings and the values given by the CFC metric. For each subject, the correlation coefficient r_S is given.

Based on data from and taking into consideration α_1, the values of r_S are greater than 0.586 for 84% of the subjects; therefore, we reject the null hypothesis. Taking into consideration α_2, all the values of r_S are greater than 0.425; therefore, we also reject the null hypothesis. For α_1, our confidence level is 95%, and for α_2, our confidence level is 99.5%.

Table 5. Correlation coefficients

		rs	α_1	α_2
Subject	1	0,74[illegible]	Reject H_0	Reject H_0
	2	0,578	Accept H_0	Reject H_0
	3	0,4[illegible]	Accept H_0	Reject H_0
	4	0,[illegible]74	Reject H_0	Reject H_0
	5	0,732	Reject H_0	Reject H_0
	6	0,[illegible]	Reject H_0	Reject H_0
	7	0,733	Reject H_0	Reject H_0
	8	0,[illegible]18	Reject H_0	Reject H_0
	9	[illegible]	Reject H_0	Reject H_0
	10	0,[illegible]38	Reject H_0	Reject H_0
	11	0,720	Reject H_0	Reject H_0
	12	0,[illegible]	Reject H_0	Reject H_0
	13	0,[illegible]33	Reject H_0	Reject H_0
	14	0,[illegible]87	Accept H_0	Reject H_0
	15	0,707	Reject H_0	Reject H_0
	16	0,704	Reject H_0	Reject H_0
	17	0,[illegible]36	Reject H_0	Reject H_0
	18	0,[illegible]99	Reject H_0	Reject H_0
	19	[illegible]64	Reject H_0	Reject H_0

After analyzing the data we gathered, we concluded that the obtained results reveal that there exists a high correlation between the CFC metric and the subject's rating of control-flow complexity. This leads us back to our original goal, which was to demonstrate that the CFC metric serves the purpose for which it was defined: to measure the control-flow complexity of processes. The results obtained are believable, and there are no ambiguities in our interpretation. We also believe that no external elements have influenced our results. The diffusion of the experimental results and the way they are presented are relevant so that they are really put into use. Therefore, we published our findings in this article, and we also are planning to develop a Web-based system to allow other researchers to replicate our experiment.

Our results recommend the use of the CFC metric in order to create less complex processes, thus reducing the time spent reading and understanding processes in order to remove faults or adapt the processes to changed requirements. The complexity measurement enables process managers and administrators to calculate the complexity of processes generated by others. Process designers can analyze the complexity of a particular process in development. Process consultants can contribute with new process components needing methods to analyze the complexity of the proposed solutions. End-users can inquire about the complexity of processes before starting process instances.

RELATED WORK

While a significant amount of research on the complexity of software programs has been done in the area of software engineering, the work found in the literature on complexity analysis for business processes is almost nonexistent. Since the research on process complexity is almost nonexistent, in this section we will discuss the progress made in the area of software complexity.

The last 30 years has seen a large amount of research aimed at determining measurable properties to capture the notions of software complexity. The earliest measures were based on analysis of software code, the most fundamental being a basic count of the number of Lines of Code (LOC). Despite being widely criticized as a measure of complexity, it continues to have widespread popularity, mainly due to its simplicity (Azuma & Mole, 1994). Research in software engineering has produced other important measurements for software. Among others are Halstead's measure (Halstead, 1977), McCabe's measure (McCabe, 1977), the COCOMO model (Boehm, 1981), and the Function-Point method (Garmus & Herron, 2000). There is a vast amount of literature on software metrics, which represents the result of the measurement of the development, operation, and maintenance of software in order to supply meaningful and timely management information. Zuse (1997) has found hundreds of different software metrics proposed and described for software measurement.

Misra and Misra (2004) have evaluated cognitive complexity measures in terms of Weyuker properties and have found that most of Weyuker's properties have been satisfied by the cognitive weight software complexity measure and established the cognitive complexity as a well-structured one. In Lakshmanan, Jayaprakash, and Sinha (1991), the authors attempt to formalize some properties that any reasonable control-flow complexity measure must satisfy. Their approach is directed at large software programs that often are built by sequencing and nesting of simpler constructs. The authors explore how control-flow complexity measures behave under such compositions. Please note that these last two fields of research have been carried out in the context of software engineering and not process management.

A recent area of research involving processes, workflows, and Quality of Service also can be considered related to the work in this article. Organizations operating in modern markets, such as e-commerce activities and distributed Web services interactions, require QoS management. Appropriate quality control leads to the creation of quality products and services; these, in turn, fulfill customer expectations and achieve customer satisfaction. Quality of service can be characterized according to various dimensions. For example, Cardoso, Sheth, and Miller (2002) have constructed a QoS model for processes composed of three dimensions: time, cost, and reliability. Another dimension that could be considered relevant under the QoS umbrella is the complexity of processes. Therefore, the complexity dimension could be added and integrated to the QoS model already developed (Cardoso et al., 2004).

The most important research on complexity analysis for business processes and workflows can be found in Cardoso (2005a; 2005b; 2005c; 2005d; 2005f) and Reijers and Vanderfeesten (2004). Reijers and Vanderfeesten (2004) propose a cohesion and coupling metric developed to analyze workflows. While their work does not take the viewpoint of complexity analysis, it easily can be reformulated to make cohesion and coupling a specific complexity perspective.

CONCLUSION

Our work presents an approach to carry out business process complexity analysis. The complexity of processes is intuitively connected to effects such as readability, effort, testability, reliability, and maintainability. Therefore, it is important to develop metrics in order to identify complex processes. Afterward, these processes can be reengineered, improved, or redesigned to reduce their complexity. The measure presented—the process control-flow complexity (CFC)—is a design-time measurement and can be used to evaluate the difficulty of producing a process design before implementation. When control-flow complexity analysis becomes part of the process development cycle, it has a considerable influence on the design phase of development, leading to further optimized processes. The control-flow complexity analysis also can be used in deciding whether to maintain or redesign a process. As known from software engineering, it is a fact that it is cost-effective to fix a defect earlier in the design lifecycle than later.

We have given a clear definition of the terminology and objectives of the control-flow complexity measure, and we have evaluated the measure in terms of Weyuker's properties. Weyuker's properties must be satisfied by every complexity measure in order to qualify as good and comprehensive. We have demonstrated that seven of nine of Weyuker's properties have been fully satisfied and one partially satisfied by the CFC measure and, hence, established the CFC as a well-structured one. We have introduced a new property—the interoperability property—that has significant importance in the context of process complexity analysis.

In order to demonstrate that our CFC metric serves the purpose for which it was defined, we have carried out an empirical validation by means of a controlled experiment. Our experiment involved 19 graduate students in Computer Science as part of a research project, and tested if the control-flow complexity of a set of 22 business processes could be predicted using the CFC metric. Analyzing the collected data using statistical methods, we have concluded that the CFC metric is highly correlated with the control-flow complexity of processes. This metric, therefore, can be used by business process analysts and process designers to analyze the complexity of processes and, if possible, develop simpler processes.

REFERENCES

Alonso, G., Mohan, C., Guenthoer, R., Agrawal, D., El Abbadi, A., & Kamath, M. (1994). *Exotica/FMQM: A persistent message-based architecture for distributed workflow management.* Proceedings of the IFIP WG8.1 Working Conference on Information Systems for Decentralized Organizations, Trondheim, Norway.

Anyanwu, K., Sheth, A., Cardoso, J., Miller, J.A., & Kochut, K.J. (2003). Healthcare enterprise process development and integration. *Journal of Research and Practice in Information Technology, Special Issue in Health Knowledge Management, 35*(2), 83–98.

Azuma, M., & Mole, D. (1994). Software management practice and metrics in the European community and Japan: Some results of a survey. *Journal of Systems and Software, 26*(1), 5–18.

Boehm, B. (1981). *Software engineering economics.* Englewood Cliffs, NJ: Prentice Hall.

BPEL4WS. (2002). Web services. Retrieved from http://www-106.ibm.com/developerworks/webservices/

BPML. (2004). Business process modeling language. Retrieved from http://www.bpmi.org/

BPMN. (2005). Business process modeling notation. Retrieved from http://www.bpmn.org/

Canós, J.H., Penadés, M.C., & Carsí, J.Á. (1999). *From software process to workflow process: the workflow lifecycle.* Proceedings of the International Process Technology Workshop, Grenoble, France.

Card, D., & Agresti, W. (1988). Measuring software design complexity. *Journal of Systems and Software, 8*, 185–197.

Cardoso, J. (2005a). *About the complexity of teamwork and collaboration processes.* Proceedings of the IEEE International Symposium on Applications and the Internet (SAINT 2005), Trento, Italy.

Cardoso, J. (2005b). *About the data-flow complexity of Web processes.* Proceedings of the 6th International Workshop on Business Process Modeling, Development, and Support: Business Processes and Support Systems: Design for Flexibility, Porto, Portugal.

Cardoso, J. (2005c). *Control-flow complexity measurement of processes and Weyuker's properties (accepted for publication).* Proceedings of the 6th International Enformatika Conference (IEC 2005), Budapest, Hungary.

Cardoso, J. (2005d). Evaluating workflows and Web process complexity. In L. Fischer (Ed.), *Workflow handbook 2005* (pp. 284–290). Lighthouse Point, FL: Future Strategies Inc.

Cardoso, J. (2005e). Path mining in Web processes using profiles. In J. Wang (Ed.), *Encyclopedia of data warehousing and mining* (pp. 896–901). Hershey, PA: Idea Group Inc.

Cardoso, J. (2005f). *Process control-flow complexity metric: An empirical validation (submitted).* Proceedings of the 1st International Conference on Management Systems for Process Improvement, Karlsruhe, Germany.

Cardoso, J. (2006). *Process control-flow complexity metric: An empirical validation.* Proceedings of the IEEE International Conference on Services Computing (IEEE SCC 06), Chicago.

Cardoso, J., Bostrom, R.P., & Sheth, A. (2004). Workflow management systems and ERP systems: Differences, commonalities, and applications. *Information Technology and Management Journal. Special issue on Workflow and E-Business, 5*(3-4), 319–338.

Cardoso, J., & Cravo, C. (2006). *Verifying the logical termination of workflows.* Proceedings of the 5th Annual Hawaii International Conference on Statistics, Mathematics and Related Fields, Honolulu, Hawaii.

Cardoso, J., Miller, J., Sheth, A., Arnold, J., & Kochut, K. (2004). Modeling quality of service for workflows and Web service processes. *Web Semantics: Science, Services and Agents on the World Wide Web Journal, 1*(3), 281–308.

Cardoso, J., Sheth, A., & Miller, J. (2002). *Workflow quality of service.* Proceedings of the International Conference on Enterprise Integration and Modeling Technology and International Enterprise Modeling Conference (ICEIMT/IEMC'02), Valencia, Spain.

Cherniavsky, J.C., & Smith, C.H. (1991). On Weyuker's axioms for software complexity measures. *IEEE Transactions on Software Engineering, 17*(6), 636–638.

Curtis, B. (1980). Measurement and experimentation in software engineering. *Proceedings of the IEEE, 68*(9), 1144–1157.

Davenport, T. (1993). *Process innovation: Reengineering work through information technology.* Harvard Business School Press.

Du, W., Davis, J., Huang, Y., & Shan, M. (1999). *Enterprise workflow resource management.* Proceedings of the International Workshop on Research Issues in Data Engineering, Sydney, Australia.

Fenton, N. (1991). *Software metrics: A rigorous approach.* London: Chapman & Hall, 1991.Garmus, D., & Herron, D. (2000). *Function point analysis: Measurement practices for successful software projects.* Boston, MA: Addison Wesley.

Fenton, N. (1994). Software measurement: A necessary scientific basis. *IEEE Transactions on Software Engineering, 20*(3).

Halstead, M.H. (1977). *Elements of software science, operating, and programming systems series* (Vol. 7). New York: Elsevier.

Hammer, M., & Champy, J. (1993). *Re-engineering the corporation. A manifesto for business revolution.* New York: Harper Collins.

Harrington, H. (1993). Process breakthrough: Business process improvement. *Journal of Cost Management (Fall)*, 30–43.

IEEE. (1992). *IEEE 610, standard glossary of software engineering terminology.* New York: Institute of Electrical and Electronic Engineers.

Jablonski, S. (1994). *MOBILE: A modular workflow model and architecture.* Proceedings of the 4th International Working Conference on Dynamic Modelling and Information Systems, Noordwijkerhout, Netherlands.

Jones, T.C. (1986). *Programming productivity.* New York: McGraw-Hill.

Kitchenham, B., Pfleeger, S.L., & Fenton, N. (1996). Toward a framework for measurement validation. *IEEE Transactions of Software Engineering, 21*(12), 929–944.

Kochut, K.J. (1999). *METEOR model version 3.* Athens, GA: Large Scale Distributed Information Systems Lab, Department of Computer Science, University of Georgia.

Kochut, K.J., Sheth, A.P., & Miller, J.A. (1999). *ORBWork: A CORBA-based fully distributed, scalable and dynamic workflow enactment service for METEOR.* Athens, GA: Large Scale Distributed Information Systems Lab, Department of Computer Science, University of Georgia.

Lakshmanan, K.B., Jayaprakash, S., & Sinha, P.K. (1991). Properties of control-flow complexity measures. *IEEE Transactions on Software Engineering Archive, 17*(12), 1289–1295.

Lanning, D.L., & Khoshgoftaar, T.M. (1994). Modeling the relationship between source code complexity and maintenance difficulty. *Computer, 27*(9), 35–41.

Leymann, F. (2001). Web services flow language (WSFL 1.0). Retrieved from http://www-4.ibm.com/software/solutions/webservices/pdf/WSFL.pdf

McCabe, T. (1976). A complexity measure. *IEEE Transactions of Software Engineering, SE-2*(4), 308–320.

McCabe, T.J. (1977). A complexity measure. *Transactions on Software Engineering, 13*(10), 308–320.

McCabe, T.J., & Watson, A.H. (1994). Software complexity. *Crosstalk, Journal of Defense Software Engineering, 7*(12), 5–9.

Menzel, C., Mayer, R.J., & Edwards, D.D. (1994). IDEF3 process descriptions and their semantics. In C.H. Dagli & A. Kusiak (Eds.), *Intelligent systems in design and manufacturing* (pp. 172-212). New York: ASME.

Miller, G. (1956). The magical number seven, plus or minus two: Some limits on our capacity for processing information. *The Psychological Review.*

Miller, J.A., Palaniswami, D., Sheth, A.P., Kochut, K.J., & Singh, H. (1998). WebWork: METEOR2's Web-based workflow management system. *Journal of Intelligence Information Management Systems: Integrating Artificial Intelligence and Database Technologies (JIIS), 10*(2), 185–215.

Misra, S., & Misra, A.K. (2004). *Evaluating cognitive complexity measure with Weyuker properties.* Proceedings of the Third IEEE International Conference on Cognitive Informatics (ICCI'04), Victoria, Canada.

Morasca, S., Briand, L., Weyuker, E., & Zelkowitz, M. (1997). Comments on "towards a framework for software measurement validation.". *IEEE Transactions on Software Engineering, 23*(3), 187–188.

Ould, M.A. (1995). *Business processes: Modelling and analysis for re-engineering and improvement.* Chichester, England: John Wiley & Sons.

Perry, D.E., Porter, A.A., & Votta, L.G. (2000). Empirical studies of software engineering: A roadmap. In A. Finkelstein (Ed.), *The future of software engineering*: ACM Press.

Reijers, H.A., & Vanderfeesten, I.T.P. (2004). Cohesion and coupling metrics for workflow process design. In J. Desel, B. Pernici, & M. Weske (Eds.), *BPM 2004 (LNCS 3080)* (Vol. LNCS 3080, pp. 290–305). Berlin: Springer-Verlag.

Sheth, A.P., van der Aalst, W., & Arpinar, I.B. (1999). Processes driving the networked economy. *IEEE Concurrency, 7*(3), 18–31.

Siegel, S., & Castellan, J. (1988). *Nonparametric statistics for the behavioral sciences*: McGraw-Hill.

Singh, M.P. (1995). *Semantical considerations on workflows: An algebra for intertask dependencies.* Proceedings of the Fifth International Workshop on Database Programming Languages, Umbria, Italy.

Smith, H., & Fingar, P. (2003). *Business process management (BPM): The third wave.* Meghan-Kiffer Press.

Tsai, W.T., Lopex, M.A., Rodriguez, V., & Volovik., D. (1986). *An approach measuring data structure complexity.* Proceedings of the COMPSAC 86.

van der Aalst, W.M.P. (1998). The application of petri nets to workflow management. *The Journal of Circuits, Systems and Computers, 8*(1), 21–66.

van der Aalst, W.M.P. (2000). Workflow verification: Finding control-flow errors using petri-net-based techniques. In W.M.P. van der Aalst, J. Desel, & A. Oberweis (Eds.), *Business process management: Models, techniques, and empirical studies* (Vol. 1806, pp. 161–183). Berlin: Springer-Verlag.

van der Aalst, W.M.P., & Hofstede, A.H.M. (2003). *YAWL: Yet another workflow language (revised version).* (QUT Technical report No. FIT-TR-2003-04). Brisbane: Queensland University of Technology.

van der Aalst, W.M.P., Hofstede, A.H.M., Kiepuszewski, B., & Barros, A.P. (2003). Workflow patterns. *Distributed and Parallel Databases, 14*(3), 5–51.

Ward, W. (1989). Software defect prevention using McCabe's complexity metric. *Hewlett Packard Journal, 40*(2), 64–69.

Wastell, D., White, P., & Kawalek, P. (1994). A methodology for business process re-design: Experiences and issues. *Journal of Strategic Information Systems, 3*(1), 23–40.

Weyuker, E.J. (1988). Evaluating software complexity measures. *IEEE Transactions on Software Eng., 14*(9), 1357–1365.

Wodtke, D., Weissenfels, J., Weikum, G., & Dittrich, A.K. (1996). *The MENTOR project: Steps towards enterprise-wide workflow management.* Proceedings of the IEEE International Conference on Data Engineering, New Orleans, LA.

WS-BEPL. (2005). Business process execution language for Web services.

Zelkowitz, M.V., & Wallace, D.R. (1998). Experimental models for validating technology. *IEEE Computer, 31*(5), 23–31.

zur Mühlen, M. (1999). *Resource modeling in workflow applications.* Proceedings of the Workflow Management Conference, Muenster, Germany.

Zuse, H. (1990). *Software complexity measures and models*. New York: de Gruyter & Co.

Zuse, H. (1997). *A framework of software measurement.* Berlin: Walter de Gruyter Inc.

This work was previously published in the International Journal of Web Services Research, Vol. 5, Issue 2, edited by L. Zhang, pp. 49-76, copyright 2008 by IGI Publishing (an imprint of IGI Global).

Chapter 23
Pattern-Based Translation of BPMN Process Models to BPEL Web Services

Chun Ouyang
Queensland University of Technology, Australia

Marlon Dumas
Queensland University of Technology, Australia and University of Tartu, Estonia

Arthur H.M. ter Hofstede
Queensland University of Technology, Australia

Wil M.P. van der Aalst
Queensland University of Technology, Australia and Eindhoven University of Technology, The Netherlands

ABSTRACT

The business process modeling notation (BPMN) is a graph-oriented language primarily targeted at domain analysts and supported by many modeling tools. The business process execution language for Web services (BPEL) on the other hand is a mainly block-structured language targeted at software developers and supported by several execution platforms. Translating BPMN models into BPEL code is a necessary step towards standards-based business process development environments. This translation is challenging since BPMN and BPEL represent two fundamentally different classes of languages. Existing BPMN-to-BPEL translations rely on the identification of block-structured patterns in BPMN models that are mapped onto structured BPEL constructs. This article advances the state of the art in BPMN-to-BPEL translation by defining methods for identifying not only perfectly block-structured fragments in BPMN models, but quasi-structured fragments that can be turned into perfectly structured ones and flow-based acyclic fragments that can be mapped onto a combination of structured constructs and control links. Beyond its direct relevance in the context of BPMN and BPEL, this article addresses issues that arise generally when translating between graph-oriented and block-structured flow definition languages.

INTRODUCTION

The *business process execution language for Web services* (BPEL) (OASIS, 2006) is emerging as a *de facto* standard for implementing business processes on top of Web services technology. Numerous platforms support the execution of BPEL processes.[1] Some of these platforms also provide graphical editing tools for defining BPEL processes. However, these tools directly follow the syntax of BPEL without elevating the level of abstraction to make them usable during the analysis and design phases of the development cycle. On the other hand, the *business process modeling notation* (BPMN) (Object Management Group, 2006) has attained some level of adoption among business analysts and system architects as a language for defining business process blueprints for subsequent implementation. Despite being a recent proposal, BPMN is already supported by more than 30 tools.[2] Consistent with the level of abstraction targeted by BPMN, none of these tools supports the execution of BPMN models directly. Instead, some of them support the translation of BPMN to BPEL.

Close inspection of existing translations from BPMN to BPEL, for example the one sketched in (Object Management Group, 2006), shows that these translations fail to fulfill the following key requirements: (i) completeness, that is applicable to BPMN model with arbitrary topology; (ii) automation, that is capable of producing target code without requiring human intervention to identify patterns in the source model; and (iii) readability, that is consistently producing target code that is understandable by humans. The latter requirement is important since the BPEL definitions produced by the translation are likely to require refinement (e.g., to specify partner links and data manipulation expressions) as well as testing and debugging. If BPEL was only intended as a language for machine consumption and not for human use, it could be replaced by mainstream programming languages or even (virtual) machine languages, but this would defeat the purpose of BPEL as a language for service composition.

The limitations of existing BPMN-to-BPEL translations are not surprising given that BPMN and BPEL belong to two fundamentally different classes of languages. BPMN is graph-oriented while BPEL is mainly block-structured (albeit providing graph-oriented constructs with syntactical limitations). Mapping between graph-oriented and block-structured process definition languages is notoriously challenging. In the case of flowcharts, mapping unstructured charts to structured ones is a well-understood problem. However, graph-oriented process definition languages extend flowcharts with parallelism (i.e., AND-splits and AND-joins) and other constructs such as deferred choice (Van der Aalst, ter Hofstede, Kiepuszewski, & Barros, 2003).

In prior work (Ouyang, Dumas, Breutel, & ter Hofstede, 2006), we proposed a translation that achieves the completeness and automation requirements outlined above for a core subset of BPMN models. However, the code produced by this translation lacks readability. Essentially, the BPMN process model is translated into a set of event-condition-action rules, and these rules are then encoded using BPEL event handlers. Thus, the translation does not exploit the block-structured constructs of BPEL, which would clearly lead to more readable code.

This article presents a complementary technique to translate BPMN to BPEL that emphasizes the readability requirement. The proposal is based on the identification of structural patterns of BPMN models which can be translated into block-structured BPEL code. The patterns are divided into: (i) well-structured patterns, which can be directly mapped onto block-structured BPEL constructs; (ii) quasi-structured patterns, which can be re-written into perfectly structured ones and then mapped onto block-structured BPEL constructs; and (iii) flow-based acyclic fragments which can be mapped onto combinations of block-structured BPEL constructs and additional control links to capture dependencies between activities located in different blocks.

Beyond their direct relevance in the context of BPMN-to-BPEL mapping, the translation patterns and algorithm presented in this paper address issues that arise generally when translating from graph-oriented process languages (e.g., UML Activity Diagrams, EPCs, YAWL, or Petri nets) to block-structured ones.

The rest of the article is structured as follows. The second and third sections provide an overview of BPMN and BPEL respectively. Next, the fourth section presents the identification of patterns in a given BPMN process model and their mappings onto BPEL. The overall translation approach is then illustrated through a case study in the fifth section. Finally, the sixth section discusses related work while the last section concludes and outlines future work.

BUSINESS PROCESS EXECUTION LANGUAGE FOR WEB SERVICES (BPEL)

BPEL (OASIS, 2006) can be seen as an extension of imperative programming languages with constructs specific to Web service implementation. These extensions are mainly inspired from business process modeling languages. Accordingly, the top-level concept of BPEL is that of *process definition*. A BPEL process definition relates a number of *activities* that need to be performed by a Web service. An activity is either a basic or a structured activity. *Basic activities* correspond to atomic actions such as: *invoke*, invoking an operation on a Web service; *receive*, waiting for a message from a partner; *exit*, terminating the entire service instance; *empty*, doing nothing; and so on. To enable the presentation of complex structures the following *structured activities* are defined: *sequence*, for defining an execution order; *flow*, for parallel routing; *switch*, for conditional routing; *pick*, for race conditions based on timing or external triggers; *while*, *repeat* and *sequential for-each*, for structured iteration; and *scope*, for grouping activities into blocks to which event, fault and compensation handlers may be attached. An event handler is an *event-action rule* that may fire at any time during the execution of a scope, and *fault* and *compensation handlers* are designed for catching and handling exceptions. Finally, the *parallel for-each* construct enables multiple instances of a given scope to be executed multiple times concurrently.

In addition, BPEL provides a non-structured construct known as *control link* which, together with the associated notions of *join condition* and *transition condition*, allows the definition of directed graphs. The graphs can be nested but must be acyclic. A control link between activities A and B indicates that B cannot start before A has either completed or has been skipped. Moreover, B can only be executed if its associated join condition evaluates to true, otherwise B is skipped. This join condition is expressed in terms of the tokens carried by control links leading to B. These tokens may take either a *positive* (true) or a *negative* (false) value. An activity X propagates a token with a positive value along an outgoing link L *if and only if* (*iff* for short) X was executed (as opposed to being skipped) and the transition condition associated to L evaluates to true. Transition conditions are Boolean expressions over the process variables (just like the conditions in a *switch* activity). The process by which positive and negative tokens are propagated along control links, causing activities to be executed or skipped, is called *dead path elimination*. Control links must not create cyclic control dependencies and must not cross the boundary of a *while* activity.

There are over 20 execution engines supporting BPEL. Many of them come with an associated graphical editing tool. However, the notation supported by these tools directly reflects the underlying code, thus forcing users to reason in terms of BPEL constructs (e.g., block-structured activities and syntactically restricted links). Current practice suggests that the level of abstraction of BPEL is unsuitable for business process analysts and designers. Instead, these user categories rely on languages perceived as "higher-level" such as BPMN and various UML diagrams, thus justifying the need for mapping languages such as BPMN onto BPEL.

BPEL process definitions can be either fully executable or they can be left underspecified. Executable BPEL process definitions are intended to be deployed into an execution engine, while underspecified BPEL definitions, also called *abstract processes*, capture a non-executable set of interactions between a given service and several other "partner services." Our BPMN-to-BPEL mapping focuses on the control flow perspective, and does not deal with data manipulation and other implementation details. Accordingly, the BPEL definitions generated by the proposed mapping correspond to abstract processes, which can be used as templates and enriched with additional details to obtain executable processes. This approach is in line with the difference in abstraction between BPMN and BPEL: BPMN is intended as a modelling language for analysis and design, while BPEL is an implementation language. Thus, one way or another BPMN models need to undergo some form of refinement to yield executable BPEL processes. This refinement is outside the scope of this article.

BUSINESS PROCESS MODELLING NOTATION (BPMN)

BPMN (Object Management Group, 2006) essentially provides a graphical notation for business process modeling, with an emphasis on control-flow. It defines a *business process diagram* (BPD), which is a kind of flowchart incorporating constructs tailored to business process modeling, such as AND-split, AND-join, XOR-split, XOR-join, and deferred (event-based) choice. In the following we first introduce BPDs and then define an abstract syntax for it.

Business Process Diagrams (BPD)

BPMN uses BPDs to describe business processes. A BPD is made up of BPMN elements. We consider a core subset of BPMN elements that can be used to build BPDs covering the fundamental control flows in BPMN. These elements are shown in Figure 1. There are *objects* and *sequence flows*. A sequence flow links two objects in a BPD and shows the control flow relation (i.e., execution order). An object can be an *event*, a *task* or a *gateway*. An event may signal the start of a process (*start event*), the end of a process (*end event*), a message that arrives, or a specific time-date being reached during a process (*intermediate message/timer event*). A task is an atomic activity and stands for work to be performed within a process. There are seven task types: *service*, *receive*, *send*, *user*, *script*, *manual*, and *reference*. For example, a receive task is used when the process waits for a message to arrive from an external partner. Also, a task may be none of the above types, which we refer to as a *blank* task. A gateway is a routing construct used to control the divergence and convergence of sequence flow. There are: *parallel fork gateways* (i.e., AND-splits) for creating concurrent sequence flows, *parallel join gateways* (i.e., AND-joins) for synchronizing concurrent sequence flows, *data/event-based XOR decision gateways* for selecting one out of a set of mutually exclusive alternative sequence flows where the choice is based on either the process data (data-based, i.e., XOR-splits) or external events (event-based, i.e., deferred choice), and *XOR merge gateways* (i.e., XOR-joins) for joining a set of mutually exclusive alternative sequence flows into one sequence flow. It is important to note that an event-based XOR decision gateway must be followed by either receive tasks or intermediate events to capture race conditions based on timing or external triggers (e.g., the receipt of a message from an external partner).

BPMN defines several other control-flow constructs. These include: (1) *task looping*, (2) *multi-*

Figure 1. A core subset of BPMN elements

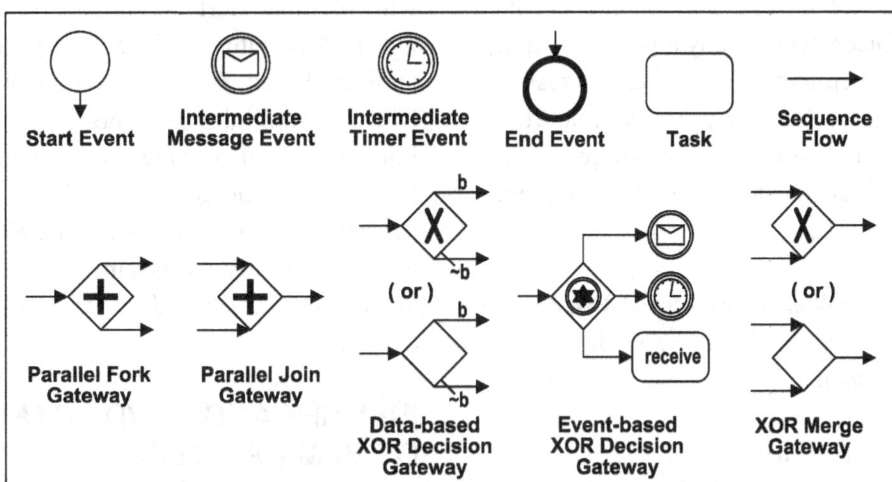

instance task, (3) *exception flow*, (4) *sub-process invocation*, (5) *inclusive OR decision gateway*—also called OR-split—and (6) *inclusive OR merge gateway* —also called OR-join. The mapping of the first five of these non-core constructs onto BPEL does not entail additional challenges. Task looping, which corresponds to "while-do" and "repeat-until" structured loops, can be directly mapped onto the corresponding BPEL structured activities. Similarly, a multi-instance task can be directly mapped onto a "parallel for-each" activity. Sub-processes can be mapped onto separate BPEL processes which call one another. Any OR-split gateway can be expanded into a combination of AND-split and XOR-split gateways (van der Aalst, ter Hofstede, Kiepuszewski, & Barros, 2003). Hence, it does not require a separate mapping rule. On the other hand, the mapping of OR-joins requires a special treatment and will be briefly discussed in the last section.

Abstract Syntax of a BPD

A BPD, which is made up of the core subset of BPMN elements shown in Figure 1, is hereafter referred to as a *core BPD*.

Definition 1 (Core BPD): *A core BPD is a tuple* $BPD = (O, T, E, G, T^R, E^S, E^I, E^E, E^I_M, E^I_T, G^F, G^J, G^D, G^V, G^M, F, Cond)$ *where:*

- *O is a set of objects which is divided into disjoint sets of tasks T, events E, and gateways G,*
- $T^R \subseteq T$ *is a set of receive tasks,*
- *E is divided into disjoint sets of start events* E^S*, intermediate events* E^I *and end events* E^E*,*
- E^I *is divided into disjoint sets of intermediate message events* E^I_M *and timer events* E^I_T*,*
- *G is divided into disjoint sets of parallel fork gateways* G^F*, parallel join gateways* G^J*, data-based XOR decision gateways* G^D*, event-based XOR decision gateways* G^V*, and XOR merge gateways* G^M*,*
- $F \subseteq O \times O$ *is the control flow relation, i.e., a set of sequence flows connecting objects,*
- *Cond:* $F \cap G^D \times O$ *is a function mapping sequence flows emanating from data-based XOR decision gateways to the set of all possible conditions (B).*[3]

The relation F defines a directed graph with nodes (objects) O and arcs (sequence flows) F. For any node $x \in O$, input nodes of x are given by $\text{in}(x) = \{y \in O \mid yF\, x\}$ and output nodes of x are given by $\text{out}(x) = \{y \in O \mid xF\, y\}$.

Definition 1 allows for graphs which are unconnected, not having start or end events, containing objects without any input and output, and so forth. Therefore, it is necessary to restrict the definition to *well-formed core BPDs*. Note that these restrictions are without loss of generality and are to facilitate the definition of the mapping of BPMN to BPEL.

Definition 2 (Well-formed core BPD) *A core BPD is well formed iff relation F satisfies the following requirements:*

- $\forall s \in E^S$, $|in(s)| = 0 \wedge |out(s)| = 1$, *i.e., start events have an indegree of zero and an outdegree of one,*
- $\forall e \in E^E$, $|out(s)| = 0 \wedge |in(e)| = 1$, *i.e. end events have an outdegree of zero and an indegree of one,*
- $\forall x \in T \cup E^I$, $|in(e)| = |out(e)| = 1$, *i.e., tasks and intermediate events have an indegree of one and an outdegree of one,*
- $\forall g \in G^F \cup G^D \cup G^V$, $|in(g)| = 1 \wedge |out(g)| > 1$, *i.e., fork or decision gateways have an indegree of one and an outdegree of more than one,*
- $\forall g \in G^J \cup G^M$, $|out(g)| = 1 \wedge |in(g)| > 1$, *i.e., join or merge gateways have an outdegree of one and an indegree of more than one,*
- $\forall g \in G^V$, $out(g) \subseteq E^I \cup T^R$, *i.e., event-based XOR decision gateway must be followed by intermediate events or receive tasks,*
- $\forall g \in G^D$, $\exists$ *an order* $<_g$ *which is a strict total order over the set of flows* $\{g\} \times out(g)$, *and for* $x \in out(g)$ *such that* $\neg \exists_{f \in \{g\} \times out(g)} ((g, x) <_g f)$, (g, x) *is the default flow among all the outgoing flows from g,*[4]
- $\forall x \in O$, $\exists s \in E^S$, $\exists e \in E^E$, $sF^* x \wedge x F^* e$,[5] *i.e., every object is on a path from a start event to an end event.*

For the translation of BPMN to BPEL in this article, we only consider well-formed core BPDs, and will use a simplified notation $BPD = (O, F, Cond)$ for their representation. Moreover, a BPD with multiple start events can be transformed into a BPD with a unique start event by using an event-based XOR decision gateway, while a BPD with multiple end events can be transformed into a BPD with a unique end event by using an inclusive OR merge gateway (i.e., OR-join, see discussion in the last section). Therefore, without loss of generality, we assume that both E^S and E^E are singletons, that is $E^S = \{s\}$ and $E^E = \{e\}$.

IDENTIFICATION AND TRANSLATION OF BPMN PATTERNS

We would like to achieve two goals when mapping BPMN onto BPEL. One is to define an algorithm which allows us to translate any well-formed core BPD into a valid BPEL process; the other is to generate readable and compact BPEL code. In prior work (Ouyang, Dumas, Breutel, & ter Hofstede, 2006), we proposed a complete translation from well-formed core BPDs to BPEL. However, the code produced by this translation lacks readability. In the following, we exploit the block-structured constructs of BPEL to address the readability requirement. The translation is based on the identification of three categories of patterns of BPMN fragments which can be mapped onto block-structured BPEL code: (i) *well-structured patterns*, (ii) *quasi-structured patterns*, and (iii) *generalized* FLOW*-patterns*. The well-structured pattern-based translation is intended to cover the class of BPMN corresponding to structured workflow models as defined in (Kiepuszewski, ter Hofstede, & Bussler, 2000). Quasi-structured patterns introduce some level of unstructured, but still, they can be expanded into well-structured components. Finally, the generalised FLOW-pattern-based translation caters for the class of acyclic BPMN models consisting of tasks, events, sequence flows, and parallel gateways only. Models in this latter class do not contain decision points (whether event-driven or data-driven) but they can be unstructured. The translations of these three categories of patterns can be combined with our prior work (Ouyang, Dumas, Breutel, & ter Hofstede, 2006). The resulting combined translation approach, as discussed in (Ouyang, Dumas, van der Aalst, & ter Hofstede, 2006), can deal with BPMN models containing all parallel gateways and XOR (event-based and data-based) gateways and with arbitrary topology.

Decomposing a BPD into Components

To map a BPD onto readable BPEL code, we need to transform a graph structure into a block structure. For this purpose, we decompose a BPD into "components" which refer to subsets of the BPD. We then try to identify "patterns" which resemble different groups of components that can be mapped onto suitable "BPEL blocks" in a systematic way. For example, a component holding a purely sequential structure should be mapped onto a BPEL *sequence* construct while a component holding a parallel structure should be mapped onto a *flow* construct.

A component is a subset of a BPD that has one entry point and one exit point. Before identifying patterns in the remaining subsections, it is necessary to formalize the notion of components in a BPD. Note that we adopt similar notations for representing an entire BPD and a component thereof. Also, to formulate the definitions, we specify an auxiliary function elt over a domain of singletons, that is, if $X = \{x\}$, then $\text{elt}(X) = x$.

Definition 3 (Component): *Let BPD = (O, F, Cond) be a well-formed core BPD. A subset of BPD, as given by* $C = (O_c, F_c, Cond_c)$, *is a component iff:*

- $O_c \subseteq O \backslash (E^S \cup E^E)$, *that is, a component does not contain any start or end event,*
- $|(\cup_{x \in Oc}\, in(x)) \backslash O_c| = 1$, *that is, there is a single entry point into the component,*[6] *which can be denoted as* $entry(C) = \text{elt}((\cup_{x \in Oc}\, in(x)) \backslash O_c)$,
- $|(\cup_{x \in Oc}\, out(x)) \backslash O_c| = 1$, *that is, there is a single exit point out of the component, which can be denoted as* $exit(C) = \text{elt}((\cup_{x \in Oc}\, out(x)) \backslash O_c)$,
- *there exists a unique source object* $i_c \in O_c$ *and a unique sink object* $o_c \in O_c$ *and* $i_c \neq o_c$, *such that* $entry(C) \in in(i_c)$ *and* $exit(C) \in out(o_c)$,
- $F_c = F \cap (O_c \times O_c)$,
- $Cond_c = Cond[F_c]$, *that is, the Cond function where the domain is restricted to* F_c.

Note that all event objects in a component are intermediate events. Also, a component contains at least two objects: the source object and the sink object. A BPD without any component, which is referred to as a *trivial BPD*, has only a single task or intermediate event between the start event and the end event. Hence, translating a trivial BPD into BPEL is straightforward.

The decomposition of a BPD helps to define an iterative approach which allows us to incrementally transform a "componentized" BPD to a block-structured BPEL process. In the following we define the function Fold that replaces a component by a single task object in a BPD. This function can be used to perform iterative reduction of a componentized BPD until no component is left in the BPD. It will play a crucial role in the mapping where we incrementally replace BPD components by BPEL constructs.

Definition 4 (Fold): *Let BPD = (O, F, Cond) be a well-formed core BPD and* $C = (O_c, F_c, Cond_c)$ *be a component of BPD. The function Fold replaces C in BPD by a blank task object* $t_c \notin O$, *i.e.,* $Fold(BPD, C, t_c) = (O', F', Cond')$ *with:*

- $O' = (O \backslash O_c) \cup \{t_c\}$,
- T_c *is the set of tasks in C, i.e.,* $T_c = O_c \cap T$,

- $T' = (T \setminus T_c) \cup \{t_c\}$ is the set of tasks in Fold (BPD,C, t_c),
- $T^{R'} = T^R \setminus T_c$ is the set of receive tasks in Fold(BPD,C, t_c), that is, t_c is not a receive task,
- $F' = (F \cap (O \setminus O_c \times O \setminus O_c)) \cup \{(entry(C), t_c), (t_c, exit(C))\}$,
- if $entry(C) \in G^D$, $Cond' = Cond[F'] \cup \{((entry(C), t_c), Cond(entry(C), i_c))\}$, otherwise, $Cond' = Cond[F']$.

Well-Structured Pattern-Based Translation

Since one of our goals for mapping BPMN onto BPEL is to generate readable BPEL code, BPEL structured activities comprising *sequence*, *flow*, *switch*, *pick* and *while*, have the first preference if the corresponding structures appear in the BPD. Components that can be suitably mapped onto any of these five structured constructs are identified as *well-structured patterns*. Here, we classify different types of well-structured patterns resembling these five structured constructs.

Definition 5 (Well-structured patterns) *Let BPD = (O, F, Cond) be a well-formed core BPD and C = (O_c, F_c, $Cond_c$) be a component of BPD. i_c is the source object of C and o_c is the sink object of C. The following components are identified as well-structured patterns:*

(a) *C exhibits a* SEQUENCE*-pattern iff $O_c \subseteq T \cup E^I$ (i.e., $\forall x \in O_c$, $|in(x)| = |out(x)| = 1$) and $entry(C) \notin G^V$. C is a maximal* SEQUENCE*-pattern if and if C is a* SEQUENCE*-pattern and there is no other* SEQUENCE*-pattern C' such that $O_c \subseteq O'_c$ where O'_c is the set of objects in C',*

(b) *C is identified as a* FLOW*-pattern iff*
- $i_c \in G^F \wedge o_c \in G^J$,
- $O_c \subseteq T \cup E^I \cup \{i_c, o_c\}$,
- $\forall x \in O_c \setminus \{i_c, o_c\}$, $in(x) = \{i_c\}$, $out(x) = \{o_c\}$.

(c) *C is identified as a* SWITCH*-pattern iff*
- $i_c \in G^D \wedge o_c \in G^M$,
- $O_c \subseteq T \cup E^I \cup \{i_c, o_c\}$,
- $\forall x \in O_c \setminus \{i_c, o_c\}$, $in(x) = \{i_c\}$, $out(x) = \{o_c\}$.

(d) *C is identified as a* PICK*-pattern iff*
- $i_c \in G^V \wedge o_c \in G^M$,
- $O_c \subseteq T \cup E^I \cup \{i_c, o_c\}$,
- $\forall x \in O_c \setminus (\{i_c, o_c\} \cup out(i_c))$, $in(x) \subset out(i_c) \wedge out(x) = \{o_c\}$.[7]

(e) *C is identified as a* WHILE*-pattern iff*
- $i_c \in G^M \wedge o_c \in G^D \wedge x \in T \cup E^I$,
- $O_c = \{i_c, o_c, x\}$,
- $F_c = \{(i_c, o_c), (o_c, x), (x, i_c)\}$.

(f) *C is identified as a* REPEAT*-pattern iff*
- $i_c \in G^M \wedge o_c \in G^D \wedge x \in T \cup E^I$,
- $O_c = \{i_c, o_c, x\}$,
- $F_c = \{(i_c, x), (x, o_c), (o_c, i_c)\}$.

(g) *C is identified as a* REPEAT+WHILE*-pattern iff*
- $i_c \in G^M \wedge o_c \in G^D \wedge x_1, x_2 \in T \cup E^I \wedge x_1 \neq x_2$,
- $O_c = \{i_c, o_c, x_1, x_2\}$,
- $F_c = \{(i_c, x_1), (x_1, o_c), (o_c, x_2), (x_2, i_c)\}$.

Figure 2 illustrates how to map each of these patterns onto the corresponding BPEL structured activities. Using the function Fold of Definition 4, a component *C* is replaced by a single task t_c attached with the BPEL translation of *C*. Note that the BPEL code for the mapping of each task t_i (*i*=1,...,*n*) is denoted as Mapping(t_i). Based on the nature of these task objects they are mapped onto the corresponding types of BPEL activities. For example, a *service* task is mapped to an invoke activity, a *receive* task (like t_r in Figure 2(d)) is mapped to a receive activity, and a *user* task may be mapped to an invoke activity followed by a receive activity.[8] Also, a task t_i may result from the folding of a previous component *C*, in which case, Mapping(t_i) is the code for the mapping of component *C*.

In Figure 2(a) to (e), the mappings of the five patterns, SEQUENCE, FLOW, SWITCH, PICK and WHILE, are straightforward. In a PICK-pattern (Figure 2(d)),

Figure 2. Mapping a well-structured pattern C onto a BPEL structured activity and folding C into a single task object t_c attached with the resulting BPEL code

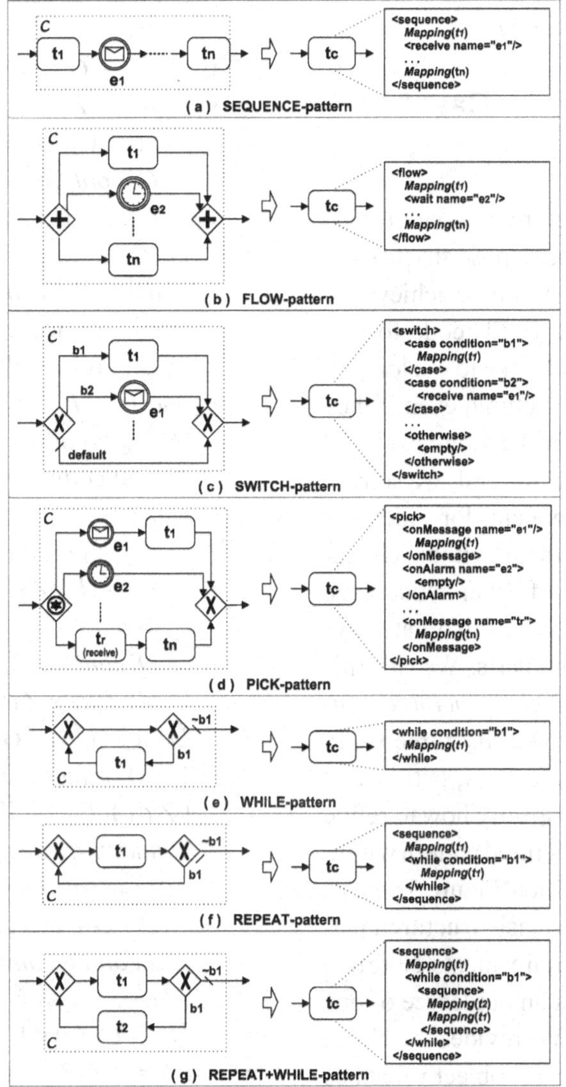

an event-based XOR decision gateway must be followed by receive tasks or intermediate message or timer events. For this reason, a SEQUENCE-pattern (Figure 2(a)) cannot be preceded by an event-based XOR decision gateway.

In Figure 2(f) and (g), two patterns, REPEAT and REPEAT+WHILE, represent *repeat* loops. *Repeat* loops are the opposite of *while* loops. A *while* loop (see WHILE-pattern in Figure 2(e)) evaluates the loop condition *before* the body of the loop is executed, so that the loop is never executed if the condition is initially false. In a *repeat* loop, the condition is checked *after* the body of the loop is executed, so that the loop is always executed at least once. In Figure 2(f), a *repeat* loop of task t_1 is equivalent to a single execution of t_1 followed by a *while* loop of t_1. In Figure 2(g), a *repeat* loop of task t_1 is combined with a *while* loop of task t_2, and both share one loop condition. In this case, task t_1 is always executed once before the initial evaluation of the condition, which is then followed by a *while* loop of sequential execution of t_2 and t_1.

Quasi-Structured Pattern-Based Translation

It can be observed from the previous subsection that well-structured patterns impose strict structural restrictions on BPDs. Again, to achieve the goal of producing readable BPEL code for the mapping of BPMN, we would like to exploit patterns with potential well-structured even if they do not strictly satisfy the restrictions captured in the previous patterns. To this end, we start to identify some of those components for which it is easy to temporarily extend them (without changing semantics) to allow for further reductions, for example split a gateway into two gateways to separate the incompatible parts. We call this category of components *quasi-structured patterns*. In the following, we classify three types of quasi-structured patterns for FLOW, SWITCH, and PICK, respectively. Also, we specify how to refine them to construct a well-structured pattern within them. To illustrate this definition, Figure 3 depicts examples of three types of quasi-structured patterns and the corresponding refinements. Note that for a given object x that has an outdegree of one (e.g., a join gateway), *succ*(x) provides the object that follows x. Similarly, for any object y that has an indegree of one (e.g., a fork gateway), *pred*(x) provides the object that precedes y (this will be used in the next subsection).

Definition 6 (Quasi-structured patterns) *Let BPD = (O, F, Cond) be a well-formed core BPD and* $TE = T \cup E$. *We may identify three types of quasi-structured patterns as follows:*

(a) *Let* $x \in G^F$, $y \in G^J$, $X = out(x)$, $Y = in(x)$, *and* $Z = X \cap Y$. *If* $X \neq Y$ *and* $|Z \cap TE| > 1$, *we can identify a subset of BPD as* $Q = (O_q, F_q, \Phi)$ *where* $O_q = \{x, y\} \cup X \cup Y$ *and* $F_q = F \cap (O_q \times O_q)$. *Q is called a quasi-FLOW-pattern, and can be converted to* $Q' = (O'_q, F'_q, \Phi)$ *where:*
- $O'_q = O_q \cup \{x', y'\}$,
- $F'_q = (F_q \backslash ((\{x\} \times Z) \cup (Z \times \{y\}))) \cup \{(x, x'), (y', y)\} \cup (\{x'\} \times Z) \cup (Z \times \{y'\})$, *and*
- *Q' contains a FLOW-pattern* $C = (Z \cup \{x', y'\}, (\{x'\} \times Z) \cup (Z \times \{y'\}), \Phi)$.

(b) *Let* $x \in G^D$, $y \in G^M$, $X = out(x) \backslash \{y\}$, $Y = in(x)$, *and* $Z = X \cap Y$. *If* $X \subset Y$ *and* $|Z \cap TE| + |Y \cap \{x\}| > 1$, *we can identify a subset of BPD as* $Q = (O_q, F_q, \Phi)$ *where* $O_q = \{x, y\} \cup X \cup Y$ *and* $F_q = F \cap (O_q \times O_q)$, *and* $Cond_q = Cond[F_q]$. *Q is called a quasi-SWITCH-pattern, and can be converted to* $Q' = (O'_q, F'_q, Cond_q)$ *where:*
- $O'_q = O_q \cup \{y'\}$,
- $F'_q = (F_q \backslash (Z \times \{y\})) \cup \{(y', y)\} \cup (Z \times \{y'\})$, *and*
- *Q' contains a SWITCH-pattern* $C = (Z \cup \{x, y'\}, (\{x\} \times Z) \cup (Z \times \{y'\}), Cond_q)$.

(c) *Let* $x \in G^V$, $y \in G^M$, $X = \cup_{z \in out(x)} \{succ(z)\} \backslash \{y\}$, $Y = in(x)$, *and* $Z = X \cap Y$. *If* $X \subset Y$ *and* $|Z \cap TE| + |Y \cap (\cup_{z \in out(x)} \{z\})| > 1$, *we can identify a subset of BPD as* $Q = (O_q, F_q, \Phi)$ *where* $O_q = \{x, y\} \cup X \cup Y$ *and* $F_q = F \cap (O_q \times O_q)$. *Q is called a quasi-PICK-pattern, and can be converted to* $Q' = (O'_q, F'_q, \Phi)$ *where:*
- $O'_q = O_q \cup \{y'\}$,
- $F'_q = (F_q \backslash (Z \times \{y\})) \cup \{(y', y)\} \cup (Z \times \{y'\})$, *and*
- *Q' contains a PICK-pattern* $C = (Z \cup \{x, y'\}, (\{x\} \times Z) \cup (Z \times \{y'\}), \Phi)$.

From this definition, it should be mentioned that for quasi-SWITCH and quasi-PICK-patterns, we decided not to consider the situation when there are additional outgoing flows from decision gateways. For quasi-SWITCH-patterns, due to the fact that the conditional flows emanating from an XOR-decision gateway are evaluated in order, it would become quite complicate and error-prone

Figure 3. Refining a quasi-structured pattern Q to construct a well-structured pattern C in Q'

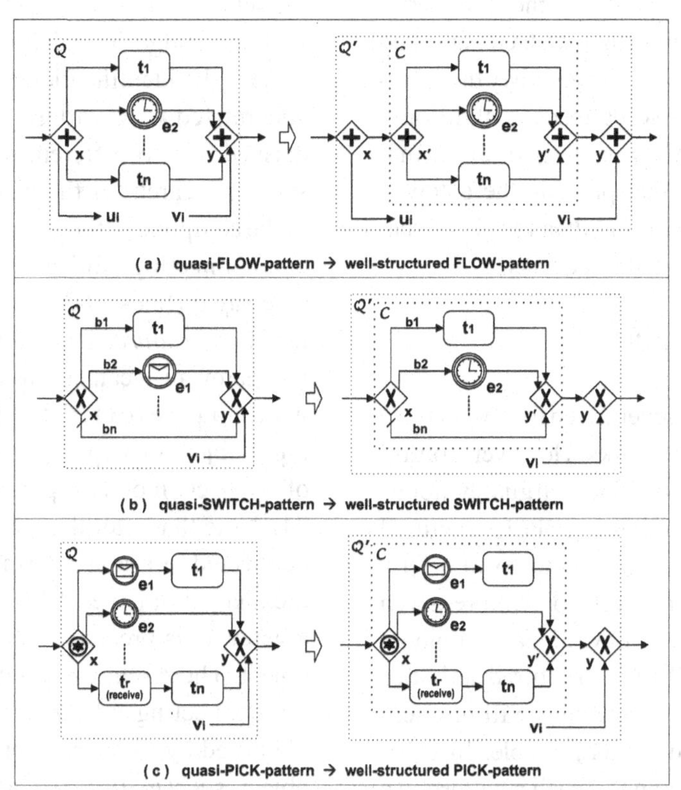

to refine the conditions on the outgoing flows when splitting XOR-decision gateways. For quasi-PICK-patterns, since we cannot decompose race conditions, it is not possible to split an event-based decision gateway.

(a) quasi-FLOW-pattern → well-structured FLOW-pattern
(b) quasi-SWITCH-pattern → well-structured SWITCH-pattern
(c) quasi-PICK-pattern → well-structured PICK-pattern

Generalized FLOW-Pattern-Based Translation

As mentioned before, we are interested in exploring more patterns which preserve structure to a certain extent such that they can always be mapped onto block-structured BPEL code. In this subsection, we look into another group of components which are acyclic and contain parallelism only. We name this group of components *generalized FLOW-patterns.*

Definition 7 (Generalized FLOW-pattern): *Let* $C = (O_c, F_c, Cond_c)$ *be a component of a well-formed core BPD.* C *is a generalized FLOW-pattern iff:*

- C *contains no cycles,*
- *all the gateways in* C *are either parallel fork or join gateways (i.e.,* $G_c = G^F_c \cup G^J_c$*), and*
- *there is no other component* $C' = (O'_c, F'_c, Cond')$ *such that* $O'_c \subset O_c$.

The reason for restricting this pattern to acyclic fragments is that we intend to map occurrences of this pattern using BPEL control links. BPEL control links can be used to define directed graphs of activities provided that these graphs are acyclic. In addition, the graphs in question must be *sound* and *safe*, which means that it should not have deadlocks (*sound*) and that there should be no cases where multiple instances of the same activity are executed concurrently (*safe*). Generalized FLOW-patterns as defined above satisfy these two properties. Indeed, these patterns contain only AND-gateways, and AND-gateways are such that every time the nodes that precede the gateway are executed once (each), and then the nodes that follow it are also executed once (each).

Translation Algorithm

We could easily map a generalized FLOW-pattern into BPEL using control links. However, control links lead to BPEL code that is arguably not as readable as equivalent code using BPEL structured activities. Many BPEL tools do not even offer a way of visualizing control links. Therefore, given a generalized FLOW-pattern, we aim at mapping it onto a combination of BPEL structured activities (only *flow* and *sequence* activities will be used) with as few control links as possible. In other words, during the mapping of such a pattern, we need to preserve as much as possible the well-structured within the pattern, by incrementally deriving and removing the links from the pattern. Based on this, Figure 4 defines an algorithm for mapping generalized FLOW-patterns to BPEL. To illustrate the algorithm, Figure 5 provides an example of applying the algorithm to the mapping of a generalised FLOW-pattern.

First, we introduce a couple of functions used in the algorithm. The function STRUCTUREDMAP translates a well-structured pattern into the corresponding BPEL structured construct according to Figure 2. It outputs a string of BPEL code. The function QUASI2STRUCTURED takes as input a well-formed BPD *W* and a quasi-structured pattern *Q* in *W*, refines *Q* to construct the corresponding well-structure pattern *C* according to Figure 3, and finally produces as output the updated BPD with the refined pattern *Q'*. Also, apart from pred and succ, we apply another auxiliary function CompIn. For any well-formed BPD *W*, CompIn(*W*) returns the set of components contained in *W*.

For our algorithm defined in Figure 4, the key issue is the identification of control links from a generalized FLOW-pattern. The control links are derived at two different stages. First, before it starts to search for the well-structured patterns in the component, the algorithm checks for all the arcs connecting a fork gateway *x* directly to a join gateway *g* (lines 19-28). If such an arc does not lead from a *source* fork gateway nor lead to a *sink* join gateway, it can be explicitly viewed as a link which imposes causal dependencies between the input object of *x* (pred(*x*)) and the output object of *g* (succ(*g*)) on two parallel threads (lines 22-24). Note that after the reduction of sequentially connected fork/join gateways at the beginning of the algorithm (lines 9-17), it is always true that a gateway is preceded/followed by a task/event object. Therefore, we can derive from the above arc connecting *x* to *g* (written as (*x*,*g*)), a link identified by its source object pred(*x*) and target object succ(*g*) (written as (pred(*x*), succ(*g*))). Then, each arc connecting a fork gateway to a join gateway is removed from the component (line 25). After the removal of these arcs, there may appear gateways with an indegree of one and an outdegree of one. These gateways do not perform any routing functions, and thus can be further reduced from the component (lines 30-33). After the above reductions, the component is now ready for the next stage of the mapping.

In the second stage, to facilitate the mapping of the entire component *C*, we construct a well-formed BPD *W* by simply adding a start event and an end event to wrap *C* (lines 35-36). *W* is a non-trivial BPD unless *C* is folded into a task object. Thus, the mapping of *W* is repeated until the whole component *C* is translated into BPEL (lines 38-61). For a non-trivial BPD *W*, the mapping always starts from a well-structured SEQUENCE-pattern or FLOW-pattern after each iteration. Such a pattern *C'* will be mapped to BPEL via

Figure 4. Algorithm for translating a generalized FLOW*-pattern into a BPEL flow construct with control links*

```
1:  input C = (O_c, F_c, Cond_c): a generalised FLOW-pattern
2:  output Blocks: {(t_c: task object, bpelcode: string)};
3:          Links: {(s_1: task/event object, t_1: task/event object)}
4:  begin
5:    let O_c = T_c ∪ E_c ∪ G_c
6:        f_c ∈ G^F_c is the source (fork gateway) object of C
7:        j_c ∈ G^J_c is the sink (join gateway) object of C
8:    // reduction of two sequentially connected fork gateways into one fork gateway
9:    while ∃ g∈G^F_c\{f_c} such that pred(g)∈G^F_c do
10:       G^F_c := G^F_c\{g}
11:       F_c := F_c ∪ ({pred(g)} × out(g))\ ({pred(g), g} ∪ ({g} × out(g)))
12:   end while
13:   // reduction of two sequentially connected join gateways into one join gateway
14:   while ∃ g∈G^J_c\{ j_c } such that pred(g)∈G^J_c do
15:      G^J_c := G^J_c\{g}
16:      F_c := F_c ∪ (in(g) × {succ(g)})\ ({g, succ(g) } ∪ (in(g) × {g}))
17:   end while
18:   // deriving links from arcs connecting a fork gateway directly to a join gateway
19:   for all g∈G^J_c such that in(g) ∩G^F_c ≠ Φ
20:      while | in(g) | > 1 do
21:         select any x ∈ in(g) ∩G^F_c such that | out(x) | > 1
22:           if x ≠ f_c and g ≠ j_c
23:           then Links := Links ∪ {pred(g), succ(g)}
24:           end if
25:           F_c := F_c\{(x, g)}
26:        end select
27:      end while
28:   end for
29:   // reduction of gateways with an indegree and an outdegree of one
30:   while ∃ g∈G_c\{ f_c, j_c } such that | in(g) | = | out(x) | = 1 do
31:      G_c := G_c\{g}
32:      F_c := (F_c\{(pred(g), g), (g, succ(g))}) ∪ {(pred(g), succ(g))}
33:   end while
34:   // construction of a BPD W containing only component C
35:   let s be a start event and e be an end event
36:   W := (O_c ∪ {s, e}, F_c ∪ {(s, f_c), (j_c, e)}, Cond [F_c])
37:   // mapping of component C
38:   while CompIn(W) ≠ Φ do
39:     if ∃ a maximal SEQUENCE-pattern or a FLOW-pattern C' ∈ CompIn(W)
40:     then t := a new task object
41:          Blocks := Blocks ∪ {(t, STRUCTUREDMAP (C'))}
42:          W := Fold(W, C', t)
43:     else if ∃ a quasi-FLOW-pattern Q ∈ W
44:          then W := QAUSI2STRUCTURED (W, Q)
45:          else // deriving an additional link from any arc connecting a task/event to a join gateway
46:               begin
47:                  select any g∈G^J_c\{ j_c }
48:                    select any x∈in(g)
49:                       Links := Links ∪ {x, succ(g)}
50:                       F_c := (F_c\{(x, g)}) ∪ {(x, j_c)}
51:                    end select
52:                  if | in(g) | = 1
53:                  then G^J_c := G^J_c\{g}
54:                       F_c := (F_c\{(pred(g), g), (g, succ(g))}) ∪ {(pred(g), succ(g))}
55:                    end if
56:                 end select
57:              end
58:          end if
59:     end if
60:   end while
61: end
```

the function STRUCTUREDMAP and then be folded into a new task object t_C (lines 39-42). Next, when there are no well-structured patterns, the algorithm tries to search for a quasi-structured pattern and then re-writes it into a well-structured one via the function QUASI2STRUCTURED (lines 43-44). Finally, when none of the above patterns can be identified, the algorithm starts to derive an additional link

Figure 5. Example of applying the algorithm shown in Figure 4 to the translation of a generalized FLOW*-pattern*

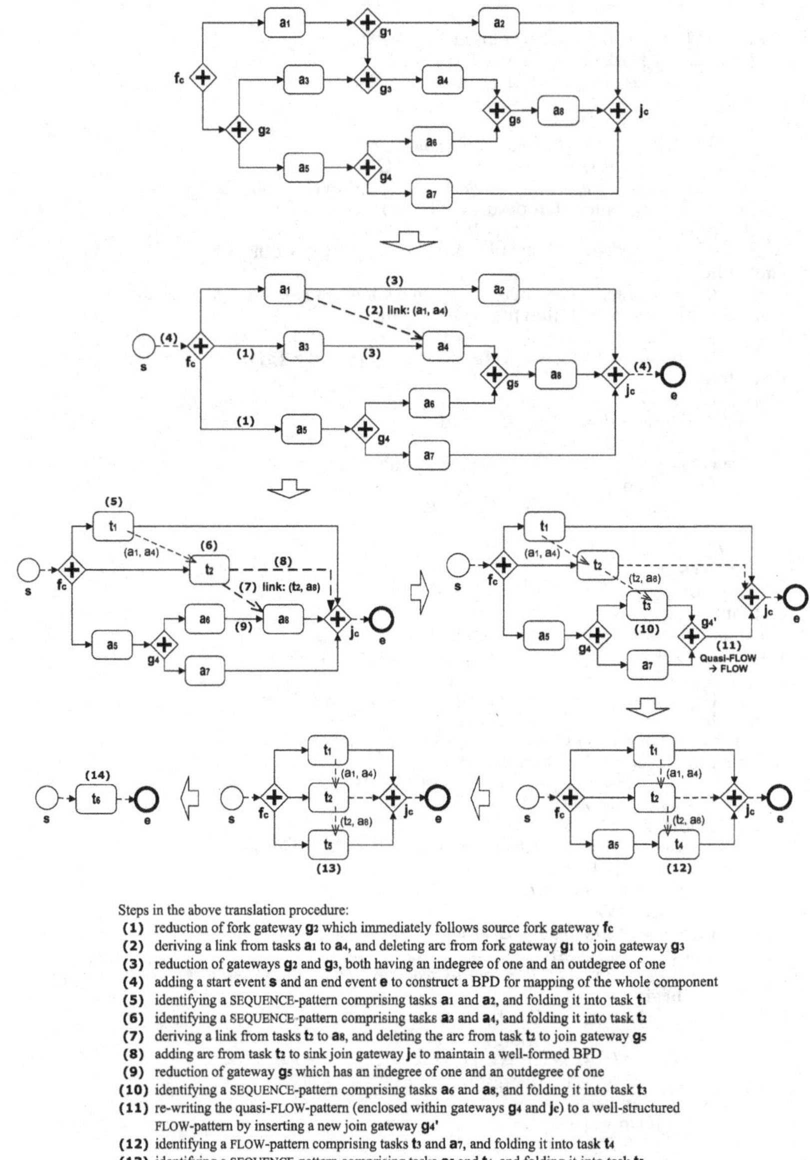
Steps in the above translation procedure:
(1) reduction of fork gateway g_2 which immediately follows source fork gateway f_c
(2) deriving a link from tasks a_1 to a_4, and deleting arc from fork gateway g_1 to join gateway g_3
(3) reduction of gateways g_2 and g_3, both having an indegree of one and an outdegree of one
(4) adding a start event s and an end event e to construct a BPD for mapping of the whole component
(5) identifying a SEQUENCE-pattern comprising tasks a_1 and a_2, and folding it into task t_1
(6) identifying a SEQUENCE-pattern comprising tasks a_3 and a_4, and folding it into task t_2
(7) deriving a link from tasks t_2 to a_8, and deleting the arc from task t_2 to join gateway g_5
(8) adding arc from task t_2 to sink join gateway j_c to maintain a well-formed BPD
(9) reduction of gateway g_5 which has an indegree of one and an outdegree of one
(10) identifying a SEQUENCE-pattern comprising tasks a_6 and a_8, and folding it into task t_3
(11) re-writing the quasi-FLOW-pattern (enclosed within gateways g_4 and j_c) to a well-structured FLOW-pattern by inserting a new join gateway g_4'
(12) identifying a FLOW-pattern comprising tasks t_3 and a_7, and folding it into task t_4
(13) identifying a SEQUENCE-pattern comprising tasks a_5 and t_4, and folding it into task t_5
(14) identifying a FLOW-pattern comprising tasks t_1, t_2 and t_5, and folding it into task t_6

from any arc connecting a task/event object x to a join gateway g (except the sink join gateway) in W (lines 46-57). Similarly, after the arc (x, g) is selected and mapped onto a link $(x, \text{succ}(g))$, it is then removed from the component. However, in this case, the source task/event object x will lose its outgoing flow and thereby the resulting BPD will not be well-formed any more. In order to maintain the well-formedness of the BPD without changing its behavior, the algorithm adds an arc from the task/event x to the end join gateway j_C. Next, if the join gateway g has only one incoming arc left, it can be deleted. Note that in the above procedure, conducting the identification of additional control links (one at a time) only as a last resort, reflects the desire to produce structured BPEL code with as few control links as possible.

Complexity Analysis

We now analyze the complexity of the shown algorithm. In this analysis, we use the following notations. Symbol $k_{n,m}$ denotes the worst-case complexity of the fragment of the algorithm contained between lines n and m. Symbols ind or outd denote functions that take as input an object x and return the indegree and the outdegree of x respectively, that is ind(x) = |in(x)|, outd(x) = |out(x)|. Meanwhile, app is a higher-level function that applies a function given as first parameter (e.g., ind or outd) to each element of a set $S=\{x_1, \ldots, x_n\}$ given as second parameter, for example app(ind, S) = {ind(x_1), …, ind(x_n)}. Finally, function max takes as input a set of integers, and returns the integer with the maximal value among the set. We use $\text{ind}_{max}(S)$ as a shorthand notation for max(app(ind, S)), and $\text{outd}_{max}(S)$ for max(app(outd, S)).

Consider the body of the algorithm (lines 5 to 60) in Figure 4. Lines 5 to 7 do not contribute to the asymptotic worst-case complexity. In lines 9 to 12, a reduction is performed for every two sequentially connected fork gateways in C. For each reduction, the set operations (lines 10 to 11) are performed, leading to a complexity of $O(\text{outd}_{max}(G^F_c))$. In the extreme case, all fork gateways in G^F_c are sequentially connected, and to reduce them into one fork gateway, $|G^F_c| - 1$ reductions needs to be performed. Thus, the complexity of lines 9 to 12 is bounded by $k_{9,12} = O(|G^F_c| * \text{outd}_{max}(G^F_c))$. Similarly, the complexity of lines 14 to 17 for reducing join gateways is $k_{14,17} = O(|G^J_c| * \text{ind}_{max}(G^J_c))$. In lines 19 to 28, the number of join gateways that directly follow fork gateways is bounded by $|G^J_c|$, and for each of these join gateways, the number of its preceding fork gateways is bounded by $O(\text{ind}_{max}(G^J_c))$. Given that mapping an arc between a join gateway and its preceding fork gateway onto a control link is trivial, the complexity of lines 19 to 28 is given by $k_{19,28} = O(|G^J_c| * \text{ind}_{max}(G^J_c))$. In lines 30 to 33, gateways with only one incoming arc and one outgoing arc are removed, hence a complexity of $k_{30,33} = O(|G_c|)$.

The construction of a BPD W around component C in lines 35 and 36 is trivial and does not contribute to the asymptotic worst-case complexity. Within W, the entire component C is then gradually mapped onto BPEL block constructs in lines 38 to 60. First, in the *if*-clause (line 39), to identify a maximal SEQUENCE-pattern, one may need to explore all tasks and events in linear time, and to identify a FLOW-pattern, one may need to go through all parallel fork gateways. As a result, the complexity of line 39 is bounded by $k_{39} = O(|T_c \cup E^I| + |G^F_c| + \text{outd}_{max}(G^F_c))$. Next, in the *then*-clause (lines 40 to 42), both the BPEL code translation (line 41) and the pattern folding operation (line 42) can be performed in linear time and thus the complexity of this *then*-clause is dominated by the pattern identification in the *if*-clause. The *else*-clause contains a nested *if-then-else* structure. Again, the complexity of the pattern identification in the nested *if*-clause (line 43) dominates the complexity of the pattern refinement in the nested *then*-clause (line 44) as well as the complexity of the link derivation in the nested *else*-clause (lines 46 to 57). Thus, we can focus on analyzing the complexity of the *if*-clause. A quasi-FLOW-pattern is similar to a well-structured FLOW-pattern but it allows additional outputs from the starting (fork) gateway and additional inputs to the closing (join) gateway. When identifying such a pattern, an additional step is required to check that at least two output task/event objects of the fork gateway share one same output join gateway. Given a fork gateway $g \in G^F_c$, this additional step can be implemented by using an algorithm that detects if there is a duplicate in the set of second-degree successors of g, i.e., $\{\text{outd}(x) \mid x \in \text{outd}(g)\}$. This duplicate detection can be achieved for example using a sorting algorithm. Hence, the complexity of identifying a quasi- FLOW-pattern is $O(|G^F_c$

$|*\text{outd}_{max}(G^F{}_c)*log(\text{outd}_{\max}(G^F{}_c)))$. This is also the value of $k_{43,58.}$ Next, based on the fact that a maximum of $|O_c|/2$ patterns may be identified in component C, the complexity of lines 38 to 60 is $k_{38,60} = O(|O_c|*(k_{39}+k_{43,58}))$. Finally, the complexity of the algorithm shown in Figure 5 can be obtained as a sum of the above worst-case complexity bounds, i.e., $k_{9,12}+k_{14,17}+k_{19,28}+k_{30,33}+k_{38,60}$.

OVERALL TRANSLATION APPROACH: AN EXAMPLE

In this section, we describe and illustrate the overall translation approach. Given a well-formed BPD, the basic idea of each step of the approach is to identify an occurrence of a pattern, to generate its BPEL translation, and then to fold the component or fragment of the model matched by the pattern into a single task object. This is repeated until no pattern is left in the BPD. The process of identifying which pattern to apply next always starts from a maximal SEQUENCE-pattern after each folding. When there are no occurrences of the sequence pattern left in the BPD, occurrences of other well-structured patterns are searched for. If one such occurrence is found, it will be processed, leading to the folding of a component or fragment of the model. The search for patterns then starts again with the sequence pattern. Since all well-structured non-sequence components are disjoint, the order of identifying these patterns is irrelevant. Next, when no well-structured patterns are left, any quasi-structured patterns are processed—again, the identification of an occurrence of any of these pattern leads to part of the model being folded and the search restarts again from the sequence pattern. Finally, if neither well-structured nor quasi-structured patterns are left, the approach searches for a generalized FLOW-pattern as a last resort. Note that a BPD comprising only the patterns defined in the previous section can be fully translated into a BPEL process. For other BPDs, we can use the general translation approach described in our prior work (Ouyang et al., 2006).

Consider the complaint handling process model shown in Figure 7 which is a well-formed core BPD. First the complaint is registered (task *register*), then in parallel a questionnaire is sent to the complainant (task *send questionnaire*) and the complaint is evaluated (task *evaluate*). If the complainant returns the questionnaire within two weeks (event *returned-questionnaire*), task *process questionnaire* is executed. Otherwise (event *time-out*), the result of the questionnaire is discarded. After either the questionnaire is processed or a time-out has occurred, the result needs to be archived (task *archive*), and in parallel, if the complaint evaluation has been completed, the actual processing of the complaint (task *process complaint*) can start. Next, the processing of the complaint is checked via task *check processing*. If the check result is NOT OK, the complaint requires

Figure 6. A complaint handling process model

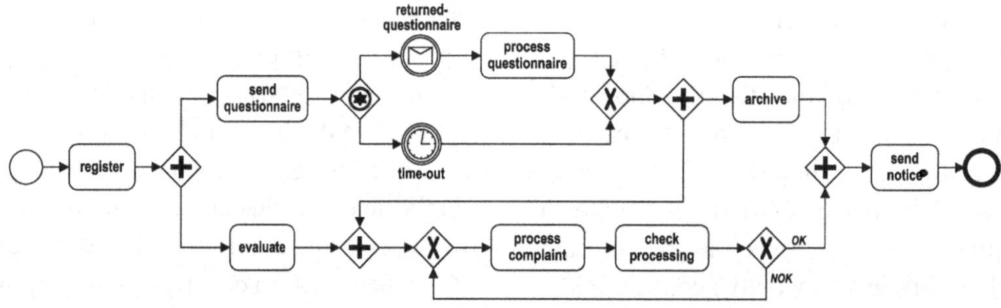

re-processing. Otherwise, if the check result is OK and also the questionnaire has been archived, a notice will be sent to inform the complainant about the completion of the complaint handling (task *send notice*). Note that labels OK and NOK on the outgoing flows of a data-based XOR decision gateway, are abstract representations of conditions on these flows.

Following the pattern-based translation approach in the previous section, we map the discussed BPD onto a BPEL process. Figure 7 sketches the translation procedure which shows how this BPD can be reduced to a trivial BPD. Each component is named C_i where i specifies in what order the components are processed, and C_i is folded into a task object named t^i_c. In Figure 7,

Figure 7. Translating the complaint handling process model in Figure 6 into BPEL.

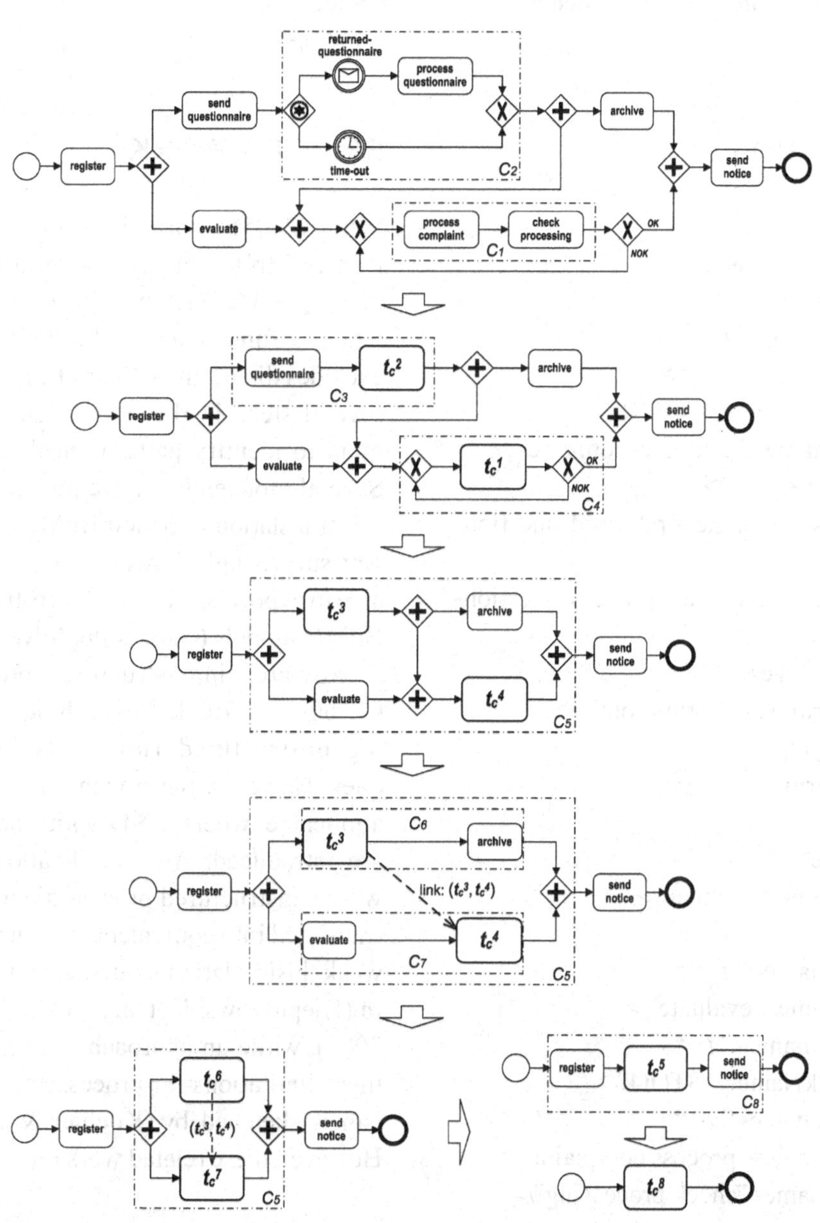

seven components are identified. All these components except C_5 capture well-structured patterns. In particular, C_1, C_3, C_6, C_7 and C_8 are identified as SEQUENCE-patterns and are folded into *sequence* activities t^1_c, t^3_c, t^6_c, t^7_c, and t^8_c, respectively; C_2 exhibits a PICK-pattern and is folded into a *pick* activity t^2_c ; and C_4 exhibits a REPEAT-pattern and is folded into a sequence of activity t^1_c followed by a *while* activity t^4_c. C_5 exhibits a generalized FLOW-pattern, and is folded into t^5_c which is a *flow* activity with a control link connecting t^3_c to t^4_c. The resulting BPEL process is sketched as:

```
<process>
 <links>
  <link name="t3TOt4"/>
 </links>
 <sequence name=" t^8_c ">
  <invoke name="register"/>
  <flow name=" t^5_c ">
   <sequence name=" t^5_c ">
    <sequence name=" t^3_c ">
     <source linkName="t3TOt4"/>
     <invoke name="send questionnaire"/>
     <pick name=" t^2_c ">
      <onMessage name="returned-questionnaire">
        <invoke name="process questionnaire"/>
      </onMessage>
      <onAlarm name="time-out">
       <empty/>
      </onAlarm>
     </pick>
    </sequence>
    <invoke name="archive"/>
   </sequence>
   <sequence name=" t^7_c ">
    <invoke name="evaluate"/>
    <sequence name=" t^4_c ">
    <target linkName="t3TOt4"/>
    <sequence name=" t^1_c ">
     <invoke name="process complaint"/>
     <invoke name="check processing"/>
    </sequence>
    <while condition="NOK">
     <sequence name=" t^1_c ">
      <invoke name="process complaint"/>
      <invoke name="check processing"/>
     </sequence>
    </while>
   </sequence>
  </sequence>
 </flow>
 <invoke name="send notice"/>
</sequence>
</process>
```

RELATED WORK

White (2005) informally sketches a translation from BPMN to BPEL. However, as acknowledged in (Object Management Group, 2006) this translation is fundamentally limited, for example it excludes diagrams with arbitrary topologies and several steps in the translation require human input to identify patterns in the source model. Several tool vendors have integrated variants of this translation into their BPMN modeling tools. Not surprisingly however, these tools are only able to export BPEL code for restricted classes of BPMN models (Gao, 2006; Silver, 2006).

Research into structured programming in the 60s and 70s led to techniques for translating unstructured flowcharts into structured ones. However, these techniques are no longer applicable when AND-splits and AND-joins are introduced. An identification of situations where unstructured process diagrams cannot be translated into equivalent structured ones (under weak bisimulation equivalence) can be found in (Kiepuszewski et al., 2000; Liu & Kumar, 2005), while an approach to overcome some of these limitations for processes without parallelism is sketched by (Koehler & Hauser, 2004). However, these related work only address a piece of the puzzle of translating from graph-oriented process modeling languages to BPEL.

This article is an extended version of (Ouyang et al., 2006) which in turn draws upon insights from one of our previous publications (Lassen & van der Aalst, 2006). Lassen and van der Aalst (2006) implement a semi-automated mapping from Colored Petri nets to BPEL. This semi-automated mapping is based on the identification of structural patterns that have commonalities with the set of well-structured translation patterns discussed in the present article.

In other complementary work (Ouyang et al., 2006), we presented a mapping from a graph-oriented language supporting AND-splits, AND-joins, XOR-splits, and XOR-joins, into BPEL. This mapping can deal with any BPMN model composed of elementary activities and these four types of gateways. However, the generated BPEL code relies heavily on BPEL event handlers, while in this article we make use of BPEL's block-structured constructs, thus obtaining more readable code. It is possible to combine these two methods by iteratively applying first the method presented in this article, and when this method can not be applied to any component of the model, applying the method in (Ouyang et al., 2006) on a minimal-size component, and so on until the process model is reduced to one single component. The technical details of this combined translation procedure are discussed in (Ouyang et al., 2006) which also introduces another translation approach that can deal with any acyclic BPMN graph containing AND and XOR gateways.

In parallel with our work, Mendling et al. (2006) have developed four strategies to translate from graph-oriented process modeling languages (such as BPMN) to BPEL. The first of these strategies, namely *structure-identification strategy*, works by identifying perfectly well-structured components and folding them incrementally. The second and third strategies, namely the *element-preservation strategy* and the *element-minimization strategy* translate acyclic graph-oriented models into BPEL process definitions that rely intensively on control links, as opposed to relying on BPEL structured activities. These strategies are similar to one of the translation procedures formalized in (Ouyang et al., 2006). Finally, the *structure-maximization strategy* tries to derive a BPEL process with as many structured activities as possible and for the remaining unstructured fragments, it tries to apply the strategies that rely on control links. None of the translation strategies by Mendling et al. (2006) are able to identify quasi-structured and generalized flow-patterns as discussed in this article.

Finally, it is interesting to mention the work conducted on the translations in the opposite direction, that is from BPEL to graph-oriented process modeling languages. One typical example is a toolset, namely *Tools4BPEL*, which consists of two main tools: *BPEL2oWFN* and *Fiona*. BPEL2oWFN maps BPEL specifications onto open Workflow nets using an algorithm described in (Hinz, Schmidt, & Stahl, 2005). The resulting nets can be loaded into a tool called Fiona that can check for various properties both for standalone and for inter-connected processes (Lohmann, Massuthe, Stahl, & Weinberg, 2006). Driven by the same motivation of enabling static analysis of BPEL processes, Brogi and Popescu (2006) present a translation from BPEL to YAWL (a graph-oriented process definition language inspired by Petri nets). Arguably, this latter BPEL-to-YAWL translation could be adapted to yield a BPEL-to-BPMN translation.

CONCLUSION

In this article, we presented an algorithm to translate models captured in a core subset of BPMN into BPEL. The translation algorithm is capable of generating readable and structured BPEL code by discovering structural patterns in the BPMN models. The proposal advances the state of the art in BPMN-to-BPEL translations by formally defining not only perfectly block-structured patterns of BPMN models, but also quasi-structured patterns and flow-based acyclic patterns. We have shown how well-structured and quasi-structured model fragments can be mapped into block-structured BPEL constructs, while flow-based acyclic fragments can be mapped into block-structured BPEL constructs with some additional control links to capture dependencies between activities located in different blocks.

An implementation of the proposed pattern-based translation algorithm is available as an open-source tool called BPMN2BPEL9. The current tool implementation covers the well-structured patterns presented in this paper as well as other complementary translation algorithms presented in (Ouyang et al., 2006; Ouyang et al., 2006). Ongoing work aims at extending the tool with the ability to detect quasi-structured patterns and flow-based acyclic patterns.

The translation technique described in this paper focuses on mapping a core subset of BPMN's control-flow constructs. For the translation to be complete, it needs to be extended to cover: (i) mappings of individual tasks and events such as send and receive tasks, user tasks, message events, timer events, and so on; and (ii) mappings of other constructs. The first point is covered in some details by (Object Management Group, 2006; White, 2005) and by other ongoing work in the context of the BPMN standardization process. The second point brings up some challenges which require special attention. In particular, mapping the OR-join gateway is likely to prove challenging especially for BPMN models containing arbitrary cycles. Indeed, this construct has a non-local semantics (Kindler, 2006), meaning that the firing behavior of an OR-join gateway may depend on other gateways in the model located far away from the OR-join gateway, as opposed to only depending on the tokens available on its input arcs. In future, we plan to investigate under which conditions can a BPMN model containing OR-join gateways be transformed into an equivalent BPMN model containing only AND and XOR gateways, so that the resulting models can be translated into BPEL using the algorithms described in this and related papers.

ACKNOWLEDGMENT

This research is supported by the Australian Research Council under the Discovery Grant "Expressiveness Comparison and Interchange Facilitation between Business Process Execution Languages" (DP0451092).

REFERENCES

Brogi, A., & Popescu, R. (2006). From BEL processes to YAWL workflows. In *Proceedings of the 3rd International Workshop on Web Services and Formal Methods* (*LNCS* 4184, pp. 107–122). Berlin: Springer-Verlag.

Gao, Y. (2006). *BPMN-BPEL transformation and round trip engineering. eClarus Software*. Retrieved March 1, 2007, from http://www.eclarus.com/pdf/BPMN_BPEL_Mapping.pdf

Hinz, S., Schmidt, K., & Stahl, C. (2005). Transforming BPEL to Petri nets. In *Proceedings of the 3rd International Conference on Business Process Management* (*LNCS* 3649, pp. 220–235). Berlin: Springer-Verlag.

Kiepuszewski, B., ter Hofstede, A.H.M., & Bussler, C. (2000). On structured workflow modelling. In *Proceedings of 12th International Conference on Advanced Information Systems Engineering* (*LNCS* 1789, pp. 431–445). Berlin: Springer-Verlag.

Kindler, E. (2006). On the semantics of EPCs: Resolving the vicious circle. *Data & Knowledge Engineering*, *56*(1), 23–40.

Koehler, J., & Hauser, R. (2004). Untangling Unstructured Cyclic Flows — A Solution Based on Continuations. In *On the Move to Meaningful Internet Systems 2004: CoopIS, DOA, and ODBASE* (LNCS 3290, pp. 121–138). Berlin: Springer-Verlag.

Lassen, K.B., & van der Aalst, W.M.P. (2006). WorkflowNet2BPEL4WS: A tool for translating unstructured workflow processes to readable BPEL. In *On the Move to Meaningful Internet Systems 2006: CoopIS, DOA, and ODBASE* (*LNCS* 4275, pp. 127–144). Berlin: Springer-Verlag.

Liu, R., & Kumar, A. (2005). An analysis and taxonomy of unstructured workflows. In *Proceedings of the 3rd International Conference on Business Process Management* (*LNCS* 3649, pp. 268–284). Berlin: Springer-Verlag.

Lohmann, N., Massuthe, P., Stahl, C., & Weinberg, D. (2006). Analyzing interacting BPEL processes. In *Proceedings of the 4th International Conference on Business Process Management* (*LNCS* 4102, pp. 17–32). Berlin: Springer-Verlag.

Mendling, J., Lassen, K.B., & Zdun, U. (2006). Transformation strategies between block-oriented and graph-oriented process modelling languages. In *Multikonferenz Wirtschaftsinformatik 2006, Band 2* (pp. 297–312). Berlin: GITO-Verlag.

OASIS (2006). Web Services Business Process Execution Language Version 2.0 (Committee Draft).

Object Management Group (2006). Business Process Modeling Notation (BPMN) Version 1.0 (OMG Final Adopted Specification).

Ouyang, C., Dumas, M., Breutel, S., & ter Hofstede, A.H.M. (2006). Translating standard process models to BPEL. In *Proceedings of 18th International Conference on Advanced Information Systems Engineering* (*LNCS* 4001, pp. 417–432). Berlin: Springer-Verlag.

Ouyang, C., Dumas, M., ter Hofstede, A.H.M., & van der Aalst, W.M.P. (2006). From BPMN process models to BPEL Web services. In *Proceedings of the 4th International Conference on Web Services* (pp. 285–292). IEEE Computer Society.

Ouyang, C., Dumas, M., van der Aalst, W.M.P., & ter Hofstede, A.H.M. (2006). *From business process models to process-oriented software systems: The BPMN to BPEL way.* (Tech. Rep. BPM-06-27, BPMcenter.org). Retrieved March 1, 2007, from http://is.tm.tue.nl/staff/wvdaalst/BPMcenter/reports/2006/ BPM-06-27.pdf

Silver, B. (2006). *The next step in process modeling.* Retrieved March 1, 2007 from http://www.brsilver. com/wordpress/2006/02/03/the-next-step-in-process-modeling. BPMSWatch

van der Aalst, W.M.P., ter Hofstede, A.H.M., Kiepuszewski, B., & Barros, A. P. (2003). Workflow patterns. *Distributed and Parallel Databases, 14*(3), 5–51.

White, S. (2005). Using BPMN to model a BPEL process. *BPTrends, 3*(3), 1–18.

ENDNOTES

1. See http://en.wikipedia.org/wiki/BPEL
2. See http://www.bpmn.org
3. A condition is a Boolean function operating over a set of propositional variables that can be abstracted out of the control flow definition. The condition may evaluate to true or false, which determines whether or not the associated sequence flow is taken during process execution.
4. The total order defined over the set of outgoing flows of an XOR decision gateway is to capture the fact that these flows are evaluated in order and the "default flow" is the one evaluated at last. This is part of

the semantics of XOR decision gateways as defined in the BPMN specification.

5 F * is the reflexive transitive closure of F, that is, x F^*y iff there is a path from x to y in BPD.

6 Note that in(x) is not defined with respect to the component but refers to the whole BPD. Similarly, this also applies to out(x) in this definition.

7 Note that $out(i_c) \subseteq T^R \cup E^I$ is the set of receive tasks and intermediate events following the event-based XOR decision gateways i_c. Between the merge gateway o_c and each of the objects in $out(i_c)$ there is at most one task or event object.

8 Since the goal of this article is to define an approach for translating BPDs to BPEL processes, we do not discuss further how to map simple tasks in BPMN to BPEL. Interested readers may refer to (Object Management Group, 2006) for some guidelines on mapping BPMN tasks into BPEL activities.

9 BPMN2BPEL is available at http://www.bpm.fit.qut.edu.au/projects/babel/tools

This work was previously published in the International Journal of Web Services Research, Vol. 5, Issue 1, edited by L. Zhang, pp. 42-62, copyright 2008 by IGI Publishing (an imprint of IGI Global).

Chapter 24
DSCWeaver:
Synchronization-Constraint Aspect Extension to Procedural Process Specification Languages

Qinyi Wu
Georgia Institute of Technology, USA

Calton Pu
Georgia Institute of Technology, USA

Akhil Sahai
HP Labs, USA

Roger Barga
Microsoft Research, USA

ABSTRACT

Correct synchronization among activities is critical in a business process. Current process languages such as BPEL specify the control flow of processes procedurally, which can lead to inflexible and tangled code for managing a crosscutting aspect—synchronization constraints that define permissible sequences of execution for activities. In this article, we present DSCWeaver, a tool that enables a synchronization-aspect extension to procedural languages. It uses DSCL (directed-acyclic-graph synchronization constraint language) to achieve three desirable properties for synchronization modeling: fine granularity, declarative syntax, and validation support. DSCWeaver then automatically generates executable code for synchronization. We demonstrate the advantages of our approach in a service deployment process written in BPEL and evaluate its performance using two metrics: lines of code (LoC) and places to visit (PtV). Evaluation results show that our approach can effectively reduce the development effort of process programmers while providing performance competitive to unwoven BPEL code.

INTRODUCTION

As more organizations adapt their execution models to become process oriented, it is increasingly important to support process modeling with expressive specification languages. This article focuses on the specification of process synchronization (Schmidt & Assmann, 1998). The recent trends in synchronization modeling have adopted a procedural style in which sequencing constructs (e.g., and-split and and-join) are used to specify the control flow of a process. In languages such as BPEL (business process execution language; *Specification: Business Process Execution Language for Web Services Version 1.1*, 2003) and XPDL (extensible markup language [XML] process definition language; Workflow Management Coalition [WMC], 2002), recurring synchronization patterns of different processes are factored out as primitives for specifying the execution order of activities (van der Aalst, ter Hofstede, Kiepuszewski, & Barros, 2003). While this sequencing, construct-based approach is good at specifying well-structured processes from the perspective of a single endpoint, it has difficulties with synchronization needs outside of recurring patterns; for example, activities in distributed parallel subprocesses require synchronization.

This article describes an aspect-oriented programming (AOP) approach to synchronization modeling in which synchronization constraints are declaratively expressed in relationship statements between activities in a process. The goal of this approach is to minimize the dependencies between process-specific functionality and synchronization control. It has been observed that synchronization control described procedurally can lead to tangled and fragile code for both process maintenance and adaptation (Lopes & Lieberherr, 1994; Pesic & van der Aalst, 2006; Singh, 2003). The challenge here is to find appropriate high-level primitives to express various synchronization behaviors that alleviate the synchronization difficulties in procedural languages. Another challenge is to automatically combine the synchronization constraints with other aspects of a process so that the result of applying this method is both compatible with the existing procedural programming environments and suitable for service-oriented environments.

Our method is based on DSCWeaver, a tool that offers a synchronization-aspect extension to procedural languages such as BPEL. The first contribution of DSCWeaver is the DAG (directed acyclic graph) synchronization constraint language (DSCL; Wu, Pu, & Sahai, 2006), which can be used to declaratively specify synchronization constraints for a process. DSCL detangles synchronization code from the base code of a process and provides flexible and expressive primitives to describe synchronization relationships for complex and evolving processes. DSCL draws on synchronization research in parallel programming (Campbell & Habermann, 1974; Salomaa & Yu, 1999), from which we adopt three desirable properties. First, DSCL provides fine granularity control on synchronization constraints. Instead of being regarded as an atomic unit, the life cycle of an activity is a sequence of states. It synchronizes with other activities based on its current states. Second, DSCL has a declarative syntax so that designers only need to specify what to be synchronized instead of how to implement it. As a result, additional synchronization constraints can be incrementally specified. Services invocated by the process can also specify their synchronization constraints declaratively and submit them to the process execution engine. Third, DSCL provides validation support to verify the correct synchronization behavior of processes by translating DSCL into Petri nets (Murata, 1989). Problems such as deadlock and an infinite synchronization sequence in a process can be detected by tools, for example, CPN (colored Petri nets) Tools (Ratzer et al., 2003).

The second contribution of DSCWeaver is the generation of an executable program from the DSCL synchronization constraints and other aspects of a process that correctly implements the original constraints. DSCWeaver translates the constraints into a set of synchronization messages with the ordering information. The code for sending and receiving these messages is inserted at the beginning and the end of each activity. At run time, activities are synchronized by exchanging these messages in order. These synchronization messages are generic and applicable to any process programming language that supports the basic messaging primitives (i.e., send and receive). We believe that messaging is well suited for synchronization control in service-oriented architectures where a process may need to be distributed for performance or implementation reasons (Chafle, Chandra, Mann, & Nanda, 2004; Schmidt & Assmann, 1998). A concrete implementation of DSCWeaver generates correctly synchronized BPEL code from DSCL specifications.

The rest of the article is organized as follows. We first present a motivating example to illustrate the synchronization constraints in a nontrivial service deployment process. We then present an overview of the DSCWeaver implementation, followed by a brief introduction to DSCL and the explanation of each submodule in DSCWeaver. After that, we explain how to apply DSCWeaver to BPEL, revisit the motivating example, and show our evaluation results. Related work and conclusions are presented last.

A MOTIVATING EXAMPLE

Consider a service deployment process for the PetStore e-commerce application, which is an online store where customers browse and purchase their favorite pets. The PetStore application consists of a database tier and an application server tier. To meet performance goals, the database server and the application server are installed on different hosts. The deployment process consists of a set of installation activities (each represented by $\boldsymbol{a}$), which interact with their target host to perform part of the installation task. This process consists of three steps.

1. **Middleware installation:** This step includes installing the database (MySQL), run-time environment (Java, Ant), and application server (Tomcat; denoted $\boldsymbol{a}_{\text{sql}}$, $\boldsymbol{a}_{\text{java}}$, $\boldsymbol{a}_{\text{ant}}$, and $\boldsymbol{a}_{\text{tomcat}}$, respectively).
2. **Application installation:** This step includes installing the application (PetStore) and its dependent libraries (Jdbc, Struts, Dao, and SQLMap), propagating the database with PetStore workload data (configure MySQL), and configuring PetStore with database server information (configure PetStore; denoted $\boldsymbol{a}_{\text{petstore}}$, $\boldsymbol{a}_{\text{jdbc}}$, $\boldsymbol{a}_{\text{struts}}$, $\boldsymbol{a}_{\text{dao}}$, $\boldsymbol{a}_{\text{sqlmap}}$, $\boldsymbol{a}_{\text{c\_sql}}$, and $\boldsymbol{a}_{\text{c\_petstore}}$, respectively).
3. **Application ignition:** This step includes starting the database and the application server (denoted $\boldsymbol{a}_{\text{s\_sql}}$ and $\boldsymbol{a}_{\text{s\_tomcat}}$, respectively).

The deployment process is orchestrated by a BPEL engine on the deployment host. The target hosts for the database and the application server are preinstalled with a Web service, InstallWS, which accepts installation instructions from activities and performs the installation tasks. Figure 1a depicts the centralized control scenario. In this topology, all synchronization logics are managed by the deployment machine (Host A), which interacts with target machines (Host B and Host C) by sending them installation instructions in order. The disadvantage of this approach is that Host A may become overloaded by the synchronization traffic if it has to simultaneously manage numerous process instances. However, we can reduce a portion of the workload for Host A by distributing deployment activities according to their target hosts. This modification leads to the decentralized deployment topology shown in Figure 1b. In the decentralized approach, the process is split into two subprocesses. All activities related to database installation form a subprocess to be deployed at

Figure 1. PetStore deployment topology

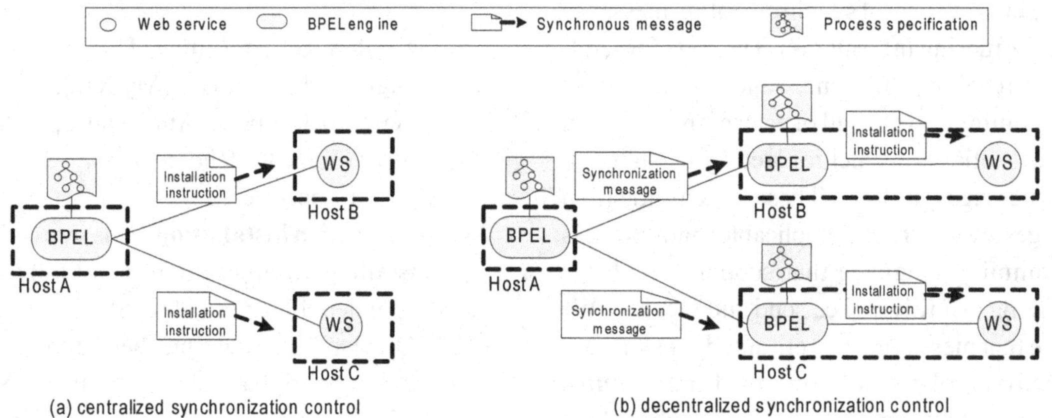

Host B, and all activities related to application server installation form another subprocess to be deployed at Host C. Each subprocess is deployed on a target host with which it interacts to fulfill the installation task. These two subprocesses interact with Host A only when they require intermediate synchronization. In the experiment section, we provide run-time performance measurements for both topologies.

Synchronization constraints are created via installation dependencies or user requirements. For example, an installation dependency arises when the installation of one software package should be placed at a specific location within the directory structure of another software package. In PetStore, the PetStore servlet code should be placed in the directory $Tomcat/webapp. User requirements may come from design strategies; for example, the application installation step is required to finish before the middleware installation step.

Instead of describing the constraints procedurally, we use two relations to specify them: HappenBefore (→) and Barrier (↔). Unlike other synchronization expression languages (Campbell & Habermann, 1974; Salomaa & Yu, 1999), the two relations operate on an activity state. The life cycle of an activity consists of three states: start (*S*), run (*R*), and finish (*F*). Activities synchronize with each other based on their current states. Figure 2 illustrates the synchronization constraints of the PetStore deployment. To give a HappenBefore example, $\boldsymbol{F}_{\mathrm{sql}} \rightarrow \boldsymbol{S}_{c\_sql}$ means the *finish* state of $\boldsymbol{a}_{\mathrm{sql}}$ should occur before the *start* state of $\boldsymbol{a}_{\mathrm{c\_sql}}$. In addition, the designer requires the run-time environment to be properly set up before the application server installation can begin, which adds $\boldsymbol{F}_{\mathrm{java}} \rightarrow \boldsymbol{S}_{tomcat}$ and $\boldsymbol{F}_{\mathrm{ant}} \rightarrow \boldsymbol{S}_{tomcat}$. To give a Barrier example, $\boldsymbol{F}_{\mathrm{sql}} \leftrightarrow \boldsymbol{F}_{tomcat}$ means that $\boldsymbol{a}_{\mathrm{sql}}$ and $\boldsymbol{a}_{\mathrm{tomcat}}$ should both be finished before the installation process moves forward.

DSCWeaver IMPLEMENTATION OVERVIEW

As an integrated tool, DSCWeaver contains three submodules to automate the translation from high-level specification to low-level executable code. The input to DSCWeaver is a process specification containing activities and their associated synchronization constraints in DSCL. Figure 3 illustrates its architecture. During the multistage translation procedure, intermediate outputs are formatted in XML for further processing:

Figure 2. Synchronization constraints in the PetStore deployment process

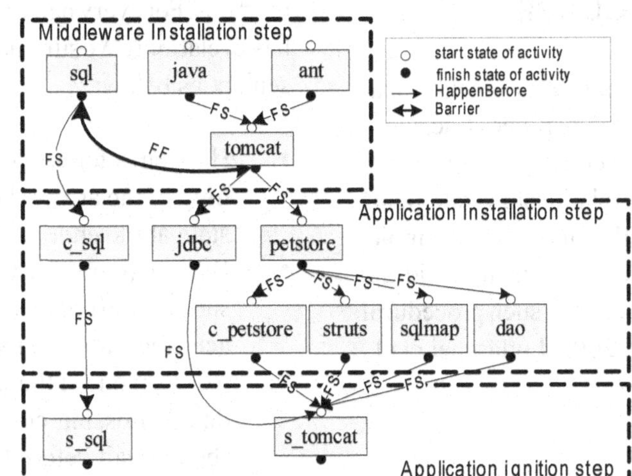

Figure 3. DSCWeaver implementation architecture

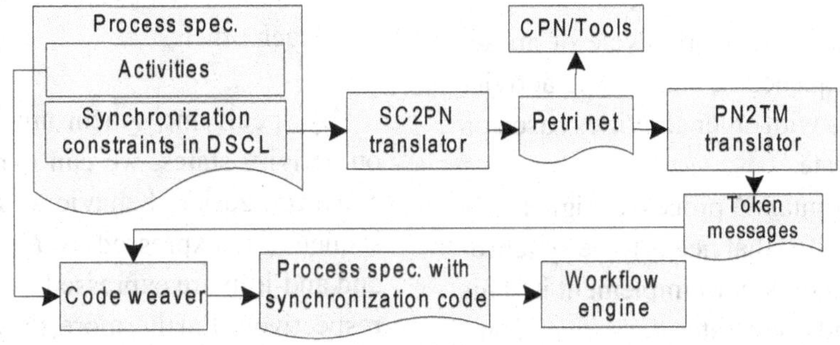

- Synchronization Constraints to Petri Net (SC2PN). This submodule takes the synchronization constraints as an input and translates them into a Petri net. The Petri net is not only an input for the CPN Tools for validation, but also an input for the next submodule.
- Petri Net to Token Message (PN2TM). This submodule consumes the Petri net from the previous submodule and maps the transition firing logic of the Petri net into token messages. These messages consist of token information such as which transition is going to consume this token or to which transition this token should be delivered.
- Code Weaver. The weaver collects information from the token messages about which messages must be sent or received for the state transitions of an activity. To weave the messages correctly, the activities are tagged in the original process specification. These tags are AOP join points that introduce hooks in the base code (Kiczales & Mezini, 2005). We demonstrate the weaving procedure by using BPEL later.

DAG SYNCHRONIZATION CONSTRAINT LANGUAGE

DSCL is designed to describe DAG synchronization behavior for activities. A process designer can use it to declaratively specify synchronization constraints in the form of relationship statements informally introduced in the motivating example. DSCL omits loop synchronizations to avoid the typical problems associated with such procedural facilities (Churches et al., 2005; Ludäscher et al., 2005).

DSCL Features

The design of DSCL adopts three features from parallel programming research (Campbell & Habermann, 1974; Salomaa & Yu, 1999):

- Fine granularity: The life cycle of an activity is a sequence of states. The activity synchronizes with other activities based on its current state.
- Declarative syntax: A process designer only needs to specify what needs to be synchronized instead of how to implement it. This simplifies and accelerates the service composition task (Benatallah, Dumas, Sheng, & Ngu, 2002).
- Validation support: Synchronization constraints are formalized in Petri nets for validation.

Fine granularity is accomplished by synchronizing an activity at different states of its life cycle. In a process, each activity goes through three states: start, run, and finish (states related to exception handling such as abort and failure are the subject of ongoing research and beyond the scope of this article). The activities interact and synchronize their execution from one state to another (in order). This brings more expressive power for synchronization behavior than state-unaware approaches.

DSCL declarative syntax defines three state relations. For every pair of states, we observe three basic relations. We summarize their notations and semantics below:

- HappenBefore (→): The state at the beginning of the arrow should happen before the state at the end.
- Barrier (↔): The two states at both ends should both be reached eventually before the activities move to their next states. In other words, if one of the states cannot be reached due to missing conditions, the other state should wait before further state transitions occur.
- Exclusive (O): The states at both ends must not be concurrent. Note that this only applies to *run* states because they are the only states where activities can actually interfere with each other.

By specifying synchronization relationships on activity states, we can express a rich set of synchronization behaviors. For instance, the sequence is expressed as $\boldsymbol{F}_i \rightarrow \boldsymbol{S}_j$. The and-split and and-join are expressed as $\boldsymbol{S}_i \leftrightarrow \boldsymbol{S}_j$ and $\boldsymbol{F}_i \leftrightarrow \boldsymbol{F}_j$, respectively. Furthermore, they can describe synchronization on two activities whose life spans are partially overlapping; for example, $\boldsymbol{S}_i \rightarrow \boldsymbol{F}_j$ means activity $\boldsymbol{a}_j$ should not finish until activity $\boldsymbol{a}_i$ starts. A concrete example is that the send-customer-satisfactory-survey activity should start before the close-a-purchasing-order activity finishes. Let us revisit the PetStore example. The synchronization constraints are the following:

1. middleware installation
   $\boldsymbol{F}_{java} \rightarrow \boldsymbol{S}_{tomcat}$, $\boldsymbol{F}_{ant} \rightarrow \boldsymbol{S}_{tomcat}$, $\boldsymbol{F}_{mysql} \leftrightarrow \boldsymbol{F}_{tomcat}$
2. application installation
   $\boldsymbol{F}_{sql} \rightarrow \boldsymbol{S}_{c\_sql}$, $\boldsymbol{F}_{tomcat} \rightarrow \boldsymbol{S}_{jdbc}$, $\boldsymbol{F}_{tomcat} \rightarrow \boldsymbol{S}_{petstore}$, $\boldsymbol{F}_{petstore} \rightarrow \boldsymbol{S}_{c\_petstore}$, $\boldsymbol{F}_{petstore} \rightarrow \boldsymbol{S}_{struts}$, $\boldsymbol{F}_{petstore} \rightarrow \boldsymbol{S}_{sqlmap}$, $\boldsymbol{F}_{petstore} \rightarrow \boldsymbol{S}_{dao}$

3. application ignition
   $\boldsymbol{F}_{c\_mysql} \rightarrow \boldsymbol{S}_{s\_mysql}$, $\boldsymbol{F}_{jdbc} \rightarrow \boldsymbol{S}_{s\_tomcat}$, $\boldsymbol{F}_{c\_petstore} \rightarrow \boldsymbol{S}_{s\_tomcat}$, $\boldsymbol{F}_{struts} \rightarrow \boldsymbol{S}_{s\_tomcat}$, $\boldsymbol{F}_{sqlmap} \rightarrow \boldsymbol{S}_{s\_tomcat}$, $\boldsymbol{F}_{dao} \rightarrow \boldsymbol{S}_{s\_tomcat}$

DSCWeaver offers validation support by translating state relationships into a Petri net. The translated Petri net is formatted to the input of CPN Tools, which is a graph editor and simulator of CPN (Jensen, 1992). It provides toolkits to identify dead transitions and infinite-occurrence sequences.

DSCL Properties

Before explaining the properties of DSCL, we first give the definition for the state relations. We use $\boldsymbol{a}$ to denote an activity in a process. We denote the state space of $\boldsymbol{a}$ by $N=\{S, R, F\}$, and X as the range of N. X_i refers to the state X of activity $\boldsymbol{a}_i$.

Definition 1: *A state relation is defined by* $(X_i, X_j) \in \psi$, *where* $X_i, X_j \in N$, $\psi = \rightarrow | \leftrightarrow | O$ *(| means or). Domain* $(\rightarrow)=\{S, F\}$, *Domain* $(\leftrightarrow)=\{S, F\}$, *and Domain* $(O)=\{R\}$.

From the definition, ψ contains three types of relations: $\rightarrow$ and $\leftrightarrow$ are used to specify relationships on the *start* or *finish* state of activities, and O is used to specify relationships on the *run* state. Since ψ describes the primitive relationship between activities, it is able to simulate all the static workflow patterns such as sequence, parallel split, synchronization, interleave parallel routing, and milestone, but not dynamic ones such as exclusive choice or arbitrary circle (van der Aalst et al., 2003). Therefore, the expressiveness of ψ is restricted to static synchronization constraints. Next, we declare two properties of ψ. We use them to define the correctness criteria of synchronization constraints in terms of state relations, and to reduce the complexity of mapping from state relations to Petri nets.

Property 1:

i. Transitivity

$(X_i, X_j) \in \psi_{\rightarrow} \wedge (X_j, X_z) \in \psi_{\rightarrow} \Rightarrow (X_i, X_z) \in \psi_{\rightarrow}$

$(X_i, X_j) \in \psi_{\leftrightarrow} \wedge (X_j, X_z) \in \psi_{\leftrightarrow} \Rightarrow (X_i, X_z) \in \psi_{\leftrightarrow}$

ii. Symmetry

$(X_i, X_j) \in \psi_{\leftrightarrow} \Rightarrow (X_j, X_i) \in \psi_{\leftrightarrow}$

Property 1 implies that $\rightarrow$ or $\leftrightarrow$ only defines a pair-wise relationship between two states. We need to form a global view to maintain the correct synchronization behavior. For example, if $\boldsymbol{S}_i \leftrightarrow \boldsymbol{S}_j$ and $\boldsymbol{S}_j \leftrightarrow \boldsymbol{S}_z$, it means that the *start* state of $\boldsymbol{a}_i$ and $\boldsymbol{a}_z$ should also be synchronized in a barrier. One abbreviation is $\boldsymbol{S}_i \leftrightarrow \boldsymbol{S}_j \leftrightarrow \boldsymbol{S}_z$. We use $\{X_i\}^+_{\rightarrow}$ to denote the transitive closure of $\rightarrow$ and $\{X_i\}^+_{\leftrightarrow}$ to denote the transitive closure of $\leftrightarrow$.

Property 2: *Given* $X_1 \leftrightarrow X_2 \ldots \leftrightarrow X_k$ *and their transitive closure* $\{X_i\}^+_{\leftrightarrow}$, $\leftrightarrow$ *can be simulated in* $\rightarrow$ *by creating a coordination activity* $\boldsymbol{a}_c$ *and replacing* $\{X_1\}^+_{\leftrightarrow}$ *with new state relationships as follows.*

i. $\forall X_i \in N(\psi)$, where $N(\psi)$ denotes all the states occurring in ψ; if $\exists X_j \in \{X_1\}^+_{\leftrightarrow}$ and $X_i \rightarrow X_j$, then $\psi = \psi \cup \{X_i \rightarrow \boldsymbol{S}_c\} - \{X_i \rightarrow X_j\}$.
ii. If $\forall X_j \in \{X_1\}^+_{\leftrightarrow}$, let $\psi = \psi \cup \{\boldsymbol{F}_c \rightarrow X_j\}$.

This property is best explained by an example. Consider the relationship statements $\boldsymbol{F}_1 \rightarrow \boldsymbol{S}_2$, $\boldsymbol{F}_3 \rightarrow \boldsymbol{S}_4$, and $\boldsymbol{S}_2 \leftrightarrow \boldsymbol{S}_4 \leftrightarrow \boldsymbol{S}_5$ for activities $\boldsymbol{a}_1$, $\boldsymbol{a}_2$, $\boldsymbol{a}_3$, $\boldsymbol{a}_4$, and $\boldsymbol{a}_5$. They require that $\boldsymbol{a}_3$, $\boldsymbol{a}_4$, and $\boldsymbol{a}_5$ only start after $\boldsymbol{a}_1$ and $\boldsymbol{a}_2$ have finished their execution. We can replace $\boldsymbol{S}_2 \leftrightarrow \boldsymbol{S}_4 \leftrightarrow \boldsymbol{S}_5$ by introducing $\boldsymbol{a}_c$, removing $\boldsymbol{F}_1 \rightarrow \boldsymbol{S}_2$ and $\boldsymbol{F}_3 \rightarrow \boldsymbol{S}_4$, and finally adding the additional relationships $\boldsymbol{F}_1 \rightarrow \boldsymbol{S}_c$, $\boldsymbol{F}_3 \rightarrow \boldsymbol{S}_c$, $\boldsymbol{F}_c \rightarrow \boldsymbol{S}_2$, $\boldsymbol{F}_c \rightarrow \boldsymbol{S}_4$, and $\boldsymbol{F}_c \rightarrow \boldsymbol{S}_5$ as shown in Figure 4.

Property 2 implies that $\leftrightarrow$ is a "syntax sugar"; we can represent $\leftrightarrow$ with $\rightarrow$ by introducing a coordination activity. Thus, without loss of generality, the translation method in the next section discusses $\rightarrow$ and O only.

Finally, we define the correctness criteria for the state relationships in a process. It considers two error situations. One is the dead end, in

Figure 4. Simulate ↔ by →

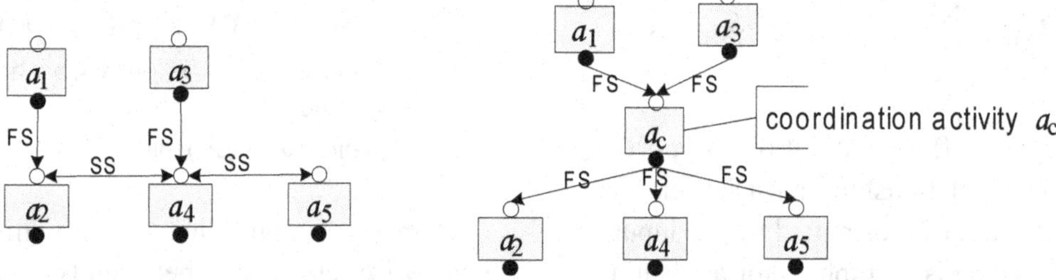

which an activity is unreachable. The other is an infinite-synchronization sequence. Definition 2 gives the formal definition.

Definition 2: *Given a process* $P = \{a_0, a_1 ... a_n\}$ *with* a_0 *as the starting activity and the associated state relationships* ψ*,* ψ *is correct for process P if and only if it satisfies the following conditions.*

1. $\forall a_i \in A, \{S_i, R_i, F_i\} \subseteq \{S_0\}^+_{\to}$
2. $\forall X_i \in \psi, X_i \notin \{X_i\}^+_{\to}$

By Condition 1, there is no dead end in synchronization. All the states of activities are reachable from the start state (S_0) of the root activity. By Condition 2, the synchronization constraints are acyclic. There is no deadlock, and an infinite-occurrence sequence cannot occur. In other words, the state of an activity is not allowed to have a HappenBefore relationship with itself. Notice that the Exclusive relation O is not considered in the correctness criteria in that it only impacts the scheduling time of associated activities and not their reachability.

TRANSLATION OF DSCL TO PETRI NETS

As a descriptive language, DSCL acquires its formal foundation by establishing a mapping to Petri nets. Petri nets are a formal and graphical language for modeling system behavior with concurrency. Following the notations in Murata (1989), a Petri net is defined as follows.

Definition 3: *A Petri net is a four-tuple* $C = (P, T, I, O)$.

i. *P* is a finite set of places.
ii. *T* is a finite set of transitions.
iii. $I: T \to P^\infty$ is the input function, a mapping from transitions to bags of places.
iv. $O: T \to P^\infty$ is the output function, a mapping from transitions to bags of places.

Places hold tokens and represent predicates about the world state. Transitions represent actions to be executed when all the places inbound to it contain adequate tokens. We use μ to denote a marking of *C*, and $R(C, \mu)$ to denote the reachability set of *C* with initial marking μ. We introduce the concept of "liveness" and explain how it can be used to validate our synchronization correctness criteria. Liveness has been considered in studies of deadlock and categorized at four levels (Murata, 1989). For the purpose of this article, we are interested in Level 1 and Level 4 only. For a Petri net $C = (P, T, I, O)$ with initial token μ, the following applies.

Definition 4: *A transition is live at Level 1 if it is potentially fireable, that is, if there exists* $\mu' \in R(C, \mu)$ *such that the transition is enabled in* μ'.

Figure 5. Translation from state relationships to Petri net

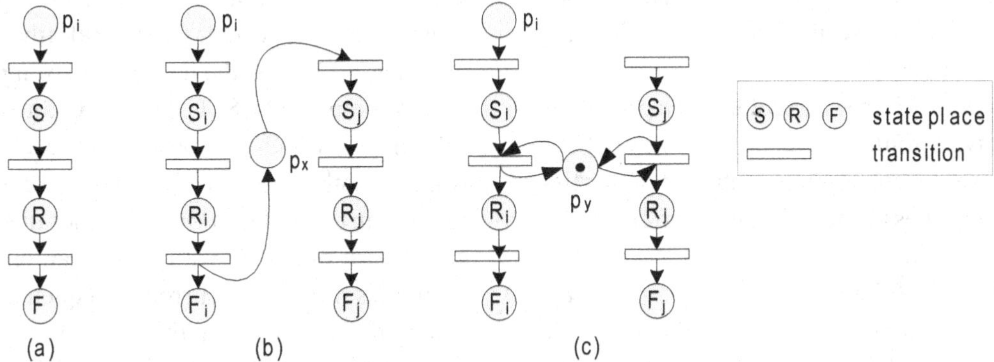

Definition 5: *A transition is live at Level 4 if for each μ′ ∈ R(C, μ) there is a firing sequence σ such that the transition is enabled in μ′.*

Liveness Level 4 is stronger than Level 1. Liveness Level 1 is used to identify whether there are unreachable transitions. Liveness Level 4 is used to identify whether there is an infinite firing sequence in the Petri net. Both of them are used to verify the correctness of state relationships, which will be explained in the next section. We also use the following proposition.

Proposition 1: *If a Petri net C = (P, T, I, O) with marking μ is at Level 4, an infinite-occurrence sequence exists.*

Proof: *We prove this by contradiction. If no infinite-occurrence sequence exists, C must halt at a marking μ′, at which no transition is enabled. This contradicts Definition 5.*

Translation from State Relationships to Petri Nets

This section describes a method to derive a Petri net from the state relationships of a process. The method follows three steps: the intrastate relation construction, which manages the state relations within an activity; the interstate relation construction, which establishes the state relations between activities; and finally, the exclusive relation construction, which handles the Exclusive relation. During the mapping, a place represents an activity state. Each transition controls the conditions that need to be satisfied before the activity can reach that state.

Step 1: Intrastate Relation Construction

Intrastate relations reflect the state transition of an activity in its life span. Each activity sequentially goes through three states: *S*, *R*, and *F*. Its Petri net is shown in Figure 5a. If there is a token at the initial place p_i, the token will be propagated to the states of *S*, *R*, and *F* in order.

Step 2: Interstate Relation Construction

For each $X_i \rightarrow X_j$, i≠j, a place and two arcs are created to connect the outbound transition corresponding to X_i and the inbound transition corresponding to X_j. For example, the state relation $\boldsymbol{F_i \rightarrow S_j}$ is connected by place p_x as illustrated in Figure 5b.

Step 3: Exclusive Relationship Construction

For the Exclusive relation O, a place with a shared token is added to the transitions that correspond to the running state of all involved activities. The shared token at place p_y guarantees that only one of the activities is executed at any point in time, as seen in Figure 5c.

In order to infer the correctness of a process in terms of synchronization relations by way of Petri net, we need to correlate the Petri net properties to the correctness criteria (Definition 2).

Proposition 2: *Given a process* $\boldsymbol{P} = \{\boldsymbol{a}_0, \boldsymbol{a}_1, ..., \boldsymbol{a}_n\}$ *and its associated state relationships* ψ*,* ψ *are correct if and only if the corresponding Petri net is at liveness Level 1, and there is no transition at liveness Level 4.*

Proof: *A Petri net at liveness Level 1 implies that every state is potentially fireable from the start state. This satisfies the correctness criterion in Definition 2. The absence of transitions at liveness Level 4 implies no state will be enabled by itself. This means no cyclic triggering sequences exist. This satisfies the correctness criterion in Definition 2.*

Validation in CPN Tools

We choose CPN Tools as the validation tool for three reasons. First, CPN is more expressive than Petri nets to describe a system (Jensen, 1992). It allows tokens to carry complex data structures. This leaves us more flexibility if DSCL will be extended to accommodate richer synchronization behaviors, for instance, conditional state transitions. Second, CPN Tools provides substantial support for verifying various properties like liveness, boundedness, and fairness. CPN Tools constructs an occurrence graph (OG) in which each node stands for a reachable marking, and an arc for each firing of a transition. Based on the occurrence graph, CPN Tools generates a report about the number of nodes in the graph, the bound for each place, and the dead and live transitions. In the report, we are particularly interested in two aspects. One is the dead transitions, which corresponds to liveness Level 1. If the dead transitions are nonexistent, the Petri net satisfies liveness Level 1. The second is the number of nodes in OG and the number of strongly connected components (SCCs). An SCC is a maximal subgraph in which it is possible to reach a node from any other node. If the number of SCCs is fewer than the nodes in OG, it implies that the net has at least one SCC with more than one node. It implies infinite-occurrence sequences exist among the nodes within this SCC (Ratzer et al., 2003), which satisfies liveness Level 4.

We use two processes to illustrate how DSCWeaver translates state relationships into a Petri net and uses CPN Tools for validation. The first process is artificially constructed to demonstrate the validation procedure. The second process revisits the PetStore deployment process.

Process 1

Process 1 contains four activities a_1, a_2, a_3, and a_4. It has three synchronization constraints:

- $\boldsymbol{S}_{a1}\rightarrow\boldsymbol{S}_{a2}$: a_2 can start immediately after a_1 starts. a_2 does not have to wait for a_1 to finish.
- $\boldsymbol{S}_{a1}\rightarrow\boldsymbol{F}_{a3}$: a_3 can only finish after a_1 starts.
- $\boldsymbol{F}_{a3}\rightarrow\boldsymbol{S}_{a4}$: a_3 finishes first, and then a_4 starts.

To make the example more interesting, suppose that the synchronization constraint $\boldsymbol{F}_{a4}\rightarrow\boldsymbol{S}_{a3}$ is mistakenly added to the process. The synchronization constraint graph is portrayed in Figure 6.

Petri net translation and simulation result. SC2PN reads the state relationships and translates them into a Petri net. For each a_i, we name the Petri net places s_i, r_i, and f_i corresponding to its *start, run,* and *finish* states respectively. The transitions between places are named S_i, R_i, and F_i respectively. For a transition *i*, if it has more than one outbound place, we number the places $x_{i0}, x_{i1} \ldots x_{in}$, $x \in \{s, r, f\}$, respectively. For a Barrier relation-

Figure 6. Synchronization constraints of Process 1

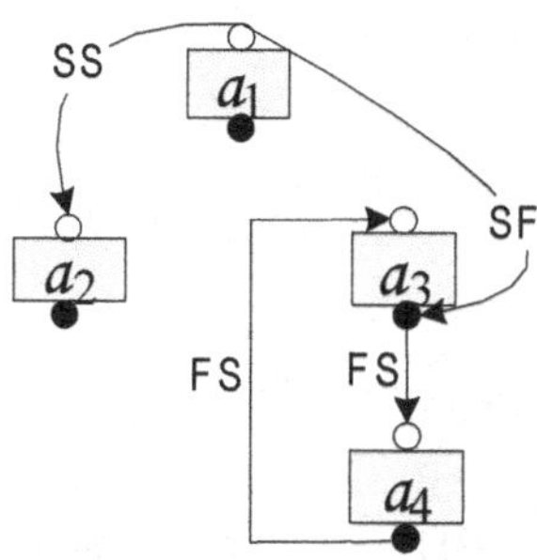

ship between a_i and a_j, we name the coordinator activity a_{ij}. Figure 7a is a screenshot of CPN Tools. We can see that there are three places and three transitions for each activity. The place s_0 with the initial marking 1\`*e* (1\`*e* represents one token with the color type *e*) is used to trigger a_1 and a_3 concurrently. Figure 7b is part of the state-space report generated by CPN Tools. The report says that transitions F3, F4, R3, R4, S3, and S4 are dead, as highlighted in the dashed rectangle in Figure 7a. This is caused by the cyclic synchronization constraints in the state relations, which violates Definition 2. Therefore, the state relationships are incorrect; $\boldsymbol{F}_{a4} \rightarrow \boldsymbol{S}_{a3}$ must be removed.

Process 2

Based on the process specification described in the motivating example, the synchronization constraint graph is reshown in Figure 8.

Petri net translation and simulation result. Figure 9a is a screenshot of CPN Tools. Due to space limitations, we omit the labels for places and transitions. From the report in Figure 9b, we can see that the size of the state space is equal to that of SCC, and no dead transitions exist. Therefore, the synchronization behavior of the PetStore process is correct.

TRANSLATION OF PETRI NET TO TOKEN MESSAGES

The PN2TM submodule translates a Petri net to a set of token messages carrying the firing information. These messages are then exchanged among activities to enforce synchronization constraints. There are two types of token messages: the *receive* token message (<receive place=p value=e />), which tells from which place *p* a transition receives a message with value *e*, and the *send* token message (<send place=p value=e />), which tells to which place *p* the transition sent a message with value *e*. A transition should receive all inbound messages before sending outbound messages. Figure 10 shows the translation result. Using Petri nets to automatically generate token messages for enforcing synchronization constraints is a distinctive feature of our approach. Most other works use formal techniques for verification only (Narayanan & McIlraith, 2002; Ouyang, van der Aalst, Breutel, Dumas, ter Hofstede, & Verbeek, 2005).

Figure 7. Process 1 (a) Petri net translation and (b) simulation report

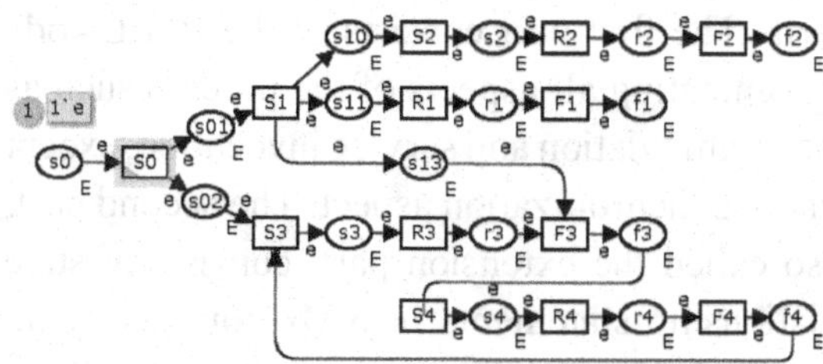

Statistics

... ...

Dead Transitions Instances
F3 1
F4 1
R3 1
R4 1
S3 1
S4 1

Figure 8. Synchronization constraints of the PetStore deployment process

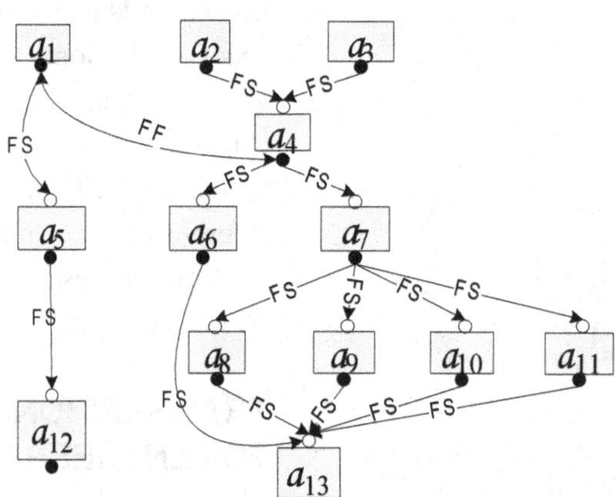

Figure 9. PetStore deployment process (a) Petri net translation and (b) simulation report

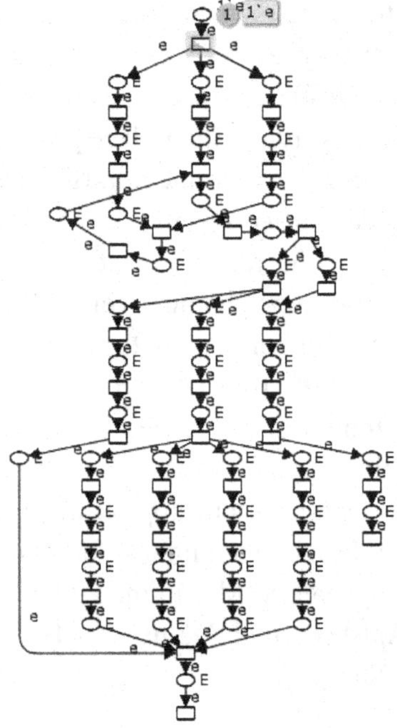

```
Statistics
------------------------------------
 State Space
   Nodes: 7298
   Arcs: 33325
   Secs: 121
   Status: Full

 Scc Graph
   Nodes: 7298
   Arcs: 33325
   Secs: 3

Home Properties
------------------------------------
 Home Markings [7298]

Liveness Properties
------------------------------------
 Dead Markings [7298]
 Dead Transition Instances: None
 Live Transition Instances: None

Fairness Properties
------------------------------------
No infinite occurrence sequences.
```

BPEL EXTENSION WITH DSCL

Because synchronization constraints specified in DSCL can be enforced by exchanging a set of token messages, our approach is applicable to any process specification language supporting basic messaging primitives (i.e., send and receive). We demonstrate how to extend BPEL with DSCL. For a given process, its specification consists of two parts. The first part consists of the BPEL code implementing all aspects of the process such as data manipulation and service invocation, except for the synchronization aspect. The second part, also called the extension part, consists of state relationship statements in XML for specifying the missing constraints in the first part. We use

Figure 10. Translation from Petri nets to token messages

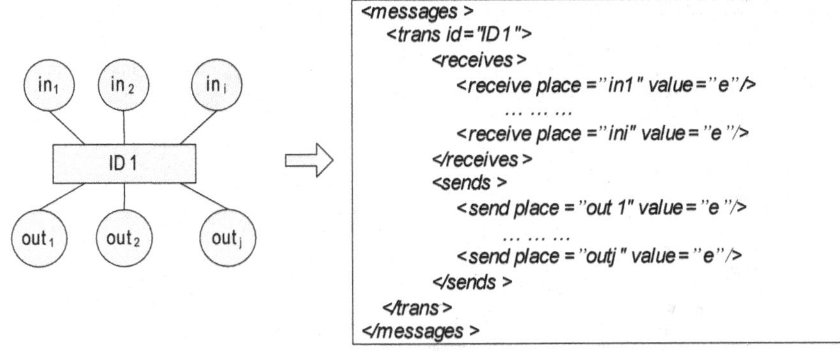

Table 1. New tags for DSCL+

Tag	Semantics	Syntax
Activity	It demarcates the boundary of an activity with a unique ID.	<activity aid="qname"> Activity </activity>
HappenBefore	It defines →. <begin> specifies the activity at the head of →, and <end> is the activity at the end of →.	<happenBefore> <begin aid="A1" state="ncname" /> <end aid="A2" state="ncname" /> </happenBefore>
Barrier	It defines ↔. <end> specifies activities at both ends of ↔.	<barrier> <end aid="A1" state=" ncname " /> ... ... <end aid="A2" state=" ncname " /> </barrier >
Exclusive	It defines O. <end> specifies activities at both ends of O.	<exclusive> <end aid="A1" state=" ncname " /> ... ... <end aid="A2" state=" ncname " /> </exclusive>
DSCL	It demarcates the extension part for DSCL.	<dscl> ... synchronization constraints ... </dscl>

DSCL+ to name the BPEL specification with the DSCL extension. DSCWeaver parses the DSCL+ code and infers the token messages. Then, it inserts BPEL code for exchanging these token messages to produce a pure BPEL specification. In order to locate the right place for insertion, the BPEL code is first instrumented with special tags to identify activities. We first introduce new XML tags for DSCL+ and then use PetStore to illustrate the weaving procedure.

DSCL+ Tags

Table 1 summarizes the syntax and semantics of new XML tags used in DSCL+.

Figure 11 shows a DSCL+ code snippet for the PetStore process. Each activity is delineated by the tag <activity> with the unique attribute *aid*. The tag <activity> is similar to a join point in AOP by which DSCWeaver knows where to insert the aspect-related code. The code for the activity of installing MySQL is given as an example. Recall

Figure 11. Code snippet for DSCL+ specification

```
<process name ="deploymentProcess " suppressJoinFailure ="yes" .../>
   <sequence>
      <receive createInstance ="yes" operation ="processCall "
      partnerLink ="ProcessCallerPL " portType ="pld:ProcessCallerPT "
      variable ="processStartMessage " />

      <flow>
         <activity aid ="Sql">
            <sequence >
               <assign>
                  <copy>
                     <from expression ="'http://ScriptHost /installMySQL .sh'"/>
                     <to part ="instruction " variable ="SqlInputMessage "/>
                  </copy>
               </assign>
               <invoke inputVariable ="SqlInputMessage "
                       operation ="execute" outputVariable ="SqlOutputMessage "
                       partnerLink ="Sql " portType ="InstallWS :InstallWS "/>
            </sequence>
         </activity>
         <activity aid ="C_Sql">
            <-- code for configuring MySQL -->
         </activity>

         <activity aid ="Tomcat ">
            <-- code for installing Tomcat -->
         </activity>
         <activity aid ="PetStore ">
            <-- code for installing PetStore -->
         </activity>

      </flow>
      <reply operation ="processCall " partnerLink ="ProcessCallerPL "
         portTyp ="pld:ProcessCallerPT " variable ="processFinishMessage " />
   </sequence>
   <dscl>
      <happenBefore >
         <begin aid ="Sql" state="finish " />
         <end aid ="C_Sql" state="start " />
      </happenBefore >
      <barrier>
         <begin aid ="Tomcat" state="finish" />
         <end aid ="PetStore " state="start " />
      </barrier>

      <happenTogether >
         <end aid ="Tomcat" state="finish" />
         <end aid ="Sql" state="finish" />
      </happenTogether >
   </dscl>
</process>
```

Instantiate a process

Define a set of activities

Call back to the invoker

DSCL code

in the section of the motivating example that the target host is preinstalled with a Web service, InstallWS, that accepts instructions from the deployment host and executes them. InstallWS has a port *execute*, which has one parameter *instruction*. The *instruction* parameter is a string with the value of a URL (uniform resource locator) where the installation script is downloaded. The function of port *execute* is to start a system shell and run the script. The extension part <dscl> is where the state relationships between activities are defined. Only three state relationships are illustrated due to space limitations. For instance, the activity with ID *Sql* should happen before activity with ID *C_Sql*. In the complete specification, all the constraints in Figure 2 are listed.

BPEL Code Weaving

DSCWeaver starts the code weaving procedure by (a) inferring the token messages to be exchanged by activities at each state, (b) querying the location of each activity in the process specification by the XPath expression //activity[@aid='*aid*'], and (c)

Figure 12. Weave code for message exchange into a process specification

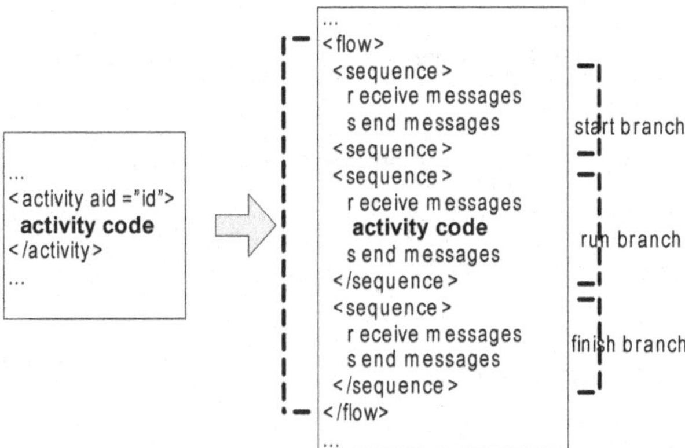

inserting the code for exchanging token messages before and after the activity code. This section explains the third step in detail. The following built-in primitives in BPEL are used:

- <invoke>: invoke the operation of a Web service
- <receive>: specify a message expected to be received
- <sequence>: provide sequential execution for all nested subprocesses
- <flow>: provide concurrency and synchronization, and exits when all branches (subprocesses) in the flow have completed

For each activity identified by the <activity> tag and its *aid*, DSCWeaver removes the block <activity>...</activity>, and adds a new block <flow>...</flow>. Within this new block, there are three branches, each of which imitates a state. The branches are called the *start* branch, *run* branch, and *finish* branch. The *start* and *finish* branches contain the code for message exchange. The *run* branch contains the code for both message exchange and activity execution. DSCWeaver uses <invoke>, <receive>, and <sequence> to implement the message exchange. <sequence> is used for bundling the code for assigning message variables and the code for sending messages. Figure 12 illustrates the weaving structure.

To better understand how the weaving procedure works, we also give the BPEL code for a simple Petri net in Figure 13. A transition T1 is waiting for the arrival of message M1 to be triggered. After T1 fires, it sends M2 to T2. Remember that the message exchange for each state corresponds to the token propagation in the Petri net. Understanding how to generate BPEL code for this net essentially explains how to generate BPEL code for more complex synchronization constraints because other situations like multiple input and output places are merely adding extra code for manipulating additional messages.

Figure 14 is the woven result. There are two partnerLinks defining the invocations between T1 waiting for M1 and T1 sending M2. The correlationSet is used to correlate T1's query for M1 and the arrival of M1. This is required by BPEL to perform an invocation in synchronous mode. T1's query is sent to a Web service MsgQueue, which will be explained next. There is a list of

Figure 13. A simple unit in a Petri net

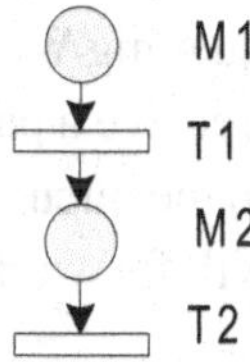

Figure 14. Snippet code after code weaving

Code for receiving message M1

Code for transition. firing

Code for sending message M2

```
<process >
  <partnerLinks >
    <partnerLink myRole ="Queryee" name="T1Wait" partnerLinkType ="psd:MQQueryPLT " partnerRole ="Queryer "/>
    <partnerLink myRole ="Queryee" name="T1send" partnerLinkType ="psd:MQQueryPLT " partnerRole ="Queryer "/>
        ...
  </partnerLinks >
  <correlationSets >
    <correlationSet name ="T1CS" properties ="psd:queryCorrelationData " />
        ...
  </correlationSets >
  <variables >
    <variable messageType ="mq:queryRequest " name="T1RevQueryMsg " />
    <variable messageType ="psd:queryResponseMessag " name="T1RevRespMsg " />
    <variable messageType ="mq:registerRequest " name="T1SendMsg"/>
          ...
  </variables >
  <sequence >
    <receive createInstance ="yes" operation ="processCall " partnerLink ="ProcessCallerPL "
        portType ="p1d:ProcessCallerPT " variable ="processStartMessage " />
    <flow>
      <flow >
        <sequence >
                <!-- code for assigning values toT 1RevQueryMsg -->
          <invoke inputVariable ="T1RevQueryMsg " operation ="query"
                partnerLink ="T1Wait" portType ="mq:MsgQueueWS ">
            <correlationSets >
              <correlationSet initiate ="yes" pattern ="out" set="T1CS"/>
            </correlationSets >
          </invoke >
          <receive operation ="queryResponse " partnerLink ="T1Wait"
                portType ="psd:QueryCallBackPT  variable ="T1RevRespMsg ">
            <correlationSets >
              <correlationSet set ="T1CS"/>
            </correlationSets >
          </receive >
        </sequence >
        <sequence >
          < !--code for firing a transition . It does nothing if this transition stands for a
            start or finish state -->
        </sequence >
        <sequence >
                <!-- code for assigning values toT 1SendMsg -->
          <invoke inputVariable ="T1SendMsg" operation ="register "
               partnerLin ="T1Send" portType ="mq:MsgQueueWS " />
        </sequence >
      </flow>
          ...
    </flow >
    <reply operation ="processCall " partnerLink ="ProcessCallerPL "
        portType ="p1d:ProcessCallerPT "        variable ="processFinishMessage " />
  </sequence >
</process >
```

variables serving as input parameters for the invocation of MsgQueue. In this example, variable T1RevQueryMsg is assigned with value M1, and variable T1SendMsg with value M2.

We would be able to exchange these messages directly if it were not for the race conditions between activities when exchanging messages. If a receiver is not active by the time a sender begins sending a message, the message is lost. We need a persistent queue for storing it until the receiver becomes ready. Therefore, a sender sends its token to a queuing Web service. When a receiver is ready to receive a particular message, it sends its request to the queue. If the message is present, the queue will forward it to the receiver. Otherwise, the receiver blocks until the arrival of the message. We implemented the MsgQueue Web service that has two ports: register, which queues a message, and query, which accepts a query for the existence of a particular message and notifies the receiver when it becomes available. Notice that the MsgQueue is slightly different from the standard message brokers in that the message delivery is dependent. Only when all the messages corresponding to the inbound places of a transition have arrived will they be delivered together to the subscribers. In a standard persistent message broker, the messages are delivered to the requester as soon as they arrive, independent of other messages.

Table 2. Number of LoCs in PetStore process

	BPEL	Centralized DSCL+	Decentralized DSCL+
Specification	10	16	16
Spec. Adaptation	7	1	1
Sync. Control Decentralization	N/A	N/A	16

EVALUATION

Development Effort Evaluation

Similar to the programming language community that typically compares programming languages in terms of lines of code, ease of use, and so forth (Prechelt, 2000), we introduce two metrics to measure the development effort of a process programmer. One is the number of lines of code (LoC) that the programmer uses to express the synchronization constraints of a process. The second metric is the number of places to visit (PtV), which is the number of places the programmer has to jump back and forth between to specify the synchronization constraints.

For LoC, we consider three situations: the effort in specifying the original process specification, the effort in modifying the original specification, and the effort in implementing synchronization control decentralization. In BPEL, each structured construct, like <sequence> and <flow>, counts as one LoC, and each unstructured construct, like <link>, counts as two LoCs because they require extra code to declare. In DSCL+, each relationship statement counts as one LoC. Notice that we do not use LoC exactly as it is used in measuring the effort for general programming languages in which each line of code is counted as one. This is because XML has a block structure where each tag has one line of code for block start and one line of code for block end. We count them as one since we feel it matches more for XML programming. The result for our PetStore example is shown in Table 2.

Original process specification. BPEL requires 10 LoC (four from <flow>, four from <sequence>, and two from <link>), shown in Figure 15, while DSCL+ requires 16 LoC for each relationship statement, shown in Figure 8. DSCL+ requires more code than BPEL because DSCL+ uses finer grained primitives than structured constructs. For example, to specify the parallel between $\boldsymbol{a}_{\text{java}}$ and $\boldsymbol{a}_{\text{ant}}$, we need only one <flow> in BPEL. However, we need four relationship statements in DSCL+. There is a trade-off between the flexibility of DSCL and the ease of expression obtained from the macro constructs of BPEL. Language choice depends on the requirements of particular processes. In our opinion, when describing a process with a simple thread of flow, BPEL is preferred due to its effectiveness in describing well-structured processes without much interprocess synchronization. Otherwise, DSCL+ is better.

Process adaptation. The advantage of DSCL+ becomes obvious during adaptation. Assume that the restriction "the middleware installation subprocess should finish before the application installation subprocess" has been removed. In BPEL, we must remove the <flow> for the middleware installation subprocess, insert $\boldsymbol{a}_{\text{sql}}$ into the database subprocess, and insert $\boldsymbol{a}_{\text{java}}$, $\boldsymbol{a}_{\text{ant}}$, and $\boldsymbol{a}_{\text{tomcat}}$ into the application server subprocess. To manage the constraint between $\boldsymbol{a}_{\text{tomcat}}$, $\boldsymbol{a}_{\text{petstore}}$, and $\boldsymbol{a}_{\text{jdbc}}$, we need one <sequence> to execute $\boldsymbol{a}_{\text{tomcat}}$ first, and one <flow> for the parallel execution between $\boldsymbol{a}_{\text{petstore}}$ and $\boldsymbol{a}_{\text{jdbc}}$. That is seven LoCs in total. In DSCL+, we simply remove the statement $\boldsymbol{F}_{\text{mysql}} \leftrightarrow \boldsymbol{F}_{tomcat}$, which is one LoC.

Figure 15. PetStore process in BPEL

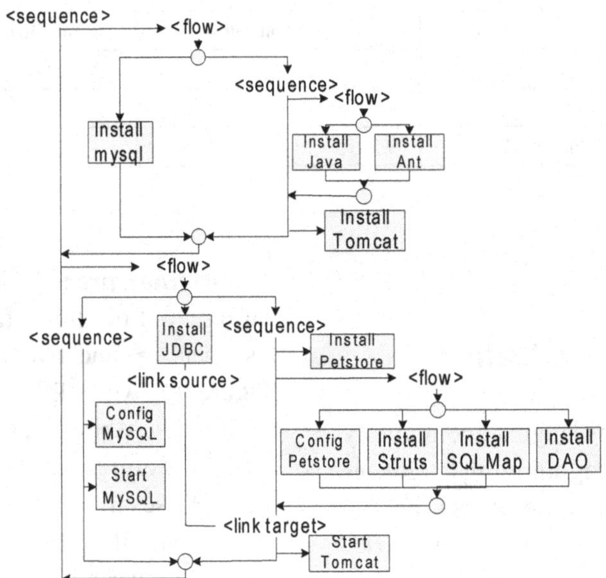

Synchronization control decentralization. It is hard to coordinate activities nested in distributed processes in BPEL because there is no easy way to universally identify an intermediate activity in a process and to specify its synchronization constraints to the activities in other processes. One way is to split the BPEL specification according to the approach in Chafle et al. (2004), but that would result in the creation of a subprocess for each intermediate activity to be synchronized. Furthermore, BPEL cannot handle exclusive synchronization constraints. In comparison, in decentralized DSCL+, each activity is uniquely tagged with its ID. A programmer only needs to specify the constraint for each subprocess and rely on DSCWeaver to weave the synchronization code for exchanging token messages across the distributed subprocesses. Therefore, the LoC remains the same as the centralized version.

For the PtV metric, one PtV is counted each time a designer has to jump to a different place in a process specification when implementing a task. The result is shown in Table 3. For the centralized DSCL+, all synchronization constraints can be specified at one place. Therefore, it is only one PtV for both the process design stage and the adaptation stage. However, the programmer has to edit two subprocess specifications (i.e., application tier and database tier) in the decentralized scenario. Therefore two PtVs are required for the decentralized deployment of PetStore. In comparison, the development effort in BPEL increases a lot in regard to the PtV metric. For example, in order to specify the original specification, each structured construct requires two PtVs. Each unstructured construct requires three PtVs. Since we have eight structured constructs and one unstructured construct, the total is 19 PtVs. The reduction from 19 PtVs to 1 PtV represents a significant reduction in development effort. Similar results can be observed during process adaptation.

Performance

There are two purposes for the performance experiment. One is to evaluate the overhead brought by DSCL+ for token message exchange. We deployed and compared the PetStore process by using standard BPEL constructs and the instrumented code generated by DSCWeaver. The

Table 3. Number of PtVs in PetStore process

	BPEL	Centralized DSCL+	Decentralized DSCL+
Specification	19	1	2
Spec. Adaptation	7	1	1
Sync. Control Decentralization	N/A	N/A	2

Table 4. Deployment time for PetStore

	ActiveBPEL	Centralized DSCL+	Decentralized DSCL+
Time (s)	75	83	75

other purpose is to demonstrate that DSCL+ can describe synchronization constraints for distributed processes and coordinate them in a decentralized manner. We also generated the decentralized DSCL code and measured its performance in terms of deployment time.

Experiment setup. Our experiment uses a cluster of Intel Pentium machines (2x 3 GHz Pentium 4, 1 GB memory) in Redhat Linux 9. The BPEL engine is ActiveBPEL. The Web service engine is Axis. We call the machine that starts the process the deployment machine, and the machine that hosts the PetStore application the target machine. In the centralized setup (Figure 1a), the deployment machine is installed with the ActiveBPEL engine for orchestrating processes and Axis for providing the MsgQueue Web service. Two client machines for the database and application servers are configured with Axis as the Web service engine. In the decentralized setup (Figure 1b), three of the machines were set up with ActiveBPEL and Axis engines. The role of the deployment machine is to coordinate with the two processes running on the two client machines. The ActiveBPEL engine on the client machine interacts with the local Axis to execute those activities that perform the tasks on the local host. We ran the experiments five times to average the deployment time. From Table 4, we can see that centralized DSCL requires more time than BPEL, but decentralized DSCL is as good as ActiveBPEL.

RELATED WORK

Modeling a process from multiple aspects has the advantages of reduced complexity and increased robustness (Schmidt & Assmann, 1998). DSCWeaver is capable of providing synchronization-aspect extension to general-purpose process languages. In this sense, our work is similar to Jeeg, which models synchronizations in temporal logic and weaves them into the rest of Java code (Milicia & Sassone, 2005). Bachmendo and Unland (2001) described an approach using aspects to control the workflow evolution by changing the behavior of structured constructs (e.g., sequence and and-split) at run time. However, it does not address implementation issues. The AO4BPEL project (Charfi & Mezini, 2004) uses aspects for service composition and collects auditing information at run time. It defines *before*, *after*, and *around* advice and uses XPath for point-cut definitions. AO4BPEL uses AOP in the traditional way. Our work separates the crosscutting concern, the synchronization aspect, and applies a different code generation technique in the weaving procedure to make it suitable for distributed synchronization applications.

Several synchronization modeling languages have been proposed in the literature, such as path expressions (Campbell & Habermann, 1974), synchronization expressions (Salomaa & Yu, 1999), and interactive expressions (Heinlein, 2001). Singh (2003) discussed the limitation of procedural specification languages and proposed a declarative approach in the context of multiagent systems by specifying synchronization constraints on the significant events of activities such as commit and abort. Though they can express more complicated synchronization behaviors, DSCL intends to make the basic primitives concise and simple in such a way that many applications can adapt our approach readily, especially in distributed cases. Different from early work, DSCL models the process state explicitly. Synchronization at the granularity of activity states is important in interactive systems (van der Aalst et al., 2003). For example, service deployment workflows are specified by putting synchronization constraints on the states of installation activities (Sahai, Singhal, Machiraju, & Joshi, 2004). In Salomaa and Yu, activities are split into two parts—the start part and the termination part—for inferring the correctness of synchronization histories. Furthermore, DSCL uses synchronization constraints over states to infer the correctness of processes. Synchronization expressions were mapped into Petri nets (Lauer & Campbell, 1975), but they did not address the correctness issue.

Different techniques have been proposed to understand the synchronization behaviors of processes such as Petri nets (Murata, 1989), π-calculus (Milner, 1999), and model checking (Betin-Can, Bultan, & Fu, 2005; Foster, Kramer, Magee, & Uchitel, 2003). We choose Petri nets as the formalization language because Petri nets model states explicitly. We also use Petri nets to generate synchronization code. The translation from a Petri net to executable code can be seen in the early work. Grid-Flow (Guan et al., 2005) provides a Petri-net-based user interface for workflow modeling in grids and automatically translates a net to the Grid-Flow description language. Instead of targeting a particular domain language, our approach can be easily integrated into different workflow languages because it only requires basic messaging facilities. Van der Aalst and Lassen (2005) introduced a tool for translating Petri nets to BPEL. Instead of establishing a mapping between a Petri net and the structured constructs in BPEL, we translate the Petri net to token messages. Synchronization in messages facilitates the task of converting BPEL from centralized control to decentralized control, which is a significant advantage in service-oriented architectures.

CONCLUSION

In this article, we address the limitations of modeling synchronization constraints in procedural process specification languages such as BPEL. We describe DSCWeaver, a software tool that implements a synchronization-aspect extension called DSCL to procedural process specification languages. DSCL is a domain-specific synchronization constraint language with three good properties: fine granularity, declarative syntax, and validation support. Syntactically, DSCL provides three state relations—HappenBefore, Barrier, and Exclusive—for a process designer to declaratively specify what the synchronization constraints are instead of how to implement them. The DSCL specification is translated into CPN for automated detection of synchronization problems such as deadlocks using CPN Tools. A concrete implementation of DSCWeaver demonstrates the combination of DSCL with BPEL. DSCL constraints are validated and woven into the base BPEL code to form a complete and correct process specification. DSCWeaver demonstrates the practicality and feasibility of providing a synchronization-aspect extension to general-purpose process specification languages in both centralized and decentralized environments.

The current design of DSCL captures only static synchronization dependencies that are known at compilation time. The synchronization requirements of services loaded and composed during run time, including issues such as exception handling and reconfiguration, are interesting research challenges for future work. For example, if an activity crashes, how should the system specify and enforce the dependencies of the recovery action, and how should the system treat the "dangling" dependencies of the crashed activity? Another question is, if an activity is replaced at run time, with the introduction of new dependencies and removal of old ones, how should the system adapt? These are a small sample of current and future research topics.

ACKNOWLEDGMENT

This research has been partially funded by the National Science Foundation Grants CISE/IIS-0242397, CISE/ITR-0219902, ENG/EEC-0335622, and CISE/CNS-0646430; the DARPA/IPTO Grant FA8750-05-1-0253; the AFOSR Grant FA9550-06-1-0201; IBM SUR grants; Hewlett-Packard; and Georgia Tech Foundation through the John P. Imlay, Jr., chair endowment.

REFERENCES

ActiveBPEL. (n.d.). Retrieved from http://www.activebpel.org

Axis. (n.d.) Retrieved from http://ws.apache.org/axis

Bachmendo, B., & Unland, R. (2001). *Aspect-based workflow evolution.* Paper presented at the Workshop on Aspect-Oriented Programming and Separation of Concerns, Lancaster, United Kingdom.

Benatallah, B., Dumas, M., Sheng, Q. Z., & Ngu, A. H. H. (2002). Declarative composition and peer-to-peer provisioning of dynamic Web services. In *Proceedings of the 18th International Conference on Data Engineering* (ICDE'02). IEEE Computer Society.

Betin-Can, A., Bultan, T., & Fu, X. (2005). Design for verification for asynchronously communicating Web services. In *Proceedings of the 14th International Conference on World Wide Web*, Chiba, Japan (pp. 750-759). ACM Press.

Campbell, R. H., & Habermann, A. N. (1974). The specification of process synchronization by path expressions. In *Lecture notes in computer science* (Vol. 16, pp. 89-102). Springer-Verlag.

Chafle, G., Chandra, S., Mann, V., & Nanda, M. G. (2004). Decentralized orchestration of composite Web services. In *Proceedings of the 13th International World Wide Web Conference*, New York.

Charfi, A., & Mezini, M. (2004). Aspect-oriented Web service composition with AO4BPEL. In *Proceedings of the European Conference on Web Services ECOWS 2004*, Erfurt, Germany (LNCS 3250).

Churches, D., Gombas, G., Harrison, A., Maassen, J., Robinson, C., Shields, M., et al. (2005). Programming scientific and distributed workflow with Triana services. *Concurrency and Computation: Practice and Experience.*

Foster, H., Kramer, J., Magee, J., & Uchitel, S. (2003). *Model-based verification of Web service compositions.* Paper presented at the IEEE ASE 2003, Montreal, Canada.

Guan, Z., Hernandez, F., Bangalore, P., Gray, J., Skjellum, A., Velusamy, V., et al. (2005). Gridflow: A grid-enabled scientific workflow system with a Petri net-based interface. *Concurrency and Computation: Practice and Experience, 18*(10), 1115-1140.

Heinlein, C. (2001). Workflow and process synchronization with interaction expressions and graphs. In *Proceedings of 17th International Conference on Data Engineering.*

Jensen, K. (1992). Colored Petri nets. In *Basic concepts.* Springer-Verlag.

Kiczales, G., & Mezini, M. (2005). Aspect-oriented programming and modular reasoning. In *Proceedings of the 27th International Conference on Software Engineering*, St. Louis, MO. ACM Press.

Lauer, P. E., & Campbell, R. H. (1975). A description of path expressions by Petri nets. In *Proceedings of the Second ACM SIGACT-SIGPLAN Symposium on Principles of Programming Languages*, Palo Alto, CA. ACM Press.

Lopes, C., & Lieberherr, K. (1994). Abstracting function-to-process relations in concurrent object-oriented applications. In *Proceedings of the European Conference on Object-Oriented Programming (ECOOP'94)* (LNCS 821). Springer-Verlag.

Ludäscher, B., Altintas, I., Berkley, C., Higgins, D., Jaeger-Frank, E., Jones, M., et al. (2005). Scientific workflow management and the Kepler system. *Concurrency and Computation: Practice and Experience.*

Milicia, G., & Sassone, V. (2005). Jeeg: Temporal constraints for the synchronization of concurrent objects. *Concurrency and Computation: Practice and Experience, 17*(5-6), 539-572.

Milner, R. (1999). *Communicating and mobile systems: The pi-calculus* (1st ed.). Cambridge University Press.

Murata, T. (1989). Petri nets: Properties, analysis and applications. In *Proceedings of the IEEE, 77*(4), 541-580.

Narayanan, S., & McIlraith, S. A. (2002). Simulation, verification and automated composition of Web services. In *Proceedings of the 11th International Conference on World Wide Web*, Honolulu, HI. ACM Press.

Ouyang, C., van der Aalst, W. M. P., Breutel, S., Dumas, M., ter Hofstede, A. H. M., & Verbeek, H. M. W. (2005). *Formal semantics and analysis of control flow in WS-BPEL* (Rep. No. BPM-05-13). BPM Center. Retrieved from http://BPMcenter.org

Pesic, M., & van der Aalst, W. M. P. (2006). DecSerFlow: Towards a truly declarative service flow language. In F. Leymann, W. Reisig, S. R. Thatte, & W. M. P. van der Aalst (Eds.), *Dagstuhl Seminar Proceedings: The Role of Business Processes in Service Oriented Architectures* (Vol. 6291).

Prechelt, L. (2000). An empirical comparison of seven programming languages. *IEEE Computer, 33*(10), 23-29.

Ratzer, A. V., Wells, L., Lassen, H. M., Laursen, M., Qvortrup, J. F., Stissing, M. S., et al. (2003). CPN tools for editing, simulating, and analysing coloured Petri nets. In W. v. d. Aaalst & E. Best (Eds.), *Application and theory of Petri nets.*

Sahai, A., Singhal, S., Machiraju, V., & Joshi, R. (2004). Automated generation of resource configurations through policy. In *Policy.* New York.

Salomaa, K., & Yu, S. (1999). Synchronization expressions and languages. *Journal of Universal Computer Science, 5*, 610-621.

Schmidt, R., & Assmann, U. (1998). Extending aspect-oriented-programming in order to flexibly support workflows. In *Proceedings of Aspect-Oriented Programming Workshop.*

Singh, M. P. (2003). Distributed enactment of multiagent workflows: Temporal logic for Web service composition. In *Proceedings of the Second International Joint Conference on Autonomous Agents and Multiagent Systems*, Melbourne, Australia. ACM Press.

Specification: Business process execution language for Web services version 1.1. (2003). Retrieved from http://www-106.ibm.com/developerworks/webservices/library/ws-bpel

van der Aalst, W. M. P., & Lassen, K. B. (2005). *Translating workflow nets to BPEL4WS* (Rep. No. BPM-05-16). BPM Center.

van der Aalst, W. M. P., ter Hofstede, A. H. M., Kiepuszewski, B., & Barros, A. P. (2003). Workflow patterns. *Distributed and Parallel Databases, 14*(3), 5-51.

Workflow Management Coalition. (2002). *Workflow process definition interface: XML process definition language* (No. WFMC-TC-1025).

Wu, Q., Pu, C., & Sahai, A. (2006). DAG synchronization constraint language for business processes. In *Proceedings of the IEEE Conference on E-Commerce Technology (CEC'06).*

This work was previously published in the International Journal of Web Services Research, Vol. 5, Issue 3, edited by L. Zhang, pp. 96-117, copyright 2008 by IGI Publishing (an imprint of IGI Global).

Chapter 25
A Reservation-Based Extended Transaction Protocol for Coordination of Web Services within Business Activities

Wenbing Zhao
Cleveland State University, USA

Firat Kart
University of California, Santa Barbara, USA

L. E. Moser
University of California, Santa Barbara, USA

P. M. Melliar-Smith
University of California, Santa Barbara, USA

ABSTRACT

This chapter describes a novel reservation-based extended transaction protocol for coordination of tasks within a business activity. With the advance of Web Services, it is anticipated that the implementation of business activities as Web Services, and the automation of business activities across multiple enterprises over the Internet, will become a reality. Classical extended transaction protocols are not well suited for this new breed of business activity, because of their use of compensating transactions. The reservation-based extended transaction protocol, described in this chapter, eliminates the need for compensating transactions by using an explicit reservation phase and an explicit confirmation/cancellation phase. This chapter provides a mapping of the reservation-based extended transaction protocol onto the Web Services Coordination Specification, and describes an implementation of the protocol.

INTRODUCTION

The Service Oriented Architecture and Web Services make it possible for enterprises to conduct business over the Internet in real-time without human supervision or intervention (Booth, Haas et al. 2004, Moser and Melliar-Smith 2009). Such business operations are often organized as business activities. A business activity consists of one or more related tasks that are carried out over a potentially long period of

DOI: 10.4018/978-1-61520-684-1.ch025

time in a loosely-coupled distributed environment. Such direct and automated computer-to-computer interactions can provide speed improvements and cost reductions for many enterprises.

Because of the nature of business activities, some extended transaction protocols, most notably sagas (Garcia-Molina and Salem 1987), are often used to coordinate the tasks of a business activity, where each individual task is executed as a classical transaction that satisfies the ACID properties, namely, Atomicity, Consistency, Isolation and Durability (Gray and Reuter 1993). If an error occurs during a business activity, the entire business activity is rolled back by applying one or more compensating transactions to reverse the committed transactions. Although useful in many cases, compensating transactions have their limitations. One problem is the cascading compensations that result from relaxation of the isolation property, *i.e.*, before the compensating transaction is applied, other transactions might see the results of the committed transaction and, therefore, must also be compensated. Identifying such transactions is difficult, because there is no way to find them a priori. Furthermore, it might be difficult or impossible to compensate a committed transaction. For example, if an end-of-quarter audit transaction is executed immediately after a sales task is committed in a publicly traded company, the sales are included in the total revenue reported to the public. The completion of the audit transaction, followed by the compensation of the sales task, can result in inconsistencies. In general, the programming of compensating transactions is very difficult and prone to error.

In this chapter, we present a novel reservation-based extended transaction protocol that avoids the use of compensating transactions while achieving atomicity and consistency similar to or better than other existing extended transaction protocols. Each task within a business activity is executed as two steps. The first step involves an explicit reservation of resources according to the business logic. For example, if the task involves reserving two seats, out of 200 available seats, on an airline flight, those two seats are explicitly reserved in a separate step. In the interests of the airline, a fee that is proportional to the duration of the reservation can be associated with the reservation. The second step involves the confirmation or cancellation of the reservation. Each of the steps is executed as a separate traditional short-running transaction, as in the sagas strategy (Garcia-Molina and Salem 1987). However, because of the explicit reservation, other transactions cannot interfere with the business activity. Thus, degree 3 isolation (Gray and Reuter 1993) is achieved and, if a business activity must be abandoned, recovery involves only the cancellation of the reservations for participants in that business activity.

In subsequent sections, we show how the reservation-based extended transaction protocol (hereafter referred to as the Reservation Protocol) can be implemented on top of the Web Services Coordination Specification, in a similar manner to WS-C and WS-BA (Cabrera, Copeland et al. 2005a, 2005c). We describe our implementation of the Reservation Protocol as middleware libraries that are linked into the application processes at the client and the server. We compare the response time, throughput and completion time of the Reservation Protocol with that of the Two Phase Commit Protocol and the Optimistic Two Phase Commit Protocol, obtained from experimental measurements based on our implementations of the protocols.

SYSTEM MODEL

A *business activity* is a unit of work that spans two or more enterprises and consists of one or more tasks. A *task* is a short-duration unit of work that is executed as a traditional transaction within a single enterprise. The tasks in a business activity are partially ordered. Tasks that are not causally related can be executed concurrently, and causally related tasks are executed according to the partial order.

Figure 1. A business activity that comprises multiple tasks that span multiple enterprises. Each task is executed as a traditional transaction within one of the enterprises

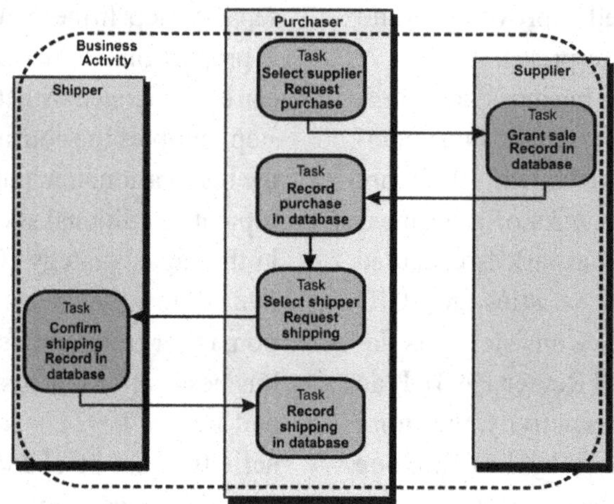

A task can be modeled as an operation on one or more resources, and typically modifies some of the attributes of those resources. For example, the task of purchasing/selling certain kinds of goods (application-defined resources), such as automobiles, can be modeled as an operation on those resources in which the owner attribute of the resource is changed from the supplier to the buyer. An operation can be read-only, in which case the task is a read-only task.

Figure 1 shows an example business activity, highly simplified, of purchasing a product (resource) from a supplier and shipping that product. The purchaser proceeds with the purchase only if both the product and the shipping are available. The purchaser first places an order for the product and then arranges for shipping. However, if the shipper cannot deliver the product in time (*e.g.,* no trucks are available), the purchaser must reverse the previous purchase and apply a compensating transaction. Later in the chapter, we show how the Reservation Protocol deals with this situation without the need for compensating transactions.

A business activity can be modeled as a *business transaction*, where there is a coordinator and multiple participants. In a business transaction, the ACID properties of traditional transactions are not appropriate for the following reasons. First, it is not necessary that all of the participants see the same result. For example, if two suppliers are competing, one might see the reservation committed, while the other sees the reservation cancelled. Second, the failure of a task does not need to result in the rollback of the entire business transaction, particularly if there are multiple alternative suppliers. Third, the effect of executing a task might not be completely reversible, because of the business logic. For example, a reservation fee might be imposed even if the business transaction is abandoned.

The coordinator and the participants in a business transaction (including the client and the server applications and/or middleware components) are subject to crash faults but not arbitrary (Byzantine) faults. In the Reservation Protocol, the coordinator for the business transaction is strongly coupled with the client application that initiated the business transaction. The coordinator runs in the same process as the client application. Therefore, the coordinator is regarded as a representative of the client, and the client is held accountable for any financial cost incurred if the client coordinator fails. However, the Reservation Protocol provides protection against failure of the client coordinator by a counterpart server coordinator, as discussed later in the Implementation section.

The communication between the coordinator and the participants in a business transaction is assumed to be reliable. We discuss the consequence of unreliable communication and how to work around that problem in the next section.

THE RESERVATION PROTOCOL

Except for read-only tasks, each task is executed as two steps and is controlled directly by the application. In the first step, the resource involved in the task is reserved in a single traditional transaction. In the second step, the reservation is either confirmed or cancelled according to the business rules, also in a single traditional transaction.

To understand how a reservation is carried out, consider the example of purchasing goods (application-defined resources). The goods to be purchased are reserved at the supplier as a result of a request by the purchaser. For example, the attribute for the amount of goods to be sold shows “reserved” rather than “available” or “sold”.

By explicitly reserving the resources involved in a task, the application has the flexibility of going forward or backward after the first step, without concern for the effects of the transaction, because a reservation allows either outcome. However, the application is not free to use the resource until after the reservation is committed. Even if other client transactions see the intermediate result of the reservation, they see only resources that are available to them and not resources that have been reserved by other clients. All operations at the server, including for example augmenting the available resources, are undertaken as local transactions at the server.

In general, the reservation and commitment/ cancellation steps imply that some form of service or work has been carried out. Consequently, an enterprise may impose a fee for the reservation and the associated service and work.

The coordination of different tasks within a business transaction is achieved in two phases, as shown in Figure 2 (where we use the same business activity as in Figure 1). In the first phase, the coordinator at the client sends reservation requests to all of the participants, in an order determined by the business rules. Reservation requests for independent tasks can be sent concurrently. In the second phase, the client coordinator determines which reservations to confirm and which reservations to cancel, and then sends the confirmation/cancellation requests to the appropriate participants. The criteria, that determine which reservations to confirm and which to cancel, are application-dependent and, thus, out-of-scope of this work.

In a traditional distributed transaction based on the Two Phase Commit Protocol or the Optimistic Two Phase Commit Protocol, if a fault occurs, each participant can decide unilaterally whether to abort and rollback the transaction. In contrast, with the Reservation Protocol, only the client coordinator is authorized to commit or cancel the transaction. A fault at other participants might affect the client's decision and, thus, the outcome of the transaction; however, it does not necessarily result in the rollback of the transaction.

Resource Reservation vs. Locking Resource vs. Resource Request Retry

At an abstract level, resource reservation in the Reservation Protocol, locking a resource in the Two Phase Commit Protocol, and resource request retry in the Optimistic Two Phase Commit Protocol are similar in that they all put the resource on hold temporarily. However, there are significant differences in the three protocols, as shown in Figure 3 and discussed below.

In the Reservation Protocol, the reservation of a resource and the confirmation or cancellation of the reservation, are executed as traditional ACID transactions. Between the reservation and the

Figure 2. A business activity executed using the Reservation Protocol

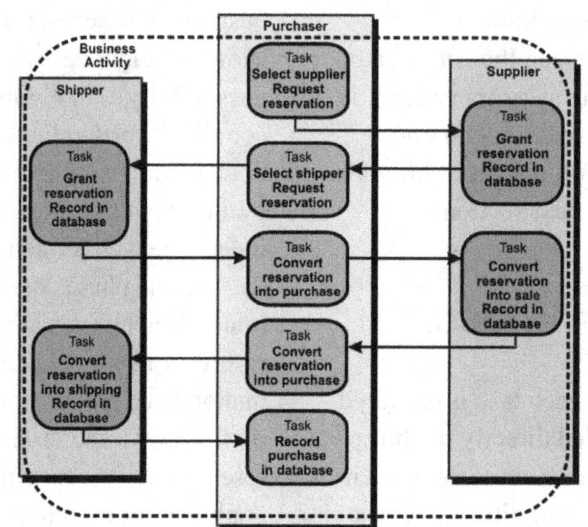

confirmation, the database records are unlocked and are available to other business activities. The application has control over the reservation, how much of the resource is reserved, and how long the resource is reserved.

In the Two Phase Commit Protocol with conservative concurrency control for database systems (Bernstein, Hadzilacos et al. 1987), the locking of a resource is internal to the database system and is transparent to the application. The resource is locked by the database system, and the application has no control over how long the resource is locked. In practice, a timeout is used to control how long a transaction lasts and to

Figure 3. Comparison of resource reservation in the Reservation Protocol, locking in the Two Phase Commit Protocol, and request retry in the Optimistic Two Phase Commit Protocol

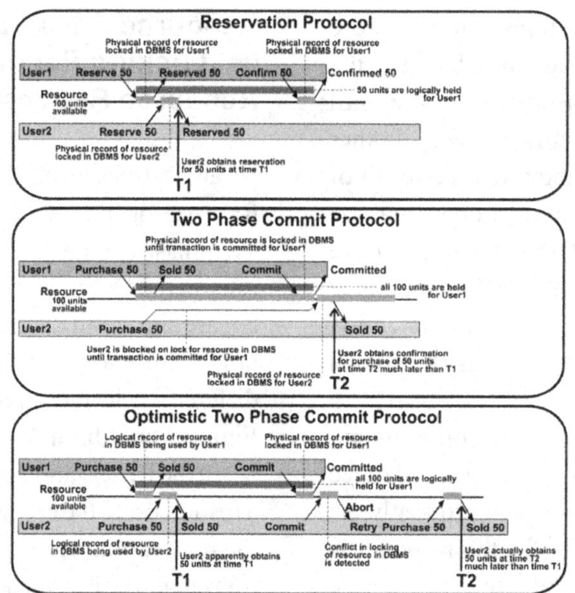

prevent a resource from being locked too long. However, expiration of the timeout can result in inconsistencies within or between the databases. The timeout used in a database system is quite distinct from the reservation period and timeouts used in the Reservation Protocol.

In the Optimistic Two Phase Commit Protocol (Herlihy 1986, Kung and Robinson 1981, Thomasian 1998), the database records are not physically locked during a transaction. Rather, when a transaction is committed, its database accesses are checked against those of other transactions. If a conflict exists, the conflicting transaction is aborted and the client of the failing transaction starts over. The Optimistic Two Phase Commit Protocol provides the same strong atomicity and isolation properties as the conservative Two Phase Commit Protocol, with lower overheads when no conflicts occur, at the price of higher overheads and longer delays when a conflict occurs.

Another difference between resource reservation and locking is the effect on other transactions that need to access the resource. If a resource is reserved and another transaction wants to access it, the transaction can acquire a lock on the resource and the application can be immediately informed of the state of the resource (*i.e.,* although some of the resource has been reserved, a sufficient quantity remains available to satisfy the reservation). Thus, the application can take an appropriate action without delay. However, if the resource is locked by the database system and another transaction wants to access it, the new transaction must wait until the lock is released. The waiting time can be long, in which case the application cannot take immediate action.

Yet another difference between resource reservation and locking of resources is whether the owner of the resource can be paid for the resource reservation. In the Reservation Protocol, the reservation of a resource forms a contract between the client and the resource owner, which explicitly reflects the fee that the resource provider can charge. The fee for the reservation can be proportional to the duration of the reservation to discourage clients from reserving resources for excessively long periods of time. It is not obvious how to associate such a fee with the locking mechanism that is internal to the database system.

To understand better this benefit of resource reservation, consider the seats on an airline flight as a resource. A transaction might need to reserve, say, two seats on a flight while it checks other legs of the trip, the availability of a hotel room, etc. The database record is locked only briefly, for the time required to indicate that two seats are reserved, and then the lock is released. Another customer (transaction) might also need to reserve seats on the same flight, and it can do so as soon as the first transaction releases its briefly held lock. If the last seat on the flight has already been reserved, the transaction can acquire the lock for the flight, look at the seat record, and immediately inform the application that no seats are available. The application, or rather the customer, might then look for available seats on other flights. On the other hand, if the seat record is locked by the database system, the late-coming transaction is simply blocked until the lock is released. When the transaction finally obtains the lock for the seat record, it provides the application with the same information, but at a (much) later time.

Operation under Fault Conditions

Under fault-free conditions, the Reservation Protocol ensures consistent results among the participants in a business transaction that have confirmed their tasks and, thus, it achieves a form of atomicity for the business transaction.

The behavior of the Reservation Protocol under fault conditions is shown in the flow chart in Figure 4. The first phase of the protocol consists of reservation actions. Once a participant (resource holder) has granted a reservation for a resource, it is committed to that reservation until the client (through the coordinator) explicitly cancels the reservation. For this to work in the business world, the participant can associate a fee with the reservation. To encourage a customer to decide quickly to confirm or cancel a reservation, the participant can use an exponentially increasing fee, *i.e.,* a long-duration reservation costs much more than a short-duration reservation.

In the second phase, if the client coordinator wishes to confirm or cancel a reservation but fails to communicate with a participant, all it must do is note the current time and then it can continue. Once a participant has granted a reservation for a resource, it is committed to honoring that reservation. The coordinator need not be concerned about the failure of a participant and can retain its current confirmation/cancellation. At the end of the second phase, the coordinator might re-attempt to communicate with the participants that were not reachable during the second phase.

If a fault occurs during the first phase, the effect is minor, *i.e.*, the fault limits the number of business partners from which the client coordinator can choose. If a critical business partner is not available and an alternative partner cannot be found, the coordinator stops the first phase and starts the second phase by canceling all existing reservations. In this case, the coordinator might still incur a fee for the reservations it made during the first phase, even though the entire business transaction has been rolled back. To avoid such a fee, the coordinator might make a reservation with a critical business partner first (knowing it does not have an alternative), or better yet, establish business relationships with other partners that provide similar services or goods.

Although we have assumed that a task within a business activity is a short-duration traditional transaction, the Reservation Protocol works equally well if a task is itself a business activity. That is, the Reservation Protocol naturally supports the notion of scopes (parent-child relations) defined by the Web Services Transaction Specification (Cabrera, Copeland et al. 2005a, 2005b, 2005c).

Mapping to the Web Services Coordination Specification

The Web Services Coordination (WS-C) Specification (Cabrera, Copeland et al. 2005a) describes an extensible framework that allows a variety of protocols for coordinating the interactions of distributed applications. The WS-C Framework enables a service to create a context needed to propagate an action to other services and to register for coordination protocols.

The Reservation Protocol can be implemented on top of the WS-C Framework in a manner similar to the business agreement protocols defined in the

Figure 4. Fault handling flow chart for the Reservation Protocol

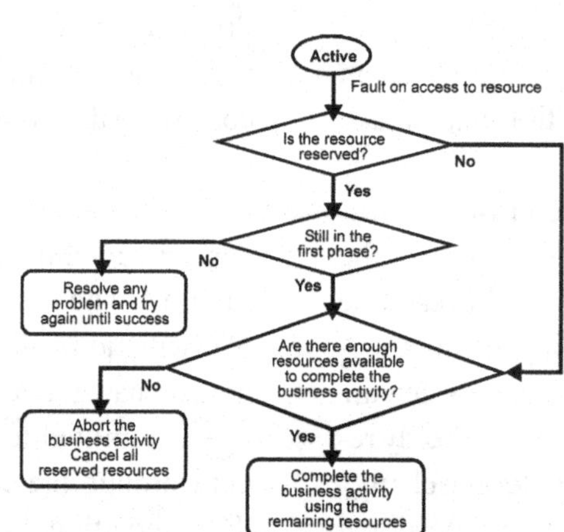

WS-BA Specification (Cabrera, Copeland et al. 2005c). In this section, we define the Reservation Protocol in terms of states and protocol message types. The state diagram given in Figure 5 shows the state of an individual participant in a business activity, on receiving and sending protocol messages. The coordination logic among the participants is under the control of the application logic and, thus, is not defined at this level. Due to space constraints, we omit technical details related to the XML schema, the related WSDL declarations, and the content of the business activity coordination context.

The coordinator sends the Cancel, Close, Forget, ExitReply, Reserve, Confirm and Cancel messages. The participant sends the Register, CancelReply, CloseReply, FaultReply, Exit, ReserveReply, ConfirmReply and CancelReply messages. The Reserve, ReserveReply, Confirm, ConfirmReply, Cancel and CancelReply messages carry application payloads that must be delivered to the appropriate applications. The message types and the states are described below.

- **Cancel/CancelReply** - The coordinator can remove a participant from a business activity while it is in the Active state by sending the participant a Cancel message. On receiving such a message, if the participant is in the correct state, it transitions to the Canceling state. The participant transitions to the Ended state when it sends a CancelReply message to the coordinator.
- **Exit/ExitReply** - A participant can leave a business activity by sending the coordinator an Exit message. Subsequently, it transitions to the Exiting state. On receiving an Exit message, the coordinator removes the corresponding participant from the business activity and responds with an ExitReply message. The participant transitions to the Ended state when it receives the ExitReply message sent by the coordinator.
- **Fault/FaultReply** - A participant can encounter a fault while it is in the Active or Reserving state. It sends a Fault message to the coordinator reporting the fault. On receiving a Fault message, the coordinator invokes an exception handler registered by the application, so that the application becomes aware of the fault. When the exception handling is completed, the coordinator removes the participant from the business activity and sends the participant a FaultReply message. The faulty participant transitions to the Ended state when it receives the FaultReply message.

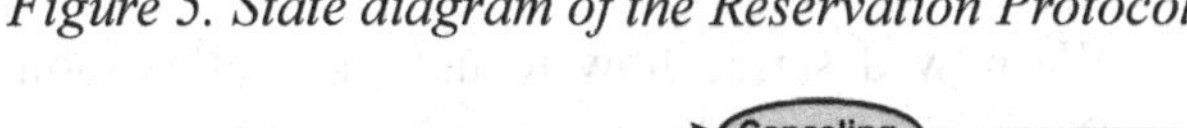
Figure 5. State diagram of the Reservation Protocol

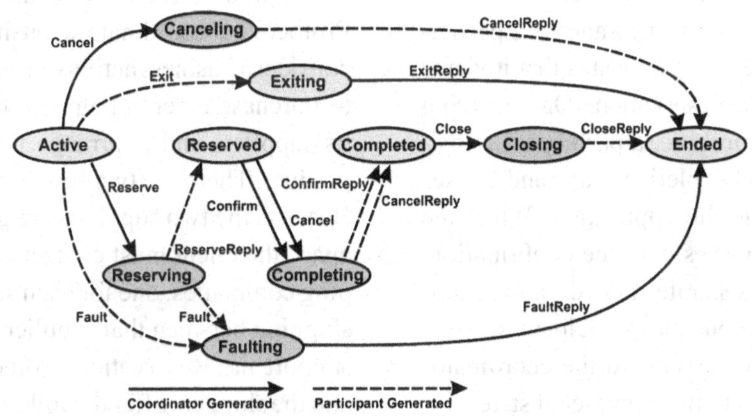

- **Reserve/ReserveReply** - The coordinator sends a Reserve message (with application payload to provide details about the reservation) when the client indicates that it wants to place a reservation with a participant. The Reserve message includes a reservation time (duration) by which the coordinator must send a Confirm/Cancel message after receiving the ReserveReply from the server. The coordinator must ensure that the reservation time is long enough, compared to the normal execution time for the business activity, so that the business activity semantics are not violated (*e.g.*, the coordinator sends a Confirm message for task A, assuming that there is enough time to confirm the reservation for task B but, by the time it sends the Confirm message for task B, the reservation for task B has timed out). On receiving the Reserve message, a participant transitions to the Reserving state and passes the message to the application, so that the order can be filled. When the application indicates that the reservation has been completed, the participant sends a ReserveReply message to the coordinator. If the application declines the reservation request, a Fault message is generated and sent to the coordinator. On sending the ReserveReply message, the participant transitions to the Reserved state.
- **Confirm/ConfirmReply** - The coordinator sends a Confirm message to a participant when the client indicates that it wants to confirm the reservation. On receiving the Confirm message, a participant transitions to the Completing state and passes the message to the application. When the application finishes with the confirmation, typically as a separate short-duration traditional transaction, the participant sends a ConfirmReply message to the coordinator and transitions to the Completed state.
- **Cancel/CancelReply** - The coordinator sends a Cancel message to a participant when the client indicates that it wishes to cancel the reservation placed earlier. On receiving the Cancel message, a participant transitions to the Completing state and passes the message to the application. When the application finishes canceling the previous reservation, the participant sends a CancelReply message to the coordinator and transitions to the Completed state.
- **Close/CloseReply** - When the two phases of the Reservation Protocol have been carried out, the coordinator sends a Close message to each of the participants. On receiving the Close message, a participant transitions to the Closing state and responds with a CloseReply message. The participant subsequently transitions to the Ended state.

Like the WS-BA protocols, the coordinator and the participants in the Reservation Protocol also accept the GetStatus and Status messages for query and response related to the current state. These operations are read-only and do not change the state. Furthermore, the Reservation Protocol requires that the coordinator and the participants are capable of handling duplicate messages.

Use Case

We now describe how to use the Reservation Protocol to coordinate a business activity. We consider a business activity in which a client wants to purchase a certain amount of a product from its suppliers and to arrange for shipment of the product. There are two suppliers for the product. Because the two suppliers are geographically far apart, the client must contact two different shipping companies, one for each supplier to provide shipping between that supplier and the client. To support the Reservation Protocol, the suppliers and the shippers offer the following Web Services operations: Reserve, Confirm and Cancel. In addition, they offer a RequestForQuote Web Service operation. First, we describe a scenario in which all of the resources are available and no fault occurs during the business activity.

As illustrated in Figure 6, at the beginning of the business transaction, the client (*i.e.*, the initiator of the transaction) asks the coordinator to create a new coordination context for the Reservation Protocol using the activation service provided by the coordinator (Step 1). The coordinator then creates a coordination context and returns it to the client (Steps 1 and 2). The coordination context contains an endpoint reference for the registration service so that the participants in the business activity can use the registration service to register for the Reservation Protocol. All messages exchanged between the client and each participant, and between the coordinator and each participant, include the coordination context created for the business activity.

During the business transaction, the client conducts a number of read-only tasks such as RequestForQuote tasks from each of the suppliers and each of the shipping companies (Step 3). Note that these steps are optional and that the client might start by going directly to the reservation phase. Because the RequestForQuote message contains the coordination context for the business transaction, the transaction participants register with the coordinator (Step 4). The Web Service responds to the RequestForQuote by sending the quotes to the client (Step 5). After having retrieved enough information from its business partners, the client asks the coordinator to start the reservation phase (Step 6).

The client coordinator then sends Reserve messages to the participants (Step 7). Subsequently, the participants respond positively with ReserveReply messages to the coordinator (Step 8). Then, the coordinator passes the reservation

Figure 6. An example of a business transaction that uses the Reservation Protocol

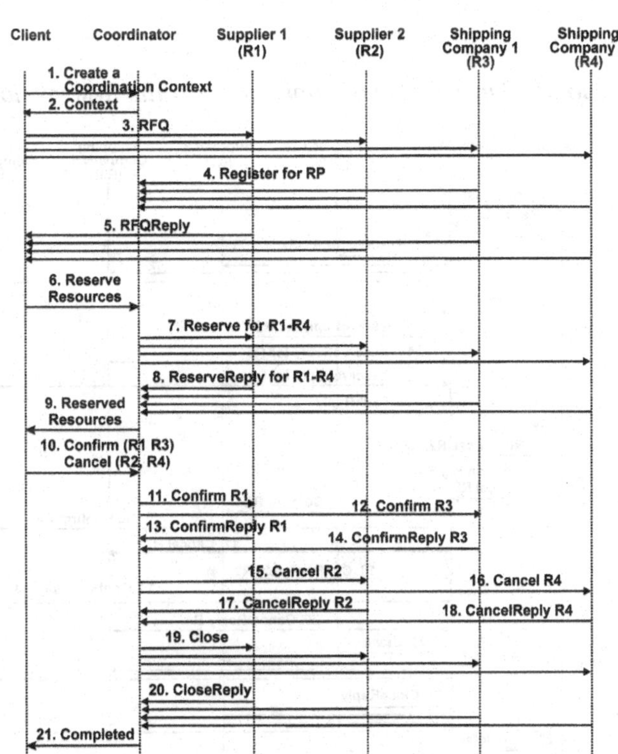

results to the client application for selection (Step 9). Next, the client directs the coordinator to start the second phase by confirming (Confirm) the reservations for supplier 1 and shipping company 1 and by canceling (Cancel) the reservations for supplier 2 and shipping company 2 (Step 10). The coordinator then does so (Steps 11-12 and Steps 15-16). As a result, the infrastructure at supplier 1 and the infrastructure at shipping company 1 send ConfirmReply messages to the client coordinator (Steps 13-14), and the infrastructure at supplier 2 and the infrastructure at shipping company 2 send CancelReply messages to the client coordinator (Steps 17-18). The coordinator then sends Close messages to all of the transaction participants (Step 19), and they respond by sending CloseReply messages to the coordinator (Step 20). The coordinator then informs the client that the business transaction has completed successfully (Step 21).

In another scenario shown in Figure 7, supplier 1 rejects the reservation request (by sending a Fault message) and supplier 2 accepts the reservation request. Thus, the client is forced to use shipping company 2. If shipping company 2 accepts the reservation request, the client confirms the reservation with supplier 2 and shipping company 2. If shipping company 1 accepts the reservation request, the client asks shipping company 1 (through the coordinator) to cancel the reservation. If shipping company 2 cannot satisfy the reservation request (*e.g.*, because there are not enough trucks available to ship the product on the required date), it rejects the reservation request and the client is forced either to find another shipping company or to rollback the business transaction. To rollback the business transaction, the client asks the coordinator to send a cancellation request to supplier 2.

If the coordinator cannot reach one or more participants during either of the two phases, the coordinator retries several times until a timeout occurs. If this happens during the reservation phase, it limits the choices of the client, and might force the rollback of the business transaction.

If a participant becomes unavailable during the confirmation/cancellation phase, the coordinator

Figure 7. Another scenario of a business transaction that uses the Reservation Protocol

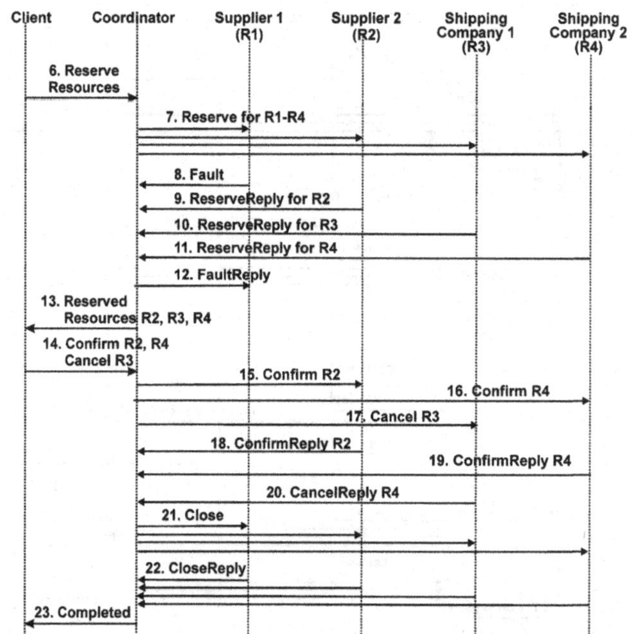

reports an exception to the client. The client can then try to communicate with the partner using different communication channels, *e.g.*, by telephone or fax, and/or can establish a dedicated communication channel with that partner.

In practice, reliable messaging (Bilorusets, Box et al. 2005) between the client coordinator and the Web Services providers must be used. Consider the following scenario which involves the raising and handling of an exception. A Web Service (a participant in a business transaction) might crash immediately after it has handled a reservation request but before it sends the corresponding reply. As part of the recovery process, when the Web Service restarts, it looks for a record of the reply message and checks if the client has received it. If no such record is found, the Web Service has the option of canceling the reservation that it made (without charging the client). Alternatively, it can proceed to regenerate the reply for the reservation request if the time that elapsed since the initial request is fairly short. The client coordinator must be ready to receive such reply messages out-of-sequence. If it has advanced to the second phase of the business transaction, the coordinator responds with a Cancel message. If it is still in the first phase, the coordinator has the option to accept the reservation even if it timed out the request earlier.

If a fault occurs after the participant has committed the reservation and the business transaction has advanced to the second phase, the coordinator cannot abandon the reservation. Moreover, the fault does not cause the coordinator to remove the participant from the participant list, because only the client is authorized to confirm or cancel the reservation explicitly. Instead, the ConfirmReply message or the CancelReply message contains an indication that an exception occurred. The coordinator invokes an exception handler registered by the client and the client makes a decision on how to proceed based on the business logic. For example, the client can cancel the reservation placed earlier with the faulty participant and confirm the reservation with another participant, if one is available. If such actions are not possible, the client corrects the problem on its side and retries the confirmation request with the faulty participant until it is eventually committed successfully.

In practice, it is desirable for a participant to mask or handle properly a transient fault by using existing fault tolerance technology such as replication, checkpointing, message logging and replay (Zhao, Moser et al. 2005). The fee-based reservation policy also encourages an enterprise to ensure that its Web Services are highly available.

IMPLEMENTATION

We have implemented the Reservation Protocol as several Java packages. The implementation includes client and server middleware, with APIs that make it easy for the client application and the server application to use the Reservation Protocol. Figure 8 illustrates the overall architecture of our implementation of the Reservation Protocol, showing the client and server components of the middleware. The client and the server middleware are designed with modularity in mind, so that the client and server applications can be developed on top of these modules.

Client Middleware

The client middleware provides APIs for the client application and facilitates the location of Web Services. As shown in Figure 8, the client middleware consists of the following components:

- Client Coordinator
- Activity Controller
- Service Group Manager
- Communication Controller.

To fulfill the functionality of the middleware, the components of the client middleware interact with each other as shown in Figure 8 and perform the functions described below.

Figure 8. The Reservation Protocol architecture

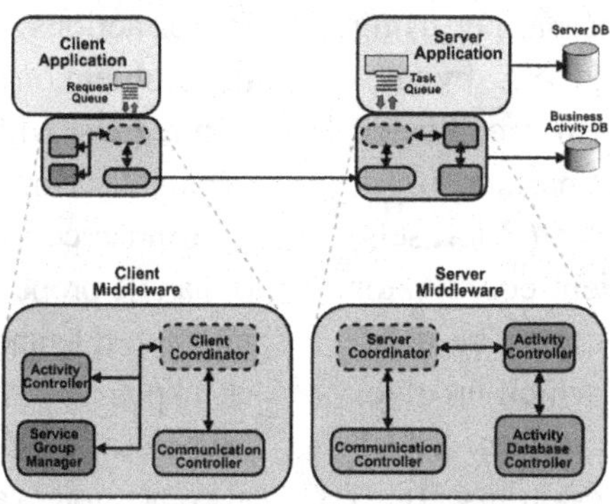

The *Client Coordinator* allows the client application to invoke API calls on it and coordinates the other components and information flow within the client middleware. The *Activity Controller* controls the lifecycle of the business activities of the client and informs the client application of activity information. The *Service Group Manager*, via the Communication Controller, obtains service information from the available servers and provides this information to the client application. The *Communication Controller* handles communication with its counterpart at the servers to which it is connected. For each server, there exists a separate handler for server communication. The communication between the client and the server is via SOAP messages.

Server Middleware

The server middleware provides APIs for the server application and keeps track of business activities and handles client connections. As shown in Figure 8, the server middleware consists of the following components:

- Server Coordinator
- Activity Controller
- Activity Database Controller
- Communication Controller.

To fulfill the functionality of the middleware, the components of the server middleware interact with each other as shown in Figure 8 and perform the functions described below.

The *Server Coordinator* invokes API callbacks on the server application, coordinates the other components and controls the information and message flow within the server middleware. The *Activity Controller* manages client business activities. When there is an update in a client activity, the Activity Controller informs the server application and the client middleware of that update. The Activity Controller keeps a timer for the reservation duration of the activity. The *Activity Database Controller* keeps information about the client activities and their status in the Business Activity Database. It provides the ability to recover and restart the server, if a fault occurs. The *Communication Controller* accepts client connections, handles communication with the client, and passes messages to the Server Coordinator.

Reservation Protocol Interactions

Figure 9 shows the Reservation Protocol interactions between the client and server applications and middleware.

When a client application wants to make a reservation with one or more Web Services, it makes a call to the client middleware, specifically to the Client Coordinator which communicates with the Service Group Manager. The Service Group Manager looks for available servers for each of the Web Services that the client requested and informs the Client Coordinator. There might be more than one server for each service type. The Client Coordinator then communicates with the Communication Controller, which sends the service requests to the respective servers and waits for replies from those servers.

When the server receives a Reserve message from the Communication Controller at the client, it informs the Server Coordinator, which interacts with the Activity Controller. The Activity Database Controller creates an entry in the Business Activity Database and then the Server Coordinator makes a call to the server application. The server application reserves its resources and replies, through a call to the Server Coordinator, which communicates with the Activity Database Controller and the Communication Controller. The Activity Database Controller updates the status of the activity in the Business Activity Database, and the Communication Controller sends a ReserveReply message to the respective client. At this point, the ActivityContoller starts the timer for the reservation, with the timeout value $T_{reserve} + T_{delay}$.

The duration T_{delay} covers the time for network delays, and is configurable. The duration $T_{reserve}$ is the amount of time that the client application has requested in its Reserve message to reply to the server, with the confirmed amount of reserved items, after it has received the ReserveReply message from the server. The Activity Controller at the server controls this time by maintaining a timer for each reservation. The client must send a Confirm/Cancel message to the respective server before the expiration of the timeout at that server's Activity Controller.

In the implementation, there is a coordinator component at both the client and the server, which work in concert with each other. The Client Coordinator decides and coordinates the lifecycle of the business activity. However, if the client fails or is unreachable (due to an application error, network failure, etc or because it is closed willingly), the Server Coordinator takes over control from the Client Coordinator. If the client has asked for a reservation time $T_{reserve}$, the Client Coordinator determines that the reservation time is $T_{reserve}$ and the Server Coordinator determines that the reservation time is $T_{reserve} + T_{delay}$. Note that T_{delay} is a kind of lead time, which ensures that the Server Coordinator does not take over

Figure 9. Reservation Protocol interactions

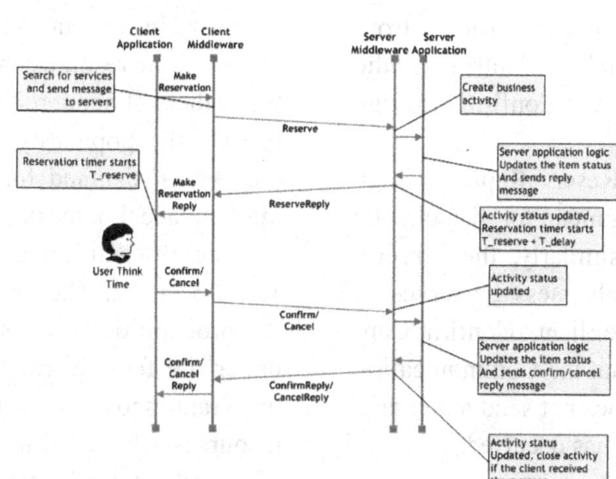

control from the Client Coordinator prematurely if a fault occurs.

Note that the amount that the client confirms must not exceed the amount that the client reserved, which is enforced by the client application. If the client application sends a Confirm message with a confirmed amount of 0, the value 0 indicates that the client does not want to purchase any of the amount it reserved, in effect, it is canceling its reservation.

Note also that, when the client application makes a reservation request, it does not specify any particular server. The Service Group Manager is responsible for choosing an appropriate server to provide the service or product and for informing the Communication Controller at the client to make the necessary request calls. The Confirm message includes the server ID, which the Communication Controller uses to find the addresses of the relevant servers.

On receiving the Confirm message, the Activity Database Controller at the server updates the status of the reservation, unless it has already timed out. When a reservation times out, the Activity Database Controller at the server updates the Business Activity Database accordingly and informs both the client and the server applications about the cancellation through the Server Coordinator and the Communication Controller, respectively. If the client application sends the Confirm message just before it receives the cancellation notice from the server, the Activity Database Controller at the server is consulted before the Confirm message is sent.

Note that the server's ReserveReply message serves as an acknowledgment for the client's Reserve message and, similarly, the server's ConfirmReply/CancelReply message serves as an acknowledgment for the client's Confirm/Cancel message. Note also that the Communication Controller at the client does not send a message to the server, if a timeout has occurred.

PERFORMANCE EVALUATION

We have implemented the Reservation Protocol, the Two Phase Commit Protocol and an Optimistic Two Phase Commit Protocol, and have conducted measurements of the protocols based on our implementations. For the experiments, we have also written a driver program that generates, and controls, the clients' requests. Here we compare the performance of the protocols. The performance metrics that we use are the mean response time seen by the clients, the mean throughput at the server, and the mean completion time at the server. For the experiments, we used a simple business activity without dependencies or chains, because we are interested in comparing the performance of the various protocols. We conducted the experiments on 3.2 GHz Pentium 4 PCs with 2 GBytes of memory and a 100 Mbit/s local-area network.

Request Distributions

We consider two different distributions of resource requests:

- Uniform random distribution
- Preferential distribution.

With the uniform random distribution, all resources have the same probability of being requested by a client. With the preferential distribution, some resources have higher probabilities than others of being requested by a client, which reflects the popularity of those resources and the clients' demand for those resources in the marketplace. For the preferential distribution, we consider three different resource request factors, 1.1, 1.5 and 2. The graph in Figure 10 shows the probabilities for resources being requested under the four distributions. For convenience, the graph shows 20 resources (instead of 100 resources which we used in our experiments). The horizontal axis represents the indices of the resources, and the vertical axis represents the probability of requesting a particular resource. For the preferential distribution with factor 2, for example, the first resource is requested with probability 0.5, the second resource is requested with probability 0.25, etc and, similarly, for the other preferential distributions.

Parameters for the Experiments

In our experiments there are 100 resources for which a client can make a request; the load on the server is increased by increasing the number of clients. In the experiments we set T_{delay} to 100 ms, where T_{delay} covers the time for network delays, as mentioned previously. The duration T_{next} is the duration of the interval between the client's completing a request and making its next request. In the experiments we set T_{next} = 60 seconds.

The "think" time T_{think} of the client is the duration of the interval between the client's receiving a ReserveReply message from the server, indicating that the server has reserved the amount of the resource requested by the client and the client's sending a Confirm/Cancel message to the server. In the experiments we set T_{think} = 100 ms, 1000 ms and 5000 ms.

Note that the client's think time does not affect the performance of the Reservation Protocol, but it is significant for the Two Phase Commit Protocol and the Optimistic Two Phase Commit Protocol, as discussed below.

Reservation Protocol

Figure 11 shows the Reservation Protocol interactions and the times for those interactions. The client sends a Reserve message to the server, requesting a reservation. The server receives the Reserve message, processes the request, and informs the client about the availability of the resource it requested in a ReserveReply message. After receiving the client's Reserve message, to avoid database inconsistencies, the server must first claim a lock on the database record for the requested resource. If the database record is already locked, the server thread is blocked and must wait in a FIFO queue for the lock until the lock is released. When it obtains the lock, the server thread checks and updates the database record to reflect the reservation of the resource for that client, and then releases the lock. The Activity Database Controller at the server inserts an entry into the Business Activity Database to record an outstanding reservation, before it passes information to the server application. The server performs the same steps when a client sends a Confirm/Cancel message to the server.

Figure 10. Resource request distributions

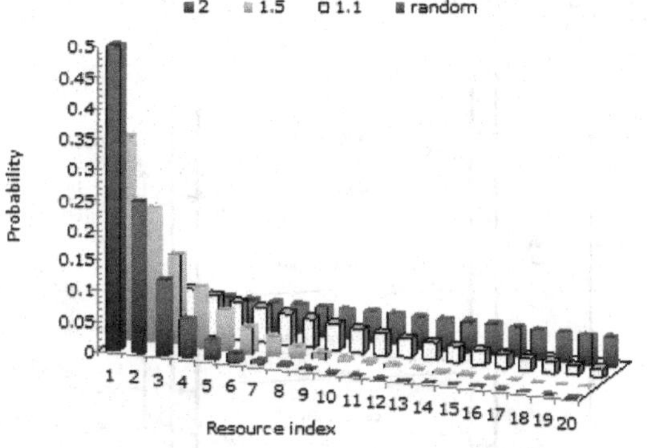

Figure 11. Times for the Reservation Protocol interactions

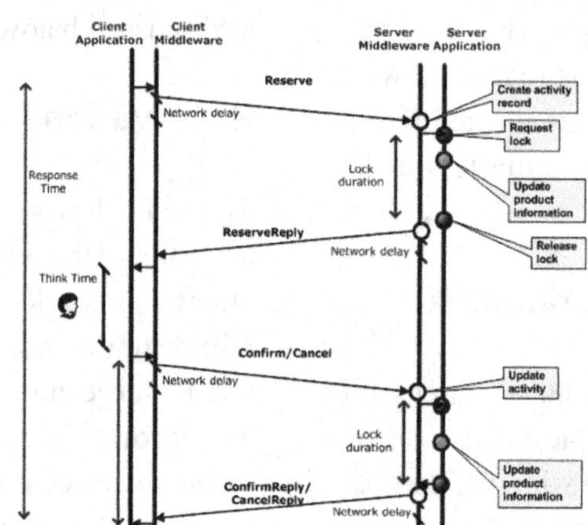

For the Reservation Protocol, the response time of the client includes the network delay for two pairs of message exchanges, the lock request delay, the message processing time, and the database access time (two database record updates, four lock updates, and four activity record updates). The think time of the client does not affect the response time seen by the client.

Two Phase Commit Protocol

Figure 12 shows the Two Phase Commit Protocol interactions and the times for those interactions. When a client requests a resource, first the server gets the lock on the database record for the resource and then makes the necessary updates to the database record. After the client commits the transaction, the server releases the lock on the database record. Note that, for the Two Phase Commit Protocol, the server exchanges several additional messages with the client before it releases the lock on the database record.

For the Two Phase Commit Protocol, the response time seen by the client includes the network delay of three pairs of message exchanges, the lock request delay, the database access time (two database record updates and two lock updates), and the think time at the client.

Optimistic Two Phase Commit Protocol

Figure 13 shows the Optimistic Two Phase Commit Protocol interactions and the times for those

Figure 12. Times for the Two Phase Commit Protocol interactions

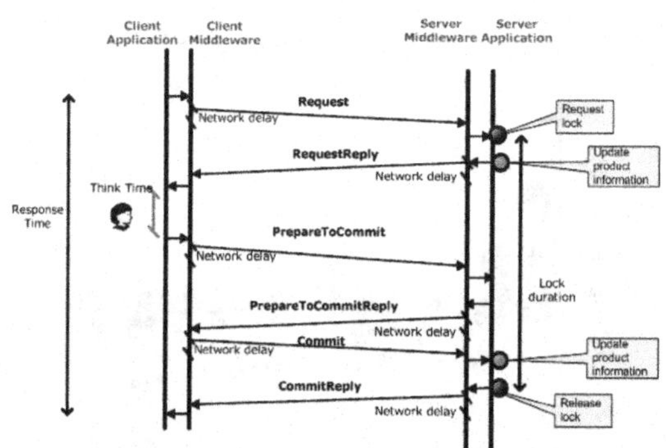

Figure 13. Times for the Optimistic Two Phase Commit Protocol interactions

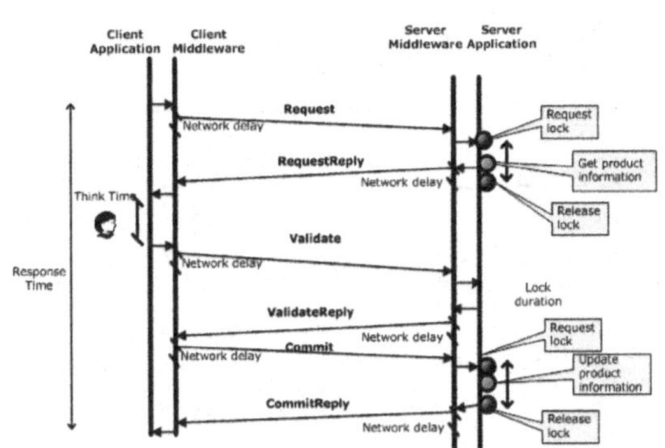

interactions. When a client makes a request, the server gets a lock on the database record, obtains information from the record, releases the lock and returns the information to the client, typically with a timestamp. The data in the database record are not modified, and the record is not locked.

When the client is ready to complete the transaction, the client requests the various servers involved to validate its prior requests. Each of the servers determines from the timestamps that the database record has not been updated by some other business activity, and returns a validate reply confirming the validity of the request. If all of the servers confirm the validity of the request, the client commits the transaction, as shown in Figure 13, and each server locks, updates, and unlocks its database record. If any server returns a negative validate reply, because the database record has been updated by some other transaction, the client aborts the current transaction and restarts it from the beginning, as shown in Figure 3.

The Optimistic Two Phase Commit Protocol is clearly similar to the Two Phase Commit Protocol, the difference being that, with the Optimistic Two Phase Commit Protocol, the database records are not held locked for long periods. If no conflict is detected during the validation phase, the Optimistic Two Phase Commit Protocol might have slightly lower overheads than the more conservative Two Phase Commit Protocol. If a conflict is detected and the transaction must be restarted, the Optimistic Two Phase Commit Protocol incurs higher overheads than the Two Phase Commit Protocol.

Response Time

As Figure 14 shows, under the uniform random distribution with think time 100 ms, the response times are almost constant as the number of concurrent requests (clients) increases. The response times of the Two Phase Commit Protocol and the Optimistic Two Phase Commit Protocol are almost identical and about twice the response time of the Reservation Protocol. The reasons for the higher response times are lock contention for the Two Phase Commit Protocol and retries for the Optimistic Two Phase Commit Protocol, and also because more messages are exchanged which results in additional network delays.

As Figure 15 shows, for the uniform random distribution with think time 1000 ms, the response time of the Reservation Protocol increases slightly as the number of concurrent requests (clients) increases, but it is still less than the response times of the Two Phase Commit Protocol and the Optimistic Two Phase Commit Protocol, which are almost constant.

As Figure 16 shows, for the uniform random distribution with think time 5000 ms, the response time of the Reservation Protocol increases slightly as the number of concurrent requests (clients)

Figure 14. Response times for the uniform random distribution with think time 100 ms

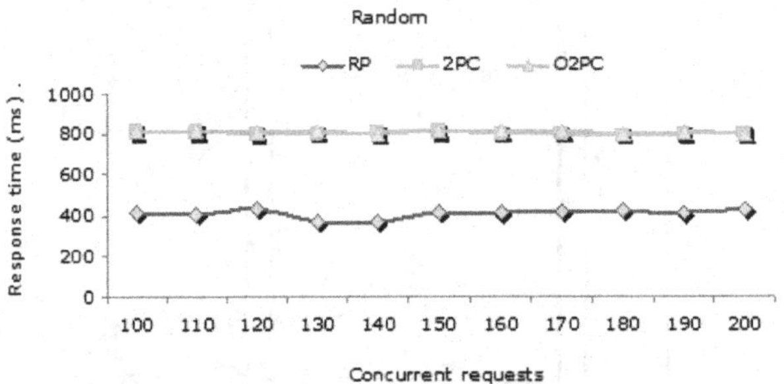

Figure 15. Response times for the uniform random distribution with think time 1000 ms

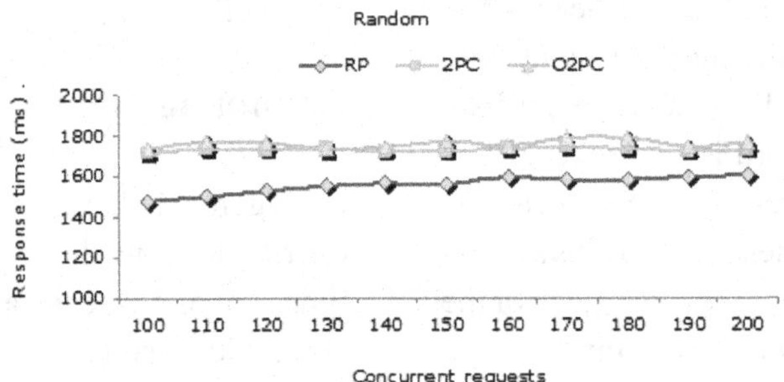

Figure 16. Response times for the uniform random distribution with think time 5000 ms

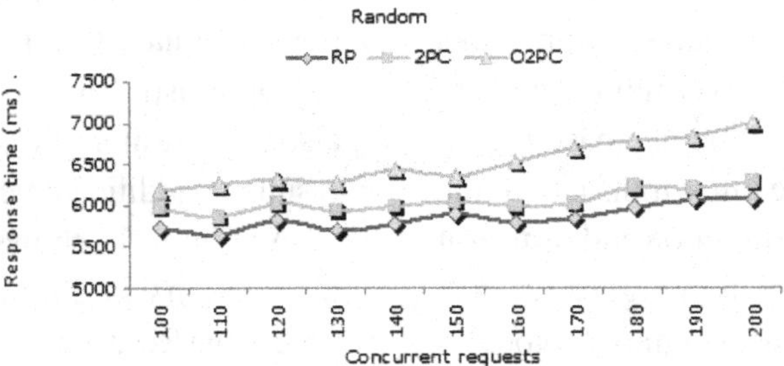

increases, but it is still less than the response times of the Two Phase Commit Protocol and the Optimistic Two Phase Commit Protocol. The Optimistic Two Phase Commit Protocol has a higher response time due to increased retries of the transactions.

Next, we investigated the response time seen by the clients for think time 100 ms under the preferential distribution with resource request factors of 1.1, 1.5 and 2.0.

As Figure 17 shows, for the preferential distribution with resource request factor 1.1 and think

Figure 17. Response times for the preferential distribution with resource request factor 1.1 and think time 100 ms

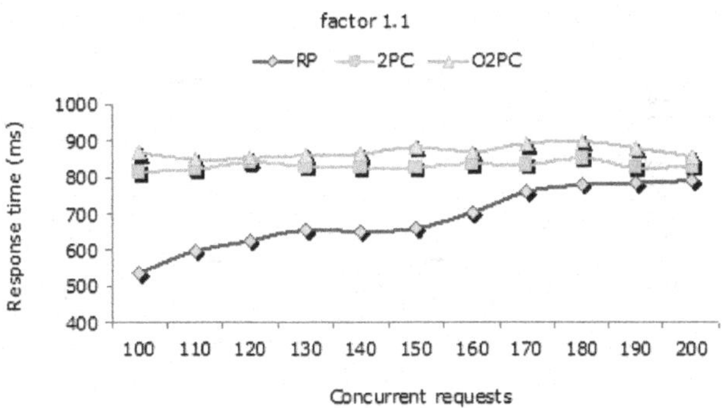

Figure 18. Response times for the preferential distribution with resource request factor 1.5 and think time 100 ms

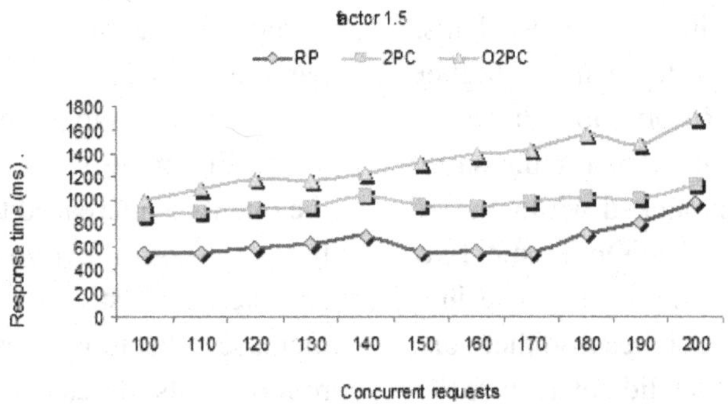

time 100 ms, the response time of the Reservation Protocol increases as the number of concurrent requests increases and almost approaches the response times of the other two protocols when the number of concurrent requests is 200. The response times of the Two Phase Commit Protocol and the Optimistic Two Phase Commit Protocol are almost constant as the number of concurrent requests (clients) increase, but are greater than the corresponding response times of the Reservation Protocol.

As Figure 18 shows, for the preferential distribution with resource request factor 1.5 and think time 100 ms, the response time of the Optimistic Two Phase Commit Protocol increases more than the response times of the other two protocols, as the number of concurrent requests increases. The response times of both the Two Phase Commit Protocol and the Optimistic Two Phase Commit Protocol are greater than the response time of the Reservation Protocol.

As Figure 19 shows, for the preferential distribution with resource request factor 2 and think time 100 ms, under increasing load, the response time of the Optimistic Two Phase Commit Protocol is considerably greater than that of the other two protocols.

For the preferential distribution with resource request factor 2, some of the resources (and the corresponding database records) have a much

Figure 19. Response times for the preferential distribution with resource request factor 2 and think time 100 ms

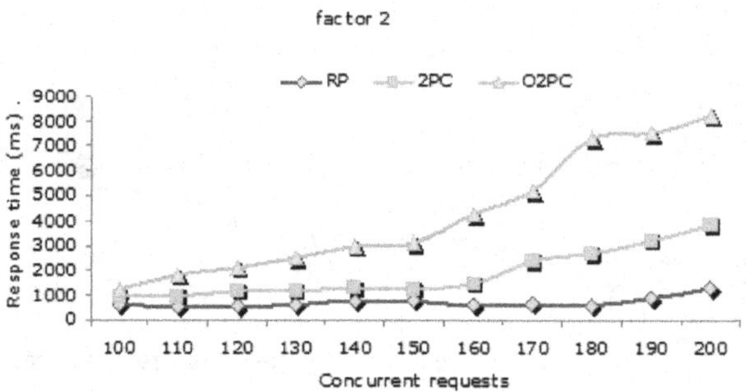

higher probability of being requested and, thus, the requests for those resources have a higher lock waiting time, before the server thread acquires the lock and continues processing the request. Thus, the Two Phase Commit Protocol has a higher response time than the Reservation Protocol, because there is more contention for the same resource, and a resource is locked while one of the clients is being served. The Optimistic Two Phase Commit Protocol has a higher response time than the Reservation Protocol, because there are many retries at the clients that did not acquire the resource in the validation phase. In the Optimistic Two Phase Commit Protocol, the client initiates the transaction and goes through the process until it succeeds. Although the client does not wait to acquire the lock for the resource as it does in the Two Phase Commit Protocol, it still needs to pass the validation phase successfully.

For a longer think time, the performance comparison of the protocols is even more striking, as the following graphs illustrate.

As Figure 20 shows, when the think time of the clients is increased to 1000 ms, the response times for both the Two Phase Commit Protocol and the Optimistic Two Phase Commit Protocol increase substantially as the number of concurrent requests increases. The Two Phase Commit Protocol holds the resources longer, resulting in a longer response time. The Optimistic Two Phase Commit Protocol results in the clients going into the retry phase later if they are not able to pass

Figure 20. Response times for the preferential distribution with resource request factor 2 and think time 1000 ms. The response time of the Reservation Protocol ranges from 1433 ms to 1697 ms

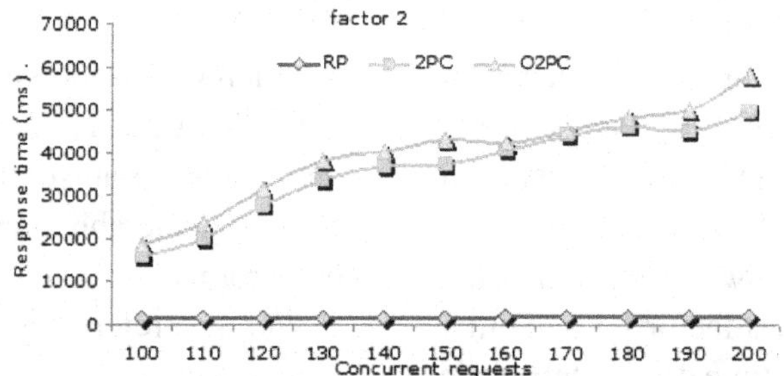

the validation phase. The Reservation Protocol does not suffer from this increased think time because there are no locks on resources as in the Two Phase Commit Protocol, and no retries as in the Optimistic Two Phase Commit Protocol.

As Figure 21 shows, when the think time of the clients is increased to 5000 ms, the response time for the Reservation Protocol remains low but, for the Two Phase Commit Protocol and the Optimistic Two Phase Commit Protocol, the response times are significantly higher. The response time of the Two Phase Commit Protocol reaches as high as 300 seconds and is worse than that of the Optimistic Two Phase Commit Protocol.

If the network delay is longer, the Optimistic Two Phase Commit Protocol is affected more than the Two Phase Commit Protocol. The reason is that, once the Two Phase Commit Protocol sends a message to the server, there are no retries and each retry of the Optimistic Two Phase Commit Protocol is affected by the longer network delay.

Throughput

We also investigated the throughput at the server for different think times of the clients and the random and preferential distributions with different resource selection factors. The throughput curves are most interesting when the clients contend for

Figure 21. Response times for the preferential distribution with resource request factor 2 and think time 5000 ms. The response time of the Reservation Protocol ranges from 5897 ms to 8317 ms

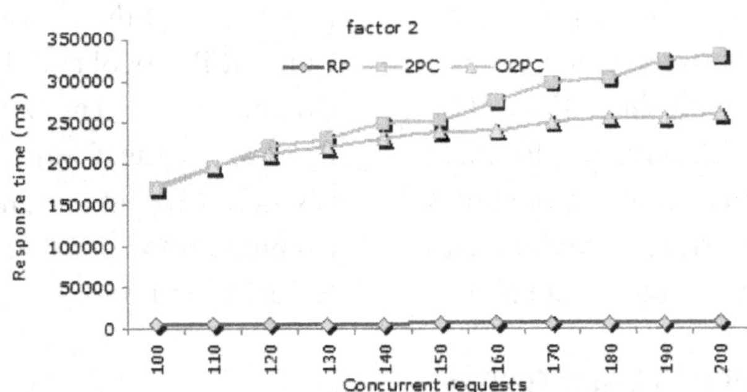

Figure 22. Throughputs for the preferential distribution with resource request factor 2 and think time 100 ms

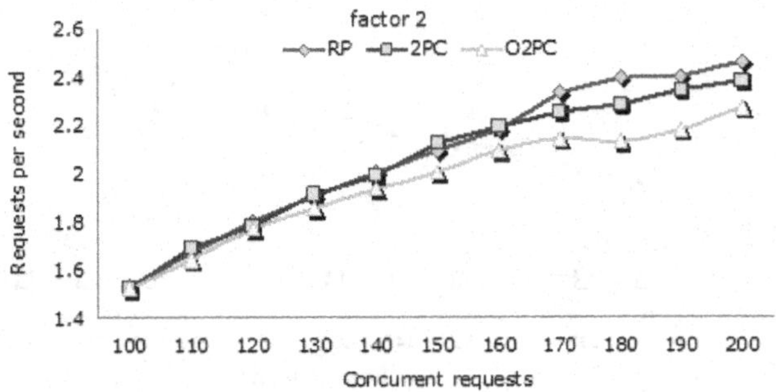

Figure 23. Throughputs for the preferential distribution with resource request factor 2 and think time 1000 ms

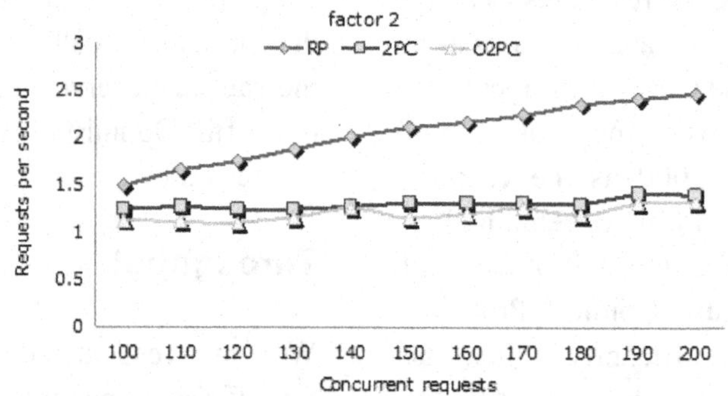

the resources; thus, we present the throughput curves only for the preferential distribution with resource request factor 2.

As Figure 22 shows, with think time 100 ms, as the number of concurrent requests increases, the throughput of all three protocols increases, without much difference between them.

As Figure 23 shows, with think time 1000 ms, the throughput of the Reservation Protocol continues to increase, whereas the throughputs of the Two Phase Commit Protocol and the Optimistic Two Phase Commit Protocol are almost constant.

As Figure 24 shows, with think time 5000 ms, the difference in throughput of the Reservation Protocol and the throughputs of the Two Phase Commit Protocol and the Optimistic Two Phase Commit Protocol is even more striking. Again, the throughput of the Reservation Protocol continues to increase as the number of concurrent requests increases, but the throughputs of the Two Phase Commit Protocol and the Optimistic Two Phase Commit Protocol remain almost constant. Again, the Two Phase Commit Protocol suffers from resource locking and the Optimistic Two Phase Commit Protocol suffers from retries, whereas the Reservation Protocol is not so affected.

Figure 24. Throughputs for the preferential distribution with resource request factor 2 and think time 5000 ms

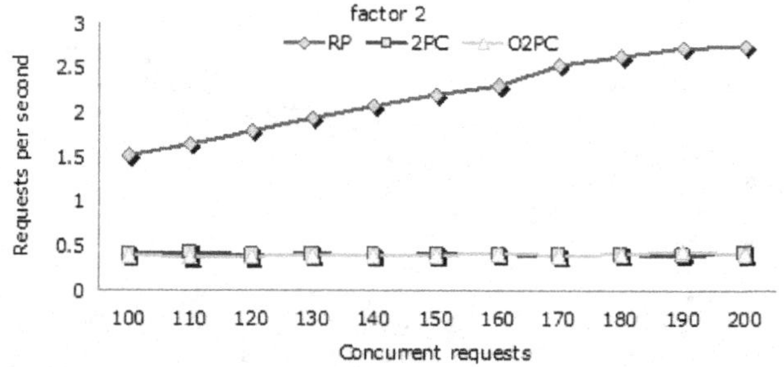

Completion Time

We have also investigated the completion time at the server as the number of concurrent requests increases, for different think times. In this experiment, there is one resource at the server and all of the clients request the same resource. When the server receives the first request, we start a timer at the server. Once the server has completed the requests for all of the clients, we stop the timer and determine the time it took the server to complete those requests.

As Figure 25 shows, for think time 100 ms, the completion time for the Reservation Protocol is better than that for the Two Phase Commit Protocol and the Optimistic Two Phase Commit Protocol. At 200 concurrent requests, the contention for the resource is high, but the Reservation Protocol is able to complete the requests in about 1/3 the time that it takes the Two Phase Commit Protocol and the Optimistic Two Phase Commit Protocol.

As Figure 26 shows, for think time 1000 ms, the completion time of the Reservation Protocol is almost 10 times better than the completion times of the Two Phase Commit Protocol and the Optimistic Two Phase Commit Protocol.

As Figure 27 shows, for think time 5000 ms, the ratio of the completion times of the Reservation Protocol to the Two Phase Commit Protocol and the Reservation Protocol to the Optimistic Two Phase Commit Protocol is about 40.

Considering all three metrics (response time, throughput, completion time), the Reservation Protocol performs better than the Two Phase Commit Protocol and the Optimistic Two Phase Commit Protocol, particularly if they think time of the clients is long. The reason is that, when the think time is long and the clients contend for the same resource, the performance of the Two Phase Commit Protocol and the Optimistic Two Phase Commit Protocol are adversely affected by the locking of resources and repeated retries, respectively. The Reservation Protocol does not suffer from such adverse effects.

Web Services, and business activities that span multiple enterprises, have relatively long think times, ranging from seconds to minutes, particularly if humans are involved. Our experiments indicate that the Reservation Protocol ought to perform better than the Two Phase Commit Protocol or the Optimistic Two Phase Commit Protocol, for Web Services and business activities that span multiple enterprises.

RELATED WORK

Broadly speaking, our Reservation Protocol is related to the extended transaction model and associated concurrency control mechanisms (Bernstein, Hadzilacos et al. 1987, Gray and Reuter 1993). The concept of reservation has been widely used in practical systems that support business services, such as hotel, airline and car rental reservations.

The business agreement protocols defined in the Web Services Business Activity Framework (Cabrera, Copeland et al. 2005c) are flexible enough to support many types of business activities. In particular, the BusinessAgreementWith-CoordinatorCompletion Protocol with the Mixed Outcome Coordination Logic is compatible with the Reservation Protocol. However, the protocols in that framework are not explicitly two-phase, and they depend on the use of compensating transactions to handle exceptions. These properties create some issues that must be circumvented to apply the Reservation Protocol in the Web Services Business Activity Framework.

The most closely related work to the Reservation Protocol is the OASIS Business Transaction Protocol (BTP) (Furniss, Dalal et al. 2004), in particular, the BTP Cohesion Protocol. The BTP Cohesion Protocol is a two-phase protocol, in which the business transaction participants have explicit control over the two phases. In the first phase, all of the transaction participants are required to prepare, *i.e.*, they must ensure that the

Figure 25. Completion times with a single resource and think time 100 ms

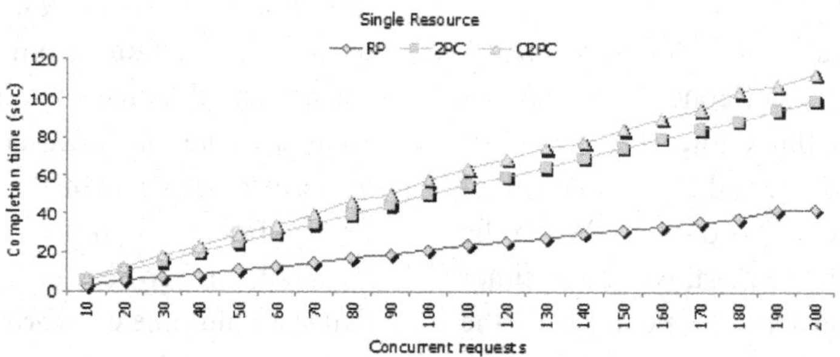

Figure 26. Completion times with a single resource and think time 1000 ms

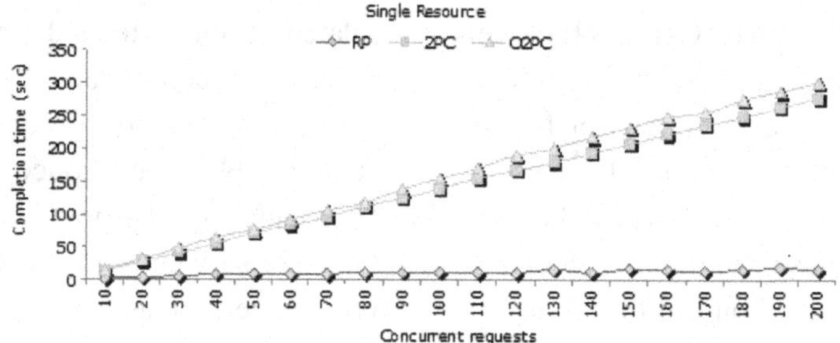

Figure 27. Completion times with a single resource and think time 5000 ms

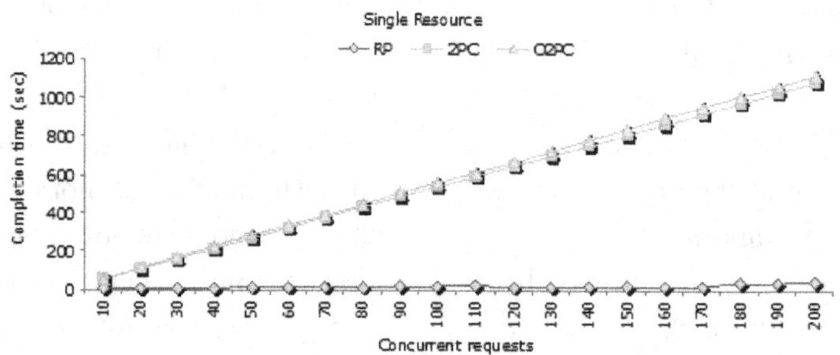

task can be committed or rolled back if a fault occurs. In the second phase, the transaction coordinator issues confirmation or cancellation requests to the participants. It is possible that only some of the participants have consistent results. One might argue that our reservation step is a special form of the prepare action and, thus, that the Reservation Protocol is a special implementation of the BTP Cohesion Protocol. However, the BTP Specification mentions only a reservation-like action as one of several ways to provide provisional or tentative state changes. The BTP Specification does not pursue the concept of reservation to the extent that we do, and does not elaborate the benefits of the reservation approach.

Another closely related work is the atomic reservation protocol for reserving resources in a free market (Ginis and Chandy 2000). In their protocol, a consumer makes timed-reservation requests to the service providers in the form of purchasing options for the use of resources provided by the service providers. In the second phase, the confirmation/cancellation requests are sent to the service providers. Compensating transactions are used to nullify the effect of a partially fulfilled plan and to start with the next plan and to cope with failures and the expiration of options acquired during the first phase. The duration of the start of the first phase and the completion of the second phase are assumed to be short (on the order of a few seconds or minutes). Thus, the term "micro-option" is used to refer to the options acquired during the first phase. Their atomic reservation protocol is not necessarily appropriate for use in loosely-coupled, long-running distributed business activities for which our Reservation Protocol is specifically designed.

The sagas strategy (Garcia-Molina and Salem 1987) allows a long-running transaction to be executed as a number of ACID transactions. Sagas can see intermediate results of other sagas; they rely on compensating transactions to handle exceptions; and they provide relaxed ACID properties for long-running transactions. The ConTract Model (Wachter and Reuter 1992) is intended for defining and controlling complex long-lived activities at a level above ACID transactions. It includes the properties of persistency, consistency, recovery, synchronization, cooperation, and the use of assertions as invariants on entry to and exit from activities.

The Tentative Holding Protocol (THP) (Roberts and Srinivasan 2001, Roberts, Collier et al. 2001), which has been considered for Web Services composition (Limthanmaphon and Zhang 2004), is used to exchange information between enterprises before a transaction begins. THP allows tentative non-blocking holds (reservations to be requested) for a business resource. The primary benefit of THP is that it minimizes the possibility of rolling back committed transactions by providing more accurate information on the availability of the business resource to the client. Unlike the Reservation Protocol, THP allows multiple clients to hold the same resource temporarily. When one of the clients places an order, the remaining clients receive notifications of the unavailability of the resource. However, nothing prevents a client from placing an order for a resource immediately, at which point another client might have taken the resource. In such a case, business rules require the rollback of the business activity, and the client must apply a compensating transaction to cancel the previously committed transaction. In the Reservation Protocol, the reservation phase is part of the business transaction and the reservation is granted exclusively to a client. Blocking reservations avoid the need for compensating transactions.

Several researchers (Alonso, Agrawal et al. 1996, Kamath and Ramamritham 1998, Worah and Sheth 1997) have considered extended transaction models in the context of workflow management systems. In many ways the issues that arise in loosely-coupled distributed systems are more complex variations of the issues that arise in such systems.

Other researchers (Fekete, Greenfield et al. 2003, Greenfield, Fekete et al. 2003a and 2003b2003b) have been engaged in a project that focuses on maintaining consistency in loosely-coupled distributed environments. They have proposed a research agenda based on an infrastructure that includes a language to express consistency conditions, tools to check whether the system maintains consistency, and guidance in using the infrastructure properly.

The Two Phase Commit Protocol (Gray and Reuter 1993) for atomic commitment of distributed transactions and the Reservation Protocol both use two phases in which the first phase involves an exclusive blocking hold of a resource and the second phase involves confirmation or cancellation of the reservation placed in the first phase. However, the protocols differ in that the Reservation Protocol requires the holding of a resource as a traditional atomic transaction, which does not prevent other transactions from being executed. To compensate the blocking hold of the resource, the Reservation Protocol allows the resource provider to require the client to pay a fee, based on the duration of the reservation. Furthermore, the Reservation Protocol allows a proper subset of the participants to see a consistent outcome, while the Two Phase Commit Protocol requires all participants to see the same outcome. As shown by our performance measurements, the Reservation Protocol performs better than the Two Phase Commit Protocol, in terms of response time seen by the client, throughput of the server, and completion time of the server because the Reservation Protocol does not require the locking of resources.

The Optimistic Two Phase Commit Protocol (Kung and Robinson 1981, Herlihy 1986, Thomasian 1998) optimistically assumes that conflicts for resources will not occur. It requires a client to retry if another client already holds a lock on the resource, rather than waiting for that client to release the lock. As shown by our performance measurements, the Reservation Protocol performs better than the Optimistic Two Phase Commit Protocol, in terms of response time seen by the client, throughput of the server, and completion time of the server because the Reservation Protocol does not involve repeated retries.

Finally, we have studied other aspects of the Reservation Protocol. In (Melliar-Smith and Moser 2007), we investigated how to use the Reservation Protocol to achieve atomicity for Web Services by exploiting the commutativity of actions. In (Zhao, Moser et al. 2008), we presented extensive analyses of the Reservation Protocol and showed its advantages over other extended transaction models. In (Kart, Moser et al. 2008), we used the Reservation Protocol in a Service Oriented Architecture for a supply chain management system.

CONCLUSION AND FUTURE WORK

In this chapter, we have described a novel reservation-based extended transaction protocol that can be used to coordinate business activities that span multiple enterprises over the Internet. Instead of resorting to compensating transactions, our Reservation Protocol employs an explicit reservation phase as a means of providing for later changes. The Reservation Protocol comprises two steps. The first step involves an exclusive blocking reservation of the resource. The second step involves the confirmation or cancellation of the reservation. We have shown that the Reservation Protocol has a number of advantages over other approaches. In particular:

The advantages of the Reservation Protocol over distributed transactions that use compensating transactions are:

- The risk of inconsistency of the databases of different enterprises is reduced.
- The programming of reservations is easier than the programming of compensating transactions.

The advantages of the Reservation Protocol over distributed transactions based on the Two Phase Commit Protocol or the Optimistic Two Phase Commit Protocol are:

- The database records are locked, both physically and logically, for only the durations of the local transactions.
- Reservations are made for only the required amount of a resource, instead of locking the database record for the entire resource for an extended period of time.
- Better response times for the clients and better throughputs and completion times at the server are achieved, particularly when there is contention among the clients for the same resources.

Beyond the current work, there are several issues worth pursuing. First, the fee-based mechanism could be studied so that the Reservation Protocol is more in line with the practice of reservations in the business world, e.g., one can reserve a hotel room for some amount of time without a fee. Another issue is how to handle a reservation for a business that imposes a deadline, if the client does not confirm or cancel the reservation before the deadline. Given its resource-centric approach, the Reservation Protocol could be augmented with mechanisms for application-level resource discovery and reservation. The Reservation Protocol could also be enhanced with mechanisms that capture and handle the dependencies and nesting of the tasks of a business activity. Integrating the Reservation Protocol into a generic Service Oriented Architecture would also be a worthwhile and challenging endeavor.

ACKNOWLEDGMENT

This research was partially supported by UC Discovery Grant/QAD COM05-10194 and by MURI/AFOSR Contract F49620-00-1-0330 for the authors at the University of California, Santa Barbara, and by a faculty startup award for the author at Cleveland State University.

REFERENCES

Alonso, G., Agrawal, D., El Abbadi, A., Kamath, M., Gunthor, R., & Mohan, C. (1996). Advanced transaction models in workflow contexts. In *Proceedings of the IEEE International Conference on Data Engineering*. New Orleans, LA (pp. 574-581).

Bernstein, P. A., Hadzilacos, V., & Goodman, N. (1987). *Concurrency Control and Recovery in Database Systems*. Reading, MA: Addison Wesley.

Bilorusets, R., Box, D., Cabrera, L. F., Davis, D., Ferguson, D., Ferris, C., et al. (2005). Web Services Reliable Messaging Protocol. Retrieved March 1, 2009 from http://download.boulder.ibm.com/ibmdl/pub/software/dw/specs/ws-rm/ws-reliablemessaging200502.pdf

Booth, D., Haas, H., McCabe, F., Newcomer, E., Champion, M., Ferris, C., & Orchard, D. (2004). Web Services Architecture. Retrieved March 1, 2009 from http://www.w3.org/TR/ws-arch

Cabrera, L. F., Copeland, G., Feingold, M., Freund, R. W., & Freund, T. Johnson, Joyce, S., J., Kaler, C., Klein, J., Langworthy, D., Little, M., Nadalin, A., Newcomer, E., Orchard, D., Robinson, I., Shewchuk, J., & Storey, T. (2005a). Web Services Coordination, Version 1.0. Retrieved March 1, 2009 from http://download.boulder.ibm.com/ibmdl/pub/software/dw/specs/ws-tx/WS-Coordination.pdf

Cabrera, L. F., Copeland, G., Feingold, M., Freund, R. W., Freund, T., Johnson, J., et al. (2005b). Web Services Atomic Transaction, Version 1.0. Retrieved March 1, 2009 from http://download.boulder.ibm.com/ibmdl/pub/software/dw/specs/ws-tx/WS-AtomicTransaction.pdf

Cabrera, L. F., Copeland, G., Feingold, M., Freund, R. W., Freund, T., Joyce, S., et al. (2005c). Web Services Business Activity Framework, Version 1.0. Retrieved March 1, 2009 from http://download.boulder.ibm.com/ibmdl/pub/software/dw/specs/ws-tx/WS-BusinessActivity.pdf

Fekete, A., Greenfield, P., Kuo, D., & Jang, J. (2003). Transactions in loosely coupled distributed systems. In *Proceedings of the 14th Australasian Database Conference*, Adelaide, Australia (pp. 7-12).

Furniss, P., Dalal, S., Fletcher, T., Green, A., Haugen, B., Ceponkus, A., & Pope, B. (2004). OASIS Business Transaction Protocol, Version 1.1. Retrieved March 1, 2009 from http://xml.coverpages.org/BTPv11-200411.pdf

Garcia-Molina, H., & Salem, K. (1987). Sagas, In *Proceedings of the ACM SIGMOD Conference*, San Francisco, CA (pp. 249-259).

Ginis, R., & Chandy, K. M. (2000). Micro-option: A method for optimal selection and atomic reservation of distributed resources in a free market environment. In *Proceedings of the ACM Conference on Electronic Commerce*, New York, NY (pp. 207-214).

Gray, J., & Reuter, A. (1993). *Transaction Processing: Concepts and Techniques*. San Francisco, CA: Morgan Kaufmann Publishers, Inc.

Greenfield, P., Fekete, A., Jang, J., & Kuo, D. (2003a). What are the consistency requirements for B2B systems? In *Proceedings of the High Performance Transaction Systems Workshop*, Asilomar, CA.

Greenfield, P., Fekete, A., Jang, J., & Kuo, D. (2003b). Compensation is not enough. In *Proceedings of the 7th IEEE International Enterprise Distributed Object Computing Conference*, Brisbane, Australia (pp. 232-239).

Herlihy, M. (1986). Optimistic concurrency control for abstract data types. In *Proceedings of the Fifth Annual ACM Symposium on Principles of Distributed Computing*, Calgary, Alberta, Canada (pp. 206-217).

Kamath, M., & Ramamritham, K. (1998). Failure handling and coordinated execution of concurrent workflows. In *Proceedings of the IEEE International Conference on Data Engineering*, Orlando, FL (pp. 334-341).

Kart, F., Moser, L. E., & Melliar-Smith, P. M. (2008). Managing and integrating supply and demand using Web Services and the Service Oriented Architecture. In Y. Huo and F. Jia (Eds.), *Supply Chain, The Way to Flat Organization* (pp. 259-282). Vienna, Austria: IN-TECH Education and Publishing.

Kung, H. T., & Robinson, J. T. (1981). On optimistic methods for concurrency control. *ACM Transactions on Database Systems*, *6*(2), 213–226. doi:10.1145/319566.319567

Limthanmaphon, B., & Zhang, Y. (2004). Web Service composition transaction management. In *Proceedings of the 15th Australasian Database Conference, Conferences in Research and Practice in Information Technology*, 27, Dunedin, New Zealand (pp. 171-179).

Melliar-Smith, P. M., & Moser, L. E. (2007). Achieving atomicity for Web Services using commutativity of actions. *Journal of Universal Computer Science*, *13*(8), 1094–1109.

Moser, L. E., & Melliar-Smith, P. M. (2009). Service Oriented Architecture and Web Services. In Ben Wah (Ed.), *Encyclopedia of Computer Science and Engineering* (pp. 2504-2511). Hoboken, NJ: John Wiley & Sons.

Roberts, J., Collier, T., Malu, P., & Srinivasan, K. (2001). Tentative hold protocol part 2: Technical specification. Retrieved March 1, 2009 from http://www.w3.org/TR/tenthold-2

Roberts, J., & Srinivasan, K. (2001). Tentative hold protocol part 1: White paper. Retrieved March 1, 2009 2006 from http://www.w3.org/TR/tenthold-1

Thomasian, A. (1998). Concurrency control: Methods, performance, and analysis. *ACM Computing Surveys*, *30*(1), 70–119. doi:10.1145/274440.274443

Wachter, H., & Reuter, A. (1992). The ConTract model. In A. K. Elmagarmid (Ed.), *Database Transaction Models for Advanced Applications* (pp. 219-263). San Francisco, CA: Morgan Kaufmann Publishers, Inc.

Worah, D., & Sheth, A. (1997). Transactions in transactional workflows. In S. Jajodia and L. Kershberg (Eds.), *Advanced Transaction Models and Architectures* (pp. 3-34).

Zhao, W., Moser, L. E., & Melliar-Smith, P. M. (2005). Fault tolerance for distributed and networked applications. In *Encyclopedia of Information Science and Technology* (pp. 1190-1196). Hershey, PA: IGI Global.

Zhao, W., Moser, L. E., & Melliar-Smith, P. M. (2008). A reservation-based extended transaction protocol. *IEEE Transactions on Parallel and Distributed Systems, 19*(2), 49–56. doi:10.1109/TPDS.2007.70727

Compilation of References

Abbott, M. (2005). *Business transaction protocol.*

ActiveBPEL. (2007). ActiveBPEL project website. Retrieved November 30, 2007, from http://www.active-endpoints.com/active-bpel-engine-overview.htm

ActiveBPEL. (n.d.). Retrieved from http://www.activebpel.org

Adorni, M., Arcelli, F., Ardagna, D., Baresi, L., Batini, C., Cappiello, C., et al. (2005). The MAIS approach to web service design. In *EMMSAD '05: Proceeding of Tenth International Workshop on Exploring Modeling Methods in Systems Analysis and Design*, Porto, Portugal (pp. 387-398).

Afandi, R., Zhang, J., & Gunter, C. A. (2006). Ampol-q: Adaptive middleware policy to support qos. In *ICSOC '06: Proceeding of the 4th International Conference on Service-Oriented Computing*, Chicago, IL, USA (pp.165–178).

Agarwal, V., Dasgupta, K., Karnik, N., Kumar, A., Kundu, A., Mittal, S., & Srivastava, B. (2005), A service creation environment based on end to end composition of web services. In *Proceedings of the WWW conference* (pp. 128-137). Chiba, Japan

Agrawal, A., et al. (2007). Web Services Human Task (WS-HumanTask), Version 1.0. Retrieved from http://www.adobe.com/devnet/livecycle/pdfs/ws_humantask_spec.pdf

Agrawal, A., et al. (2007). WS-BPEL Extension for People (BPEL4People), Version 1.0. Retrieved from http://www.adobe.com/devnet/livecycle/pdfs/bpel4people_spec.pdf

Agrawal, R., Gunopulos, D., & Leymann, F. (1998). Mining Process Models from Workflow Logs. In *Proceedings of the 6th International Conference on Extending Database Technology* (pp. 469-498). Valencia, Spain.

Ahn, G.-J., Sandhu, R., Kang, M. H., & Park, J. S. (2000). Injecting RBAC to secure a web-based workflow system. In *Proceedings of the 5th ACM Workshop on Role-Based Access Contro* (pp. 1-10). Berlin, Germany. Retrieved from http://portal.acm.org/citation.cfm?doid=344287.344295

Aho, A. V., Sethi, R., & Ullman, J. D. (1988). *Compilers: Principles, Techniques and Tools.* New York: Addison-Wesley.

Ajanta. (2002). *Ajanta project website.* Retrieved December 4, 2005, from http://www.cs.umn.edu/Ajanta/

Akkiraju, R., & Goodwin, R. (2003). *A method for semantically enhancing the service discovery capabilities of UDDI.* Proceedings of the Workshop on Information Integration on the Web, IJCAI 2003, Acapulco, Mexico, 87–92.

Akkiraju, R., Farrell, J., Miller, J., Nagarajan, M., Schmidt, M.-T., Sheth, A., Verma, K., (2005) Web Service Semantics, WSDL-S, W3C Submission, http://www.w3.org/Submission/WSDL-S/

Al Sairaf, S., Emmanouil, F. S., Ghanem, M., Giannadakis, N., Guo, Y., Kalaitzopoulos D., Osmond M., Rowe, A., Syed, J., Wendel, P. (2003). The design of discovery net: Towards open grid services for knowledge discovery. *International Journal of High Performance Computing Applications.*

Albin, S. (2003). *The Art of Software Architecture: Design Methods and Techniques.* New York: John Wiley & Sons.

Allcock, W., Bresnahan, J., Kettimuthu, R., Link, M., Dumitrescu, C., Raicu, I., & Foster, I. (2005). The Globus striped GridFTP framework and server. *ACM Super Computing.*

Allen, G., Davis, K., Dolkas, K., Doulamis, N., Goodale, T., Kielmann, T., Merzky, A., Nabrzyski, J., Pukacki, J., Radke, T., Russell, M., Seidel, E., Shalf, J., and Taylor, I., (2003), Enabling Applications on the Grid: A GridLab Overview, International Journal of High Performance Computing Applications: Special issue on Grid Computing: Infrastructure and Applications, August 2003

Alonso, G., Agrawal, D., El Abbadi, A., Kamath, M., Gunthor, R., & Mohan, C. (1996). Advanced transaction models in workflow contexts. In *Proceedings of the IEEE International Conference on Data Engineering*. New Orleans, LA (pp. 574-581).

Alonso, G., Mohan, C., Guenthoer, R., Agrawal, D., El Abbadi, A., & Kamath, M. (1994). *Exotica/FMQM: A persistent message-based architecture for distributed workflow management.* Proceedings of the IFIP WG8.1 Working Conference on Information Systems for Decentralized Organizations, Trondheim, Norway.

Alves, A., Arkin, A., Askary, A., Bloch, B., Curbera, F., Ford, M., Goland, Y., Guízar, A., Kartha, N., Liu, C. K., Khalaf, R., König, D., Marin, M., Mehta, V., Thatte, S., Rijn, D., Yendluri, P., Yiu, A., (2006), Web Services Business Process Execution Language Version 2.0 Public Review Draft, 23rd August 2006, available at http://docs.oasis-open.org/wsbpel/2.0/

Amin, M. (2001). Towards Self-Healing Energy Infrastructure Systems. *IEEE Computer Applications in Power, 14*(1), 20–28. doi:10.1109/67.893351

Amir, R., & Zeid, A. (2004). A UML profile for service oriented architectures. *ACM Object-Oriented Programming, Systems, Languages, and Applications Poster session.*

Amir, Y., Danilov, C., Miskin-Amir, M., Schultz, J., & Stanton, J. (2004). *The Spread Toolkit: Architecture and Performance* (Technical Report CNDS-2004-1). Johns Hopkins University, April. Retrieved April 4, 2008, from http://www.cnds.jhu.edu/pub/papers/cnds-2004-1.pdf

Amsden, J., Gardner, T., Griffin C., & Iyengar, S. (2005). UML 2.0 profile for software services. IBM developerWorks.

Anbazhagan, M., & Arun, N. (2002). Use SOAP-based intermediaries to build chains of Web service functionality. Retrieved September 1, 2002 from http://www.ibm.com/developerworks/java/library/ws-soapbase/?loc=dwmain.

Anderson, A. (2005). Core and Hierarchical Role Based Access Control (RBAC) Profile of XACML, Version 2.0. OASIS Standard. Retrieved from http://docs.oasis-open.org/xacml/2.0/access_control-xacml-2.0-rbac-profile1-spec-os.pdf

Andrews, T., Curbera, F., Dholakia, H., Goland, Y., Klein, J., Leymann, F., et al. (2003). *Business Process Execution Language for Web Services Version 1.1.* Retrieved December 4, 2005, from ftp://www6.software.ibm.com/software/developer /library/ws-bpel.pdf.

Anton, H., & Rorres, C. (1994). *Elementary Linear Algebra: Applications.* John Wiley & Sons.

Anyanwu, K., Sheth, A., Cardoso, J., Miller, J.A., & Kochut, K.J. (2003). Healthcare enterprise process development and integration. *Journal of Research and Practice in Information Technology, Special Issue in Health Knowledge Management, 35*(2), 83–98.

Apache Axis. (2006). Apache AXIS project website. Retrieved February 23, 2009, from http://ws.apache.org/axis/

Apache Axis2 (2008). Apache AXIS2 project website. Retrieved February 23, 2009, from http://ws.apache.org/axis2/

Apollo (2005). Apache Apollo project website. Retrieved February 24, 2009, from http://incubator.apache.org/projects/apollo.html

Appel, A. W. (1992). *Compiling with continuations.* Cambridge University Press.

Arcelli, F., Raibulet, C., Tisato, F., & Adorni, M. (2004). Architectural Reflection in Adaptive Systems. In *SEKE '04: Proceeding of the International Conference on Software Engineering & Knowledge Engineering,* Banff, Canada (pp. 74-79).

Ardagna, D., Comerio, M., De Paoli, F., & Grega, S. (2005). An Hybrid Approach to QoS Evaluation. In *EMMSAD '05: Proceeding of the International Workshop on Exploring Modeling Methods in Systems Analysis and Design,* Porto, Portugal, (pp. 581-592).

Argyroudis, P. G., Verma, R., Tewari, H., & O'Mahony, D. (2004). Performance analysis of cryptographic protocols on handheld devices. In *Third IEEE International Symposium on Network Computing and Applications* (pp. 169-174).

Armstrong, R., et al. (1999). Toward a common component architecture for high-performance scientific computing. *HPDC.*

Arsanjani A., Zhang L., Ellis M., Allam A., & Channabasavaiah K. (2007) S3: A service-oriented reference architecture. *IT Professional, 9*(3).

Arsanjani, A. (2005). Toward a Pattern Language for Service-Oriented Architecture and Integration. IBM developerWorks. Retrieved from http://www.ibm.com/developerworks/webservices/library/ws-soa-soi/

Arsanjani, A., Zhang, L.-J., Ellis, M., Allam, A., & Channabasavaiah, K. (2007). S3: A Service-Oriented Reference Architecture. *IT Professional, 9*(3), 10–17. doi:10.1109/MITP.2007.53

Atluri, V., & Huang, W. (1996). An authorization model for workflows. In *Proceedings of the 4th European Symposium on Research in Computer Security* (LNCS 1146, pp. 4-64).

Attie, P., Singh, M. P., Sheth, A. P., & Rusinkiewicz, M. (1993). Specifying and enforcing intertask dependencies. In *Proceedings of the International Conference on Very Large Databases (VLDB)*, August (pp.134-145).

Awan, A., Jagannathan, S., & Grama, A. (2007) Macroprogramming Heterogeneous Sensor Networks using COSMOS. In *Proceedings of the 2007 EuroSys Conference*, March (pp. 159-172).

Axis. (n.d.) Retrieved from http://ws.apache.org/axis

Azuma, M., & Mole, D. (1994). Software management practice and metrics in the European community and Japan: Some results of a survey. *Journal of Systems and Software, 26*(1), 5–18.

Bacchus, F., & Kabanza, F. (1996). Using temporal logic to control search in a forward chaining planner. In M. Ghallab & A. Milani (Eds.), *New Directions in Planning* (pp. 141-153). IOS Press.

Bachmendo, B., & Unland, R. (2001). *Aspect-based workflow evolution.* Paper presented at the Workshop on Aspect-Oriented Programming and Separation of Concerns, Lancaster, United Kingdom.

Bae, J., Bae, H., Kang, S., & Kim, Y. (2004). Automatic control of workflow process using ECA rules. *IEEE Transactions on Knowledge and Data Engineering, 16*(8), 1010–1023. doi:10.1109/TKDE.2004.20

Bajaj, S., Box, D., Chappell, D., Curbera, F., Daniels, G., Hallam-Baker, P. et al. (2006). *Web Services Policy Framework (WS-Policy).* Version, 1.2, March. Retrieved March 28, 2006 from: http://download.boulder.ibm.com/ibmdl/pub/software/dw/specs/ws-polfram/ws-policy-2006-03-01.pdf

Bajaj, S., Box, D., Chappell, D., Curbera, F., Daniels, G., Hallam-Baker, P. et al. (2006). *Web Services Policy Attachment (WS-PolicyAttachment).* Version, 1.2, March. Retrieved March 28, 2006 from: http://download.boulder.ibm.com/ibmdl/pub/software/dw/specs/ws-polatt/ws-polat-2006-03-01.pdf

Bajaj, S., Box, D., Chappell, D., Curbera, F., Daniels, G., Hallam-Baker, P., Hondo, M., Kaler, C., Langworthy, D., Nadalin, A., Nagaratnam, N., Prafullchandra, H., Riegen, C., Roth, D., Schlimmer, J., Sharp, C., Shewchuk, J., Vedamuthu, A., Yalçinalp, Ü., Orchard, D., (2006), Web Services Policy 1.2 - Framework (WS-Policy), W3C Member Submission April 2006, available at http://www.w3.org/Submission/2006/SUBM-WS-Policy-20060425/

Bakker, J. L., & Jain, R. (2002, April). Next generation service creation using XML scripting language. In *Proceedings of the IEEE International Conference on Communications (ICC2002), New York, USA* (pp. 2001-2007). Washington: IEEE Computer Society.

Baligand, F., & Monfort, V. (2004). A concrete solution for web services adaptability using policies and aspects. *Proceedings of UNITN/Springer International Conference on Service Oriented Computing.*

Ballinger, K., Ehnebuske, D., Ferris, C., Gudgin, M., Nottingham, M., Yendluri, P., (2004) Basic Profile Version 1.1, WS-I specification, 8 August 2004, http://www.ws-i.org/Profiles/BasicProfile-1.1-2004-07-21.html

Banavar, G., Chandra, T., Mukherjee, B., Nagarajarao, J., Strom, R., & Sturman, D. (1999). An Efficient Multicast Protocol for Content-Based Publish-Subscribe Systems. In *Proceedings of the 19th IEEE international Conference on Distributed Computing Systems* (May 31 - June 04, 1999) (p. 262). ICDCS. IEEE Computer Society.

Banks, D., Carley, K. (1994). Metric inference for social networks, *Journal of classification, 11*(1), 121-149.

Baravaglio, A., Licciardi, C. A., & Venezia, C. (2005, August). Web Service Applicability in telecommunications Service Platforms. In *Proceedings of the International Conference on Next Generation Web Services Practices (NWeSP), Seoul, Korea* (pp. 39-44). Washington: IEEE Computer Society.

Barendregt, H. P. (1984). *The Lambda Calculus, Its Syntax and Semantics.* North-Holland.

Barrere, F., Benzekri, A., Grasset, F., Laborde, R., & Nasser, B. (2003). Inter-Domains Policy Negotiation. In *Proceedings of the 4th International Workshop on Policies for Distributed Systems and Networks (POLICY'03),* (pp. 239-242), Lake Como, Italy.

Bass, L., Clements, P., & Kazman, R. (1998). *Software Architecture in Practice.* Massachusetts: Addison Wesley.

Bass, L., Clements, P., & Kazman, R. (2003). *Software Architecture in Practice* (2nd ed.). Addison Wesley.

BEA Systems, IBM Corporation, Microsoft Corporation, SAP AG, & Siebel Systems (2003). Business process execution language for Web services (BPEL 1.1). *Technical Report.*

Beck, K. (2000). *Extreme Programming Explained: Embrice Change.* Boston, MA: Addison-Wesley.

Beckett, D., McBride, B., (2004), RDF/XML Syntax Specification (Revised), W3C Recommendation, February 2004, available at: http://www.w3.org/TR/rdf-syntax-grammar/

Beizer, B. (1990). *Software Testing Techniques.* New York: Van Nostrand Reinhold.

Belaunde, M., & Falcarin, P. (2008, June). Realizing an MDA and SOA Marriage for the Development of Mobile Services. In *4th European Conference on Model Driven Architecture (ECMDA-2008), Berlin, Germany* (pp. 393-405). Springer-Verlag.

Bellare, M., Canetti, R., & Krawczyk, H. (1996). Keying hash functions for message authentication. In *Advances in Cryptology: CRYPTO 1996* (LNCS 1109, pp. 1-15). Santa Barbara, CA: Springer-Verlag.

Benatallah, B., Dumas, M., and Sheng, Q. Z.,(2003), The SELF-SERV Environment for Web Services Composition, IEEE Internet Computing Jan/Feb Issue, Vol. 7 (1). IEEE Society 2003

Benatallah, B., Dumas, M., Sheng, Q. Z., & Ngu, A. H. H. (2002). Declarative composition and peer-to-peer provisioning of dynamic Web services. In *Proceedings of the 18th International Conference on Data Engineering* (ICDE'02). IEEE Computer Society.

Benatallah, B., Hacid, M., Leger, A., Rey, C., & Toumani, F. (2005). On automating Web Services Discovery. *The VLDB Journal, 14*(1), 84–96. doi:10.1007/s00778-003-0117-x

Benatallah, B., Sheng, Q. Z., & Dumas, M. (2003). The Self-Serv Environment for Web Services Composition. *IEEE Internet Computing, 7*(1), 40–48. doi:10.1109/MIC.2003.1167338

Berardi, D., De Giacomo, G., Lenzerini, M., Mecella, M., & Calvanese. D. (2004). Synthesis of underspecified composite e-services based on automated reasoning. *Proceedings of the 2nd International Conference on Service Oriented Computing (ICSOC),* pp. 105–114.

Berkman Center for Internet & Society at Harvard Law School. (2007). *Rss2.0.* Retrieved from http://blogs.law.harvard.edu/tech/rss

Bermudez, L., Bogden, P., Bridger, E., Creager, G., Forrest, D., & Graybeal, J. (2006). Toward an ocean observing system of systems. *MTS/IEEE Oceans.*

Bernstein, A., Kaufmann, E., Burki, C., & Klein M. (2005). How similar is it? Towards personalized similarity measures in ontologies. In *7. Tag. Wirt. Informatik*

Bernstein, P. A., Hadzilacos, V., & Goodman, N. (1987). *Concurrency Control and Recovery in Database Systems.* Reading, MA: Addison Wesley.

Bertino, E., Castano, S., & Ferrari, E. (2001). On Specifying Security Policies for Web Documents with an XML-Based Language. In *Proceedings of the Sixth ACM Symposium on Access Control Models and Technologies,* (pp. 57-65), Chantilly, Virginia.

Bertino, E., Ferrari, E., & Atluri, V. (1999). The specification and enforcement of authorization constraints in workflow management systems. *ACM Transactions on Information and System Security, 2*(1), 65–104. doi:10.1145/300830.300837

Bertino, E., Ferrari, E., & Squicciarini, A. (2004). Trust negotiation: Concepts, systems, and languages. *Computing in Science and Engineering, July/August,* 27-34.

Betin-Can, A., Bultan, T., & Fu, X. (2005). Design for verification for asynchronously communicating Web services. In *Proceedings of the 14th International Conference on World Wide Web,* Chiba, Japan (pp. 750-759). ACM Press.

Bharadwaj, R. (2002). SOL: a verifiable synchronous language for reactive systems. In *Proceedings of Synchronous Languages, Applications, and Programming (SLAP'02).* Retrieved December 4, 2005, from http://chacs.nrl.navy.mil/publications/CHACS/2002/2002bharadwaj-entcs.pdf

Bharadwaj, R. (2003). Secure middleware for situation-aware naval C^2 and combat systems. In *Proceedings of the 9th International Workshop on Future Trends of Distributed Computing System (FTDCS'03),* 2003, May (pp. 233-240).

Bhargavan, K., Fournet, C., Gordon, A., & O'Shea, G. (2005). An Advisor for Web Services Security Policies. In *Proceedings of the 2005 Workshop on Secure Web Services (SWS '05),* (pp. 1-9), Fairfax, Virginia, USA.

Bhiri, S., Gaaloul, W., & Godart, C. (2008). Mining and Improving Composite Web Services Recovery Mechanisms. *International Journal of Web Services Research, 5*(2), 23–48.

Bhiri, S., Godart, C., & Perrin, O. (2006). Transactional patterns for reliable web services compositions, In *Proceedings of the 6th international conference on Web engineering* (pp. 137-144). Palo Alto.

Bhiri, S., Perrin, O., & Godart, C. (2005). Ensuring required failure atomicity of composite Web services, In *Proceedings of the 14th International World Wide Web Conference* (pp. 138-147). Chiba, Japan.

Bichler, M., & Lin, K. (2006). Service-oriented computing. *IEEE Computer, 39*(6).

Bieberstein N., Bose S., Fiammante M., Jones K., & Shah R. (2005). *Service-oriented architecture (SOA) compass: Business value, planning, and enterprise roadmap.* IBM Press.

Bilorusets, R., Box, D., Cabrera, L. F., Davis, D., Ferguson, D., Ferris, C., et al. (2005). Web Services Reliable Messaging Protocol. Retrieved March 1, 2009 from http://download.boulder.ibm.com/ibmdl/pub/software/dw/specs/ws-rm/ws-reliablemessaging200502.pdf

Birman, K. P., Chen, J., Hopkinson, E. M., Thomas, R. J., Thorp, J. S., & van Renesse, R. (2005). Overcoming Communications Challenges in Software for Monitoring and Controlling Power Systems. *Proceedings of the IEEE, 93*(5), 1028–1041. doi:10.1109/JPROC.2005.846339

Biron, P., & Malhotra, A. (2004). XML Schema Part 2: Datatypes, W3C Recommendation. Retrieved from http://www.w3.org/TR/xmlschema-2/

Blackburn, P., deRijke, M., & Venema, Y. (2003). *Modal Logic.* Cambridge University Press.

Bloomberg, J. (2002). Testing Web services today and tomorrow. Retrieved from http://www-106.ibm.com/developerworks/rational/library/content/rationaledge/oct02/webtesting_therationaledge_oct02.pdf.

Boehm, B. (1981). *Software engineering economics.* Englewood Cliffs, NJ: Prentice Hall.

Bolchini, D., Paolini, P. (2004). Goal-Driven Requirements Analysis for Hypermedia-intensive Web Applications. *Requirements Engineering Journal, RE03 Special Issue (9),* 85-103.

Booth, D., Haas, H., McCabe, F., Newcomer, E., Champion, M., Ferris, C., Orchard, D., (2004), Web Services Architecture, W3C Working Group Note, February 2004, available at http://www.w3.org/TR/ws-arch/

Booth, D., Haas, H., McCabe, F., Newcomer, E., Champion, M., Ferris, C., & Orchard, D. (2004). Web Services Architecture. Retrieved March 1, 2009 from http://www.w3.org/TR/ws-arch

Bose, R., & Frew, J. (2004). Composing lineage metadata with XML for custom satellite-derived data products. *SS-DBM.*

Bose, R., & Frew, J. (2005). Lineage retrieval for scientific data processing: A survey. *ACM Computing Surveys, 37,* 1–28.

Bose, R., Foster, I., & Moreau. L. (2006). Report on the international provenance and annotation workshop. *SIGMOD Record, 35*(3), 51–53.

Botha, R. A., & Elofi, J. H. P. (2001). Separation of duties for access control enforcement in workflow environments. *IBM Systems Journal, 40*(3), 666–682.

Box, D., Cabrera, L. F., Critchley, C., Curbera, D., Ferguson, D., Geller, A., et al. (2004). Web Services Eventing (WS-Eventing). Retrieved December 9, 2006, from http://www.ibm.com/developerworks/webservices/library/specification/ws-eventing/

Box, D., et al. (2004). Web services eventing (WS-eventing). *Technical Report.*

BPEL. (2003). *Business Process Execution Language for Web Services (Version 1.1).* Retrieved December 5, 2007, from http://www.ibm.com/developerworks/library/specification/ws-bpel/

BPEL4WS. (2002). Web services. Retrieved from http://www-106.ibm.com/developerworks/webservices/

BPML. (2004). Business process modeling language. Retrieved from http://www.bpmi.org/

BPMN. (2005). Business process modeling notation. Retrieved from http://www.bpmn.org/

Brandes, U., Eiglsperger, M., Herman, I., Himsolt, M., & Marshall, M.S. (2002). GraphML progress report: Structural layer proposal. *LNCS, 2265*, 501–512.

Bray, T., Paoli, J., Sperberg-McQueen, C. M., Maler, E., Yergeau, F., (2004), Extensible Markup Language (XML) 1.0 (Third Edition), W3C Recommendation 04 February 2004, http://www.w3.org/TR/2004/REC-xml-20040204/

Brittenham, P., Cubrera, F., Ehnevuske, D., & Graham, S. (2001). Understanding WSDL in a UDDI Registry. Retrieved from http://www-106.ibm.com/developerworks/webservices/library/ws-wsdl/ .

Broemmer, D. (2002). *J2EE Best Practices: Java Design Patterns, Automation, and Performance.* Massachusetts: John Wiley & Sons.

Brogi, A., & Popescu, R. (2006). From BEL processes to YAWL workflows. In *Proceedings of the 3rd International Workshop on Web Services and Formal Methods* (*LNCS* 4184, pp. 107–122). Berlin: Springer-Verlag.

Brooks, C., Lee, E. A., Liu, X., Neuendorffer, S., Zhao, Y., & Zheng, H. (2005). Heterogeneous Concurrent Modeling and Design in Java, Volume 3: Ptolemy II Domains. *Tech. Report UCB/ERL M05/21, University of California, Berkeley.* July 15.

Bruijn, J., Bussler, C., Domingue, J., Fensel, D., Kifer, M., Kopecky, J., Lara, R., Oren, E., Polleres, A., Stollberg, M., (2005), Web Service Modeling Ontology (WSMO), WSMO Final Draft February 2005, available at http://www.wsmo.org/TR/d2/v1.1/

Buchmann, F., & Bass, L. (2001). Introduction to the attribute driven design method. In *ICSE '01: Proceeding of the 23rd international Conference on Software Engineering*, Toronto, Ontario, Canada.

Bultan, T., Fu, X., Hull, R., & Su, J. (2003). Conversation specification: a new approach to design and analysis of e-service composition. In *Proceedings of the 12th International World Wide Web Conference* (pp. 403-410). Budapest, Hungary.

Bunke, H., & Shearer, K. (1998). A Graph Distance Metric based on the Maximal Common Subgraph. *Pattern Recognition Letters, 19*(3-4), 255–259. doi:10.1016/S0167-8655(97)00179-7

Burgy, L., Consel, C., Latry, F., Lawall, J., Palix, N., & Reveillere, L. (2006, June). Language Technology for Internet-Telephony Service Creation. In *Proceedings of the IEEE International Conference on Communications (ICC2006), vol. 4, Istanbul, Turkey* (pp. 1795–1800). Washington: IEEE Computer Society.

Burstein, M., Bussler, C., Zaremba, M., Finin, T., Huhns, N. M., Paolucci, M., Sheth, P. A., Williams, S., (2005), A semantic web service architecture, In IEEE Internet Computing, vol 9 issue 5, Sept.-Oct. 2005, 72-81

Cabrera, L. F., Copeland, G., Feingold, M., Freund, R. W., & Freund, T. Johnson, Joyce, S., J., Kaler, C., Klein, J., Langworthy, D., Little, M., Nadalin, A., Newcomer, E., Orchard, D., Robinson, I., Shewchuk, J., & Storey, T. (2005). Web Services Coordination, Version 1.0. Retrieved March 1, 2009 from http://download.boulder.ibm.com/ibmdl/pub/software/dw/specs/ws-tx/WS-Coordination.pdf

Cabrera, L. F., Copeland, G., Feingold, M., Freund, R. W., Freund, T., Johnson, J., et al. (2005). Web Services Atomic Transaction, Version 1.0. Retrieved March 1, 2009 from http://download.boulder.ibm.com/ibmdl/pub/software/dw/specs/ws-tx/WS-AtomicTransaction.pdf

Cabrera, L. F., Copeland, G., Feingold, M., Freund, R. W., Freund, T., Joyce, S., et al. (2005). Web Services Business Activity Framework, Version 1.0. Retrieved March 1, 2009 from http://download.boulder.ibm.com/ibmdl/pub/software/dw/specs/ws-tx/WS-BusinessActivity.pdf

Campbell, R. H., & Habermann, A. N. (1974). The specification of process synchronization by path expressions. In *Lecture notes in computer science* (Vol. 16, pp. 89-102). Springer-Verlag.

Canós, J.H., Penadés, M.C., & Carsí, J.Á. (1999). *From software process to workflow process: the workflow lifecycle.* Proceedings of the International Process Technology Workshop, Grenoble, France.

Cappiello, C., Missier, P., Pernici, B., Plebani, P., & Batini, C. (2004). QoS in Multichannel IS: The MAIS Approach. In *ICWE Workshops '04: Proceeding of the International Conference on Web Engineering*, Munich, Germany (pp. 255-268).

Capra, L., Emmerich, W., & Mascolo, C. (2001). Reflective Middleware Solutions for Context-Aware Applications. In *REFLECTION '01: Proceeding of the Third International Conference on Metalevel Architectures and Separation of Crosscutting Concerns*, London, UK (pp. 126-133).

Carbone, J. A. (2004). *IT Architecture Toolkit*. New Jersey: Prentice Hall PTR.

Card, D., & Agresti, W. (1988). Measuring software design complexity. *Journal of Systems and Software, 8*, 185–197.

Cardelli, L., & Gordon, A. D. (2000). Mobile ambients. *Theoretical Computer Science, 240*(1), 177–213. doi:10.1016/S0304-3975(99)00231-5

Cardoso, J. (2005). *About the complexity of teamwork and collaboration processes.* Proceedings of the IEEE International Symposium on Applications and the Internet (SAINT 2005), Trento, Italy.

Cardoso, J. (2005). *About the data-flow complexity of Web processes.* Proceedings of the 6th International Workshop on Business Process Modeling, Development, and Support: Business Processes and Support Systems: Design for Flexibility, Porto, Portugal.

Cardoso, J. (2005). *Control-flow complexity measurement of processes and Weyuker's properties (accepted for publication).* Proceedings of the 6th International Enformatika Conference (IEC 2005), Budapest, Hungary.

Cardoso, J. (2005). Evaluating workflows and Web process complexity. In L. Fischer (Ed.), *Workflow handbook 2005* (pp. 284–290). Lighthouse Point, FL: Future Strategies Inc.

Cardoso, J. (2005). How to Measure the Control-flow Complexity of Web processes and Workflows. In L. Fischer (Ed.), *Workflow Handbook 2005* (pp. 199-212). Lighthouse Point, FL: WfMC.

Cardoso, J. (2005). Path mining in Web processes using profiles. In J. Wang (Ed.), *Encyclopedia of data warehousing and mining* (pp. 896–901). Hershey, PA: Idea Group Inc.

Cardoso, J. (2006). *Process control-flow complexity metric: An empirical validation.* Proceedings of the IEEE International Conference on Services Computing (IEEE SCC 06), Chicago.

Cardoso, J., & Cravo, C. (2006). *Verifying the logical termination of workflows.* Proceedings of the 5th Annual Hawaii International Conference on Statistics, Mathematics and Related Fields, Honolulu, Hawaii.

Cardoso, J., Bostrom, R.P., & Sheth, A. (2004). Workflow management systems and ERP systems: Differences, commonalities, and applications. *Information Technology and Management Journal. Special issue on Workflow and E-Business, 5*(3-4), 319–338.

Cardoso, J., Miller, J., Sheth, A., & Arnold, J. (2004). Modeling Quality of Service for Workflows and Web Service Processes. *Web Semantics Journal, 1*(3), 281–308.

Cardoso, J., Miller, J., Sheth, A., Arnold, J., & Kochut, K. (2004). Modeling quality of service for workflows and Web service processes. *Web Semantics: Science, Services and Agents on the World Wide Web Journal, 1*(3), 281–308.

Cardoso, J., Sheth, A., & Miller, J. (2002). *Workflow quality of service.* Proceedings of the International Conference on Enterprise Integration and Modeling Technology and International Enterprise Modeling Conference (ICEIMT/IEMC'02), Valencia, Spain.

Caromel, D., & Henrio, L. (2005). *A Theory of Distributed Objects.* Springer Verlag.

Casati, F., Castano, S., & Fugini, M. (2001). Managing workflow authorization constraints through active database technology. *Information Systems Frontiers, 3*(3), 319–338. doi:10.1023/A:1011461409620

Catlett, C. (2002). The TeraGrid: A primer. Retrieved from www.teragrid.org

CCXML. (2007). *W3C, Voice Browser Call Control: CCXML version 1.0 specification.* Retrieved December 5, 2007, from http://www.w3.org/TR/ccxml/

Chafle, G., Chandra, S., Mann, V., & Nanda, M. G. (2004). Decentralized orchestration of composite Web services. In *Proceedings of the 13th International World Wide Web Conference*, New York.

Chan, A. T. S., & Chuang, S. N. (2003). MobiPADS: a reflective middleware for context-aware computing. *IEEE Transactions on Software Engineering, 29*(12), 1072–1085. doi:10.1109/TSE.2003.1265522

Chan, F. T., Chen, T. Y., Cheung, S. C., Lau, M. F., & Yiu, S. M. (1998). Application of Metamorphic Testing in Numerical Analysis. In *Proceedings of IASTED International Conference on Software Engineering (SE 1998)* (pp. 191–197). Calgary. Canada: ACTA Press.

Chan, W. K., & Chen, T. Y. Lu, Heng, Tse, T. H., & Yau, S. S. (2005). A metamorphic approach to integration testing of context-sensitive middleware-based applications. In *Proceedings of the Fifth Annual International Conference on Quality Software (QSIC 2005)* (pp. 241-249). Los Alamitos, California: IEEE Computer Society Press.

Chan, W. K., & Chen, T. Y., Lu, Heng, Tse, T. H., & Yau, S. S. (2006). Integration testing of context-sensitive middleware-based applications: a metamorphic approach. *International Journal of Software Engineering and Knowledge Engineering, 16*(5), 677–703. doi:10.1142/S0218194006002951

Chan, W. K., Cheung, S. C., & Leung, K. R. P. H. (2005). Towards a Metamorphic Testing Methodology for Service-Oriented Software Applications. The First International Workshop on Services Engineering (SEIW 2005), in *Proceedings of the 5th Annual International Conference on Quality Software (QSIC 2005)* (pp. 470–476). Los Alamitos, California: IEEE Computer Society.

Chan, W. K., Cheung, S. C., & Leung, K. R. P. H. (2007). A Metamorphic Testing Approach for Online Testing of Service-Oriented Software Applications. *International Journal of Web Services Research, 4*(2), 60–80.

Chan, W. K., Cheung, S. C., & Tse, T. H. (2005). Fault-based testing of database application programs with conceptual data model. In *Proceedings of the 5th Annual International Conference on Quality Software (QSIC 2005)* (pp. 187-196). Los Alamitos, California: IEEE Computer Society Press.

Chang, T.-K., & Hwang, G.-H. (2004). Using the extension function of XSLT and DSL to secure XML documents. In *18th International Conference on Advanced Information Networking and Applications* (pp. 556-561).

Chappell, D. (2004). *Enterprise service bus.* O'Reilly.

Chappell, D. (2005) The case against BPEL: Why the language is less important than you think. *Opinari Blog*, Number 14, October 2005. Last accessed December 15, 2006 from http://www.davidchappell.com/HTML_email/Opinari_No14_10_05.html

Charfi, A., & Mezini, M. (2004). Aspect-oriented Web service composition with AO4BPEL. In *Proceedings of the European Conference on Web Services ECOWS 2004*, Erfurt, Germany (LNCS 3250).

Chen, F., Ryder, B., Milanova, A., & Wannacott, D. (2004). Testing of Java Web Services for Robustness. In *Proceedings of the International Symposium on Software Testing and Analysis (ISSTA 2004)* (pp. 23–34). New York: ACM Press.

Chen, T. Y., Cheung, S. C., & Yiu, S. M. (1998). *Metamorphic testing: a new approach for generating next test cases* (Technical Report HKUST-CS98-01). Hong Kong: Department of Computer Science, Hong Kong University of Science and Technology.

Chen, T. Y., Huang, D. H., Tse, T. H., & Zhou, Z. Q. (2004). Case studies on the selection of useful relations in metamorphic testing, in *Proceedings of the 4th Ibero-American Symposium on Software Engineering and Knowledge Engineering (JIISIC 2004)* (pp. 569–583). Madrid, Spain: Polytechnic University of Madrid.

Chen, T. Y., Tse, T. H., & Zhou, Z. Q. (2002). Semi-proving: an integrated method based on global symbolic evaluation and metamorphic testing. In *Proceedings of the ACM SIGSOFT International Symposium on Software Testing and Analysis (ISSTA 2002)* (pp. 191–195). New York: ACM Press.

Chen, T. Y., Tse, T. H., & Zhou, Z. Q. (2003). Fault-based testing without the need of oracles. *Information and Software Technology, 45*(1), 1–9. doi:10.1016/S0950-5849(02)00129-5

Cheney, J. (2001). Compressing XML with multiplexed hierarchical PPM models. In *Data Compression Conference, Snowbird, USA* (pp. 163–172).

Cherniavsky, J.C., & Smith, C.H. (1991). On Weyuker's axioms for software complexity measures. *IEEE Transactions on Software Engineering, 17*(6), 636–638.

Chinnici, R., Gudgin, M., Moreau, J.-J., Weerawarana, S., (2003), Web Services Description Language (WSDL) Version 2.0 Part 1: Core Language, W3C Candidate Recommendation, 27 March 2006, available at http://www.w3.org/TR/wsdl20/

Chou, W. (2002, July-August). Inside SSL: The secure sockets layer protocol. *IT Pro*, 47-52.

Christensen, E., Curbera, F., Meredith, G., & Weerawarana, S. (2001). Web Services Description Language (WSDL) Version 1.1, W3C Note. Retrieved from http://www.w3.org/TR/2001/NOTE-wsdl-20010315.

Christensen, E., Curbera, F., Meredith, G., Weerawarana, S., (2001) Web Services Description Language (WSDL) 1.1 W3C Note 15 March 2001, available at: http://www.w3.org/TR/wsdl

Chung, J.-Y., Lin, K.-J., & Mathieu, R. G. (2003). Web Services Computing: Advancing Software Interoperability. *IEEE Computer, 36*(10), 35–37.

Churches, D., et al. (2006). Programming scientific and distributed workflow with Triana Services. *Concur-*

rency and Computation: Practice and Experience, 18(10), 1021–1037.

Clark, J., & DeRose, S. (1999). XML Path Language (XPath) Version 1.0, W3C Recommendation. Retrieved from http://www.w3.org/TR/1999/REC-xpath-19991116.

Clark, J., & Murata, M. (2001). Definitive specification for RELAX NG using the XML syntax. Retrieved March 17, 2009, from http://www.relaxng.org/spec-20011203.html

Cohen-Boulakia, S., Cohen, S., & Davidson, S. (2007). Addressing the provenance challenge using zoom. *Concurrency and Control: Practice and Experience.*

Colan, M. (2004). Service-Oriented Architecture expands the vision of Web Services, Part 1: Characteristics of Service-Oriented Architecture. Retrieved from http://www-128.ibm.com/developerworks/webservices/library/ws-soaintro.html.

Colgrave, J., Akkiraju, R., & Goodwin, R. (2004). *External Matching in UDDI.* Proceedings of the International Conference on Web Services, 2004.

Comerio, M., De Paoli, F., & Grega, S. (2006). Quality Composition in Web-Service Design. In *ICDCSW '06: Proceeding of the International Conference on Distributed Computing Systems-Workshops*, Lisbon, Portugal.

Comerio, M., De Paoli, F., Grega, S., Batini, C., Di Francesco, C., & Di Pasquale, A. (2004). A Service Re-design Methodology for Multi-channel Adaptation. In *ICSOC '04: Proceeding of the International Conf. of Service Oriented Computing*, New York, NY, USA (pp.11-20).

Comerio, M., De Paoli, F., Maurino, A., & Palmonari, M. (2007). NFP-aware Semantic Web Services Selection. In *EDOC '07: Proceeding of the 11th IEEE International Enterprise Distributed Object Computing Conference*, Annapolis, Maryland, USA (pp. 70-78).

Cook, J. E., & Wolf, A. L. (1998). Discovering models of software processes from event-based data. [TOSEM]. *ACM Transactions on Software Engineering and Methodology, 7*(3), 215–249. doi:10.1145/287000.287001

Cook, J. E., & Wolf, A. L. (1998). Event-based detection of concurrency. In *Proceedings of 6th ACM SIGSOFT FSE conference* (pp. 35-45). Florida, USA.

Cook, J. E., & Wolf, A. L. (1999). Software Process Validation: Quantitatively Measuring the Correspondence of a Process to a Model. *ACM Transactions on Software Engineering and Methodology, 8*(2), 147–176. doi:10.1145/304399.304401

Crampton, J. (2005). A reference monitor for workflow systems with constrained task execution. In *Proceedings of the 10th ACM Symposium on Access Control Models and Technologies*, Stockholm, Sweden (pp. 38-47).

Crampton, J. (2005). XACML and role-based access control. Presentation at *DIMACS Workshop on Security of Web Services and e-Commerce, DIMACS Center, CoRE Building, Rutgers University, Piscataway, NJ.*

Curbera, F., Duftler, M., Khalaf, R., Nagy, W., Mukhi, N., & Weerawarana, S. (2002). Unraveling the Web services web: An introduction to SOAP, WSDL, and UDDI. [Los Alamitos, California: IEEE Computer Society Press.]. *IEEE Internet Computing, 6*(2), 86–93. doi:10.1109/4236.991449

Curbera, F., Khalaf, R., Mukhi, N., Tai, S., & Weerawarana, S. (2003). The next step in web services. *Communications of the ACM, 46*(10), 29–34. doi:10.1145/944217.944234

Curtis, B. (1980). Measurement and experimentation in software engineering. *Proceedings of the IEEE, 68*(9), 1144–1157.

Czajkowski, K., Ferguson. D., Foster, I., Frey, J., Graham, S., Maguire, T., Snelling, D., Tuecke, S., (2004), From Open Grid Services Infrastructure to WS-Resource Framework: Refactoring & Evolution, Version 1.0, Whitepaper, February 2004.

Davenport, T. (1993). *Process innovation: Reengineering work through information technology.* Harvard Business School Press.

Davulcu, H., Mukhopadhyay, S., Singh, P., & Yau, S. S. (2009). Default α-Logic for Modeling Customizable Failure Semantics in Workflow Systems Using Dynamic Reconfiguration Constraints. In *Proceedings of International Conference on Grid and Distributed Computing (GDC)*, December (pp. 49-56).

Dayal, U., Hsu, M., & Ladin, R. (1990). Organizing long running activities with triggers and transactions. In *Proceedings of the 1990 ACM SIGMOD International Conference on Management of Data*, May (pp. 204-214).

De Labey, S., & Steegmans, E. (2008, Sept.). Extending WS-Notification with an Expressive Event Notification Broker. In *IEEE International conference on Web Services (ICWS'08), Beijing, China* (pp. 312-319). IEEE Computer Society.

de Medeiros, A. K. A., van der Aalst, W. M. P., & Weijters, A. J. M. M. (2008). Quantifying process equivalence based on observed behavior. *Data & Knowledge Engineering, 64*(1), 55–74. doi:10.1016/j.datak.2007.06.010

de Medeiros, A. K. A., Weijters, A. J. M. M., & van der Aalst, W. M. P. (2007). Genetic process mining: an experimental evaluation. *Data Mining and Knowledge Discovery, 14*(2), 245–304. doi:10.1007/s10618-006-0061-7

de Rose, L.A., & Reed, D.A. (1999). SvPablo: A multi-language architecture-independent performance analysis system. *ICPP.*

Degwekar, S., Su, S.Y.W., & Lam, H. (2004). *Constraint specification and processing in Web services publication and discovery.* Proceedings of the IEEE International Conference on Web Services (ICWS 04), 210–217.

Della-Libera, G., Gudgin, M., Hallam-Baker, P., Hondo, M., Granqvist, H., Kaler, C. et al. (2005). *Web Services Security Policy Language (WS-SecurityPolicy).* Version 1.1, July. Retrieved July 28, 2006 from: ftp://www6.software.ibm.com/software/developer/library/ws-secpol.pdf

DeMichiel, L., Keith, M., (2006), Enterprise Java Beans, Version 3.0: EJB Core Contracts and Requirements, Release 8 May 2006, available at http://java.sun.com/

Deng, Y., Frankl, P., & Wang, J. (2004). Testing web database applications. Workshop on testing, analysis and verification of web services (TAV-WEB), *SIGSOFT Software Engineering Notes, 29*(5), 1-10. New York: ACM Press.

Dey, A. K., & Abowd, G. D. (2001). A conceptual framework and a toolkit for supporting the rapid prototyping of context-aware applications. *Human-Computer Interaction (HCI) Journal, 16*(2-4), 97–166.

Dietterich, T.G., & Lathrop, R.H. (1997). Solving the multiple-instance problem with axis-parallel rectangles. *Artificial Intelligence, 89*(1-2), 31–71.

Dinsmore, P., Balenson, D., Heyman, M., Kruus, P., Scace, C., & Sherman, A. (2000). Policy-Based Security Management for Large Dynamic Groups: An Overview of the DCCM Project. In *Proceedings, DARPA Information Survivability Conference and Exposition (DISCEX'00),* Vol. 1, (pp. 64-73). Hilton Head, South Carolina.

DLNA. (2006). Digital Living Network Alliance. Retrieved from http://www.dlna.org

DOLMEN. (1997). *Bridging and wireless access for terminal mobility in CORBA* (Rep. No. LK-OMG01). Paper presented at the DOLMEN Consortium.

Dong, X., Halevy, A., Madhavan, J., Nemes, E., & Zhang. J. (2004). Similarity search for Web services. *Proceedings of the 30th VLDB Conference,* Toronto, Canada

Doug, B., Martin, C., Oisin, H., Mark, L., Jeff, M., Eric, N., et al. (2003). Web Services Composite Application Framework (WS-CAF). Retrieved July 28, 2003 from http://www.arjuna.com/standards/ws-caf/

Droegemeier, K.K., et al. (2005). Service-oriented environments for dynamically interacting with mesoscale weather. *Computing in Science and Engineering, 7*(6), 12–29.

Du, W., Davis, J., Huang, Y., & Shan, M. (1999). *Enterprise workflow resource management.* Proceedings of the International Workshop on Research Issues in Data Engineering, Sydney, Australia.

Dubray, J. J., Amand, S., Martin, J. M., (2006), ebXML Business Process Specification Schema Technical Specification v2.0.4, Committee Specification, 13 October 2006, available at http://www.oasis-open.org/committees/documents.php?wg_abbrev=ebxml-bp

Duflos, S. (2002). An Architecture for Policy-Based Security Management for Distributed Multimedia Services.In *Proceedings of the 10th ACM International Conference on Multimedia,* (pp. 653-655), Juan-les-Pins, France.

Duftler, J. M., Mukhi, K. N., Slominski, A., Weerawarana, S., (2001), Web Services Invocation Framework (WSIF), OOPSLA 2001 Workshop on Object-Oriented Web Services: Supporting the Development, Deployment and Evolution of Web Services, October 2001 - Tampa, Florida, USA

Duigou, M., (2006), JXTA v2.0 Protocols Specification, IETF Working Group Draft Specification, August 2006

Dustar, S., & Haslinger, S. (2004). Testing of Service-Oriented Architectures: A Practical Approach. In *Proceedings of the 5th Annual International Conference on Object-Oriented and Internet-Based Technologies, Concepts, and Applications for a Networked World (NODe 2004)* (LNCS 3263, pp. 97–112).

Dustdar, S., Gall, H., & Schmidt, R. (2004). Web Services for Groupware in Distributed and Mobile Collaboration. *12th IEEE Euromicro Conference on Parallel, Distributed and Network-Based Processing (PDP 2004)* (p. 241).

ECHONET. (2006). ECHONET Consortium. Retrieved from http://www.echonet.gr.jp/

Eclipslee (2007). Eclipslee project website. Retrieved December 30, 2007, from, https://eclipslee.dev.java.net/

Elenius, D. and Ingmarsson, M. 2004. Ontology-based service discovery in p2p networks. In Proceedings of the First International Workshop on Peer-to-Peer Knowledge Management, Boston, Massachusetts, USA, August 2004, CEUR-WS, August 2004, Vol. 108.

Elmagarmid, A. K. (1992). *Database Transaction Models for Advanced Applications*. Morgan Kaufmann.

Elmagarmid, A. K. (Ed.). (1992). *Database transaction models for advanced applications*. San Francisco: Morgan Kaufmann Publishers Inc.

Endrei, M., Ang, J., Arsanjani, A., Chua, S., Comte, P., Krogdahl, P., et al., (2004). *Patterns: Service-oriented architecture and Web services*. IBM Red Books.

Erl, T. (2004). *Service-Oriented Architecture: A Field Guide to Integrating XML and Web Services*. New Jersey: Prentice Hall PTR.

Ermagan, V., & Krüger, H. (2007). A UML2 profile for service modeling. *Proceedings of ACM/IEEE International Conference on Model Driven Engineering Languages and Systems*.

ETSI. (2002). *The ETSI OSA Parlay-X 3.0 Specifications*. Retrieved December 5, 2007, from http://portal.etsi.org/docbox/TISPAN/Open/OSA/ParlayX30.html.

Eugster, P.T., Felber, P.A., Guerraoui, R., & Kermarrec, A.M. (2003). The many faces of publish/subscribe. *ACM Computing Surveys, 35*, 114–131.

Faheem, H. (2005). A Multiagent-Based Approach for Managing Security Policy. In *Proceedings of the 2nd IFIP International Conference on Wireless and Optical Communications Networks (WOCN 2005)*, (pp. 351-356), Dubai, UAE.

Fang, J., Hu, S., Han Y., (2004), A Service Interoperability Assessment Model for Service Composition, In Proceedings of the 2004 IEEE International Conference on Services Computing (SCC'04), Sept. 2004, Shanghai, China

Farrell, J., Lausen, H., (2006), Semantic Annotations for WSDL, W3C Working Draft 28, Sept. 2006

Fauvet, M.-C., Dumas, M., & Benatallah, B. (2002). Collecting and Querying Distributed Traces of Composite Service Executions. In *Proceedings of the 14th International Conference on Cooperative Information Systems* (pp. 373-390). California.

Fekete, A., Greenfield, P., Kuo, D., & Jang, J. (2003). Transactions in loosely coupled distributed systems. In *Proceedings of the 14th Australasian Database Conference*, Adelaide, Australia (pp. 7-12).

Fensel, D., & Bussler, C. (2002). The Web Service Modeling Framework WSMF. *Electronic Commerce Research and Applications, 1*(2), 113–137. doi:10.1016/S1567-4223(02)00015-7

Fenton, N. (1991). *Software metrics: A rigorous approach*. London: Chapman & Hall, 1991.Garmus, D., & Herron, D. (2000). *Function point analysis: Measurement practices for successful software projects*. Boston, MA: Addison Wesley.

Fenton, N. (1994). Software measurement: A necessary scientific basis. *IEEE Transactions on Software Engineering, 20*(3).

Fielding, R., Gettys, J., Mogul, J., Nielsen, H. F., Masinter, L., Leach, P., et al. (1999). *RFC 2616: Hypertext transfer protocol: HTTP/1.1*. Internet Engineering Task Force.

Filho, R. S. S., de Souza, C. R. B., & Redmiles, D. F. (2003, June). The design of a configurable, extensible and dynamic notification service. In *Proceedings of the 2nd international workshop on Distributed event-based systems* (pp. 1-8). San Diego, USA.

Floyd, S., Jacobson, V., Liu, C., McCanne, S., & Zhang, L. (1996). A Reliable Multicast Framework for Light-weight Sessions and Application Level Framing. *IEEE/ACM Transactions on Networking, 5*(6), 784-803.

Foster, H., Kramer, J., Magee, J., & Uchitel, S. (2003). *Model-based verification of Web service compositions*. Paper presented at the IEEE ASE 2003, Montreal, Canada.

Foster, I. (2005). Service-oriented computing. *Science, 308*(5723).

Foster, I., Kesselman, C., Nick, J., & Tuecke S. (2002). The physiology of the grid: An open grid services architecture for distributed systems integration. *Global Grid Forum*.

Foster, I.T., Vöckler, J., Wilde, M., & Zhao, Y. (2003). The virtual data grid: A new model and architecture for data-intensive collaboration. *CIDR*.

Fowler, M. (2003). *Patterns of Enterprise Application Architecture*. Massachusetts: Addison Wesley.

Frankel, D. S. (2003). *Model Driven Architecture: Applying MDA to Enterprise Computing*. New York: John Wiley & Sons.

Frankl, P. G., & Weyuker, E. J. (1988). An Applicable Family of Data Flow Testing Criteria. *IEEE Transactions on Software Engineering, 14*(10), 1483–1498. doi:10.1109/32.6194

Freier, A. O., Karlton, P., & Kocher, P. C. (1996). *The SSL protocol version 3.0*. Netscape Communications.

Freund, T., & Little, M. (Eds.). (2007). *Web Service Business Activity Version 1.1*. Retrieved April 16, 2007 from http://docs.oasis-open.org/ws-tx/wstx-wsba-1.1-spec-os.pdf

Fuentes, L., & Vallecillo, A. (2004). An introduction to UML profiles. *The European Journal for the Informatics Professional, 5*(2).

Furniss, P., Dalal, S., Fletcher, T., Green, A., Haugen, B., Ceponkus, A., & Pope, B. (2004). OASIS Business Transaction Protocol, Version 1.1. Retrieved March 1, 2009 from http://xml.coverpages.org/BTPv11-200411.pdf

Gaaloul, W., Baïna, K., & Godart, C. (2008). Log-based mining techniques applied to Web service composition reengineering. [SOCA]. *Service Oriented Computing and Applications, 2*(2-3), 93–110. doi:10.1007/s11761-008-0023-6

Gaaloul, W., Bhiri, S., & Godart, C. (2004). Discovering Workflow Patterns from Timed Logs. In *Proceedings of Informationssysteme im E-Business und E-Government, Beiträge des Workshops derGI-Fachgruppe EMISA* (pp. 84-94). LNI, Luxemburg.

Gaaloul, W., Bhiri, S., & Godart, C. (2004). Discovering Workflow Transactional Behavior from Event based Log. In *Proceedings of the 12th International Conference on Cooperative Information Systems*, Cyprus, October 2004, 25-29.

Gamma, E., Helm, R., Johnson, R., & Vlissides, J. M. (1994) *Design Patterns: Elements of Reusable Object-Oriented Software*. Addison-Wesley.

Gannon, D., et al. (2005). Service oriented architectures for science gateways on grid systems. *ICSOC*.

Gao, Y. (2006). *BPMN-BPEL transformation and round trip engineering. eClarus Software*. Retrieved March 1, 2007, from http://www.eclarus.com/pdf/BPMN_BPEL_Mapping.pdf

García-Fanjul, J., Tuya, J., & de la Riva, C. (2006). Generating Test Cases Specifications for BPEL Compositions of Web Services Using SPIN. In *International Workshop on Web Services Modeling and Testing* (*WS-MaTe 2006*) (pp. 83-94). Berlin: Springer-Verlag.

Garcia-Molina, H., & Salem, K. (1987). Sagas, In *Proceedings of the ACM SIGMOD Conference*, San Francisco, CA (pp. 249-259).

Gardner, T. (2003). UML modeling of automated business processes with a mapping to BPEL4WS. *Proceedings of European Conference on Object-Oriented Programming Workshop on Object Orientation and Web Services.*

Gay, D., Philip, L., von Behren, R., Welsh, M., Brewer, E., & Culler, D. (2003). The nesC Language: A Holistic Approach to Networked Embedded Systems. In *Proceedings of ACM SIGPLAN 2003 Conference on Programming Language Design and Implementation*, June (pp. 1-11).

Geer, D. (2006). Nanotechnology: The Growing Impact of Shrinking Computers. *IEEE Pervasive Computing / IEEE Computer Society [and] IEEE Communications Society, 5*(1), 7–11. doi:10.1109/MPRV.2006.10

Gelgi. F. (2005). *Embedding AI planning techniques into single machine total weighted tardiness problem* (Technical Report), Arizona State University. Retrieved December 4, 2005, from http://www.public.asu. edu/~fgelgi/ai/atoc/smtwt-report.pdf

Georgakopoulos, D., Hornick, M., & Sheth, A. (1995). An overview of workflow management: from process modeling to workflow automation infrastructure. *Journal on Distributed and Parallel Databases, 3*(2), 119–153. doi:10.1007/BF01277643

Giaglis, G. M. (2001). A Taxonomy of Business Process Modeling and Information Systems Modeling Techniques. *International Journal of Flexible Manufacturing Systems, 13*(2), 209–228. doi:10.1023/A:1011139719773

Gibbons, P., Karp, B., Ke, Y., Nath, S., Seshan, S., (2003), IrisNet: An Architecture for a World-Wide Sensor Web, IEEE Pervasive Computing, V(2), N(4), October-December 2003

Ginis, R., & Chandy, K. M. (2000). Micro-option: A method for optimal selection and atomic reservation of distributed resources in a free market environment. In *Proceedings of the ACM Conference on Electronic Commerce*, New York, NY (pp. 207-214).

Girardot, M., & Sundaresan, N. (2000). Millau: An encoding format for effcient representation and exchange of XML over the web. In *9th International World Wide Web Conference, May 2000, Amsterdam, Netherlands* (pp. 747–765).

Glitho, R. H., Khendek, F., & De Marco, A. (2003). Creating Value Added Services in Internet Telephony: An Overview and a Case Study on a High-Level Service Creation Environment. *IEEE Transactions on Systems, Man and Cybernetics. Part C, Applications and Reviews, 33*(4), 446–457. doi:10.1109/TSMCC.2003.818499

Global Environment Fund. (2005). *The Emerging Smart Grid: Investment and Entrepreneurial Potential in the Electric Power Grid of the Future*, October. Retrieved from: http://www.globalenvironmentfund.com/GEF%20white%20paper_Electric%20Power%20Grid.pdf

Goble, C. (2002). Position statement: Musings on provenance, workflow and (semantic Web) annotations for bioinformatics. *Workshop on Data Derivation and Provenance.*

Goderis, A., Brooks, C., Altintas, I., Lee, E.A., & Goble, C.A. (2007). Composing different models of computation in Kepler and Ptolemy II. *Proceedings of the International Conference on Computational Science (ICCS) 2007*, Beijing, China, May 27-30.

Goderis, A., Li, P., & Goble, C.A. (2006). Workflow discovery: The problem, a case study from escience and a graph-based solution. *Proceedings of the IEEE International Conference on Web Services (ICWS)*, Chicago, USA, September 18-22.

Goderis, A., Sattler, U., Lord P., & Goble C. (2005). Applying DLs to workflow reuse and repurposing. *International Description Logics workshop*, Edinburgh, Scotland, July 24-26.

Goderis, A., Sattler, U., Lord, P., & Goble, C. (2005). Seven bottlenecks to workflow reuse and repurposing. *Proceedings of the 4th International Semantic Web Conference (ISWC 2005)*, LNCS volume 3792, pages 323–337, Galway, Ireland.

Gomez-Perez, A., Gonzalez-Cabero, R., & Lama, M. (2004). A Framework for Design and Composition of Semantic Web Services. *IEEE Intelligent Systems, 19*(4), 24–31. doi:10.1109/MIS.2004.32

Gönczy, L., & Varró, D. (2006). Modeling of reliable messaging in service oriented architecture. *Proceedings of Telcert International Workshop on Web Services Modeling and Testing.*

Gong, L., (2001). JXTA: a network programming environment, IEEE Internet Computing, May/Jun 2001, Vol. 5 (3), pp. 88-95.

Graham, S., Niblett, P., Chappell, D., Lewis, A., Nagaratnam, N., Parikh, J., et al. (2004). Web Services Brokered Notification (WS-BrokeredNotification). Retrieved December 9, 2006, from http://www.ibm.com/developerworks/library/specification/ws-notification/

Gramm, M., Ritter, A., Schiller, J. H., (2004). Efficient selection and monitoring of QoS-aware web services with the WS-QoS framework. In Proceedings of 2004 IEEE/WIC/ACM International Conference on Web Intelligence, Beijing, China, September 2004, 152-158.

Gray, J., & Reuter, A. (1993). *Transaction Processing: Concepts and Techniques.* San Francisco, CA: Morgan Kaufmann Publishers, Inc.

Graziani, P., Billi, R., Burzagli, L., Gabbanini, A., Palchetti, B., Bertini, E., Kimani, S., Sbattella, L., Barbieri, T., Bianchi, C., Batini, C. (2003). Definition of User Typologies. *MAIS internal report R 7.3.1.*

Greenfield, P., Fekete, A., Jang, J., & Kuo, D. (2003). Compensation is not enough. In *Proceedings of the 7th International Enterprise Distributed Object Computing Conference (EDOC'03)*, 232. Brisbane, Australia.

Greenfield, P., Fekete, A., Jang, J., & Kuo, D. (2003). What are the consistency requirements for B2B systems? In *Proceedings of the High Performance Transaction Systems Workshop*, Asilomar, CA.

Greenfield, P., Fekete, A., Jang, J., & Kuo, D. (2003). Compensation is not enough. In *Proceedings of the 7th IEEE International Enterprise Distributed Object Computing Conference*, Brisbane, Australia (pp. 232-239).

Greenwood, M., et al. (2003). Provenance of e-science experiments—experience from Bioinformatics. *UK OST e-Science 2nd AHM.*

Grigori, D., Casati, F., Castellanos, M., Dayal, U., Sayal, M., & Shan, M.-C. (2004). Business process intelligence. *Computers in Industry, 53*(3), 321–343. doi:10.1016/j.compind.2003.10.007

Grigori, D., Corrales, J., & Bouzeghoub, M. (2006). Behavioral matchmaking for service retrieval. *Proceedings of the IEEE International Conference on Web Services (ICWS)*, Chicago, USA, September 18-22.

Gronmo, R., & Solheim, I. (2004). Towards Modeling Web Service Composition in UML. In *Proceedings of the 2nd International Workshop on Web Services: Modeling, Architecture and Infrastructure* (WSMAI 2004) (pp. 72-86). Porto, Portugal, April 13-14, 2004.

Groth, P., Luck, M., & Moreau, L. (2004). A protocol for recording provenance in service-oriented grids. *OPODIS*.

Groth, P., Miles, S., Fang, W., Wong, S.C., Zauner, K.-P., & Moreau, L. (2005). Recording and using provenance in a protein compressibility experiment. *HPDC*.

Gruber, R. E., Krishnamurthy, B., & Panagos, E. (2001), Corba notification service: Design challenges and scalable solutions. In *Proceedings of the 17th International Conference on Data Engineering*,(pp. 13–20), *Washington, DC, USA*. IEEE Computer Society.

Guan, Z., Hernandez, F., Bangalore, P., Gray, J., Skjellum, A., Velusamy, V., et al. (2005). Grid-flow: A grid-enabled scientific workflow system with a Petri net-based interface. *Concurrency and Computation: Practice and Experience, 18*(10), 1115-1140.

Gudgin, M. (2004), Secure, reliable, transacted; innovation in web services architecture, In*Proceedings of the ACM International Conference on Management of Data* (pp. 879-880).

Gulzar, M., & Ganeshan, K. (2003). *Practical J2EE Application Architecture*. California: McGraw-Hill Osborne Media.

Gunter, D., Tierney, B., Jackson, K., Lee, J., & Stoufer, M. (2002). Dynamic monitoring of high-performance distributed applications. *HPDC*.

Gunthor, R. (1993). Extended transaction processing based on dependency rules. *International Workshop on Research Issues in Data Engineering: Interoperability in Multidatabase Systems (RIDE-IMS'93)*, April (pp.207-214).

Gupta, V., & Gupta, S. (2001). Securing the wireless Internet. *IEEE Communications Magazine, 39*(12), 68-74.

Ha, B.-H., Reijers, H. A., Bae, J., Bae, H. (2006). An Approximate Analysis of Expected Cycle Time in Business Process Execution (LNCS 4103, pp. 65-74).

Haines, R., Mckeown, M., Pickles, S. M., Pinning, R. L., Porter A. R., & Riding, M. (2005). The service architecture of the TeraGyroid experiment, *Phil. Trans. R. Soc., 363*, 1743–1755

Hale, J., Galiasso, P., Papa, M., & Shenoi, S. (1999). Security Policy Coordination for Heterogeneous Information Systems. In *Proceedings of the 15th Annual Computer Security Applications Conference (ACSAC '99)*, (pp. 219-228), Scottsdale, Arizona.

Halstead, M.H. (1977). *Elements of software science, operating, and programming systems series* (Vol. 7). New York: Elsevier.

Hamadi, R., & Benatallah, B. (2003). A Petri net-based model for web service composition. In *Proceedings of the Australasian Database Conference* (pp. 191-200). Adelaide, Australia.

Hammer, M., & Champy, J. (1993). *Re-engineering the corporation. A manifesto for business revolution*. New York: Harper Collins.

Hammouda, K. M., & Kamel, M. S. (2004). Efficient Phrase-Based Document Indexing for Web Document Clustering. *IEEE Transactions on Knowledge and Data Engineering, 16*(10), 1279–1296. doi:10.1109/TKDE.2004.58

Harrington, H. (1993). Process breakthrough: Business process improvement. *Journal of Cost Management (Fall)*, 30–43.

Hawthorne, J. (1996). On the Logic of Nonmonotonic Conditionals and Conditional Probabilities. *Journal of Philosophical Logic, 25*(2), 185–218. doi:10.1007/BF00247003

Heckel, R., Lohmann, M., & Thöne, S. (2003). Towards a UML profile for service-oriented architectures. *Proceedings of Workshop on Model Driven Architecture: Foundations and Applications.*

Heinlein, C. (2001). Workflow and process synchronization with interaction expressions and graphs. In *Proceedings of 17th International Conference on Data Engineering.*

Heitmeyer, C. L., Jeffords, R. D., & Labaw, B. G. (1996). Automated Consistency Checking of Requirements Specifications. *ACM Transactions on Software Engineering and Methodology, 5*(3), 231–261. doi:10.1145/234426.234431

Helander, J., & Xiong, Y. (2005). Secure Web services for low-cost devices. In *Eighth IEEE International Symposium on Object-Oriented Real-Time Distributed Computing* (pp. 130-139).

Herbest, J. (2000). A Machine Learning Approach to Workflow Management. In *Proceedings of the 11th European Conference on Machine Learning* (pp. 183-194). Barcelona, Spain.

Herbest, J. (2000). Dealing with Concurrency in Workflow Induction. In *Proceedings of the European Concurrent Engineering Conference*, Leicester, United Kingdom.

Herlihy, M. (1986). Optimistic concurrency control for abstract data types. In *Proceedings of the Fifth Annual ACM Symposium on Principles of Distributed Computing*, Calgary, Alberta, Canada (pp. 206-217).

Hey, T., & Trefethen, A. (2002). The UKe-Science core program and the Grid. *International Conference on Computational Science, 1*(3), 21.

Hinz, S., Schmidt, K., & Stahl, C. (2005). Transforming BPEL to Petri nets. In *Proceedings of the 3rd International Conference on Business Process Management* (*LNCS* 3649, pp. 220–235). Berlin: Springer-Verlag.

Ho, S., & Kwok, S. (2003). The attraction of personalized service for users in mobile commerce: An empirical study. *ACM SIGecom Exchanges, 3*(4),10-18,.

Hoff, H., Gronmo, R., Skogan, D., Strand, A., (2005), D7 Specification of the Visual Composition Language (VSCL), SODIUM (IST-FP6-004559) Project's Deliverable, June 2005

Hopkinson, K. M., Birman, K. P., Giovanini, R., Coury, D. V., Wang, X., & Thorp, J. S. (2003). EPOCHS: Integrated COTS Software For Agent-based Electric Power and Communication Simulation. In *Proceedings of 2003 Winter Simulation Conference*, December (pp. 1158-1166).

HORIBA. (2000). Tsuichau-mon – Light Right. Retrieved from http://www.jp.horiba.com/products_e/hip08/hip08_04.htm#6

Hsu, M. (1993). Special issue on workflow and extended transaction systems. *Bulletin of the IEEE Technical Committee on Data Engineering, 16*(2).

Huang, Y., Slominski, A., Herath, C., & Gannon, D. (2006). WS-Messenger: A Web services based messaging system for service-oriented grid computing. *CCGrid.*

Huffman, D. A. (1952). A method for the construction of minimum-redundancy codes. *Proceedings of the Institute of Radio Engineers, 40*(9), 1098–1101.

Hull, D., Zolin, E., Bovykin, A., Horrocks, I., Sattler, U., & Stevens, R. (2006). Deciding semantic matching of stateless services. *Proceedings of the 21st National Conference on Artificial Intelligence AAAI*

Hundal, S. S., & Brown, F. M. (1991). A Theory of Nonmonotonic Planning. *Proceedings of the 19th Annual Conference on Computer Science*, March (pp. 247-254).

IBM (2005). Web services data collector. Retrieved from www.alphaworks.ibm.com/tech/wsdatacollector

IBM. (2006). *IBM Rational Software Development Platform.* Retrieved August 17, 2007, from http://www.ibm.com/software/developmentplatform.

IBM. (2007). *WebSphere Telecom Web Services Server.* Retrieved December 5, 2007, from http://www-306.ibm.com/software/pervasive/serviceserver/.

IBM. (2008). *WebSphere Application Server.* Retrieved March 20, 2008, from http://www-306.ibm.com/software/webservers/appserv/was/.

IEEE. (1992). *IEEE 610, standard glossary of software engineering terminology.* New York: Institute of Electrical and Electronic Engineers.

IFEAD. The Institute for Enterprise Architecture Developments (2004). *Extended Enterprise Architecture Framework.* Retrieved February 8, 2008 from http://enterprise-architecture.info

Igaki, H., Nakamura, M., & Matsumoto, K. (2005). A Service-Oriented Framework for Networked Appliances to Achieve Appliance Interoperability and Evolution in Home Network System (short paper). In *Proc. of International Workshop on Principles of Software Evolution (IWPSE 2005)* (pp. 61-64).

IM. (2005). *Web services secure conversation language (WS-SecureConversation).* IBM, Microsoft, et al.

IMS. (2006). *3GPP TS 23.228: IP multimedia subsystem (Stage 2) standard specification.* Retrieved December 5, 2007, from http://www.3gpp.org/ftp/Specs/html-info/23228.htm

Inoue, K., Yokomori, R., Yamamoto, T., Matsushita, M., & Kusumoto, S. (2005). Ranking significance of software components based on use relations. *IEEE Transactions on Software Engineering, 31*(3), 213–225.

International Organization for Standardization. (n.d.). ISO 7498-2, *Information Processing Systems – Open Systems Interconnection – Basic Reference Model – Part 2: Security Architecture.* Retrieved Feb. 11, 2004 from http://www.iso.org/

Internet Engineering Task Force (IETF). (2004). *RFC 3851: Secure/multipurpose Internet mail extensions (S/MIME) version 3.1 message specification.* Author.

ISO. (n.d.). *Open System Interconnection- Distributed Transaction Processing (OSI-TP) Model, ISO IS 100261.*

ITU-T. (n.d.). *Recommendation X.800, Security Architecture for OSI.* Retrieved Feb. 11, 2004 from: http://www.itu.int/rec/recommendation.asp?type=items&lang=e&parent=T-REC-X.800-199103-I

Ivkovic, I., (2001), Improving Gnutella Protocol: Protocol Analysis and Research Proposals, LimeWire Gnutella Research Contest, September 2001

Jablonski, S. (1994). *MOBILE: A modular workflow model and architecture.* Proceedings of the 4th International Working Conference on Dynamic Modelling and Information Systems, Noordwijkerhout, Netherlands.

Jaeger, M. C., Rojec-Goldmann, G., & Muhl, G. (2004). QoS Aggregation for Web Service Composition using Workflow Patterns. In *EDOC '04: Proceeding of the Enterprise Distributed Object Computing Conference*, Washington, DC, USA, (pp. 149-159).

Jansen-Vullers, M. H., van der Aalst, W. M. P., & Rosemann, M. (2006). Mining Configurable Enterprise Information Systems. *Data & Knowledge Engineering, 56*(3), 195–244. doi:10.1016/j.datak.2005.03.007

Java Community Process. (2001). UML profile for Enterprise Java Beans.

Jensen, K. (1992). Colored Petri nets. In *Basic concepts.* Springer-Verlag.

Johnston, S. (2004). UML 1.4 profile for software services with a mapping to BPEL 1.0. *IBM developerWorks.*

Jones, T.C. (1986). *Programming productivity.* New York: McGraw-Hill.

Jordan, D., & Evdemon, J. (2007). Web Services Business Process Execution Language, Version 2.0, OASIS Standard. Retrieved from http://docs.oasis-open.org/wsbpel/2.0/OS/wsbpel-v2.0-OS.pdf.

Jorstad, I., Thanh, D. V., & Dustdar, S. (2004). An Analysis of Service Continuity in Mobile Services. In *Proceedings of the 2nd International Workshop on Distributed and Mobile Collaboration (DMC 2004)* (pp. 121-126). Modena, Italy, June 14-16, 2004.

Joshi, J., Aref, W., Ghafoor, A., & Spafford, E. (2001). Security models for Web-based applications. *Communications of the ACM, 44*(2), 38-44.

JSR-240. (2008). *JAIN™ SLEE API Specification.* Retrieved March 19, 2009, from http://jcp.org/aboutJava/communityprocess/final/jsr240/index.html.

Jünger, M.A., Rintelen, F., Stocker, H., Wasserman, J.D., Végh, M., Radimerski, T., Greenberg, M.E., Hafen, E. (2003). The Drosophila forkhead transcription factor FOXO mediates the reduction in cell number associated with reduced insulin signaling. *Journal Biol., 2*(3), 20.

Jürjens, J. (2002). UMLsec: Extending UML for secure systems development. *Proceedings of ACM/IEEE International Conference on Unified Modeling Language.*

JXTA Org, (2006) Project JXTA, available at http://www.jxta.org/, accessed 21 December 2006

Kaden Control Lab. (2006). AVT Series. Retrieved from http://d-purasu.hp.infoseek.co.jp/

Kahn, G. & MacQueen, D. B. (1977). Coroutines and Networks of Parallel Processes, *Information Processing* 77, B. Gilchrist, editor, North-Holland Publishing Co.

Kamath, M., & Ramamritham, K. (1998). Failure handling and coordinated execution of concurrent workflows. In *Proceedings of the IEEE International Conference on Data Engineering,* Orlando, FL (pp. 334-341).

Kandaswamy, G., Fang, L., Huang, Y., Shirasuna, S., Marru, S., & Gannon, D. (2006). Building Web services for scientific grid applications. *IBM Journal of Research and Development, 50*(2/3), 249–260.

Kangasharju, J. (2007). Efficient implementation of XML security for mobile devices. In *IEEE International Conference on Web Services* (pp. 134-141). Salt Lake City, UT: Institute of Electrical and Electronic Engineers.

Kangasharju, J., Tarkoma, S., & Lindholm, T. (2005). Xebu: A binary format with schema-based optimizations for XML data. In A. H. H. Ngu, M. Kitsuregawa, E. Neuhold, J.-Y. Chung, & Q. Z. Sheng (Eds.), *Sixth International Conference on Web Information Systems Engineering* (LNCS 3806, pp. 528-535). New York: Springer-Verlag.

Kapfhammer, G. M., & Soffa, M. L. (2003). A family of test adequacy criteria for database-driven applications. In *Proceedings of the 9th European software engineering con-*

ference held jointly with 11th ACM SIGSOFT international symposium on Foundations of software engineering (ESEC/FSE 2003) (pp. 98–107). New York: ACM Press.

Kart, F., Moser, L. E., & Melliar-Smith, P. M. (2008). Managing and integrating supply and demand using Web Services and the Service Oriented Architecture. In Y. Huo and F. Jia (Eds.), *Supply Chain, The Way to Flat Organization* (pp. 259-282). Vienna, Austria: IN-TECH Education and Publishing.

Kavantzas, N., Burdett, D., Ritzinger, G., Fletcher, T., Lafon, Y.,Barreto, C., (2005), Web Service Choreography Description Language (WS-CDL) ver 1.0, Nov 2005, http://www.w3.org/TR/ws-cdl-10/

Keckel, R., & Lohmann, M. (2005). Towards contract-based testing of Web services. *Electronic Notes in Theoretical Computer Science, 116*, 145–156. doi:10.1016/j.entcs.2004.02.073

Keidar, I., & Dolev, D. (1995). Increasing the Resilience of Atomic Commit, at No Additional Cost. In *Proceedings of the Fourteenth ACM SIGACT-SIGMOD-SIGART Symposium on Principles of Database Systems* (San Jose, California, United States, May 22 - 25, 1995). PODS '95 (pp. 245-254). New York: ACM Press.

Keidar, I., Sussman, J., Marzullo, K., & Dolev, D. (2002). Moshe: A group membership service for WANs. *ACM Transactions on Computer Systems, 20*(3), 191–238. doi:10.1145/566340.566341

Kent, S., & Atkinson, R. (1998). *RFC 2401: Security architecture for the Internet protocol.* Internet Engineering Task Force.

Khurana, H., Gavrilal, S., Bobba, R., Koleva, R., Sonalker, A., Dinu, E., Gligor, V., & Baras, J. (2003). Integrated Security Services for Dynamic Coalitions. In *Proceedings of the DARPA Information Survivability Conference and Exposition (DISCEX'03),* Vol. 2, (pp. 38-40), Washington D.C..

Kiczales, G., & Mezini, M. (2005). Aspect-oriented programming and modular reasoning. In *Proceedings of the 27th International Conference on Software Engineering,* St. Louis, MO. ACM Press.

Kiepuszewski, B., ter Hofstede, A.H.M., & Bussler, C. (2000). On structured workflow modelling. In *Proceedings of 12th International Conference on Advanced Information Systems Engineering* (*LNCS* 1789, pp. 431–445). Berlin: Springer-Verlag.

Kindler, E. (2006). On the semantics of EPCs: Resolving the vicious circle. *Data & Knowledge Engineering, 56*(1), 23–40.

Kitchenham, B., Pfleeger, S.L., & Fenton, N. (1996). Toward a framework for measurement validation. *IEEE Transactions of Software Engineering, 21*(12), 929–944.

Klein, J. (1991). Advanced Rule-driven Transaction Management. In . *Proceedings of IEEE COMPCON, 1991*(February), 562–567.

Klien, E., Einspanier, U., Lutz, M., & Hübner, S. (2004). An Architecture for Ontology-based Discovery and Retrieval of Geographic Information. In *AGILE '04: Proceeding of the 7th Conference on Geographic Information Science,* Heraklion, Greece (pp. 179-188).

Kochut, K.J. (1999). *METEOR model version 3.* Athens, GA: Large Scale Distributed Information Systems Lab, Department of Computer Science, University of Georgia.

Kochut, K.J., Sheth, A.P., & Miller, J.A. (1999). *ORBWork: A CORBA-based fully distributed, scalable and dynamic workflow enactment service for METEOR.* Athens, GA: Large Scale Distributed Information Systems Lab, Department of Computer Science, University of Georgia.

Koehler, J., & Hauser, R. (2004). Untangling Unstructured Cyclic Flows — A Solution Based on Continuations. In *On the Move to Meaningful Internet Systems 2004: CoopIS, DOA, and ODBASE* (LNCS 3290, pp. 121–138). Berlin: Springer-Verlag.

Kojo, M., Raatikainen, K., Liljeberg, M., Kiiskinen, J., & Alanko, T. (1997). An efficient transport service for slow wireless telephone links. *IEEE Journal on Selected Areas in Communication, 15*(7), 1337-1348.

Kolberg, M., Magill, E. H., & Wilson, M. (2003). Compatibility Issues between Services Supporting Networked Appliances. *IEEE Communications Magazine, 41*(11), 136–147. doi:10.1109/MCOM.2003.1244934

Koshutanski, H., & Massacci, F. (2003). An Access Control Framework for Business Processes for Web Services. In *Proceedings of ACM Workshop on XML Security* (pp. 15-24). George W. Johnson Center at George Mason University, Fairfax, Va, USA.

Kreger, H. (2003). Fulfilling the web services promise. *Communications of the ACM, 46*(6), 29–34. doi:10.1145/777313.777334

Kritikos, K., & Plexousakis, D. (2006). Semantic QoS Metric Matching. In *ECOWS '06: Proceeding of the European Conference on Web Services*, Washington, DC, USA (pp. 265–274).

Kruchten, P. (2003). *The Rational Unified Process: An Introduction* (3rd ed.). Massachusetts: Addison Wesley.

Kulchenko, P. Reese. B. (2004). SOAP:Lite - Client and server side SOAP implementation. Retrieved from http://www.soaplite.com/

Kung, H. T., & Robinson, J. T. (1981). On optimistic methods for concurrency control. *ACM Transactions on Database Systems, 6*(2), 213–226. doi:10.1145/319566.319567

Lakshmanan, K.B., Jayaprakash, S., & Sinha, P.K. (1991). Properties of control-flow complexity measures. *IEEE Transactions on Software Engineering Archive, 17*(12), 1289–1295.

Langworthy, D. (2005). *WS-AtomicTransaction.*

Langworthy, D. (2005). *WS-BusinessActivity.*

Langworthy, D. (2005). *WS-Coordination.*

Lanning, D.L., & Khoshgoftaar, T.M. (1994). Modeling the relationship between source code complexity and maintenance difficulty. *Computer, 27*(9), 35–41.

Lassen, K.B., & van der Aalst, W.M.P. (2006). WorkflowNet-2BPEL4WS: A tool for translating unstructured workflow processes to readable BPEL. In *On the Move to Meaningful Internet Systems 2006: CoopIS, DOA, and ODBASE* (*LNCS* 4275, pp. 127–144). Berlin: Springer-Verlag.

Lauer, P. E., & Campbell, R. H. (1975). A description of path expressions by Petri nets. In *Proceedings of the Second ACM SIGACT-SIGPLAN Symposium on Principles of Programming Languages*, Palo Alto, CA. ACM Press.

Lee, A.J., Winslett, M., Basney, J., & Welch, V. (2006). Traust: A Trust Negotiation-Based Authorization Service for Open Systems. In *Proceedings of the 11th ACM Symposium on Access Control Models and Technologies,* (pp. 39-48), Lake Tahoe, California.

Lewis, G., Morris, E., O'Brien, L., Smith, D., & Wrage, L. (2005). *SMART: The Service-Oriented Migration and Reuse Technique* (Tech Rep CMU/SEI-2005-TN-029). Software Engineering Institute.

Leymann, F. (2001). Web services flow language (WSFL 1.0). IBM Software Group. Retrieved from http://www-306.ibm.com/software/solutions/webservices/pdf/WSFL.pdf

Leymann, F., & Roller, D. (2000). *Production workflow: concepts and techniques*. New Jersey: Prentice Hall PRT.

LG Electronics (2008). LGE Home Network. Retrieved from http://www.lge.com/products/homenetwork/html/lge_homenetwork.jsp

Li P., Chen Y., & Romanovsky A. (2006). Measuring the dependability of Web services for use in e-Science experiments. *Proceedings of 3rd International Service Availability Symposium*, Helsinki, Finland, May 15-16.

Li, L., Liu, C., & Wang, J. (2005). Deriving Transactional Properties of CompositeWeb Services. In *Proceedings of IEEE International Conference on Web Services* (pp. 631-638). Salt Lake City, USA.

Li, P., Hayward, K., Jennings, C. et al. (2004). Association of variations in I kappa b-epsilon with Graves' disease using classical methodologies and myGrid methodologies. In *UK e-Science All Hands Meeting.*

Li, Y., Pan, Y., Zhang, L., Xie, B., & Sun, J.S. (2006). *Ranking component retrieval results by leveraging user history information.* Proceedings of the 18th International Conference on Software Engineering and Knowledge Engineering (SEKE), 284–289.

Li, Z. Sun, W., Jiang, Z., & Zhang, X (2005). BPEL4WS unit testing: framework and implementation. In *Proceedings of Internatonal Conference on Web Services (ICWS 2005)* (pp. 103-110). Los Alamitos, California: IEEE Computer Society.

Lian, W., Cheung, W. W., Mamoulis, N., & Yiu, S. (2004). An Efficient and Scalable Algorithm for Clustering XML Documents by Structure. *IEEE Transactions on Knowledge and Data Engineering, 16*(1), 82–96. doi:10.1109/TKDE.2004.1264824

Liang, F. (2007). On the Robustness of Metamorphic Testing. MSc Thesis. Department of Computer Science, The University of Hong Kong.

Licciardi, C. A., & Falcarin, P. (2003). Analysis of NGN Service Creation Technologies. In *IEC Annual Review of Communications, 56* (pp. 537-551). Chicago: IEC (International Engineering Consortium).

Liefke, H., & Suciu, D. (2000). XMill: an efficient compressor for XML data. In *Proceedings of the 2000 ACM SIGMOD International Conference on Management of Data, Dallas, USA* (pp. 153–164).

Limthanmaphon, B., & Zhang, Y. (2004). Web Service composition transaction management. In *Proceedings of the 15th Australasian Database Conference, Conferences in Research and Practice in Information Technology*, 27, Dunedin, New Zealand (pp. 171-179).

List, B., & Korherr, B. (2005). A UML 2 profile for business process modelling. *Proceedings of ACM International Conference on Conceptual Modeling Workshop on Best Practices of UML at the International Conference on Conceptual Modeling.*

Little, M. (2003). Transactions and web services. *Communications, 46*(10), 49–54.

Little, M., & Wilkinson, A. (Eds.). (2007). Web Service Atomic Transaction Version 1.1. Retrieved April 16, 2007 from http://docs.oasis-open.org/ws-tx/wstx-wsat-1.1-spec-os.pdf.

Liu, D.T., Franklin, M.J., Garlick, J., & Abdulla, G.M. (2005). Scaling up data-centric middleware on a cluster computer. *Technical Report, Lawrence Livermore National Laboratory.*

Liu, R., & Kumar, A. (2005). An analysis and taxonomy of unstructured workflows. In *Proceedings of the 3rd International Conference on Business Process Management* (*LNCS* 3649, pp. 268–284). Berlin: Springer-Verlag.

Lodderstedt, T., Basin, D., & Doser, J. (2002). SecureUML: A UML-based modeling language for model-driven security. *Proceedings of ACM/IEEE International Conference on Unified Modeling Language.*

Lohmann, N., Massuthe, P., Stahl, C., & Weinberg, D. (2006). Analyzing interacting BPEL processes. In *Proceedings of the 4th International Conference on Business Process Management* (*LNCS* 4102, pp. 17–32). Berlin: Springer-Verlag.

Loke, S. W. (2003). Service-Oriented Device Echology Workflows. In *Proc. of 1st Int'l Conf. on Service-Oriented Computing (ICSOC2003)* (LNCS 2910, pp. 559-574).

Long, D. T., & Page, D. C. (2007). Supporting Portable Applications with JAIN SLEE. In Telecommunications Networks and Applications Conference (pp. 454-459). Australasian: ATNAC.

Looker, N., & Xu, J. (2003). Assessing the Dependability of SOAP RPC based Web Services by Fault Injection. In *Proceedings of IEEE International Workshop on Object-Oriented, Real-Time and Dependable Systems* (pp 163-170). Los Alamitos, California: IEEE Computer Society Press.

Lopes, C., & Lieberherr, K. (1994). Abstracting function-to-process relations in concurrent object-oriented applications. In *Proceedings of the European Conference on Object-Oriented Programming (ECOOP'94)* (LNCS 821). Springer-Verlag.

Lord, P., Alper, P., Wroe, C., & Goble C. (2005). Feta: A lightweight architecture for user oriented semantic service discovery. *Proceedings of the European Semantic Web Conference (ESWC).*

LP. (2005). *LP_SOLVE: Linear Programming Code.* Retrieved March 1, 2006, from http://www.cs.sunysb.edu/~algorith/implement/lpsolve/implement.shtml

Ludäscher, B., et al. (2006). Scientific workflow management and the Kepler system. *Concurrency and Computation: Practice and Experience, 18*(10), 1039–1065.

Lum, W. Y., & Lau, F. C. M. (2003). User-Centric Content Negotiation for Effective Adaptation Service in Mobile Computing. *IEEE Transactions on Software Engineering, 29*(12), 1000–1111.

Maarek, Y.S., Berry, D.M., & Kaiser, G.E. (1991). An information retrieval approach for automatically constructing software libraries. *IEEE Transactions on Software Engineering, 17*(8), 800–813.

Manasce, D. (2004). Composing Web Service: A QoS View. *IEEE Internet Computing, 8*(6), 88–90. doi:10.1109/MIC.2004.57

Marcos, E., Castro, V., & Vela, B. (2003). Representing Web services with UML: A case study. *Proceedings of UNITN/Springer International Conference on Service Oriented Computing.*

Maron, O, & Lozano-Pérez, T. (1998). A framework for multiple-instance learning. *Advances in Neural Information Processing Systems 10*, 570–576.

Maron, O., & Ratan, A.L. (1998). *Multiple-instance learning for natural scene classification.* Proceedings of the 15th International Conference on Machine Learning, Madison, WI, 341–349.

Martin, D., Burstein, M., Hobbs, J., Lassila, O., McDermott, D., McIlraith, S., Narayanan, S., Paolucci, M., Parsia, B., Payne, T., Sirin, E., Srinivasan, N., Sycara, K., (2004) OWL-S: Semantic Markup for Web Services, W3C submission, Nov. 2004 http://www.w3.org/Submission/OWL-S/

Martin, E., Basu, S., & Xie, T. (2007). Automated Testing and Response Analysis of Web Services. In *Proceedings of 2007 IEEE International Conference on Web Services (ICWS 2007)* (pp. 647-654). Los Alamitos, California: IEEE Computer Society Press.

Matheus, C. J., Kokar, M. M., & Baclawski, K. (2003). A core ontology for situation awareness. In *Proceedings of 6th International Conference on Information Fusion,* July (pp. 545-552).

Matheus, C. J., Kokar, M. M., Baclawski, K., & Letkowski, J. (2003). Constructing RuleML-based domain theories on top of OWL ontologies. In *Proceedings of 2nd International Workshop on Rules and Rule Markup Languages for the Semantic Web*, October (pp. 81-94).

Maurino, A., Pernici, B., & Schreiber, F. A. (2003). Adaptive channel behavior in financial information system. In *CAiSE '03: Proceeding of the Conference on Advanced Information System Engineering,* Klagenfurt/Velden, Austria (pp. 109-112).

Maximilien, E., & Singh, M. P. (2004). A framework and ontology for dynamic web services selection. *IEEE Internet Computing, 8*(5), 84–93. doi:10.1109/MIC.2004.27

May, D., & Shepherd, R. (1984). The transputer implementation of occam. In *Proceedings of the International Conference on Fifth, Generation Computer Systems, Tokyo,* 1984.

McCabe, T. (1976). A complexity measure. *IEEE Transactions of Software Engineering, SE-2*(4), 308–320.

McCabe, T.J. (1977). A complexity measure. *Transactions on Software Engineering, 13*(10), 308–320.

McCabe, T.J., & Watson, A.H. (1994). Software complexity. *Crosstalk, Journal of Defense Software Engineering, 7*(12), 5–9.

McCarthy, J. (2001). *Situation calculus with concurrent events and narrative.* Retrieved December 4, 2005, from http://www-formal.stanford.edu/jmc/narrative.html

McCarthy, J., & Hayes, P. J. (1969). Some philosophical problems from the standpoint of artificial intelligence. *Machine Intelligence, 4,* 463–502.

McGovern, J. (2003). *Java Web Services Architecture.* New York: Morgan Kaufmann.

McGovern, J., Ambler, S. W., Stevens, M. E., Linn, J., Sharan, V., & Jo, E. K. (2003). *A Practical Guide to Enterprise Architecture.* New Jersey: Prentice Hall PTR.

McGuinness, D., Harmelen, F. (2004), OWL Web Ontology Language Overview, W3C Recommendation, February 2004, available at http://www.w3.org/TR/owl-features/

Mecella, M., & Pernici, B. (2003). Designing wrapper components for e-services in integrating heterogeneous systems . *The VLDB Journal, 10*(1), 2–15.

Medeiros, C. B., Perez-Alcazar, J., Digiampietri, L., Pastorello Jr, G. Z., Santanche, A., Torres, R. S., Madeira, E., & Bacarin, E. (2005). WOODSS and the Web: Annotating and reusing scientific workflows. *SIGMOD Record Special Issue on Scientific Workflows, 34*(3), September.

Medvidovic, N., Rosenblum, D., Gamble, R., (1999), Bridging Heterogeneous Software Interoperability Platforms, Technical Report, USC-CSE-99-529, Center for Software Engineering, USC, November 1999

Mehrotra, S., Rastogi, R., Korth, H. F., & Silberschatz, A. (1992). A Transaction Model for Multidatabase Systems. In *Proceedings of International Conference on Distributed Computing Systems* (pp. 56-63). Yokohama, Japan.

Mehrotra, S., Rastogi, R., Silberschatz, A., & Korth, H. (1992), A transaction model for multidatabase systems. In *Proceedings of the 12th IEEE International Conference on Distributed Computing Systems (ICDCS92)* (pp. 56-63). Yokohama, Japan.

Mei, L., Chan, W. K., & Tse, T. H. (2008). Data flow testing of service-oriented workflow applications. In *Proceedings of the 30th International Conference on Software Engineering (ICSE 2008).* New York, NY, USA: ACM Press.

Melliar-Smith, P. M., & Moser, L. E. (2007). Achieving atomicity for Web Services using commutativity of actions. *Journal of Universal Computer Science, 13*(8), 1094–1109.

Mendling, J., Lassen, K.B., & Zdun, U. (2006). Transformation strategies between block-oriented and graph-oriented process modelling languages. In *Multikonferenz Wirtschaftsinformatik 2006, Band 2* (pp. 297–312). Berlin: GITO-Verlag.

Menzel, C., Mayer, R.J., & Edwards, D.D. (1994). IDEF3 process descriptions and their semantics. In C.H. Dagli & A. Kusiak (Eds.), *Intelligent systems in design and manufacturing* (pp. 172-212). New York: ASME.

Messmer, B.T., & Bunke, H. (2000). Efficient subgraph isomorphism detection: A decomposition approach. *IEEE Transaction on Knowledge and Data Engineering, 12*(2), 307–323.

Metzger, A. (2004). Feature Interactions in Embedded Control Systems. *Computer Networks, 45*(5), Special Issue on Directions in Feature Interaction Research, 625-644.

Microsoft Corporation (1996), Distributed Component Object Model Protocol-DCOM/1.0, draft, November 1996, available at http://www.microsoft.com/Com/resources/comdocs.asp

Miers, D., Harmon, P., & Hall., C. (2006). The 2006 BPM suites report, September. Retrieved from http://www.bptrends.com

Miles, S., Groth, P., Branco, M., & Moreau, L. (2005). The requirements of recording and using provenance in e-science experiments. *Technical Report, Electronics and Computer Science, University of Southampton.*

Mili, A., Mili, R., & Mittermeier, R. (1997). Storing and retrieving software components: A refinement-based system. *IEEE Transactions on Software Engineering, 23*(7), 445–460.

Mili, H., Valtchev, P., Di Sciullo, A.-M., & Gabrini, P. (2001). *Automating the indexing and retrieval of reusable software components.* Proceedings of the 6th International Workshop (NLDB 01), Madrid, Spain, 75–86.

Milicia, G., & Sassone, V. (2005). Jeeg: Temporal constraints for the synchronization of concurrent objects. *Concurrency and Computation: Practice and Experience, 17*(5-6), 539-572.

Miller, G. (1956). The magical number seven, plus or minus two: Some limits on our capacity for processing information. *The Psychological Review.*

Miller, J.A., Palaniswami, D., Sheth, A.P., Kochut, K.J., & Singh, H. (1998). WebWork: METEOR2's Web-based workflow management system. *Journal of Intelligence Information Management Systems: Integrating Artificial Intelligence and Database Technologies (JIIS), 10*(2), 185–215.

Milner, R. (1999). *Communicating and Mobile Systems: the π-Calculus.* Cambridge University Press.

Ming, L., Xiao-Bing, X., & Zhou, Z. (2004). Chinese Web index page recommendation based on multi-instance learning. *Journal of Software, 15*(9), 1328–1335.

Misra, S., & Misra, A.K. (2004). *Evaluating cognitive complexity measure with Weyuker properties.* Proceedings of the Third IEEE International Conference on Cognitive Informatics (ICCI'04), Victoria, Canada.

MobiCents Project. (2007). *MobiCents: The Open Source VoIP Middleware Platform.* Retrieved December 5, 2007, from https://mobicents.dev.java.net/

Montagut, F., Molva, R., & Golega, S. T. (2008). Automating the Composition of transactional Web Services. *International Journal of Web Services Research, 5*(1), 24–41.

Morasca, S., Briand, L., Weyuker, E., & Zelkowitz, M. (1997). Comments on "towards a framework for software measurement validation.". *IEEE Transactions on Software Engineering, 23*(3), 187–188.

Moreau, L., & Foster, I. (2006). *Provenance and annotation of data.* Proceedings of the International Provenance and Annotation Workshop, *LNCS* 4145.

Moreau, L., & Ludascher, B. (2007). The first provenance challenge. *Concurrency and Control: Practice and Experience.*

Moser, L. E., & Melliar-Smith, P. M. (2009). Service Oriented Architecture and Web Services. In Ben Wah (Ed.), *Encyclopedia of Computer Science and Engineering* (pp. 2504-2511). Hoboken, NJ: John Wiley & Sons.

Moses, T. (2005). Extensible Access Control Markup Language (XACML), Version 2.0, OASIS Standard, 2005. Retrieved from http://docs.oasis-open.org/xacml/2.0/access_control-xacml-2.0-core-spec-os.pdf

Mukhi, N. K., Konuru, R., & Curbera, F. (2004). Cooperative middleware specialization for service oriented architectures. In *Proceedings of the 13th international World Wide Web conference on Alternate track papers & posters (WWW 2004)* (pp.206–215). New York: ACM Press.

Murata, M., Lee, D., & Mani, M. (2001). Taxonomy of XML schema languages using formal language theory. In *Proceedings of Extreme Markup Languages, August 2001, Montreal, Canada* (pp. 153-166).

Murata, T. (1989). Petri nets: Properties, analysis and applications. In *Proceedings of the IEEE, 77*(4), 541-580.

Murer, T., Scherer, D., Wuertz, A., (1996), Improving component interoperability information, Proceedings of Workshop on Component-Oriented Programming (WCOP'96) at 10th European Conference on Object-Oriented Programming (ECOOP'96), pp. 150–158, dpunkt, July 1996

Muse (2007). Apache Muse project website. Retrieved February 23, 2009, from http://ws.apache.org/muse/

Mylopoulos, J., & Lau, D. (2004). Designing Web Services with Tropos. In *ICWS '04: Proceeding of the IEEE International Conference on Web Services*, Washington, DC, USA (p. 306).

Nakamura, M., Fukuoka, Y., Igaki, H., & Matsumoto, M. (2008). Implementing Multi-Vendor Home Network System with Vendor-Neutral Services and Dynamic Service Binding. In *IEEE International Conference on Services Computing (SCC 2008)* (pp. 275-282).

Nakamura, M., Igaki, H., & Matsumoto, K. (2005). Feature Interactions in Integrated Services ofNetworked Home Appliances -An Object-Oriented Approach-. In *Proc. of Int'l. Conf. on Feature Interactions in Telecommunication Networks and Distributed Systems (ICFI'05)* (pp. 236-251).

Nakamura, M., Tanaka, A., Igaki, H., Tamada, T., & Matsumoto, K. (2008). Constructing Home Network Systems and Integrated Services Using Legacy Home Appliances and Web Services. [JWSR]. *International Journal of Web Services Research*, *5*(1), 82–98.

Nakamura, Y., Tatsubori, M., Imamura, T., & Ono, K. (2005). Model-driven security based on a Web services security architecture. *Proceedings of IEEE International Conference on Services Computing.*

NANO Media Inc. (2005). App-rimo-con. Retrieved from http://www.nanomedia.jp/english/service/s02.html

Narayanan, S, & McIlraith, S. (2003). Analysis and Simulation of Web Services. *Computer Networks*, *42*(5), 675-693.

Narayanan, S., & McIlraith, S. A. (2002). Simulation, verification and automated composition of Web services. In *Proceedings of the 11th International Conference on World Wide Web*, Honolulu, HI. ACM Press.

Nejdl, W., Wolf, B., Qu, C., Decker, S., Sintek, M., Naeve, A., Nilsson, M., Palmer, M., Risch, T., (2001), EDUTELLA: A P2P Networking Infrastructure Based on RDF, Edutella White Paper, November 2001, available at http://edutella.jxta.org/reports/edutella-whitepaper.pdf

Newmarch, J. (2005) UPnP services and Jini clients. In Proceedings of the 2005 Conference on Information Systems: Next Generations, ISNG 2005, Las Vegas, Nevada, USA.

News On Feeds. (2008). List of news aggregators. Retrieved from http://www.newsonfeeds.com/faq/aggregators

Newton, R., Morrisett, G., & Welsh, M. (2007). The regiment macroprogramming system. In *Proceedings of the 6th International Conference on Information Processing in Sensor Networks (IPSN'07)*, April (pp. 489-498).

Nezhad, H.R. M., Benatallah, B., Casati, F., Toumani, F., (2006), Web service interoperability specifications, IEEE Computer, vol. 39 no. 5, May 2006, pp 24-32

Niedermeier, U., Heuer, J., Hutter, A., Stechele, W., & Kaup, A. (2002). An MPEG-7 tool for compression and streaming of XML data. In *Proceedings of the IEEE International Conference on Multimedia and Expo, August 2002, Lausanne, Switzerland* (pp. 521–524).

Noy, N. F., Fergerson, R. W., & Musen, M. A. (2000). The Knowledge Model of Protégé-2000: Combining Interoperability and Flexibility. In *EKAW '00: Proceeding of the 12th European Workshop on Knowledge Acquisition, Modeling and Management*, London, UK (pp. 17–32).

Noy, N. F., Sintek, M., Decker, S., Crubezy, M., Fergerson, R. W., & Musen, M. A. (2001). Creating semantic web contents with protege-2000. *IEEE Intelligent Systems*, *16*, 60–71. doi:10.1109/5254.920601

O'Grady, S. (2004). *SOA meets compliance: compliance oriented architecture.* White paper, RedMonk.

O'Neill, M., Hallam-Baker, P., Cann, S.M., Sherma, M., Simon, E., Watters, P.A. & White, A. (2003). *Web Services Security.* McGraw-Hill/Osborne.

OASIS (2006). Web Services Business Process Execution Language Version 2.0 (Committee Draft).

OASIS (2006). *Web Services Security: SOAP Message Security 1.1 (WS-Security 2004).* OASIS Standard Specification, February 1. Retrieved March 28, 2006 from http://www.oasis-open.org/committees/download.php/16790/wss-v1.1-spec-os-SOAPMessageSecurity.pdf

OASIS. (2005). Universal Description, Discovery and Integration (UDDI) version 3.0.2. Retrieved from http://uddi.org/pubs/uddi_v3.htm.

Oba, K., Hashimoto, M., Fujikura, S., & Munehira, T. (2005). The status quo and challenges of service-oriented architecture based application design. *Proceedings of IPSJ Workshop on Software Engineering.*

Object Management Group (2006). Business Process Modeling Notation (BPMN) Version 1.0 (OMG Final Adopted Specification).

Object Management Group (OMG). (2005). *Wireless access and terminal mobility in CORBA, version 1.2.* Needham, MA: Author.

Object Management Group. (2003). Common warehouse metamodel, version 1.1.

Object Management Group. (2004). UML 2.0 super structure specification.

Object Management Group. (2005). Business process definition metamodel.

Object Management Group. (2005). UML profile for modeling quality of service and fault tolerance characteristics and mechanisms.

Object Management Group. (2006). Business process modeling notation, version 1.0.

Object Management Group. (2006). UML profile and metamodel for services, request for proposal.

Object Management Group. (2006) UML profile for data distribution service, request for proposal.

Object Management Group. (2007) Data Distribution Service for Real-time Systems, version 1.2.

Offutt, J., & Xu, W. (2004). Generating test cases for Web services using data perturbation. Workshop on testing, analysis and verification of web services (TAV-WEB), *SIGSOFT Software Engineering Notes, 29*(5), 1-10.

Oinn, T., Greenwood, M., Addis, M,. Alpdemir, M., Ferris, J., Glover, K., et al. (2005). Taverna: Lessons in creating a workflow environment for the life sciences. *Concurrency and Computation: Practice and Experience Special issue on Scientific Workflows.*

OMA. (2007). *Open Mobile Alliance.* Retrieved December 5, 2007, from http://www.openmobilealliance.org

OMG (2006). CORBA component model v4.0. *Technical Report, OMG.*

OMG. (2004). *UML Profile for Modeling Quality of Service, Fault Tolerance Characteristics, Mechanisms.* Retrieved June 14, 2005, from http://www.omg.org/docs/ptc/04-06-01.pdf

OMG. Object Management Group (2002). *Model Driven Architecture.* http://www.omg.org/mda. (February 8 2008).

OpenCloud. (2008). *Rhino 2.0 Developer Preview Release.* Retrieved December 5, 2007, from http://www.opencloud.com/products/rhino-kit/dp1/docs/index.html

Organization for the Advancement of Structured Information Standards. (2003). Web services business process execution language.

Organization for the Advancement of Structured Information Standards. (2004). Web service reliability 1.1.

Organization for the Advancement of Structured Information Standards. (2004). Web service reliable messaging.

Organization for the Advancement of Structured Information Standards. (2005). Web services security policy language.

Organization for the Advancement of Structured Information Standards (OASIS). (2004). *Web services security: SOAP message security 1.0.* Billerica, MA: Author.

Oriol, M. (2002) Peer Services: From Description to Invocation. In Proceedings of the 2002 International Workshop on Agents and Peer-to-Peer Computing, July 2002, Bologna, Italy, Springer Berlin / Heidelberg, LNCS 2530/2003, 21-32

Ortiz, G., & Hernández, J. (2006). Toward UML profiles for Web services and their extra-functional properties. *Proceedings of IEEE International Conference on Web Services.*

OSGi. (2007). OSGi™ - The Dynamic Module System for Java. Retrieved February 23, 2009, from http://www.osgi.org/

Ostertag, E., Hendler, J., Prieto-Diaz, R., & Braun, C. (1992). Computing similarity in a reuse library system: An AI-based approach. *ACM Transactions on Software Engineering and Methodology, 1*(3), 205–228.

Ostrowski, K., & Birman, K. P. (2006). Extensible Web Services Architecture for Notification in Large-Scale Systems. In *Proceedings of the IEEE international Conference on Web Services (ICWS'06) - Volume 00* (September 18 - 22, 2006). ICWS (pp. 383-392). IEEE Computer Society.

Ostrowski, K., & Birman, K. P. (2006). Scalable Group Communication System for Scalable Trust. In *Proceedings of the First ACM Workshop on Scalable Trusted Computing*

(Alexandria, Virginia, USA, November 3, 2006). STC '06 (pp. 3-6). New York: ACM Press.

Ostrowski, K., & Birman, K. P. (2006). *Scalable Publish-Subscribe in a Managed Framework.* Cornell University Technical Report.

Ostrowski, K., Birman, K. P., & Dolev, D. (2006). *Properties Framework and Typed Endpoints for Scalable Group Communication.* Cornell University Technical Report.

Ostrowski, K., Birman, K. P., Dolev, D., & Ahnn, J.-H. (2008). *Programming with Live Distributed Objects.* Submitted to the European Conference on Object-Oriented Programming (ECOOP'08).

Ould, M.A. (1995). *Business processes: Modelling and analysis for re-engineering and improvement.* Chichester, England: John Wiley & Sons.

Ouyang, C., Dumas, M., Breutel, S., & ter Hofstede, A.H.M. (2006). Translating standard process models to BPEL. In *Proceedings of 18th International Conference on Advanced Information Systems Engineering* (*LNCS* 4001, pp. 417–432). Berlin: Springer-Verlag.

Ouyang, C., Dumas, M., ter Hofstede, A.H.M., & van der Aalst, W.M.P. (2006). From BPMN process models to BPEL Web services. In *Proceedings of the 4th International Conference on Web Services* (pp. 285–292). IEEE Computer Society.

Ouyang, C., Dumas, M., van der Aalst, W.M.P., & ter Hofstede, A.H.M. (2006). *From business process models to process-oriented software systems: The BPMN to BPEL way.* (Tech. Rep. BPM-06-27, BPMcenter.org). Retrieved March 1, 2007, from http://is.tm.tue.nl/staff/wvdaalst/BPMcenter/reports/2006/ BPM-06-27.pdf

Ouyang, C., van der Aalst, W. M. P., Breutel, S., Dumas, M., ter Hofstede, A. H. M., & Verbeek, H. M. W. (2005). *Formal semantics and analysis of control flow in WS-BPEL* (Rep. No. BPM-05-13). BPM Center. Retrieved from http://BPMcenter.org

OWL Services Coalition. (2003). *OWL-S: Semantic Markup for Web Services.*

Pactolus (2001). RapidFLEX™ Service Creation Environment. Retrieved December 5, 2007, from http://www.pactolus.com/

Pahl, C., & Casey, M. (2003). Ontology support for web service processes. In ESEC/FSE-11: Proceeding of the 9th European software engineering conference held jointly with 11th ACM SIGSOFT international symposium on Foundations of software engineering, New York, NY, USA (pp. 208–216).

Pallickara, S., Fox, G., Yildiz, B., Pallickara, S.L., Patel, S., & Yemme, D. (2005). On the costs for reliable messaging in Web/grid service environments. *e-Science.*

Pan, Y., Wang, L., Zhang, L., Xie, B., & Yang, F.Q. (2004). *Relevancy based semantic interoperation of reuse repositories.* Proceedings of the 12th ACM SIGSOFT Symposium on Foundations of Software Engineering (FSE), 211–220.

Panasonic Electric Works, Ltd. (2008). Lifinity. Retrieved from http://denko.panasonic.biz/Ebox/kahs/index.html (in Japanese)

Pantazoglou, M., Tsalgatidou, A., and Athanasopoulos, G. (2006), Discovering Web Services and JXTA Peer-to-Peer Services in a Unified Manner, In Proceedings of the 4th International Conference on Service Oriented Computing, December 2006, Chicago, USA, Eds. A. Dan and W. Lamersdorf, 104-115

Paolucci, M., & Kawamura, T. (2002). *Importing the Semantic Web in UDDI.* Proceedings of the E-Services Semantic Web Workshop (ESSW 2002), 225–236.

Paolucci, M., Kawamura, T., Payne, T.R., & Sycara, K. (2002). *Semantic matching of Web services capabilities.* Proceedings of the First International Semantic Web Conference (ISWC), Sardinia, Italy, 333–347.

Papazoglou, M. (2003). Service-oriented computing: concepts, characteristics and directions. *Proceedings of IEEE International Conference on Web Information Systems Engineering.*

Papazoglou, M. P., & Georgakopoulos, D. (2003). Service-Oriented Computing. *Communications of the ACM, 46*(10), 25–28. doi:10.1145/944217.944233

Papazoglou, M., Krämer, B., Yang, J., (2004), Leveraging Web Services and Peer-to-Peer Networks, Book Chapter in Advanced Information Systems, Feb 2004, Springer Berlin / Heidelberg 2681/2003, 485-501

Papazoglou, M., Traverso, P., Dustdar, S., Leymann, F., & Krämer, B. (2006). Service-oriented computing: A research roadmap. In *Service Oriented Computing (SOC) Dagstuhl Seminar Proceeding.*

Parasoft Corporation. (2005). SOATest. Available at http://www.parasoft.com/jsp/products/home.jsp?product=SOAP&itemId=101.

Parastatidis, S., Woodman, S., Webber, J., Kuo, D., & Greenfield, P. (2006). Asynchronous messaging between Web services using SSDL. *IEEE Internet Computing, 10*(1), 26–39. doi:10.1109/MIC.2006.3

Park, J., & Chung, J. (2003). Design of SPS Model Using Mobile Agent System. In *Proceedings of the IEEE 37th Annual 2003 International Carnahan Conference on Security Technology*, (pp. 38-42), Taipei, Taiwan.

Paul, S., Sabnani, K. K., Lin, J. C.-H., & Bhattacharyya, S. (1997). Reliable Multicast Transport Protocol. *IEEE Journal on Selected Areas in Communications, 15*(3), 407–421. doi:10.1109/49.564138

Pautasso, C., Alonso, G., (2004) "From Web Service Composition to Megaprogramming" In Proceedings of the 5th VLDB Workshop on Technologies for E-Services (TES-04), Toronto, Canada, August 29-30, 2004

Penta, M., Bruno, M., & Esposito, G. V., Mazza, & Canfora, G. (2007). Test and Analysis of Web Services. In *Web Services Regression Testing* (pp. 205-234). Berlin: Springer.

Perkins, C. (1996). *RFC 2002: IP mobility support.* Internet Engineering Task Force.

Pernici, B. (2006). *Mobile Information Systems – Infrastructure and Design for Adaptivity and Flexibility (the MAIS approach).* Springer.

Perry, D.E., Porter, A.A., & Votta, L.G. (2000). Empirical studies of software engineering: A roadmap. In A. Finkelstein (Ed.), *The future of software engineering*: ACM Press.

Pesic, M., & van der Aalst, W. M. P. (2006). DecSerFlow: Towards a truly declarative service flow language. In F. Leymann, W. Reisig, S. R. Thatte, & W. M. P. van der Aalst (Eds.), *Dagstuhl Seminar Proceedings: The Role of Business Processes in Service Oriented Architectures* (Vol. 6291).

Pinto, J. A. (1994). *Temporal Reasoning in the Situation Calculus.* PhD Thesis, University of Toronto, Toronto.

Plaisted, D. (2003). *A hierarchical situation calculus.* Retrieved December 4, 2005, from http://arxiv.org/abs/cs/0309053

Plale, B. (2005). Resource requirements study for LEAD storage repository. *Technical Report 001, Linked Environments for Atmospheric Discovery.*

Pollet, T., Maas, G., Marien, J., & Wambecq, A. (2006, April). Telecom services delivery in a SOA. In *Proceedings of 20th International Conference on Advanced Information Networking and Applications (AINA 2006), 2* (pp. 529-533). Los Alamitos: IEEE Computer Society.

Ponnekanti, S., & Fox, A. (2002). Sword: A developer toolkit for web service composition. In *Proceedings of the 11th International World Wide Web Conference (WWW 2002).*

Potlapally, N. R., Ravi, S., Raghunathan, A., & Jha, N. K. (2006). A study of the energy consumption characteristics of cryptographic algorithms and security protocols. *IEEE Transactions on Mobile Computing, 5*(2), 128-143.

Prechelt, L. (2000). An empirical comparison of seven programming languages. *IEEE Computer, 33*(10), 23-29.

Priest, G. (2001). *An Introduction to Non-Classical Logic.* Cambridge University Press.

Prieto-Diaz, R., & Freeman, P. (1987). Classifying software for reuse. *IEEE Software*, *4*(1), 6–16.

Provost, W. (2003). *UML for Web services.* Retrieved March 1, 2006, from http://www.xml.com/lpt/a/ws/2003/08/05/uml.html

Punin, J., Krishnamoorthy, M., & Zaki, M. (2001). Web Usage Mining: Languages and Algorithms. In *Proceedings of Studies in Classification, Data Analysis, and Knowledge Organization.* Springer-Verlag.

Python (2009). Python language's official website. Retrieved March 2 from http://www.python.org/

Qu, C., and Nejdl, W. (2004) Interacting the Edutella/JXTA Peer-to-Peer Network with Web Services. In Proceedings of the 2004 Symposium on Applications and the Internet, IEEE Computer Society.

Radhakrishnan, R., & Wookey, M. (2004). *Model driven Architecture enabling Service oriented architectures.* Retrieved March 3, 2005, from http://www.omg.org/news/whitepapers/mdasoa.pdf

Rajasekaran, P., Miller, J. A., Verma, K., & Sheth, A. P. (2004). Enhancing Web Services Description and Discovery to Facilitate Composition. In *Proceeding of The First International Workshop on Semantic Web Services and Web Process Composition (SWSWPC 2004)* (LNCS 3387, pp. 55-68).

Ranganathan, A., & Campbell, R. H. (2003). A middleware for context-aware agents in ubiquitous computing environments. In *Proceedings of 5th ACM/IFIP/USENIX International Middleware Conference*, October (pp. 143-161).

Rannenberg, K. (2001). Multilateral Security a Concept and Examples for Balanced Security. In *Proceedings of the 2000 Workshop on New Security Paradigms*, (pp. 151-162), Ballycotton, County Cork, Ireland.

Rao, J., Kungas, P., & Matskin, M. (2003). Application of linear logic to web service composition. In *Proceedings of the 1st International Conference on Web Services (ICWS'03)*, June (pp. 3-9).

Ratzer, A. V., Wells, L., Lassen, H. M., Laursen, M., Qvortrup, J. F., Stissing, M. S., et al. (2003). CPN tools for editing, simulating, and analysing coloured Petri nets. In W. v. d. Aaalst & E. Best (Eds.), *Application and theory of Petri nets*.

Ravichandran, T. (2003). Special issue on component-based software development. *The DATA BASE for Advances in Information Systems*, *34*(4), 45–46.

Ray, I., & Xin, T. (2006). Analysis of dependencies in advanced transaction models. *Distributed and Parallel Databases*, *20*(1), 5–27. doi:10.1007/s10619-006-8593-9

Reijers, H.A., & Vanderfeesten, I.T.P. (2004). Cohesion and coupling metrics for workflow process design. In J. Desel, B. Pernici, & M. Weske (Eds.), *BPM 2004 (LNCS 3080)* (Vol. LNCS 3080, pp. 290–305). Berlin: Springer-Verlag.

Renesse, R., Birman, K. P., & Vogels, W. (2003). Astrolable: A Robust and Scalable Technology for Distributed System Monitoring, Management and Data Mining. *ACM Transactions on Computer Systems*, *21*(2), 164–206. doi:10.1145/762483.762485

Ribler, R.L., Vetter, J.S., Simitci, H., & Reed, D.A. (1998). Autopilot: Adaptive control of distributed applications. *HPDC*.

Roberts, D., & Johnson, R. (1997). *Evolving frameworks: A pattern language for developing object-oriented frameworks*. Pattern Languages of Program Design 3, Chapter 26. Addison Wesley.

Roberts, J., & Srinivasan, K. (2001). Tentative hold protocol part 1: White paper. Retrieved March 1, 2009 2006 from http://www.w3.org/TR/tenthold-1

Roberts, J., Collier, T., Malu, P., & Srinivasan, K. (2001). Tentative hold protocol part 2: Technical specification. Retrieved March 1, 2009 from http://www.w3.org/TR/tenthold-2

Roman, M., Hess, C., Cerqueira, R., Ranganathan, A., Campbell, R. H., & Nahrstedt, K. (2002). A middleware infrastructure for active spaces. *IEEE Pervasive Computing / IEEE Computer Society [and] IEEE Communications Society*, *1*(4), 74–83. doi:10.1109/MPRV.2002.1158281

Rosenberg, J., Lennox, J., & Schulzrinne, H. (1999). Programming Internet telephony services. *IEEE Network*, *13*(3), 42–49. doi:10.1109/65.767138

Rosenberg, J., Schulzrinne, H., Camarillo, G., Johnston, A., Peterson, J., Sparks, R., et al. (2002). *SIP: Session Initiation Protocol, RFC 3261*. Retrieved November 21, 2007, from http://www.ietf.org/rfc/rfc3261.txt.

RosettaNet (n.d.). RosettaNet Standard (RosettaNet Partner Interface Processes). Retrieved from http://www.rosettanet.org

Rouached, M., Gaaloul, W., van der Aalst, W. M. P., Bhiri, S., & Godart, C. (2006). Web Service Mining and verification of Properties: An approach based on Event Calculus. In *Proceedings of the International Cooperative Information Systems* (pp. 408-425). Montpellier, France.

Rouse, W. B. (2005). A Theory of Enterprise Transformation . *Systems Engineering*, *8*(4), 279–295. doi:10.1002/sys.20035

Rozinat, A., & van der Aalst, W. M. P. (2005). Conformance testing: measuring the fit and appropriateness of event logs and process models. In *Proceedings* of *Business Process Management Workshops* (pp. 163–176). Nancy, France.

RSS-DEV Working Group. (2000). Rss1.0. Retrieved from http://web.resource.org/rss/1.0/

Ruiz, A., Corchuelo, R., Martín,O., Durán, A., Toro, M., (2000), Addressing Interoperability in Multi-Organisational Web-Based Systems, Proceedings of the 2nd ECOOP Workshop on Object Interoperability (WOI'2000), Sophia Antipolis, France, June 12, 2000

Rush, R., & Wallace, W. A. (1997). Elicitation of knowledge from multiple experts using network inference. *IEEE Transactions on Knowledge and Data Engineering*, *9*(5), 688–698. doi:10.1109/69.634748

Rusinkiewicz, M., & Sheth, A. P. (1995). Specification and execution of transactional workflows. In *Modern Database Systems: The Object Model, Interoperability, and Beyond* (pp. 592-620). Addison-Wesley.

Ryan, N., (2005), Smart Environments for Cultural Heritage, In *Proceedings of 24th International Symposium on Reading the Historical Spatial Information in the World*, pp 17-33, Kyoto, Japan, February 2005.

Ryutov, T., Zhou, L., Neuman, C., Leithead, T., & Seamons, K.E. (2005). Adaptive Trust Negotiation and Access Control. In *Proceedings of the 10 ACM Symposium on Access Control Models and Technologies*, (pp. 139-146), Stockholm, Sweden.

Sahai, A., Machiraju, V., Ouyang, J., & Wurster, K. (2001). *Message tracking in SOAP-based Web services* (Tech Rep HPL-2001-199). Retrieved 2001 from http://www.hpl.hp.com/techreports/2001/HPL-2001-199.html.

Sahai, A., Singhal, S., Machiraju, V., & Joshi, R. (2004). Automated generation of resource configurations through policy. In *Policy*. New York.

Sakamoto, H., Igaki, H., & Nakamura, M. (2008). Integrating Networked Home Appliances and Information Resources on the Internet Using RSS. ([in Japanese]. *Tech Rep, IEICE, 108*(136), 47–52.

Salomaa, K., & Yu, S. (1999). Synchronization expressions and languages. *Journal of Universal Computer Science, 5*, 610-621.

Sandoz, P., Triglia, A., & Pericas-Geertsen, S. (2004). Fast infoset. Retrieved March 17, 2009, from http://java.sun.com/developer/technicalArticles/xml/fastinfoset/

Satyanarayanan, M. (2001). Pervasive computing: Vision and challenges. *IEEE Personal Communications, 8*(4), 10-17.

Sayal, M., Casati, F., Shan, M., & Dayal, U. (2002). Business Process Cockpit. In *Proceedings of 28th International Conference on Very Large Data Bases* (pp. 880-883). Hong Kong, China.

Sayood, K. (2000). *Introduction to data compression* (2nd ed.). San Francisco: Morgan Kaufmann Publishers Inc.

Schekkerman, J. (2003). *How to Survive in the Jungle of Enterprise Architecture Framework: Creating or Choosing an Enterprise Architecture Framework*. North Carolina: Trafford Publishing.

Schimm, G. (2004). Mining exact models of concurrent workflows . *Computers in Industry, 53*(3), 265–281. doi:10.1016/j.compind.2003.10.003

Schmidt, R., & Assmann, U. (1998). Extending aspect-oriented-programming in order to flexibly support workflows. In *Proceedings of Aspect-Oriented Programming Workshop*.

Schneider, J. (2003). Theory, benefits and requirements for efficient encoding of XML documents. In *W3C Workshop on Binary Interchange of XML Information Item Sets*. World Wide Web Consortium.

Schneier, B. (1990). *Applied cryptography* (2nd ed.). New York: John Wiley & Sons.

Schülke, A., Abbadessa, D., & Winkler, F. (2006, April). Service Delivery Platform: Critical Enabler to Service Providers' New Revenue Streams. In *Proceedings of World Telecommunications Congress (WTC 2006), Budapest, Hungary*.

Schuldt, H., Alonso, G., & Schek, H. (1999) Concurrency control and recovery in transactional process management. In *Proceedings of the Conference on Principles of Database Systems* (pp. 316-326). Philadelphia, Pennsylvania.

Scott, D. & Sharp, R. (2003). Specifying and enforcing application-level Web security policies. *IEEE Transactions on Knowledge and Data Engineering, 15*(4), 771-783.

Segoufin, L., & Vianu, V. (2002). Validating streaming xml documents. In *Proceedings of the 21st ACM SIGMOD-SIGACT-SIGART symposium on Principles of database systems, New York, USA* (pp. 53–64).

Sekimoto, J., Nakamura, M., Igaki, H., & Matsumoto, K. (2008). *Supporting End-Users for Creating Integrated Services in Home Network System* (Technical Report of IEICE, Volume 107, Number 525, 289-294) (in Japanese)

Sessions, R., & Sickler, J. V. (2003). *Software Fortresses: Modeling Enterprise Architectures*. Massachusetts: Addison Wesley.

ShaikhAli, A., & Rana, O.F. (2003). *UDDIe: An extended registry for Web services*. Proceedings of the 2003 Symposium on Applications and the Internet Workshops, 85–89.

Shan, T. C., & Hua, W. W. (2005). High-performance Data Caching Mechanisms. 2005 *Web Information and System Application Conference (WISA 2005)*.

Shan, T. C., & Hua, W. W. (2006). Solution Architecture of N-Tier Applications. In *Proceedings of 3rd IEEE International Conference on Services Computing* (pp. 349-356). California: IEEE Computer Society.

Shan, T. C., et al. (2004). *Websphere Business Integration for SAP*. New York: IBM Corporation.

Shan, T. C., et al. (2004). *WebSphere MQ Solutions in a Microsoft. NET Environment*. New York: IBM Corporation.

Sheth, A.P., van der Aalst, W., & Arpinar, I.B. (1999). Processes driving the networked economy. *IEEE Concurrency, 7*(3), 18–31.

Shirasuna, S., & Gannon, D. (2006). XBaya: A graphical workflow composer for the Web services architecture. *Technical Report 004, Linked Environments for Atmospheric Discovery*.

Shirasuna, S., Slominski, A., Fang, L., & Gannon, D. (2004). Performance comparison of security mechanisms for grid services. In R. Buyya (Ed.), *Fifth IEEE/ACM International Workshop on Grid Computing* (pp. 360-364).

Shuping, R. (2003). A Framework for Discovering Web Services with Desired Quality of Services Attributes. In *ICWS '03: Proceedings of the International Conference on Web Services*, Las Vegas, Nevada, USA (pp. 208-213).

Siegel, J., (1996), CORBA Fundamentals and Programming, Wiley, 1996

Siegel, S., & Castellan, J. (1988). *Nonparametric statistics for the behavioral sciences*: McGraw-Hill.

Silver, B. (2006). *The next step in process modeling*. Retrieved March 1, 2007 from http://www.brsilver. com/wordpress/2006/02/03/the-next-step-in-process-modeling. BPMSWatch

Simmhan, Y., Plale, B., & Gannon, D. (2005). A survey of data provenance in e-science. *SIGMOD Record, 34*(3), 31–36.

Simmhan, Y.L., Pallickara, S.L., Vijayakumar, N.N., & Plale, B. (2006). *Data management in dynamic environment-driven computational science*. Proceedings of the IFIP Working Conference on Grid-Based Problem Solving Environments (WoCo9).

Simmhan, Y.L., Plale, B., & Gannon, D. (2006). *Towards a quality model for effective data selection in collaboratories*. Proceedings of the IEEE Workflow and Data Flow for Scientific Applications (SciFlow) Workshop.

Simmhan, Y.L., Plale, B., & Gannon, D. (2007). Query capabilities of the Karma provenance framework. *Concurrency and Control: Practice and Experience*.

Simmhan, Y.L., Plale, B., Gannon, D., & Marru, S. (2006c). Performance evaluation of the Karma provenance framework for scientific workflows. *IPAW* and *LNCS* 4145.

Singh, M. P. (1995). Semantical considerations on workflows: an algebra for intertask dependencies. In *Proceedings of the 5th International Workshop on Database Programming Languages (DBPL-5)*, September (pp. 5-19).

Singh, M. P. (2003). Distributed enactment of multiagent workflows: Temporal logic for Web service composition. In *Proceedings of the Second International Joint Conference on Autonomous Agents and Multiagent Systems*, Melbourne, Australia. ACM Press.

Singh, P., Gelgi, F., Davulcu, H., Yau, S. S., & Mukhopadhyay, S. (2008). A Risk Reduction Framework for Dynamic Workflows. In *Proceedings of 2008 IEEE International Conference on Services Computing*, July (pp. 381-388).

Sirin, E., Hendler, J. A., & Parsia, B. (2003). Semi-automatic composition of web services using semantic descriptions. In *Proceedings of the Web Services: Modeling, Architecture and Infrastructure (WSMAI) Workshop in conjunction with the 5th International Conference on Enterprise Information Systems (ICEIS 2003)*, April (pp. 17-24).

Skogan, D., Groenmo, R., & Solheim, I. (2004). Web Service Composition in UML. In *EDOC '04: Proceeding of the IEEE Enterprise Distributed Object Computing*, Monterey, USA (pp. 47-57).

Slominski, A. (2006). Adapting BPEL to scientific workflows. *Workflows for e-Science*.

Smith, D. J., & Meyers, B. C. (2005). *Exploiting Programmatic Interoperability: Army Future Force Workshop* (Tech Rep CMU/SEI-2005-TN-042). Software Engineering Institute.

Smith, H., & Fingar, P. (2003). *Business process management (BPM): The third wave*. Meghan-Kiffer Press.

SOAP-JMS. (2008). *Simple Object Access Protocol, version 1.2*. Retrieved February 23, 2009, from http://www.w3.org/TR/2008/WD-soapjms-20081121/

Soler, E., Villarroel, R., Trujillo, J., Medina, E., & Piattini, M. (2006). Representing security and audit rules for data warehouses at the logical level by using the common warehouse metamodel. *Proceedings of IEEE International Conference on Availability, Reliability and Security*.

Sorensen, M. H., & Urzyczyn, P. (2006). *Lectures on the Curry-Howard Isomorphism,* Elsevier.

Specification: Business process execution language for Web services version 1.1. (2003). Retrieved from http://www-106.ibm.com/developerworks/webservices/library/ws-bpel

Stephenson, J. (2003). *Service Oriented Architecture, OptimalJ, CBDI Report.* Retrieved March 1, 2006, from http://www.omg.org/mda/mda_files/CBDI-SOAOptimalJ-US2003.pdf.

Stevens, R., Tipney, H., Wroe, C., Oinn T., Senger, M., Lord, P., et al. (2004). Exploring Williams-Beuren Syndrome Using [my]Grid. *Bioinformatics, 20*(i), 303–i310.

Stevens, R., Glover, K., Greenhalgh, C., Jennings, C., Pearce, S., Li, P., et al. (2003). Performing in silico experiments on the Grid: A users perspective. *Proceedings of UK e-Science All Hands Meeting,* 43-50.

Storer, J., & Szymanski, T. (1982). Data compression via textural substitution. *Journal of the ACM, 29*(4), 928–951. doi:10.1145/322344.322346

Strang, T., Linnhoff-Popien, C. (2003), Service Interoperability in Ubiquitous Computing Environments, Proceedings of International Conference on Advances in Infrastructure for Electronic Business, Education, Science, Medicine, and Mobile Technologies on the Internet (SSGRR2003w), L'Aquila, Italy, January,2003

Sun Microsystems, (2005), "JXTA v2.3.x: Java Programmers Guide", available at: http://www.jxta.org, April 2005

Szomszor, M., & Moreau, L. (2003). Recording and reasoning over data provenance in Web and grid services. *ODBASE.*

Tan, J.J., Poslad, S., & Xi, Y. (2004). Policy Driven Systems for Dynamic Security Reconfiguration. *Proceedings of the 3rd International Joint Conference on Autonomous Agents and Multiagent Systems,* Vol. 3, (pp. 1274-1275), New York, New York.

Tanenbaum, A. S., (2003), Computer Networks, Prentice Hall, fourth edition, 2003, ISBN: 0-13-066102-3

Tang, S. Liebetruth, C., & Jaeger, M. C. (2003) The OWL-S matcher software. Retrieved from http://flp.cs.tu-berlin.de/

Telecom Italia Lab. (n.d.). *JADE (Java Agent Development Framework).* Retrieved Feb. 14, 2005 from http://jade.tilab.com/

Thatte, S. (2001). XLANG Web Services for Business Process Design. Microsoft Corporation. Retrieved from http://www.gotdotnet.com/team/xml wsspecs/xlang-c/default.htm

Thatte, S. (2003). *Business Process Execution Language for Web Services Version 1.1 (BPEL).*

Thomasian, A. (1998). Concurrency control: Methods, performance, and analysis . *ACM Computing Surveys, 30*(1), 70–119. doi:10.1145/274440.274443

Thompson, H. S., Beech, D., Maloney, M., & Mendelsohn, N. (2004). XML Schema Part 1: Structures, W3C Recommendation. Retrieved from http://www.w3.org/TR/xmlschema-1/

Timm, J. T. E., & Gannod, G. C. (2005). A Model-Driven Approach for Specifying Semantic Web Services. In *ICWS '05: Proceeding of the IEEE International Conference on Web Services,* Washington, DC, USA (pp. 313–320).

TOGAF. The Open Group (2003). The Open Group Architecture Framework Version 9 ("Enterprise Edition"). Retrieved February 8, 2008 from http://www.opengroup.org/togaf

Tolani, P., & Haritsa, J. R. (2002). XGRIND: A query-friendly XML compressor. In *Proceedings of the International Conference on Data Engineering, February 2000, San Jose, USA,* (pp. 225–234).

Toman, V. (2004). Syntactical compression of XML data. In *Proceedings of the International Conference on Advanced Information Systems Engineering, June 2004, Riga, Latvia,* (pp. 273–282).

Torrellas, G.A.S. & Vargas, L.A.V. (2003). Modelling a Flexible Network Security Systems Using Multi-Agents Systems: Security Assessment Considerations. In *Proceedings of the 1st International Symposium on Information and Communication Technologies (ISICT 03),* pp. 365-371, Dublin, Ireland.

Toshiba (2008). *Toshiba home network – Feminity.* Retrieved from http://feminity.toshiba.co.jp/feminity/feminity_eng/index.html

Tosic, V., Patel, K., & Pagurek, B. (2002). WSOL - Web Service Offerings Language. In *CAiSE '02/ WES '02: Revised Papers from the International Workshop on Web Services, E-Business, and the Semantic Web,* London, UK (pp. 57–67).

Tsai, W. T., Chen, Y., & Cao, Z. Bai, X., Hung, H., & Paul, R. (2004). Testing Web services using progressive group testing. In *Proceedings of Advanced Workshop on Content Computing (AWCC 2004)*, (LNCS 3309, pp. 314–322).

Tsai, W. T., Chen, Y., Paul, R., Huang, H., Zhou, X., & Wei, X. (2005). Adaptive Testing, Oracle Generation, and Test Case Ranking for Web Services. In *Proceedings of the 29th Annual International Computer Software and Applications conference (COMPSAC 2005)* (pp. 101–106). Los Alamitos, California: IEEE Computer Society Press.

Tsai, W. T., Paul, R., Song, W., & Cao, Z. (2002). Coyote: An XML-Based Framework for Web Services Testing. In *Proceedings of The 7th IEEE International Symposium on High-Assurance Systems Engineering (HASE 2002)* (pp. 173–176). Los Alamitos, California: IEEE Computer Society Press.

Tsai, W. T., Paul, R., Wang, Y., Fan, C., & Wang, D. (2002). Extending WSDL to facilitate Web services testing. In *Proceedings of The 7th IEEE International Symposium on High-Assurance Systems Engineering (HASE 2002)* (pp. 171–172). Los Alamitos, California: IEEE Computer Society Press.

Tsai, W.T., Lopex, M.A., Rodriguez, V., & Volovik., D. (1986). *An approach measuring data structure complexity.* Proceedings of the COMPSAC 86.

Tsalgatidou, A. Athanasopoulos, G., Pantazoglou, M., Pautasso, C., Heinis, T., Gronmo, R., Hoff, H., Berre, A-J., Glittum, M., Topouzidou, S. (2006) Developing Scientific Workflows from Heterogeneous Services, ACM SIGMOD-RECORD v(35) n(2) 22-28, June 2006

Tsalgatidou, A., Athanasopoulos, G., Pantazoglou, M., (2005), Generic Service Model Specification, Technical Report, available at: http://www.di.uoa.gr/~gathanas/TR/gesmo-1.0-report.pdf

Tse, T. H., Yau, S. S., Chan, W. K., Lu, H., & Chen, T. Y. (2004), Testing context-sensitive middleware-based software applications, in *Proceedings of the 28th Annual International Computer Software and Applications Conference (COMPSAC 2004)*, pp. 458–466. Los Alamitos, California: IEEE Computer Society Press.

Tsesmetzis, D., Roussaki, I., Papaioannou, I., & Anagnostou, M. (2006). Qos awareness support in web-service semantics. In *AICT/ICIW '06: Proceeding of the Advanced International Conference on Telecommunications and International Conference on Internet and Web Applications and Services*, Guadeloupe, French Caribbean, (pp. 128–135).

Turi, D., Missier, P., De Roure, D., Goble C., & Oinn, T. (2007). Taverna workflows: Syntax and semantics. *Proceedings of the 3rd e-Science conference*, Bangalore, India, December.

UDDI Technical Committee. About UDDI. OASIS UDDI Member Section. Retrieved from http://www.uddi.org/about.html .

UDDI. (2007). *UDDI Specification version 3.0.2.* Retrieved December 5, 2007, from http://uddi.xml.org/specification

Ulbrich, A., Weis, T., & Geihs, K. (2003). QoS Mechanism Composition at Design-Time and Runtime. In *ICDCSW '03: Proceeding of the 23rd International Conference on Distributed Computing Systems, Washington*, DC, USA (pp. 118-136).

Umar, A. (1997). *Application Reengineering: Building Web-Based Applications and Dealing with Legacy.* Englewood, Cliffs, NJ: Prentice-Hall.

UMT SINTEF. (2005). *UML Model Transformation Tool.* Retrieved March 1, 2006, from http://umt-qvt.sourceforge.net

UPnP. (2007). *Universal Plug and Play Device Standards*, UPnP Forum, September. Retrieved April 4, 2008, from http://upnp.org/standardizeddcps/default.asp

Vallecillo, A., Hernandez, J., Troya J., (2000), Woi'00: New issues in object interoperability, LNCS (1964): ECOOP'2000 Workshop Reader, pp. 256–269, Springer

van der Aalst, W. M. P., & Lassen, K. B. (2005). *Translating workflow nets to BPEL4WS* (Rep. No. BPM-05-16). BPM Center.

van der Aalst, W. M. P., & Weijters, A. J. M. M. (2004). Process Mining: a Research Agenda. *Computers in Industry, 53*(3), 231–244. doi:10.1016/j.compind.2003.10.001

van der Aalst, W. M. P., Dumas, M., Ouyang, C., Rozinat, A., & Verbeek, H. M. W. (2008). Conformance checking of service behaviour. [TOIT]. *ACM Transactions on Internet Technology, 8*(3), 13.

van der Aalst, W. M. P., Hofstede, A.H.M., ter, , & Kiepuszewski, B. Barros, A.P. (2003). Workflow Patterns. *Distributed and Parallel Databases, 14*(3), 5–51. doi:10.1023/A:1022883727209 van der Aalst, W. M. P., van Dongen, B. F., Herbst, J., Maruster, L., Schimm, G., & Weijters, A. J. M. M. (2003). Workflow Mining: A Survey of Issues and Approaches. *Data & Knowledge Engineering, 47*(2), 237–267. doi:10.1016/S0169-023X(03)00066-1

van der Aalst, W. M. P., Weijters, A. J. M. M., & Maruster, L. (2004). Workflow Mining: Discovering Process Models from Event Logs. *IEEE Transactions on Knowledge and Data Engineering, 16*(9), 1128–1142. doi:10.1109/TKDE.2004.47

van der Aalst, W.M.P. (1998). The application of petri nets to workflow management. *The Journal of Circuits, Systems and Computers, 8*(1), 21–66.

van der Aalst, W.M.P. (2000). Workflow verification: Finding control-flow errors using petri-net-based techniques. In W.M.P. van der Aalst, J. Desel, & A. Oberweis (Eds.), *Business process management: Models, techniques, and empirical studies* (Vol. 1806, pp. 161–183). Berlin: Springer-Verlag.

van der Aalst, W.M.P., & Hofstede, A.H.M. (2003). *YAWL: Yet another workflow language (revised version).* (QUT Technical report No. FIT-TR-2003-04). Brisbane: Queensland University of Technology.

van der Aalst, W.M.P., Hofstede, A.H.M., Kiepuszewski, B., & Barros, A.P. (2003). Workflow patterns. *Distributed and Parallel Databases, 14*(3), 5–51.

van der Aalst, W.M.P., ter Hofstede, A.H.M., Kiepuszewski, B., & Barros, A. P. (2003). Workflow patterns. *Distributed and Parallel Databases, 14*(3), 5–51.

Varadharajan, V. (1990). A Multilevel Security Policy Model for Networks. In *Proceedings of the 9th Annual Joint Conference of the IEEE Computer and Communication Societies (INFOCOM 90),* Vol. 2, (pp. 710-718), San Francisco, California.

Venezia, C., & Falcarin, P. (2006, September). Communication Web Services Composition and Integration. In *Proceedings of International Conference on Web Services (ICWS-06), Chicago, USA* (pp. 523-530). IEEE Press.

Ventuneac, M., Coffey, T., & Salomie, I. (2003). A Policy-Based Security Framework for Web-Enabled Applications. In *Proceedings 1st International Symposium on Information and Communication Technologies,* (pp. 487-492), Dublin, Ireland.

Vinoski, S. (2003). Integration with Web services. *IEEE Internet Computing, 7*(6).

Vogels, W., (2003), Web Services Are Not Distributed Objects, IEEE Internet Computing, Nov.-Dec. 2003

Vokäc, M. (2005). Using a domain-specific language and custom tools to model a multi-tier service-oriented application: Experiences and challenges. *Proceedings of ACM/IEEE International Conference on Model Driven Engineering Languages and Systems.*

W3C (2001). XML Schema. Retrieved from http://www.w3.org/xml/schema.

W3C (2002). *Web Service Activity.* Retrieved from http://www.w3.org/2002/ws/

W3C (2003). SOAP Version 1.2 Part 1: Messaging Framework. Retrieved from http://www.w3.org/tr/soap12-part1/

W3C (2004). Extensible Markup Language (XML) 1.0 (3rd ed.). Retrieved from http://www.w3.org/TR/2004/REC-xml-20040204/.

W3C (2005). Web Services Description Language (WSDL) version 2.0 Part 1: Core Language. Retrieved from http://www.w3.org/tr/wsdl20/

W3C (2005). Working group note: XML binary characterization. Retrieved March 17, 2009, from http://www.w3.org/TR/xbc-characterization/

W3C (2005). Charter of the efficient XML interchange working group. Retrieved March 17, 2009, from http://www.w3.org/2005/09/exi-charter-final.html

W3C (2007). World Wide Web Consortium. Retrieved December 5, 2007, from http://www.w3.org

W3C (2008). Working Draft: Efficient XML Interchange (EXI) Format 1.0. Retrieved March 17, 2009, from http://www.w3.org/TR/2008/WD-exi-20080919/

W3C. (2002). *Web Services Description Language (WSDL).*

W3C. (2004). *OWL Web Ontology Language: Overview.* Retrieved December 4, 2005, from http://www.w3.org/TR/owl-features

W3C. (2004). *Web services architecture.* Retrieved December 4, 2005, from http://www.w3.org/TR/2004/NOTE-ws-arch-20040211/

Wachter, H., & Reuter, A. (1992). The ConTract model. In A. K. Elmagarmid (Ed.), *Database Transaction Models for Advanced Applications* (pp. 219-263). San Francisco, CA: Morgan Kaufmann Publishers, Inc.

Wada, H. & Suzuki, J. (2006). *Designing ecological observation systems using service oriented architecture.* Elsevier/ISEI International Conference on Ecological Informatics, poster paper.

Wada, H., Suzuki, J., & Oba K. (2006). A model-driven development framework for non-functional aspects in service oriented grids. *Proceedings of IEEE International Conference on Autonomic and Autonomous Systems.*

Wada, H., Suzuki, J., & Oba K. (2006). Modeling non-functional aspects in service oriented architecture. *Proceedings of IEEE International Conference on Services Computing..*

Wada, H., Suzuki, J., & Oba K. (2006). A service-oriented design framework for secure network applications. *Proceedings of IEEE International Conference on Computer Software and Applications Conference.*

Wainer, J., Barthelmess, P., & Kumar, A. (2005). W-RBAC A workflow security model incorporating controlled overriding of constraints. *International Journal of Cooperative Information Systems, 12*(4), 455–486. doi:10.1142/S0218843003000814

Waldinger, R. J. (2000). Web agents cooperating deductively. In *Proceedings of the 1st International Workshop on Formal Approach to Agent-Based Systems*, April (pp. 250-262).

Wang, G., Chen, A., Wang, C., Fung, C., & Uczekaj, S. (2004). Integrated quality of service (QoS) management in service-oriented enterprise architectures. *Proceedings of IEEE Enterprise Distributed Object Computing Conference.*

Wang, J., & Zucker, J.-D. (2000). *Solving the multiple-instance problem: A lazy learning approach.* Proceedings of the 17th International Conference on Machine Learning, San Francisco, California, 1119–1125.

Wang, L., & Lee, L. (2005). *UML-based modeling of Web services security.* IEEE European Conference on Web Services, poster paper.

Wang, Y.Q., & Stroulia, E. (2003). Flex*ible interface matching for Web Services discovery.* Proceedings of the Fourth International Conference on Web Information Systems Engineering (WISE 03), 147–156.

WAP Forum. (2001). *Wireless application protocol: Architecture specification.*

WAP Forum. (2001). *Wireless transport layer security specification.*

Ward, W. (1989). Software defect prevention using McCabe's complexity metric. *Hewlett Packard Journal, 40*(2), 64–69.

Wastell, D., White, P., & Kawalek, P. (1994). A methodology for business process re-design: Experiences and issues. *Journal of Strategic Information Systems, 3*(1), 23–40.

Weerawarana, S., & Curbera, F. (2002). Business process with BPEL4WS: Understanding BPEL4WS, Part1. Retrieved from http://www-106.ibm.com/developerworks/webservices/\\library/ws-bpelcol1

Weinsberg, Y., Dolev, D., Anker, T., & Wyckoff, P. (2006). Hydra: A Novel Framework for Making High-Performance Computing Offload Capable. In *Proceedings of the 31st IEEE Conference on Local Computer Networks (LCN 2006).* Tampa, November 2006.

Weiser, M. (1993). Some computer science issues in ubiquitous computing. *Communications of the ACM, 36*(7), 75-84.

Weiss, M., & Esfandiari, B. (2005). On Feature Interactions Among Web Services. *International Journal of Web Services Research, 2*(4), 22–47.

Werner, C., Buschmann, C., & Fischer, S. (2007). Advanced Data Compression Techniques for SOAP Web Services. In L.-J. Zhang (Ed.), *Modern Technologies in Web Services Research* (pp. 76–97). Hershey: IGI Publishing.

Werner, C., Buschmann, C., Jäcker, T., & Fischer, S. (2006). Bandwidth and Latency Considerations for Efficient SOAP Messaging. *International Journal of Web Services Research, 3*(1), 49–67.

West, K. (2005). Scoping out the planet. *Scientific American.*

Weyuker, E.J. (1988). Evaluating software complexity measures. *IEEE Transactions on Software Eng., 14*(9), 1357–1365.

WfMC (2005). Workflow Management Coalition Workflow Standard Process Definition Interface -- XML Process Definition Language, Document Number WFMC-TC-1025 Version 1.13.

WFMC. (1996). *WorkFlow Management Coalition. Terminology and glossary.* Retrieved December 4, 2005, from http://www.wfmc.org/standards/docs/TC-1011_term_glossary_v3.pdf

White, S. (2005). Using BPMN to model a BPEL process. *BPTrends, 3*(3), 1–18.

Wilson, M., Kolberg, M., & Magill, E. H. (2008). Considering Side Effects in Service Interactions in Home Automation – an Online Approach. In *Proc. of Int'l. Conf. on Feature Interactions in Software and Communication Systems (ICFI'08)* (pp. 172-187).

Winsborough, W., & Li, N. (2004). Safety in Automated Trust Negotiation. In *Proceedings, 2004 IEEE Symposium on Security and Privacy (S&P'04),* (pp. 147-160), Oakland, California.

Winslett, M., Yu, T., Seamons, K., Hess, A., Jacobson, J., Jarvis, R. et al. (2002). Negotiating trust on the web. *IEEE Internet Computing, November/December*, 30-37,.

Wodtke, D., Weissenfels, J., Weikum, G., & Dittrich, A.K. (1996). *The MENTOR project: Steps towards enterprise-wide workflow management.* Proceedings of the IEEE International Conference on Data Engineering, New Orleans, LA.

Wohed, P., van der Aalst, W. M. P., Dumas, M., & ter Hofstede, A. H. M. (2003, October). Analysis of Web Services Composition Languages: The Case of BPEL4WS. In *Proceedings of the 22nd International Conference on Conceptual Modeling (ER), Chicago, USA* (LNCS 2813, pp. 200-215).

Wolstencroft, K., Oinn, T., Goble, C., Ferris, J., Wroe, C., Lord, P., et al. (2005, December). Panoply of utilities in Taverna. In *First International Conference on e-Science and Grid Computing (e-science), Melbourne, Australia,* (pp. 156-162). Washington: IEEE Computer Society.

Wombacher, A. (2006). Evaluation of technical measures for workflow similarity based on a pilot study. *Proceedings of CoopIS*, Montpellier, France, November 1-3.

Wombacher, A., Fankhauser, P., Mahleko, B., & Neuhold, E. (2004). Matchmaking for Business Processes Based on Choreographies. *International Journal of Web Services, 1*(4), 14–32.

Woodman, S. J., Palmer, D. J., Shrivastava, S. K., & Wheater, S. M. (2004). Notations for the specification and verification of composite web services. In *Proceedings of the 8th IEEE International Enterprise Distributed Object Computing Conference (EDOC'04)*, September (pp. 35-46).

Worah, D., & Sheth, A. (1997). Transactions in transactional workflows. In S. Jajodia and L. Kershberg (Eds.), *Advanced Transaction Models and Architectures* (pp. 3-34).

Workflow Management Coalition. (2002). *Workflow process definition interface: XML process definition language* (No. WFMC-TC-1025).

World Wide Web Consortium (W3C) (n.d.). *Extensible Markup Language (XML).* Retrieved March 18, 2006 at http://www.w3.org/XML/

World Wide Web Consortium (W3C). (1999). *WAP binary XML content format.* Cambridge, MA: Author.

World Wide Web Consortium (W3C). (2001). *Canonical XML version 1.0.* Cambridge, MA: Author.

World Wide Web Consortium (W3C). (2002). *XML Encryption Syntax and Processing.* Cambridge, MA: Author.

World Wide Web Consortium (W3C). (2002). *XML signature syntax and processing.* Cambridge, MA: Author.

World Wide Web Consortium (W3C). (2003). *SOAP version 1.2 part 1: Messaging framework.* Cambridge, MA: Author.

World Wide Web Consortium (W3C). (2003). *SOAP version 1.2 part 2: Adjuncts.* Cambridge, MA: Author.

World Wide Web Consortium (W3C). (2005). *XML-binary optimized packaging.* Cambridge, MA: Author.

World Wide Web Consortium (W3C). (2007). *Efficient XML interchange (EXI) format 1.0.* Cambridge, MA: Author.

World Wide Web Consortium (W3C). (2007). *Efficient XML interchange measurements note.* Cambridge, MA: Author.

World Wide Web Consortium (W3C). (2007). *XQuery 1.0: An XML query language.* Cambridge, MA: Author.

World Wide Web Consortium (W3C). (2007). *XSL transformations (XSLT) version 2.0.* Cambridge, MA: Author.

World Wide Web Consortium. (2002). XML encryption syntax and processing.

World Wide Web Consortium. (2002). XML signature syntax and processing.

World Wide Web Consortium. (2006). Web services policy framework.

Wroe, C., Goble, C., Goderis, A., Lord, P., Miles, S., Papay, J., et al. (2007). Recycling workflows and services through discovery and reuse. *Concurrency and Computation: Practice and Experience, 19*(2), 181-194.

Wroe, C., Stevens, R., Goble, C., Roberts, A., & Greenwood, M. (2003). A suite of DAML+OIL ontologies to describe bioinformatics Web services and data. *International Journal of Cooperative Information Systems, 12*(2), 197–224.

WS-Addressing. (2004). *W3C WS-Addressing specification.* Retrieved February 23, 2009, from http://www.w3.org/Submission/ws-addressing/

WS-BEPL. (2005). Business process execution language for Web services.

WS-Brokered Notification. (2006). *OASIS WS-Brokered Notification version 1.3 specification.* Retrieved February 23, 2009, from http://docs.oasis-open.org/wsn/wsn-ws_brokered_notification-1.3-spec-os.pdf

WS-CDL. (2005). *Web Services Choreography Description Language Version 1.0.* Retrieved December 5, 2007, from http://www.w3.org/TR/ws-cdl-10/

WSDL. (2001). *Web services description language.* Retrieved December 4, 2005, from http://www.w3.org/TR/wsdl

WSDL. (2007). *Web Service Description Language version 1.1 specification.* Retrieved December 5, 2007, from http://www.w3.org/TR/wsdl

WSDM. (2006). *OASIS Web Services Distributed Management standard specification.* Retrieved February 23, 2009, from http://www.oasis-open.org/committees/wsdm/

WSIF Org, (2006), Web Service Invocation Framework, accessed at 21 December 2006, available at http://ws.apache.org/wsif/

WSMO. (2005). *Web Services Modeling Ontology.* Retrieved March 1, 2006, from http://www.wsmo.org/TR/d2/v1.2/

WSN. (2007). *OASIS Web Service Notification specifications version 1.3.* Retrieved February 23, 2009, from http://www.oasis-open.org/committees/wsn

WS-ReliableMessaging. (2007). *OASIS WS-Reliable Messaging version 1.1 standard.* Retrieved February 23, 2009, from http://docs.oasis-open.org/ws-rx/wsrm/200702/wsrm-1.1-spec-os-01.pdf

WS-Resource Framework. (2004). Globus Alliance website. Retrieved February 25, 2009, from http://www.globus.org/wsrf/specs/ws-wsrf.pdf

WSRF. (2007). *OASIS Web Service Resource Framework standard specification.* Retrieved February 23, 2009, from http://www.oasis-open.org/committees/wsrf

WS-Topics. (2006). *OASIS Web Services Topics version 1.3 specification.* Retrieved February 23, 2009, from http://docs.oasis-open.org/wsn/wsn-ws_topics-1.3-spec-os.pdf

Wu, Q., Pu, C., & Sahai, A. (2006). DAG synchronization constraint language for business processes. In *Proceedings of the IEEE Conference on E-Commerce Technology (CEC'06).*

Wu, X., & Schulzrinne, H. (2003, May). Programmable end system services using SIP. In *Proceedings of The IEEE International Conference on Communications (ICC 2003), Anchorage, Alaska, USA* (pp. 789-793). IEEE Press.

Xiangpeng, Z., Cerone, A., & Krishnan, P. (2006). Verifying BPEL Workflows Under Authorisation Constraints. In *Proceedings of Fourth International Conference on Business Process Management* (BPM 2006), Vienna, Austria, September.

XMethods. http://www.xmethods.com/

XPDL. (2007). Workflow Management Coalition: XML Process Description Language, version 2.0 standard. Retrieved December 5, 2007, from http://www.wfmc.org/standards/xpdl.htm

Yan, J., Li, Z., Yuan, Y., Sun, W., & Zhang, J. (2006). BPEL4WS Unit Testing: Test Case Generation Using a Concurrent Path Analysis Approach. In *Proceedings of the 17th International Symposium on Software Reliability Engineering* (ISSRE 2006) (pp. 75-84). Los Alamitos, California: IEEE Computer Society Press. Chunyang Ye, S.C. Cheung & W.K. Chan (2006). Publishing and composition of atomicity-equivalent services for B2B collaboration. In *Proceedings of the 28th International Conference on Software Engineering (ICSE 2006)* (pp. 351-360). Los Alamitos, California: IEEE Computer Society Press.

Yang, Y., Fu, Z., & Wu, S. (2003). Bands: An Inter-Domain Internet Security Policy Management System for IPSEC/

VPN. In *Proceedings of the IFIP/IEEE 8th International Symposium on Integrated Network Management,* (pp. 231-244), Colorado Springs, Colorado.

Yau, S. S., Davulcu, H., Mukhopadhyay, S., Huang, D., Gong, H., & Singh, P. (2007). Automated situation-aware service composition in service-oriented computing. [IJWSR]. *International Journal of Web Services Research, 4*(4), 59–82.

Yau, S. S., Gong, H., Huang, D., Gao, W., & Zhu, L. (2006) Automated agent synthesis for situation awareness in service-based systems. In *Proceedings of the 30th IEEE International Computer Software and Applications Conference (COMPSAC'06),* September (pp. 503-510).

Yau, S. S., Gong, H., Huang, D., Gao, W., & Zhu, L. (2008). Specification, decomposition and agent synthesis for situation-aware service-based systems. *Journal of Systems and Software, 81*(10), 1663–1680. doi:10.1016/j.jss.2008.02.035

Yau, S. S., Huang, D., & Zhu, L. (2007) An approach to adaptive distributed execution monitoring for workflows in service-based systems. In *Proceedings of the 4th IEEE International Workshop on Software Cybernetics (IWSC'07),* July (pp. 211-216).

Yau, S. S., Huang, D., Gong, H., & Davulcu, H. (2005) Situation-awareness for adaptable service coordination in service-based systems. In *Proceedings of the 29th Annual International Computer Software and Application Conference (COMPSAC' 05),* July (pp.107-112).

Yau, S. S., Huang, D., Zhu, L., & Cai, K.-Y. (2007) A software cybernetic approach to deploying and scheduling workflow applications in service-based systems. In *Proceedings of the 11th International Workshop on Future Trends of Distributed Computing Systems (FTDCS'07),* March (pp. 149-156).

Yau, S. S., Karim, F., Wang, Y., Wang, B., & Gupta, S. K. S. (2002). Reconfigurable context-sensitive middleware for pervasive computing. *IEEE Pervasive Computing / IEEE Computer Society [and] IEEE Communications Society, 1*(3), 33–40. doi:10.1109/MPRV.2002.1037720

Yau, S. S., Mukhopadhyay, S., & Bharadwaj, R. (2005) Specification, analysis and implementation of architectural patterns for dependable software systems. In *Proceedings of the 10th IEEE International Workshop on Object-oriented Real-time Dependable Systems (WORDS 2005),* February (pp. 197-204).

Yau, S. S., Mukhopadhyay, S., Huang, D., Gong, H., Davulcu, H., & Zhu, L. (2005). Automated agent synthesis for situation-aware service coordination in service-based systems. Retrieved December 4, 2005, from http://dpse.eas.asu.edu /as3/papers/ASU-CSE-TR-05-009.pdf

Yau, S. S., Wang, Y., & Karim, F. (2002). Development of situation-aware application software for ubiquitous computing environments. In *Proceedings of the 26th IEEE International Computer Software and Applications Conference (COMPSAC'02),* August (pp. 233-238).

Yau, S. S., Zhu, L., Huang, D., & Gong, H. (2007). An approach to automated agent deployment in service-based systems. In *Proceedings of the 10th IEEE Symposium on Object-oriented Real-time distributed Computing (ISORC'07),* May (pp. 257-264).

Yau, S., Yao, Y., Chen, Z., & Zhu, L. (2005). An Adaptable Security Framework for Service-based Systems. In *Proceedings 10th IEEE International Workshop on Object-Oriented Real-Time Dependable Systems (WORDS2005),* (pp. 28-35), Sedona, Arizona.

Yee, G., & Korba, L. (2003). Bilateral E-services Negotiation Under Uncertainty. In *Proceedings of the 2003 International Symposium on Applications and the Internet (SAINT2003),* (pp. 352-355), Orlando, Florida.

Yee, G., & Korba, L. (2003). The Negotiation of Privacy Policies in Distance Education. In *Proceedings of the 14th IRMA International Conference,* (pp. 702-705), Philadelphia, Pennsylvania.

Yee, G., & Korba, L. (2005). Semi-automatic derivation and use of personal privacy policies in e-business. *International Journal of E-Business Research, 1*(1), 54-69.

Yee, G., & Korba, L. (2005). Negotiated Security Policies for E-Services and Web Services. In *Proceedings of the 2005 IEEE International Conference on Web Services (ICWS 2005),* Vol. 2, (pp. 605-612), Orlando, Florida.

Yee, G., & Korba, L. (2005). Context-Aware Security Policy Agent for Mobile Internet Services. In *Proceedings of the 2005 IFIP International Conference on Intelligence in Communication Systems (INTELLCOMM 2005),* (pp. 249-259), Montreal, Quebec, Canada.

Yu, J., & Buyya, R. (2005). A taxonomy of scientific workflow systems for grid computing. *SIGMOD Record, 34*(3), 44–49.

Zachman, J. (2002). *Zachman Framework*. Retrieved February 8, 2008 from http://www.zifa.com.

Zaremski, A.M., & Wing, J.M. (1995). Signature matching: A tool for using software libraries. *ACM Transactions on Software Engineering and Methodology*, *4*(2), 146–170.

Zaremski, A.M., & Wing, J.M. (1997). Specification matching of software components. *ACM Transactions on Software Engineering and Methodology*, 333–369.

Zelkowitz, M.V., & Wallace, D.R. (1998). Experimental models for validating technology. *IEEE Computer*, *31*(5), 23–31.

Zeng, L., Benatallah, B., Ngu, A., Dumas, M., Kalagnanam, J., & Chang, H. (2004). QoS-aware middleware for Web Service Composition. *IEEE Transactions on Software Engineering*, *30*(5), 311–327. doi:10.1109/TSE.2004.11

Zhang, C., & Chen, X. (2005). *A multiple instance learning approach for content based image retrieval using one-class support vector machine*. Proceedings of the IEEE International Conference on Multimedia and Expo (ICME 2005), 1142–1145.

Zhang, C., Chen, S.-C., & Shyu, M.-L. (2004). *Multiple object retrieval for image databases using multiple instance learning and relevance feedback*. Proceedings of the 2004 IEEE International Conference on Multimedia and Expo (ICME), Taipei, Taiwan, 775–778.

Zhang, K., & Shasha, D. (1989). Simple Fast Algorithms for the Editing Distance between Trees and Related Problems. *SIAM Journal on Computing*, *18*(6), 1245–1262. doi:10.1137/0218082

Zhang, L.-J., Zhang, J., & Allam, A. (2008). A Method and Case Study of Designing Presentation Module in an SOA-based Solution Using Configurable Architectural Building Blocks (ABBs). In *Proceedings of the 2008 IEEE International Conference on Services Computing (SCC 2008)*, Jul. 8-11, 2008, Honolulu, HI, USA (pp. 459-467).

Zhang, Z., & Yang, H. (2004). Incubating services in legacy systems for architectural migration. *Proceedings of IPSJ/IEEE Asia-Pacific Software Engineering Conference*.

Zhao, J., Wroe, C., Goble, C.A., Stevens, R., Quan, D., & Greenwood, R.M. (2004). Using semantic Web technologies for representing e-science provenance. *ISWC*.

Zhao, W., Moser, L. E., & Melliar-Smith, P. M. (2005). Fault tolerance for distributed and networked applications. In *Encyclopedia of Information Science and Technology* (pp. 1190-1196). Hershey, PA: IGI Global.

Zhao, W., Moser, L. E., & Melliar-Smith, P. M. (2008). A reservation-based extended transaction protocol. *IEEE Transactions on Parallel and Distributed Systems*, *19*(2), 49–56. doi:10.1109/TPDS.2007.70727

Zhao, Y., Wilde, M., & Foster. I. (2006). Applying the virtual data provenance model. *Proceedings of the International Provenance and Annotation Workshop (IPAW)*, Chicago, USA, May 3-5.

Zhao, Z, Booms, S., Belloum, A., de Laat, C, & Hertzberger, B. (2006). VLE-WVBus: A scientific workflow bus for multi e-Science domains. *Proceedings of the 2nd IEEE Iint. Conference on E-Science and Grid Computing (e-Science 2006)* Amsterdam, Netherlands.

Zhou, Z.-H., Jiang, K., & Li, M. (2005). Multi-instance learning based web mining. *Applied Intelligence*, *22*(2), 135–147.

Zhu, H. (2006). A framework for service-oriented testing of Web services. In Proceedings of 30th *Annual International Computer Software and Applications Conference (COMPSAC 2006), Vol 2.* Los Alamitos, California: IEEE Computer Society Press.

Zhu, H., Hall, P. A. V., & May, J. H. R. (1997). Software unit test coverage and adequacy. *ACM Computing Surveys*, *29*(4), 366–427. doi:10.1145/267580.267590

Zhu, L., & Gorton, I. (2007). UML profiles for design decisions and non-functional requirements. *Proceedings of ACM/IEEE International Conference on Software Engineering Workshop on Sharing and Reusing Architectural Knowledge - Architecture, Rationale, and Design Intent.*

Zimmermann, O., Tomlinson, M., & Peuser, S. (2003). *Perspectives on Web Services*. Heidelberg: Springer.

Zou, J., & Pavlovski, C. (2006). Modeling architectural non functional requirements: From use case to control case. *Proceedings of IEEE International Conference on e-Business Engineering.*

Zou, Y.Z., Zhang, L.J., Zhang, L., Xie, B., & Mei, H. (2006). *User feedback-based refinement for Web services retrieval using multiple instance learning*. Proceedings of the International Conference on Web Services, Chicago, 18–22.

zur Mühlen, M. (1999). *Resource modeling in workflow applications*. Proceedings of the Workflow Management Conference, Muenster, Germany.

Zuse, H. (1990). *Software complexity measures and models*. New York: de Gruyter & Co.

Zuse, H. (1997). *A framework of software measurement*. Berlin: Walter de Gruyter Inc.

About the Contributors

Liang-Jie (LJ) Zhang is a Research Staff Member and Program Manager of Application Architectures and Realization at IBM T.J. Watson Research Center. He has made significant original contributions to Services Computing innovations and interactive media systems. Zhang is the founding chair of IBM Research's Services Computing Professional Interest Community and has been leading an IBM Service-Oriented Architecture (SOA) tooling and architecture research project for years. He has been co-leading IBM's SOA Solution Stack (a.k.a SOA Reference Architecture: Solution View) project since 2004. His new book Services Computing has been published by Springer. He has received 2 IBM Outstanding Technical Achievement Awards, 9 IBM Creative Contribution Awards, an Outstanding Achievement Award by the World Academy of Sciences, and an Innovation Leadership Award from Chinese Institute of Electronics. Dr. Zhang has 36 granted patents and 20 pending patent applications. As the lead inventor, he holds federated Web services discovery and dynamic services composition patents. He is the chair of IEEE Computer Society Technical Committee on Services Computing. He has been appointed as the Editor-in-Chief of IEEE Transactions on Services Computing.

* * *

Wil van der Aalst is a full Professor of Information Systems at the Technische Universiteit Eindhoven having a position in both the Department of Mathematics and Computer Science and the department of Technology Management. Currently he is also an adjunct professor at Queensland University of Technology working within the BPM group. His research interests include workflow management, process mining, Petri nets, business process management, process modelling, and process analysis.

George Athanasopoulos is currently a researcher and member of the S3 Laboratory (www.s3lab.com) and a Ph.D. candidate student at the Department of Informatics and Telecommunications of the National and Kapodistrian University of Athens (www.di.uoa.gr). He has a diploma from Department of Computer Engineering and Informatics of the University of Patras (www.ceid.upatras.gr) and has participated in various research and development projects during his work experience. His research interests include service-oriented computing with a focus on the context-adaptable composition of heterogeneous services comprising various types of services such Web services (either stateless or stateful), P2P services, sensor and actuator services, etc. Additional research interests are related to distributed systems and software architecture modeling as well as modern programming methodologies.

Hyerim Bae is an assistant professor in the Industrial Engineering Department at Pusan National University (PNU), Korea. He received PhD, MS, and BS degrees from the Industrial Engineering Department at Seoul National University, Korea. He had been a manager for information strategic planning at Samsung Card Corporation before he joined PNU. He is interested in the areas of Business Process Management (BPM), process-based B2B integration, and ubiquitous business computing. His current research activities include analysis of business process efficiency, controlling of logistics processes with context awareness, and convenient modeling of business processes.

Joonsoo Bae is an Assistant Professor of Department of Industrial and Information Systems Engineering in Chonbuk National University. He received PhD, MS, and BS degrees in Industrial Engineering from Seoul National University, South Korea in 2000, 1995, and 1993, respectively. He also completed one year postdoctoral course in College of Computing of Georgia Institute of Technology at 2006. He had industry experience in LG-EDS as a technical consultant of SCM & CRM team from 2000 to 2002. He is interested in system design and integration of management information system and e-Business technology. His research topics include business processes management using workflow systems and advanced internet application.

Roger Barga works for the Microsoft Corporation as lead architect for External Research in Microsoft Research (MSR). Prior to assuming this role, Roger was a researcher in the database group at Microsoft Research since 1997. He is a member of the ACM and IEEE. Contact him at barga@microsoft.com.

Carlo Batini is full professor of Computer Engineering at Università di Milano Bicocca. His research interests include cooperative information systems, information systems and data base systems modeling and design, usability of information systems, data and information quality. He has published over 30 papers in international journals and books, about 80 papers at the international level, including IEEE and ACM Transactions, co-edited five books, and published 15 books. Formerly, since 1995 to 2003 in Italy he was a member of the board of directors of the Authority for Information Technology in the Public Administration, where he headed several large scale projects for the modernization of the public administration.

José Felipe Mejia Bernal is PhD student in software engineering at Politecnico di Torino, where he received his M.S. degree in Computer Engineering in 2006, and he worked as research assistant in Department of Computer Science and Automation. His current research interests include dynamic business process, Rule-based programming and context-aware systems.

Elisa Bertino is professor of computer science at Purdue University and Research Director of the Center for Information and Research in Information Assurance and Security. Prior to joining Purdue, she was a professor and department head at the Department of Computer Science and Communication of the University of Milan. She has been a visiting researcher at the IBM Research Laboratory (now Almaden) in San Jose, at the Microelectronics and Computer Technology Corporation, at Rutgers University, at Telcordia Technologies. Her recent research focuses on privacy techniques for databases, digital identity management, policy systems, and security for web service. She is a Fellow of ACM and of IEEE. She received the IEEE Computer Society 2002 Technical Achievement Award and the IEEE Computer Society 2005 Kanai Award. She a member of the editorial board of IEEE Transactions on Dependable and Secure Computing, and IEEE Security & Privacy.

Ramesh Bharadwaj is currently a member of the Software Engineering Section of NRLNaval Research Laboratory's Center for High Assurance Computer Systems. He also served as an adjunct associate professor of computer science at the George Washington University. His research interests include methods and tools for engineering software for high assurance systems, secure agents and agent based software engineering, languages and tools for model-driven development of mission-critical systems, computational logic. He received a Ph.D. in software engineering from McMaster University. He is a member of IEEE and ACM.

Sami Bhiri is a senior researcher at DERI - the National University of Ireland, Galway, where he is leading the SOA research unit and managing several EU projects. Before joining DERI, he was a research and teaching assistant in the University of Nancy 1 and in the ECOO team of the LORIA-INRIA research laboratory. His research interests are in the area of applying semantics to B2B Integration, Service Oriented Computing and Business Process Management.

Ken Birman is Professor of Computer Science at Cornell University. He currently heads the QuickSilver project, which is developing the world's fastest and most scalable publish-subscribe system and a new, highly automated, platform aimed at making it dramatically easier to build scalable clustered applications. Previously he worked on fault-tolerance, security, and reliable multicast. In 1987 he founded a company, Isis Distributed Systems, which developed robust software solutions for stock exchanges, air traffic control, and factory automation. For example, Isis currently operates the New York and Swiss Stock Exchanges, the French air traffic control system, and the US Navy AEGIS warship. The technology permits these and other systems to automatically adapt themselves when failures or other disruptions occur, and to replicate critical services so that availability can be maintained even while some system components are down. In contrast to his past work, Birman's recent work has focused on issues of scale, self-management and self-repair mechanisms for complex distributed systems, such as large data centers and wide-area publish-subscribe. The very large scale of these kinds of applications poses completely new challenges. For example, while protocols for data replication on a small scale are closely tied to dahabase concepts such as two-phase commit, these large scale applications are best viewed as probabilistic systems, and the most appropriate technologies are similar to techniques seen in peer-to-peer file sharing applications. Birman is the author of several books. His most recent textbook, "Reliable Distributed Computing: Technologies, Web Services, and Applications", was published by Springer-Verlag in May of 2005. Previously he wrote two other books and more than 200 journal and conference papers, including one that appeared in Scientific American in May, 1996. Dr. Birman was also Editor in Chief of ACM Transactions on Computer Systems from 1993-1998 and is a Fellow of the ACM.

Ylva Brandt finished her studies at the Braunschweig University of Technology, Germany, with a diploma (equivalent to a Master's Degree) in computer science in September 2005. The main focus of her studies was directed at distributed systems, data bases and E-Learning. In July 2007 she earned a second Master's Degree (Master of Arts in Education) at the Georg-August-University in Göttingen, Germany. In her master thesis, she explored the influence of gender on students' academic self-concept. Currently, she is continuing her studies at the teacher training college in Göttingen. Furthermore, she teaches mathematics and computer science at the Max-Planck-Gymnasium in Göttingen. Her current research focuses on new design concepts for computer science learning materials.

Carsten Buschmann received his Master of Computer Science from the Braunschweig University of Technology, Germany, in 2002. He conducted research at the Braunschweig University of Technology and the University of Lübeck in the area of wireless sensor networks. Besides exploring middleware support for application development for distributed pervasive computing within the SWARMS project, he developed context awareness protocols for wireless sensor networks. He received his PhD in January 2009 from the University of Lübeck. Serving as General Manager and CTO of the coalesenses GmbH, a startup company founded in 2005 as a spin-off of the University of Lübeck, he is the leading force behind the development of iSense, a modular hardware and software platform for wireless sensor networks.

Jorge Cardoso joined the University of Madeira (Portugal) in March 2003. He previously gave lectures at University of Georgia (USA) and at the Instituto Politécnico de Leiria (Portugal). Dr. Cardoso received his Ph.D. in Computer Science from the University of Georgia in 2002. While at the University of Georgia, he was part of the LSDIS Lab. where he did extensive research on workflow management systems. In 1999, he worked at the Boeing Company on enterprise application integration. Dr. Cardoso is the organizer of the International Workshop on Semantic and Dynamic Web Processes series. He has published over 80 refereed papers in the areas of workflow management systems, semantic Web, and related fields. He has also edited 4 books on semantic Web and Web services. He is on the Editorial Board of the Enterprise Information Systems Journal, the International Journal on Semantic Web and Information systems, and the International Journal of Information Technology. He is also member of the Editorial Advisory Review Board of Idea Group Inc. Prior to joining the University of Georgia, he worked for two years at CCG, Zentrum für Graphische Datenverarbeitung, where is did research on Computer Supported Cooperative Work.

James Caverlee is a Ph.D. candidate in the College of Computing at Georgia Tech and a member of the multidisciplinary Tennenbaum Institute for enterprise transformation. His research interests are generally in the areas of Web and Distributed Information Management, with an emphasis on: (1) Enterprise Computing and Workflow Management; (2) Spam-Resilient Web-Scale Computing; and (3) Web Information Retrieval and Management. James graduated magna cum laude from Duke University in 1996 with a B.A. in Economics. He received the M.S. degree in Engineering-Economic Systems & Operations Research in 2000, and the M.S. degree in Computer Science in 2001, both from Stanford University.

W.K. Chan received this Ph.D. degree in Software Engineering from The University of Hong Kong, Hong Kong in 2004. He is a Lecturer of City University of Hong Kong. He publishes service computing research results actively in ICSE and FSE. He serves on the program committee of international conferences and reviews papers of many software engineering conferences and journals such as TSE, TOSEM, ASEJ, JSS, ICSE, FSE, ISSTA, ASE, COMPSAC, QSIC, APSEC, and ISSRE. He has practiced software engineering in the industry for more than 10 years before completing his PhD study. His research interests include solving software engineering issues in embedded system, applications of pervasive computing and service computing. He is a member of ACM and IEEE.

S.C. Cheung received his Ph.D. degree in Computing from the Imperial College of Science, Technology and Medicine, University of London, London, U.K in 1994. He is an Associate Professor of Computer Science and Engineering, and Associate Director of CyberSpace Center at the Hong Kong University of

Science and Technology. He is an associate editor of the IEEE Transactions on Software Engineering, and participates actively into the program and organizing committees of many major international conferences on software engineering, distributed systems and web technologies. His work has been reported by more than 100 publications at international journals and conferences, which include TOSEM, TSE, ASE, DSS, TR, ICSE, FSE, ESEC and ER. He is a Chartered Fellow of the British Computer Society and a senior member of the IEEE. He co-found the first International Workshop on Services Computing (SEIW) in 2005, the first International Workshop on Automation of Software Testing (AST) in 2006, and was the tutorials chair of ICSE 2006. He has co-edited special issues for the Computer Journal and the International Journal of Web Services Research (JWSR), such as ICSE, FSE, ISSTA, ASE, ICDCS, ER, COMPSAC, APSEC, QSIC, EDOC, SCC and CEC. His research interests include software engineering, services computing, ubiquitous computing, and embedded software engineering.

Marco Comerio is a PhD student at Università di Milano Bicocca. He received his laurea degree in Computer Science at the same University in 2006. His PhD thesis regards the definition of a novel approach for semantic web service selection based on the evaluation of non-functional properties. His research interests are mainly in semantic web services, service oriented design methodologies and non-functional properties (NFP). He has published about 10 papers in international conferences and journals. He is currently working in the European IST project n. 27347 SEEMP (Single European Employment Market-Place) and in the Italian FIRB project RBNE05XYPW NeP4B (Networked Peers for Business).

Jason Crampton is a Reader in Information Security in the Information Security Group (ISG) at Royal Holloway, University of London, United Kingdom. He joined the ISG having completed his PhD in 2002. His research is mainly concerned with the development of formal models for access control in computerized systems, with particular interest in the management of authorization policies. He is an associate editor of ACM Transactions on Information and System Security and has been a programme committee member for numerous security-related conferences.

Hasan Davulcu has been an assistant professor in the Department of Computer Science and Engineering at Arizona State University since 2002. He received a Ph.D. in computer science from the State University of New York at Stony Brook. His research interests include logic-based workflow modeling, Web mining, and information integration.

Flavio De Paoli is an associate professor at Università di Milano Bicocca; he received a laurea degree in Electronic Engineering, and a PhD in Computer Science from the Politecnico di Milano. His research interests include software engineering, programming languages, software architecture, and cooperative distributed systems. His main current activities deal with the definition of service-based models and architecture for the development of collaborative Web applications to support communities of interest, and quality-based development of service-based business processes. He is co-author of three books and several papers in international journals and conference proceedings.

Danny Dolev received his B.Sc. degree in mathematics and physics from the Hebrew University, Jerusalem in 1971. His M.Sc. thesis in Applied Mathematics was completed in 1973, at the Weizmann Institute of Science, Israel. His Ph.D. thesis was on Synchronization of Parallel Processors (1979). He was a Post-Doctoral fellow at Stanford University, 1979-1981, and IBM Research Fellow 1981-1982. He joined the Hebrew University in 1982. From 1987 to 1993 he held a joint appointment as a professor at the Hebrew University and as a research staff member at the IBM Almaden Research Center. He is currently a professor at the Hebrew University of Jerusalem. His research interests are all aspects of distributed computing, fault tolerance, security and networking -- theory and practice.

Marlon Dumas is an Associated Professor at Queensland University of Technology and Fellow of the Queensland Government (``Smart State'' Fellow). He received a PhD from University of Grenoble (France) in 2000. His research interests are in the areas of business process management, application integration and e-commerce technology.

Paolo Falcarin is research assistant in the Software Engineering Group at the Department of Computer Science and Automation of Politecnico di Torino, one of the leading engineering universities in Italy. He received his M.S. degree in Computer Science Engineering in 2000, and his PhD in Software Engineering, in 2004, from Politecnico di Torino.

Stefan Fischer is a full professor in computer science at the University of Lübeck, Germany, and the director of the Institute for Telematics. He got his diploma degree in "Wirtschaftsinformatik" and his doctoral degree from the University of Mannheim, Germany, in 1992 and 1996, respectively. After a postdoctoral year at the University of Montreal, Canada, he joined the newly founded International University in Germany, one of the first private universities in Germany, as an assistant professor in 1998. In 2001, he became an associate professor in computer science at the Braunschweig University of Technology, where he stayed until 2004, when he joined Lübeck University. His research interest is currently focused on new network and distributed system structures such as ad-hoc and sensor networks. He has (co-)authored about 100 scientific books and articles. Dr Fischer is a member of ACM, IEEE and the German Gesellschaft für Informatik (GI).

Walid Gaaloul is an assistant professor in TELECOM & Management SudParis . He was an adjunct lecturer in the National University of Ireland, Galway (NUIG) and a postdoctoral researcher at the Digital Enterprise Research Institute (DERI). He holds an M.S. (2002) and a Ph.D. (2006) in computer science from the University of Nancy-France. His research interests lie in the area of Business Process Management, Process intelligence, Process reliability, Service Oriented Computing and semantics for B2B Integration.

Dennis Gannon is a Professor of Computer Science and Science Director of Pervasive Technology Labs at Indiana University. His research interests include programming systems and tools, distributed computing, computer networks, parallel programming, computational science, problem solving environments and performance analysis of Grid and MPP systems. IEEE member.

Carole Goble is a Professor in the School of Computer Science in the University of Manchester. She is Director of the myGrid project, a software toolkit for Life Science services that has produced the Taverna workflow workbench, and pioneered the use of semantic web technologies for service management and provenance collection. She is technical director of the OntoGrid project, which has developed, S-OGSA, the first reference architecture for metadata management in Grid middleware. She is the current chair of the Open Middleware Infrastructure Institute UK (OMII-UK), which provides software and support for the UK e-Science community, including the prototyping of the myExperiment. org portal for sharing and reusing experiments on-line. Her research interests include Grid computing, the Semantic Grid, the Semantic Web, e-Science and Bioinformatics.

Claude Godart is full time Professor at Nancy University, France and scientific director of the INRIA ECOO project. His centre of interest concentrates on the consistency maintenance of the data mediating the cooperation between several partners. This encompasses advanced transaction models, user centric workflow and web services composition models. He has been implicated in several transfer projects with industries (France, Europe, and Japan) for a wide range of applications including e-commerce, software processes and e-learning.

Antoon Goderis received his undergraduate degree in Applied Economics from K.U. Leuven, Belgium, in 2000, the M.Sc. in Computer Science from University of Manchester, UK, in 2001, and the M.Sc. in Artificial Intelligence from the University of Edinburgh, UK, in 2003. He is finishing a Ph.D. in the School of Computer Science at the University of Manchester. His research interests are in workflow reuse, discovery and similarity, e-Science, the Semantic Web and Bioinformatics.

Silvan Tecumseh Golega is a master student at the Hasso-Platner-Institut of the Universität Potsdam, Germany. Silvan received a B.Sc. from the Hasso-Platner-Institut in 2006 after spending one year at the Universidad Rey Juan Carlos in Madrid, Spain. Silvan performed the practical work of his master thesis under the supervision of Frederic Montagut at SAP Research, France on the topic Composition and Coordination of Transactional Business Processes. He contributed to the work presented in this chapter during his stay at SAP Research.

Simone Grega is a young researcher at Università di Milano Bicocca; he received a laurea degree in Computer Science from the same University in 2006. His research interests include service-oriented methodologies, information systems and data quality. His main current activities deal with the definition of a service modeling design methodology to project Web service characterized by an high-level of quality (Quality of Service). Moreover, his activities deal with the definition of a methodology that allows the improvement of data quality by considering different types of information (structured, semi-structured and unstructured data). He is author of several papers in international journals and conference proceedings. He is currently working in the European IST project n. 27347 SEEMP (Single European Employment Market-Place) and in the Italian FIRB project RBNE0358YR eG4M (eGovernment for Mediterranean Countries). He was involved in European projects, part of the FP6 EU research program on service engineering, working on service creation technologies and service description languages. He was the program chair of the first Telecom Service Oriented Architectures Workshop (TSOA) in 2007. His current research interests include model driven engineering, service engineering, distributed systems.

Arthur ter Hofstede received his PhD in Computer Science from the University of Nijmegen in The Netherlands in 1993. Currently he works as an Associate Professor at the School of Information Systems of the Faculty of Information Technology of Queensland University of Technology in Brisbane, Australia. He is co-leader of the BPM group in the Faculty. His main research interests are in the conceptual and formal foundations of workflow. He is committed to the Workflow Patterns Initiative (www.workflowpatterns.com) and the YAWL (Yet Another Workflow Language) Initiative (http://yawlfoundation.org/).

Dazhi Huang is a Ph.D. student in the Department of Computer Science and Engineering at Arizona State University. His research interests include middleware, mobile and ubiquitous computing, and workflow scheduling in service-oriented computing environments. He received his B.S. in computer science from Tsinghua University in China.

Hiroshi Igaki {received the B.E. degree (2000) in Department of Electrical and Electronics Engineering from Kobe University, Japan, and the M.E. degree (2002) and D.E. degree (2005) in Information Science from Nara Institute of Science and Technology, Japan. From 2006 to 2007, he worked for Faculty of Mathematical Sciences and Information Engineering, Nanzan University, Japan. He is currently an Assistant Professor of Graduate School of Engineering at Kobe University. His research interests include communication support in software development, web services and service-oriented architecture. He is a member of the IEEE, ACM, IEICE and IPSJ.

Jaakko Kangasharju is a doctoral student at the University of Helsinki, and working as a researcher at the Helsinki Institute for Information Technology. His PhD dissertation focuses on enabling XML messaging and processing on mobile devices. He is currently a member of the Efficient XML Interchange Working Group at the World Wide Web Consortium.

Firat Kart received the Ph.D. degree in Electrical and Computer Engineering at the University of California, Santa Barbara. He received the B.S. degree in Computer Science from Bilkent University in Ankara, Turkey. Currently, he is a principal engineer / architect at Tibco in Palo Alto, California. His research interests include distributed systems, computer networks, Service Oriented Architectures, Web Services, database transactions, and supply chain and healthcare applications.

Oba Katsuya Oba received the Batchelor of Arts degree from Osaka University, Osaka, Japan, in 1989. He joined Osaka Gas Information System Research Institute Co., Ltd. (OGIS-RI) as a systems engineer. From 2000 to 2005, he worked for OGIS International, Inc. in Palo Alto, California as General Manager and leaded several software product development and R&D projects. He returned to OGIS-RI in 2006, and is leading R&D and business development relating to Service Oriented Architecture (SOA). His research interests include software architecture, business and systems modeling and software development processes. He is a member of Information Processing Society of Japan.

Larry Korba is a Principal Research Officer with the National Research Council Canada. He is the Group Leader of the Information Security Group in the Institute for Information Technology (http://www.iit-iti.nrc-cnrc.gc.ca/) and involved in the research and development of security and privacy enhancing technologies for applications ranging from gaming to ad hoc wireless systems.

Leung is a Chartered Fellow of the British Computer Society, a Fellow of the Institute of Print-media Professionals, a Fellow of the Hong Kong Institutions of Engineer, a Fellow of the Hong Kong Computer Society, a Senior Member of the IEEE and IEEE Computer Society, and has been an Executive Committee member (1990-1993), General Secretary (1994), Vice-Chair (1995-1997) and Chair (1998-1999), Past Chair since 2000, of the IEEE Hong Kong Section Computer Chapter. The Chapter won the IEEE Most Outstanding Computer Society Chapter Award in 1998. Dr. Leung is also a C.Eng., an Ir., a Chartered IT Professional, a RPE (Information), and a member of ACM and ACS.

Karl R.P.H. Leung is a Principal Lecturer in the Department of Information & Communications Technology at the Hong Kong Institute of Vocational Education (IVE) and the Director of the Compuware Software Testing Laboratory of IVE. Dr. Leung is also an Adjunct Professor of the University of Queensland, Australia and an Advisor of the Shunde Polytechnic, P.R. China, and an Advisor & Adjunct Professor of the Panyu Polytechnic, P.R. China. Dr. Leung is also a reviewer of many major journals and conferences and has participated in the organization of many major international conferences. His research areas include: Domain Modeling, Mission Critical Software Engineering Methodology, Secure Workflow Systems, Software Testing, Mobile Location Estimation, Ubiquitous & Location Based Systems and QoS of Video Streaming.

Peter Li gained a Masters in Research in Bioinformatics from the University of Leeds, UK in 2002. He is currently a Research Associate at the Manchester Interdisciplinary Building, University of Manchester, UK. His research focus is on the application of e-Science technologies in systems biology.

Yan Li is currently a Ph.D. candidate in software institute at Peking University, P.R. China. His current research interests include component-based software development, reuse repository and component retrieval.

Tancred Lindholm is a doctoral student at the Helsinki University of Technology, and working as a researcher at the Helsinki Institute for Information Technology. His research is concentrated on structured data access and synchronization on limited devices.

Ling Liu is an associate professor at the College of Computing at Georgia Tech. There, she directs the research programs in Distributed Data Intensive Systems Lab (DiSL), examining research issues and technical challenges in building large scale distributed computing systems that can grow without limits. Dr. Liu and the DiSL research group have been working on various aspects of distributed data intensive systems, ranging from distributed computing systems, enterprise systems to business workflow management systems. Prof. Liu has published more than 160 technical papers in the areas of Internet Computing systems, Internet data management, distributed systems, and information security. She is the recipient of best paper award of WWW 2004 and best paper award of IEEE ICDCS 2003, and a recipient of 2005 Pat Goldberg Memorial Best Paper Award. Her research group has produced a number of software systems that are either open sources or directly accessible online, among which the most popular ones are WebCQ and XWRAPElite. Dr. Liu is currently on the editorial board of several international journals, including IEEE Transactions on Knowledge and Data Engineering, International Journal of Very large Database systems (VLDBJ), International Journal of Web Services Research, and has chaired a number of conferences as a PC chair, a vice PC chair, or a general chair, including IEEE International Conference on Data Engineering (ICDE 2004, ICDE 2006, ICDE 2007), IEEE International Conference on Distributed Computing (ICDCS 2006), IEEE International Conference on Collaborative Computing (CollaborateCom 2005, 2006), IEEE International Conference on Web Services (ICWS 2004). She is a recipient of IBM Faculty Award (2003, 2006). Prof. Liu's current research is partly sponsored by grants from NSF CISE CSR, ITR, CyberTrust, AFOSR, and IBM.

Ken-ichi Matsumoto received the BE, ME, and PhD degrees in Information and Computer sciences from Osaka University, Japan, in 1985, 1987, 1990, respectively. Dr. Matsumoto is currently a professor in the Graduate School of Information Science at Nara Institute of Science and Technology, Japan. His research interests include software metrics and measurement framework. He is a senior member of the IEEE, and a member of the ACM, IEICE, IPSJ and JSSST.

Andrea Maurino is a research associate at Università di Milano Bicocca. He received his laurea degree and PhD from the Politecnico di Milano; his research fields include orchestration of mobile information systems, methodologies for developing multichannel information systems, quality of web applications and data quality. He has published about 20 papers in international conferences and journals.

Hong Mei is currently a professor in the School of Electronics Engineering and Computer Science, Peking University, P.R. China. He received a Bachelor's degree and a Master's degree in Computer Science from Nanjing University of Aeronautics & Astronautics (NUAA) in 1984 and 1987 respectively, and a Doctorate degree in Computer Science from Shanghai Jiao Tong University in 1992. From 1987 to 1989, he was working at NUAA as a research assistant. In 1992, he joined in Peking University (PKU) as a post-doctoral research fellow. From 1994 to present, he was working at the Department of Computer Science and Technology and the School of Electronics Engineering and Computer Science in PKU, and became associate professor in 1994 and full professor in 1997. His current research interests include: Software Engineering and Software Engineering Environment, Software Reuse and Software Component Technology, Distributed Object Technology, Software Production Technology, and Programming Language.

P. M. Melliar-Smith is a professor in the Department of Electrical and Computer Engineering at the University of California, Santa Barbara. Previously, he worked as a research scientist at SRI International in Menlo Park. His research interests encompass the fields of distributed systems and applications, and network architectures and protocols. He has published more than 250 conference and journal papers in computer science and engineering. Dr. Melliar-Smith is a pioneer in the field of fault-tolerant distributed computing. He received the Ph.D. in Computer Science from the University of Cambridge, England.

Refik Molva is a full professor and the head of the Computer Communications Department at Eurecom Institute in Sophia Antipolis, France. His current research interests are in security protocols for self-organizing systems and privacy. He has been responsible for research projects on multicast and mobile network security, anonymity and intrusion detection. Beside security, he worked on distributed multimedia applications over high speed networks and on network interconnection. Prior to joining Eurecom, he worked as a Research Staff Member in the Zurich Research Laboratory of IBM where he was one of the key designers of the KryptoKnight security system. He also worked as a network security consultant in the IBM Consulting Group in 1997. Refik Molva has a Ph.D. in Computer Science from the Paul Sabatier University in Toulouse (1986) and a B.Sc. in Computer Science (1981) from Joseph Fourier University, Grenoble, France.

Frederic Montagut is a Senior Researcher with SAP Research in Zurich, Switzerland. Frederic obtained his engineering diploma from Telecom INT, France, the Diploma of Advanced Studies (M.Sc.) in Network and Distributed Systems from Nice University, France in 2004 and a PhD in Computer Science from Telecom Paristech, France in 2007. He joined SAP Research in October 2004 as a PhD candidate working under the supervision of Pr Refik MOLVA, Eurecom Institute before moving to Switzerland. His research interests range from distributed workflow systems, workflow coordination to workflow security.

Louise E. Moser is a professor in the Department of Electrical and Computer Engineering at the University of California, Santa Barbara. Her research interests span the fields of computer networks, distributed systems and software engineering. Dr. Moser has authored or coauthored more than 250 conference and journal publications. She has served as an associate editor for the IEEE Transactions on Services Computing and the IEEE Transactions on Computers and as an area editor for IEEE Computer in the area of networks. She received the Ph.D. in Mathematics from the University of Wisconsin, Madison.

Supratik Mukhopadhyay has been an assistant professor of Computer Science at Utah State University University since 2006. He received the Ph.D. degree in computer science at the Max Planck Institute Germany in 2001. During the year 2001-2002, he did postdoctoral research at the University of Pennsylvania, and was an Assistant Professor in computer science at West Virginia University. His research interests include formal methods for developing dependable systems.

Masahide Nakamura received the B.E., M.E., and Ph.D. degrees in Information and Computer Sciences from Osaka University, Japan, in 1994, 1996, 1999, respectively. From 1999 to 2000, he has been a post-doctoral fellow in SITE at University of Ottawa, Canada. He joined Cybermedia Center at Osaka University from 2000 to 2002. From 2002 to 2007, he worked for the Graduate School of Information Science at Nara Institute of Science and Technology, Japan. He is currently an associate professor in the Graduate School of Engineering at Kobe University. His research interests include the service-oriented architecture, Web services, the feature interaction problem, V&V techniques and software security. He is a member of the IEEE, ACM, IEICE, and IPSJ.

Richi Nayak is a senior lecturer in the School of Information System, Queensland University of Technology, Brisbane, Australia. Her research interests are data mining and Web intelligence. She has published over 50 papers in journals, conference proceedings and books. She has developed various innovative mining techniques and applications related to XML, Software Engineering, e-commerce, m-commerce and Web services.

Krzysztof Ostrowski is a Ph.D. candidate in the Computer Science department at Cornell University. He is currently building Live Distributed Objects, a new programming model and a platform, in which instances of distributed protocols are modeled as components with an object-oriented look and feel that can be composed in a type-safe manner to build complex distributed applications using a simple, intuitive drag and drop interface. Before joining Cornell, Krzys spent four years in the industry.

Chun Ouyang received her PhD in Computer Systems Engineering from the University of South Australia in 2004. She currently works as a post-doctoral research fellow at the Faculty of Information Technology in Queensland University of Technology, Australia. Her research interests are in the areas of workflow management, process modelling and analysis, Web services, Petri nets, and formal specification and verification.

Federica Paci is now a post-doctoral research associate at the Department of Information Engineering and Computer Science, Università degli Studi di Trento. From Febraury 2008 to March 2009, Federica Paci was a post-doctoral research associate at Purdue University. Paci's main research interests include access control for service oriented architectures and for virtual organizations, digital identity management, and trust negotiations. Currently, she is exploring privacy issues in the context of social networks. Paci earned her Ph.D. in Computer Science from the University of Milan, Italy, in Febraury 2008. In Febraury 2004, she received the equivalent of a combined bachelor's/master's degree in Computer Science, also from the University of Milan. During Spring Semester of 2005 and 2006, Paci was a visiting research scholar at CS Department of Purdue University, West Lafayette, IN. Paci is the author or co-author of more than 10 conference chapters and journal articles. Currently, she is co-authoring a book on Web services security. She served as a program committee member for APWeb 2008, IEEE CollaborateCom 2008, WWW 2009 Poster Session and ICPS 2009.

Michael Pantazoglou is currently a Ph.D. student at the Department of Informatics and Telecommunications of the National and Kapodistrian University of Athens. He holds a diploma degree in Informatics and Telecommunications from the same institution. He joined the S3 Laboratory in 2004 as a research scientist. During the last 3 years, he has participated in the SODIUM and SeCSE research & development projects. His research interests include service-oriented technologies with focus on service discovery and composition, information retrieval, natural language processing, and data processing.

Beth Plale is an Associate Professor of Computer Science and Director of the Data Search Institute at Indiana University. Her research interest is in the broad area of large-scale data management, specifically stream mining and event processing, distributed metadata and integration, provenance, grid and service-oriented architectures, and petascale databases. IEEE member.

Calton Pu is the John P. Imlay Jr. Chair in Software at Georgia Tech. His research interests include operating systems, transaction processing, and Internet data management. Pu received a PhD in computer science from the University of Washington. He is a member of the ACM, a senior member of the IEEE, and a fellow of the AAAS. Contact him at calton@cc.gatech.edu.

Akhil Sahai is a senior research scientist at HP Laboratories and is currently researching the areas of policy management and resource utility architectures. He has in the recent past researched the areas of web service and business process management. Contact him at akhil.sahai@hp.com.

Krishna Shenai is professor and chair at the Electrical Engineering and Computer Science Department at University of Toledo. He has more than 300 papers in IEEE journals and conferences, 4 books, 10 book chapters, and 15 patents. He is an IEEE Fellow, an AAAS Fellow, an IETE (India) Fellow, and an IEEE Distinguished lecturer. Before joining academia in 1995, he has held leadership positions in industry for 10 years (COMSAT, GE, Intel). He received his PhD. from Sanford University in electrical engineering in 1986.

Yogesh L. Simmhan is a doctoral candidate at Indiana University, working on distributed data and metadata management for large scale, data driven applications based on Grid and web-service paradigms. He is particularly interested in issues related to efficient provenance tracking, discovery, quality evaluation, and long term preservation of data generated from scientific workflows, with the overarching goal of building scalable information systems to effectively manage data end-to-end. IEEE member.

Junichi Suzuki Junichi Suzuki received a Ph.D. in computer science from Keio University, Japan, in 2001. He joined the University of Massachusetts, Boston in 2004, where he is currently an Assistant Professor of computer science. From 2001 to 2004, he was with the School of Information and Computer Science, the University of California, Irvine (UCI), as a postdoctoral research fellow. Before joining UCI, he was with Object Management Group Japan, Inc., as Technical Director. His research interests include model-driven software development, autonomous adaptive distributed systems, biologically-inspired software adaptation and self-organizing sensor networks. He is an editor of International Journal of Software Patterns, International Journal of Software Architecture and International Journal of Software Reuse. He was the Program Co-Chair of the 2008 IEEE International Workshop on Methodologies for Non-functional Properties in Services Computing. He served on over 35 conference program committees, and served as a workshop co-chair for the ACM/IEEE/ICST/Create-Net BIONETICS 2007 conference. He is an active participant and contributor in the ISO SC7/WG19 and the Object Management Group, Super Distributed Objects SIG. He is a member of IEEE and ACM.

Haruaki Tamada received the B.E. and M.E. in Information and Communication Engineering from Kyoto Sangyo University, Japan in 1999, 2001. He received D.E. degree from information science from Nara Institute of Science and Technology, Japan in 2006. He is currently an assistant professor in Faculty of Computer Science and Engineering at Kyoto Sangyo University, Japan. His research interests include software security, software measurement. He is a member of the IEICE, IPSJ and IEEE.

Akihiro Tanaka received the B.E. in Information and Mathematical from Nara University of Education, Japan in 2005. He received M.E. degree from Nara Institute of Science and Technology, Japan in 2007. He is currently working for Hitachi, Ltd. His research interests include service oriented architecture, Web service, home network system, legacy appliances.

Sasu Tarkoma received his MSc and PhD degrees in Computer Science from the University of Helsinki, Department of Computer Science. He has managed and participated in national and international research projects at the University of Helsinki, Helsinki University of Technology, and Helsinki Institute for Information Technology. He has also lectured several courses on middleware and data communications. He has over 40 scientific publications and has also contributed to several books on mobile middleware. His research interests include middleware and distributed computing.

Aphrodite Tsalgatidou is a permanent member of the Academic Staff at the Department of Informatics and Telecommunications of the National and Kapodistrian University of Athens since 1999. She holds a diploma degree in Chemistry from the same institution and an M.Sc. and a Ph.D in Computer

Science from the University of Manchester, England. Previously she was with the Hellenic Telecom Organization and a Research Director in a private company. Aphrodite is the director of the S3 Laboratory (www.s3lab.com) which pursues research in service engineering, software engineering and software development; she has participated in and/or managed a large number of projects in these areas and has published relevant papers. Her current research focuses on service interoperability, service discovery and composition, peer to peer systems and business process management and interoperability.

Claudio Venezia is researcher at Telecom Italia Lab since 2002. He received a degree in Economics with an experimental addressing in computer science along with further computer science certifications from University of Turin (Italy) in July 1998. He worked for three years in Ernst and Young critical technologies in several domains (Banking, Automotive, and E-commerce). He has been contributing to standardization activities (JAIN-SLEE, W3C) and internal and international Projects. His research interests include enhanced SOA paradigms meshing up IT and telecom capabilities, (Semantic) Web Services technologies and XML-based languages towards Web 2.0.

Hiroshi Wada Hiroshi Wada received his M.S. degree in computer science from Keio University, Japan, in 2002. He started the Ph.D. program in the University of Massachusetts, Boston in 2005. His research interests include model-driven software development, and service oriented architecture. Before enrolling in the Ph.D. program, he worked for Object Technology Institute, Inc., and engaged in consulting and educational services in the field of object oriented technologies, distributed systems and software modeling.

Christian Werner is an assistant professor for Distributed Systems at the Institute of Telematics at the University of Lübeck, Germany. Before, he was a researcher at the Braunschweig University of Technology and at the L3S research lab in Hannover, Germany. He is author of two books, several book chapters and more than 20 publications in conference and workshop proceedings. He received his diploma (equivalent to Master Degree) from the Humboldt-University in Berlin in July 2002. He received a doctoral degree from the University of Lübeck in August 2006. His research activities are focused on efficient approaches for implementing service-oriented architectures and other Internet-based services. This includes technologies for enhancing web services performance, particularly XML compression techniques, enhancing services reliability for medical applications, using web services on resource-constrained devices as well as new methods for transmitting audio and video data with ultra-low delays in the Internet.

Qinyi Wu is a PhD student at Georgia Tech, where she is also a member of the Distributed Data Intensive Systems Lab in the university's College of Computing. Her technical interests include workflows, transaction processing, and web services. She is a member of the IEEE. Contact her at qxw@cc.gatech.edu.

Bing Xie is currently an associate professor in the School of Electronics Engineering and Computer Science, Peking University, P.R. China. He received his Ph.D. degree in 1998. His current research interests include software engineering, component-based software development, formal methods and distributed systems.

Stephen S. Yau is currently the director of Information Assurance Center and a professor in the Department of Computer Science and Engineering at Arizona State University, Tempe, Arizona, USA. He served as the chair of the department from 1994 to 2001. He was previously with the University of Florida, Gainesville and Northwestern University, Evanston, Illinois. He served as the president of the Computer Society of the IEEE (Institute of Electrical and Electronics Engineers) and the editor-in-chief of IEEE Computer magazine. His current research is in distributed and service-oriented computing, adaptive middleware, software engineering and trustworthy computing. He received the Ph.D. degree in electrical engineering from the University of Illinois, Urbana. He is a life fellow of the IEEE and a fellow of American Association for the Advancement of Science.

George O.M. Yee (www.georgeyee.ca) is a Senior Research Officer in the Information Security Group, Institute for Information Technology, National Research Council Canada (NRC). Prior to joining the NRC in late 2001, he spent over 20 years at Bell-Northern Research and Nortel Networks. George received his PhD (Electrical Engineering) from Carleton University, Ottawa, Canada, where he is currently an Adjunct Research Professor. He is on the Editorial Review Board of several journals and has published over 50 papers within the last five years. George is a Senior Member of IEEE, and member of ACM and Professional Engineers Ontario. His research interests include security and privacy for e-services, using software agents to enhance reliability, security, and privacy, and engineering software for reliability, security, and performance.

Jia Zhang is an Assistant Professor of Department of Computer Science at Northern Illinois University. Zhang co-authors the book titled "Services Computing". She has published over 80 refereed journal articles, book chapters, and conference papers. Zhang is serving as Associate Editor of IEEE Transactions on Services Computing (TSC), International Journal of Web Services Research (JWSR), and the Advances in Web Services Research (AWSR) Book Series, IGI Global. She also serves on Editorial Board of IEEE IT Professional. Zhang serves as Program Vice Chair of IEEE International Conference on Web Services (ICWS 2009, 2008, 2007, & 2006). Her current research interests center around Services Computing, with a focus on QoS testing, data management, mobile learning, and collaborative learning. Zhang received her Ph.D. in Computer Science from University of Illinois at Chicago in 2000. She is a member of the IEEE.

Lu Zhang received the B.S. and the Ph.D. degrees in Computer Science both from Peking University, P.R. China. He was a postdoctoral researcher with the Department of Computer Science, the University of Liverpool. He is now an associate professor with the School of Electronics Engineering and Computer Science, Peking University, P.R. China. His current research interests include program comprehension, reverse engineering, component-based software development, software modeling, and software testing.

Wenbing Zhao received the Ph.D. degree in Electrical and Computer Engineering from the University of California, Santa Barbara, in 2002. Currently, he is an assistant professor in the Department of Electrical and Computer Engineering at Cleveland State University. His current research interests include distributed systems, computer networks, fault tolerance and security. In the past, he has conducted research in the fields of superconducting materials and quantum optics. Dr. Zhao has more than 60 academic publications.

Yanzhen Zou is currently a Ph.D. student of the School of Electronics Engineering and Computer Science of Peking University, P.R. China. Her current research interests include component-based software development, reuse repository, Web Services retrieval, Web Services trustworthiness assessment and trust management in service-oriented environments.

Index

Symbols

A

B

C

E

H

I

J

K

L

M

N

O

P

Q

R

S

U

V

W

X

Y

Z